Teaching Composition
Background Readings

Teaching Composition

Background Readings

Second Edition

T. R. Johnson

Tulane University

Bedford/St. Martin's   Boston   ◆   New York

For Bedford/St. Martin's
Developmental Editor: Karin Halbert
Production Editor: Deborah Baker
Senior Production Supervisor: Joe Ford
Senior Marketing Manager: Richard Cadman
Editorial Assistant: Stefanie Wortman
Copyeditor: Tara Masih
Text Design: Claire Seng-Niemoeller
Cover Design: Donna Lee Dennison
Composition: Karla Goethe, Orchard Wind Graphics
Printing and Binding: Haddon Craftsmen, Inc., an R. R. Donnelley & Sons Company

President: Joan E. Feinberg
Editorial Director: Denise B. Wydra
Editor in Chief: Karen S. Henry
Director of Marketing: Karen Melton Soeltz
Director of Editing, Design, and Production: Marcia Cohen
Managing Editor: Elizabeth M. Schaaf

Manufactured in the United States of America.

9 8 7 6 5 4
f   e   d   c   b   a

For information, write: Bedford/St. Martin's, 75 Arlington Street, Boston, MA 02116 (617-399-4000)

ISBN: 0–312–41529–X
EAN: 978–0–312–41529–7

Acknowledgments
Chris M. Anson, "Portfolios for Teachers: Writing Our Way to Reflective Practice" from *New Directions in Portfolio Assessment: Reflective Practice, Critical Theory, and Large Scale Scoring,* edited by Laurel Black, et al. Copyright © 1994 by Boynton/Cook Publishers, Inc. Reprinted with the permission of the author.
Arnetha Ball and Ted Lardner, "Dispositions toward Language: Teacher Constructs of Knowledge and the Ann Arbor Black English Case" from *College Composition and Communication* 48:4 (December 1997). Copyright © 1997 by the National Council of Teachers of English. Reprinted with permission.
David Bartholomae, "Inventing the University" from *When a Writer Can't Write: Studies in Writer's Block and Other Composing-Process Problems,* edited by Mike Rose. Copyright © 1985. Reprinted with the permission of The Guilford Press.
James A. Berlin, "Rhetoric and Ideology in the Writing Class" from *College English* (September 1988). Copyright © 1988 by the National Council of Teachers of English. Reprinted with permission.

Preface

This selection of readings is designed to help you acquire or broaden a theoretical and practical background as you prepare to teach college-level composition. Although I've selected the readings with first-time instructors in mind, I also hope that veteran instructors in community colleges and four-year institutions will find in this volume helpful perspectives, important ideas, and practical suggestions.

The thirty readings in this edition of *Teaching Composition: Background Readings* (twelve of them new) address major concerns of composition theory and practice. Chapter 1, "Teaching Writing: Key Concepts and Philosophies for Reflective Practice," examines, describes, and reflects on the beliefs and assumptions that inform writing pedagogies. The readings in Chapter 2, "Thinking about the Writing Process," discuss ways that writers shape thought into words when they explore ideas, plan, draft, consider (or ignore) audiences, and revise. This chapter also contains completely revised subsections on the increasingly important topics of integrating technology and visual literacy into the writing classroom, as well as a new section on sentence-level pedagogies. Chapter 3, "Responding to and Evaluating Student Writing," focuses on teachers' strategies for responding to writers' needs and working with students at diverse writing sites. Chapter 4, "Issues in Writing Pedagogy: Institutional Politics and the Other," focuses on classroom and faculty diversity. Throughout this volume, many of the readings include helpful citations, and at the end of the volume an updated annotated bibliography lists other relevant and important articles that could not be included in this preface. These citations offer the opportunity for further reflection and research on composition and its artful teaching.

You can, of course, jump in anywhere and read the article that best suits your needs at the moment. Know, however, that there are rich interconnections among the readings that build a recursivity into the collection. The articles by Peter Elbow and Nancy Sommers, for example, are referenced frequently in other readings in this collection; in "The Erasure of the Sentence," Robert J. Connors examines and evaluates the sentence-level rhetoric that Francis Christensen sets forth in "A Generative Rhetoric of the Sentence." So you may find yourself stopping in the middle of one reading to refer to another one. The readings have also been thoughtfully organized so as to logically build upon, and segue into, important concepts.

Because teachers are the primary audience for each writer in this collection, you will find very practical recommendations about teaching strategies. A headnote to each reading focuses on the selection writer's key assumptions and consistent themes. Two kinds of reflective question sets follow each selection: "The Writer's Insights as a Resource for Your Teaching" and "The Writer's Insights as a Resource for Your Writing Classroom." I wrote the first set of recommendations to prompt you into reflective practice as a writing teacher. I based these recommendations on my experience working with writers, my training and supervision of novice writing instructors, and my work with colleagues across the curriculum. The second set of suggestions describe strategies that have worked for professors and graduate writing instructors alike as they apply the insights of a reading to their actual practice in the classroom.

Our discipline's conversations have always been spirited, whether about philosophical issues, learning and writing theory, or pedagogical assumptions that influence our work with writers. From such conversations — public and private, in scholarly journals, faculty lounges, and on listservs — and from our own classroom experience and reflection, we gain confidence and clarity in our vision of the nature and purpose of writing courses. I hope your "conversation" with these readings will help you to become an adept and creative teacher of writing.

The revision of *Teaching Composition: Background Readings* owes much to the helpful suggestions of the following instructors: Renee Bangerter, Fullerton College; Aaron Goldweber, Broome Community College; Tom Pace, John Carroll University; Matthew Parfitt, Boston University; and Dawn Skorczewski, Emerson College. Thanks also go to the staff at Bedford/St. Martin's, especially Joan Feinberg, Denise Wydra, Karen Henry, Beth Castrodale, Karin Halbert, Stefanie Wortman, Elizabeth Schaaf, and Deb Baker.

Teaching Composition: Background Readings — compiled to accompany composition texts — includes both theoretical background and practical advice for writing instructors. Each Bedford/St. Martin's composition text is also accompanied by its own instructor's manual, which provides such practical resources as chapter overviews, sample syllabi, teaching tips, discussion prompts, additional assignments, and recommendations about using the electronic ancillary package. I recommend that you use this volume of background readings in tandem with the instructor's manual for the text you and your students are using to take best advantage of the information and possibilities offered by the textbook.

Other Bedford/St. Martin's Professional Resources

Background Readings

Teaching Argument in the Composition Course

Teaching Developmental Reading

Teaching Developmental Writing, Second Edition

Teaching Technical Communication

Bibliographies

The Bedford Bibliography for Teachers of Basic Writing

The Bedford Bibliography for Teachers of Writing, Sixth Edition

Teaching Advice

Assigning, Responding, Evaluating, Third Edition

The Elements of Teaching Writing: A Resource for Instructors in All Disciplines

A TA's Guide to Teaching Writing in All Disciplines

Portfolio Teaching

The St. Martin's Guide to Teaching Writing, Fifth Edition

For more information, contact your local sales representative, e-mail us at sales_support@bfwpub.com, or visit our Web site at <bedfordstmartins.com>.

Contents

"To composition scholars, teachers, and administrators who have campaigned vigorously for student portfolios, the teaching portfolio makes good sense. Yet we still have much to learn about the method, both as a tool for appraising teachers' performance and as a way to encourage faculty development, collaboration, and professionalism."

"[S]ince language is a social phenomenon that is a product of a particular historical moment, our notions of the observing self, the communities in which the self functions, and the very structures of the material world are social constructions — all specific to a particular time and culture. These social constructions are thus inscribed in the very language we are given to inhabit in responding to our experience."

"[The student] has to invent the university by assembling and mimicking its language while finding some compromise between idiosyncrasy, a personal history, on the one hand, and the requirements of convention, the history of a discipline, on the other hand."

"[I]nstead of thinking bigger and wider, as composition has typically done — using large imagined geographies to situate and validate composition studies as a discipline — now it is time to think smaller and more locally."

"Education must begin with the solution of the teacher-student contradiction, by reconciling the poles of the contradiction so that both are simultaneously teachers *and* students."

"'In a certain sense, the current generation of students needs to reinvent the university itself, not by replacing one department or methodology with another, but by building broad connections across areas of knowledge that still remain in relative isolation.'"

"All the writers I have observed, skilled and unskilled alike, use the process of retrospective structuring while writing. Yet the degree to which they do so varies and seems, in fact, to depend upon the model of the writing process that they have internalized. Those who realize that writing can be a recursive process have an easier time with waiting, looking, and discovering."

"This paper, too, treats writing as a problem-solving process, focusing, however, on what happens when the process dead-ends in writer's block.

It will further suggest that . . . blockers may well be stymied by possessing rigid or inappropriate rules, or inflexible or confused plans. Ironically enough, these are occasionally instilled by the composition teacher or gleaned from the writing textbook."

"The common ingredient that I find in all of the writing I admire . . . is something that I shall reluctantly call the rhetorical stance, a stance which depends on discovering and maintaining in any writing situation a proper balance among the three elements that are at work in any communicative effort: the available arguments about the subject itself, the interests and peculiarities of the audience, and the voice, the implied character, of the speaker."

"An audience is a field of force. The closer we come — the more we think about these readers — the stronger the pull they exert on the contents of our minds. The practical question, then, is always whether a particular audience functions as a helpful field of force or one that confuses or inhibits us."

"But student writers constantly struggle to bring their essays into congruence with a predefined meaning. The experienced writers do the opposite: they seek to discover (to create) meaning in the engagement with their writing, in revision."

"[I]ntentions are shaped by the community the writer wants to make his or her way into, and the revision process is not a simple matter of making a text 'better' or 'clearer.' Revision is instead the very complicated matter of struggle between a full, excess-ive life and the seemingly strict limits of what can be written and understood within a particular discourse community."

"The sentence itself as an element of composition pedagogy is hardly mentioned today outside of textbooks. But we can learn as much from watching the working out of Darwinian intellectual failures as from participating in the self-congratulatory normal science of the current winners, and so I offer this history of syntactic methods since 1960 in the spirit of the old New England gravestone: 'As you are now, so once was I; as I am now, so you shall be.'"

"We need a rhetoric of the sentence that will do more than combine the ideas of primer sentences. We need one that will *generate* ideas."

"Students can learn to write by learning the uses of chaos, which is to say, rediscovering the power of language to generate the sources of meaning. Our job is to design sequences of assignments that let our students discover what language can do, what they can do with language."

"I believe composition studies faculty have a much larger and more complicated obligation to fulfill — that of trying to understand and make sense of, to *pay attention* to, how technology is now inextricably linked to literacy and literacy education in this country."

"[O]ur findings do suggest that the instructional uses of CMC in undergraduate writing courses can be complicated by a variety of factors that instructors may have to consider. Moreover, while our findings do lend some credence to those who call for caution in extolling the virtues of CMC, they also suggest that online environments differ in intriguing ways from more traditional classroom environments and provide spaces of opportunity and risk for teachers and students who use them."

"I am after a clearer understanding of what can happen when the visual is very consciously brought into the composition classroom as a form of communication worth both examining *and* producing. What, for example, might it mean to ask, as I did of the students whose work opens this paper, for a visual argument? Are we posing a new relationship between composition and communication or resurrecting an older one? How does the visual both promise and threaten to change the composition course?"

"Recognizing the hybrid literacies our students now bring to our classrooms, we need a better understanding of the increasingly visual and interactive rhetorical features of digital documents. As writing technologies change, they require changes in our understanding of writing and rhetoric and, ultimately, in our writing pedagogy."

"Instead of finding errors or showing students how to patch up parts of their texts, we need to sabotage our students' conviction that the drafts they have written are complete and coherent. Our comments need to offer students revision tasks of a different order of complexity and sophistication from the ones that they themselves identify, by forcing students back into the chaos, back to the point where they are shaping and restructuring their meaning."

Peter Elbow

"So the most important point, then, is that *I am not arguing against judgment or evaluation*. I'm just arguing against that crude, oversimple way of *representing* judgment — distorting it, really — into a single number, which means ranking people and performances along a single continuum."

Douglas D. Hesse

"Unlike individual paper grading, portfolio evaluation involves judging a collection of texts written by a writer. The grade reflects an overall assessment of the writer's ability to produce varied kinds of texts, not an average of grades on individual papers."

Joseph Harris

"Language is not only a means of communicating but a form of identification, a badge that seems to define its wearer and yet, paradoxically, can be changed. It is the fear and hope of such change that so powerfully charges the debate on error."

Patrick Hartwell

"[W]e need to attempt some massive dislocation of our traditional thinking, to shuck off our hyperliterate perception of the value of formal rules, and to regain the confidence in the tacit power of unconscious knowledge that our theory of language gives us."

Muriel Harris and Tony Silva

"ESL writers often come to the writing center seeking an editor, someone who will mark and correct their errors and help them fix the paper. On one hand, as tutors we are collaborators who listen to the student's concerns when setting the tutorial agenda. On the other hand, as tutors we also want to begin with rhetorical concerns before looking at sentence-level matters."

"Because of cultural differences in patterns of language use, and because of differences in styles of interaction used to demonstrate knowledge, many students from diverse social and linguistic backgrounds are entering urban classrooms where teachers still have a difficult time recognizing and fully utilizing the wealth of language resources students use effectively outside school."

"It is my contention that feminist pedagogy, although compelling, may reinforce rather than critique or transform patriarchal structures by reinscribing what Magda Lewis calls the 'woman as caretaker ideology.' . . ."

"Writing instruction should enable students to recognize the writerly self as a *persuasive instrument* that can be strategically deployed and to learn to make effective use of their own multiple locations to take personal stands on public issues *that transcend the confessional.*"

"[O]ur writing classes do become the setting for argument about capital punishment, euthanasia, abortion, women's rights. If we regard these discussions as having at most only 'situational' weight — a 'this time and place' payoff — then the dynamics of shared ideas is not allowed its proper role in the *necessary directionality* for the human condition and the condition of the planet we inhabit — that of alleviating suffering and cruelty. . . ."

"In this essay I set out a case for why the concept of sponsorship is so richly suggestive for exploring economies of literacy and their effects. Then, through use of extended case examples, I demonstrate the practical application of this approach for interpreting current conditions of literacy teaching and learning, including persistent stratification of opportunity and escalating standards for literacy achievement."

Teaching Writing: Key Concepts and Philosophies for Reflective Practice

E very choice you make as a writing instructor is informed by some philosophy of composition and of teaching composition, even if you're not fully aware of the philosophy you hold. The more aware you become of your assumptions and premises, the more you can rethink and improve your teaching. Each of the writers in this chapter challenges us to examine the assumptions that govern the ways we teach. To begin this process of reflection, we recommend that — before you start to teach a writing course or early in the semester — you sit down and freewrite or brainstorm for about fifteen minutes, listing your "I believes" about writing and about the teaching of writing. Periodically shape those beliefs into a coherent format that you can refer to as you plan assignments, structure sequences of assignments, build or redesign a syllabus, ponder a writing curriculum, propose support services for writers across the curriculum, or discuss your pedagogy with colleagues.

After each of the readings in this text, you will find questions and suggestions that help link the piece to your professional development and classroom practice. You may find it useful to reflect on these prompts in a reflective teaching journal. Many first-year instructors keep a journal in which they log and reflect on what occurs in class and how students respond to assignments. Those instructors use the journal to describe their own reactions and responses to the class dynamic, to the process of building a writing community, and to the connections they are making between what they are reading outside the classroom and actual events within their classroom. Two or three times a semester they read over their entries and chart their own learning and growth as instructors. By the end of the first semester, most new instructors can see some dramatic changes in confidence, attitudes about writing communities and student writing, use of teaching strategies, and understanding of how the parts of the syllabus or the course connect. The journal is a very useful resource for writing about teaching, for developing a final draft of a philosophy for teaching writing, and for designing syllabi for second-semester or second-year courses. It could be an important part of a teaching portfolio, a collection of products that demonstrate your practice and improvement as an instructor. For a practical discussion of creating a teaching portfolio, turn to Chris M. Anson's "Portfolios for Teachers: Writing Our Way to Reflective Practice," which follows.

Portfolios for Teachers: Writing Our Way to Reflective Practice

Chris M. Anson

When teachers assemble portfolios of materials that document and tell stories about their teaching, they create not only a tool for others to evaluate their performance in the classroom but also an invaluable resource for their own professional reflection. In this essay, which was published in New Directions in Portfolio Assessment: Reflective Practice, Critical Theory, and Large-Scale Scoring *(1994), Chris M. Anson suggests that reflection reinforces several important roles: the teacher as writer, scholar, and professional. While Anson explores how the teaching portfolio may be adapted to the unique characteristics and goals of individual writing programs, he argues that in any form, portfolios help "raise the intellectual stature of narratives about classroom experience" in a field that generally privileges more formal and abstract types of inquiry. An archive of firsthand teaching experience can support more rigorous and expansive scholarship, and, in turn, contribute to better-informed abstract models upon which, as Anson puts it, "living, breathing teachers can, in all their complexity, act."*

n 1986, George Hillocks published his now well-known work, *Research on Written Composition*. This was the first "metaanalysis" in a maturing field, a sign that the study of writing had reached a critical mass sufficient to let us stand back and assess how far we had come and to find out what works in the teaching of writing. The result was a useful set of delivery modes that described the dominant ways in which composition classrooms are organized and taught, followed by an empirical assessment of these modes' effectiveness.

If Hillocks's painstaking synthesis clearly reflected our preoccupations, then formal inquiry into composition had been driven by a hunger for abstractions, not by a desire to understand what happens in the minds of individual teachers who are influenced by personal experiences and act on self-constructed theory. As Susan Miller characterizes this focus on the abstract, it has left little room for "interpretive theory in composition, an approach that privileges the subject in, and the subjectivity of, composition as an intellectual pursuit" (120). Such an approach relies on accounts of teaching that weave through the thoughts, ambitions, and struggles of individual teachers as they breathe life into their own personal curriculum.

Unfortunately, the scholarly research community often devalues storytelling as a type of inquiry. In *The Making of Knowledge in Composition,* North defends the practice even as he acknowledges that "its credibility, its power vis-a-vis other kinds of knowledge, has gradually, steadily diminished" (21). In an effort to raise the intellectual stature of narratives about classroom experience, Brannon argues that it is primarily through storytelling that we come to know about teaching. Proposing a dialectic between the "softness" of classroom narratives and the "hardness" of scientific truth that has dominated our scholarly journals, she argues that it is time for each to inform the other, time to rediscover "reliability" of our own reflected practice. Brannon is not alone in this belief. Recent work such as Witherell and Noddings' collection, *Stories Lives Tell: Narrative and Dialogue in Education*, as well as extensive research by Lee Shulman, suggest a growing awareness of teachers' reflected practice as an arena of authentic study. These voices challenge us to redefine what should count as knowledge of the writing classroom and ask why it is that teachers' stories are not widely written and heard.

Recently, through such organizations as the American Association of Higher Education, teachers and administrators have taken a keen interest in an innovation that places personal accounts of teaching at the center of instructional development: the *teaching portfolio* (see Edgerton, Hutchings, and Quinlan). Teaching portfolios invite teachers to tell the story of their work and in doing so to become more reflective of their own practice. As such, teaching portfolios respond directly to calls, like Brannon's, to legitimize classroom experience and wed teaching and instructional inquiry.

To composition scholars, teachers, and administrators who have campaigned vigorously for student portfolios, the teaching portfolio makes good sense. Yet we still have much to learn about the method, both as a tool for appraising teachers' performance and as a way to encourage faculty development, collaboration, and professionalism. This chapter describes the teaching portfolio and its goals, offers a rationale for its centrality to our profession, suggests some ways in which it can be adapted to specific kinds of writing programs, and raises questions for further exploration and study.

The Nature and Structure of Teaching Portfolios

Most approaches to teaching portfolios define them as a collection of materials, assembled by a faculty member, that document or reflect teaching performance. Some approaches emphasize the "communicative" goals of portfolios as a way to share one's teaching, others stress its role in assessment, still others its potential to encourage development. Wolf's description in "The Schoolteacher's Portfolio" perhaps best sums up these various functions:

> A [teaching] portfolio can be defined as a container for storing and displaying evidence of a teacher's knowledge and skills. However, this definition is incomplete. A portfolio is more than a container — a portfolio also represents an attitude that assessment is dynamic, and that the richest portrayals of teaching (and student) performance are based upon multiple sources of evidence collected over time in authentic settings.

While the portfolio may seem at first glance like a typical faculty "file," it differs from standard dossiers in important ways. First, although it can contain personal material, it benefits from agreements among a community of teachers about what it should contain and what purposes it should serve. Individual faculty dossiers, by contrast, represent mostly private efforts (often symbolically "off-limits" in a locked department file). Second, the teaching portfolio is not simply a repository of the outcomes of teaching; it contains documents that show teachers in action, both creating their teaching and reflecting on it during moments of introspection. Finally, the teaching portfolio may contain much more material than might be forwarded to a hiring committee or faculty evaluation team. The portfolio may become several portfolios, each displaying different materials depending on its purpose and audience.

Ideally, a teaching portfolio should contain both primary and secondary documents. Primary documents are actual materials from classroom instruction, including, but by no means limited to, the following:

- Syllabi
- Course overviews or descriptions
- Assignments of all kinds
- Exams
- Study Guides
- Student papers, perhaps with teacher comments
- Classroom materials such as overheads or handouts
- Innovative instructional materials (computer programs, etc.)

- Logs from class visits
- Student evaluations

Secondary documents are materials that demonstrate active, critical thinking about instructional issues and materials. They might include the following:

- Reflections on peer-observations or videotapes
- Reflections on course evaluations
- Self-evaluations of all kinds
- Narrative accounts of problem-solving
- Responses to case studies and scenarios about teaching
- Journals documenting thoughtfulness about instructional issues
- Goal statements and philosophies
- Letters of assessment from others

From a developmental perspective, these secondary documents are essential if portfolios are to be used for something more than what Wolf, in *Teaching Portfolios,* calls "amassing papers." Instead, they must be "*structured* around key dimensions of teaching, such as planning, teaching, evaluating students, and professional activities. . . . [T]he portfolio should be more than a few snapshots, but should reflect a person's accomplishments over time and in a variety of contexts" (2).

Most published descriptions of teaching portfolios also stress their collaborative potential. Portfolios should not only bring teachers together to talk about and share in the activity of teaching, but should also represent the influences of colleagues, students, and theorists. They should, then, be understood first as something programmatic or anchored in a community, not as a "file" stored away in a department cabinet.

Teaching Portfolios at the Center of Writing Programs

Teaching portfolios seem especially well-suited to the field of composition, whose scholars and teachers are experts in writing assessment just as they understand and strongly promote the use of writing as a mode of learning. Three important subject positions of teachers among our community nicely match the less discipline-specific goals of the teaching portfolio.

Teacher as Writer

More than in any other teaching-oriented field, composition celebrates the value of writing for improved instruction and deeper reflection. In most nationally prominent workshops on the teaching of writing, participants' experiences drafting, sharing, and revising their own texts become the seeds of personal and professional growth. Such experiences "enact the belief that the best writing teachers are teachers who write" (Faery); participants learn how to teach writing "from the inside out" (Healy).

As Durst points out, however, many teachers write less than their own students:

> For most elementary, secondary, and community college teachers . . . writing is not a necessary part of the job. On the contrary, the responsibilities of their jobs generally work *against* finding time and energy for writing. And, of course, there are few job-related rewards for being a teacher who writes. (262)

Institutions that expect publication do, of course, encourage their faculty to write. Yet to survive in these settings, the faculty may end up working exclusively on articles and books unrelated to teaching.

Teaching portfolios must be *written*. While most primary documents placed in a portfolio have an independent life as part of classroom instruction, the portfolio casts a new light on such documents and gives their creators a different sense of audience. Through the imagined eyes of a colleague or administrator, the college teacher now rethinks the overly dictatorial tone in her course syllabus. Anticipating the scrutiny of a hiring committee looking at his portfolio, the recent Ph.D. wonders whether his sample assignment seems clear enough to demonstrate his best work. Knowing she will soon be sharing her comments on student papers with her peer teaching team, the instructor at a community college begins reflecting on her style of response. The various audiences invited into these teachers' portfolios inspire them to think in more principled ways about how their teaching materials are written, and this process leads to revision, new thought, and new action where perhaps otherwise there would be little change.

But it is the secondary documents that really encourage teachers to write. Teaching philosophies, observation reports, discussions of course designs, explanations of assignments, analyses of comments of student papers, reflections on sets of student evaluations — these become the threads of a narrative, a kind of professional autobiography of a teacher's classroom life. It is difficult to imagine anyone invested in their daily work as a teacher giving short shrift to a statement of their beliefs about how best students learn and how best we might teach them. Ideally, teachers can meet in small focus groups to circulate and discuss drafts of their reflections and philosophies. Revisions of primary or secondary documents can then lead to changed attitudes and improved teaching strategies.

Teacher as Scholar

The dominant rhetoric in higher education unnecessarily splits teaching and scholarship, often through systems that reward one more richly than the other. "Research universities" stand in stark contrast to "teaching colleges." In spelling out the criteria for success, promotion and tenure codes usually separate the activities of "research and scholarship" or "publishing" from the activities of "teaching and advising students," as if the two were unrelated. In its report on the rising costs of higher education, the U.S. House Select Committee on Children, Youth, and Families argues that "the focus on higher education today is on research, not teaching" (3). Offering statistics that show the decline of attention to teaching and advising relative to the rise in emphasis on research, the report suggests that

> conducting research has become such an overwhelming focus on today's campuses that those professors who still manage to teach more than a few hours a day are actually looked down upon by their peers, to say nothing of the negative effect teaching has on their chances for tenure, pay, and promotion. (3–4)

Such dichotomizing characterizes teaching as a deliberately unscholarly kind of work requiring the endurance of tedium in contrast to the more demanding and intellectually rewarding work of research. In a valiant effort to tear down this barrier between the personal life of the laboratory or office and the public life of the classroom, Ernest Boyer offers four specific ways in which teachers can be scholars: through the scholarship of discovery (such as research), the scholarship of integration (such as writing a textbook), the scholarship of application (such as consulting), and the scholarship of teaching. Uniting all the professional activities of college faculty under the banner of scholarship restores teaching to its rightful intellectual place. "At bottom," Edgerton, Hutchings, and Quinlan claim, "the concept entails a view that teaching, like other scholarly activities . . . relies on a base of expertise, a 'scholarly knowing' that needs to and *can* be identified, made public, and evaluated; a scholarship that faculty themselves must be responsible for monitoring" (1).

By creating and developing teachers' base of expertise through inquiry into the real problems and experiences of the classroom, teaching portfolios encourage this scholarly view of teaching. In the field of composition, "teacher research" has already gained prestige as a kind of inquiry rooted in classroom experience but branching into the world of theory and investigation. As William Schubert argues, even the teacher lore so often denigrated as unprincipled chit-chat is actually highly relevant to "the theory and practice of curriculum, teaching, supervision, and school improvement. . . . To assume that scholarship can focus productively on what teachers learn recognizes teachers as important partners in the creation of knowledge about education" (207).

Teacher as Professional

Faculty members in higher education, particularly at research-oriented universities, often define their professional lives in terms of scholarship. In spite of the increased demand for a stronger commitment to teaching in American universities, the public itself perpetuates the image of experts in disciplines whose intellectual missions exist at some remove from teaching. The popular press stereotypes "absent-minded professors" as intellectuals immersed in the stuff of their disciplines. TV shows and movies depict faculty as distant, hard-to-reach scholars who hurry from their lectures for fear of being harassed by students. Much rarer are images of compassionate teachers willing to sit down with students and help them to learn, and who think conscientiously about their own instruction.

This tendency to privilege field-specific knowledge as the gist of one's professional life systematically devalues teachers (especially in public schools) whose professions are necessarily rooted in classrooms. Howard Gardner has described this situation as a paradox: "Few societies have paid as much lip service to the importance of education . . . yet it seems necessary to say as well that education — and particularly the schools — have often held a dubious position in the value scheme of the larger society" (98). Perhaps no sign more strongly defines the belief in professionalism-as-scholarship than the organization of the faculty vita. Publications, research grants, conference papers, and other artifacts of scholarship almost always appear before (and more prominently than) lists of courses, names of advisees, instructional innovations, and other outcomes of teaching.

Teaching portfolios not only display a teacher's best work but invite readers into the teacher's studio, where strategies for principled instruction are conceived and created. Portfolios provide glimpses — and sometimes longer, studied gazes — of teachers at work as professionals. In this sense, the portfolio encourages teachers to think of themselves as experts whose decisions are reflected in the professional artifacts of their instruction. Their expertise as *conveyors and orchestrators* of special knowledge stands side-by-side with that specialized knowledge itself.

Adapting Teaching Portfolios to Specific Contexts

Most of the literature on teaching portfolios agrees that portfolios give teachers a way to work on and document not just the outcome of their efforts but also their reflection, improvement, and growing expertise. Individuals or committees charged with evaluating teachers (for performance appraisals, merit pay, or hiring) come away from a portfolio with a much clearer and more comprehensive picture of a teacher's work than brief testimonials and statistics from student evaluations. And, in composition, portfolios define a space for teachers to work on their own writing or, with other teachers, collectively focus on a large area of their professional lives.

Yet in spite of this conceptual agreement about teaching portfolios, important practical questions remain. Without decisions about the contents and uses of portfolios, they can become merely random repositories — haphazardly organized collections of student evaluations, old syllabi, and hastily photocopied handouts. And if they are used solely for assessment, teachers may soon look on them with feelings of fear and doubt rather than a sense of personal ownership in their work.

To be effective, portfolios must be adapted to teachers' and administrators' specific needs. If a program of faculty development wants to emphasize teaching style, the documents might go so far as to include a videotape of all or part of a class session along with a self-analysis. If participants in a writing-across-the-curriculum program want to improve the way they read students' work, then the portfolio might contain some examples of students' final and/or draft papers representing a range of quality, along with the teacher's commentary on those and an accompanying reflection on the nature of the teacher's responses. Specific questions can be designed as prompts ("Characterize your response style by examining a classful of your papers, and include a sample; what are your goals in responding to student writing? How do your comments achieve those goals?"). If a department wants to work in a given year on the principles of effective writing assignments, the portfolio might include three sample assignments with accompanying descriptions of their place in the scheme of a course and a rationale for their design. The following year, the focus might shift to advising students — and the portfolio contents for that year should reflect the shift. Central to the adaptation of portfolio contents is the constant need to guide reflection and encourage change in keeping with the missions of particular departments and institutions.

To illustrate this adaptive potential further, let's consider three fictitious writing programs where teaching portfolios play a role in faculty development and the evaluation of teaching. Each site uses portfolios for different purposes among quite different teachers.

Site 1 is Jonesville College, a small liberal arts school with a strong writing-across-the-curriculum program. The program is supported by teaching portfolios among all faculty assigned to "writing-intensive" (WI) courses. WI courses have a smaller class size than most other courses and also carry a special incentive bonus paid by the central administration. New teachers of WI courses meet monthly throughout their first year to participate in workshops, discuss the integration of writing into their coursework, and share ideas and samples of student writing. Coordinators of the WI program use portfolios initially to support faculty development. However, because competition to teach WI courses is keen, faculty are reappointed to these courses yearly. An evaluation committee coordinated by the director of writing across the curriculum examines the portfolios of present WI teachers who wish to continue teaching the following year. Criteria for reappointment include evidence of principled assignment design, integration of writing fully into the coursework, reflections on the nature of students' writing, and year-end self-assessments with commentary for further improvement. At Jonesville, therefore, the portfolios begin cumulatively and developmentally for teachers-in-training, and turn recursive and evaluative in future years. Model portfolios from experienced WI teachers provide ideas and techniques for teachers new to the program and demonstrate the principles of reflective practice.

Site 2 is the English department at Smithtown Community College, a midsize campus near a major metropolitan area. The department coordinates a single first-year composition course staffed largely by annually renewed instructors, some of whom teach at other local colleges and spend little extra time on campus. Five years ago, the instructors lobbied the department to examine its rather haphazard process of faculty evaluation after several younger instructors were eliminated following a budget cut. The chair decided to begin a teaching portfolio program as a way to assess the instructors' performance and create a better community of more committed teachers.

The model he chose is recursive: each portfolio must include, at a minimum, a full syllabus for each course taught, along with a two- or three-page rationale for its design; three samples of student writing from each course in the categories "strong," "typical," and "weak," along with the original responses and a one-page analysis explaining the papers' relative strengths and weaknesses and how the responses encouraged revision or further learning; two-page post-course self-assessments for all classes taught, with accompanying student evaluations from one of those classes; and a cover essay articulating a philosophy of teaching. Optional but strongly encouraged are informal write-ups of conference sessions, workshops, or readings relating to teaching.

The portfolios represent Smithtown's mission by focusing on student performance relative to strong, student-centered teaching. In successive years, teachers must revise or replace these documents but must refer to the changes they have made in their methods or beliefs. The chair discusses the portfolio with each instructor at the time of reappointment. It is generally understood that seniority will not count as much as a continued commitment, demonstrated in the portfolio, to change, renewal, and improvement in teaching. While the instructors continue to lobby against the inequities of annual renewals, they feel that the portfolios more fairly reflect their abilities at the time of reappointment.

Site 3 is a large composition program at Johnson State University, staffed almost entirely by teaching assistants pursuing Ph.D.s in the Department of English. As part of its TA development program, the program begins teaching portfolios in the first year of the TAs' five-year appointments. The model shown in Figure 1 is cumulative: the directors feel that as TAs move through their teaching appointments, they naturally attend to different concerns at different levels of instructional sophistication. Since most of their new TAs have never taught before, Year 1 focuses on strategies for leading discussions, running small groups, working individually with students, and managing

Figure 1   A Cumulative Model for Teaching Portfolios

	FOCUS	ENTRIES
Year 1	Experiential	Reflections on visits Teaching reflections Responses to student writing
Year 2	Logistical	Syllabus with rationale Extended descriptions of assignments with rationales Narrative philosophy of teaching
Year 3	Theoretical	Revised philosophy of teaching New rationales based on theory Student surveys of techniques, with analysis and reflection
Year 4	Experimental	Post-course self-assessments Analyses of experimental techniques Revised philosophy of teaching
Year 5	Professional	Best samples of all work (new portfolio for job search)

time. All TAs are given a common course design that they may slightly modify after consultation. During the year, each TA must visit another instructor's class at least twice and be visited at least twice. Small teams discuss, revise, and enter into the portfolio their write-ups of these visits, as well as reflections on samples of student writing. At several points during the year, the instructors write "teaching reflections" in which they analyze specific successes and failures in their classroom instruction. The writing program administrators and their assistants respond to the portfolio entries as they are cycled into the portfolio.

In Year 2, the TAs begin designing their own versions of the composition courses offered at JSU. Now the focus is logistical. Documents placed in the portfolio include a full syllabus, an accompanying rationale, and extended descriptions of each assignment along with explanations of its goal, contents, and sequence in the course. Instructors also write narrative-like philosophies of teaching. By the time they move to Year 3, the TAs must begin reading more extensively in the area of composition theory and research. A graduate course optionally supports this new theoretical focus. Now the TAs must reinterpret their classroom activities, course design, and philosophy through the new perspectives offered in their readings. Documents include revised statements of philosophy, deeper rationales for pedagogical choices, and at least one carefully administered student survey focusing on a specific technique in the classroom, along with an analysis of the results.

In Year 4, TAs move into a more experimental stage during which they try out new and often innovative ideas in the classroom. In addition to post-course self-assessments, each TA must place into her portfolio at least two analyses of experimental or innovative instructional strategies. The best of these are photocopied and circulated among all the instructors. Finally, between Years 4 and 5, TAs prepare a professional teaching dossier from the materials they have accumulated in their teaching portfolios. These include the very best examples of syllabi, assignments, descriptions of innovations, reflections, post-course self-assessments of students' evaluations, and teaching philosophies. In this way, JSU's program uses teaching portfolios initially as a development tool and gradually "professionalizes" them to support teachers' job searches when they complete their graduate programs.

Clearly, each of these sketches raises concerns just as it suggests innovations. Most such concerns, however, will not arise from the "developmental" potential of teaching portfolios but from their use in the evaluation of teaching. No one will argue against creating a space for deeper reflection, greater collaboration, and more effective instruction. But many will question the method as a way to make judgments about teaching ability. To this issue we now briefly turn.

The Problem of Assessment

At the heart of the teaching portfolio lies the belief that excellent teachers possess a special expertise, what Shulman calls the "pedagogy of substance," that allows them to transform discipline-specific material into learnable concepts and methods. Shulman's research suggests that it is possible to gauge or measure this expertise and the attempt to achieve it. Because it provides rich descriptions and actual materials from teachers' instruction, the teaching portfolio opens up that possibility for measurement in a way that has excited many educators concerned about the public cry for accountability in higher education.

As experts in the assessment of student writing and thinking, compositionists interested in teaching portfolios as an evaluation tool face the mixed blessing of working out criteria for successful performance. Primary documents appear to be the easiest to codify in this way: most teachers can distinguish between an especially strong course syllabus and an undeveloped or quickly drafted one. The unimaginative or thoughtlessly written assignment stands in stark contrast to the assignment that reflects clear goals and will interest and motivate students. Secondary documents, on the other hand, present more interesting puzzles. How might we measure "the ability to reflect"? What really counts for good response to students' in-process drafts? How might we sort strong from weak rationales for specific writing assignments?

Consider, for example, excerpts from the observation logs of two teaching assistants in the early years of their teaching careers. The teachers, both women, have observed the class of a colleague, kept a descriptive log of what happened during the class, and met briefly with the teacher to discuss the log.

Excerpt 1

[The teacher has visited a colleague's class on a day when the students worked on rough drafts of papers in small groups.]

Four of the five students apparently had little difficulty with the assignment, although not having read the papers I could only judge by watching their interaction. The fifth was out of her element, a high-school student who did not understand the assignment or seemed unable to carry it through. The teacher was extremely empathetic to her and gave her many openings to verbalize her understanding of the assignment and the essay she was analyzing; however, she was unable to do so. He finally excused her by saying she was apparently just "letting it sit for a while."

The quality of the students' comments varied, but they stayed quite general. The high-school student offered no contribution, except to say that she could not read one copy of the rough draft that she had been given. The teacher, unquestioningly the main critic here, offered comments and questions to each of the writers. All of the information flowed through him, rather than from student to student.

Paper I. The paper was more analytical than evaluative. Student comments were made on clarifying audience, using more detail, and asking for elaboration and expansion at specific points. The best student response came for this paper, which was apparently quite funny. The teacher pointed out that the rhetorical strategies needed clarification. . . .

Paper III. This "undeveloped" paper has already been mentioned. The instructor's tact was impeccable, and he gave her a chance to start over if she needed it. In the postobservation conference, the instructor related that this student did not ever take his offers of extra help. Her attendance is good, although she is in over her head. *I would infer that because this student is in high school she probably thinks that if she continues to come to class she will pass, regardless of her written performance.* . . .

Excerpt 2

[The teacher has visited a colleague's class on a day when the students have brought in short responses to a chapter about journal writing.]

. . . At this juncture, X solicited responses from the class. "Ok, what did you think about the reading? How did you react to it?" There is general silence; students flipping through the pages. X tries again. "Was this useful, do you think, as a way to start writing?" Students seem to nod in assent, but still no response. X starts talking about the concepts in the chapter. Two ways to use the techniques, as learning tool to explore material, and as writing tool to gather thoughts and draft. 7 minutes; X still talking. Then he asks if there are any questions. A student says she keeps a journal anyway, and can she turn in pages from it in this journal or somehow do both at the same time. X cracks a joke that loosens up the class a little. Then he sobers, advises her to do more academic kind of work in the course journal. Leave other stuff out. One student doesn't see the difference. He explains; focus is always on

course or paper. Then quickly moves to transition into his explanation of
the next assignment.

*Two issues emerged for me from this part of the observation. The first
is the questioning style and the silence. I find this so typical in my own
teaching. You throw out a questions and . . . nothing. I think X lost a
chance to capitalize on the s's freewrites. Maybe by prefacing: "Take a
look for a minute at your freewrites about the chapter, and star or circle
any responses that stand out for you." Give them 30 seconds or so, then
follow up. If the response seems limited, maybe just call on them, or do a
safe-circle round-robin kind of thing, so everyone has a voice. X filled in
the silence, but in our pre-ob he said he was trying to make his course as
active as possible. So this wasn't a case of mini-lecture, of presenting
vital information, but it came off like a lecture.*

*The other issue (a little thornier?) is the journal. The most exciting
part of the first part of the class came when the student asked about her
own journal writing. Then #10 thought there wasn't difference between
the two types (actually he asked, but it was almost an implication). I
might have to let this run a bit. The journal is slippery; maybe X could
have asked #6 to describe what sort of stuff she writes in her personal
journal, to gauge if it could fit into the course journal. Also, if the initial
class discussion had been richer, the question might have come up in
that context, instead of a "Is it ok to do such-and-such" question. I know
how X felt. There hadn't been any discussion, he was put off, had other
stuff to cover, and maybe just shut down a potential theoretical problem
with the journal. He did loosen them up, which seemed a wise move if
you're uncertain yourself. I'm not sure. But the openness he wanted didn't
seem to be there. In my own use of journals in the classroom, I try to . . .
[paragraph].*

After describing the next assignment, X asked students . . .

As shown in the italicized material, the first teacher provides almost no reflection on her observation. She is witness to, but not interpreter of, the classroom she observed. In contrast, the second teacher
stops in the middle of her account to discuss her own use of journals
and how she might have handled a moment of silence. If we assume
that the presence of such meta-commentary reflects positively on a
teacher's ability to monitor her own teaching and continually improve
her instruction, the second teacher would seem far ahead of the first.

Anyone who uses such material for assessment, however, will soon
have the gnawing suspicion that the presence or absence of reflection
may not predict teaching ability — just as talking a lot in class may
not predict a student's intellectual acumen, ability to write, or accumulated knowledge. Critics in the creative arts have long claimed that
artistic ability may be largely unconscious. Writers, painters, and com-
posers are often unable to say exactly what made them describe a scene
in such lugubrious words, choose burnt umber for the edge of the moon,
or suddenly shift to the minor key in the middle of a movement; yet
they may still create brilliant works.

Comparisons of what defines "quality" in teaching — between individual teachers, between departments, or between disciplines — can

also illustrate quite clearly the present dubiousness of specifying universal criteria or standards for such quality. Edgerton, Hutchings, and Quinlan, for example, include in their monograph *The Teaching Portfolio* a sample entry from Harvard University history teacher James Wilkinson. Wilkinson's entry includes a student's typed book review, on which Wilkinson has made marginal annotations and an end comment. In his reflective statement accompanying the student paper, Wilkinson describes his reasons for writing what he did, and what the sample tells him about his own practice. This and other examples of portfolio entries are reproduced in order to "look at the particulars that might comprise [a teaching portfolio]" (13).

From the perspective of a history department, Wilkinson's entry no doubt shows a concerned faculty member who takes the time to design good assignments, read his students' work carefully, and write useful comments. While not intended to be a model of excellence, Wilkinson's entry clearly reveals a dedicated teacher at work, someone able to stand back from his teaching enough to know that he is offering "encouragement, even where there is need for improvement," and not "writ[ing] out what [students] should have said, but instead giv[ing] them general guidelines" (39). Most advocates of writing across the curriculum would react enthusiastically to such an entry, inspired that writing can be used effectively in all disciplines.

But if we switch the setting for purposes of illustration, the history department's criteria seem more localized. From the perspective of a faculty member teaching advanced composition, Wilkinson's commentary may seem inadequate, or "differently adequate," lacking developmental insight or advice about the writing process in order to draw the student's attention to the material of history. Once we acknowledge such multiple perspectives coming from widely different disciplinary, departmental, or institutional settings, the problem of establishing universal criteria for "good teaching" takes on considerable complexity. Perhaps evaluating teaching using documents in a portfolio (especially secondary ones) may have to remain the responsibility of individual departments within specific universities.

To release themselves of such dilemmas, most administrators argue that specifying exactly what should be in the portfolio and then describing strong and weak examples of those contents *encourages certain kinds of thinking* conducive to good teaching. This privileges neither the "science" of teaching, which assumes an objectivist and sometimes clinical view, nor the "art" of teaching, which often resigns ability to intuition, magic, and God-given dispositions. Reflection blends the two approaches by assuming that teaching can be discussed and improved consciously even if it can never be understood entirely clinically. If the ability to reflect on and problematize teaching activities really is associated with expertise, then evaluation programs can play a powerful role in improving instruction across entire campuses by raising to consciousness at least some of those decisions, actions, and experiences that lead to success in the classroom.

Without explicit, theoretically informed criteria for such portfolio contents as observation logs, reflections on student evaluations, or rationales for assignments, teaching portfolios can still encourage accountability, which in turn can be linked to assessment. A program of faculty or TA development, for example, can list documents that must be placed into a teaching portfolio over a certain time period. More ambitious programs can provide models of well-written, reflective documents, and can encourage faculty collaboration, perhaps by setting up small teams or pairing novice teachers with mentors. In such a context, both Teacher A and Teacher B above could carry on a useful discussion of their observations. Teacher A might express some interest in Teacher B's feelings about journal writing, or strategies for engaging the class when a question to students meets with deafening silence. Both teachers could profit from such interaction. In responding to Teacher B's questions about her observation, Teacher A might begin expressing her own values and ideas more fully. Did she think that the teacher was treating the high school student differently? What might this suggest about the "levels" of students in mixed classrooms and how to deal with such differences in small groups? What might one do in a small group when the discussion is staying too "general"? What happens when students find a peer's paper "funny" or enjoyable but the teacher thinks it needs more work on "rhetorical strategies"? Simply establishing Teacher A's interpretation and evaluation of the classroom scene might then lead into substantive issues of classroom organization, interaction, and teaching style. Good *reflection* may naturally follow from good *discussion,* and vice versa.

An agenda of research and development for the teaching portfolio within the field of composition might begin by acknowledging that no monolithic concept of "good teaching" exists; indeed, the entire field devotes most of its energy to this very question, without ever reaching closure. Having put aside the trepidation of such a totalized view, discussions within departments might turn to principled ways of achieving established goals. Such a situation already exists, though not always explicitly, across different writing programs around the country. One school's philosophy and goals may justify a heavy emphasis on the relationship between reading and writing, especially in traditional library research, while another's emphasizes the development of critical awareness of cultural difference, using a major "ethnographic" paper as its pivotal writing assignment. Within each context, however, there are certainly better and worse ways to teach the research paper or the ethnographic exploration. Open discussion of such methods can, in turn, raise questions about the program's larger goals, creating curricular change just as it changes and improves the teaching of individual faculty.

Whether or not the field can ever reach consensus about "good teaching," the evaluative criteria for performance should be shaped in the context of each teacher's work. A good teacher may not be someone who consistently uses small-group conferencing just because a national board of consultants or a group of composition scholars have deemed them crucial to the development of students' writing abilities. Rather, a good teacher may be someone who tried small-group conferences early on, abandoned them because they didn't seem to be working, and now, urged on by the portfolio, is revisiting this method, experimenting with it, and asking sensible questions about its role in the classroom. Administrators, merit-pay committees, and others charged with evaluating teaching may have to *intuit* improvement and hard work from the available documents — a prospect that itself might encourage teachers to be more explicit about their goals, methods, and reflections as teachers.

Clearly, much work remains to be done — most of it fortuitous for the field. In the need to establish standards for such seemingly routine tasks as responding to and evaluating student writing, designing a theoretically informed composition course, or integrating reading and writing in a principled way, we may as a field push our own investigations of writing curriculums and teaching methods a bit further. And that, in turn, will create better abstract models upon which living, breathing teachers can, in all their complexity, act.

Bibliography

Boyer, Ernest. *Scholarship Reconsidered: Priorities of the Professoriate.* Princeton, NJ: Princeton UP, 1990.

Brannon, Lil. "Knowing Our Knowledge: A Case for Teacher Research." Keynote Address, Annual Summer Conference of the Council of Writing Program Administrators. Breckenridge, CO. July 1992.

Durst, Russel K. "A Writer's Community: How Teachers Can Form Writing Groups." *Teacher as Writer: Entering the Professional Conversation.* Ed. Karin L. Dahl. Urbana, IL: National Council of Teachers of English, 1992. 261–271.

Edgerton, Russell, Patricia Hutchings, and Kathleen Quinlan. *The Teaching Portfolio: Capturing the Scholarship in Teaching.* Washington, D.C.: American Association of Higher Education, 1991.

Faery, Rebecca B. "Teachers *and* Writers: The Faculty Writing Workshop and Writing Across the Curriculum." Midwest Modern Language Association. St. Louis, MO. November 1992.

Gardner, Howard. "The Difficulties of School." *Literacy: An Overview by 14 Experts.* Ed. Stephen R. Graubard. New York: Noonday Press, 1991. 85–114.

Healy, Mary K. "Writing Communities: One Historical Perspective." *Teacher as Writer: Entering the Professional Conversation.* Ed. Karin L. Dahl. Urbana, IL: National Council of Teachers of English, 1992. 253–260.

Hillocks, George, Jr. *Research on Written Composition: New Directions for Teaching.* Urbana, IL: National Council of Teachers of English, 1986.

Miller, Susan. *Textual Carnivals: The Politics of Composition.* Carbondale, IL: Southern Illinois UP, 1992.

North, Stephen. *The Making of Knowledge in Composition: Portrait of an Emerging Field.* Portsmouth, NH: Boynton/Cook, 1987.

Schubert, William H. "Teacher Lore: A Basis for Understanding Praxis." *Stories Lives Tell: Narrative and Dialogue in Education*. Eds. Carol Witherell and Ned Noddings. New York: Teachers College Press, 1991. 207–233.

Shulman, Lee. "Paradigms and Research Programs in the Study of Teaching: A Contemporary Perspective." *Handbook of Research on Teaching*. Ed. Merlin C. Whitrock. New York: Macmillan, 1986. 3–36.

United States. Cong. House Select Committee on Children, Youth, and Families. *College Education: Paying More and Getting Less*. 102nd Cong. Washington: GPO, 1992.

Witherell, Carol, and Ned Noddings. Eds. *Stories Lives Tell: Narrative and Dialogue in Education*. New York: Teachers College Press, 1991.

Wolf, Kenneth P. "The Schoolteacher's Portfolio: Practical Issues in Design, Implementation and Evaluation." *Phi Delta Kappan*, October 1991. 129–136.

———. *Teaching Portfolios: Synthesis of Research and Annotated Bibliography*. San Francisco: Far West Laboratory for Educational Research and Development, 1991.

Anson's Insights as a Resource for Your Teaching

1. Consider compiling a teaching portfolio and reflect on the context in which you would create and use it. Who will be your audience? What do you think their foremost questions will be as they study your portfolio? What primary messages do you want your portfolio to convey?

2. What will you include in your portfolio, and why? How will you arrange its contents? What broader principles will provide the basis for assembling these materials?

Anson's Insights as a Resource for Your Writing Classroom

1. Anson suggests that "an agenda of research and development for the teaching portfolio within the field of composition might begin by acknowledging that no monolithic concept of 'good teaching' exists." Ask students how they define "good teaching." In a journal entry for your teaching portfolio, reflect on your own teaching practices in light of the discussion. In what ways do you meet — or fail to meet — your students' expectations of a good teacher? How might you change your practices to better meet their needs?

2. Create a discussion group in which colleagues share each other's portfolios. Dialogue about classroom practices can lead to the

discovery of new practices or twists on familiar activities to add to your repertoire. Experiment with at least one teaching strategy or classroom activity that you learned from a colleague and reflect on the results in your portfolio.

Rhetoric and Ideology in the Writing Class

James A. Berlin

This classic essay provides an introduction to the theories that Berlin developed fully in his 1987 book Rhetoric and Reality: Writing Instruction in American Colleges, 1900–1985. *According to Berlin, an ideology addresses three questions: What exists? What is good? What is possible? Berlin suggests that there are three competing ideologies of writing instruction in our time: (1) cognitivist, (2) expressionist, and (3) social-epistemic. Each of these three ideologies carries its own notion of what writing is, what good writing and teaching are, and what we should aspire to accomplish with our students. Each of the three also represents a political stance, a take on the power relations that exist among author, audience, and text, as well as between teacher and student. This valuable essay can be used as a bibliography for further reading about these different approaches.*

The question of ideology has never been far from discussions of writing instruction in the modern American college. It is true that some rhetorics have denied their imbrication in ideology, doing so in the name of a disinterested scientism — as seen, for example, in various manifestations of current-traditional rhetoric. Most, however, have acknowledged the role of rhetoric in addressing competing discursive claims of value in the social, political, and cultural. This was particularly evident during the sixties and seventies, for example, as the writing classroom became one of the public areas for considering such strongly contested issues as Vietnam, civil rights, and economic equality. More recently the discussion of the relation between ideology and rhetoric has taken a new turn. Ideology is here foregrounded and problematized in a way that situates rhetoric within ideology, rather than ideology within rhetoric. In other words, instead of rhetoric acting as the transcendental recorder or arbiter of competing ideological claims, rhetoric is regarded as always already ideological. This position means that any examination of a rhetoric must first consider the ways its very discursive structure can be read so as to favor one version of economic, social, and political arrangements over other versions. A rhetoric then considers competing claims in these three realms from an ideological perspective made possible both by its constitution and by its application — the dialectical interaction between the rhetoric as text and the interpretive practices brought to it. A rhetoric can never be innocent, can never be a disinterested arbiter of the ideological claims of others because it is always already serving certain ideological claims. This perspective on ideology and rhetoric will be discussed in greater detail later. Here I merely wish to note that it has been forwarded most recently by such figures as Patricia Bizzell, David Bartholomae, Greg Myers, Victor Vitanza, and John Clifford and John Schilb. I have also called upon it in my monograph on writing instruction in twentieth-century American colleges. I would like to bring the discussion I began there up to date, focusing on ideology in the three rhetorics that have emerged as most conspicuous in classroom practices today: the rhetorics of cognitive psychology, of expressionism, and of a category I will call social-epistemic.

Each of these rhetorics occupies a distinct position in its relation to ideology. From the perspective offered here, the rhetoric of cognitive psychology refuses the ideological question altogether, claiming for itself the transcendent neutrality of science. This rhetoric is nonetheless easily preempted by a particular ideological position now in ascendancy because it encourages discursive practices that are compatible with dominant economic, social, and political formations. Expressionistic rhetoric, on the other hand, has always openly admitted its ideological predilections, opposing itself in no uncertain terms to the scientism of current-traditional rhetoric and the ideology it encourages. This rhetoric is, however, open to appropriation by the very forces it opposes in contradiction to its best intentions. Social-epistemic rhetoric is an alternative that is self-consciously aware of its ideological stand, making the very question of ideology the center of classroom activities, and in so doing providing itself a defense against preemption and a strategy for self-criticism and self-correction. This third rhetoric is the one I am forwarding here, and it provides the ground of my critique of its alternatives. In other words, I am arguing from ideology, contending that no other kind of argument is possible — a position that must first be explained.

Ideology is a term of great instability. This is true whether it is taken up by the Left or Right — as demonstrated, for example, by Raymond Williams in *Keywords* and *Marxism and Literature* and by Jorge Larrain in *The Concept of Ideology*. It is thus necessary to indicate at the outset the formulation that will be followed in a given discussion. Here I will rely on Göran Therborn's usage in *The Ideology of Power and the Power of Ideology*. Therborn, a Marxist sociologist at the University of Lund, Sweden, calls on the discussion of ideology found in Louis Althusser and on the discussion of power in Michel Foucault. I have chosen Therborn's adaptation of Althusser rather than Althusser himself because Therborn so effectively counters the ideology-science distinction of his source, a stance in which ideology is always false consciousness while a particular version of Marxism is defined as its scientific alternative in possession of objective truth. For Therborn, no position can lay claim to absolute, timeless truth, because finally all formulations are historically specific, arising out of the material conditions of a particular time and place. Choices in the economic, social, political, and cultural are thus always based on discursive practices that are interpretations, not mere transcriptions of some external, verifiable certainty. The choice for Therborn then is never between scientific truth and ideology, but between competing ideologies, competing discursive interpretations. Finally, Therborn calls upon Foucault's "micropolitics of power" (7) without placing subjects within a seamless web of inescapable, wholly determinative power relations. For Therborn, power can be identified and resisted in a meaningful way.

Therborn offers an especially valuable discussion for rhetoricians because of his emphasis on the discursive and dialogic nature of ideology. In other words, Therborn insists that ideology is transmitted through language practices that are always the center of conflict and contest:

> The operation of ideology in human life basically involves the constitution and patterning of how human beings live their lives as conscious, reflecting initiators of acts in a structured, meaningful world. Ideology operates as discourse, addressing or, as Althusser puts it, interpellating human beings as subjects. (15)

Conceived from the perspective of rhetoric, ideology provides the language to define the subject (the self), other subjects, the material world, and the relation of all of these to each other. Ideology is thus inscribed in language practices, entering all features of our experience.

Ideology for Therborn addresses three questions: "What exists? What is good? What is possible?" The first deals with epistemology, as Therborn explains: "what exists, and its corollary, what does not exist: that is, who we are, what the world is, what nature, society, men and women are like. In this way we acquire a sense of identity, becoming conscious of what is real and true; the visibility of the world is thereby structured by the distribution of spotlights, shadows, and darkness." Ideology thus interpellates the subject in a manner that determines what is real and what is illusory, and, most important, what is experienced and what remains outside the field of phenomenological experience, regardless of its actual material existence. Ideology also provides the subject with standards for making ethical and aesthetic decisions: "*what is good,* right, just, beautiful, attractive, enjoyable, and its opposites. In this way our desires become structured and normalized." Ideology provides the structure of desire, indicating what we will long for and pursue. Finally, ideology defines the limits of expectation: "*what is possible* and impossible; our sense of the mutability of our being-in-the-world and the consequences of change are hereby patterned, and our hopes, ambitions, and fears given shape" (18). This last is especially important since recognition of the existence of a condition (poverty, for example) and the desire for its change will go for nothing if ideology indicates that a change is simply not possible (the poor we have always with us). In other words, this last mode of interpellation is especially implicated in power relationships in a group or society, in deciding who has power and in determining what power can be expected to achieve.

Ideology always carries with it strong social endorsement, so that what we take to exist, to have value, and to be possible seems necessary, normal, and inevitable — in the nature of things. Ideology also, as we have seen, always includes conceptions of how power should — again, in the nature of things — be distributed in a society. Power here means political force but covers as well social forces in everyday contacts. Power is an intrinsic part of ideology, defined and reinforced by it, determining, once again, who can act and what can be accomplished. These power relationships, furthermore, are inscribed in the discursive practices of daily experience — in the ways we use language and are used (interpellated) by it in ordinary parlance. Finally, it should be noted that ideology is always pluralistic, a given historical moment displaying a variety of competing ideologies and a given individual reflecting one or another permutation of these conflicts, although the overall effect of these permutations tends to support the hegemony of the dominant class.

Cognitive Rhetoric

Cognitive rhetoric might be considered the heir apparent of current-traditional rhetoric, the rhetoric that appeared in conjunction with the new American university system during the final quarter of the last century. As Richard Ohmann has recently reminded us, this university was a response to the vagaries of competitive capitalism, the recurrent cycles of boom and bust that characterized the nineteenth-century economy. The university was an important part of the strategy to control this economic instability. Its role was to provide a center for experts engaging in "scientific" research designed to establish a body of knowledge that would rationalize all features of production, making it more efficient, more manageable, and, of course, more profitable. These experts were also charged with preparing the managers who were to take this new body of practical knowledge into the marketplace. The old nineteenth-century college had prepared an elite to assume its rightful place of leadership in church and state. The economic ideal outside the college was entirely separate, finding its fulfillment in the self-made, upwardly mobile entrepreneur who strikes it rich. The academic and the economic remained divided and discrete. In the new university, the two were joined as the path to success became a university degree in one of the new scientific specialities proven to be profitable in the world of industry and commerce. The new middle class of certified meritocrats had arrived. As I have indicated in my monograph on the nineteenth century, current-traditional rhetoric with its positivistic epistemology, its pretensions to scientific precision, and its managerial orientation was thoroughly compatible with the mission of this university.

Cognitive rhetoric has made similar claims to being scientific, although the method called upon is usually grounded in cognitive psychology. Janet Emig's *The Composing Process of Twelfth Graders* (1971), for example, attempted an empirical examination of the way students compose, calling on the developmental psychology of Jean Piaget in guiding her observations. In studying the cognitive skills observed in the composing behavior of twelve high school students, Emig was convinced that she could arrive at an understanding of the entire rhetorical context — the role of reality, audience, purpose, and even language in the composing act. Richard Larson was equally ambitious as throughout the seventies he called upon the developmental scheme of Jerome Bruner (as well as other psychologists) in proposing a problem-solving approach to writing, once again focusing on cognitive structures in arriving at an understanding of how college students compose. James Moffett and James Britton used a similar approach in dealing with the writing of students in grade school. For cognitive rhetoric, the structures of the mind correspond in perfect harmony with the structures of the material world, the minds of the audience, and the units of language (see my *Rhetoric and Reality* for a fuller discussion of this history). This school has been the strongest proponent of addressing the "process" rather than the "product" of writing in the classroom — although other theories have also supported this position even as they put forward a different process. Today the cognitivists continue to be a strong force in composition studies. The leading experimental research in this area is found in the work of Linda Flower and John Hayes, and I would like to focus the discussion of the relation of ideology and cognitive rhetoric on their contribution.

There is no question that Flower considers her work to fall within the domain of science, admitting her debt to cognitive psychology (Hayes's area of specialization), which she describes as "a young field — a reaction, in part, against assumptions of behaviorism" (vii). Her statements about the composing process of writing, furthermore, are based on empirical findings, on "data-based" study, specifically the analysis of protocols recording the writing choices of both experienced and inexperienced writers. This empirical study has revealed to Flower and Hayes — as reported in "A Cognitive Process Theory of Writing" — that there are three elements involved in composing: the task environment, including such external constraints as the rhetorical problem and the text so far produced; the writer's long-term memory, that is, the knowledge of the subject considered and the knowledge of how to write; and the writing processes that go on in the writer's mind. This last is, of course, of central importance to them, based as it is on the invariable structures of the mind that operate in a rational, although not totally predictable, way.

The mental processes of writing fall into three stages: the planning stage, further divided into generating, organizing, and goal setting; the translating stage, the point at which thoughts are put into words; and the reviewing stage, made up of evaluating and revising. This process is hierarchical, meaning that "components of the process [are] imbedded within other components" (Flower and Hayes 375), and it is recursive, the stages repeating themselves, although in no predetermined order. In other words, the elements of the process can be identified and their functions described, but the order of their operation will vary from task to task and from individual to individual, even though the practices of good writers will be very similar to each other (for a rich critique, see Bizzell). The "keystone" of the cognitive process theory, Flower and Hayes explain, is the discovery that writing is a goal-directed process: "In the act of composing, writers create a hierarchical network of goals and these in turn guide the writing process." Because of this goal-directedness, the protocols of good writers examined consistently "reveal a coherent underlying structure" (377).

It is clear from this brief description that Flower and Hayes focus on the individual mind, finding in the protocol reports evidence of cognitive structures in operation. Writing becomes, as Flower's textbook indicates, just another instance of "problem-solving processes people use every day," most importantly the processes of experts, such as "master chess players, inventors, successful scientists, business managers, and artists" (Flower 2–3). Flower's textbook says little about artists, however, focusing instead on "real-world" writing. She has accordingly called upon the help of a colleague from the School of Industrial Management (vi), and she includes a concern for consulting reports and proposals as well as ordinary academic research reports — "the real world of college and work" (4). This focus on the professional activity of experts is always conceived in personal and managerial terms: "In brief, the goal of this book is to help you gain more control of your own composing process: to become more efficient as a writer and more effective with your readers" (2). And the emphasis is on self-made goals, "on your own goals as a writer, on what you want to do and say" (3).

As I said at the outset, the rhetoric of cognitive psychology refuses the ideological question, resting secure instead in its scientific examination of the composing process. It is possible, however, to see this rhetoric as being eminently suited to appropriation by the proponents of a particular ideological stance, a stance consistent with the modern college's commitment to preparing students for the world of corporate capitalism. And as we have seen above, the professional orientation of *Problem-Solving Strategies for Writing* — its preoccupation with "analytical writing" (4) in the "real world" of experts — renders it especially open to this appropriation.

For cognitive rhetoric, the real is the rational. As we observed above, for Flower and Hayes the most important features of composing are those which can be analyzed into discrete units and expressed in linear, hierarchical terms, however unpredictably recursive these terms may be. The mind is regarded as a set of structures that performs in a rational manner, adjusting and reordering functions in the service of the goals of the individual. The goals themselves are considered unexceptionally apparent in the very nature of things, immediately identifiable as worthy of pursuit. Nowhere, for example, do Flower and Hayes question the worth of the goals pursued by the manager, scientist, or writer. The business of cognitive psychology is to enable us to learn to think in a way that will realize goals, not deliberate about their value: "I have assumed that, whatever your goals, you are interested in discovering better ways to achieve them" (Flower and Hayes 1). The world is correspondingly structured to foreground goals inherently worth pursuing — whether these are private or professional, in writing or in work. And the mind is happily structured to perceive these goals and, thanks to the proper cognitive development of the observer — usually an expert — to attain them. Obstacles to achieving these goals are labelled "problems," disruptions in the natural order, impediments that must be removed. The strategies to resolve these problems are called "heuristics," discovery procedures that "are the heart of problem solving" (36). Significantly, these heuristics are not themselves rational, are not linear and predictable — "they do not come with a guarantee" (37). They appear normally as unconscious, intuitive processes that problem solvers use without realizing it, but even when formulated for conscious application they are never foolproof. Heuristics are only as good or bad as the person using them, so that problem solving is finally the act of an individual performing in isolation, solitary and alone (see Brodkey). As Flower explains: "Good writers not only have a large repertory of powerful strategies, but they have sufficient self-awareness of their own process to draw on these alternative techniques as they need them. In other words, they guide their own creative process" (37). The community addressed enters the process only after problems are analyzed and solved, at which time the concern is "adapting your writing to the needs of the reader" (1). Furthermore, although the heuristics used in problem solving are not themselves rational, the discoveries made through them always conform to the mensurable nature of reality, displaying "an underlying hierarchical organization" (10) that reflects the rationality of the world. Finally, language is regarded as a system of rational signs that is compatible with the mind and the external world, enabling the "translating" or "transforming" of the nonverbal intellectual operations into the verbal. There is thus a beneficent correspondence between the structures of the mind, the structures of the world, the structures of the minds of the audience, and the structures of language.

This entire scheme can be seen as analogous to the instrumental method of the modern corporation, the place where members of the meritocratic middle class, the 20 percent or so of the work force of certified college graduates, make a handsome living managing a capitalist economy (see Braverman ch. 18). Their work life is designed to turn goal-seeking and problem-solving behavior into profits. As we have seen in Flower, the rationalization of the writing process is specifically designated an extension of the rationalization of economic activity. The pursuit of self-evident and unquestioned goals in the composing process parallels the pursuit of self-evident and unquestioned profit-making goals in the corporate marketplace: "whatever your goals are, you are interested in achieving better ways to achieve them" (Flower 12). The purpose of writing is to create a commodified text (see Clines) that belongs to the individual and has exchange value — "problem solving turns composing into a goal-directed journey — writing my way to where I want to be" (4) — just as the end of corporate activity is to create a privately-owned profit. Furthermore, while all problem solvers use heuristic procedures — whether in solving hierarchically conceived writing problems or hierarchically conceived management problems — some are better at using them than are others. These individuals inevitably distinguish themselves, rise up the corporate ladder, and leave the less competent and less competitive behind. The class system is thus validated since it is clear that the rationality of the universe is more readily detected by a certain group of individuals. Cognitive psychologists specializing in childhood development can even isolate the environmental features of the children who will become excellent problem solvers, those destined to earn the highest grades in school, the highest college entrance scores, and, finally, the highest salaries. Middle-class parents are thus led to begin the cultivation of their children's cognitive skills as soon as possible — even in utero — and of course there are no shortage of expert-designed commodities that can be purchased to aid in the activity. That the cognitive skills leading to success may be the product of the experiences of a particular social class rather than the perfecting of inherent mental structures, skills encouraged because they serve the interests of a ruling economic elite, is never considered in the "scientific" investigation of the mind.

Cognitive rhetoric can be seen from this perspective as compatible with the ideology of the meritocratic university described in Bowles and Gintis's *Schooling in Capitalist America*. Power in this system is relegated to university-certified experts, those individuals who have the cognitive skills and the training for problem solving. Since social, political, and cultural problems are, like the economic, the result of failures in rational goal-seeking behavior, these same experts are the best prepared to address these matters as well. Furthermore, the agreement of experts in addressing commonly shared problems in the economic and political arenas is additional confirmation of their claim to power: all trained observers, after all, come to the same conclusions. Once again, the possibility that this consensus about what is good and possible is a product of class interest and class experience is never seriously entertained. Cognitive rhetoric, then, in its refusal of the ideological question leaves itself open to association with the reification of technocratic science characteristic of late capitalism, as discussed, for example, by Georg Lukács, Herbert Marcuse, and Jürgen Habermas (see Larrain ch. 6). Certain structures of the material world, the mind, and language, and their correspondence with certain goals, problem-solving heuristics, and solutions in the economic, social, and political are regarded as inherent features of the universe, existing apart from human social intervention. The existent, the good, and the possible are inscribed in the very nature of things as indisputable scientific facts, rather than being seen as humanly devised social constructions always remaining open to discussion.

Expressionistic Rhetoric

Expressionistic rhetoric developed during the first two decades of the twentieth century and was especially prominent after World War I. Its earliest predecessor was the elitist rhetoric of liberal culture, a scheme arguing for writing as a gift of genius, an art accessible only to a few, and then requiring years of literary study. In expressionistic rhetoric, this gift is democratized, writing becoming an art of which all are capable. This rhetoric has usually been closely allied with theories of psychology that argued for the inherent goodness of the individual, a goodness distorted by excessive contact with others in groups and institutions. In this it is the descendant of Rousseau on the one hand and of the romantic recoil from the urban horrors created by nineteenth-century capitalism on the other. Left to our own devices, this position maintains, each of us would grow and mature in harmony. Unfortunately, hardly anyone is allowed this uninhibited development, and so the fallen state of society is both the cause and the effect of its own distortion, as well as the corrupter of its individual members. In the twenties, a bowdlerized version of Freud was called upon in support of this conception of human nature. More recently — during the sixties and after — the theories of such figures as Carl Rogers, Abraham Maslow, Eric Fromm, and even Carl Jung have been invoked in its support. (For a fuller discussion of the history and character of expressionistic rhetoric offered here, see my "Contemporary Composition," and *Rhetoric and Reality* 43–46, 73–81, 159–65.)

For this rhetoric, the existent is located within the individual subject. While the reality of the material, the social, and the linguistic are never denied, they are considered significant only insofar as they serve the needs of the individual. All fulfill their true function only when being exploited in the interests of locating the individual's authentic nature. Writing can be seen as a paradigmatic instance of this activity. It is an art, a creative act in which the process — the discovery of the true self — is as important as the product — the self discovered and expressed. The individual's use of the not-self in discovering the self takes place in a specific way. The material world provides sensory images that can be used in order to explore the self, the sensations leading to the apprehending-source of all experience. More important, these sense impressions can be coupled with language to provide metaphors to express the experience of the self, an experience which transcends ordinary non-metaphoric language but can be suggested through original figures and tropes. This original language in turn can be studied by others to understand the self and can even awaken in readers the experience of their selves. Authentic self-expression can thus lead to authentic self-experience for both the writer and the reader. The most important measure of authenticity, of genuine self-discovery and self-revelation, furthermore, is the presence of originality in expression; and this is the case whether the writer is creating poetry or writing a business report. Discovering the true self in writing will simultaneously enable the individual to discover the truth of the situation which evoked the writing, a situation that, needless to say, must always be compatible with the development of the self, and this leads to the ideological dimension of the scheme.

Most proponents of expressionistic rhetoric during the sixties and seventies were unsparingly critical of the dominant social, political, and cultural practices of the time. The most extreme of these critics demanded that the writing classroom work explicitly toward liberating students from the shackles of a corrupt society. This is seen most vividly in the effort known as "composition as happening." From this perspective, the alienating and fragmenting experience of the authoritarian institutional setting can be resisted by providing students with concrete experiences that alter political consciousness through challenging official versions of reality. Writing in response to such activities as making collages and sculptures, listening to the same piece of music in different settings, and engaging in random and irrational acts in the classroom was to enable students to experience "structure in unstructure; a random series of ordered events; order in chaos; the logical illogicality of dreams" (Lutz 35). The aim was to encourage students to resist the "interpretations of experience embodied in the language of others [so as] to order their own experience" (Paull and Kligerman). This more extreme form of political activism in the classroom was harshly criticized by the moderate wing of the expressionist camp, and it is this group that eventually became dominant. The names of Ken Macrorie, Walker Gibson, William Coles, Jr., Donald Murray, and Peter Elbow were the most visible in this counter effort. Significantly, these figures continued the ideological critique of the dominant culture while avoiding the overt politicizing of the classroom. In discussing the ideological position they encouraged, a position that continues to characterize them today, I will focus on the work of Murray and Elbow, both of whom explicitly address the political in their work.

From this perspective, power within society ought always to be vested in the individual. In Elbow, for example, power is an abiding concern — apparent in the title to his recent textbook *(Writing with Power)*, as well as in the opening pledge of his first to help students become "less helpless, both personally and politically" by enabling them to get "control over words" *(Writing without Teachers* vii). This power is consistently defined in personal terms: "power comes from the words somehow fitting the *writer* (not necessarily the reader) . . . power comes from the words somehow fitting *what they are about*" *(Writing with Power* 280). Power is a product of a configuration involving the individual and her encounter with the world, and for both Murray and

Elbow this is a function of realizing one's unique voice. Murray's discussion of the place of politics in the classroom is appropriately titled "Finding Your Own Voice: Teaching Composition in an Age of Dissent," and Elbow emphasizes, "If I want power, I've got to use *my* voice" (*Embracing Contraries* 202). This focus on the individual does not mean that no community is to be encouraged, as expressionists repeatedly acknowledge that communal arrangements must be made, that, in Elbow's words, "the less acceptable hunger for participation and merging is met" (98). The community's right to exist, however, stands only insofar as it serves all of its members as individuals. It is, after all, only the individual, acting alone and apart from others, who can determine the existent, the good, and the possible. For Murray, the student "must hear the contradictory counsel of his readers, so that he learns when to ignore his teachers and his peers, listening to himself after evaluating what has been said about his writing and considering what he can do to make it work" ("Finding Your Own Voice"). For Elbow, the audience can be used to help improve our writing, but "the goal should be to move toward the condition where we don't necessarily need it in order to speak or write well." Since audiences can also inhibit us, Elbow continues, "we need to learn to write what is true and what needs saying even if the whole world is scandalized. We need to learn eventually to find in *ourselves* the support which — perhaps for a long time —we must seek openly from others" (*Writing with Power* 190).

Thus, political change can only be considered by individuals and in individual terms. Elbow, for example, praises Freire's focus on the individual in seeking the contradictions of experience in the classroom but refuses to take into account the social dimension of this pedagogy, finally using Freire's thought as an occasion for arriving at a personal realization of a "psychological contradiction, not an economic one or political one," at the core of our culture (*Embracing Contraries* 98). The underlying conviction of expressionists is that when individuals are spared the distorting effects of a repressive social order, their privately determined truths will correspond to the privately determined truths of all others: my best and deepest vision supports the same universal and eternal laws as everyone else's best and deepest vision. Thus, in *Writing without Teachers* Elbow admits that his knowledge about writing was gathered primarily from personal experience, and that he has no reservations about "making universal generalizations upon a sample of one" (16). Murray is even more explicit in his first edition of *A Writer Teaches Writing:* "the writer is on a search for himself. If he finds himself he will find an audience, because all of us have the same common core. And when he digs deeply into himself and is able to define himself, he will find others who will read with a shock of recognition what he has written" (4).

This rhetoric thus includes a denunciation of economic, political, and social pressures to conform — to engage in various forms of corporate-sponsored thought, feeling, and behavior. In indirectly but unmistakably decrying the dehumanizing effects of industrial capitalism, expressionistic rhetoric insists on defamiliarizing experience, on getting beyond the corruptions of the individual authorized by the language of commodified culture in order to re-experience the self and through it the external world, finding in this activity possibilities for a new order. For expressionistic rhetoric, the correct response to the imposition of current economic, political, and social arrangements is thus resistance, but a resistance that is always construed in individual terms. Collective retaliation poses as much of a threat to individual integrity as do the collective forces being resisted, and so is itself suspect. The only hope in a society working to destroy the uniqueness of the individual is for each of us to assert our individuality against the tyranny of the authoritarian corporation, state, and society. Strategies for doing so must of course be left to the individual, each lighting one small candle in order to create a brighter world.

Expressionistic rhetoric continues to thrive in high schools and at a number of colleges and universities. At first glance, this is surprising, unexpected of a rhetoric that is openly opposed to establishment practices. This subversiveness, however, is more apparent than real. In the first place, expressionistic rhetoric is inherently and debilitatingly divisive of political protest, suggesting that effective resistance can only be offered by individuals, each acting alone. Given the isolation and incoherence of such protest, gestures genuinely threatening to the establishment are difficult to accomplish. Beyond this, expressionistic rhetoric is easily co-opted by the very capitalist forces it opposes. After all, this rhetoric can be used to reinforce the entrepreneurial virtues capitalism most values: individualism, private initiative, the confidence for risk taking, the right to be contentious with authority (especially the state). It is indeed not too much to say that the ruling elites in business, industry, and government are those most likely to nod in assent to the ideology inscribed in expressionistic rhetoric. The members of this class see their lives as embodying the creative realization of the self, exploiting the material, social, and political conditions of the world in order to assert a private vision, a vision which, despite its uniqueness, finally represents humankind's best nature. (That this vision in fact represents the interests of a particular class, not all classes, is of course not acknowledged.) Those who have not attained the positions which enable them to exert this freedom have been prevented from doing so, this ideology argues, not by economic and class constraints, but by their own unwillingness to pursue a private vision, and this interpretation is often embraced by those excluded from the ruling elite as well as by the ruling elite itself. In other words, even those most constrained by their positions in the class structure may support the ideology found in expressionistic rhetoric in some form. This is most commonly done by divorcing the self from the alienation of work, separating work experience from other experience so that self-discovery and -fulfillment take place away from the job. For some this may lead to the pursuit of self-expression in intellectual or aesthetic pursuits. For most this quest results in a variety of forms of consumer behavior, identifying individual self-expression with the consumption of some commodity. This separation of work from authentic human activity is likewise reinforced in expressionistic rhetoric, as a glance at any of the textbooks it has inspired will reveal.

Social-Epistemic Rhetoric

The last rhetoric to be considered I will call social-epistemic rhetoric, in so doing distinguishing it from the psychological-epistemic rhetoric that I am convinced is a form of expressionism. (The latter is found in Kenneth Dowst and in Cyril Knoblauch and Lil Brannon, although Knoblauch's recent *College English* essay displays him moving into the social camp. I have discussed the notion of epistemic rhetoric and these two varieties of it in *Rhetoric and Reality* 145–55, 165–77, and 184–85.) There have been a number of spokespersons for social-epistemic rhetoric over the last twenty years: Kenneth Burke, Richard Ohmann, the team of Richard Young, Alton Becker and Kenneth Pike, Kenneth Bruffee, W. Ross Winterowd, Ann Berthoff, Janice Lauer, and, more recently, Karen Burke Lefevre, Lester Faigley, David Bartholomae, Greg Myers, Patricia Bizzell, and others. In grouping these figures together I do not intend to deny their obvious disagreements with each other. For example, Myers, a Leftist, has offered a lengthy critique of Bruffee, who — along with Winterowd and Young, Becker and Pike — is certainly of the Center politically. There are indeed as many conflicts among the members of this group as there are harmonies. They are brought together here, however, because they share a notion of rhetoric as a political act involving a dialectical interaction engaging the material, the social, and the individual writer, with language as the agency of mediation. Their positions, furthermore, include an historicist orientation, the realization that a rhetoric is an historically specific social formation that must perforce change over time; and this feature in turn makes possible reflexiveness and revision as the inherently ideological nature of rhetoric is continually acknowledged. The most complete realization of this rhetoric for the classroom is to be found in Ira Shor's *Critical Teaching and Everyday Life.* Before considering it, I would like to discuss the distinguishing features of a fully articulated social-epistemic rhetoric.

For social-epistemic rhetoric, the real is located in a relationship that involves the dialectical interaction of the observer, the discourse community (social group) in which the observer is functioning, and the material conditions of existence. Knowledge is never found in any one of these but can only be posited as a product of the dialectic in which all three come together. (More of this in a moment.) Most important, this dialectic is grounded in language: the observer, the discourse community, and the material conditions of existence are all verbal constructs. This does not mean that the three do not exist apart from language: they do. This does mean that we cannot talk and write about them — indeed, we cannot know them — apart from language. Furthermore, since language is a social phenomenon that is a product of a particular historical moment, our notions of the observing self, the communities in which the self functions, and the very structures of the material world are social constructions — all specific to a particular time and culture. These social constructions are thus inscribed in the very language we are given to inhabit in responding to our experience. Language, as Raymond Williams explains in an application of Bakhtin (*Marxism and Literature* 21–44), is one of the material and social conditions involved in producing a culture. This means that in studying rhetoric — the ways discourse is generated — we are studying the ways in which knowledge comes into existence. Knowledge, after all, is an historically bound social fabrication rather than an eternal and invariable phenomenon located in some uncomplicated repository — in the material object or in the subject or in the social realm. This brings us back to the matter of the dialectic.

Understanding this dialectical notion of knowledge is the most difficult feature of social-epistemic rhetoric. Psychological-epistemic rhetoric grants that rhetoric arrives at knowledge, but this meaning-generating activity is always located in a transcendent self, a subject who directs the discovery and arrives through it finally only at a better understanding of the self and its operation — this self-comprehension being the end of all knowledge. For social-epistemic rhetoric, the subject is itself a social construct that emerges through the linguistically circumscribed interaction of the individual, the community, and the material world. There is no universal, eternal, and authentic self that beneath all appearances is at one with all other selves. The self is always a creation of a particular historical and cultural moment. This is not to say that individuals do not ever act as individuals. It is to assert, however, that they never act with complete freedom. As Marx indicated, we make our own histories, but we do not make them just as we wish. Our consciousness is in large part a product of our material conditions. But our material conditions are also in part the products of our consciousness. Both consciousness and the material conditions influence each other, and they are both imbricated in social relations defined and worked out through language. In other words, the ways in which the subject understands and is affected by material conditions is circumscribed by socially devised definitions, by the community in which the subject lives. The community in turn is influenced by the subject and the material conditions of the moment. Thus, the perceiving subject, the discourse communities of which the subject is a part, and the material world itself are all the constructions of an historical discourse, of the ideological formulations inscribed in the language-mediated practical activity of a particular time and place. We are lodged within a hermeneutic circle, although not one that is impervious to change.

This scheme does not lead to an anarchistic relativism. It does, however, indicate that arguments based on the permanent rational structures of the universe or on the evidence of the deepest and most profound personal intuition should not be accepted without question. The material, the social, and the subjective are at once the producers and the products of ideology, and ideology must continually be challenged so as to reveal its economic and political consequences for individuals. In other words, what are the effects of our knowledge? Who benefits from a given version of truth? How are the material benefits of society distributed? What is the relation of this distribution to social relations? Do these relations encourage conflict? To whom does our knowledge designate power? In short, social-epistemic rhetoric views knowledge as an arena of ideological conflict: there are no arguments from transcendent truth since all arguments arise in ideology. It thus inevitably supports economic, social, political, and cultural democracy. Because there are no "natural laws" or "universal truths" that indicate what exists, what is good, what is possible, and how power is to be distributed, no class or group or individual has privileged access to decisions on these matters. They must be continually decided by all and for all in a way appropriate to our own historical moment. Finally, because of this historicist orientation, social-epistemic rhetoric contains within it the means for self-criticism and self-revision. Human responses to the material conditions of existence, the social relations they encourage, and the interpellations of subjects within them are always already ideological, are always already interpretations that must be constantly revised in the interests of the greater participation of all, for the greater good of all. And this of course implies an awareness of the ways in which rhetorics can privilege some at the expense of others, according the chosen few an unequal share of power, perquisites, and material benefits.

Social-epistemic rhetoric thus offers an explicit critique of economic, political, and social arrangements, the counterpart of the implicit critique found in expressionistic rhetoric. However, here the source and the solution of these arrangements are described quite differently. As Ira Shor explains, students must be taught to identify the ways in which control over their own lives has been denied them, and denied in such a way that they have blamed themselves for their powerlessness. Shor thus situates the individual within social processes, examining in detail the interferences to critical thought that would enable "students to be their own agents for social change, their own creators of democratic culture" (48). Among the most important forces preventing work toward a social order supporting the student's "full humanity" are forms of false consciousness — reification, pre-scientific thought, acceleration, mystification — and the absence of democratic practices in all areas of experience. Although Shor discusses these forms of false consciousness in their relation to working-class students, their application to all students is not hard to see, and I have selected for emphasis those features which clearly so apply.

In falling victim to reification, students begin to see the economic and social system that renders them powerless as an innate and unchangeable feature of the natural order. They become convinced that change is impossible, and they support the very practices that victimize them — complying in their alienation from their work, their peers, and their very selves. The most common form of reification has to do with the preoccupation with consumerism, playing the game of material acquisition and using it as a substitute for more self-fulfilling behavior. In pre-scientific thinking, the student is led to believe in a fixed human nature, always and everywhere the same. Behavior that is socially and self-destructive is then seen as inevitable, in the nature of things, or can be resisted only at the individual level, apart from communal activity. Another form of pre-scientific thinking is the belief in luck, in pure chance, as the source of social arrangements, such as the inequitable distribution of wealth. The loyalty to brand names, the faith in a "common sense" that supports the existing order, and the worship of heroes, such as actors and athletes, are other forms of this kind of thought, all of which prevent "the search for rational explanations to authentic problems" (66). Acceleration refers to the pace of everyday experience — the sensory bombardment of urban life and of popular forms of entertainment — which prevents critical reflection. Mystifications are responses to the problems of a capitalist society which obscure their real sources and solutions, responses based on racism, sexism, nationalism, and other forms of bigotry. Finally, students are constantly told they live in the most free, most democratic society in the world, yet they are at the same time systematically denied opportunities for "self-discipline, self-organization, collective work styles, or group deliberation" (70), instead being subjected at every turn to arbitrary authority in conducting everyday affairs.

Shor's recommendations for the classroom grow out of an awareness of these forces and are intended to counter them. The object of this pedagogy is to enable students to *"extraordinarily reexperience the ordinary"* (93), as they critically examine their quotidian experience in order to externalize false consciousness. (Shor's use of the term "critical" is meant to recall Freire as well as the practice of the Hegelian Marxists of the Frankfurt School.) The point is to "address self-in-society and social-relations-in-self" (95). The self then is regarded as the product of a dialectical relationship between the individual and the social, each given significance by the other. Self-autonomy and self-fulfillment are thus possible not through becoming detached from the social, but through resisting those social influences that alienate and disempower, doing so, moreover, in and through social activity. The liberatory classroom begins this resistance process with a dialogue that inspires "a democratic model of social relations, used to problematize the undemocratic quality of social life" (95). This dialogue — a model inspired by Paulo Freire — makes teacher and learner equals engaged in a joint practice that is "[l]oving, humble, hopeful, trusting, critical" (95). This is contrasted with the unequal power relations in the authoritarian classroom, a place where the teacher holds all power and knowledge and the student is the receptacle into which information is poured, a classroom that is "[l]oveless, arrogant, hopeless, mistrustful, acritical" (95). Teacher and student work together to shape the content of the liberatory classroom, and this includes creating the materials of study in the class — such as textbooks and media. Most important, the students are to undergo a conversion from "manipulated objects into active, critical subjects" (97), thereby empowering them to become agents of social change rather than victims. Shor sums up these elements: "social practice is studied in the name of freedom for critical consciousness; democracy and awareness develop through the form of dialogue; dialogue externalizes false consciousness, changing students from re-active objects into society-making subjects: the object-subject switch is a social psychology for empowerment; power through study creates the conditions for reconstructing social practice" (98).

This approach in the classroom requires interdisciplinary methods, and Shor gives an example from the study of the fast-food hamburger: "Concretely my class's study of hamburgers not only involved English and philosophy in our use of writing, reading, and conceptual analysis, but it also included economics in the study of the commodity relations which bring hamburgers to market, history and sociology in an assessment of what the everyday diet was like prior to the rise of the hamburger, and health science in terms of the nutritional value of the ruling burger" (114). This interdisciplinary approach to the study of the reproduction of social life can also lead to "the unveiling of hidden social history" (115), the discovery of past attempts to resist self-destructive experience. This in turn can lead to an examination of the roots of sexism and racism in our culture. Finally, Shor calls upon comedy to reunite pleasure and work, thought and feeling, and upon a resourceful use of the space of the classroom to encourage dialogue that provides students with information withheld elsewhere on campus — "informational, conceptual, personal, academic, financial" (120) — ranging from the location of free or inexpensive services to the location of political rallies.

This survey of the theory and practice of Ira Shor's classroom is necessarily brief and reductive. Still, it suggests the complexity of the behavior recommended in the classroom, behavior that is always open-ended, receptive to the unexpected, and subversive of the planned. Most important, success in this classroom can never be guaranteed. This is a place based on dialectical collaboration — the interaction of student, teacher, and shared experience within a social, interdisciplinary framework — and the outcome is always unpredictable. Yet, as Shor makes clear, the point of this classroom is that the liberated consciousness of students is the only educational objective worth considering, the only objective worth the risk of failure. To succeed at anything else is no success at all.

It should now be apparent that a way of teaching is never innocent. Every pedagogy is imbricated in ideology, in a set of tacit assumptions about what is real, what is good, what is possible, and how power ought to be distributed. The method of cognitive psychology is the most likely to ignore this contention, claiming that the rhetoric it recommends is based on an objective understanding of the unchanging structures of mind, matter, and language. Still, despite its commitment to the empirical and scientific, as we have seen, this rhetoric can easily be made to serve specific kinds of economic, social, and political behavior that works to the advantage of the members of one social class while disempowering others — doing so, moreover, in the name of objective truth. Expressionistic rhetoric is intended to serve as a critique of the ideology of corporate capitalism, proposing in its place an ideology based on a radical individualism. In the name of empowering the individual, however, its naivete about economic, social, and political arrangements can lead to the marginalizing of the individuals who would resist a dehumanizing society, rendering them ineffective through their isolation. This rhetoric also is easily co-opted by the agencies of corporate capitalism, appropriated and distorted in the service of the mystifications of bourgeois individualism. Social-epistemic rhetoric attempts to place the question of ideology at the center of the teaching of writing. It offers both a detailed analysis of dehumanizing social experience and a self-critical and overtly historicized alternative based on democratic practices in the economic, social, political, and cultural spheres. It is obvious that I find this alternative the most worthy of emulation in the classroom, all the while admitting that it is the least formulaic and the most difficult to carry out. I would also add that even those who are skeptical of the Marxian influence found in my description of this rhetoric have much to learn from it. As Kenneth Burke has shown, one does not have to accept the Marxian premise in order to realize the value of the Marxian diagnosis (109). It is likewise not necessary to accept the conclusions of Ira Shor about writing pedagogy in order to learn from his analysis of the ideological practices at work in the lives of our students and ourselves. A rhetoric cannot escape the ideological question, and to ignore this is to fail our responsibilities as teachers and as citizens.

Works Cited

Bartholomae, David. "Inventing the University." *When a Writer Can't Write: Research on Writer's Block and Other Writing Problems.* Ed. Mike Rose. New York: Guilford, 1986.

Berlin, James A. "Contemporary Composition: The Major Pedagogical Theories." *College English* 44 (1982): 765–77.

———. *Rhetoric and Reality: Writing Instruction in American Colleges, 1900–1985.* Carbondale: Southern Illinois UP, 1987.

———. *Writing Instruction in Nineteenth-Century American Colleges.* Carbondale: Southern Illinois UP, 1984.

Bizzell, Patricia. "Cognition, Convention, and Certainty: What We Need to Know about Writing." *PRETEXT* 3 (1982): 213–43.

Bowles, Samuel, and Herbert Gintis. *Schooling in Capitalist America.* New York: Basic, 1976.

Braverman, Harry. *Labor and Monopoly Capital: The Degradation of Work in the Twentieth Century.* New York: Monthly Review P, 1974.

Brodkey, Linda. "Modernism and the Scene of Writing." *College English* 49 (1987): 396–418.

Bruner, Jerome S. *The Process of Education*. Cambridge: Harvard UP, 1960.

Burke, Kenneth. *A Rhetoric of Motives*. Berkeley: U of California P, 1969.

Clifford, John, and John Schilb. "A Perspective on Eagleton's Revival of Rhetoric." *Rhetoric Review* 6 (1987): 22–31.

Clines, Ray. "Composition and Capitalism." *Progressive Composition* 14 (Mar. 1987): 4–5.

Dowst, Kenneth. "The Epistemic Approach: Writing, Knowing, and Learning." *Eight Approaches to Teaching Composition*. Ed. Timothy Donovan and Ben W. McClelland. Urbana: NCTE, 1980.

———. "An Epistemic View of Sentence Combining: A Rhetorical Perspective." *Sentence Combining: A Rhetorical Perspective*. Eds. Donald A. Daiker, Andrew Kerek, and Max Morenberg. Carbondale: Southern Illinois UP, 1986. 321–33.

Elbow, Peter. *Embracing Contraries: Explorations in Learning and Teaching*. New York: Oxford, 1981.

———. *Writing without Teachers*. New York: Oxford UP, 1973.

———. *Writing with Power: Techniques for Mastering the Writing Process*. New York: Oxford UP, 1981.

Emig, Janet. *The Composing Process of Twelfth Graders*. Research Report No. 13. Urbana: NCTE, 1971.

Flower, Linda. *Problem-Solving Strategies for Writing*. 2nd ed. San Diego: Harcourt, 1985.

Flower, Linda, and John R. Hayes. "A Cognitive Process Theory of Writing." *College Composition and Communication* 32 (1981): 365–87.

Knoblauch, C. H. "Rhetorical Constructions: Dialogue and Commitment." *College English* 50 (1988): 125–40.

Knoblauch, C. H., and Lil Brannon. *Rhetorical Traditions and the Teaching of Writing*. Upper Montclair: Boynton, 1984.

Larrain, Jorge. *The Concept of Ideology*. Athens: U of Georgia P, 1979.

Larson, Richard. "Discovery through Questioning: A Plan for Teaching Rhetorical Invention." *College English* 30 (1968): 126–34.

———. "Invention Once More: A Role for Rhetorical Analysis." *College English* 32 (1971): 665–72.

———. "Problem-Solving, Composing, and Liberal Education." *College Composition and Communication* 23 (1972): 208–10.

Lutz, William D. "Making Freshman English a Happening." *College Composition and Communication* 22 (1971): 35–38.

Murray, Donald. "Finding Your Own Voice: Teaching Composition in an Age of Dissent." *College Composition and Communication* 20 (1969): 118–23.

———. *A Writer Teaches Writing*. Boston: Houghton, 1968.

Myers, Greg. "Reality, Consensus, and Reform in the Rhetoric of Composition Teaching." *College English* 48 (1986): 154–74.

Ohmann, Richard. "Literacy, Technology, and Monopoly Capital." *College English* 47 (1985): 675–89.

Paull, Michael, and Jack Kligerman. "Invention, Composition, and the Urban College." *College English* 33 (1972): 651–59.

Shor, Ira. *Critical Teaching and Everyday Life*. 1980. Chicago: U of Chicago P, 1987.

Therborn, Göran. *The Ideology of Power and the Power of Ideology*. London: Verso, 1980.

Vitanza, Victor. "'Notes' towards Historiographies of Rhetorics; or, Rhetorics of the Histories of Rhetorics: Traditional, Revisionary, and Sub/Versive." *PRETEXT* 8 (1987): 63–125.

Williams, Raymond. *Keywords: A Vocabulary of Culture and Society.* Rev. ed. New York: Oxford UP, 1977.

———. *Marxism and Literature.* New York: Oxford UP, 1977.

Berlin's Insights as a Resource for Your Teaching

1. Make some notes on the ideology that dominates your own teaching. Which moments in your classroom practice most clearly illustrate your commitment to this ideology? What moments suggest that your classroom practice incorporates more than one ideology? While Berlin's tripartite model is a powerful tool for organizing our sense of what goes on in our classroom, actual practice is far too "messy" to be contained and fully delineated by such a simplistic model. Explore ways in which certain aspects of your teaching advance more than one ideology. Are some of your assignments driven by all three modes?

2. Which of Berlin's approaches to writing instruction do your students seem most inclined to accept? Do you have some budding expressionists in your classroom? Do you have any cognitivists on board? Consider ways of using ideological differences among your students as the basis for class discussion, even for writing.

Berlin's Insights as a Resource for Your Writing Classroom

1. Classroom reality is always more complex than any clear-cut taxonomy or model. Monitor your teaching for a few weeks to see how the more successful moments in class discussion are grounded in ideology. If you find that you get the best results when you are an expressivist, then examine what within this approach causes the success. Can it be combined with the more appealing elements of other ideologies?

2. Have students write brief, informal accounts of how they see themselves as writers. Read through these accounts with Berlin's taxonomy in mind. Which ideologies rule your students' self-conceptions? Do ideological patterns emerge in the accounts of strong students as opposed to weak students? How might you use Berlin's thinking to address weaker students?

Inventing the University

David Bartholomae

First published in 1985, David Bartholomae argues, in what is now considered to be a classic statement about the overall aims of the composition classroom, that we must, above all, enable our students to participate in the discourses of the academy. These discourses embody the "conventional" ideals of skepticism and critique and require those who participate in them to move beyond what have traditionally been considered, by comparison, naïve clichés and commonplaces that more often characterize personal writing. Bartholomae is chiefly interested in bringing students to share in the authority that the academic institution makes available; in order to do so, he argues, we must teach students to acquire those particular habits of mind that are the mark of that authority.

Education may well be, as of right, the instrument whereby every individual, in a society like our own, can gain access to any kind of discourse. But we well know that in its distribution, in what it permits and in what it prevents, it follows the well-trodden battle-lines of social conflict. Every educational system is a political means of maintaining or of modifying the appropriation of discourse, with the knowledge and the powers it carries with it.

— Foucault, *The Discourse on Language*

. . . the text is the form of the social relationships made visible, palpable, material.

— Bernstein, *Codes, Modalities and the Process of Cultural Reproduction: A Model*

I

Every time a student sits down to write for us, he has to invent the university for the occasion — invent the university, that is, or a branch of it, like history or anthropology or economics or English. The student has to learn to speak our language, to speak as we do, to try on the peculiar ways of knowing, selecting, evaluating, reporting, concluding, and arguing that define the discourse of our community. Or perhaps I should say the *various* discourses of our community, since it is in the nature of a liberal arts education that a student, after the first year or two, must learn to try on a variety of voices and interpretive schemes — to write, for example, as a literary critic one day and as an experimental psychologist the next; to work within fields where the rules governing the presentation of examples or the development of an argument are both distinct and, even to a professional, mysterious.

The student has to appropriate (or be appropriated by) a specialized discourse, and he has to do this as though he were easily and comfortably one with his audience, as though he were a member of the academy or an historian or an anthropologist or an economist; he has to invent the university by assembling and mimicking its language while finding some compromise between idiosyncrasy, a personal history, on the one hand, and the requirements of convention, the history of a discipline, on the other hand. He must learn to speak our language. Or he must dare to speak it or to carry off the bluff, since speaking and writing will most certainly be required long before the skill is "learned." And this, understandably, causes problems.

Let me look quickly at an example. Here is an essay written by a college freshman.

> In the past time I thought that an incident was creative was when I had to make a clay model of the earth, but not of the classical or your everyday model of the earth which consists of the two cores, the mantle and the crust. I thought of these things in a dimension of which it would be unique, but easy to comprehend. Of course, your materials to work with were basic and limited at the same time, but thought help to put this limit into a right attitude or frame of mind to work with the clay.
>
> In the beginning of the clay model, I had to research and learn the different dimensions of the earth (in magnitude, quantity, state of matter, etc.). After this, I learned how to put this into the clay and come up with something different than any other person in my class at the time. In my opinion, color coordination and shape was the key to my creativity of the clay model of the earth.
>
> Creativity is the venture of the mind at work with the mechanics relay to the limbs from the cranium, which stores and triggers this action. It can be a burst of energy released at a precise time a thought is being transmitted. This can cause a frenzy of the human body, but it depends on the characteristics of the individual and how they can relay the message clearly enough through mechanics of the body to us as an observer. Then we must determine if it is creative or a learned process varied by the individuals thought process. Creativity is indeed a tool which has to exist, or our world will not succeed into the future and progress like it should.

I am continually impressed by the patience and goodwill of our students. This student was writing a placement essay during freshman orientation. (The problem set to him was: "Describe a time when you did something you felt to be creative. Then, on the basis of the incident you have described, go on to draw some general conclusions about 'creativity.'") He knew that university faculty would be reading and evaluating his essay, and so he wrote for them.

In some ways it is a remarkable performance. He is trying on the discourse even though he doesn't have the knowledge that would make the discourse more than a routine, a set of conventional rituals and gestures. And he is doing this, I think, even though he *knows* he doesn't have the knowledge that would make the discourse more than a routine. He defines himself as a researcher working systematically, and not as a kid in a high school class: "I thought of these things in a dimension of . . .";"I had to research and learn the different dimensions of the earth (in magnitude, quantity, state of matter, etc.)." He moves quickly into a specialized language (his approximation of our jargon) and draws both a general, textbook-like conclusion — "Creativity is the venture of the mind at work . . ." — and a resounding peroration — "Creativity is indeed a tool which has to exist, or our world will not succeed into the future and progress like it should." The writer has even picked up the rhythm of our prose with that last "indeed" and with the qualifications and the parenthetical expressions of the opening paragraphs. And through it all he speaks with an impressive air of authority.

There is an elaborate but, I will argue, a necessary and enabling fiction at work here as the student dramatizes his experience in a "setting" — the setting required by the discourse — where he can speak to us as a companion, a fellow researcher. As I read the essay, there is only one moment when the fiction is broken, when we are addressed differently. The student says, "Of course, your materials to work with were basic and limited at the same time, but thought help to put this limit into a right attitude or frame of mind to work with the clay." At this point, I think, we become students and he the teacher giving us a lesson (as in, "You take your pencil in your right hand and put your paper in front of you"). This is, however, one of the most characteristic slips of basic writers. (I use the term "basic writers" to refer to university students traditionally placed in remedial composition courses.) It is very hard for them to take on the role — the voice, the persona — of an authority whose authority is rooted in scholarship, analysis, or research. They slip, then, into a more immediately available and realizable voice of authority, the voice of a teacher giving a lesson or the voice of a parent lecturing at the dinner table. They offer advice or homilies rather than "academic" conclusions. There is a similar break in the final paragraph, where the conclusion that pushes for a definition ("Creativity is the venture of the mind at work with the mechanics relay to the limbs from the cranium") is replaced by a conclusion that speaks in the voice of an elder ("Creativity is indeed a tool which has to exist, or our world will not succeed into the future and progress like it should").

It is not uncommon, then, to find such breaks in the concluding sections of essays written by basic writers. Here is the concluding section of an essay written by a student about his work as a mechanic. He had been asked to generalize about work after reviewing an on-the-job experience or incident that "stuck in his mind" as somehow significant.

> How could two repairmen miss a leak? Lack of pride? No incentive? Lazy? I don't know.

At this point the writer is in a perfect position to speculate, to move from the problem to an analysis of the problem. Here is how the paragraph continues, however (and notice the change in pronoun reference).

> From this point on, I take *my* time, do it right, and don't let customers
> get under *your* skin. If they have a complaint, tell them to call your boss
> and he'll be more than glad to handle it. Most important, worry about
> yourself, and keep a clear eye on everyone, for there's always someone
> trying to take advantage of you, anytime and anyplace. (Emphasis
> added)

We get neither a technical discussion nor an "academic" discussion but
a Lesson on Life.[1] This is the language he uses to address the general
question, "How could two repairmen miss a leak?" The other brand of
conclusion, the more academic one, would have required him to speak
of his experience in our terms; it would, that is, have required a special
vocabulary, a special system of presentation, and an interpretive scheme
(or a set of commonplaces) he could have used to identify and talk about
the mystery of human error. The writer certainly had access to the
range of acceptable commonplaces for such an explanation: "lack of
pride," "no incentive," "lazy." Each commonplace would dictate its own
set of phrases, examples, and conclusions; and we, his teachers, would
know how to write out each argument, just as we know how to write
out more specialized arguments of our own. A "commonplace," then, is
a culturally or institutionally authorized concept or statement that
carries with it its own necessary elaboration. We all use commonplaces
to orient ourselves in the world; they provide points of reference and a
set of "prearticulated" explanations that are readily available to organize and interpret experience. The phrase "lack of pride" carries with it
its own account of the repairman's error, just as at another point in
time a reference to "original sin" would have provided an explanation,
or just as in certain university classrooms a reference to "alienation"
would enable writers to continue and complete the discussion. While
there is a way in which these terms are interchangeable, they are not
all permissible: A student in a composition class would most likely be
turned away from a discussion of original sin. Commonplaces are the
"controlling ideas" of our composition textbooks, textbooks that not only
insist on a set form for expository writing but a set view of public life.[2]

   When the writer says, "I don't know," then, he is not saying that he
has nothing to say. He is saying that he is not in a position to carry on
this discussion. And so we are addressed as apprentices rather than as
teachers or scholars. In order to speak as a person of status or privilege, the writer can either speak to us in our terms — in the privileged
language of university discourse — or, in default (or in defiance) of that,
he can speak to us as though we were children, offering us the wisdom
of experience.

   I think it is possible to say that the language of the "Clay Model"
paper has come *through* the writer and not from the writer. The writer
has located himself (more precisely, he has located the self that is represented by the "I" on the page) in a context that is finally beyond him,
not his own and not available to his immediate procedures for invent-

ing and arranging text. I would not, that is, call this essay an example of "writer-based" prose. I would not say that it is egocentric or that it represents the "interior monologue or a writer thinking and talking to himself" (Flower, 1981, p. 63). It is, rather, the record of a writer who has lost himself in the discourse of his readers. There is a context beyond the intended reader that is not the world but a way of talking about the world, a way of talking that determines the use of examples, the possible conclusions, acceptable commonplaces, and key words for an essay on the construction of a clay model of the earth. This writer has entered the discourse without successfully approximating it.

Linda Flower (1981) has argued that the difficulty inexperienced writers have with writing can be understood as a difficulty in negotiating the transition between "writer-based" and "reader-based" prose. Expert writers, in other words, can better imagine how a reader will respond to a text and can transform or restructure what they have to say around a goal shared with a reader. Teaching students to revise for readers, then, will better prepare them to write initially with a reader in mind. The success of this pedagogy depends on the degree to which a writer can imagine and conform to a reader's goals. The difficulty of this act of imagination and the burden of such conformity are so much at the heart of the problem that a teacher must pause and take stock before offering revision as a solution. A student like the one who wrote the "Clay Model" paper is not so much trapped in a private language as he is shut out from one of the privileged languages of public life, a language he is aware of but cannot control.

II

Our students, I've said, have to appropriate (or be appropriated by) a specialized discourse, and they have to do this as though they were easily or comfortably one with their audience. If you look at the situation this way, suddenly the problem of audience awareness becomes enormously complicated. One of the common assumptions of both composition research and composition teaching is that at some "stage" in the process of composing an essay a writer's ideas or his motives must be tailored to the needs and expectations of his audience. Writers have to "build bridges" between their point of view and the reader's. They have to anticipate and acknowledge the reader's assumptions and biases. They must begin with "common points of departure" before introducing new or controversial arguments. Here is what one of the most popular college textbooks says to students.

> Once you have your purpose clearly in mind, your next task is to define and analyze your audience. A sure sense of your audience — knowing who it is and what assumptions you can reasonably make about it — is crucial to the success of your rhetoric. (Hairston, 1978, p. 107)

It is difficult to imagine, however, how writers can have a purpose before they are located in a discourse, since it is the discourse with its projects and agendas that determines what writers can and will do. The writer who can successfully manipulate an audience (or, to use a less pointed language, the writer who can accommodate her motives to her reader's expectations) is a writer who can both imagine and write from a position of privilege. She must, that is, see herself within a privileged discourse, one that already includes and excludes groups of readers. She must be either equal to or more powerful than those she would address. The writing, then, must somehow transform the political and social relationships between students and teachers.

If my students are going to write for me by knowing who I am — and if this means more than knowing my prejudices, psyching me out — it means knowing what I know; it means having the knowledge of a professor of English. They have, then, to know what I know and how I know what I know (the interpretive schemes that define the way I would work out the problems I set for them); they have to learn to write what I would write or to offer up some approximation of that discourse. The problem of audience awareness, then, is a problem of power and finesse. It cannot be addressed, as it is in most classroom exercises, by giving students privilege and denying the situation of the classroom — usually, that is, by having students write to an outsider, someone excluded from their privileged circle: "Write about 'To His Coy Mistress,' not for your teacher but for the students in your class"; "Describe Pittsburgh to someone who has never been there"; "Explain to a high school senior how best to prepare for college"; "Describe baseball to an Eskimo." Exercises such as these allow students to imagine the needs and goals of a reader, and they bring those needs and goals forward as a dominant constraint in the construction of an essay. And they argue, implicitly, what is generally true about writing — that it is an act of aggression disguised as an act of charity. What these assignments fail to address is the central problem of academic writing, where a student must assume the right of speaking to someone who knows more about baseball or "To His Coy Mistress" than the student does, a reader for whom the general commonplaces and the readily available utterances about a subject are inadequate.

Linda Flower and John Hayes, in an often quoted article (1981), reported on a study of a protocol of an expert writer (an English teacher) writing about his job for readers of *Seventeen* magazine. The key moment for this writer, who seems to have been having trouble getting started, came when he decided that teenage girls read *Seventeen*; that some teenage girls like English because it is tidy ("some of them will have wrong reasons in that English is good because it's tidy — can be a neat tidy little girl"); that some don't like it because it is "prim" and that, "By God, I can change that notion for them." Flower and Hayes's conclusion is that this effort of "exploration and consolidation" gave the writer "a new, relatively complex, rhetorically sophisticated working goal, one which encompasses plans for topic, a persona, and the audience" (p. 383).[3]

Flower and Hayes give us a picture of a writer solving a problem, and the problem as they present it is a cognitive one. It is rooted in the way the writer's knowledge is represented in the writer's mind. The problem resides there, not in the nature of knowledge or in the nature of discourse but in a mental state prior to writing. It is possible, however, to see the problem as (perhaps simultaneously) a problem in the way subjects are located in a field of discourse.

Flower and Hayes divide up the composing process into three distinct activities: "planning or goal-setting," "translating," and "reviewing." The last of these, reviewing (which is further divided into two subprocesses, "evaluating" and "revising"), is particularly powerful, for as a writer continually generates new goals, plans, and text, he is engaging in a process of learning and discovery. Let me quote Flower and Hayes's conclusion at length.

> If one studies the process by which a writer uses a goal to generate ideas, then consolidates those ideas and uses them to revise or regenerate new, more complex goals, one can see this learning process in action. Furthermore, one sees why the process of revising and clarifying goals has such a broad effect, since it is through setting these new goals that the fruits of discovery come back to inform the continuing process of writing. In this instance, some of our most complex and imaginative acts can depend on the elegant simplicity of a few powerful thinking processes. We feel that a cognitive process explanation of discovery, toward which this theory is only a start, will have another special strength. By placing emphasis on the inventive power of the writer, who is able to explore ideas, to develop, act on, test, and regenerate his or her own goals, we are putting an important part of creativity where it belongs — in the hands of the working, thinking writer. (1981, p. 386)

While this conclusion is inspiring, the references to invention and creativity seem to refer to something other than an act of writing — if writing is, finally, words on a page. Flower and Hayes locate the act of writing solely within the mind of the writer. The act of writing, here, has a personal, cognitive history but not a history as a text, as a text that is made possible by prior texts. When located in the perspective afforded by prior texts, writing is seen to exist separate from the writer and his intentions; it is seen in the context of other articles in *Seventeen*, of all articles written for or about women, of all articles written about English teaching, and so on. Reading research has made it possible to say that these prior texts, or a reader's experience with these prior texts, have bearing on how the text is read. Intentions, then, are part of the history of the language itself. I am arguing that these prior texts determine not only how a text like the *Seventeen* article will be read but also how it will be written. Flower and Hayes show us what happens in the writer's mind but not what happens to the writer as his motives are located within our language, a language with its own requirements and agendas, a language that limits what we might say and that makes us write and sound, finally, also like someone else. If you think of other accounts of the composing process — and I'm thinking of accounts as diverse as Richard Rodriguez's *Hunger of Memory* (1983) and Edward Said's *Beginnings* (1975) — you get a very different account of what happens when private motive enters into public discourse, when a personal history becomes a public account. These accounts place the writer in a history that is not of the writer's own invention; and they are chronicles of loss, violence, and compromise.

It is one thing to see the *Seventeen* writer making and revising his plans for a topic, a persona, and an audience; it is another thing to talk about discovery, invention, and creativity. Whatever plans the writer had must finally have been located in language and, it is possible to argue, in a language that is persistently conventional and formulaic. We do not, after all, get to see the *Seventeen* article. We see only the elaborate mental procedures that accompanied the writing of the essay. We see a writer's plans for a persona; we don't see that persona in action. If writing is a process, it is also a product; and it is the product, and not the plan for writing, that locates a writer on the page, that locates him in a text and a style and the codes or conventions that make both of them readable.

Contemporary rhetorical theory has been concerned with the "codes" that constitute discourse (or specialized forms of discourse). These codes determine not only what might be said but also who might be speaking or reading. Barthes (1974), for example, has argued that the moment of writing, where private goals and plans become subject to a public language, is the moment when the writer becomes subject to a language he can neither command nor control. A text, he says, in being written passes through the codes that govern writing and becomes "'de-originated,' becomes a fragment of something that has always been *already* read, seen, done, experienced" (p. 21). Alongside a text we have always the presence of "off-stage voices," the oversound of all that has been said (e.g., about girls, about English). These voices, the presence of the "already written," stand in defiance of a writer's desire for originality and determine what might be said. A writer does not write (and this is Barthes's famous paradox) but is, himself, written by the languages available to him.

It is possible to see the writer of the *Seventeen* article solving his problem of where to begin by appropriating an available discourse. Perhaps what enabled that writer to write was the moment he located himself as a writer in a familiar field of stereotypes: Readers of *Seventeen* are teenage girls; teenage girls think of English (and English teachers) as "tidy" and "prim," and, "By God, I can change that notion for them." The moment of eureka was not simply a moment of breaking through a cognitive jumble in that individual writer's mind but a moment of breaking into a familiar and established territory — one with insiders and outsiders; one with set phrases, examples, and conclusions.

I'm not offering a criticism of the morals or manners of the teacher who wrote the *Seventeen* article. I think that all writers, in order to write, must imagine for themselves the privilege of being "insiders" — that is, the privilege both of being inside an established and powerful discourse and of being granted a special right to speak. But I think that right to speak is seldom conferred on us — on any of us, teachers or students — by virtue of the fact that we have invented or discovered an original idea. Leading students to believe that they are responsible for something new or original, unless they understand what those words mean with regard to writing, is a dangerous and counterproductive practice. We do have the right to expect students to be active and engaged, but that is a matter of continually and stylistically working against the inevitable presence of conventional language; it is not a matter of inventing a language that is new.

When a student is writing for a teacher, writing becomes more problematic than it was for the *Seventeen* writer (who was writing a version of the "Describe baseball to an Eskimo" exercise). The student, in effect, has to assume privilege without having any. And since students assume privilege by locating themselves within the discourse of a particular community — within a set of specifically acceptable gestures and commonplaces — learning, at least as it is defined in the liberal arts curriculum, becomes more a matter of imitation or parody than a matter of invention and discovery.

To argue that writing problems are also social and political problems is not to break faith with the enterprise of cognitive science. In a recent paper reviewing the tremendous range of research directed at identifying general cognitive skills, David Perkins (1985) has argued that "the higher the level of competence concerned," as in the case of adult learning, "the fewer *general* cognitive control strategies there are." There comes a point, that is, where "field-specific" or "domain-specific" schemata (what I have called "interpretive strategies") become more important than general problem-solving processes. Thinking, learning, writing — all these become bound to the context of a particular discourse. And Perkins concludes:

> Instruction in cognitive control strategies tends to be organized around problem-solving tasks. However, the isolated problem is a creature largely of the classroom. The nonstudent, whether operating in scholarly or more everyday contexts, is likely to find himself or herself involved in what might be called "projects" — which might be anything from writing a novel to designing a shoe to starting a business.

It is interesting to note that Perkins defines the classroom as the place of artificial tasks and, as a consequence, has to place scholarly projects outside the classroom, where they are carried out by the "nonstudent." It is true, I think, that education has failed to involve students in scholarly projects, projects that allow students to act as though they were colleagues in an academic enterprise. Much of the written work that students do is test-taking, report, or summary — work that places them outside the official discourse of the academic community, where they are expected to admire and report on what we do, rather than inside that discourse, where they can do its work and participate in a common enterprise.[4] This, however, is a failure of teachers and curriculum designers, who speak of writing as a mode of learning but all too often represent writing as a "tool" to be used by an (hopefully) educated mind.

It could be said, then, that there is a bastard discourse peculiar to the writing most often required of students. Carl Bereiter and Marlene Scardamalia (1985) have written about this discourse (they call it "knowledge-telling"; students who are good at it have learned to cope with academic tasks by developing a "knowledge-telling strategy"), and they have argued that insistence on knowledge-telling discourse undermines educational efforts to extend the variety of discourse schemata available to students.[5] What they actually say is this:

> When we think of knowledge stored in memory we tend these days to think of it as situated in three-dimensional space, with vertical and horizontal connections between sites. Learning is thought to add not only new elements to memory but also new connections, and it is the richness and structure of these connections that would seem . . . to spell the difference between inert and usable knowledge. On this account, the knowledge-telling strategy is educationally faulty because it specifically avoids the forming of connections between previously separated knowledge sites.

It should be clear by now that when I think of "knowledge" I think of it as situated in the discourse that constitutes "knowledge" in a particular discourse community, rather than as situated in mental "knowledge sites." One can remember a discourse, just as one can remember an essay or the movement of a professor's lecture; but this discourse, in effect, also has a memory of its own, its own rich network of structures and connections beyond the deliberate control of any individual imagination.

There is, to be sure, an important distinction to be made between learning history, say, and learning to write as an historian. A student can learn to command and reproduce a set of names, dates, places, and canonical interpretations (to "tell" somebody else's knowledge); but this is not the same thing as learning to "think" (by learning to write) as an historian. The former requires efforts of memory; the latter requires a student to compose a text out of the texts that represent the primary materials of history and in accordance with the texts that define history as an act of report and interpretation.

Let me draw on an example from my own teaching. I don't expect my students to *be* literary critics when they write about *Bleak House*.

If a literary critic is a person who wins publication in a professional journal (or if he or she is one who could), the students aren't critics. I do, however, expect my students to be, themselves, invented as literary critics by approximating the language of a literary critic writing about *Bleak House*. My students, then, don't invent the language of literary criticism (they don't, that is, act on their own) but they are, themselves, invented by it. Their papers don't begin with a moment of insight, a "by God" moment that is outside of language. They begin with a moment of appropriation, a moment when they can offer up a sentence that is not theirs as though it were their own. (I can remember when, as a graduate student, I would begin papers by sitting down to write literally in the voice — with the syntax and the key words — of the strongest teacher I had met.)

What I am saying about my students' essays is that they are approximate, not that they are wrong or invalid. They are evidence of a discourse that lies between what I might call the students' primary discourse (what the students might write about *Bleak House* were they not in my class or in any class, and were they not imagining that they were in my class or in any class — if you can imagine any student doing any such thing) and standard, official literary criticism (which is imaginable but impossible to find). The students' essays are evidence of a discourse that lies between these two hypothetical poles. The writing is limited as much by a student's ability to imagine "what might be said" as it is by cognitive control strategies.[6] The act of writing takes the student away from where he is and what he knows and allows him to imagine something else. The approximate discourse, therefore, is evidence of a change, a change that, because we are teachers, we call "development." What our beginning students need to learn is to extend themselves, by successive approximations, into the commonplaces, set phrases, rituals and gestures, habits of mind, tricks of persuasion, obligatory conclusions and necessary connections that determine the "what might be said" and constitute knowledge within the various branches of our academic community.[7]

Pat Bizzell is, I think, one of the most important scholars writing now on "basic writers" (and this is the common name we use for students who are refused unrestrained access to the academic community) and on the special characteristics of academic discourse. In a recent essay, "Cognition, Convention, and Certainty: What We Need to Know about Writing" (1982a), she looks at two schools of composition research and the way they represent the problems that writing poses for writers.[8] For one group, the "inner-directed theorists," the problems are internal, cognitive, rooted in the way the mind represents knowledge to itself. These researchers are concerned with discovering the "universal, fundamental structures of thought and language" and with developing pedagogies to teach or facilitate both basic, general cognitive skills and specific cognitive strategies, or heuristics, directed to serve more specialized needs. Of the second group, the "outer-directed theorists," she says that they are "more interested in the social processes whereby language-learning and thinking capacities are shaped and used in particular communities."

> The staple activity of outer-directed writing instruction will be analysis of the conventions of particular discourse communities. For example, a main focus of writing-across-the-curriculum programs is to demystify the conventions of the academic discourse community. (1982a, p. 218)

The essay offers a detailed analysis of the way the two theoretical camps can best serve the general enterprise of composition research and composition teaching. Its agenda, however, seems to be to counter the influence of the cognitivists and to provide bibliography and encouragement to those interested in the social dimension of language learning.

As far as basic writers are concerned, Bizzell argues that the cognitivists' failure to acknowledge the primary, shaping role of convention in the act of composing makes them "particularly insensitive to the problems of poor writers." She argues that some of those problems, like the problem of establishing and monitoring overall goals for a piece of writing, can be

> better understood in terms of the unfamiliarity with the academic discourse community, combined, perhaps, with such limited experience outside their native discourse communities that they are unaware that there is such a thing as a discourse community with conventions to be mastered. What is underdeveloped is their knowledge both of the ways experience is constituted and interpreted in the academic discourse community and of the fact that all discourse communities constitute and interpret experience. (1982a, p. 230)

One response to the problems of basic writers, then, would be to determine just what the community's conventions are, so that those conventions could be written out, "demystified" and taught in our classrooms. Teachers, as a result, could be more precise and helpful when they ask students to "think," "argue," "describe," or "define." Another response would be to examine the essays written by basic writers — their approximations of academic discourse — to determine more clearly where the problems lie. If we look at their writing, and if we look at it in the context of other student writing, we can better see the points of discord that arise when students try to write their way into the university.

The purpose of the remainder of this chapter will be to examine some of the most striking and characteristic of these problems as they are presented in the expository essays of first-year college students. I will be concerned, then, with university discourse in its most generalized form — as it is represented by introductory courses — and not with the special conventions required by advanced work in the various disciplines. And I will be concerned with the difficult, and often violent accommodations that occur when students locate themselves in a discourse that is not "naturally" or immediately theirs.

III

I have reviewed 500 essays written, as the "Clay Model" essay was, in response to a question used during one of our placement exams at the University of Pittsburgh: "Describe a time when you did something you felt to be creative. Then, on the basis of the incident you have described, go on to draw some general conclusions about 'creativity.'" Some of the essays were written by basic writers (or, more properly, those essays led readers to identify the writers as basic writers); some were written by students who "passed" (who were granted immediate access to the community of writers at the university). As I read these essays, I was looking to determine the stylistic resources that enabled writers to locate themselves within an "academic" discourse. My bias as a reader should be clear by now. I was not looking to see how a writer might represent the skills demanded by a neutral language (a language whose key features were paragraphs, topic sentences, transitions, and the like — features of a clear and orderly mind). I was looking to see what happened when a writer entered into a language to locate himself (a textual self) and his subject; and I was looking to see how, once entered, that language made or unmade the writer.

Here is one essay. Its writer was classified as a basic writer and, since the essay is relatively free of sentence-level errors, that decision must have been rooted in some perceived failure of the discourse itself.

> I am very interested in music, and I try to be creative in my interpretation of music. While in high school, I was a member of a jazz ensemble. The members of the ensemble were given chances to improvise and be creative in various songs. I feel that this was a great experience for me, as well as the other members. I was proud to know that I could use my imagination and feelings to create music other than what was written.
>
> Creativity to me, means being free to express yourself in a way that is unique to you, not having to conform to certain rules and guidelines. Music is only one of the many areas in which people are given opportunities to show their creativity. Sculpting, carving, building, art, and acting are just a few more areas where people can show their creativity.
>
> Through my music I conveyed feelings and thoughts which were important to me. Music was my means of showing creativity. In whatever form creativity takes, whether it be music, art, or science, it is an important aspect of our lives because it enables us to be individuals.

Notice the key gesture in this essay, one that appears in all but a few of the essays I read. The student defines as his own that which is a commonplace. "Creativity, *to me*, means being free to express yourself in a way that is unique to you, not having to conform to certain rules and guidelines." This act of appropriation constitutes his authority; it constitutes his authority as a writer and not just as a musician (that is, as someone with a story to tell). There were many essays in the set that told only a story — where the writer established his presence as a musician or a skier or someone who painted designs on a van, but not as a person at a remove from that experience interpreting it, treating it as a metaphor for something else (creativity). Unless those stories were long, detailed, and very well told — unless the writer was doing more than saying, "I am a skier" or a musician or a van-painter — those writers were all given low ratings.

Notice also that the writer of the "Jazz" paper locates himself and his experience in relation to the commonplace (creativity is unique expression; it is not having to conform to rules or guidelines) regardless of whether the commonplace is true or not. Anyone who improvises "knows" that improvisation follows rules and guidelines. It is the power of the commonplace — its truth as a recognizable and, the writer believes, as a final statement — that justifies the example and completes the essay. The example, in other words, has value because it stands within the field of the commonplace.[9] It is not the occasion for what one might call an "objective" analysis or a "close" reading. It could also be said that the essay stops with the articulation of the commonplace. The following sections speak only to the power of that statement. The reference to "sculpting, carving, building, art, and acting" attests to the universality of the commonplace (and it attests the writer's nervousness with the status he has appropriated for himself — he is saying, "Now, I'm not the only one here who has done something unique"). The commonplace stands by itself. For this writer, it does not need to be elaborated. By virtue of having written it, he has completed the essay and established the contract by which we may be spoken to as equals: "In whatever form creativity takes, whether it be music, art, or science, it is an important aspect of *our* lives because it enables *us* to be individuals." (For me to break that contract, to argue that *my* life is not represented in that essay, is one way for me to begin as a teacher with that student in that essay.)

All of the papers I read were built around one of three commonplaces: (1) creativity is self-expression, (2) creativity is doing something new or unique, and (3) creativity is using old things in new ways. These are clearly, then, key phrases from the storehouse of things to say about creativity. I've listed them in the order of the students' ratings: A student with the highest rating was more likely to use number three than number one, although each commonplace ran across the range of possible ratings. One could argue that some standard assertions are more powerful than others, but I think the ranking simply represents the power of assertions within our community of readers. Every student was able to offer up an experience that was meant as an example of "creativity"; the lowest range of writers, then, was not represented by students who could not imagine themselves as creative people.[10]

I said that the writer of the "Jazz" paper offered up a commonplace regardless of whether it was true or not; and this, I said, was an instance of the power of a commonplace to determine the meaning of an example. A commonplace determines a system of interpretation that can be used to "place" an example within a standard system of belief. You can see a similar process at work in this essay.

> During the football season, the team was supposed to wear the same type of cleats and the same type socks, I figured that I would change this a little by wearing my white shoes instead of black and to cover up the team socks with a pair of my own white ones. I thought that this looked better than what we were wearing, and I told a few of the other people on the team to change too. They agreed that it did look better and they changed their combination to go along with mine. After the game people came up to us and said that it looked very good the way we wore our socks, and they wanted to know why we changed from the rest of the team.
>
> I feel that creativity comes from when a person lets his imagination come up with ideas and he is not afraid to express them. Once you create something to do it will be original and unique because it came about from your own imagination and if any one else tries to copy it, it won't be the same because you thought of it first from your own ideas.

This is not an elegant paper, but it seems seamless, tidy. If the paper on the clay model of the earth showed an ill fit between the writer and his project, here the discourse seems natural, smooth. You could reproduce this paper and hand it out to a class, and it would take a lot of prompting before the students sensed something fishy and one of the more aggressive ones said something like, "Sure he came up with the idea of wearing white shoes and white socks. Him and Billy 'White-Shoes' Johnson. Come on. He copied the very thing he said was his own idea, 'original and unique.'"

The "I" of this text — the "I" who "figured," "thought," and "felt" — is located in a conventional rhetoric of the self that turns imagination into origination (I made it), that argues an ethic of production (I made it and it is mine), and that argues a tight scheme of intention (I made it because I decided to make it). The rhetoric seems invisible because it is so common. This "I" (the maker) is also located in a version of history that dominates classrooms, the "great man" theory: History is rolling along (the English novel is dominated by a central, intrusive narrative presence; America is in the throes of a Great Depression; during football season the team was supposed to wear the same kind of cleats and socks) until a figure appears, one who can shape history (Henry James, FDR, the writer of the "White Shoes" paper), and everything is changed. In the argument of the "White Shoes" paper, the history goes "I figured . . . I thought . . . I told . . . They agreed . . ." and, as a consequence, "I feel that creativity *comes from when* a person lets his imagination come up with ideas and he is not afraid to express them." The act of appropriation becomes a narrative of courage and conquest. The writer was able to write that story when he was able to imagine himself in that discourse. Getting him out of it will be a difficult matter indeed.

There are ways, I think, that a writer can shape history in the very act of writing it. Some students are able to enter into a discourse but, by stylistic maneuvers, to take possession of it at the same time. They don't originate a discourse, but they locate themselves within it aggressively, self-consciously. Here is another essay on jazz, which for sake of convenience I've shortened. It received a higher rating than the first essay on jazz.

> Jazz has always been thought of as a very original creative field in music. Improvisation, the spontaneous creation of original melodies in a piece of music, makes up a large part of jazz as a musical style. I had the opportunity to be a member of my high school's jazz ensemble for three years, and became an improvisation soloist this year. Throughout the years, I have seen and heard many jazz players, both professional and amateur. The solos performed by these artists were each flavored with that particular individual's style and ideas, along with some of the conventional premises behind improvisation. This particular type of solo work is creative because it is done on the spur of the moment and blends the performer's ideas with basic guidelines.
>
> I realized my own creative potential when I began soloing. . . .
>
> My solos, just as all the solos generated by others, were original because I combined and shaped other's ideas with mine to create something completely new. Creativity is combining the practical knowledge and guidelines of a discipline with one's original ideas to bring about a new, original end result, one that is different from everyone else's. Creativity is based on the individual. Two artists can interpret the same scene differently. Each person who creates something does so by bringing out something individual in himself.

The essay is different in some important ways from the first essay on jazz. The writer of the second is more easily able to place himself in the context of an "academic" discussion. The second essay contains an "I" who realized his "creative potential" by soloing; the first contained an "I" who had "a great experience." In the second essay, before the phrase, "I had the opportunity to be a member of my high school's jazz ensemble," there is an introduction that offers a general definition of improvisation and an acknowledgment that other people have thought about jazz and creativity. In fact, throughout the essay the writer offers definitions and counterdefinitions. He is placing himself in the context of what has been said and what might be said. In the first paper, before a similar statement about being a member of a jazz ensemble, there was an introduction that locates jazz solely in the context of this individual's experience: "I am very interested in music." The writer of this first paper was authorized by who he is, a musician, rather than by what he can say about music in the context of what is generally said. The writer of the second essay uses a more specialized vocabulary; he talks about "conventional premises," "creative potential," "musical style," and "practical knowledge." And this is not just a matter of using bigger words, since these terms locate the experience in the context of a recognizable interpretive scheme — on the one hand there is tradition and, on the other, individual talent.

It could be said, then, that this essay is also framed and completed by a commonplace: "Creativity is combining the practical knowledge and guidelines of a discipline with one's original ideas to bring about a new, original end result, one that is different from everyone else's." Here, however, the argument is a more powerful one; and I mean "powerful" in the political sense, since it is an argument that complicates a "naïve" assumption (it makes scholarly work possible, in other words), and it does so in terms that come close to those used in current academic debates (over the relation between convention and idiosyncrasy or between rules and creativity). The assertion is almost consumed by the pleas for originality at the end of the sentence; but the point remains that the terms "original" and "different," as they are used at the end of the essay, are problematic, since they must be thought of in the context of "practical knowledge and guidelines of a discipline."

The key distinguishing gesture of this essay, that which makes it "better" than the other, is the way the writer works against a conventional point of view, one that is represented within the essay by conventional phrases that the writer must then work against. In his practice he demonstrates that a writer, and not just a musician, works within "conventional premises." The "I" who comments in this paper (not the "I" of the narrative about a time when he soloed) places himself self-consciously within the context of a conventional discourse about the subject, even as he struggles against the language of that conventional discourse. The opening definition of improvisation, where improvisation is defined as spontaneous creation, is rejected when the writer begins talking about "the conventional premises behind improvisation." The earlier definition is part of the conventional language of those who "have always thought" of jazz as a "very original creative field in music." The paper begins with what "has been said" and then works itself out against the force and logic of what has been said, of what is not only an argument but also a collection of phrases, examples, and definitions.

I had a teacher who once told us that whenever we were stuck for something to say, we should use the following as a "machine" for producing a paper: "While most readers of _____ have said _____, a close and careful reading shows that _____." The writer of the second paper on jazz is using a standard opening gambit, even if it is not announced with flourish. The essay becomes possible when he sets himself against what must become a "naïve" assumption — what "most people think." He has defined a closed circle for himself. In fact, you could say that he has laid the groundwork for a discipline with its own key terms ("practical knowledge," "disciplinary guidelines," and "original ideas"), with its own agenda and with its own investigative procedures (looking for common features in the work of individual soloists).

The history represented by this student's essay, then, is not the history of a musician and it is not the history of a thought being worked out within an individual mind; it is the history of work being done within and against conventional systems.

In general, as I reviewed essays for this study, I found that the more successful writers set themselves in their essays against what they defined as some more naïve way of talking about their subject — against "those who think that . . ." — or against earlier, more naïve versions of themselves — "once I thought that. . . ." By trading in one set of commonplaces at the expense of another, they could win themselves status as members of what is taken to be some more privileged group. The ability to imagine privilege enabled writing. Here is one particularly successful essay. Notice the specialized vocabulary, but notice also the way in which the text continually refers to its own language and to the language of others.

> Throughout my life, I have been interested and intrigued by music. My mother has often told me of the time, before I went to school, when I would "conduct" the orchestra on her records. I continued to listen to music and eventually started to play the guitar and the clarinet. Finally, at about the age of twelve, I started to sit down and to try to write songs. Even though my instrumental skills were far from my own high standards, I would spend much of my spare time during the day with a guitar around my neck, trying to produce a piece of music.
>
> Each of these sessions, as I remember them, had a rather set format. I would sit in my bedroom, strumming different combinations of the five or six chords I could play, until I heard a series of which sounded particularly good to me. After this, I set the music to a suitable rhythm, (usually dependent on my mood at the time), and ran through the tune until I could play it fairly easily. Only after this section was complete did I go on to writing lyrics, which generally followed along the lines of the current popular songs on the radio.
>
> At the time of the writing, I felt that my songs were, in themselves, an original creation of my own; that is, I, alone, made them. However, I now see that, in this sense of the word, I was not creative. The songs themselves seem to be an oversimplified form of the music I listened to at the time.
>
> In a more fitting sense, however, I *was* being creative. Since I did not purposely copy my favorite songs, I was, effectively, originating my songs from my own "process of creativity." To achieve my goal, I needed what a composer would call "inspiration" for my piece. In this case the inspiration was the current hit on the radio. Perhaps, with my present point of view, I feel that I used too much "inspiration" in my songs, but, at that time, I did not.
>
> Creativity, therefore, is a process which, in my case, involved a certain series of "small creations" if you like. As well, it is something, the appreciation of which varies with one's point of view, that point of view being set by the person's experience, tastes, and his own personal view of creativity. The less experienced tend to allow for less originality, while the more experienced demand real originality to classify some-

thing a "creation." Either way, a term as abstract as this is perfectly correct and open to interpretation.

This writer is consistently and dramatically conscious of herself form-ing something to say out of what has been said *and* out of what she has been saying in the act of writing this paper. "Creativity" begins in this paper as "original creation." What she thought was "creativity," how-ever, she now says was imitation; and, as she says, "in a sense of the word" she was not "creative." In another sense, however, she says that she *was* creative, since she didn't purposefully copy the songs but used them as "inspiration."

While the elaborate stylistic display — the pauses, qualifications, and the use of quotation marks — is in part a performance for our ben-efit, at a more obvious level we as readers are directly addressed in the first sentence of the last paragraph: "Creativity, therefore, is a process which, in my case, involved a certain series of 'small creations' if you like." We are addressed here as adults who can share her perspective on what she has said and who can be expected to understand her terms. If she gets into trouble after this sentence, and I think she does, it is because she doesn't have the courage to generalize from her assertion. Since she has rhetorically separated herself from her younger "self," and since she argues that she has gotten smarter, she assumes that there is some developmental sequence at work here and that, in the world of adults (which must be more complete than the world of chil-dren) there must be something like "real creativity." If her world is imperfect (if she can only talk about creation by putting the word in quotation marks), it must be because she is young. When she looks beyond herself to us, she cannot see our work as an extension of her project. She cannot assume that we too will be concerned with the prob-lem of creativity and originality. At least she is not willing to challenge us on those grounds, to generalize her argument, and to argue that even for adults creations are really only "small creations." The sense of privilege that has allowed her to expose her own language cannot be extended to expose ours.

The writing in this piece — that is, the work of the writer within the essay — goes on in spite of, or against, the language that keeps pressing to give another name to her experience as a songwriter and to bring the discussion to closure. (In comparison, think of the quick clo-sure of the "White Shoes" paper.) Its style is difficult, highly qualified. It relies on quotation marks and parody to set off the language and attitudes that belong to the discourse (or the discourses) that it would reject, that it would not take as its own proper location.

David Olson (1981) has argued that the key difference between oral language and written language is that written language separates both the producer and the receiver from the text. For my student writ-ers, this means that they had to learn that what they said (the code) was more important than what they meant (the intention). A writer, in other words, loses his primacy at the moment of writing and must begin to attend to his and his words' conventional, even physical presence on the page. And, Olson says, the writer must learn that his authority is not established through his presence but through his absence — through his ability, that is, to speak as a god-like source behind the limitations of any particular social or historical moment; to speak by means of the wisdom of convention, through the oversounds of official or authoritative utterance, as the voice of logic or the voice of the community. He concludes:

> The child's growing competence with this distinctive register of language in which both the meaning and the authority are displaced from the intentions of the speaker and lodged "in the text" may contribute to the similarly specialized and distinctive mode of thought we have come to associate with literacy and formal education. (1981, p. 110)

Olson is writing about children. His generalizations, I think I've shown, can be extended to students writing their way into the academic community. These are educated and literate individuals, to be sure, but they are individuals still outside the peculiar boundaries of the academic community. In the papers I've examined in this chapter, the writers have shown an increasing awareness of the codes (or the competing codes) that operate within a discourse. To speak with authority they have to speak not only in another's voice but through another's code; and they not only have to do this, they have to speak in the voice and through the codes of those of us with power and wisdom; and they not only have to do this, they have to do it before they know what they are doing, before they have a project to participate in, and before, at least in terms of our disciplines, they have anything to say. Our students may be able to enter into a conventional discourse and speak, not as themselves, but through the voice of the community; the university, however, is the place where "common" wisdom is only of negative values — it is something to work against. The movement toward a more specialized discourse begins (or, perhaps, best begins) both when a student can define a position of privilege, a position that sets him against a "common" discourse, and when he or she can work self-consciously, critically, against not only the "common" code but his or her own.

IV

Pat Bizzell, you will recall, argues that the problems of poor writers can be attributed both to their unfamiliarity with the conventions of academic discourse and to their ignorance that there are such things as discourse communities with conventions to be mastered. If the latter is true, I think it is true only in rare cases. All the student writers I've discussed (and, in fact, most of the student writers whose work I've seen) have shown an awareness that something special or something different is required when one writes for an academic classroom. The essays that I have presented in this chapter all, I think, give evidence of writers trying to write their way into a new community. To some degree, however, all of them can be said to be unfamiliar with the conventions of academic discourse.

Problems of convention are both problems of finish and problems of substance. The most substantial academic tasks for students, learning history or sociology or literary criticism, are matters of many courses, much reading and writing, and several years of education. Our students, however, must have a place to begin. They cannot sit through lectures and read textbooks and, as a consequence, write as sociologists or write literary criticism. There must be steps along the way. Some of these steps will be marked by drafts and revisions. Some will be marked by courses, and in an ideal curriculum the preliminary courses would be writing courses, whether housed in an English department or not. For some students, students we call "basic writers," these courses will be in a sense the most basic introduction to the language and methods of academic writing.

Our students, as I've said, must have a place to begin. If the problem of a beginning is the problem of establishing authority, of defining rhetorically or stylistically a position from which one may speak, then the papers I have examined show characteristic student responses to that problem and show levels of approximation or stages in the development of writers who are writing their way into a position of privilege.

As I look over the papers I've discussed, I would arrange them in the following order: the "White Shoes" paper; the first "Jazz" essay; the "Clay Model" paper; the second "Jazz" essay; and, as the most successful paper, the essay on "Composing Songs." The more advanced essays for me, then, are those that are set against the "naïve" codes of "everyday" life. (I put the terms "naïve" and "everyday" in quotation marks because they are, of course, arbitrary terms.) In the advanced essays one can see a writer claiming an "inside" position of privilege by rejecting the language and commonplaces of a "naïve" discourse, the language of "outsiders." The "I" of those essays locates itself against the specialized language of what is presumed to be a more powerful and more privileged community. There are two gestures present then — one imitative and one critical. The writer continually audits and pushes against a language that would render him "like everyone else" and mimics the language and interpretive systems of the privileged community.

At a first level, then, a student might establish his authority by simply stating his own presence within the field of a subject. A student, for example, writes about creativity by telling a story about a time he went skiing. Nothing more. The "I" on the page is a skier, and skiing stands as a representation of a creative act. Neither the skier nor skiing are available for interpretation; they cannot be located in an essay that is not a narrative essay (where skiing might serve metaphorically as an example of, say, a sport where set movements also allow for a personal style). Or a student, as did the one who wrote the "White Shoes" paper, locates a narrative in an unconnected rehearsal of commonplaces about creativity. In both cases, the writers have finessed the requirement to set themselves against the available utterances of the world outside the closed world of the academy. And, again, in the first "Jazz" paper, we have the example of a writer who locates himself within an available commonplace and carries out only rudimentary procedures for elaboration, procedures driven by the commonplace itself and not set against it. Elaboration, in this latter case, is not the opening up of a system but a justification of it.

At a next level I would place student writers who establish their authority by mimicking the rhythm and texture, the "sound," of academic prose, without there being any recognizable interpretive or academic project under way. I'm thinking, here, of the "Clay Model" essay. At an advanced stage, I would place students who establish their authority as *writers*; they claim their authority, not by simply claiming that they are skiers or that they have done something creative, but by placing themselves both within and against a discourse, or within and against competing discourses, and working self-consciously to claim an interpretive project of their own, one that grants them their privilege to speak. This is true, I think, in the case of the second "Jazz" paper and, to a greater degree, in the case of the "Composing Songs" paper.

The levels of development that I've suggested are not marked by corresponding levels in the type or frequency of error, at least not by the type or frequency of sentence-level error. I am arguing, then, that a basic writer is not necessarily a writer who makes a lot of mistakes. In fact, one of the problems with curricula designed to aid basic writers is that they too often begin with the assumption that the key distinguishing feature of a basic writer is the presence of sentence-level error. Students are placed in courses because their placement essays show a high frequency of such errors, and those courses are designed with the goal of making those errors go away. This approach to the problems of the basic writer ignores the degree to which error is less often a constant feature than a marker in the development of a writer. A student who can write a reasonably correct narrative may fall to pieces when faced with a more unfamiliar assignment. More important, however, such courses fail to serve the rest of the curriculum. On every campus there is a significant number of college freshmen who require a course to introduce them to the kinds of writing that are required for a university education. Some of these students can write correct sentences and some cannot; but, as a group, they lack the facility other freshmen possess when they are faced with an academic writing task.

The "White Shoes" essay, for example, shows fewer sentence-level errors than the "Clay Model" paper. This may well be due to the fact that the writer of the "White Shoes" paper stayed well within safe, familiar territory. He kept himself out of trouble by doing what he could easily do. The tortuous syntax of the more advanced papers on my list is a syntax that represents a writer's struggle with a difficult and unfamiliar language, and it is a syntax that can quickly lead an inexperienced writer into trouble. The syntax and punctuation of the "Composing Songs" essay, for example, shows the effort that is required when a writer works against the pressure of conventional discourse. If the prose is inelegant (although I confess I admire those dense sentences) it is still correct. This writer has a command of the linguistic and stylistic resources — the highly embedded sentences, the use of parentheses and quotation marks — required to complete the act of writing. It is easy to imagine the possible pitfalls for a writer working without this facility.

There was no camera trained on the "Clay Model" writer while he was writing, and I have no protocol of what was going through his mind, but it is possible to speculate on the syntactic difficulties of sentences like these: "In the past time I thought that an incident was creative was when I had to make a clay model of the earth, but not of the classical or your everyday model of the earth which consists of the two cores, the mantle and the crust. I thought of these things in a dimension of which it would be unique, but easy to comprehend." The syntactic difficulties appear to be the result of the writer's attempt to use an unusual vocabulary and to extend his sentences beyond the boundaries of what would have been "normal" in his speech or writing. There is reason to believe, that is, that the problem was with *this* kind of sentence, in this context. If the problem of the last sentence is that of holding together the units "I thought," "dimension," "unique," and "easy to comprehend," then the linguistic problem was not a simple matter of sentence construction. I am arguing, then, that such sentences fall apart not because the writer lacked the necessary syntax to glue the pieces together but because he lacked the full statement within which these key words were already operating. While writing, and in the thrust of his need to complete the sentence, he had the key words but not the utterance. (And to recover the utterance, I suspect, he would need to do more than revise the sentence.) The invisible conventions, the prepared phrases remained too distant for the statement to be completed. The writer would have needed to get inside of a discourse that he could in fact only partially imagine. The act of constructing a sentence, then, became something like an act of transcription in which the voice on the tape unexpectedly faded away and became inaudible.

Shaughnessy (1977) speaks of the advanced writer as one who often has a more facile but still incomplete possession of this prior discourse. In the case of the advanced writer, the evidence of a problem is the presence of dissonant, redundant, or imprecise language, as in a sentence such as this: "No education can be *total*, it must be *continuous*."

Such a student, Shaughnessy says, could be said to hear the "melody of formal English" while still unable to make precise or exact distinctions. And, she says, the pre-packaging feature of language, the possibility of taking over phrases and whole sentences without much thought about them, threatens the writer now as before. The writer, as we have said, inherits the language out of which he must fabricate his own messages. He is therefore in a constant tangle with the language, obliged to recognize its public, communal nature and yet driven to invent out of this language his own statements. (1977, pp. 207–08)

For the unskilled writer, the problem is different in degree and not in kind. The inexperienced writer is left with a more fragmentary record of the comings and goings of academic discourse. Or, as I said above, he or she often has the key words without the complete statements within which they are already operating.

Let me provide one final example of this kind of syntactic difficulty in another piece of student writing. The writer of this paper seems to be able to sustain a discussion only by continually repeating his first step, producing a litany of strong, general, authoritative assertions that trail quickly into confusion. Notice how the writer seems to stabilize his movement through the paper by returning again and again to recognizable and available commonplace utterances. When he has to move away from them, however, away from the familiar to statements that would extend those utterances, where he, too, must speak, the writing — that is, both the syntax and the structure of the discourse — falls to pieces.

> Many times the times drives a person's life depends on how he uses it. I would like to think about if time is twenty-five hours a day rather than twenty-four hours. Some people think it's the boaring or some people might say it's the pleasure to take one more hour for their life. But I think the time is passing and coming, still we are standing on same position. We should use time as best as we can use about the good way in our life. Everything we do, such as sleep, eat, study, play and doing something for ourselves. These take the time to do and we could find the individual ability and may process own. It is the important for us and our society. As time going on the world changes therefor we are changing, too. When these situation changes we should follow the suitable case of own. But many times we should decide what's the better way to do so by using time. Sometimes like this kind of situation can cause the success of our lives or ruin. I think every individual of his own thought drive how to use time. These affect are done from environmental causes. So we should work on the better way of our life recognizing the importance of time.

There is a general pattern of disintegration when the writer moves off from standard phrases. This sentence, for example, starts out coherently and then falls apart: "*We should use time as best as we can* use about the good way in our life." The difficulty seems to be one of extending those standard phrases or of connecting them to the main subject reference, "time" (or "the time," a construction that causes many of the problems in the paper). Here is an example of a sentence that shows, in miniature, this problem of connection: *"I think every individual of his own thought drive how to use time."*

One of the remarkable things about this paper is that, in spite of all the syntactic confusion, there is the hint of an academic project here. The writer sets out to discuss how to creatively use one's time. The text seems to allude to examples and to stages in an argument, even if in the end it is all pretty incoherent. The gestures of academic authority, however, are clearly present, and present in a form that echoes the procedures in other, more successful papers. The writer sets himself against what "some people think"; he speaks with the air of authority: "But I think. . . . Everything we do. . . . When these situation changes. . . ." And he speaks as though there were a project underway, one where he proposes what he thinks, turns to evidence, and offers a conclusion: "These affect are done from environmental causes. So we should work. . . ." This is the case of a student with the ability to imagine the general outline and rhythm of academic prose but without the ability to carry it out, to complete the sentences. And when he gets lost in the new, in the unknown, in the responsibility of his own commitment to speak, he returns again to the familiar ground of the commonplace.

The challenge to researchers, it seems to me, is to turn their attention again to products, to student writing, since the drama in a student's essay, as he or she struggles with and against the languages of our contemporary life, is as intense and telling as the drama of an essay's mental preparation or physical production. A written text, too, can be a compelling model of the "composing process" once we conceive of a writer as at work within a text and simultaneously, then, within a society, a history, and a culture.

It may very well be that some students will need to learn to crudely mimic the "distinctive register" of academic discourse before they are prepared to actually and legitimately do the work of the discourse, and before they are sophisticated enough with the refinements of tone and gesture to do it with grace or elegance. To say this, however, is to say that our students must be our students. Their initial progress will be marked by their abilities to take on the role of privilege, by their abilities to establish authority. From this point of view, the student who wrote about constructing the clay model of the earth is better prepared for his education than the student who wrote about playing football in white shoes, even though the "White Shoes" paper is relatively error-free and the "Clay Model" paper is not. It will be hard to pry loose the writer of the "White Shoes" paper from the tidy, pat discourse that allows him to dispose of the question of creativity in such a quick and efficient manner. He will have to be convinced that it is better to write sentences he might not so easily control, and he will have to be convinced that it is better to write muddier and more confusing prose (in order that it may sound like ours), and this will be harder than convincing the "Clay Model" writer to continue what he has already begun.

Acknowledgments

Preparation of this chapter was supported by the Learning Research and Development Center of the University of Pittsburgh, which is supported in part by the National Institute of Education.

Notes

1. David Olson (1981) has made a similar observation about school-related problems of language learning in younger children. Here is his conclusion: "Hence, depending upon whether children assumed language was primarily suitable for making assertions and conjectures or primarily for making direct or indirect commands, they will either find school texts easy or difficult" (p. 107).

2. For Aristotle, there were both general and specific commonplaces. A speaker, says Aristotle, has a "stock of arguments to which he may turn for a particular need."

   > If he knows the *topoi* (regions, places, lines of argument) — and a skilled speaker will know them — he will know where to find what he wants for a special case. The general topics, or *common*places, are regions containing arguments that are common to all branches of knowledge. . . . But there are also special topics (regions, places, *loci*) in which one looks for arguments appertaining to particular branches of knowledge, special sciences, such as ethics or politics. (1932, pp. 154–55)

   And, he says, "the topics or places, then, may be indifferently thought of as in the science that is concerned, or in the mind of the speaker." But the question of location is "indifferent" *only* if the mind of the speaker is in line with set opinion, general assumption. For the speaker (or writer) who is not situated so comfortably in the privileged public realm, this is indeed not an indifferent matter at all. If he does not have the commonplace at hand, he will not, in Aristotle's terms, know where to go at all.

3. Pat Bizzell has argued that the *Seventeen* writer's process of goal-setting

   > can be better understood if we see it in terms of writing for a discourse community. His initial problem . . . is to find a way to include these readers in a discourse community for which he is comfortable writing. He places them in the academic discourse community by imagining the girls as students. . . . Once he has included them in a familiar discourse community, he can find a way to address them that is common in the community: he will argue with them, putting a new interpretation on information they possess in order to correct misconceptions. (1982a, p. 228)

4. See Bartholomae (1979, 1983) and Rose (1983) for articles on curricula designed to move students into university discourse. The movement to extend writing "across the curriculum" is evidence of a general concern for locating students within the work of the university; see Bizzell (1982a) and Maimon *et al.* (1981). For longer works directed specifically at basic writing, see Ponsot and Deen (1982) and Shaughnessy (1977). For a book describing a course for more advanced students, see Coles (1978).

5. In spite of my misgivings about Bereiter and Scardamalia's interpretation of the cognitive nature of the problem of "inert knowledge," this is an essay I regularly recommend to teachers. It has much to say about the dangers of what seem to be "neutral" forms of classroom discourse and provides, in its final section, a set of recommendations on how a teacher might undo discourse conventions that have become part of the institution of teaching.

6. Stanley Fish (1980) argues that the basis for distinguishing novice from expert readings is the persuasiveness of the discourse used to present and defend a given reading. In particular, see the chapter, "Demonstration vs. Persuasion: Two Models of Critical Activity" (pp. 356–73).

7. Some students, when they come to the university, can do this better than others. When Jonathan Culler says, "the possibility of bringing someone to see that a particular interpretation is a good one assumes shared points of departure and common notions of how to read," he is acknowledging that teaching, at least in English classes, has had to assume that students, to be students, were already to some degree participating in the structures of reading and writing that constitute English studies (quoted in Fish, 1980, p. 366).

     Stanley Fish tells us "not to worry" that students will violate our enterprise by offering idiosyncratic readings of standard texts:

> The fear of solipsism, of the imposition by the unconstrained self of its own prejudices, is unfounded because the self does not exist apart from the communal or conventional categories of thought that enable its operations (of thinking, seeing, reading). Once we realize that the conceptions that fill consciousness, including any conception of its own status, are culturally derived, the very notion of an unconstrained self, of a consciousness wholly and dangerously free, becomes incomprehensible. (1980, p. 335)

     He, too, is assuming that students, to be students (and not "dangerously free"), must be members in good standing of the community whose immediate head is the English teacher. It is interesting that his parenthetical catalogue of the "operations" of thought, "thinking, seeing, reading," excludes writing, since it is only through written records that we have any real indication of how a student thinks, sees, and reads. (Perhaps "real" is an inappropriate word to use here, since there is certainly a "real" intellectual life that goes on, independent of writing. Let me say that thinking, seeing, and reading are valued in the academic community *only* as they are represented by extended, elaborated written records.) Writing, I presume, is a given for Fish. It is the card of entry into this closed community that constrains and excludes dangerous characters. Students who are excluded from this community are students who do poorly on written placement exams or in freshman composition. They do not, that is, move easily into the privileged discourse of the community, represented by the English literature class.

8. My debt to Bizzell's work should be evident everywhere in this essay. See also Bizzell (1978, 1982b) and Bizzell and Herzberg (1980).

9. Fish says the following about the relationship between student and an object under study:

> we are not to imagine a moment when my students "simply see" a physical configuration of atoms and *then* assign that configuration a

significance, according to the situation they happen to be in. To be in the situation (this or any other) is to "see" with the eyes of its interests, its goals, its understood practices, values, and norms, and so to be conferring significance *by* seeing, not after it. The categories of my students' vision are the categories by which they understand themselves to be functioning as students . . . and objects will appear to them in forms related to that way of functioning rather than in some objective or preinterpretive form. (1980, p. 334)

10. I am aware that the papers given the highest rankings offer arguments about creativity and originality similar to my own. If there is a conspiracy here, that is one of the points of my chapter. I should add that my reading of the "content" of basic writers' essays is quite different from Lunsford's (1980).

References

Aristotle. (1932). *The rhetoric of Aristotle* (L. Cooper, Trans.). Englewood Cliffs, NJ: Prentice-Hall.

Barthes, R. (1974). S/Z (R. Howard, Trans.). New York: Hill & Wang.

Bartholomae, D. (1979). Teaching basic writing: An alternative to basic skills. *Journal of Basic Writing*, 2, 85–109.

Bartholomae, D. (1983). Writing assignments: Where writing begins. In P. Stock (Ed.), *Forum* (pp. 300–12). Montclair, NJ: Boynton/Cook.

Bereiter, C., & Scardamalia, M. (1985). Cognitive coping strategies and the problem of "inert knowledge." In S. S. Chipman, J. W. Segal, & R. Glaser (Eds.), *Thinking and learning skills: Research and open questions* (Vol. 2). Hillsdale, NJ: Erlbaum.

Bizzell, P. (1978). The ethos of academic discourse. *College Composition and Communication*, 29, 351–55.

Bizzell, P. (1982a). Cognition, convention, and certainty: What we need to know about writing. *Pre/text*, 3, 213–44.

Bizzell, P. (1982b). College composition: Initiation into the academic discourse community. *Curriculum Inquiry*, 12, 191–207.

Bizzell, P., & Herzberg, B. (1980). "Inherent" ideology, "universal" history, "empirical" evidence, and "context-free" writing: Some problems with E. D. Hirsch's *The Philosophy of Composition. Modern Language Notes*, 95, 1181–1202.

Coles, W. E., Jr. (1978). *The plural I.* New York: Holt, Rinehart & Winston.

Fish, S. (1980). *Is there a text in this class? The authority of interpretive communities.* Cambridge, MA: Harvard University Press.

Flower, L. S. (1981). Revising writer-based prose. *Journal of Basic Writing*, 3, 62–74.

Flower, L., & Hayes, J. (1981). A cognitive process theory of writing. *College Composition and Communication*, 32, 365–87.

Hairston, M. (1978). *A contemporary rhetoric.* Boston: Houghton Mifflin.

Lunsford, A. A. (1980). The content of basic writers' essays. *College Composition and Communication*, 31, 278–90.

Maimon, E. P., Belcher, G. L., Hearn, G. W., Nodine, B. F., & O'Conner, F. X. (1981). *Writing in the arts and sciences.* Cambridge, MA: Winthrop.

Olson, D. R. (1981). Writing: The divorce of the author from the text. In B. M. Kroll & R. J. Vann (Eds.), *Exploring speaking–writing relationships: Con-*

nections and contrasts. Urbana, IL: National Council of Teachers of English.

Perkins, D. N. (1985). General cognitive skills: Why not? In S. S. Chipman, J. W. Segal, & R. Glaser (Eds.), *Thinking and learning skills: Research and open questions* (Vol. 2). Hillsdale, NJ: Erlbaum.

Ponsot, M., & Deen, R. (1982). *Beat not the poor desk*. Montclair, NJ: Boynton/ Cook.

Rodriguez, R. (1983). *Hunger of memory*. New York: Bantam.

Rose, M. (1983). Remedial writing courses: A critique and a proposal. *College English*, 45, 109–28.

Said, E. W. (1975). *Beginnings: Intention and method*. Baltimore: The Johns Hopkins University Press.

Shaughnessy, M. (1977). *Errors and expectations*. New York: Oxford University Press.

Bartholomae's Insights as a Resource for Your Teaching

1. Make a brief list of the particular features of academic discourse. How does academic discourse differ from the sorts of mental and verbal habits that characterize students who are new to the university?

2. Consider the social and political implications of Bartholomae's argument. Will some students be at a distinct advantage or disadvantage in terms of appropriating "authoritative discourse" because of their social or cultural backgrounds? How might you level the playing field for your students?

Bartholomae's Insights as a Resource for Your Writing Classroom

1. Share with your students the student essays that Bartholomae uses as examples. After they have had time to think and form their own opinions about the essays, share with them Bartholomae's ideas about the essays. Ask students to compare and contrast their own sense of what's interesting about this student work with Bartholomae's ideas. What do they like or dislike about Bartholomae's vision of the composition classroom?

2. Have students explore the social implications of Bartholomae's theory. Will certain groups be excluded from appropriating this discourse, or at least face significant barriers to doing so? Ask students whether they feel that Bartholomae's views of helping students master this academic discourse are pragmatic, laden with cultural values, or both. What do they feel should be standards for valid discourse? Valued discourse?

Composition's Imagined Geographies: The Politics of Space in the Frontier, City, and Cyberspace

Nedra Reynolds

Certain spatial metaphors have figured prominently in the ways composition has come to understand itself. As the world shrinks and we hear more and more talk of a "global village," we need to reflect carefully on these terms rather than persist uncritically in thinking that space is merely neutral or transparent or devoid of powerful social significance. We initially thought of our discipline in terms of the frontier; later, we came to see it more and more as a contact zone or a city; as we look to the future, we find ourselves increasingly concerned with our work in cyberspace. In this essay, first published in a 1998 issue of College Composition and Communication, *Nedra Reynolds argues that we should be especially alert to the actual material conditions of our working lives and those of our students, for these contexts inform our process of making and communicating meaning and self-understanding quite powerfully and with considerable complexity — complexity that is often masked by a too-casual reliance on abstract, general metaphors.*

> We must be insistently aware of how space can be made to hide conse-
> quences from us, how relations of power and discipline are inscribed
> into the apparently innocent spatiality of social life, how human
> geographies become filled with politics and ideology.
>
>   — Edward W. Soja (6)

> It is helpful to remind ourselves that one of the things a university does
> is alter one's sense of geography.
>
>   — Mary N. Muchiri et al. (178)

In their recent article on "Importing Composition: Teaching and Researching Academic Writing beyond North America," Mary N. Muchiri and her coauthors challenge our assumptions that composition is "universal" in its uses and applications, and that writing instructors and writing students do not occupy particular geographic locations. Muchiri et al. remind readers that composition is very much a product of North America and of capitalism and illustrate what happens to composition research when it is exported — how it changes in a different, de-localized context of its origination. "Importing Composition" highlights some of the assumptions that form the basis of U.S. research on academic writing — assumptions that sometimes seem "bizarre" in a new context (176). In our limited notions of geography, we make assumptions about serving the world in our writing classes: "The teacher in New York or Los Angeles may look out over a classroom and think, 'The whole world is here.' It isn't" (195).

In its analysis of contemporary writing instruction — informed by imports and exports, journeys, the local and the global — "Importing

Composition" contributes to a geographic study of composition that asks us to confront many of our assumptions about place and space. My purpose here is to extend that contribution by using concepts from postmodern geography to explore how spaces and places are socially produced through discourse and how these constructed spaces can then deny their connections to material reality or mask material conditions.[1] Cultural geography invites us to question the relationships between material conditions and imagined territories, a relationship I identify here as the politics of space, and asks us to attend to the negotiations of power that take place across and within a number of spaces: regional or topographical, domestic or institutional, architectural or electronic, real or imagined. Making a geographic turn enables me to examine the politics of space in composition with three general aims: (1) to interpret some of composition's most enduring spatial metaphors as "imagined geographies" responsible, in part, for composition's disciplinary development and identity; (2) to illustrate the effects of time-space compression on composition's workers; (3) and to argue for a spatial politics of writing instruction that denies transparent space and encourages the study of neglected places where writers work.

Attending to the politics of space can begin with simple observations about where writers and writing instructors work — in a variety of institutional, public, and private spaces (some of them difficult to categorize as either public or private): the academic buildings of our offices, computer labs, and writing centers; the cafeterias, libraries, and classrooms of our campuses; the large conference hotels where we meet to exchange ideas and socialize; the kitchen table, desks, or computer corners in our homes. These actual locations for the work of writing and writing instruction coexist with several metaphorical or imaginary places where we write, study writing, or create theories about writing: webs of meaning, research paradigms, home departments, discourse communities, frontiers, cities, and cyberspaces.

Composition workers have long had to deal with the politics of space, whether this has involved trying to reduce section sizes, find a room to establish a writing center, or stake our disciplinary territory. In carving out areas to call its own, composition has created imagined geographies that hold a number of implications. A writing center, for example, occupies a certain number of square feet in a campus building, but it also occupies an imaginary place where writing is taught, learned, or talked about very differently than in a lecture hall or around a seminar table. Edward Soja, in *Postmodern Geographies: The Reassertion of Space in Critical Social Theory*, defines postmodern geography as the study of the social production of spaces or studying the linkages among space, knowledge, and power (20). The social production of spaces takes place in all discourse arenas, wherever rhetors are "inventing" the boundaries of inquiry, the agendas of research, or the languages of arguments. How have composition theorist-practitioners imagined the spaces of writing, writers, and writing instruction? "Where" have they placed the work of composition studies as a field or discipline, and what implications do these real or imaginary placements hold? After demonstrating the endurance of one of composition's most important imagined geographies, the *frontier*, and the emergence of two more, the *city* and *cyberspace*, I argue that these imaginary places for writing and writing instruction have been rendered benign, or anesthetized by the influence of transparent space; that we have neglected the relationship between material spaces and actual practices; and that we need to attend to the effects of time-space compression on composition's workers.

Spatial Metaphors in the Discourses of Composition Studies

Spatial metaphors have long dominated our written discourse in this field ("field" being one of the first spatial references we can name) because, first, writing itself is spatial, or we cannot very well conceive of writing in ways other than spatial. In "The Limits of Containment: Text-as-Container in Composition Studies," Darsie Bowden asserts that composition "is especially rife with metaphors because composing involves complex cognitive activities . . . that are difficult to talk about and understand" (364). As Bowden's analysis suggests, many of our metaphors in writing and composition studies involve or depend on imaginary conceptions of space. From bound texts to pages to paragraphs, sentences, and words, we read and write in distinctly spatial ways. We read from left to right (in most languages), and we scan pages up and down or rifle through a stack of pages from top to bottom. We are accustomed to margins and borders that frame texts for us and page numbers or arrow icons that mark our place. (How often have you found a remembered passage by its placement on a page, its position in the text?) Academic and professional writers are comfortable with manipulating textual spaces and now that the tasks of organizing and presenting information — with spatial constraints all around — constitute one of a writer's biggest challenges. Techno-revolutions are changing our notions of texts on pages, most of us realize, and the days of container metaphors for texts may be numbered.

Jay David Bolter's *Writing Space: The Computer, Hypertext, and the History of Writing* thoroughly demonstrates that writing specialists would be hard pressed to imagine or explain writing in terms other than spatial. From *topoi* to transitions, we make decisions throughout the writing process based on spatial relationships; for example, where an example goes or what point connects to what claim. To control textual space *well* is to be a good writer; in fact, controlling textual spaces is very much tied to both literacy and power. Chris Anson identifies some commonly accepted practices that are really about writing teachers' efforts to assert control over textual space — rules about margins and double-spacing, about where the staple or paper clip goes, about where the writer's name and the date belong — all of these practices or rules are about control, which as he points out, might slip away from us in the age of electronic writing.

When created via computer interfaces, texts burst out of their containers, as Cynthia Selfe and Richard Selfe have argued. One of the reasons that word processing has been so revolutionary to writers is that it allows for easier, faster manipulation of space: sentences, chunks, or paragraphs can be deleted or moved in seconds. Because readers orient themselves spatially within printed texts — "How many more pages?" — Bolter explains that spatial disorientation is, in fact, one of the problems or challenges of electronic writing, where "the reader seldom has a sense of where he or she is in the book" (87).

Because writing teachers recognize both the spatial nature of writing and the importance of controlling textual as well as disciplinary space, compositionists have developed a rich repertoire of memorable spatial images and referents, everything from webs of meaning to turf wars. Spatial metaphors have served to establish what composition should be or to lament what composition has become. For example, claims of composition as a discipline have called on the lofty spatial metaphors of paradigms and "domains" (Phelps) or on the more mundane: inside Stephen North's sprawling, junky house of lore resides a group of sad occupants who live in the basement (Miller). Feminist readings of the field have concentrated on the domestic spaces of composition, where underpaid women are assigned primarily chores and housekeeping tasks (Slagle and Rose; Neel). In our discussions of economic and political issues about composition, we refer to heavy courseloads as teaching "in the trenches" because composition occupies the "low" position in the academy, akin to a carnival (Miller).

Generally, as composition has encountered postmodernism, metaphors of inside and outside, margin and center, boundaries and zones have become increasingly familiar, appealing, even comfortable. Mike Rose's *Lives on the Boundary;* Carolyn Ericksen Hill's *Writing from the Margins;* and Mary Louise Pratt's "Arts of the Contact Zone" identify three of the most popular spatial metaphors for discussing issues of difference and diversity or for asserting where the work of composition studies should concentrate. Perhaps the most appealing spatial metaphor right now is Gloria Anzaldúa's "borderlands" (*La Frontera*), where cultures are mixed and mingled and where geographic borders do not hold. Imagining spaces where differences mingle is important to a field characterized by interdisciplinarity and populated with some of the most marginalized members of the academy: per-course instructors, teaching assistants, and first-year students.

Despite composition's affinity for spatial metaphors, and despite rhetoric's attention to spaces for public discourse, there has not yet been a concerted effort to examine composition's geographies, nor have composition scholars typically looked to the disciplinary area of geography studies. Composition and geography have undergone similar changes in recent decades due to the impact of new technologies, and both fields are pursuing a growing interest in spatial theories.[2]

Geographic Literacy: Yet Another Crisis

Geography is, literally or etymologically, *writing the earth*, yet composition studies has not drawn much from it, exploring instead the terrains of history, philosophy, linguistics, and cognitive psychology. The lack of engagement so far between composition and geography is particularly striking in light of the fact that both fields remain so marginalized among academic disciplines and that both have been targeted by media-driven campaigns regarding literacy, composition in the mid-1970s and geography in the mid-1980s.

Like composition studies, geography has experienced the national media attention of a declared "literacy crisis." Approximately a decade after the claims that schoolchildren could not read or write, the media began reporting on survey and test results showing that college students guessed wildly on geography tests and were unable to read a map, identify important countries, or name boundary rivers or mountains.[3] With the collapse of several subjects into "social studies," American students had become geographically illiterate. Surveys confirmed that nearly 70% of all secondary students had no formal course work in geography, and the media were eager to report the most egregious examples of ignorance; for example, the belief that Canada was a state ("Teachers Lament").

In 1985, in response to "deterioration of geographic knowledge," two professional organizations set forth new guidelines for the teaching of geography in elementary and secondary schools, and Congress designated a "National Geography Awareness Week" in 1988 "to combat a widespread ignorance of geography" ("Redoubling"). The National Geographic Society pumped over two million dollars into the D.C. public school system alone, for teacher-training, a high-tech classroom, atlases, maps, and software (Horwitz A8).

Now, just ten years after the nationwide concern with geographic ignorance, interest in geography is said to be soaring, with a declared "Renaissance" in geographic education (ABC World News). From inflatable globes to such popular programs and games as "Where in the World is Carmen Sandiego?" American schoolchildren have improved test scores. Geography's fortunes are changing because of a new push towards geographic education — complete with corporate sponsorship — and because of near-revolutionary changes in map-making technology (Hitt).

A driving force behind geography's renaissance is economics: the interest in geography aligns sharply with the expansion of multinational capitalism across the globe. Satellites, cable, NAFTA, and the information superhighway — all of these developments have motivated politicians and educators to argue that American students need to be able to navigate these new horizons for commercialism. Functional illiteracy is bad for the goals of capitalism, and educators recognize the urgency of knowing more about other places and cultures in order to be competitive in the world market. A new urgency about geographic literacy accompanies other signs of the impact of time-space compression, or the belief that the planet is shrinking, with a general speed-up in the pace of everyday life.

Time-Space Compression

> Our daily life, our psychic experience, our cultural languages, are today dominated by categories of space rather than by categories of time.
> — Fredric Jameson (16)

The huge campaign to remedy the geography literacy crisis gained momentum, in part, by changing conceptions of space in our late-capitalist economy. With technologies that allow the rapid, almost instantaneous, transmission of information and ever-faster modes of transportation, our world is perceived to be "smaller" than it used to be, a phenomenon known as *time-space compression*. First named by Marx as the annihilation of space through time, time-space compression means more time to work and thus more profit (Massey 146; Harvey 293; Soja 126). As spaces seem to shrink, time seems to expand — and the illusion that there is more time would allow capitalists to get more out of workers. "Time-space compression refers to movement and communication across space, to the geographical stretching-out of social relations, and to our experience of all this" (Massey 147). The perception that the earth is shrinking to the size of a "global village" — a perception that benefits the expansion of capitalism — is important to contemporary geography studies and to any examination of the spatial turn in postmodernism.

The general sensations of a shrinking planet — busier, noisier, and more crowded — triggers the temptation to look out over urban classrooms and think "the whole world is here." Other examples of time-space compression include: (1) satellites beaming events "around the globe"; (2) the weird sense of mobility that comes from "surfing the net" or from exchanging e-mail with someone in Johannesburg or Berlin or Seoul; (3) the "really there" feeling enhanced by big-screen televisions or expensive sound systems in theaters; (4) Microsoft's slogan "Where do you want to go today?" and (5) the IBM slogan "solutions for a small planet." Notably, these examples are from business, the media, and technology — forces that have combined to give us an onslaught of everyday images about how small our world is and how easily traversed.

In *The Condition of Postmodernity*, geographer David Harvey claims that the history of capitalism has been characterized by this speed-up in the pace of life. Harvey explains that time-space compression forces us "to alter, sometimes in quite radical ways, how we represent the world to ourselves" (240), the consequences of which "have particular bearing on postmodern ways of thinking, feeling, and doing" (285). These postmodern effects have by now become quite familiar: a dominance of images, where the images themselves become more real than reality: "reality gets created rather than interpreted under conditions of stress and time-space compression" (306). We get the false sense of going somewhere when we log on and having been somewhere after we log off. Through the ability of technology to simulate travel, we think we're "experiencing" a different culture, otherness, or diversity, but we're not even leaving the comfortable (or crowded) confines of our homes or offices.

As technology and capitalism have combined to make time-space compression more common and familiar, one alarming result has been the idea that space is negligible or transparent. This consequence is related to what Jameson identifies as "a new kind of flatness or depthlessness, a new kind of superficiality, . . . perhaps the most supreme formal feature of all the postmodernisms" (9). As space flattens out, time becomes both harder to notice *and* more important; the masking of *time* through the changing boundaries for *space* has consequences for workers, students, women, for all of us. Time-space compression masks the politics of space by producing the illusion that, for example, electronic gadgets can overcome space and create more time. There are distinct dangers in believing that space does not matter, and a number of geographers or spatial theorists have named this threat *transparent space*.

Transparent Space

> Transparent space assumes that the world can be seen as it really is
> and that there can be unmediated access to the truth of objects it sees;
> it is a space of mimetic representation.
> — Alison Blunt and Gillian Rose (5)

It is easy to take space and time for granted because they are such an obvious part of our everyday existence; they become routine because there doesn't seem to be anything we can do about them. However, it is important to challenge the idea of a single and objective sense of time or space, against which we attempt to measure the diversity of human conceptions and perceptions. Time-space compression leads us to believe that space is no big deal, that every divide is smaller than it seems, but feminist and other cultural geographers insist that divides are real, that differences are material and concrete, and that space cannot be treated as transparent or "innocent."

In *Space, Place, and Gender*, Doreen Massey explains that the "usual" explanation for time-space compression is internationalized capitalism, but that such an explanation is "insufficient" for women:

> The degree to which we can move between countries, or walk about the
> streets at night, or venture out of hotels in foreign cities, is not just
> influenced by "capital." Survey after survey has shown how women's
> mobility . . . is restricted — in a thousand different ways, from physical
> violence to being ogled at or made to feel quite simply "out of place" —
> not by "capital," but by men. (147–48)

Time-space compression is a "high theory" concept that feminist geographers have tried to make more practical and more concerned with the everyday. As Elizabeth Wilson notes, feminists are more interested in policy issues related to space — women's safety, street lighting, or the dearth of public transport — than in theoretical or conceptual considerations (148). Massey and other feminist geographers are working towards notions of space as paradoxical, provisional, contradictory, fragmented. A notion of paradoxical spaces helps feminists to resist "transparent space," which is a particularly dangerous notion for women and other minorities because it denies differences or neglects the politics of space, especially in domestic or everyday environments. Documenting women's relationships to space has resulted in numerous studies of the home or neighborhoods — locales particularly important for women. Whether women find themselves in public space or private homes, real or imagined communities, they often experience those spaces as oppressive (Gillian Rose 143–50). Their experiences and emotions in domestic spaces are so geographically rooted, they can vary with the floor plan — women can get angry in the kitchen, for example, but not in the bedroom (Blunt and Rose 2).

Even spaces presumed to be safe are often a threat to women. College campuses provide a good example of this image, especially as they are represented in typical media shots (especially recruitment or fundraising videos or photographs). The stately buildings, wide green lawns, and gatherings of people, presumably engaged in collegial exchanges, give the impression of harmonious intellectual activity in a tranquil environment. I spent four years on one of the most attractive college campuses ever to appear in a brochure, Miami University of Oxford, Ohio. The buildings match. Framed in buildings of southern Georgian architecture, red brick with large windows trimmed in the (exact) same shade of creamy yellow, the campus is famous for its gardens and landscaping. The serene appearance, however, masks the politics of space; for example, the numerous "keep off the grass" signs that dot the lush green lawns or the threat to women who dare to walk alone at night.

I began to think more about the politics of space after Jane Marcus visited Miami University and, struck by its wealth and privilege, spoke about the material conditions at her institution, City College, where instructors were lucky to have an office with a desk at all; forget about photocopying, a phone, chalk, or paper. If your walls weren't covered with graffiti and you had a chair, you were truly lucky. Then I read Jonathan Kozol's *Savage Inequalities* with an undergraduate course, a book which details the educational injustices done to students in cold, damp, dark classrooms, with falling plaster and trashy playgrounds. Place does matter; surroundings do have an effect on learning or attitudes towards learning, and material spaces have a political edge. In short, *where* writing instruction takes place has everything to do with *how*. When, for example, open admissions' policies went into effect, writing-center directors found themselves fighting for the most modest of spaces. Hard-won writing centers were often located in basements or tiny rooms, far from the heart of campus activity.

Some composition scholars *have* recognized issues of transparent space. In the February 1996 *CCC*, Ellen Cushman uses photographs and community history to show how "the Approach," a granite walkway leading up the hill to RPI in Troy, NY, illustrates "deeply rooted sociological distances" between the university and the community (8). The Approach is not simply a set of steps and pillars in disrepair — not transparent space — but a symbol of the wide gap between town and gown, a gap that is economic and political. Cushman's material analysis of a physical location resists the notion of transparent space. It is more typical in composition texts, however, to find notions of space that reach beyond the physical confines of classrooms or campuses, to think bigger and wider, to imagine frontiers, cities, and cyberspaces.

Imagined Geographies: Frontier, City, and Cyberspace

In what follows, I offer three extended examples of sites where time-space compression and transparent space have played out in the discourses of composition studies. While I hesitate to make the argument that time-space compression "causes" the creation of these imagined geographies, these three sites offer powerful examples of the social production of spaces in composition. In addition, their features and metaphors illustrate how material conditions can be ignored when a pioneering spirit takes hold.

The Frontier of Basic Writing

As composition workers struggled with the impact of open admissions and the demands of an expanding population, they faced working in crowded, inadequate building space populated by speakers and writers of many languages or dialects, few of them closely resembling traditional academic discourse. The feeling of "foreignness" and claustrophobia led to the construction, in discursive terms, of spaces where their struggles could be enacted. The only space big enough for such a struggle was a *frontier*.

From the first day of Open Admissions at City College, more space was needed for writing instruction. *The New York Times* reported in October of 1970 that tutoring was taking place in coat rooms while classes were being held in former ice skating rinks and supermarkets. At John Jay College, the square feet per student shrunk from 93 in 1969 to 31 the following year. "With lounge space scarce and college cafeterias jammed, many students study, do homework and eat their lunches sitting on corridor floors and stairways," and this crowding was reported in October, before the weather forced all students inside (Buder). Nearly everyone associated with the Open Admissions program has commented on the overcrowded conditions; Adrienne Rich's famous essay on "Teaching Language in Open Admissions" refers to the "overcrowded campus where in winter there is often no place to sit between classes" (60), and she gives another account to Jane Maher: "the overcrowding was acute. In the fall of 1970 we taught in open plywood cubicles set up in Great Hall [where] you could hear the noise from other cubicles; concentration was difficult for the students" (109).

The crowded and otherwise inadequate material conditions at City College led to composition's first imagined geography — and perhaps its most enduring spatial metaphor for arguing composition's legitimacy as a discipline. Mina Shaughnessy's *Errors and Expectations* opens with pointed attention to the local environment and to a very concrete physical space: she sits "alone in [a] worn urban classroom," reading with shock and dismay the folder of "alien" student essays (*vii*). The worn urban classroom, however, is soon replaced by a metaphoric location, larger and more romantic — the frontier: "the territory I am calling basic writing . . . is still very much of a frontier, unmapped, except for . . . a few blazed trails" (4). Instead of concentrating on the worn urban classroom as a site for the study of basic writing, Shaughnessy creates a guide for teachers "heading to [a] pedagogical West" (4). She admits the flaws of her map — "it is certain to have the shortcomings of other frontier maps, with doubtless a few rivers in the wrong place and some trails that end nowhere" — but what is important here is that she does not map the classroom, or the urban college spaces, or the city of New York (4). A concrete physical location, then, is erased by the more powerful American metaphor of the frontier.

Shaughnessy's early reviewers eagerly picked up on this frontier imagery because it allowed inexperienced, tentative, even resistant writing teachers to feel like brave, noble conquerors. Harvey Wiener, for example, describes Shaughnessy's book as the map, compass, and guide for those who dare to venture — or who would be sent — into the "jungle of trial and error" where teachers must "hack branches" through students' tortuous prose (715).

One way to read Shaughnessy's construction of the frontier metaphor is to see it romantically as desire for the open space of the frontier, in reaction to the crowded, chaotic conditions of City College in an Open Admissions system. Shaughnessy was undoubtedly surrounded by overwhelming needs and demands, and all of her biographers or reviewers connect her frontier imagery to her regional identity, formed in the Black Hills of South Dakota. For example, Janet Emig writes in her eulogy for Shaughnessy, "Mina could not be understood without understanding that she came from the West" (37). To read Shaughnessy's work through the lens of the Western motif is tempting not only because of her family roots in the West, but also because of the contrast provided by her move to New York City and her major life's work spent in crowded, urban classrooms. Imagining her homeland and her own identity as a strong prairie-dweller gave her a form of escape from the multiple and oppressive institutional structures of City College. In this version, sustaining her practical, perhaps even vocational, emphasis can be draining and frustrating because of the enormity of the task; thus, Shaughnessy looks to the West for energy and a sense of mission.

Others have interpreted Shaughnessy's frontier metaphor through the realities of her workload and the crowded material spaces of City College. Robert Lyons claims that "her frequent allusions to the pioneer role of basic writing teachers and to the 'frontier' experience of such work had more to do with her sense of taxing workloads than with nostalgia for her Western past" (175). Indeed, Shaughnessy worked herself to exhaustion, suffering a brief physical collapse in 1971 (Lyons 175). For teachers in the trenches, hard work defines their experience more accurately than large expanses of hope and possibility.

Metaphors of the frontier result from dominant ideologies of space, place, and landscape in the United States: the more the better; own as much as possible; keep trespassers off; if it looks uninhabited, it must be. Canonical in American studies, F. J. Turner's thesis, "The Significance of the Frontier in American History" (1893), claimed that pushing west into the frontier was the most defining aspect of the American spirit, that the social, political, and intellectual development of the United States can be traced along the line of Western expansion. Settling the frontier, according to Turner, reenacted the history of social evolution. Turner's thesis, along with more recent studies from literature and film, can help to explain the power of the frontier metaphor in composition studies. As critics have shown, Western films capture the harshness and supposed "emptiness" of the landscape. One cinematic shot of rock and desert puts into place "an entire code of values," especially the lure of "infinite access": "the openness of the space means that domination can take place. . . . The blankness of the plain implies — without ever stating — that this is a field where a certain kind of mastery is possible" (Tompkins 74–75).

The frontier metaphor appears again and again in the literature of composition studies, often as a way of establishing or confirming composition's disciplinary status. Janice Lauer, for example, in an article which begins by asking, "Is this study a genuine discipline?" reinscribes Shaughnessy's frontier imagery. Lauer traces "the field's pioneer efforts" as it "staked out [the] territory [of writing] for investigation" (21). She characterizes composition's early theorists in "their willingness to take risks, to go beyond the boundaries of their traditional training into foreign domains" (21). According to Lauer, composition's "dappled" character as a discipline holds both advantages and risks: composition can be a "rich field of inquiry" or "a terrain of quicksand":

> The immensity of unexplored land presents a subtle seduction, drawing newcomers by promising not to relegate them to tiny plots in which to work out the arcane implications of already established scholarship. But once committed, some individuals have difficulty finding entries or end up losing their way because the role of pathfinder is challenging and

thus ill-suited to everyone. The field's largely unmapped territory, therefore, has rewarded some handsomely but been fatal to others. (25)

To construct composition as a risky venture, not for the fainthearted, as Lauer does, gives composition studies a tough image: if only the fittest can survive, then it must be worthy of the status of a discipline. Joseph Harris has argued that Shaughnessy mistakenly assumed the frontier of basic writing was unoccupied, and the frontier metaphor has problematic colonialist echoes that are fairly obvious (79). Harris also makes the case that the frontier metaphor is actually quite innocuous; it gave teachers of literature a dose of missionary zeal about teaching writing to underprepared students, but also allowed them to imagine that they were not changing but simply extending the reach of the curriculum (80). Naming basic writing a frontier served to mask the politics of space — the real material conditions that crowded students into classrooms with overworked and underpaid teachers.

The frontier metaphor endures because composition's professional development was dependent on sounding "new," bold, untamed, and exciting without really changing the politics of space at all. Frontier was an important imaginary space for the early days of Open Admissions because it seemed to invite "vision," hope, and wide expanses of possibility, but the frontier metaphor was also a reaction against the overwhelming work and responsibility that went along with educating larger, more diverse populations of college writers. Composition's development and growth meant changes in its imagined geographies, and after a brief investment in the geography of "community," composition needed a more powerful and diverse space in which to imagine its work, subjects, and practices — the *city*.

Composition as City: Postmodern and Rhetorical Spaces

As composition grew and developed, different settlements sprang up all across the wide frontier, communities characterized by differences in philosophy, political allegiances, or research methods. Acknowledgment of the diverse communities within composition was one way of demonstrating its legitimacy, but the appeal of the community metaphor soon wore thin, replaced by evocations of the city. Naming composition a city marks a moment of maturity in its history, but there are consequences to any imagined geography, and the politics of space can be either illuminated or disguised by images of the modern city.

As a second generation imagined geography, "community" offered tremendous rhetorical power. As Joseph Harris explicates, the metaphor of community is "both seductive and powerful" and "makes a claim on us that is hard to resist" (99). However, like the notion of frontier, community too often assumed transparent space — where there are clear insiders or outsiders; where differences may not be so welcomed or encouraged; or where the goal of consensus silences productive dissensus (Trimbur 608–10).

Composition scholars were quick to recognize that a warm, fuzzy notion of composition — where like-minded peoples cooperate harmoniously — would not serve the diverse populations of composition dwellers. If the frontier metaphor characterized composition as a tough field, community sounded too "wimpy," and composition continued to need authority or legitimacy within the academy. "Community" was also not geographically loaded enough to be appealing and enduring, not in the ways that frontier and city are geographically expansive and symbolically romantic. In other words, community did not last long as an imagined geography in composition because its spaces were just too limited. An imagined geography big enough to hold composition's ambitions was that of the city. Cities offer diversity of peoples and places, models of cooperation, more sites for public gathering, and more feelings of exhilaration, sometimes a keen sense of "survival of the fittest." A city metaphor seems richer and more exciting; the bustle of a city implies that work is getting done.

Seeing composition as a city also invokes the places where rhetoric flourishes — the agora, marketplace, theater, or coffeehouse. The city, therefore, offers at least two ideologies or dominant sets of images and metaphors: 1) city as an embodiment of postmodernism; 2) city as a reflection of democratic ideals. The material conditions of the city are more "in your face" than those of the frontier, which assumes a blank plain; the politics of space, therefore, seem more obvious in the city or less difficult to identify. Still, notions of the city differ ideologically, and too many views of the city glamorize its appeal.

Contemporary geographers often turn to the city to illustrate their claims about postmodernism. Edward Soja reads Los Angeles as the perfect example of "the dynamics of capitalist spatialization"; L.A. is *the* capitalist city (191). One view of the city emphasizes simultaneous stimulation and terror, where postmodern subjects feel most keenly a kind of twenty-first-century panic: the fear of being crowded; that all the space is being taken up; that the planet is overpopulated and toxic. Simultaneously, however, caught between contradictory desires, we also want the excitement and exhilaration of a city. The goal of postmodern city life is not to achieve stable orientation, but to accept disorientation as a way of life.

To invoke a city is, on one hand, to identify composition with postmodernism since crowded urban streets, like busy visual images, are more postmodern. On the other hand, unlike postmodern geographers, Harris and Lester Faigley want to claim the democratic, rhetorical, or public images of the city; for example, the idea that cities revolve around a center (Soja 234–35). In contrast to the frontier, cities have a central location, a "polis," or a "heart" (as in "in the heart of the city"). Thus, the city seems a more appropriate, more invigorating site for the exchange of ideas: there is a central place to meet, an especially appealing notion for rhetorical scholars interested in the gathering places of ancient cultures and in public spheres for communication.[4]

The city seems a more sophisticated image for composition's maturity than that of the frontier because it invites a more paradoxical notion of space and represents a different kind of work. Composition as a city invites more diversity because many different activities can go on simultaneously and, following the logic of traffic lights, no one will cause accidents or pile-ups; everyone cooperates. To navigate a city requires more experience, skill, or wits than to navigate a small community, and the alienation or anonymity are outweighed by the opportunities or stimulation. The frontier signifies the hard physical labor of sod-busting and planting and harvesting, with a landscape of plains or rolling hills, capped by big skies. The city holds bolder or more complicated signifiers, but corporate work images come to mind: high-rise office buildings, with photocopiers and air-conditioning and water coolers, where the politics of space are both enhanced and complicated by modern architecture and technologies.

In representing the city as a place of either postmodern exhilaration or democratic participation, scholars and theorists may be glamorizing the city and overlooking some of the material realities — the same problem that exists with the frontier metaphor. Visitors to cities almost never see the ghettos, for example, and tourists are herded — through promotional materials, transportation routes, and hotel locations — to the most attractive sites. In addition, time-space compression works to make city-dwellers believe that technologies to shrink space have actually resulted in more time. As most commuters will attest, however, "having more time" is not exactly their experience. As cultural geographer Peter Jackson points out, ideologies of city and frontier do not differ all that much: "frontier ideologies are extraordinarily persistent even in the contemporary city, where they reappear as ideologies of 'pioneering' or 'homesteading' in the urban 'wilderness'" (111). Thus, Turner's thesis is once again reinforced — that the pioneering spirit is deeply American, and that American ideologies celebrate pioneering myths.

While the appeal of frontier turns on the American fantasies of space and place (that it is endless; the more the better; that space can be mastered), the appeal of the city turns on busy visual images, heightened adrenaline, movement, and a desire for public space or mutual co-existence with others. As Shaughnessy found out, however, work in the city was just as hard and taxing. Both of these appeals are present in a potent geographic site — *cyberspace*. Cyberspace is an imagined geography where visitors or homesteaders can be simultaneously stimulated and terrified, where order and disorder co-exist, and where the frontier metaphor continues its hold over our collective imagination. Cyberspace and its attendant electronic technologies also offer the most representative example of time-space compression, where space seems to shrink as time seems to expand.

Cyberspace and the New Frontier

> Space is not a scientific object removed from ideology and politics; it has always been political and strategic.
>
> — Henri Lefebvre (qtd. in Soja 80)

As electronic writing technologies radicalize the work of our field once again, with an impact probably as large as that of Open Admissions, the pattern repeats itself: in the face of some confusion and an overwhelming sense of responsibility, the frontier beckons. It is tempting to call cyberspace "the new frontier" because it offers a sense of excitement and possibility in the face of otherwise frightening changes, and those influences combine to make cyberspace the latest imagined geography.

The frontier metaphor served well during the Kennedy Administration to justify the space program; now the frontier extends beyond space, into new imaginary territory called cyberspace. Without NASA-level technology and equipment — with only a PC and Internet access — "anyone" can go there, making it far more accessible. It is not difficult to illustrate the dominance of the frontier metaphor in discourses of electronic technologies. A core course in the telecommunications MA at George Mason University is titled "Taming the Electronic Frontier" (Cox). The Electronic Frontier Foundation lobbies to stop legislation limiting the freedom of computer users. Howard Rheingold's *The Virtual Community: Homesteading on the Electronic Frontier* addresses the idea of domesticating space — making a home in unfamiliar territory, staking a claim, naming it ours. Even the moral code of the frontier is reproduced: "The Internet has been like the Wild West before law and order was brought to it" (Vitanza 133). When two hackers meet in the OK corral for a shoot-out, the good guy usually wins (Markoff 121).

Composition, like *Star Trek* and NASA, is so completely "American," as the Muchiri essay argues, that the temptation to claim a new final frontier is strong and appealing. Despite the attractiveness of naming cyberspace a new frontier, cyberspace is not transparent space, as several scholars have recognized. Emily Jessup says it quite succinctly: "The land of computing is a frontier country, and, as in the development of most frontier countries, there are many more men than women" (336). Women and other disenfranchised groups will have to follow the maps, tracks, and instructional manuals written by the techies, mostly men who got to the colony first. Concerns of colonialism have been addressed by invoking democracy — claims that cyberspace offers more opportunities for voices to be heard, that "anyone" can participate. This view has its critics, too; for example, Mark Poster claims that promotions of Internet news groups and other virtual communities as "nascent public spheres that will renew democracy" are "fundamentally misguided" because they "overlook the profound differences between Internet 'cafes' and the agoras of the past" (135). Cyberspace is not transparent space, and dominant sexual-social politics are reproduced on the Net (Tannen, Bruckman): crimes have been committed in MUDs and MOOs, with rape and death in "the Bungle case" on Lambdamoo (Dibbell).

Granted, much about cyberspace is hugely inviting: chat rooms and emoticons and a "web" of access to information (and to "community"). The notion of the web, familiar to composition through both Janet Emig and Marilyn Cooper, touches on ecological metaphors that many writing teachers found more inviting than other mechanistic metaphors for the writing process. The World Wide Web has the same inviting ecological tenor, and the implication is that strands seem to connect the whole world, stretching across and enveloping many sites. At odds with these "warm and fuzzy" notions of the WWW are some material realities: the whole world is *not* in the Web. Issues of access aside, the metaphor of a web also evokes entrapment. Webs, as any fly knows, can be sticky traps for the negligent or gullible; not all of us are safe in a web. A web has thousands, if not millions, of intersecting strands. What I want to know is, how do I get around in here? And how do I get out when I want to leave? (If it weren't for the "Back" and "Home" icons on the newer Web browsers, I would still be lost in cyberspace!)

A lot of Net users find it hard to leave — not only from confusion but from a sense that virtual spaces are more inviting or attractive. When they devote themselves to screens and keyboards, online participants are removing their actual bodies from physical spaces, and that creates another set of problems for geopolitics. As Stephen Doheny-Farina argues in *The Wired Neighborhood*, participation in online communities removes people from their geophysical communities — the streets and schools, sidewalks and shops that make up a neighborhood. People have understandably turned to virtual communities to fulfill some of their needs not being met by physical communities, but Doheny-Farina claims that the Internet's chat rooms are new public spaces. Admitting his own fascination with MediaMOO, in one chapter, Doheny-Farina shows how the supposedly public spaces are more accurately a maze of private rooms, where one's participation ("socialization") is dependent upon one's technical expertise, including one's skill as a typist (61). Settling upon the analogy of virtual communities being like airport bars, Doheny-Farina admits to the compelling nature of these online enterprises, but repeatedly notes the seduction, even the danger, of ignoring the politics of space in our daily environments.

While I am no expert on computers and writing or electronic technologies, my lack of expertise is precisely the point: Most people aren't, and we are the ones entering frontierland well behind the first settlers. The material spaces have changed but the challenges and responsibilities have not. Much as Shaughnessy sat in her worn urban classroom wondering how to help her stunningly unskilled students through the tangle of academic discourse, I sit in a new, well-equipped computer classroom and wonder how I can guide my students through the maze of electronic writing technologies — or if I should turn my composition classes into Computer Literacy 101, Advanced Word Processing, or Introduction to the Internet. Our field is beginning to feel very keenly the responsibility for educating students about electronic writing technologies, and that creates a new level of anxiety (and stimulation) akin to city life. From my experience at a fairly large state university in the Northeast, most of my first-year students are not computer-literate or computer-comfortable. Their high schools in this and surrounding states did not exactly pass out laptops as students walked through the security terminals. Most literacy workers are more affected by budget constraints than by a technology explosion, so expectations to educate students in electronic discourses and computer technologies — while also helping them to think more critically, write more fluently and persuasively, and edit more carefully — becomes an overwhelming responsibility.

The frontier, city, and cyberspace are three imagined geographies that illustrate how composition's socially produced spaces have served to give composition vision and a sense of mission but have also served to mask the politics of space. In the concluding section below, I want to turn to more unfamiliar material places that need our attention, especially in their implications for workers and working conditions.

Between Spaces and Practices: Geographic Possibilities for Studying Composition

As this section suggests, time-space compression affects composition's workers on a daily basis, in concrete ways that need our attention. A spatial politics of writing instruction works to deny transparent space and to attend to neglected places, in their material rather than their imaginary forms, where writers and writing teachers work, live, talk, daydream, or doodle. I'm particularly interested in the increased demands on *time* because technologies have shifted *space*, along with the ways in which technology has increased responsibilities and workloads while material spaces for writing instruction continue to crowd or deteriorate. Composition needs to develop ways to study space differently that might close the gap between imagined geographies and material conditions for writing, between the spaces and practices, or that might confront the way that time-space compression creates illusions about "more time" and "overcoming" spatial barriers.

First, instead of thinking bigger and wider, as composition has typically done — using large imagined geographies to situate and validate composition studies as a discipline — now it is time to think smaller and more locally. And while there have been plenty of studies of classrooms or writing centers or writing programs, a geographic emphasis would insist on more attention to the connection between spaces and practices, more effort to link the material conditions to the activities of particular spaces, whether those be campuses, classrooms, office, computer labs, distance-learning sites, or hotels.

The material spaces of campuses, schoolyards, and classrooms across the country — especially those in economically devastated areas — are marked by ceiling tiles falling onto unswept floors, in rooms with graffiti, trash, and no chalk, or no chalkboard. Classrooms are crowded and too hot or too cold, or with badly filtered air. Certain buildings on many campuses are said to be "poison," where a disproportionate number of illnesses develop, including cancer.[5] To neglect these material realities in qualitative studies of writing instruction is to ignore the politics of space, the ways in which our surroundings or location affect the work that is done there. In research studies of all types, there is scant attention to the conditions and context affecting participants and researchers alike: the weather, the room, the amount or quality of space.

To illustrate, the teaching assistant offices at my institution are referred to, variously, as the pit, the rat's nest, or the hole, where the walls are paper-thin dividers; where there's only one phone for roughly twenty-four instructors; and where occupants last winter had to dodge buckets and trash cans strategically placed to catch rain leaks and falling plaster. Any outsider would immediately recognize the status of the teaching assistants based only on the appearance of their office space. Moving beyond a "thick description," a qualitative study of this space would have to account, in the fullest possible ways, for the material conditions of this office which have everything to do with the work that gets done there. Even newcomers to the academy recognize that the larger or nicer the office, the more senior its occupant, and they don't need a member of a space allocation committee to tell them that.

Perhaps more important than a spatial-politics approach to qualitative research, understanding more about how time-space compression works would enable us to both acknowledge and address working conditions in writing instruction, an issue of the 1990s that will not go away in the new century. Time-space compression creates the illusion that we have "shrunk" space or overcome wide distances; with such a notion comes the conclusion that without travel time, workers can produce more. The capitalist equation — less space equals more time — makes issues of worker exploitation even more complicated for writing instruction.

Issues of working conditions are near the top of the agendas of our professional organizations, with CCCC and MLA having passed or considering resolutions committed to the improvement of the status of non–tenure-track faculty in composition studies. Given the complexity of trying to make any concrete or measurable changes, it seems that one way to improve the status of non–tenure-track faculty in composition is to examine closely the spaces in which we ask them to work, the conditions of those spaces, and the assumptions about time and space that control workers' daily environments.

With laptop computers, around-the-clock access, and the option of asynchronous dialogue, the idea that workers can be productive from "anywhere" at "any time" permeates our culture. Composition workers are just now beginning to recognize how new technologies have affected our workdays, as this passage illustrates:

> In theory, email should create more time. But even though readers can chug along at their own paces, individual paces may not always be in sync. . . . [In participating in Portnet, an online discussion], I was desperate for time. Because of my teaching and professional schedule, my email communication had to wait until evening — late evening. My commitment to Portnet faltered somewhat the first time I turned on my computer at eleven o'clock p.m. and discovered more than forty Portnet messages waiting for me. The next night over eighty Portnet messages appeared on the screen . . . between . . . more than twenty posts from my students . . . and another ten from local colleagues on various matters. (Dickson, qtd. in Allen et al. 377)

Questions about working conditions multiply, too, when considering the impact of distance-learning, the latest rage in the competitive world of higher education, especially in areas of the West and Midwest where towns and cities are far apart. Questions should arise for composition programs about how distance-learning changes our ideas about writing instruction and our common practices involving, as just one example, peer response groups (that is, f2f meetings between writers). What happens to classrooms, libraries, "memorial unions," or lecture halls, especially on some already-deteriorating campuses, many built on the cheap in the late 1960s and early 70s? Should colleges invest more in electronic technologies than in buildings that invite gatherings? Some colleges, in an effort to combine community outreach, distance-learning, and keen competitiveness, have all but eliminated central campuses. For example, Rio Salado Community College in Tempe, Arizona, "has no campus and educates 34,000 students in places like churches and shopping malls, and, increasingly, at home on their computers" (Applebome 24). What happens, then, to the geopolitical spaces of university campuses, especially in light of Doheny-Farina's concerns?

Despite the growing attention to new spaces for the work of our profession, the material sites for composition extend beyond offices, classrooms, computer labs, or cyberspaces. Many of the debates, discussions and conversations about writing instruction take place in hotels or on conference sites distinguished by huge buildings in the downtown areas of major cities, and these sites are especially prone to being treated as transparent space. With the growth of CCCC in the last fifty years, our meeting sites have had to expand and change to accommodate the growing numbers, and site selection for our annual meetings has become the most highly charged, time-consuming, and hotly politicized issue of the CCCC Executive Committee in recent years.

First, on a very practical level, CCCC's annual meeting, held in the spring months of every year, requires thirty-five contiguous meeting rooms and 1,500 sleeping rooms for a four-day gathering of over 3,000 members. Those numbers and needs alone make it difficult to find cities that can serve our membership, and the equation is complicated by the desire to represent fairly or sensitively every diverse constituency within CCCC — to attend to a complicated variety of geographic, economic, and political concerns. While the effort to rotate the locations by region has been in place for years, increasing efforts to accommodate political concerns have made the process of site selection fraught with difficult decisions about "whose" interests count more or which cities have the least offensive laws or statutes. An inept process of site selection was finally challenged after the Executive Committee decided to go to Atlanta for the 1999 convention. Some members of the Gay and Lesbian Caucus announced, in response, that they would boycott that convention, citing in particular their exclusion from the process of selecting convention cities. Since then, the CCCC Officers and Executive Committee have worked to institutionalize the voices and concerns of various caucuses within the organization, making communication across the membership a more integral part of the site selection process (culminating in a recently named "Convention Concerns Committee").

What does it matter where we meet? First, convention sites are tangible examples of the politics of space in composition — where discourses, practices, and people meet in a geopolitical space — and convention hotels and cities also represent some of the neglected places where the work of writing instruction is impacted by geophysical factors. Second, beyond the large concerns about the personal safety of CCCC members, there are many small material realities that affect many things about the success of a conference site. For example, when we are occupied with transportation woes, the cost of a meal in a hotel, or the lack of women's bathroom stalls, time and energy are taken away from conversation about writing, about students, about our programs and ideas. When hotels don't have a central meeting place, or the main lobby is hard to find, or the levels are oddly numbered, members waste time finding each other and sacrifice time talking or listening or engaging.

Imagined geographies have served their purpose in composition's identity-formation and will continue to shape a sense of vision and possibility for writing teachers and researchers. However, the imaginary visions must be more firmly grounded in material conditions: traveling through cyberspace, for example, does require hardware and software, and meeting in hotels does mean that workers must serve and clean up after us.

A spatial politics of writing instruction would not call for a new frontier but for a more paradoxical sense of space to inform our research and practices and to approach the study of the social production of spaces in a field already committed to examining the production of discourse. Most importantly, a spatial politics of writing instruction would resist notions of transparent space that deny the connections to material conditions and would account for the various ways in which time-space compression affects composition's workers.

Acknowledgments

Thanks to those who read, responded, and made me think harder: Kristen Kennedy, Arthur Riss, Nancy Cook, and the two *CCC* reviewers, John Trimbur and Gregory Clark.

Notes

1. Many of the geographers I have been reading have been influenced by Henri Lefebvre and by Foucault's later writings, particularly "Questions on Geography" and "Of Other Spaces." Michel de Certeau's *The Practice of Everyday Life* has been tremendously helpful in thinking about the rhetoric of negotiating space (see esp. "Walking in the City" 91–110) and the connection between spaces and practices. Feminist geographers draw from a range of landscape studies, women's travel writing, and colonialist theories, and urban geographers are likely to frame their work with postmodernist architecture; the fascination with Los Angeles is particularly striking (Jameson; Soja; Harvey). My turn to geography is one response to John Schilb's challenge to rhetoricians: that we should be explaining and illustrating postmodernism for those who cannot (or will not) read Fredric Jameson. In an RSA presentation in May, 1994, Schilb demonstrated this claim through a reading of a Clint Eastwood film, set at the Hotel Bonaventure in Los Angeles.

2. Composition scholarship is increasingly interested in spatial theories and the importance of locations. A quick review of the program for the 1998 CCCC Annual Convention yields at least a dozen panel or forum titles with such keywords as space, place, landscapes, the politics of space, the public sphere, postmodern geography, or travel. See also Gregory Clark's 1998 *CCC* essay, "Writing as Travel, or Rhetoric on the Road."

3. For example, a 1988 Gallup survey showed that 75% of Americans age 18–24 couldn't locate the Persian Gulf on a world map and 25% couldn't find the Pacific Ocean (Horwitz A8).

4. Most recently, Harris has offered *public* as a better keyword than *community*. See *A Teaching Subject*, pp. 107–10.

5. The campus building I work in is just plain filthy, one result of severe budget cuts, and the conditions do affect the morale of workers. The state of the bathroom, while it may "bond" the women on my floor, does not exactly promote worker loyalty or productivity.

Works Cited

Allen, Michael, et al. "Portfolios, WAC, Email, and Assessment: An Inquiry on Portnet." *Situating Portfolios.* Ed. Kathleen Blake Yancey and Irwin Weiser. Logan: Utah State UP, 1997. 370–84.

Anson, Chris. "Assigning and Responding to Student Writing." Colgate U, Hamilton, NY, Aug. 1995.

Anzaldúa, Gloria. *Borderlands / La Frontera.* San Francisco: Aunt Lute, 1987.

Applebome, Peter. "Community Colleges at the Crossroads: Which Way Is Up?" *New York Times* 3 Aug. 1997: 4A; 24–26; 30.

Blunt, Alison, and Gillian Rose, eds. *Writing Women and Space: Colonial and Postcolonial Geographies.* NY: Guilford, 1994.

Bolter, Jay David. *Writing Space: The Computer, Hypertext, and the History of Writing.* Mahwah: Erlbaum, 1991.

Bowden, Darsie. "The Limits of Containment: Text-as-Container in Composition Studies." *CCC* 44 (1993): 364–79.

Bruckman, Amy S. "Gender Swapping on the Internet." Vitanza. 441–47.

Buder, Leonard. "Open-Admissions Policy Taxes City U. Resources." *New York Times* 12 Oct. 1970: A1+.

Certeau, Michel de. *The Practice of Everyday Life.* Berkeley: U of California P, 1984.

Clark, Gregory. "Writing as Travel, or Rhetoric on the Road." *CCC* 49 (1998): 9–23.

Cooper, Marilyn M. "The Ecology of Writing." *College English* 48 (1986): 364–75.

Cox, Brad. "Taming the Electronic Frontier." http://gopher.gmu.edu/bcox/LRN6372/00LRNG572.html.

Cushman, Ellen. "Rhetorician as Agent of Social Change." *CCC* 47 (1996): 7–28.

Dibbell, Julian. "A Rape in Cyberspace." Vitanza. 448–65.

Doheny-Farina, Stephen. *The Wired Neighborhood.* New Haven: Yale UP, 1996.

Emig, Janet. "Mina Pendo Shaughnessy." *CCC* 30 (1979): 37–8.

Faigley, Lester. *Fragments of Rationality: Postmodernity and the Subject of Composition.* U of Pittsburgh P, 1992.

Harris, Joseph. *A Teaching Subject: Composition since 1966.* Upper Saddle River: Prentice, 1997.

Harvey, David. *The Condition of Postmodernity: An Enquiry into the Origins of Cultural Change.* Cambridge: Blackwell, 1989.

Hill, Carolyn Ericksen. *Writing from the Margins: Power and Pedagogy for Teachers of Composition.* New York: Oxford UP, 1990.

Hitt, Jack. "Atlas Shrugged: The New Face of Maps." *Lingua Franca* 5.5 (1995): 24–33.

Horwitz, Sari. "No Longer a World Apart: Grant Brings Geography Home to District Students." *Washington Post* 19 Mar. 1994: A1; A8.

Jackson, Peter. *Maps of Meaning: An Introduction to Cultural Geography.* New York: Routledge, 1989.

Jameson, Fredric. *Postmodernism, or, The Cultural Logic of Late Capitalism.* Durham: Duke UP, 1991.

Jessup, Emily. "Feminism and Computers in Composition Instruction." *Evolving Perspectives on Computers and Composition Studies: Questions for the 1990s.* Ed. Gail E. Hawisher and Cynthia L. Selfe. Urbana: NCTE, 1991. 336–55.

Kozol, Jonathan. *Savage Inequalities: Children in America's Schools.* New York: Crown, 1991.

Lauer, Janice M. "Composition Studies: A Dappled Discipline." *Rhetoric Review* 3 (1984): 20–29.

Lyons, Robert. "Mina Shaughnessy." *Traditions of Inquiry.* Ed. John Brereton. New York: Oxford UP, 1985. 171–89.

Maher, Jane. *Mina P. Shaughnessy: Her Life and Work.* Urbana: NCTE, 1997.

Markoff, John. "Hacker and Grifter Duel on the Net." Vitanza. 119–21.

Massey, Doreen. *Space, Place, and Gender.* Minneapolis: U of Minnesota P, 1994.

Miller, Susan. *Textual Carnivals: The Politics of Composition.* Southern Illinois UP, 1991.

Muchiri, Mary N., Nshindi G. Mulamba, Greg Myers, and Deoscorous B. Ndoloi. "Importing Composition: Teaching and Researching Academic Writing beyond North America." *CCC* 46 (1995): 175–98.

Nash, Catherine. "Remapping the Body/Land: New Cartographies of Identity, Gender, and Landscape in Ireland." *Writing Women and Space: Colonial and Postcolonial Geographies.* Ed. Alison Blunt and Gillian Rose. 227–50.

Neel, Jasper. "The Degradation of Rhetoric; Or, Dressing Like a Gentleman, Speaking Like a Scholar." *Rhetoric, Sophistry, Pragmatism.* Ed. Steven Mailloux. New York: Cambridge UP, 1995. 61–81.

North, Stephen M. *The Making of Knowledge in Composition: Portrait of an Emerging Field.* Upper Montclair: Boynton, 1987.

Phelps, Louise Wetherbee. "The Domain of Composition." *Rhetoric Review* 4 (1986): 182–95.

Poster, Mark. "The Net as a Public Sphere?" *Wired* Nov. 1995: 135–36.

Pratt, Mary Louise. "Arts of the Contact Zone." *Profession* 91 (1991): 33–40.

"Redoubling the Efforts at Teaching Geography." *New York Times* 19 Nov. 1993: C, 11:1.

Rheingold, Howard. *The Virtual Community: Homesteading on the Electronic Frontier.* New York: Harper, 1993.

Rich, Adrienne. "Teaching Language in Open Admissions." *On Lies, Secrets, and Silence: Selected Prose 1966–1978.* New York: Norton, 1979. 51–68.

Rose, Gillian. *Feminism and Geography: The Limits of Geographical Knowledge.* Minneapolis: U of Minnesota P, 1993.

Rose, Mike. *Lives on the Boundary.* New York: Free P, 1989.

Schilb, John. "Articulating the Discourses of Postmodernism." Rhetoric Society of America, Norfolk, VA, May 1994.

Selfe, Cynthia, and Richard J. Selfe, Jr. "The Politics of the Interface: Power and Its Exercise in Electronic Contact Zones." *CCC* 45 (1994): 480–504.

Shaughnessy, Mina. *Errors and Expectations.* New York: Oxford UP, 1977.

Slagle, Diane Buckles, and Shirley K. Rose. "Domesticating English Studies." *Journal of Teaching Writing* 13 (1994): 147–68.

Soja, Edward W. *Postmodern Geographies: The Reassertion of Space in Critical Social Theory.* New York: Verso, 1989.

Tannen, Deborah. "Gender Gap in Cyberspace." Vitanza. 141–43.

"Teachers Lament Geography Scores." *New York Times* 12 Mar. 1985: III, 11:1.

Tompkins, Jane. *West of Everything: The Inner Life of Westerns.* New York: Oxford UP, 1992.

Trimbur, John. "Consensus and Difference in Collaborative Learning." *College English* 51 (1989): 602–16.

Turner, Frederick Jackson. "The Significance of the Frontier in American History (1893)." *History, Frontier, and Section.* Albuquerque: U of New Mexico P, 1993. 59–91.

Vitanza, Victor, ed. *CyberReader.* Boston: Allyn, 1996.

Wiener, Harvey S. Rev. of *Errors and Expectations,* by Mina P. Shaughnessy. *College English* 38 (1977): 715–17.

Wilson, Elizabeth. "The Rhetoric of Urban Space." *New Left Review* 209 (1995): 146–60.

Reynolds's Insights as a Resource for Your Teaching

1. After reading Reynolds's essay, the question "Where do you work?" resonates with particular complexity. Try brainstorming some distinguishing features of the student body at the institution where you teach. What sorts of regional influences or economic factors shape their experience in your classroom? In what ways do these influences shape the administration under which you work?

2. While the essay's three dominant metaphors (frontier, city, cyberspace) have a certain value, they also are undoubtedly loaded with myths and assumptions that mask key aspects of your distinctive environment. Explore the limitations of these metaphors as models for understanding your classroom. Can you identify actual moments or imagine possible scenarios where this masking proceeds with particularly destructive results?

Reynolds's Insights as a Resource for Your Writing Classroom

1. Summarize Reynolds's ideas about the metaphor of the frontier and the city for your students. What concerns do they have about this way of looking at the classroom? What potential problems do they envision?

2. In considering the increased accessibility that telecommunications technology offers to regions and people on a global scale, do students think that this access emphasizes the perception and understanding of cultural, social, and regional differences, or do they think that it is contributing to an increasingly homogenized worldview?

The Banking Concept of Education

Paulo Freire

The classroom functions as a microcosm of the larger society, and thus the power dynamics and forms of authority that rule a classroom are perhaps the primary lessons that most students learn in school. In this chapter from his seminal 1970 work, Pedagogy of the Oppressed, *Paulo Freire uses banking as a metaphor to describe teaching that treats students as passive containers for their teachers' knowledge. In order to restore equality to the classroom, educators must do away with hierarchy and engage in meaningful dialogue with their fellow learners. According to Freire, students can free themselves from structures of domination by actively collaborating on solutions to real-world problems, a practice by which they embark on open-ended humanist revolution.*

A careful analysis of the teacher-student relationship at any level, inside or outside the school, reveals its fundamentally *narrative* character. This relationship involves a narrating Subject (the teacher) and patient, listening objects (the students). The contents, whether values or empirical dimensions of reality, tend in the process of being narrated to become lifeless and petrified. Education is suffering from narration sickness.

The teacher talks about reality as if it were motionless, static, compartmentalized, and predictable. Or else he expounds on a topic completely alien to the existential experience of the students. His task is to "fill" the students with the contents of his narration — contents which are detached from reality, disconnected from the totality that engendered them and could give them significance. Words are emptied of their concreteness and become a hollow, alienated, and alienating verbosity.

The outstanding characteristic of this narrative education, then, is the sonority of words, not their transforming power. "Four times four is sixteen; the capital of Pará is Belém." The student records, memorizes, and repeats these phrases without perceiving what four times four really means, or realizing the true significance of "capital" in the affirmation "the capital of Pará is Belém," that is, what Belém means for Pará and what Pará means for Brazil.

Narration (with the teacher as narrator) leads the students to memorize mechanically the narrated content. Worse yet, it turns them into "containers," into "receptacles" to be "filled" by the teacher. The more completely he fills the receptacles, the better a teacher he is. The more meekly the receptacles permit themselves to be filled, the better students they are.

Education thus becomes an act of depositing, in which the students are the depositories and the teacher is the depositor. Instead of communicating, the teacher issues communiqués and makes deposits which the students patiently receive, memorize, and repeat. This is the "banking" concept of education, in which the scope of action allowed to the students extends only as far as receiving, filing, and storing the deposits. They do, it is true, have the opportunity to become collectors or cataloguers of the things they store. But in the last analysis, it is men themselves who are filed away through the lack of creativity, transformation, and knowledge in this (at best) misguided system. For apart from inquiry, apart from the praxis, men cannot be truly human. Knowledge emerges only through invention and re-invention, through the restless, impatient, continuing, hopeful inquiry men pursue in the world, with the world, and with each other.

In the banking concept of education, knowledge is a gift bestowed by those who consider themselves knowledgeable upon those whom they consider to know nothing. Projecting an absolute ignorance onto others, a characteristic of the ideology of oppression, negates education and knowledge as processes of inquiry. The teacher presents himself to his students as their necessary opposite; by considering their ignorance absolute, he justifies his own existence. The students, alienated like the slave in the Hegelian dialectic, accept their ignorance as justifying the teacher's existence — but, unlike the slave, they never discover that they educate the teacher.

The *raison d'être* of libertarian education, on the other hand, lies in its drive towards reconciliation. Education must begin with the solution of the teacher-student contradiction, by reconciling the poles of the contradiction so that both are simultaneously teachers *and* students.

This solution is not (nor can it be) found in the banking concept. On the contrary, banking education maintains and even stimulates the contradiction through the following attitudes and practices, which mirror oppressive society as a whole:

a. the teacher teaches and the students are taught;
b. the teacher knows everything and the students know nothing;
c. the teacher thinks and the students are thought about;
d. the teacher talks and the students listen — meekly;
e. the teacher disciplines and the students are disciplined;
f. the teacher chooses and enforces his choice, and the students comply;
g. the teacher acts and the students have the illusion of acting through the action of the teacher;
h. the teacher chooses the program content, and the students (who were not consulted) adapt to it;
i. the teacher confuses the authority of knowledge with his own professional authority, which he sets in opposition to the freedom of the students;
j. the teacher is the Subject of the learning process, while the pupils are mere objects.

It is not surprising that the banking concept of education regards men as adaptable, manageable beings. The more students work at storing the deposits entrusted to them, the less they develop the critical consciousness which would result from their intervention in the world as transformers of that world. The more completely they accept the passive role imposed on them, the more they tend simply to adapt to the world as it is and to the fragmented view of reality deposited in them.

The capability of banking education to minimize or annul the students' creative power and to stimulate their credulity serves the interests of the oppressors, who care neither to have the world revealed nor to see it transformed. The oppressors use their "humanitarianism" to preserve a profitable situation. Thus they react almost instinctively against any experiment in education which stimulates the critical faculties and is not content with a partial view of reality but always seeks out the ties which link one point to another and one problem to another.

Indeed, the interests of the oppressors lie in "changing the consciousness of the oppressed, not the situation which oppresses them";[1] for the more the oppressed can be led to adapt to that situation, the more easily they can be dominated. To achieve this end, the oppressors use the banking concept of education in conjunction with a paternalistic social action apparatus, within which the oppressed receive the euphemistic title of "welfare recipients." They are treated as individual cases, as marginal men who deviate from the general configuration of a "good, organized, and just" society. The oppressed are regarded as the pathology of the healthy society, which must therefore adjust these "incompetent and lazy" folk to its own patterns by changing their mentality. These marginals need to be "integrated," "incorporated" into the healthy society that they have "forsaken."

The truth is, however, that the oppressed are not "marginals," are not men living "outside" society. They have always been "inside" — inside the structure which made them "beings for others." The solution is not to "integrate" them into the structure of oppression, but to transform that structure so that they can become "beings for themselves." Such transformation, of course, would undermine the oppressors' purposes; hence their utilization of the banking concept of education to avoid the threat of student *conscientização*.

The banking approach to adult education, for example, will never propose to students that they critically consider reality. It will deal instead with such vital questions as whether Roger gave green grass to the goat, and insist upon the importance of learning that, on the contrary, *R*oger gave green grass to the *r*abbit. The "humanism" of the banking approach masks the effort to turn men into automatons — the very negation of their ontological vocation to be more fully human.

Those who use the banking approach, knowingly or unknowingly (for there are innumerable well-intentioned bank-clerk teachers who do not realize that they are serving only to dehumanize), fail to perceive that the deposits themselves contain contradictions about reality. But, sooner or later, these contradictions may lead formerly passive students to turn against their domestication and the attempt to domesticate reality. They may discover through existential experience that their present way of life is irreconcilable with their vocation to become fully human. They may perceive through their relations with reality that reality is really a *process,* undergoing constant transformation. If men are searchers and their ontological vocation is humanization, sooner or later they may perceive the contradiction in which banking education seeks to maintain them, and then engage themselves in the struggle for their liberation.

But the humanist, revolutionary educator cannot wait for this possibility to materialize. From the outset, his efforts must coincide with those of the students to engage in critical thinking and the quest for mutual humanization. His efforts must be imbued with a profound trust in men and their creative power. To achieve this, he must be a partner of the students in his relations with them.

The banking concept does not admit to such partnership — and necessarily so. To resolve the teacher-student contradiction, to exchange the role of depositor, prescriber, domesticator, for the role of student among students would be to undermine the power of oppression and serve the cause of liberation.

Implicit in the banking concept is the assumption of a dichotomy between man and the world: man is merely *in* the world, not *with* the world or with others; man is spectator, not re-creator. In this view, man is not a conscious being (*corpo consciente*); he is rather the possessor of *a* consciousness: an empty "mind" passively open to the reception of deposits of reality from the world outside. For example, my desk, my books, my coffee cup, all the objects before me — as bits of the world which surrounds me — would be "inside" me, exactly as I am inside my study right now. This view makes no distinction between being accessible to consciousness and entering consciousness. The distinction, however, is essential: the objects which surround me are simply accessible to my consciousness, not located within it. I am aware of them, but they are not inside me.

It follows logically from the banking notion of consciousness that the educator's role is to regulate the way the world "enters into" the students. His task is to organize a process which already occurs spontaneously, to "fill" the students by making deposits of information which he considers to constitute true knowledge.[2] And since men "receive" the world as passive entities, education should make them more passive still, and adapt them to the world. The educated man is the adapted man, because he is better "fit" for the world. Translated into practice, this concept is well suited to the purposes of the oppressors, whose tranquility rests on how well men fit the world the oppressors have created, and how little they question it.

The more completely the majority adapt to the purposes which the dominant minority prescribe for them (thereby depriving them of the right to their own purposes), the more easily the minority can continue to prescribe. The theory and practice of banking education serve this end quite efficiently. Verbalistic lessons, reading requirements,[3] the methods for evaluating "knowledge," the distance between the teacher and the taught, the criteria for promotion: everything in this ready-to-wear approach serves to obviate thinking.

The bank-clerk educator does not realize that there is no true security in his hypertrophied role, that one must seek to live *with* others in solidarity. One cannot impose oneself, nor even merely co-exist with one's students. Solidarity requires true communication, and the concept by which such an educator is guided fears and proscribes communication.

Yet only through communication can human life hold meaning. The teacher's thinking is authenticated only by the authenticity of the students' thinking. The teacher cannot think for his students, nor can he impose his thought on them. Authentic thinking, thinking that is concerned about *reality,* does not take place in ivory tower isolation, but only in communication. If it is true that thought has meaning only when generated by action upon the world, the subordination of students to teachers becomes impossible.

Because banking education begins with a false understanding of men as objects, it cannot promote the development of what Fromm calls "biophily," but instead produces its opposite: "necrophily."

> While life is characterized by growth in a structured, functional manner, the necrophilous person loves all that does not grow, all that is mechanical. The necrophilous person is driven by the desire to transform the organic into the inorganic, to approach life mechanically, as if all living persons were things. . . . Memory, rather than experience; having, rather than being, is what counts. The necrophilous person can related to an object — a flower or a person — only if he possesses it; hence a threat to his possession is a threat to himself; if he loses possession he loses contact with the world. . . . He loves control, and in the act of controlling he kills life.[4]

Oppression — overwhelming control — is necrophilic; it is nourished by love of death, not life. The banking concept of education, which serves the interests of oppression, is also necrophilic. Based on a mechanistic, static, naturalistic, spatialized view of consciousness, it transforms students into receiving objects. It attempts to control thinking and action, leads men to adjust to the world, and inhibits their creative power.

When their efforts to act responsibly are frustrated, when they find themselves unable to use their faculties, men suffer. "This suffering due to impotence is rooted in the very fact that the human equilibrium has been disturbed."[5] But the inability to act which causes men's anguish also causes them to reject their impotence, by attempting

> . . . to restore [their] capacity to act. But can [they], and how? One way is to submit to and identify with a person or group having power. By this symbolic participation in another person's life, [men have] the illusion of acting, when in reality [they] only submit to and become a part of those who act.[6]

Populist manifestations perhaps best exemplify this type of behavior by the oppressed, who, by identifying with charismatic leaders, come to feel that they themselves are active and effective. The rebellion they express as they emerge in the historical process is motivated by that desire to act effectively. The dominant elites consider the remedy to be more domination and repression, carried out in the name of freedom, order, and social peace (that is, the peace of the elites). Thus they can condemn — logically, from their point of view — "the violence of a strike by workers and [can] call upon the state in the same breath to use violence in putting down the strike."[7]

Education as the exercise of domination stimulates the credulity of students, with the ideological intent (often not perceived by educators) of indoctrinating them to adapt to the world of oppression. This accusation is not made in the naïve hope that the dominant elites will thereby simply abandon the practice. Its objective is to call the attention of true humanists to the fact that they cannot use banking educational methods in the pursuit of liberation, for they would only negate that very pursuit. Nor may a revolutionary society inherit these methods from an oppressor society. The revolutionary society which practices banking education is either misguided or mistrusting of men. In either event, it is threatened by the specter of reaction.

Unfortunately, those who espouse the cause of liberation are themselves surrounded and influenced by the climate which generates the banking concept, and often do not perceive its true significance or its dehumanizing power. Paradoxically, then, they utilize this same instrument of alienation in what they consider an effort to liberate. Indeed, some "revolutionaries" brand as "innocents," "dreamers," or even "reactionaries" those who would challenge this educational practice. But one does not liberate men by alienating them. Authentic liberation — the process of humanization — is not another deposit to be made in men. Liberation is a praxis: the action and reflection of men upon their world in order to transform it. Those truly committed to the cause of liberation can accept neither the mechanistic concept of consciousness as an empty vessel to be filled, nor the use of banking methods of domination (propaganda, slogans — deposits) in the name of liberation.

Those truly committed to liberation must reject the banking concept in its entirety, adopting instead a concept of men as conscious beings, and consciousness as consciousness intent upon the world. They must abandon the educational goal of deposit-making and replace it with the posing of the problems of men in their relations with the world. "Problem-posing" education, responding to the essence of consciousness — *intentionality* — rejects communiqués and embodies communication. It epitomizes the special characteristic of consciousness: being *conscious of,* not only as intent on objects but as turned in upon itself in a Jasperian "split" — consciousness as consciousness *of* consciousness.

Liberating education consists in acts of cognition, not transferrals of information. It is a learning situation in which the cognizable object (far from being the end of the cognitive act) intermediates the cognitive actors — teacher on the one hand and students on the other. Accordingly, the practice of problem-posing education entails at the outset that the teacher-student contradiction be resolved. Dialogical relations — indispensable to the capacity of cognitive actors to cooperate in perceiving the same cognizable object — are otherwise impossible.

Indeed, problem-posing education, which breaks with the vertical patterns characteristic of banking education, can fulfill its function as the practice of freedom only if it can overcome the above contradiction. Through dialogue, the teacher-of-the-students and the students-of-the-teacher cease to exist and a new term emerges: teacher-student with students-teacher. The teacher is no longer merely the-one-who-teaches, but one who is himself taught in dialogue with the students, who in turn while being taught also teach. They become jointly responsible for a process in which all grow. In this process, arguments based on "authority" are no longer valid; in order to function, authority must be *on the side of* freedom, not *against* it. Here, no one teaches another, nor is anyone self-taught. Men teach each other, mediated by the world, by the cognizable objects which in banking education are "owned" by the teacher.

The banking concept (with its tendency to dichotomize everything) distinguishes two stages in the action of the educator. During the first, he cognizes a cognizable object while he prepares his lessons in his study or his laboratory; during the second, he expounds to his students about that object. The students are not called upon to know but to memorize the contents narrated by the teacher. Nor do the students practice any act of cognition, since the object towards which that act should be directed is the property of the teacher rather than a medium evoking the critical reflection of both teacher and students. Hence in the name of the "preservation of culture and knowledge" we have a system which achieves neither true knowledge nor true culture.

The problem-posing method does not dichotomize the activity of the teacher-student: he is not "cognitive" at one point and "narrative" at another. He is always "cognitive," whether preparing a project or engaging in dialogue with the students. He does not regard cognizable objects as his private property, but as the object of reflection by himself and the students. In this way, the problem-posing educator constantly re-forms his reflections in the reflection of the students. The students — no longer docile listeners — are now critical co-investigators in dialogue with the teacher. The teacher presents the material to the students for their consideration, and re-considers his earlier considerations as the students express their own. The role of the problem-posing educator is to create, together with the students, the conditions under which knowledge at the level of the *doxa* is superseded by true knowledge, at the level of the *logos*.

Whereas banking education anesthetizes and inhibits creative power, problem-posing education involves a constant unveiling of reality. The former attempts to maintain the *submersion* of consciousness; the latter strives for the *emergence* of consciousness and *critical intervention* in reality.

Students, as they are increasingly posed with problems relating to themselves in the world and with the world, will feel increasingly challenged and obliged to respond to that challenge. Because they apprehend the challenge as interrelated to other problems within a total context, not as a theoretical question, the resulting comprehension tends to be increasingly critical and thus constantly less alienated. Their response to the challenge evokes new challenges, followed by new understandings; and gradually the students come to regard themselves as committed.

Education as the practice of freedom — as opposed to education as the practice of domination — denies that man is abstract, isolated, independent, and unattached to the world; it also denies that the world exists as a reality apart from men. Authentic reflection considers neither abstract man nor the world without men, but men in their relations with the world. In these relations consciousness and world are simultaneous: consciousness neither precedes the world nor follows it.

> La conscience et le monde sont donnés d'un même coup: extérieur par essence à la conscience, le monde est, par essence relatif à elle.[8]

In one of our culture circles in Chile, the group was discussing (based on a codification) the anthropological concept of culture. In the midst of the discussion, a peasant who by banking standards was completely ignorant said: "Now I see that without man there is no world." When the educator responded: "Let's say, for the sake of argument, that all the men on earth were to die, but that the earth itself remained, together with trees, birds, animals, rivers, seas, the stars . . . wouldn't all this be a world?" "Oh no," the peasant replied emphatically. "There would be no one to say: 'This is a world.'"

The peasant wished to express the idea that there would be lacking the consciousness of the world which necessarily implies the world of consciousness. *I* cannot exist without a *not-I*. In turn, the *not-I* depends on that existence. The world which brings consciousness into existence becomes the world *of* that consciousness. Hence, the previously cited affirmation of Sartre: *"La conscience et le monde sont donnés d'un même coup."*

As men, simultaneously reflecting on themselves and on the world, increase the scope of their perception, they begin to direct their observations towards previously inconspicuous phenomena:

> In perception properly so-called, as an explicit awareness [*Gewahren*], I
> am turned towards the object, to the paper, for instance. I apprehend it
> as being this here and now. The apprehension is a singling out, every
> object having a background in experience. Around and about the paper
> lie books, pencils, ink-well, and so forth, and these in a certain sense are
> also "perceived," perceptually there, in the "field of intuition"; but whilst
> I was turned towards the paper there was no turning in their direction,
> nor any apprehending of them, not even in a secondary sense. They
> appeared and yet were not singled out, were not posited on their own
> account. Every perception of a thing has such a zone of background

> intuitions or background awareness, if "intuiting" already includes the
> state of being turned towards, and this also is a "conscious experience,"
> or more briefly a "consciousness of" all indeed that in point of fact lies in
> the co-perceived objective background.[9]

That which had existed objectively but had not been perceived in its
deeper implications (if indeed it was perceived at all) begins to "stand
out," assuming the character of a problem and therefore of challenge.
Thus, men begin to single out elements from their "background
awarenesses" and to reflect upon them. These elements are now objects of men's consideration, and, as such, objects of their action and
cognition.

In problem-posing education, men develop their power to perceive
critically *the way they exist* in he world *with which* and *in which* they
find themselves; they come to see the world not as a static reality, but
as a reality in process, in transformation. Although the dialectical relations of men with the world exist independently of how these relations
are perceived (or whether or not they are perceived at all), it is also
true that the form of action men adopt is to a large extent a function of
how they perceive themselves in the world. Hence, the teacher-student
and the students-teachers reflect simultaneously on themselves and
the world without dichotomizing this reflection from action, and thus
establish an authentic form of thought and action.

Once again, the two educational concepts and practices under analysis come into conflict. Banking education (for obvious reasons) attempts,
by mythicizing reality, to conceal certain facts which explain the way
men exist in the world; problem-posing education sets itself the task of
demythologizing. Banking education resists dialogue; problem-posing
education regards dialogue as indispensable to the act of cognition which
unveils reality. Banking education treats students as objects of assistance; problem-posing education makes them critical thinkers. Banking education inhibits creativity and domesticates (although it cannot
completely destroy) the *intentionality* of consciousness by isolating consciousness from the world, thereby denying men their ontological and
historical vocation of becoming more fully human. Problem-posing education bases itself on creativity and stimulates true reflection and action upon reality, thereby responding to the vocation of men as beings
who are authentic only when engaged in inquiry and creative transformation. In sum: banking theory and practice, as immobilizing and fix-
ating forces, fail to acknowledge men as historical beings; problem-
posing theory and practice take men's historicity as their starting point.

Problem-posing education affirms men as beings in the process of
becoming — as unfinished, uncompleted beings in and with a likewise
unfinished reality. Indeed, in contrast to other animals who are unfinished, but not historical, men know themselves to be unfinished; they
are aware of their incompletion. In this incompletion and this awareness lie the very roots of education as an exclusively human manifes-

tation. The unfinished character of men and the transformational character of reality necessitate that education be an ongoing activity.

Education is thus constantly remade in the praxis. In order to *be,* it must *become.* Its "duration" (in the Bergsonian meaning of the word) is found in the interplay of the opposites *permanence* and *change.* The banking method emphasizes permanence and becomes reactionary; problem-posing education — which accepts neither a "well-behaved" present nor a predetermined future — roots itself in the dynamic present and becomes revolutionary.

Problem-posing education is revolutionary futurity. Hence it is prophetic (and, as such, hopeful). Hence, it corresponds to the historical nature of man. Hence, it affirms men as beings who transcend themselves, who move forward and look ahead, for whom immobility represents a fatal threat, for whom looking at the past must only be a means of understanding more clearly what and who they are so that they can more wisely build the future. Hence, it identifies with the movement which engages men as beings aware of their incompletion — an historical movement which has its point of departure, its Subjects and its objective.

The point of departure of the movement lies in men themselves. But since men do not exist apart from the world, apart from reality, the movement must begin with the men-world relationship. Accordingly, the point of departure must always be with men in the "here and now," which constitutes the situation within which they are submerged, from which they emerge, and in which they intervene. Only by starting from this situation — which determines their perception of it — can they begin to move. To do this authentically they must perceive their state not as fated and unalterable, but merely as limiting — and therefore challenging.

Whereas the banking method directly or indirectly reinforces men's fatalistic perception of their situation, the problem-posing method presents this very situation to them as a problem. As the situation becomes the object of their cognition, the naïve or magical perception which produced their fatalism gives way to perception which is able to perceive itself even as it perceives reality, and can thus be critically objective about that reality.

A deepened consciousness of their situation leads men to apprehend that situation as an historical reality susceptible of transformation. Resignation gives way to the drive for transformation and inquiry, over which men feel themselves to be in control. If men, as historical beings necessarily engaged with other men in a movement of inquiry, did not control that movement, it would be (and is) a violation of men's humanity. Any situation in which some men prevent others from engaging in the process of inquiry is one of violence. The means used are not important; to alienate men from their own decision-making is to change them into objects.

This movement of inquiry must be directed towards humanization — man's historical vocation. The pursuit of full humanity, however, cannot be carried out in isolation or individualism, but only in fellowship and solidarity; therefore it cannot unfold in the antagonistic relations between oppressors and oppressed. No one can be authentically human while he prevents others from being so. Attempting *to be more* human, individualistically, leads to *having more,* egotistically: a form of dehumanization. Not that it is not fundamental *to have* in order *to be* human. Precisely because it *is* necessary, some men's *having* must not be allowed to constitute an obstacle to others' *having,* must not consolidate the power of the former to crush the latter.

Problem-posing education, as a humanist and liberating praxis, posits as fundamental that men subjected to domination must fight for their emancipation. To that end, it enables teachers and students to become Subjects of the educational process by overcoming authoritarianism and an alienating intellectualism; it also enables men to overcome their false perception of reality. The world — no longer something to be described with deceptive words — becomes the object of that transforming action by men which results in their humanization.

Problem-posing education does not and cannot serve the interests of the oppressor. No oppressive order could permit the oppressed to begin to question: Why? While only a revolutionary society can carry out this education in systematic terms, the revolutionary leaders need not take full power before they can employ the method. In the revolutionary process, the leaders cannot utilize the banking method as an interim measure, justified on grounds of expediency, with the intention of *later* behaving in a genuinely revolutionary fashion. They must be revolutionary — that is to say, dialogical — from the outset.

Notes

1. Simone de Beauvoir, *La Pensée de Droite, Aujord'hui* (Paris); ST, *El Pensamiento político de la Derecha* (Buenos Aires, 1963), p. 34.
2. This concept corresponds to what Sartre calls the "digestive" or "nutritive" concept of education, in which knowledge is "fed" by the teacher to the students to "fill them out." See Jean-Paul Sartre, "Une idée fundamentale de la phénoménologie de Husserl: L'intentionalité," *Situations I* (Paris, 1947).
3. For example, some professors specify in their reading lists that a book should be read from pages 10 to 15 — and do this to "help" their students!
4. Eric Fromm, *The Heart of Man* (New York, 1966), p. 41.
5. *Ibid.,* p. 31.
6. *Ibid.*
7. Reinhold Niebuhr, *Moral Man and Immoral Society* (New York, 1960), p. 130.
8. Sartre, *op. cit.,* p. 32.
9. Edmund Husserl, *Ideas — General Introduction to Pure Phenomenology* (London, 1969), pp. 105–06.

Freire's Insights as a Resource for Your Teaching

1. In the opening paragraph of the essay, Freire argues that knowledge becomes "lifeless and petrified" in traditional banking education; he labels this problem "narration sickness." Does all lecture-based teaching inevitably suffer from narration sickness? How might you tailor your own more extensive remarks to students in ways that maximize their potential for "problem-posing"?

2. Consider Freire's theory in light of James A. Berlin's classifications of cognitivist, expressionist, and social-epistemic ideologies of writing instruction (pp. 19–38). Which pattern does Freire's approach most closely follow? Which type of ideology would most likely result in teaching that suffers from "narration sickness"?

Freire's Insights as a Resource for Your Writing Classroom

1. Outline Freire's concepts of "banking" and "problem-posing" for students. Ask them to describe a particularly positive or negative experience in their development as student writers, analyzing the experience in terms of Freire's theory.

2. Experiment with different degrees of "banking" and "problem-posing" during a particular phase of your class. To evaluate and fine-tune your approach, reflect on the results in your teaching journal and share your ideas with colleagues.

Can Teaching, Of All Things, Prove to Be Our Salvation?

Kurt Spellmeyer

The power academic institutions wield is, paradoxically, also a weakness. Their extraordinary authority over the intellectual legacies and traditions we inherit can also articulate itself as a debilitating slowness in responding to cultural change and pressing international crises. How can we narrow the gap that separates the "ivory tower" from the lives of those struggling today in a world that — perhaps more desperately than ever — needs meaningful intellectual and cultural leadership?

In this chapter from Arts of Living: Reinventing the Humanities for the Twenty-First Century *(2003), Kurt Spellmeyer describes one university's attempt to create a curriculum that would provide students with essential knowledge and skills. The administration devised a plan*

*that, rather than decide what young people needed to know — which is
the aim of the great books courses — instead attempted to anticipate the
problems they would have to solve. Spellmeyer reports that within the
rigid structure and demands of the academy, this interdisciplinary
initiative was almost doomed from the start. It succeeded, however, in
finding an accommodating home in the writing program.*

Just before noon on September 11, 2001, while I was working at home
on revisions to this book, my wife Barbara phoned to tell me that
New York City was under siege. Of course I thought she was joking.
Like millions of Americans that morning, I sat speechless as the World
Trade Towers burned and fell, again and again in endless televised
replays.

In the immediate aftermath, it become commonplace to say that
nothing would ever be the same, and in a certain sense this was true.
Candidate Bush had eschewed "nation building," but President Bush
found himself preoccupied with the forging of multicontinental coalitions while sending many thousands of troops overseas — the exact
figure still remains under wraps — to a semiarid plateau more than
seven thousand miles away from his "ranch" in Crawford, Texas. But
this was not the only change. Long regarded with suspicion by most
Americans west of the Hudson, New Yorkers were suddenly transformed
into global ambassadors of a nation that had shown it could "pull together in crisis," its police and fire squads hailed as heros, its abrasive
and scandal-tainted mayor elevated to *Time*'s "Person of the Year," in
the company of Gandhi and Winston Churchill. And if the memory of
massacres at My Lai and Kent State had soured aging boomers on the
use of armed forces, the popular press compared troops landing in Kabul
to the liberating armies of D-Day. At this moment, no one can even
begin to foresee the ramifications of such developments.

Yet at the same time, nothing has changed in at least one important sense. The education most Americans now receive is essentially
the same as a century ago, in form if not in content. Yes, more Americans finish high school, more get to college and take degrees, but the
organization of basic knowledge, the stock-in-trade of the humanities,
assumed its current appearance well before the invention of airplanes
and cars, before the two World Wars, before people understood the structure of the atom, before the United Nations, before the discovery of
penicillin, and before the mapping of space beyond our solar system.
For many people working in the humanities, however, the failure to
address such developments is not a failure at all: as they see it, their
purpose is to keep the past alive for its own sake and not because it
might happen to have some utility now. They might agree that people
need to know a bit about world politics, contemporary geography, advances in science, and so on, but they might say that all of this is eva-
nescent and superficial. Anyone can keep track of current events simply by reading the papers, but the knowledge that really matters stays

the same no matter what the future brings. We humanists value foundations, traditions, and canons, whether we wish to preserve them in amber or subversively explode them. This is why eleventh graders in the state where I live — who may someday bear arms in Africa or Indonesia — still read Hawthorne's "Young Goodman Brown" and memorize events from U.S. history that get forgotten the day after the exam. My guess is that the current innovation of national standardized testing will only make matters worse: students will get better at standardized tests, but nothing will have altered the enormous disparity between the world that young Americans actually inhabit and the image of the world preserved and purveyed by the knowledge apparatus.

After 9/11 at my university there were teach-ins and a special lecture series, but no one in the flurry of information seemed to recall a debate that flamed up and then died out less than a decade earlier, a debate that had consumed the time and energy of key faculty for several years on end. It had begun in response to the "Qualls Report," a document that called for fundamental change in undergraduate education here at Rutgers. Under the direction of Barry Qualls, chair of the English Department and later Dean of the Humanities, a committee had acknowledged openly what everyone knew but seldom vocalized: that college students across the United States graduate without an adequate understanding of their society, their world, and their times. But agreement about the problem did not produce agreement about potential remedies. If the committee had begun its discussions by attempting to define a core curriculum, it soon ran up against an immovable wall: no one could concur about whose knowledge counted as "essential." Very quickly every discipline and subdiscipline made the claim that its particular specialization could not be cut from the list. Students needed to know about Reconstruction, the nature-versus-nurture debate, Quattrocento painting, Aristotle on politics, Wordsworth and Keats, as well as recent achievements in psychology, philosophy, and the sciences. Not only did the members of the committee disagree about what constituted "cultural literacy," but they could not even reach consensus on the definition of culture itself, in spite of their evident respect for one another and the good intentions they all shared.

After many fruitless hours stuck at this impasse, the committee took a radically different tack: instead of beginning with the effort to define the kinds of knowledge educated people ought to have, it tried to identify the problems that college graduates might be expected to face in the next twenty years or so, not as doctors or lawyers or Indian chiefs, but as ordinary citizens. And here, it turned out, agreement came more readily. Of course, a list of this sort would look different now. No committee member ten years ago could have foreseen how quickly human cloning might become a reality, just as no one could have anticipated the machinations of al-Qaeda. The committee overlooked other matters as well. Since 1990, the ruination of the world's environment has continued to accelerate, and the growing convergence of opinion on global warming has failed to produce any meaningful response. In 1990, the Kyoto Agreement lay seven years ahead. Today, it has apparently died and gone to heaven reserved for noble but stillborn ideas. Who would have guessed ten years ago that the next world war might begin, not in the Middle East as so many have suspected, but on the border between India and Pakistan? And who then could have predicted bioterrorism? The list drawn up by the Qualls committee might look distinctly dated now. Yet to point out that the present moment's urgencies will become tomorrow's old news is not to deny the importance of events as they unfold in the here and now. I would say the committee had exactly the right idea.

What Qualls and his associates concretely proposed instead of a core curriculum were courses designed around "dialogues" on the issues of consequence to society as a whole. The idea was to give students the intellectual tools — the information and the interpretive paradigms — to explore both the problems of the coming century and their possible solutions. As originally imagined, the "dialogues courses" were supposed to instigate a rich cross mixing of the disciplines, as enticing to the faculty as they would be to students. According to the final plan, the Dean's office would release a list of dialogues courses for each coming year, and on the way to graduation all our students were supposed to complete several of these special courses. While the conventional divisions of knowledge would remain in place, supported by the iron scaffolding of departments and disciplines, the dialogues courses would eventually become the centerpiece of undergraduate intellectual life.

What actually happened? Initially, very little. As the report circulated downward from the deaconal level to individual faculty, they quickly grasped that nothing in the university's structure of promotion and reward would compensate them for the special efforts they would have to make if they got involved. They felt uncomfortable, as well, teaching out of their field: historians knew little about ecology, English professors might explore "economies of signs" but in fact they knew next to nothing about economies of dollars. To make matters worse, the teaching done in the dialogues courses would seldom translate easily into publication, and the willingness of some faculty to participate might keep them locked below decks with the undergraduates instead of mounting freely to the vistas of graduate study. Besides, they would have to work with strangers from other departments who might look at them askance, or at whom they might look in much the same manner. The faculty responded, in other words, with all the reservations inculcated by their long and arduous training, and by the culture of the University itself, which would, indeed, punish them through benign neglect when raises were handed out. No one at our Research 1 institution gets a raise for better teaching. Ultimately, the administration, which had called for the report and convened the committee, distanced itself from the whole debate, preferring not to squander its political capital on a contest so clearly destined to end with the innovators' defeat.

More was at stake, however, than the dreams of a few idealists and the intransigence of the professoriate. Consider 9/11. Consider, too, that right now, by most estimates, species are disappearing at a rate without precedent since mammals first appeared on earth. Should global warming become a reality, we are not likely to enjoy a future of springlike weather at Christmas. Years of record drought in Afghanistan, record cold in Mongolia, record floods in Bangladesh — these may offer us a foretaste of things to come, not outright cataclysm but a slow, steady, and irreparable deterioration of the natural order. On its own, this deterioration might pose mortal challenges to many societies around the globe, but it is just now intersecting with an orgy of first-world-style consumption and first-world-style pollution to match, combined with a projected fivefold increase in the world population since 1900. While the triumph of Western democracy, such as it is, may seem virtually assured, environmental degradation could easily undermine not only economic progress but political stability as well. If people are willing to fight wars over oil, they will surely spill blood over water when that resource becomes desperately scarce, as many observers now predict. We may assume that the extensiveness and redundancy of our social systems will safeguard us against disaster, but the world's economy in 1929 collapsed within a few weeks, while the Soviet Union fell apart just as fast and just as unexpectedly.

What have we done to prepare the next generation for these problems and possibilities? At my institution six or seven years ago, the great majority of the faculty apparently resolved that we couldn't do much, and probably shouldn't. For the soundest of institutional and historical reasons, we were quite willing to perpetuate an arrangement guaranteeing that *none* of the coming century's major problems will be studied formally at the university: for the most part, whatever students happened to learn about these matters they will have to learn on their own. As for their professors, we continue to believe — or at least to claim — that a knowledge of Plato, a reading of Shakespeare, a brush with current historiography, an immersion in possible world theory, or an acquaintance with the New York Fluxus artists circa 1960, will somehow enable young Americans to make better decisions than if they actually had more pertinent information at their ready command. As far as I'm concerned, this is the sheerest superstition.

But the story does not end with the shelving of the Qualls report. The one place at our university where the proposal could be instituted was our writing program. That it happened there, and only there, was no accident. Although housed in an English department, the program had a long record of interdisciplinary instruction. In fact, it drew its teachers, for the most part TAs or adjunct instructors, from across the spectrum of the humanities and social sciences. Its marginal status, without so much as a budget line of its own, and its position at the bottom of the ladder of prestige, made it an ideal place for innovation. With so few tenured faculty employed in the teaching of writing, and with such poor compensation for those engaged with that work, the stakes were too low to spark much of a fight. One day, with few dust-ups to speak of, English 101 became the foundation course for a program of interdisciplinary study that reached about eleven thousand undergraduates every year.

Most students in college composition classes nationwide do exactly what they did in high school, writing about short stories, novels, poetry, and plays — literary pseudo-scholarship masquerading as something else. Or the students read "short essays" that might have appeared originally as opinion pieces in the major daily papers, something by Shelby Steele on affirmative action, for instance, or by Katie Roiphe on the perfidy of various feminists, or a classic from the archives like E. B. White's "Once More to the Lake" or Nora Ephron's infamous "Breasts." Alternately, students learn to practice cultural critique, unmasking class anxieties in *ER* or celebrating gangsta rap as counterhegemonic. The thinking behind such absurdities, which only the force of long tradition can obscure, is that English 101 should somehow bridge the gap between the home world of the students themselves and the specialized concerns of the university. But what an image of that "home world" most courses conjure up! Can the students or their instructors really bring themselves to believe in it?

The teaching of E. B. White in 2002 is the product of an all-too-familiar compromise in English 101: the students pretend to learn, and will do so in good humor so long as little effort is required from them, while the faculty, often indifferent and underpaid, pretend to teach. The same might be said, however, of lower-level courses across the curriculum. Complaints about this predicament have become a permanent fixture of university life, much like statues of forgotten Confederate generals in empty, sun-baked Southern parks. But the champions of teaching have misunderstood why it might have value for us once again: not because teaching possesses some intrinsic merit, like hard manual labor or cold morning baths. Teaching has lost its value precisely because the humanities no longer see their fate as linked to the future lives of ordinary citizens. Instead of asking how we might enable those citizens to act in the world that is likely to emerge ten or fifteen years from now, we have imagined ourselves as our society's principle actors, while those citizens, our students, have become superfluous in our eyes. But what should really matter, and what might really save us, is our attention to the problems they will have to address, and the skills they will need in order to improve on our common life. Our job is not to lead, but to prepare and support.

After several years of trial and error, it became possible for beginning students at my institution to read Benjamin Barber on civil society, Martha Nussbaum on women and human rights, Malcolm Gladwell on the dynamics of change in commercial culture, and Michael Pollan on Monsanto's genetic engineering. Students had the opportunity to write papers on health care in the Third World, global trade and environmental decline, the Internet and rates of voter turnout, artificial intelligence and religious tradition. Certainly, the writing classes taught students how to write; but more important, these classes taught them how to use academic knowledge, fixed and formalized as it probably has to be, in order to make sense of a perpetually shifting real-world terrain. As texts for reading and writing, Benjamin Barber or Karen Armstrong demand a great deal more than a four-page theme on teenagers and abortion, and not simply because the prose is conceptually difficult and presupposes a wide range of background knowledge. Instead of urging students to take sides on an issue whose contours are already familiar and well-defined, thinkers like Barber and Armstrong expect those who engage with their ideas to move beyond the accustomed contours. Barber and Armstrong enact synthetic thinking, and they require it as well.

These demands we acknowledged openly in the preface to the reader we assembled for the writing program's flagship course, which still carries the antiquated title of "Expository Writing." Here's one part of what we told the students themselves:

> Although the articles and essays in this book deal with subjects as diverse as the anthropology of art and the ethics of science, the book is not really "about" art or science or any of the other subjects explored by the readings. Instead this book is about the need for new ways of thinking, and it does not pretend that those ways of thinking already exist. Never before have people faced uncertainty in so many different areas. How, for instance, will the information technologies affect our personal lives? As corporations spread across the continents, will our identity as Americans continue to be important, or will we need to see ourselves in other ways? Will genetic technology lead to a Brave New World of "designer babies" and made-to-order soldier-clones or will its breakthroughs revolutionize food production and eliminate genetic disease?
>
> Unlike most questions posed by textbooks, the right answers to these questions aren't waiting for us in the teacher's edition. Not even the best educated and the most experienced can foresee with certainty how the life of our times will turn out. Our problems today are not only much more sweeping than humankind has encountered before, they are also more complex. Globalization is not just an issue for economists, or political scientists, or historians, or anthropologists; it is an issue for all of them together. The degradation of the biosphere is not just an ecological matter, but a political, social, and cultural matter as well. The uniqueness of our time requires us to devise new understandings of ourselves and the world. One purpose of this course is to provide a place for these understandings to emerge.
>
> It may seem strange, perhaps, that we would have such lofty goals in a course for undergraduates. Surely the experts are better equipped than college students to respond to the issues our world now confronts. But this assumption may be unjustified. In a certain sense, the current generation of students needs to reinvent the university itself, not by replacing one department or methodology with another, but by building

broad connections across areas of knowledge that still remain in
relative isolation.

Clearly, this is a manifesto and not the innocuous course description it
pretends to be. It tells students that the university's knowledge has
reached its historical and institutional limits, and that their role as
social actors after graduation will require them to think and act in
ways beyond the imaginings of most of their professors.

Earlier, I claimed that English 101 had become "the foundation
course for a program of interdisciplinary study that reached about
eleven thousand undergraduates every year." While that figure is entirely accurate, and even a bit conservative, the foundation stands alone
as of this writing, uncrowned by the soaring architecture of any new
curriculum. Perhaps this is how change always has to come. In a certain sense, after all, the situation of the academic humanities is nothing short of hopeless: few of those ensconced within the institution's
cocoon have any pressing reason to pursue systemic change. For this
very reason, however, any future life the humanities might enjoy will
depend on our students — those raw, unlettered citizen-dilettantes —
and on our efforts to prepare them for their world, not ours, should we
make such effort at all. And this too we said, more or less, in the preface to our book:

> The humanities will have succeeded in their work only when students
> take the knowledge of the university beyond the university itself. In a
> certain sense, this means that students have to become their own best
> teachers: they need to find in their own lives — their own goals, values,
> and commitments — an organizing principle for a learning experience
> which is bound to seem disorganized. The great, unspoken secret of the
> university now is that the curriculum has no center: specialization
> makes sure of that. Historians write primarily for historians; literary
> critics for other literary critics. As students shuttle back and forth
> between these specialized domains, the only coherence they can take
> away from their education is a coherence they have made for them-
> selves.

Ironically the humanities may find themselves better off if they abandon all hope of recovering a centrality they have never really had, not
in Plato's time nor Shakespeare's nor Lionel Trilling's. The very effort
to protect something called "the past" from something called "the
present" already testifies to the limitations of our temporal perspective. When we gaze a thousand years into the past, or a thousand years
into the future, the worlds we envision there are only reflections of our
world right now, and it is to this fragile, fearful world that we must
turn with all our energy, intelligence, and care.

Spellmeyer's Insights as a Resource for Your Teaching

1. Consider Spellmeyer's critique of college composition classes. How closely does his indictment of the typical composition course apply to what goes on in your own class? Which elements of your course might Spellmeyer favor? How might you expand those elements?

2. Consider the quote from Spellmeyer's preface to the collection of readings that he and his colleagues prepared for a writing course. Although he admits that "such lofty goals" might seem strange, he holds that "building broad connections across areas of knowledge" is the paramount purpose of education in our times. What do you make of his goals? How are your teaching goals similar to or different from Spellmeyer's? What connections might you seek to build in your composition classroom, and how might you go about doing so?

Spellmeyer's Insights as a Resource for Your Writing Classroom

1. Sketch Spellmeyer's argument for your students and then ask them to freewrite about their reactions to Spellmeyer's ideas for ten minutes. Follow this freewriting session with a class discussion about their responses.

2. After outlining Spellmeyer's argument to students, ask them about their hopes for your course: What, ideally, will the course enable them to do outside the classroom for themselves and for their community?

2

Thinking about the Writing Process

A s a result of the paradigm shift in composition studies from viewing writing as product to viewing writing as process, we now know much more about what writers do when they generate texts. The first sections in this chapter are designed to address the individual and complex nature of the inevitably intertwined processes of generating a draft, considering audience, revising, and crafting sentences. Although each writer's highly individualized and recursive processes of composing and constructing meaning cannot be fit easily or appropriately into these neat categories, the essays in this chapter are grouped and sequenced to logically progress through the major elements of the composing process. As with all the readings in this volume, they interconnect: One may modify, challenge, or confirm the insights of other essays. The readings were also chosen to offer a balance of theoretical framework and practical classroom strategies.

The chapter also includes a section on teaching with computers. Computer literacy is no longer optional; writers need computer literacy to succeed at the university and beyond. Today, teaching writing with computers has moved beyond teaching students how to use word processing features — like "cut and paste" — as an alternative to pencil and paper drafting and revising. Students' increasing aptitude and experience with computers prior to coming to the university, as well as increased access to technology, demand that we change the way we think about integrating computers into the writing classroom. Nevertheless, gaps in access still remain, and the writers in this section offer practical strategies for teaching with computers as well as critical insights on the socioeconomic implications of the complex link between technology and literacy.

Finally, the chapter concludes with two perspectives on teaching visual literacy. Images surround us — on television, in magazines, and in myriad other forms. This continuous influx of visual imagery inevitably contributes to shaping and structuring our views of reality. Just as we teach students to actively read print texts, we must teach them to actively "read" and analyze visual texts. Conversely, we should also be aware of how our students can use and manipulate visuals in their own processes of composing. Not only do we want students to read both print and visual texts critically, but we also want them to think critically about the texts that they themselves produce. The selections in this section of the chapter explore these issues from two different but complementary perspectives — shifting the focus of visual literacy from analysis to design, and teaching key features of visual rhetoric as they operate in digital writing environments.

Generating a Draft

Understanding Composing

Sondra Perl

Most writing teachers and theorists share Sondra Perl's belief that writing is a recursive process and that writers engage in "retrospective structuring" as they generate drafts. In this 1990 article from College Composition and Communication, *Perl uses her own observations of the composing processes of a variety of writers to analyze the significance of those processes. She defines a "felt sense" that may be a very rich and necessary resource for the writer even as it may be one that the writer (and his or her audience) has difficulty describing and consciously triggering.*

Perl believes that "skilled writers" rely on a felt sense even when they don't know it, and she implies that "unskilled writers" might come to use this felt sense and to engage in "retrospective structuring" more productively. She theorizes that writers who have internalized a model of writing as a recursive process rather than a linear process may have an easier time attending to their inner reflections.

You may well find "new thoughts" about composing as you read Perl's conjectures about "felt sense." In particular, you may be interested in the link of "felt sense" with "projective structuring," Perl's name for the process in which writers make what they intend to say intelligible to others.

Any psychological process, whether the development of thought or voluntary behavior, is a process undergoing changes right before one's eyes. . . . Under certain conditions it becomes possible to trace this development.[1]

— L. S. Vygotsky

> It's hard to begin this case study of myself as a writer because even
> as I'm searching for a beginning, a pattern of organization, I'm watching
> myself, trying to understand my behavior. As I sit here in silence, I can
> see lots of things happening that never made it onto my tapes. My mind
> leaps from the task at hand to what I need at the vegetable stand for
> tonight's soup to the threatening rain outside to ideas voiced in my
> writing group this morning, but in between "distractions" I hear myself
> trying out words I might use. It's as if the extraneous thoughts are a
> counterpoint to the more steady attention I'm giving to composing. This
> is all to point out that the process is more complex than I'm aware of,
> but I think my tapes reveal certain basic patterns that I tend to follow.
> — Anne, New York City teacher

Anne is a teacher of writing. In 1979, she was among a group of twenty teachers who were taking a course in research and basic writing at New York University.[2] One of the assignments in the course was for the teachers to tape their thoughts while composing aloud on the topic "My Most Anxious Moment as a Writer." Everyone in the group was given the topic in the morning during class and told to compose later on that day in a place where they would be comfortable and relatively free from distractions. The result was a tape of composing aloud and a written product that formed the basis for class discussion over the next few days.

One of the purposes of this assignment was to provide teachers with an opportunity to see their own composing processes at work. From the start of the course, we recognized that we were controlling the situation by assigning a topic and that we might be altering the process by asking writers to compose aloud. Nonetheless we viewed the task as a way of capturing some of the flow of composing and, as Anne later observed in her analysis of her tape, she was able to detect certain basic patterns. This observation, made not only by Anne, then leads me to ask "What basic patterns seem to occur during composing?" and "What does this type of research have to tell us about the nature of the composing process?"

Perhaps the most challenging part of the answer is the recognition of recursiveness in writing. In recent years, many researchers including myself have questioned the traditional notion that writing is a linear process with a strict plan-write-revise sequence.[3] In its stead, we have advocated the idea that writing is a recursive process, that throughout the process of writing, writers return to substrands of the overall process, or subroutines (short successions of steps that yield results on which the writer draws in taking the next set of steps); writers use these to keep the process moving forward. In other words, recursiveness in writing implies that there is a forward-moving action that exists by virtue of a backward-moving action. The questions that then need to be answered are "To what do writers move back?" "What exactly is being repeated?" "What recurs?"

To answer these questions, it is important to look at what writers do while writing and what an analysis of their processes reveals. The descriptions that follow are based on my own observations of the composing processes of many types of writers including college students, graduate students, and English teachers like Anne.

Writing does appear to be recursive, yet the parts that recur seem to vary from writer to writer and from topic to topic. Furthermore, some recursive elements are easy to spot while others are not.

1. The most visible recurring feature or backward movement involves rereading little bits of discourse. Few writers I have seen write for long periods of time without returning briefly to what is already down on the page.

For some, like Anne, rereading occurs after every few phrases; for others, it occurs after every sentence; more frequently, it occurs after a "chunk" of information has been written. Thus, the unit that is reread is not necessarily a syntactic one, but rather a semantic one as defined by the writer.

2. The second recurring feature is some key word or item called up by the topic. Writers consistently return to their notion of the topic throughout the process of writing. Particularly when they are stuck, writers seem to use the topic or a key word in it as a way to get going again. Thus many times it is possible to see writers "going back," rereading the topic they were given, changing it to suit what they have been writing or changing what they have written to suit their notion of the topic.

3. There is also a third backward movement in writing, one that is not so easy to document. It is not easy because the move, itself, cannot immediately be identified with words. In fact, the move is not to any words on the page nor to the topic but to feelings or nonverbalized perceptions that *surround* the words, or to what the words already present evoke in the writer. The move draws on sense experience, and it can be observed if one pays close attention to what happens when writers pause and seem to listen or otherwise react to what is inside of them. The move occurs inside the writer, to what is physically felt. The term used to describe this focus of writers' attention is *felt sense*. The term "felt sense" has been coined and described by Eugene Gendlin, a philosopher at the University of Chicago. In his words, felt sense is

> the soft underbelly of thought . . . a kind of bodily awareness that . . . can be used as a tool . . . a bodily awareness that . . . encompasses everything you feel and know about a given subject at a given time. . . . It is felt in the body, yet it has meanings. It is body *and* mind before they are split apart.[4]

This felt sense is always there, within us. It is unifying, and yet, when we bring words to it, it can break apart, shift, unravel, and become something else. Gendlin has spent many years showing people how to work with their felt sense. Here I am making connections between what he has done and what I have seen happen as people write.

When writers are given a topic, the topic itself evokes a felt sense in them. This topic calls forth images, words, ideas, and vague fuzzy feelings that are anchored in the writer's body. What is elicited, then, is not solely the product of a mind but of a mind alive in a living, sensing body.

When writers pause, when they go back and repeat key words, what they seem to be doing is waiting, paying attention to what is still vague and unclear. They are looking to their felt experience, and waiting for an image, a word, or a phrase to emerge that captures the sense they embody.

Usually, when they make the decision to write, it is after they have a dawning awareness that something has clicked, that they have enough of a sense that if they begin with a few words heading in a certain direction, words will continue to come which will allow them to flesh out the sense they have.

The process of using what is sensed directly about a topic is a natural one. Many writers do it without any conscious awareness that that is what they are doing. For example, Anne repeats the words "anxious moments," using these key words as a way of allowing her sense of the topic to deepen. She asks herself, "Why are exams so anxiety provoking?" and waits until she has enough of a sense within her that she can go in a certain direction. She does not yet have the words, only the sense that she is able to begin. Once she writes, she stops to see what is there. She maintains a highly recursive composing style throughout and she seems unable to go forward without first going back to see and to listen to what she has already created. In her own words, she says:

> My disjointed style of composing is very striking to me. I almost never move from the writing of one sentence directly to the next. After each sentence I pause to read what I've written, assess, sometimes edit and think about what will come next. I often have to read the several preceding sentences a few times as if to gain momentum to carry me to the next sentence. I seem to depend a lot on the sound of my words and . . . while I'm hanging in the middle of this uncompleted thought, I may also start editing a previous sentence or get an inspiration for something which I want to include later in the paper.

What tells Anne that she is ready to write? What is the feeling of "momentum" like for her? What is she hearing as she listens to the "sound" of her words? When she experiences "inspiration," how does she recognize it?

In the approach I am presenting, the ability to recognize what one needs to do or where one needs to go is informed by calling on felt sense. This is the internal criterion writers seem to use to guide them when they are planning, drafting, and revising.

The recursive move, then, that is hardest to document but is probably the most important to be aware of is the move to felt sense, to what is not yet *in words* but out of which images, words, and concepts emerge.

The continuing presence of this felt sense, waiting for us to discover it and see where it leads, raises a number of questions.

Is "felt sense" another term for what professional writers call their "inner voice" or their feeling of "inspiration"?

Do skilled writers call on their capacity to sense more readily than unskilled writers?

Rather than merely reducing the complex act of writing to a neat formulation, can the term "felt sense" point us to an area of our experience from which we can evolve even richer and more accurate descriptions of composing?

Can learning how to work with felt sense teach us about creativity and release us from stultifyingly repetitive patterns?

My observations lead me to answer "yes" to all four questions. There seems to be a basic step in the process of composing that skilled writers rely on even when they are unaware of it and that less skilled writers can be taught. This process seems to rely on very careful attention to one's inner reflections and is often accompanied with bodily sensations.

When it's working, this process allows us to say or write what we've never said before, to create something new and fresh, and occasionally it provides us with the experience of "newness" or "freshness," even when "old words" or images are used.

The basic process begins with paying attention. If we are given a topic, it begins with taking the topic in and attending to what it evokes in us. There is less "figuring out" an answer and more "waiting" to see what forms. Even without a predetermined topic, the process remains the same. We can ask ourselves, "What's on my mind?" or "Of all the things I know about, what would I most like to write about now?" and wait to see what comes. What we pay attention to is the part of our bodies where we experience ourselves directly. For many people, it's the area of their stomachs; for others, there is a more generalized response and they maintain a hovering attention to what they experience throughout their bodies.

Once a felt sense forms, we match words to it. As we begin to describe it, we get to see what is there for us. We get to see what we think, what we know. If we are writing about something that truly interests us, the felt sense deepens. We know that we are writing out of a "centered" place.

If the process is working, we begin to move along, sometimes quickly. Other times, we need to return to the beginning, to reread, to see if we captured what we meant to say. Sometimes after rereading we move on again, picking up speed. Other times by rereading we realize we've gone off the track, that what we've written doesn't quite "say it," and we need to reassess. Sometimes the words are wrong and we need to change them. Other times we need to go back to the topic, to call up the sense it initially evoked to see where and how our words led us astray. Sometimes in rereading we discover that the topic is "wrong," that the direction we discovered in writing is where we really want to go. It is important here to clarify that the terms "right" and "wrong" are not necessarily meant to refer to grammatical structures or to correctness.

What is "right" or "wrong" corresponds to our sense of our intention. We intend to write something, words come, and now we assess if those words adequately capture our intended meaning. Thus, the first question we ask ourselves is "Are these words right for me?" "Do they capture what I'm trying to say?" "If not, what's missing?"

Once we ask "what's missing?" we need once again to wait, to let a felt sense of what is missing form, and then to write out of that sense.

I have labeled this process of attending, of calling up a felt sense, and of writing out of that place, the process of *retrospective structuring*. It is retrospective in that it begins with what is already there, inchoately, and brings whatever is there forward by using language in structured form.

It seems as though a felt sense has within it many possible structures or forms. As we shape what we intend to say, we are further structuring our sense while correspondingly shaping our piece of writing.

It is also important to note that what is there implicitly, without words, is not equivalent to what finally emerges. In the process of writing, we begin with what is inchoate and end with something that is tangible. In order to do so, we both discover and construct what we mean. Yet the term "discovery" ought not lead us to think that meaning exists fully formed inside of us and that all we need do is dig deep enough to release it. In writing, meaning cannot be discovered the way we discover an object on an archeological dig. In writing, meaning is crafted and constructed. It involves us in a process of coming-into-being. Once we have worked at shaping, through language, what is there inchoately, we can look at what we have written to see if it adequately captures what we intended. Often at this moment discovery occurs. We see something new in our writing that comes upon us as a surprise. We see in our words a further structuring of the sense we began with and we recognize that in those words we have discovered something new about ourselves and our topic. Thus when we are successful at this process, we end up with a product that teaches us something, that clarifies what we know (or what we knew at one point only implicitly), and that lifts out or explicates or enlarges our experience. In this way, writing leads to discovery.

All the writers I have observed, skilled and unskilled alike, use the process of retrospective structuring while writing. Yet the degree to which they do so varies and seems, in fact, to depend upon the model of the writing process that they have internalized. Those who realize that writing can be a recursive process have an easier time with waiting, looking, and discovering. Those who subscribe to the linear model find themselves easily frustrated when what they write does not immediately correspond to what they planned or when what they produce leaves them with little sense of accomplishment. Since they have relied on a formulaic approach, they often produce writing that is formulaic as well, thereby cutting themselves off from the possibility of discovering something new.

Such a result seems linked to another feature of the composing process, to what I call *projective structuring,* or the ability to craft what one intends to say so that it is intelligible to others.

A number of concerns arise in regard to projective structuring; I will mention only a few that have been raised for me as I have watched different writers at work.

1. Although projective structuring is only one important part of the composing process, many writers act as if it is the whole process. These writers focus on what they think others want them to write rather than looking to see what it is they want to write. As a result, they often ignore their felt sense and they do not establish a living connection between themselves and their topic.

2. Many writers reduce projective structuring to a series of rules or criteria for evaluating finished discourse. These writers ask, "Is what I'm writing correct?" and "Does it conform to the rules I've been taught?" While these concerns are important, they often overshadow all others and lock the writer in the position of writing solely or primarily for the approval of readers.

Projective structuring, as I see it, involves much more than imagining a strict audience and maintaining a strict focus on correctness. It is true that to handle this part of the process well, writers need to know certain grammatical rules and evaluative criteria, but they also need to know how to call up a sense of their reader's needs and expectations.

For projective structuring to function fully, writers need to draw on their capacity to move away from their own words, to decenter from the page, and to project themselves into the role of the reader. In other words, projective structuring asks writers to attempt to become readers and to imagine what someone other than themselves will need before the writer's particular piece of writing can become intelligible and compelling. To do so, writers must have the experience of being readers. They cannot call up a felt sense of a reader unless they themselves have experienced what it means to be lost in a piece of writing or to be excited by it. When writers do not have such experiences, it is easy for them to accept that readers merely require correctness.

In closing, I would like to suggest that retrospective and projective structuring are two parts of the same basic process. Together they form the alternating mental postures writers assume as they move through the act of composing. The former relies on the ability to go inside, to attend to what is there, from that attending to place words upon a page, and then to assess if those words adequately capture one's meaning. The latter relies on the ability to assess how the words on that page will affect someone other than the writer, the reader. We rarely do one without the other entering in; in fact, again in these postures we can see the shuttling back-and-forth movements of the composing process, the move from sense to words and from words to sense, from inner experience to outer judgment and from judgment back to experience. As we move through this cycle, we are continually composing and recomposing our meanings and what we mean. And in doing so, we display some of the basic recursive patterns that writers who observe themselves closely seem to see in their own work. After observing the process for a long time we may, like Anne, conclude that at any given moment the process is more complex than anything we are aware of; yet such insights, I believe, are important. They show us the fallacy of reducing the composing process to a simple linear scheme and they leave us with the potential for creating even more powerful ways of understanding composing.

Notes

1. L. S. Vygotsky, *Mind in Society,* trans. M. Cole, V. John-Steiner, S. Scribner, and E. Souberman (Cambridge: Harvard UP, 1978) 61.
2. [I team-taught this course with] Gordon Pradl, Associate Professor of English Education at New York University.
3. See Janet Emig, *The Composing Processes of Twelfth-Graders,* NCTE Research Report No. 13 (Urbana: NCTE, 1971); Linda Flower and J. R. Hayes, "The Cognition of Discovery," *CCC* 31 (Feb. 1980): 21–32; Nancy Sommers, "The Need for Theory in Composition Research," *CCC* 30 (Feb. 1979): 46–49.
4. Eugene Gendlin, *Focusing* (New York: Everest, 1978) 35, 165.

Perl's Insights as a Resource for Your Teaching

1. Perl models a "holistic perspective" on the composing process and pays careful attention to the composing processes of the students she teaches. As you read this article and reflect on it, jot down your own memories of this experience of a "felt sense" as well as statements your students have made about such experiences. Save those notes for use in your discussions of getting started with a writing task.

2. Explore your own writing process in your reflective teaching journal. Which steps recur most frequently in your own writing? Try to articulate your own processes of restrospective and projective structuring.

Perl's Insights as a Resource for Your Writing Classroom

1. Perl insists that to craft accessible and intelligible writing, writers have to project themselves as readers of the work. They must anticipate the needs of readers even before and while the writing is in process. This sort of "decentering" is difficult for many students. Perl recommends reading as a major resource for such positive structuring. To assist students in calling up a "felt sense" of their readers, ask them to discuss, in journals or in small groups, experiences they have had of being excited by something they read.

   You might also organize a related class discussion of a "difficult" reading. Ask students to discuss any experiences of feeling overwhelmed by the reading, or "lost" in parts of it. Ask them to use sensory description, if appropriate to their experience.

   In helping students to recognize an awareness of themselves as critical readers, this discussion also encourages students to think about the particular readers' needs that they may have anticipated in the essays that they are currently drafting.

2. Many generating strategies — those used by individual writers as well as the more formally described heuristics like freewriting, brainstorming, and the reporter's questions — help students start to pay attention to inner reflections and accompanying physical sensations. After they have practiced with several formal heuristics, ask your students to describe, either in journal entries or in fifteen-minute writing sessions, what they notice about their "getting started" and their "beginning again."

Rigid Rules, Inflexible Plans, and the Stifling of Language: A Cognitivist Analysis of Writer's Block

Mike Rose

What's really going on when a student writer can't write, even when an assignment's deadline looms closer and closer? In this study, which first appeared in his influential 1989 book Lives on the Boundary: The Struggles and Achievements of America's Underprepared, *Mike Rose finds ten students at UCLA who struggle with writer's block and compares their composing processes with those of students who do not have writer's block. Students are often blocked by very specific cognitive objects: They are stifled by rigid "dos and don'ts" that they have internalized from past teachers and textbooks, and what they finally, painstak-*

ingly produce inevitably never matches their inflexible plans. Writers who do not struggle with writer's block, on the other hand, are unimpeded by any such hypersensitivity to rules and plans: They just write, knowing that they can revise or retract later. In the next section of this chapter, Considering Audience, Peter Elbow focuses on how writers' concerns about audience — particularly in the generating and drafting stages — can inhibit or "block" writing (see pp. 145–67, "Closing My Eyes as I Speak"), in that students may feel bound by their preconceived ideas of audience expectation and thus conform their writing to "fit" these. It is when we try to fit our writing into predetermined molds that we become stymied by self-consciousness, making it nearly impossible to tap the resources of our imagination.

R uth will labor over the first paragraph of an essay for hours. She'll write a sentence, then erase it. Try another, then scratch part of it out. Finally, as the evening winds on toward ten o'clock and Ruth, anxious about tomorrow's deadline, begins to wind into herself, she'll compose that first paragraph only to sit back and level her favorite exasperated interdiction at herself and her page: "No. You can't say that. You'll bore them to death."

Ruth is one of ten UCLA undergraduates with whom I discussed writer's block, that frustrating, self-defeating inability to generate the next line, the right phrase, the sentence that will release the flow of words once again. These ten people represented a fair cross-section of the UCLA student community: lower-middle-class to upper-middle-class backgrounds and high schools, third-world and Caucasian origins, biology to fine arts majors, C+ to A– grade point averages, enthusiastic to blasé attitudes toward school. They were set off from the community by the twin facts that all ten could write competently, and all were currently enrolled in at least one course that required a significant amount of writing. They were set off among themselves by the fact that five of them wrote with relative to enviable ease while the other five experienced moderate to nearly immobilizing writer's block. This blocking usually resulted in rushed, often late papers and resultant grades that did not truly reflect these students' writing ability. And then, of course, there were other less measurable but probably more serious results: a growing distrust of their abilities and an aversion toward the composing process itself.

What separated the five students who blocked from those who didn't? It wasn't skill; that was held fairly constant. The answer could have rested in the emotional realm — anxiety, fear of evaluation, insecurity, etc. Or perhaps blocking in some way resulted from variation in cognitive style. Perhaps, too, blocking originated in and typified a melding of emotion and cognition not unlike the relationship posited by Shapiro between neurotic feeling and neurotic thinking.[1] Each of these was possible. Extended clinical interviews and testing could have teased out the answer. But there was one answer that surfaced readily in brief explorations of these students' writing processes. It was not profoundly emotional, nor was it embedded in that still unclear construct of cognitive style. It was constant, surprising, almost amusing if its results weren't so troublesome, and, in the final analysis, obvious: the five students who experienced blocking were all operating either with writing rules or with planning strategies that impeded rather than enhanced the composing process. The five students who were not hampered by writer's block also utilized rules, but they were less rigid ones, and thus more appropriate to a complex process like writing. Also, the plans these non-blockers brought to the writing process were more functional, more flexible, more open to information from the outside.

These observations are the result of one to three interviews with each student. I used recent notes, drafts, and finished compositions to direct and hone my questions. This procedure is admittedly non-experimental, certainly more clinical than scientific; still, it did lead to several inferences that lay the foundation for future, more rigorous investigation: (a) composing is a highly complex problem-solving process[2] and (b) certain disruptions of that process can be explained with cognitive psychology's problem-solving framework. Such investigation might include a study using "stimulated recall" techniques to validate or disconfirm these hunches. In such a study, blockers and non-blockers would write essays. Their activity would be videotaped and, immediately after writing, they would be shown their respective tapes and questioned about the rules, plans, and beliefs operating in their writing behavior. This procedure would bring us close to the composing process (the writers' recall is stimulated by their viewing the tape), yet would not interfere with actual composing.

In the next section I will introduce several key concepts in the problem-solving literature. In section three I will let the students speak for themselves. Fourth, I will offer a cognitivist analysis of blockers' and non-blockers' grace or torpor. I will close with a brief note on treatment.

Selected Concepts in Problem Solving: Rules and Plans

As diverse as theories of problem solving are, they share certain basic assumptions and characteristics. Each posits an *introductory period* during which a problem is presented, and all theorists, from Behaviorist to Gestalt to Information Processing, admit that certain aspects, stimuli, or "functions" of the problem must become or be made salient and attended to in certain ways if successful problem-solving processes are to be engaged. Theorists also believe that some conflict, some stress, some gap in information in these perceived "aspects" seems to trigger problem-solving behavior. Next comes a *processing period,* and for all the variance of opinion about this critical stage, theorists recognize the necessity of its existence — recognize that man, at the least, somehow "weighs" possible solutions as they are stumbled upon and, at the most, goes through an elaborate and sophisticated information-processing routine to achieve problem solution. Furthermore, theorists believe — to varying degrees — that past learning and the particular "set," direction, or orientation that the problem solver takes in dealing with past experience and present stimuli have critical bearing on the efficacy of solution. Finally, all theorists admit to a *solution period,* an end-state of the process where "stress" and "search" terminate, an answer is attained, and a sense of completion or "closure" is experienced.

These are the gross similarities, and the framework they offer will be useful in understanding the problem-solving behavior of the students discussed in this paper. But since this paper is primarily concerned with the second stage of problem-solving operations, it would be most useful to focus this introduction on two critical constructs in the processing period: rules and plans.

Rules

Robert M. Gagné defines "rule" as "an inferred capability that enables the individual to respond to a class of stimulus situations with a class of performances."[3] Rules can be learned directly[4] or by inference through experience.[5] But, in either case, most problem-solving theorists would affirm Gagné's dictum that "rules are probably the major organizing factor, and quite possibly the primary one, in intellectual functioning."[6] As Gagné implies, we wouldn't be able to function without rules; they guide response to the myriad stimuli that confront us daily, and might even be the central element in complex problem-solving behavior.

Dunker, Polya, and Miller, Galanter, and Pribram offer a very useful distinction between two general kinds of rules: algorithms and heuristics.[7] Algorithms are precise rules that will always result in a specific answer if applied to an appropriate problem. Most mathematical rules, for example, are algorithms. Functions are constant (e.g., pi), procedures are routine (squaring the radius), and outcomes are completely predictable. However, few day-to-day situations are mathematically circumscribed enough to warrant the application of algorithms. Most often we function with the aid of fairly general heuristics or "rules of thumb," guidelines that allow varying degrees of flexibility when approaching problems. Rather than operating with algorithmic precision and certainty, we search, critically, through alternatives, using our heuristic as a divining rod — "if a math problem stumps you, try working backwards to solution"; "if the car won't start, check X, Y, or Z," and so forth. Heuristics won't allow the precision or the certitude afforded by algorithmic operations; heuristics can even be so "loose" as to be vague. But in a world where tasks and problems are rarely mathematically precise, heuristic rules become the most appropriate, the most functional rules available to us: "a heuristic does not guarantee the optimal solution or, indeed, any solution at all; rather, heuristics offer solutions that are good enough most of the time."[8]

Plans

People don't proceed through problem situations, in or out of a laboratory, without some set of internalized instructions to the self, some program, some course of action that, even roughly, takes goals and possible paths to that goal into consideration. Miller, Galanter, and Pribram have referred to this course of action as a plan: "A plan is any hierarchical process in the organism that can control the order in which a sequence of operations is to be performed" (16). They name the fundamental plan in human problem-solving behavior the TOTE, with the initial T representing a *test* that matches a possible solution against the perceived end-goal of problem completion. O represents the clearance to *operate* if the comparison between solution and goal indicates that the solution is a sensible one. The second T represents a further, post-operation, *test* or comparison of solution with goal, and if the two mesh and problem solution is at hand the person *exits* (E) from problem-solving behavior. If the second test presents further discordance between solution and goal, a further solution is attempted in TOTE-fashion. Such plans can be both long-term and global and, as problem solving is underway, short-term and immediate.[9] Though the mechanicality of this information-processing model renders it simplistic and, possibly, unreal, the central notion of a plan and an operating procedure is an important one in problem-solving theory; it at least attempts to metaphorically explain what earlier cognitive psychologists could not — the mental procedures . . . underlying problem-solving behavior.

Before concluding this section, a distinction between heuristic rules and plans should be attempted; it is a distinction often blurred in the literature, blurred because, after all, we are very much in the area of gestating theory and preliminary models. Heuristic rules seem to function with the flexibility of plans. Is, for example, "If the car won't start, try X, Y, or Z" a heuristic or a plan? It could be either, though two qualifications will mark it as heuristic rather than plan. (A) Plans subsume and sequence heuristic and algorithmic rules. Rules are usually "smaller," more discrete cognitive capabilities; plans can become quite large and complex, composed of a series of ordered algorithms, heuristics, and further planning "sub-routines." (B) Plans, as was mentioned earlier, include criteria to determine successful goal-attainment and, as well, include "feedback" processes — ways to incorporate and use information gained from "tests" of potential solutions against desired goals.

One other distinction should be made: that is, between "set" and plan. Set, also called "determining tendency" or "readiness,"[10] refers to the fact that people often approach problems with habitual ways of reacting, a predisposition, a tendency to perceive or function in one way rather than another. Set, which can be established through instructions or, consciously or unconsciously, through experience, can assist performance if it is appropriate to a specific problem,[11] but much of the literature on set has shown its rigidifying, dysfunctional effects.[12] Set differs from plan in that set represents a limiting and narrowing of response alternatives with no inherent process to shift alternatives. It is a kind of cognitive habit that can limit perception, not a course of action with multiple paths that directs and sequences response possibilities.

The constructs of rules and plans advance the understanding of problem solving beyond that possible with earlier, less developed formulations. Still, critical problems remain. Though mathematical and computer models move one toward more complex (and thus more real) problems than the earlier research, they are still too neat, too rigidly sequenced to approximate the stunning complexity of day-to-day (not to mention highly creative) problem-solving behavior. Also, information-processing models of problem solving are built on logic theorems, chess strategies, and simple planning tasks. Even Gagné seems to feel more comfortable with illustrations from mathematics and science rather than with social science and humanities problems. So although these complex models and constructs tell us a good deal about problem-solving behavior, they are still laboratory simulations, still invoked from the outside rather than self-generated, and still founded on the mathematico-logical.

Two Carnegie-Mellon researchers, however, have recently extended the above into a truly real, amorphous, unmathematical problem-solving process — writing. Relying on protocol analysis (thinking aloud while solving problems), Linda Flower and John Hayes have attempted to tease out the role of heuristic rules and plans in writing behavior.[13] Their research pushes problem-solving investigations to the real and complex and pushes, from the other end, the often mysterious process of writing toward the explainable. The latter is important, for at least since Plotinus many have viewed the composing process as unexplainable, inspired, infused with the transcendent. But Flower and Hayes are beginning, anyway, to show how writing generates from a problem-solving process with rich heuristic rules and plans of its own. They show, as well, how many writing problems arise from a paucity of heuristics and suggest an intervention that provides such rules.

This paper, too, treats writing as a problem-solving process, focusing, however, on what happens when the process dead-ends in writer's block. It will further suggest that, as opposed to Flower and Hayes's students who need more rules and plans, blockers may well be stymied by possessing rigid or inappropriate rules, or inflexible or confused plans. Ironically enough, these are occasionally instilled by the composition teacher or gleaned from the writing textbook.

"Always Grab Your Audience" — The Blockers

In high school, *Ruth* was told and told again that a good essay always grabs a reader's attention immediately. Until you can make your essay do that, her teachers and textbooks putatively declaimed, there is no need to go on. For Ruth, this means that beginning bland and seeing what emerges as one generates prose is unacceptable. The beginning is everything. And what exactly is the audience seeking that reads this beginning? The rule, or Ruth's use of it, doesn't provide for such investigation. She has an edict with no determiners. Ruth operates with another rule that restricts her productions as well: if sentences aren't grammatically "correct," they aren't useful. This keeps Ruth from toying with ideas on paper, from the kind of linguistic play that often frees up the flow of prose. These two rules converge in a way that pretty effectively restricts Ruth's composing process.

The first two papers I received from *Laurel* were weeks overdue. Sections of them were well written; there were even moments of stylistic flair. But the papers were late and, overall, the prose seemed rushed. Furthermore, one paper included a paragraph on an issue that was never mentioned in the topic paragraph. This was the kind of mistake that someone with Laurel's apparent ability doesn't make. I asked her about this irrelevant passage. She knew very well that it didn't fit, but believed she had to include it to round out the paper. "You must always make three or more points in an essay. If the essay has less, then it's not strong." Laurel had been taught this rule both in high school and in her first college English class; no wonder, then, that she accepted its validity.

As opposed to Laurel, *Martha* possesses a whole arsenal of plans and rules with which to approach a humanities writing assignment, and, considering her background in biology, I wonder how many of them were formed out of the assumptions and procedures endemic to the physical sciences.[14] Martha will not put pen to first draft until she has spent up to two days generating an outline of remarkable complexity. I saw one of these outlines and it looked more like a diagram of protein synthesis or DNA structure than the time-worn pattern offered in composition textbooks. I must admit I was intrigued by the aura of process (vs. the static appearance of essay outlines) such diagrams offer, but for Martha these "outlines" only led to self-defeat: the outline would become so complex that all of its elements could never be included in a short essay. In other words, her plan locked her into the first stage of the composing process. Martha would struggle with the conversion of her outline into prose only to scrap the whole venture when deadlines passed and a paper had to be rushed together.

Martha's "rage for order" extends beyond the outlining process. She also believes that elements of a story or poem must evince a fairly linear structure and thematic clarity, or — perhaps bringing us closer to the issue — that analysis of a story or poem must provide the linearity or clarity that seems to be absent in the text. Martha, therefore, will bend the logic of her analysis to reason ambiguity out of existence. When I asked her about a strained paragraph in her paper on Camus' "The Guest," she said, "I didn't want to admit that it [the story's conclusion] was just hanging. I tried to force it into meaning."

Martha uses another rule, one that is not only problematical in itself, but one that often clashes directly with the elaborate plan and obsessive rule above. She believes that humanities papers must scintillate with insight, must present an array of images, ideas, ironies gleaned from the literature under examination. A problem arises, of course, when Martha tries to incorporate her myriad "neat little things," often inherently unrelated, into a tightly structured, carefully sequenced essay. Plans and rules that govern the construction of impressionistic, associational prose would be appropriate to Martha's desire, but her composing process is heavily constrained by the non-impressionistic and nonassociational. Put another way, the plans and rules that govern her exploration of text are not at all synchronous with the plans and rules she uses to discuss her exploration. It is interesting to note here, however, that as recently as three years ago Martha was absorbed in creative writing and was publishing poetry in high school magazines. Given what we know about the complex associational, often non-neatly-sequential nature of the poet's creative process, we can infer that Martha was either free of the plans and rules discussed earlier or they were not as intense. One wonders, as well, if the exposure to three years of university physical science either established or intensified Martha's concern with structure. Whatever the case, she now is hamstrung by conflicting rules when composing papers for the humanities.

Mike's difficulties, too, are rooted in a distortion of the problem-solving process. When the time of the week for the assignment of writing topics draws near, Mike begins to prepare material, strategies, and plans that he believes will be appropriate. If the assignment matches his expectations, he has done a good job of analyzing the professor's intentions. If the assignment *doesn't* match his expectations, however, he cannot easily shift approaches. He feels trapped inside his original plans, cannot generate alternatives, and blocks. As the deadline draws near, he will write something, forcing the assignment to fit his conceptual procrustean bed. Since Mike is a smart man, he will offer a good deal of information, but only some of it ends up being appropriate to the assignment. This entire situation is made all the worse when the time between assignment of topic and generation of product is attenuated further, as in an essay examination. Mike believes (correctly) that one must have a plan, a strategy of some sort in order to solve a problem. He further believes, however, that such a plan, once formulated, becomes an exact structural and substantive blueprint that cannot be violated. The plan offers no alternatives, no "sub-routines." So, whereas Ruth's, Laurel's, and some of Martha's difficulties seem to be rule-specific ("always catch your audience," "write grammatically"), Mike's troubles are more global. He may have strategies that are appropriate for various writing situations (e.g., "for this kind of political science assignment write a compare/contrast essay"), but his entire approach to formulating plans and carrying them through to problem solution is too mechanical. It is probable that Mike's behavior is governed by an explicitly learned or inferred rule: "Always try to 'psych out' a professor." But in this case this rule initiates a problem-solving procedure that is clearly dysfunctional.

While Ruth and Laurel use rules that impede their writing process and Mike utilizes a problem-solving procedure that hamstrings him, *Sylvia* has trouble deciding which of the many rules she possesses to use. Her problem can be characterized as cognitive perplexity: some of her rules are inappropriate, others are functional; some mesh nicely with her own definitions of good writing, others don't. She has multiple rules to invoke, multiple paths to follow, and that very complexity of choice virtually paralyzes her. More so than with the previous four students, there is probably a strong emotional dimension to Sylvia's blocking, but the cognitive difficulties are clear and perhaps modifiable.

Sylvia, somewhat like Ruth and Laurel, puts tremendous weight on the crafting of her first paragraph. If it is good, she believes the rest of the essay will be good. Therefore, she will spend up to five hours on the initial paragraph: "I won't go on until I get that first paragraph down." Clearly, this rule — or the strength of it — blocks Sylvia's production. This is one problem. Another is that Sylvia has other equally potent rules that she sees as separate, uncomplementary injunctions: one achieves "flow" in one's writing through the use of adequate transitions; one achieves substance to one's writing through the use of evidence. Sylvia perceives both rules to be "true," but several times followed one to the exclusion of the other. Furthermore, as I talked to Sylvia, many other rules, guidelines, definitions were offered, but none with conviction. While she *is* committed to one rule about initial paragraphs, and that rule is dysfunctional, she seems very uncertain about the weight and hierarchy of the remaining rules in her cognitive repertoire.

"If It Won't Fit My Work, I'll Change It" — The Non-blockers

Dale, Ellen, Debbie, Susan, and Miles all write with the aid of rules. But their rules differ from blockers' rules in significant ways. If similar in content, they are expressed less absolutely — e.g., "*Try* to keep audience in mind." If dissimilar, they are still expressed less absolutely, more heuristically — e.g., "I can use as many ideas in my thesis paragraph as I need and then develop paragraphs for each idea." Our non-blockers do express some rules with firm assurance, but these tend to be simple injunctions that free up rather than restrict the composing process, e.g., "When stuck, write!" or "I'll write what I can." And finally, at least three of the students openly shun the very textbook rules that some blockers adhere to: e.g., "Rules like 'write only what you know about' just aren't true. I ignore those." These three, in effect, have formulated a further rule that expresses something like: "If a rule conflicts with what is sensible or with experience, reject it."

On the broader level of plans and strategies, these five students also differ from at least three of the five blockers in that they all possess problem-solving plans that are quite functional. Interestingly, on first exploration these plans seem to be too broad or fluid to be useful and, in some cases, can barely be expressed with any precision. Ellen, for example, admits that she has a general "outline in [her] head about how a topic paragraph should look" but could not describe much about its structure. Susan also has a general plan to follow, but, if stymied, will quickly attempt to conceptualize the assignment in different ways: "If my original idea won't work, then I need to proceed differently." Whether or not these plans operate in TOTE-fashion, I can't say. But they do operate with the operate-test fluidity of TOTEs.

True, our non-blockers have their religiously adhered-to rules: e.g., "When stuck, write," and plans, "I couldn't imagine writing without this pattern," but as noted above, these are few and functional. Otherwise, these non-blockers operate with fluid, easily modified, even easily discarded rules and plans (Ellen: "I can throw things out") that are sometimes expressed with a vagueness that could almost be interpreted as ignorance. There lies the irony. Students that offer the least precise rules and plans have the least trouble composing. Perhaps this very lack of precision characterizes the functional composing plan. But perhaps this lack of precision simply masks habitually enacted alternatives and sub-routines. This is clearly an area that needs the illumination of further research.

And then there is feedback. At least three of the five non-blockers are an Information-Processor's dream. They get to know their audience, ask professors and T.A.s specific questions about assignments, bring half-finished products in for evaluation, etc. Like Ruth, they realize the importance of audience, but unlike her, they have specific strategies for obtaining and utilizing feedback. And this penchant for testing writing plans against the needs of the audience can lead to modification of rules and plans. Listen to Debbie:

> In high school I was given a formula that stated that you must write a thesis paragraph with *only* three points in it, and then develop each of those points. When I hit college I was given longer assignments. That stuck me for a bit, but then realized that I could use as many ideas in my thesis paragraph as I needed and then develop paragraphs for each one. I asked someone about this and then tried it. I didn't get any negative feedback, so I figured it was o.k.

Debbie's statement brings one last difference between our blockers and non-blockers into focus; it has been implied above, but needs specific formulation: the goals these people have, and the plans they generate to attain these goals, are quite mutable. Part of the mutability comes from the fluid way the goals and plans are conceived, and part of it arises from the effective impact of feedback on these goals and plans.

Analyzing Writer's Block

Algorithms Rather Than Heuristics

In most cases, the rules our blockers use are not "wrong" or "incorrect" — it is good practice, for example, to "grab your audience with a catchy opening" or "craft a solid first paragraph before going on." The problem is that these rules seem to be followed as though they were algorithms, absolute dicta, rather than the loose heuristics that they were intended to be. Either through instruction, or the power of the textbook, or the predilections of some of our blockers for absolutes, or all three, these useful rules of thumb have been transformed into near-algorithmic urgencies. The result, to paraphrase Karl Dunker, is that these rules do not allow a flexible penetration into the nature of the problem. It is this transformation of heuristic into algorithm that contributes to the writer's block of Ruth and Laurel.

Questionable Heuristics Made Algorithmic

Whereas "grab your audience" could be a useful heuristic, "always make three or more points in an essay" is a pretty questionable one. Any such rule, though probably taught to aid the writer who needs structure, ultimately transforms a highly fluid process like writing into a mechanical lockstep. As heuristics, such rules can be troublesome. As algorithms, they are simply incorrect.

Set

As with any problem-solving task, students approach writing assignments with a variety of orientations or sets. Some are functional, others are not. Martha and Jane (see note 14), coming out of the life sciences and social sciences respectively, bring certain methodological orientations with them — certain sets or "directions" that make composing for the humanities a difficult, sometimes confusing, task. In fact, this orientation may cause them to misperceive the task. Martha has formulated a planning strategy from her predisposition to see processes in terms of linear, interrelated steps in a system. Jane doesn't realize that she can revise the statement that "committed" her to the direction her essay has taken. Both of these students are stymied because of formative experiences associated with their majors — experiences, perhaps, that nicely reinforce our very strong tendency to organize experiences temporally.

The Plan That Is Not a Plan

If fluidity and multi-directionality are central to the nature of plans, then the plans that Mike formulates are not true plans at all but, rather, inflexible and static cognitive blueprints.[15] Put another way, Mike's "plans" represent a restricted "closed system" (vs. "open system") kind of thinking, where closed system thinking is defined as focusing on "a limited number of units or items, or members, and those properties of the members which are to be used are known to begin with and do not change as the thinking proceeds," and open system thinking is characterized by an "adventurous exploration of multiple alternatives with strategies that allow redirection once 'dead ends' are encountered."[16] Composing calls for open, even adventurous thinking, not for constrained, no-exit cognition.

Feedback

The above difficulties are made all the more problematic by the fact that they seem resistant to or isolated from corrective feedback. One of the most striking things about Dale, Debbie, and Miles is the ease with which they seek out, interpret, and apply feedback on their rules, plans, and productions. They "operate" and then they "test," and the testing is not only against some internalized goal, but against the requirements of external audience as well.

Too Many Rules — "Conceptual Conflict"

According to D. E. Berlyne, one of the primary forces that motivate problem-solving behavior is a curiosity that arises from conceptual conflict — the convergence of incompatible beliefs or ideas. In *Structure and Direction in Thinking*,[17] Berlyne presents six major types of conceptual conflict, the second of which he terms "perplexity":

> This kind of conflict occurs when there are factors inclining the subject toward each of a set of mutually exclusive beliefs. (257)

If one substitutes "rules" for "beliefs" in the above definition, perplexity becomes a useful notion here. Because perplexity is unpleasant, people are motivated to reduce it by problem-solving behavior that can result in "disequalization":

> Degree of conflict will be reduced if either the number of competing . . . [rules] or their nearness to equality of strength is reduced. (259)

But "disequalization" is not automatic. As I have suggested, Martha and Sylvia hold to rules that conflict, but their perplexity does *not* lead to curiosity and resultant problem-solving behavior. Their perplexity, contra Berlyne, leads to immobilization. Thus "disequalization" will have to be effected from without. The importance of each of, particularly, Sylvia's rules needs an evaluation that will aid her in rejecting some rules and balancing and sequencing others.

A Note on Treatment

Rather than get embroiled in a blocker's misery, the teacher or tutor might interview the student in order to build a writing history and profile: How much and what kind of writing was done in high school? What is the student's major? What kind of writing does it require? How does the student compose? Are there rough drafts or outlines available? By what rules does the student operate? How would he or she define "good" writing? etc. This sort of interview reveals an incredible amount of information about individual composing processes. Furthermore, it often reveals the rigid rule or the inflexible plan that may lie at the base of the student's writing problem. That was precisely what happened with the five blockers. And with Ruth, Laurel, and Martha (and Jane) what was revealed made virtually immediate remedy possible. Dysfunctional rules are easily replaced with or counter-balanced by functional ones if there is no emotional reason to hold onto that which simply doesn't work. Furthermore, students can be trained to select, to "know which rules are appropriate for which problems."[18] Mike's difficulties, perhaps because plans are more complex and pervasive than rules, took longer to correct. But inflexible plans, too, can be remedied by pointing out their dysfunctional qualities and by assisting the student in developing appropriate and flexible alternatives. Operating this way, I was successful with Mike. Sylvia's story, however, did not end as smoothly. Though I had three forty-five minute contacts with her, I was not able to appreciably alter her behavior. Berlyne's theory bore results with Martha but not with Sylvia. Her rules were in conflict, and perhaps that conflict was not exclusively cognitive. Her case keeps analyses like these honest; it reminds us that the cognitive often melds with, and can be overpowered by, the affective. So while Ruth, Laurel, Martha, and Mike could profit from tutorials that explore the rules and plans in their writing behavior, students like Sylvia may need more extended, more affectively oriented counseling sessions that blend the instructional with the psychodynamic.

Notes

1. David Shapiro, *Neurotic Styles* (New York: Basic, 1965).
2. Barbara Hayes-Ruth, a Rand cognitive psychologist, and I are currently developing an information-processing model of the composing process. A good deal of work has already been done by Linda Flower and John Hayes (see note 13 and surrounding text). I have just received — and recommend — their "Writing as Problem Solving" (paper presented at American Educational Research Association, April 1979).
3. Robert M. Gagné, *The Conditions of Learning* (New York: Holt, 1970) 193.
4. E. James Archer, "The Psychological Nature of Concepts," *Analysis of Concept Learning*, ed. H. J. Klausmeirer and C. W. Harris (New York: Academic P, 1966) 37–44; David P. Ausubel, *The Psychology of Meaningful Verbal Behavior* (New York: Grune, 1963); Robert M. Gagné, "Problem Solving," *Categories of Human Learning*, ed. Arthur W. Melton (New York:

Academic P, 1964) 293–317; George A. Miller, *Language and Communication* (New York: McGraw, 1951).

5. George Katona, *Organizing and Memorizing* (New York: Columbia UP, 1940); Roger N. Shepard, Carl I. Hovland, and Herbert M. Jenkins, "Learning and Memorization of Classifications," *Psychological Monographs,* 75.13 (1961) (entire no. 517); Robert S. Woodworth, *Dynamics of Behavior* (New York: Holt, 1958) chs. 10–12.

6. Gagné, *The Conditions of Learning,* 190–91.

7. Karl Dunker, "On Problem Solving," *Psychological Monographs,* 58.5 (1945) (entire no. 270); George A. Polya, *How to Solve It* (Princeton: Princeton UP, 1945); George A. Miller, Eugene Galanter, and Karl H. Pribram, *Plans and the Structure of Behavior* (New York: Holt, 1960).

8. Lyle E. Bourne, Jr., Bruce R. Ekstrand, and Roger L. Dominowski, *The Psychology of Thinking* (Englewood Cliffs: Prentice, 1971).

9. John R. Hayes, "Problem Topology and the Solution Process," *Thinking: Current Experimental Studies,* ed. Carl P. Duncan (Philadelphia: Lippincott, 1967) 167–81.

10. Hulda J. Rees and Harold E. Israel, "An Investigation of the Establishment and Operation of Mental Sets," *Psychological Monographs,* 46 (1925) (entire no. 210).

11. Ibid.; Melvin H. Marx, Wilton W. Murphy, and Aaron J. Brownstein, "Recognition of Complex Visual Stimuli as a Function of Training with Abstracted Patterns," *Journal of Experimental Psychology* 62 (1961): 456–60.

12. James L. Adams, *Conceptual Blockbusting* (San Francisco: Freeman, 1974); Edward DeBono, *New Think* (New York: Basic, 1958); Ronald H. Forgus, *Perception* (New York: McGraw, 1966) ch. 13; Abraham Luchins and Edith Hirsch Luchins, *Rigidity of Behavior* (Eugene: U of Oregon Books, 1959); N. R. F. Maier, "Reasoning in Humans. I. On Direction," *Journal of Comparative Psychology* 10 (1920): 115–43.

13. Linda Flower and John Hayes, "Plans and the Cognitive Process of Writing," paper presented at the National Institute of Education Writing Conference, June 1977; "Problem-Solving Strategies and the Writing Process," *College English* 39 (1977): 449–61. See also note 2.

14. Jane, a student not discussed in this paper, was surprised to find out that a topic paragraph can be rewritten after a paper's conclusion to make that paragraph reflect what the essay truly contains. She had gotten so indoctrinated with Psychology's (her major) insistence that a hypothesis be formulated and then left untouched before an experiment begins that she thought revision of one's "major premise" was somehow illegal. She had formed a rule out of her exposure to social science methodology, and the rule was totally inappropriate for most writing situations.

15. Cf. "A plan is flexible if the order of execution of its parts can be easily interchanged without affecting the feasibility of the plan . . . the flexible planner might tend to think of lists of things he had to do; the inflexible planner would have his time planned like a sequence of cause-effect relations. The former could rearrange his lists to suit his opportunities, but the latter would be unable to strike while the iron was hot and would generally require considerable 'lead-time' before he could incorporate any alternative sub-plans" (Miller, Galanter, and Pribram, 120).

16. Frederic Bartlett, *Thinking* (New York: Basic, 1958) 74–76.

17. *Structure and Direction in Thinking* (New York: Wiley, 1965) 255.

18. Flower and Hayes, "Plans and the Cognitive Process of Writing," 26.

Rose's Insights as a Resource for Your Teaching

1. Consider the risks in teaching students how to write: Invariably, a few students will be cowed by your authority and will internalize even the most idle and perfunctory observations that you make. Worse yet, they will treat those observations not simply as useful tips but as some sort of holy edict. When they do, their ability to compose will be curtailed. In a journal, reflect on ways to prevent your overly earnest students from damaging themselves this way. What are some strategies you might devise to teach in a way that minimizes this risk?

2. How do you help students who have come into your classroom blocked by mishandled writing advice? What can you say to them? Can you use some of Rose's theory when giving advice to students who have already mishandled the advice given them in the past?

Rose's Insights as a Resource for Your Writing Classroom

1. Consider how you respond to grammar errors in student writing. Could thorough marking of "incorrect" spots in a paper contribute to what Rose identifies as an overly zealous conscientiousness about following the rules? Hold a class discussion about students' reactions to your written comments on their papers. Based on the discussion and on Rose's insights, how might you modify the ways you comment on student writing?

2. Ask students to meet in small groups, and make a list of the five most important dos and don'ts of writing. Then have them write their lists on the board. As you discuss these rules, emphasize their tentative nature, and encourage students to take all of them with a grain of salt. Explain to them that to be overly concerned with such matters can undermine the process of getting thoughts down on paper.

Considering Audience

The Rhetorical Stance

Wayne C. Booth

Although this essay was written over forty years ago, it continues to enjoy frequent reprinting and much discussion among those who teach writing.

Wayne C. Booth mixes casual anecdotes about his classroom practice with a sophisticated study of traditional rhetoric. Booth's central insight is that the success or failure of a piece of writing hinges on how the writer stages the author-subject-audience relationships within the text. He defines the ideal balance, or "rhetorical stance," by contrasting it with several "corruptions"—unbalanced stances that result in dry, obscure, or vacuous writing. Booth includes practical strategies to help students achieve the rhetorical stance, the proper balance that underlies all effective, persuasive writing.

Last fall I had an advanced graduate student, bright, energetic, well-informed, whose papers were almost unreadable. He managed to be pretentious, dull, and disorganized in his paper on *Emma,* and pretentious, dull, and disorganized on *Madame Bovary.* On *The Golden Bowl* he was all these and obscure as well. Then one day, toward the end of term, he cornered me after class and said, "You know, I think you were all wrong about Robbe-Grillet's *Jealousy* today." We didn't have time to discuss it, so I suggested that he write me a note about it. Five hours later I found in my faculty box a four-page polemic, unpretentious, stimulating, organized, convincing. Here was a man who had taught freshman composition for several years and who was incapable of committing any of the more obvious errors that we think of as characteristic of bad writing. Yet he could not write a decent sentence, paragraph, or paper until his rhetorical problem was solved — until, that is, he had found a definition of his audience, his argument, and his own proper tone of voice.

The word *rhetoric* is one of those catch-all terms that can easily raise trouble when our backs are turned. As it regains a popularity that it once seemed permanently to have lost, its meanings seem to range all the way from something like "the whole art of writing on any subject," as in Kenneth Burke's *The Rhetoric of Religion,* through "the special arts of persuasion," on down to fairly narrow notions about rhetorical figures and devices. And of course we still have with us the meaning of "empty bombast," as in the phrase "merely rhetorical."

I suppose that the question of the role of rhetoric in the English course is meaningless if we think of rhetoric in either its broadest or its narrowest meanings. No English course could avoid dealing with rhetoric in Burke's sense, under whatever name, and on the other hand nobody would ever advocate anything so questionable as teaching "mere rhetoric." But if we settle on the following, traditional, definition, some real questions are raised: "Rhetoric is the art of finding and employing the most effective means of persuasion on any subject, considered independently of intellectual mastery of that subject." As the students say, "Prof. X knows his stuff but he doesn't know how to put it across." If rhetoric is thought of as the art of "putting it across," considered as quite distinct from mastering an "it" in the first place, we are immediately landed in a bramble bush of controversy. Is there such an art? If so, what does it consist of? Does it have a content of its own? Can it be taught? Should it be taught? If it should, how do we go about it, head on or obliquely?

Obviously it would be foolish to try to deal with many of these issues in twenty minutes. But I wish that there were more signs of our taking all of them seriously. I wish that along with our new passion for structural linguistics, for example, we could point to the development of a rhetorical theory that would show just how knowledge of structural linguistics can be useful to anyone interested in the art of persuasion. I wish there were more freshman texts that related every principle and every rule to functional principles of rhetoric, or, where this proves impossible, I wish one found more systematic discussion of why it is impossible. But for today, I must content myself with a brief look at the charge that there is nothing distinctive and teachable about the art of rhetoric.

The case against the isolability and teachability of rhetoric may look at first like a good one. Nobody writes rhetoric, just as nobody ever writes writing. What we write and speak is always *this* discussion of the decline of railroading and *that* discussion of Pope's couplets and the other argument for abolishing the poll-tax or for getting rhetoric back into English studies.

We can also admit that like all the arts, the art of rhetoric is at best very chancy, only partly amenable to systematic teaching; as we are all painfully aware when our 1:00 section goes miserably and our 2:00 section of the same course is a delight, our own rhetoric is not entirely under control. Successful rhetoricians are to some extent like poets, born, not made. They are also dependent on years of practice and experience. And we can finally admit that even the firmest of principles about writing cannot be taught in the same sense that elementary logic or arithmetic or French can be taught. In my first year of teaching, I had a student who started his first two essays with a swear word. When I suggested that perhaps the third paper ought to start with something else, he protested that his high school teacher had taught him always to catch the reader's attention. Now the teacher was right, but the application of even such a firm principle requires reserves of tact that were somewhat beyond my freshman.

But with all of the reservations made, surely the charge that the art of persuasion cannot in any sense be taught is baseless. I cannot think that anyone who has ever read Aristotle's *Rhetoric* or, say, Whateley's *Elements of Rhetoric* could seriously make the charge. There is more than enough in these and the other traditional rhetorics to provide structure and content for a year-long course. I believe that such a course, when planned and carried through with intelligence and flexibility, can be one of the most important of all educational experiences. But it seems obvious that the arts of persuasion cannot be learned in one year, that a good teacher will continue to teach them regardless of his subject matter, and that we as English teachers have a special responsibility at all levels to get certain basic rhetorical principles into all of our writing assignments. When I think back over the experiences which have had any actual effect on my writing, I find the great good fortune of a splendid freshman course, taught by a man who believed in what he was doing, but I also find a collection of other experiences quite unconnected with a specific writing course. I remember the instructor in psychology who pencilled one word after a peculiarly pretentious paper of mine: *bull*. I remember the day when P. A. Christensen talked with me about my Chaucer paper, and made me understand that my failure to use effective transitions was not simply a technical fault but a fundamental block in my effort to get him to see my meaning. His off-the-cuff pronouncement that I should never let myself write a sentence that was not in some way explicitly attached to preceding and following sentences meant far more to me at that moment, when I had something I wanted to say, than it could have meant as part of a pattern of such rules offered in a writing course. Similarly, I can remember the devastating lessons about my bad writing that Ronald Crane could teach with a simple question mark on a graduate seminar paper, or a pencilled "Evidence for this?" or "Why this section here?" or "Everybody says so. Is it true?"

Such experiences are not, I like to think, simply the result of my being a late bloomer. At least I find my colleagues saying such things as "I didn't learn to write until I became a newspaper reporter," or "The most important training in writing I had was doing a dissertation under old *Blank*." Sometimes they go on to say that the freshman course was useless; sometimes they say that it was an indispensable preparation for the later experience. The diversity of such replies is so great as to suggest that before we try to reorganize the freshman course, with or without explicit confrontations with rhetorical categories, we ought to look for whatever there is in common among our experiences, both of good writing and of good writing instruction. Whatever we discover in such an enterprise ought to be useful to us at any level of our teaching. It will not, presumably, decide once and for all what should be the content of the freshman course, if there should be such a course. But it might serve as a guideline for the development of widely different programs in the widely differing institutional circumstances in which we must work.

The common ingredient that I find in all of the writing I admire — excluding for now novels, plays and poems — is something that I shall reluctantly call the rhetorical stance, a stance which depends on discovering and maintaining in any writing situation a proper balance among the three elements that are at work in any communicative effort: the available arguments about the subject itself, the interests and peculiarities of the audience, and the voice, the implied character, of the speaker. I should like to suggest that it is this balance, this rhetorical stance, difficult as it is to describe, that is our main goal as teachers of rhetoric. Our ideal graduate will strike this balance automatically in any writing that he considers finished. Though he may never come to the point of finding the balance easily, he will know that it is what makes the difference between effective communication and mere wasted effort.

What I mean by the true rhetorician's stance can perhaps best be seen by contrasting it with two or three corruptions, unbalanced stances often assumed by people who think they are practicing the arts of persuasion.

The first I'll call the pedant's stance; it consists of ignoring or underplaying the personal relationship of speaker and audience and depending entirely on statements about a subject — that is, the notion of a job to be done for a particular audience is left out. It is a virtue, of course, to respect the bare truth of one's subject, and there may even be some subjects which in their very nature define an audience and a rhetorical purpose so that adequacy to the subject can be the whole art of presentation. For example, an article on "The relation of the ontological and teleological proofs," in a recent *Journal of Religion,* requires a minimum of adaptation of argument to audience. But most subjects do not in themselves imply in any necessary way a purpose and an audience and hence a speaker's tone. The writer who assumes that it is enough merely to write an exposition of what he happens to know on the subject will produce the kind of essay that soils our scholarly journals, written not for readers but for bibliographies.

In my first year of teaching I taught a whole unit on "exposition" without ever suggesting, so far as I can remember, that the students ask themselves what their expositions were *for.* So they wrote expositions like this one — I've saved it, to teach me toleration of my colleagues: the title is "Family Relations in More's *Utopia.*" "In this theme I would like to discuss some of the relationships with the family which Thomas More elaborates and sets forth in his book, *Utopia.* The first thing that I would like to discuss about family relations is that overpopulation, according to More, is a just cause of war." And so on. Can you hear that student sneering at me, in this opening? What he is saying is something like "you ask for a meaningless paper, I give you a meaningless paper." He knows that he has no audience except me. He knows that I don't want to read his summary of family relations in *Utopia,* and he knows that I know that he therefore has no rhetorical purpose. Because he has not been led to see a question which he considers worth answering, or an audience that could possibly care one way or the other, the paper is worse than no paper at all, even though it has no grammatical or spelling errors and is organized right down the line, one, two, three.

An extreme case, you may say. Most of us would never allow ourselves that kind of empty fencing? Perhaps. But if some carefree foundation is willing to finance a statistical study, I'm willing to wager a month's salary that we'd find at least half of the suggested topics in our freshman texts as pointless as mine was. And we'd find a good deal more than half of the discussions of grammar, punctuation, spelling, and style totally divorced from any notion that rhetorical purpose to some degree controls all such matters. We can offer objective descriptions of levels of usage from now until graduation, but unless the student discovers a desire to say something to somebody and learns to control his diction for a purpose, we've gained very little. I once gave an assignment asking students to describe the same classroom in three different statements, one for each level of usage. They were obedient, but the only ones who got anything from the assignment were those who intuitively imported the rhetorical instructions I had overlooked — such purposes as "Make fun of your scholarly surroundings by describing this classroom in extremely elevated style," or "Imagine a kid from the slums accidentally trapped in these surroundings and forced to write a description of this room." A little thought might have shown me how to give the whole assignment some human point, and therefore some educative value.

Just how confused we can allow ourselves to be about such matters is shown in a recent publication of the Educational Testing Service, called "Factors in Judgments of Writing Ability." In order to isolate those factors which affect differences in grading standards, ETS set six groups of readers — businessmen, writers and editors, lawyers, and teachers of English, social science and natural science — to reading the same batch of papers. Then ETS did a hundred-page "factor analysis" of the amount of agreement and disagreement, and of the elements which different kinds of graders emphasized. The authors of the report express a certain amount of shock at the discovery that the median correlation was only .31 and that 94 percent of the papers received either seven, eight, or nine of the nine possible grades.

But what *could* they have expected? In the first place, the students were given no purpose and no audience when the essays were assigned. And then all these editors and businessmen and academics were asked to judge the papers in a complete vacuum, using only whatever intuitive standards they cared to use. I'm surprised that there was any correlation at all. Lacking instructions, some of the students undoubtedly wrote polemical essays, suitable for the popular press; others no doubt imagined an audience, say, of *Reader's Digest* readers, and others wrote with the English teachers as implied audience; an occasional student with real philosophical bent would no doubt do a careful analysis of the pros and cons of the case. This would be graded low, of course, by the magazine editors, even though they would have graded it high if asked to judge it as a speculative contribution to the analysis of the problem. Similarly, a creative student who has been getting A's for his personal essays will write an amusing colorful piece, failed by all the social scientists present, though they would have graded it high if asked to judge it for what it was. I find it shocking that tens of thousands of dollars and endless hours should have been spent by students, graders, and professional testers analyzing essays and grading results totally abstracted from any notion of purposeful human communication. Did nobody protest? One might as well assemble a group of citizens to judge students' capacity to throw balls, say, without telling the students or the graders whether altitude, speed, accuracy or form was to be judged.

The judges would be drawn from football coaches, jai-lai experts, lawyers, and English teachers, and asked to apply whatever standards they intuitively apply to ball throwing. Then we could express astonishment that the judgments did not correlate very well, and we could do a factor analysis to discover, lo and behold, that some readers concentrated on altitude, some on speed, some on accuracy, some on form — and the English teachers were simply confused.

One effective way to combat the pedantic stance is to arrange for weekly confrontations of groups of students over their own papers. We have done far too little experimenting with arrangements for providing a genuine audience in this way. Short of such developments, it remains true that a good teacher can convince his students that he is a true audience, if his comments on the papers show that some sort of dialogue is taking place. As Jacques Barzun says in *Teacher in America,* students should be made to feel that unless they have said something to someone, they have failed; to bore the teacher is a worse form of failure than to anger him. From this point of view we can see that the charts of grading symbols that mar even the best freshman texts are not the innocent time savers that we pretend. Plausible as it may seem to arrange for more corrections with less time, they inevitably reduce the student's sense of purpose in writing. When he sees innumerable W13s and P19s in the margin, he cannot possibly feel that the art of persuasion is as important to his instructor as when he reads personal comments, however few.

This first perversion, then, springs from ignoring the audience or overreliance on the pure subject. The second, which might be called the advertiser's stance, comes from *under*valuing the subject and overvaluing pure effect: how to win friends and influence people.

Some of our best freshman texts — Sheridan Baker's *The Practical Stylist,* for example — allow themselves on occasion to suggest that to be controversial or argumentative, to stir up an audience is an end in itself. Sharpen the controversial edge, one of them says, and the clear implication is that one should do so even if the truth of the subject is honed off in the process. This perversion is probably in the long run a more serious threat in our society than the danger of ignoring the audience. In the time of audience-reaction meters and pre-tested plays and novels, it is not easy to convince students of the old Platonic truth that good persuasion is honest persuasion, or even of the old Aristotelian truth that the good rhetorician must be master of his subject, no matter how dishonest he may decide ultimately to be. Having told them that good writers always to some degree accommodate their arguments to the audience, it is hard to explain the difference between justified accommodation — say changing *point one* to the final position — and the kind of accommodation that fills our popular magazines, in which the very substance of what is said is accommodated to some preconception of what will sell. "The publication of *Eros* [magazine] represents a major breakthrough in the battle for the liberation of the human spirit."

At a dinner about a month ago I sat between the wife of a famous civil rights lawyer and an advertising consultant. "I saw the article on your book yesterday in the *Daily News*," she said, "but I didn't even finish it. The title of your book scared me off. Why did you ever choose such a terrible title? Nobody would buy a book with a title like that." The man on my right, whom I'll call Mr. Kinches, overhearing my feeble reply, plunged into a conversation with her, over my torn and bleeding corpse. "Now with my *last* book," he said, "I listed twenty possible titles and then tested them out on four hundred businessmen. The one I chose was voted for by 90 percent of the businessmen." "That's what I was just saying to Mr. Booth," she said. "A book title ought to grab you, and *rhetoric* is not going to grab anybody." "Right," he said. "My *last* book sold fifty thousand copies already; I don't know how this one will do, but I polled two hundred businessmen on the table of contents, and . . ."

At one point I did manage to ask him whether the title he chose really fit the book. "Not quite as well as one or two of the others," he admitted, "but that doesn't matter, you know. If the book is designed right, so that the first chapter pulls them in, and you *keep* 'em in, who's going to gripe about a little inaccuracy in the title?"

Well, rhetoric is the art of persuading, not the art seeming to persuade by giving everything away at the start. It presupposes that one has a purpose concerning a subject which itself cannot be fundamentally modified by the desire to persuade. If Edmund Burke had decided that he could win more votes in Parliament by choosing the other side — as he most certainly could have done — we would hardly hail this party-switch as a master stroke of rhetoric. If Churchill had offered the British "peace in our time," with some laughs thrown in, because opinion polls had shown that more Britishers were "grabbed" by these than by blood, sweat, and tears, we could hardly call his decision a sign of rhetorical skill.

One could easily discover other perversions of the rhetorician's balance — most obviously what might be called the entertainer's stance — the willingness to sacrifice substance to personality and charm. I admire Walker Gibson's efforts to startle us out of dry pedantry, but I know from experience that his exhortations to find and develop the speaker's voice can lead to empty colorfulness. A student once said to me, complaining about a colleague, "I soon learned that all I had to do to get an A was imitate Thurber."

But perhaps this is more than enough about the perversions of the rhetorical stance. Balance itself is always harder to describe than the clumsy poses that result when it is destroyed. But we all experience the balance whenever we find an author who succeeds in changing our minds. He can do so only if he knows more about the subject than we do, and if he then engages us in the process of thinking — and feeling — it through. What makes the rhetoric of Milton and Burke and Churchill great is that each presents us with the spectacle of a man passionately involved in thinking an important question through, in the company of an audience. Though each of them did everything in his power to make his point persuasive, including a pervasive use of the many emotional appeals that have been falsely scorned by many a freshman composition text, none would have allowed himself the advertiser's stance; none would have polled the audience in advance to discover which position would get the votes. Nor is the highly individual personality that springs out at us from their speeches and essays present for the sake of selling itself. The rhetorical balance among speakers, audience, and argument is with all three men habitual, as we see if we look at their non-political writings. Burke's work on the Sublime and Beautiful is a relatively unimpassioned philosophical treatise, but one finds there again a delicate balance: though the implied author of this work is a far different person, far less obtrusive, far more objective, than the man who later cried *sursum corda* to the British Parliament, he permeates with his philosophical personality his philosophical work. And though the signs of his awareness of his audience are far more subdued, they are still here: every effort is made to involve the *proper* audience, the audience of philosophical minds, in a fundamentally interesting inquiry, and to lead them through to the end. In short, because he was a man engaged with men in the effort to solve a human problem, one could never call what he wrote dull, however difficult or abstruse.

Now obviously the habit of seeking this balance is not the only thing we have to teach under the heading of rhetoric. But I think that everything worth teaching under that heading finds its justification finally in that balance. Much of what is now considered irrelevant or dull can, in fact, be brought to life when teachers and students know what they are seeking. Churchill reports that the most valuable training he ever received in rhetoric was in the diagramming of sentences. Think of it! Yet the diagramming of a sentence, regardless of the grammatical system, can be a live subject as soon as one asks not simply "How is this sentence put together," but rather "Why is it put together in this way?" or "Could the rhetorical balance and hence the desired persuasion be better achieved by writing it differently?"

As a nation we are reputed to write very badly. As a nation, I would say, we are more inclined to the perversions of rhetoric than to the rhetorical balance. Regardless of what we do about this or that course in the curriculum, our mandate would seem to be, then, to lead more of our students than we now do to care about and practice the true arts of persuasion.

Booth's Insights as a Resource for Your Teaching

1. Read any piece of writing by a student, and track the ways the author appeals to you as a reader. Where does the author adopt the pedant's stance? The advertiser's stance? How might these terms help you to comment on student work that needs improvement?

2. Consider the stance that you model for your students. Do you alternate between pedant and advertiser, or do you strike a rhetorical stance most of the time? How do the students respond to the various stances we model for them?

Booth's Insights as a Resource for Your Writing Classroom

1. Assign Booth's essay to your students. Once they've read it, have them explore it according to the terms Booth himself presents. Does Booth effectively balance the audience-subject-author relationships? If so, how and where does he manage to strike this balance? Are there any places where the stance seems imbalanced and starts to lean in one direction or another?

2. Ask students to examine their own work or each other's in light of Booth's essay. Have them focus on passages in their own writing that lean toward a pedant, advertiser, or entertainer stance. Can they use Booth's terms to diagnose and fix problems?

Closing My Eyes as I Speak: An Argument for Ignoring Audience

Peter Elbow

In the following selection, first published in College English *in 1987, Peter Elbow argues that writers often need simply to ignore audience. Even though he credits several arguments for audience awareness and agrees that a consideration of audience can invite and enable the writer to generate thought and feeling, he cautions that audience awareness can sometimes inhibit and even block writing. In particular, attention to audience in the earliest stages of writing may confuse and inhibit the writer, whereas during revision it may enlighten and liberate the writer.*

Elbow asserts that when attention to audience complicates thinking so much that student writers short out, we should suggest that the students ignore the audience and pay attention to their own thinking. He disagrees that writers who shape "reader-based prose" are ipso facto more cognitively mature than those who produce "writer-based prose." Instead, he insists that the ability to turn off audience awareness when it is distracting or confusing is a higher skill. Writers who can switch off audience awareness and sustain quiet, thoughtful reflection — who can in private reflection make meaning for themselves and shape a discourse from such thinking alone — are independent and mature thinkers. Once these writers work out through drafts and "internal conversation" what they think, they can turn their attention back to audience. Elbow insists that "ignoring audience can lead to worse drafts but better revisions."

> Very often people don't listen to you when you speak to them. It's only when you talk to yourself that they prick up their ears.
>
> — John Ashbery

When I am talking to a person or a group and struggling to find words or thoughts, I often find myself involuntarily closing my eyes as I speak. I realize now that this behavior is an instinctive attempt to blot out awareness of audience when I need all my concentration for just trying to figure out or express what I want to say. Because the audience is so imperiously present in a speaking situation, my instinct reacts with this active attempt to avoid audience awareness. This behavior — in a sense impolite or antisocial — is not so uncommon. Even when we write, alone in a room to an absent audience, there are occasions when we are struggling to figure something out and need to push aside awareness of those absent readers. As Donald Murray puts it, "My sense of audience is so strong that I have to suppress my conscious awareness of audience to hear what the text demands" (Berkenkotter and Murray 171). In recognition of how pervasive the role of audience is in writing, I write to celebrate the benefits of ignoring audience.[1]

It will be clear that my argument for writing without audience awareness is not meant to undermine the many good reasons for writing *with* audience awareness some of the time. (For example, that we are liable to neglect audience because we write in solitude; that young people often need more practice in taking into account points of view different from their own; and that students often have an impoverished sense of writing as communication because they have only written in a school setting to teachers.) Indeed I would claim some part in these arguments for audience awareness — which now seem to be getting out of hand.

I start with a limited claim: even though ignoring audience will usually lead to weak writing at first — to what Linda Flower calls "writer-based prose" — this weak writing can help us in the end to better writing than we would have written if we'd kept readers in mind from the start. Then I will make a more ambitious claim: writer-based prose is sometimes better than reader-based prose. Finally I will explore some of the theory underlying these issues of audience.

A Limited Claim

It's not that writers should never think about their audience. It's a question of when. An audience is a field of force. The closer we come — the more we think about these readers — the stronger the pull they exert on the contents of our minds. The practical question, then, is always whether a particular audience functions as a helpful field of force or one that confuses or inhibits us.

Some audiences, for example, are *inviting* or *enabling*. When we think about them as we write, we think of more and better things to say — and what we think somehow arrives more coherently structured than usual. It's like talking to the perfect listener: we feel smart and come up with ideas we didn't know we had. Such audiences are helpful to keep in mind right from the start.

Other audiences, however, are powerfully *inhibiting* — so much so, in certain cases, that awareness of them as we write blocks writing altogether. There are certain people who always make us feel dumb when we try to speak to them: we can't find words or thoughts. As soon as we get out of their presence, all the things we want to say pop back into our minds. Here is a student telling what happens when she tries to follow the traditional advice about audience:

> You know _____ [author of a text] tells us to pay attention to the audience that will be reading our papers, and I gave that a try. I ended up without putting a word on paper until I decided the hell with _____; I'm going to write to who I damn well want to; otherwise I can hardly write at all.

Admittedly, there are some occasions when we benefit from keeping a threatening audience in mind from the start. We've been putting off writing that letter to that person who intimidates us. When we finally sit down and write *to* them — walk right up to them, as it were, and look them in the eye — we may manage to stand up to the threat and grasp the nettle and thereby find just what we need to write.

Most commonly, however, the effect of audience awareness is somewhere between the two extremes: the awareness disturbs or disrupts our writing and thinking without completely blocking it. For example, when we have to write to someone we find intimidating (and of course students often perceive teachers as intimidating), we often start thinking wholly defensively. As we write down each thought or sentence, our mind fills with thoughts of how the intended reader will criticize or object to it. So we try to qualify or soften what we've just written — or write out some answer to a possible objection. Our writing becomes tangled. Sometimes we get so tied in knots that we cannot even figure out what we *think*. We may not realize how often audience awareness has this effect on our students when we don't see the writing process behind their papers: we just see texts that are either tangled or empty.

Another example. When we have to write to readers with whom we have an awkward relationship, we often start beating around the bush and feeling shy or scared, or start to write in a stilted, overly careful style or voice. (Think about the cute, too-clever style of many memos we get in our departmental mailboxes — the awkward self-consciousness academics experience when writing to other academics.) When students are asked to write to readers they have not met or cannot imagine, such as "the general reader" or "the educated public," they often find nothing to say except clichés they know *they* don't even quite believe.

When we realize that an audience is somehow confusing or inhibiting us, the solution is fairly obvious. We can ignore that audience altogether during the *early* stages of writing and direct our words only to ourselves or to no one in particular — or even to the "wrong" audience, that is, to an *inviting* audience of trusted friends or allies. This strategy often dissipates the confusion; the clenched, defensive discourse starts to run clear. Putting audience out of mind is of course a traditional practice: serious writers have long used private journals for early explorations of feeling, thinking, or language. But many writing teachers seem to think that students can get along without the private writing serious writers find so crucial — or even that students will *benefit* from keeping their audience in mind for the whole time. Things often don't work out that way.

After we have figured out our thinking in copious exploratory or draft writing — perhaps finding the right voice or stance as well — *then* we can follow the traditional rhetorical advice: Think about readers and revise carefully to adjust our words and thoughts to our intended audience. For a particular audience it may even turn out that we need to *disguise* our point of view. But it's hard to disguise something while engaged in trying to figure it out. As writers, then, we need to learn when to think about audience and when to put readers out of mind.

Many people are too quick to see Flower's "writer-based prose" as an analysis of what's wrong with this type of writing and miss the substantial degree to which she was celebrating a natural, and indeed developmentally enabling, response to cognitive overload. What she doesn't say, however, despite her emphasis on planning and conscious control in the writing process, is that we can *teach* students to notice when audience awareness is getting in their way — and when this happens, consciously to put aside the needs of readers for a while. She seems to assume that when an overload occurs, the writer-based gear will, as it were, automatically kick into action to relieve it. In truth, of course, writers often persist in using a malfunctioning *reader*-based gear despite the overload — thereby mangling their language or thinking. Though Flower likes to rap the knuckles of people who suggest a "correct" or "natural" order for steps in the writing process, she implies such an order here: When attention to audience causes an overload, start out by ignoring them while you attend to your thinking; after you work out your thinking, turn your attention to audience.

Thus if we ignore audience while writing on a topic about which we are not expert or about which our thinking is still evolving, we are likely to produce exploratory writing that is unclear to anyone else — perhaps even inconsistent or a complete mess. Yet by doing this exploratory "swamp work" in conditions of safety, we can often coax our thinking through a process of new discovery and development. In this way we can end up with something better than we could have produced if we'd tried to write to our audience all along. In short, ignoring audience can lead to worse drafts but better revisions. (Because we are professionals and adults, we often write in the role of expert: we may know what we think without new exploratory writing; we may even be able to speak confidently to critical readers. But students seldom experience this confident professional stance in their writing. And think how much richer *our* writing would be if we defined ourselves as *in*expert and allowed ourselves private writing for new explorations of those views we are allegedly sure of.)

Notice then that two pieties of composition theory are often in conflict:

1. Think about audience as you write (this stemming from the classical rhetorical tradition).

2. Use writing for *making new meaning,* not just transmitting old meanings already worked out (this stemming from the newer epistemic tradition I associate with Ann Berthoff's classic explorations).

It's often difficult to work out new meaning while thinking about readers.

A More Ambitious Claim

I go further now and argue that ignoring audience can lead to better writing — immediately. In effect, writer-based prose can be *better* than reader-based prose. This might seem a more controversial claim, but is there a teacher who has not had the experience of struggling and struggling to no avail to help a student untangle his writing, only to discover that the student's casual journal writing or freewriting is untangled and strong? Sometimes freewriting is stronger than the essays we get only because it is expressive, narrative, or descriptive writing and the student was not constrained by a topic. But teachers who collect drafts with completed assignments often see passages of freewriting that are strikingly stronger *even* when they are expository and constrained by the assigned topic. In some of these passages we can sense that the strength derives from the student's unawareness of readers.

It's not just unskilled, tangled writers, though, who sometimes write better by forgetting about readers. Many competent and even professional writers produce mediocre pieces *because* they are thinking too much about how their readers will receive their words. They are acting too much like a salesman trained to look the customer in the eye and to think at all times about the characteristics of the "target audience." There is something too staged or planned or self-aware about such writing. We see this quality in much second-rate newspaper or magazine or business writing: "good-student writing" in the awful sense of the term. Writing produced this way reminds us of the ineffective actor whose consciousness of self distracts us: he makes us too aware of his own awareness of us. When we read such prose, we wish the writer would stop thinking about us — would stop trying to "adjust" or "fit" what he is saying to our frame of reference. "Damn it, put all your attention on what you are saying," we want to say, "and forget about us and how we are reacting."

When we examine really good student or professional writing, we can often see that its goodness comes from the writer's having gotten sufficiently wrapped up in her meaning and her language as to forget all about audience needs: the writer manages to "break through." The Earl of Shaftesbury talked about writers needing to escape their audience in order to find their own ideas (Cooper 1:109; see also Griffin). It is characteristic of much truly good writing to be, as it were, on fire with its meaning. Consciousness of readers is burned away; involvement in subject determines all. Such writing is analogous to the performance of the actor who has managed to stop attracting attention to her awareness of the audience watching her.

The arresting power in some writing by small children comes from their obliviousness to audience. As readers, we are somehow sucked into a more-than-usual connection with the meaning itself because of the child's gift for more-than-usual concentration on what she is saying. In short, we can feel some pieces of children's writing as being very writer-based. Yet it's precisely that quality which makes it powerful for us as readers. After all, why should we settle for a writer's entering our point of view, if we can have the more powerful experience of being sucked out of our point of view and into her world? This is just the experience that children are peculiarly capable of giving because they are so expert at total absorption in their world as they are writing. It's not just a matter of whether the writer "decenters," but of whether the writer has a sufficiently strong focus of attention to make the *reader* decenter. This quality of concentration is what D. H. Lawrence so admires in Melville:

> [Melville] was a real American in that he always felt his audience in front of him. But when he ceases to be American, when he forgets all audience, and gives us his sheer apprehension of the world, then he is wonderful, his book [*Moby Dick*] commands a stillness in the soul, an awe. (158)

What most readers value in really excellent writing is not prose that is right for readers but prose that is right for thinking, right for language, or right for the subject being written about. If, in addition, it is clear and well suited to readers, we appreciate that. Indeed we feel insulted if the writer did not somehow try to make the writing *available* to us before delivering it. But if it succeeds at being really true to language and thinking and "things," we are willing to put up with much difficulty as readers:

> Good writing is not always or necessarily an adaptation to communal norms (in the Fish/Bruffee sense) but may be an attempt to construct (and instruct) a reader capable of reading the text in question. The

literary history of the "difficult" work — from Mallarmé to Pound, Zukofsky, Olson, etc. — seems to say that much of what we value in writing we've had to learn to value by learning how to read it. (Trimbur)

The effect of audience awareness on voice is particularly striking — if paradoxical. Even though we often develop our voice by finally "speaking up" to an audience or "speaking out" to others, and even though much dead student writing comes from students not really treating their writing as a communication with real readers, nevertheless, the opposite effect is also common: we often do not really develop a strong, authentic voice in our writing till we find important occasions for *ignoring* audience — saying, in effect, "To hell with whether they like it or not. I've got to say this the way I want to say it." Admittedly, the voice that emerges when we ignore audience is sometimes odd or idiosyncratic in some way, but usually it is stronger. Indeed, teachers sometimes complain that student writing is "writer-based" when the problem is simply the idiosyncrasy — and sometimes in fact the *power* — of the voice. They would value this odd but resonant voice if they found it in a published writer (see Elbow, "Real Voice," *Writing with Power*). Usually we cannot *trust* a voice unless it is unaware of us and our needs and speaks out in its own terms (see the Ashbery epigraph). To celebrate writer-based prose is to risk the charge of *romanticism:* just warbling one's woodnotes wild. But my position also contains the austere *classic* view that we must nevertheless *revise* with conscious awareness of audience in order to figure out which pieces of writer-based prose are good as they are — and how to discard or revise the rest.

To point out that writer-based prose can be *better* for readers than reader-based prose is to reveal problems in these two terms. Does *writer-based* mean:

1. That the text doesn't work for readers because it is too much oriented to the writer's point of view?

2. Or that the writer was not thinking about readers as she wrote, although the text *may* work for readers?

Does *reader-based* mean:

3. That the text works for readers — meets their needs?

4. Or that the writer was attending to readers as she wrote although her text *may* not work for readers?

In order to do justice to the reality and complexity of what actually happens in both writers and readers, I was going to suggest four terms for the four conditions listed above, but I gradually realized that things are even too complex for that. We really need to ask about what's going on in three dimensions — in the *writer,* in the *reader,* and in the *text* — and realize that the answers can occur in virtually any combination:

Was the writer thinking about readers or oblivious to them?

Is the *text* oriented toward the writer's frame of reference or point of view, or oriented toward that of readers? (A writer may be thinking about readers and still write a text that is largely oriented toward her own frame of reference.)

Are the readers' needs being met? (The text may meet the needs of readers whether the writer was thinking about them or not, and whether the text is oriented toward them or not.)

Two Models of Cognitive Development

Some of the current emphasis on audience awareness probably derives from a model of cognitive development that needs to be questioned. According to this model, if you keep your readers in mind as you write, you are operating at a higher level of psychological development than if you ignore readers. Directing words to readers is "more mature" than directing them to no one in particular or to yourself. Flower relates writer-based prose to the inability to "decenter," which is characteristic of Piaget's early stages of development, and she relates reader-based prose to later more mature stages of development.

On the one hand, of course this view must be right. Children do decenter as they develop. As they mature they get better at suiting their discourse to the needs of listeners, particularly to listeners very different from themselves. Especially, they get better at doing so *consciously* — thinking *awarely* about how things appear to people with different viewpoints. Thus much unskilled writing is unclear or awkward *because* the writer was doing what it is so easy to do — unthinkingly taking her own frame of reference for granted and not attending to the needs of readers who might have a different frame of reference. And of course this failure is more common in younger, immature, "egocentric" students (and also more common in writing than in speaking since we have no audience present when we write).

But on the other hand, we need the contrary model that affirms what is also obvious once we reflect on it, namely that the ability to *turn off* audience awareness — especially when it confuses thinking or blocks discourse — is also a "higher" skill. I am talking about an ability to use language in "the desert island mode," an ability that tends to require learning, growth, and psychological development. Children, and even adults who have not learned the art of quiet, thoughtful, inner reflection, are often unable to get much cognitive action going in their heads unless there are other people present to have action *with*. They are dependent on live audience and the social dimension to get their discourse rolling or to get their thinking off the ground.

For in contrast to a roughly Piagetian model of cognitive development that says we start out as private, egocentric little monads and grow up to be public and social, it is important to invoke the opposite model that derives variously from Vygotsky, Bakhtin, and Meade. According to this model, we *start out* social and plugged into others and only gradually, through learning and development, come to "unplug" to any significant degree so as to function in a more private, individual and differentiated fashion: "Development in thinking is not from the individual to the socialized, but from the social to the individual" (Vygotsky 20). The important general principle in this model is that we tend to *develop* our important cognitive capacities by means of social interaction with others, and having done so we gradually learn to perform them alone. We fold the "simple" back-and-forth of dialogue into the "complexity" (literally, "foldedness") of individual, private reflection.

Where the Piagetian (individual psychology) model calls our attention to the obvious need to learn to enter into viewpoints other than our own, the Vygotskian (social psychology) model calls our attention to the equally important need to learn to produce good thinking and discourse *while alone*. A rich and enfolded mental life is something that people achieve only gradually through growth, learning, and practice. We tend to associate this achievement with the fruits of higher education.

Thus we see plenty of students who lack this skill, who have nothing to say when asked to freewrite or to write in a journal. They can dutifully "reply" to a question or a topic, but they cannot seem to *initiate* or *sustain* a train of thought on their own. Because so many adolescent students have this difficulty, many teachers chime in: "Adolescents have nothing to write about. They are too young. They haven't had significant experience." In truth, adolescents don't lack experience or material, no matter how "sheltered" their lives. What they lack is practice and help. Desert island discourse is a learned cognitive process. It's a mistake to think of private writing (journal writing and freewriting) as merely "easy" — merely a relief from trying to write right. It's also hard. Some exercises and strategies that help are Ira Progoff's "Intensive Journal" process, Sondra Perl's "Composing Guidelines," or Elbow's "Loop Writing" and "Open Ended Writing" processes (*Writing with Power* 50–77).

The Piagetian and Vygotskian developmental models (language-begins-as-private vs. language-begins-as-social) give us two different lenses through which to look at a common weakness in student writing, a certain kind of "thin" writing where the thought is insufficiently developed or where the language doesn't really explain what the writing implies or gestures toward. Using the Piagetian model, as Flower does, one can specify the problem as a weakness in audience orientation. Perhaps the writer has immaturely taken too much for granted and unthinkingly assumed that her limited explanations carry as much meaning for readers as they do for herself. The cure or treatment is for the writer to think more about readers.

Through the Vygotskian lens, however, the problem and the "immaturity" look altogether different. Yes, the writing isn't particularly clear or satisfying for readers, but this alternative diagnosis suggests a failure of the private desert island dimension: the writer's explanation is too thin because she didn't work out her train of thought fully enough *for herself.* The suggested cure or treatment is *not* to think more about readers but to think more for herself, to practice exploratory writing in order to learn to engage in that reflective discourse so central to mastery of the writing process. How can she engage readers more till she has engaged herself more?

The current emphasis on audience awareness may be particularly strong now for being fueled by *both* psychological models. From one side, the Piagetians say, in effect, "The egocentric little critters, we've got to *socialize* 'em! Ergo, make them think about audience when they write!" From the other side, the Vygotskians say, in effect, "No wonder they're having trouble writing. They've been bamboozled by the Piagetian heresy. They think they're solitary individuals with private selves when really they're just congeries of voices that derive from their discourse community. Ergo, let's intensify the social context — use peer groups and publication: make them think about audience when they write! (And while we're at it, let's hook them up with a better class of discourse community.)" To advocate ignoring audience is to risk getting caught in the crossfire from two opposed camps.

Two Models of Discourse: Discourse as Communication and Discourse as Poesis or Play

We cannot talk about writing without at least implying a psychological or developmental model. But we'd better make sure it's a complex, paradoxical, or spiral model. Better yet, we should be deft enough to use two contrary models or lenses. (Bruner pictures the developmental process as a complex movement in an upward reiterative spiral — not a simple movement in one direction.)

According to one model, it is characteristic of the youngest children to direct their discourse to an audience. They learn discourse *because* they have an audience; without an audience they remain mute, like "the wild child." Language is social from the start. But we need the other model to show us what is also true, namely that it is characteristic of the youngest children to use language in a *nonsocial* way. They use language not only because people talk to them but also because they have such a strong propensity to play and to build — often in a *nonsocial* or non-audience-oriented fashion. Thus although one paradigm for discourse is social communication, another is private exploration or solitary play. Babies and toddlers tend to babble in an exploratory and reflective way — to themselves and not to an audience — often even with no one else near. This archetypally private use of discourse is strikingly illustrated when we see a pair of toddlers in "parallel play" alongside each other — each busily talking but not at all trying to communicate with the other.

Therefore, when we choose paradigms for discourse, we should think not only about children using language to communicate, but also about children building sandcastles or drawing pictures. Though children characteristically show their castles or pictures to others, they just as characteristically trample or crumple them before anyone else can see them. Of course sculptures and pictures are different from words. Yet discourse implies more media than words; and even if you restrict discourse to words, one of our most mature uses of language is for building verbal pictures and structures for their own sake — not just for communicating with others.

Consider this same kind of behavior at the other end of the life cycle: Brahms staggering from his deathbed to his study to rip up a dozen or more completed but unpublished and unheard string quartets that dissatisfied him. How was he relating to audience here — worrying too much about audience or not giving a damn? It's not easy to say. Consider Glenn Gould deciding to renounce performances before an audience. He used his private studio to produce recorded performances for an audience, but to produce ones that satisfied *himself* he clearly needed to suppress audience awareness. Consider the more extreme example of Kerouac typing page after page — burning each as soon as he completed it. The language behavior of humans is slippery. Surely we are well advised to avoid positions that say it is "always X" or "essentially Y."

James Britton makes a powerful argument that the "making" or poesis function of language grows out of the expressive function. Expressive language is often for the sake of communication with an audience, but just as often it is only for the sake of the speaker — working something out for herself (66–67, 74ff). Note also that "writing to learn," which writing-across-the-curriculum programs are discovering to be so important, tends to be writing for the self or even for no one at all rather than for an outside reader. You throw away the writing, often unread, and keep the mental changes it has engendered.

I hope this emphasis on the complexity of the developmental process — the limits of our models and of our understanding of it — will serve as a rebuke to the tendency to label students as being at a lower stage of cognitive development just because they don't yet write well. (Occasionally they *do* write well — in a way — but not in the way that the labeler finds appropriate.) Obviously the psychologistic labeling impulse started out charitably. Shaughnessy was fighting those who called basic writers *stupid* by saying they weren't dumb, just at an earlier developmental stage. Flower was arguing that writer-based prose is a natural response to a cognitive overload and indeed developmentally enabling. But this kind of talk can be dangerous since it labels students as literally "retarded" and makes teachers and administrators start to think of them as such. Instead of calling poor writers *either* dumb or slow (two forms of blaming the victim), why not simply call them poor writers? If years of schooling haven't yet made them good writers, perhaps they haven't gotten the kind of teaching and support they need. Poor students are often deprived of the very thing they need most to write well (which is given to good students): lots of extended and adventuresome writing for self and for audience. Poor students are often asked to write only answers to fill-in exercises.

As children get older, the developmental story remains complex or spiral. Though the first model makes us notice that babies start out with a natural gift for using language in a social and communicative fashion, the second model makes us notice that children and adolescents must continually learn to relate their discourse better to an audience — must struggle to decenter better. And though the second model makes us notice that babies also start out with a natural gift for using language in a *private,* exploratory and playful way, the first model makes us notice that children and adolescents must continually learn to master this solitary, desert island, poesis mode better. Thus we mustn't think of language only as communication — nor allow communication to claim dominance either as the earliest or as the most "mature" form of discourse. It's true that language is inherently communicative (and without communication we don't develop language), yet language is just as inherently the stringing together of exploratory discourse for the self — or for the creation of objects (play, poesis, making) for their own sake.

In considering this important poesis function of language, we need not discount (as Berkenkotter does) the striking testimony of so many witnesses who think and care most about language: professional poets, writers, and philosophers. Many of them maintain that their most serious work is *making,* not *communicating,* and that their commitment is to language, reality, logic, experience, not to readers. Only in their willingness to cut loose from the demands or needs of readers, they insist, can they do their best work. Here is William Stafford on this matter:

> I don't want to overstate this . . . but . . . my impulse is to say I don't think of an audience at all. When I'm writing, the satisfactions in the process of writing are my satisfactions in dealing with the language, in being surprised by phrasings that occur to me, in finding that this miraculous kind of convergent focus begins to happen. That's my satisfaction, and to think about an audience would be a distraction. I try to keep from thinking about an audience. (Cicotello 176)

And Chomsky:

> I can be using language in the strictest sense with no intention of communicating. . . . As a graduate student, I spent two years writing a lengthy manuscript, assuming throughout that it would never be published or read by anyone. I meant everything I wrote, intending nothing as to what anyone would [understand], in fact taking it for granted that there would be no audience. . . . Communication is only one function of language, and by no means an essential one. (Qtd. in Feldman 5–6)

It's interesting to see how poets come together with philosophers on this point — and even with mathematicians. All are emphasizing the "poetic" function of language in its literal sense — "poesis" as "making." They describe their writing process as more like "getting something right" or even "solving a problem" for its own sake than as communicating with readers or addressing an audience. The task is not to satisfy readers but to satisfy the rules of the system: "[T]he writer is not thinking of a reader at all; he makes it 'clear' as a contract with *language*" (Goodman 164).

Shall we conclude, then, that solving an equation or working out a piece of symbolic logic is at the opposite end of the spectrum from communicating with readers or addressing an audience? No. To draw that conclusion would be a fall again into a one-sided position. Sometimes people write mathematics *for* an audience, sometimes not. The central point in this essay is that we cannot answer audience questions in an *a priori* fashion based on the "nature" of discourse or of language or of cognition — only in terms of the different *uses* or *purposes* to which humans put discourse, language, or cognition on different occasions. If most people have a restricted repertoire of uses for writing — if most people use writing only to send messages to readers, that's no argument for constricting the *definition* of writing. It's an argument for helping people expand their repertoire of uses.

The value of learning to ignore audience while writing, then, is the value of learning to cultivate the private dimension: the value of writing in order to make meaning to oneself, not just to others. This involves learning to free oneself (to some extent, anyway) from the enormous power exerted by society and others, to unhook oneself from external prompts and social stimuli. We've grown accustomed to theorists and writing teachers puritanically stressing the *problem* of writing: the tendency to neglect the needs of readers because we usually write in solitude. But let's also celebrate this same feature of writing as one of its glories: writing *invites* disengagement too, the inward turn of mind, and the dialogue with self. Though writing is deeply social and though we usually help things by enhancing its social dimension, writing is also the mode of discourse best suited to helping us develop the reflective and private dimension of our mental lives.

"But Wait a Minute, ALL Discourse Is Social"

Some readers who see *all* discourse as social will object to my opposition between public and private writing (the "trap of oppositional thinking") and insist that *there is no such thing as private discourse.* What looks like private, solitary mental work, they would say, is really social. Even on the desert island I am in a crowd.

> By ignoring audience in the conventional sense, we return to it in another sense. What I get from Vygotsky and Bakhtin is the notion that audience is not really out there at all but is in fact "always already" (to

use that poststructuralist mannerism . . .) inside, interiorized in the conflicting languages of others — parents, former teachers, peers, prospective readers, whomever — that writers have to negotiate to write, and that we do negotiate when we write whether we're aware of it or not. The audience we've got to satisfy in order to feel good about our writing is as much in the past as in the present or future. But we experience it (it's so internalized) as *ourselves*. (Trimbur)

(Ken Bruffee likes to quote from Frost: "'Men work together, . . . / Whether they work together or apart'" ["The Tuft of Flowers"]). Or — putting it slightly differently — when I engage in what seems like private non-audience-directed writing, I am really engaged in communication with the "audience of self." For the self is multiple, not single, and discourse to self is communication from one entity to another. As Feldman argues, "The self functions as audience in much the same way that others do" (290).

Suppose I accept this theory that all discourse is really social — including what I've been calling "private writing" or writing I don't intend to show to any reader. Suppose I agree that all language is essentially communication directed toward an audience — whether some past internalized voice or (what may be the same thing) some aspect of the self. What would this theory say to my interest in "private writing"?

The theory would seem to destroy my main argument. It would tell me that there's no such thing as "private writing"; it's impossible *not* to address audience; there are no vacations from audience. But the theory might try to console me by saying not to worry, because we don't *need* vacations from audience. Addressing audience is as easy, natural, and unaware as breathing — and we've been at it since the cradle. Even young, unskilled writers are already expert at addressing audiences.

But if we look closely we can see that in fact this theory doesn't touch my central practical argument. For even if all discourse is naturally addressed to *some* audience, it's not naturally addressed to the *right* audience — the living readers we are actually trying to reach. Indeed the pervasiveness of past audiences in our heads is one more reason for the difficulty of reaching present audiences with our texts. Thus even if I concede the theoretical point, there still remains an enormous practical and phenomenological difference between writing "public" words for others to read and writing "private" words for no one to read.

Even if "private writing" is "deep down" social, the fact remains that, as we engage in it, we don't have to worry about whether it works on readers or even makes sense. We can refrain from doing all the things that audience-awareness advocates advise us to do ("keeping our audience in mind as we write" and trying to "decenter"). Therefore this social-discourse theory doesn't undermine the benefits of "private writing" and thus provides no support at all for the traditional rhetorical advice that we should "always try to think about (intended) audience as we write."

In fact this social-discourse theory reinforces two subsidiary arguments I have been making. First, even if there is no getting away from *some* audience, we can get relief from an inhibiting audience by writing to a more inviting one. Second, audience problems don't come only from *actual* audiences but also from phantom "audiences in the head" (Elbow, *Writing with Power* 186ff). Once we learn how to be more aware of the effects of both external and internal readers and how to direct our words elsewhere, we can get out of the shadow even of a troublesome phantom reader.

And even if all our discourse is *directed to* or *shaped by* past audiences or voices, it doesn't follow that our discourse is *well directed to* or *successfully shaped for* those audiences or voices. Small children *direct* much talk to others, but that doesn't mean they always *suit* their talk to others. They often fail. When adults discover that a piece of their writing has been "heavily shaped" by some audience, this is bad news as much as good: often the writing is crippled by defensive moves that try to fend off criticism from this reader.

As teachers, particularly, we need to distinguish and emphasize "private writing" in order to teach it, to teach that crucial cognitive capacity to engage in extended and productive thinking that doesn't depend on audience prompts or social stimuli. It's sad to see so many students who can reply to live voices but cannot engage in productive dialogue with voices in their heads. Such students often lose interest in an issue that had intrigued them — just because they don't find other people who are interested in talking about it and haven't learned to talk reflectively to *themselves* about it.

For these reasons, then, I believe my main argument holds force even if I accept the theory that all discourse is social. But, perhaps more tentatively, I resist this theory. I don't know all the data from developmental linguistics, but I cannot help suspecting that babies engage in *some* private poesis — or "play-language" — some private babbling in addition to social babbling. Of course Vygotsky must be right when he points to so much social language in children, but can we really trust him when he denies *all* private or nonsocial language (which Piaget and Chomsky see)? I am always suspicious when someone argues for the total nonexistence of a certain kind of behavior or event. Such an argument is almost invariably an act of definitional aggrandizement, not empirical searching. To say that *all* language is social is to flop over into the opposite one-sidedness that we need Vygotsky's model to save us from.

And even if all language is *originally* social, Vygotsky himself emphasizes how "inner speech" becomes more individuated and private as the child matures. "Egocentric speech is relatively accessible in three-year-olds but quite inscrutable in seven-year-olds: the older the child, the more thoroughly has his thought become inner speech" (Emerson 254; see also Vygotsky 134). "The inner speech of the adult represents his 'thinking for himself' rather than social adaptation. . . . Out of context, it would be incomprehensible to others because it omits to mention what is obvious to the 'speaker'" (Vygotsky 18).

I also resist the theory that all private writing is really communication with the *audience of self.* ("When we represent the objects of our thought in language, we intend to make use of these representations at a later time. . . . [T]he speaker-self must have audience directed intentions toward a listener-self" [Feldman 289].) Of course private language often is a communication with the audience of self:

- When we make a shopping list. (It's obvious when we can't decipher that third item that we're confronting *failed* communication with the self.)

- When we make a rough draft for ourselves but not for others' eyes. Here we are seeking to clarify our thinking with the leverage that comes from standing outside and reading our own utterance as audience — experiencing our discourse as receiver instead of as sender.

- When we experience ourselves as slightly split. Sometimes we experience ourselves as witness to ourselves and hear our own words from the outside — sometimes with great detachment, as on some occasions of pressure or stress.

But there are other times when private language is not communication with audience of self:

- Freewriting to no one: for the *sake* of self but not *to* the self. The goal is not to communicate but to follow a train of thinking or feeling to see where it leads. In doing this kind of freewriting (and many people have not learned it), you don't particularly plan to come back and read what you've written. You just write along and the written product falls away to be ignored, while only the "real product" — any new perceptions, thoughts, or feelings produced in the mind by the freewriting — is saved and looked at again. (It's not that you don't experience your words *at all* but you experience them only as speaker, sender, or emitter — not as receiver or audience. To say that's the same as being audience is denying the very distinction between "speaker" and "audience.")

As this kind of freewriting actually works, it often *leads* to writing we look at. That is, we freewrite along to no one, following discourse in hopes of getting somewhere, and then at a certain point we often sense that we have *gotten* somewhere: we can tell (but not because we stop and read) that what we are now writing seems new or intriguing or important. At this point we may stop writing; or we may keep on writing, but in a new audience-relationship, realizing that we *will* come back to this passage and read it as audience. Or we may take a new sheet (symbolizing the new audience-relationship) and try to write out for ourselves what's interesting.

- Writing as exorcism is a more extreme example of private writing *not* for the audience of self. Some people have learned to write in order to get rid of thoughts or feelings. By freewriting what's obsessively going round and round in our head we can finally let it go and move on.

I am suggesting that some people (and especially poets and freewriters) engage in a kind of discourse that Feldman, defending what she calls a "communication-intention" view, has never learned and thus has a hard time imagining and understanding. Instead of always using language in an audience-directed fashion for the sake of communication, these writers unleash language for its own sake and let it function a bit on its own, without much *intention* and without much need for *communication,* to see where it leads — and thereby end up with some intentions and potential communications they didn't have before.

It's hard to turn off the audience-of-self in writing — and thus hard to imagine writing to no one (just as it's hard to turn off the audience of *outside* readers when writing an audience-directed piece). Consider "invisible writing" as an intriguing technique that helps you become less of an audience-of-self for your writing. Invisible writing prevents you from seeing what you have written: you write on a computer with the screen turned down, or you write with a spent ballpoint pen on paper with carbon paper and another sheet underneath. Invisible writing tends to get people not only to write faster than they normally do, but often better (see Blau). I mean to be tentative about this slippery issue of whether we can really stop being audience to our own discourse, but I cannot help drawing the following conclusion: just as in freewriting, suppressing the *other* as audience tends to enhance quantity and sometimes even quality of writing; so in invisible writing, suppressing the *self* as audience tends to enhance quantity and sometimes even quality.

Contraries in Teaching

So what does all this mean for teaching? It means that we are stuck with two contrary tasks. On the one hand, we need to help our students enhance the social dimension of writing: to learn to be *more* aware of audience, to decenter better and learn to fit their discourse better to the needs of readers. Yet it is every bit as important to help them learn the private dimension of writing: to learn to be *less* aware of audience, to put audience needs aside, to use discourse in the desert island mode. And if we are trying to advance contraries, we must be prepared for paradoxes.

For instance if we emphasize the social dimension in our teaching (for example, by getting students to write to each other, to read and comment on each other's writing in pairs and groups, and by staging public discussions and even debates on the topics they are to write about), we will obviously help the social, public, communicative dimension of writing — help students experience writing not just as jumping through hoops for a grade but rather as taking part in the life of a community of discourse. But "social discourse" can also help private writing by getting students sufficiently involved or invested in an issue so that they finally want to carry on producing discourse alone and in private — and for themselves.

Correlatively, if we emphasize the private dimension in our teaching (for example, by using lots of private exploratory writing, freewriting, and journal writing and by helping students realize that of course they may need practice with this "easy" mode of discourse before they can use it fruitfully), we will obviously help students learn to write better reflectively for themselves without the need for others to interact with. Yet this private discourse can also help public, social writing — help students finally feel full enough of their *own* thoughts to have some genuine desire to *tell* them to others. Students often feel they "don't have anything to say" until they finally succeed in engaging themselves in private desert island writing for themselves alone.

Another paradox: Whether we want to teach greater audience awareness or the ability to ignore audience, we must help students learn not only to "try harder" but also to "just relax." That is, sometimes students fail to produce reader-based prose because they don't *try* hard enough to think about audience needs. But sometimes the problem is cured if they just relax and write *to* people — as though in a letter or in talking to a trusted adult. By unclenching, they effortlessly call on social discourse skills of immense sophistication. Sometimes, indeed, the problem is cured if the student simply writes in a more social *setting* — in a classroom where it is habitual to share lots of writing. Similarly, sometimes students can't produce sustained private discourse because they don't try hard enough to keep the pen moving and forget about readers. They must persist and doggedly push aside those feelings of, "My head is empty, I have run out of anything to say." But sometimes what they need to learn through all that persistence is how to relax and let go — to unclench.

As teachers, we need to think about what it means to *be an audience* rather than just be a teacher, critic, assessor, or editor. If our only response is to tell students what's strong, what's weak, and how to improve it (diagnosis, assessment, and advice), we actually *undermine* their sense of writing as a social act. We reinforce their sense that writing means doing school exercises, producing for authorities what they already know — *not* actually trying to say things to readers. To help students experience us as *audience* rather than as assessment machines, it helps to respond by "replying" (as in a letter) rather than always "giving feedback."

Paradoxically enough, one of the best ways teachers can help students learn to turn off audience awareness and write in the desert island mode — to turn off the babble of outside voices in the head and listen better to quiet inner voices — is to be a special kind of private audience to them, to be a reader who nurtures by trusting and believing in the writer. Britton has drawn attention to the importance of teacher as "trusted adult" for school children (67–68). No one can be good at private, reflective writing without some *confidence and trust in self.* A nurturing reader can give a writer a kind of permission to forget about other readers or to be one's own reader. I have benefited from this special kind of audience and have seen it prove useful to others. When I had a teacher who believed in me, who was interested in me and interested in what I had to say, I wrote well. When I had a teacher who thought I was naive, dumb, silly, and in need of being "straightened out," I wrote badly and sometimes couldn't write at all. Here is an interestingly paradoxical instance of the social-to-private principle from Vygotsky and Meade: We learn to listen better and more trustingly to *ourselves* through interaction with trusting *others.*

Look for a moment at lyric poets as paradigm writers (instead of seeing them as aberrant), and see how they heighten *both* the public and private dimensions of writing. Bakhtin says that lyric poetry implies "the absolute certainty of the listener's sympathy" (113). I think it's more helpful to say that lyric poets learn to create more than usual privacy in which to write *for themselves* — and then they turn around and let *others overhear.* Notice how poets tend to argue for the importance of no-audience writing, yet they are especially gifted at being public about what they produce in private. Poets are revealers — sometimes even grandstanders or showoffs. Poets illustrate the need for opposite or paradoxical or double audience skills: on the one hand, the ability to be private and solitary and tune out others — to write only for oneself and not give a damn about readers, yet on the other hand, the ability to be more than usually interested in audience and even to be a ham.

If writers really need these two audience skills, notice how bad most conventional schooling is on both counts. Schools offer virtually no privacy for writing: everything students write is collected and read by a teacher, a situation so ingrained students will tend to complain if you don't collect and read every word they write. Yet on the other hand, schools characteristically offer little or no social dimension for writing. It is *only* the teacher who reads, and students seldom feel that in giving their writing to a teacher they are actually communicating something they really want to say to a real person. Notice how often they are happy to turn in to teachers something perfunctory and fake that they would be embarrassed to show to classmates. Often they feel shocked and insulted if we want to distribute to classmates the assigned writing they hand in to us. (I think of Richard Wright's realization that the naked white prostitutes didn't bother to cover themselves when he brought them coffee as a black bellboy because they didn't really think of him as a man or even a person.) Thus the conventional school setting for writing tends to be the least private and the least public — when what students need, like all of us, is practice in writing that is the most private and also the most public.

Practical Guidelines about Audience

The theoretical relationships between discourse and audience are complex and paradoxical, but the practical morals are simple:

1. Seek ways to heighten both the *public* and *private* dimensions of writing. (For activities, see the previous section.)

2. When working on important audience-directed writing, we must try to emphasize audience awareness *sometimes*. A useful rule of thumb is to start by putting the readers in mind and carry on as long as things go well. If difficulties arise, try putting readers out of mind and write either to no audience, to self, or to an inviting audience. Finally, always *revise* with readers in mind. (Here's another occasion when orthodox advice about writing is wrong — but turns out right if applied to revising.)

3. Seek ways to heighten awareness of one's writing process (through process writing and discussion) to get better at taking control and deciding when to keep readers in mind and when to ignore them. Learn to discriminate factors like these:

    a. The writing task. Is this piece of writing *really* for an audience? More often than we realize, it is not. It is a draft that only we will see, though the final version will be for an audience; or exploratory writing for figuring something out; or some kind of personal private writing meant only for ourselves.

    b. Actual readers. When we put them in mind, are we helped or hindered?

    c. One's own temperament. Am I the sort of person who tends to think of what to say and how to say it when I keep readers in mind? Or someone (as I am) who needs long stretches of forgetting all about readers?

    d. Has some powerful "audience-in-the-head" tricked me into talking to it when I'm really trying to talk to someone else — distorting new business into old business? (I may be an inviting teacher-audience to my students, but they may not be able to pick up a pen without falling under the spell of a former, intimidating teacher.)

    e. Is *double audience* getting in my way? When I write a memo or report, I probably have to suit it not only to my "target audience" but also to some colleagues or supervisor. When I write something for publication, it must be right for readers, but it won't be published unless it is also right for the editors — and if it's a book it won't be much read unless it's right for reviewers. Children's stories won't be bought unless they are right for editors and reviewers *and* parents. We often tell students to write to a particular "real-life" audience — or to peers in the class — but of course they are also writing for us as graders. (This problem is more common as more teachers get interested in audience and suggest "second" audiences.)

f. Is *teacher-audience* getting in the way of my students' writing? As teachers we must often read in an odd fashion: in stacks of twenty-five or fifty pieces all on the same topic; on topics we know better than the writer; not for pleasure or learning but to grade or find problems (see Elbow, *Writing with Power* 216–36).

To list all these audience pitfalls is to show again the need for thinking about audience needs — yet also the need for vacations from readers to think in peace.

Acknowledgments

I benefited from much help from audiences in writing various drafts of this piece. I am grateful to Jennifer Clarke, with whom I wrote a collaborative piece containing a case study on this subject. I am also grateful for extensive feedback from Pat Belanoff, Paul Connolly, Sheryl Fontaine, John Trimbur, and members of the Martha's Vineyard Summer Writing Seminar.

Note

1. There are many different entities called audience: (a) The actual readers to whom the text will be given; (b) the writer's conception of those readers — which may be mistaken (see Ong; Park; Ede and Lunsford); (c) the audience that the text implies — which may be different still (see Booth); (d) the discourse community or even genre addressed or implied by the text (see Walzer); (e) ghost or phantom "readers in the head" that the writer may unconsciously address or try to please (see Elbow, *Writing with Power* 186ff. Classically, this is a powerful former teacher. Often such an audience is so ghostly as not to show up as actually "implied" by the text). For the essay I am writing here, these differences don't much matter: I'm celebrating the ability to put aside the needs or demands of *any* or all of these audiences. I recognize, however, that we sometimes cannot fight our way free of unconscious or tacit audiences (as in b or e above) unless we bring them to greater conscious awareness.

Works Cited

Bakhtin, Mikhail. "Discourse in Life and Discourse in Poetry." Appendix. *Freudianism: A Marxist Critique.* By F. N. Volosinov. Trans. I. R. Titunik. Ed. Neal H. Bruss. New York: Academic, 1976. (Holquist's attribution of this work to Bakhtin is generally accepted.)

Berkenkotter, Carol, and Donald Murray. "Decisions and Revisions: The Planning Strategies of a Publishing Writer and the Response of Being a Rat — or Being Protocoled." *College Composition and Communication* 34 (1983): 156–72.

Blau, Sheridan. "Invisible Writing." *College Composition and Communication* 34 (1983): 297–312.

Booth, Wayne. *The Rhetoric of Fiction.* Chicago: U Chicago P, 1961.

Britton, James. *The Development of Writing Abilities, 11–18.* Urbana: NCTE, 1977.

Bruffee, Kenneth A. "Liberal Education and the Social Justification of Belief." *Liberal Education* 68 (1982): 95–114.

Bruner, Jerome. *Beyond the Information Given: Studies in the Psychology of Knowing.* Ed. Jeremy Anglin. New York: Norton, 1973.

———. *On Knowing: Essays for the Left Hand.* Expanded ed. Cambridge: Harvard UP, 1979.

Chomsky, Noam. *Reflections on Language.* New York: Random, 1975.

Cicotello, David M. "The Art of Writing: An Interview with William Stafford." *College Composition and Communication* 34 (1983): 173–77.

Clarke, Jennifer, and Peter Elbow. "Desert Island Discourse: On the Benefits of Ignoring Audience." *The Journal Book.* Ed. Toby Fulwiler. Montclair: Boynton, 1987.

Cooper, Anthony Ashley, 3rd Earl of Shaftesbury. *Characteristics of Men, Manners, Opinions, Times, Etc.* Ed. John M. Robertson. 2 vols. Gloucester, MA: Smith, 1963.

Ede, Lisa, and Andrea Lunsford. "Audience Addressed/Audience Invoked: The Role of Audience in Composition Theory and Pedagogy." *College Composition and Communication* 35 (1984): 140–54.

Elbow, Peter. *Writing with Power.* New York: Oxford UP, 1981.

———. *Writing without Teachers.* New York: Oxford UP, 1973.

Emerson, Caryl. "The Outer Word and Inner Speech: Bakhtin, Vygotsky, and the Internalization of Language." *Critical Inquiry* 10 (1983): 245–64.

Feldman, Carol Fleisher. "Two Functions of Language." *Harvard Education Review* 47 (1977): 282–93.

Flower, Linda. "Writer-Based Prose: A Cognitive Basis for Problems in Writing." *College English* 41 (1979): 19–37.

Goodman, Paul. *Speaking and Language: Defense of Poetry.* New York: Random, 1972.

Griffin, Susan. "The Internal Voices of Invention: Shaftesbury's Soliloquy." Unpublished. 1986.

Lawrence, D. H. *Studies in Classic American Literature.* Garden City: Doubleday, 1951.

Ong, Walter. "The Writer's Audience Is Always a Fiction." *PMLA* 90 (1975): 9–21.

Park, Douglas B. "The Meanings of 'Audience.'" *College English* 44 (1982): 247–57.

Perl, Sondra. "Guidelines for Composing." Appendix A. *Through Teachers' Eyes: Portraits of Writing Teachers at Work.* By Sondra Perl and Nancy Wilson. Portsmouth: Heinemann, 1986.

Progoff, Ira. *At a Journal Workshop.* New York: Dialogue, 1975.

Shaughnessy, Mina. *Errors and Expectations: A Guide for the Teacher of Basic Writing.* New York: Oxford UP, 1977.

Trimbur, John. "Beyond Cognition: Voices in Inner Speech." *Rhetoric Review* 5 (1987): 211–21.

———. Letter to the author. September 1985.

Vygotsky, L. S. *Thought and Language.* Trans. and ed. E. Hanfmann and G. Vakar. 1934. Cambridge: MIT P, 1962.

Walzer, Arthur E. "Articles from the 'California Divorce Project': A Case Study of the Concept of Audience." *College Composition and Communication* 36 (1985): 150–59.

Wright, Richard. *Black Boy.* New York: Harper, 1945.

Elbow's Insights as a Resource for Your Teaching

1. Respond to Elbow's claim that writer-based prose is sometimes better than reader-based prose. Have you ever found students' journal writing or freewriting to be stronger than their formal writing? How might you implement Elbow's ideas to help such students write more effective final drafts? Does Elbow's argument impact the way that you will address the subject of audience awareness with your students in the future?

2. Elbow's recommendation is to turn off the screen while writing with a computer. Try this and then reflect on the results. Were you better able to ignore audience? Did this exercise have an effect on your writing?

Elbow's Insights as a Resource for Your Writing Classroom

1. Elbow's "ghost reader" — a student's sense of an inflexible teacher-as-evaluator — surfaces frequently in early essays from first-year writers and most often in diagnostic essays written the first week. Photocopy a few samples of writing where the ghost reader clearly frightened the writer into dense or unclear or stuffy or inauthentic prose. Ask the class to decide where the "ghost teacher as reader" intruded and to suggest ways to exorcise the ghost reader.

2. Ask students to describe, either in journal entries or a brainstorming session, strategies that they use or habits that they have when writing or preparing to write (which they may have

dismissed as personal idiosyncrasies unrelated to writing), and how these strategies and habits are related to their personal approach to the writing process. Do these habits hinder or encourage the flow of ideas? How might students consciously adjust these habits to promote uninhibited writing?

Revising a Draft

Revision Strategies of Student Writers and Experienced Adult Writers

Nancy Sommers

First published in College Composition and Communication *in 1980, Nancy Sommers's landmark study of the revision strategies used by students and by "adult" writers concludes that student writers do not work from a holistic perspective on writing or perceive revision as a recursive process. Her categories of "student" and "experienced adult" writers can be borrowed and applied to members of a first-year composition course. Many class members already understand revising as "discovery" — a repeated process of beginning over again, starting out new. Some writers, however, need to acquire this "new" perspective on revision.*

Sommers cites or implies several reasons that students see revision only as a linear process attending to surface features of a manuscript: previous writing experiences, infrequent practice, traditional dicta about the nature of revising, and cognitive readiness. She asserts that writing teachers can assist student writers to mature and to acquire a perspective on writing as discovery and development. Furthermore, writing teachers can help student writers to realize, as experienced adult writers do, that "Good writing disturbs: it creates dissonance."

Sommers's discussion in "Responding to Student Writing" (see Chapter 3, pp. 383–92) shows us the practical effects on student writers of our written responses to their texts. She clearly demonstrates that teacher commentary can directly affect and improve the revision strategies of writers.

Although various aspects of the writing process have been studied extensively of late, research on revision has been notably absent. The reason for this, I suspect, is that current models of the writing process have directed attention away from revision. With few exceptions, these models are linear; they separate the writing process into discrete stages. Two representative models are Gordon Rohman's suggestion that the composing process moves from prewriting to writing to rewriting and James Britton's model of the writing process as a series of stages described in metaphors of linear growth, conception — incubation — production.[1] What is striking about these theories of writing is that they model themselves on speech: Rohman defines the writer

in a way that cannot distinguish him from a speaker ("A writer is a man who . . . puts [his] experience into words in his own mind" [15]); and Britton backs his theory of writing on what he calls (following Jakobson) the "expressiveness" of speech.[2] Moreover, Britton's study itself follows the "linear model" of the relation of thought and language in speech proposed by Vygotsky, a relationship embodied in the linear movement "from the motive which engenders a thought to the shaping of the thought, *first* in inner speech, *then* in meanings of words, and *finally* in words" (qtd. in Britton 40). What this movement fails to take into account in its linear structure — "first . . . then . . . finally" — is the recursive shaping of thought by language; what it fails to take into account is *revision*. In these linear conceptions of the writing process revision is understood as a separate stage at the end of the process — a stage that comes after the completion of a first or second draft and one that is temporally distinct from the prewriting and writing stages of the process.[3]

The linear model bases itself on speech in two specific ways. First of all, it is based on traditional rhetorical models, models that were created to serve the spoken art of oratory. In whatever ways the parts of classical rhetoric are described, they offer "stages" of composition that are repeated in contemporary models of the writing process. Edward Corbett, for instance, describes the "five parts of a discourse" — *inventio, dispositio, elocutio, memoria, pronuntiatio* — and, disregarding the last two parts since "after rhetoric came to be concerned mainly with written discourse, there was no further need to deal with them,"[4] he produces a model very close to Britton's conception [*inventio*], incubation [*dispositio*], production [*elocutio*]. Other rhetorics also follow this procedure, and they do so not simply because of historical accident. Rather, the process represented in the linear model is based on the irreversibility of speech. Speech, Roland Barthes says, "is irreversible":

> A word cannot be retracted, except precisely by saying that one retracts it. To cross out here is to add: if I want to erase what I have just said, I cannot do it without showing the eraser itself (I must say: "*or rather . . .*" "*I expressed myself badly . . .*"); paradoxically, it is ephemeral speech which is indelible, not monumental writing. All that one can do in the case of a spoken utterance is to tack on another utterance.[5]

What is impossible in speech is *revision:* like the example Barthes gives, revision in speech is an afterthought. In the same way, each stage of the linear model must be exclusive (distinct from the other stages) or else it becomes trivial and counterproductive to refer to these junctures as "stages."

By staging revision after enunciation, the linear models reduce revision in writing, as in speech, to no more than an afterthought. In this way such models make the study of revision impossible. Revision, in Rohman's model, is simply the repetition of writing; or to pursue Britton's organic metaphor, revision is simply the further growth of what is already there, the "preconceived" product. The absence of research on revision, then, is a function of a theory of writing which makes revision both superfluous and redundant, a theory which does not distinguish between writing and speech.

What the linear models do produce is a parody of writing. Isolating revision and then disregarding it plays havoc with the experiences composition teachers have of the actual writing and rewriting of experienced writers. Why should the linear model be preferred? Why should revision be forgotten, superfluous? Why do teachers offer the linear model and students accept it? One reason, Barthes suggests, is that "there is a fundamental tie between teaching and speech," while "writing begins at the point where speech becomes *impossible.*"[6] The spoken word cannot be revised. The possibility of revision distinguishes the written text from speech. In fact, according to Barthes, this is the essential difference between writing and speaking. When we must revise, when the very idea is subject to recursive shaping by language, then speech becomes inadequate. This is a matter to which I will return, but first we should examine, theoretically, a detailed exploration of what student writers as distinguished from experienced adult writers *do* when they write and rewrite their work. Dissatisfied with both the linear model of writing and the lack of attention to the process of revision, I conducted a series of studies over the past three years which examined the revision processes of student writers and experienced writers to see what role revision played in their writing processes. In the course of my work the revision process was redefined as *a sequence of changes in a composition — changes which are initiated by cues and occur continually throughout the writing of a work.*

Methodology

I used a case study approach. The student writers were twenty freshmen at Boston University and the University of Oklahoma with SAT verbal scores ranging from 450–600 in their first semester of composition. The twenty experienced adult writers from Boston and Oklahoma City included journalists, editors, and academics. To refer to the two groups, I use the terms *student writers* and *experienced writers* because the principal difference between these two groups is the amount of experience they have had in writing.

Each writer wrote three essays, expressive, explanatory, and persuasive, and rewrote each essay twice, producing nine written products in draft and final form. Each writer was interviewed three times after the final revision of each essay. And each writer suggested revisions for a composition written by an anonymous author. Thus extensive written and spoken documents were obtained from each writer.

The essays were analyzed by counting and categorizing the changes made. Four revision operations were identified: deletion, substitution, addition, and reordering. And four levels of changes were identified: word, phrase, sentence, theme (the extended statement of one idea). A coding system was developed for identifying the frequency of revision by level and operation. In addition, transcripts of the interviews in which the writers interpreted their revisions were used to develop what was called a *scale of concerns* for each writer. This scale enabled me to codify what were the writer's primary concerns, secondary concerns, tertiary concerns, and whether the writers used the same scale of concerns when revising the second or third drafts as they used in revising the first draft.

Revision Strategies of Student Writers

Most of the students I studied did not use the terms *revision* or *rewriting*. In fact, they did not seem comfortable using the word *revision* and explained that revision was not a word they used, but the word their teachers used. Instead, most of the students had developed various functional terms to describe the type of changes they made. The following are samples of these definitions:

> *Scratch Out and Do Over Again:* "I say scratch out and do over, and that means what it says. Scratching out and cutting out. I read what I have written and I cross out a word and put another word in; a more decent word or a better word. Then if there is somewhere to use a sentence that I have crossed out, I will put it there."
>
> *Reviewing:* "Reviewing means just using better words and eliminating words that are not needed. I go over and change words around."
>
> *Reviewing:* "I just review every word and make sure that everything is worded right. I see if I am rambling; I see if I can put a better word in or leave one out. Usually when I read what I have written, I say to myself, 'that word is so bland or so trite,' and then I go and get my thesaurus."
>
> *Redoing:* "Redoing means cleaning up the paper and crossing out. It is looking at something and saying, no that has to go, or no, that is not right."
>
> *Marking Out:* "I don't use the word rewriting because I only write one draft and the changes that I make are made on top of the draft. The changes that I make are usually just marking out words and putting different ones in."
>
> *Slashing and Throwing Out:* "I throw things out and say they are not good. I like to write like Fitzgerald did by inspiration, and if I feel inspired then I don't need to slash and throw much out."

The predominant concern in these definitions is vocabulary. The students understand the revision process as a rewording activity. They do so because they perceive words as the unit of written discourse. That is, they concentrate on particular words apart from their role in the text. Thus one student quoted above thinks in terms of dictionaries, and, following the eighteenth-century theory of words parodied in *Gulliver's Travels,* he imagines a load of things carried about to be exchanged. Lexical changes are the major revision activities of the students because economy is their goal. They are governed, like the linear model itself, by the Law of Occam's razor that prohibits logically needless repetition: redundancy and superfluity. Nothing governs speech more than such superfluities; speech constantly repeats itself precisely because spoken words, as Barthes writes, are expendable in the cause of communication. The aim of revision according to the students' own description is therefore to clean up speech; the redundancy of speech is unnecessary in writing, their logic suggests, because writing, unlike speech, can be reread. Thus one student said, "Redoing means cleaning up the paper and crossing out." The remarkable contradiction of cleaning by marking might, indeed, stand for student revision as I have encountered it.

The students place a symbolic importance on their selection and rejection of words as the determiners of success or failure for their compositions. When revising, they primarily ask themselves: can I find a better word or phrase? A more impressive, not so clichéd, or less humdrum word? Am I repeating the same word or phrase too often? They approach the revision process with what could be labeled as a "thesaurus philosophy of writing"; the students consider the thesaurus a harvest of lexical substitutions and believe that most problems in their essays can be solved by rewording. What is revealed in the students' use of the thesaurus is a governing attitude toward their writing: that the meaning to be communicated is already there, already finished, already produced, ready to be communicated, and all that is necessary is a better word "rightly worded." One student defined *revision* as "redoing"; *redoing* meant "just using better words and eliminating words that are not needed." For the students, writing is translating: the thought to the page, the language of speech to the more formal language of prose, the word to its synonym. Whatever is translated, an original text already exists for students, one which need not be discovered or acted upon, but simply communicated.[7]

The students list repetition as one of the elements they most worry about. This cue signals to them that they need to eliminate the repetition either by substituting or deleting words or phrases. Repetition occurs, in large part, because student writing imitates — transcribes — speech: attention to repetitious words is a manner of cleaning speech. Without a sense of the developmental possibilities of revision (and writing in general) students seek, on the authority of many textbooks, simply to clean up their language and prepare to type. What is curious, however, is that students are aware of lexical repetition, but not conceptual repetition. They only notice the repetition if they can "hear" it; they do not diagnose lexical repetition as symptomatic of problems on a deeper level. By rewording their sentences to avoid the lexical repetition, the students solve the immediate problem, but blind themselves to problems on a textual level; although they are using different words, they are sometimes merely restating the same idea with different words. Such blindness, as I discovered with student writers, is the inability to "see" revision as a process: the inability to "re-view" their work again, as it were, with different eyes, and to start over.

The revision strategies described above are consistent with the students' understanding of the revision process as requiring lexical changes but not semantic changes. For the students, the extent to which they revise is a function of their level of inspiration. In fact, they use the word *inspiration* to describe the ease or difficulty with which their essay is written, and the extent to which the essay needs to be revised. If students feel inspired, if the writing comes easily, and if they don't get stuck on individual words or phrases, then they say that they cannot see any reason to revise. Because students do not see revision as an activity in which they modify and develop perspectives and ideas, they feel that if they know what they want to say, then there is little reason for making revisions.

The only modification of ideas in the students' essays occurred when they tried out two or three introductory paragraphs. This results, in part, because the students have been taught in another version of the linear model of composing to use a thesis statement as a controlling device in their introductory paragraphs. Since they write their introductions and their thesis statements even before they have really discovered what they want to say, their early close attention to the thesis statement, and more generally the linear model, function to restrict and circumscribe not only the development of their ideas, but also their ability to change the direction of these ideas.

Too often as composition teachers we conclude that students do not willingly revise. The evidence from my research suggests that it is not that students are unwilling to revise, but rather that they do what they have been taught to do in a consistently narrow and predictable way. On every occasion when I asked students why they hadn't made any more changes, they essentially replied, "I knew something larger was wrong, but I didn't think it would help to move words around." The students have strategies for handling words and phrases and their strategies helped them on a word or sentence level. What they lack, however, is a set of strategies to help them identify the "something larger" that they sensed was wrong and work from there. The students do not have strategies for handling the whole essay. They lack procedures or heuristics to help them reorder lines of reasoning or ask questions about their purposes and readers. The students view their compositions in a linear way as a series of parts. Even such potentially useful concepts as "unity" or "form" are reduced to the rule that a composition, if it is to have form, must have an introduction, a body, and a conclusion, or the sum total of the necessary parts.

The students decide to stop revising when they decide that they have not violated any of the rules for revising. These rules, such as "Never begin a sentence with a conjunction" or "Never end a sentence with a preposition," are lexically cued and rigidly applied. In general, students will subordinate the demands of the specific problems of their text to the demands of the rules. Changes are made in compliance with abstract rules about the product, rules that quite often do not apply to the specific problems in the text. These revision strategies are teacher-based, directed towards a teacher-reader who expects compliance with rules — with pre-existing "conceptions" — and who will only examine parts of the composition (writing comments about those parts in the margins of their essays) and will cite any violations of rules in those parts. At best the students see their writing altogether passively through the eyes of former teachers or their surrogates, the textbooks, and are bound to the rules which they have been taught.

Revision Strategies of Experienced Writers

One aim of my research has been to contrast how student writers define revision with how a group of experienced writers define their revision processes. Here is a sampling of the definitions from the experienced writers:

> *Rewriting:* "It is a matter of looking at the kernel of what I have written, the content, and then thinking about it, responding to it, making decisions, and actually restructuring it."

> *Rewriting:* "I rewrite as I write. It is hard to tell what is a first draft because it is not determined by time. In one draft, I might cross out three pages, write two, cross out a fourth, rewrite it, and call it a draft. I am constantly writing and rewriting. I can only conceptualize so much in my first draft — only so much information can be held in my head at one time; my rewriting efforts are a reflection of how much information I can encompass at one time. There are levels and agenda which I have to attend to in each draft."

> *Rewriting:* "Rewriting means on one level, finding the argument, and on another level, language changes to make the argument more effective. Most of the time I feel as if I can go on rewriting forever. There is always one part of a piece that I could keep working on. It is always difficult to know at what point to abandon a piece of writing. I like this idea that a piece of writing is never finished, just abandoned."

> *Rewriting:* "My first draft is usually very scattered. In rewriting, I find the line of argument. After the argument is resolved, I am much more interested in word choice and phrasing."

> *Revising:* "My cardinal rule in revising is never to fall in love with what I have written in a first or second draft. An idea, sentence, or even a phrase that looks catchy, I don't trust. Part of this idea is to wait a while. I am much more in love with something after I have written it than I am a day or two later. It is much easier to change anything with time."

> *Revising:* "It means taking apart what I have written and putting it back together again. I ask major theoretical questions of my ideas, respond to those questions, and think of proportion and structure, and try to find a controlling metaphor. I find out which ideas can be developed and which should be dropped. I am constantly chiseling and changing as I revise."

The experienced writers describe their primary objective when revising as finding the form or shape of their argument. Although the metaphors vary, the experienced writers often use structural expressions such as "finding a framework," "a pattern," or "a design" for their argument. When questioned about this emphasis, the experienced writers responded that since their first drafts are usually scattered attempts to define their territory, their objective in the second draft is to begin observing general patterns of development and deciding what should be included and what excluded. One writer explained, "I have learned from experience that I need to keep writing a first draft until I figure out what I want to say. Then in a second draft, I begin to see the structure of an argument and how all the various sub-arguments which are buried beneath the surface of all those sentences are related." What is described here is a process in which the writer is both agent and vehicle. "Writing," says Barthes, unlike speech, "develops like a seed, not a line,"[8] and like a seed it confuses beginning and end, conception and production. Thus, the experienced writers say their drafts are "not determined by time," that rewriting is a "constant process," that they feel as if they "can go on forever." Revising confuses the beginning and end, the agent and vehicle; it confuses, *in order to find,* the line of argument.

After a concern for form, the experienced writers have a second objective: a concern for their readership. In this way, "production" precedes "conception." The experienced writers imagine a reader (reading their product) whose existence and whose expectations influence their revision process. They have abstracted the standards of a reader and this reader seems to be partially a reflection of themselves and functions as a critical and productive collaborator — a collaborator who has yet to love their work. The anticipation of a reader's judgment causes a feeling of dissonance when the writer recognizes incongruities between intention and execution, and requires these writers to make revisions on all levels. Such a reader gives them just what the students lacked: new eyes to "re-view" their work. The experienced writers believe that they have learned the causes and conditions, the product, which will influence their reader, and their revision strategies are geared towards creating these causes and conditions. They demonstrate a complex understanding of which examples, sentences, or phrases should be included or excluded. For example, one experienced writer decided to delete public examples and add private examples when writing about the energy crisis because "private examples would be less controversial and thus more persuasive." Another writer revised his transitional sentences because "some kinds of transitions are more easily recognized as transitions than others." These examples represent the type of strategic attempts these experienced writers use to manipulate the conventions of discourse in order to communicate to their reader.

But these revision strategies are a process of more than communication; they are part of the process of *discovering meaning* altogether. Here we can see the importance of dissonance; at the heart of revision is the process by which writers recognize and resolve the dissonance they sense in their writing. Ferdinand de Saussure has argued that meaning is differential or "diacritical," based on differences between terms rather than "essential" or inherent qualities of terms. "Phonemes," he said, "are characterized not, as one might think, by their own positive quality but simply by the fact that they are distinct."[9] In fact, Saussure bases his entire *Course in General Linguistics* on these differences, and such differences are dissonant; like musical dissonances which gain their significance from their relationship to the "key" of the composition which itself is determined by the whole language, specific language (parole) gains its meaning from the system of language (langue) of which it is a manifestation and part. The musical composition — a "composition" of parts — creates its "key" as in an overall structure which determines the value (meaning) of its parts. The analogy with music is readily seen in the compositions of experienced writers: both sorts of composition are based precisely on those structures experienced writers seek in their writing. It is this complicated relationship between the parts and the whole in the work of experienced writers which destroys the linear model; writing cannot develop "like a line" because each addition or deletion is a reordering of the whole. Explicating Saussure, Jonathan Culler asserts that "meaning depends on difference of meaning."[10] But student writers constantly struggle to bring their essays into congruence with a predefined meaning. The experienced writers do the opposite: they seek to discover (to create) meaning in the engagement with their writing, in revision. They seek to emphasize and exploit the lack of clarity, the differences of meaning, the dissonance, that writing as opposed to speech allows in the possibility of revision. Writing has spatial and temporal features not apparent in speech — words are recorded in space and fixed in time — which is why writing is susceptible to reordering and later addition. Such features make possible the dissonance that both provokes revision and promises, from itself, new meaning.

For the experienced writers the heaviest concentration of changes is on the sentence level, and the changes are predominantly by addition and deletion. But, unlike the students, experienced writers make changes on all levels and use all revision operations. Moreover, the operations the students fail to use — reordering and addition — seem to require a theory of the revision process as a totality — a theory which, in fact, encompasses the *whole* of the composition. Unlike the students, the experienced writers possess a nonlinear theory in which a sense of the whole writing both precedes and grows out of an examination of the parts. As we saw, one writer said he needed "a first draft to figure out what to say," and "a second draft to see the structure of an argument buried beneath the surface." Such a "theory" is both theoretical and strategical; once again, strategy and theory are conflated in ways that are literally impossible for the linear model. Writing appears to be more like a seed than a line.

Two elements of the experienced writers' theory of the revision process are the adoption of a holistic perspective and the perception that revision is a recursive process. The writers ask: What does my essay as a *whole* need for form, balance, rhythm, or communication? Details are added, dropped, substituted, or reordered according to their sense of what the essay needs for emphasis and proportion. This sense, however, is constantly in flux as ideas are developed and modified; it is constantly "re-viewed" in relation to the parts. As their ideas change, revision becomes an attempt to make their writing consonant with that changing vision.

The experienced writers see their revision process as a recursive process — a process with significant recurring activities — with different levels of attention and different agenda for each cycle. During the first revision cycle their attention is primarily directed towards narrowing the topic and delimiting their ideas. At this point, they are not as concerned as they are later about vocabulary and style. The experienced writers explained that they get closer to their meaning by not limiting themselves too early to lexical concerns. As one writer commented to explain her revision process, a comment inspired by the summer 1977 New York power failure: "I feel like Con Edison cutting off certain states to keep the generators going. In first and second drafts, I try to cut off as much as I can of my editing generator, and in a third draft, I try to cut off some of my idea generators, so I can make sure that I will actually finish the essay." Although the experienced writers describe their revision process as a series of different levels or cycles, it is inaccurate to assume that they have only one objective. The same objectives and sub-processes are present in each cycle, but in different proportions. Even though these experienced writers place the predominant weight upon finding the form of their argument during the first cycle, other concerns exist as well. Conversely, during the later cycles, when the experienced writers' primary attention is focused upon stylistic concerns, they are still attuned, although in a reduced way, to the form of the argument. Since writers are limited in what they can attend to during each cycle (understandings are temporal), revision strategies help balance competing demands on attention. Thus, writers can concentrate on more than one objective at a time by developing strategies to sort out and organize their different concerns in successive cycles of revision.

It is a sense of writing as discovery — a repeated process of beginning over again, starting out new — that the students failed to have. I have used the notion of dissonance because such dissonance, the incongruities between intention and execution, governs both writing and meaning. Students do not see the incongruities. They need to rely on their own internalized sense of good writing and to see their writing with their "own" eyes. Seeing in revision — seeing beyond hearing — is at the root of the word *revision* and the process itself; current dicta on revising blind our students to what is actually involved in revision. In fact, they blind them to what constitutes good writing altogether.

Good writing disturbs: it creates dissonance. Students need to seek the dissonance of discovery, utilizing in their writing, as the experienced writers do, the very difference between writing and speech — the possibility of revision.

Acknowledgments

The author wishes to express her gratitude to Professor William Smith, University of Pittsburgh, for his vital assistance with the research reported in this article and to Patrick Hays, her husband, for extensive discussions and critical help.

Notes

1. D. Gordon Rohman and Albert O. Wlecke, "Pre-writing: The Construction and Application of Models for Concept Formation in Writing," Cooperative Research Project No. 2174, U.S. Office of Education, Department of Health, Education, and Welfare; James Britton, Anthony Burgess, Nancy Martin, Alex McLeod, Harold Rosen, *The Development of Writing Abilities* (11–18) (London: Macmillan, 1975).
2. Britton is following Roman Jakobson, "Linguistics and Poetics," *Style in Language,* ed. T. A. Sebeok (Cambridge: MIT P, 1960).
3. For an extended discussion of this issue see Nancy Sommers, "The Need for Theory in Composition Research," *College Composition and Communication* 30 (Feb. 1979): 46–49.
4. *Classical Rhetoric for the Modern Student* (New York: Oxford UP, 1965) 27.
5. Roland Barthes, "Writers, Intellectuals, Teachers," *Image-Music-Text,* trans. Stephen Heath (New York: Hill, 1977) 190–91.
6. Barthes 190.
7. Nancy Sommers and Ronald Schleifer, "Means and Ends: Some Assumptions of Student Writers," *Composition and Teaching* 2 (1980): 69–76.
8. *Writing Degree Zero,* in *Writing Degree Zero and Elements of Semiology,* trans. Annette Lavers and Colin Smith (New York: Hill, 1968) 20.
9. *Course in General Linguistics,* trans. Wade Baskin (New York, 1966) 119.
10. Jonathan Culler, *Saussure,* Penguin Modern Masters Series (London: Penguin, 1976) 70.

Sommers's Insights as a Resource for Your Teaching

1. In your reflective teaching journal, reflect on the experiences that influenced you to think about revising your own texts.

2. When you work with a writer who engages in "deep revision," ask whether that writer will give you permission to use excerpts from his or her multiple drafts. With these drafts, you can demonstrate to future students what can happen when a writer moves beyond surface revision. (Any time you want to use student

writing — for teaching or research or published writing — you must receive permission.)

Sommers's Insights as a Resource for Your Writing Classroom

1. Use the categories Sommers sets up to prompt small-group discussion about revision. Ask the groups to list what they view as characteristics of good revising. Then introduce the concept of "student" and "mature or experienced student" and ask them to classify the characteristics they described as representative of one or the other. Often students will volunteer descriptions that echo those that Sommers lists. If they don't, summarize Sommers's list and ask students to consider their own revising strategies in light of Sommers's categories. If you establish with your students that a mature college writer views revision as a recursive process, you give them one criterion by which to assess their growth as writers.

2. Prepare a sampler of revision suggestions from completed peer editing checklists or from transcripts of workshop sessions. (Borrow such materials from a teaching colleague if you are teaching for the first time or find your students apprehensive about seeing their comments used anonymously.) Organize small groups to evaluate peer criticism. Students should be instructed to consider which comments encourage revisions to improve the form and substance of the writer's argument, which comments focus the writer's attention on the needs of multiple readers, and which comments address lexical concerns. Ask each group to list the comments they would welcome on working drafts and to define or describe specifically what makes those comments useful. Have them also explain, in as much detail as possible, what makes the other comments less useful or less accessible. Don't be surprised if some class members find the exercise challenging: Many have never been asked to reflect on their critical thinking or encouraged to regard peer criticism as a significant writing experience.

Toward an Excess-ive Theory of Revision

Nancy Welch

With its mix of immediately recognizable, real-life writing situations and powerful philosophical underpinnings, this excerpt, from Getting Restless: Rethinking Writing and Revision *(1997), disrupts our "continued insistence on words like* clarity, consistency, *and* completeness" *in describing what we want our students to achieve in their writing. More specifically, Nancy Welch questions the "dominant beliefs about revision as a one-way movement . . . from unruly, unsocialized first draft to socially adapted, socially meaningful final product." She describes a different idea of revision, one "in which individual identities exceed and transgress" these neat-and-tidy containers, for it is in this excess that she wants us to locate emergent identities, voices, and truly important acts of re-visioning, crafting, and shaping meaning.*

> I think there is more that I want in here. Here is where I start to feel that my ideas scatter. I feel like I need something else or that it's just missing something.
>
> — Brandie, a first-year composition
> student writing in the margins of a draft

While it's generally thought that students view revision as a mechanical activity of correcting errors or as punishment for not getting a piece of writing right the first time, my classroom and writing center experiences tell me that many of our students *do* understand revision as a rich, complex, and often dramatic life-changing process. They understand — and have experienced — the kind of revision Adrienne Rich (1979) describes: as a moment of awakening consciousness, as entering old texts and cherished beliefs from new critical directions, as seeing with fresh and troubled eyes how they've been led to name themselves and each other (pp. 34–35).

The problem: The students I've worked with don't always know how to take the next step of intervening in a draft's meanings and representations. Or, in the context of a composition classroom, they understand that "revision" means the very opposite of such work, the systematic suppression of all complexity and contradiction. Another problem: Composition teachers by and large haven't been asking questions like "Something missing, something else?" that promote revision as getting restless with familiar and constrictive ways of writing and being, as creating alternatives. We respond instead (so a look through recent classroom texts suggests) in ways that restrict revision to a "narrowing" of focus, the correction of an "inappropriate tone" or "awkward repetition," the changing of any passage that might "confuse, mislead, or irritate" readers.[1]

Historians and critics of rhetoric, composition, and literacy education like James Berlin (1984), Susan Miller (1994), and Frank Smith (1986) have traced numerous reasons for this emphasis on writing as the management of meaning. They've linked such emphasis to the rise and codification of English as a discipline, to the opening of universities to working-class and minority students judged "deficient" and in need of linguistic and social correction, and to the faith educators have placed in the tenets of behaviorism.[2] Teachers and researchers in composition, rhetoric, and women's studies have also been resisting and recasting this history: through the arguments of Ann Berthoff against behaviorist conceptions of composing, through the productive dissonance that collaborative writing can generate (Lunsford 1991, Trimbur 1989, the *JAC* Winter 1994 issue on collaboration), through experiments in blending or contrasting autobiographical and academic voices (Bloom 1992, Bridwell-Bowles 1995, Brodkey 1994, Fulwiler 1990, Tompkins 1987), and through critiques of static conceptions of genre and the privileging of argument over autobiography (Bleich 1989, Bridwell-Bowles 1992, Frey 1990, Lamb 1991, Tompkins 1992). Most recently compositionists have also engaged Mary Louise Pratt's (1991) metaphor of the *contact zone* and Gloria Anzaldúa's (1987) of *borderlands* in refiguring academic scenes of writing as dynamic sites for multiple, conflicting, and creative language practices that push against and redraw the bounds of particular communities and genres (Horner 1994, Lu 1994, Severino 1994). The work of these researchers and many others destabilizes set notions about what constitutes academic discourse, genre, and authority, and they open up a field of speculation about what forms, voices, audiences, and concerns might be available and valued as academic work in the future. "At stake," Gesa Kirsch (1993) writes, "is nothing less than a new vision of what constitutes reading and writing — our scholarly work — in the academy" (p. 134).

What we still need to examine, however, are how these critiques, experiments, and speculations might be brought to bear on our ideas about revision and, more specifically, ways of talking in classrooms about revision that, despite the displacements of postmodernity, continue to posit the ideal of a stable, clear, and complete text. We need to consider, too, what practices of revision — of seeing with fresh eyes, of entering old texts from new critical directions — we must figure into our speculations and in our pedagogies if we are to move beyond calls for change into enactments of change in our writing and in our classrooms both.

In this chapter I want to revisit composition's articulated theories of revision and consider another layer to their history that can help us understand this continued insistence on words like *clarity*, *consistency*, and *completeness* at a time when other cherished and problematic ideals have given way — a history that's underwritten first by readings of Sigmund Freud, later by readings of Jacques Lacan, and their narratives of the encounter between an individual and society.[3] In particular I'll examine how one offshoot of Freud, "ego psychology," along with Lacanian rereadings, shape composition's dominant beliefs about revision as a one-way movement from writer-based to reader-based prose; from unruly, unsocialized first draft to socially adapted, socially meaningful final product.[4] Then, turning to feminist rereadings of Freud and Lacan, I'll consider a different story of revision that highlights the ways in which individual identities always exceed and transgress the discursive formations available to them — always confuse, mislead, and irritate not only a text's readers, but oftentimes its writer as well. More, contemporary feminist theorists stress that it's in the pursuit of what exceeds, what transgresses, what is restless and irritated, that we can locate the beginnings of identity, voice, and revision — revision as getting restless with a first draft's boundaries, revision as asking, "Something missing, something else?" of our texts and of our lives.

My short story "The Cheating Kind" (1994) started with a memory from my teenage years: riding the backroads in an old, beat-up Cadillac that my best friend's father and his girlfriend loaned us along with a six-pack of Black Label beer because, even though we were only fifteen, without licenses, our presence wasn't wanted in the house. When I started the story, those memories seemed charged with rebellion, possibility, heady high-speed freedom; as the drafting continued, though, I grew more and more uneasy with the narrator's point of view. She seemed capable of just about anything for a taste of adventure. Her desires seemed to eclipse completely whatever Marla, her friend, might be feeling as they drove around in that Cadillac, banished from her house, banished from the narrator's house, too, since the narrator's mother didn't regard Marla as a "nice" girl. Though a cherished myth of the fiction workshop, as Mary Cain (1995) writes, is that a writer is in control of the text and meanings she creates, seeking the advice of workshop members only to make her text and meanings clear and unambiguous to others, I didn't feel at all in control of this story and the questions it raised: Where was this narrator taking my memories? How much did she have to do with me? And what did social class, power, and status — the narrator from an exceedingly quiet, exceedingly polite middle-class family; Marla from a working-class household and the part of town where "things happen" — have to do with this story, with the memory from which it came?

Then came the story's end — a minor car wreck, the old Cadillac skidding off the road and into a corn field — I thought I was "dreaming up" since I couldn't quite remember how my friendship with the real Marla ended:

> *It was only slender stalks of corn, ripe and ready for picking, that we hit. They gave way easily, and Marla, of course, didn't die.*
>
> *It would be an easier story to tell if she had — the stuff of high drama like Gatsby face down and bleeding in a pool, the romance of a steak knife shivering between two ribs. I couldn't simply walk away then, pretend it had all never happened, brush off my acquaintance with Marla like a fine layer of dirt . . .*
>
> *"We'll have to get a tow truck," Marla said, looking down at the Cadillac's front end shoved through rows of broken stalks, the tires dug into soft, rutted earth. She stepped carefully around the undamaged plants, shook her head, and said, "We'll need help."*
>
> *A drop of blood clung to her lip, and she touched a finger to it. Probably I should have asked her, "Are you hurt?" But I was already thinking ahead to the tow truck, the sheriff, the call to my mother. I saw Bob Crofton shaking his head and saying no, of course he didn't give two fourteen-year-olds his Cadillac to drive.*

"I'll go," I said. I took one step back. Crisp leaves and stalks crackled beneath my feet. I kicked into the road a crushed, empty can of Black Label. "You stay here. I'll get help."

I took another step back, then paused for the jagged bolt of lightning to strike me dead or for Marla to read my aura and explode, "Oh, like hell I'm going to let you leave me here to take the blame." But the sky stayed the same bruised rainless gray, and Marla remained by the car and nodded as if she believed me, as if she trusted me to do this one small, honest thing.

"You stay here," I said again, turning now to run. (p. 45)

In the end, the narrator leaves Marla with the wreck, Marla to take the blame, back to the quiet, polite, "nothing-ever-happens-here" part of town. Though this ending isn't autobiographical, didn't actually happen, it also strikes me as true.

Let me put it this way: As I drafted and revised "The Cheating Kind," and especially its last scene, I wasn't concerned with the questions, "How can I better adapt each scene to the story's central theme?" and "How can I get my message across to readers?" — questions of craft, questions of a writer detached from and in complete control of his or her meanings. I was too caught up in the questions instead, "How much of this narrator's point of view was mine, is mine?" and "What does this story say about how I am already adapted — and to what?"

The Ethics of Excess: Three Stories

Psychoanalysis, French feminism, excess: These are words, I know, that conjure up images of uncritical celebrations of "writing the body" and lead to the protest, "But it's not responsible to invite students to write to excess, given what they're asked to do in their other classes" and "This is unethical since we're not licensed in psychology and psychiatry and aren't trained to handle what might result from encouraging the excessive."[5] Following a 1994 MLA presentation in which Wendy Bishop and Hans Ostrom (1994) argued for "convention making" and "convention breaking" taught together in the classroom, one teacher remarked to another, "I don't think students need to be confused any more than they already are." These are concerns I will address directly at this chapter's end, as well as indirectly in revision narratives placed throughout this chapter. Here, to suggest why we need to address these issues of restlessness, confusion, and excess along the borders of convention and genre, I'll introduce three brief stories that will be on my mind throughout this chapter:

1. Brandie, a student in a first-year composition class is, like many students at this large Midwestern land-grant institution, viewing the university as a place of transition between her rural upbringing and an adulthood defined primarily by what she cannot do and where she cannot go. She knows that after graduation she can neither return to the farm her family no longer owns nor to

the small town where her parents met and married; its shrinking economy can't support her and the numbers of other children raised and schooled there. Her mission at the university, as she vaguely understands and writes it, is "to get a teaching certificate so I can get a decent job somewhere or maybe to meet someone and get married which is weird since my parents always knew each other growing up and that won't be true for me and whoever 'he' may be." At the start of the semester she writes essays in a consistently upbeat tone about moving to the city and adjusting to a large university, stating, "I feel that in a huge place like the university you can very easily be just a number, but just as easily be somebody," and concluding, "I am making all I can of being a college student." As she reads this last paragraph aloud to her small group, another student, her background similar to Brandie's, begins to sing, "Be all that you can be. Get an edge on life . . ." Everyone laughs, Brandie too. "But, hey," Brandie says, "this is reality, right? We got to do it." Another student asks, "But don't you miss your old friends?" Brandie nods. "Aren't you ever homesick?" Brandie nods again and says, "But I don't want to put any of that into the story. It would take away from the positive idea I'm trying to get across. I don't want people to think I'm a mess."

2. To the writing center, Moira, a sophomore taking an intermediate writing class, brings a draft about her experience of going through a pregnancy, then placing the child up for adoption. The draft begins in the doctor's office where Moira learned she was pregnant, then proceeds through the adoption and her decision to return to school. Though the draft is seven pages long, Moira doesn't get past reading aloud in the writing center the first two paragraphs, stopping frequently to explain to me about her boyfriend, her parents, the plans she'd been making to move with her sister to another state, the uncertainty she shared with her boyfriend about whether they were really in love, her worries too that this uncertainty was created by her father who insisted she was too young for a serious relationship, how she sat on the examination table waiting for the doctor, thinking of all of this, and telling herself, "There's nothing wrong, there's nothing wrong." When I ask her if all she's telling me and jotting down in the margins has a place in the draft, Moira says, "That's the problem. I feel like it does, but then I worry about boring readers with all this background. It's all set up for the doctor to come in and tell me the news, and I don't feel like I can just leave readers hanging."

3. Lisa, a composition instructor, stops me in the hallway between classes and asks me to talk to her sometime about revision. She continues:

I don't feel comfortable asking my students to revise because I don't really know how to revise either. I've got all these journals and papers that I don't do anything with because even though I know they're not perfect, I don't want to take the life out of them, "do this" or "do that" like people tell me I need to. So they just sit there, and it's the same with my students. Maybe what they write isn't perfect, but it's got life and maybe cleaning it up would kill that life.

As Lisa talks, I wonder how many teachers moving down the hall around us might voice the same ambivalence, how many also have stacks of journals and papers they've written and are afraid to touch. Strangely, I think too of Tillie Olsen's (1976) short story "I Stand Here Ironing" and especially its closing phrase, "helpless before the iron" (p. 21).

These stories are on my mind now because each suggests to me the start of revisionary consciousness — as Brandie and her group members recognize a troubling cultural narrative that may be writing their lives, as Moira considers aloud the relationships that shape her experiences and that don't fit into the shape of her draft, as Lisa notes the tension between her classroom's generative theories of composing and dominant ideas of revision as cleaning up, closing down, even killing off. These stories also suggest to me the kind of helplessness that Olsen's narrator voices as she stands at the ironing board. Brandie, Moira, and Lisa aren't sure how they can intervene in these texts, they're not sure *that* they can intervene. They stand, in other words, at the intersection between full, excessive lives and the seemingly strict limits of texts that must be ironed out, made unwrinkled and smooth.

These stories also suggest that, difficult and discomforting as it is to linger at this intersection, real irresponsibility lies in denying its existence, in trying to push past this place as quickly and neatly as possible. It's here, at this intersection, that we need, first, to question the legacy of twentieth-century psychologies with their emphasis on the clear, the consistent, and the complete, and, second, to expand our understanding of the psychoanalytic frame to include what were, at least at times, Freud and Lacan's very much *plural* aims: the movement of individual desires toward social goals; the exploration too of ideas, feelings, experiences, and identities that exceed the rules of a given language, the margins of a given genre, the boundaries of the communities in which we live and write.

Sometimes it's surprisingly easy. In the writing center I ask Moira if she were to imagine writing out some of this "background," if she were to imagine that these details won't "bore" readers — including herself as reader — where would she want to begin? She takes her pencil and draws a line between one sentence about sitting on the exam table and the next in which the doctor arrives. We talk, then, about the idea of "space breaks" — a visual interruption of four spaces on the page, opening up room for writing about the relationships, questions, and hopes her first draft left out, then another space break signaling the return to the original narrative. When Moira returns to the writing center the next week, she's tried the space break and says she was surprised to realize that what she wrote within it wasn't "background" but the "heart of it all." She still feels restless, though, about one sentence, explaining, "I say here about my father being overbearing, and that's how it felt at the time but that's not always true or completely true." She pauses, then asks, "Can I take just that one sentence and write another essay from it?"

Yes. Yes, of course.

The Ego, the Id, and Revising with Freud

As Robert Con Davis (1987) observes in his introduction to *College English*'s second of two special issues on composition and psychoanalysis, we can find in the *Collected Works* not one Freud but (at least) two: the early Freud of the instinctual "drive" theory, and the later Freud of "ego" psychoanalysis from which springs mainstream American psychoanalytic and pop psychological practice. It's that later Freud who carved the mind into three not-at-all-distinct realms — the ego, the id, and the superego — giving us a three-part topography of a self at war with its selves. According to this model, the *id* is that part of agency, part of the self, that develops from the needs and impulses of the body and is inseparably bound to sensations of pain, pleasure, deprivation, and fulfillment. Out of the id develops the *ego*, that part of the self that seeks to regulate and control chaotic id impulses, and the *superego*, that part that represents parental, social, and institutional controls — the genesis of prohibition, censorship, and guilt, but also of social awareness and responsibility.

From this later Freud grew two popular versions of psychoanalytic practice. Id psychology focuses on and privileges the instinctual drives and an individual's "private" and "personal" fantasies that escape or speak in muted form through the ego's monitor. From id psychology comes the practice of dream analysis, classical Freudian readings of literature as revelations of an author's psyche, and the idea of automatic writing. Ego psychology, on the other hand, stresses the containment of id fantasy and the construction and maintenance of a social identity.[6] Defining psychoanalysis as an "instrument to enable the ego to achieve a progressive conquest of the id" (Freud 1962b, XIX, p. 56), ego psychology underwrites behaviorism (which places the superego outside the individual in external punishments and rewards that shape the ego's functioning), literature's reader-response theories (which follow an individual among others as he or she develops personal reactions into culturally shared interpretations), and, I'd like to argue, composition's dominant ideas about writing and revision.[7] Consider:

> Revision is by nature a strategic, adaptive process. . . . One revises only when the text needs to be better. (Flower, and colleagues 1986, p. 18)

Perhaps the best definition of revising is this: revising is whatever a writer does to change a piece of writing for a particular reader or readers — whoever they may be. . . . (Elbow and Belanoff 1989, p. 166)

[H]e must become like us. . . . He must become someone he is not. . . . The struggle of the student writer is not the struggle to bring out that which is within; it is the struggle to carry out those ritual activities that grant one entrance into a closed society. (Bartholomae 1983, p. 300)

These compositionists, usually divided into the separate realms of *cognitivist, expressivist,* and *social constructionist,* share *in common* an understanding of revision as movement from the individual (or writer-based) to the social (or reader-based), the increasingly strategized, adapted, socially integrated and socially meaningful finished product. Though Flower and colleagues have been criticized for ignoring the social dimensions of writing in their seemingly interior cognitivist model, they actually highlight the social in their definition of revision — the need for writers to reread and adapt their texts according to very much social ideas of what they should say, how a piece of writing should appear, what would make it "better." Similarly, though the pedagogy of Elbow and Belanoff has been labeled "expressivist" and might be read as a pedagogy of the id, they too construct revision (albeit with some discomfort) as changes made toward a social text and social functioning; they too (within *Community of Writers,* that is) share in common with ego psychology the belief that movement from individual to social, private fantasy to public meaning, is desirable or, at least, unavoidable.

But it's David Bartholomae especially who makes visible for me the intersections between our understandings of composing and the ideas of ego psychology, showing how Freud's tripartite model of the mind has been further codified into separate, distinct realms: the student as "id" who must not bring out that which is within — or rather, that which is formed by social languages and communities deemed unintelligible within academe, deemed "other" than academic discourse; the draft as developing, regulatory "ego"; the teacher as "superego," the embodiment of the closed society and its rituals for meaning. Bartholomae doesn't tone down this process as entirely natural and as always positive and progressive. Rather, noting that stories of learning to write in academic settings are often "chronicles of loss, violence, and compromise" (1985, p. 142), his construction of the writing scene suggests that revision has much more to do with politics than with brain biology or liberal humanism. In this construction, intentions are shaped by the community the writer wants to make his or her way into, and the revision process is not a simple matter of making a text "better" or "clearer." Revision is instead the very complicated matter of struggle between a full, excess-ive life and the seemingly strict limits of what can be written and understood within a particular discourse community. Here, Bartholomae and other social constructionists like Patricia Bizzell and Thomas Recchio share much in common with Jacques Lacan, his rereading of Freud, and his view that the making of identity and meaning are social acts from the very start.

At a midterm conference, Rachel, a student in my first-year compo-sition course, tells me, "I'm learning a lot from your class." I cock my head, puzzled. Rachel is always in class, never late, always has a draft, neatly typed, never handwritten, for workshops. A model student. Dis-turbingly so. (I can't remember now, looking back, what Rachel wrote about, only that her drafts were always clear and concise, a thesis stated in the first paragraph and stuck to through the very end.) "Is there any-thing missing for you in class?" I ask. "Anything we're not doing that you wish we would or something we could be doing more of?" I'm fum-bling about, trying to get at my sense that there's something that could be and isn't in Rachel's writing for class or that could be and isn't in the class for Rachel. But Rachel shakes her head. "No, everything's great. It really makes a lot of sense, you know: free write, think about what's at the center, free write some more, get some feedback, go with a new ques-tion. It's great." Maybe, I think, my sense of something missing is wrong; she's identifying what she's learning after all. Maybe I'm only imagin-ing an underground, unarticulated frustration she feels with this class, and maybe I just can't see something that really is happening in her writing.

Then at the semester's end Rachel writes her evaluation for the course in a voice I hadn't heard from her before — one of anger, of frustration, and of intense involvement with this writing task: "Supposedly this was a course in composition, but I'll tell you I didn't learn one thing about composition from it."

Mirror-Mirror *or* Revising with Lacan

With Lacan's rereading of Freud and, particularly, his reading of Freud's early thinking on the development of ego in "Narcissism" (Freud 1962b, XIV), that sense of the inevitability of the movement from self to other, individual sensation to social codification, is both reinforced and ren-dered as troubling. Beginning with the infant in an amorphous and boundaryless state, just a "l'hommelette" or "omelette" (little man, mass of egg), Lacan explores the advent of the largely metaphoric "mirror stage" in which individuals confront and seek to connect with a smooth and consistent reflection of themselves (1977b, p. 197). The mirror im-ages they find can be gratifying — giving a sense of shape and whole-ness to what was before a chaotic jumble of needs and sensations — but such images are also a source of discord and anxiety. The outer image of containment and completion is at odds with the inner sensa-tions of fragmentation and incoherence; it leads to conflict between the "Ideal-I" reflected in the mirror and the "turbulent movements that the subject feels are animating him [or her]," and it asks an individual to combat and contain those sensations increasingly in order to as-sume an identity that's outside, other, and alienating (1977a, p. 2). "It is this moment," Lacan writes, "that decisively tips the whole of human knowledge into mediatization through the desire of the other" (1977a, p. 5). It is at this moment, in other words, when American ego psychology's clear distinctions between individual and society break down, revealing how an individual sense of self, meaning, and reality is thoroughly mediated by social mirrors and the images of wholeness and coherence they reflect.

The story of Lacan's mirror stage helps me to understand why professional writers are so often reluctant to talk about revision and show to others early drafts of their work. Fiction writer Tobias Wolff, for instance, destroys all early versions of his stories, explaining, "They embarrass me, to tell you the truth. . . . I only want people to see my work at its very best" (quoted in Woodruff 1993, p. 23). "When I finish a piece of writing," says Joyce Carol Oates, notorious for her reticence about the subject of her own writing, "I try my best to forget the preliminary stages, which involve a good deal of indecision, groping, tension" (quoted in Woodruff 1993, p. 167). Those early drafts may not match up at all to social mirrors that tell us what a short story ought to look like or what a good writer's sentences ought to sound like. They may even pose a threat to the writer's sense of himself or herself as a good writer at all, a threat to the belief that this draft can ever be finished and published. (This is something against which students in my fiction-writing classes particularly struggle, saying that they want or need to put their story drafts aside "to cool," when, in fact, I suspect that they fear the unsettling images these drafts reflect, images they see not in terms of possibility, but of failure to match up and fit in.) Lacan's analysis of the mirror stage tells me, too, why students often respond in conferences and in peer groups (as Richard Beach observed in a 1986 essay) with "Oh, I feel pretty good [about this draft]" or "I don't feel good about it at all but I don't want to revise it." It makes sense, I think, especially in an environment of evaluation, of grades, to respond to dissonance and disjuncture by insisting, "No, this is clear enough, good enough" or to worry that any intervention might make a sense of misfit and distortion even worse.

In my view, the story of Lacan's mirror stage is the story that underwrites social constructionist understandings of writing and revision. "[I]t is evident," Thomas Recchio (1991) writes, "that we all have to find ways to function in a language [or languages] . . . that have already been configured" (p. 446). "[H]e must become like us," Bartholomae (1983) writes. ". . . He must become someone he is not" (p. 300). Like Lacan, both Recchio and Bartholomae stress how from the very first word, the very first draft, a student in the composition classroom encounters, grapples with, and tries to accommodate an alien, even alienating, way of writing. Both stress that a notion of revision as a clean movement from writer-based to reader-based prose is also fiction, since languages and contexts for writing are already social, already reader based. A writer doesn't create language in isolation and out of thin air, then work toward involving others; one's words are already deeply involved in the work and words of others, come from without rather than from within, and can seem, as Lacan writes, like "the assumption of the armour of an alienating identity . . ." (1977a, p. 4).

This isn't to say that Recchio, Bartholomae, and other social constructionists postulate a writer who has no agency within this armor. Through "orchestrating and subordinating" the multiple social discourses of a text, Recchio (1991) states, a student may "begin to find her own voice" (pp. 452–453). "The person writing," Bartholomae (1990) says, "can be found in the work, the labor, the deployment and deflection . . ." (p. 130). Still, here, as in the usual reading of Lacan, there is that overriding sense of inevitability: We can resist this narrative of being subsumed and written by the assumptions and rituals of a single community — through deployment and deflection, subordination and control — but we cannot fundamentally alter it.[8]

In "Fighting Words: Unlearning to Write the Critical Essay," Jane Tompkins (1988) examines the narratives — of movie westerns, of the biblical David and Goliath — that underwrite traditional forms of academic writing: critics gunning each other's readings down; a graduate student standing up at her first conference with her slingshot-of-a-paper, hoping to smite the big voices in her field so she has the right to speak. That's also the narrative of my first academic publication: Set up this authority, set up that, then tear them down, get on with what you want to say. I was shaken when, one year later, I met one of those authorities face to face. It occurred to me then, and should have occurred to me before, that she was more than the few words on the page I chose to quote: a living breathing person leading a complex life, asking complex questions — who she is and what her work is far exceeding the boundaries I'd drawn.

In this chapter, too, I'm doing it again, choosing quotations from writers whose work exceeds the space I'm giving them and the narrow focus of revision I've selected. This is a problem — one to which I have to keep returning, not skipping over with the gesture of a "However" or "Yet it's easy to see . . . ," creating a text that's problematically concise, simply clear.

The Trouble with Mirrors

Freud and Lacan are not figures I want to dismiss, and I don't think, either, that compositionists can or should shrug off the influence of twentieth-century psychologies. Freud remains appealing to me if for no other reason than because he located his research in narrative. Though he wasn't always a critical reader of his narratives with their traces of sentimental romance, Victorian melodrama, and the mechanistic metaphors of industrial capitalism, he illustrates why forms of narrative research — case studies, ethnographies, autobiographical literacy narratives — are crucial to the making of knowledge in composition: They make visible what is "uncanny" in our thinking and in our practices; they reveal the slips and contradictions that disrupt our broad generalizations (or we might say "wishes") about what's happening in our classrooms and in our discipline. Stories, as Mary Ann Cain (1995) observes, don't merely "mirror" our assumptions and expectations; they "talk back."

Similarly, all the slips and contradictions of a classroom text like Elbow and Belanoff's (1989) *Community of Writers* — with its conflicting id-based and ego-based assertions, "You write for yourself; you write for others" — make visible and talk back to my own slips, my own contradictions when I try to talk with students about revision. As for Lacan, though his theories may appear grim and deterministic, he does tell me why my students and I are sometimes so unsettled when we look back on our early drafts, those drafts distorting what we wished to see, declining to mirror back ideas smooth-surfaced and well-mannered, the gratifying images of a graceful writer, a good teacher. Composition's social constructionists have also worked to disturb the discipline's harmonious image of the writing process as natural, asocial, and apolitical; they stress that no classroom and no piece of writing can ever be free from the problematic encounter between an individual and society, the pressures and desires to see one's text neatly reflect a preplanned intention, a pleasing image, the certainty of one's membership in a closed society.

But no social mirror — and this is what usual readings of Lacan leave out — can ever reflect back to us, whole and complete, an image of ourselves and the true nature of things. There is always something missing, something else, or, as feminist critic Sheila Rowbotham (1973) writes, misfit and distortion as we lumber around "ungainly-like" in "borrowed concepts" that do not "fit the shapes we [feel] ourselves to be" (p. 30). This has to be the case as well for the mirrors that our readings of Freud and Lacan provide. Those mirrors offer some ideas about writing and revision, individual identity and social meaning, that we want and need. Those mirrors ought to make us restless with what they distort, what they miss, what else they imply.

My restlessness begins when I consider how both our Freudian and Lacanian constructions of revision position the teacher as superego, the representative of the "us" students must learn to write like or as the regulatory voice in the margins telling students where and how their texts need to adapt and change. As philosopher Michele Le Dœuff (1989) considers, the position of superego sets teachers up for a "tic"-like approach to responding to students' texts: "systematically correcting [any] infidelities" and "castigating the language of the student . . . by writing in red in the margin . . ." (p. 57). That castigation may be overt with insistent commands like "Be specific!" or "Focus!"; it can also take the seemingly benign forms of "Does this paragraph really belong here?" or "Some readers might be offended by this." Either way, this relationship between teacher and student, teacher and text, doesn't set us up for questioning the textual ideals we and our students are writing/responding to match. It doesn't set us up for understanding the encounter between teacher and text as a potentially rich "contact zone" or "borderland" for questioning, speculating, and, possibly, revising the teacher's response. It constructs instead (Le Dœuff's point as she examines the grading of doctoral exams in philosophy) a position of complete submission for the student, of utter mastery for the teacher. Meanwhile, the question doesn't even come up: *Just who or what has mastered the teacher?*

My restlessness increases when I recall that Lacan's thinking about the mirror stage, so influential to social constructionism, began with his reading of Freud's essay on narcissism — suggesting some disturbing answers to that question: Just who or what has mastered the teacher? In Lacan, the experience of the mirror stage sends an individual in a "fictional direction," toward an imaginary idea of an "us," of a community and its practices into which an individual wants to fit. As compositionist Kurt Spellmeyer observed in his 1994 MLA presentation, "Lost in the Funhouse: The Teaching of Writing and the Problem of Professional Narcissism," this fictional direction is also a *narcissistic* one. It can lead us to seek — in our own writing and in others', in academic journal articles, dissertations, and students' compositions — gratifying images of ourselves, and it can lead us to feel frustrated and annoyed when a piece of writing doesn't reflect such an image. These imaginary identifications don't always lead us to question what's being gratified when we write an article that others call graceful, witty, or astute or when we write in the margins of a student's essay "Nice work" or "Very smoothly written." These imaginary identifications don't always lead us to question, either, the longing among compositionists within their departments and institutions to project certain images of themselves to the exclusion and debasement of others — as in "I teach a cultural studies classroom [rather than a mere writing class]" or "I'm in rhetoric [not composition]" or "I'm a post-process theorist [disassociated, that is, from composition's research of the past twenty years]."

Stressing at the start and end of his presentation that our academic lives are carried out under powerful institutional gazes, very often within English departments that value literature over composition, the high and sweeping theoretical over the narrative, detailed, and everyday, Spellmeyer suggests that compositionists do have some means for resistance. We can shift our attention from texts by a Beckett or a Joyce to texts by students; we can, as Spellmeyer demonstrated in his presentation, deploy French terms in ironic tones and with raised eyebrows, calling for light laughter and an edge of skepticism. These forms of resistance aside, however, we cannot fundamentally revise the forms, voices, and subjects of the texts we write — not according to this story of the formation of academic identity.

Here my restlessness is most extreme as social constructionism (slipping into social determinism), which began with a radical intervention in too-smooth notions of "the writing process," ends with a denial of possibilities for further intervention, as it replaces questions with absolute statements of what must be, and so repeats the move of ego psychology, asserting the need to adapt to a prefigured principle of (institutional) reality: *He must learn to write like us; narratives of academic socialization will always be narratives of loss, violence, compromise, and alienation; academic production is the production of anxiety, narcissism, and neurosis — this is just the way things are.*

I thought about Tompkins's (1988) essay "Fighting Words" and my own David-and-Goliath article this past week while reading poems in Prairie Schooner. *I read poems by T. Alan Broughton that meditate on letters written by Vincent Van Gogh to his brother Theo, one by Cornelius Eady written from a photograph of Dexter Gordon, another by Adrienne Su that takes its occasion from a sentence in* Alice's Adventures in Wonderland: *"Everything is queer today." Funny that poets are often charged with sequestering themselves in silent garrets or with suffering the most from the anxiety of influence. These three poets model for me ways of beginning to write, of working with the words of others, and of finding a voice — ways that don't involve setting up and knocking down. They suggest we might revise our usual forms of academic production by remaining at, rather than trying to get past, that border between one's text and others. Maxine Hong Kingston also offers me an example of this border work between one's voice and another's. In* The Woman Warrior *Kingston (1976) creates, continually returns to, and enriches a portrait of her mother, making places in her text for the both of them, even where — or especially where — their voices, their views, aren't at all one and the same.*

"Too Much": Revising to Death

In "Professional Narcissism," Kurt Spellmeyer focuses on the anxious, even neurotic relationships that form between writer and text, text and reader, when we write to adapt to institutional mirrors. Two fictional stories about revision as adaptation — Margaret Atwood's "The Bog Man" (1991) and Paule Marshall's *Praisesong for the Widow* (1984) — also focus on those powers of social mirrors and suggest more chilling consequences still. In "The Bog Man," there is Julie who revises again and again the tale of her long-ago affair with Connor, a married archeology professor who brought her as his "assistant" on an excavation in Scotland. Throughout the story Julie revises Connor, revises herself, even revises the setting where they broke up because "Julie broke up with Connor in the middle of a swamp" sounds "mistier, more haunted" than "Julie broke up with Connor in the middle of a bog" or, the truth, in a pub (p. 77). In her revisions of the story, told "late at night, after the kids were in bed and after a few drinks, always to women," Julie works to shut out any details that might be less than amusing, too hard to figure out (p. 94). She "skims over the grief," "leaves out entirely any damage she may have caused," thinks that this or that fact "does not really fit into the story" (pp. 94–95). Connor, like the bog man they go to Scotland to excavate, "loses in substance every time she forms him in words" (p. 95). In the end, Julie has an ironic, consistent, and lifeless tale of an episode from her life. In the end, Connor is "almost an anecdote" and Julie is "almost old" (p. 95).

Avey, the main character in Paule Marshall's novel *Praisesong for the Widow*, is also "almost old" when she begins, with great restlessness and resistance, to look back on the narrative of middle-class socialization she and her now-dead husband, Jerome, followed as they moved "out" and "up" from a fifth-floor walk-up in Harlem to a suburban house in White Plains, New York. She remembers the "small rituals" they left behind: a coffee ring on Sunday morning, gospel choirs on the Philco, Jerome (who then called himself "Jay," even his name changing with their move) reciting the poetry of Langston Hughes (pp. 124–126). She remembers their "private lives," their lovemaking, that had seemed "inviolable" but that also "fell victim to the strains. . . . Love like a burden [Jerome] wanted to get rid of" (p. 129). And she remembers the dances Jerome led her in across their small living room, "declaring it to be the Rockland Palace or the Renny," in the days before his voice began to change to one that said, "If it was left to me I'd close down every dancehall in Harlem and burn every drum! That's the only way these Negroes out here'll begin making any progress!" (pp. 95, 132). *"Too much!"* That's what Avey cries out as she finally lets herself remember and mourn the changes in her husband, in herself, the cost of their "progress." She doesn't romanticize the years on Halsey Street in Harlem and doesn't erase the grim hardship; she does ask herself, "Hadn't there perhaps been another way?" She thinks, "They had behaved, she and Jay, as if there had been nothing about themselves worth honoring" (p. 139).

Julie, Jerome, and Avey are cast within narratives of accommodation and change that point toward the not-always-acknowledged implications of composition's dominant theories and practices of revision. Julie, for instance, strategizes and adapts, alters and omits, so that her story's "effect" matches her "intention." She revises with the aim of better functioning within an already configured language — here, the already configured and even clichéd language of college girls who get into affairs with married professors, of a middle-aged, middle-class woman who makes light of younger, wilder days. While Recchio considers that an individual voice may be formed through the work of orchestration and subordination, coherence and control, Atwood's story dramatizes the opposite case as Julie's orchestrations and subordination lead, in the end, to no voice at all. The same is true and much more disturbing in Marshall's story of Jerome. His work to adapt his life and his words to a single course of action, one proper tone, ends with his lying in a coffin while everyone congratulates his widow "on how well she had held up in the face of her great loss" (pp. 132–133).

In feminist readings of psychoanalysis the revision process involves both *dream-work* (the exploration of identifications and meanings along the border of consciousness) and *death-work* (the critique and dismantling of beliefs and identifications we experience as our selves, making their loss a kind of death). Joining the work of discovering and questioning, dis-orienting and re-orienting, revision becomes that process Winnicott (1971) calls "creative living" and that Kristeva (1986a) calls "dissidence": a process through which one recognizes how he or she has been situated, the process through which one negotiates with reality "out there" to change that situation. In Marshall's depiction of Jerome's brief life, however, there is no room for dream-work, dissidence, and negotiation with reality "out there." While Lacan (1977a) defines death-work as working one's way toward a "new truth" that is "always disturbing" (p. 169), in Marshall's representation of Jerome there is no work, no activity, no confrontation with and reflection on what in these life changes are disturbing; there is only the literal and complete killing off of a whole history, a whole host of attachments, every one of his daily rituals for meaning, as he works to adapt his life to one principle of reality. It's a story not of *re-vision* but of assimilation.

With Julie, Jerome, and Avey's narratives in mind, we might reconsider resistance to revision and that fear Lisa expressed of revision taking the "life" from a piece of writing just as Jerome's process of change literally took the life from him. Lisa, unlike Jerome, is not marginalized by race; however, as an untenured instructor in the university, a Jewish woman in the predominantly Christian and Protestant Nebraskan culture, a woman who came to feminism in her forties and after an impoverishing divorce, Lisa is aware each time she sits down to write of working against the grain of the dominant culture, a working-against she's only recently found the confidence to try. Viewing revision as the work of toning down and fitting in, the work of moving away from, not into, disturbing new positions and truths, she fears the silencing of a voice she's only just begun to use. In some instances at least, Lisa persuades me, a refusal to revise may arise from an intuitive understanding of the intimate link between language and identity, an intuitive understanding that we really can revise a story, revise ourselves, to death.

That is, unless we return to that intersection between a full and excess-ive life and the limits of a particular society, asking, with Marshall's Avey, if there isn't another way.

Sometimes relationships in the classroom — to reading, to other students — can recast, rather than reinforce, the usual social mirrors teachers and students write and respond within. In an intermediate composition class, Scott, a senior in his midtwenties, reads aloud in class a narrative of a ski trip in which he and his friends abandon another friend, new to skiing, on the beginner's slope. In his draft, Scott represents this friend as "whining" and "annoying," comedically clumsy and inept, deserving, so the story implies, to be left behind. The students in class laugh as Scott reads. Except Amanda, Scott's journal partner, who writes to him in her next journal, "What about you? Weren't you a beginner on that trip too? Did you worry about being left?"

   Meanwhile, Scott is also reading Tim O'Brien's (1990) semiauto-biographical novel The Things They Carried *in which the narrator, Tim, recreates his decision to go to Vietnam, feeling as though there were "an audience" to his life, an audience shouting "Traitor!" and "Pussy!" as he tries to imagine swimming for Canada (p. 60). Later O'Brien's narrator considers what happened when he sent one of his published stories to Norman, a foot soldier who was with him in Vietnam on the night when Kiowa, another foot soldier, was killed in a "shit field." About the story, Norman writes back, "It's not terrible . . . but you left out Vietnam. Where's Kiowa? Where's the shit?" (p. 181). With O'Brien's words in mind, Scott considers the audiences to his own life who expect him to be amusing, to keep it light, to skip the shit. He considers that in his latest draft, about canoeing on the Niobrara River, he's repeated the move that Amanda noticed in his ski trip draft — displacing his confusion and fear onto others, setting them up as comedic and inept, almost writing himself out of the story altogether. During an in-class glossing activity, Scott lists in the margins of his draft, as O'Brien does in his short story "The Things They Carried," some of the events, problems, and questions that he carried on this trip. He writes, "We were all having problems, and I want to bring those out" and "What's really going on here? Where's my trip?"*

   With his glosses, Scott begins to revise, adding a scene in which he and his friend Chuck, riding down the Niobrara one afternoon in a slowly meandering canoe, talk seriously about their lives, relationships, and futures — the kind of serious and meandering talk between two men that isn't usually represented in social (and classroom) discourse. This and other revised passages don't present a version of Scott as whole and complete, who he really is, the way it really was. In the margins of the revision and his journal, he continues to write, "I may be using Chuck to say some of how I was feeling and perceived things" and "I'm looking for a voice I can feel comfortable with" and "I need to try this paragraph again." The revision does, though, lead him to a next step: giving the draft to Chuck to read, "fidgeting" while Chuck read "very slowly," and feeling "a great weight lifted" when Chuck responded by asking for a copy to keep. "He didn't ask 'Where's the Niobrara?'" Scott writes. "He didn't complain that I'd left out the shit."

Wrestling with Lacanian Bondage

Like Marshall's Avey, film theorist Joan Copjec (1989) also seeks another way, one out of what she calls the "realtight" bond in contemporary psychoanalytic theory between the "symbolic" and the "imaginary," between individual identity and the social gazes thought to determine, wholly, completely, who we can be and what we can say (p. 227). That real-tight bond seals us off from any consideration of the "real" or of, as Freud (1962b) puts it, that "inch of nature" that exceeds any one construction of our selves (Copjec 1989, pp. 228–229; Freud 1962b, XXI, p. 91). It leads, for instance, to film theorists positing a single (male) gaze that women are positioned within and must take pleasure from as they view a film, with no room for restlessness, resistance, another way of watching.

But this real-tight bond, Copjec writes, is also the result of a *misreading* of Lacan and, in particular, the familiar Lacanian aphorism, "Desire is the desire of the Other" (Copjec 1989, p. 238). In this misreading — one exemplified not only in film theory but also in composition's social-constructionist theories of writing — writers and their texts are viewed as entirely determined by the social mirrors that surround them, by actual and identifiable "Others" to which we can point and say, "Yes, there's the locus of my desire, the mirror I want to match." According to this (mis)reading, Copjec writes, individuals take on social representations as images of their own "ideal being" — that "Ideal I" from Lacan's mirror stage. As we take a "narcissistic pleasure" from such images (because they offer us shape and symmetry), we become "cemented" or "glued" to them, coming to call them (no longer an alienating armor) our selves — or, in the classroom, our definition of good writing, what we want our teaching and our students' texts to reflect (Copjec 1989, p. 229; this is likewise Spellmeyer's point in "Professional Narcissism" [1994]).

The problem with this construction of desire and the formation of identity is that it overlooks the capital "O" Lacan places here on "Other." In Lacan, there are "others" — small "o" — who are the people, communities, histories, social representations, and social discourses with whom and with which we interact, influence, and are influenced by — that "mediatization" the end of the mirror stage tips us toward, others with identifiable shapes, locations, and limits. There is also a persistent sense of *Otherness* (capital "O") beyond the limits of those people, communities, and discourses, a persistent sense we can't quite see and name that we might call the "real," the "inch of nature" that exceeds, overflows, cannot be contained and copied. "[W]e *have no image* of the Other's desire . . . ," Copjec writes, no single representation that can bring "reunion"; there is always "something more, something indeterminate, some question of meaning's reliability" (pp. 236–238, my emphasis).

In Copjec's reading of Lacan, identity is produced "not in conformity to social laws," but "in response to our inability to conform" to social laws and discursive limits (p. 242): with the recognition of limits there's restlessness, movement, a desire that can't be satisfied with determined gazing into the reflection of one social mirror.[9] Copjec's reading takes us back to that intersection between individual and society, between excess and limits, with the understanding that a sense of something missing, something else isn't a mistake to be corrected, isn't an unruly id to be suppressed, but is instead the start of revisionary activity by a self that is neither singular and static nor entirely composed by a fixed set of social determinants.

In an introductory fiction-writing class, the instructor says to me, "Technically, your story is very good. Clear. Logical, Complete. Good details." He pauses. "It's just that — " He smiles, starts again. "I think maybe you haven't found your material yet. You need to let yourself be a little messy." He adds, handing me back my story, handing me another story too, "Read this. Maybe it'll say what I mean." I nod, make my exit, frustrated, angry, ready to write on an end-of-semester evaluation, "Supposedly this was a course in fiction writing, but I'll tell you . . ." My material? What is that? And why were none of the routines I'd followed to write news stories (I was then working for a daily paper) working for me now? How did Mona Simpson, the writer of the story this instructor handed me, manage to make her stuff sound so, well, real? Home now, I head straight to my computer, turn it on, then do something else: turn off the lighted screen. This semester I'm also taking a seminar for writing tutors. We're reading Mikhail Bakhtin (1981), who claims that words hold within them whole lives and histories, the suggestions of relationships, of conflicts, of resolutions that can't last for long. We're also reading Peter Elbow (1987), who advocates shutting off the computer screen, writing in the dark. Do I believe it? Try it? Let the words run along, then reread to see what story is being written there, one I hadn't planned and controlled? I begin to write, thinking that whatever happens will prove to my instructor that a mess is exactly what will come of this, thinking too about the last time I felt this mute, pent-up, and confused — when I was sixteen years old and running away from home. I write, "In Cincinnati the snow turned to rain . . ." Half an hour later I stop, print it out, and without looking at the pages, mail them to the instructor with an irritable note, "So. Is this my material?"

"Yes," he said.

This is not the story "How I Came to Discover My Own True Voice." (The fiction that came from writing in the dark, "The Road from Prosperity" [1996], ended up being seven years in the making — seven years of trusting, doubting, then trying to trust again Elbow and Bakhtin, seven years of discovering how to read and work with the Otherness of my own words, the unruliness of my writing.) It's a story instead about coming up against the limits of my writing, traveling over the curricular boundaries into another class (a so-called theory class), coming back, learning to write — maybe for the first time.

Writing in the "Chinks and Cracks"

One way of starting the kind of revision, Copjec's essay suggests, is through exploring practices of "prodigality" that can both highlight and take us beyond a particular community or genre's discursive limits. In an essay that begins with the either/or choice feminists face between "silence and cooptation," Jerry Aline Flieger (1990) considers that beyond the position of "dutiful daughter" to institutional forms of living and writing or that of "illegitimate mother's daughter" who rejects institutions (and voice, power, authority), there is the possibility of another position: that of the "Prodigal Daughter" (pp. 57–59). The prodigal daughter "is a daughter still" who "acknowledges her heritage," but who also "goes beyond the fold of restrictive paternal law" and returns not castigated and repentant, ready to settle down and fit in, but "enriched" (pp. 59–60). The prodigal daughter "is lush, exceptional, extravagant, and affirmative"; her participation in one community (like feminism) creates for her an identity that exceeds the limits of another (like psychoanalysis). That excess-iveness allows her to take exception to a community's limits and laws; it enables her to introduce new questions and rituals, to "enlarge its parameters" and "recast its meanings," changing the bounds of "what is permissible" (p. 60), changing, indeed, what constitutes that community and the practices of those within it.

Enlarging the parameters and reenvisioning limits also concerns Michele Le Dœuff as she reworks static notions of rationality in philosophy into practices of "migration" — writing with and through other social discourses and needs rather than positioning philosophy apart from and above others. "I am seeking the greatest possibility of movement," Le Dœuff writes, a practice of writing that migrates into and creates authority from "different fields of knowledge, 'disciplines' or discursive formations, between different periods of thought and between supposedly different 'levels' of thought, from everyday opinions to the original metaphysical system" (1991, p. 51). For Le Dœuff this means bringing her experiences with the Women's Movement in France into her work as a philosopher, rather than choosing a focus on one or the other. In this way Le Dœuff recasts her role from a "precious admirer" of and careful commentator on the texts of male philosophers (1989, p. 120). Migration shows her the limits of those texts, creates new questions and possibilities of projects beyond philosophy's usual bounds: critiques of philosophy's strategy for authority through displacing "theoretical incapacity" onto others in order to create its meanings (1989, p. 126); examination of the "erotico-theoretical transference" that has historically defined women's relationships to philosophy; exploration, too (since the prodigal daughter is also "affirmative"), of "plural work" with other writers and other disciplines that reconnects philosophy to daily social concerns.[10]

Flieger and Le Dœuff's practices of migration and prodigality aren't pendulum swings away from the social and back to the purely private and personal: an uncritical celebration of an untamed id, the mirage of an essentialized female language. Quite the opposite, the experience of migration, Le Dœuff writes, works to "exile" a writer from the conventions of a discipline and the assumptions of doctrinal bases, and by doing so denaturalizes those conventions and assumptions, preventing them from becoming commonplace, essential, the way it must be (1991, p. 222). Similarly, plural work, instead of promising escape and freedom, offers Le Dœuff a "continuing sense" of "limits," "the recognition that 'I do not do everything on my own,'" and that this incompleteness is not a "tragedy," but the opportunity to continue revising along that border of "the unknown and the unthought" (1989, pp. 126, 128). As

Julia Kristeva writes, also working with these notions of migration and exile, the experience of traveling beyond disciplinary limits and comfortable ways of knowing and writing can take us out of "the mire of common sense" and enable us to become a "stranger" to the daily communities, discursive formations, and rituals for meaning we would otherwise take for granted, their limits and implications invisible to us (1986a, p. 298). Neither advocating a search for a singular self nor attachment to one social identity, these theorists seek instead the formation and recognition of multiple attachments, bringing *all* of one's identities to the scene of writing, working for a voice of lushness that's a powerful means of critique and creation both.

The writings of Teresa de Lauretis, Trinh T. Minh-ha, and Minnie Bruce Pratt also demonstrate the creative, critical, and socially responsive uses of migration and prodigality. In *Technologies of Gender*, de Lauretis (1987) argues for migration away from a focus on the "positions made available by hegemonic discourses" and toward "social spaces carved in the interstices of institutions," in the "chinks and cracks" where one can find — already in existence, not needing to be longed for, a utopian future not yet come — "new forms of community" and "micropolitical practices of daily life and daily resistances that afford both agency and sources of power . . ." (pp. 25–26). Writing away from the prevailing discourses and the positions they allow is what Trinh (1989) does in *Woman, Native, Other* as she moves away from the word *author* with its implications of a solitary genius and toward the word *storyteller* with its connection to dailiness, community, and collectivity. The essays of poet and lesbian activist Minnie Bruce Pratt (1991) also stress that the work of crossing limits isn't the trivial and apolitical pursuit of an ivory-towered class of writers, without consequence for the better or worse. In claiming her identity as a lesbian, "step[ping] over a boundary into the forbidden," Pratt lost her children to her husband's custody, the court ruling that she had committed a "crime against nature" (p. 24). In claiming that identity, she writes, she also gained the ability to keep crossing boundaries, connect her struggles as a lesbian to those of others subordinated by race, gender, or class, and take her poetry "beyond the bounds of law and propriety into life" (pp. 23–24, 241).

In the here and now, these writers offer examples of writing that seeks to name, understand, and transgress the limits of prefigured texts, understandings, and ways of living. They demonstrate revision not as that one-way movement from writer-based to reader-based prose, but instead as that moment of looking back on a text, asking how it's already reader based, already socialized and reproducing the limits of a given society, and whether there's something missing, something else. Doing so, they radically question Lacanian (and social constructionist) notions that coming into language always and only means compromise and alienation. In these writings there's a refusal to leave the intersection with a quick and uneasy compromise; there's the work of revision as seeking other options and attachments, as expanding one's focus, and as learning to write to excess.

That's true too for Paule Marshall's Avey in *Praisesong for the Widow* (1984) who does not remain within White Plains' bounds of middle-class propriety and within the narrative of loss, violence, and compromise that marked her husband's death. Moving instead into another story of revision, Avey abandons the security and strict itinerary of a middle-class cruise ship. She travels — disoriented, ill, weary from mourning her husband Jay and their early life together — to the island of Carriacou. There, in the company of others making their yearly excursion to this island of their birth and of their ancestors, Avey begins to dance, "[a]ll of her moving suddenly with a vigor and passion she hadn't felt in years," her feet picking up the rhythm of the Carriacou Tramp, "the shuffle designed to stay the course of history" (1984, pp. 249–250). At the novel's end Avey, like Flieger's prodigal daughter, is on her way back to New York — exceptional, extravagant, and prepared now to alter the former limits of her life.

In class, Brandie reads her draft and writes back to her words in the margins. She writes "Spark!" and "I was amazed when I wrote this" next to the first paragraph that ends, "I can't believe that it took me nineteen years, one month, and six days to realize that I, Brandie Marie Anderson, have no idea whatsoever what I want to do with the rest of my life." She writes, "Here is where I start to feel that my ideas scatter . . ." next to the final paragraph that concludes "I have learned that I can do anything I want in this world, or I can do nothing." In between these paragraphs she's told the story of bringing a college friend, who grew up in a large city, home to visit her family. She's described feeling proud ("I felt like I was the man who invented the whole farming system itself") and defensive ("I wanted to destroy her feelings that my house was like that on Little House on the Prairie*") and confused ("I don't know why I thought my life was the only kind there was. I don't know why I never questioned my future"). In the margins she writes, "But is that really so bad?"*

Then Brandie turns to her journal partner, Meg, and says, "Do you want to trade?" Brandie reads and writes back to Meg's draft, which is about growing up with two families — her mother, stepfather, and their children together; her father, stepmother, and their children together. Meg reads and writes back to Brandie's draft, responding primarily to Brandie's marginal glosses: "I think this paragraph is perfect!" and "Brandie, what exactly was different about your background, and what made you think June's was so exciting? There's the obvious — bigger town, more to do, but tell me in your own words!" and "You ask yourself if that [not questioning the future] is so bad. Can you try to answer the question?" Reading this, Brandie nods and starts to make a list called "Differences" at the bottom of the page. By the end of class when she gives the draft to me, its margins — top, bottom, right, and left — are filled with conversation, arrows, directions, questions. Next to the glosses

I write, "Yes," "Yes," and "I'd like to hear about this too," then respond to one sentence near the end that says, "I can really see myself teaching . . . except to teach you have to know everything, and I know I don't." I write: "I'd like to hear more about what you see when you see yourself teaching. What creates the view that a teacher must know everything? . . . Let's talk about this — maybe in a journal?"

Brandie does choose this draft to revise, responding to Meg's questions and her own. There are other kinds of revision taking place, too, of which this particular essay, by itself, is only a part: revision as Brandie strays from writing essays in a consistently upbeat tone with one "positive idea" she wants to "get across"; revision as Brandie and Meg carry their conversation from the margins of each others' drafts into their journals, writing about the differences in their lives and families; revision as Brandie and I write in journals back and forth about the images of teachers we've grown up with and what it can mean to see one's self as a teacher. There's revision too as I no longer reserve the space in the margins for my pen. Have I eliminated teacher as "superego," as regulatory voice? No. But just as Freud didn't posit the id, the ego, and the superego as absolute, distinct realms, I'm trying to blur the boundaries and populate this space with multiple voices, relationships, and tones.

Toward an Excess-ive Theory of Revision

"[A]t every point of *opposition*," writes Gayle Elliott (1994) in an essay about the tensions between feminist theory and creative writing, "is a point — an *opportunity* — of *intersection*" (p. 107, Elliott's emphases). "Limits," Ann Berthoff (1981) writes, "make choice possible and thus free the imagination" (p. 77). These words also apply to that opposition between the fullness of a life and the limits of genre and community. Yes, writers do confront languages already configured for them. Yes, we do write within powerful institutional gazes that can seem as impervious and punishing as the barbed wire that lines this country's southern border, and yes, identities do exceed the bounds of what's called permissible and appropriate in a given genre, discipline, or classroom, creating narratives of loss and of compromise. But Copjec, Fleiger, Pratt, Le Dœuff, Trinh, Marshall, and a great many writers more demonstrate that opposition *can* become intersection, a contact zone populated with activity, meaning, and the kind of revision that comes from working at the borders of community, writing to exceed the limits of a given language and form.

These writers also demonstrate that the first-person narrative, accompanied by practices of re-vision, doesn't necessarily produce "the ideology of sentimental realism" and reification of "a single authoring point of view" — the troubling limits of an "expressivist" conception of composing that David Bartholomae (1995) argues convincingly against (p. 69). When we understand with Joan Copjec that the "real" can't be inhabited, that even the most seemingly "complete" and "authentic" narrative has its limits and inexpressible excesses, we can begin to read at the limits. We can value not so much the "genuine voice" of a personal narrative, or its "candor" or "unique sensibility," but rather the activity of this writer at the border between text and context, between the fullness of experience and the limits of language that can be worked, transgressed, and radically revised.

When I return to composition studies from this migration into psychoanalysis, feminism, philosophy, and fiction, I find plenty of examples of working at the borders and transforming opposition into intersection. Histories of rhetoric, for example, show the historical specificity, the historical *limits*, of conventional forms for teaching writing like the five-paragraph essay and the rhetorical modes. In making visible the boundaries those forms describe, these histories open up the possibility of — and need for — migration.[11] Teachers of creative writing like Gayle Elliott show how the borders separating composition, creative writing, and critical theory can be redrawn, urging the greatest possibility of movement across "creative" and "critical" genres and identities. Alice Gillam (1991) redefines writing centers from a "battleground" (where students must choose between either focusing, cutting, and controlling or leaving a first draft as is) to a site where writers "*flesh out* the contradictions" and "*puzzle over* the off-key shifts in voice," as a way of discovering rather than imposing focus (p. 7, my emphases). In "Dialogic Learning across Disciplines," Marilyn Cooper (1994b), like Gillam, migrates toward the theories of Mikhail Bakhtin to consider that disciplinary conventions aren't fixed entities to be acquired by students, but are subject to "the forces of unification and the forces of diversification," making it possible for students to participate in the work of diversification as well (p. 532). Min-Zhan Lu (1994) dramatizes how that participation takes place when members of her first-year composition class examine an apparent "error" in a student's text *as* a richly nuanced and meaningful stylistic choice. Through this revision, they create a contact zone between the official codes of school and other languages students bring to this setting; they reconsider academic production as involving "approximating, negotiating, and revising" among contending codes — *including* those traditionally excluded from academic discourse (p. 447).

Lu especially helps me respond to teachers who fear that encouraging an excess-ive understanding of revision will confuse and even harm students both struggling with alien academic discourses and writing for professors who value neatly managed and monovocal meanings. Forces of unification, as well as of diversification, are always present in a classroom as students and teachers bring with them a range of histories, experiences, and assumptions about the limits and possibilities of writing in classrooms.[12] Rather than taking academic conventions as natural or as unquestionably superior to other language practices, rather than ignore these varied histories and varied understandings of just what the limits are, Lu writes that "the process of negotiation encourages students to struggle with such unifying forces" (p. 457) — to resist for a moment the work of subordination, coherence, and control; to pause, reflect, and consider the complexities of their choices; to realize that there *are* choices. Instead of confusing or misleading students, this renaming of error as style to be *puzzled over, thought through* (the same way teachers and students would puzzle over and think through the stylistic choices of a Gertrude Stein) offers those who want to resist a single official style, the community-based practices of revision, reflection, and argumentation they need to do so; it also offers those familiar with the discourses of school a view of that style's limits, as well as a view of the chinks and the cracks through which they might stray.

In composition's process legacy we can also find, I believe, practices of revision and reflection that can guide students and teachers as they consider revision as getting restless with a draft's initial meanings and representations, as seeking alternatives. Ann Berthoff's philosophy and practices, for instance, have always sought to engage the "form-finding and form-creating powers of the mind" in the "possibility of changing" a reality (1981, pp. 85, 92). Her practice of glossing invites students to reflect and revise along the borders of their texts — to "think about their thinking" and "interpret their interpretations," to see the limits and the choices there — while her practice of interpretive paraphrase offers a writer the means to write toward what exceeds. The double-entry notebook creates a visible space of critical exile where one can look back on, name, and rename initial meanings and representations; the question, "What's the opposite case?" encourages migrating from and complicating a first draft's focus.

I could continue — migrating from Berthoff's revisionary pedagogy to considering Elbow and Belanoff's loop writing as prodigality, Sondra Perl's open-ended composing process as creating a contact zone between forces of unification and diversification. But my point is this: These theorists tell me we need to remain at the intersection between "process" and "post-process" conceptions of composing, not quickly push past that intersection, not call one side the "past" and the other the "present." We need more border talk between the classroom practices and detailed case studies of the 1970s and 1980s, and current calls for institutionwide revisions of community, genre, academic discourse, and academic authority. (It's Flower and Hayes, I realize, who first showed me what I could learn about my classrooms through writing and reflecting on case studies; Elbow continues to invite me to turn off the computer screen as I draft.) Investigating the borders, we can refuse the gesture of projecting theoretical incapacity onto others; we resist *that* mirror for establishing authority. At the intersection, process pedagogies can be revitalized through examining how race, class, gender, ethnicity, sexual orientation — students' and teachers' many and varied cultural and personal histories — inform their writing, reading, and revising. And at the intersection teachers can both question and reclaim practices of revision we and our students need if we are to enact our many visions of change, if we are to be able, on a day-to-day basis, to question, intervene, and create; if we are to be able, on a day-to-day basis, to confront confusion, turn opposition into intersection, and create from the experience of limits the experience of choice.

Taking the sentence about her father from her adoption draft, Moira revises, creating another essay that considers her father's beliefs about what her decisions should be. With that draft comes another source of restlessness, though, as Moira considers that her responses, her beliefs, aren't in this writing. In the writing center she places another sheet of paper beside the draft and, asking of each paragraph, "Where am I in this?" she begins to write back to her draft on the new page — a kind of excess-ive version of glossing. "I think," she says after twenty minutes of this writing, "that the thing is this: My father always taught me that the decisions we make should bring us peace. But what we both have to learn is that we may have different ideas about what peace is, what decisions are right for me." It's close to the end of our meeting in the writing center and Moira checks her syllabus to see when her draft is due. She talks about leaving the draft as is or cutting up the paragraphs of both writings seeing what would happen if she tried to put them together. She talks about rewriting the first paragraph with a new emphasis on what she and her father need to learn, and she talks too about taking both pieces of writing to her composition class' next draft workshop, asking her small-group members what they think.

Moira talks too, as she's packing up, about her father's uneasy childhood, how he dropped out of school, why it's so important to him that her life be perfect. "Is that history a part of what you're talking about in your draft?" I ask, and Moira nods. "It should be," she says. "It says why. It tells me why."

Something Missing, Something Else

When Moira, like Brandie, whose words began this chapter, dares to consider that there's something missing in her text, something more, she recognizes the limits of that text and there, at the limit, she imagines what might happen next. What happens next is talking and writing on the borders of a neat and tidy draft, recognizing that its incompleteness isn't a tragedy at all, but a site of choice including the choice to stop for now, including the choice to continue. What happens is Moira and I both know that in a few weeks some of this writing will be graded, that she will decide which. Meanwhile there's time, here and there, in the chinks and cracks of her work and school schedule, for Moira to migrate toward questions other than: *What will get me an A?*

But this kind of work can only happen — *really happen* — within settings like Moira's writing class that promote and support an excess-ive understanding of revision: one that questions the ideal of the complete, contained, and disciplined body, the complete, contained, and disciplined text; one that takes the double perspective that revision involves both movement toward social goals *and* questioning what's being perpetuated or omitted in the process. Those questions can return a writer to invention as marginal glosses carry into other writings, as an interpretive paraphrase grows into something too big, too complicated to be easily integrated into the paper from which it came. So that students don't feel overwhelmed by the reflections these texts-in-progress mirror back, we also need to situate these practices in relationships that offer challenge and support like Brandie's with her journal partner and Scott with his reading of Tim O'Brien. Because investigating limits and straying from what may have been comfortable boundaries can be disorienting, dismaying, a threat to one's sense of self and to the life of a draft, students need the greatest possibility of choices about when to ask: *Something missing, something else?* In my classes this has meant that some students revise a particular draft by taking the same general topic, migrating into another genre, seeing how an autobiographical narrative, for instance, might look as a poem, a collage, a research project, a letter, or a fictional story. Meanwhile, others revise not by returning to a particular draft but to a journal entry (a kind of revision advocated by Ken Macrorie), seeing its limits and how this writing might be carried on. In one case a student struggling with the idea of revision reread a favorite book from his adolescence; his revision took the form of writing about that experience of rereading. In institutional settings, including my classrooms, revision *does* become another limit, another constraint, a social ideal to which students feel they must adapt. Around that word *revision*, though, there are borders students and teachers can name, question, negotiate, and rename, creating excess-ive understandings of what revisionary work can mean.

This kind of revision, however, depends on teachers supporting students' work at the intersection. It asks teachers to practice forms of response and evaluation that make sense of such work instead of operating out of a double standard that allows many of us to feel confident reading the excess-ive writings of a Joyce, Dickinson, or Foucault, but dismayed before a student who is writing at the line between what's comfortable and familiar and what's challenging, strange, and new.[13] This kind of revision depends on a teacher's ability to revise as well, to turn that question — Something missing, something else? — back on his or her reading of a student's draft, on what the limits of that reading are, what other ways of reading there might be.

Here, though, I come to the limits of this chapter and of this book, with a recognition that there's a great deal missing, a great deal more. Or I come to an intersection between this project I'm trying to finish and future projects I imagine, including:

- Where and when do teachers begin to feel restless with their ways of responding to students' texts, suggesting an intersection between a full, excess-ive experience of reading and the limits of prefigured forms for response? Where and when do teachers begin to ask, "Something missing, something else?" of their responses?

- What happens when teachers bring their reading of students' texts into dialogue with their reading of other writers whose work pushes against any single "Ideal Text" (to borrow Knoblauch and Brannon's apt and Lacanian phrase)?[14] Or, given that many teachers have argued precisely for such an intersection, what works against this happening or against this happening more?

- What would it mean to bring an excess-ive understanding of revision into dialogue with current research in the use of portfolios and of contract grading? To what extent do these practices of assessment in particular institutional contexts continue to perpetuate the ideal of complete, contained, disciplined texts? To what extent do these practices, again in particular institutional contexts, work to subvert such an ideal, pointing toward the excess-ive instead?

- What would it mean to alter the question, "How is this piece of writing finished?" into "What work does this writing suggest that might be carried on?" and "What are the future projects that might arise from it?"

- What would it mean to consider the literature classroom as a place that's also very much concerned with the investigation of "Something missing, something else?" Can we locate the work of interpretation in a literature class, as in the composition class, at the intersection between full, excess-ive experiences of reading and the limits of prefigured forms for response?

- What would happen in a fiction workshop if students and their teacher investigated, examined, and revised the limits of cultural notions of who a fiction writer or poet is and how he or she works? What would it mean to create such a workshop that actively seeks to address, as fiction writer Eve Shelnutt puts it, "the myth that works of the imagination and full consciousness are anti-thetical" (1989, p. 5)? What difference would this make to students' writing and to their reading of each others' work?[15]

- And since some ideas about just what "full consciousness" means in contemporary critical and literary theory make me restless, what intersections can I discover between my own excess-ive experiences as a writer of fiction and the limits of the theories through which I make sense of those experiences? How can Le Dœuff's project of working between philosophy and feminism become my own as I migrate between fiction and feminism, teacher and writer?

But all of these questions are, really, various versions of, departures from, and returns to this: What will happen when we begin to read, write, and teach at that tense, problematic, and fascinating boundary between *individual* and *society* — reading, writing, and teaching with an excess-ive and pluralized understanding of these terms and of the intricate braids that make it impossible for us to distinguish between the two? What if we read to see boundaries our texts and our students are getting restless within? What if we learned to watch for places where a text begins to resist, get unruly, and maybe even stray? What will happen when we read with the belief that our students do have, as Ross Winterowd wrote in 1965, *"restless minds"* that we can glimpse and encourage in their writing — if we get restless with static ways of reading, conventional forms of response (p. 93)?

Which suggests yet another question: What will happen when we begin to read to discover not *whether* a student needs to revise (suggesting the responses of no or yes, finished or not, still within that frame that values the complete and the contained), but to discover instead where and how, in or around this writing, he or she *has already started* to revise? That's work we can notice, work we can value, work that might continue within or beyond this not-so-single text. What would this mean for our students' writing? For how teachers and students talk about writing? For how students and teachers understand what revision can be?

As an undergraduate in an advanced composition class (before I migrated over into the fiction workshop, before I'd come up hard against the limits of my writing), I turned in an essay every Friday, got it back every Monday with an A. Especially since I then worked for a daily paper, I was a practiced writer — maybe too practiced and I knew it too. "Wonderfully wrought throughout" the professor wrote beside those A's. "Graceful." "Lovely." I felt gratified by those comments and A's. Restless too. Not so sure these essays really were so perfect and complete. Not sure what to do about it either, what questions to ask and where. At the semester's end the professor told us to return to the essay that received the lowest grade, revise it for a higher one.

"Mine were all A's," I told him after class. "What should I do?"

"You don't have to do anything," he said. "Your work is fine as is."

It wasn't, it isn't, not at all — but that's another story. Or the story of why I'm writing now, still restless, not satisfied.

Notes

1. I've taken these constructions of revision from three current composition textbooks but want to avoid attaching authors' names to them, since I found a dozen other textbooks that offered similar understandings of revision, telling me that none of these constructions can be attributed to a single author.

2. Michele Le Dœuff's (1989) *The Philosophical Imaginary*, which ties philosophy's systematic suppression of its own contradictions to its desire to gain and maintain academic status, also offers a way to read composition's history and particularly its history of teaching revision as the containment, rather than exploration, of dissonance. Likewise Mikhail

Bakhtin's (1968) *Rabelais and His World* traces the ideological history of an emphasis on the text as a "classical body" that is "entirely finished, completed, strictly limited" — and, so, seemingly divorced from "living practice and class struggle" (pp. 320, 471).

3. In this chapter, I'll be looking at the most prominent and frequently cited constructions of revision from composition's *expressivist, cognitivist,* and *social constructionist* orientations. There are crucial differences, though, among composition teachers within these orientations and individual voices that have argued for or suggested different constructions of revision. Susan Osborn (1991), for instance, seeks to "provide a context in which revision and revision are explicated as both integral to the writing process and a way of knowing ourselves as readers and writers" (p. 270). Min-Zhan Lu (1994) also stresses "writing as a process of re-seeing" — including re-seeing, negotiating, and revising the conventions of academic discourse (p. 449). Recent articles in the *Writing Center Journal* — by, for instance, Alice Gillam (1991) and Cynthia Haynes-Burton (1994) — likewise work against the grain of revision as a one-way movement from writer-based to reader-based prose. In this chapter, then, I have the double aims of (1) explicating the construction of revision against which these teachers write and (2) writing toward the construction of revision their work suggests.

4. The terms *writer-based* and *reader-based* prose come from Linda Flower's (1979) essay "Writer-Based Prose: A Cognitive Basis for Problems in Writing," and her terms have given compositionists ways of thinking about the kind of audience for whom a piece of writing might be intended. This book, for instance, is decidedly intended for others to read and so it might be called *reader-based*, while the journal in which I considered the questions, problems, and breakthroughs of this book's writing is decidedly intended for me alone and so might be called *writer-based*. The problem I'm working with in this essay, though, is how these terms have been lifted from their original context, *writer-based* becoming increasingly used as synonymous with *solipsistic*, while *reader-based* is increasingly reduced to meaning *clear, concise, and instantly, easily understandable* and reduced to the single, unquestioned goal of revision.

5. The most thoughtful and searching critique I've found of the psychoanalytic frame, particularly the Lacanian psychoanalytic frame, in the classroom is Ann Murphy's (1989) "Transference and Resistance in the Basic Writing Classroom: Problematics and Praxis." Though I read that essay as underwritten by the assumptions of ego psychology — the need for students and teachers to adapt to and function within a social reality, a belief in stable and socially rewarding roles students can write toward, along with a promise to students that mastery of writing conventions can be "congruent with her or his own needs" (p. 185) — this statement from Murphy remains central to my thinking about revision in this book and in my teaching: "[A] process which seeks further to decenter [students] can be dangerous" (p. 180). Like Murphy's students in basic writing classrooms, the students I meet are already (often in ways that aren't readily apparent) decentered, divided, disoriented. They don't need or want a teacher, from her position of relative security and power, to create decentering experiences for them. What needs to be decentered instead, I think, is the view that learning and writing can ever be safe, neat, and tidy, leading us to be surprised, dismayed, and totally unprepared when we find again

and again that no, learning and writing are not safe and neat at all. What needs to be decentered, too, I think, is the view that essays, unlike our lives, should contain nothing of disorientation, uncertainty, and division.

6. In *Dora* (Freud 1962a), for example, Freud contrasts the hysterical patient's "inability to give an ordered history" of her life with that of a patient whose "story came out perfectly clearly and connectedly" and whose case, Freud thus concluded, could not be one of hysteria (p. 31). In other words, Freud equates the unruly, disorderly, and discontinuous with emotional illness, and the clear, calm, and perfectly connected with emotional health. Ironically, Freud's own text might be called hysterical, then, with its many and sometimes acknowledged incompletenesses, contradictions, and omissions.

7. Elizabeth Wright (1989) takes a closer look at the forms of psychoanalysis that have influenced literary studies and theories and (by implication) composition, too.

8. Recently, however, Recchio (1994) suggests a much more dialogic and recursive process of revision in which society shapes individuals' texts, but in which many individuals in turn speak back to and shape society. "Realizing [this] potential of the essay in the Freshman English classroom, however," he writes, "is a thorny problem, for writing pedagogy has been dominated by formalized self-contained systematic thought where play, discovery, and recursiveness are squeezed out of discourse, and subordinated to a misleading formalist consistency and clarity" (p. 224).

9. Copjec's figuring of an unsatisfiable and restless desire runs against the grain of consumer culture that depends on our believing that if we can acquire the right sweater/car/hand cream/theoretical frame/language/publication/degree we will be satisfied, reunited with our complete being. There is no "Other" that can complete us, no matter what advertisements, textbooks, how-to guides, and academic programs may promise. She suggests to me that a classroom that seeks to understand this and at least question the ideal of the whole, complete, unified, and nothing-left-to-say text is also a classroom that prepares students and teachers to see themselves as critics and creators, rather than frustrated consumers, of culture.

10. For further exploration see Le Dœuff's essay "Long Hair, Short Ideas" in *The Philosophical Imaginary* (1989) and the "Second Notebook" in *Hipparchia's Choice* (1991).

11. See, for example, Sharon Crowley (1991) and James Berlin (1984).

12. Carrie Leverenz (1994) offers a careful and disturbing examination of such forces of unification at work in students' responses to each others' writing in a composition classroom.

13. I'm indebted to Wendy Bishop and Hans Ostrom (1994) who made this point in their 1994 MLA presentation, "Letting the Boundaries Draw Themselves."

14. Freud's *Dora* (1962a) or *Interpretation of Dreams* (1962b, IV), with all of their assertions, examples, clarifications, contradictions, caveats, and footnotes that continue for a page or more, strike me as excellent choices for disrupting stable notions of what can constitute "academic" writing. Try reading one of these, then telling someone, "Writing in academia must be clear, consistent, and concise." I don't think such an assertion is possible after Freud.

15. I think of these questions especially because recently a teacher remarked to me that students in her class who name themselves as "Writers" — capital "W" — also produce the most "writer-based" and "egocentric" work

she's ever seen. I suspect, though, that the writing of such a student isn't at all writer based, individualistic, divorced from readers and the social realm. Instead, that writing and that writer are probably very much caught up in and overdetermined by those social myths of the solitary, misunderstood, at-odds-with-society poetic genius — "a breath-mist," poet and fiction writer Fred Chappell (1992) writes, that one needs to clear away in order to begin to write (p. 21).

Works Cited

Ahlschwede, Margrethe. 1992. "No Breaks, No Time-Outs, No Place to Hide: A Writing Lab Journal." *Writing on the Edge* 3: 21–40.

Alton, Cheryl. 1993. Comment on "Crossing Lines," *College English* 6: 666–69.

Anzaldúa, Gloria. 1987. *Borderlands / La Frontera: The New Mestiza.* San Francisco, CA: Spinsters/Aunt Lute.

Atwell, Nancie. 1987. *In the Middle.* Portsmouth, NH: Boynton/Cook.

Atwood, Margaret. 1991. "The Bog Man." In *Wilderness Tips.* New York: Doubleday.

Bakhtin, Mikhail. 1968. *Rabelais and His World.* Translated by Helene Iswolsky. Cambridge, MA: MIT Press.

———. 1981. *The Dialogic Imagination.* Translated by Caryl Emerson and Michael Holquist. Edited by Michael Holquist. Austin, TX: University of Texas Press.

Bartholomae, David. 1983. "Writing Assignments: Where Writing Begins." In *Forum.* Edited by Patricia L. Stock. Upper Montclair, NJ: Boynton/Cook. 300–12.

———. 1985. "Inventing the University." In *When a Writer Can't Write.* Edited by Mike Rose. New York: Guilford Press. 134–65.

———. 1990. Response to "Personal Writing, Professional Ethos, and the Voice of 'Common Sense.'" *Pre /Text* 11.1–2: 122–30.

———. 1995. "Writing with Teachers: A Conversation with Peter Elbow." *College Composition and Communication* 46: 62–71.

Beach, Richard. 1986. "Demonstrating Techniques for Assessing Writing in the Writing Conference." *College Composition and Communication* 37: 56–65.

Berlin, James. 1984. *Writing Instruction in Nineteenth-Century American Colleges.* Carbondale, IL: Southern Illinois University Press.

Berthoff, Ann E. 1981. *The Making of Meaning.* Portsmouth, NH: Boynton/Cook.

Bigras, Julien. 1978. "French and American Psychoanalysis." In *Psychoanalysis, Creativity, and Literature.* Edited by Alan Roland. New York: Columbia University Press. 11–21.

Bishop, Wendy. 1990. *Something Old, Something New: College Writing Teachers and Classroom Change.* Carbondale, IL: Southern Illinois University Press.

———. 1993. "Writing Is/And Therapy?: Raising Questions about Writing Classrooms and Writing Program Administration." *Journal of Advanced Composition* 13: 503–516.

———, and Hans Ostrom. 1994. "Letting the Boundaries Draw Themselves: What Theory and Practice Have Been Trying to Tell Us." MLA Convention. San Diego, CA. 29 December.

Bizzell, Patricia. 1984. "William Perry and Liberal Education." *College English* 46: 447–454.

Bleich, David. 1988. *The Double Perspective: Language, Literacy, and Social Relations.* New York: Oxford University Press.

———. 1989. "Genders of Writing." *Journal of Advanced Composition* 9: 10–25.

Bloom, Lynn Z. 1992. "Teaching College English as a Woman." *College English* 54: 818–825.

Brand, Alice. 1991. "Social Cognition, Emotions, and the Psychology of Writing." *Journal of Advanced Composition* 11: 395–407.

Brannon, Lil, and C. H. Knoblauch. 1982. "On Students' Rights to Their Own Texts: A Model of Teacher Response." *College Composition and Communication* 33: 157–166.

Brannon, Lil. 1993. "M[other]: Lives on the Outside." *Written Communication* 10: 457–465.

———. 1994. "Rewriting the Story: Expressivism and the Problem of Experience." Conference on College Composition and Communication, Washington, DC. 23 March.

Bridwell-Bowles, Lillian. 1992. "Discourse and Diversity: Experimental Writing within the Academy." *College Composition and Communication* 43: 349–368.

———. 1995. "Freedom, Form, Function: Varieties of Academic Discourse." *College Composition and Communication* 46: 46–61.

Brodkey, Linda. 1994. "Writing on the Bias." *College English* 56: 527–547.

Brooke, Robert. 1987. "Lacan, Transference, and Writing Instruction." *College English* 49: 679–691.

———. 1988. "Modeling a Writer's Identity: Reading and Imitation in the Writing Classroom." *College Composition and Communication* 39: 23–41.

———, Judith Levin, and Joy Ritchie. 1994. "Teaching Composition and Reading Lacan: An Exploration in Wild Analysis." *Writing Theory and Critical Theory.* Edited by John Clifford and John Schilb. New York: MLA. 159–175.

Broughton, T. Alan. 1993. "Preparing the Way," "On This Side of the Canvas," "Death as a Cloudless Day," and "Refuge." *Prairie Schooner* 67 (Fall): 51–55.

Bruffee, Kenneth A. 1984. "Peer Tutoring and the 'Conversation of Mankind.'" In *Writing Centers: Theory and Administration.* Edited by Gary A. Olson. Urbana, IL: NCTE. 3–15.

Cain, Mary Ann. 1995. *Revisioning Writers' Talk: Gender and Culture in Acts of Composing.* Albany, NY: State University of New York Press.

Chappell, Fred. 1992. "First Attempts." In *My Poor Elephant: 27 Male Writers at Work.* Edited by Eve Shelnutt. Atlanta, GA: Longstreet. 17–29.

Clark, Beverly Lyon, and Sonja Weidenhaupt. 1992. "On Blocking and Unblocking Sonja: A Case Study in Two Voices." *College Composition and Communication* 43: 55–74.

Clark, Irene L. 1993. "Portfolio Grading and the Writing Center." *The Writing Center Journal* 13: 48–62.

Clark, Suzanne. 1994. "Rhetoric, Social Construction, and Gender: Is It Bad to Be Sentimental?" In *Writing Theory and Critical Theory.* Edited by John Clifford and John Schilb. New York: MLA. 96–108.

Con Davis, Robert. 1987. "Pedagogy, Lacan, and the Freudian Subject." *College English* 49: 749–755.

Cooper, Marilyn. 1994a. "Really Useful Knowledge: A Cultural Studies Agenda for Writing Centers." *The Writing Center Journal* 14: 97–111.

———. 1994b. "Dialogic Learning across Disciplines." *Journal of Advanced Composition* 14: 531–546.

Copjec, Joan. 1989. "Cutting Up." In *Between Feminism and Psychoanalysis.* Edited by Teresa Brennan. London: Routledge. 227–246.

Crowley, Sharon. 1991. "A Personal Essay on Freshman English." *Pre/Text* 12.3–4: 156–176.

Daniell, Beth. 1994. "Composing (as) Power." *College Composition and Communication* 45: 238–246.

de Beauvoir, Simone. 1959. *Memoirs of a Dutiful Daughter.* Translated by James Kirkup. Cleveland, OH: World Publishing.

———. 1962. *The Prime of Life.* Translated by Peter Green. Cleveland, OH: World Publishing.

de Lauretis, Teresa. 1987. *Technologies of Gender.* Bloomington, IN: Indiana University Press.

Deletiner, Carole. 1992. "Crossing Lines." *College English* 54: 809–817.

Eady, Cornelius. 1993. "Photo of Dexter Gordon, About to Solo, 1965." *Prairie Schooner* 67 (Fall): 11.

Ebert, Teresa L. 1991. "The 'Difference' of Postmodern Feminism," *College English* 53: 886–904.

Ede, Lisa. 1994. "Reading the Writing Process." In *Taking Stock: The Writing Process Movement in the 90s.* Edited by Lad Tobin and Thomas Newkirk. Portsmouth, NH: Boynton/Cook. 31–43.

Elbow, Peter. 1973. *Writing without Teachers.* New York: Oxford University Press.

———. 1981. *Writing with Power.* New York: Oxford University Press.

———. 1987. "Closing My Eyes as I Speak: An Argument for Ignoring Audience." *College English* 49: 50–69.

———, and Pat Belanoff. 1989. *Community of Writers.* New York: McGraw-Hill.

———. 1990. *What Is English?* New York: MLA.

Elliott, Gayle. 1994. "Pedagogy in Penumbra: Teaching, Writing, and Feminism in the Fiction Workshop." In *Colors of a Different Horse: Rethinking Creative Writing Theory and Pedagogy.* Edited by Wendy Bishop and Hans Ostrom. Urbana, IL: NCTE. 100–126.

Ellsworth, Elizabeth. 1989. "Why Doesn't This Feel Empowering? Working through the Repressive Myths of Critical Pedagogy." *Harvard Educational Review* 59: 297–324.

Faigley, Lester. 1992. *Fragments of Rationality: Postmodernity and the Subject of Composition.* Pittsburgh, PA: University of Pittsburgh Press.

———, and Stephen Witte. 1981. "Analyzing Revision." *College Composition and Communication* 32: 400–414.

Felman, Shoshana. 1987. *Jacques Lacan and the Adventure of Insight: Psychoanalysis in Contemporary Culture.* Cambridge, MA: Harvard University Press.

———. 1993. *What Does a Woman Want?: Reading and Sexual Difference.* Baltimore, MD: Johns Hopkins University Press.

Flax, Jane. 1990. *Thinking Fragments: Psychoanalysis, Feminism, and Postmodernism in the Contemporary West.* Berkeley, CA: University of California Press.

Flieger, Jerry Aline. 1990. "The Female Subject: (What) Does Woman Want?" In *Psychoanalysis and . . .* Edited by Richard Feldstein and Henry Sussman.

New York: Routledge. 54–63.

Flower, Linda. 1979. "Writer-Based Prose: A Cognitive Basis for Problems in Writing." *College English* 41: 19–37.

———, John Hayes, Linda Carey, et al. 1986. "Detection, Diagnosis, and the Strategies of Revision." *College Composition and Communication* 37: 16–55.

Freire, Paulo. 1992 (1970). *Pedagogy of the Oppressed.* New York: Continuum.

Freud, Sigmund. 1962a. *Dora: An Analysis of a Case of Hysteria.* New York: Collier/Macmillan.

———. 1962b (1958). *The Standard Edition of the Complete Psychological Works of Sigmund Freud.* Edited and translated by James Strachey. London: Hogarth.

Frey, Olivia. 1990. "Beyond Literary Darwinism: Women's Voices and Critical Discourse." *College English* 52: 507–526.

Fuller, Margaret. 1992. *The Essential Margaret Fuller.* Edited by Jeffrey Steele. New Brunswick, NJ: Rutgers University Press.

Fulwiler, Toby. 1990. "Looking and Listening for My Voice." *College Composition and Communication* 41: 214–220.

Gallop, Jane. 1982. *The Daughter's Seduction: Feminism and Psychoanalysis.* Ithaca, NY: Cornell University Press.

———. 1988. "The Seduction of an Analogy." In *Thinking through the Body.* New York: Columbia University Press.

Gere, Anne Ruggles. 1994. "Kitchen Tables and Rented Rooms: The Extracurriculum of Composition." *College Composition and Communication* 45: 75–92.

Gillam, Alice M. 1991. "Writing Center Ecology: A Bakhtinian Perspective." *The Writing Center Journal* 11: 3–11.

Glass, James M. 1993. *Shattered Selves: Multiple Personality in a Postmodern World.* Ithaca, NY: Cornell University Press.

Gore, Jennifer. 1993. *The Struggle for Pedagogies: Critical and Feminist Discourses as Regimes of Truth.* New York: Routledge.

Harris, Muriel. 1995. "Talking in the Middle: Why Writers Need Writing Tutors." *College English* 57: 27–42.

Haynes-Burton, Cynthia. 1994. "'Hanging Your Alias on Their Scene': Writing Centers, Graffiti, and Style." *Writing Center Journal* 14: 112–124.

Heath, Shirley Brice. 1982. *Ways with Words: Language, Life, and Work in Communities and Classrooms.* Cambridge, MA: Cambridge University Press.

———. 1994. "Finding in History the Right to Estimate." *College Composition and Communication* 45: 97–102.

Helmers, Marguerite H. 1994. *Writing Students: Composition Testimonials and Representations of Students.* Albany, NY: State University of New York Press.

Herzberg, Bruce. 1994. "Community Service and Critical Teaching." *College Composition and Communication* 45: 307–319.

hooks, bell. 1989. *Talking Back.* Boston, MA: South End Press.

Horner, Bruce. 1994. "Mapping Errors and Expectations for Basic Writing: From the 'Frontier Field' to 'Border Country.'" *English Education* 26: 29–51.

Hunter, Ian. 1988. *Culture and Government: The Emergence of Literacy Education.* London: Macmillan.

Jardine, Alice. 1989. "Notes for an Analysis." In *Between Feminism and Psychoanalysis.* Edited by Teresa Brennan. London: Routledge. 73–85.

Jouve, Nicole Ward. 1991. *White Woman Speaks with Forked Tongue: Criticism as Autobiography.* London: Routledge.

Kalpakian, Laura. 1991. "My Life as a Boy." In *The Confidence Woman: 26 Women Writers at Work.* Edited by Eve Shelnutt. Atlanta, GA: Longstreet. 43–57.

Kingston, Maxine Hong. 1976. *The Woman Warrior: Memories of a Girlhood among Ghosts.* New York: Knopf.

Kirsch, Gesa B. 1993. *Women Writing the Academy: Audience, Authority, and Transformation.* Carbondale, IL: Southern Illinois University Press.

Knoblauch, C. H. 1990. "Literacy and the Politics of Education." In *The Right to Literacy.* Edited by Andrea A. Lunsford, Helene Moglen, and James Slevin. New York: MLA. 74–80.

———. 1991. "Critical Teaching and Dominant Culture." In *Composition and Resistance.* Edited by C. Mark Hurlbert and Michael Blitz. Portsmouth, NH: Heinemann. 12–21.

———, and Lil Brannon. 1993. *Critical Teaching and the Idea of Literacy.* Portsmouth, NH: Boynton/Cook.

Kristeva, Julia. 1986a. "A New Type of Intellectual: The Dissident." Translated by Sean Hand. In *The Kristeva Reader.* Edited by Toril Moi. New York: Columbia University Press.

———. 1986b. "Women's Time." Translated by Alice Jardine and Harry Blake. *The Kristeva Reader.* Edited by Toril Moi. New York: Columbia University Press.

———. 1987. *In the Beginning Was Love: Psychoanalysis and Faith.* Translated by Arthur Goldhammer. New York: Columbia University Press.

Lacan, Jacques. 1977a. *Ecrits: A Selection.* Translated by Alan Sheridan. New York: Norton.

———. 1977b. *The Four Fundamental Concepts of Psychoanalysis.* Translated by Alan Sheridan. London: Hogarth.

Lamb, Catherine. 1991. "Beyond Argument in Feminist Composition." *College Composition and Communication* 42: 11–24.

Le Dœuff, Michele. 1989. *The Philosophical Imaginary.* Translated by Colin Gordon. Stanford, CA: Stanford University Press.

———. 1990. "Women, Reason, Etc." *Differences: A Journal of Feminist Cultural Studies* 2: 1–13.

———. 1991. *Hipparchia's Choice: An Essay Concerning Women, Philosophy, etc.* Translated by Trista Selous. Oxford: Blackwell.

———. 1993. "Harsh Times." *New Left Review* 199 (May–June): 127–139.

Leverenz, Carrie Shively. 1994. "Peer Response in the Multicultural Composition Classroom: Dissensus — A Dream (Deferred)." *Journal of Advanced Composition* 14: 167–186.

Lorde, Audre. 1980. *The Cancer Journals.* Argyle, NY: Spinsters.

Lu, Min-Zhan. 1994. "Professing Multiculturalism: The Politics of Style in the Contact Zone." *College Composition and Communication* 45: 442–458.

Lunsford, Andrea. 1991. "Collaboration, Control, and the Idea of a Writing Center." *The Writing Center Journal* 12: 3–10.

———, Helene Moglen, and James Slevin, eds. 1990. *The Right to Literacy.* New York: MLA.

Macrorie, Ken. 1970. *Telling Writing.* Rochelle Park, NJ: Hayden.

Marshall, Paule. 1984. *Praisesong for the Widow.* New York: Dutton.

Miller, Susan. 1994. "Composition as Cultural Artifact: Rethinking History as Theory." In *Writing Theory and Critical Theory.* Edited by John Clifford and

John Schilb. New York: MLA. 19–32.

Moi, Toril. 1989. "Patriarchal Thought and the Drive for Knowledge." In *Between Feminism and Psychoanalysis*. Edited by Teresa Brennan. London: Routledge. 189–205.

Morrison, Toni. 1970. *The Bluest Eye*. New York: Washington Square.

Morson, Gary Saul. 1994. *Narrative and Freedom: The Shadows of Time*. New Haven, CT: Yale University Press.

Mortensen, Peter, and Gesa E. Kirsch. 1993. "On Authority in the Study of Writing." *College Composition and Communication* 44: 556–572.

Murphy, Ann. 1989. "Transference and Resistance in the Basic Writing Classroom: Problematics and Praxis." *College Composition and Communication* 40: 175–187.

Murray, Donald M. 1982. "Teaching the Other Self: The Writer's First Reader." *College Composition and Communication* 33: 140–147.

———. 1995 (1991). *The Craft of Revision*. 2nd ed. Fort Worth, TX: Harcourt Brace.

North, Stephen. 1984. "The Idea of a Writing Center." *College English* 46: 433–446.

———. 1990. "Personal Writing, Professional Ethos, and the Voice of 'Common Sense.'" *Pre/Text* 11.1–2: 105–119.

O'Brien, Tim. 1990. *The Things They Carried*. New York: Penguin.

———. 1994. "The Vietnam in Me." *The New York Times Magazine* October 2: 48–57.

O'Connor, Frank. 1988. "Guests of the Nation." In *Fiction 100*, 5th ed. Edited by James H. Pickering. New York: Macmillan. 1227–1235.

Ohmann, Richard. 1976. *English in America: A Radical View of the Profession*. New York: Oxford University Press.

Olsen, Tillie. 1976 (1956). "I Stand Here Ironing." In *Tell Me a Riddle*. New York: Dell.

Osborn, Susan. 1991. "'Revision/Re-Vision': A Feminist Writing Class." *Rhetoric Review* 9: 258–273.

Pontalis, J. B. 1978. "On Death-Work in Freud, in the Self, in Culture." In *Psychoanalysis, Creativity, and Literature*. Edited by Alan Roland. New York: Columbia University Press. 85–95.

Pratt, Mary Louise. 1991. "Arts of the Contact Zone." In *Profession*. New York: MLA. 33–40.

Pratt, Minnie Bruce. 1991. *Rebellion: Essays 1980–1991*. Ithaca, NY: Firebrand.

Quandahl, Ellen. 1994. "The Anthropological Sleep of Composition." *Journal of Advanced Composition* 14: 413–429.

Ragland-Sullivan, Ellie. 1987. *Jacques Lacan and the Philosophy of Psychoanalysis*. Urbana and Chicago, IL: University of Illinois Press.

Recchio, Thomas. 1991. "A Bakhtinian Reading of Student Writing." *College Composition and Communication* 42: 446–454.

———. 1994. "On the Critical Necessity of 'Essaying.'" In *Taking Stock: The Writing Process Movement in the 90s*. Edited by Lad Tobin and Thomas Newkirk. Portsmouth, NH: Boynton/Cook. 219–235.

Rich, Adrienne. 1979. "When We Dead Awaken: Writing as Re-Vision." In *On Lies, Secrets, and Silence*. New York: Norton.

Ritchie, Joy. 1990. "Between the Trenches and the Ivory Towers: Divisions between University Professors and High School Teachers." In *Farther Along: Transforming Dichotomies in Rhetoric and Composition*. Edited by Kate Ronald and Hephzibah Roskelly. Portsmouth, NH: Boynton/Cook. 101–121.

Robinson, Marilynne. 1982. *Housekeeping.* New York: Bantam.

Rorty, Richard. 1991. "Feminism and Pragmatism." *Michigan Quarterly Review* 30 (Spring): 231–258.

Rose, Mike. 1989. *Lives on the Boundary: The Struggles and Achievements of America's Underprepared.* New York: Free Press; London: Collier Macmillan.

Rosenblatt, Louise. 1983 (1938). *Literature as Exploration.* 4th ed. New York: MLA.

———. 1993. "The Transactional Theory: Against Dualisms." *College English* 55: 377–386.

Rowbotham, Sheila. 1973. *Woman's Consciousness, Man's World.* London: Penguin.

Rushdie, Salman. 1990. *Haroun and the Sea of Stories.* New York: Viking.

Schuster, Charles I. 1985. "Mikhail Bakhtin as Rhetorical Theorist." *College English* 47: 594–607.

Severino, Carol. 1994. "Writing Centers as Linguistic Contact Zones and Borderlands." *The Writing Lab Newsletter* 19 (December): 1–5.

Shelnutt, Eve. 1989. *The Writing Room: Keys to the Craft of Fiction and Poetry.* Marietta, GA: Longstreet.

Silko, Leslie Marmon. 1977. *Ceremony.* New York: Viking Press.

Smith, Frank. 1986. *Insult to Intelligence: The Bureaucratic Invasion of Our Classrooms.* New York: Arbor House.

Sommers, Nancy. 1980. "Revision Strategies of Student Writers and Experienced Adult Writers." *College Composition and Communication* 31: 378–388.

Spellmeyer, Kurt. 1994. "Lost in the Funhouse: The Teaching of Writing and the Problem of Professional Narcissism." Division on the Teaching of Writing. MLA Convention. San Diego, CA. 29 December.

Sperling, Melanie, and Sarah Warshauer Freedman. 1987. "A Good Girl Writes Like a Good Girl." *Written Communication* 4: 343–369.

Spivak, Gayatri Chakravorty. 1989. "Feminism and Deconstruction Again: Negotiating with Unacknowledged Masculinism." In *Between Feminism and Psychoanalysis.* Edited by Teresa Brennan. London: Routledge. 206–223.

Stone, Leo. 1984. *Transference and Its Context: Selected Papers on Psychoanalysis.* New York: J. Aronson.

Su, Adrienne. 1993. "Alice Descending the Rabbit-Hole." *Prairie Schooner* 67 (Fall): 34–35.

Sunstein, Bonnie. 1994. *Composing a Culture: Inside a Summer Writing Program with High School Teachers.* Portsmouth, NH: Boynton/Cook.

Tobin, Lad. 1993. *Writing Relationships: What Really Happens in the Composition Class.* Portsmouth, NH: Boynton/Cook.

Tompkins, Jane. 1987. "Me and My Shadow." *New Literary History* 19: 169–178.

———. 1988. "Fighting Words: Unlearning to Write the Critical Essay." *Georgia Review* 42: 585–590.

———. 1992. "The Way We Live Now." *Change* 24 (November/December): 15–19.

Trimbur, John. 1989. "Consensus and Difference in Collaborative Learning." *College English* 51: 602–616.

———. 1994. "Taking the Social Turn: Teaching Writing Post-Process." *College Composition and Communication* 45: 108–118.

Trinh, T. Minh-ha. 1989. *Woman, Native, Other: Writing Postcoloniality and*

Feminism. Bloomington, IN: Indiana University Press.

Warnock, Tilly, and John Warnock. 1984. "Liberatory Writing Centers: Restoring Authority to Writers." In *Writing Centers: Theory and Administration*. Edited by Gary A. Olson. Urbana, IL: NCTE. 16–23.

Weesner, Theodore. 1987 (1967). *The Car Thief.* New York: Vintage.

Welch, Nancy. 1993. "Resisting the Faith: Conversion, Resistance, and the Training of Teachers." *College English* 55: 387–401.

———. 1994. "The Cheating Kind." *Other Voices* 20 (Spring): 37–45.

———. 1996. "The Road from Prosperity." *Threepenny Review* 64 (Winter): 14–16.

Winnicott, D. W. 1971. *Playing and Reality*. London: Tavistock.

Winterowd, W. Ross. 1965. *Rhetoric and Writing*. Boston, MA: Allyn and Bacon.

Woodruff, Jay, ed. 1993. *A Piece of Work: Five Writers Discuss Their Revisions*. Iowa City, IA: University of Iowa Press.

Woolbright, Meg. 1992. "The Politics of Tutoring: Feminism with the Patriarchy." *The Writing Center Journal* 13: 16–30.

Wright, Elizabeth. 1989 (1984). *Psychoanalytic Criticism: Theory in Practice*. London: Routledge.

Welch's Insights as a Resource for Your Teaching

1. Welch values a vision of writing that runs counter to mainstream academic discourse. What practical difficulties might this vision present in your teaching, and how might you work around them?

2. What do you make of Welch's use of psychoanalytic concepts to understand revision? How might some of these tools be helpful in understanding other phases of composing and other aspects of teaching writing?

Welch's Insights as a Resource for Your Writing Classroom

1. Ask your students to reconsider a "finished" piece of writing. What would they add to it if they were to lengthen it a great deal? What digressions would they undertake? Help them to realize that they are not simply tacking on more prose but are free to explore digressions that may entirely change the focus and thrust of the paper.

2. Ask your students to reflect on some of the potential digressions they delineated in question 1 as potential topics for future essays. Would they want to pursue any of these further? If so, which ones, and why?

Crafting Sentences

The Erasure of the Sentence

Robert J. Connors

During the 1970s, the field of composition was briefly dominated by sentence-level pedagogies. In this article from the September 2000 issue of College Composition and Communication, *Robert J. Connors describes the emergence and reception of three teaching methods that focused on improving students' syntactical skills: Francis Christensen's generative rhetoric, exercises in imitation, and sentence combining. Connors goes on to account for several changes in teacher attitudes — including negative reactions to formalism, behaviorism, and empiricism — that contributed to the quick disappearance of sentence rhetorics. The discrediting of these methods owed little to a well-developed critique; in fact, the experimental results that supported sentence pedagogies were never disproved. Connors suggests that we re-evaluate the usefulness of sentence-level rhetorics and our reasons for neglecting them.*

In the 1980s, as composition studies matured, theoretical and critical interrogation of much of the field's received wisdom began in earnest. The field of composition studies, increasingly in the hands of the new generation of trained specialist Ph.D.'s, began to do more and more effectively what intellectual fields have always done: define, subdivide, and judge the efforts of members. Some elements of the older field of composition teaching became approved and burgeoned, while others were tacitly declared dead ends: lore-based and therefore uninteresting, scientistic and therefore suspect, mechanistic and therefore destructive. Little attention has been paid to these preterite elements in the older field of composition; they have been dropped like vestigial limbs, and most of those who once practiced or promoted those elements have retired or moved to more acceptable venues, maintaining a circumspect silence about their earlier flings with now-unpopular ideas such as paragraph theory, or structural linguistics, or stage-model developmental psychology. Of all of the inhabitants of this limbo of discarded approaches, there is no more dramatic and striking exemplar than what was called the school of syntactic methods. These sentence-based pedagogies rose from older syntax-oriented teaching methods to an extraordinary moment in the sun during the 1970s bidding fair to become methodologically hegemonic. But like the mayfly, their day was brief though intense, and these pedagogies are hardly mentioned now in mainstream composition studies except as of faint historical interest. The sentence itself as an element of composition pedagogy is hardly mentioned today outside of textbooks. But we can learn as much from watching the working out of Darwinian intellectual failures as from participating in the self-congratulatory normal science of the current winners, and so I offer this history of syntactic methods since 1960 in the spirit of the old New England gravestone: "As you are now, so once was I; as I am now, so you shall be."

From the earliest point in American composition-rhetoric, the sentence was a central component of what students were asked to study, practice, and become conversant with. From the 1890s onward, chapters on The Sentence in most textbooks were fairly predictable. Western rhetorical theories about the sentence date back to classical antiquity, with roots in Latin grammar and in the oral rhetorical theories of the classical period, and they came to their nineteenth-century form by a long process of accretion. Traditional sentence pedagogy assumed grammatical knowledge of the sort inculcated by Reed and Kellogg diagrams, but the prime elements in these textbook chapters were taxonomic, all this time focused on their place in sentence construction. Along with the breakdown of sentences by grammatical types — simple, compound, complex, and compound-complex — which was usually taken up in the grammar chapters of textbooks, the traditional classification of sentences is by function: declarative, imperative, interrogative, and exclamatory sentences. The traditional rhetorical classifications of sentences were also covered: long and short, loose and periodic, and balanced. In addition, sentence pedagogy nearly always included coverage of the old abstractions that informed modern composition-rhetoric from 1890 through the present: those of Adams Sherman Hill (clearness, energy, force), Barrett Wendell (unity, coherence, emphasis), or C. S. Baldwin (clearness and interest).[1]

All of these traditional sentence pedagogies included many exercises and much practice, and we fail to understand them if we think of them only as defined by their abstractions and classifications. Most sentence chapters in textbooks asked students to create many sentences, and indeed, sentence-level pedagogy was an important part of traditional writing courses. It became even more central during the 1950s, a period when composition teachers were looking to structural linguistics with expectation and sentence-writing was much discussed. But as I have discussed in more detail elsewhere (*Composition-Rhetoric* 162–70), it was just as structural linguistics was gaining a serious foothold in composition pedagogy that its theoretical bases came under sustained and successful attack from Noam Chomsky and the theory of transformational-generative grammar.

Here we enter a more familiar modern territory, the post-1960 era of composition and composition studies. And it is here that we find the beginnings of the three most important of the sentence-based rhetorics that were to seem so promising to writing teachers of the New Rhetoric era: the generative rhetoric of Francis Christensen, imitation exercises, and sentence-combining. I want to take up these three more modern syntactic methods in roughly chronological order, beginning with the ideas of Francis Christensen.

Christensen Rhetoric

Francis Christensen, a professor of English at the University of Southern California, began to publish essays in the early 1960s complaining that traditional theories of the sentence widely taught throughout the first sixty years of this century were primarily taxonomic rather than generative or productive. Except in providing examples, they were not of much real help to teachers in showing students how to write good sentences. In 1963, Christensen published what is arguably his most important article, "A Generative Rhetoric of the Sentence." In this article and in other works published up to his death in 1970, Christensen described a new way of viewing sentences and a pedagogical method that could be used to teach students how to write longer, more mature, more varied and interesting sentences.

In the opening sentence of "A Generative Rhetoric of the Sentence," he announced his intentions: "If a new grammar is to be brought to bear on composition, it must be brought to bear on the rhetoric of the sentence" (155). Christensen was certain that the sentence is the most important element in rhetoric because it is "a natural and isolable unit" ("Course" 168). Complaining that the traditional conceptions of the sentence were merely descriptive, Christensen argued that traditional sentence pedagogy simply did not help students learn to write. "We do not really teach our captive charges to write better — we merely expect them to" ("Generative" 155). Christensen indicated that both the grammatical and rhetorical classifications of sentences are equally barren in the amount of real assistance they give to students. "We need a rhetoric of the sentence that will do more than combine the ideas of primer sentences. We need one that will generate ideas" ("Generative" 155).

Christensen rhetoric did not follow the traditional canons of rhetoric, which begin with conceptualization or invention; instead it opted for a view that all other skills in language follow syntactic skills naturally. According to Christensen, you could be a good writer if you could learn to write a good sentence. His pedagogy consisted of short base-level sentences to which students were asked to attach increasingly sophisticated systems of initial and final modifying clauses and phrases — what he called "free modifiers." Effective use of free modifiers would result in effective "cumulative sentences," and Christensen's most famous observation about teaching the cumulative sentence was that he wanted to push his students "to level after level, not just two or three, but four, five, or six, even more, as far as the students' powers of observation will take them. I want them to become sentence acrobats, to dazzle by their syntactic dexterity" ("Generative" 160).

For some years after 1963, Christensen's syntactic rhetoric was widely discussed, praised, and damned. His few short articles — and all of them were contained in *Notes toward a New Rhetoric,* a book of 110 pages — created an intense interest in syntactic experimentation and innovation. Several experiments confirmed the effectiveness of using generative rhetoric with students. During the early 1970s, two published reports appeared on the use of the *Christensen Rhetoric Program* (an expensive boxed set of overhead transparencies and workbooks that had appeared in 1968). Charles A. Bond, after a rather loosely controlled experiment, reported that there was a "statistically significant difference" between the grades of a group of students taught using Christensen methods and those of a control group taught by conventional methods; he also mentioned that his students were enthusiastic about cumulative sentences. R. D. Walshe, teaching a group of adult night-class students in Australia (it is hard to imagine two groups of native-speaking English students as far removed from one another as Bond's American first-year students and Walshe's Australian working people), found that although some of Christensen's claims for his system were inflated, the *Christensen Rhetoric Program* generally worked well and was liked by his students.

These tests of Christensen's program were unscientific and anecdotal, and it was not until 1978 that a full-scale empirical research test was done on the Christensen system. The experiment's creator, Lester Faigley, began with two hypotheses: First, that the Christensen sentence method would increase syntactic maturity in those who used it (for a fuller discussion of the concept of syntactic maturity, see the next section of this paper), and second, that the Christensen rhetoric program as a whole would produce a measurable qualitative increase in writing skill. Faigley tested four experimental sections and four control sections in his experiment. The experimental sections used Christensen's *A New Rhetoric,* and the control sections used a well-known content-oriented rhetoric textbook, McCrimmon's *Writing with a Purpose.* Faigley proved both of his hypotheses; he found that the writing produced by the Christensen program not only was measurably more mature but also received better average ratings (.63 on a six-point scale; statistically significant) from blind holistic readings ("Generative" 179). Faigley's experiment showed that the Christensen method does produce measurable classroom results.

Imitation

The argument about Christensen rhetoric was in full swing during the middle 1960s when another syntactic method was first popularized: imitation exercises. Unlike Christensen rhetoric, imitation was part of the rediscovered trove of classical rhetorical theory that was coming to light in English departments. From the time of Isocrates and Aristotle, exercises in direct imitation and in the copying of structures had been recommended by theorists and teachers of rhetoric, and after Edward P. J. Corbett published his essay "The Uses of Classical Rhetoric" in 1963 and his *Classical Rhetoric for the Modern Student* in 1965, the use of imitation exercises in composition classes enjoyed a renaissance of popularity. There are, of course, different meanings for the term *imitation,* but in rhetoric it has always meant one thing: the emulation of the syntax of good prose models by students wishing to improve their writing or speaking styles. The recurring word used by the ancients concerning imitation, according to Corbett, was *similis;* the objective of imitation exercises was to make the student's writing similar to that of a superior writer ("Theory" 244). This similarity does not imply that the student's writing will be identical to the writing she imitates; the similarity that imitation promotes is not of content, but of form. Corbett recommends several different sorts of exercises, the first and simplest of which involved "copying passages, word for word from admired authors" ("Theory" 247). For students who have spent some time copying passages, Corbett recommends a second kind of imitation exercise: pattern practice. In this exercise, the student chooses or is given single sentences to use as patterns after which he or she is to design sentences of his or her own. "The aim of this exercise," says Corbett, "is not to achieve a word-for-word correspondence with the model but rather to achieve an awareness of the variety of sentence structure of which the English language is capable" ("Theory" 249). The model sentences need not be followed slavishly, but Corbett suggests that the student observe at least the same kind, number, and order of phrases and clauses.

After Corbett's initial arguments for imitation, other scholars took the method up as an important technique. As Winston Weathers and Otis Winchester put it in their 1969 textbook on imitation, *Copy and Compose,* writing "is a civilized art that is rooted in tradition" (2). The assumption that imitation makes about contemporary student writing is that it is often stylistically barren because of lack of familiarity with good models of prose style and that this barrenness can be remedied by an intensive course in good prose models. Weathers and Winchester — whose *Copy and Compose* and *The New Strategy of Style,* as well as Weathers's *An Alternate Style: Options in Composition,* recommended imitation as a primary exercise — became the most notable proponents of imitation. Weathers and Winchester used a slightly more complex model of imitation that did Corbett: They asked their students first to copy a passage, then to read a provided analysis of the model's structure, and finally to compose an imitation. During the 1970s, Frank D'Angelo, William Gruber, Penelope Starkey, S. Michael Halloran, and other writers all supported classically based imitation exercises as effective methods for attaining improved student sentence skills. A second set of imitation exercises proposed during the late 1960s and early 1970s were called "controlled composition exercises," and were actually a hybrid, melding some aspects of imitation and some aspects of sentence-combining. Controlled composition, according to Edmund Miller, is "the technique of having students copy a passage as they introduce some systematic change" (ii).

From the middle 1960s onward, a small but significant number of voices kept reproposing the value of imitation. Frank D'Angelo noted that imitation connoted counterfeiting and stereotyping in most people's minds, when it should connote originality and creativity. A student who practices imitation, he suggests, "may be spared at least some of the fumblings of the novice writer" for forms in which to express his thoughts (283). A "student will become more original as he engages in creative imitation," claimed D'Angelo (283). Weathers and Winchester took the argument further: "Originality and individuality are outgrowths of a familiarity with originality in the work of others, and they emerge from a knowledge of words, patterns, constructions and procedures that all writers use" (*Copy and Compose* 2).

Like Christensen rhetoric, imitation was put to the test, in this case by Rosemary Hake and Joseph Williams, who performed an experiment in 1977 that compared sentence-combining pedagogy with an imitation pedagogy that they evolved under the term "sentence expansion." Hake and Williams found that the students in their imitation group learned to write better expository prose with fewer flaws and errors than students using sentence-combining pedagogies ("Sentence" 143). Since sentence-combining was known by the late seventies to produce better syntactic results than non-sentence methods, this finding was important. Imitation, proponents claimed, provided students with practice in the "ability to design" that is the basis of a mature prose style. The different imitation techniques, whether they consist of direct copying of passages, composition of passages using models, or controlled mutation of sentence structures, all have this in common: They cause students to internalize the structures of the piece being imitated; as Corbett points out, internalization is the key term in imitation. With those structures internalized, a student is free to engage in the informed processes of choice, which are the wellspring of real creativity. William Gruber, writing in 1977, argued that imitation assists in design: "Standing behind imitation as a teaching method is the simple assumption that an inability to write is an inability to design — an inability to shape effectively the thought of a sentence, a paragraph, or an essay" (493–94). Gruber argued that imitation liberates students' personalities by freeing them of enervating design decisions, at least temporarily. Without knowledge of what has been done by others, claimed proponents of imitation exercises, there can be no profound originality.

The Sentence-Combining Juggernaut

Sentence-combining in its simplest form is the process of joining two or more short, simple sentences to make one longer sentence, using embedding, deletion, subordination, and coordination. In all probability sentence-combining was taught by the grammaticus of classical Rome, but such exercises have tended to be ephemera, and none has come down to us. Shirley Rose's article of 1983, "One Hundred Years of Sentence-Combining," traced the use of similar techniques back to the nineteenth century and argued that teachers asking students to combine short sentences into long ones was a pedagogy growing out of school-book grammar and structural grammar as well as more modern grammatical ideas (483).

While combining exercises can be found in the 1890s, it was not until 1957, when Noam Chomsky revolutionized grammatical theory with his book *Syntactic Structures,* that the theoretical base was established upon which modern sentence-combining pedagogies would be founded. This base was, of course, Chomskian transformational-generative (TG) grammar, which for a while caused tremendous excitement in the field of composition. TG grammar, which quickly swept both traditional and structural grammar aside in linguistics between 1957 and 1965, seemed at that time to present to composition the possibility of a new writing pedagogy based on the study of linguistic transformations. In 1963, Donald Bateman and Frank J. Zidonis of the Ohio State University conducted an experiment to determine whether teaching high-school students TG grammar would reduce the incidence of errors in their writing. They found that students taught TG grammar both reduced errors and developed the ability to write more complex sentence structures. Despite some questionable features in the Bateman and Zidonis study, it did suggest that learning TG grammar had an effect on student writing.

The Bateman and Zidonis study was published in 1964, and in that same year a study was published that was to have far more importance for sentence-combining: Kellogg Hunt's *Grammatical Structures Written at Three Grade Levels.* Francis Christensen had been using the term "syntactic fluency" since 1963, but Christensen's use of it was essentially qualitative and impressionistic. Hunt's work would become the basis for most measurements of "syntactic maturity," a quantitative term that came to be an important goal of sentence-combining. To recap Hunt's study quickly: He wished to find out what elements of writing changed as people matured and which linguistic structures seemed to be representative of mature writing. To this end he studied the writings of average students in the fourth, eighth, and twelfth grades and expository articles in *Harper's* and *The Atlantic.* At first Hunt studied sentence length, but he quickly became aware that the tendency of younger writers to string together many short clauses with "and" meant that sentence length was not a good indicator of maturity in writing. He studied clause length, and as he says, he "became more and more interested in what I will describe as one main clause plus whatever subordinate clauses happen to be attached to or embedded within it" ("Synopsis" 111). This is Hunt's most famous concept, the "minimal terminable unit" or "T-unit." "Each T-unit," says Hunt, is "minimal in length and each could be terminated grammatically between a capital and a period" (112).

The T-unit, Hunt found, was a much more reliable index of stylistic maturity than sentence length. Eventually he determined the three best indices of stylistic maturity: the average number of words per T-unit, the average number of clauses per T-unit, and the average number of words per clause. When applied to writing at different grade levels, he found that these numbers increased at a steady increment. [In Table 1] is a chart that Frank O'Hare adapted from Hunt's work and from similar work by Roy O'Donnell, William Griffin, and Raymond Norris. As you can see, the rise in these three indices over time is obvious. Although these preliminary studies of Bateman and Zidonis and of Hunt used no sentence-combining at all, they did represent the bases from which high-modern sentence-combining sprang: the methodological linguistic base of TG grammar and the empirical quantitative base of Hunt's studies of syntactic maturity.

These two bases were brought together in the first important experiment involving sentence-combining exercises, that of John Mellon in 1965. Mellon called the 1969 report of his experiment *Transformational Sentence-Combining: A Method for Enhancing the Development of Syntactic Fluency in English Composition,* and his was the first study actually asking students to practice combining kernel sentences rather than merely to learn grammar. "Research," wrote Mellon, ". . . clearly shows that memorized principles of grammar, whether conventional or modern, clearly play a negligible role in helping students achieve 'correctness' in their written expression" (15). What *could* help students do this, reasoned Mellon, was instruction in TG grammar plus practice exercises in combining short "kernel sentences" into longer, more complex sentences.

With Mellon's initial publication of his work in 1967 and then with the national publication by NCTE in 1969, sentence-combining was established as an important tool in helping students write more mature sentences. But the grammar question still remained open. Since Mellon had to spend so much time teaching the principles of TG grammar in order to allow his students to work on his complex exercises, there was doubt as to which activity — learning the grammar or doing the exercises — had gotten the results. After all, Bateman and Zidonis had gotten error reduction — though admittedly not scientifically measured growth — from mere TG grammar instruction alone. How much importance did the sentence-combining exercises really have?

These questions were put to rest once again and for all in 1973 with the publication of Frank O'Hare's research monograph *Sentence-Combining: Improving Student Writing without Formal Grammar Instruction.* This study, which was the spark that ignited the sentence-combining boom of the late 1970s, showed beyond a doubt that sentence-combining exercises, without any grammar instruction at all, could achieve important gains in syntactic maturity for students who used them. Testing seventh graders, O'Hare used sentence-combining exercises with his experimental group over a period of eight months without ever mentioning any of the formal rules of TG grammar. The control group was not exposed to sentence-combining at all.

O'Hare's test measured six factors of syntactic maturity and found that "highly significant growth had taken place on all six factors" (55). His experimental group of seventh graders, after eight months of

Table 1. Words per T-unit, clauses per T-unit, words per clause

| | **Grade Level** | | | | | | **Superior Adults** |
	3	**4**	**5**	**7**	**8**	**12**	
Words/T-unit	7.67	8.51	9.34	9.99	11.34	14.4	20.3
Clauses/T-unit	1.18	1.29	1.27	1.30	1.42	1.68	1.74
Words/Clause	6.5	6.6	7.4	7.7	8.1	8.6	11.5

O'Hare (22).

sentence-combining, now wrote an average of 15.75 words per T-unit, which was 9 percent higher than the 14.4 words per T-unit Hunt had reported as the average of twelfth graders. The other factors were similarly impressive. Just as important as the maturity factors, though, were the results of a second hypothesis O'Hare was testing: whether the sentence-combining group would write compositions that would be judged better in overall quality than those of the control group. Eight experienced English teachers rated 240 experimental and control essays written after the eight-month test period, and when asked to choose between matched pairs of essays, chose an experimental-group essay 70 percent of the time. The results suggested that sentence-combining exercises not only improved syntactic maturity but also affected perceived quality of writing in general.

The O'Hare study focused interest in sentence-combining, which had been associated with Mellon's complex directions, as a pedagogic tool. A follow-up study by Warren E. Combs found that the gains in writing quality that were produced by O'Hare's methods persisted over time and were still notable as long as two months after the sentence-combining practice had been discontinued. Textbooks began to appear using sentence-combining exercises, notably William Strong's *Sentence-Combining: A Composing Book* in 1973, which used "open" exercises, and O'Hare's own *Sentencecraft* of 1975. There remained now only one important question about sentence-combining: Was it useful for first-year students in college, or were they too old to be helped by the practice it gave? There was no doubt that it worked at the secondary-school level, but an article by James Ney in 1975 describing his attempts to use sentence-combining in a first-year class cast doubt of the technique's usefulness for eighteen year olds. Some teachers who had tried small doses of sentence-combining in first-year classes anecdotally reported no noticeable change in student writing.

Were college students too old for syntactic methods? This last question was answered in 1978 by the publication of the first results of a large and impressively rigorous study conducted under an Exxon grant at Miami University of Ohio by Donald A. Daiker, Andrew Kerek, and Max Morenberg. This college-level study used ninety of William Strong's "open" exercises and others created by the Miami researchers. These "open" exercises, some of which were lengthy and gave considerable stylistic and creative leeway to students, gave no directions on how best to complete them, and thus there was no "correct" answer or combination. Daiker, Kerek, and Morenberg's experimental and control groups each consisted of six sections of first-year college students, and their experiment was conducted over a fifteen-week semester (245–48). The Miami researchers found that their experimental group, like O'Hare's, evidenced both statistically meaningful gains in syntactic maturity and a gain in overall quality of the writing they produced. Daiker, Kerek, and Morenberg's sentence-combining group moved during the experiment from a high-twelfth-grade-level of syntactic maturity to a level approximating high-sophomore- or junior-level college writing skills. In addition, their experimental group showed statistically significant gains in three qualitative measures of general essay quality: holistic, forced-choice, and analytic (Morenberg, Daiker, and Kerek 250–52).

The late 1970s, just after the Miami experiment, were the high-water mark for sentence-combining. The literature grew so fast it was difficult to keep up with it; Daiker and his colleagues hosted an entire large conference devoted to sentence-combining at Miami in 1978 and another in 1983; scores of normal-science experiments were conducted using it in classrooms across the nation during the early 1980s. The lesson of sentence-combining was simple but compelling; as O'Hare said, "writing behavior can be changed fairly rapidly and with relative ease" (68). The result: Sentence-combining was a land-rush for a time. Between 1976 and 1983, there were no fewer than 49 articles in major journals about sentence-combining and hundreds of papers and conference presentations.[2] The success of the method provoked nasty quarrels about who "owned" it or had a moral right to profit from it. Revisionist narratives about development of the technique were published. Everyone, it seemed, wanted a piece of the pie now that it had been proven so tasty.

With the potency during the early 1980s of the movement toward empirical research — a movement that had been materially strengthened by the popularity of some of the sentence-combining research — we might expect that sentence-combining would have continued as a potent force in the developing field of composition studies. The research was there; the pedagogy was usable by almost any teacher and provided results that could be seen impressionistically as well as measured; the method had powerful champions. It had been long assumed that sentence-combining could be a useful part of a complete rhetoric program, but by the late 1970s, the venerable Kellogg Hunt was suggesting that sentence-combining was so useful that it should take up all class time in a first-year course, that "in every sense, sentence-combining can be [a] comprehensive writing program in and of itself, for at least one semester" ("Anybody" 156).

Look upon my works, ye mighty, and despair.

The Counterforces

In an astonishing reversal of fortune for sentence rhetorics, the triumphalism, the quarrels, and the debates of the early 1980s — now mostly forgotten — died away after 1983 or so. The articles on sentence issues fell away radically, and those that were written were more and more about applications to learning disabilities, or English as a second language, or special education. Erstwhile syntactic rhetoricians turned to other issues. The devaluation of sentence-based rhetorics is a complex phenomenon, and we need to approach it with circumspection. Let me first try to establish the reality of what I'm calling the "erasure of the sentence" in clearly numerical terms. Table 2 lists raw numbers of books and articles appearing in general-composition journals about the three sentence rhetorics discussed in this essay.

While I can't claim that this chart, which I derived from a combination of ERIC searching and my own research, is exhaustive or even directly replicable, the numbers themselves are less important than the trends they show. And these numerical trends strongly match our intuitive sense of what has been going on. We see, starting with Christensen's first articles in the early 1960s, a strong interest in sentence-writing that was mostly taken up with generative rhetoric and imitation during the early period of the New Rhetoric, say, 1963–1975. After 1976, the interest in Christensen begins to peter out as sentence-combining gathers momentum; a truly extraordinary burst of activity occurred in the late 1970s and early 1980s. But after 1984, general articles on sentence-combining died out, and more and more of the essays published had to do with use of sentence-combining in classes in English as a second language or with behaviorally disordered or autistic students; an ERIC search shows only three essays published on general-composition sentence-combining after 1986. The few general articles that were published after 1986 came more and more to be critical, but even the criticisms died away. After the mid-1980s, the sentence rhetorics of the 1960s and 1970s were gone, at least from books and journals.[3] Shirley Rose's 1983 article on the history of sentence-combining, which probably felt when she wrote it like a historical background to a vital part of the field, now looks more like the *ave atque vale* of the field to sentence-combining.

What iceberg did this *Titanic* meet? It was not a sudden ending, certainly; there had been criticism of sentence rhetorics going back to the 1960s. There had been some sentence-combining studies reporting equivocal results. There had been arguments over the differences between Christensen's "syntactic fluency" and Hunt's "syntactic maturity." And there had been ongoing questions about the meaning and validity of T-units and the relationship between syntactic maturity and holistically rated writing quality. But all of these had been essentially

	Christensen	Imitation	Sentence-combining
Table 2. Books and composition journal articles about sentence rhetorics, 1960–1998			
1960–1965	4	1	1
1966–1970	13	2	2
1971–1975	12	5	3
1976–1980	6	4	31
1981–1985	2	3	23
1986–1990	2	5	3
1991–1998	1	2	2

in-house issues, methodological or pragmatic, mostly waged in the pages of *Research in the Teaching of English.* By the early 1980s, sentence rhetorics had been criticized by some theorists for over fifteen years — but finally the criticisms were coming to bite.

That this devaluation of sentence rhetorics took place slowly meant that it was not noticeable as such by most people in the field. But once noted, it stands out as quite an extraordinary phenomenon. The story of sentence rhetorics is analogous, perhaps, to that of the U.S. space exploration effort of the 1960s. John F. Kennedy determined in 1961 that we would beat the Russians to the moon, and as a result of amazing effort, technological breakthrough, heart-rending sacrifice, and incalculable spondulix, *Apollo 11* landed on the Mare Tranquilitatis in 1969. We went back a few more times, put up flags, drove about in dune-buggies, collected dusty gray rocks, and came home. We had seen what it had to offer. And after a while, we did not go back anymore.

Similarly, in the early 1960s, a few scholars in composition determined to update the ages-old notion that students needed to be able to write good sentences before they could write good essays. Through new discovery, imaginative application of literary ideas, grammatical theory, and empirical research breakthroughs, methods and measurements were evolved that could determine whether student writers were writing better sentences. Teaching methods relating to the measurements were tested, and they succeeded, repeatedly and incontrovertibly, in producing better sentence writers. In addition, researchers determined that there was indeed a correlation between sentence skill and general perceived writing skill, discovering repeatedly that experimental sentence-writing groups were also holistically rated better writers. The techniques were honed and refined for different levels, and they finally appear in easily usable textbooks available to all. We had said we wanted newer and better teaching techniques, and the sentence rhetorics of the 1960s and 1970s provided them. And, as a discipline, we then peered quizzically at what we had wrought, frowned, and declared that no, this was not what we had really wanted. We had seen what it had to offer. And after a while, we did not go back any more.

To understand the reasons for the erasure of sentence rhetorics, we need to look at the kinds of criticism that were leveled at them almost as soon as they demonstrated any success. It will become apparent, doing this, that sentence rhetorics were not dragged under by any sudden radical uprising in the early 1980s, but rather finally succumbed to an entire line of criticism that had been ongoing for at least fifteen years. The reasons for the erasure of the sentence are multiple and complex, but as we look back over the varied critiques of syntactic rhetorics that were leveled beginning with Johnson, I think we can induce some general themes — themes that I would argue represent an important, if sometimes tacit, set of underlife definitions for composition studies in the past two decades.

The first and most obvious of the lines of criticism that would engulf sentence rhetorics was what we might call anti-formalism — the idea that any pedagogy based in form rather than in content was automatically suspect. Some part of this anti-formalist position is a result of distrust of traditional textbook pedagogies, what we might call the reaction against rhetorical atomism. For much of rhetorical history, and certainly for all of the history of composition, the pedagogical method of taking discourse apart into its constituent components and working on those components separately had been accepted almost absolutely. In American composition-rhetoric, this meant the familiar textbook breakdown of the "levels" of discourse — the word, the sentence, the paragraph, the essay. The great difference between the early New Rhetoric of the 1960s and 1970s and the work that came after it is largely found in the New-Rhetoric acceptance of atomistic formal levels up until the late 1970s and the later rejection of them. The first exposition of this point was by James Moffett in his classic 1968 book *Teaching the Universe of Discourse,* in which Moffett surveyed sentence rhetorics (including Christensen and early [Mellon] sentence-combining) and concluded that teachers must "leave the sentence within its broader discursive context" (186). Teachers can help students relate to syntactic options only in the context of a whole discourse, Moffett believed, and thus a teacher can only help a student "if the units of learning are units larger than the hindsight sentence." He criticized traditional writing pedagogy for moving from "little particle to big particle" toward the whole composition. "For the learner," Moffett wrote, "basics are not the small-focus technical things but broad things like meaning and motivation, purpose and point, which are precisely what are missing from exercises" (205). This was a line of attack that came to be heard more and more often.

We first see it in responses to Francis Christensen's work, which began to draw criticism almost as soon as it was formulated. The ink was hardly dry on the large and ambitious *Christensen Rhetoric Program,* Christensen's expensive boxed set of workbooks and projector overlays, when the first serious critique of his theory was published in 1969. Sabina Thorne Johnson, in an article called "Some Tentative Strictures on Generative Rhetoric," admitted that Christensen offered "a revolution in our assessment of style and in our approach to the teaching of composition" (159), but she also had some important reservations about the *generative* nature of the cumulative sentence. Johnson's critique was essential: "Christensen seems to believe that form can generate content (*Program*, p. vi). I don't believe it can, especially if the content is of an analytical or critical nature" (159). Johnson went on to criticize Christensen's reliance upon narrative and descriptive writing for his examples and as the basis for his theory, complaining that narrative and descriptive skills seldom carry over to exposition. She initiated a line of argument against syntactic methods that later came to seem conclusive: that students need training in higher-level skills such as invention and organization more than they need to know how to be "sentence acrobats."

Christensen himself died (of natural causes) shortly after Johnson's article appeared, and the attack on his theory led to a colorful exchange between Johnson and Christensen's widow Bonniejean that can be surveyed in back issues of *College English*. This debate was joined by A. M. Tibbetts, who made several telling points. Although Christensen is useful in the classroom, said Tibbetts, the claims he made for his system are simply "not empirically true as stated" (142). It is true that pattern practice with cumulative sentences can help students learn to use free modifiers, Tibbetts continued, but that is only one of the skills writers need. While he admitted that Christensen's method produced clever sentences from students, Tibbetts complained that that was part of the problem. "What we are generally after in expository writing," Tibbetts warned, "is accuracy rather than cleverness" (144). He rearticulated Johnson's reservations about the formal generativity of the Christensen rhetoric program. Christensen's theory, argued Tibbetts, is not designed to teach young people how to do the most valuable things any grammar-rhetoric should be designed to teach — how to think; how to separate and define issues; how to isolate fallacies; how to make generalizations and value judgments — in brief, how to express the truths and realities of our time and how to argue for improvements. He criticizes, as did Johnson, Christensen's "fiction fallacy," as he calls it: the idea that students should learn to write like Welty and Faulkner. Narrative and descriptive writing, Tibbetts claims, require no logical analysis and lead to "arty, false descriptions of adolescent mental states" (143). If you want nothing but "sentence acrobats," Tibbetts warned, "you are likely to get what you deserve — dexterous rhetorical acrobats who dexterously tell untruths" (143).

W. Ross Winterowd, no enemy to linguistic issues in composition, also questioned Christensen's work in 1975, when he pointed out that Christensen rhetoric exercises "take sentences out of the living content of the rhetorical situation and make them into largely meaningless dry runs" (338). Although he was himself trained in linguistics, Winterowd had deep reservations about large claims made for formalist "technologies":

> I can envision no "technology" of composition, no effective programming of students for efficiency in learning to write — nor would most composition teachers want such efficiency. From my point of view, "efficient" exercises in sentence-building, for instance, are downright morbid because they miss the point concerning the creative act of producing meaningful language in a rhetorical situation. (90)

And when James Moffett reacted to the formalist orientation of early sentence-combining, his Parthian shot — "It's about time the sentence was put in its place" (187) — could have been the watchword on syntactic rhetorics for a whole group of theorists whose work was gaining power.

The two *loci classici* of this anti-formalist position were the papers given at the second Miami sentence-combining conference in 1983 by Donald Murray and by Peter Elbow (their invitation by the Miami group seems in retrospect not unlike Brutus's decision to allow Antony to speak at Caesar's funeral).[4] Murray's essay is one of the wildest and most subtle he ever wrote, an almost unreadable melange of brainstorming lists, poem drafts, and endless badly combined sentences that commit formal mayhem on sentence-combining while never mentioning the technique, inviting students to write as badly as he does here in order to learn to write well. Elbow was much more open in his challenges to the formalist assumptions of sentence-combining, and he deserves to be quoted at length:

> I think sentence-combining is vulnerable to attack for being so a-rhetorical — so distant from the essential process of writing. In sentence-combining the student is not engaged in figuring out what she wants to say or saying what is on her mind. And because it provides prepackaged words and ready-made thoughts, sentence-combining reinforces the push-button, fast-food expectations in our culture. As a result the student is not saying anything to anyone: The results of her work are more often "answers" given to a teacher for correction — not "writing" given to readers for reactions. (233)

Though Elbow followed up this frontal barrage with a quick statement that these were his misgivings in their most extreme form, the remainder of his essay is a careful assessment of the dangers of making sentence-based work any very important part of writing instruction. Believing that "every one of our students at every moment is *capable* of generating a perfectly intelligible, lively sentence," Elbow says that the way to bring student skills out most usefully is "by leaving syntax more alone — that is, by learning to do a better job of writing down words in the order in which they come to mind" (241). Indeed, the whole thesis of Elbow's essay is that students do better and are truer to their own language when they leave their syntax alone. Elbow's final word on form-based work is that it is not, cannot be, genuinely generative. "[Sentence-combining] gives the wrong model for generating by implying that when we produce a sentence we are making a package for an already completed mental act" (245).[5]

The second strand of criticism leveled against syntactic rhetorics is related to anti-formalism; we might call it anti-automatism or anti-behaviorism. This set of critiques was based in the idea that pedagogies that meant to tap into non-conscious behavioral structures and to manipulate them for a specific end were inherently demeaning to students. The debate on behaviorism had been raging since the 1950s, of course, but it was given new impetus in composition in 1969 with the notorious publication of Robert Zoellner's "Talk-Write: A Behavioral Pedagogy for Composition" in *College English*. Zoellner's open plea for consideration of behavioral aspects to writing pedagogy struck a powerful nerve; *College English* printed no fewer than eight passionate rejoinders to Zoellner in 1969 and 1970. Behaviorism in psychology was the subject of deep distrust on the part of most humanists, and any proposal for pedagogical uses of it was bound to be regarded with suspicion. It was here that syntactic pedagogies were problematical, because they all used exercises to build "skills" in a way that was not meant to be completely conscious. These skills would then be on tap for all conscious student-writing purposes. What most syntactic theorists wanted from their pedagogies was a systematic and intense exposure of student writers to models and activities that would not only teach them "correct structure," but would rather, as W. Ross Winterowd suggests, "activate their competence" in language so that it "spills over into the area of performance" (253). Effective generation, imitation, or combination would be praised, and incorrect syntactic manipulation could be corrected and criticized. But for many critics, the behaviorist, exercise-based formats of these pedagogies were deeply troubling. They were perceived as a-rhetorical, uncreative, and in some senses destructive of individuality.

Imitation exercises in particular were perceived as actively insulting to the creativity of student writers. Probably the most controversial of the syntactic methods in the 1970s, imitation exercises seemed to ask their team to play defense from the beginning. Objections to imitation were made on several grounds, and most theorists who discussed imitation even in the 1970s felt compelled to defend their interest in it. Frank D'Angelo claimed in 1973 that popular feeling against imitation existed because it was perceived as drudgery, "dull, heavy, and stultifying" (283), and spent his essay explicating how imitation was actually close to invention. But the complaint about drudgework was only a part of the reason that imitation was a pedagogy besieged from its inception. The main reason for the unpopularity of imitation was that it was perceived as "mere servile copying," destructive of student individuality and contributory to a mechanized, dehumanizing, Skinnerian view of writing. The romanticism of the age, seen clearly in much of the anti-Zoellner criticism, would grow more and more potent as the 1970s segued into the 1980s. Teachers and theorists reacted against any form of practice that seemed to compromise originality and the expression of personal feelings, and imitation exercises were among the most obvious indoctrinations to "tradition" and "the system." As a result of this fear of loss of individuality and originality in student writing, those who recommended imitation were fighting a battle that they were the first to join and, ultimately, the first to lose.

Although imitation's defenders sought to clear it of the charges of automatism leveled against it by the age, arguments against imitation never disappeared, even during its heyday, since it was the most overtly anti-romantic of the sentence-based writing pedagogies. D'Angelo noted in 1973 that imitation connotes counterfeiting and stereotyping in most people's minds, when it should connote originality and creativity. William Gruber, whose essay is titled " 'Servile Copying' and the Teaching of English Composition," knew that imitation was distrusted by many teachers when he argued that imitation does not affect creativity. Gruber argued that imitation exercises liberate students' personalities by freeing them of enervating design decisions, at least temporarily. Without knowledge of what has been done by others, he claimed, there can be no profound originality: "Self-expression is possible only when the self has a defined area to work in" (497). But Gruber admitted that imitation "seems, I suppose, an 'inorganic' way of teaching writing" (495) and that his students initially seemed suspicious of it. "The greater part of students' mistrust of imitation . . . seems to derive more from emotional factors than from intellectual ones: for they grew up during the sixties, and they seem either to balk at any extreme formalization of the process of education, or to want one instant set of rules for all writing" (496). Gruber was indeed up against the powerful psychological backwash of the 1960s, as were, eventually, all proponents of sentence rhetorics.

The problem was in the exercises. Critics pointed out that sentence-combining exercises were quintessentially *exercises,* context-stripped from what students really wanted to say themselves. James Britton and his colleagues called such exercises "dummy runs," a term Britton's group evolved to describe tasks unrelated to the larger issues of creative composing in which a student is "called upon to perform a writing task in order (a) to exercise his capacity to perform that kind of task, and/or (b) to demonstrate to the teacher his proficiency in performing it" (104–05). And, as early as 1968, James Moffett was defining exercises as the central definition of old and discredited pedagogy:

> An exercise, by my definition, is any piece of writing practiced only in schools — that is, an assignment that stipulates arbitrary limits that leave the writer with no real relationships between him and a subject and an audience. I would not ask a student to write anything other than an authentic discourse, because the learning process proceeds from intent and content down to the contemplation of technical points, not the other way. (205)

Moffett was primarily attacking the old workbook "drill and kill" exercises that had stultified students since the 1920s, but he reports here on a keen resentment that had been building against all pedagogies based in the older ideas of exercises as "mental discipline." The wholesale (and heartfelt) assault on the teaching of grammar in composition that had been set off by Richard Braddock, Richard Lloyd-Jones, and Lowell Schoer's *Research in Written Composition* in 1963 was a related phenomenon. Many teachers had simply come to disbelieve in the efficacy of any exercise-based teaching. By 1980, this attack on the "from parts to the whole" tradition associated with exercises and textbooks had become much more general. Despite the flashy research claims to the contrary, many people felt that syntactic rhetorics were really not that much different from the old-time "grammar workbook" exercises whose usefulness had been aggressively challenged.

The final line in the congeries of criticism that brought down syntactic rhetorics was anti-empiricism. Now we are in complex territory, and I must be careful to limit my claims. The empirical-research strand in English studies had existed since the 1920s, when educational psychometricians first began to try testing classroom pedagogies against one another. Modern empirical research in composition, however, was much newer, dating back primarily to the potent critiques of Braddock, Lloyd-Jones, and Schoer in *Research in Written Composition,* which had pointed to serious methodological problems in most extant English research and laid the ground for defensible studies. In 1966, Braddock had founded the journal *Research in the Teaching of English* to publish the newer and better work he envisioned, and most compositionists cheered. For the next two decades the empirical strand in composition waxed powerful, with syntactic methods as its first great success and with the cognitive psychology-based research associated mainly with Carnegie-Mellon as its second. In the Big Tent atmosphere of the New Rhetoric era of the 1960s and early 1970s, there was a general air of good feeling produced by the vision, widely shared, that all — rhetoricians, process-based teachers, linguists, stylisticians, experimenters, psychologists — could work together to reform and improve the teaching of writing; workers in different vineyards need not be enemies. Once sentence rhetorics began to get serious ink in the late 1970s, however, a number of teachers looked at them more closely and began to feel some discomfort, especially with their pre- and post-test scientism, their quantifications, their whole atmosphere of horse race experimentalism. This discomfort was not eased by the huge success of sentence-combining, with its Huntian movement toward a possible pedagogical hegemony. So in the late 1970s, we see the first serious signals of an open anti-empiricism movement within the coalescing field of composition studies.

Anti-scientism and anti-empiricism were not completely novel in the field, of course. We saw a sort of prequel to the movement in the point-counterpoint debate about psychology and invention heuristics in 1971 and 1972 between Janice Lauer and Ann Berthoff.[6] In its modern form, however, the movement probably begins with Susan Wells's and Patricia Bizzell's work in the late 1970s. Wells looked carefully at Christensen's work, arguing that it was empiricist in both method and epistemology, with an asocial contemplation of static phenomena at its center. The natural attitude for a student doing Christensen exercises, said Wells, is

> minute and unquestioning attention to his or her own perceptions, passive receptivity to the messages of sensation, and the desire to work in isolation. . . . These characteristics amount to a sort of contemplation. . . . Contemplation is not distinguished by its objects, but by the relation of thinker to thought, and Christensen's rhetoric enforces a contemplative relation. (472)

And, in an important essay in 1979, Pat Bizzell made the point, which she and others would sharpen over the next decade, that cultural and community traditions would be "as important — if not more important — in shaping the outcome of our debate, as any empirical evidence adduced and interpreted by the competing schools of thought" (768).

This humanist- and theory-based criticism found its first voice in the late 1970s and early 1980s in attacks on the most obvious and successful empirical research going: syntactic pedagogical research.[7] We can see echoes of the anti-empirical position in some of the arguments I've mentioned against generative rhetoric and imitation, but the real edge of this criticism was directed at sentence-combining, whose basis in quantitative methods was almost total. One criticism resulting from this reliance on empiricism was that sentence-combining was a practice without a theory, a method without a principle, an *ars* without an *exercitatio*. As Winterowd complained in 1975, "in our self-made ghetto, compositionists have neglected theory, opting to concern ourselves with the pragmatics of everyday teaching" (90–91). James Kinneavy brought this complaint down to specifics in 1978, noting that ". . . few efforts have been made to place sentence-combining into a larger curricular framework," and that it still awaited a philosophic rationale (60, 76). This lack of a general theory was not seen at first as a particular problem, since the new research strand of sentence-combining was so novel and powerful that it submerged other questions.[8] But by 1983, when Miami held its second sentence-combining conference, the problem of theory had become obvious to many participants. The book that emerged from that conference, *Sentence-Combining: A Rhetorical Perspective,* is a fascinating collection, the last major statement made by the discipline about sentence rhetorics, and as a collection it shows clear awareness of the changing weather around sentence rhetorics.

By 1983, it was no longer enough to report that sentence-combining "worked" if no one could specify *why* it worked. Stars of the 1978 Miami conference Rosemary Hake and Joseph Williams were back, this time with more questions than answers. "Sentence-combining is at this moment operating at a very crude level of sophistication," they claimed, ". . . interesting theoretical speculation about sentence-combining has been very infrequent" ("Some" 100–01). Kenneth Dowst, in his essay "An Epistemic View of Sentence-Combining: Practice and Theories," takes on directly the popular perception that sentence-combining was "a practice devoid of a theory" (333). After examining the relation of sentence-combining to epistemic rhetoric, Dowst comes to the conclusion that sentence-combining *has* a theory, but that it is "a theory that many teachers are finding problematic and many students inadequately relevant. To wit: formalism" (333). The connection with formalism is not the only one possible, says Dowst, but other connections, to rhetoric or epistemic theory, "remain only to be enacted" (333). Despite the hopes expressed at the 1983 conference, they never were. And in the increasingly theoretical world of composition studies post-1985, practice without theory was increasingly associated with the lore-world of earlier composition and condemned.

Another criticism was that sentence-combining represented methodological hegemony of a kind destructive to a truly humanistic epistemology. Michael Holzman, in his "Scientism and Sentence Combining" in 1983, dry-gulches sentence-combining with such energy that he almost appears paranoid about its possibilities. After slashing and burning all the research findings down to the affirmation that "sentence-combining exercises do appear to help students learn how to combine sentences (although this skill deteriorates rapidly)" (77), Holzman makes his central claim for an end to "scientistic" research. "The humanities are the sciences of man," he writes, ". . . It would be a serious mistake to allow the fascination of methodologies for social scientific research to bring us to doubt that literacy is primarily a humanistic attainment" (78–79). Holzman's fear — that the clear-cut successes of the sentence-combining research might slant the whole evolving discipline of composition studies away from traditional humanistic/rhetorical lines and into the camp of social sciences and psychology — was beginning to be widely shared in the early 1980s and came to its real fruition four years later, with the wholesale reaction against cognitive approaches and empiricism in general that marked the beginning of the Social-Construction Era.[9] The best-known example of this methodological critique was Stephen North's famous chapter on the experimentalists in his *Making of Knowledge in Composition* in 1987, which calls out the Miami researchers in particular for criticism (although not as harshly as it does some other experimentalists).

The result of all of these lines of criticism of syntactic methods was that they were stopped almost dead in their tracks as a research program and ceased being a popular teaching project just a little later. The degree to which the attacks succeeded can be seen in the curious growth of the truly lore-oriented conception that "research has shown that sentence-combining doesn't work." When preparing to write this essay, I asked a number of friends and colleagues in composition studies what had ever happened to sentence-combining. At least half of them replied that it had lost currency because it had been shown not to work, not to help students write better. So far as I can determine, this is simply not true. Outside of a few essays, including Marzano's and Holzman's, that really did take a slash-and-burn attitude toward reporting balanced opinions of the research, I can find no work that genuinely "disproved" the gains created for students through sentence practice. It is true that Lester Faigley showed, in two essays in 1979 and 1980, that Hunt's concept of syntactic maturity did not correlate with generally perceived writing quality ("Problems"; "Names"). But Faigley himself did not question the holistic quality gains of the sentence-combining students, stating that the answer must be that sentence-combining and generative rhetoric "affect some part of the writing process more fundamental than the enhancement of syntactic maturity" ("Problems" 99).[10]

Warren Combs and Richard Smith published an essay in 1980 that reported that students would write demonstrably longer sentences if simply told to do so by the teacher ("Overt and Covert Cues"), but their experiment was short-term, and they specifically stated that their "findings in no way call the efficacy of SC [sentence-combining] instruction into question" (35).[11] It is true that the Miami group's last report, which appeared in the non-mainstream *Perceptual and Motor Skills,* found that absent other writing work, the gains made by the sentence-combiners were self-sustaining, but that the advantage that the experimental group had shown over the control group disappeared after two years. The control group, in other words, caught up to the sentence-combiners after twenty-eight months. This shows, as the Miami researchers comment, that the sentence-combining practice "simply accelerated the positive changes that would have occurred after a longer period of normal maturation and experience" (Kerek, Daiker, and Morenberg 1151). In other words, syntactic gains, if not practiced, only persisted for two years. But by this criterion, if our methods in any given first-year composition course don't measurably put our students ahead of other students *forever,* they don't work and are not worth doing. That's a high hurdle for any pedagogy to clear. There were, finally, a few articles published with "Questions" in their titles: Mary Rosner's "Putting 'This and That Together' to Question Sentence-Combining Research" in 1984 and Aviva Freedman's "Sentence Combining: Some Questions" in 1985, but these essays were concerned with specific queries about technical style and abstracting ability. Neither questioned the general writing success of students using the technique.

It really does seem that the current perception that somehow sentence rhetorics "don't work" exists as a massive piece of wish-fulfillment. Leaving aside the question of syntactic fluency or maturity entirely, the data from holistic and analytic general essay readings are unequivocal. George Hillocks, reviewing the research in 1986, looked closely into all the major sentence-combining research and found many lines of inquiry that needed to be followed up. But after his careful dissection, he still concluded his section on sentence rhetorics with a quote that recognized the value of the technique: "Even with so many questions left unanswered, one is tempted to agree with Charles Cooper (1975c) that 'no other single teaching approach has ever consistently been shown to have a beneficial effect on syntactic maturity and writing quality' (p. 72)" (151). In other words, if people believe that research has shown that sentence rhetorics don't work, their belief exists not because the record bears it out but because it is what people want to believe.

Why we want to believe it is the interesting part.

So what was it that erased the sentence, wiped what had been the "forefront in composition research today . . . at the cutting edge of research design" in 1980[12] off the radar screen of composition studies? What reduced it from a vital, if unfinished, inquiry into why a popular stylistic method worked so well to a half-hidden and seldom-discussed classroom practice on the level of, say, vocabulary quizzes? It was not, as we have seen, that sentence rhetorics were proved useless. Neither was this erasure the simple playing out of a vein of material before the onslaughts of the normal scientists who followed the major researchers of sentence rhetorics. If the last important work in sentence-combining, Daiker, Kerek, and Morenberg's *Rhetorical Perspective,* shows anything, it is that many of the most interesting questions about sentence rhetorics were still being raised and not answered.[13]

I think that we have, to a large extent, already seen what it was. The sentence was erased by the gradual but inevitable hardening into disciplinary form of the field of composition studies as a subfield of English studies. The anti-formalism, anti-behaviorism, and anti-empiricism that marked the criticism of sentence rhetorics can be found in some earlier writers and thinkers in the older field of composition, but not with the hegemony they gradually achieved as disciplinary structures were formed after 1975. These three attitudinal strands are hallmarks of English studies and not of works in the other fields — speech, psychology, education — from which composition grew after 1950. Departmental structures are lasting and durable, and as it became apparent that composition studies as a field would almost universally find its departmental home in the same place its primary course identity — first-year composition — resided, cross-disciplinary elements in the older composition-rhetoric world were likely to fade. The graduate students after 1975 who would make up the core of composition studies were, for better or worse, English graduate students, and they would go on to become English professors.

On a sheer demographic basis, it is not strange to see many default attitudes based around English departments — textuality, holism, stratification by status, theory-desire, distrust of scientism — gradually come to define composition studies. However complex the feelings composition people had and have about English departments, such departments are usually our native lands. Even if we reject much of the culture, we still speak the language. And one result of the increasing English-identification of composition studies has been a gradual movement away from connections that had helped define an earlier, looser version of composition that arose in the 1950s. We have dropped much of our relationship with non-English elements — with education and with high school teachers, with speech and communications and with oral rhetoric, with psychology and with quantitative research.

This is not the place for a complete discussion of the changing demographics of composition studies as it became a clear subfield of English. In this article I wanted to show, in a very delimited instance, evidence of the movement's power and potency by examining one part of its effects. When a phenomenon is hard to see or define, looking at what it has done may point to important realities about it. In this case, as in a tornado documentary, the effects exist as a trail of destruction. There was indeed much destruction in the wake of the disciplinary formation of composition studies, but since most of it was destruction of things few people after 1980 had ever believed in or fought for, the destruction was not noticed by many. Who remembers a vital NCTE College Section? Who mourns for the Four Communications Skills or the modes of discourse? But we should remember that swept away with the modes and the five types of paragraphs were other, newer, and potentially more valuable things. The loss of all defense of formalism has left some curious vacuums in the middle of our teaching. Rejection of all behaviorist ideas has left us with uncertainties about any methodology not completely rationalistic or any system of pedagogical rewards. Distrust of scientistic empiricism has left us with few proofs or certainties not ideologically based. More has been lost than sentence-combining here, but it seems somehow part of human nature to forget about the preterite. Many people still professionally active today have deep background as generative rhetoricians or imitation adepts or sentence-combining pioneers, but they have lost most of their interest; they do not do that much anymore. They have cut their losses and gone on. We all must.

Notes

1. C. S. Baldwin's terms, clearness and interest, were not used in his earlier textbook, *A College Manual of Rhetoric,* in 1902, which adopted Hill's version of Whately's terms. They are found in his later text, *Composition: Oral and Written,* from 1909.

2. These numbers do *not* include conference papers at the two Miami sentence-combining conferences, which became 45 separate essays in the two proceeding books.

3. Notice I'm not claiming that sentence rhetorics were gone from teaching. Anecdotal evidence seems to suggest that some teachers have continued to use sentence-combining and Christensen rhetoric even absent any mention of them in books or journals. They have thus become part of what Stephen North calls teacher lore. But isn't it ironic that such techniques, which made strong moves toward grammatical analyses and empirical proofs, have ended up as lore, which North defines (23) as being driven by pragmatic logic and experiential structure?

4. William Strong attempted to respond to Murray and Elbow in a heart-breaking piece with which the 1983 Miami conference (and collection) closes. Strong has read their papers, and his essay is an attempt to explain to them, and to the world at large, that sentence-combining is both more and less than they think and fear. Called "How Sentence Combining Works," Strong's essay admits that sentence-combining is not, cannot be, "real writing," and that it cannot and should never take the place of naturalistic experience. Still, though, Strong will not admit that sentence-combining is a-rhetorical or non-naturalistic, and he believes that "the language in sentence combining often triggers metalinguistic thinking beyond its own discursive content" and "helps students transfer power from oral language performance to writing" (350). Strong's is an extraordinary rhetorical performance, struggling at the end of the Era of Good Feelings for tolerance from a group that was moving inevitably away from him. But finally, his plea for compromise and understanding fell on stony ground. Composition studies after 1980 did not like or trust exercises. Any kind of exercises.

5. Today, more than fifteen years after the first carronades were fired at the various movements associated with the term "process," we are used to thinking of our world as "post-process" and of "expressivism" as a devil term and a dead letter. As an intellectual field, we have managed with considerable success to marginalize that movement, at least insofar as it existed as ongoing intellectual or non-pedagogical discourse. Its greatest champions — Moffett, Britton, Garrison, Emig, Murray, Macrorie, Stewart, Rohmann — have died or retired, leaving Peter Elbow nearly alone to carry the banner. Many people see expressivism today — not unlike sentence-combining, ironically — as a hoary pedagogical survival, *exercitatio* with *ars*, old-time staffroom lore and instructor prejudice, the body still moving after the head has been cut off. It is difficult, on first consideration, to imagine the writing-process movement as a potent destructive force, or to think that we, in our shining theoretical plumage, are still living in the backwash of its great primary act of pedagogical creation/destruction: the wreck of formalism in all its versions.

But the powerful revolutionary doctrine of the process movement was, finally, terribly simple. It wished to do away with whatever was not authentic in writing and teaching writing. Its great enemy was modern composition-rhetoric, that huge carpetbag of textbook nostrums about modes and forms and methods and sentences and rules and paragraphs and vocabulary and punctuation and exercises and unity and coherence and emphasis. If rhetoric was a fox that knew many small things, process was a hedgehog that knew one great thing: you learn to write by writing and rewriting things important to you with the help of a sympathetic reader/teacher. Everything else is, finally, flummery. Formalism and atomism were huge and inescapable parts of modern composition-rhetoric, and the writing process movement laid down a constant challenge to them from 1960 onward. If, as was the case, formalism or atomism were charges that could be applied even to New Rhetoric ideas such as syntactic rhetorics, then applied they must be. Sadly, regretfully applied, yes, since many sentence-combiners had been friends. But when you build a set of positions based completely on authenticity and anti-formalism, you cannot easily choose some formalism you will be friends with.

Max Morenberg of the Miami sentence-combining group certainly had no doubt who had burnt his topless tower. In two conference presentations, in 1990 and 1992, he surveyed the wreckage and protested against the attitudes that had wrought it. His somewhat bitter titles tell the story: In 1990 he delivered "Process/Schmocess: Why Not Combine a Sentence or Two?" and in 1992 he delivered " 'Come Back to the Text Ag'in, Huck Honey!' " Both blamed dichotomizing process/product thinking for the demise of sentence rhetorics. Unfortunately, Morenberg never published either talk outside of ERIC.

6. This whole argument can be seen most easily in Winterowd's *Contemporary Rhetoric* (99–103), along with Winterowd's thoughtful commentary on it.

7. Only a few people saw then that this movement would a few years later in 1987 enlarge the criticism to include the equally powerful cognitive-psychology strand of research; in retrospect it seems clear that the real relation between sentence research and cognitive research lay in their common nemesis. The enlarging reaction against quantitative research would eventually come to include all but the most narrative and humanistic qualitative research as well, and the results would, in the end, be the same: the effective ending of whole lines of research within mainstream composition studies. Of course, much research is still carried on, but it tends to be reported at NCTE and American Educational Research Association, rather than at CCCC. See Charney for the reaction of many researchers to this movement within composition studies.

8. As late as 1981, even such a noted practitioner of theory as the late James Berlin was co-authoring purely practical essays on sentence-combining containing such statements as, "In sum, the 'sentence skills' unit should not be relegated to a few hours devoted to 'style,' but should be seen as central to some of a writer's major concerns" (Broadhead and Berlin 306).

9. In my "Composition Studies and Science," published just a month before Holzman's essay, I made almost the exact plea for the primacy of humanities-based (which I called rhetorical) inquiry over social-science inquiry. Although I made my own howlers in that piece (lumping Pat Bizzell in with all other Kuhn-quoters as an advocate of empirical science!), I was not, I hope, slanting evidence as obviously as Holzman seems to do in his condemnation of sentence-combining, whose whole train of successes he dismisses with a sneer.

10. Faigley's and Holzman's work led to Forrest Houlette's 1984 article on reliability and validity in external criteria and holistic scoring, a piece that seems to suggest that neither criterion can be considered empirically dependable under all conditions without the context of the other. This was the level of epistemological humility syntactic research had reached by 1984: There was no longer any dependable way to determine what writing was actually good.

11. Richard Haswell and his co-authors recently mentioned the study of Combs and Smith as a rare example of replication of research in composition studies (5), and in terms of careful numerical enumeration of syntactic growth, this is true. But Combs and Smith studied their students over a much shorter period (six days) than did O'Hare or the Miami researchers and made no attempt to cover holistic writing-quality issues. (There is also some evidence that the overtly cued students [those told that their teacher would grade long sentences more favorably] simply began to string

long sentences together in a few simple ways, since their T-unit numbers went up but their clause numbers did not [see pp. 33–35].)

12. This rather embarrassing quote is from my dissertation, written in 1979 and 1980. It's humbling to watch your own doxa turn into historical grist.

13. Janice Neuleib suggested, after hearing an earlier version of this paper, that another possible reason for the decline of sentence-combining was not that all of the research had been done, but that all of the impressive and groundbreaking research had been done. No one is much interested in the quotidian mopping-up work of normal science, especially in social science-based fields. The specialized and smaller scale studies that were called for (but not done) after 1983 were not career-makers. Although I thought at first that this idea might be too cynical, I have been gradually forced to admit its possibility.

Works Cited

Bateman, Donald R., and Frank J. Zidonis. *The Effect of a Study of Transformational Grammar on the Writing of Ninth and Tenth Graders.* Urbana: NCTE, 1966.

Bizzell, Patricia. "Thomas Kuhn, Scientism, and English Studies." *College English* 40 (1979): 764–71.

Bond, Charles A. "A New Approach to Freshman Composition: A Trial of the Christensen Method." *College English* 33 (1972): 623–27.

Braddock, Richard, Richard Lloyd-Jones, and Lowell Schoer. *Research in Written Composition.* Urbana: NCTE, 1963.

Britton, James, Tony Burgess, Nancy Martin, Alex McLeod, and Harold Rosen. *The Development of Writing Abilities (11–18).* Basingstoke: Macmillan, 1975.

Broadhead, Glenn J., and James A. Berlin. "Twelve Steps to Using Generative Sentences and Sentence Combining in the Composition Classroom." *College Composition and Communication* 32 (1981): 295–307.

Charney, Davida. "Empiricism Is Not a Four-Letter Word." *College Composition and Communication* 47 (1996): 567–93.

Christensen, Francis. "A Generative Rhetoric of the Sentence." *College Composition and Communication* 14 (1963): 155–61.

———. *Notes toward a New Rhetoric: Six Essays for Teachers.* New York: Harper, 1967.

———. "The Course in Advanced Composition for Teachers." *College Composition and Communication* 24 (1973): 163–70.

Christensen, Francis, and Bonniejean Christensen. *A New Rhetoric.* New York: Harper, 1975.

Combs, Warren E. "Sentence-Combining Practice: Do Gains in Judgments of Writing 'Quality' Persist?" *Journal of Educational Research* 70 (1977): 318–21.

Combs, Warren E., and William L. Smith. "The Effects of Overt and Covert Cues on Written Syntax." *Research in the Teaching of English* 14 (1980): 19–38.

Connors, Robert J. "Composition Studies and Science." *College English* 45 (1983): 1–20.

———. *Composition-Rhetoric: Backgrounds, Theory, and Pedagogy.* Pittsburgh: U of Pittsburgh P, 1997.

Cooper, Charles R. "Research Roundup: Oral and Written Composition." *English Journal* 64 (1975): 72–74.

Corbett, Edward P. J. *Classical Rhetoric for the Modern Student.* New York: Oxford UP, 1965.

———. "The Theory and Practice of Imitation in Classical Rhetoric." *College Composition and Communication* 22 (1971): 243–50.

Daiker, Donald A., Andrew Kerek, and Max Morenberg. "Sentence-Combining and Syntactic Maturity in Freshman English." *College Composition and Communication* 29 (1978): 36–41.

———, eds. *Sentence-Combining: A Rhetorical Perspective.* Carbondale: Southern Illinois UP, 1985.

———, eds. *Sentence-Combining and the Teaching of Writing.* Conway, AR: L&S Books, 1979.

———. *The Writer's Options: College Sentence-Combining.* New York: Harper and Row, 1979.

D'Angelo, Frank. "Imitation and Style." *College Composition and Communication* 24 (1973): 283–90.

Dowst, Kenneth. "An Epistemic View of Sentence-Combining: Practice and Theories." Daiker et al. *Sentence-Combining: A Rhetorical Perspective.* 321–33.

Elbow, Peter. "The Challenge for Sentence Combining." Daiker et al. *Sentence-Combining: A Rhetorical Perspective.* 232–45.

Faigley, Lester L. "Generative Rhetoric as a Way of Increasing Syntactic Fluency." *College Composition and Communication* 30 (1979): 176–81.

———. "Problems in Analyzing Maturity in College and Adult Writing." Daiker et al. *Sentence-Combining and the Teaching of Writing.* 94–100.

———. "Names in Search of a Concept: Maturity, Fluency, Complexity, and Growth in Written Syntax." *College Composition and Communication* 31 (1980): 291–300.

Freedman, Aviva. "Sentence Combining: Some Questions." *Carleton Papers in Applied Language Studies* 2 (1985): 17–32.

Graves, Richard L., ed. *Rhetoric and Composition: A Sourcebook for Teachers.* Rochelle Park, NJ: Hayden, 1976.

Gruber, William E. " 'Servile Copying' and the Teaching of English Composition." *College English* 39 (1977): 491–97.

Hake, Rosemary, and Joseph M. Williams. "Sentence Expanding: Not Can, or How, but When." Daiker et al. *Sentence-Combining and the Teaching of Writing.* 134–46.

———. "Some Cognitive Issues in Sentence Combining: On the Theory that Smaller Is Better." Daiker et al. *Sentence-Combining: A Rhetorical Perspective.* 86–106.

Halloran, S. Michael. "Cicero and English Composition." Conference on College Composition and Communication. Minneapolis. 1978.

Haswell, Richard H., Terri L. Briggs, Jennifer A. Fay, Norman K. Gillen, Rob Harrill, Andrew M. Shupala, and Sylvia S. Trevino. "Context and Rhetorical Reading Strategies." *Written Communication* 16 (1999): 3–27.

Hillocks, George, Jr. *Research on Written Composition: New Directions for Teaching.* Urbana: NCTE, 1986.

Holzman, Michael. "Scientism and Sentence Combining." *College Composition and Communication* 34 (1983): 73–79.

Houlette, Forrest. "Linguistics, Empirical Research, and Evaluating Composition." *Journal of Advanced Composition* 5 (1984): 107–14.

Hunt, Kellogg W. *Grammatical Structures Written at Three Grade Levels.* Urbana: NCTE, 1965.

———. "A Synopsis of Clause-to-Sentence Length Factors." Graves 110–17.

———. "Anybody Can Teach English." Daiker et al. *Sentence-Combining and the Teaching of Writing.* 149–56.

Johnson, Sabina Thorne. "Some Tentative Strictures on Generative Rhetoric." *College English* 31 (1969): 155–65.

Kinneavy, James L. "Sentence Combining in a Comprehensive Language Framework." Daiker et al. *Sentence-Combining and the Teaching of Writing.* 60–76.

Kerek, Andrew, Donald A. Daiker, and Max Morenberg. "Sentence Combining and College Composition." *Perceptual and Motor Skills* 51 (1980): 1059–1157.

Marzano, Robert J. "The Sentence-Combining Myth." *English Journal* 65 (1976): 57–59.

Mellon, John. *Transformational Sentence-Combining: A Method for Enhancing the Development of Syntactic Fluency in English Composition.* Urbana: NCTE, 1969.

———. "Issues in the Theory and Practice of Sentence-Combining: A Twenty-Year Perspective." Daiker et al. *Sentence-Combining and the Teaching of Writing.* 1–38.

Miller, Edmund. *Exercises in Style.* Normal, IL: Illinois SUP, 1980.

Moffett, James. *Teaching the Universe of Discourse.* Boston: Houghton Mifflin, 1968.

Morenberg, Max. "Process/Schmocess: Why Not Combine a Few Sentences?" Conference on College Composition and Communication. Chicago. March 1990. ERIC ED 319040.

———. " 'Come Back to the Text Ag'in, Huck Honey!' " NCTE Convention. Louisville. November 1992. ERIC ED 355557.

Morenberg, Max, Donald Daiker, and Andrew Kerek. "Sentence-Combining at the College Level: An Experimental Study." *Research in the Teaching of English* 12 (1978): 245–56.

Murray, Donald. "Writing Badly to Write Well: Searching for the Instructive Line." Daiker et al. *Sentence-Combining: A Rhetorical Perspective.* 187–201.

Ney, James. "The Hazards of the Course: Sentence-Combining in Freshman English." *The English Record* 27 (1976): 70–77.

North, Stephen M. *The Making of Knowledge in Composition.* Upper Montclair, NJ: Heinneman-Boynton/Cook, 1987.

O'Donnell, Roy C., William J. Griffin, and Raymond C. Norris. *Syntax of Kindergarten and Elementary School Children: A Transformational Analysis.* Urbana: NCTE, 1967.

O'Hare, Frank. *Sentence-Combining: Improving Student Writing without Formal Grammar Instruction.* Urbana: NCTE, 1973.

———. *Sentencecraft.* Lexington: Ginn, 1975.

Rose, Shirley K. "Down from the Haymow: One Hundred Years of Sentence-Combining." *College English* 45 (1983): 483–91.

Rosner, Mary. "Putting 'This and That Together' to Question Sentence-Combining Research." *Technical Writing Teacher* 11 (1984): 221–28.

Starkey, Penelope. "Imitatio Redux." *College Composition and Communication* 25 (1974): 435–37.

Strong, William. "How Sentence Combining Works." Daiker et al. *Sentence-Combining: A Rhetorical Perspective.* 334–50.

———. *Sentence-Combining: A Composing Book.* New York: Random House, 1973.

Tibbetts, A. M. "On the Practical Uses of a Grammatical System: A Note on Christensen and Johnson." *Rhetoric and Composition: A Sourcebook for Teachers.* E. Richard Graves. Rochelle Park, NJ: Hayden Books, 1976. 139–49.

Walshe, R. D. "Report on a Pilot Course on the Christensen Rhetoric Program." *College English* 32 (1971): 783–89.

Weathers, Winston. *An Alternate Style: Options in Composition.* Rochelle Park, NJ: Hayden Books, 1980.

Weathers, Winston, and Otis Winchester. *Copy and Compose.* Englewood Cliffs, NJ: Prentice-Hall, 1969.

———. *The New Strategy of Style.* New York: McGraw-Hill, 1978.

Wells, Susan. "Classroom Heuristics and Empiricism." *College English* 39 (1977): 467–76.

Winterowd, W. Ross. *Contemporary Rhetoric: A Conceptual Background with Readings.* New York: Harcourt Brace, 1975.

Zoellner, Robert. "Talk-Write: A Behavioral Pedagogy for Composition." *College English* 30 (1969): 267–320.

Connors's Insights as a Resource for Your Teaching

1. Beyond a purely grammatical perspective, what lessons about the construction of sentences have figured in your own development as a writer? Do you hold any general rules of thumb about crafting sentences that you share with your students? How might careful attention to the sentence — again, beyond a strict interest in grammatical correctness — benefit students?

2. In your view, which aspects of the sentence-based pedagogies that Connors describes seem most worth retaining? Which seem less valuable? Of the three pedagogies he sketches, which would you be most likely to adopt with your students, and why?

Connors's Insights as a Resource for Your Writing Classroom

1. In a recent batch of student drafts, identify sentences that you think could benefit from revision. Put students in small groups and assign each group a problem sentence; then have each group explain why their sentence is weak and how it could be improved.

2. Develop some sentence-combining or imitation exercises. You could have students work on these as a class, or you could require them as homework assignments, perhaps for extra credit. Talk with your students about their experiences with the exercises. Did students find them worthwhile? Why or why not?

A Generative Rhetoric of the Sentence

Francis Christensen

In the following chapter from his essay collection Notes Toward a New
Rhetoric *(1963), Francis Christensen proposes that we train students to
write the dynamic "cumulative sentence," a structure that invigorates
writing by challenging students to reflect their minds at work. Teaching
them to "grow" sentences by adding multiple levels of modifiers before,
after, or within a base clause not only results in a mature, lively style, but
it also gives students the sophistication and confidence to mimic the ebb-
and-flow movement of thought. To cultivate "syntactical ingenuity,"
Christensen suggests breaking example sentences into their various layers
of structure and discussing the relationships between the modifiers. This
in turn opens the way for discussions of style in terms of four key principles: addition, direction, rhythm, and texture. Although critics may
argue that cumulative sentences are too long for most first-year college
students to handle, Christensen disagrees: "I try in narrative sentences to
push to level after level, not just two or three, but four, five, or six, even
more, as far as the students' powers of observation will take them. I want
them to become sentence acrobats, to dazzle by their syntactic dexterity.
I'd rather have to deal with hyperemia than anemia."*

We do not have time in our classes to teach everything about the
rhetoric of the sentence. I believe in "island hopping," concentrating on topics where we can produce results and leaving the rest,
including the "comma splice" and the "run-on sentence," to die on the
vine. The balanced sentence deserves some attention in discursive writing, and the enormous range of coordinate structures deserves a bit
more. The rhythm of good modern prose comes about equally from the
multiple-tracking of coordinate constructions and the downshifting and
backtracking of free modifiers. But the first comes naturally; the other
needs coaxing along.

This coaxing is the clue to the meaning of *generative* in my title. (It
is not derived from generative grammar; I used it before I ever heard of
Chomsky.) The teacher can use the idea of levels of structure to urge
the student to add further levels to what he has already produced, so
that the structure itself becomes an aid to discovery.

This system of analysis by levels is essentially an application of
immediate constituent analysis. IC analysis reveals what goes with
what. The order in which initial, medial, and final elements are cut off
is immaterial, but one might as well start at the beginning. Thus, in
sentence 2 below [p. 252], the first cut would take off the whole set of
initial modifiers. Then the members of a coordinate set are separated
and, if the dissection is to be carried out to the ultimate constituents,
analyzed one by one in order. In sentence 1 [252], the first cut would
come at the end of the base clause, taking off levels 2, 3, and 4 together
since they are dependent on one another. Another cut would come at

the end of level 2, taking off levels 3 and 4 together since 4 is a modifier of 3. Medial modifiers have to be cut *out* rather than *off.*

If the new grammar is to be brought to bear on composition, it must be brought to bear on the rhetoric of the sentence. We have a workable and teachable, if not a definitive, modern grammar; but we do not have, despite several titles, a modern rhetoric.

In composition courses we do not really teach our captive charges to write better — we merely *expect* them to. And we do not teach them how to write better because we do not know how to teach them to write better. And so we merely go through the motions. Our courses with their tear-out workbooks and four-pound anthologies are elaborate evasions of the real problem. They permit us to put in our time and do almost anything else we'd rather be doing instead of buckling down to the hard work of making a difference in the student's understanding and manipulation of language.

With hundreds of handbooks and rhetorics to draw from, I have never been able to work out a program for teaching the sentence as I find it in the work of contemporary writers. The chapters on the sentence all adduce the traditional rhetorical classification of sentences as loose, balanced, and periodic. But the term *loose* seems to be taken as a pejorative (it sounds immoral); our students, no Bacons or Johnsons, have little occasion for balanced sentences; and some of our worst perversions of style come from the attempt to teach them to write periodic sentences. The traditional grammatical classification of sentences is equally barren. Its use in teaching composition rests on a semantic confusion, equating complexity of structure with complexity of thought and vice versa. But very simple thoughts may call for very complex grammatical constructions. Any moron can say "I don't know who done it." And some of us might be puzzled to work out the grammar of "All I want is all there is," although any chit can think it and say it and act on it.

The chapters on the sentence all appear to assume that we think naturally in primer sentences, progress naturally to compound sentences, and must be taught to combine the primer sentences into complex sentences — and that complex sentences are the mark of maturity. We need a rhetoric of the sentence that will do more than combine the ideas of primer sentences. We need one that will *generate* ideas.

For the foundation of such a generative or productive rhetoric I take the statement from John Erskine, the originator of the Great Books courses, himself a novelist. In the essay "The Craft of Writing" (*Twentieth Century English,* Philosophical Library, 1946) he discusses a principle of the writer's craft which, though known he says to all practitioners, he has never seen discussed in print. The principle is this: "When you write, you make a point, not by subtracting as though you sharpened a pencil, but by adding." We have all been told that the formula for good writing is the concrete noun and the active verb. Yet Erskine says, "What you say is found not in the noun but in what you add to qualify the noun. . . . The noun, the verb, and the main clause serve merely as the base on which meaning will rise. . . . The modifier is the essential part of any sentence." The foundation, then, for a generative or productive rhetoric of the sentence is that composition is essentially a process of *addition.*

But speech is linear, moving in time, and writing moves in linear space, which is analogous to time. When you add a modifier, whether to the noun, the verb, or the main clause, you must add it either before the head or after it. If you add it before the head, the direction of modification can be indicated by an arrow pointing forward; if you add it after, by an arrow pointing backward. Thus we have the second principle of a generative rhetoric — the principle of *direction of modification* or *direction of movement.*

Within the clause there is not much scope for operating with this principle. The positions of the various sorts of close, or restrictive, modifiers are generally fixed and the modifiers are often obligatory — "The man who came to dinner remained till midnight." Often the only choice is whether to add modifiers. What I have seen of attempts to bring structural grammar to bear on composition usually boils down to the injunction to "load the patterns." Thus "pattern practice" sets students to accreting sentences like this: "The small boy on the red bicycle who lives with his happy parents on our shady street often coasts down the steep street until he comes to the city park." This will never do. It has no rhythm and hence no life; it is tone-deaf. It is the seed that will burgeon into gobbledegook. One of the hardest things in writing is to keep the noun clusters and verb clusters short.

It is with modifiers added to the clause — that is, with sentence modifiers — that the principle comes into full play. The typical sentence of modern English, the kind we can best spend our efforts trying to teach, is what we may call the *cumulative sentence.* The main clause, which may or may not have a sentence modifier before it, advances the discussion; but the additions move backward, as in this clause, to modify the statement of the main clause or more often to explicate or exemplify it, so that the sentence has a flowing and ebbing movement, advancing to a new position and then pausing to consolidate it, leaping and lingering as the popular ballad does. The first part of the preceding compound sentence has one addition, placed within it; the second part has 4 words in the main clause and 49 in the five additions placed after it.

The cumulative sentence is the opposite of the periodic sentence. It does not represent the idea as conceived, pondered over, reshaped, packaged, and delivered cold. It is dynamic rather than static, representing the mind thinking. The main clause ("the additions move backward" above) exhausts the mere fact of the idea; logically, there is nothing more to say. The additions stay with the same idea, probing its bearings and implications, exemplifying it or seeking an analogy or metaphor for it, or reducing it to details. Thus the mere form of the sentence generates ideas. It serves the needs of both the writer and the reader, the writer by compelling him to examine his thought, the reader by letting him into the writer's thought.

Addition and direction of movement are structural principles. They involve the grammatical character of the sentence. Before going on to other principles, I must say a word about the best grammar as the foundation for rhetoric. I cannot conceive any useful transactions between teacher and students unless they have in common a language for talking about sentences. The best grammar for the present purpose is the grammar that best displays the layers of structure of the English sentence. The best I have found in a textbook is the combination of immediate constituent and transformation grammar in Paul Roberts's *English Sentences*. Traditional grammar, whether oversimple as in the school tradition or overcomplex as in the scholarly tradition, does not reveal the language as it operates; it leaves everything, to borrow a phrase from Wordsworth, "in disconnection dead and spiritless." *English Sentences* is oversimplified and it has gaps, but it displays admirably the structures that rhetoric must work with — primarily sentence modifiers, including nonrestrictive relative and subordinate clauses, but, far more important, the array of noun, verb, and adjective clusters. It is paradoxical that Professor Roberts, who has done so much to make the teaching of composition possible, should himself be one of those who think that it cannot be taught. Unlike Ulysses, he does not see any work for Telemachus to work.

Layers of structure, as I have said, is a grammatical concept. To bring in the dimension of meaning, we need a third principle — that of *levels of generality* or *levels of abstraction*. The main or base clause is likely to be stated in general or abstract or plural terms. With the main clause stated, the forward movement of the sentence stops, the writer shifts down to a lower level of generality or abstraction or to singular terms, and goes back over the same ground at this lower level.[1] There is no theoretical limit to the number of structural layers or levels, each[2] at a lower level of generality, any or all of them compounded, that a speaker or writer may use. For a speaker, listen to Lowell Thomas; for a writer, study William Faulkner. To a single independent clause he may append a page of additions, but usually all clear, all grammatical, once we have learned how to read him. Or, if you prefer, study Hemingway, the master of the simple sentence: "George was coming down in the telemark position, kneeling, one leg forward and bent, the other trailing, his sticks hanging like some insect's thin legs, kicking up puffs of snow, and finally the whole kneeling, trailing figure coming around in a beautiful right curve, crouching, the legs shot forward and back, the body leaning out against the swing, the stick accenting the curve like points of light, all in a wild cloud of snow." Only from the standpoint of school grammar is this a simple sentence.

This brings me to the fourth, and last, principle, that of texture. *Texture* provides a descriptive or evaluative term. If a writer adds to few of his nouns or verbs or main clauses and adds little, the texture may be said to be thin. The style will be plain or bare. The writing of most of our students is thin — even threadbare. But if he adds frequently or much or both, then the texture may be said to be dense or rich. One of the marks of an effective style, especially in narrative, is variety in the texture, the texture varying with the change in pace, the variation in texture producing the change in pace. It is not true, as I have seen it asserted, that fast action calls for short sentences; the action is fast in the sentence by Hemingway above. In our classes, we have to work for greater density and variety in texture and greater concreteness and particularity in what is added.

I have been operating at a fairly high level of generality. Now I must downshift and go over the same points with examples. The most graphic way to exhibit the layers of structure is to indent the word groups of a sentence and to number the levels. The first three sentences illustrate the various positions of the added sentence modifiers — initial, medial, and final. The symbols mark the grammatical character of the additions: SC, subordinate clause; RC, relative clause; NC, noun cluster; VC, verb cluster; AC, adjective cluster; A + A, adjective series; Abs, absolute (i.e., a VC with a subject of its own); PP, prepositional phrase. The elements set off as on a lower level are marked as sentence modifiers by junctures or punctuation. The examples have been chosen to illustrate the range of constructions used in the lower levels; after the first few they are arranged by the number of levels. The examples could have been drawn from poetry as well as from prose. Those not attributed are by students.

1

1 He dipped his hands in the bichloride solution and shook them,
  2 a quick shake, (NC)
    3 fingers down, (Abs)
      4 like the fingers of a pianist above the keys. (PP)

Sinclair Lewis

2

  2 Calico-coated, (AC)
  2 small-bodied, (AC)
    3 with delicate legs and pink faces in which their mismatched eyes rolled wild and subdued, (PP)
1 they huddled,
  2 gaudy motionless and alert, (A + A)
  2 wild as deer, (AC)
  2 deadly as rattlesnakes, (AC)
  2 quiet as doves. (AC)

William Faulkner

3

1 The bird's eye, / , remained fixed upon him;
   2 / bright and silly as a sequin (AC)
1 its little bones, / , seemed swooning in his hand.
   2 / wrapped . . . in a warm padding of feathers (VC)

                                                Stella Benson

4

1 The jockeys sat bowed and relaxed,
   2 moving a little at the waist with the movement of their horses.
     (VC)

                               Katherine Anne Porter

5

1 The flame sidled up the match,
   2 driving a film of moisture and a thin strip of darker grey before it.
     (VC)

6

1 She came among them behind the man,
   2 gaunt in the gray shapeless garment and the sunbonnet, (AC)
   2 wearing stained canvas gymnasium shoes. (VC)

                                           Faulkner

7

1 The Texan turned to the nearest gatepost and climbed to the top of
  it,
   2 his alternate thighs thick and bulging in the tight trousers, (Abs)
   2 the butt of the pistol catching and losing the sun in pearly gleams.
     (Abs)

                                         Faulkner

8

1 He could sail for hours,
   2 searching the blanched grasses below him with his telescopic eyes,
     (VC)
   2 gaining height against the wind, (VC)
   2 descending in mile-long, gently declining swoops when he curved
     and rode back, (VC)
   2 never beating a wing. (VC)

                              Walter Van Tilburg Clark

9

1 They regarded me silently,
   2 Brother Jack with a smile that went no deeper than his lips, (Abs)
     3 his head cocked to one side, (Abs)
     3 studying me with his penetrating eyes; (VC)
   2 the other blank-faced, (Abs)
     3 looking out of eyes that were meant to reveal nothing and to
       stir profound uncertainty. (VC)

                                Ralph Ellison

10

1 He stood at the top of the stairs and watched me,
  2 I waiting for him to call me up, (Abs)
  2 he hesitating to come down, (Abs)
    3 his lips nervous with the suggestion of a smile, (Abs)
    3 mine asking whether the smile meant come, or go away. (Abs)

11

1 Joad's lips stretched tight over his long teeth for a moment, and
1 he licked his lips,
  2 like a dog, (P)
    3 two licks, (NC)
      4 one in each direction from the middle. (NC)

Steinbeck

12

1 We all live in two realities:
  2 one of seeming fixity, (NC)
    3 with institutions, dogmas, rules of punctuation, and routines, (PP)
      4 the calendared and clockwise world of all but futile round on round; (NC) and
  2 one of whirling and flying electrons, dreams, and possibilities, (NC)
    3 behind the clock. (PP)

Sidney Cox

13

1 It was as though someone, somewhere, had touched a lever and shifted gears, and
1 the hospital was set for night running,
  2 smooth and silent, (A + A)
  2 its normal clatter and hum muffled, (Abs)
  2 the only sounds heard in the whitewalled room distant and unreal: (Abs)
    3 a low hum of voices from the nurses' desk, (NC)
      4 quickly stifled, (VC)
    3 the soft squish of rubber-soled shoes on the tiled corridor; (NC)
    3 starched white cloth rustling against itself, (NC) and, outside,
    3 the lonesome whine of wind in the country night (NC) and
    3 the Kansas dust beating against the windows. (NC)

14

1 The beach sounds are jazzy,
  2 percussion fixing the mode — (Abs)
    3 the surf cracking and booming in the distance, (Abs)
    3 a little nearer dropped bar-bells clanking, (Abs)
    3 steel gym rings, / , ringing, (Abs)
    / 4 flung together, (VC)
    3 palm fronds rustling above me, (Abs)
      4 like steel brushes washing over a snare drum, (PP)
    3 troupes of sandals splatting and shuffling on the sandy cement, (Abs)

        4 their beat varying, (Abs)
           5 syncopation emerging and disappearing with changing
              paces. (Abs)
                              15
1 A small Negro girl develops from the sheet of glare-frosted walk,
   2 walking barefooted, (VC)
      3 her bare legs striking and coiling from the hot cement, (Abs)
         4 her feet curling in, (Abs)
            5 only the outer edges touching. (Abs)
                              16
1 The swells moved rhythmically toward us,
   2 irregularly faceted, (VC)
   2 sparkling, (VC)
   2 growing taller and more powerful until the shining crest bursts,
      (VC)
      3 a transparent sheet of pale green water spilling over the top,
         (Abs)
         4 breaking into blue-white foam as it cascades down the front
            of the wave, (VC)
         4 piling up in a frothy mound that the diminishing wave pushes
            up against the pilings, (VC)
            5 with a swishsmash, (PP)
         4 the foam drifting back, (Abs)
            5 like a lace fan opened over the shimmering water as the
               spent wave returns whispering to the sea. (PP)

The best starting point for a composition unit based on these four
principles is with two-level narrative sentences, first with one second-
level addition (sentences 4, 5), then with two or more parallel ones (6,
7, 8). Anyone sitting in his room with his eyes closed could write the
main clause of most of the examples; the discipline comes with the
additions, provided they are based at first on immediate observation,
requiring the student to phrase an exact observation in exact language.
This can hardly fail to be exciting to a class: it is life, with the variety
and complexity of life; the workbook exercise is death. The situation is
ideal also for teaching diction — abstract-concrete, general-specific,
literal-metaphorical, denotative-connotative. When the sentences begin to come out right, it is time to examine the additions for their grammatical character. From then on the grammar comes to the aid of the
writing and the writing reinforces the grammar. One can soon go on to
multilevel narrative sentences (1, 9–11, 15, 16) and then to brief narratives of three to six or seven sentences on actions with a beginning, a
middle, and an end that can be observed over and over again — beating eggs, making a cut with a power saw, or following a record changer's
cycle or a wave's flow and ebb. (Bring the record changer to class.) Description, by contrast, is static, picturing appearance rather than behavior. The constructions to master are the noun and adjective clusters
and the absolute (13, 14). Then the descriptive noun cluster must be

taught to ride piggyback on the narrative sentence, so that description and narration are interleaved: "In the morning we went out into a new world, a glistening crystal and white world, each skeleton tree, each leafless bush, even the heavy, drooping power lines sheathed in icy crystal." The next step is to develop the sense for variety in texture and change in pace that all good narrative demands.

In the next unit, the same four principles can be applied to the expository paragraph. But this is a subject for another paper.

I want to anticipate two possible objections. One is that the sentences are long. By freshman English standards they are long, but I could have produced far longer ones from works freshmen are expected to read. Of the sentences by students, most were written as finger exercises in the first few weeks of the course. I try in narrative sentences to push to level after level, not just two or three, but four, five, or six, even more, as far as the students' powers of observation will take them. I want them to become sentence acrobats, to dazzle by their syntactic dexterity. I'd rather have to deal with hyperemia than anemia. I want to add my voice to that of James Coleman (*CCC*, December 1962) deploring our concentration on the plain style.

The other objection is that my examples are mainly descriptive and narrative — and today in freshman English we teach only exposition. I deplore this limitation as much as I deplore our limitation to the plain style. Both are a sign that we have sold our proper heritage for a pot of message. In permitting them, the English department undercuts its own discipline. Even if our goal is only utilitarian prose, we can teach diction and sentence structure far more effectively through a few controlled exercises in description and narration than we can by starting right off with exposition (Theme One, 500 words, precipitates *all* the problems of writing). There is no problem of invention; the student has something to communicate — his immediate sense impressions, which can stand a bit of exercising. The material is not already verbalized — he has to match language to sense impressions. His acuteness in observation and in choice of words can be judged by fairly objective standards — is the sound of a bottle of milk being set down on a concrete step suggested better by *clink* or *clank* or *clunk?* In the examples, study the diction for its accuracy, rising at times to the truly imaginative. Study the use of metaphor, of comparison. This verbal virtuosity and syntactical ingenuity can be made to carry over into expository writing.

But this is still utilitarian. What I am proposing carries over of itself into the study of literature. It makes the student a better reader of literature. It helps him thread the syntactical mazes of much mature writing, and it gives him insight into that elusive thing we call style. Last year a student told of rereading a book by her favorite author, Willa Cather, and of realizing for the first time *why* she liked reading her: she could understand and appreciate the style. For some students, moreover, such writing makes life more interesting as well as giving them a way to share their interest with others. When they learn how to put concrete details into a sentence, they begin to look at life with more alertness. If it is liberal education we are concerned with, it is just possible that these things are more important than anything we can achieve when we set our sights on the plain style in expository prose.

I want to conclude with a historical note. My thesis in this paragraph is that modern prose like modern poetry has more in common with the seventeenth than with the eighteenth century and that we fail largely because we are operating from an eighteenth century base. The shift from the complex to the cumulative sentence is more profound than it seems. It goes deep in grammar, requiring a shift from the subordinate clause (the staple of our trade) to the cluster and the absolute (so little understood as to go almost unnoticed in our textbooks). And I have only lately come to see that this shift has historical implications. The cumulative sentence is the modern form of the loose sentence that characterized the anti-Ciceronian movement in the seventeenth century. This movement, according to Morris W. Croll,[3] began with Montaigne and Bacon and continued with such men as Donne, Browne, Taylor, Pascal. To Montaigne, its art was the art of being natural; to Pascal, its eloquence was the eloquence that mocks formal eloquence; to Bacon, it presented knowledge so that it could be examined, not so that it must be accepted.

But the Senecan amble was banished from England when "the direct sensuous apprehension of thought" (T. S. Eliot's words) gave way to Cartesian reason or intellect. The consequences of this shift in sensibility are well summarized by Croll:

> To this mode of thought we are to trace almost all the features of modern literary education and criticism, or at least of what we should have called modern a generation ago: the study of the precise meaning of words; the reference to dictionaries as literary authorities; the study of the sentence as a logical unit alone; the careful circumscription of its limits and the gradual reduction of its length; . . .[4] the attempt to reduce grammar to an exact science; the idea that forms of speech are always either correct or incorrect; the complete subjection of the laws of motion and expression in style to the laws of logic and standardization — in short, the triumph, during two centuries, of grammatical over rhetorical ideas. (*Style, Rhetoric and Rhythm,* p. 232.)

Here is a seven-point scale any teacher of composition can use to take stock. He can find whether he is based in the eighteenth century or in the twentieth and whether he is consistent — completely either an ancient or a modern — or is just a crazy mixed-up kid.

Postscript

I have asserted that "syntactical ingenuity" can best be developed in narrative-descriptive writing and that it can be made to carry over into discursive writing. The count made for the article on sentence openers included all sentence modifiers — or free modifiers, as I prefer to call them. In the total number of free modifiers, the 2000 word samples were almost identical — 1545 in the fiction and 1519 in the nonfiction, roughly one in three sentences out of four. But they differ in position:

| Nonfiction | initial 575 | medial 492 | final 452 |
| Fiction | initial 404 | medial 329 | final 812 |

And they differ in some of the grammatical kinds used in the final position:

| Nonfiction | NC 123 | VC 63 | Abs 9 |
| Fiction | NC 131 | VC 218 | Abs 108 |

Thus the differences are not in the structures used, only in the position and in the frequency of the various kinds of structures. It will be well to look at a few more sentences of discursive prose.

17

1 His [Hemingway's] characters, / , wander through the ruins of
    Babel,
  2/ expatriates for the most part, (NC)
  2 smattering many tongues (VC) and
  2 speaking a demotic version of their own. (VC)

Harry Levin

18

1 From literal to figurative is one range that a word may take:
  2 from *foot* of a person to *foot* of a mountain, (PP)
    3 a substituted or metaphoric use. (NC)

1 From concrete to abstract is another range:
  2 from *foot* to *extremity,* (PP)
    3 stressing one of the abstract characteristics of foot, (VC)
      4 a contrast for which the terms *image* and *symbol* as distin-
        guished from *concept* are also used. (NC)

Josephine Miles

19

  2 Going back to his [Hemingway's] work in 1944, (VC)
1 you perceive his kinship with a wholly different group of novelists,
  2 let us say with Poe and Hawthorne and Melville: (PP)
    3 the haunted and nocturnal writers, (NC)
    3 the men who dealt in images that were symbols of an inner
      world. (NC)

Malcolm Cowley

20

1 Even her style in it is transitional and momentous,
  2 a matter of echoing and reminiscing effects, and of little clarion notes of surprise and prophecy here and there; (NC)
    3 befitting that time of life which has been called the old age of youth and the youth of old age, (AC or VC)
    4 a time fraught with heartache and youthful tension. (NC)
Glenway Wescott, of Colette's Break of Day

21

  2 Aglow with splendor and consequence, (AC)
1 he [Sterne] rejoined his wife and daughter,
  2 whom he presently transferred to his new parsonage at Coxwold, (RC)
    3 an old and rambling house, (NC)
    4 full of irregular, comfortable rooms, (AC)
    4 situated on the edge of the moors, (VC)
      5 in a neighborhood much healthier than the marshy lands of Sutton. (PP)
Peter Quennell

22

1 It is with the coming of man that a vast hole seems to open in nature,
  2 a vast black whirlpool spinning faster and faster, (NC)
    3 consuming flesh, stones, soil, minerals, (VC)
    3 sucking down the lightning, (VC)
    3 wrenching power from the atom, (VC)
      4 until the ancient sounds of nature are drowned out in the cacophony of something which is no longer nature, (SC)
        5 something instead which is loose and knocking at the world's heart, (NC)
        5 something demonic and no longer planned — (NC)
          6 escaped, it may be — (VC)
          6 spewed out of nature, (VC)
          6 contending in a final giant's game against its master. (VC)
Loren Eiseley

The structures used in prose are necessarily the structures used in poetry, necessarily because prose and poetry use the same language. Poets may take more liberties with the grammar than prose writers are likely to do; but their departures from the norm must all be understood by reference to the norm. Since poets, like the writers of narrative, work more by association than by logical connection, their sentences are likely to have similar structures. They seem to know the values of the cumulative sentence.

The first example here consists of the first two stanzas of "The Meadow Mouse"; the slashes mark the line ends. The other example constitutes the last four of the five stanzas of "The Motive for Metaphor." It shows well how structural analysis of the sentence reveals the tactics of a difficult poem.

23

1 In a shoebox stuffed in an old nylon stocking / Sleeps the baby mouse I found in the meadow, /
  2 Where he trembled and shook beneath a stick / Till I caught him up by the tail and brought him in, / (RC)
    3 Cradled in my hand, / (VC)
    3 a little quaker, (NC)
      4 the whole body of him trembling, / (Abs)
    3 His absurd whiskers sticking out like a cartoon mouse, / (Abs)
    3 His feet like small leaves, / (Abs)
      4 Little lizard-feet, / (NC)
      4 Whitish and spread wide when he tried to struggle away, / (AC)
        5 Wriggling like a minuscule puppy. (VC)

1 Now he's eaten his three kinds of cheese and drunk from his bottle-cap watering trough — /
  2 So much he just lies in one corner, / (AC)
    3 His tail curled under him, (Abs)
    3 his belly big / As his head, (Abs)
    3 His bat-like ears / Twitching, (Abs)
      4 tilting toward the least sound. (VC)

Theodore Roethke

24

  2 In the same way, (PP)
1 you were happy in spring,
  2 with the half colors of quarter-things, (PP)
    3 The slightly brighter sky, (NC)
    3 the melting clouds, (NC)
    3 the single bird, (NC)
    3 the obscure moon — (NC)
      4 The obscure moon lighting an obscure world of things that would never be quite expressed, (NC)
        5 where you yourself were never quite yourself and did not want nor have to be, (RC)
          6 desiring the exhilarations of changes: (VC)
            7 the motive for metaphor, (NC)
          6 shrinking from the weight of primary noon, (VC)
            7 the ABC of being, (NC)
            7 the ruddy temper, (NC)
            7 the hammer of red and blue, (NC)
            7 the hard sound — (NC)
              8 steel against intimation — (NC)
            7 the sharp flash, (NC)
            7 the vital, arrogant, fatal, dominant X. (NC)

Wallace Stevens

Notes

1. Cf. Leo Rockas, "Abstract and Concrete Sentences," *CCC,* May 1963. Rockas describes sentences as abstract or concrete, the abstract implying the concrete and vice versa. Readers and writers, he says, must have the knack of apprehending the concrete in the abstract and the abstract in the concrete. This is true and valuable. I am saying that within a single sentence the writer may present more than one level of generality, translating the abstract into the more concrete in added levels.

2. This statement is not quite tenable. Each helps to make the idea of the base clause more concrete or specific, but each is not more concrete or specific than the one immediately above it.

3. "The Baroque Style in Prose," *Studies in English Philology: A Miscellany in Honor of Frederick Klaeber* (1929), reprinted in *Style, Rhetoric, and Rhythm: Essays by Morris W. Croll* (1966) and A. M. Witherspoon and F. J. Warnke, *Seventeenth-Century Prose and Poetry,* 2nd ed. (1963). I have borrowed from Croll in my description of the cumulative sentence.

4. The omitted item concerns punctuation and is not relevant here. In using this scale, note the phrase "what we should have called modern a generation ago" and remember that Croll was writing in 1929.

Christensen's Insights as a Resource for Your Teaching

1. Consider Christensen's essay alongside the excerpts from Ann E. Berthoff's *The Making of Meaning* (pp. 262–73). How might Berthoff's conceptual framework aid you in implementing Christensen's pedagogy? Have you ever worked with language in this way or taught this sort of sentence analysis to your students? What were the results?

2. With Robert J. Connors's critique in mind ("The Erasure of the Sentence," pp. 219–47), consider what we might lose by ignoring Christensen's ideas and other sentence-level pedagogies. How might you guide your students in practicing Christensen's "generative rhetoric" as part of the composing process?

Christensen's Insights as a Resource for Your Writing Classroom

1. Ask your students to bring to class their most recent drafts of essay writing. Instruct students to isolate one of the shortest sentences in a draft and then work with them to "build upon" the sentence by adding modifiers to its various parts. Discuss how these changes to one small, isolated moment in the essay might necessitate adjustments to other parts of the drafted essay.

2. Share with your students the point that Christensen makes about the "tone-deaf" sentence that can burgeon into "gobbledegook" (p. 250), and then share with them the formula that Christensen describes next, the formula for the cumulative sentence. Have students work in small groups to identify and reshape some of the longer, "tone-deaf" sentences in their drafts into cumulative sentences — that is, sentences that are, after revision, perhaps just as long as the original but much more elegant, readable, and meaningful.

From The Making of Meaning

Ann E. Berthoff

Though teachers have embraced the concept of writing as process, Ann E. Berthoff argues that most have not incorporated it productively into their classroom practices. In The Making of Meaning: Metaphors, Models, and Maxims for Writing Teachers *(1981), she suggests that teachers can begin to improve writing by alerting students to how their minds work with language, imposing order on fundamentally ambiguous signs and abstracting from experience to establish categories and relationships. When students recognize the cognitive steps that underlie standard draft stages, they will be better equipped to make free and productive revisions of their work.*

Learning the Uses of Chaos

I t is, perhaps, a measure of our sophistication that we English teachers can boldly set about discussing the topic *learning to write*, identifying an issue in nonpretentious terms while realizing that it isn't as simple a matter as it sounds. Holding a conference on the topic suggests an awareness that learning to write is a matter for theoretical consideration, not just recipe swapping; that the difficulties we must confront in teaching students how to write deserve something other than high-minded expressions of dismay. We need theory in order to find out what can be done about teaching composition and to define what it is we think we are doing. No theoretical premise is of greater importance to all the new rhetorics, from "free writing" to tagmemics, than that composing is a process; however, this idea, which is already on the way to becoming conventional wisdom, is not helping us as it should. That is to say, the idea that there is not just *composition* but *composing* is becoming dogma, an idea being handed on to teachers and students alike before the implications it might have for pedagogy and course design have been explored or understood.

What does it mean to say that composing is a process? Why is it important that, at all levels of development and in all grades, students of writing should understand that composing is a process? How do we design courses — sequences of assignments — which can make that understanding something other than received dogma? For unless composing as a process is what we actually teach, not just what we proclaim, the idea cannot be fruitful. In many instances, the language of the new rhetoric is used when there is no correspondingly new attitude towards what we are teaching, to say nothing of how we are teaching it. There may be talk of "pre-writing," but the term is misleading if it is taken to mean getting a thesis statement. (I have seen a writing lab manual for tutors that defines pre-writing as a matter of learning to outline.) A textbook that exhorts students in the first chapter to carry through discovery procedures and in the second discusses the rhetorical modes as they were defined in the eighteenth century has not encouraged students to understand the relationship of earlier and later phases of composing.

It is not instructive to talk about "the composing process" unless we have a conception of the kind of process writing is — or, at least, the kind of process it is not. Thus writing is *not* like cooking a particular dish; writing may resemble, at one stage or another, some phase of, say, making a cream sauce, but it is not sequential or "linear"; it is not measurement, followed by amalgamation and transformation. An analogy for writing that is based on culinary experience would have to include ways of calculating the guests' preferences, as well as ways of determining what's on the shelf — the cook's and the grocer's — and what's in the purse. Nor is the composing process like playing games or developing various motor skills. Such analogies leave out of account language, or they conceive of it in mechanistic or merely behavioral terms. But language is not merely a tool; it is not a set of counters to be moved about nor a set of conventions to be manipulated in order to express one or another idea. We don't have ideas that we put into words; we don't think of what we want to say and then write. In composing, we make meanings. We find the forms of thought by means of language, and we find the forms of language by taking thought. If we English teachers are to understand composing as the kind of process it is, we will need a philosophy of language that can account for this dialectic of forming. A hopeful sign that this is beginning to happen is that English teachers are beginning to study Vygotsky, a developmental psychologist who knew that language and thought do not bear one another a sequential relationship, but that they are simultaneous and correlative.

I believe we can best teach the composing process by conceiving of it as a continuum of making meaning, by seeing writing as analogous to all those processes by which we make sense of the world. It is generally a surprise to students to learn that writing has anything in common with anything else they have ever done — and for the very good reason that, as it has generally been taught them, it has indeed nothing much to do with anything they have ever done. But writing, taught as a process of making meanings, can be seen to be like taking in a happening, forming an opinion, deciding what's to be done, construing a text, or reading the significance of a landscape. Thinking, perceiving, writing are all acts of composing: any composition course should insure that students learn the truth of this principle, that making meanings is the work of the active mind and is thus within their natural capacity.

Meanings don't just happen: we make them; we find and form them. In that sense, all writing courses are creative writing courses. Learning to write is learning to do deliberately and methodically with words on the page what we do all the time with language. Meanings don't come out of the air; we make them out of a chaos of images, half-truths, remembrances, syntactic fragments, from the mysterious and unformed. The most useful slogan for the composition course — along with "how do I know what I mean 'till I hear what I say?" — is *ex nihilo nihil fit:* out of nothing, nothing can be made. When we teach pre-writing as a phase of the composing process, what we are teaching is not how to get a thesis statement but the generation and uses of chaos; when we teach revision as a phase of the composing process, we are teaching just that — reseeing the ways out of chaos.

Our students, because they are language animals, because they have the power of naming, can generate chaos; they can find ways out of chaos because language creates them. Language itself is the great heuristic. Any name implies generalization; any cluster of names implies classification; any classification implies statement. As Kenneth Burke says, to name something *A* is to declare simultaneously that it is not *not-A*.^Δ All rhetorical functions can be derived from that most profound of linguistic facts, that words, in Vygotsky's formulation, come into being as verbal generalizations. It is the *discursive* character of language, its tendency to "run along," to be syntactical, which brings thought along with it. It is the discursive, generalizing, forming power of language that makes meanings from chaos.

Students can learn to write by learning the uses of chaos, which is to say, rediscovering the power of language to generate the sources of meaning. Our job is to design sequences of assignments that let our students discover what language can do, what they can do with language. Kenneth Koch got poetry out of his youngsters because he gave them syntactic structures to play with; Sylvia Ashton-Warner's "key vocabulary" became what she called "the captions of the dynamic life itself"; Paulo Freire's "generative words" provided the means by which the peasants in his literacy classes — "culture circles" — could name the world. Our students can learn to write only if we give them back their language, and that means playing with it, working with it, using it instrumentally, making many starts. We want them to learn the truth of Gaston Bachelard's observation that "in the realm of mind, to begin

---

Δ: As noted on p. 272, throughout *The Making of Meaning,* Berthoff uses this symbol to indicate source materials that she draws on repeatedly. The cited passages follow the article in the section titled "More Maxims."

is to know you have the right to begin again." Our students cannot learn the uses of chaos if we continue to make assignments appropriate not to these beginnings but to the final phases of the composing process. Beginnings, for instance, should never be graded: identifying mistakes is irrelevant when we are teaching making a start at the process of making meanings.

Now, chaos is scary: the meanings that can emerge from it, which can be discerned taking shape within it, can be discovered only if students who are learning to write can learn to tolerate ambiguity. It is to our teacherly advantage that the mind doesn't like chaos; on the other hand, we have to be alert to the fact that meanings can be arrived at too quickly, the possibility of other meanings being too abruptly foreclosed. What we must realize ourselves and make dramatically evident to our students is what I. A. Richards means when he calls ambiguities "the hinges of thought."

Learning to write is a matter of learning to tolerate ambiguity, of learning that the making of meaning is a dialectical process determined by perspective and context. Meanings change as we think about them; statements and events, significances and interpretations can mean different things to different people at different times. Meanings are not prebaked or set for all time; they are created, found, formed, and re-formed. Even dictionary definitions change: that is a brand new discovery for most students, that language has a history. How we see something — a relationship between word and idea or object, or between two words or statements — depends on our experience, and on our purposes, our perspective, "where we're coming from." We know reality not directly but by means of the meanings we make. (The role of critical thinking is, of course, to review and revise those meanings.) What we know, we know in some form — perceptual or conceptual. We see relationships not in isolation but in a field of other relationships: as a text has a context, so events and ideas and objects have a "context of situation," in Malinowski's formulation. It is the nature of signifiers to be unclear, multivalent, polysemous, ambiguous, until perspective and context are determined. I consider it the most important advance of the semester if a student moves from "Webster tell us . . ." to "what this situation means depends on how you look at it." *It depends* is a slogan I would add to *ex nihilo nihil fit.*

For students to discover that ambiguities are "the hinges of thought," we surely will have to move from the inert, passive questions that we inscribe in the margins of papers and which we direct to student readers: "What do you mean here?" "What is the author trying to say?" Those are not critically useful questions; they elicit insubstantial responses or "I-thought-that-was-what-you-wanted" or, on occasion, students simply cast their eyes heavenward. We should focus on the shifting character of meaning and the role of perspective and context, and we can do so by raising such questions as these: "How does it change your meaning if you put it this way?" "If the author is saying *X,* how does that go with the *Y* we heard him saying in the preceding chapter — or stanza?"

"What do you make of passage *A* in the light of passage *B?*" Students learn to use ambiguities as "the hinges of thought" as they learn to formulate alternate readings; to say it again, watching how the "it" changes. In my view, from my perspective, *interpretive paraphrase* is another name for the composing process itself. It is the means by which meanings are hypothesized, identified, developed, modified, discarded, or stabilized. And, furthermore, it is the only way I know to teach students how to edit their compositions. Interpretive paraphrase enacts the dialogue that is at the heart of all composing: a writer is in dialogue with his various selves and with his audience. And here is where the classroom hour can actively help us. The composition classroom ought to be a place where the various selves are heard and an audience's response is heard — listened to and responded to. Language is an exchange: we know what we've said and what can be understood from it when we get a response; we come to know what we mean when we hear what we say. It is this critical, reflexive character of language that allows us to think about thinking. Learning to write involves us all in many such unvicious circles whereby we interpret our interpretations.

Interpretive paraphrase — continually asking, "How does it change the meaning if I put it this way?" — is, of course, the principal method of all critical inquiry, but its importance for us in the composition classroom is that it teaches students to see relationships and to discover that that is what they do with their minds. It does not seem so to them: isolation and absurdity, not connectedness and meaningfulness, are for our students the characterizing qualities of most experience. Perhaps it's time to stop when one reaches the point of huge sociological generalization, but I think that this one is true; it is, after all, only another way of speaking of the alienation that is recognizably the mark of our era. If we can make the composition classroom a forum, a culture circle, a theatre, a version of Tolstoy's armchair aswarm with children questioning, talking, and arguing — if the composition classroom is the place where dialogue is the mode of making meaning, then we will have a better chance to dramatize not only the fact that language itself changes with the meanings we make from it and that its powers are generative and developmental, but also that it is the indispensable and unsurpassable means of reaching others and forming communities with them. The ability to speak is innate, but language can only be realized in a social context. Dialogue, that is to say, is essential to the making of meaning and thus to learning to write. The chief use of chaos is that it creates the need for that dialogue.

Discovering Limits

Our panel topic is rather less compelling than the convention slogan. The idea of the human mind as the supreme resource is more inspiriting than the notion of one more innovative this or that, and certainly the concept of mind is no more problematic than the notion of "students with learning and language difficulties." Of course, some difficulties are more difficult than others: you can't expect to teach someone to read a paragraph if he can't read a sentence, or a sentence if he can't read words, or words if he can't construe letters or letter groups. And yet that is not to say that we teach reading by teaching the alphabet. I realize that it is casuistry of a sort to stretch the idea of difficulty, but I do want to claim that "students with language and learning difficulties" is a pretty fair description of students entering college. If our freshmen were not burdened with such difficulties, if they encountered no such difficulties, we would not have to labor to teach them to write coherently, to read critically, and to think cogently. I believe that what is good for the best and brightest is essential for students who have difficulties. Those we used to call slow learners need the freedom and the opportunities we trouble to offer our prize students. And, in turn, what is important and worthwhile for disadvantaged students will prove to be useful and valuable for the good readers and the practiced writers.

If we tap this supreme resource, the minds of our students, we will find powerful, profoundly rooted capacities that cannot be identified solely in quantifiable terms and quotients, but which we can learn to identify and train. Mind in this sense is not reducible to what has been called "intelligence" by psychologists looking for something to measure; intelligence is a culture-bound concept as mind is not. Socrates demonstrated his method not with the head of the class but with an illiterate slave boy. Montessori's first school in Rome was for children who had been certified by the state as cretini — morons. It was Brazilian peasants who gained the experience of freedom in attending Paulo Freire's literacy classes. The point from which these great teachers of the disadvantaged begin is the mind's operation, the human mind in action. Now our convention slogan — Let the Minds of Our Students Be the Supreme Resource — is a sound point of departure for the composition teacher because composing *is* the mind in action! The composing process that involves writing down words requires the same acts of mind as the composing process by which we make sense of the world. Jargon like "nonverbal communication" masks the fact that all perception, all communication, takes place in a world built by language. Man is the language animal and the operation of his mind is a linguistic operation, whether words are spoken or not.

It's very refreshing to have the NCTE and its affiliates publicly declaring an interest in mind. It's a welcome change from the pseudoscientific concepts we've grown used to: verbal behavior, communication skills, input and feedback, encoding and decoding. But we should be on our guard against becoming ensnared in the problem of defining what "mind" is; and, be warned, this is the game that psychologists and philosophers who deplore what they call "mentalism" like to play and win. (They do not equally enjoy the game of deciding what is "behavior.") Laboring under the delusion that they are being "scientific," English teachers have all too often asked such questions as, "What *is* creativity?" What *is* communication?" You may remember that the theme song of the Dartmouth Conference was, "What *is* English?" That kind of questioning gets us nowhere; it is neither pragmatic nor scientific. J. Robert Oppenheimer explains in discussing this misconception of scientific inquiry that Einstein did not ask, "What is a clock?" Rather, he framed questions about how we would measure time over immense distances. We will have to learn to ask not "what *is* mind?" but "what happens when we use our minds in writing that is comparable to what happens when we make sense of the world?" and "what happens in the composing process?" Josephine Miles has entitled one discussion of composition, "What Do We Compose?" and another, "How What's What in the English Language?" Such questions as these will help us develop a working concept of mind. A good name for the mind in action is *imagination:* Coleridge called the imagination "the prime agent of all human perception."[Δ] That is an epistemological concept that English teachers should make their own. I suggest, then, that this panel topic could be restated as follows: *Teaching the composing process by liberating the imagination.*

I will try in this talk to suggest what that might mean when we set about developing "innovative composition courses for students with learning and language difficulties."

The one sure principle of composition, as of imagination, is that nothing comes of nothing; *ex nihilo nihil fit:* nothing can be made from nothing. Recent textbooks in composition have begun to show signs of an interest in the subject of invention, though the process seems still unclear, if not misconceived. The first use of language that a student of composition has to learn, I think, is in the generation of chaos. If we don't begin there, we falsify the composing process because composition requires choosing all along the way, and you can't choose if there are no perceived alternatives: chaos is the source of alternatives. If we are unwilling to risk chaos, we won't have provided our students with the opportunity to discover that ambiguities are, as I. A. Richards has said, "the hinges of thought."[Δ]

Once we encourage the generation of chaos, however, we are morally as well as pedagogically bound to present very carefully the ways of emerging from it. Happily, the process of generating chaos provides, itself, the means of emerging from chaos by making something of it. I like to demonstrate how this can be so by having everybody in class name what he sees, what comes to mind in response to, say, a photograph from Steichen's *Family of Man,* with everyone writing down everybody else's word. Twice around the room and there begin to be repetitions; names group themselves like so many birds flocking; three times around the room and the blackboard is full, the sheet of paper covered. (That can illustrate the psychological advantage of having a full page rather than an empty sheet, and it suggests that chaos might be better than nothing.) The chaos begins to take shape: classifying, which is organized comparing, proceeds without the stimulus of prefabricated, loaded "study questions." The primary compositional modes of amalgamation and elimination begin to operate. All this happens more or less without guidance, though if there is a roadblock it can be exploded by asking the only study question anyone ever needs: How does who do what?

The reason that this natural ordering process takes place in the very act of naming is that the mind naturally abstracts. The human mind — but that is a redundancy: the mind naturally orders by comparing and differentiating. (That process of selection apparently goes on in the retinal cells at an electrochemical level.) We see in terms of classes and types; everything we see is seen as an example of a kind of thing. Perception is contingent on the mind's capacity for analogizing.

My point is that we do not have to teach our students *how* to abstract but *that* they abstract. What we do teach is how to listen in on the dialogue in progress when they are looking and classifying in the act of perception. That dialogue is thinking; it is dialectical. *Dialogue* and *dialectic* are cognate: learning to see what you're looking at really means learning to question and questioning is the life of thought. The composing process, I think we can say, is empowered from beginning to end by the dialectic of question and answer. The way to bring this fact to life for our students is to encourage writing from the start — not topic sentences and thesis statements of course, but lists, class names, questions, and tentative answers and new questions. This "pre-writing" is writing; a cluster of names is a protoparagraph; a cluster of clusters is a nascent composition.

To suggest the formal nature of this emergence from chaos I used to employ rather elaborate schematic devices — bits and pieces of signs from symbolic logic, tagmemic grids, flowcharts, and so on, but the trouble is — and it's not a problem peculiar to students with learning and language difficulties — the relationship of the sign to its referent is easily misconceived and the signs themselves become the focus of interest. I've collected pre-writing sheets covered with diagrams and charts that bore no relationship to the words employed, with whatever concepts might have emerged totally obscured by a mass of lines and boxes. Students have submitted first drafts with the appearance of sketches for a painting of the Martyrdom of St. Sebastian, because they were under the impression that "she likes arrows." Just as we can't teach reading by simply teaching the alphabet, so we can't teach composition by laying out unintelligible floor plans.

The alternative, I've come to believe, is a line drawn down the middle of the page. Overschematizing is no more conducive to the definition of choices than the formal outline, but opposition as an organizing concept, one which has been borrowed from linguistics by structuralists in all disciplines, can be very helpful to us in teaching composition. Opposition is a highly generalized term covering juxtapositions, alignments, echoes as well as antitheses, opposites, and counterpoint. Figure and ground are in opposition; beginning and end are in opposition; character and plot are in opposition. The ends of a scale and the banks of a river represent two kinds of opposition. It is a concept to think with; it is quickly grasped by all students because it is a name for what they are already doing when they judge size and distance and degrees of all kinds. Opposition is the principle informing every phrase they utter, every step they take. I have seen many a student weighed down with learning and language difficulties come to life smiling at the brand new discovery that composing has anything whatsoever to do with anything else he has ever done. Exercises in forming and developing oppositions not only provide the steps out of chaos; they also become the means of discovering that composing is a dialectical process: it starts and stops and starts again; it can proceed in circles; it is tentative, hypothetical, and recapitulative. Our students can learn, when they use the concept of opposition to think with, that composing means naming, differentiating, comparing, classifying, selecting, and thus defining; that composing means getting it together. Isn't that what we want to teach them?

"A composition is a bundle of parts": that is Josephine Miles' very useful definition.[Δ] Composing means identifying the parts and bundling them; in the composing process we recreate wholes by establishing relationships between the parts. All our innovative powers in designing composition courses should go to assuring that writing is involved at all stages of this process. The textbooks that warn glibly or sternly, "Don't begin to write until you know what you want to say," ought to be returned to the publishers. The motto of every composition course should be, "How do I know what I mean until I hear what I say?" I'm very fond of that old chestnut; here is a more weighty formulation: I. A. Richards, recalling Plato as usual, declares that "dialectic is the continuing audit of meaning."[Δ]

Some experienced writers can keep track of what they are saying in that interior dialogue and thus can audit their meanings in their heads, but students with learning and language difficulties should write it down, continually. In that way they can learn to recognize the interior dialogue and keep the dialectic going. Writing at all stages of composition brings to full consciousness the experience of the mind at work, the imagination in action. Writing can counter the notion that ideas fall from heaven, that some people just "have" them and others just don't. Writing at all stages is a way of seeing ideas develop. We want to assure that the student continually discovers that it is his mind that is giving form to chaos; that his language is ordering chaos; that his imagination is just what Coleridge tells him it is, "a shaping spirit."

We encourage that experience of writing and thereby the auditing of meaning by providing linguistic forms, syntactical and rhetorical structures, not for imitation but for use as speculative instruments. Forms are not cookie cutters superimposed on some given, rolled-out reality dough; forms are not alien structures that are somehow made appropriate to "what you want to say." Forms are our means of abstracting; or, rather, forming *is* abstracting. Abstracting is what the mind does; abstracting, forming is the work of imagination. But this can rapidly become more interesting as metaphysics than as pedagogy. I suggest that we think of forms by considering what they do: they provide limits. "A poet," in Allen Tate's definition, "is a man willing to come under the bondage of limitations — if he can find them." Limits make choice possible and thus free the imagination.

Consider what Kenneth Koch calls the "poetry idea" in his experimental writing assignments: that's the conception of form we need. Koch gets poetry out of his third graders by making forms available to them. He doesn't say, "Tell me what it would feel like to be a geranium in a sunny window." He reads poetry with them and then offers a form that can answer to their experience, their perceptions. "I used to be a _____, but now I am a _____." Or he says, "Talk to something that isn't a person; ask it a question":

> Dog, where did you get that bark?
> Dragon, where do you get that flame?
> Kitten, where did you get that meow?
> Rose, where did you get that red?
> Bird, where did you get those wings?

At first, Koch was apologetic about his dependence on form, but he soon came to see that it was the limits the forms provided that allowed the kids to discover their feelings and to shape their insights.

This conception of form as limit-providing structure can help us see more clearly that throughout the composing process the writer is engaged in limiting: selecting and differentiating are ways of limiting; we limit when we compare, classify, amalgamate, and discard; defining is, by definition, a setting of limits. How we limit is how we form. It is an idea that can help us develop sequences in our innovative composition courses. I. A. Richards has said that all learning depends upon a sequence of "partially parallel tasks." Any composition course should be organized so that learning something about syntactical structure prepares for learning something about paragraph structure. As it is, the new rhetorics every year lay out what the old rhetorics have been explaining since the eighteenth century; that, for instance, there are three modes of writing, called "exposition," "description," and "narrative." Do we create the occasions for our students to discover that argument can take the form of narrative, as in fable? that there is a logic of metaphor, in Robert Frost's sonnets as well as in Donne's? that description and analysis are both essential to definition? How many advanced composition courses incorporate so-called creative writing? It's time our composition courses were themselves composed, that we ask of them unity, coherence, and emphasis.

I have quoted I. A. Richards throughout because he has thought more deeply than anyone I know about the pedagogical implications of a philosophy of mind that stresses the shaping power of imagination. If we let the minds of our students be the supreme resource, it means we will be recognizing that language is "the supreme organ of the mind's self-ordering growth."[Δ] It is language — not vocabulary or a sophisticated repertory of syntactical structures, though we can work on this;

not the students' very own language and not the teacher's — it is language as a form-finder and form-creator that makes possible naming and opposition and definition; it is the power of language as a form that creates order from chaos; it is language that frames the dialectic, limits the field, forms the questions and answers, starts the dialectic and keeps it going; it is language that makes choice possible. That is why we can say that to learn to compose is to discover both the power of the mind and the meaning of human freedom.

More Maxims

I have depended on certain formulations in trying to make the case for reclaiming the imagination in order to teach the composing process as a matter of making meaning. Throughout the talks and articles that constitute Part II, I have cited a few statements repeatedly. They are indicated in the text by this sign:$^{\Delta}$ For convenience's sake, I've gathered them here with bibliographic data.

> Implied in the use of the negative, there is both the ability to generalize and the ability to specify. That is, you cannot use the negative properly without by the same token exemplifying the two basic dialectical resources of merger and division. For you can use "no" properly insofar as you can classify under one head many situations that are, in their positive details, quite distinct from one another. In effect, you group them under the head of "Situations all of which are classes in terms of the negative." And in the very act of so classifying, you distinguish them from another class of situations that are "not No-Situations."
>
> > Kenneth Burke, *Language as Symbolic Action*
> > (Berkeley: University of California Press, 1968), p. 425.

> The primary IMAGINATION I hold to be the living Power and prime Agent of all human Perception, and as a repetition in the finite mind of the eternal act of creation in the infinite I AM.
>
> > Samuel Taylor Coleridge, *Biographia Literaria,* Chap. XIII.

> *Questioner:* Like a whole composition, then, a word is a bundle of parts?
> Speaker: A bundle, a life, with a life history. . . .
>
> > Josephine Miles, "English: A Colloquy; or, How What's What in the Language," *California English Journal,* 2 (1966), 3–14.

> Language . . . is an organ — the supreme organ of the mind's self-ordering growth.

> Corresponding to all these studies [Mathematics, Physics, Chemistry, Biology, Sociology, Anthropology, Poetics, Dialectic] are characteristic uses of language. Poetics, I suggest, is faced by the most complex of them. Above Poetics I would put only Dialectic as being concerned with the relations of Poetics with all other studies and with their relations to one another. Dialectics would thus be the supreme study, with Philosophy as its Diplo-

matic Agent. All of them are both subject matter and language studies. That is the chief point here; there is no study which is not a language study, concerned with the speculative instruments it employs.

> I. A. Richards, *Speculative Instruments*
> (N.Y.: Harcourt, 1955), p. 9; pp. 115–16.

In general we will find that the more important a word is, and the more central and necessary its meanings are in our pictures of ourselves and the world, the more ambiguous and possibly deceiving the word will be. Naturally these words are also those which have been most used in philosophy. But it is not the philosophers who have made them ambiguous; it is the position of their ideas, as the very hinges of all thought. Our archproblem . . . has been "What should guide the reader's mind?" Our answer was "Our awareness of interdependence, of how things hang together, which makes us able to give and audit an account of what may be meant in a discussion — that highest activity of REASON which Plato named "Dialectic."

> I. A. Richards, *How to Read a Page*
> (1942; rpt. Boston: Beacon Press, 1959), p. 24; p. 240.

Berthoff's Insights as a Resource for Your Teaching

1. Some of Berthoff's key terms — for example, *chaos, dialogue, meaning, process,* and *ambiguity* — are fairly generalized and abstract, and therefore invite the reader to link them to his or her own sense of practical contexts. How might you paraphrase Berthoff's ideas to students, and what sorts of classroom activities might enable your students to benefit from an understanding of these terms?

2. What might Berthoff mean by the extraordinarily concise assertion, "forming is abstracting"? As you elaborate the variety of implications of this assertion, consider ways that you could help students to understand, practice, and cultivate the skill of making meaning.

Berthoff's Insights as a Resource for Your Writing Classroom

1. Berthoff explains that when she teaches writing, she "offers linguistic forms, syntactical and rhetorical structures, not for imitation but for use as speculative instruments." Develop some of these structures for your students to work with. How will you introduce these forms, how will you grade them, and what role would you expect them to play in your students' composing processes?

2. Berthoff suggests that we would do well to show students how writing is closely akin to other activities that they perform constantly. Develop ways to illustrate this point for your students, and then ask them to describe everyday activities that function as metaphors for key aspects of the composing process.

Teaching Writing with Computers

Technology and Literacy: A Story about the Perils of Not Paying Attention

Cynthia L. Selfe

In this essay, Cynthia L. Selfe explores difficult questions about student access to technology and, more specifically, advocates for writing teachers to think about technology in ways that will allow educators to relearn important lessons about literacy. The revolution in computer technology, if not carefully watched and regularly criticized — even redirected — will only function in a conservative, reproductive fashion that entrenches and exacerbates the inequities of economic class. Selfe first presented this essay as her Chair's Address to the 1997 Conference on College Composition and Communication, and it was later published in a 1999 issue of CCC. *Selfe also wrote a longer text on the subject,* Technology and Literacy in the Twenty-First Century: The Perils of Not Paying Attention *(1999).*

> Technological literacy — meaning computer skills and the ability to use computers and other technology to improve learning, productivity and performance — has become as fundamental to a person's ability to navigate through society as traditional skills like reading, writing, and arithmetic. . . . In explicit acknowledgment of the challenges facing the education community, on February 15, 1996, President Clinton and Vice President Gore announced the Technology Literacy Challenge, envisioning a 21st century where all students are technologically literate. The challenge was put before the nation as a whole, with responsibility . . . shared by local communities, states, the private sector, educators, local communities, parents, the federal government, and others. . . .
> — *Getting America's Students Ready for the 21st Century* (5)

> We know, purely and simply, that every single child must have access to a computer. . . .
> — Bill Clinton, qtd. in *Getting America's Students Ready for the 21st Century* (4)

A central irony shaping my experience with the CCCC as a professional organization goes something like this: I consider it a fortunate occurrence and a particular point of pride that many of the best ideas about teaching and learning writing, the most powerfully explanatory theoretical insights about language and discourse and literacy that inform education today, grow directly out of conversations among CCCC members. Given this situation, however, I find it compellingly unfortunate that the one topic serving as a focus for my own professional involvement — that of computer technology and its use in teaching composition — seems to be the single subject best guaranteed to inspire glazed eyes and complete indifference in that portion of the CCCC membership which does not immediately sink into snooze mode.

This irony, I am convinced, has nothing to do with collegial good will. CCCC colleagues have been unerringly polite in the 17 years of discussions we have had about technology. After all this time, however, I can spot the speech acts that follow a turn of the conversation to computers — the slightly averted gaze, the quick glance at the watch, the panicky look in the eyes when someone lapses into talk about microprocessors, or gigabytes, or ethernets. All these small potent gestures, as Michel de Certeau would say, signify pretty clearly — technology is either boring or frightening to most humanists; many teachers of English composition feel it antithetical to their primary concerns and many believe it should not be allowed to take up valuable scholarly time or the attention that could be best put to use in teaching or the study of literacy. I have, believe me, gotten the message — as subtle as it is.

These attitudes toward technology issues, of course, aren't shared by everyone in this organization — there are pockets of technology studies scholars and teachers here and there among us; notable occasions when an individual CCCC leader does speak about technology; and, every now and again, a professional conversation among us about the array of challenges associated with technology. These occasions remain exceptions, however, and anybody familiar with the values of traditional humanism knows that, as a group, we tend to hold in common a general distrust of the machine, that a preference for the non-technological still characterizes our community.

Our tendency to avoid focusing on the technological means that — while we are tolerant of those colleagues interested in the "souls of machines," to use Bruno Latour's term — we assign them to a peculiar kind of professional isolation "in their own separate world" of computer sessions and computer workshops and computers and writing conferences that many CCCC members consider influenced more by the concerns of "engineers, technicians, and technocrats" (vii) than those of humanists. It is this same set of historically and professionally determined beliefs, I think, that informs our actions within our home departments, where we generally continue to allocate the responsibility of technology decisions — and oftentimes the responsibility of technology studies — to a single faculty or staff member who doesn't mind wrestling with computers or the thorny, and the unpleasant issues that can be associated with their use. In this way, we manage to have the best of both worlds — we have computers available to use for our own studies, in support of our classes and our profession — but we have also relegated these technologies into the background of our professional lives. As a result, computers are rapidly becoming invisible, which is how we like our technology to be. When we don't have to pay attention to machines, we remain free to focus on the theory and practice of language, the stuff of real intellectual and social concern.

Why We Allow Ourselves to Ignore Technology

As humanists, we prefer things to be arranged this way because computer technology, when it is too much in our face (as an unfamiliar technology generally is), can suggest a kind of cultural strangeness that is off-putting. We are much more used to dealing with older technologies like print, a technology conventional enough so that we don't have to think so much about it, old enough so that it doesn't call such immediate attention to the social or material conditions associated with its use. Books, for example, are already and always — almost anyway — there. At this point in history, books are relatively cheap, they are generally accessible to students and to us, and they are acknowledged by our peers to be the appropriate tools of teaching and learning to use. As a result, our recognition of the material conditions associated with books have faded into the background of our imagination. Thus, although we understand on a tacit level that the print technology in which we invest so readily (and in which we ask students to invest) contributes to our own tenure and promotion, to our own wallets, and to our own status in the profession and in the public eye — this understanding is woven into the background of our professional attention, and we seldom pay attention to it on a daily basis. If we did, we'd go mad.

There are other things that don't occur to us, as well. When we use the more familiar technology of books, for instance, it is mostly within a familiar ideological system that allows us to ignore, except for some occasional twinges of conscience, the persistence of print and our role in this persistence. It allows us to ignore the understanding that print literacy functions as a cultural system — as Lester Faigley noted two years ago — not only to carry and distribute enlightened ideas, but also as a seamless whole to support a pattern of continuing illiteracy in this country.

I provide this example to suggest that composition studies faculty, educated in the humanist tradition, generally prefer our technologies and the material conditions associated so closely with them to remain in the background for obvious reasons, and the belief systems we construct in connection with various technologies allow us to accomplish this comfortable process of naturalization.

In the case of computers — we have convinced ourselves that we and the students with whom we work are made of much finer stuff than the machine in our midst, and we are determined to maintain this state of affairs. This ideological position, however, has other effects, as well. As a result of the inverse value we generally assign to discussions about computers, our professional organizations continue to deal with technology in what is essentially a piecemeal fashion. We now think of computers, for instance, as a simple tool that individual faculty members can use or ignore in their classrooms as they choose, but also one that the profession, as a collective whole — and with just a few notable exceptions — need not address too systematically. And so we have paid technology issues precious little focused attention over the years.

Why Composition Specialists Need to Pay Attention to Technology Issues

Allowing ourselves the luxury of ignoring technology, however, is not only misguided at the end of the 20th century, it is dangerously short-sighted. And I do not mean, simply, that we are all — each of us — now teaching students who must know how to communicate as informed thinkers and citizens in an increasingly technological world — although this is surely so. This recognition has led composition faculty only to the point of *using* computers — or having students do so — but not to the point of *thinking* about what we are doing and understanding at least some of the important implications of our actions.

I believe composition studies faculty have a much larger and more complicated obligation to fulfill — that of trying to understand and make sense of, to *pay attention* to, how technology is now inextricably linked to literacy and literacy education in this country. As a part of this obligation, I suggest that we have some rather unpleasant facts to face about our own professional behavior and involvement. To make these points more persuasively, I offer a real-life story about what has happened in American schools and literacy instruction as a result of our unwillingness to attend to technological issues.

An honest examination of this situation, I believe, will lead composition studies professionals to recognize that these two complex cultural formations — technology and literacy — have become linked in ways that exacerbate current educational and social inequities in the United States rather than addressing them productively. The story will lead us to admit, I believe, that we are, in part, already responsible for a bad — even a shameful — situation, and, I hope, will inspire us to do something more positive in the future.

I'll provide readers the moral of this story up front so that no one misses it. *As composition teachers, deciding whether or not to use technology in our classes is simply not the point — we have to pay attention to technology.* When we fail to do so, we share in the responsibility for sustaining and reproducing an unfair system that, scholars such as Elspeth Stuckey and Mike Rose have noted in other contexts, enacts social violence and ensures continuing illiteracy under the aegis of education.

I know, however, that it is not easy for composition teachers to pay attention to technology. As Anthony Giddens would say, our tendency to ignore technology — to focus on humans rather than on machines —

is "deeply sedimented" (22) in our culture, in the history of our humanist profession. And the sedimentation of this belief system is so deep that it has come to comprise a piece of what Pierre Bordieu might call *doxa* (166) — a position everyone takes so much for granted, is so obvious, that people no longer even feel the need to articulate it. But by subscribing to this attitude, we may also be allowing ourselves to ignore the serious social struggles that continue to characterize technology as a cultural formation in this country.

Nowhere are these struggles and debates rendered in more complex terms in the United States — and nowhere are they more influential on our own work — than they are in the link between literacy and computer technology that has been established in increasingly direct ways over the last decade. This potent linkage is sustained and reproduced by a complexly related set of cultural influences: workplaces in which approximately 70% of jobs requiring a bachelors degree or an advanced college degree now require the use of computers (*Digest of Education Statistics* 458); a corporate sector focused on exploiting the 89% of "teachers and the public" who believe that the Internet adds value to teaching and learning specifically because it "reduces the costs teachers spend on classroom activities" ("MCI Nationwide Poll"); schools in which 87% of high school students are now writing on computers by Grade 11 (Coley, Crandler, and Engle 27); and homes in which 86% of parents are convinced that a computer is *the* one "most beneficial and effective product that they can buy to expand their children's opportunities" for education, future success, and economic prosperity (*Getting America's Students Ready* 10).

The tendential force generated by these complexly related formations — which magnify our country's economic dependence on technology — is considerable. However, because it is always easier to ascribe responsibility for such a situation to others — to blame the greed of the corporate representatives who sell computers, or the blindness of school administrators who mandate the use of computers, or the shortsightedness of parents who consider technology a guarantor of learning for their children, I want to focus primarily on our own professional roles and responsibilities associated with this social dynamic.

It is, after all, partly a result of the involvement of English composition specialists, or lack of involvement, in some cases, that the linkage between literacy and technology has come to inform most of the official instruction that goes on within the United States' educational system, most official definitions and descriptions of literacy featured in the documents we write and read, and many of the criteria used to gauge literacy levels within this country. Few government documents about educational goals; few documents outlining national or state educational standards, including our own NCTE standards document; and few corporate job descriptions now fail to acknowledge a citizen's need to read, write, and communicate in electronic environments.

And certainly, like most Americans, we have not felt a responsibility to involve ourselves directly in some of the more public discussions about technology and educational policy because many of us unconsciously subscribe to a belief — both culturally and historically determined — that technology is a productive outgrowth of Science and Innovation (cf. Winner; Virilio; Feenberg; Johnson-Eilola). As a result, we take comfort when the linkage between literacy and computer technology is portrayed as a socially progressive movement, one that will benefit American citizens generally and without regard for their circumstances or backgrounds. Such a belief releases us from the responsibility to pay attention.

It is this last point, however, that makes the American cultural narrative about technology and literacy a particularly potent force in our lives, and that provides a jumping off point for our real-life story about technology.

An American Narrative about Computer Technology and Its Growing Links to Literacy Instruction

This story about technology and literacy could be dated by any number of historical events, but for the purposes of this paper, we turn to June of 1996, when the Clinton-Gore administration — with direct reference to the larger cultural narrative of social-progress-through-technology that I have just identified — published a document entitled *Getting America's Students Ready for the Twenty-First Century,* which announced an official national project to expand *technological literacy,* the "ability to use computers and other technology to improve learning, productivity and performance" (5).

The purpose of this large-scale project — as outlined by Secretary of Education Richard Riley — was, and is, to help "all of our children to become technologically literate" so that each "will have the opportunity to make the most of his or her own life," to "grow and thrive" within the "new knowledge- and information-driven economy" (3–4). By "technologically literate," this document refers to the use of computers not only for the purposes of calculating, programming, and designing, but also for the purposes of reading, writing, and communicating (15–19) — at least for the officially sponsored academic tasks required in schools across the country.

Estimates indicate that this particular literacy project may cost up to $109 billion dollars — averaging either $11 billion annually for a decade or between $10 and $20 billion annually for five years — from a variety of sources at the national, state, and local levels (*Getting America's Students Ready* 6). Where has this money come from and where has it gone? As Todd Oppenheimer notes:

> New Jersey cut state aid to a number of school districts this past year and then spent $10 million on classroom computers. In Union City, California, a single school district is spending $27 million to buy new gear for a mere eleven schools. . . . in Mansfield, Massachusetts, admin-

istrators dropped proposed teaching positions in art, music and physical education, and then spent $333,000 on computers. (46)

Secretary of Education Richard Riley, in *Getting America's Students Ready,* lists other funded projects from various states — here is a sampling:

California

$279 million (one time, State Board) for "instructional materials, deferred maintenance, technology. . . ."

$13.4 million (State Board) for educational technology.

$10 million (State budget) to "refurbish and update used or donated computers."

$100 million (current year, Governor Wilson) for "educational technology."

$35 million (Pacific Telesis) for rate overcharges. (60)

Delaware

$30 million (State, three years) to fund "infrastructure initiative." (61)

District of Columbia

$9 million for "hardware and software purchases." (61)

Idaho

$10.4 million (Idaho Educational Technology Initiative) for "technology in the classroom." (62)

Maine

$15 million (Governor) to "establish a distance learning network." (63)

Montana

$2.56 million (NSF) to support "SummitNet."

$100,000 (State) "for technology." (65)

Texas

$150 million (State, Telecommunications Infrastructure Fund).

$30/student (State) for "purchasing electronic textbooks or technological equipment . . . , training educational personnel directly involved in student learning, . . . access to technological equipment." (67)

Wisconsin

$10 million (State) for "improve[d] access to advanced telecommunications and distance education technologies." (68)

[Telecommunications providers] have provided unidentified funds for Advanced Telecommunications Foundation. (68)

In comparison to the miserly federal funding this country is allocating to other literacy and education projects, these amounts stagger the imagination.

To put these expenditures for technology into perspective, we can look at the 1999 budget for the Department of Education that President Clinton has recently sent to the United States Congress. In this budget, the President has requested $721 million of direct federal funding for educational technology but less than half of that amount, $260 million, for the America Reads Challenge and less than one-tenth of that amount, $67 million, for teacher recruitment and preparation (US Dept. of Education, p. 3).

And we are already in the midst of this project — the administration's deadline for creating such a technologically literate citizenry, one that will think of official, school-sponsored literacy practices as occurring primarily in technological contexts, is "early in the 21st century" (*Getting America's Students Ready* 3).

This project, and the extensive influence it has had on our national understanding of officially-sponsored literacy practices, is a phenomenon that deserves close study not only because of the considerable attention that individual teachers and school districts around the country have already paid to its goals, but, interestingly and conversely, because of the utter lack of systematic and considered attention that our profession as a whole and our professional organizations have accorded it. And so I will move the story forward a bit more.

Since 1996, although our professional standards documents now reflect the core values of this project in that they assume the necessity of computer *use* by communicators in the 21st century, they do not provide adequate guidance about how to get teachers and students *thinking critically about such use*. Moreover, in a curious way, neither the CCCC, nor the NCTE, nor the MLA, nor the IRA — as far as I can tell — have ever published a single word about our own professional stance on this particular nationwide technology project: not one statement about how we think such literacy monies should be spent in English composition programs; not one statement about what kinds of literacy and technology efforts should be funded in connection with this project or how excellence should be gauged in these efforts; not one statement about the serious need for professional development and support for teachers that must be addressed within the context of this particular national literacy project.

Nor have these organizations articulated any official or direct response to the project's goals or the ways in which schools and teachers are already enacting these goals within classrooms. And this is true despite the fact that so many literacy educators in a range of situations — including all English and Language Arts teachers in primary, secondary, and college/university classrooms — have been broadly affected by the technology-literacy linkage for the past decade and will continue to be so involved well into the next century.

In other words, as members of these professional organizations, we need to do a much better job of paying critical attention to technology issues that affect us. Now why is this particular task so important? By paying critical attention to lessons about *technology,* we can re-learn important lessons about *literacy.* It is the different perspective on literacy that technology issues provide us that can encourage such insights. In the sections that follow, I point out just a few of these lessons.

Remembering the Truth about Large-Scale Literacy Projects and the Myth of Literacy

The first lesson that the national project to expand technological literacy can teach us has to do with the efficacy of large-scale literacy projects, in general, and with the myth of literacy. One of the primary arguments for the project to expand technological literacy rests on the claim that such an effort will provide all Americans with an education enriched by technology, and, thus, equal opportunity to access high-paying, technology-rich jobs and economic prosperity after graduation. The truth of this claim, however, has not been borne out and is not likely to be so. This fact is one of the primary reasons why we need to pay attention to technology issues.

Scholars such as Brian Street, Harvey Graff, and James Paul Gee note that such claims are not unusual in connection with large-scale, national literacy projects. Indeed, our willingness to believe these claims contributes to the potency of what Graff has called the "literacy myth," a widely held belief that literacy and literacy education lead autonomously, automatically, and directly to liberation, personal success, or economic prosperity. This myth, however, is delusory in its simplicity, as Street says:

> The reality [of national literacy movements] is more complex, is harder to face politically. . . . when it comes to job acquisition, the level of literacy is less important than issues of class, gender, and ethnicity; lack of literacy is more likely to be a symptom of poverty and deprivation than a cause. (18)

In the specific case of the project to expand technological literacy, the claim is that a national program will provide all citizens equal access to an improved education and, thus, equal opportunity for upward social mobility and economic prosperity. If we *pay attention* to the facts surrounding the project's instantiation, however, we can remind ourselves of the much harder lesson: in our educational system, and in the culture that this system reflects, computers *continue to be distributed differentially along the related axes of race and socioeconomic status* and this distribution contributes to ongoing patterns of racism and to the continuation of poverty.

It is a fact, for instance, that schools primarily serving students of color and poor students continue to have less access to computers, and access to less sophisticated computer equipment than do schools primarily serving more affluent and white students (Coley et al. 3). And it is a fact that schools primarily serving students of color and poor students continue to have less access to the Internet, less access to multimedia equipment, less access to CD-ROM equipment, less access to local area networks, less access to video-disc technology than do schools primarily serving more affluent and white students (Coley et al. 3).

This data, which is profoundly disturbing, becomes all the more problematic if we trace the extended effects of the technology-literacy linkage into the country's workplaces and homes. There, too, the latest census figures indicate, the linkage is strongly correlated to both race and socioeconomic status. It is a fact, for instance, that Black employees or Hispanic employees are *much* less likely than white employees to use a range of computer applications in their workplace environments (*Digest* 458). It is also a fact that employees who have not graduated from high school are much less likely to use a range of computer applications than are employees who have a high school degree or have some college experience (*Digest* 458). And it is a fact that poor families in both urban and rural environments and Black and Hispanic Americans are much less likely to own and use computers than individuals with higher family incomes and white families (*Smith* 212; *Digest 1996* 458; *Getting* 36).

In other words, the poorer you are and the less educated you are in this country — both of which conditions are correlated with race — the less likely you are to have access to computers and to high-paying, high-tech jobs in the American workplace.

The challenges associated with the unequal distribution and use of computer technology along the related axes of socioeconomic status, education, and race have proven embarrassingly persistent for a number of related reasons. Secretary of Education Richard Riley, for example, citing a 1995 General Accounting Office Survey, notes that

> half of all schools do not have adequate wiring (such as outlets) to handle their technology needs. More than half do not have sufficient telephone lines, and 60 percent consider the number of conduits for network cable unsatisfactory. Schools that have all of these infrastructure elements are clearly the exception to the rule. Strikingly, schools in large central cities are even less equipped to meet the demands of technology than other schools; more than 40 percent do not even have enough electrical power to use computers on a regular basis. . . . Classrooms in older buildings, for example, may require expensive renovations to improve electrical systems before computers and networks can be installed, discouraging the community from making a commitment. (*Getting America's Students Ready* 34–35)

As a result of this overdetermined system, the differential distribution of technology and technological literacy continues — albeit, with some complex new variations. In a recent article published in *Science,* for example, Hoffman and Novak identified the following findings:

- Overall whites were significantly more likely than African Americans to have a home computer in their household. Whites were also slightly more likely to have access to a PC at work. (390)
- Proportionately, more than twice as many whites as African Americans had used the Web in the past week. As of January 1997, we estimate that 5.2 million (±1.2 million) African Americans and 40.8 million whites (±2.1 million) have ever used the Web, and that 1.4 million (±0.5 million) African Americans and 20.3 million (±1.6 million) whites used the Web in the past week. (390)
- As one would expect . . . increasing levels of income corresponded to an increased likelihood of owning a home computer, regardless of race. In contrast, adjusting for income did not eliminate the race differences with respect to computer access at work. . . . Notably . . . , race differences in Web use vanish at household incomes of $40,000 and higher. (390)
- 73% of white students owned a home computer, only 32% of African American students owned one. "This difference persisted when we statistically adjusted for students' reported household income." (390)
- White students were significantly more likely than African American students to have used the Web, especially in the past week. (391)
- White students lacking a home computer, but not African American students, appear to be accessing the Internet from locations such as homes of friends and relatives, libraries, and community centers. (391)

Acknowledging these facts, we might understand better why the rhetoric associated with national literacy projects serves to exacerbate the dangers that they pose. When Secretary of Education Richard Riley states, for example, that "Computers are the 'new basics' of education . . ." or that the project of technological literacy can help us give "all of our young people" an "opportunity to grow . . . and thrive" in the "new knowledge- and information-driven economy" (*Getting* 3), he erroneously suggests, in Brian Street's words, "that the acquisition of literacy" will by itself "lead to 'major' impacts in terms of social and cognitive skills and 'development' " within a population (14). As Street reminds us, these "simple stories" that "both politicians and the press" tell about literacy to justify and sustain the momentum of such major programs, frequently "deflect attention from the complexity and real political difficulties" (17). The ultimate effect, according to Street, is an overly narrow understanding of literacy — usually in terms of a single official literacy — and the development of accompanying "patronizing assumptions about what it means to have difficulties with reading and writing in contemporary society. Such rhetoric also serves to raise false hopes about what the acquisition of literacy means for job prospects, social mobility, and personal achievement" (17).

In the specific case of computers and literacy, these stories serve to deflect our attention from the fact that "every single child" does *not* now have access to technology, and some students, especially those who are poor and of color, have less access than others. And so, *if* access to, and use of, technology in school-based settings *is* now a fundamental skill of literacy and *if* such skills *do* help prepare graduates for the jobs they will be asked to do, these same students can expect less opportunity to assume high-tech and high-paying jobs, not more. As Richard Ohmann described the underlying dynamic in a prescient 1985 *College English* article about the general relationship between technology, literacy, and economic conditions:

> Of course there will be more jobs in the computer field itself. But . . . the field is layered into specialties, which will be dead ends for most people in them. . . . Graduates of MIT will get the challenging jobs; community college grads will be technicians; those who do no more than acquire basic skills and computer literacy in high school will probably find their way to electronic workstations at McDonald's. I see every reason to expect that the computer revolution, like other revolutions from the top down, will indeed expand the minds and the freedom of an elite, meanwhile facilitating the degradation of labor and the stratification of the workforce that have been hallmarks of monopoly capitalism from its onset. (683)

The frustrating cycle associated with this situation is so dismally clear and sickeningly familiar because it mirrors exactly the dynamics associated with more traditional literacy efforts in our country. As Graff notes, official literacies usually function in a conservative, and reproductive, fashion — in favor of dominant groups and in support of the existing class-based system:

> Hegemonic relationships have historically involved processes of group and class formation, recruitment, indoctrination, and maintenance at all levels of society. For most of literacy's history, these functions have centered upon elite groups and their cohesion and power. For them, the uses of literacy have been diverse but have included common education, culture, and language. . . . shared interests and activities; control of scarce commodities, such as wealth, power, and even literacy; and common symbols and badges, of which literacy could be one. (*Legacies* 12)

Thus, the national project to expand technological literacy has *not* served to reduce illiteracy — or the persistent social problems that exacerbate illiteracy. Rather, it has simply changed the official criteria for both "literate" and "illiterate" individuals, while retaining the basic ratio of both groups.

In sum, we have little evidence that any large-scale project focusing on a narrowly defined set of officially sanctioned literacy skills will result in fundamental changes in the ratio of people labeled as literate or illiterate. These categories are socially constructed identities which our current educational system reproduces rather than addresses. Similarly, we have no specific evidence that the current project to expand technological literacy will change the patterns of literacy and illiteracy in this country. Rather, this project is likely to support persistent patterns of economically-based literacy acquisition because citizens of color and those from low socioeconomic backgrounds continue to have less access to high-tech educational opportunities and occupy fewer positions that make multiple uses of technology than do white citizens or those from higher socioeconomic backgrounds.

Literacy Education Is a Political Act

Given the effects we have just described, the national project to expand technological literacy can also serve to re-teach us a second lesson — that literacy is always a political act as well as an educational effort. In this context, we can understand that the national project to expand technological literacy is motivated as much by political and economic agenda as it is by educational values and goals. To trace the concrete forms of political agenda, one relatively easy starting place is 1992. At that time in history, the Clinton-Gore team was preparing to enter Washington, and this administration had already identified technology as a key factor in both its domestic and international economic policies. At home, the Clinton-Gore team was facing a long-standing slowdown in manufacturing and productivity, persistent poverty, and an increasing income gap between the rich and the poor. As the 1997 *Economic Report to the President* tells the story:

> For more than two decades America has faced serious problems: productivity growth has been slower than in the past, income inequity has increased, and poverty has persisted. In addition, serious challenges loom for the future, such as the aging of the baby boom, which threatens to create severe fiscal strains in the next century. (Council 18)

The administration knew well that its ability to address these problems and to inject new vigor into the domestic economy — or to convince the American public that it had done so — would be a deciding factor in the way the effectiveness of their administration was judged. On the international scene, the Clinton-Gore team faced three important and related changes in the world's economic picture: the end of the Cold War and the fall of Communism in the Soviet Union, the emergence of growing markets among the developing countries of East Asia and Latin America that threatened to capture an increasingly large percentage of the world's consumers, and the threatening increase in competition due to the global scope of the international economy.

To kill these two economic birds with one stone, the Clinton-Gore administration focused on the idea of expanding America's technology efforts — the design, manufacturing, and consumption of both technology and technological expertise. On the international scene, the administration took three steps to expand technology efforts. The first step involved defining America's focused area of specialization in the world marketplace as technology and information services:

> The Administration's economic policy has been an aggressive effort to increase exports through the opening of markets abroad . . . The United States will certainly gain, both as a major exporter of information technology and as an importer, as American industries take advantage of new foreign technologies that will lower their costs and increase their productivity. (*Council* 27)

The second and third steps involved exerting leadership in the development of a Global Information Infrastructure (GII) built on the back of the country's own National Information Infrastructure (NII). As part of this effort, the United States offered other countries — especially those with emerging markets that were hungry for technological involvement — the opportunity to buy American goods and services exported in connection with the GII. As Gore described the plan to the International Telecommunications Union in Buenos Aires in 1994:

> We can use the Global Information Infrastructure for technical collaboration between industrialized nations and developing countries. All agencies of the U.S. government are potential sources of information and knowledge that can be shared with partners across the globe. . . . The U.S. can help provide the technical know-how needed to deploy and use these new technologies. USAID and U.S. businesses have helped the U.S. Telecommunications Training Institute train more than 3500 telecommunications professionals from the developing world, including many in this room.

Such a system also set up the possibility of continued reliance on American goods and services. Technicians trained in the deployment and use of American technology and American-designed operating systems, and American software, and American networks, for example, would tend to continue to rely on — and purchase — those products and components with which they were most familiar. Gore articulated the economic reasoning behind this plan:

> For us in the United States, the information infrastructure already is to the U.S. economy of the 1990s what transportation infrastructure was to the economy of the mid-20th century.

> The integration of computing and information networks into the economy makes U.S. manufacturing companies more productive, more competitive, and more adaptive to changing conditions. . . .

The benefits associated with the GII expansion had political as well as economic effects. If the GII was constructed according to the Clinton-Gore plan, it would not only re-vitalize the American economy, it would also help promote the spread of democracy and capitalism around the globe within the context of a liberalized global economic system. The GII would accomplish this goal by providing forums for democratic involvement and expanded freedom of speech, by increasing privatization of technology resources, and by decreasing government regulation. As Gore noted:

> The GII will not only be a metaphor for a functioning democracy, it will in fact promote the functioning of democracy by greatly enhancing the participation of citizens in decision-making. And it will greatly promote the ability of nations to cooperate with each other. I see a new Athenian age of democracy forged in the fora the GII will create. . . .

> The integration of computing and information networks into the economy makes U.S. manufacturing companies more productive, more competitive, and more adaptive to changing conditions and it will do the same for the economies of other nations. . . .

> To promote, to protect, to preserve freedom and democracy, we must make telecommunications development an integral part of every nation's development. Each link we create strengthens the bonds of liberty and democracy around the world. By opening markets to stimulate the development of the global infrastructure, we open lines of communication.

> By opening lines of communication, we open minds.

The international effort to expand technology, however, was only one part of the Clinton-Gore agenda. The other — and, in some ways, the more important — effort occurred in the domestic arena and focused on the revitalization of the American domestic economy through the expansion of the American computer industry. The Clinton-Gore team saw this particular industry as an economic "engine" (Gore, *Global Information* 3) that would, by increasing technological efforts at home, in turn, jump-start the international effort: providing the resources — the additional technology and the technological expertise — required to exploit emerging world markets.

To carry out this complex plan, the domestic engine of technology had to be cranked up and, to accomplish this goal, the Clinton-Gore administration knew that it had to accomplish two tasks:

- educate a pool of technologically sophisticated workers and technology specialists would could assist in the effort to reach new global markets and export more American manufactured equipment and specialized technology services to the rest of the world; and

- provide an influx of resources into the domestic computer industry so that it could simultaneously support the international effort and assume an increasingly important role in re-vitalizing the domestic economy.

And it was in response to these complexly related economic and political agendas that the national project to expand technological literacy was born. The dynamics that underlie this project were ideally and specifically suited to the economic and political goals we have just sketched out. Touted as an educational effort designed to improve citizens' literacy levels and, thus, their opportunities for future prosperity, the project was targeted at producing a continuing supply of educated workers who both had the skills necessary to design and manufacture increasingly sophisticated technological goods at home, and could offer sophisticated and specialized technological services in international arenas. Central to the task of achieving these targeted goals, the Clinton-Gore team recognized, was its ability to levy the power of the national educational system to reach large numbers of Americans in relatively short order. It was only within such a national system, they recognized, that an appropriately large proportion of the country's population could quickly acquire the training necessary to boost high-tech industries.

Importantly, such a plan was pretty close to self-fueling — citizens who learned the habits of reading, writing, and communicating on computers early in their lives within high-tech schools would tend to demand and consume such goods later in life when they graduated, thus injecting an increasingly continuous flow of money into the computer industry. And the plan's effects in the public sector promised to resonate effectively with its effects in the private sector: when citizens used, or were exposed to, cutting-edge technologies in their workplaces, or in school settings, they would desire them, as well, in their homes — and they would purchase updated technologies more frequently. Further, to ensure the continuation of the same high-tech careers and industries that have served them so well, such citizens would also tend to vote in support of political and economic programs that involved the further expansion of technology markets both domestically and internationally. Such citizens, moreover, would recognize the key role that technological literacy plays in their own success, and, so, demand a similar education for their children.

From our perspective today, of course, we can see a darker side of this dynamic. The economic engine of technology must be fueled by — and produce — not only a continuing supply of individuals who are highly *literate* in terms of technological knowledge, but also an ongoing supply of individuals who fail to acquire technological literacy, those who are termed *"illiterate"* according to the official definition. These latter individuals provide the unskilled, low-paid labor necessary to sustain the system I have described — their work generates the surplus labor that must be continually re-invested in capital projects to produce more sophisticated technologies.

The people labeled as "illiterate" in connection with technology — as expected — are those with the least power to effect a change in this system. They come from families who attend the poorest schools in this country and they attend schools with the highest populations of students of color. In part because of such facts, these students have less access to technology, in general, and less access to more sophisticated technology during their educational years. Partially as a result of their educational backgrounds, such individuals are hired into less desirable, lower-paid positions that demand fewer official technological literacy skills.

Moreover, because skills in *technological* communication environments are so closely linked with literacy instruction *in general,* and because students who come from such backgrounds are afforded the poorest efforts of the educational system and the lowest expectations of many teachers, the label of "illiterate" has broader implications for these individuals' ability to acquire other skills through their formal schooling years.

Remembering Our Own Role in the Literacy/Illiteracy Cycle

The danger associated with such an extensive ideological system, as Terry Eagleton points out, is the effective processes of naturalization that it engenders. Successful ideological systems "render their beliefs natural and self-evident" by so closely identifying them with "common sense" of a society so that nobody could imagine how they might ever be different (58). More importantly, as Eagleton continues,

> This process, which Pierre Bordieu calls *doxa,* involves the ideology in creating as tight a fit as possible between itself and social reality, thereby closing the gap into which the leverage of critique could be inserted. Social reality is redefined by the ideology to become coextensive with itself, in a way which occludes the truth that the reality in fact generated the ideology. . . . The result, politically speaking, is an apparently vicious circle: the ideology could only become transformed if the reality was such as to allow it to become objectified; but the ideology processes reality in ways which forestall this possibility. The two are thus mutually self-confirming. On this view, a ruling ideology does not so much combat alternative ideas as thrust them beyond the very bounds of the thinkable. (58)

It is within this effectively naturalized matrix of interests, I would argue, that English teachers all over this country have become the unwitting purveyors of technology and technological literacy — even as we try to avoid a technological focus by attending to more traditionally conceived topics within the humanities.

The paradoxical dynamics at the heart of this situation are difficult to wrap our minds around especially because they function at so many different levels. Because we fail to address the project to expand technological literacy in focused, systematic, and critical ways within the professional arenas available to us, English composition teachers have come to understand technology as "just another instructional tool" that they can choose either to use or ignore. And, working from this context, we divide ourselves into two perfectly meaningless camps — those who use computers to teach classes and those who don't. Both groups feel virtuous about their choices, and both manage to lose sight of the real issue. Computer-using teachers instruct students in how to *use* technology — but all too often, they neglect to teach students how *to pay critical attention* to the issues generated by technology use. Teachers who choose *not* to use technology in their classes content themselves with the mistaken belief that their choice to avoid technology use absolves them and the students in their classes from *paying critical attention* to technology issues. In other words, both groups contribute to the very same end. And when such things happen, when we allow ourselves to ignore technological issues, when we take technology for granted, when it becomes invisible to us, when we forget technology's material bases — regardless of whether or not we use technology — we participate unwittingly in the inequitable literacy system I have just described.

Paying Attention to Action

So can composition teachers address the complex linkages among technology, literacy, poverty, and race? The primary factors determining any individual's involvement, of course, must necessarily start with the local and specific — with social agents' own deep and penetrating knowledge of the specific colleges and universities in which they work; the particular families, communities, cultures within which we live and form our own understanding of the world; the individual students, teachers, administrators, board members, politicians, and parents whose lives touch ours.

As Donna Haraway reminds us, this kind of "situated knowledges-approach" (175) leads to a kind of "coyote" (189) way of knowing — one different from the traditional perspective of Science, but in that difference, capable of offering a "more adequate, richer, better account of the world" that makes it possible to "live in it well and in critical, reflexive relation to our own as well as others' practices" (178). Such an approach may provide "only partial perspective" (181), Haraway cautions, but it allows us to avoid the trap of claiming a scientific objectivity that invites a false sense of closure and overly simple answers.

This kind of paying attention can serve as a collective effort to construct a "larger vision" of our responsibilities as a profession, one that depends on a strong sense of many *somewheres* (e.g., schools, classrooms, districts, communities) "in particular" (187) — especially when such a project is undertaken with a critical understanding of what we are trying to accomplish with such work and a collective commitment to seeing social problems "faithfully from another's point of view" (181) and even when it is clear that such a vision must remain partial, distorted, and incomplete. In this way, our profession can assemble, from many local understandings "stitched together imperfectly" (183), a picture of technological literacy — as it now functions within our culture — that might allow us to act with more strategic effectiveness and force, both collectively and individually.

A situated knowledges-approach to paying attention also honors a multiplicity of responses to technological literacy. Given the constraints of local and specific contexts, and a commitment to engaging with the lives of individual students, for example, some teachers will find their best avenue of involvement to reside in individual agency, others will find increasing effectiveness when they work with other colleagues. Some educators will find work within their own classroom to be the most immediately pressing and others will find the action in local communities to offer the most immediate and successful venue for their work. Indeed, the appreciation of local situations and variations may help composition studies professionals understand the power of large-scale projects when they are built on the critical understandings and active participation of a diverse group of educators.

Operating from this understanding of the local and particular, suggestions for critical engagement with technological literacy issues must allow for wide variations in social, political, economic, and ideological positionings, and wide variations in teachers, students, administrators, citizens, and communities. In deference to this approach, the suggestions that follow focus on the typical *sites* for critically informed action on technological literacy (and on general areas of attention within such sites) rather than on specific projects that should be undertaken within these sites. Individual teachers and groups of teachers, students, parents, and school administrators must determine within such sites how best to pay increased and critical attention to the linkage between technology and literacy — recognizing as fully as possible the local conditions affecting the work they do.

In Curriculum Committees, Standards Documents, and Assessment Programs

We need to pursue opportunities for resisting projects and systems that serve to establish an overly narrow, official version of literacy practices or skills. Such projects and systems simply serve to reward the literacy practices of dominant groups and punish the practices of others. They serve to reproduce a continuing and oppressive cycle of illiteracy, racism, and poverty in this country and in others.

Within these venues, composition specialists can lead the way in insisting on a diverse range of literacy practices and values, rather than one narrow and official form of literacy. We have made a start at this effort in the 1996 NCTE *Standards for the English Language Arts,* but CCCC needs to go much further in helping both future teachers and those already in classrooms understand why this work is so important and what implications their successes and failures may have.

In Our Professional Organizations

We need to recognize that if written language and literacy practices are our professional business, so is technology. This recognition demands a series of carefully considered and very visible professional stands on a variety of technological issues now under debate in this country: for example, on the access issues we have discussed, on the issue of technology funding for schools, on the issue of multiple venues for students' literacy practices, on the national project to expand technological literacy, and so on. We need to engage in much more of this kind of professional activism, and more consistently.

In Scholarship and Research

We also need to recognize that technological literacy is our responsibility. We need not only additional examinations of the ideological systems and cultural formations currently informing the literacy-technology link, but also the historical patterns established by other literacy technologies. And we need research like that Regina Copeland has just completed in West Virginia that takes a hard look at the access that individuals in various population groups — students of color, poor students, women — have to computer-supported literacy instruction, and of the expenditure of government and schools and family funds in support of technology and literacy. We also need additional research on how various technologies influence literacy values and practices and research on how teachers might better use technologies to support a wide range of literacy goals for different populations. We need work like that Nancy Guerra Barron has completed in LA to examine the bilingual online discussions of Latino students in a Chicano studies class and trace the ways in which these students manage to shape and use electronic environments productively to mirror the linguistic richness of their lives outside the classroom. These projects represent only some of the many that we can encourage.

In Language Arts and English Studies Classrooms, and in First-Year and Advanced English Composition Courses

We need to recognize that we can no longer simply educate students to become technology users — and consumers — without also helping them learn how to become critical thinkers about technology and the social issues surrounding its use. When English/language arts faculty require students to use computers in completing a range of assignments — without also providing them the time and opportunity to explore the complex issues that surround technology and technology use in substantive ways — we may, without realizing it, be contributing to the education of citizens who are habituated to technology use but who have little critical awareness about, or understanding of, the complex relationships between humans, machines, and the cultural contexts within which the two interact.

Composition teachers, language arts teachers, and other literacy specialists need to recognize that the relevance of technology in the English studies disciplines is not simply a matter of helping students work effectively with communication software and hardware, but, rather, also a matter of helping them to understand and to be able to assess — to pay attention to — the social, economic, and pedagogical implications of new communication technologies and technological initiatives that affect their lives. Knowledgeable literacy specialists at all levels need to develop age-appropriate and level-appropriate reading and writing activities aimed at this goal. This approach — which recognizes the complex links that now exist between literacy and technology at the end of the twentieth century — constitutes a *critical technological literacy* that will serve students well.

In Computer-Based Communication Facilities

We have to put scholarship and research to work as praxis. These technology-rich facilities can serve not only as teaching environments for students completing literacy assignments — as sites within which both faculty and students can develop their own critical technological literacy — but also as sites within which students and faculty can formulate guidelines and policies for critically informed practices that put these understandings to work in complicated social situations. Feenberg offers the possibility of considering such sites in terms of their *underdetermined* potential, a potential which can be exploited by interested and knowledgeable social agents determined to make a difference in their own and others' lives. Technology-rich communication facilities are already replete with such interested agents — the English/language arts teachers involved in designing and teaching within them, the students involved in using them and learning within them, the staff members (often students) responsible for keeping them operational, and the administrators who help to fund them.

In technology-rich communication facilities, students and teachers can develop a more critically-informed sense of technology by actively confronting and addressing technology issues in contexts that matter — contexts that involve real people (peers, faculty, community members, staff members) engaged in a range of daily practices (making decisions about software and hardware purchases, hiring individuals who can help teachers and students deal more effectively with technology, setting lab fee levels for students, deciding on etiquette and use guidelines, identifying access problems) within their various lived experiences and in light of their own goals. When confronted and addressed in these complicated and often contradictory contexts, technology and technological issues become connected with social issues, human values, and material conditions — rather than naturalized and separated from such experiences.

These sets of issues and others are all part of the process of managing technology-rich environments, and each is a component of the critical technological literacy we believe students must develop as they become effective social agents and citizens. Our culture will need these activists — in school board and PTO meetings, in small businesses, on corporate boards, and in government agencies where decisions about communication technologies will influence the personal and professional lives of citizens.

In Districts and Systems and States That Have Poor Schools, Rural Schools, and Schools with Large Populations of Students of Color

We need to resist the tendential forces that continue to link technological literacy with patterns of racism and poverty. We need to insist on and support more equitable distributions of technology.

In Our Voting for School Board Elections, in Committee Meetings, in Public Hearings, at National Conventions, in the Public Relations Statements of Our Professional Organizations

We have to argue — at every change that we can get — that poor students and students of color get more access to computers and to more sophisticated computers, that teachers in schools with high populations of such students be given more support.

In Pre-Service and In-Service Educational Programs and Curricula

We need to help all English composition teachers get more education on both technology use and technology criticism. In the curricula comprising our own graduate programs and the educational programs that prepare teachers for careers in our profession, we need to make sure these programs don't simply teach young professionals to *use* computers — but rather, that we teach them how to pay attention to technology and the issues that result from, and contribute to, the technology-literacy linkage. It is no longer enough, for instance, simply to ask graduate students or colleagues to use computers in composition classes. Instead, we need to help them read in the areas of technology criticism, social theories, and computer studies and, then, provide them important opportunities to participate in making hard decisions about how to pay attention to technology issues in departments, colleges, and local communities; how to address the existing links between literacy and technology in undergraduate curricula; how to provide more access to technology for more people and how to help individuals develop their own critical consciousness about technology.

In Libraries, Community Centers, and Other Non-Traditional Public Places

We need to provide free access to computers for citizens at the poverty level and citizens of color — not only so that such individuals have access to computers and, thus, can become proficient in computer use for communication tasks, but also so that these citizens have access to the Internet and to online sites for collective political [uses] (Oppel; Hoffman and Novak).

Toward an End . . .

The lessons I have outlined in the preceding pages, as I am sure readers understand, are as much about literacy as they are about technology. But, as Bruno Latour notes, real-life stories *always* lack richness and accuracy when they are told from a single perspective. We require multiple perspectives if we hope to construct a robust and accurate understanding of the ways in which technology functions in our culture. Our profession's occasional respectful attention to technology and the social issues that surround technology may allow us to see things from a slightly different point of view, even if for only a moment in time. And from such a perspective, as Latour reminds us, our interpretations of issues "take on added density" (viii).

I might add that this occasional merging of the technological and the humanist perspectives — into a vision that is more robustly informed — has as much value for scientists and engineers as it does for humanists. Margaret Boden, an early pioneer in artificial intelligence, notes in the Introduction to her landmark 1977 books, that she was drawn to the study of artificial intelligence for its potential in "counteracting the dehumanizing influence of natural science" and for its ability to "clarify the nature of human purpose, freedom, and moral choice," those "hidden complexities of human thinking" (4) that machines cannot replicate, that have always concerned us most within this profession.

One technology writer, Mark Weiser, has said that "The most profound technologies are those that disappear," that "weave themselves into the fabric of everyday life until they are indistinguishable from it" (94). I agree, but with a slightly different interpretation — these technologies may be the most *profound* when they disappear, but — it is exactly when this happens that they also develop the most potential for being *dangerous*. We have, as a culture, watched the twin strands of technology and literacy become woven into the fabric of our lives — they are now inscribed in legislation, in the law — in the warp and woof of our culture. But, recognizing this context, we cannot allow ourselves to lose sight of either formation. We must remind ourselves that laws write the texts of people's lives, that they constantly inscribe their intent and power on individuals — as Michel de Certeau says, "making its book out of them" (140).

It is our responsibility, as educators, to commit ourselves every day that we teach to reading and analyzing these texts, these lives of students — honestly, with respect, and to the very best of our collective and personal abilities. The alternative — of ignoring them, of perceiving students only in terms of their numbers in our schools or as members of undifferentiated groups — is simply unacceptable. As Elspeth Stuckey, Mike Rose, Harvey Graff, Brian Street, James Paul Gee, and many others have told us, when we participate in unthinking ways in political agendas, legislative initiatives, or educational systems that support an overly narrow version of official literacy, we all lose, and we are all implicated in the guilt that accrues to a system of violence through literacy.

It is my hope that by paying some attention to technology, we may learn lessons about becoming better humanists, as well.

Works Cited

Barron, Nancy Guerra. "Egalitarian Moments: Computer Mediated Communications in a Chicano Studies (ChS 111) Course." MA Thesis. California State U at Los Angeles, 1998.

Boden, Margaret. *Artificial Intelligence and Natural Man.* New York: Basic, 1977.

Bordieu, Pierre. *Outline of a Theory of Practice.* New York: Cambridge UP, 1977.

Coley, R. J., J. Crandler, and P. Engle. *Computers and Classrooms: The Status of Technology in U.S. Schools.* Princeton: ETS, 1997.

Copeland, Regina. "Identifying Barriers to Computer-Supported Instruction." Diss. West Virginia U, 1997.

Council of Economic Advisors. *Economic Report of the President.* Washington, DC: US Government Printing Office, 1997.

de Certeau, Michel. *The Practice of Everyday Life.* Trans. Steven Randall. Berkeley: U of California P, 1984.

Digest of Education Statistics 1996. Washington, DC: National Center for Education Statistics, Office of Educational Research and Improvement, 1996.

Eagleton, Terry. *Ideology: An Introduction.* London: Verso, 1991.

Faigley, Lester. "Literacy After the Revolution." *CCC* 48 (1987): 30–43.

Feenberg, Andrew. *The Critical Theory of Technology.* New York: Oxford UP, 1991.

Gee, James. *Social Linguistics and Literacies: Ideology in Discourses.* New York: Falmer, 1990.

Getting America's Students Ready for the 21st Century: Meeting the Technology Literacy Challenge: A Report to the Nation on Technology and Education. Washington, DC: US Dept. of Education, 1996.

Giddens, Anthony. *The Constitution of Society: Outline of the Theory of Structuration.* Berkeley: U of California P, 1985.

Gore, Albert, Jr. "VP Remarks — International Telecommunications Union." Buenos Aires, Argentina, 21 March 1994. <http://www.whitehouse.gov/WH/EOP/OVP/html/telunion.html>.

Gore, Albert, Jr. *Global Information Infrastructure: Agency for Cooperation.* Washington, DC: US Government Printing Office, 1995.

Graff, Harvey J. *The Legacies of Literacy: Continuities and Contradictions in Western Culture and Society.* Bloomington: Indiana UP, 1987.

———. *The Literacy Myth: Cultural Integration and Social Structure in the Nineteenth Century.* New Brunswick: Transaction, 1991.

Green, Kenneth C. "The Campus Computing Project: The 1995 National Survey of Desktop Computing in Higher Education." 1996. <http://ericir.syr.edu/Projects/Campus_computing/1995/index.html>.

Haraway, Donna. "Situated Knowledges: The Science Question in Feminism and the Privilege of Partial Perspective." *Technology and the Politics of Knowledge.* Ed. Andrew Feenberg and Alastair Hannay. Bloomington: Indiana UP, 1995. 175–94.

Hoffman, Donna L., and Thomas P. Novak, "Bridging the Racial Divide on the Internet." *Science* 17 April 1998: 390–91.

Johnson-Eilola, Johndan. *Nostalgic Angels: Rearticulating Hypertext Writing.* Norwood: Ablex, 1997.

Latour, Bruno. *Aramis or the Love of Technology.* Trans C. Porter. Cambridge: Harvard UP, 1996.

"MCI Nationwide Poll on Internet in Education." National Press Club. Washington, DC, 3 March 1998.

Michigan Curriculum Framework: Content Standards and Benchmarks. Lansing: Michigan Dept. of Education, 1995.

Ohmann, Richard. "Literacy, Technology, and Monopoly Capital." *College English* 47 (1985): 675–89.

Oppel, Shelby. "Computer Lab Offers Escape from Poverty." *St. Petersburg Times* 17 Sept. 1997: 3B.

Oppenheimer, Todd. "The Computer Delusion." *Atlantic Monthly,* July 1997: 45–62.

"Public Law 102-73, the National Literacy Act of 1991." House of Representatives Bill 751, 25 July 1991. <http://novel.nifl.gov/public-law.html>.

Rose, Mike. *Lives on the Boundary: The Struggles and Achievements of America's Underprepared.* New York: Free P, 1989.

Smith, Thomas M. *Condition of Education, 1997.* Washington, DC: National Center for Education Statistics, U.S. Government Printing Office, 1997. NCES 97–388.

Standards for the English Language Arts. Urbana: NCTE, 1996.

Street, Brian V. *Social Literacies: Critical Approaches to Literacy Development, Ethnography, and Education.* London: Longman, 1995.

Stuckey, J. Elspeth. *The Violence of Literacy.* Portsmouth: Boynton, 1990.

US Dept. of Education. Community Update, No. 56. "President Clinton Sends 1999 Budget to Congress." Office of Intergovernmental and Interagency Affairs, 1998.

Virilio, Paul. *Speed and Politics: An Essay on Dromology.* Trans. Mark Polizzotti. New York: Semiotext(e), 1986.

Weiser, Mark. "The Computer for the 21st Century." *Scientific American* 265.3 (Sept. 1991): 94–104.

Winner, Langdon. *The Whale and the Reactor: A Search for Limits in an Age of High Technology.* Chicago: U of Chicago P, 1986.

Selfe's Insights as a Resource for Your Teaching

1. Selfe's argument hinges on the 1996 Clinton-Gore project *Getting America's Students Ready for the 21st Century*. What links do you see between Selfe's critique and other, more recent literacy campaigns? What is your own role in what Selfe calls the "Literacy/Illiteracy Cycle"? What forces have shaped that role, and what might be involved in revising that role?

2. Technologies, as Selfe suggests, are most profound when they "disappear" and "weave themselves into the fabric of everyday life." However, this is also when they become most dangerous, for, at this point, we no longer think critically about them. In addition to the problems of equal access that Selfe explores, what other elements of technology warrant our careful, critical scrutiny?

Selfe's Insights as a Resource for Your Writing Classroom

1. Selfe argues that we have a responsibility not only to help our students work effectively with computers, but also to help them "to understand and to be able to assess — to pay attention to — the social, economic, and pedagogical implications of new communication technologies and technological initiatives that affect their lives." Share with your students the broad outlines of Selfe's argument and point out that this argument was first presented in 1997. Discuss with them how the issues she raises have evolved since the article first appeared.

2. Consider your grading criteria for an upcoming writing assignment, and devise ways to expand it so that, in Selfe's words, you "resist . . . an overly narrow, official version of literacy practices or skills."

Computer-Mediated Communication in the Undergraduate Writing Classroom: A Study of the Relationship of Online Discourse and Classroom Discourse in Two Writing Classes

Robert P. Yagelski and Jeffrey T. Grabill

Originally published in Computers and Composition *in 1998, this article explores the complex dynamics between in-class, face-to-face dialogue and its online counterpart. The authors begin with a useful review of related studies on computer-mediated communication and then analyze the results of interviews, surveys, and samples of student discourse. They found that how instructors design, manage, and evaluate their students' online communication plays a primary role in how students approach these assignments, though other factors — including student perceptions of their own status as undergraduates in a university — can also have a complex, powerful impact.*

In 1986, Starr Roxanne Hiltz used the term "virtual classroom" to describe an instructional project at the New Jersey Institute of Technology in which classes were conducted entirely online using computer-mediated communication, or computer "conferences." Since then, *virtual classrooms* have become an increasingly common part of course offerings at many universities (see Wells, 1993). What is far more common than courses offered entirely online, however, is the use of computer-mediated communication (CMC) in conventional courses, or what Hiltz (1990) termed *mixed mode* courses (p. 136). For example, during the 1995 spring semester, when this study was conducted, approximately 200 electronic bulletin boards or newsgroups, were established for use in conventional undergraduate and graduate courses at Purdue University. Many courses also employed electronic mail and computer mailing lists. In many of these courses, newsgroups and electronic mail were used largely to supplement (and in some cases to replace) conventional classroom discussion, in effect extending classroom discourse beyond the time and space of the regular class meetings. As the burgeoning literature on distance education and computers in composition indicates, these developments at Purdue mirror trends at institutions worldwide (see Wells, 1993, p. 35).

This increase in the use of computer-mediated communication in writing classrooms at all educational levels has typically been characterized as beneficial (see Hawisher & Selfe, 1991, for a good review). As Edward P. J. Corbett (1992) wrote in his foreword to the 1989 collection *Re-Imagining Computers and Composition*, the "online interactions between students or between students and teachers . . . radically alters the atmosphere of the composition classroom for the better" (p. viii). And indeed, there is ample evidence that classroom uses of CMC can have a significant impact on student writing (e.g., Cohen & Riel, 1989) and on student learning generally (e.g., Cheng, Lehman, & Armstrong, 1991; Hiltz, 1990; Phillips & Santoro, 1989). But our collective understanding of the specific uses and effects of these technologies on instruction and learning in traditional classroom settings is limited. Although CMC technologies have been used in distance learning for a decade and a half, we are only beginning to understand the relationship between increasingly common classroom uses of CMC (especially asynchronous applications such as newsgroups and electronic mail) and traditional face-to-face classroom discourse. As Eldred and Hawisher (1995) pointed out in a recent review of research on electronic networks, "Very few studies have looked at the reciprocal relationship between CMC and the face-to-face contexts in which teachers and students meet together" (p. 353). Moreover, a growing body of scholarship suggests that CMC technologies may reproduce and/or reinforce long-standing inequities within classrooms, especially with respect to race and gender (Gruber, 1995; Herring, Johnson, & Dibenedetto, 1992; Romano, 1993; Takayoshi, 1994; see also Selfe & Hilligoss, 1994). In short, as the uses of CMC continue to expand dramatically in classrooms at all educational levels, important questions remain to be addressed about the effects of CMC on teaching and learning and the relationship between CMC and traditional classroom practices.

In this article, we report on a study of the relationship between electronic or online discourse and face-to-face discourse in two undergraduate writing classes in which computer-mediated communication was employed to supplement conventional in-class lecture and discussion. Specifically, we examined characteristics of both electronic and face-to-face discourse in these classes, especially as they related to the ways in which students and teachers perceived their respective roles within the context of each course; in addition, we explored the potential influence of in-class discourse and factors associated with the course context on the nature and rates of student participation in online discussions. Our results revealed that student participation in online discussions related in complex ways to a variety of factors associated with the face-to-face discourse in each class, the ways in which the instructor structured the course and managed the uses of CMC in the course, and the students' perceptions of CMC and its importance within the context of each course. These results complicate the findings of some previous studies that suggested increased and more equitable student participation in online discussions; they also complicate our understanding of the ways students participate in online discussions in educational settings, particularly in writing classes. In addition, they provide insight into the complex relationships among the nature of online discourse in educational settings and a variety of factors related to classroom context and undergraduate student experience.

Review of the Literature

Much of the research on uses of CMC in educational and organizational settings during the past decade or so has focused on the potential benefits of CMC. Hawisher (1992) summarized six advantages that researchers from a variety of disciplines — especially distance education and computers and composition — commonly associated with CMC, or what Hawisher termed *electronic conferences* (p. 82):

1. Electronic conferences are text-based environments in which participants are totally immersed in writing.

2. They provide a real and expanded audience for writers.

3. They encourage a sense of community.

4. They demonstrate a high degree of involvement on the part of participants.

5. They encourage equitable participation.

6. They can encourage a decrease in leader-centered communication. (pp. 84–91)

As Hawisher pointed out, these benefits are cited routinely in studies of CMC. For instance, in a study comparing online and face-to-face discussions in a university sociology course, Quinn, Mehan, Levin, & Black (1983) found that "interaction via a non-real time [electronic] message system showed multiple threads of discourse, a higher proportion of students' responses to teacher's initiations, and few teacher evaluations" (p. 326); they also found that "in the electronic message discussion, turn-allocation was more open" and not dominated by the teacher (p. 324). Levin, Kim, & Riel (1990) found that the electronic discussions on the Intercultural Learning Network (ICLN), which linked students and teachers around the world through CMC, "deviate[d] from the most common face-to-face 'whole group' instructional pattern, which is a string of alterations in turns between teacher and different students" (p. 195). Using Mehan's (1978) IRE Sequence (Initiation by the teacher, Reply by the student, Evaluation by the teacher), which Mehan found to comprise 53% of teacher-student interactions in classrooms in his study, Levin et al. found that instances of the IRE pattern in online discussions "were rare and usually embedded in a more complex pattern" (p. 201); furthermore, whereas in the Mehan study "almost all initiations and evaluations [during face-to-face classroom interactions] were by the teacher, and almost all replies were by the students," Levin et al. reported that 29% of evaluations in the online discussions in their study were made by students and "less than half (39%) of the initiations were made by adults" (p. 206). These findings of increased, more equitable, and less leader-centered participation in online discussions are supported by other studies (Bump, 1990; Feenberg, 1987; Hiltz, 1990; Hiltz & Turoff, 1978; Kiesler, Siegel, & McGuire, 1984) and by testimonials from educators (Butler & Kinneavy, 1991; Cooper & Selfe, 1990; Faigley, 1990; Kremers, 1990). As Levin et al. concluded, "There are substantial differences between face-to-face instruction and instruction conducted using electronic networks" (p. 206). Clearly, the potential for CMC to alter traditional patterns of discourse in classroom discussions is high.

However, CMC can be extremely complex, and patterns of online discourse may be affected by a variety of factors. In her review of research on CMC, Wells (1993) identified three key factors that seem to "interact" with the rates of student participation in online discussions: The educational level of the students; the amount of time students must devote to such tasks as logon procedures; and the model of online interaction to which students are exposed (p. 6). Wells also cited a number of studies indicating that the ways instructors assign and use CMC in their courses can affect participation rates. For example, McCreary and Van Duren (1987) found that assigning a percentage of final grades to the content of electronic messages influenced student participation. In addition, the ways instructors conduct online discussions may affect student participation. For instance, in a study of CMC in an introductory undergraduate education course, Ahern, Peck, and Laycock (1992) reported that "the style of discourse used by the instructor is the most important factor in determining the amount of student participation as well as improving the quality of the [student] responses" (p. 307). Eldred (1991), describing how she used electronic bulletin boards in her English classes, found that "moderating [by the instructor] was an essential part of on-line discussions, but on-line conversations were not the best means of encouraging in-class discussions" (p. 51). Such research indicates that factors such as the structure of a course, its grading policies, and the ways instructors manage both in-class and online discussions are likely to influence the nature of student participation in online discourse.[1]

At the same time, many researchers have identified a variety of difficulties associated with online discussions. Summarizing disadvantages that are commonly cited in studies of CMC, Hawisher (1992) asserted that "electronic conferences can be every bit as ineffective as traditional forums for learning" (p. 93). In reviewing research on the uses of CMC to encourage student participation and group interaction, Harasim (1989) cited studies indicating that "achieving an active membership (in which members are actively writing and reading [electronic] notes) has been a problem in on-line educational activities" (p. 52). She noted that although CMC "offers potential for active group participation and interaction, it does not guarantee it" (p. 52). Some studies indicate that the problems of teacher-dominated discussion that some researchers identify with traditional face-to-face classroom discussion can arise online. For example, Thompson (1988) reported that the instructor described in her study dominated class discussion on the electronic network as much as she had in face-to-face classroom discussions. Moreover, scholars have increasingly begun to explore the ways electronic discourse may replicate racial, gender, and other inequities that can affect traditional face-to-face classroom discussions (Gruber, 1995; Herring, Johnson, & Dibenedetto, 1992). For example, Romano (1993) described the ways students in her undergraduate writing course negotiated racial, ethnic, and gender identity in online discussions and concluded that "new technology cannot entirely dismantle old habits" (p. 21). Herring et al. described inequities in participation among men and women on a Usenet newsgroup and concluded that the electronic medium did not break down "gender barriers" (p. 21).

It is important to note that the benefits and problems associated with CMC seem to apply to asynchronous (or non-real-time) forms, such as newsgroups and listservs, as well as to synchronous (or real-time) forms such as Internet Relay Chat (IRC) and programs such as Daedalus. For example, the problems of racial and ethnic identity that Romano (1993) described arose in synchronous online discussions; Herring et al. (1992) described similar problems relating to gender on an asynchronous listserv, while Gruber (1995) reported problems in both media. However, much of the literature on computers and composition has focused on the benefits of using synchronous CMC as a way to "decenter" the classroom (see esp. Butler & Kinneavy, 1991; Faigley, 1990 and 1992, chapter 6); less attention seems to have been given to asynchronous forms of CMC in writing classes, despite evidence that these forms may be more commonly used and despite obvious differences in the two forms of CMC. For example, synchronous discussions usually take place in a computer-equipped classroom during regular class meeting times, with students and teachers physically present during online discussions. By contrast, asynchronous discussions often take place outside regular class meetings. Thus, synchronous discussions can significantly alter class meetings, whereas asynchronous discussions often serve as an "external" supplement to conventional in-class lecture and discussion. Although many researchers in computers and composition have attempted to identify the ways in which synchronous CMC encourages "more active participation than in many traditional classroom discussions" (Butler & Kinneavy, 1991, p. 409), few studies have investigated how commonly used asynchronous forms of CMC may relate to more traditionally organized classes; moreover, little attention has been focused on the ways online discussions and conventional in-class discourse may related to and influence each other.

The research summarized here indicates that a number of factors may influence student online participation in specific contexts. But specifically *how* CMC might relate to those contexts is not well understood, and the studies cited above raise a number of questions about the relationship of CMC to conventional face-to-face classroom discussion and to a variety of factors associated with the educational contexts within which CMC is used. For example, do patterns of online discourse relate in identifiable ways to patterns of face-to-face classroom discussion in mixed mode courses? Gruber (1995) concluded that uses of CMC must be understood "in connection with the goals established by the institution, the teaching approaches proposed by the instructors, and the expectations entertained by students" (p. 62). What other factors associated with a course or classroom context, such as the structure of the course or the nature of course assignments, might affect student participation in online discussions? If a teacher's online discourse style influences student participation, as Ahern, Peck, and Laycock (1992) found, how might a teacher's in-class discourse style affect online participation? Moreover, how do students understand their participation in online discussions? How might students' perceptions of CMC affect their online participation? The study described in this article was an attempt to address such questions.

Research Questions

This study addressed four central questions:

1. What was the nature of student participation in course-related online discussions in mixed mode writing courses in which CMC was employed?

2. What factors associated with the context of these mixed mode writing courses, in which CMC was used to supplement face-to-face discussion, might have affected the rates and nature of student participation in course-related online discourse?

3. How did the online discourse relate to face-to-face discourse in such a course?

4. How might students' perceptions of CMC have affected their online participation?

Design of the Study

This study employed both qualitative and quantitative techniques to collect a variety of data related to the in-class and online discourse of two undergraduate writing courses, English 306 and Communications 456, which were offered at Purdue University during the 1994–1995 academic year. We attended regular class meetings of both courses throughout the semester, during which we took field notes and coded face-to-face in-class discourse according to a scheme developed for the study (see Appendix A); we monitored the online discussions for each course and collected all electronic messages posted to the course newsgroup or mailing list; we interviewed students and instructors about their uses of CMC in the class; and we collected documents, such as syllabi, assignment prompts, and various handouts, both in paper and electronic form, related to each course. We then employed several methods to analyze these bodies of data. These techniques are described in detail in the following sections.

THE COURSES   English 306, Introduction to Professional Writing, and Communications 456, Advertising Copywriting, are writing-intensive courses offered as part of two undergraduate majors at Purdue University: English 306 is a required course in the Professional Writing emphasis within the English major, and COM 456 is one of several upper-level courses offered to communications majors. Both courses were taught in networked computer labs and both employed computer technology in a variety of ways to support writing instruction. Although both are professional writing courses, each has a different focus and different goals.

English 306 is designed to introduce undergraduate professional writing majors to issues in professional writing and to provide them with intensive practice in professional writing. During the semester we observed this course, the twice-weekly, 75-minute class meetings were conducted in a workshop-style format in which the instructor, Jordan, typically lectured or led discussion at the beginning of class for 30 minutes or less and then allowed students to devote the remaining class time to work on their projects individually or within their groups.[2] The class met in a lab equipped with 29 Apple computers networked to a server with Internet access. Twenty students enrolled in the course; one student dropped during the sixth week of the semester.

Communications 456 was a lecture-based course that introduced students to methods and concepts in advertising copywriting. Most of the 50-minute class meetings were devoted to lectures by the instructor, Debbie, during which an overhead projector was always employed. Typically, one of the three weekly class meetings, usually on Friday, was designated a "lab day," during which students worked individually or collaboratively on their assignments. The class met in a lab equipped with 21 Apple computers networked to a server with Internet access. Unlike in English 306, the server was rarely used in COM 456 to exchange course-related documents; most assignments were submitted in hard copy. Eighteen students enrolled in the course. (One student declined to participate in this study.) During the semester when this study was conducted, two sections of COM 456 were offered, both taught by the same instructor. Only one section was included in this study, but students from both sections participated in the online discussions on the newsgroup established for the course.

THE INSTRUCTORS   Both instructors were experienced computer users with a broad knowledge of Internet resources and CMC technologies. Jordan, the English 306 instructor, was a full-time faculty member in English whose professional focus was technical writing. He had used CMC in writing courses he had taught at two universities before coming to Purdue. For English 306, he established a listserv mailing list, which he intended to use primarily as a forum for discussion and as a means of communication between him and the students. Debbie, the COM 456 instructor, was a full-time faculty member in the Communications Department who had extensive professional experience in the field of advertising. She had previously used electronic mail in communications courses she had taught at another university, but she had never used CMC as an integral part of her courses. For COM 456, she established a Usenet newsgroup as a forum for discussion of course topics and issues in advertising more generally; she also introduced students to electronic mail as a means of communication for the course.

Data Collection

We employed several methods to collect data for this study.

FIELD NOTES OF CLASS MEETINGS   In order to understand the context of each course and to be able to describe and analyze the face-to-face discourse in each course, the researchers attended a majority of class meetings for each course. At least one researcher attended 37 (86%) of 43 scheduled class meetings for COM 456, and 23 (82%) of 28 meetings for English 306.[3] During these meetings, we took field notes describing in-class activities. For COM 456, two sets of field notes (taken independently by each researcher) were made for 55.8% of the class meetings and one set (when only one researcher attended class) for 86%; for English 306, two sets of field notes were made for 39% of the class meetings and one set for 82%.

During class meetings we also coded in-class discourse according to a scheme we developed for the study (see Appendix A). The purpose of this scheme was to provide data about the relative frequency of various types of face-to-face interactions that occurred in each class. Coding sheets enabled us to indicate which types of discourse were occurring at 30-second intervals. We tested the coding scheme during the first week of the semester we observed English 306 and COM 456, when the instructors were introducing their courses and handling enrollment adjustments; neither the COM 456 newsgroup nor the English 306 listserv was in use at this time. After adjusting the coding scheme slightly, we used it to code each class meeting we attended. We completed at least one coding sheet for 77.5% of COM 456 class meetings and 80.8% of English 306 class meetings; we completed two coding sheets for 55.0% of the COM 456 class meetings and for 34.6% of the English 306 meetings. Throughout the semester, we shared our field notes each week and periodically checked our coding sheets for consistency.

INTERVIEWS   We interviewed both instructors before and during the semester about their course designs, their intentions for the uses of CMC in their courses, the problems they perceived in using CMC, and their prior experiences in using CMC technologies. These interviews were conducted face-to-face and were audiotaped. We also interviewed, either face-to-face or via e-mail, seven students in COM 456 and six in English 306 about their experiences with and perceptions of the uses of CMC in these courses. All interviews were voluntary. Students were made to understand that their participation or nonparticipation in such interviews would not be made known to their instructor and would have no bearing on their course grades.

SURVEYS   We distributed two sets of surveys to all the students in each course, one set during the second week of the semester and the second set during the final week. These surveys provided data regarding students' prior experiences with CMC, their perceptions of its uses in these courses, their assessment of its value in these courses, and their attitudes toward computers in general.

MONITORING ONLINE DISCUSSIONS   Finally, we monitored all electronic discourse on the COM 456 newsgroup and the English 306 listserv. During the semester 545 messages were posted to the COM 456 newsgroup, 294 of those by students from the section of the course we studied. 114 e-mail messages were sent as part of English 306; 108 of those were posted to the 306 listserv and six were sent as private e-mail messages. All newsgroup and e-mail messages were archived on disk.

Data Analysis

Several methods were used to analyze the data described above. First, quantitative analyses were conducted using the coding sheets, the newsgroup and listserv messages, and the survey data. These analyses were then supplemented with qualitative data collected through the field notes and interviews.

ANALYSIS OF IN-CLASS DISCOURSE   All coding sheets were tabulated to arrive at percentages of each category of discourse over the entire semester. In addition, each researcher's coding sheets were tabulated separately to check for consistency.[4] These figures provide a general picture of the typical patterns of face-to-face discourse in each class — for example, percentage of in-class discourse devoted to lecture by the instructor as compared to that taken up by student questions. In addition, individual coding sheets provide a way to highlight differences in discourse patterns for COM 456 and English 306.

ANALYSIS OF ONLINE DISCOURSE   A number of quantitative measures of newsgroup and listserv messages were taken. The total number of messages posted by each student during the semester was determined; number of messages posted per week was also determined. Averages of these figures were tabulated. The average number of lines per message was determined for each student. In addition, the total number of lines posted by each student during the semester was determined, and averages were tabulated for each course. These figures provide a picture of the rates of student participation in online discourse in each class.

Content analyses of newsgroup and listserv posts were also conducted. At the end of the semester, we reviewed all online messages according to content. Because of differences in the nature of the two courses and in how each instructor used CMC, we devised two separate schemes to code the content of online messages, one for COM 456 and one for English 306 (see Appendix B). After testing the schemes on representative messages, we each coded newsgroup and listserv messages and then compared our results. For this first round of coding, we coded 254 of the 589 messages posted to the COM 456 newsgroup and agreed on 84% of these. For English 306, our rate of agreement after coding all 114 e-mail messages was 90.4%. We discussed posts on which we disagreed, made necessary adjustments, and then coded all online messages again. For the second round of coding, our rate of agreement for all 545 messages posted to the COM 456 newsgroup was 86.7%; for the English 306 listserv messages, the rate was 94.0%. After these rounds of coding, we discussed disagreements to determine final codings for each message.

We tabulated the results of the content coding to determine percentages for each category for the entire semester as well as week-by-week. We also determined the figures for each student. These figures provide a sense of the content or nature of online discussions in each course.

ANALYSIS OF THE SURVEYS   Many of the questions on the two student surveys allowed for quantitative analysis. (Others asked for students' opinions about CMC in the course and about their prior experiences with CMC.) We tabulated the results of these surveys to determine percentages for each question in each course. We also tabulated the results of the attitude scale at the beginning and end of the semester.

QUALITATIVE ANALYSES   In addition to these various quantitative measures, we reviewed field notes and interview data in an effort to identify key factors influencing the quantitative results and to examine potential relationships among these factors and the online discourse. For example, interviews with the students provided insight into how students participated in online discussions and into their perceptions of online and in-class discussions. Moreover, during interviews we often asked students about particular topics or comments in the online discussions to understand better their perceptions of those discussions. The students' responses to these questions, some of which we discuss in more detail later in this article, provide a fuller sense of the context within which the online and in-class discussions took place and help explain the results of the statistical analyses described above. Similarly, interviews with the instructors enabled us to understand their perceptions of online discourse in their classes. Finally, field notes provided a rich source of data that enabled us to understand the classroom context surrounding specific online discussions. For example, field notes indicated specific topics of in-class discussion, which could be compared to online discussion topics. Field notes also indicated the kinds of in-class activities that were taking place at a given time, which could be checked against the patterns of discourse emerging on the coding sheets or online.

Results

Results of the study reveal various patterns of in-class and online discourse in each course and suggest complex relationships between in-class and online discourse and a variety of contextual factors. First, we present results of the quantitative analyses. Then we elaborate on these results by presenting qualitative data.

Results of the quantitative analyses can be divided into analyses of in-class discourse and analyses of online discourse.

IN-CLASS DISCOURSE   For COM 456, in-class discourse tended to be dominated by the instructor (see Table 1 for study results and Appendix A for category descriptions). Results of the tabulations of coding sheets indicate that 56.9% of in-class discourse was comprised of the instructor lecturing, questioning, responding to students' questions, or giving instructions to students (Categories TL, TQ1, TQ2, TR1, TR2, and TC); lecturing (TL) was the most common form of in-class discourse, comprising 42.4% of classroom discourse. Student-centered discourse, including student responses to the instructor's questions, students' questions, and students' comments (Categories FSR, MSR, FSQ, MSQ, FSC, MSC), comprised only 9.4% of in-class discourse. Student-*initiated* discourse, which includes students' *unsolicited* questions and comments (Categories FSQ, MSQ, FSC, MSC), comprised only 3.5% of in-class discourse. In addition, 32.6% of in-class discourse was comprised of small-group activities or individual student work (SMG and ST). During such time, the instructor was often engaged in one-to-one conversations with individual students, usually regarding specific assignments or problems with the computers; these student-teacher interactions (ST) comprised 16.1% of in-class discourse.

These figures indicate the extent to which in-class discourse in COM 456 was teacher-centered. The periodic "lab days," during which the instructor allowed students to work on their assignments individually or in small groups, deviated from this pattern of teacher-centered discourse. During most class meetings, however, all but a few minutes of class time were devoted to lecture, during which few students spoke at all. Field notes indicate that even when students did speak in class, it was almost always to ask brief questions of clarification or to respond to the instructor's questions in ways that did not deviate from her predetermined lecture topics. In only a few instances during the semester did a student raise a question during a lecture that challenged the instructor's comment or proposed a topic other than what the instructor had been discussing. The following exchange during a lecture on

Table 1. Percentages of Types of Classroom Discourse

	TL	TQ1	TQ2	TR1	TR2	TC	FSR	MSR	FSQ	MSQ	FSC	MSC	SMG	ST	NVC
COM 456	42.4	6.4	0.7	4.4	2.2	0/8	4.8	1.1	2.5	0.3	0.7	<0.1	16.5	16.1	1.1
Engl. 306	28.8	3.2	0.2	1.5	1.9	0.9	0.9	1.0	1.5	0.9	0.1	<0.1	25.5	32.8	0.9

psychological principles in advertising was typical of the in-class discourse. In this case, Debbie was illustrating a point by referring to an example of an ad campaign for a hair-setter device.

Debbie:	How many of you have heard of the molecular hair-setter? [A number of students raise their hands.] I'm surprised. How did you hear about it?
Student 1:	My roommate has one.
Student 2:	I saw an infomercial about it.
Debbie:	[Nods.] There's a very interesting story about that product.

Debbie then goes on to relate the story. At times, the in-class "discussion" did involve more student input than the above example suggests, but such instances were rare.

For English 306, the numbers are somewhat different (see Table 1). Teacher-centered discourse (Categories TL, TQ1, TQ2, TR1, TR2, and TC) comprised 36.4% of total in-class discourse, while student-centered discourse (Categories FSR, MSR, FSQ, MSQ, FSC, MSC) comprised only 4.4%. However, fully 58.3% of in-class discourse was comprised of either small-group discussions (SMG) or interactions between Jordan and individual students or small groups of students (ST). Thus, well over half of the in-class discourse in English 306 was devoted to small-group discourse rather than teacher-directed discussions or lectures. Indeed, Jordan spent slightly more time (32.8%) in interactions with one or two students (ST), usually focused on an assigned project, than he did lecturing (28.8%). Thus, in English 306, although students did not participate more extensively in whole-class discussions than did their peers in COM 456, they did have more opportunities to interact with peers and the instructor.

In-class discourse in these two undergraduate writing courses, then, differed in the extent to which it tended to be dominated by the instructor (see Figure 1). In COM 456, in-class discourse was teacher-centered, with lecture by the instructor comprising the largest discourse category; in English 306, classroom discourse was characterized by less lecture and slightly lower rates of student participation in whole-class discussions but by significantly higher rates of student-teacher and small-group, student-to-student interactions. In neither course, however, was there extensive student participation in large-group face-to-face discussion, and when large-group discussion did occur, it tended to be teacher-directed and followed the IRE pattern that Mehan (1978) describes.

ONLINE DISCOURSE   Assuming that the nature of online discourse relates in some ways to in-class discourse, the figures presented above suggest that we might expect online discussions in English 306 to be more open and less teacher-directed, with higher rates of student participation, than online discourse in COM 456. However, results of the

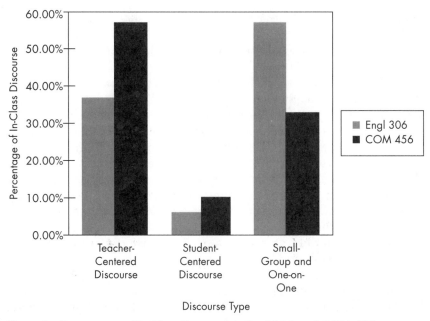

Figure 1. Comparison of In-Class Discourse in Engl 306 and COM 456

analyses of the online discussions for these two classes suggest that the relationship between online and in-class discourse was more complex.

RATES OF PARTICIPATION   In COM 456, all students posted messages to the course newsgroup during the semester. A total of 294 messages was posted by the students in this section of COM 456 over 14 weeks. (The rest of the 545 messages were posted by members of the other section of COM 456.) Students posted an average of 1.12 messages per student per week (see Table 2). All but two students posted at least 12 messages during the semester, with the average number of messages per student totaling 16 over the semester. Most messages posted by students to the COM 456 newsgroup were short, averaging 7.32 lines per message[5] (see Table 3). Debbie, the instructor, who posted 11 messages during the semester, wrote significantly longer messages than the students, averaging 59.17 lines per message; the highest student average was 13.81 lines per message.

For English 306, 114 e-mail messages were sent during the semester. Of these 108 were posted to the class mailing list; the others were "private" messages sent by an individual student to Jordan or by Jordan to an individual student. Jordan sent the highest number of messages (44). The number of messages sent during the semester by an individual student ranged from one to 11 and averaged only 3.5. As Table 2 indicates, these numbers amounted to an average of only 0.24 messages per student per week. Lines per message averaged 15.16 (see

Table 3). Jordan wrote the longest message (164 lines — a message explaining the submission guidelines for the final portfolio); the longest student message was 64 lines and was sent by Rachel, whose messages averaged 38.17 lines.

Unlike COM 456, in which weekly posts to the newsgroup remained fairly constant throughout the semester, English 306 online discourse dropped off precipitously after the fifth week of the semester. For the first four weeks after Jordan set up the class mailing list, an average of 21.7 messages per week was sent. From that point until the end of the semester, the average number of messages per week was only 2.6. In short, most of the activity on the class mailing list occurred during the second and fifth weeks of the semester, when Jordan gave students specific readings to discuss online. After the fifth week, the list ceased to be an active forum for class discussion; instead, it was used almost exclusively by Jordan as a means of distributing information about assignments (see Figure 2).

CONTENT OF ONLINE DISCUSSIONS   Just as online participation rates differed in these two courses, so too did the *nature* of the online discourse.

Discussions on the COM 456 newsgroup tended to be chatty and sometimes lively, ranging over a variety of topics, some related to the course material and some seemingly unrelated. Table 4 reveals that discussions focused on personal issues more than any other category, including course assignments and general issues in advertising (see Appendix B for explanation of content categories). During the semester, 103 of 323[6] (31.9%) messages posted focused on personal issues, which included comments about student life, references to personal situations (such as complaints about too many tests in a given week), opinions about happenings on campus or about music, and so on. By comparison, 58 messages (18.0%) focused on general issues in adver-

---

Table 2. Average Number of Messages Posted per Week per Student

	Mean	High	Low[1]	St Dev
COM 456	1.12	7	0	0.53
Engl 306	0.24	7	0	0.15

Note: [1] Not including the week of spring break.

Table 3. Average Number of Lines per Message per Student

	Mean	High	Low	St Dev
COM 456	7.32	13.81	3.92	2.86
Engl 306	15.16	38.17	4.50	7.92

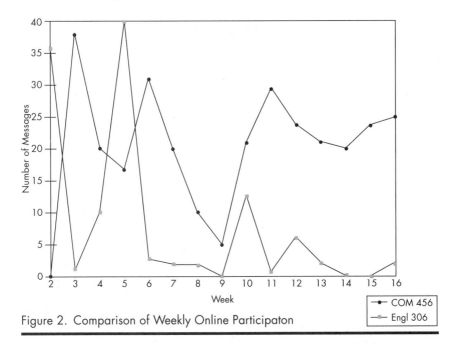

Figure 2. Comparison of Weekly Online Participaton

tising and 74 (22.9%) focused on course assignments; 32 (9.9%) focused on comments about the course in general. If categories 1 through 4 are combined, encompassing messages about advertising, the course itself, course assignments, and career issues in advertising, 60.7% of the messages posted to the newsgroup referred in some fashion to course topics, loosely defined. Still, nearly a third had little or no direct relation to course topics but focused instead on personal matters or student life.

These figures indicate that online discussions in COM 456 were not necessarily the kind of in-depth engagements with course issues that some researchers have found in studies of CMC, especially synchronous forms (Bump, 1990; Butler & Kinneavy, 1991; Faigley, 1990; Levin et al., 1990; Quinn et al., 1983). Moreover, a review of the messages indicates that even when they focused on course-related matters or issues in advertising, they were often brief and did not engage these

Table 4. Content of COM 456 Newsgroup Posts: Number of Messages by Content Category					
1 *Advts*	**2** *Course*	**3** *Assgn*	**4** *Career*	**5** *Persnl*	**6** *Techn*
Number of Messages 58	32	74	32	103	24

issues in great depth. The following message about a television advertisement was typical:

> I have to comment on the lottery ads that have the lady singing the bingo song. I know their point is to annoy the viewers and to react by buying a ticket, but I think the ad is overly annoying. Every time that commercial comes on I turn it or mute it. Now is this what the advertisers want? I don't think so. There has to be a better way to advertise this product without the risk of losing viewers.

Such a post is ostensibly "about" effectiveness in advertising, yet it is similar to the kind of brief comment students typically made during in-class discussion. In addition, although the online discourse was more interactive than in-class discourse, with several discussion threads developing over the semester, in general the newsgroup seems to have been less interactive than online discussions in other studies (e.g., Levin et al., 1990; Quinn et al., 1983). Thus, although online discourse in COM 456 was characterized by decidedly higher rates of student participation and interaction than in-class discourse, it nevertheless seemed to mirror some aspects of in-class discourse, especially in the sense that it tended to be characterized by brief comments and short threads of discussion.[7]

In English 306, online discussions were almost exclusively focused on course assignments and related issues. The six content categories (see Appendix B) in our coding scheme reflect this focus. Only 6 of 114 messages sent during the semester included content that related to what might be considered "personal" issues regarding careers in professional writing, and even those six did relate to a topic from a reading assigned by Jordan (see Table 5). All other messages were posted in direct response to the assigned readings. Unlike the COM 456 newsgroup, then, online discussions in English 306 never deviated from the course themes and included no references to student life or personal matters. In addition, online messages in English 306 were decidedly longer than newsgroup posts in COM 456, as noted above. In this sense, online discussions in English 306 were more like the in-depth student comments that some researchers have observed in online discourse (e.g., Butler & Kinneavy, 1991).

	1 Course	2 Assgn	3 Indvl	4a Disc	4b Disc	5 Other
Number of Messages	20	39	7	31	15	6

Table 5. Content of English 306 E-mail Messages: Number of Messages by Content Category

Interestingly, whereas in-class discourse in English 306 was less teacher-centered than in-class discourse in COM 456, online discourse was somewhat more teacher-centered. Jordan posted more messages than any student, although his messages tended to focus on parameters for assignments. And the results of the coding indicate that even during online discussion of the readings and related course topics, students tended to respond to Jordan's prompts rather than to each other. In Category 4, Discussion of Readings and Course Issues, 31 of 46 messages (67.4%) were sent in direct response to Jordan's assignment prompts or to questions that he posed; only 15 of those 46 messages (32.6%) were sent in response to other students' comments or questions (see Table 5). Thus, although online discourse in English 306 was certainly focused on course readings and assignments in ways that COM 456 discussions were not, it tended to be less interactive than in-class discourse and somewhat more controlled by the teacher.

Results of the quantitative measures and much of the qualitative data, then, reveal observable patterns in both the in-class and online discourse in each of these courses. These patterns suggest, as has much previous research, that use of CMC in itself, to paraphrase Harasim (1989), will not guarantee active student participation or interaction nor will it guarantee that student participation will be in-depth and engaged. Clearly, these results suggest that there was no simple correlation between in-class and online discourse in these mixed mode courses. Instead, the results raise a number of questions about the rates and nature of student participation in online discourse and about the relationship of that discourse to the in-class discussion and to other factors associated with the context of the course. For example, why did students in COM 456 devote a significant portion of their newsgroup posts to "personal" issues apparently unrelated to course matters? Why did the students in English 306 not do the same, instead devoting their longer, more formal e-mail messages almost exclusively to discussion of the assigned readings? Why were these online discussions not more interactive? How did the students in these classes understand the purpose(s) of the electronic discourse and their roles as participants in it? And how might their understandings have influenced the nature of their online discourse? What other factors associated with the context of each course might have contributed to the nature of the students' online discourse?

Answers to these questions, we believe, lie in a careful examination of the context of each course and the ways CMC was presented and used in those courses. The qualitative data provide insight into how students understood the uses of CMC and which factors might have influenced their online participation. In addition, these data provide a fuller sense of the context surrounding the in-class and online discourse and suggest tentative conclusions regarding the connections between in-class and online discourse. We discuss these findings in the next section.

Online Discourse and Course Context

The results presented above suggest that the nature of in-class discourse in these two courses may have had some influence on the online discussions, but clearly no cause-and-effect relationship existed between in-class and online discourse. Qualitative data suggest that a variety of factors related to course context and to students' and instructors' perceptions of CMC may have played significant roles in shaping online discourse in these two mixed mode courses. Among these many factors, four emerge from the data as especially important: (a) the ways in which CMC was assigned and managed by the instructor and perceived by the students; (b) the nature of the course, especially how class time was structured and how the purposes of the course were presented to and understood by students; (c) the students' perceptions in general of CMC as a communication medium; and (d) the students' sense of their roles as participants in course-related discourse, both in-class and online. These sets of factors overlapped and influenced each other in complex ways, of course, but each can be described separately in order to help explain the nature of the online discourse in these classes. In the following sections, we discuss, first, the ways in which CMC was used in each course and how the nature of the course itself may have influenced online discussions, and second, the ways in which students understood CMC and their roles in online discussions.

Assigning Electronic Discussions in Mixed Mode Courses

Data from the present study suggest that the ways each instructor presented and managed CMC in her or his course played an important role in shaping the rates and nature of student participation in online discourse. The two instructors in this study conceived of, presented, and managed the online discussions differently, and those differences seem to be reflected in differences in the online discourse we observed in each course.

Debbie, the instructor for COM 456, though an experienced participant in online discussions herself, was a novice in using CMC in her courses. As we note above, the semester in which we studied her class was her first attempt to use a newsgroup for ongoing discussion in an undergraduate course. In interviews at the beginning of the semester, she expressed her commitment to the idea of a newsgroup as a way of "providing an open forum and supplementing in-class discussions." But she also confessed to some uncertainty about using the newsgroup. During the third week of the semester, she admitted that her intention was, "frankly, mostly exploratory — to see how students tend to react and how the technology might enhance learning."

Despite her uncertainties, Debbie described the newsgroup in her course syllabus as a "fun and an interesting way to extend our coursework" and provided a list of possible ways to participate in the online discussions: for example, asking questions about course concepts; analyzing the concept under discussion; describing your experience of how course concepts are applied or misapplied in practice; discussing the ethical ramifications of current advertising practices you observe; introducing a topic of your own that you think is pertinent to advertising copywriting.

Thus, the newsgroup was initially presented to students as an interesting and straightforward way to engage in discussions about relevant issues in advertising copywriting. In addition, Debbie required students to post at least one message each week to the course newsgroup and counted this participation as 10% of the final grade. In effect, this arrangement meant that students would earn the full 10% simply by posting a message each week without regard to the content of those messages. Although Debbie explicitly described the kinds of messages she wanted the students to post, she provided neither the criteria nor the means for assessing the content of those messages.

By contrast, Jordan did not require online participation in English 306, but he expected and emphasized it. His syllabus did not include any reference to the class mailing list, but it did include a description of a "reading/discussion journal" assignment, worth 10% of the students' grades, "in which you respond to material raised in class and in the readings from the . . . text." At the beginning of the third week of class, Jordan announced in class that this "reading/discussion journal" would be replaced by electronic discussions on the class mailing list, which he had introduced during the previous week. At that point he directed students to post responses to assigned readings to the class list rather than submitting them in hard copy. Thus, at the outset, Jordan presented the online discourse as a kind of electronic version of a relatively formal, academic reading journal rather than as a more open discussion of course issues. Two weeks later, after students had begun posting their responses to the class list, Jordan announced in class that he wanted to get a "true discussion" going on e-mail, not one "moderated by me." Nevertheless, students initially seem to have understood the online discourse as a version of the reading journal. In addition, Jordan never established a clear policy regarding participation or grading. Not surprisingly, online participation began to decrease after the first few weeks and, despite his warning during the 6th week of the semester about lowering grades for lack of participation, virtually disappeared by the second half of the course.

Some previous research indicates that requiring student online participation results in higher rates of participation (Harasim, 1987; see Wells, 1993, p. 6). In the present study, participation in English 306 was mandated but not in a clear manner and not until the third week of the course. In addition, specific parameters for grading of online participation were never provided. Not surprisingly, online participation was quite low, with several students posting only a single message all semester. On the other hand, Debbie's assignment structure seems to have resulted in relatively constant student participation in the online discussions in COM 456. Students in the class averaged a little more than one message per week, which fell in line with her requirement. In fact, 13 of the 17 students earned at least 8 of the possible 10 points for the electronic discussions, with 6 of those earning the full 10 points. Nearly all students who were interviewed reported that they would not have participated regularly in the newsgroup discussions if they had not been required to do so. Thus, Debbie's grading policy seems to have had the desired effect of encouraging students to participate in the online discussions.

The *nature* of that participation, however, was a more complicated matter. In an interview conducted during the third week of the semester, Debbie expressed her hopes that the online discussions would be an opportunity for students "to actually mull over each other's comments and then respond, which may lead to (a) wider breadth of information/creative thinking about advertising and/or (b) more thoughtful discussion than might occur in the classroom." To an extent, the newsgroup did provide just such an opportunity. As the results of the content analysis (see Table 4) indicate, students did engage issues in advertising and discuss course concepts. But they did not do so to the extent Debbie had hoped, and she complained that "the threads that do emerge seem to be relatively short-lived, compared to those we see in the subscription lists." At the mid-semester break she described much of the online discourse as irrelevant chat, and soon after that she announced in class that although there had been some good discussion on the newsgroup, students' posts had wandered off to "spring break fantasies," and she wanted them to focus on course topics. A look at some representative posts reveals of the source of Debbie's disappointment:

> Although it seems like the semester just started, I am VERY ready for Spring Break. I think everyone is counting the days until they can get away from studies and classes. I know I am!

> When this semester ends and I graduate, (hopefully) I do not think that I am going to rush out and get to work immediately. I think I am going to take some time off and travel a bit. I feel like I deserve it, after all, I've been in school the majority of my life. I want to see something before I settle in. I can't wait until this is over!

Even posts that did address the kinds of issues Debbie had hoped would characterize the electronic discussions were often brief and superficial. The following message, which refers to two course assignments (a brand character description and an advertising strategy assignment), was typical:

> Hi everyone! Just some random thoughts for all of you to think about. First of all I'm not quite understanding this brand character thing if someone could explain it to me! Also, anyone know of any useful electives that I could take next year that would be beneficial to advertising; such as computer classes or art, etc. Lastly, I've been thinking a lot

about my resume lately, and I want ideas! Other than that, I hope you all have a great week, and good luck on your strategy assignment!

Furthermore, those posts that did engage issues in more depth did not typically spark many responses from other students. After the mid-semester break, Mary posted a long message addressing a complex ethical issue in advertising (see below under "Students' Perceptions of CMC and Their Online Roles"). Only five messages were posted in response to this post over the two weeks. By comparison, virtually every student posted a message about semester break activities.

Clearly, requiring and grading online participation in itself will not result in the kinds of in-depth discussions instructors might hope for. In this case, Debbie's assignment structure may even have contributed to the kind of superficiality and "irrelevant" discussion that disappointed her. Several students complained in interviews that they had difficulty coming up with things to say in their weekly posts: "I usually find myself grasping at random thoughts just so that I can write something." "Some people have a lot of trouble finding things to write about each week." A few also complained that the newsgroup wasn't really discussion. Christine noted that questions posed or comments made usually resulted in no response by other students. Gary said it was more like "reading a newspaper" than engaging in a discussion. Several students suggested that the grading policy, which gave students credit only for the number of messages they posted and not for the content of those messages, resulted in many irrelevant posts. Gary, for example, felt that students received credit for posting "five or six lines, something like that — several sentences strung together, and that's usually enough." Melissa complained that "some people aren't making use of the newsgroup. I feel as though most of us are being forced to write so people just write 'trash.' . . . A lot of the things on there are either over-repeated or doesn't pertain to anything we're doing." Holly concurred and noted that "every now and then someone actually comes up with a good point relating to advertising, then the newsgroup is beneficial for us; otherwise it's just a waste of time and space."

Perhaps even more important, although many students were excited about learning CMC technologies, they often seemed uncertain about the purpose of the newsgroup in the course. For example, Christine and Gary both commented that the students in the class were "guinea pigs" on which CMC was being tested. Christine added that "it's a good thing to learn . . . but it's not really incorporated into the class. It's just a sidebar in the class . . . I'm still unclear on so much of it." Similarly, Brian complained that "although I do feel that this technology is important . . . it really doesn't seem to integrate well into the theory of the course." He added that the newsgroup "would be better used if we had a topic to talk about . . . As far as what I would like to talk about, I really don't know." Melissa seemed to speak for many students in expressing "mixed feelings about the whole thing." This uncertainty among the students about the purpose of the course newsgroup seems to have grown out of the ways in which Debbie framed and managed the uses of CMC in her course: Her policy of grading only for posting a message and her decision not to provide students with specific topics for discussion seemed to have shaped the nature of students' participation in the online discussions. In addition, as Christine's comment suggests, students did not seem to perceive the online discussions as central to the work of the course and thus did not commit themselves to those discussions.

These conclusions are reinforced by examining similar data from English 306. In that course, issues of superficial or irrelevant online discussion did not arise. One chief reason seems to be that although Jordan did not require a minimum number of messages, he clearly limited the topics of discussion to the assigned readings and questions. Indeed, as noted above, all the messages posted to the class list involved discussion of the assigned readings and prompts supplied by Jordan or matters related to course projects; only six messages late in the semester referred to issues of job satisfaction that could be seen as unrelated to the assigned topics, though even those grew out of discussion of Jordan's prompts. In interviews, students seemed clear that the purpose of the online discussions was, as one student wrote, to provide a "means of participating in class discussions both in and out of class." No student expressed the kinds of complaints voiced by students in COM 456 about the irrelevance of the online discussions. Thus, the way in which Jordan framed the use of the mailing list as a medium for in-depth discussion of assigned readings, not as a forum for general conversation, and set expectations for its use as a kind of reading journal, which was clearly part of the work of the course, seemed to limit the nature of the online discussions. It did not, however, result in high rates of participation, which seems to have been a function of his unclear grading policy. As a result, although students did engage in the kinds of online discussions Jordan seemed to want, they did not participate regularly over the semester.

In sum, how the instructors set up, assigned, and managed the CMC components of their courses seems to have played a key role in shaping students' online participation. But the nature of students' online participation also seemed to be a function of their perceptions about and experiences with CMC in general and their own status and experience as undergraduate students. We discuss these factors in the following section.

STUDENTS' PERCEPTIONS OF CMC AND THEIR ONLINE ROLES Brian's comments, presented above, that he didn't know what to "talk about" online suggests that students' uncertainty about the online discussions in COM 456 may also relate to their lack of familiarity with the medium of asynchronous CMC. The data from the student surveys support such an explanation. These data indicate that few students had experience with newsgroups or other forms of CMC before entering

Debbie's class: Of the 16 students responding to the initial survey, eight indicated they had had some experience with e-mail but only one indicated any prior experience with a newsgroup. And once online, students had no models for how Debbie expected their newsgroup discussions to proceed: All 11 of Debbie's messages concerned requirements for course assignments; in none did she engage in discussion.

Perhaps because of the lack of models, students' online discussions at times focused on issues that rarely, if ever, surfaced in class, and such topics prompted discussions that were very different from in-class discourse. For instance, one thread that emerged during the semester concerned job-hunting. Many of the students in the course were seniors who were concerned about the prospect of seeking employment in advertising. As Table 4 indicates, 32 (or 9.9%) of the 323 messages posted to the class newsgroup focused on career issues. The first such message was posted during the sixth week of the semester by a student in Debbie's other COM 456 section and referred to a student-sponsored job-information seminar called Communications Day. This message spawned a thread that included 22 messages over three weeks in which students discussed the merits of "Comm Day" and eventually began discussing job-search strategies and difficulties, as the following two posts illustrate:

> First of all, I did not go to Comm Day because I had to work. But I also didn't go because of the rumors that it is a waste of time — and judging from everyone's comments, those rumors are true. I really get sick of everyone telling us that we'll never find jobs when we graduate. They all act like we're looking to be the CEO of the company the second we walk in the door. How ridiculous! Anyway, I can hear disheartening crap about the job market from everyone else — I don't need to pay $25 to some guy who's supposed to be helping us and decides to depress all of us.

> Unlike the majority of you, I found Comm Day '95 to be helpful and interesting. No company is going to come to Purdue and beg you for a job . . . The professionals I took the time to speak to were very helpful and if you would of took [sic] the time to stop them and ask them questions they were more than willing to give you names of other people in your field. The idea of Comm Day was networking and that's what I did.

Related threads about the job market continued throughout the semester. Field notes indicate that Debbie rarely spoke directly about such matters in class. And as we note above, the nature of in-class discourse made it difficult for students to raise such concerns during class. Even when students discussed matters on the newsgroup that fell into the category of "Advertising Issues," they often raised concerns that were not addressed in Debbie's lectures. For instance, Mary's message about a small town's public relations campaign to attract white families concerned ethical problems of a kind that Debbie referred to only briefly in one lecture much later in the semester. Mary wrote, in part:

> In yesterday's (Wed. 3/8/95) Chicago Sun-Times, there was an article about a little suburban town called Matteson, IL, and how they have hired a PR firm to try and create advertising to try and persuade white people to buy homes in that city. In case any of you are wondering, the population now stands at 49% white, 43% black, and 8% other . . . I am not trying to create an issue of black or white here . . . What I am saying, however, is that it is campaigns like this that really make me wonder about advertising and what I'm doing in this field. I forget that a portion of advertising isn't product/retail/etc., and realize that one day it might be my firm that decides to take on a client such as this. I would have a real problem with this — I mean, what do you do when your firm decides to take on a campaign that is against what you believe in?

The newsgroup thus provided students with a forum for discussing matters that grew out of course topics but were not directly related to the concepts that Debbie introduced in her lectures.[8] As Melissa put it, the newsgroup is "good because it opens up another form of communication throughout the class. Most of the things discussed are things we couldn't have discussed in class."

By contrast, Jordan's own high rate of online participation in English 306 and his use of several examples of messages from a professional communications newsgroup provided his students with specific models of online discussion. As a result, students seemed less uncertain about what they were expected to discuss online and how they were to conduct online discussions. In an interview, Rachel commented that "the e-mail discussion tends to bring out a higher level of the type of language used [than in-class discussion]. Students write in a more professional manner." Interestingly, what Rachel calls the "academic or professional" nature of the online discussions in English 306 may have contributed to the low level of student participation in those discussions after the fifth week. At least one student confessed in an interview to being a bit "intimidated" by these online discussions. Another student complained that the discussions were too limited to the assigned readings and proposed that "maybe if Jordan gave us something to critique or a quote or something relating to us, the e-mail would become a little less boring." This complaint is especially interesting in that it suggests that students may not have felt that the online discussions were the appropriate forum for discussing issues "relating to us," whereas in COM 456 the newsgroup became a forum for discussion of those very issues. For the students in English 306, it seems, the online discussions were limited to a certain kind of discussion of course topics defined by Jordan. In this sense, the nature of the instructor's online presence and her or his way of framing the CMC component of the course seem to have been key factors in influencing how students understood their online participation. Such a finding complicates the claim that CMC can lead to more egalitarian participation in class discussions: Students may opt out of online discussions when they are unsure about their roles in such discussions.

Another factor that seems to have helped shape online participation was the students' conceptions of CMC in general. On the questionnaires, students were asked whether they understood the online discussions in their course to be "talking" or "writing." In COM 456, 9 of the 14 students (64.3%) who completed the final questionnaire indicated that the newsgroup discussions were "talk," whereas 3 characterized them as "writing"; one called them "both" and another "computer writing." Students in this class seemed to conceive of the newsgroup as something akin to informal oral discussions. By contrast, only 4 of 15 students in English 306 (26.7%) characterized the online discussions as "talking," while 7 (46.7%) described them as "writing," and 4 as "other" (e.g., "like a journal," "computer work," or "a good combination of both"). In response to a question about what they liked best about the online discussions, several students in English 306 indicated that the online discussions provided an opportunity to hear what other students had to say about the readings. For these students, the online discussions seemed to be not so much "conversation" but rather a kind of focused set of written academic exchanges about assigned topics. These perceptions of the nature of online discourse seemed to shape the students' participation in the online discussions. The students in COM 456, who generally understood the course-related online discourse as talk and did not have models of online discourse, engaged in a great deal of informal "conversation" characterized by brief comments. The students in English 306 tended to see the online discussions as a form of academic writing and had models, provided by their instructor, to reinforce such a view; not surprisingly, their online discussions were characterized by longer, more focused messages related to course readings and assignments.

The nature of the online discussions in these courses may have been complicated even further by the students' sense of their status as undergraduates enrolled in courses within their majors. In a variety of ways, the factors we have been describing — the nature of in-class discourse, the structure of the courses, how the CMC components of those courses were managed by the instructors, and the instructors' online presence — seemed to have shaped the online roles that students constructed for themselves. Some of our data, especially interview transcripts, suggest that this construction was perhaps more conscious than it might seem. In other words, we think students responded to the constraints we have been describing — constraints such as Debbie's grading policies for the newsgroup discussions or Jordan's focus on using the class listserv to discuss the assigned readings — primarily *as students* and engaged in online discussions accordingly. Obviously, their decisions about how to engage in such online discussions were mediated by their own knowledge about and attitudes toward CMC, but those decisions may have had more to do with their sense of their roles *as students* than with their understanding of the technology or their experiences with online discourse. As a result, students seemed to participate in the online forums *not* as if those forums represented spaces for discourse that might deviate from or challenge "normal" in-class discourse, but rather as if those online spaces represented extensions of normal in-class discourse.

Conclusions

The nature of the online discussions in these two writing courses reflects, we believe, the complexity of course-related online discourse, especially in mixed mode courses. Our findings suggest that the rates and nature of students' online participation in such courses are related to a variety of factors associated with the context of such courses, especially the ways the instructors structured, managed, and evaluated online discussions as course assignments. It seems clear that the nature of online discussions in the courses we studied bore less relationship to the in-class discourse than to these other factors. In this sense, our findings corroborate those of other studies, suggesting that such factors as grading policies, assignment structure, and instructor participation can have a significant impact on students' online participation. At the same time, this study suggests that the nature of students' online participation is a function of other complex and sometimes conflicting factors related to students' sense of the purpose(s) of CMC within a mixed mode course and, perhaps most intriguing, to their positions as undergraduate students in traditionally organized university courses.

In this study, course-related online discourse differed from the in-class discourse we observed, but it was not necessarily more open, in-depth, engaged, egalitarian, or student-centered than in-class discourse or than the kind of online discussions described in some studies cited above. In COM 456, students' online discussions deviated from the topics and patterns of in-class discourse but, we would argue, did not seem to fall outside the bounds of "acceptable" course-related discourse. Conversely, the somewhat more lengthy and in-depth messages posted to the English 306 mailing list were part of an online discussion which was characterized by low rates of participation and a relative lack of student engagement; in this sense, the online discourse in English 306 mirrored more traditional patterns of teacher-directed in-class discourse. Our findings thus seem to support a growing body of research and commentary suggesting that simply putting students online does not necessarily increase their rates of participation in course-related discussions, significantly change the nature of that participation, or provide a more egalitarian and less leader-centered space for student voices. Clearly, the online environments provided by the use of CMC technologies such as the COM 456 newsgroup or the English 306 listserv list are complex discursive spaces that can be as difficult and complicated for students to negotiate as the more traditional classroom — perhaps more so.

Ultimately, online discourse in this study seems to have been a function of the ways in which individual participants negotiated the various constraints on their participation and understood their respective roles within that discourse. The nature of the students' online discourse might best be understood as growing in part out of their constructed roles as students in the course. Although our data suggest that the online discourse was shaped by a variety of factors, the use of CMC did not by itself seem to alter the students' sense of their roles as undergraduate students, as some research, especially on synchronous forms of CMC, might suggest (e.g., Faigley, 1990 and 1992).

These conclusions are necessarily tentative, since the design of our study did not enable us to explore more fully how students might have participated in online discussions in other settings, nor did it allow for anything other than relatively general comparisons between online and in-class discourse. Our findings, especially in terms of the comparison between English 306 and COM 456, suggest that online discourse might exhibit very different characteristics in different classroom contexts. But our research design does not enable us to draw anything more than tentative conclusions about which specific contextual factors will shape that discourse. Moreover, because we designed the study in a way that would enable us to make general comparisons between online discussions and the nature of typical in-class discourse, direct comparisons of online comments and in-class comments was not possible. In addition, this study was limited by the small number of participants and its relatively narrow scope. We have no way of knowing how factors relating to students' educational and sociocultural backgrounds might have figured into their online participation. For instance, we might find that the online discourse of a more racially heterogeneous group of students, such as Faigley (1992) and Romano (1993) observed, would differ markedly from that of the comparatively homogeneous students in our study. Nor can we do more than speculate about whether practical factors such as scheduling and access to technology might have influenced students' participation. It is possible that such factors may have had greater influence on students' online discourse than the factors we have identified.

Nevertheless, our findings do suggest that the instructional uses of CMC in undergraduate writing courses can be complicated by a variety of factors that instructors may have to consider. Moreover, while our findings do lend some credence to those who call for caution in extolling the virtues of CMC, they also suggest that online environments differ in intriguing ways from more traditional classroom environments and provide spaces of opportunity and risk for teachers and students who use them. Our study underscores a need for more inquiry into how those spaces enable and limit discourse and, more importantly, how they relate to the more conventional discursive spaces that teachers and students occupy.

Acknowledgment

The authors wish to thank the Center for Undergraduate Instructional Excellence in the School of Liberal Arts at Purdue University for a fellowship and grant that provided the time and financial support necessary to complete the research described in this article.

References

Ahern, Terence C., Peck, Kyle, & Laycock, Mary. (1992). The effects of teacher discourse on computer-mediated discussion. *Journal of Educational Computing Research, 8,* 291–309.

Bump, Jerome. (1990). Radical changes in class discussion using networked computers. *Computers and the Humanities, 24,* 49–65.

Butler, Wayne M., & Kinneavy, James L. (1991). The electronic discourse community: God, meet Donald Duck. *Focuses, 4,* 91–108.

Cheng, Hui-Chuan, Lehman, James, & Armstrong, Penny. (1991). Comparison of performance and attitude in traditional and computer conferencing classes. *American Journal of Distance Education, 5,* 51–64.

Cohen, Moshe, & Riel, Margaret. (1989). The effect of distant audiences on students' writing. *American Educational Research Journal, 26,* 143–59.

Cooper, Marilyn, & Selfe, Cynthia L. (1990). Computer conferences and learning: Authority, resistance, and internally persuasive discourse. *College English, 52,* 847–69.

Corbett, Edward P. J. (1992). Foreward. In Hawisher, Gail E., & LeBlanc, Paul (Eds.), *Re-imagining computers and composition: Teaching and research in the virtual age* (pp. vii–viii). Portsmouth, NH: Heinemann.

Eldred, Janet M. (1991). Pedagogy in the computer-networked classroom. *Computers and Composition, 8,* 46–61.

Eldred, Janet M., & Hawisher, Gail. (1995). Researching electronic networks. *Written Communication, 12,* 330–59.

Faigley, Lester. (1992). *Fragments of rationality.* Pittsburgh, PA: University of Pittsburgh Press.

Faigley, Lester. (1990). Subverting the electronic network: Teaching writing using networked computers. In Donald A. Daiker & Max Morenberg (Eds.), *The writing teacher as researcher: Essays in the theory and practice of class-based research* (pp. 290–311). Portsmouth, NH: Heinemann.

Feenberg, Andrew. (1987). Computer conferencing and the humanities. *Instructional Science, 16,* 169–86.

Gruber, Sibylle. (1995). Re: ways we contribute: Students, instructors, and pedagogies in the computer-mediated writing classroom. *Computers and Composition, 12,* 61–78.

Harasim, Linda. (1989). On-line education: A new domain. In R. Mason and A. Kaye (Eds.), *Mindweave: Communication, computers, and distance education* (pp. 50–62). Oxford: Pergamon Press.

Harasim, Linda. (1987). Teaching and learning on-line: Issues in computer-mediated graduate courses. *Canadian Journal of Educational Communication, 16* (2): 117–35.

Hawisher, Gail E. (1992). Electronic meetings of the minds: Research, electronic conferences, and composition studies. In Gail E. Hawisher & Paul LeBlanc (Eds.), *Re-imagining computers and composition: Teaching and research in the virtual age* (pp. 81–101). Portsmouth, NH: Heinemann.

Hawisher, Gail E., & LeBlanc, Paul. (1992). *Re-imagining computers and composition: Teaching and research in the virtual age.* Portsmouth, NH: Heinemann.

Hawisher, Gail E., & Selfe, Cynthia L. (1991). The rhetoric of technology and the electronic writing class. *College Composition and Communication, 42,* 55–65.

Herring, Susan, Johnson, Deborah, & Dibenedetto, Tamra. (1992). Participation in electronic discourse in a feminist field. *Proceedings from the Berkeley Women and Language Conference.*

Hiltz, Starr Roxanne. (1986). The virtual classroom: Using computer-mediated communication for university teaching. *Journal of Communication, 36,* 94–104.

Hiltz, Starr Roxanne. (1990). Evaluating the virtual classroom: In L. M. Harasim (Ed.), *Online education: Perspectives on a new environment* (pp. 133–83). New York: Praeger.

Hiltz, Starr Roxanne, & Turoff, Murray. (1978). *The network nation: Human communication via computer.* Reading, MA: Addison-Wesley.

Kiesler, Sarah, Siegel, Jane, & McGuire, Timothy W. (1984). Social psychological aspects of computer-mediated communication. *American Psychologist, 39,* 1123–1134.

Kremers, Marshall. (1990). Sharing authority on a synchronous network: The case for riding the beast. *Computers and Composition, 7,* 33–44.

Levin, James A., Kim, Haesun, & Riel, Margaret. (1990). Analyzing instructional interactions on electronic message networks. In L. M. Harasim (Ed.), *Online education: Perspectives on a new environment* (pp. 185–213). New York: Praeger.

McCreary, Elaine K., & Van Duren, J. (1987). Educational applications of computer conferencing. *Canadian Journal of Educational Communication, 16,* 107–15.

McGuire, Timothy W., Kiesler, Sarah, & Siegel, Jane. (1987). Group and computer-mediated discussion of effects in risk decision making. *Journal of Personality and Social Psychology, 52,* 917–30.

Mehan, Hugh. (1979). *Learning lesson: Social organization in the classroom.* Cambridge, MA: Harvard University Press.

Mehan, Hugh. (1978). Structuring school structure. *Harvard Educational Review, 48,* 32–64.

Quinn, Clark N., Mehan, Hugh, Levin, James A., & Black, Steven D. (1983). Real education in non-real time: The use of electronic message systems for instruction. *Instructional Science, 11,* 313–27.

Phillips, Gerald M., & Santoro, Gerald M. (1989). Teaching group discussion via computer-mediated communication. *Communication Education, 38,* 151–61.

Romano, Susan. (1993). The egalitarian narrative: Whose story? Which yardstick? *Computers and Composition, 10,* 5–28.

Selfe, Cynthia L., & Hilligoss, Susan. (1994). *Literacy and computers: The complications of teaching and learning with technology.* New York: MLA.

Takayoshi, Pamela. (1994). Building new networks from the old: Women's experiences with electronic communication. *Computers and Composition, 11,* 21–35.

Thompson, D. (1988). Conversational networking: Why the teacher gets most of the lines. *Collegiate Microcomputer, 6,* 193–201.

Wells, Rosalie. (1993). *Computer-mediated communication for distance education: An international review of design, teaching, and institutional issues.*
State College, PA: American Center for Distance Education.

Appendix A

Coding Scheme for Type of Face-to-Face Classroom Discourse

Code	Description	Definition
TL	Teacher Lecturing	Teacher is talking, explaining, providing information with no overt attempt to involve students.
TQ1	Teacher Question, 1	Teacher asks a direct question to the students as a group, expecting some sort of answer from volunteer(s).
TQ2	Teacher Question, 2	Teacher asks a direct question to a particular student, perhaps in a follow-up to a student comment.
TR1	Teacher Response, 1	Teacher responds to a student's answer to his/her direct question. This response may be an evaluation or an elaboration.
TR2	Teacher Response, 2	Teacher responds to a student's direct question to him/her.
TC	Teacher Command	Teacher gives students directions for an in-class assignment or exercise.
MSQ	Male Student Question	A male student asks a direct question of the teacher.
FSQ	Female Student Question	A female student asks a direct question of the teacher.
MSR	Male Student Response	A male student responds to a question posed by the teacher.
FSR	Female Student Response	A female student responds to a question posed by the teacher.
MSC	Male Student Comment	A male student makes a comment, not in response to the teacher's direct question, but unsolicited, perhaps as part of a classroom discussion.
FSC	Female Student Comment	A female student makes a comment, not in response to the teacher's direct question, but unsolicited, perhaps as part of a classroom discussion.
SMG	Small-Group Discussion	Students engaged in face-to-face discussion in small groups as part of a class assignment or exercise.
ST	Student Presentation	A one-on-one discussion between the teacher and one student or a small group of students that does not involve the entire class; such a discussion may be the result of a specific question about an assignment or coursework posed to the teacher by the student.

SP	Student-Teacher Discussion	A formal presentation to the class by a single student or group of students.
NVR	Student Non-Verbal Response	Student responds to teacher question with a non-verbal gesture, such as a raised hand.

Appendix B: Coding Schemes for Content of Online Messages

Content categories for posts to the COM 456 course newsgroup:

1. **Issues in Advertising, Advertising Theory.** Includes any posts focused primarily on issues or topics in the professional field of advertising. For example, art vs. advertising; creativity; Maslow; consumer research. Includes comments about specific ads (for example, Diet Coke ads on television). May also include posts related to course assignments but focused primarily on broader issues in the field of advertising.

2. **Course-Related Posts.** Posts focused primarily on the COM 456 class in a general way, including comments on in-class activities, course texts, exams, the usefulness of the course, complaints about the course, etc.

3. **Class Assignments.** Posts focused primarily on course assignments, including comments and questions about assignments.

4. **Career Issues.** Posts focused primarily on students' searches for employment in advertising and related matters. Includes concerns, questions, and comments about job-search activities.

5. **Personal.** Posts focused primarily on issues related to student life that have no obvious connection to the other four categories. Includes comments about attending parties and recreational events, spring break activities, and so on.

6. **Technology.** Comments on computer technology (and related technologies), especially comments about software used for the course and problems with computer technologies.

Content categories for e-mail messages in English 306:

1. **Course-Related.** Announcements related to course projects or assignments or comments on projects and assignments.

2. **Assignment-Related.** Messages sent as part of a specific assignment.

3. **Individual Communications.** Messages sent from Jordan to a student or from a student to Jordan regarding such matters as attendance, assignments, etc. These messages were not distributed via the class listserv but were "private" messages.

4. **Online Discussion.**

    4a. **Responses to Jordan.** Messages posted in response to Jordan's questions about assigned readings.

    4b. **Response to Other Students.** Messages posted about readings in response to comments or questions posted by other students.

5. **Other Comments.** Comments on topics not directly related to the assigned readings.

Notes

1. In addition to these studies of CMC in educational environments, a number of studies of CMC in non-academic settings indicate that CMC can sometimes be less effective for some kinds of discussion-oriented tasks. For example, several studies conducted by researchers at Carnegie Mellon University suggest that CMC may be inferior to face-to-face discourse for sustained discussion (Kiesler, Siegel, & McQuire, 1984; McGuire, Kiesler, & Siegel, 1987). McGuire et al. (1987; p. 925) concluded that in the groups they studied in a business setting, "face-to-face discussion produced more frequent, more full, and more novel arguments than computer-mediated communication did."

2. Pseudonyms are used throughout this article to refer to the instructors and the students who participated in the study.

3. Both researchers attended 24 (55.8%) of 43 scheduled meetings for COM 456 and 11 (39%) of 28 scheduled meetings for English 306. The rate was lower for English 306 because of a prior scheduling conflict for one of the researchers. Two of the COM 456 class meetings were canceled because of legal holidays. Of the six COM 456 meetings that neither of us attended, two were examination days during which the entire class meeting was devoted to test-taking. For English 306, two class meetings were canceled by the instructor.

4. For these analyses, percentages for each category were tabulated so that results were calculated for all of Bob's coding sheets and for all of Jeff's coding sheets. The results were so close that we felt confident in using either set of coding sheets in analyzing the in-class discourse. For the final figures, however, we used all coding sheets made on days when both of us attended class, supplemented by sheets that were coded by one of us on days that the other did not attend. In this way, the figures in Table 1 represent a composite of the in-class discourse as determined from both sets of coding sheets.

5. Lines per message was used as a measure in part because the mainframe Unix system in use at Purdue automatically calculated the number of lines in each message posted to a class newsgroup. As such, these numbers provided a readily available measure of the length of messages posted to the newsgroup. We amended these numbers by excluding blank lines, line representing students' "signatures," and lines reproduced from previous messages to which students were responding. Given the margins set by the system, lines averaged 11 words, so that a 7-line message contained approximately 75–80 words.

6. The discrepancy between the figure of 323 total messages presented here and reflected in Table 4 and the figure of 294 total messages is a result of the coding scheme we used to analyze message content. Most messages were coded as falling into a single category. We coded each message based on our assessments of which category best described the overall thrust of the message. As a result, a message that devoted 8 lines to a discussion of advertising and a single line to a personal comment was coded as category 1. However, several messages defied such easy classification. These were messages in which significant numbers of lines were devoted to more than one issue and could thus be seen as falling into more than one category. Of the 545 total messages posted by both sections of COM 456 to the course newsgroup, we identified 33 such messages and coded them accordingly: that is, if a message had significant content that might be classified as category 1 and significant content that might be classified as category 5, we coded the message as 1/5. (Two messages were coded as falling into three categories.) As a result, a single message coded as category 1 and category 5 would be counted twice, once as category 1 and once as category 5. Thus, for this analysis the "total" number of messages increased, as suggested in Table 4.

7. It's important to note here that small-group discourse (SMG) during class meetings was indeed "interactive" in the sense that students were engaged with each other in discussions that were not moderated or controlled by the instructor. However, as the figures provided above indicate, most COM 456 class meetings were characterized by the students "talking" to each other — much as they might during in-class small-group discussions (SMG). In this sense, we feel confident in describing online discourse as "more interactive" than in-class discourse.

8. Interestingly, in interviews students sometimes expressed the belief that such matters were not really within the purview of the course. Mary suggested that concerns such as those she raised about the town's ad campaign were not really relevant to the main purpose of COM 456: "I don't necessarily think she [Debbie] should address the subject in class, as she is teaching methods of copywriting. She might address the subject by having us write copy for an ad such as this one." Mary, like many of her classmates, believed that the purpose of COM 456 was to teach students the practical methods of advertising copywriting.

Yagelski and Grabill's Insights as a Resource for Your Teaching

1. Yagelski and Grabill suggest that students may opt out of online discussions if the egalitarian potentials of such a format ultimately make them feel confused about their roles as students. How might you manage computer-mediated communication in ways that will prevent that confusion?

2. Online discussions can develop as direct extensions of relatively formal, academic exchange, but at the same time, students are

free in these online discussions to introduce topics that time constraints prevent from arising during class. How might you balance both these tendencies to maximize the benefits of online discussion?

Yagelski and Grabill's Insights as a Resource for Your Writing Classroom

1. Divide your students into small groups. Within each group, the members will develop a written exchange of views on a course reading (or some other issue) by e-mailing each other daily for a week or so. You then have the option of having them present their exchanges as one of the course's formal writing assignments.

2. In conjunction with a reading assignment, give your students a prompt for a short, written response to that reading, and require them to post their answers to an electronic discussion board. Then, when the class meets to discuss that reading, let the posts from the electronic discussion board focus the conversation.

Teaching Visual Literacy

From Analysis to Design: Visual Communication in the Teaching of Writing

Diana George

In the following 2002 article from College Composition and Communication, *Diana George traces the history of visual literacy in the composition classroom, ultimately calling for "a new configuration of verbal/visual relationships, one that does allow for more than image analysis, image-as-prompt, or image as dumbed-down language." George argues that our current discussions of bringing visual rhetoric into the classroom often underestimate the abilities of our students who have grown up in a world rich with images and technology. By directly addressing how our students can both analyze and produce visuals, we can create new kinds of assignments and new goals for our writing courses. George, for example, describes an assignment that has been successful in her course — the "visual argument." By deeply engaging students in visual rhetoric, such assignments can move our students past deeply entrenched assumptions that words are the makings of "high culture" while mere pictures are the makings of "low culture."*

In some respects . . . words cannot compare in effectiveness with pictures. The mere outlines in a Greek vase painting will give you a more immediate appreciation of the grace and beauty of the human form than pages of descriptive writing. A silhouette in black paper will enable you to recognize a stranger more quickly than the most elaborate description in words. (166)

— John Hays Gardiner, George Lyman Kittredge, and Sarah Louise Arnold, 1902

How's this for a visual argument: In response to reading Adam Hochschild's *King Leopold's Ghost,*[1] Boikhutso Jibula, a first-year student from Botswana, reproduces three maps of Africa, each on a transparency. In the first, the continent is empty except for what look like random circles primarily in the sub-Saharan region. The circles outline areas traditionally occupied or claimed by various tribes or communities before colonization. Boikhutso then superimposes a second map — this one of colonized Africa. He points out the English, French, and German names of places that now have well-defined borders, most of which cut through the original circles, splitting traditional regions into new nations, neither named for nor controlled by the people whose places he had identified in the original map. Over that second map, Boikhutso superimposes a third — this one is postcolonial Africa. The names, he points out, are changed. German East Africa is now mainly Tanzania. The Congo Free State is, on this map at any rate, Zaire. Colonization has ended, he tells us, but the boundaries are much the same, the people dispersed or gone, the languages and kingdoms and villages still split or destroyed. It takes very few words for Boikhutso to tell the class what these maps show them: Precolonial Africa cannot be recovered. There is no possibility of going back to what was there before the colonizer. African people must work as nations within the nations now outlined on this third map.

Or picture this: In the same course, Grace VanCamp from lower Michigan creates a dinner place setting, Judy Chicago style. On a place mat, she arranges a plastic plate, knife, fork, spoon, and Coca-Cola glass. On the face of the plate, Grace has glued a map of the African continent. The place card reads, "King Leopold."

And finally: Deirdre Johns shows the class a remaking of Leopold of Belgium's Congo Free State flag. Like the original, her redesign features a bold yellow star in the center of a deep blue field. She tells the class that in her research she learned of the reasoning for the design: the star was to signify the light of Europe being brought in to the Dark Continent. In Deirdre's flag, the blue field is now covered with images of precolonial African art. The gold star is covered in images of slavery, faces of explorers, photos from the rubber and ivory trade. "This is what Europe really brought to Congo," she tells the class.

There are others I could describe — graphs and oil paintings and Web pages and digital designs and book covers and more — but they would tell much the same story. The work of these students and others like them has convinced me that current discussions of visual communication and writing instruction have only tapped the surface of possibilities for the role of visual communication in the composition class.[2] Or, even more to the point — our students have a much richer imagination for what we might accomplish with the visual than our journals have yet to address.

From W. J. T. Mitchell's claim that the second half of the twentieth century was marked by "the pictorial turn" (11–34) to the New London Group's call for a pedagogy of "multiliteracies," we are experiencing yet another push to incorporate visual language into the composition course.[3] It is, of course, true that an insistence on the importance of visual literacy is an old and perennial one. In fact, it has become common today to talk of multiple literacies, to encourage the uses of visual communication in the teaching of writing, and to argue that writing is itself a form of visual communication.

Even so, there remains much confusion over what is meant by *visual communication, visual rhetoric,* or, more simply, *the visual* and where or whether it belongs in a composition course. What's more, to the extent that this confusion remains unaddressed, visual and written communication continue to be held in a kind of tension — the visual figuring into the teaching of writing as a problematic, something added, an anomaly, a "new" way of composing, or, somewhat cynically, as a strategy for adding relevance or interest to a required course. Only rarely does that call address students as producers as well as consumers or critics of the visual. More rarely does the call acknowledge the visual as much more than attendant to the verbal.

My aim in what follows is not to define visual communication or visual rhetoric in a way that would eliminate that tension. I actually believe that some tug of war between words and images or between writing and design can be productive as it brings into relief the multiple dimensions of all forms of communication. For my purposes here, at any rate, there is little reason to argue that the visual and the verbal are the same, are read or composed in the same way, or have the same status in the tradition of communication instruction.

In place of a resolution, then, I am after a clearer understanding of what can happen when the visual is very consciously brought into the composition classroom as a form of communication worth both examining *and* producing. What, for example, might it mean to ask, as I did of the students whose work opens this paper, for a visual argument? Are we posing a new relationship between composition and communication or resurrecting an older one? How does the visual both promise and threaten to change the composition course?

At this point, I should make an important distinction. I will be examining primarily the places of visual literacy in the *composition* classroom. It is quite true that a concern for visual literacy/visual communication has been an ongoing one in the teaching of scientific, technical, and professional communication. In fact, for a number of compositionists over the years, the technical writing course was exactly where the visual belonged. (Witness, for example, Rudolph Flesch's rather Gradgrindian declaration that one mainstay of technical writing instruction, understanding the use of graphs and charts, "is not one of the three R's.") My focus is on arguments that have been made for including the visual in composition courses because these arguments are linked closely to discussions of basic literacy and even to English departments' investments in literacy studies rather than to professional communication's emphasis on the functions or uses of visual information. That is not at all to dismiss the extensive work that characterizes professional communication's engagement with the visual. Instead, it is my attempt to bring composition studies into a more thoroughgoing discussion of the place of visual literacy in the writing classroom.

In the end, I argue that the terms of debate typical in our discussions of visual literacy and the teaching of writing have limited the kinds of assignments we might imagine for composition. I do not make a claim that our students have a special talent for the visual or that their knowledge of the visual is necessarily more sophisticated than their teachers' are. Instead, I would argue that if we are ever to move beyond a basic and somewhat vague call for attention to "visual literacy" in the writing class, it is crucial to understand how very complicated and sophisticated is visual communication to students who have grown up in what by all accounts is an aggressively visual culture. Such a move must first address how relationships between visual communication and writing instruction have been typically configured.

In order to get to that argument, however, I find it necessary first to set what I'd call one curricular context through which visual literacy has entered the teaching of writing, at least as it emerges in scholarly journals and textbook assignments for more than fifty years. The history of how visual literacy has entered the teaching of writing, at least as it emerges in scholarly journals and textbook assignments for more than fifty years, is not a smooth or consistent one in which writing instruction and visual literacy move seamlessly from image analysis to design. Instead, it is one that can best be related through major themes that have dominated the English classroom since at least the 1940s. I begin, in fact, at what might seem a far remove from the college writing classroom: examining arguments in elementary and secondary education for including visual instruction alongside lessons more familiar to English language arts. It is here that we see most clearly how visual studies has been perceived as a threat to language and literature instruction.

Visual Literacy in the English Classroom

In 1946, the instructor's edition of the popular Dick and Jane elementary reader series alerted teachers to the reality that teaching reading demanded attention to more than print literacy. It meant teaching students to read pictures as well as words:

> Skill in interpreting pictures is becoming increasingly important as a means of securing pleasure and information. Adults today are exposed to "picture" magazines, cartoons, advertisements, movies, and many types of diagrammatic schemes for the presentation of facts. Children are surrounded with picture books and "read" the funnies long before they enter school. Regardless of age or situation, the individual who can "read" pictorial material effectively has access to a vast world of new ideas. (Kismaric and Hieferman 88)

Fifty years later, the New London Group issued their report through which they identified the ability both to read and *use* visual information/visual signs as primary among multiliteracies:

> [W]e argue that literacy pedagogy now must account for the burgeoning variety of text forms associated with information and multimedia technologies. *This includes understanding and competent control of representational forms* that are becoming increasingly significant in the overall communications environment, such as visual images and their relationship to the written word — for instance, visual design in desktop publishing or the interface of visual and linguistic meaning in multimedia. (61, emphasis added)

The two reports sound a common theme about visual communication that might be summed up in this way: Literacy means more than words, and visual literacy means more than play.

Coming as it did at the beginning of a media revolution of sorts, the Dick and Jane statement was repeated in a number of ways for the next thirty years or so. During much of the second half of the twentieth century, mass media became a focus for study or a problem to confront in literacy instruction, and so I turn briefly to school talk about television, the visual medium that, throughout the 1950s and 1960s, threatened (or promised) to change the English classroom permanently.

In 1961, NCTE issued its report from the Commission on the Study of Television, *Television and the Teaching of English*. Neil Postman, who twenty-five years later would publish his own critique of the culture of television (*Amusing Ourselves to Death*), was its primary author. For Postman and the members of his commission, the job at hand was to convince English teachers that television was not only a proper subject for the English classroom but a necessary one, even though "We do not mean to suggest by its use that television is the equivalent of *belles lettres* but rather that certain kinds of television programs employ language and action in ways that duplicate the functions of traditional literary forms" (39–40). The commission's incentive for bringing the study of television into the English class will likely sound somewhat dated but still very familiar: "To the extent that their responses to television are *informed, discriminating,* and *creative,* we may be assured that our language and literature, as well as the lives of our students, will be enriched by contact with television. *But taste and critical judgment are learned habits of mind*" (1, emphasis added). Here, the points of concern are explicit: Television is what our children are watching. It surrounds them daily. It is their "primary source of literary experience" (1). The English teacher's job, then, is to foster "taste and critical judgment," two qualities that lift the schooled above the unschooled. This judgment was deemed important because, according to the commission's figures, already in 1961 (only thirteen years after the 1948 postwar boom in television production) 88 percent of American households in the U.S. owned at least one television (30). It was a "literary experience" that threatened to replace those forms more common (and more comfortable) to the English class. "Teachers of English," the report states, "must help the children qualify their enthusiasm with thoughtful criticism" (73).

Though not quite the call for relevance that became common in the 1960s, this report, like the Dick and Jane instructors' manual fifteen years earlier and the New London Group's manifesto thirty-five years later, does acknowledge a changing world in which "a redefinition of 'literacy' is required, one that would extend beyond the printed page" (12). In the end, although the Commission on the Study of Television was not persuaded of the need for a new literacy, its members did accept the challenge to extend the content of the English classroom to include a new literature — television as literary text.

It is here, then, in these early lessons on the uses of visual texts in the reading and writing classroom that literacy instruction and literary studies meet. Visual (be they paintings, films, comic books, or television narratives) were to be studied in the same way as literacy texts, as subjects of close analysis — a use of the visual that continues throughout the history of writing instruction.

In 1962, only one year after the publication of the Postman report, NCTE published William Boutwell's *Using Mass Media in the Schools,* a report from The Committee on the Use of Mass Media. In it, Boutwell writes, "No rain forest in darkest Africa ever confronted men with more unknowns or a strange mixture of enthusiasm, excitement, fears, and hopes than the tangled strands of communication we call 'mass media'" (v). As Boutwell tells us in his preface to the report, mass media (everything from newspapers and magazines to radio, television, motion pictures, and comic books) "often seems to be a force beyond human control" (vi).

An air of resignation over the influence of mass media permeates this collection, even in such writing assignments as Nina T. Fleir's proposal that teachers use students' favorite television shows rather than poetry, drama, or fiction as prompts for writing (150–52). Only rarely do we encounter a suggestion that students might become producers as well as receivers or victims of mass media, especially visual media. As a tool for literacy instruction, then, this collection uses visual media as little more than a prompt for student essays and stories, a substitute for more traditional literary forms, or a subject of scrutiny.

By contrast, the 1996 New London Group report would also direct students' attention toward mass media but not as a subject of scrutiny or an invention prompt alone. Instead, the New London Group adds to the older model of media study the notion of *design* as a way of understanding literacy acquisition. What the New London Group urges, then, is not a closer relationship to media but the use of media to encourage the development of "multi-modal designs" that relate

> . . . all the other modes in quite remarkably dynamic relationships. For instance, mass media images relate the linguistic to the visual and to the gestural in intricately designed ways. Reading the mass media for its linguistic meanings alone is not enough. Magazines employ vastly different visual grammars according to their social and cultural content. A script of a sitcom such as *Roseanne* would have none of the qualities of the program if you didn't have a "feel" for its unique gestural, audio, and visual meanings. A script without this knowledge would only allow a very limited reading. Similarly, a visit to a shopping mall involves a lot of written text. However, either a pleasurable or a critical engagement with the mall will involve a multimodal reading that not only includes the design of language, but a spatial reading of the architecture of the mall and the placement and meaning of the written signs, logos, and lighting. (80–81)

What these scholars urge, then, is not simply the inclusion of mass media as objects of study but the use of media to encourage the development of multimodal designs.

I will return to this issue of design, but for the moment it is important to point out that thinking of composition as *design* shifts attention, if only momentarily, from the product to the act of production. We might say that despite their concern for the influence of television on students' writing and reading abilities, even the 1962 Boutwell collection in some ways prefigured the work of the New London Group. Yet, without a concept like the notion of design, these older media assignments seem to be stuck in a kind of literacy civil war — one that pits poetics against the popular and words against pictures.

Visual Literacy in the Writing Class: The Case of *Writing with a Purpose*

The treatment of the visual in postsecondary writing instruction has been a tentative one in many of the same ways as those early attempts to bring mass media into English classrooms. As a case in point, the story of how visual elements were incorporated into successive editions of a single and very popular twentieth-century college writing text (James McCrimmon's *Writing with a Purpose*) can serve to mirror the history of the visual in writing classes, especially as it indicates a clear impulse to include the visual but not always a consistent or stable way of doing that.[4]

Although some visual elements (primarily charts, graphs, and diagrams) were present even in 1950 in the first edition,[5] it wasn't until 1972 when *Writing with a Purpose* introduced a visual assignment, organized around eighteenth-century British artist William Hogarth's prints *Beer Street* and *Gin Lane,* that the textbook used visuals as an integral part of any writing assignment. According to Dean Johnson of Houghton Mifflin,

> The Hogarth pictures were introduced in the fifth edition (cy 1972) and used through the eighth edition (cy 1984). Originally they were the stuff of an exercise to support observation as a means of gathering material. In each edition, however, they were treated differently. In the seventh edition, for example, they were used to illustrate a so-called "three step method of interpretation" (e.g., observe, interpret, infer).[6]

By the eighth edition, the Hogarth prints were linked to lessons in the chapter on planning strategies.

In his discussion of how the 1970s editions of *Writing with a Purpose* reflected the changes in the student population, Robert Connors points to the visual design of the fifth edition as indicating a "lowered evaluation of its audience's abilities" signaled by "wide margins and a two-color format to open up the text's appearance" (107). Later editions, Connors writes, are even more prone to a visual appearance that suggests a dumbing down. The 1976 edition, for example, "goes in deeply for the 'visual observation' invention methods . . . It is filled with photos, cartoons, illustrations, all meant to add spice to the text" (108). And, while I would argue that the visual is not at all a simpler form of communication than the verbal, it seems clear that Connors is very likely correct in his assessment of the editorial motives for changing the visual format of *Writing with a Purpose* and, in particular, for adding visual like the Hogarth prints.

At the outset, the *Beer Street* and *Gin Lane* prints were meant to teach students the art of observation and develop the skill of creating vivid word images — much in the tradition of *ut pictora poesis,* popularized in literary criticism in the late 1950s and early 1960s, especially by Jean Hagstrum's *The Sister Arts.*[7] According to Johnson, the Hogarth prints remained in McCrimmon's text primarily because teachers liked them. Thus, the prints stayed on for several editions because they were popular with faculty who, no doubt, recognized them as not mere popular culture but popular culture in the literary tradition. Assignments linked to the prints changed with changing composition pedagogy.

This last bit of information is useful to keep in mind in the context of a discussion on the places of visual in the writing classroom. In many respects, the Hogarth prints were absolutely peripheral to whatever writing assignment might be attached to them. Nearly any pair of images might have been used as prompts for the same writing assignments. Within the tradition of verbal/visual communication I am outlining here, only certain kinds of "visual" assignments seem possible for a writing course. Primarily, these would be assignments that use visual images as prompts for essay writing.

Such a tactic was not new with McCrimmon, of course. Lucille Schultz found similar uses of the visual to be common in writing textbooks as far back as the nineteenth century:

> [These texts] rely heavily on illustrations as a teaching tool . . . fairly detailed and complex illustrations were used abundantly in many of the lesser known mid-19th century first books of composition; in addition to common objects, they depicted scenes of home life, school life, and work life, and the illustrations served as writing prompts for young writers who were asked to describe what they saw in the picture. In these books, the illustrations were not simply embellishment or ornament, they were an integral part of the book's instructional practice. (12)

Though these early texts commonly used pictures (often reproductions of paintings) as prompts for student compositions, the aim of each exercise was to bring students to a more vivid or accurate use of written language.[8] Often, the authors made an elaborate case for the advantage or superiority of words over pictures. The Gardiner, Kittredge, and Arnold comment that opens this paper, for example, appears at first to be an argument for the primacy of the visual over the verbal, but the authors go on to say, "what can a picture tell you about wind or heat, about sound or smell, about motion, about the feeling of roughness or moisture? Nothing *directly;* it can only *suggest*" (166, emphasis in original).

Of course, other kinds of assignments involving visuals do occur in college writing pedagogies. Visual analysis (especially advertising analysis) has been commonplace in postsecondary writing instruction for at least fifty years as a part of the post-World War II emphasis on propaganda and semantics characteristic of many composition and communication courses beginning in the 1940s,[9] but that practice did not always or consistently include careful consideration of how images, layout, or graphics actually communicated meaning. Instead, advertising was treated as a subject for critique rather than itself a form of communication that employed both word and image. A 1975 *CCC* article by D. G. Kehl describes an advertising analysis assignment typical for composition in the seventies. Though Kehl does make a brief reference to the images (the pictures) in particular ads, he does so only to suggest that the ad image functions to replicate the "controlling idea" or "central thesis" of a traditional argument essay of the sort students might be assigned to write. Like the McCrimmon assignments, Kehl used advertising as a sort of shadow essay, a form once removed from the actual written essay students would produce. Kehl's stated motive for using advertising at all is one repeated by many of his colleagues throughout this period: He argues that this is a good assignment, especially "For students who are visually but not necessarily verbally sensitive" (135). Running through much of the composition literature of the period, assignments linked to images carried with them a call for relevance, the need to make this dull, required class more interesting, and the suggestion that less verbal students would perhaps succeed with pictures where they could not with words. These were sometimes arguments for using popular culture in the writing class but not always.[10]

For many instructors during this same period, the use of visuals went hand in hand with expressivist pedagogies. In 1972, for example, Harcourt Brace Jovanovich published Joseph Frank's *You*, a trendy writing text loaded with photos, paintings, ads, drawings, and graphic designs. The basic assumption of this text was that each student was an individual who had something to say and could find a voice with which to say it. The focus is clearly on the self as Frank tells students, "*You* is also concerned with perception, for how and what you perceive determines who you are" (iii). Thus, assignments tied to visuals asked students how a particular image made them feel or of what an image reminded them. One assignment even juxtaposes a Rorschach-like inkblot with an abstract painting to get at how an image can be created "deliberately trying to expand both [the painter's] and the viewer's consciousness" (100). And, of course, Walker Gibson's *Seeing and Writing*, written around this same time, makes much the same argument for using visual media in the writing classroom.

Throughout much of the work mentioned so far, there runs an ongoing suspicion that the visual must somehow be important to writing. It just isn't entirely clear how. Are images strategies for getting students to pay attention to detail? Do they mimic the rhetoric of verbal argument? Are they a dumbing down of writing instruction making visible to nonverbal students what the verbally gifted can conceptualize? Certainly, there is the message in much of this work that images may be useful, even proper stimuli for writing, but they are no substitute for the complexity of language.

The Turn to Cultural Theory

When David Bartholomae and Anthony Petrosky reprinted a portion of John Berger's *Ways of Seeing* in their 1987 composition reader (and named their text *Ways of Reading* in a nod to Berger's work), they connected the visual arts very directly with the world of language. Berger's *Ways of Seeing* initially shook the world of art history with its insistence upon the social production of art. As a text about meaning and culture, *Ways of Seeing* has been even more important to a broader audience.[11] Berger begins his argument simply:

> Seeing comes before words. The child looks and recognizes before it can speak. But there is also another sense in which seeing comes before words. It is seeing which establishes our place in the surrounding world; we explain that world with words, but words can never undo the fact that we are surrounded by it. The relation between what we see and what we know is never settled. . . . The way we see things is affected by what we know or what we believe. In the Middle Ages when men

> believed in the physical existence of Hell the sight of fire must have
> meant something different from what it means today. (7–8)

That idea, that images are not a reflection of a fixed reality, that, instead, our ways of understanding the world around us are somehow commingled with how we represent the world visually was a notion that appealed to teachers of writing like Bartholomae and Petrosky who were searching for ways of incorporating cultural theory into the composition classroom.

What was radical about Berger's work was his insistence on breaking down the barriers that separated high culture (in this case art history) from low (advertising). Bartholomae and Petrosky's *Ways of Reading* made that message available to the writing class. In this textbook, not only was meaning no longer restricted to the verbal, the visual was also not used as a gentle step into the "more serious" world of the verbal. As an extract published in a composition reader, *Ways of Seeing* certainly did lead writing teachers to ask students to examine images as culturally informed texts. Yet, the complete written text of Berger's argument was *visually* much farther reaching than any discussion of image analysis might suggest or, at least, than the design of composition readers at the time would allow for.[12]

In a "Note to the Reader" that opens *Ways of Seeing,* Berger writes, "The form of the book is as much to do with our purpose as the arguments contained within it" (5). Berger points particularly to "essays" that consist only of images that "are intended to raise as many questions as the verbal essays" (5). And, yet, he could just as well have been talking about the text's heavy font, the cover design that reproduces the opening remarks of the first essay, or the ragged-right margins that call attention to page design. It would be many years before this very conscious attention to design and its relation to meaning would have much impact at all on college composition courses.

Instead, the push in the eighties was to continue to explore what visuals could teach students about their written compositions. In 1986, for example, William Costanzo, then chair of the NCTE Committee on Film Study, reported in *CCC* on a 1979 NEH project to teach film *as* composition. He lists four arguments for the use of film in teaching writing:

> (1) The basic steps of filmmaking can serve as a working model of the
> composing process ... (2) ... An understanding of the visual code which
> enables us to "read" a movie can help to clarify the conventions of
> English diction, syntax, punctuation, and usage. (3) Many of the rhetorical principles of film composition (for organizing inchoate experience
> into meaningful sequence, for achieving a suitable style, for selling a
> product or an idea) can be applied directly to specific writing tasks. (4)
> When students' notions of composition are widened to include these
> more familiar, visual forms, the writing class seems less remote. (79–80)

This urge to tie the use of images in any way possible to "the composing process" was a common one throughout this period.

Costanzo's report would seem rather ordinary, certainly right in line with attitudes we have already witnessed, if it weren't for an afterword he included as the article was being readied for press. In it, Costanzo acknowledges that his report was written five years earlier and that his understanding of the role of film in writing classes has changed considerably since that time. By 1986, Costanzo is no longer making a simple link between the study of film and the teaching of composing strategies. Instead, he writes: "If I once regarded film study as a path to better writing, I now see film and writing as equal partners traveling along the same road" (86). His concluding remarks signal a significant shift in the way he, at least, had begun to think of the role of visual media in the writing class:

> Much of what once seemed revelatory about the role of visual media in our students' lives is now widely accepted, even taken for granted. Film and television continue to dominate a major portion of their formative years, creating expectations, shaping attitudes, influencing language patterns, and providing a common frame of reference. . . . At the same time, groundbreaking work in semiotics, neurophysiology, and cognitive psychology has made strong connections between visual forms of thought and written language. It now appears that the act of writing involves more visual thinking than we recognized in traditional composition classes. (86)

Here, Costanzo was no longer talking about the visual as a convenient heuristic but, instead, asking that compositionists pay attention to "visual thinking" as one way of understanding the written word. Significantly, Costanzo's report appears in the same issue of *CCC* as Stephen Bernhardt's "Seeing the Text," an article arguing for the importance of teaching not images in the writing classroom but writing-as-image or, at least, of noting that the design of a text as well as the words used in the text conveyed meaning. Bernhardt's work indicated a change in the ways many compositionists began to think of "the visual" as it relates to the teaching of writing. For many, that change was most evident in attention to design.

The Influence of Design

Throughout the history of writing instruction in this country, there has been some attention to the visual nature of written compositions, if only, in the earliest textbooks, to emphasize the importance of handwriting or penmanship as a visual representation of the writer's character.[13] And, of course, even today, the one visual reproduction we can count on in even the most contemporary texts is that snapshot of the research paper, complete with title page and works cited. In these lessons on producing the research paper, such visual marks as margins, page layout, and font size take on the utmost importance, again, in visually representing the seriousness and thoroughness with which the student has approached the assignment. In effect, they become a sign of academic decorum.

For many years, in fact, the research paper section was literally the only place in a composition textbook where we might encounter any reference to page design, layout, or font choices; primarily, we found a reminder to double space, choose a readable font appropriate for serious work (12-point Times, perhaps), and use "normal" margins. That has begun to change, especially since the first edition of John Trimbur's *Call to Write,* which includes a brief chapter on document design as well as attention to visual communication throughout in genres as various as flyers, posters, Web pages, and public service ads.[14]

In his most recent scholarship, Trimbur examines the "materiality of literacy from the perspective that writing is a visible language produced and circulated in material forms" ("Delivering" 188). This attention to the production of text as visible language, emphasizing "the composer's work . . . to make the special signs we call writing" (189) is one that links literacy practice with production and distribution of text and to the history and theory of graphic design (see also Trimbur, "Composition"). Perhaps even more useful for the future of visual communication and writing studies is Trimbur's use of the work of Walter Benjamin who "offers a way to think about how the study and teaching of writing might take up the visual . . . as more than just new texts and topics . . . to write about" ("Delivering" 199–200). As this work suggests, recent emphasis on design history, research, and theory marks a turn in the way scholars and teachers might begin thinking of composition and its relation to graphic design.

Such a turn is, however, very recent. Even as late as 1987, discussion of page design was minimal and often tied to word processing technology or desktop publishing. In March 1987, for example, *College English* ran a Macintosh ad entitled "A lesson in English Composition." The ad copy suggests that a Mac can make proofreading, copyediting, and formatting easier. The sample page offered in the ad — "created on a Macintosh" — tells a very different story. This very professional looking page clearly argues that it is the visual dimension of this composition that is most intriguing — layout, graphics, fonts, pull-out quotes. "With a Macintosh your students can prepare compositions that look like classics," the ad reads. "The rest is for posterity to judge."

Perhaps more than any other technology, desktop publishing has moved writing instruction into the world of design, despite, I suspect, our best efforts to contain composition in the essay of the sort familiar in *Harper's* or *Esquire* or *The Atlantic.*[15] To talk of literacy instruction in terms of *design* means to ask writers to draw on available knowledge and, at the same time, transform that knowledge/those forms as we redesign. Design, the New London Group writes, "will never simply reproduce Available Designs. Designing transforms knowledge in producing new constructions and representations of reality" (76; see also Buchanan on the rhetoric of design).[16]

If I have given the impression that the media revolution of the fifties and sixties was a tough one for composition teachers, then I must say here that the world of graphic design, electronic text, and Web technologies certainly will prove even more difficult, though ultimately perhaps more useful for future understandings of composition as design. As with written compositions, Web pages must have an internal coherence; they must, in other words, be navigable. Unlike written compositions, the internal logic of a Web piece is likely to appear first in the visual construction of the page — not only in the images chosen but the colors, the placement of text or links, the font, the use of white space, and other elements linked more closely to the world of graphic design than to composition pedagogy. The work of Anne Wysocki is useful here as she challenges writing teachers to rethink their notions of what composition means — beyond the word and inclusive of the visual. Wysocki writes, "When we ask people in our classes to write for the Web we enlarge what we mean by composition. None of us are unaware of the visuality of the Web, of how that initial default, neutral grey has a different blankness than typing-paper" ("Monitoring Order"). And whether it is true or not that their teachers are aware of the difference between the blank screen and the blank page, our students are certainly aware of this difference. Many already compose for the Web. Many have worked in the realm of the visual (or the *virtual*) as constitutive of composing texts of all sorts years before they get to their first-year college courses.

The Place of the Visual in Composition Today

At this point (feeling just a bit like Tristram Shandy telling the story of life), I must back up once more before I go forward, this time to emphasize how much has changed in the ways we have thought about our students' work in composition over the past twenty-five years or more. In 1975, Harris K. Leonard, writing about his use of *Superman* comics to teach concepts from the classics, expresses concern over his students' request to make their own comics. This is how he describes the situation:

> Once the students realized how influential comic books were, some of them began to inquire why they could not write their own comics, reflecting their own heritage and their own reality. This was a difficult question, but as a teacher of the classics I had only one way to answer it. When they finished the course they would be able to write their own comics. However, the reason they were in college was not to learn comic book writing, but to counter the comic book mentality of our age with a more educated vision. The classics provide that vision. The classics are classics because they represent the finest and most humane statement on the universal human condition. . . . (406)

Nearly twenty-five years later, Lester Faigley, in "Material Literacy and Visual Design," describes several Web sites he has encountered that are composed by teens as young as fifteen. "I find these sites remarkable for a number of reasons," Faigley writes, "not the least of which is the considerable design talent of these adolescents" (173). He goes on to compare these teens' thought-provoking and creative uses of image, text, and technology to the dull sameness of official sites created for mainstream companies. At no point in this article does Faigley seem remotely worried that these students are not learning what they should be learning in school. He seems to be asking, instead, why it is that we (their teachers) don't seem to understand how sophisticated these literacy practices actually are.

I don't mean to target Leonard here. His response is one that had a certain currency at the time and is right in line with what I've been describing throughout this discussion. Comics might have seemed like a useful way to get students into the "real" work of the course, but the notion that students should want to create their own comics "reflecting their own heritage and their own reality" would have seemed silly to many good teachers even in the fourth quarter of the last century.

I began by claiming that our students have a much richer imagination for how the visual might enter composition than our journals have yet to address, and so I return here to those students whose work opens this paper. In my assignment (see Appendix), I simply asked for a *visual argument*. The form, medium, and aim of the argument was up to the students. The course was a first-year seminar meant to introduce students to university-level work and to make a passing nod, at any rate, in the direction of oral, written, and visual communication practices. For many faculty across campus, I suspect such a course might represent precisely what Leonard was after in 1975, an introduction to the "great works of western culture."

The visual argument is an assignment I have given for at least five years now, but, like Faigley in his encounter with student work, I was struck in the fall of 2000 by how many more students seemed comfortable in the realm of visual design than had in years before and by how very few of them asked what I meant by visual argument. Moreover, these students turned to all sorts of visual design, as the assignment sheet suggested they might, for their projects. Those less comfortable with "art work" chose to create charts, diagrams, or maps. Those like Jake Betzold or Andy Waisanen, more comfortable with digital design and Web technologies, worked with PhotoShop to make digital "paintings" or set up Web sites devoted to the course. Deirdre's flag was created by using colored construction paper, scissors, glue, and a photocopier. Not one of these students seemed to think that their visual argument was any less complicated or took less research or thought than the typical argument essay that they were also assigned in the course.

When I told other faculty teaching sections of the same course that I would be asking my students to construct a visual argument, many were more than skeptical. They wanted to know if such a genre exists and, if it does, how can it be taught, and for what reason might I use it — except, perhaps, to keep students doing "interesting projects." Primarily, faculty asked how I could evaluate visual arguments since some students, according to these faculty, are just more visual/more visually talented than others. Perhaps the most important of these questions is the first: What is a visual argument?

In 1996, analytic philosopher J. Anthony Blair, writing on "The Possibility and Actuality of Visual Arguments," just barely manages to agree that a visual argument, possessing all of the "salient properties of arguments," could actually be said to exist, and if it could be said to exist, it would have to be quite strictly "non-verbal visual communication" (26). To summarize Blair briefly, an argument must make a claim (an assertion), motivated by reasons for the claim, communicated to an audience in an attempt to convince that audience (the recipient) to accept the claim on the basis of the reasons offered (24). In this definition, drawn from the work of D. J. O'Keefe, claims must be "linguistically explicable" though not necessarily expressed linguistically. In other words, there is room here for the possibility of a nonverbal assertion.

To be faithful to Blair's position, I would have to say that, though he does acknowledge that visual argument is possible and even that visual arguments have been made, he does not hold out much hope for making one that is either propositionally complex or at all unique. Of course, in order to make his own argument, Blair must assert that the visual is open to interpretation in a way that words are not.[17] Such an assertion can only be made if one believes that the verbal and visual both involve communication of meaning. Certainly, parallels between verbal and visual communication do exist, which is why Blair finds himself agreeing, if grudgingly, that visual argument is *possible*.

My own requirements for visual argument are less rigid than Blair's, though I certainly accept his primary description of argument and ask that visual arguments make a claim or assertion and attempt to sway an audience by offering reasons to accept that claim. The simplest way for me to explain visual argument (and one I use with my own students) is to begin with visual parody, especially of the sort familiar to readers of *Adbusters* or the Guerilla Girls. Visual parody, like verbal parody, does make an overt claim, assertion, or proposition that draws particularly on comparison, juxtaposition, and intertextuality to offer the assertion to an audience for acceptance.[18] But visual arguments do not need to be parodic. All sorts of visuals make assertions and develop those assertions with visual information.

Though I would reject Blair's notion that a visual argument must be entirely nonverbal, I would say that a visual argument must make its case primarily through the visual. Deirdre's argument, for example, makes use of the flag as a visual expression of nationhood. Through research, she learned what the original Congo Free State flag was supposed to be saying about that nation. Her assertion, that what Europeans really brought to Africa was not enlightenment but slavery, is carried through visually. To make an argument that would convince her audience, she used visuals familiar to that audience, in this case, a class of first-year students in a seminar called Africa in the Popular Imagination. She drew from books the class had read and images the class had seen. In other words, her argument was visually powerful and easily read by her target audience. Though some readers might consider her assertion somewhat sentimental or oversimplified, I do not read it that way at all. The students in this course, including students from Rwanda, Botswana, and Ghana, had not heard the history of Leopold's Congo before the course — in particular, the international human rights movement generated by events of the time. The American students began the course recalling stories they had heard or read of African exploration, and most assumed that explorers had opened the Congo, as well as other areas of the continent, up to development of the best sort. Deirdre's decision to turn Leopold's flag back on him, to show it for what it was, represents an attempt on her part to ask her audience to reread the history of Congo exploration and to rethink the state of civilization and art that thrived there before Leopold's Congo Free State.

The same could be said of Boikhutso's map and Grace's place setting. Grace took from the course Leopold's statement that he meant to get for himself "a piece of this magnificent African cake" and extended that to the ludicrous: the king who sees an entire continent as his to feast upon. This, in contrast to the propaganda at the time in which Leopold represented himself as a great philanthropist taking the Congo region under his protection in order to end slavery and ensure international free trade. Her audience knew the background for her argument, and so her piece was shaped for that audience.

Boikhutso's map series aims for a much more difficult position statement. Though his argument might be read as obvious (it is obvious that we can never return to a precolonial Africa), that is not necessarily a position available to everyone involved. Boikhutso began the course by wanting to explain current Zimbabwe land disputes: why some Africans might feel that white settlers should be run off the land no matter the cost. These land disputes, which have become quite bloody, are for some involved an attempt to return Africans to land that was once theirs. As Boikhutso illustrates, theirs is a fruitless attempt if they believe that they can return to precolonial Africa. As he said in his presentation, "African people must learn to deal with what is here; not to try to recover what cannot be recovered." And, though some might see that argument as self-evident or one only useful for a first-year seminar in a small town, it is an argument Boikhutso felt needed to be made to the people involved today in actual violent and ongoing land battles.

The students in these classes were clearly very serious about the arguments they were making. They were also quite serious about how a visual argument should be evaluated. Given an opportunity to design evaluation criteria, students turned to the same criteria we would find common for written arguments: Does the visual make an argument? How well does the visual communicate that argument? Is the argument relevant to the course and to the assignment? Is it interesting? Is it clear or focused?

In other words, these students and others like them took the visual in its broadest sense as a form of communication through which they could make a sophisticated and relevant argument. And, though their evaluation criteria could certainly come under scrutiny within the context of schooling and how schooling elevates certain values/certain ways of thinking over others, I choose to offer them as one way of illustrating how the students saw these assignments fitting into their course work as it is typically evaluated.

Composition in a Visual Age

The history I have outlined clearly links words to high culture and the visual to low, words to production and images to consumption. And yet, as Cynthia Selfe has suggested, teachers of English composition have not, until very recently, had the means to produce communication that went very far beyond the word.[19] Many of us still remember producing dittos and stencils. We worked long and tedious hours armed with razor blades, correcting fluid, and as much patience as we could muster given the state of our fingers and hands covered with ink and cracking from printing chemicals. The idea of *producing* that went beyond that often blotched or botched handout would have been unthinkable. As well, most English teachers have not been trained in visual thinking beyond the level of *ut pictora poesis* or of media criticism. My own abilities in graphic design are very clearly limited by my willingness to learn software, to the clipart and borders available in that software, and to my barely tutored eye for design and page layout.[20]

Teachers who have been interested in using the visual in writing classes have generally limited their discussions to analysis because there were few ways of doing otherwise. Certainly, more recent access to the Internet and to desktop publishing has given teachers ways of incorporating visual thinking into the writing class, but even that will take time and money and equipment and training. And, again, while some teachers have access to state-of-the-art technology, many others have trouble finding an overhead projector that works or arrives in the classroom on time. My guess is that many of these difficulties will not ease up in yet another age of back-to-basics talk and threats of outcomes-based funding. Yet, our students will continue to work with whatever technology — most of it primarily visual — they can get their hands on.

For those scholars and teachers like Wysocki, Faigley, Trimbur, Johnson-Eilola, and others who are raising new questions about verbal and visual communication, the issue seems to be less one of resources than of emphasis or, rather, relationship. The question for me is not whether, "Learning to see well helps students write well," as Donald and Christine McQuade claim in their 2000 textbook *Seeing and Writing* (vii). Instead the question is much closer to one Anne Wysocki and Johndan Johnson-Eilola ask: "What are we likely to carry with us when we ask that our relationship with all technologies should be like that we have with the technology of printed words?" (349).

Whether that question will lead us, as the New London Group and others suggest, toward multiliteracies or toward composition as design or simply toward a more complete way of understanding verbal and visual communication practices is not resolved. What such a question, and others like it, does lead to, however, is a new configuration of verbal/visual relationships, one that does allow for more than image analysis, image-as-prompt, or image as dumbed-down language. For students who have grown up in a technology-saturated and an image-rich culture, questions of communication and composition absolutely will include the visual, not as attendant to the verbal but as complex communication intricately related to the world around them.

Acknowledgments

In my world, all scholarship is collaborative, and so I would like to thank the many friends and colleagues who took time to read and advise me on this article as it went through several incarnations. Among them, I particularly thank John Trimbur, Jeanette Harris, Diane Shoos, Cindy Selfe, Anne Wysocki, Julia Jasken, and Robert Johnson. Marilyn Cooper, Jack Selzer, and Joseph Harris provided careful and invaluable commentary in the final shaping of the article. I am especially grateful to MTU students Boikhutso Jibula, Deirdre Johns, Grace VanCamp, Derrick Siebert, Jake Betzold, and Andy Waisanen for permission to use or refer to their compositions in this article.

Appendix

Africa in the Popular Imagination
Making a Visual Argument

So far this term, we have talked about how popular ideas and ideals are conveyed in film and in explorers' journals and reports. As well, we have talked about how these ideas can be changed, corrected, enriched by such investigations as Hochschild's *King Leopold's Ghost* or E. D. Morel's reports on the conditions in the Congo at the turn of the century. You have also looked at maps to note how a map can convey a particular argument or idea.

For this next assignment, I want you to make a **visual argument** about Africa and its people. We have been focusing on events in the Congo and on early explorations and reports, so it will be easiest if you focus your work on the issues, people, or ideas you have found in your reading and in the films you have watched.

You'll notice, for example, that even the cover of Hochschild's history makes a visual argument by layering a photo of mutilated African villagers on top of the portrait of Leopold to suggest the two are intricately connected.

A visual argument can take any form you wish. Here are a few suggestions:

1. Make a new cover for one of the books you have read — *Tarzan* or *King Leopold's Ghost* or *Through the Dark Continent* or *Heart of Darkness* or *Travels in West Africa.*

2. Draw a map that conveys an idea of the changing nature of Africa after Leopold — changing populations, exports of raw materials vs. imports, changing political boundaries, changing transportation systems, etc.

3. Design a chart or visually powerful table to convey one or more of these changes.

4. Create a Web page (just the opening page for now) that introduces readers to the issues you think are important.

5. Make a flyer.

6. Create a collage of photos and maps you find that help you convey an argument.

7. Make a painting.

8. Draw a diagram.

You will present your argument to the class. Be sure to tell the class what decisions you made to create your argument and how well you think you got your position across.

The visual can cover any of the material from the beginning of the course through our discussions of *Heart of Darkness.*

Notes

1. *King Leopold's Ghost* is a history of Leopold of Belgium's colonization of the Congo.
2. I first began assigning visual arguments several years ago at a suggestion from John Trimbur whose work very much informs my own here.
3. The New London Group formed in September 1994 at a meeting in New London, New Hampshire. The ten women and men who make up the group are Courtney B. Cazden, Bill Cope, Norman Fairclough, James Paul Gee, Mary Kalantzis, Gunther Kress, Carmen Luke, Sarah Michaels, Martin Nakata, and Joseph Lo Bianco. Their original manifesto appeared in the *Harvard Educational Review* in 1996 and is cited here under "New London Group." A version of that original piece also appears as the first chapter of the book-length collection *Multiliteracies: Literacy Learning and the Design of Social Futures* cited here under Cope and Kalantzis. For more information on the group, see Trimbur, "Review of *Multiliteracies*."
4. I choose *Writing with a Purpose* here partially because of its popularity and long life but also because Robert Connors (*Composition-Rhetoric*) chose

it as a text illustrative of composition pedagogy from the 1950s into the 1970s. Moreover, this was in no way a media-based composition book, and so an examination of McCrimmon's inclusion of the visual for this text can serve to suggest how the visual entered many non-media-based composition classrooms for many years.

5. In Robert Connors's discussion of this text he notes that there were "no illustrations at all in the first three editions, but by the mid-1970s *Writing with a Purpose* contained over thirty pictures and photographs" (106). Actually, there were illustrations in that first edition though no photographs. The illustrations occur in the research paper assignment where McCrimmon has reproduced several graphs and charts.

6. Personal e-mail correspondence with author, April 7, 1996.

7. Jean Hagstrum argues that, though the typical rendering of the phrase came to be "Let a poem be like a painting," there is little warrant for that particular interpretation (9–10).

8. See Lucille Schultz's discussion (18–19) of John Frost's 1839 text, *Easy Exercises in Composition* and A. R. Phippen's 1854 *The Illustrated Composition Book*.

9. See Diana George and John Trimbur ("Communication Battle") for a further discussion of this period in writing instruction.

10. In fact, a brief survey of *CCC* during this period reveals a growing desire to explain how and why we might bring images into the writing class though the assignments are all slightly different, each with different aims. For example, a 1974 "Staffroom Interchange" piece reports on the benefits of assigning a cassette-slide show in required composition as a way to reach what the authors called "non-verbal/right-hemisphere-dominated" students who "find it up-to-date and relevant to their world of movies and TV" (Burnett and Thomason 430). In 1977, Jack Kligerman argued for the use of photography in the composition class to teach students to see objectively, to learn to detail what they see in an image before they try to interpret that image. Here, photography is used as a kind of heuristic aiding the art of selection, planning, arranging, and observing because, Kligerman says of students, "as writers, one of their main problems is to learn to 'capture' a scene in language, to make or re-make part of the world" (174). In his article Kligerman expressed special concern that students simply weren't ready to interpret what they saw until they could objectively list the details of the world surrounding them: "For unless we can get our students to record what they see in the most unmetaphorical, uninterpretive way," Kligerman writes, "then as teachers we are merely helping them confirm what they already believe. Moreover, we could be reinforcing habits and making it impossible for them to discover a world 'out there' and, perhaps, a basis for inductive reasoning" (176). The picture as evidence of a fixed and knowable outside reality is the lesson here.

11. *Ways of Seeing* was a BBC television series before it came out in book form.

12. Publishers have, off and on, attempted to play with the more traditional design of writing texts. Joseph Frank's *You*, mentioned above, is one example of that. However, it has not been until very recently, perhaps with the publication of Donald McQuade and Christine McQuade's *Seeing and Writing*, that design allowed the visual to take much more than an illustrative role as a supplement to the written text or as a way of making the written text more appealing to the eye.

13. See, for example, Brainard Kellogg's 1891 discussion of letter writing with its emphasis on penmanship in *A Text-Book on Rhetoric Supplementing the Development of the Science with Exhaustive Practice in Composition.*

14. The shift toward normalizing the visual in writing instruction is also one impulse behind many of the assignments in Diana George and John Trimbur's *Reading Culture,* particularly in Visual Culture, Mining the Archive, and Fieldwork sections.

15. In "Delivering the Message," John Trimbur provides a brief bibliographic sketch indicating how design studies is beginning to make itself felt in writing studies.

16. For a further discussion of design and multiliteracies, see Gunther Kress, "Design and Transformation"; Bill Cope and Mary Kalantzis, "Designs for Social Futures"; and Kress, "Multimodality."

17. See, for example, J. Anthony Blair's assertion that "the conditions of visual expression are indeterminate to a much greater degree than is the case with verbal expression" (27).

18. See Diana George and Diane Shoos for a more thorough discussion of intertextuality and George and Trimbur (*Reading Culture,* 211–15) for assignments based on visual parody.

19. As Cynthia Selfe points out, "I don't think people remain unconvinced that the visual is important, but I don't think they know how to make that turn" from words to the visual. These comments were made during a telephone conversation with the author, December 4, 2000.

20. Add to that the fact that (as we often tell each other about computers in the classroom) technology is unevenly distributed. Ten years ago, it would have been a luxury for many faculty to have consistent access to a video player and inexpensive videos not to mention the capacity for making videotapes of their own. Copyright laws have made some copying, even some video rental for classroom, difficult. Both videotapes and DVDs are now produced without any permission rights for public showing. In the end, just showing an ad or a clip of a film or television program for class discussion can be considered off-limits if some of the most conservative interpretations of copyright laws are observed.

    If a classroom is not wired for Internet use, the expense of visuals can be far beyond the reach of most English teachers. Some of the most useful tapes for teaching media analysis, for example, are extremely expensive if individual teachers must purchase them, running from as low as $19.95 to as high as $295 for tapes from such sources as Media Education Foundation. Even cheap rentals are not a wholly satisfying solution to the problem I outline here.

Works Cited

Bartholomae, David, and Anthony Petrosky. *Ways of Reading.* Boston: Bedford/ St. Martin's, 1987.

Berger, John. *Ways of Seeing.* London: BBC and Penguin, 1977.

Bernhardt, Stephen. "Seeing the Text." *College Composition and Communication* 37 (1986): 66–78.

Blair, J. Anthony. "The Possibility and Actuality of Visual Arguments." *Argumentation and Advocacy* 33 (1996): 23–39.

Boutwell, William D., ed. *Using Mass Media in the Schools.* New York: Appleton-Century-Crofts, 1962.

Buchanan, Richard. "Declaration by Design: Rhetoric, Argument, and Demonstration in Design Practice." *Design Discourse: History, Theory, Criticism.* Ed. Victor Margolin. Chicago: U Chicago P, 1989. 91–109.

Burnett, Esther, and Sandra Thomason. "The Cassette-Slide Show in Required Composition." *College Composition and Communication* 25 (1974): 426–30.

Connors, Robert J. *Composition-Rhetoric: Backgrounds, Theory, and Pedagogy.* Pittsburgh: Pittsburgh UP, 1997.

Cope, Bill, and Mary Kalantzis. *Multiliteracies: Literacy Learning and the Design of Social Futures.* London: Routledge, 2000.

———. "Designs for Social Futures." Cope and Kalantzis 203–34.

Costanzo, William. "Film as Composition." *College Composition and Communication* 37 (1986): 79–86.

Faigley, Lester. "Material Literacy and Visual Design." *Rhetorical Bodies: Toward a Material Rhetoric.* Ed. Jack Selzer and Sharon Crowley. Madison: U of Wisconsin P, 1999. 171–201.

Flesch, Rudolf. *The Art of Readable Writing.* New York: Harper, 1949.

Frank, Joseph. *You.* New York: Harcourt Brace Jovanovich, 1972.

Gardiner, John Hays, George Lyman Kittredge, and Sarah Louise Arnold. *The Mother Tongue: Elements of English Composition, Book III.* Boston: Ginn & Company, 1902.

George, Diana, and Diane Shoos. "Dropping Breadcrumbs in the Intertextual Forest: or, We Should Have Brought a Compass." Ed. Gail Hawisher and Cynthia Selfe, *Passions, Pedagogies, and Twentieth-First Century Technologies.* Logan: Utah State UP, 1999. 115–26.

George, Diana, and John Trimbur. "The Communication Battle, or Whatever Happened to the Fourth C?" *College Composition and Communication* 50 (1999): 682–98.

———. *Reading Culture: Contexts for Critical Reading and Writing.* 4th ed. New York: Longman, 2001.

Gibson, Walker. *Seeing and Writing.* 2nd ed. New York: D. McKay Co., 1974.

Hagstrum, Jean H. *The Sister Arts: The Tradition of Literary Pictorialism and English Poetry from Dryden to Gray.* Chicago: Chicago UP, 1958.

Hochschild, Adam. *King Leopold's Ghost.* Boston: Houghton Mifflin, 1998.

Kehl, D. G. "The Electric Carrot: The Rhetoric of Advertisement." *College Composition and Communication* 26 (1975): 134–40.

Kellogg, Brainerd. *A Text-Book on Rhetoric Supplementing the Development of the Science with Exhaustive Practice in Composition.* New York: Effingham Maynard, 1891.

Kismaric, Carole, and Marvin Heiferman. *Growing Up with Dick and Jane.* San Francisco: Collins, 1996.

Kligerman, Jack. "Photography, Perception, and Composition." *College Composition and Communication* 28 (1977): 174–78.

Kress, Gunther. "Design and Transformation: New Theories of Meaning." Cope and Kalantzis 153–61.

———. "Multimodality." Cope and Kalantzis 182–202.

Leonard, Harris K. "The Classics — Alive and Well with Superman." *College English* 37 (1975): 405–07.

McCrimmon, James. *Writing with a Purpose.* Boston: Houghton Mifflin, 1950.

McCrimmon, James, Joseph F. Trimmer, and Nancy Sommers. *Writing with a Purpose.* 8th ed. Boston: Houghton Mifflin, 1984.

McQuade, Donald, and Christine McQuade. *Seeing & Writing.* Boston: Bedford/St. Martin's, 2000.

Meyers, Lewis. *Seeing Writing*. New York: Harcourt Brace Jovanovich, 1980.

Mitchell, W. J. T. *Picture Theory*. Chicago: U of Chicago P, 1994.

New London Group. "A Pedagogy of Multiliteracies: Designing Social Futures." *Harvard Educational Review* 66 (1996): 60–92.

Postman, Neil. *Amusing Ourselves to Death*. New York: Penguin, 1985.

———. *Television and the Teaching of English*. New York: Appleton-Century-Crofts, Inc., 1961.

Schultz, Lucille M. "Elaborating Our History: A Look at Mid-19th Century First Books of Composition." *College Composition and Communication* 45 (1994): 10–30.

Trimbur, John. *The Call to Write*. New York: Longman, 1999.

———. "Composition and the Circulation of Writing." *College Composition and Communication* 52 (2000): 188–219.

———. "Delivering the Message: Typography and the Materiality of Writing." *Composition as Intellectual Work*. Ed. Gary Olson. Carbondale: Southern Illinois UP, 2002. 188–202.

———. "Review of *Multiliteracies: Literacy Learning and the Design of Social Futures*." *College Composition and Communication* 52 (2001): 659–62.

Willens, Anita. "TV — Lick It or Join It?" Boutwell, 254–56.

Wysocki, Anne Frances. "Monitoring Order: Visual Desire, the Organization of Web Pages, and Teaching the Rules of Design." *Kairos* 3.2 (Fall 1998). 12 Jun. 2002 <http://www.hu.mtu.edu/~awysocki>.

Wysocki, Anne Frances, and Johndan Johnson-Eilola. "Blinded by the Letter: Why Are We Using Literacy as a Metaphor for Everything Else?" *Passions, Pedagogies, and Twenty-First Century Technologies*. Ed. Gail Hawisher and Cynthia Selfe. Logan: Utah State UP, 1999. 349–68.

George's Insights as a Resource for Your Teaching

1. Reflect on your own experience of learning to write. How were you guided in thinking about the visual appearance of your work? What key virtues were you encouraged to cultivate, and how did this sense of appearances influence your experience of the content of your work? Were you, for example, more concerned with creating a "neat" paper than one that was crowded with difficult thinking? How might early schooling in penmanship have influenced your sense of what writing is all about? Given the way that new technologies have made the visual design of our texts easier to manipulate, how have your ideas about the relations between form and content, appearance and substance evolved?

2. Consider how your own course materials — the syllabus or assignment sheets, for example — make a "visual argument." What sorts of arguments do they make? Are there ways to make these visual arguments more effective?

George's Insights as a Resource for Your Writing Classroom

1. In the appendix to the essay, George describes her visual argument assignment. Consider developing a similar assignment regarding issues that your students have been reading about. Are there some aspects of George's assignment you would avoid or other aspects that you would foreground? How would you do so, and why?

2. Ask your students to define the term *visual argument*. What elements should a visual argument consist of? What makes constructing a visual argument different from constructing a verbal argument? Which task do students feel is easier, and why? Do they feel that one is more important than the other? Why or why not?

Understanding Visual Rhetoric in Digital Writing Environments

Mary E. Hocks

In the following article, first published in College Composition and Communication *in 2003, Mary E. Hocks states, "As writing technologies change, they require changes in our understanding of writing and rhetoric and, ultimately, in our writing pedagogy." Because students are increasingly both reading and producing online texts, Hocks argues that "we must help our students pay attention to the rhetorical features of these highly visual digital environments." To show how we can incorporate lessons on visual rhetoric into our writing courses, Hocks analyzes two interactive digital documents, defining and illustrating three key features of visual rhetoric: audience stance, transparency, and hybridity. By focusing on these concepts in our classes, we can teach visual rhetoric as a process, one that both overlaps with and significantly departs from more traditional, purely verbal models of the composing process.*

Scholarship in rhetoric and composition has begun to emphasize the central role of visual rhetoric for writers, especially those working in digital writing environments. Visual rhetoric, or visual strategies used for meaning and persuasion, is hardly new, but its importance has been amplified by the visual and interactive nature of native hypertext and multimedia writing. The early developers of hypertextual writing as well as the scholars who study the effect technologies have on readers and writers in various settings have all influenced our understanding of how multimedia technologies use visual rhetoric. Since the appearance of hypertext and other interactive new media, these digital writing environments make it difficult to separate words from visuals or privilege one over the other.[1] Interactive digital texts can blend words and visuals, talk and text, and authors and audiences in ways that are recognizably postmodern.[2] Hypertext theorists and software designers Jay Bolter and Michael Joyce emphasized this visual and experimental character of digital hypertextual writing when they created the hypertext writing program *Storyspace.* Richard Lanham emphasized the rhetorical nature of digital writing, defining a "digital rhetoric" that recaptures the rhetorical paideia by making explicit oral and visual rhetorical concerns that were buried in the last two centuries of print culture and conventions (30). More recent scholarly work outlines the rhetorical practices possible with hypertext and multimedia, from Gary Heba's delineation of how html authoring mirrors rhetorical processes for composition to Patricia Sullivan's arguments that expand our definitions of electronic writing to include graphics, screen design, and other media forms. While professional writers rarely complete an entire interface or graphic design, early work in professional and technical communication by James Porter and Patricia Sullivan, Edward Tufte, and Barbara Mirel all demonstrated how rhetorical decisions impact the visual design of an online document or system: this work helped alert composition scholars to the visual nature of digital writing practices.[3] And as Anne Wysocki demonstrates in "Impossibly Distinct," computer-based interactive media can now blend text and images so thoroughly that they are indistinguishable on the screen (210). By using careful rhetorical analysis that is sensitive to audience, situation, and cultural contexts, Wysocki demonstrates how new media requires a complex relationship between verbal and visual meanings. This important line of rhetorical criticism tells us that new technologies simply require new definitions of what we consider writing.

Persuaded by these arguments, many teachers of writing who were trained in print-based rhetorics now want to articulate principles of visual rhetoric for our students. We sometimes borrow elements of visual rhetoric from moving image studies and design fields as well as draw more upon the fully visual culture within which our students work, live, and learn.[4] Whenever students look at artifacts such as online games or Web sites, we can begin by teaching them to "read" critically assumptions about gender, age, nationality, or other identity categories. Visual communication theories, however, tend to draw too easy a parallel between visual grammar and verbal grammar or to posit visual literacy as easier or more holistic than verbal literacy.[5] We need to recognize that these new media and the literacies they require are hybrid forms. Historical studies of writing technologies have demonstrated how all writing is hybrid — it is an once verbal, spatial, and visual.[6] Acknowledging this hybridity means that the relationships among word and image, verbal texts and visual texts, "visual culture" and "print culture" are all dialogic relationships rather than binary opposites.[7] Recognizing the hybrid literacies our students now bring to our classrooms, we need a better understanding of the increasingly visual and interactive rhetorical features of digital documents. As writing technologies change, they require changes in our understanding of writing and rhetoric and, ultimately, in our writing pedagogy.

With access to digital technologies increasing (or simply assumed) in our college writing courses, interactive digital media have increasingly become part of what we analyze and teach when we teach writing. Writers now engage in what Porter calls "internetworked writing" — writing that involves the intertwining of production, interaction, and publication in the online classroom or professional workplace as well as advocating for one's online audiences (12). Those of us who teach writing online find that we must help our students pay attention to the rhetorical features of these highly visual digital environments. I want to highlight the visual nature of these rhetorical acts and, conversely, the rhetorical nature of these visual acts as hybrid forms of reading and authoring in the digital medium of the World Wide Web. To explain visual rhetoric online to our students, we can begin by carefully articulating the rhetorical features we see in various interactive digital media. In our classrooms, we can also begin to break down the processes for creating successful digital documents, first by simply looking at the computers around us and analyzing them as intensely visual artifacts. The screen itself is a tablet that combines words, interfaces, icons, and pictures that invoke other modalities like touch and sound. But because modern information technologies construct meaning as simultaneously verbal, visual, and interactive hybrids, digital rhetoric *simply assumes* the use of visual rhetoric as well as other modalities.

This essay defines and illustrates some key features of visual rhetoric as they operate in two interactive digital documents designed for the World Wide Web. I first analyze features from two examples of academic hypertextual essays to demonstrate how visual and verbal elements work together to serve the rhetorical purposes and occasions for these publications. I then turn to how writing teachers can teach visual rhetoric by discussing work created by students and the strategies they used to create a visually persuasive and rhetorically effective Web site for Shakespeare studies. These examples demonstrate how analyzing interactive digital media can help students develop rhetorical abilities and become more reflective authors. I believe that teaching digital rhetoric requires profound changes in how all of us think about both writing and pedagogy: Critiquing and producing writing in digital environments actually offers a welcome return to rhetorical principles and an important new pedagogy of writing as design.

A Visual Digital Rhetoric

Any rhetorical theory works as a dynamic system of strategies employed for creating, reacting to, and receiving meaning. An individual author typically operates within multiple social and cultural contexts and, hopefully, advocates ethically for his or her audiences. Thus, digital rhetoric describes a system of ongoing dialogue and negotiations among writers, audiences, and institutional contexts, but it focuses on the multiple modalities available for making meaning using new communication and information technologies. I want to introduce some key features of digital rhetoric by analyzing two scholarly hypertexts by Anne Wysocki and Christine Boese. The following terms help us describe how visual rhetoric operates in digital writing environments:

Audience Stance: The ways in which the audience is invited to participate in online documents and the ways in which the author creates an *ethos* that requires, encourages, or even discourages different kinds of interactivity for that audience.

Transparency: The ways in which online documents relate to established conventions like those of print, graphic design, film, and Web pages. The more the online document borrows from familiar conventions, the more transparent it is to the audience.

Hybridity: The ways in which online documents combine and construct visual and verbal designs. Hybridity also encourages both authors and audiences to recognize and construct multifaceted identities as a kind of pleasure.

Wysocki's and Boese's texts were published on the World Wide Web in 1998. The last decade marked a time when academic institutions and forms of writing began to change dramatically in their relationships to technology. Bolter called this period the "late age of print" in 1992 to describe how hypertext and multimedia technologies had brought us into an era where both print and digital forms are important to readers (10). When these two texts appeared during 1998, academics had been increasingly exposed to hypertexts (especially on the Web) as the publication opportunities and other institutional support grew for online academic work. Wysocki and Boese each had an interested readership and online community for their work, but each also clearly used the opportunities to educate a wider audience of academics and fans about the strategies important for design on the Web. Readers encountering this work brought with them the similarly postmodern hybridity of their own reading experiences, including experiences with linear print texts, changing scholarly conventions, online communities, and a growing familiarity with online texts. The authors of these documents met these readers' needs by using rhetorical features appropriate to a digital reading and writing environment, while also making concessions to the needs of their readers in a time of transition.

Although my analysis focuses on Web sites in relation to our changing academic conventions during a particular time period, I believe that these terms can help us develop an understanding of most interactive digital media as they change or reproduce more familiar forms. The kinds of features and categories I offer here focus on native hypertextual writing and reading processes, but they are hardly exhaustive categories. In these two works, the authors also bring up the subjects of changing literacies and the medium of the Web explicitly. Perhaps because these two authors have some experience (though no formal training) with digital graphic design and have taught visual communication, they offer both an execution of visual strategies and a self-conscious commentary that is inherently instructive for a visual rhetoric — what *Tristram Shandy* as experimental narrative was for early narrative theory. Each example uses these visual and interactive strategies in ways that are appropriate to the rhetorical situation and the hypertextual medium, but they go beyond formal innovation to help audiences take more conscious responsibility for making meaning out of the text. Audiences can experience the pleasures of agency and an awareness of themselves as constructed identities in a heterogeneous medium. How that agency gets played out, however, depends on the purpose and situation for the text in relation to the audience's need for linearity and other familiar forms.

Published in the online journal *Kairos* <http://english.ttu.edu/kairos/> in fall 1998, Wysocki's "Monitoring Order" is intended for teachers of writing in online environments who are experienced with Web-based hypertexts but are not as familiar with histories of design, the subject of her essay. This essay provides an important overview of the continuities between book design and Web page design, persuading us to be sensitive to the historical and cultural specificity of our current conventions for all designs, both book pages and Web browsers. Wysocki discusses how the order of designs and the contexts for reading all come from culturally framed experiences with literacy. We all "encoun-

Monitoring Order:
Visual desire, the Organization of web pages, and Teaching the rules of design

by Anne Frances Wysocki
Michigan Technological University

Abstract

Monitoring Order looks at two potential sources -- writings about book design and writings about visual arrangement in painting -- for helping teachers of writing think about teaching visual composition for Web pages; both sources are problematic but suggest directions for further study.

This web was peer-reviewed by Johndan Johnson-Eilola, Pam Takayoshi, and Cindy Wambeam of the *Kairos* Editorial Board.

Contact the author.

Anne Frances Wysocki is completing her dissertation in the Rhetoric and Technical Communication program at Michigan Technological University, where she teaches classes in multimedia development, visual communication, and digital photography.

Note: There are no external links in this webtext.

http://english.ttu.edu/kairos/3.2/features/wysocki/bridge.html

ter designs individually, based on our particular bodily histories and presents" ("Monitoring Order"). She explains that, because the Web inherits book page design, it embeds the cultural assumptions about order on a page that come from our history with print texts: "[V]isual designs can (as is most evident in what I've written about books) be expressions of and means for reproducing cultural and political structures, and . . . such visual orderings are likely to be those that are repeated. . . ." ("Monitoring Order"). The history of typography demonstrates that, because book design strives to be transparent, we don't necessarily think of it as designed or discuss the embedded assumptions about reading. Two-dimensional graphic design offers some guidance for designing Web pages but is also limited in its formalism. Ultimately, Wysocki wants readers to ask themselves "what the arrangement of images and words on a web page asks us to desire: what order is reinforced by a design, and what designs give us chances to re-order? ("Monitoring Order"). The Web, while borrowing from both print and graphics design traditions, lends itself to looking again at the digital texts and pages whose structures and margins can change. Wysocki's argument and visual strategies work together to motivate readers and change their ways of seeing design.

Audience stance describes how the work visually gives readers a sense of agency and possibilities for interactive involvement. Wysocki's essay works visually by enacting in the interface the concepts about design and desire that it discusses while constructing the screen as page. The *ethos* created by Wysocki addresses the expected academic conventions for linear argument and also challenges those expectations. Wysocki, an experienced designer of interactive media, originally delivered this piece at the Computers and Writing Conference, and she kept it within the linear format when designing this talk into an essay for *Kairos*.[8] When "Monitoring Order" appeared in September 1998, *Kairos* as a whole averaged 137,000 hits with 7,500 unique visitors per month, while today it averages 240,000 hits and 10,000 unique visitors per month.[9] Most direct involvement between this audience and the author in 1998 occurred in forms prescribed by the journal — the linear Web-text structure, the "Contact the author" e-mail link, and the discussion forum included in another section of the journal. But Wysocki uses the interface and the tone of her essay to create arguments using pages of texts and illustrations readers are familiar with, while subtly making readers construct a reading and a way of seeing the essay. She thus fulfills, and also plays with, the desire for ordered readings, using the essay itself to challenge the audience while also giving them the linearity they might want or even need.

The essay is divided into sections, or nodes, and the length of text in each node varies, but tiles in the upper frame allow readers to access the nodes, which are subsections of the argument, in any order. Each node can be read autonomously but also works to develop the overall argument of the essay. Some screens require scrolling to find all the examples; some screens are short, emphatic transitional and summary paragraphs. The final tile brings up the anticipated list of sources. The shape of each section thus develops and stresses points of the argument for readers familiar with academic arguments but also familiar with basic Web conventions like scrolling and clicking on buttons. If one clicks on a tile to navigate through the piece, subtle changes on the screen indicate movement through the document and reinforce the audience's sense of agency and interaction. The design of the essay invites readers to think beyond the familiar linear structure, to playfully reflect on the self-consciously linear structure. Readers are offered the pleasure of consciously "monitoring order" themselves by clicking on tiles and pursuing different orders as they read or re-read the essay. By creating this kind of interactive and reflective stance, Wysocki reminds readers of themselves as active readers and helps them be attentive to the features of design on the page. For readers with the ability to access its graphics and frames, the essay offers an interactive experience where color, shape, and text cannot be separated. The interface leaves these readers with a renewed sense of how design choices become contextualized in arguments, in this case about the changes in page and book designs throughout history.

Transparency refers to how the writer designs a document in ways familiar and clear to readers. Wysocki demonstrates how screen design of any new media document might use strategies borrowed from historically specific approaches to page design, graphic design, and the changing conventions (such as frames) for Web pages. "Monitoring Order" uses forms, color, and a familiar page layout to create a fairly transparent interface that quickly teaches a novice reader how to navigate

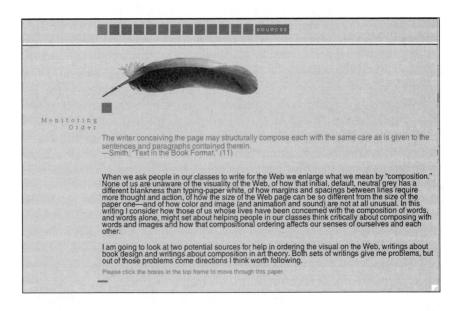

it, relying primarily on repeated forms and colors as visual tools of organization.

Wysocki provides navigation through the text with the sequence of color tiles in the top frame. The tiles are different colors that correspond to the sections of the essay — blues for the sections on book design, reds for the sections on graphic design, and greens for the introduction and conclusion. These colors are repeated in the opening figure of the quill feather, an appropriately antiquated image of writing's material history represented on the computer screen. The quotations, subheadings, and reading instructions appear in slightly different colored text that stands out typographically. The feather and the graphic representing the subsection — here, a single green tile for the first node — appear at the top left of the main frame to orient the reader as if on a printed page. The bottom of this first page instructs us to click on the tiles to move through the paper. In this same location on subsequent pages, the tiles are repeated as a set of lines at the bottom of each screen so that we can visually identify the end of a section by its corresponding tiles. The tiles provide a navigational device and a kind of footprint of each screen. The forms on the screen are thus decorative and interactive, painterly, and significant representations for information. The screen is visually coherent primarily through the strategy of repetition — here, the use of repeated colors and forms. On the surface, this coherence provides a calm sense of modernist order that is simultaneously visual and navigational. Order reassures readers that they won't get lost and that the text has a structure that can be tracked visually as well as verbally.

The **hybridity** of the Web medium refers to the interplay between the visual and the verbal in one constructed, heterogeneous semiotic space. Wysocki's site takes advantage of this hybridity to combine pictures and text in thoughtful and unconventional ways. The sections of text incorporate quotes and pictures and reproductions of texts as evidence for the arguments about visual design and its historical specificity. This strategy uses the juxtaposition of pictures, words, and unconventional margins to transform our understanding of the visual through the reading experience. For example, in the following screen [at the top of page 366], Wysocki plays with the conventional relationships between texts and pictures on pages: the margins expand outward slightly on the left, reminding readers of how the digital page is not fixed but mutable. The illustration, a pictorial history book, is a startling example of how the production of such books served as an excuse for political oppression by conquerors who valued only verbal texts. Finally, the illustration is placed within the sentence without figure captions in the same way that verbal evidence supporting an argument might be.

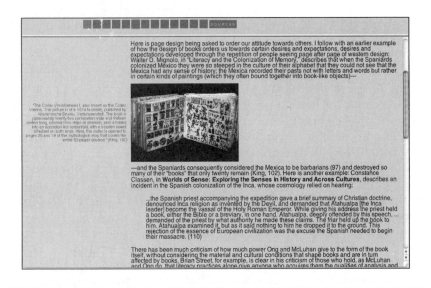

Because of Wysocki's skillful use of examples like these to visually challenge the reader's sense of order and design, the readers of this journal leave this essay having actually experienced a new way of seeing what was previously invisible. An early example of what has become a hallmark of Wysocki's work, "Monitoring Order" uses colors, visual metaphors, and graphical repetitions to guide us through a meditation about our own perceptions, expectations, and attitudes regarding the visual in relation to text. In response, readers can imagine themselves as more thoughtful about designs or even as capable designers themselves.

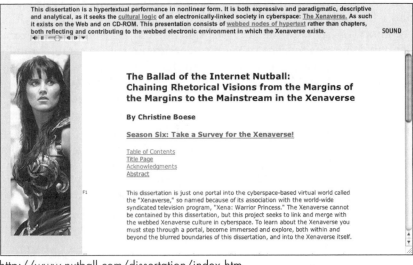

http://www.nutball.com/dissertation/index.htm

Self-published and updated since 1998, Christine Boese's "The Ballad of the Internet Nutball" was the first hypertextual dissertation accepted by Rensselaer Polytechnic University. Boese's project is a participation/observer ethnography and analysis of the fans and online culture surrounding the popular fantasy television show, *Xena: Warrior Princess*. The original audiences for this site included the dissertation committee members and the *Xena* fans. Boese explains the goal in her dissertation is to

> explore the constellations of social forces in cyberspace, which have led to the success of a noncommercial, highly trafficked, dynamic culture or what is sometimes called a "community." . . . This research examines how the <u>rhetorical visions</u> of this culture are used to write the narratives of its ongoing existence, in a way that is increasingly independent of the dominant narratives of the television program itself.

Boese's ethnographic project analyzes show episodes, photographs, fan-authored fantasy narratives about the implicit lesbian subplot between Xena and her warrior-poet sidekick Gabrielle, surveys, and more than 1,100 Web sites devoted to the show and its fans online, and face-to-face interactions at fan conventions. This comprehensive study of a fan culture, or fandom, offers fresh definitions of both online community and hypertextual structure.

The **audience stance** is established on the opening screen as music, images, text, and hypertextual structure all set the stage for a highly interactive experience. With the freedom to design her own interface and the support of committee members to explore new techniques for hypertextual structure, Boese created a complex collage of visual and navigational strategies. Similarly, the kinds of agency presented to readers are complex and multifaceted, allowing many choices for interaction, including several ways to read the document. The *ethos* Boese creates is at once that of engaged insider, co-participant, and scholarly investigator, one that assumes an engaged online audience of fans. She emphasizes these multiple stances by providing equal amounts of narrative, analysis, personal reflection, and interaction. The familiar academic contexts for a dissertation, including title page and acknowledgments, are included as links from this first screen, as well as a traditional table of contents. But this document actively invites participation from those whom Boese calls in her acknowledgments "my co-authors" of the study, the fan audience for the site. These co-participants not only completed the expected surveys and interviews, but they have added online materials and interpretations to the site over time. Boese thus creates an experience of open-ended possibility with these proliferating texts and interpretations. When it first appeared on the Web, the site saw about 500 visits a month by these fans, but it continues to get a growing amount of traffic — up to 22,200 hits and 6,155 unique visitors a month at the time of this study. Its audience has apparently grown as academics and online journals have referenced Boese's study as a cult fan site and a course resource.[10]

Like Wysocki's visual strategies, Boese's are integral to her argument, in this case to motivate and engage readers in the complex web of texts and interactions that make up the online culture called the Xenaverse. Boese's interface design is not very **transparent,** offering instead an unfamiliar, multidimensional structure that includes complex linking and several forms of navigation:

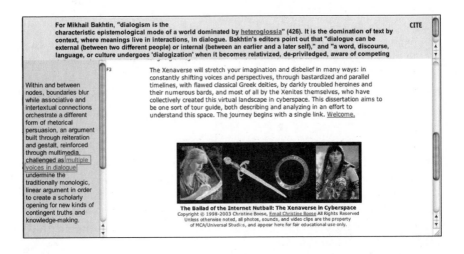

For Mikhail Bakhtin, "dialogism is the characteristic epistemological mode of a world dominated by heteroglossia" (426). It is the domination of text by context, where meanings live in interactions, in dialogue. Bakhtin's editors point out that "dialogue can be external (between two different people) or internal (between an earlier and a later self)," and "a word, discourse, language, or culture undergoes 'dialogization' when it becomes relativized, de-priviledged, aware of competing

CITE

F3

The Xenaverse will stretch your imagination and disbelief in many ways: in constantly shifting voices and perspectives, through bastardized and parallel timelines, with flawed classical Greek deities, by darkly troubled heroines and their numerous bards, and most of all by the Xenites themselves, who have collectively created this virtual landscape in cyberspace. This dissertation aims to be one sort of tour guide, both describing and analyzing in an effort to understand this space. The journey begins with a single link. Welcome.

Within and between nodes, boundaries blur while associative and intertextual connections orchestrate a different form of rhetorical persuasion, an argument built through reiteration and gestalt, reinforced through multimedia, challenged as multiple voices in dialogue undermine the traditionally monologic, linear argument in order to create a scholarly opening for new kinds of contingent truths and knowledge-making.

The Ballad of the Internet Nutball: The Xenaverse in Cyberspace
Copyright © 1998-2003 Christine Boese, Email Christine Boese All Rights Reserved
Unless otherwise noted, all photos, sounds, and video clips are the property
of MCA/Universal Studios, and appear here for fair educational use only.

Boese's interface takes full advantage of nonlinear hypertextual form by using multiple frames, linking strategies, and multiple media in ways that draw attention to the constructed interface. Boese provides three frames, four navigational paths, and an image map to accommodate many kinds of readers. The use of three simultaneous frames in the screens gives an experience of nonhierarchical depth and multidimensionality to the screen space. Each frame is marked by a different color — blue at the top, pink at the side, and white in the middle — and the screen is assembled as a collage of contrasting colors, photographs, and links within the text and at the right margins of texts. Text appears organized by its graphical and spatial presentation in all frames. These texts also interact with one another to a great degree. Hypertextual links, when clicked, bring up explanations and citations in the other frames or in additional pop-up windows. Thus, one experiences many changes taking place through this cross-linking on what appears to be one level of information, creating what Janet Murray refers to as an experience of immersion that leads to increased agency (162).

To enhance that agency and also offer concessions to more linear readers, Boese uses several methods of navigation that provide multiple paths through the text. The picture of Gabrielle, the poet, leads to a narrative reading of the text. The sword, one of Xena's weapons, moves one to the argumentative theoretical portion of the text, while Xena's other weapon, the disc-shaped Shockrum, leads to a pop-up window that provides the image map — a clickable collage of photos offering a nonlinear path through the document. Finally, the picture of Xena leads to a discussion of interconnecting themes in the study. At every turn, then, readers are offered multiple choices, allowing them to construct very different readings of the text. At the same time, readers experience a dissonance between this text and other familiar forms (like linear fantasy narratives or academic arguments) that defamiliarizes their experiences with print narrative, argumentative forms, and even with other, simpler hypertexts. This process of awareness is what Bolter and Grusin call "hypermediation," because the historical relationship of media forms becomes apparent in the structure. In fact, Boese's aim, as she explains in her section on design, is to create what Joyce called "constructive hypertext," thereby encouraging audiences to actively construct their own readings and meanings (42–43). Boese's readers are highly aware of the interface as a Web-based, experimental structure that bears little resemblance to print forms.

The **hybridity** of the Web interface allows Boese to swap different kinds of media — texts, pictures, sounds, links, data sources, and citations — in and out of the various sections of the screen and pop up windows. She juxtaposes textual explanations with purely visual arguments. For example, this visual representation of the Xenaverse —

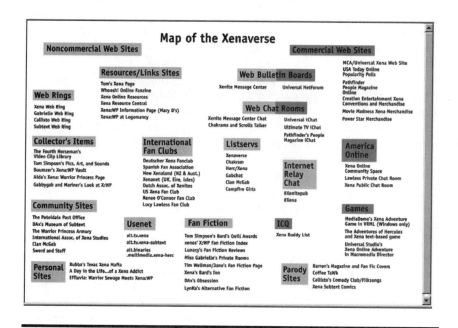

uses what Tufte would call an "information-rich" interface to present a large amount of data on a single level, with colors distinguishing the data (blue for noncommercial on the left, yellow for commercial on the right) and boxes and columns regularizing the data. While displaying many formal characteristics common to any two-dimensional design (alignment and clustering of similar data, highlighted headings, use of white space), the page asks readers to appreciate the depth and breadth of the online communities and to observe that noncommercial sites coded blue outnumbered commercial sites in yellow almost two to one. Readers, by grasping the scope of the Xenaverse and immersing themselves in the many sites and media included in the project, can help create the fan culture and construct themselves as fans, critics, or storytellers as they see fit.

Several important rhetorical features emerge from looking at both of these documents. First, each piece establishes an **audience stance** by offering readers different forms of interactivity and agency. This stance results largely from the author creating an *ethos* and a connection with readers that encourages different kinds of audience participation. Each author thus uses the interactive and performative potential of the hypertextual medium, encouraging the audience to explore the space created by the digital document and to reflectively participate in their own explorations and construction of the text. Secondly, each piece uses formal structures that mix old and new forms of reading and viewing conventions to create the audience's perception of **transparency.** The document's historical relationship to familiar conventions helps create a sense of familiar structure and allows the audience to recognize desired information quickly. Transparency is also created by defamiliarizing the audience's experiences with reading and writing conventions by drawing explicit and sometimes playful attention to both the discontinuities and the continuities between older and newer forms of reading, writing, and viewing information. This process can allow the audience to experience the pleasure of constructing their own readings and playing with form. In the two examples, both documents make concession to and also disrupt the expectations of academic readers accustomed to traditional print and other media forms, but in quite different ways appropriate to the rhetorical context. Finally, each author uses the **hybridity** of the digital medium to capitalize on its constructed nature and also to encourage readers to be aware of their own hybrid identities. In a space where multifaceted identities can be constructed, experienced, and even performed, this experience of hybridity works to the audience's advantage by increasing the experience of pleasure through identification and multiplicity.

Although they obviously overlap, these categories provide a starting point for talking about the rhetorical and visual features of Web-based digital documents together, the contexts for designing these documents as visual arguments, and the potential impact of these designs on audiences, particularly through the use of interface designs and interactivity. Both essays use hypertextual form to underscore reflexively the arguments they make about conventions and about cultures. Both authors use the visual interactive medium to persuade their audiences to participate in and be changed by the reading experience. "Monitoring Order" uses academic readers' expectations about linearity and visual page design in a traditional "page" format and then subtly challenges those conventions using page designs and pictures as self-explanatory pieces of evidence to embody Wysocki's arguments about the historical specificity of all designs. Boese's dissertation immerses readers in a multidimensional structure that disrupts expectations about linearity up front but still provides many choices that lead to a linear path. The invitations to participate and be transformed by the online Xena cultures abound, driven by the agency offered to readers throughout the document. Analyzing professional models like this helps us demonstrate good techniques for how multimedia writing can then be taught as visual and verbal rhetorical practice.

Teaching Visual Digital Rhetoric

When we bring an understanding of digital rhetoric to our electronic classrooms, we need to expand our approach not only to rhetorical criticism but also to text production. Digital technologies can encourage what the New London School theorists call a multimodal approach to literacy, where using communication technologies engages students in a multisensory experience and active construction of knowledge. To use multimedia technologies effectively, writers have to use practices that are not just verbal but visual, spatial, aural, and gestural to meaning (Cope and Kalantzis 26; Kress, "Multimodality" 182). These theorists make a powerful case for redefining literacy practice and attending to the political and social impact made possible by technologies as complex artifacts that can help transform our lived experience. Their approach to pedagogy suggests that students can work from within their diverse cultures and multiple identities using their own languages as well as their everyday lived experiences to design new kinds of knowledge. This definition of literacy and its implications for teaching echo what Cynthia Selfe has called "critical technological literacy" in its recognition of the political implications of technological literacies and its commitment to diversity. This approach to literacy education reinforces the value of teaching students to think of themselves not just as critics but as designers of knowledge. Gunther Kress distinguishes how critique and design are two knowledge-making processes that manifest different social environments and epistemologies. Critique occurs when "existing forms, and the social relations of which they are manifestations, are subjected to a distanced, analytical scrutiny to reveal the rules of their constitution. . . . In periods of relative social stability critique has the function of introducing a dynamic into the system" ("'English' at" 87). Design becomes essential in times of intense social change: "While critique looks at the present through the means of past production, Design shapes the future through deliberate deployment of representational resources in the designer's interest" (77). In other words, design moves us from rhetorical criticism to invention and production. The "shaping" of resources gives students' work social and political impact and allows them to learn how to represent new forms of knowledge. To establish a balanced rhetorical approach, then, we must offer students experiences both in the analytic process of critique, which scrutinizes conventional expectations and power relations, and in the transformative process of design, which can change power relations by creating a new vision of knowledge.

In terms of visual rhetoric, students need to learn the "distanced" process of how to critique the saturated visual and technological landscape that surrounds them as something structured and written in a set of deliberate rhetorical moves. They then need to enact those visual moves on their own. Kress's notion of multimodal design helps to underscore how helpful design projects can be for learning visual rhetoric. If we can teach students to critique the rhetorical and visual features of professional hypertexts — the audience stance, presentations of *ethos,* transparency of the interface for readers, and the hybridity of forms and identities — we can also teach them to design their own technological artifacts that use these strategies but are more speculative or activist in nature. This approach to pedagogy asks teachers not only to incorporate new kinds of texts into our classrooms but new kinds of multimodal compositional processes that ask students to envision and create something that perhaps does not yet exist.

http://www.wcenter.spelman.edu/ENG310_F98proj/Shake.html

To illustrate the transformative process of design, I want to turn to a student online project from a Shakespeare course at Spelman College, also self-published in 1998 when many students were designing their first Web-based documents.[11] The project focused on collecting professional and student opinions on colorblind casting in Shakespeare performances. The class Web site became an ongoing collaboration and a new experience for the English professor and the students. The professor explains that she hoped that students would "test their own ideas against those of a wide variety of people concerned with the study of Shakespeare" and "express their opinions to persons outside of their own school environment" (McDermott 2). She gave students the topic of colorblind casting, used by theaters to create more diversity in traditional theater, and cited the controversies regarding these casting practices. Students then identified key arguments about race and collected professional opinions online to create the first Web site that explicitly addresses race and casting practices in Shakespearean studies. They constructed an activist stance, using their identities as individual Black women and as a Spelman College community. Furthermore, publishing their work online highlighted the students' perceived impact on audiences and underscored the rhetorical ethics of internetworked writing emphasized by Porter. Students became designers of knowledge about Shakespeare by weaving together and visually representing their own perspectives and the perspectives of others on the Web. On the page, these voices become enacted as a visual mix of colored text, commercial and homemade visuals, seriousness and fun, as the students explain the occasion for their site and the controversies surrounding their topic, asking "Should Non-European Actors Be Cast in Major Roles?"

To construct the project, the students used **audience stance** to offer an engaging site with a layout and tone that would appeal to other students studying Shakespeare while also being responsible to the professionals with whom they had been communicating. The site includes interactive and inviting features that students designed specifically for other students. For example, the "guestbook" link visually marks a place where the students invite other students to respond to this controversial topic. Quotes in the guestbook compliment the students' work on the site, including a supporting quote by actor Raul Julia on his Shakespearean role. A student from another school wrote a deliberately informal note of recognition: "well i think that casting blacks and other colors into Shakespeare's work is very essential. as a student studying his arts i enjoyed acting out the parts that would of been issued to a white person. colorblindness is a great approach because then all can feel into the theme and not left out. thank you for your time and god bless." While few in number, these responses enhanced the class's sense of audience and purpose for designing the site.[12]

Another way students designed interactivity was to create a space where they could publish the ideas they collected from surveys. Students used the playful feature of a "thought bubble," an inherently visual/verbal semiotic space borrowed from comic book traditions, to represent their audience of professionals and their opinions culled from the surveys. Each thought bubble offers an opinion in its own unique color and a sense of incompleteness is suggested in the title's ellipsis:

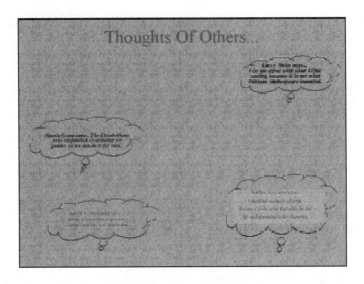

Students use these familiar forms to represent meaning for other students and professionals. The Spelman site works rhetorically to draw students into a dialogue about Shakespeare and race through its simple but engaging interface while also presenting research on the topic of Shakespeare to fulfill their responsibilities as researchers. By keeping these audience representations relatively separate, students hoped to persuade both audiences of the impact of colorblind casting. The students create an *ethos* of the collective voice of their class community that strikes a balance between professional academic discourse and authoritative self-identification, what Stephen Knadler, writing about online projects by students from the same college, calls a *"felt re-embodiment* online" (238). For example, on the next screen [at the top of page 375], the students describe the "unanswered questions" they have and cite Errol Hill, a noted Caribbean scholar, as an authority, before they announce the purpose of their project. The clash between personal voice and professional discourse in this site exhibits the same kind of "double-consciousness" that Knadler saw in his students' portfolios and that teachers often find in students working to assimilate personal voices with distanced and objective academic discourse.

Students used a variety of familiar techniques to create a **transparent** interface appropriate for their rhetorical situation and for the audience. Keeping the site simple and straightforward for multiple audiences was a primary goal for the class as they were learning Web design. They use basic and familiar conventions for the Web at that time — linear arrangements and horizontal rules on pages, traditional book-style layout of pictures alongside text, and short nodes of explanatory text to help keep readers oriented. Students avoided using frames or other more complex hypertextual lining, opting instead for a few

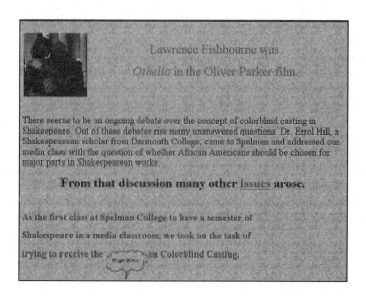

conventional in-text links. The pages use these familiar conventions but still take some advantage of the digital medium to go beyond traditional print-page format. Prompted by the idea of color, the students use multicolored text to provide a visual pun and argument to remind audiences that color is indeed visible. Students also playfully invite readers to explore the thoughts of others with the thought bubbles. The page is deceptively simple: It has a depth of resources offered through the few hypertextual links here, including the survey results linked to the "Thoughts of Others" box, a link to other Shakespeare sites, and a link to a class bulletin board with pictures, news, and reviews of ongoing productions.

While these pages appear "messy" in that they have less design continuity, onscreen spatial structure, and interface features than the professional examples, they illustrate the process of students learning to bring visual and verbal arguments together. The text on this page aims to balance opinions objectively, using black text for the opening summary and green text for their explicit purpose in making the site, thus establishing a firm sense of the class community as the occasion for this design. At the same time, commercial pictures with captions alongside them open the page and emphasize depictions of familiar Black actors cast in recent productions. Blue links lead to other issues from the class and opinions on the topic. The students thus build a visual argument about the track record of successful casting practices through the pictures as they introduce the controversy. They then work to balance perspectives and research about the topic. The **hybridity** of the medium thus lets students use texts, pictures, and other illustrations interchangeably to illustrate their learning and also to encourage engagement and responses from their dual audiences of students and theater professionals. Students can take on the role of offering professional perspectives and still be students.

If we understand this site as epistemic rhetoric (see James Berlin), it demonstrates how students can make their ongoing work and learning purposeful by directing it toward this particular situation and their audience of both professionals and students. By publishing it online as public discourse and new knowledge in the field, students have an immediate sense of their impact on audiences. The "Shakespeare in Color" Web site "makes an actual contribution to Shakespeare studies" while teaching students "investigative technique, analytical skills, and something about the process of publishing and taking responsibility for one's scholarly work" (McDermott 4). It thus becomes an authentic learning experience that has brought students in touch with a new experience of literature, of performance, and of theater culture through contact with their broader audience of professionals. Students themselves recognized the value of these activities and described their projects as "extremely creative," and including "alternate ways" of representing their understanding of the course material. Most importantly, students were extremely proud of their accomplishments, saw themselves as talented, and appreciated the "hands-on learning" and the opportunity to present their work in a public forum for an actual audience.[13] Design projects such as this not only bring the concept of multiliteracy squarely into the middle of the composition process but also help students design an activist academic project that represents new knowledge for a real audience.

How do we begin to help students enact their understanding of visual and digital rhetoric? Teachers must first develop assignments and projects that complement the goals of their courses. In this case, the professor wanted a multimodal experience of literary texts, interactions with professionals, and collaborative active learning experiences using multimedia technology. After these students looked critically at the visual elements of Web sites and other media, they then planned out their project together and designed the site for their two audiences. Students created a Web site and a PowerPoint project in this course and presented their preliminary designs in an oral presentation to other students and faculty from the department. When teaching design, I also begin by analyzing media and encouraging students to think broadly about visual elements and interactivity. I show them published new media titles and ask them to look for the rhetorical features like audience stance, *ethos*, transparency of the interface, and hybridity. They come to understand these features by analyzing the visual details: the use of elements like color, space, linearity; the use of conventions from film, print, advertisements, and typical Web sites; and the use of forms of agency for audiences. Students then draw conclusions about visual arguments and the purposes of interactivity. I have them sketch out or illustrate "borrowed" features they'd like to include in their projects. I do this so they will not limit their designs to their own production skills or to the technologies available at any one time in our classrooms. My students conduct research by starting with their own understandings of visual representations and their own perspectives as users of familiar and not-so-familiar technologies. This process of speculative design encourages students to think both creatively and rhetorically about everything from cell phones to online games, while paradoxically not limiting them to the time and place of particular software programs.

The next step is to teach students to map out or storyboard their projects. Storyboarding is a visual technique borrowed from documentary video production where every shot is planned out to correspond to a narrative script. In multimedia productions, storyboarding refers to planning and sketching out each screen of the digital production. To teach students the storyboarding process, I give them sheets of paper and ask them to draw every media element, each navigational link, and all text that appears on the screen. They also note the colors and any other graphics that will be used on each screen. This process makes them pay careful attention to visual arguments, to spatial placement on the screen, and to the consistency of the interface. It also forces them to narrow the scope of their projects in collaboration with one another and their audience. They think carefully about what the audience will see and how audience members will interact with the information in their projects. When students learn to storyboard a sequence of screens, they learn to think carefully about how visual information gets structured as part of the design. Their design and drawing skills can be minimal because storyboarding teaches students to *think through* the elements of design and navigation that meet the audience's needs. The speculative design process can be accomplished in a couple of weeks, and students don't need any specific technical skills to complete the assignments. I sometimes go on and teach students to use a scanner and an image software program that allows them to alter an already existing still image and change its meaning. If time permits, students can then create their own graphics and import them into a Web authoring program to be combined with links and other interactive features. This authoring of the project can take more weeks to accomplish, but it is well worth the time and effort if the ultimate goal is to have students publish a permanent Web site. Students in the Shakespeare class benefited from interacting with the target audience online and in oral presentations to other students as they decided how to design the content of the site. The oral critique of the site by other students is a very important part of the process — not only did students feel compelled to impress their audience of peers, but they also had the opportunity to revise their site before making it accessible online.

While this discussion offers only a starting point for teaching design, it shows how valuable all stages of design projects can be for students. Design projects require writers to look at successful models, to think deeply about audience, to design visual and verbal arguments together, and to actively construct new knowledge. Because the process of design is fundamentally visual and multimodal, it can be challenging, but it leads students to a new understanding of how designed spaces and artifacts impact audiences. Teaching design allowed these students to try to shape the social and cultural environment in which they found themselves by bringing together research and their own perspectives online to define a concept of English Studies. Nancy Kaplan ("Literacy and Technology"), Craig Stroupe ("Visualizing English"), and Randy Bass ("Story and Archive") have all demonstrated that the design of artifacts is an essential part of literacy and of enacting disciplinary knowledge in English Studies because those artifacts will ultimately determine how knowledge is received and perpetuated for our field. When designing digital documents and also seeing how people use and interpret them, our students can then see themselves as active producers of knowledge in their discipline.

Acknowledgments

I am grateful to Marilyn Cooper, Gary Bays, and the *CCC* reviewers for their helpful comments on this article. Special thanks to Jeff Grabill for his many readings and insights throughout the revision process. Thanks also to Chris Boese, Kristine McDermott, and Anne Wysocki for their contributions to this work, and to the Spelman students who allowed me to discuss their course work.

Notes

1. At the time that the hypertext theorists developed theories about electronic writing in the 1980s, they were primarily referring to elements of early hypertextual systems and the interactions in online communication before widespread use of graphical browsers on the World Wide Web. The early hypertext theorists focused immediately on both the visual and spatial character of electronic writing. For example, Jay Bolter defined the new writing technologies as "the visual writing space" (11) and outlined how they require a new visual literacy. Nancy Kaplan explained that "hypertextual writing systems [could] provide a graphic representation of textual structures, a dynamic map of the textual system in play" that "remain dynamic pictures of an evolving text" ("E-Literacies"). Michael Joyce highlighted Bolter's description of hypertext as "topographic writing" that implied its visual quality (47) and stated eloquently: "hypertext is, before anything else, a visual form" (19).

2. See, for example, Lester Faigley on the postmodern composing online self, George Landow on the connections between hypertext and postmodern literary theory, and Nancy Baym on the conversational features of online discourse. See Stuart Moulthrop and Peter Elbow on the postmodern forms of rhizome and collage for hypertext and for home pages. Hypertext seems to embody postmodern forms of writing, as Jane Yellowlees Douglass states: "The beauty of hypertext is . . . that it propels us from the straightened 'either/or' world that print has come to represent and into a universe where the 'and/and/and' is always possible" (146).

3. James Porter and Patricia Sullivan's early collaborative essay ends with a renewed emphasis on the visual challenges of electronic text (422). Barbara Mirel has demonstrated how database design has become an essential part of communication in the workplace and includes a "visual rhetoric" for effective data design (95). Similarly, Edward Tufte describes a successful computer interface as having a well-crafted parallelism and clustering of images that allows "visual reasoning" by the user. In two practical guides for authors, Domenic Stansberry points out in his guidelines for writers that designing content for new media focuses mostly on interactive design — the structure and flow of information pathways (17), while Karen Schriver includes chapters on interactive document design.

4. Not surprisingly, useful connections have been made between teaching writing and the visual arts as mutually reinforcing literacies in the classroom (e.g., Childers, Hobson, and Mullin). Theories for analyzing visual communication and visual culture have been highlighted in cross-disciplinary studies of culture and design, for example, the collections *The Visual Culture Reader* and *Design Discourse*. Industrial design discourse has been shown by Richard Buchanan as having a fully demonstrative rhetoric, drawing on the past and showing possibilities for the future in everyday objects (107). Hanno Ehses analyzes the visual rhetoric of performance posters, pointing out how the design medium of the poster collapses "visual and verbal" representation as the "structure itself becomes semiotic, since each of the two forms contains information over and above that pertaining to its own set" (193). The collection *Page to Screen* (Snyder) is a good example of cross-disciplinary scholarship that looks at the design processes involved in digital linguistic acts.

5. For examples of these parallels, see Michael Gibson and Donis Dondis. For critiques of these approaches to visual literacy and visual communication, see Mary Hocks, "Toward," and Anne Wysocki, "Seriously Visible."

6. See, for example, Jay Bolter, Richard Lanham, Christina Hass, and Michael Joyce.

7. See Mary Hocks and Michelle Kendrick for a complete discussion of hybridity in the history of visual and verbal language systems.

8. Personal communication with the author.

9. Personal communication with Doug Eyman, co-editor of *Kairos*. As Eyman explains it, the approximations of unique visitors, while more accurate than numbers of visits or hits, are probably underestimated due to technological constraints.

10. Personal communication with the author. As Christine Boese explains it, the increased traffic seems to correspond to moments when the site has been listed in articles or resources on cult fandoms. She adds that number of hits does indicate that some people might be reading fairly deep the thirty or so main screens and other pop-up data windows in the site.

11. I did not teach this course, but as director of a faculty development program in communication across the curriculum I worked with a group of teachers from many disciplines who integrated multimedia design projects into their courses (see Mary Hocks and Daniele Bascelli). Faculty used an intensive summer workshop to develop online instructional resources like this site for their courses and to design writing-intensive assignments for their students that capitalized on the resources in the multimedia-equipped classroom.

12. I was unable to obtain data on visits to the Spelman College Writing Center site.
13. Results from an anonymous focus group of students, Spelman College, Atlanta, GA, May 2, 1992.

Works Cited

Bass, Randy. "Story and Archive in the Twenty-First Century." *College English* 61.6 (1999): 659–70.

Baym, Nancy. "From Practice to Culture on Usenet." In *The Cultures of Computing.* Ed. Susan Leigh Star. Oxford: Basil Blackwell, 1995. 29–52.

Berlin, James A. *Rhetorics, Poetics, and Cultures: Refiguring College English Studies.* Urbana, IL: NCTE, 1996.

Boese, Christine. "The Ballad of the Internet Nutball: Chaining Rhetorical Visions from the Margins to the Mainstream in the Xenaverse." Diss. online 1998 <http://www.nutball.com/dissertation/index.htm>.

Bolter, Jay David. *Writing Space: The Computer, Hypertext, and the History of Writing.* Hillsdale, NJ: Lawrence Erlbaum, 1991.

Bolter, Jay David, and Richard Grusin. *Remediation: Understanding New Media.* Cambridge: MIT P, 1999.

Buchanan, Richard. "Declaration by Design: Rhetoric, Argument, and Demonstration in Design Practice." In *Design Discourse: History, Theory, Criticism.* Ed. Victor Margolin. Chicago: U of Chicago P, 1989. 91–109.

Childers, Pamela B., Eric Hobson, and Joan A. Mullin. *ARTiculating: Teaching Writing in a Visual World.* Portsmouth, NH: Heinemann, 1998.

Cope, Bill, and Mary Kalantzis, eds. *Multiliteracies: Literacy Learning and the Design of Social Futures.* New York: Routledge, 2000.

Dondis, Donis A. *A Primer of Visual Literacy.* Cambridge: MIT P, 1973.

Douglass, Jane Yellowlees. "Will the Most Reflexive Relativist Please Stand Up: Hypertext, Argument, and Relativism." In *Page to Screen: Taking Literacy into the Electronic Era.* Ed. Ilana J. Snyder. London: Routledge, 1998. 144–62.

Ehses, Hanno H. J. "Representing MacBeth: A Case Study in Visual Rhetoric." In *Design Discourse: History, Theory, Criticism.* Ed. Victor Margolin. Chicago: U of Chicago P, 1989. 187–97.

Elbow, Peter. "Collage: Your Cheatin' Art." *Writing on the Edge* 9.1 (Fall/Winter 1997–98): 26–40.

Faigley, Lester. *Fragments of Rationality: Postmodernity and the Subject of Composition.* Pittsburgh, PA: U of Pittsburgh P, 1992.

Gibson, Michael. "Teaching Critical Analytical Methods in the Digital Typography Classroom." *Visible Language* 31.1 (1997): 300–25.

Hass, Christina. *Writing Technology: Studies on the Materiality of Literacy.* Mahwah, NJ: Lawrence Erlbaum, 1996.

Heba, Gary. "HyperRhetoric: Multimedia, Literacy, and the Future of Composition." *Computers and Composition* 14.1 (January 1997): 19–44.

Hocks, Mary E. "Toward a Visual Critical Electronic Literacy." *Works and Days* 17.1 & 2 (Spring/Fall 1999): 157–72.

Hocks, Mary E., and Daniele Bascelli. "Building a Multimedia Program across the Curriculum." In *Electronic Communication across the Curriculum.* Ed. Richard A. Selfe, Donna Reiss, and Art Young. Urbana, IL: NCTE. 40–56.

Hocks, Mary E., and Michelle Kendrick. "Introduction: Eloquent Images." In *Eloquent Images: Word and Image in the Age of New Media.* Cambridge: MIT P, 2003.

Joyce, Michael. *Of Two Minds: Hypertext Pedagogy and Poetics.* Ann Arbor: U of Michigan P, 1995.

Kaplan, Nancy. "E-Literacies: Politexts, Hypertexts, and Other Cultural Formations in the Late Age of Print." 1997 <http://iat.ubalt.edu/kaplan/lit/>.

———. "Literacy and Technology: Beyond the Book." <http://raven.ubalt.edu/staff/kaplan/parc/>.

Knadler, Stephen. "E-Racing Difference in E-Space: Black Female Subjectivity and the Web-Based Portfolio." *Computers and Composition* 18.3 (2001): 235–55.

Kress, Gunther. " 'English' at the Crossroads: Rethinking Curricula of Communication in the Context of the Turn to the Visual." *Passions, Pedagogies and 21st Century Technologies.* Ed. Gail E. Hawisher and Cynthia L. Selfe. Logan: Utah UP, 1999. 66–88.

———. "Multimodality." *Multiliteracies: Literacy Learning and the Design of Social Futures.* Ed. Bill Cope and Mary Kalantzis. New York: Routledge, 2000. 182–202.

Landow, George P. *Hypertext: The Convergence of Contemporary Critical Theory and Technology.* Baltimore: Johns Hopkins UP, 1992.

Lanham, Richard A. *The Electronic Word: Democracy, Technology, and the Arts.* Chicago: U of Chicago P, 1993.

McDermott, Kristine. "Report on Teaching and Technology Workshop for the Shakespeare Association of America." Unpublished manuscript. Atlanta, GA: Spelman College, 1998. 1–5.

Mirel, Barbara. "Writing and Database Technology: Extending the Definition of Writing in the Workplace." *Electronic Literacies in the Workplace: Technologies of Writing.* Ed. Patricia Sullivan and Jennie Dautermann. Urbana, IL: NCTE, 1996. 91–114.

Mirzoeff, Nicholas, ed. *The Visual Culture Reader.* New York: Routledge, 1998.

Mitchell, William J. *The Reconfigured Eye: Visual Truth in the Post-Photographic Era.* Cambridge: MIT P, 1992.

Moulthrop, Stuart. "Beyond the Electronic Book: A Critique of Hypertext Rhetoric." *Hypertext '91 Proceedings.* New York: The Association for Computing Machinery. 291–98.

Mullet, Kevin, and Darrell Sano. *Designing Visual Interfaces: Communication Oriented Techniques.* Mountain View, CA: Sun Microsystems, 1995.

Murray, Janet Horowitz. *Hamlet on the Holodeck: The Future of Narrative in Cyberspace.* Cambridge: MIT P, 1998.

Porter, James E. *Rhetorical Ethics and Internetworked Writing.* Greenwich, CT: Ablex, 1998.

Porter, James, and Patricia Sullivan. "Remapping Curricular Geography: Professional Writing in/and English Studies." *Journal of Business and Technical Communication* 7 (1993): 389–422.

Schriver, Karen A. *Dynamics in Document Design: Creating Text for Readers.* New York: John Wiley and Sons, 1997.

Selfe, Cynthia L. "Technology and Literacy: A Story about the Perils of Not Paying Attention." *College Composition and Communication* 50.3 (February 1999): 411–36.

Snyder, Ilana, ed. *Page to Screen: Taking Literacy into the Electronic Era.* London: Routledge, 1998.

Stansberry, Domenic. *Labyrinths: The Art of Interactive Writing and Design.* Belmont, CA: Wadsworth Publishing, 1998.

STORYSPACE™. Computer Software. Watertown, MA: Eastgate Systems, Inc. December 2, 2002 <http://www.eastgate.com/Storyspace.html>.

Stroupe, Craig. "Visualizing English: Recognizing the Hybrid Literacy of Visual and Verbal Authorship on the Web." *College English* 62.5 (May 2000): 607–32.

Tufte, Edward. *Visual Explanations: Images and Quantities, Evidence and Narrative.* Cheshire, CT: Graphics Press, 1997.

Wysocki, Anne Frances. "Impossibly Distinct: On Form/Content and Word/Image in Two Pieces of Computer-Based Interactive Multimedia." *Computers and Composition* 18 (2001): 209–34.

———. "Monitoring Order." *Kairos* 3.2 (Fall 1998). Online <http://english.ttu.edu/kairos/3.2/indx_f.html>.

———. "Seriously Visible." *Eloquent Images: Word and Image in the Age of New Media.* Ed. Mary E. Hocks and Michelle Kendrick. Cambridge: MIT P, 2003.

Hocks's Insights as a Resource for Your Teaching

1. Consider your students' level of preparedness for engaging the issues of visual rhetoric and new technology. What about your own level of comfort with the rhetoric that Hocks describes? Make a list of the aspects of visual rhetoric that feel familiar to you and those aspects that you would like to know more about. What resources are available at your school for teachers who want to learn more about technology?

2. How might certain features of your composition course, as currently configured, lend themselves particularly well to an online project? What about some of your own course materials? Would you consider asking your students to produce an online text? Why or why not?

Hocks's Insights as a Resource for Your Writing Classroom

1. Devise for your students a set of guidelines for analyzing the visual rhetoric of an online document. You might organize your guidelines around Hocks's concepts of audience stance, transparency, and hybridity.

2. Discuss with your students Hocks's concept of hybridity, and, in particular, how it can be used as a rhetorical strategy. Ask students to write a paper that explains the power of visual and verbal interplay in an online document of their choosing.

3

Responding to and
Evaluating Student Writing

Teachers' responses to student texts are continuously cited as the most significant influence — positive or negative — on students' concepts of themselves as writers. Although to many students "teacher response" signifies grades and summary comments, teachers may respond to student writing in several other ways: inside and outside the classroom, through structured feedback and spontaneously, and as both ally and gatekeeper.

Careful reflection on classroom practice prompted the articles in this chapter. Each essay is, of course, informed by philosophical perspectives, but all these readings focus very specifically on practical strategies for working with students at different skill levels in a variety of writing sites. You'll find many connections among the readings and a high degree of "intertextuality." Although you may be tempted to turn to just one of these readings only as a strong need arises, we recommend that you read them all and that you read them against the other pieces in this collection. These articles all resonate with a strong concern for student growth and empowerment, and from them you can carry away new ideas about ways of responding to student writing.

Responding to Student Writing

Nancy Sommers

In the conclusion of this landmark essay, first published in College Composition and Communication *in 1982, Nancy Sommers describes what continues to be a major responsibility for writing teachers: "The challenge we face as teachers is to develop comments which will provide an inherent reason for students to revise; it is a sense of revision as discovery, as a repeated process of beginning again, as starting out new, that our students have not learned. We need to show our students how to seek, in the possibility of revision, the dissonances of discovery — to show them through our comments why new choices would positively change their texts, and thus to show them the potential for development implicit in their own writing."*

Sommers's article reports the findings and the significance to teaching practice of collaborative research on the nature and effects of teachers' comments on first and second drafts. Lil Brannon, Cyril Knoblauch, and Sommers learned that instructor commentary can "appropriate" student texts — that is, distract writers from their own purposes in writing texts and focus them instead on responding to what they perceive the instructor wants in future drafts. They also found that instructor commentary was rarely text-based but rather exemplified the abstract, vague, and generic writing that we ask our students to avoid.

The article prompts writing teachers to analyze how they respond to student writing in all its stages, to adapt their comments on each draft to the needs and purpose of the writer, and to demonstrate through text-based comments the "thoughtful commentary" of attentive readers.

More than any other enterprise in the teaching of writing, responding to and commenting on student writing consumes the largest proportion of our time. Most teachers estimate that it takes them at least twenty to forty minutes to comment on an individual student paper, and those twenty to forty minutes times twenty students per class, times eight papers, more or less, during the course of a semester add up to an enormous amount of time. With so much time and energy directed to a single activity, it is important for us to understand the nature of the enterprise. For it seems, paradoxically enough, that although commenting on student writing is the most widely used method for responding to student writing, it is the least understood. We do not know in any definitive way what constitutes thoughtful commentary or what effect, if any, our comments have on helping our students become more effective writers.

Theoretically, at least, we know that we comment on our students' writing for the same reasons professional editors comment on the work of professional writers or for the same reasons we ask our colleagues to read and respond to our own writing. As writers we need and want thoughtful commentary to show us when we have communicated our ideas and when not, raising questions from a reader's point of view that may not have occurred to us as writers. We want to know if our writing has communicated our intended meaning and, if not, what questions or discrepancies our reader sees that we, as writers, are blind to.

In commenting on our students' writing, however, we have an additional pedagogical purpose. As teachers, we know that most students find it difficult to imagine a reader's response in advance, and to use such responses as a guide in composing. Thus, we comment on student writing to dramatize the presence of a reader, to help our students to become that questioning reader themselves, because, ultimately, we believe that becoming such a reader will help them to evaluate what they have written and develop control over their writing.[1]

Even more specifically, however, we comment on student writing because we believe that it is necessary for us to offer assistance to student writers when they are in the process of composing a text, rather than after the text has been completed. Comments create the motive for revising. Without comments from their teachers or from their peers, student writers will revise in a consistently narrow and predictable way. Without comments from readers, students assume that their writing has communicated their meaning and perceive no need for revising the substance of their text.[2]

Yet as much as we as informed professionals believe in the soundness of this approach to responding to student writing, we also realize that we don't know how our theory squares with teachers' actual practice — do teachers comment and students revise as the theory predicts they should? For the past year my colleagues, Lil Brannon, Cyril Knoblauch, and I have been researching this problem, attempting to discover not only what messages teachers give their students through their comments, but also what determines which of these comments the students choose to use or to ignore when revising. Our research has been entirely focused on comments teachers write to motivate revisions. We have studied the commenting styles of thirty-five teachers at New York University and the University of Oklahoma, studying the comments these teachers wrote on first and second drafts, and interviewing a representative number of these teachers and their students. All teachers also commented on the same set of three student essays. As an additional reference point, one of the student essays was typed into the computer that had been programmed with the "Writer's Workbench," a package of twenty-three programs developed by Bell Laboratories to help computers and writers work together to improve a text rapidly. Within a few minutes, the computer delivered editorial comments on the student's text, identifying all spelling and punctuation errors, isolating problems with wordy or misused phrases, and suggesting alternatives, offering a stylistic analysis of sentence types, sentence beginnings, and sentence lengths, and finally, giving our freshman essay a Kincaid readability score of eighth grade which, as the computer program informed us, "is a low score for this type of document." The sharp contrast between the teachers' comments and those of the computer highlighted how arbitrary and idiosyncratic most of our teachers' comments are. Besides, the calm, reasonable language of the computer provided quite a contrast to the hostility and mean-spiritedness of most of the teachers' comments.

The first finding from our research on styles of commenting is that *teachers' comments can take students' attention away from their own purposes in writing a particular text and focus that attention on the teachers' purpose in commenting.* The teacher appropriates the text from the student by confusing the student's purpose in writing the text with her own purpose in commenting. Students make the changes the teacher wants rather than those that the student perceives are necessary, since the teachers' concerns imposed on the text create the reasons for the subsequent changes. We have all heard our perplexed students say to us when confused by our comments: "I don't understand how you want me to change this" or "Tell me what *you* want me to do." In the beginning of the process there was the writer, her words, and her desire to communicate her ideas. But after the comments of the teacher are imposed on the first or second draft, the student's attention dramatically shifts from "This is what I want to say," to "This is what *you* the teacher are asking me to do."

This appropriation of the text by the teacher happens particularly when teachers identify errors in usage, diction, and style in a first draft and ask students to correct these errors when they revise; such comments give the student an impression of the importance of these errors that is all out of proportion to how they should view these errors at this point in the process. The comments create the concern that these "accidents of discourse" need to be attended to before the meaning of the text is attended to.

It would not be so bad if students were only commanded to correct errors, but, more often than not, students are given contradictory messages; they are commanded to edit a sentence to avoid an error or to condense a sentence to achieve greater brevity of style, and then told in the margins that the particular paragraph needs to be more specific or to be developed more. An example of this problem can be seen in the following student paragraph:

       wordy; be precise — which Sunday?   ✓*comma needed*

Every year [on one Sunday in the middle of January] tens of
                 word choice
millions of people <u>cancel</u> all events, plans or work to watch the
                                   wordy
Super Bowl. This audience includes [little boys and girls, old
                 be specific — what reasons?
people, and housewives and men.] <u>Many reasons</u> have been

given to explain why the Super Bowl has become so popular
and why   *(what spots?)*   *awkward*
t̶h̶a̶t̶commercial spots cost up to $100,000.00. <u>One explanation</u>
                                  another what?
<u>is that people</u> like to take sides and root for a team. <u>Another is</u>
            spelling✓
that some people like the pagentry and excitement of the event.

These reasons alone, however, do not explain
too colloquial
<u>a happening</u> as big as the Super Bowl.

Left margin: You need to do more research.

Right margin: This paragraph needs to be expanded in order to be more interesting to a reader.

In commenting on this draft, the teacher has shown the student how to edit the sentences, but then commands the student to expand the paragraph in order to make it more interesting to a reader. The interlinear comments and the marginal comments represent two separate tasks for this student; the interlinear comments encourage the student to see the text as a fixed piece, frozen in time, that just needs some editing. The marginal comments, however, suggest that the meaning of the text is not fixed, but rather that the student still needs to develop the meaning by doing some more research. Students are commanded to edit and develop at the same time; the remarkable contradiction of developing a paragraph after editing the sentences in it represents the confusion we encountered in our teachers' commenting styles. These different signals given to students, to edit and develop, to condense and elaborate, represent also the failure of teachers' comments to direct genuine revision of the text as a whole.

Moreover, the comments are worded in such a way that it is difficult for students to know what is the most important problem in the text and what problems are of lesser importance. No scale of concerns is offered to a student, with the result that a comment about spelling or a comment about an awkward sentence is given weight equal to a comment about organization or logic. The comment that seemed to represent this problem best was one teacher's command to his student: "Check your commas and semicolons and think more about what you are thinking about." The language of the comments makes it difficult for a student to sort out and decide what is most important and what is least important.

When the teacher appropriates the text for the student in this way, students are encouraged to see their writing as a series of parts — words, sentences, paragraphs — and not as a whole discourse. The comments encourage students to believe that their first drafts are finished drafts, not invention drafts, and that all they need to do is patch and polish their writing. That is, teachers' comments do not provide their students with an inherent reason for revising the structure and meaning of their texts, since the comments suggest to students that the meaning of their text is already there, finished, produced, and all that is necessary is a better word or phrase. The processes of revising, editing, and proofreading are collapsed and reduced to a single trivial activity, and the students' misunderstanding of the revision process as a rewording activity is reinforced by their teachers' comments.

It is possible, and it quite often happens, that students follow every comment and fix their texts appropriately as requested, but their texts are not improved substantially, or, even worse, their revised drafts are inferior to their previous drafts. Since the teachers' comments take the students' attention away from their own original purposes, students concentrate more, as I have noted, on what the teachers commanded them to do than on what they are trying to say. Sometimes students do not understand the purpose behind their teachers' comments and take these comments very literally. At other times students understand the comments, but the teacher has misread the text and the comments, unfortunately, are not applicable. For instance, we repeatedly saw comments in which teachers commanded students to reduce and condense what was written, when in fact what the text really needed at this stage was to be expanded in conception and scope.

The process of revising always involves a risk. But, too often revision becomes a balancing act for students in which they make the changes that are requested but do not take the risk of changing anything that was not commented on, even if the students sense that other changes are needed. A more effective text does not often evolve from such changes alone, yet the student does not want to take the chance of reducing a finished, albeit inadequate, paragraph to chaos — to fragments — in order to rebuild it, if such changes have not been requested by the teacher.

The second finding from our study is that *most teachers' comments are not text-specific and could be interchanged, rubber-stamped, from text to text*. The comments are not anchored in the particulars of the students' texts, but rather are a series of vague directives that are not text-specific. Students are commanded to "Think more about [their] audience, avoid colloquial language, avoid the passive, avoid prepositions at the end of sentences or conjunctions at the beginning of sentences, be clear, be specific, be precise, but above all, think more about what [they] are thinking about." The comments on the following student paragraph illustrate this problem:

> *Begin by telling your reader
> what you are going to write about.*
>
> In the sixties it was drugs, in the seventies it was rock and roll.
> *avoid "one of the"*
> Now in the eighties, one of the most controversial subjects is
> *elaborate*
> nuclear power. The United States is in great need of its own
> source of power. Because of environmentalists, coal is not an
> *be specific*
> acceptable source of energy. [Solar and wind power have not
> *avoid "it seems"*
> yet received the technology necessary to use them] It seems that
> nuclear power is the only feasible means right now for obtain-
> ing self-sufficient power. However, too large a percentage of the
> population are against nuclear power claiming it is unsafe.
> *be precise*
> With as many problems as the United States is having concern-
> ing energy, it seems a shame that the public is so quick to "can"
> a very feasible means of power. Nuclear energy should not be
> given up on, but rather, more nuclear plants should be built.

Think more about your reader.

Thesis sentence needed.

One could easily remove all the comments from this paragraph and rubber-stamp them on another student text, and they would make as much or as little sense on the second text as they do here.

We have observed an overwhelming similarity in the generalities and abstract commands given to students. There seems to be among teachers an accepted, albeit unwritten canon for commenting on student texts. This uniform code of commands, requests, and pleadings demonstrates that the teacher holds license for vagueness while the student is commanded to be specific. The students we interviewed admitted to having great difficulty with these vague directives. The students stated that when a teacher writes in the margins or as an end comment, "choose precise language," or "think more about your audience," revising becomes a guessing game. In effect, the teacher is saying to the student, "Somewhere in this paper is imprecise language or lack of awareness of an audience and you must find it." The problem presented by these vague commands is compounded for the students when they are not offered any strategies for carrying out these commands. Students are told that they have done something wrong and that there is something in their text that needs to be fixed before the text is acceptable. But to tell students that they have done something wrong is not to tell them what to do about it. In order to offer a useful revision strategy to a student, the teacher must anchor that strategy in the specifics of the student's text. For instance, to tell our student, the author of the above paragraph, "to be specific," or "to elaborate," does not show our student what questions the reader has about the meaning of the text, or what breaks in logic exist, that could be resolved if the writer supplied specific information; nor is the student shown how to achieve the desired specificity.

Instead of offering strategies, the teachers offer what is interpreted by students as rules for composing; the comments suggest to students that writing is just a matter of following the rules. Indeed, the teachers seem to impose a series of abstract rules about written products even when some of them are not appropriate for the specific text the student is creating.[3] For instance, the student author of our sample paragraph presented above is commanded to follow the conventional rules for writing a five-paragraph essay — to begin the introductory paragraph by telling his reader what he is going to say and to end the paragraph with a thesis sentence. Somehow these abstract rules about what five-paragraph products should look like do not seem applicable to the problems this student must confront when revising, nor are the rules specific strategies he could use when revising. There are many inchoate ideas ready to be exploited in this paragraph, but the rules do not help the student to take stock of his (or her) ideas and use the opportunity he has, during revision, to develop those ideas.

The problem here is a confusion of process and product; what one has to say about the process is different from what one has to say about the product. Teachers who use this method of commenting are formulating their comments as if these drafts were finished drafts and were not going to be revised. Their commenting vocabularies have not been adapted to revision and they comment on first drafts as if they were justifying a grade or as if the first draft were the final draft.

Our summary finding, therefore, from this research on styles of commenting is that the news from the classroom is not good. For the most part, teachers do not respond to student writing with the kind of thoughtful commentary which will help students to engage with the issues they are writing about or which will help them think about their purposes and goals in writing a specific text. In defense of our teachers, however, they told us that responding to student writing was rarely stressed in their teacher-training or in writing workshops; they had been trained in various prewriting techniques, in constructing assignments, and in evaluating papers for grades, but rarely in the process of reading a student text for meaning or in offering commentary to motivate revision. The problem is that most of us as teachers of writing have been trained to read and interpret literary texts for meaning, but, unfortunately, we have not been trained to act upon the same set of assumptions in reading student texts as we follow in reading literary texts.[4] Thus, we read student texts with biases about what the writer should have said or about what he or she should have written, and our biases determine how we will comprehend the text. We read with our preconceptions and preoccupations, expecting to find errors, and the result is that we find errors and misread our students' texts.[5] We find what we look for; instead of reading and responding to the meaning of a text, we correct our students' writing. We need to reverse this approach. Instead of finding errors or showing students how to patch up parts of their texts, we need to sabotage our students' conviction that the drafts they have written are complete and coherent. Our comments need to offer students revision tasks of a different order of complexity and sophistication from the ones that they themselves identify, by forcing students back into the chaos, back to the point where they are shaping and restructuring their meaning.[6]

For if the content of a student text is lacking in substance and meaning, if the order of the parts must be rearranged significantly in the next draft, if paragraphs must be restructured for logic and clarity, then many sentences are likely to be changed or deleted anyway. There seems to be no point in having students correct usage errors or condense sentences that are likely to disappear before the next draft is completed. In fact, to identify such problems in a text at this early first-draft stage, when such problems are likely to abound, can give a student a disproportionate sense of their importance at this stage in the writing process.[7] In responding to our students' writing, we should be guided by the recognition that it is not spelling or usage problems that we as writers first worry about when drafting and revising our texts.

We need to develop an appropriate level of response for commenting on a first draft, and to differentiate that from the level suitable to a second or third draft. Our comments need to be suited to the draft we are reading. In a first or second draft, we need to respond as any reader would, registering questions, reflecting befuddlement, and noting places where we are puzzled about the meaning of the text. Comments should point to breaks in logic, disruptions in meaning, or missing information. Our goal in commenting on early drafts should be to engage students with the issues they are considering and help them clarify their purposes and reasons in writing their specific text.

For instance, the major rhetorical problem of the essay written by the student who wrote the first paragraph (the paragraph on nuclear power) quoted above was that the student had two principal arguments running through his text, each of which brought the other into question. On the one hand, he argued that we must use nuclear power, unpleasant as it is, because we have nothing else to use; though nuclear energy is a problematic source of energy, it is the best of a bad lot. On the other hand, he also argued that nuclear energy is really quite safe and therefore should be our primary resource. Comments on this student's first draft need to point out this break in logic and show the student that if we accept his first argument, then his second argument sounds fishy. But if we accept his second argument, his first argument sounds contradictory. The teacher's comments need to engage this student writer with this basic rhetorical and conceptual problem in his first draft rather than impose a series of abstract commands and rules upon his text.

Written comments need to be viewed not as an end in themselves — a way for teachers to satisfy themselves that they have done their jobs — but rather as a means for helping students to become more effective writers. As a means for helping students, they have limitations; they are, in fact, disembodied remarks — one absent writer responding to another absent writer. The key to successful commenting is to have what is said in the comments and what is done in the classroom mutually reinforce and enrich each other. Commenting on papers assists the writing course in achieving its purpose; classroom activities and the comments we write to our students need to be connected. Written comments need to be an extension of the teacher's voice — an extension of the teacher as reader. Exercises in such activities as revising a whole text or individual paragraphs together in class, noting how the sense of the whole dictates the smaller changes, looking at options, evaluating actual choices, and then discussing the effect of these changes on revised drafts — such exercises need to be designed to take students through the cycles of revising and to help them overcome their anxiety about revising: that anxiety we all feel at reducing what looks like a finished draft into fragments and chaos.

The challenge we face as teachers is to develop comments which will provide an inherent reason for students to revise; it is a sense of revision as discovery, as a repeated process of beginning again, as starting out new, that our students have not learned. We need to show our students how to seek, in the possibility of revision, the dissonances of discovery — to show them through our comments why new choices would positively change their texts, and thus to show them the potential for development implicit in their own writing.

Notes

1. C. H. Knoblauch and Lil Brannon, "Teacher Commentary on Student Writing: The State of the Art," *Freshman English News* 10 (Fall 1981): 1–3.
2. For an extended discussion of revision strategies of student writers see Nancy Sommers, "Revision Strategies of Student Writers and Experienced Adult Writers," *College Composition and Communication* 31 (Dec. 1980): 378–88.
3. Nancy Sommers and Ronald Schleifer, "Means and Ends: Some Assumptions of Student Writers," *Composition and Teaching* 2 (Dec. 1980): 69–76.
4. Janet Emig and Robert P. Parker, Jr., "Responding to Student Writing: Building a Theory of the Evaluating Process," paper, Rutgers University.
5. For an extended discussion of this problem see Joseph Williams, "The Phenomenology of Error," *College Composition and Communication* 32 (May 1981): 152–68.
6. Ann Berthoff, *The Making of Meaning* (Upper Montclair: Boynton, 1981).
7. W. U. McDonald, "The Revising Process and the Marking of Student Papers," *College Composition and Communication* 24 (May 1978): 167–70.

Sommers's Insights as a Resource for Your Teaching

1. Examine your comments on several pieces of student writing. Analyze your commenting style on both early drafts and final papers. Do your comments clarify the papers' most important problems? Are your responses text-specific — that is, "anchored in the particulars of the students' texts" — or could they easily be "rubber-stamped" on any number of student essays? With Sommers's findings in mind, consider ways your comments might better help students engage in meaningful revision.

2. Ask a colleague teaching the same course to work with you on some early student drafts. Trade a set of drafts. Write your comments about revision on a separate sheet of paper; exchange and compare your comments, paying particular attention to the specificity of each comment and to precision of language. You'll both profit from the discussion and may find your reading of the text enhanced by this "external assessor."

   You might also use this technique when you evaluate final drafts. The ensuing conversation about your evaluative comments and criteria for evaluation will certainly give you both perspective on and confidence about your process of evaluating and grading.

Sommers's Insights as a Resource for Your Writing Classroom

1. Conduct an in-class session analyzing students' evaluative comments. After students have completed a shared writing task, ask them to respond using a peer editing checklist from the class text or one that you've constructed with the class. Ask students to write sentence-length, specific comments about issues of meaning and about attention to audience concerns. As a class, discuss specific comments, evaluating how well they do or do not promote substantive revision.

2. Ask class members to identify commentary that has assisted them in deep revision when they write a self-assessment to accompany a submitted draft. Ask questions like "What advice did your peer readers give?" and "What did you do with the advice?"

Ranking, Evaluating, and Liking: Sorting Out Three Forms of Judgment

Peter Elbow

By distinguishing among the activities involved in grading student work, we cannot only do a better job of grading but can also keep grading from getting in the way of teaching and learning. In this article from a 1993 issue of College English, *Peter Elbow argues for the inadequacy of ranking, or "summing up one's judgment of a performance or person into a single, holistic number or score." In contrast, evaluating involves thoughtfully commenting on the strengths and weaknesses of different parts or dimensions of a work. He suggests shifting the emphasis from ranking to evaluating, making assessments of writing more informative and reliable. However, even evaluation, in large quantities, can hinder learning, so Elbow proposes that we consider how to create "evaluation free zones" in our classrooms, encouraging students to take risks and learn in ways that they otherwise might not. Finally, Elbow looks to redeem the undervalued reaction of "liking" student writing. By paying attention to what we like, we can connect with student work and discover its richest potential for growth.*

This essay is my attempt to sort out different acts we call assessment — some different ways in which we express or frame our judgments of value. I have been working on this tangle not just because it is interesting and important in itself but because assessment tends so much to drive and control *teaching*. Much of what we do in the classroom is determined by the assessment structures we work under.

Assessment is a large and technical area and I'm not a professional. But my main premise or subtext in this essay is that we nonprofessionals can and should work on it because professionals have not reached definitive conclusions about the problem of how to assess writing (or anything else, I'd say). Also, decisions about assessment are often made by people even less professional than we, namely legislators. Pat Belanoff and I realized that the field of assessment was open when we saw the harmful effects of a writing proficiency exam at Stony Brook and worked out a collaborative portfolio assessment system in its place (Belanoff and Elbow; Elbow and Belanoff). Professionals keep changing their minds about large-scale testing and assessment. And as for classroom grading, psychometricians provide little support or defense of it.

The Problems with Ranking and the Benefits of Evaluating

By ranking I mean the act of summing up one's judgment of a performance or person into a single, holistic number or score. We rank every time we give a grade or holistic score. Ranking implies a single scale or continuum or dimension along which all performances are hung.

By evaluating I mean the act of expressing one's judgment of a performance or person by pointing out the strengths and weaknesses of different features or dimensions. We evaluate every time we write a comment on a paper or have a conversation about its value. Evaluation implies the recognition of different criteria or dimensions — and by implication different contexts and audiences for the same performance. Evaluation requires going *beyond* a first response that may be nothing but a kind of ranking ("I like it" or "This is better than that"), and instead looking carefully enough at the performance or person to make distinctions between parts or features or criteria.

It's obvious, thus, that I am troubled by ranking. But I will resist any temptation to argue that we can get rid of all ranking — or even should. Instead I will try to show how we can have *less* ranking and *more* evaluation in its place.

I see three distinct problems with ranking; it is inaccurate or unreliable; it gives no substantive feedback; and it is harmful to the atmosphere for teaching and learning.

(1) First the unreliability. To rank reliably means to give a *fair* number, to find the single quantitative score that readers will agree on. But readers don't agree.

This is not news — this unavailability of agreement. We have long seen it on many fronts. For example, research in evaluation has shown many times that if we give a paper to a set of readers, those readers tend to give it the full range of grades (Diederich). I've recently come across new research to this effect — new to me because it was published in 1912. The investigators carefully showed how high school English teachers gave different grades to the same paper. In response to criticism that this was a local problem in English, they went on the next year to discover an even greater variation among grades given by high school geometry teachers and history teachers to papers in their subjects. (See the summary of Daniel Starch and Edward Elliott's 1913 *School Review* articles in Kirschenbaum, Simon, and Napier 258–59.)

We know the same thing from literary criticism and theory. If the best critics can't agree about what a text means, how can we be surprised that they disagree even more about the quality or value of texts? And we know that nothing in literary or philosophical theory gives us any agreed-upon rules for settling such disputes.

Students have shown us the same inconsistency with their own controlled experiments of handing the same paper to different teachers and getting different grades. This helps explain why we hate it so when students ask us their favorite question, "What do you want for an A?": it rubs our noses in the unreliability of our grades.

Of course champions of holistic scoring argue that they get *can* get agreement among readers — and they often do (White). But they get that agreement by "training" the readers before and during the scoring sessions. What "training" means is getting those scorers to stop reading the way they normally read — getting them to stop using the conflicting criteria and standards they normally use outside the scoring sessions. (In an impressive and powerful book, Barbara Herrnstein Smith argues that whenever we have widespread inter-reader reliability, we have reason to suspect that difference has been suppressed and homogeneity imposed — almost always at the expense of certain groups.) In short, the reliability in holistic scoring is not a measure of how texts are valued by real readers in natural settings, but only of how they are valued in artificial settings with imposed agreements.

Defenders of holistic scoring might reply (as one anonymous reviewer did), that holistic scores are not perfect or absolutely objective readings but just "judgments that most readers will agree are the appropriate ones given the purpose of the assessment and the system of communication." But I have been in and even conducted enough holistic scoring sessions to know that even that degree of agreement doesn't occur unless "purpose" and "appropriateness" are defined to mean acceptance of the single set of standards imposed on that session. We know too much about the differences among readers and the highly variable nature of the reading process. Supposing we get readings only from academics, or only from people in English, or only from respected critics, or only from respected writing programs, or only from feminists, or only from sound readers of my tribe (white, male, middle-class, full professors between the ages of fifty and sixty). We *still* don't get agreement. We can sometimes get agreement among readers from some subset, a particular community that has developed a strong set of common values, perhaps *one* English department or *one* writing program. But what is the value of such a rare agreement? It tells us nothing about how readers from other English departments or writing programs will judge — much less how readers from other domains will judge.

(From the opposite ideological direction, some skeptics might object to my skeptical train of thought: "So what else is new?" they might reply. "Of *course* my grades are biased, 'interested' or 'situated' — always partial to my interests or the values of my community or culture. There's no other possibility." But how can people consent to give grades if they feel that way? A single teacher's grade for a student is liable to have substantial consequences — for example on eligibility for a scholarship or a job or entrance into professional school. In grading, surely we must not take anything less than genuine fairness as our goal.)

It won't be long before we see these issues argued in a court of law, when a student who has been disqualified from playing on a team or rejected from a professional school sues, charging that the basis for his plight — teacher grades — is not reliable. I wonder if lawyers will be able to make our grades stick.

(2) Ranking or grading is woefully uncommunicative. Grades and holistic scores are nothing but points on a continuum from "yea" to "boo" — with no information or clues about the criteria behind these noises. They are 100 percent evaluation and 0 percent description or information. They quantify the degree of approval or disapproval in readers but tell nothing at all about what the readers actually approve or disapprove of. They say nothing that couldn't be said with gold stars or black marks or smiley-faces. Of course our first reactions are often nothing but global holistic feelings of approval or disapproval, but we need a system for communicating our judgments that nudges us to move beyond these holistic feelings and to articulate the basis of our feeling — a process that often leads us to change our feeling. (Holistic scoring sessions sometimes use rubrics that explain the criteria — though these are rarely passed along to students — and even in these situations, the rubrics fail to fit many papers.) As C. S. Lewis says, "People are obviously far more anxious to express their approval and disapproval of things than to describe them" (7).

(3) Ranking leads students to get so hung up on these oversimple quantitative verdicts that they care more about scores than about learning — more about the grade we put on the paper than about the comment we have written on it. Have you noticed how grading often forces us to write comments to justify our grades? — and how these are often *not* the comment we would make if we were just trying to help the student write better? ("Just try writing several favorable comments on a paper and then giving it a grade of D" [Diederich 21].)

Grades and holistic scores give too much encouragement to those students who score high — making them too apt to think they are already fine — and too little encouragement to those students who do badly. Unsuccessful students often come to doubt their intelligence. But oddly enough, many "A" students also end up doubting their true ability and feeling like frauds — because they have sold out on their own judgment and simply given teachers whatever yields an A. They have too often been rewarded for what they don't really believe in. (Notice that there's more cheating by students who get high grades than by those who get low ones. There would be less incentive to cheat if there were no ranking.)

We might be tempted to put up with the inaccuracy or unfairness of grades if they gave good diagnostic feedback or helped the learning climate; or we might put up with the damage they do to the learning climate if they gave a fair or reliable measure of how skilled or knowledgeable students are. But since they fail dismally on both counts, we are faced with the striking question of why grading has persisted so long.

There must be many reasons. It is obviously easier and quicker to express a global feeling with a single number than to figure out what the strengths and weaknesses are and what one's criteria are. (Though I'm heartened to discover, as I pursue this issue, how troubled teachers are by grading and how difficult they find it.) But perhaps more important, we see around us a deep *hunger to rank* — to create pecking orders: to see who we can look down on and who we must look up to, or in the military metaphor, who we can kick and who we must salute. Psychologists tell us that this taste for pecking orders or ranking is associated with the authoritarian personality. We see this hunger graphically in the case of IQ scores. It is plain that IQ scoring does not represent a commitment to looking carefully at people's intelligence; when we do that, we see different and frequently uncorrelated *kinds* or *dimensions* of intelligence (Gardner). The persistent use of IQ scores represents the hunger to have a number so that everyone can have a rank. ("Ten!" mutter the guys when they see a pretty woman.)

Because ranking or grading has caused so much discomfort to so many students and teachers, I think we see a lot of confusion about the process. It is hard to think clearly about something that has given so many of us such anxiety and distress. The most notable confusion I notice is the tendency to think that if we renounce ranking or grading, we are renouncing the very possibility of judgment and discrimination — that we are embracing the idea that there is no way to distinguish or talk about the difference between what works well and what works badly.

So the most important point, then, is that *I am not arguing against judgment or evaluation.* I'm just arguing against that crude, oversimple way of *representing* judgment — distorting it, really — into a single number, which means ranking people and performances along a single continuum.

In fact I am arguing *for evaluation.* Evaluation means looking hard and thoughtfully at a piece of writing in order to make distinctions as to the quality of different features or dimensions. For example, the process of evaluation permits us to make the following kinds of statements about a piece of writing:

- The thinking and ideas seem interesting and creative.
- The overall structure or sequence seems confusing.

- The writing is perfectly clear at the level of individual sentences and even paragraphs.

- There is an odd, angry tone of voice that seems unrelated or inappropriate to what the writer is saying.

- Yet this same voice is strong and memorable and makes one listen even if one is irritated.

- There are a fair number of mistakes in grammar or spelling: more than "a sprinkling" but less than "riddled with."

To rank, on the other hand, is to be forced to translate those discriminations into a single number. What grade or holistic score do these judgments add up to? It's likely, by the way, that more readers would agree with those separate, "analytic" statements than would agree on a holistic score.

I've conducted many assessment sessions where we were not trying to impose a set of standards but rather to find out how experienced teachers read and evaluate, and I've had many opportunities to see that good readers give grades or scores right down through the range of possibilities. Of course good readers sometimes agree — especially on papers that are strikingly good or bad or conventional, but I think I see difference more frequently than agreement when readers really speak up.

The process of evaluation, because it invites us to articulate our criteria and to make distinctions among parts or features or dimensions of a performance, thereby invites us further to acknowledge the main fact about evaluation: that different readers have different priorities, values, and standards.

The conclusion I am drawing, then, in this first train of thought is that we should do less ranking and more evaluation. Instead of using grades or holistic scores — single number verdicts that try to sum up complex performances along only one scale — we should give some kind of written or spoken evaluation that discriminates among criteria and dimensions of the writing — and if possible that takes account of the complex context for writing: who the writer is, what the writer's audience and goals are, who we are as readers and how we read, and how we might differ in our reading from other readers the writer might be addressing.

But how can we put this principle into practice? The pressure for ranking seems implacable. Evaluation takes more time, effort, and money. It seems as though we couldn't get along without scores on writing exams. Most teachers are obliged to give grades at the end of each course. And many students — given that they have become conditioned or even addicted to ranking over the years and must continue to inhabit a ranking culture in most of their courses — will object if we don't put grades on papers. Some students, in the absence of the crude gold star or black mark, may not try hard enough (though how hard is "enough" — and is it really our job to stimulate motivation artificially with grades — and is grading the best source of motivation?).

It is important to note that there are certain schools and colleges that do *not* use single-number grades or scores, and they function successfully. I taught for nine years at Evergreen State College, which uses only written evaluations. This system works fine, even down to getting students accepted into high quality graduate and professional schools.

Nevertheless we have an intractable dilemma: that grading is unfair and counterproductive but that students and institutions tend to want grades. In the face of this dilemma there is a need for creativity and pragmatism. Here are some ways in which I and others use *less ranking* and *more evaluation* in teaching — and they suggest some adjustments in how we score large-scale assessments. What follows is an assortment of experimental compromises — sometimes crude, seldom ideal or utopian — but they help.

(a) Portfolios. Just because conventional institutions oblige us to turn in a single quantitative course grade at the end of every marking period, it doesn't follow that we need to grade individual papers. Course grades are more trustworthy and less damaging because they are based on so many performances over so many weeks. By avoiding frequent ranking or grading, we make it *somewhat* less likely for students to become addicted to oversimple numerical rankings — to think that evaluation always translates into a simple number — in short, to mistake ranking for evaluation. (I'm not trying to defend conventional course grades since they are still uncommunicative and they still feed the hunger for ranking.) Portfolios permit me to refrain from grading individual papers and limit myself to writerly evaluative comments — and help students see this as a positive rather than a negative thing, a chance to be graded on a body of their best work that can be judged more fairly. Portfolios have many other advantages as well. They are particularly valuable as occasions for asking students to write extensive and thoughtful explorations of their own strengths and weaknesses.

A midsemester portfolio is usually an informal affair, but it is a good occasion for giving anxious students a ballpark estimate of how well they are doing in the course so far. I find it helpful to tell students that I'm perfectly willing to tell them my best estimate of their course grade — but only if they come to me in conference and only during the second half of the semester. This serves somewhat to quiet their anxiety while they go through seven weeks of drying out from grades. By midsemester, most of them have come to enjoy not getting those numbers and thus being able to think better about more writerly comments from me and their classmates.

Portfolios are now used extensively and productively in larger assessments, and there is constant experimentation with new applications (Belanoff and Dickson; *Portfolio Assessment Newsletter*; *Portfolio News*).

(b) Another useful option is to make a strategic retreat from a wholly negative position. That is, I sometimes do a *bit* of ranking even on individual papers, using two "bottom-line" grades: H and U for "Honors" and "Unsatisfactory." I tell students that these translate to about A or A- and D or F. This practice may seem theoretically inconsistent with all the arguments I've just made, but (at the moment, anyway) I justify it for the following reasons.

First, I sympathize with a *part* of the students' anxiety about not getting grades: their fear that they might be failing and not know about it — or doing an excellent job and not get any recognition. Second, I'm not giving *many* grades; only a small proportion of papers get these H's or U's. The system creates a "non-bottom-line" or "non-quantified" atmosphere. Third, these holistic judgments about best and worst do not seem as arbitrary and questionable as most grades. There is usually a *bit* more agreement among readers about the best and worst papers. What seems most dubious is the process of trying to rank that whole middle range of papers — papers that have a mixture of better and worse qualities so that the numerical grade depends enormously on a reader's priorities or mood or temperament. My willingness to give these few grades goes a long way toward helping my students forgo most bottom-line grading.

I'm not trying to pretend that these minimal "grades" are truly reliable. But they represent a very small amount of ranking. Yes, someone could insist that I'm really ranking every single paper (and indeed if it seemed politically necessary, I could put an OK or S [for satisfactory] on all those middle range papers and brag, "Yes, I grade everything"). But the fact is that I am doing *much less sorting* since I don't have to sort them into five or even twelve piles. Thus there is a huge reduction in the total amount of unreliability I produce.

(It might seem that if I use only these few minimal grades I have no good way for figuring out a final grade for the course — since that requires a more fine-grained set of ranks. But I don't find that to be the case. For I also give these same minimal grades to the many other important parts of my course such as attendance, meeting deadlines, peer responding, and journal writing. If I want a mathematically computed grade on a scale of six or A through E, I can easily compute it when I have such a large number of grades to work from — even though they are only along a three-point scale.)

This same practice of crude or minimal ranking is a big help on larger assessments outside classrooms, and needs to be applied to the process of assessment in general. There are two important principles to emphasize. On the one hand we must be prudent or accommodating enough to admit that despite all the arguments against ranking, there *are* situations when we need that bottom-line verdict along one scale: which student has not done satisfactory work and should be denied credit for the course? which student gets the scholarship? which candidate to hire or fire? We often operate with scarce resources. But on the other hand we must be bold enough to insist that we do far more ranking than is really needed. We can get along not only with fewer occasions for assessment but also with fewer gradations in scoring. If we decide what the *real* bottom-line is on a given occasion — perhaps just "failing" or perhaps "honors" too — then the reading of papers or portfolios is enormously quick and cheap. It leaves time and money for evaluation — perhaps for analytic scoring or some comment.

At Stony Brook we worked out a portfolio system where multiple readers had only to make a binary decision: acceptable or not. Then individual teachers could decide the actual course grade and give comments for their own students — so long as those students passed in the eyes of an independent rater (Elbow and Belanoff; Belanoff and Elbow). The best way to begin to wean our society from its addiction to ranking may be to permit a tiny bit of it (which also means less unreliability) — rather than trying to go "cold turkey."

(c) Sometimes I use an analytic grid for evaluating and commenting on student papers. An example is given in Figure 1. I often vary the criteria in my grid (e.g. "connecting with readers" or "investment") depending on the assignment or the point in the semester.

Grids are a way I can satisfy the students' hunger for ranking but still not give in to conventional grades on individual papers. Sometimes I provide nothing but a grid (especially on final drafts), and this is a very quick way to provide a response. Or on midprocess drafts I sometimes use a grid in addition to a comment: a more readerly comment that often doesn't so much tell them what's wrong or right or how to improve things but rather tries to give them an account of what is *happening to me* as I read their words. I think this kind of comment is really the most useful thing of all for students, but it frustrates some students for a while. The grid can help these students feel less anxious and thus pay better attention to my comment.

I find grids extremely helpful at the end of the semester for telling students their strengths and weaknesses in the course — or what they've done well and not so well. Besides categories like the ones above, I use categories like these: "skill in giving feedback to others," "ability to meet deadlines," "effort," and "improvement." This practice makes my final grade much more communicative.

(d) I also help make up for the absence of ranking — gold stars and black marks — by having students share their writing with each other

Strong	OK	Weak	
			CONTENT, INSIGHTS, THINKING, GRAPPLING WITH TOPIC
			GENUINE REVISION, SUBSTANTIVE CHANGES, NOT JUST EDITING
			ORGANIZATION, STRUCTURE, GUIDING THE READER
			LANGUAGE: SYNTAX, SENTENCES, WORDING, VOICE
			MECHANICS: SPELLING, GRAMMAR, PUNCTUATION, PROOFREADING
			OVERALL [Note: this is not a sum of the other scores.]

Figure 1.

a great deal both orally and through frequent publication in class magazines. Also, where possible, I try to get students to give or send writing to audiences outside the class. At the University of Massachusetts at Amherst, freshmen pay a ten dollar lab fee for the writing course, and every teacher publishes four or five class magazines of final drafts a semester. The effects are striking. Sharing, peer feedback, and publication give the best reward and motivation for writing, namely, getting your words out to many readers.

(e) I sometimes use a kind of modified *contract grading*. That is, at the start of the course I pass out a long list of all the things that I most want students to do — the concrete activities that I think most lead to learning — and I promise students that if they do them *all* they are guaranteed a certain final grade. Currently, I say it's a B — it could be lower or higher. My list includes these items: not missing more than a week's worth of classes; not having more than one late major assignment; *substantive* revising on all major revisions; good copy editing on all final revisions; good effort on peer feedback work; keeping up the journal; and substantial effort and investment on each draft.

I like the way this system changes the "bottom-line" for a course: the intersection where my authority crosses their self-interest. I can tell them, "You have to work very hard in this course, but you can stop worrying about grades." The crux is no longer that commodity I've always hated and never trusted: a numerical ranking of the quality of their writing along a single continuum. Instead the crux becomes what I care about most: the *concrete behaviors* that I most want students to engage in because they produce more learning and help me teach better. Admittedly, effort and investment are not concrete observable behaviors, but they are no harder to judge than overall quality of writing. And since I care about effort and investment, I don't mind the few arguments I get into about them; they seem fruitful. ("Let's try and figure out why it looked to me as though you didn't put any effort in here.") In contrast, I hate discussions about grades on a paper and find such arguments fruitless. Besides, I'm not making fine distinctions about effort and investment — just letting a bell go off when they fall palpably low.

It's crucial to note that I am *not* fighting evaluation with this system. I am just fighting ranking or grading. I still write evaluative comments and often use an evaluative grid to tell my students what I see as strengths and weaknesses in their papers. My goal is not to get rid of evaluation but in fact to emphasize it, enhance it. I'm trying to get students to listen *better* to my evaluations — by uncoupling them from a grade. In effect, I'm doing this because I'm so fed up with students *following* or *obeying* my evaluations too blindly — making whatever changes my comments suggest but doing it for the sake of a grade; not really taking the time to make up their own minds about whether they think my judgments or suggestions really make sense to them. The worst part of grades is that they make students obey us without carefully thinking about the merits of what we say. I love the situation this system so often puts students in: I make a criticism or suggestion about their paper, but it doesn't matter to their grade whether they go along with me or not (so long as they genuinely revise in some fashion). They have to think; to decide.

Admittedly this system is crude and impure. Some of the really skilled students who are used to getting A's and desperate to get one in this course remain unhelpfully hung up about getting those H's on their papers. But a good number of these students discover that they can't get them, and they soon settle down to accepting a B and having less anxiety and more of a learning voyage.

The Limitations of Evaluation and the Benefits of Evaluation-free Zones

Everything I've said so far has been in praise of evaluation as a substitute for ranking. But I need to turn a corner here and speak about the *limits* or *problems* of evaluation. Evaluating may be better than ranking, but it still carries some of the same problems. That is, even though I've praised evaluation for inviting us to acknowledge that readers and contexts are different, nevertheless the very word *evaluation* tends to imply fairness or reliability or getting beyond personal or subjective preferences. Also, of course, evaluation takes a lot more time and work. To rank you just have to put down a number; holistic scoring of exams is cheaper than analytic scoring.

Most important of all, evaluation harms the climate for learning and teaching — or rather *too much* evaluation has this effect. That is, if we evaluate *everything* students write, they tend to remain tangled up in the assumption that their whole job in school is to give teachers "what they want." Constant evaluation makes students worry more about psyching out the teacher than about what they are really learning. Students fall into a kind of defensive or on-guard stance toward the teacher: a desire to hide what they don't understand and try to impress. This stance gets in the way of learning. (Think of the patient trying to hide symptoms from the doctor.) Most of all, constant evaluation by someone in authority makes students reluctant to take the risks that are needed for good learning — to try out hunches and trust their own judgment. Face it: if our goal is to get students to exercise their own judgment, that means exercising an immature and undeveloped judgment and making choices that are obviously wrong to us.

We see around us a widespread hunger to be evaluated that is often just as strong as the hunger to rank. Countless conditions make many of us walk around in the world wanting to ask others (especially those in authority), "How am I doing, did I do OK?" I don't think the hunger to be evaluated is as harmful as the hunger to rank, but it can get in the way of learning. For I find that the greatest and most powerful breakthroughs in learning occur when I can get myself and others to *put aside* this nagging, self-doubting question ("How am I doing? How am I doing?") — and instead to take some chances, trust our instincts or hungers. When everything is evaluated, everything counts. Often the most powerful arena for deep learning is a kind of "time out" zone from the pressures of normal evaluated reality: make-believe, play, dreams — in effect, the Shakespearian forest.

In my attempts to get away from too much evaluation (not from all evaluation, just from too much of it), I have drifted into a set of teaching practices which now feel to me like the *best* part of my teaching. I realize now what I've been unconsciously doing for a number of years: creating "evaluation-free zones."

(a) The paradigm evaluation-free zone is the ten minute, nonstop freewrite. When I get students to freewrite, I am using my authority to create unusual conditions in order to contradict or interrupt our pervasive habit of always evaluating our writing. What is essential here are the two central features of freewriting: that it be private (thus I don't collect it or have students share it with anyone else); and that it be nonstop (thus there isn't time for planning, and control is usually diminished). Students quickly catch on and enter into the spirit. At the end of the course, they often tell me that freewriting is the most useful thing I've taught them (see Belanoff, Elbow, and Fontaine).

(b) A larger evaluation-free zone is the single unevaluated assignment — what people sometimes call the "quickwrite" or sketch. This is a piece of writing that I ask students to do — either in class or for homework — without any or much revising. It is meant to be low stakes writing. There is a bit of pressure, nevertheless, since I usually ask them to share it with others and *I* usually collect it and read it. But I don't write any comments at all — except perhaps to put straight lines along some passages I like or to write a phrase of appreciation at the end. And I ask students to refrain from giving evaluative feedback to each other — and instead just to say "thank you" or mention a couple of phrases or ideas that stick in mind. (However, this writing-without-feedback can be a good occasion for students to discuss the *topic* they have written about — and thus serve as an excellent kick-off for discussions of what I am teaching.)

(c) These experiments have led me to my next and largest evaluation-free zone — what I sometimes call a "jump start" for my whole course. For the last few semesters I've been devoting the first three weeks *entirely* to the two evaluation-free activities I've just described: freewriting (and also more leisurely private writing in a journal) and quickwrites or sketches. Since the stakes are low and I'm not asking for much revising, I ask for *much more* writing homework per week than usual. And every day we write in class: various exercises or games. The emphasis is on getting rolling, getting fluent, taking risks. And every day all students read out loud something they've written — sometimes a short passage even to the whole class. So despite the absence of feedback, it is a very audience-filled and sociable three weeks.

At first I only dared do this for two weeks, but when I discovered how fast the writing improves, how good it is for building community, and what a pleasure this period is for me, I went to three weeks. I'm curious to try an experiment with teaching a whole course this way. I wonder, that is, whether all that evaluation we work so hard to give really does any more good than the constant writing and sharing (Zak).

I need to pause here to address an obvious rejoinder: "But withholding evaluation is not normal!" Indeed, it is *not* normal — certainly not normal in school. We normally tend to emphasize evaluations — even bottom-line ranking kinds of evaluations. But I resist the argument that if it's not normal we shouldn't do it.

The best argument for evaluation-free zones is from experience. If you try them, I suspect you'll discover that they are satisfying and bring out good writing. Students have a better time writing these unevaluated pieces; they enjoy hearing and appreciating these pieces when they don't have to evaluate. And *I* have a much better time when I engage in this astonishing activity: reading student work when I don't have to evaluate and respond. And yet the writing improves. I see students investing and risking more, writing more fluently, and using livelier, more interesting voices. This writing gives me and them a higher standard of clarity and voice for when we move on to more careful and revised writing tasks that involve more intellectual pushing — tasks that sometimes make their writing go tangled or sodden.

The Benefits and Feasibility of Liking

Liking and disliking seem like unpromising topics in an exploration of assessment. They seem to represent the worst kind of subjectivity, the merest accident of personal taste. But I've recently come to think that the phenomenon of liking is perhaps the most important evaluative response for writers and teachers to think about. In effect, I'm turning another corner in my argument. In the first section I argued against ranking — with evaluating being the solution. Next I argued not *against* evaluating — but for no-evaluation zones in *addition* to evaluating. Now I will argue neither against evaluating nor against no-evaluation zones, but for something very different in addition, or perhaps underneath, as a foundation: liking.

Let me start with the germ story. I was in a workshop and we were going around the circle with everyone telling a piece of good news about their writing in the last six months. It got to Wendy Bishop, a good poet (who has also written two good books about the teaching of writing), and she said, "In the last six months, I've learned to *like* everything I write." Our jaws dropped; we were startled — in a way scandalized. But I've been chewing on her words ever since, and they have led me into a retelling of the story of how people learn to write better.

The old story goes like this: We write something. We read it over and we say, "This is terrible. I *hate* it. I've got to work on it and improve it." And we do, and it gets better, and this happens again and again, and before long we have become a wonderful writer. But that's not really what happens. Yes, we vow to work on it — but we don't. And next time we have the impulse to write, we're just a *bit* less likely to start.

What really happens when people learn to write better is more like this: We write something. We read it over and we say, "This is terrible. . . . But I *like* it. Damn it, I'm going to get it good enough so that others will like it too." And this time we don't just put it in a drawer, we actually work hard on it. And we try it out on other people too — not just to get feedback and advice but, perhaps more important, to find someone else who will like it.

Notice the two stories here — two hypotheses. (a) "First you improve the faults and then you like it." (b) "First you like it and then you improve faults." The second story may sound odd when stated so baldly, but really it's common sense. Only if we like something will we get involved enough to work and struggle with it. Only if we like what we write will we write again and again by choice — which is the only way we get better.

This hypothesis sheds light on the process of how people get to be published writers. Conventional wisdom assumes a Darwinian model: poor writers are unread; then they get better; as a result, they get a wider audience; finally they turn into Norman Mailer. But now I'd say the process is more complicated. People who get better and get published really tend to be driven by how much *they* care about their writing. Yes, they have a small audience at first — after all, they're not very good. But they try reader after reader until finally they can find people who like and appreciate their writing. I certainly did this. If someone doesn't like her writing enough to be pushy and hungry about finding a few people who also like it, she probably won't get better.

It may sound so far as though all the effort and drive comes from the lonely driven writer — and sometimes it does (Norman Mailer is no joke). But, often enough, readers play the crucially active role in this story of how writers get better. That is, the way writers *learn* to like their writing is by the grace of having a reader or two who likes it — even though it's not good. Having at least a few appreciative readers is probably indispensable to getting better.

When I apply this story to our situation as teachers I come up with this interesting hypothesis: *good writing teachers like student writing* (and like students). I think I see this borne out — and it is really nothing but common sense. Teachers who hate student writing and hate students are grouchy all the time. How could we stand our work and do a decent job if we hated their writing? Good teachers see what is only *potentially* good, they get a kick out of mere possibility — and they encourage it. When I manage to do this, I teach well.

Thus, I've begun to notice a turning point in my courses — two or three weeks into the semester: "Am I going to like these folks or is this going to be a battle, a struggle?" When I like them everything seems to go better — and it seems to me they learn more by the end. When I don't and we stay tangled up in struggle, we all suffer — and they seem to learn less.

So what am I saying? That we should like bad writing? How can we see all the weaknesses and criticize student writing if we just like it?

But here's the interesting point: if I *like* someone's writing it's *easier* to criticize it.

I first noticed this when I was trying to gather essays for the book on freewriting that Pat Belanoff and Sheryl Fontaine and I edited. I would read an essay someone had written, I would want it for the book, but I had some serious criticism. I'd get excited and write, "I really like this, and I hope we can use it in our book, but you've got to get rid of this and change that, and I got really mad at this other thing." I usually find it hard to criticize, but I began to notice that I was a much more critical and pushy reader when I liked something. It's even fun to criticize in those conditions.

It's the same with student writing. If I like a piece, I don't have to pussyfoot around with my criticism. It's when I don't like their writing that I find myself tiptoeing: trying to soften my criticism, trying to find something nice to say — and usually sounding fake, often unclear. I see the same thing with my own writing. If I like it, I can criticize it better. I have faith that there'll still be something good left, even if I train my full critical guns on it.

In short — and to highlight how this section relates to the other two sections of this essay — liking is not the same as ranking or evaluating. Naturally, people get them mixed up: when they like something, they assume it's good; when they hate it, they assume it's bad. But it's helpful to uncouple the two domains and realize that it makes perfectly good sense to say, "This is terrible, but I like it." Or, "This is good, but I hate it." In short, I am not arguing here *against* criticizing or evaluating. I'm merely arguing *for* liking.

Let me sum up my clump of hypotheses so far:

- It's not improvement that leads to liking, but rather liking that leads to improvement.

- It's the mark of good writers to like their writing.

- Liking is not the same as evaluating. We can often criticize something better when we like it.

- We learn to like our writing when we have a respected reader who likes it.

- Therefore, it's the mark of good teachers to like students and their writing.

If this set of hypotheses is true, what practical consequences follow from it? How can we be better at liking? It feels as though we have no choice — as though liking and not-liking just happen to us. I don't really understand this business. I'd love to hear discussion about the mystery of liking — the phenomenology of liking. I sense it's some kind of putting oneself out — or holding oneself open — but I can't see it clearly. I have a hunch, however, that we're not so helpless about liking as we tend to feel.

For in fact I can suggest some practical concrete activities that I have found fairly reliable at increasing the chances of liking student writing:

(a) I ask for lots of private writing and merely shared writing, that is, writing that I don't read at all, and writing that I read but don't comment on. This makes me more cheerful because it's so much easier. Students get *better* without me. Having to evaluate writing — especially bad writing — makes me more likely to hate it. This throws light on grading: it's hard to like something if we know we have to give it a D.

(b) I have students share lots of writing with each other — and after a while respond to each other. It's easier to like their writing when I don't feel myself as the only reader and judge. And so it helps to build community in general: it takes pressure off me. Thus I try to use peer groups not only for feedback, but for other activities too, such as collaborative writing, brainstorming, putting class magazines together, and working out other decisions.

(c) I increase the chances of my liking their writing when I get better at finding what *is* good — or *potentially* good — and learn to praise it. This is a skill. It requires a good eye, a good nose. We tend — especially in the academic world — to assume that a good eye or fine discrimination means *criticizing*. Academics are sometimes proud of their tendency to be bothered by what is bad. Thus I find I am sometimes looked down on as dumb and undiscriminating: "He likes bad writing. He must have no taste, no discrimination." But I've finally become angry rather than defensive. It's an act of discrimination to see what's good in bad writing. Maybe, in fact, this is the secret of the mystery of liking: to be able to see potential goodness underneath badness.

Put it this way. We tend to stereotype liking as a "soft" and sentimental activity. Mr. Rogers is our model. Fine. There's nothing wrong with softness and sentiment — and I love Mr. Rogers. But liking can also be hard-assed. Let me suggest an alternative to Mr. Rogers: B. F. Skinner. Skinner taught pigeons to play ping-pong. How did he do it? Not by moaning, "Pigeon standards are falling. The pigeons they send us these days are no good. When I was a pigeon . . ." He did it by a careful, disciplined method that involved close analytic observation. He put pigeons on a ping-pong table with a ball, and every time a pigeon turned his head 30 degrees toward the ball, he gave a reward (see my "Danger of Softness").

What would this approach require in the teaching of writing? It's very simple . . . but not easy. Imagine that we want to teach students an ability they badly lack, for example how to organize their writing or how to make their sentences clearer. Skinner's insight is that we get nowhere in this task by just telling them how much they lack this skill: "It's disorganized. Organize it!" "It's unclear. Make it clear!"

No, what we must learn to do is to read closely and carefully enough to show the student little bits of *proto*-organization or *sort of* clarity in what they've already written. We don't have to pretend the writing is wonderful. We could even say, "This is a terrible paper and the worst part about it is the lack of organization. But I will teach you how to organize it. Look here at this little organizational move you made in this sentence. Read it out loud and try to feel how it pulls together this stuff here and distinguishes it from that stuff there. Try to remember what it felt like writing that sentence — creating that piece of organization. Do it some more." Notice how much more helpful it is if we can say, "Do *more* of what you've done here," than if we say, "Do something *different* from anything you've done in the whole paper."

When academics criticize behaviorism as crude it often means that they aren't willing to do the close careful reading of student writing that is required. They'd rather give a cursory reading and turn up their nose and give a low grade and complain about falling standards. No one has undermined behaviorism's main principle of learning: that reward produces learning more effectively than punishment.

(d) I improve my chances of liking student writing when I take steps to get to know them a bit as people. I do this partly through the assignments I give. That is, I always ask them to write a letter or two to me and to each other (for example about their history with writing). I base at least a couple of assignments on their own experiences, memories, or histories. And I make sure some of the assignments are free choice pieces — which also helps me know them.

In addition, I make sure to have at least three conferences with each student each semester — the first one very early. I often call off some classes in order to keep conferences from being too onerous (insisting nevertheless that students meet with their partner or small group when class is called off). Some teachers have mini-conferences with students during class — while students are engaged in writing or peer group meetings. I've found that when I deal only with my classes as a whole — as a large group — I sometimes experience them as a herd or lump — as stereotyped "adolescents"; I fail to experience them as individuals. For me, personally, this is disastrous since it often leads me to experience them as that scary tribe that I felt rejected by when *I* was an eighteen-year-old — and thus, at times, as "the enemy." But when I sit down with them face to face, they are not so stereotyped or alien or threatening — they are just eighteen-year-olds.

Getting a glimpse of them as individual people is particularly helpful in cases where their writing is not just bad, but somehow offensive — perhaps violent or cruelly racist or homophobic or sexist — or frighteningly vacuous. When I know them just a bit I can often see behind their awful attitude to the person and the life situation that spawned it, and not hate their writing so much. When I know students I can see that they are smart behind that dumb behavior; they are doing the best they can behind that bad behavior. Conditions are keeping them from acting decently; something is holding them back.

(e) It's odd, but the more I let myself show, the easier it is to like them and their writing. I need to share some of my own writing — show some of my own feelings. I need to write the letter to them that they write to me — about my past experiences and what I want and don't want to happen.

(f) It helps to work on my own writing — and work on learning to *like* it. Teachers who are most critical and sour about student writing are often having trouble with their own writing. They are bitter or unforgiving or hurting toward their own work. (I think I've noticed that failed PhDs are often the most severe and difficult with students.) When we are stuck or sour in our own writing, what helps us most is to find spaces free from evaluation such as those provided by freewriting and journal writing. Also, activities like reading out loud and finding a supportive reader or two. I would insist, then, that if only for the sake of our teaching, we need to learn to be charitable and to like our own writing.

A final word. I fear that this sermon about liking might seem an invitation to guilt. There is enough pressure on us as teachers that we don't need someone coming along and calling us inadequate if we don't *like* our students and their writing. That is, even though I think I am right to make this foray into the realm of feeling, I also acknowledge that it is dangerous — and paradoxical. It strikes me that we also need to have permission to hate the dirty bastards and their stupid writing.

After all, the conditions under which they go to school bring out some awful behavior on their part, and the conditions under which we teach sometimes make it difficult for us to like them and their writing. Writing wasn't meant to be read in stacks of twenty-five, fifty, or seventy-five. And we are handicapped as teachers when students are in our classes against their will. (Thus high school teachers have the worst problem here, since their students tend to be the most sour and resentful about school.)

Indeed, one of the best aids to liking students and their writing is to be somewhat charitable toward ourselves about the opposite feelings that we inevitably have. I used to think it was terrible for teachers to tell those sarcastic stories and hostile jokes about their students: "teacher room talk." But now I've come to think that people who spend their lives teaching *need* an arena to let off this unhappy steam. And certainly it's better to vent this sarcasm and hostility with our buddies than on the students themselves. The question, then, becomes this: do we help this behavior function as a venting so that we can move past it and not be trapped in our inevitable resentment of students? Or do we tell these stories and jokes as a way of staying stuck in the hurt, hostile, or bitter feelings — year after year — as so many sad teachers do?

In short I'm not trying to invite guilt, I'm trying to invite hope. I'm trying to suggest that if we do a sophisticated analysis of the difference between liking and evaluating, we will see that it's possible (if not always easy) to like students and their writing — without having to give up our intelligence, sophistication, or judgment.

Let me sum up the points I'm trying to make about ranking, evaluating, and liking:

- Let's do as little ranking and grading as we can. They are never fair and they undermine learning and teaching.

- Let's use evaluation instead — a more careful, more discriminating, fairer mode of assessment.

- But because evaluating is harder than ranking, and because too much evaluating also undermines learning, let's establish small but important evaluation-free zones.

- And underneath it all — suffusing the whole evaluative enterprise — let's learn to be better likers: liking our own and our students' writing, and realizing that liking need not get in the way of clear-eyed evaluation.

Works Cited

Belanoff, Pat, and Marcia Dickson, eds. *Portfolios: Process and Product.* Portsmouth, NH: Boynton/Cook-Heinemann, 1991.

Belanoff, Pat, and Peter Elbow. "Using Portfolios to Increase Collaboration and Community in a Writing Program." *WPA: Journal of Writing Program Administration* 9.3 (Spring 1986): 27–40. (Also in *Portfolios: Process and Product.* Ed. Pat Belanoff and Marcia Dickson. Portsmouth, NH: Boynton/Cook-Heinemann, 1991.)

Belanoff, Pat, Peter Elbow, and Sheryl Fontaine, eds. *Nothing Begins with N: New Investigations of Freewriting.* Carbondale, Southern Illinois UP, 1991.

Bishop, Wendy. *Released into Language: Options for Teaching Creative Writing.* Urbana: NCTE, 1990.

———. *Something Old, Something New: College Writing Teachers and Classroom Change.* Carbondale: Southern Illinois UP, 1990.

Diederich, Paul. *Measuring Growth in English.* Urbana: NCTE, 1974.

Elbow, Peter. "The Danger of Softness." *What Is English?* New York: MLA, 1990. 197–210.

Elbow, Peter, and Pat Belanoff. "State University of New York: Portfolio-Based Evaluation Program." *New Methods in College Writing Programs: Theory into Practice.* Ed. Paul Connolly and Teresa Vilardi. New York: MLA, 1986. 95–105. (Also in *Portfolios: Process and Product.* Ed. Pat Belanoff and Marcia Dickson. Portsmouth, NH: Boynton/Cook-Heinemann, 1991.)

Gardner, Howard. *Frames of Mind: The Theory of Multiple Intelligences.* New York: Basic, 1983.

Kirschenbaum, Howard, Sidney Simon, and Rodney Napier. *Wad-Ja-Get? The Grading Game in American Education.* New York: Hart Publishing, 1971.

Lewis, C. S. *Studies in Words.* 2d ed. London: Cambridge UP, 1967.

Portfolio Assessment Newsletter. Five Centerpointe Drive, Suite 100, Lake Oswego, Oregon 97035.

Portfolio News. c/o San Dieguito Union High School District, 710 Encinitas Boulevard, Encinitas, CA 92024.

Smith, Barbara Herrnstein. *Contingencies of Value: Alternative Perspectives for Critical Theory.* Cambridge: Harvard UP, 1988.

White, Edward M. *Teaching and Assessing Writing.* San Francisco: Jossey-Bass, 1985.

Zak, Frances. "Exclusively Positive Responses to Student Writing." *Journal of Basic Writing* 9.2 (1990): 40–53.

Elbow's Insights as a Resource for Your Teaching

1. Reflect on your own grading procedures: Which of Elbow's three activities — ranking, evaluating, or liking — have influenced them the most? Why?

2. Consider what Elbow says about liking, and trace the ups and downs of your enjoyment of student writing. Can you imagine ways to like it more, and, more important, to articulate this liking more effectively?

Elbow's Insights as a Resource for Your Writing Classroom

1. How might your composition course make more room for what Elbow calls "evaluation-free zones"? Try to make such moments become a regular feature of your students' drafting and revising processes.

2. As you respond to your next batch of student drafts, strive to make at least one sincere, positive comment on each of them. When you receive the final drafts, try to determine whether the positive reinforcement appreciably altered the ways your students approached the task of final revision.

Portfolio Standards for English 101

Douglas D. Hesse

Douglas D. Hesse developed the following guidelines, reprinted in Strategies for Teaching First-Year Composition *(2002), for instructors at Illinois State University. Provided to English 101 students as well as to the teachers, this set of standards for assessing portfolios offers detailed discussion of exactly what distinguishes the best portfolios from the merely good ones, and the good ones from those that are flawed. A carefully stated rubric can be a useful dimension of any syllabus for any writing course, for it gives both students and teachers a clear and explicit set of guidelines for evaluating student work.*

Unlike individual paper grading, portfolio evaluation involves judging a collection of texts written by a writer. The grade reflects an overall assessment of the writer's ability to produce varied kinds of texts, not an average of grades on individual papers. Raters will choose the description that best fits the portfolio. In other words, not all of the criteria in a selected grade range may apply to a given set of papers, but that cluster of criteria more accurately describes the portfolio than any other. Feedback to student portfolios will usually consist of some indication to the students of how their work measures against these various criteria, plus a few sentences of written response to the portfolio as a whole. Individual papers are not marked.

The "A" Portfolio

"A" portfolios demonstrate the writer's skillful ability to perform in a variety of rhetorical situations. "A" portfolios suggest that the writer will be able to adroitly handle nearly any task an undergraduate student writer might encounter, in both academic and public forums. The papers, the drafting materials, and, most important, the reflective introduction demonstrate the writer's sense of his or her development through the semester, his or her ability to reflect analytically and critically on his or her writing, and the relations among works submitted in the portfolio.

Individual works in "A" portfolios tend consistently to be appropriate to their intended audiences, audiences who are characterized as well read or knowledgeable on the topics and ideas addressed. These readers would often be struck by the freshness of ideas, strategies, perspective, or expression in the work. Writers are usually able to bridge knowledge or opinion gaps between themselves and their readers and effectively create a context for the writing.

The quality of thought in "A" portfolios is generally ambitious and mature. Not only is the writer able to state claims or ideas clearly and effectively, but also he or she is generally able to provide support and discuss warrants for those claims in a manner that reflects the complexity of issues and yet still takes a plausible position. Not only is the writer able to describe phenomena or events clearly and effectively, but also he or she is able to analyze and interpret their possible meanings, going beyond the obvious. "A" writers usually have a keen eye for detail. Individual works are most often characterized by an effective texture of general and specific ideas or by such compelling specific ideas or accounts that generalizations are implicit.

Through allusions, interpretive strategies, and stylistic sophistication, "A" portfolios often suggest that their authors read or have read widely, not only materials assigned for courses but also a variety of public texts: newspapers, magazines, and books. These writers are able to incorporate ideas and insights gained from reading into their texts, sometimes critically, sometimes generatively, sometimes as support or illustration of ideas. This is not to suggest, however, that all works in portfolios must be documented. Indeed, reference to outside sources in many papers would be contrived, inappropriate, and undesirable.

"A" portfolios frequently show how their writers are able to draw on personal experience and direct observations of the world around them. They are able to connect these experiences and observations to readings or to new situations. Their writing often displays analogical or metaphorical thinking.

"A" portfolios may show frequent evidence of the writer's ability to make conceptual or global revisions — wide-ranging changes at the idea level — as well as local revisions — changes that affect meaning primarily in sentences and paragraphs. The writer is often able to use the entire range of revision operations: addition, subtraction, transposition. The writer is frequently able to use teacher and peer response generatively, moving beyond a single, narrow comment to revise other aspects of the paper — or to initiate revisions on her or his own.

"A" portfolios are generally marked by a range of sophisticated stylistic features appropriate to a given writing situation, perhaps including sentences of various types and lengths (especially cumulative and other subordinated structures), striking word choices that are appropriate to the situation of the paper, and the effective use of metaphor and analogy, often extended. Papers often reflect a distinctive voice. The opening strategies of "A" papers are generally creative and engaging, the conclusions more than simple restatements of preceding ideas.

"A" portfolios, although not necessarily perfect, are virtually free of the kinds of errors that compromise the effectiveness of the piece, and have virtually no stigmatized errors.

"A" portfolios are neatly printed and organized as described in "Guidelines for Turning in Portfolios."

Incomplete portfolios may not be graded "A."

The "B" Portfolio

"B" portfolios generally suggest the writer's skillful ability to perform in a variety of rhetorical situations, though a few areas may not be as strong as others. "B" portfolios suggest that the writer will be able successfully to handle nearly any task an undergraduate student writer might encounter, in both academic and public forums. The papers, the drafting materials, and, most important, the reflective introduction suggest progress toward the writer's becoming conversant with his or her development, toward an ability to reflect analytically and critically on his or her writing, and toward understanding the relations among works submitted in the portfolio.

Individual works in "B" portfolios are usually appropriate to their intended audiences, audiences who are characterized as well read or knowledgeable on the topics and ideas addressed. "B" portfolios may be less ambitious in their choice of intended topics or audience, or may be less sophisticated in the way they address their readers than "A" portfolios. "B" writers are often able to bridge knowledge or opinion gaps between themselves and their readers and to create a plausible context for the writing.

The quality of thought in "B" portfolios is often ambitious and mature. Not only is the writer able to state claims or ideas clearly and effectively, but also he or she is frequently able to provide support and discuss warrants for those claims in a manner that frequently reflects the complexity of issues. Not only is the writer able to describe phenomena or events clearly and effectively, but also he or she is generally able to analyze and interpret their meaning. Individual works are often characterized by an effective texture of general and specific ideas.

Through allusions, interpretive strategies, and stylistic sophistication, "B" portfolios suggest that their authors read widely, not only materials assigned for courses but also a variety of public texts: newspapers, magazines, and books. These writers are able to incorporate ideas and insights from reading into their texts, sometimes critically, sometimes generatively, sometimes as support or illustration of ideas, although this is often done less fluently or facilely than in "A" portfolios. This is not to suggest, however, that all works must be documented. Indeed, reference to outside sources in many papers would be contrived, inappropriate, and undesirable.

"B" portfolios occasionally show how their writers are able to draw on personal experience and observations of the world around them. They suggest that their writers are able to connect experience and direct observations to readings or to new situations. Occasionally, their writing may display analogical or metaphorical thinking.

"B" portfolios show occasional evidence of the writer's ability to make conceptual or global revision (or frequent evidence of such revisions that are not always fully successful). They show the writer's ability to make effective local revisions and to use a variety of revision strategies. The writer is sometimes able to use teacher and peer response generatively, moving beyond a single, narrow comment to revise other aspects of the paper.

"B" portfolios display a variety of sophisticated stylistic features, including sentences of various types and lengths (perhaps including cumulative and other subordinated structures), word choices that are appropriate to the rhetorical situation of the paper, and the occasional use of metaphor and analogy, though sometimes these features may not be fully controlled or appropriate. There is frequently a distinctive voice to the papers, although this may be uneven. The opening strategies of "B" papers are creative and engaging, the conclusions more than simple restatements of preceding ideas.

"B" portfolios, although not necessarily perfect, are virtually free of the kinds of errors that compromise the rhetorical effectiveness of the piece, and have virtually no stigmatized errors.

"B" portfolios are neatly printed and organized as described in "Guidelines for Turning in Portfolios."

Incomplete portfolios may not be graded "B."

The "C" Portfolio

"C" portfolios demonstrate the writer's ability to perform competently in a variety of rhetorical situations, perhaps even showing skills in some writings. The set of papers, the drafting materials, and, most important, the writer's reflective introduction suggest progress toward the writer's becoming conversant with his or her development, toward an ability to reflect analytically and critically on his or her writing, and toward understanding the relations among works submitted in the portfolio. "C" writers, however, may not be nearly as perceptive as "B" writers in making connections between projects, in discussing and illustrating general tendencies in their writing, or in critically analyzing their drafting processes. These portfolios may seem to be more compilations of isolated works than at least partially connected wholes. Again, the reflective introduction will be most useful in making this judgment.

Writing in "C" portfolios adequately addresses knowledge and attitudes of peers. While this writing may often successfully address a well-read and knowledgeable outside audience, the context and occasion for the writing tend to be confined more to the classroom situation itself.

The quality of thought in "C" portfolios is competent and sometimes compelling, though often standard or familiar. Not only is the writer able to state claims or ideas clearly and effectively, but also he or she is able to provide support and discuss warrants for those claims, although the complexities of the issues involved may be suggested rather than fully treated — or perhaps dealt with very little. Not only is the writer able to describe phenomena or events clearly and effectively, but also he or she is able to analyze and interpret their meaning, although the interpretations may be obvious or sometimes perfunctory. Individual works are often characterized by a texture of general and specific elements, but paraphrase and repetition may often take the place of development. Papers may be developed more by partition or addition, in the mode of the five-paragraph theme, rather than by logical or organic development of a central idea.

"C" portfolios demonstrate the writer's ability to read course materials critically and analytically and to incorporate ideas from reading into his or her texts. There may be some suggestions of the writer's facility with outside readings, but they may not be well integrated into papers, used rather in a more cut-and-paste fashion than a more organic one.

"C" writers may be able to draw on personal experience and observations of the world around them and connect these to readings or to new situations. The connections, however, may not be as fully integrated, explored, or subtle as in "B" portfolios.

"C" portfolios demonstrate the writer's ability to make local revisions, perhaps with one dominant strategy (addition, for example). While these portfolios may suggest the writer's ability to make global revisions, this ability is not clearly demonstrated. Revisions are frequently tied narrowly to specific comments made by the teacher or peers; the writer is less clearly a self-starter when it comes to revision than the "A" or "B" student.

"C" portfolios display a reasonable range of stylistic features, although sentences tend to be of a fairly uniform type (usually subject-

verb-complement) and sentence length is mostly a function of coordination rather than subordination. There is infrequent use of metaphor
and analogy. The voice of these papers is perhaps generic, competent
but largely indistinct from other student prose. The opening strategies
of writings in "C" portfolios may rely fairly directly on the assignment
sheets or use some version of a funnel strategy. Conclusions tend to
summarize the preceding ideas.

"C" portfolios are virtually free of the kinds of errors that compromise the rhetorical effectiveness of the piece, and they have few stigmatized errors and no consistent patterns of stigmatized errors.

"C" portfolios are neatly printed and organized as described in
"Guidelines for Turning in Portfolios."

Incomplete portfolios may not be graded "C."

The "D" Portfolio

"D" portfolios suggest the writer's inability to write competently in several rhetorical situations. Writers of "D" portfolio work will likely have
difficulty in other college or public writing situations. The set of papers, the drafting materials, and, most important, the writer's reflective introduction suggest that the writer is not fairly conversant with
his or her development as a writer and is fairly unable to reflect analytically and critically on his or her writing. These portfolios generally
seem to be more compilations of isolated works than partially connected
wholes.

While the writing is sometimes appropriate to an audience that is
knowledgeable on the topics and ideas addressed, frequently the writer
assumes less — or more — of his or her readers than is appropriate.
There are considerable knowledge or opinion gaps between the writer
and his or her reader, and the context for the writing is usually limited
to the classroom assignments themselves.

The quality of thought in "D" portfolios is frequently stock or perfunctory. The writer may be able to state claims or ideas clearly but is
able to provide only minimal support and discuss virtually no warrants for that support. The writer may be able to describe phenomena
or events clearly, but his or her interpretations may be obvious or perfunctory. While works may sometimes display a texture of general and
specific elements, paraphrase and repetition may often take the place
of development. "D" portfolios may contain papers that are consistently
shorter than is needed to successfully engage the tasks.

"D" portfolios suggest their authors' difficulties in reading course
materials critically and analytically. These writers may have some difficulty summarizing complex ideas. Or they may be able to summarize
but unable to respond critically or interpretively. They incorporate ideas
from reading into their texts in ways that are frequently not well integrated, in more of a cut-and-paste fashion than an organic one.

"D" portfolios suggest the writer's ability to make local revisions,
but these are often infrequent or do not substantially improve the pa-

per from draft to draft. Revisions may take the form primarily of proof-reading or direct responses only to the teacher's or peers' comments.

"D" portfolios may display a narrow range of stylistic features, with most sentences of a fairly uniform type. The result may be an overly predictable text, at levels all the way from the sentence, to paragraphs, to openings and closings.

"D" portfolios may display some of the kinds of errors that compromise the rhetorical effectiveness of individual works and may have some stigmatized errors, even a pattern of one such error.

"D" portfolios may not be neatly printed, or they may not be neatly organized as described in "Guidelines for Turning in Portfolios."

"D" portfolios may be incomplete.

The "F" Portfolio

"F" portfolios demonstrate the writer's inability to write competently in various aims (persuasive, explanatory, and narrative), although the writer may be better in some than in others; writers of "F" portfolio work will have difficulty in most writing situations. The set of papers, the drafting materials, and, most important, the writer's reflective introduction generally indicate that the writer is not conversant with his or her development as a writer and that he or she is unable to reflect analytically and critically on his or her writing. These portfolios generally seem to be more compilations of isolated works than at least partially connected wholes.

The writing is almost never appropriate to an audience that is knowledgeable on the topics and ideas addressed; the writer assumes less — or more — of his or her readers than is appropriate, expecting readers to fill in all the gaps, to make all the connections, and automatically agree with the writer's perspective.

The quality of thought in "F" portfolios is perfunctory, obvious, or unclear. The writer may offer claims or ideas but be unable to provide much support. The writer may be able to describe phenomena or events but be unable to analyze or interpret them. Paraphrase and repetition often take the place of development. "F" portfolios may contain papers that are consistently shorter than is needed to successfully engage the tasks.

"F" portfolios demonstrate their authors' difficulties in reading course materials critically and analytically. These writers may have considerable difficulty summarizing complex ideas. They are unable to respond critically or interpretively. They incorporate ideas from reading into their texts in a cut-and-paste fashion rather than a more organic one.

"F" portfolios show relatively little evidence of revision, and what is there is frequently done at the sentence level or narrowly in response to a teacher's comment.

"F" portfolios may display the kinds of errors that compromise the rhetorical effectiveness of individual works; they may have patterns of stigmatized errors.

"F" portfolios may not be neatly printed, or they may not be neatly organized as described in "Guidelines for Turning in Portfolios."

"F" portfolios may be incomplete.

English 101 Final Portfolio Cover Sheet and Checklist, Spring 1999

Please provide the following information, which will help make sure you submit all the appropriate materials with your final portfolio. Turn this sheet in with your final portfolio. Thank you.

Name _____ Social Security Number _____
Instructor and Section Number _____
Local Address and Phone:

_____

Permanent Address:

_____

I. A check on the right numbers and kinds of works
_____ This portfolio contains a total of 20–30 pages.
_____ This portfolio contains a reflective introduction (Part I, Course Guide, p. 8).
_____ This portfolio contains at least 17 pages of revised writing from the course, appx. 5000–7500 words (Part II, p. 8).
_____ The writings in Part II consist of at least 4 but not more than 8 papers.
Note: It's acceptable to list a paper in more than one category below:
One persuasive paper in the portfolio is titled:
One paper that has analysis or critique as its primary aim is titled:
One paper that makes substantial use of readings is titled:
_____ This portfolio contains an analysis of writing done for another course and a copy of that paper (Part III, p. 8).

II. A check of format for the portfolio
_____ I have included drafts for each paper. These are arranged exactly as described in step 3 on page 11 of the English 101 Course Guide. I understand that the Writing Program strongly urges me to keep a photocopy.
_____ I have provided an electronic second copy of the portfolio exactly as described in step 7 on page 11.
_____ I have turned in all materials in a two-pocket folder. On the outside of the folder is the information requested in step 9 on page 11 of the Course Guide. I understand that I can pick up my portfolio from my teacher at the beginning of next semester.

III. Permission: Choosing to give or withhold permission will not affect your grade in any way. Report any concerns or irregularities to the director of Writing Programs or the program ombudsperson.

I give my permission to the English Department to reproduce writings from this portfolio in future editions of Language and Composition I Course Guide: _____ yes _____ no

I give permission to my instructor or to the English Department to reproduce or otherwise use my writings for teaching training or research purposes. This includes permission to quote from my work in published articles or books. I understand that I will not be identified in any way, that my participation is completely voluntary, and that I may withdraw my permission, in writing, at any time. _____ yes _____ no

IV. Certification

The works submitted in this portfolio do not violate the plagiarism policy stated in the Course Guide. I understand that plagiarism will result in an F for the course.

_____

(signed)   (date)

Hesse's Insights as a Resource for Your Teaching

1. Look closely at the criteria Hesse sets forth for the "A" portfolio, the "B" portfolio, and so on. How would adopting Hesse's set of standards change your course? What challenges or obstacles might they create in your particular institution? How might you revise these standards to fit your own situation?

2. Consider the potential uses — beyond evaluation — of student portfolios. How might you use them when you yourself are evaluated by supervisors? How might they function, systematically, in your own ongoing "reflective practice" as a teacher? Try to devise some particular ways of tracking broad trends in student portfolios over a couple of semesters.

Hesse's Insights as a Resource for Your Writing Classroom

1. Hesse suggests that the reflective portfolio introduction that students must write at the end of the semester is quite important. What guidelines would you offer your students to assist them in this task? How long should the introduction be? What sorts of terms are they expected to use as conceptual tools for understanding their work over the semester? How directly must they refer to your own evaluative commentary on their work?

2. Early in the semester, distribute a set of criteria among your students for grading portfolios and discuss with them, in detail, what these criteria mean. Another possibility is to devote the first week of the semester to discussing standards with your students so that they have significant input into the terms by which their work will be evaluated. Take careful notes throughout the discussion, and at the next class meeting present a draft of the criteria for revision. As a class, work together to finalize the standards by way of ending the introduction to the course. Beginning the course in this way can enable broad discussion about the definition of good writing, what sorts of things first-year students should learn, and so on. It will also give students a crucial sense of responsibility for the class, since they will have had a hand in developing the grading criteria.

Error

Joseph Harris

In this chapter from his 1997 book A Teaching Subject: Composition Since 1966, *Joseph Harris situates the discussion of error historically, looking closely at the debate between John Rouse and Gerald Graff over the meaning of Mina Shaughnessy's widely known work,* Errors and Expectations, *and detailing the broader politics that make this such a heated debate. Harris argues that we are obligated to teach students to write correctly, not because of any naïve faith in the transcendent value of the "standard" but because these issues are inextricably linked to the need for authority and credibility that brings students to the university in the first place. Supporting a shift from issues of phrasing and correctness to matters of stance and argument, Harris's beliefs complement David Bartholomae's overall goal — to help students gain the authority in their discourse that will provide them access to academic and professional communities (see "Inventing the University," Chapter 1).*

"How Rouse makes his living is none of my business, but I venture that if he manages a decent livelihood it is only because he has somewhere or other submitted to enough socialization to equip him to do something for which somebody is willing to pay him" (852). So thundered Gerald Graff in the pages of *College English* in 1980, as part of a response to an article John Rouse had published in the same journal a year before. Not only was Graff's tone here sententious and overbearing, his question was also rhetorical to the point of being disingenuous, since how Rouse made his living should have been clear to anyone who had read his article, which was on the teaching of college writing and included a standard biographical note on its title page identifying him as "a teacher of English and an administrator in public schools" as well as the author of previous pieces in *College English* and of a book called *The Completed Gesture: Myth, Character, and Education* ("Politics" 1). So Rouse was a teacher and writer, "managing his livelihood" in much the same way as Graff, and probably drawing on much the same sort of skills and "socialization" in order to do so. Except not quite. For what Graff — who was identified by a similar note on the first page of his response as the chair of the English department at Northwestern University, as well as the author of articles in several prestigious literary journals and of a book published by the University of Chicago Press (851) — was hinting rather broadly at was that he didn't know who this guy was, that Rouse (schoolteacher rather than professor; articles in *College English* rather than *Salmagundi*; book published by trade rather than university press) was not a player in the academic world that Graff moved about in. And perhaps why this seemed so important was that Rouse had presumed to criticize the work of someone who was such a player, someone who by then had in fact become a kind of revered figure in the literary establishment, its sanctioned representative of the good teacher — and that was Mina Shaughnessy.

Although in many ways, Rouse had seemed to ask for precisely the sort of response he got from Graff and others.[1] His article on "The Politics of Composition" offered what I still see as a trenchant critique of Shaughnessy's 1977 *Errors and Expectations*, a book on the teaching of "basic" or underprepared college writers that had almost immediately gained the status of a classic. Rouse argued that Shaughnessy's relentless focus on the teaching of grammar might in many cases actually hinder the attempts of anxious and inexperienced students to elaborate their thoughts effectively in writing. I agree. But his criticism was couched in language that sometimes seemed deliberately aimed to provoke: Rouse failed to acknowledge, for instance, the crucial political importance and difficulty of the role that Shaughnessy took on in the late 1960s when she set up the first Basic Writing Program at City College of New York, and thus found herself in charge of diagnosing and responding to the academic needs of thousands of newly admitted and severely underprepared open admissions students. He also failed to note the clear sympathy and respect for such students that runs throughout *Errors and Expectations* and which all of her many admirers argue was central to Shaughnessy's work as a teacher and intellectual. And he was either unaware of or did not see the need to mention her tragic and early death from cancer the year before in 1978. Instead, Rouse went ferociously on the attack, arguing that Shaughnessy's "overriding need to socialize these young people in a manner politically acceptable accounts, I think, for her misinterpretations of student work and her disregard of known facts of language learning" (1–2). This rabble-rousing tone led right into Graff's magisterial response, and a much needed argument over teaching aims and strategies became clouded with competing accusations of elitism and pseudoradicalism, as snide guesses about Mina Shaughnessy's psychopolitical needs or John Rouse's means of earning a living were followed by insinuations about who *really* had the best interests of students in mind. "Is this submission with a cheerful smile? 'Mrs. Shaughnessy, we do know our verbs and adverbs,'" sneered Rouse (8). "John Rouse's article . . . illustrates the predicament of the thoughtful composition teacher today," replied Graff, who then went on to explain that it was the very conscientiousness of such teachers that left them "open to attack from critics of Rouse's persuasion" (851).

I want to do two things in this chapter: First, to work through what might actually be at stake in this argument over error and socialization, to sort out what competing views of the aims and practices of teaching are being offered in it, and, second, to try to understand why this particular issue in teaching, more than any other that I know of, seems to spark such strong feeling. I begin by looking more closely at Mina Shaughnessy, who figures in this debate, I think, less as an advocate of a position which many people now find very compelling than as a kind of icon, a model of what it might mean to be, in Graff's words, a "thoughtful composition teacher."

Shaughnessy was an elegant but evidently also rather slow writer. Her entire body of work consists of a few essays and talks along with a single book, *Errors and Expectations*. This has been enough, though, to secure her place in the history of the field. *Errors and Expectations* showed how students who had often been presumed uneducable, hopelessly unprepared for college work, could in fact be helped to compose reasonably correct academic prose — that their problems with college writing stemmed not from a lack of intelligence but from inexperience. As Shaughnessy put it, "BW students write the way they do, not because they are slow or non-verbal, indifferent to or incapable of academic excellence, but because they are beginners and must, like all beginners, learn by making mistakes" (5). The students whom Shaughnessy worked with (she calls them "BWs" or "basic writers"), and whose writings fill the pages of her book, were for the most part blacks and Hispanics who had been given the chance to attend City through its (then) new and controversial program of open admissions for graduates of New York high schools.[2] Shaughnessy's work with these students was thus an intrinsic part of one of the most ambitious democratic reforms of American higher education — as the glowing reviews of her book in popular liberal magazines like *The Nation* and *Atlantic Monthly* attested.

But while politically liberal, the plan of work sketched out in *Errors and Expectations* is in many ways quite intellectually conservative. What people tend to remember and admire about *Errors and Expectations* is Shaughnessy's early defense of the aims of open admissions, her attentiveness throughout to the language of students, and her analysis late in the book of the difficulties students often have in taking on the critical and argumentative stance of much academic writing. What tends to be forgotten or glossed over is that the bulk of *Errors and Expectations* is a primer on teaching for correctness, pure and simple, as the titles of its Chapters 2 through 6 show: Handwriting and Punctuation, Syntax, Common Errors, Spelling, and Vocabulary. And even the much more celebrated seventh chapter on Beyond the Sentence offers what seems to me a distressingly formulaic view of academic writing and how to teach it. For instance, an extraordinarily detailed "sample lesson" on helping students write about reading (251–55) offers students an extended list of quotations culled from the book they are reading (*Black Boy*), followed by a set of procedures (Observation, Idea, and Analysis — the three of which are themselves broken into substeps) that they are to use in analyzing this list of details, and ends up by instructing them to

> Follow the steps given above. Make observations on parts, repetitions, omissions, and connections. Write down the main idea you get from your observations. Develop that main idea into an essay that makes a general statement, an explanation of the statement, an illustration of the statement, and a concluding statement. (255)

Follow the steps given above. I can't imagine a less compelling representation of the work of a critic or intellectual. Students are not asked in this assignment to say anything about what they thought or felt about their reading, or to connect what the author is writing about with their own experiences, or to take a stand on what he has to say; rather, they are simply told to generate and defend "a main idea" about a list of details that their teacher has given them from the book. What is the point of having students read books (like *Black Boy*) that might speak to their situations and concerns if they are not then encouraged to draw on their life experiences in speaking back to it? The tame parody of critical analysis sketched out in this assignment is "academic" in the worst sense: its form predetermined, its aim less to say something new or interesting than to demonstrate a competence in a certain kind of school writing.

Errors and Expectations thus argues for a new sort of student but not a new sort of intellectual practice. It says that basic writers can also do the kind of work that mainstream students have long been expected to do; it doesn't suggest this work be changed in any significant ways. This is a strong part of its appeal. Throughout her writings Shaughnessy offers a consistent image of herself as an *amateur* and a *reformer*. Even as she helped to set up the new field of "basic writing," Shaughnessy identified herself less with composition than with mainstream literary studies. Few of her admirers miss the chance to note how she was the product of a quite traditional education (B.A. in speech from Northwestern, M.A. in literature from Columbia) or to mark her love of Milton and drama.[3] Her method in *Errors and Expectations* is essentially that of the literary critic: a close and careful explication of difficult texts — except that in this case the difficulty springs from the inexperience of students rather than from the virtuosity of professionals. And her list of references and suggested readings at the end of her book has an undisciplined and eclectic quality: some literature, some criticism, some linguistics, some psychology, some work on second language learning and on the writing process — whatever, it seems, that could be found which might help with the task at hand.

This image of the autodidact or amateur was carefully constructed. Shaughnessy often depicts herself and her colleagues as "pioneers" working on a new "frontier," who need to "dive in" and explore previously uncharted waters (the metaphor varies a bit) so they can form a new kind of knowledge and expertise to use in teaching a new kind of college student. In "Mapping Errors and Expectations for Basic Writing," Bruce Horner points to the troubling (indeed, almost unconsciously racist) implications of describing teachers and students in terms of pioneers and natives. I would add that the "frontier" Shaughnessy claimed to stumble upon was already quite well developed, that even though the field of composition was not disciplined or professionalized in the same ways it is now, many teachers and writers had for some time been dealing with much the same sorts of issues.

There is no question that Shaughnessy brought a new sense of urgency to the problem of teaching underprepared writers. But it wasn't a new problem. In 1961, for instance, David Holbrook had written his moving book on *English for the Rejected* (still perhaps the bluntest and most accurate name for "basic" writers); in 1967, John Dixon was writing in *Growth through English* about students like Joan, the third grader with an IQ of 76 who wrote her poem about "the yellow bird." (It is this British and school-based tradition that John Rouse identifies himself with in his response to Shaughnessy.) And in America, in 1977, the same year that *Errors and Expectations* came out, Geneva Smitherman published *Talkin and Testifyin*, a book that urged teachers to spend less time correcting the language of black students and more time responding to what they had to say. And throughout the 1970s, the very time that Shaughnessy was most active in the profession, what remains perhaps the liveliest and most vehement debate in the history of CCCC was going on around the drafting and eventual approval of its 1974 statement on "The Students' Right to Their Own Language," a document which militantly asserted the need for teachers to move beyond a simple concern with having students write standard written English. None of these texts or authors can be placed in easy agreement with the approach taken by Shaughnessy in *Errors and Expectations*, which remains, again, after everything else is said about it, a book on teaching grammar. What Shaughnessy depicts as a sparse and unpopulated frontier of inquiry, then, looks from another perspective (to make use of a competing cliché) more like a marketplace of ideas as contending factions hawk their positions and argue against the views of others.

But this contrast also shows the appeal of the metaphor of the frontier, which allowed Shaughnessy to present herself less as criticizing than *extending* the reach of English studies. (Contrast this with critics, like Rouse, who positioned themselves as outsiders arguing *against* the status quo.) Even at her angriest moments (as in her article on "The English Professor's Malady," in which she complains of her colleagues' unwillingness to take on the hard work of teaching students not already familiar with their preferred ways of reading and writing), Shaughnessy's argument was for the profession to live up to its own stated values. Her message was consistently one of *inclusion* — that we can (and should) teach a kind of student, the "basic writer," who has too often slipped beneath the notice of the professoriate. And not only that, but she also showed how this sort of teaching could draw on precisely the sort of skills that people trained in English were likely to have, as well as to offer them much the sort of intellectual rewards which they most valued. The pleasures of *Errors and Expectations* are strikingly like that of good literary criticism: Passages of student writing that seem almost impossibly convoluted and obscure are patiently untangled and explicated. Shaughnessy thus offered the profession of English studies a useful image of one of its own best selves: The teacher who happily takes on the class of boneheads that the rest of us dread encountering and who patiently teaches them the very "basics" which we want to be able to assume they already know.

But *what* Shaughnessy argues can (and should) be taught to these new students is dismaying. Here, for instance, is the plan she offers for a basic writing course near the end of *Errors and Expectations*:

Weeks 1–5	Combined work on syntax and punctuation, following recommendations in Chapters 2 and 3.
Weeks 6–7	Spelling — principles of word formation, diagnostic techniques. (After this, spelling instruction should be individualized.)
Weeks 8–12	Common errors — verb inflections for number, noun inflections for number, verb tenses, agreement.
Weeks 13–15	Vocabulary — prefixes, suffixes, roots, abstract-concrete words, precision. (289)

Fifteen weeks and the focus never moves past correctness. Nowhere here (or anywhere else in her book) do we get a sense that the work of a basic writing course might be not only to train students in the mechanics of writing correct sentences but also to engage them in the life of the mind, to offer them some real experience in testing out and elaborating their views in writing. At no point in *Errors and Expectations* does Shaughnessy talk about how teachers might respond to the gist or argument of student writings, or about how to help students use writing to clarify or revise what they think. Indeed, as Rouse pointed out, Shaughnessy does not even seem to notice how many of the students whose work she cites change what they actually have to say in the process of trying to write more correct sentences.[4] Coupled with this is her nearly complete lack of interest in revision. Almost all of the student writings that Shaughnessy analyzes are timed first drafts; her goal in teaching was not to have students go back to edit and revise what they had written but to write new impromptu pieces with fewer mistakes in them. Her measures of good writing, that is to say, centered on fluency and correctness at the almost total expense of meaning. A footnote near the end of her book strikingly shows this mechanistic emphasis. Comparing some pieces written early in the term with those composed later on by the same students, Shaughnessy remarks,

> In all such before-and-after examples, the "after" samples bear many marks of revision (crossed-out words, corrected punctuation, etc.), suggesting that students have acquired the important habit of going back over their sentences with an eye to correctness. (277)

Revision here is pictured simply as a habit of proofreading. *Errors and Expectations* is thus the sort of book that tells you everything but why — as students and teachers labor together to perfect the form of prose whose actual or possible meanings they never seem to talk about.

Compare this to the sort of work that, at precisely the same time, Geneva Smitherman was arguing ought to go on in writing classes. A sociolinguist active in political and legal debates over the schooling of black children, Smitherman was also a strong influence in the framing of the 1974 CCCC statement on the "Students' Right to Their Own Language." (Shaughnessy was conspicuously absent from this debate.) Her 1977 *Talkin and Testifyin* is an impassioned and lucid defense of the richness and complexity of black English. In its final chapter, Smitherman turns to language education, which she argues should center (for both black and white students) on skills in reading and writing that are "intellectual competencies that can be taught in any dialect or language" (228). To teach such a "communicative competence," teachers need to move beyond a fetishizing of correctness and instead focus on the more substantive, difficult, and rhetorical

> aspects of communication such as content and message, style, choice of words, logical development, originality of thought and expression, and so forth. Such are the real components of language power, and they cannot be measured by narrow conceptions of "correct grammar." While teachers frequently correct student language on the basis of such misguided conceptions, saying something correctly, and saying it well, are two entirely different Thangs. (229)

This emphasis on forming something to say and working to say it well could hardly be more different than Shaughnessy's focus on error. Smitherman continues to drive this emphasis home by comparing her responses to two student pieces: one a vacuous (and stylistically bland) comment on Baraka's *Dutchman* by a white student teacher, and the other a poorly developed paragraph on the evils of war by a black ninth grader. What I find striking is how Smitherman uses much the same strategy in responding to both writers, challenging them to articulate their positions more fully before working to correct their phrasings. To the white student, Smitherman said,

> as kindly as I could, that his "essay" was weak in content and repetitious, and that it did not demonstrate command of the literary critical tools that teachers of literature are supposed to possess, *plus it didn't really say nothing!* (229)

While in responding to the black ninth grader writing on war, she asked things like:

> "Some say . . ." Who is "some"? . . .
> Exactly who are the two sides you're talking about here? What category of people? Name them and tell something about them. . . .
> Give me an example showing when and how such a disagreement leads to war. . . . (230)

While these two responses show some differences in tone (and perhaps appropriately so, given the varying situations of the writers), their aim is quite similar: to get students to think about what they want to say in their writing and about the effects their words have on readers. Smitherman is quick to say that she is not advocating an "off-the-deep-end permissiveness of letting their kids get away with anything," but rather that she is teaching toward a rhetorical and stylistic awareness that is "deeper and more expansive" than that encouraged by a focus on norms of correctness (233). Her position is much the same as that taken by Rouse in his response to Shaughnessy, and indeed something like it has become in recent years the consensus view of the profession, at least as represented in the pages of *CCC* and *College English* and at the annual meetings of CCCC: Students must learn not simply how to avoid mistakes but how to write in ways that engage the attention of educated readers. Teachers need then to respond to what students are trying to say, to the effectiveness of their writing as a whole, and not simply to the presence or absence of local errors in spelling, syntax, or usage. Correctness thus becomes not the single and defining issue in learning how to write but simply one aspect of developing a more general communicative competence.

This shift in focus was given articulate and moving expression by Mike Rose in his 1989 *Lives on the Boundary*, a book which, like *Errors and Expectations*, gained almost immediate acclaim both within and outside the profession. Like Shaughnessy, Rose argues for the intelligence and promise of students who are too often dismissed as unprepared or even unfit for college work, and like her too, his work and writing speaks to the linkings between education and politics, since the underprepared students he works with are so often also (and not coincidentally) people of color or from lower socioeconomic classes. And, certainly, even though the students Rose works with in Los Angeles in the 1980s often seem to live in an almost completely different world than those Shaughnessy worked with in New York in the 1970s, what both groups most need to learn is how to find their way into a system of education that seems at many points purposely designed to exclude them. But rather than assuming, like Shaughnessy, that what such students need is yet more training in the "basics," Rose argues that an unremitting focus on the more routine and dull aspects of intellectual work can instead act to dim their ambitions and limit their chances of success. One of the most telling bits of evidence Rose has to offer for this view comes from his own life, since as a boy he was placed in the vocational track of his local schools and so learned of the boredom and condescension of such classrooms firsthand. He was only retracked into college prep when a teacher noticed he was doing suspiciously well in biology. You don't know what you don't know, Rose suggests: "The telling thing is how chancy both my placement into and exit from Voc. Ed. was; neither I nor my parents had anything to do with it" (30). We can't expect students to grow proficient at kinds of intellectual work that they don't know about, that they've never really been given a chance to try their hands at.

What struggling students need, then, is not more of the basics but a sense of what others find most exciting and useful about books, writing, and ideas. Here's how Rose describes how he began to form his own aims for teaching while working with a group of Vietnam veterans studying to return to college:

> Given the nature of these men's needs and given the limited time I would have with them, could I perhaps orient them to some of the kinds of reading and writing and ways of thinking that seem essential to a liberal course of study, some of the habits of mind that Jack MacFarland and the many [of Rose's own teachers] that followed him helped me develop? . . . I was looking for a methodical way to get my students to think about thinking. Thinking. Not a fussbudget course, but a course about thought. I finally decided to build a writing curriculum on four of the intellectual strategies my education had helped me develop — some of which, I later learned were as old as Aristotle — strategies that kept emerging as I reflected on the life of the undergraduate: summarizing, classifying, comparing, and analyzing. (138)

The crucial words here are *habits of mind*, a phrasing even older than Aristotle, at least as it is often used to translate the Greek notion of *arete*, those "virtues" or "excellences" required by the citizens of a democracy.[5] There is an admirable hardheadedness in this teaching project that is reminiscent of Shaughnessy; like her, Rose wants to demystify the workings of the academy for his students. But a course on habits or strategies of thinking is in practice quite different from one focused on issues of correctness in language. As Rose outlines his course,

> Each quarter, I began by having the students summarize short
> simple readings, and then moved them slowly through classifying and
> comparing to analyzing. . . . I explained and modeled, used accessible
> readings, tried to incorporate what the veterans learned from one
> assignment to the next, slowly increased difficulty, and provided a lot of
> time for the men to talk and write. (143)

Malcolm Kiniry and Rose offer a more elaborate version of such a course
in their 1990 *Critical Strategies for Academic Writing*, a text whose
aim is to engage students in reading and writing, at a beginning and
approximate level, about the kinds of issues and questions that academics in various fields take on. Similarly, in their 1986 *Facts, Artifacts, and Counterfacts*, David Bartholomae and Anthony Petrosky
sketch out a plan for a basic writing course that is set up very much
like a graduate seminar: Students read, write, and talk together about
a particular intellectual issue over the course of a term, coming at the
same topic from a number of different angles, reading one another's
writings, seeing how the individual concerns they bring to their common subject influence what each of them has to say about it. The trick
of such teaching is, of course, to find a set of readings that underprepared
students will find accessible, and not only speak to their concerns but
also push their ways of understanding and talking about them. (Some
of the classes described in *Facts, Artifacts*, for instance, had students
read and write on "Growth and Adolescence," or "Work," or "Creativity.") But what's more important is how this sort of teaching signals a
shift in focus from *error* to *academic discourse*, from issues of phrasing
and correctness to matters of stance and argument.

I support this shift myself, and, again, feel that Shaughnessy's failure to attend in any sustained way to issues beyond the sentence is
what now makes her work, less than twenty years after its appearance, seem of merely historical interest rather than of practical use.
(There is a dark irony here: The subtitle of *Errors and Expectations* is
A Guide for the Teacher of Basic Writing, and Shaughnessy is often
invoked as a model practitioner whose scholarship was deeply rooted
in her day-to-day work with students. And yet I can't now imagine
giving *Errors and Expectations* as a guide to a beginning teacher of
basic writing, although I still often offer new teachers other writings
from the 1960s and 1970s by people like Moffett, Britton, Elbow, and
Coles.) Still one can see how this downplaying of error might seem to
outsiders simply a way of slipping past the difficulty and drudgery of
actually teaching writing. "Students and parents complain that they
are being patronized, that the more relaxed, more personalist pedagogy fails to teach anybody how to write" (852), was how Graff (who is
no cultural reactionary) put it in 1980. Given his distrust of Rouse and
defense of Shaughnessy, it seems clear that for Graff learning "how to
write" involves strong attention to issues of correctness, and his complaint about "relaxed" standards has been echoed in countless ways
not only by students and parents but also by college faculty and ad-

ministrators, as well as by writers in the popular press.[6] As one of my colleagues, a biologist, said to me recently after a curriculum meeting in which I argued for a new structuring of introductory writing courses at my college: "The thing is, most of us think that too many students can't write worth a damn, and we wish you'd just do something about it."

It's tempting to dismiss such complaints as misinformed, as in many ways they surely are. But that is also precisely the problem. Again, for some time now, most compositionists have held that a focus on error can often block the attempts of beginning writers to form their thoughts in prose, and indeed that the explicit teaching of grammatical forms usually has little effect on the abilities of students to write fluently or correctly.[7] But ask anyone *outside* the field (and this includes many writing teachers who are not active in CCCC) what they expect students to learn in a composition course, and you are likely to hear a good bit about issues of proper form and correctness. As even someone like the distinguished liberal philosopher Richard Rorty put it, when asked in an interview about what the aims of a writing course might be,

> I think the idea of freshman English, mostly, is just to get them to write complete sentences, get the commas in the right place, and stuff like that — the stuff we would like to think the high schools do and, in fact, they don't. But as long as there's a need for freshman English, it's going to be primarily a matter of the least common denominator of all the jargon. (Olson 6–7)

Although Rorty's interviewer, Gary Olson, expresses surprise at this response (since Rorty's views on language have influenced many progressive composition theorists), it seems to me both familiar and reasonable enough. What I find more distressing has been the ongoing inability of compositionists (myself among them) to explain ourselves to people like Graff and Rorty. Instead we have too often retreated behind the walls of our professional consensus, admonishing not only our students and university colleagues but the more general public as well when they fail to defer to our views on language learning — answering their concerns about correctness by telling them, in effect, that they should not want what they are asking us for.

This is an unfortunate stance for a field that defines itself through its interest in teaching and the practical workings of language. I am not advocating a return to Shaughnessy-like focus on error, but I do think we can learn from her responsiveness to the concerns of people outside our field. Rather than either meekly acceding to or simply dismissing what Smitherman called "the national mania for correctness" (229), we need to argue for a view of literacy that clearly recognizes and includes such concerns but is not wholly defined by them.

A first step might be to reinterpret worries about "grammar" or "correctness" in a more generous and expansive way. Rather than reading them as moves to trivialize the issues involved in learning to write, to turn everything into a simple matter of proofreading, we might see such remarks as somewhat clumsy attempts to voice concerns about how one gains or loses authority in writing. For even if mistakes do not interfere with what a writer has to say, they can still do serious harm to her credibility. Indeed, it is precisely because many mistakes (lapses in spelling or punctuation, for instance) seem so trivial that their appearance in a writer's text can seem to speak of a lack of care or ability. People don't want to be caught out in their writing or to have their students or children caught out. And so many struggling writers speak of their "problems with grammar" as a kind of shorthand for a whole set of difficulties they have with writing that are much harder to name, much as many readers will begin to complain about fairly trivial errors in a text they have grown impatient with for other less easily defined reasons. It is one thing to feel that in a particular classroom your language will not be held up for ridicule; it is another to feel confidence in your abilities to write to an indifferent or even hostile reader — to a different sort of teacher or examiner, perhaps, or to an applications committee or potential employer. Something like this is, I think, what lies behind many worries about "relaxed" or "permissive" forms of teaching. To gloss over such concerns is to dodge questions about the workings of power in language at their most naked.

Not that responding to them is all that easy either. As I've noted before, simply drilling students in proper forms has been shown to have little effect — and besides, the problem of gaining authority is not merely a matter of getting rid of error; students must also and at the same time acquire a rhetorical ease and power, an ability to write persuasively as well as correctly. And standards of correctness vary from one context to the other, along with the readiness of readers to look for mistakes, as Joseph Williams points out in his stunning 1981 article on "The Phenomenology of Error," in which he shows how the authors of writing handbooks often commit the same errors they decry, and sometimes in the very act of stating them — as when, for instance, while inveighing against the use of negative constructions, one text declares that "the following example . . . is not untypical"; or when in "Politics and the English Language" Orwell casts his famous polemic against the passive voice *in the passive voice*; or when yet another handbook advises that "Emphasis is often achieved . . . by the use of verbs in the active rather than in the passive voice" (158). The reason we don't tend to notice such problems, Williams argues, is that we're not looking for them. And, conversely, why we find so many mistakes in student papers is because we expect to, we're on the watch for them. (Williams clinches his case by revealing, at the end of his article, that he has deliberately inserted about a hundred "errors" in his own text. I have never met a reader who claimed to notice more than two or three on a first reading.)

Williams's point is not that we should downplay the significance of error but that we should focus our attention and energies on those mistakes which really count, on those that seriously impugn a writer's authority. (Maxine Hairston added to this line of thinking in a piece that appeared that same year in *College English*, "Not All Errors Are Created Equal: Nonacademic Readers in the Professions Respond to Lapses in Usage.") This makes good sense, but even more important is how Williams locates "error" as something that exists not simply as marks on a page but also as a part of the consciousness of writers, readers, and (in the form of handbooks and such) the culture at large. A mistake is not a mistake unless it's noticed as one, is how the argument goes, and it's a line of thought that sheds light both on why some writers have such difficulty proofreading their work and on the role that readers play in creating a mania of correctness. For what is involved in detecting errors seems to be not only an awareness of rules but a shift in attentiveness: One needs to learn how to read for mistakes as well as meaning.[8] This suggests the need for a kind of double approach to the issue of error, one that deals frankly with the practical politics of the situation: What writers need to learn is how to read their work for those lapses that will send many readers into a tailspin; what readers (and the culture) need to learn is to lighten up, to recognize the writing of reasonably correct prose as a fairly complex intellectual achievement and to be a little less quick to damn a writer for a few mistakes.

In practice one often sees this sort of double approach. In the *Facts, Artifacts* course, for instance, students are asked to revise and edit one of their writings for publication in a class book, a process which requires them to carefully proofread and correct their prose. And while his *Lives on the Boundary* is a plea to reform education in America, to make it more forgiving of error and more willing to work with difference, the picture Mike Rose offers of himself *as a teacher* throughout the book is of someone who wants to help students claim whatever power they can in the system as it stands. As one woman tells him,

> You know, Mike, people always hold this shit over you, make you . . . make you feel stupid with their fancy talk. But now *I've* read it, I've read Shakespeare, I can say I, *Olga*, have read it. I won't tell you I like it, 'cause I don't know if I do or I don't. But I like knowing what it's about. (223)

While in another context, I might want to quibble with the term *fancy talk*, what is crucial to realize here, I think, is that unless you already feel at home in the workings of critical or intellectual discourse, that's all it's likely to seem to you: fancy talk. And I don't see how you could possibly begin to feel at ease in any sort of fancy talk unless you also felt sure both that what you had to say would be listened to seriously and that you weren't likely to commit any egregious nails-on-the-chalkboard kinds of mistakes (*c'est je*, that sort of thing) in trying to speak or write it. So while we can't teach for correctness alone, we also can't *not* teach for it either. I think of the joke in Calvin Trillin's 1977 novel

Runestruck, when a lawyer goes out "on a drive to relax from the pressures of a civil liberties case he was arguing in a nearby town — the case of an elementary school teacher of progressive views who claimed that she was fired by the local school board solely because she had refused to teach her students to spell" (23). "Better watch my grammar" versus "won't really teach kids how to write." Some choice. (And Trillin probably actually knew something about the debate over error in the 1970s, since he is married to Alice Trillin, who taught basic writing with Shaughnessy at City College.) We need to make sure that in distancing ourselves from poor practice (a focus on error alone) we don't seem to advocate an equally unconvincing stance (no concern with error at all).

In the mid-1980s, a number of teachers and theorists tried to break out of this rhetorical bind by arguing that the job of writing teachers was to initiate students into the workings of the academic discourse community, to learn the specific conventions of college writing. I comment more about this move in Chapter 5. For now, I simply want to say that the power of this view has much to do with the elasticity of the term *convention* — which can describe almost anything from a critical habit of mind to a preferred form of citing sources to specific usages and phrasings. Using a term like *convention*, you can argue (and indeed I would) that in learning to write at college, students need to work on everything from spelling and punctuation to active verbs to self-reflexivity — and to do all this at once. Nothing can ruin the credibility of an academic piece more than poor proofreading (I know from hard experience as both a writer and journal editor), but errorless typing doesn't make up for a lack of critical insight either. To gain control over academic discourse, writers need to work on several levels at once — as do their teachers.

There is both a conceptual and rhetorical problem, though, I think, with a stress on specifically academic writing. In her 1991 rereading of *Errors and Expectations*, Min-Zhan Lu criticizes Shaughnessy's tendency to pit the ways with words that students bring with them to college against a seemingly neutral "language of public transactions" (*Errors* 125), a move which Lu argues allows Shaughnessy to gloss over the fact that academic writing is both characterized by the use of certain linguistic forms and often associated with a particular set of political values. We do not teach a contextless Standard Written English, Lu argues, but a specific kind of writing closely tied to the particular aims and needs of university work. We thus need to recognize there are other Englishes, tied to other contexts or communities, which are not simply underdeveloped or less public versions of academic discourse, but that work toward different ends and whose use may express a competing or oppositional politics — as when, for instance, Geneva Smitherman draws on the forms and phrasings of black English throughout *Talkin and Testifyin*. This view of academic discourse as a limited and specific *use* of language, whose characteristic forms and gestures can thus be defined and taught, has proven a powerful tool in sharpening our sense of what might go on in a college writing class. But it can also seem once more to cast its advocates in the role of simply teaching a professional jargon. For instance, when asked by Gary Olson if writing teachers should try to teach students the "normal discourse" of the academic fields they are studying, Richard Rorty replies,

> It strikes me as a terrible idea. . . . I think that America has made itself a bit ridiculous in the international academic world by developing distinctive disciplinary jargon. It's the last thing we want to inculcate in the freshmen. (Olson 6–7)

Rorty's tone here is sneering, but even still the issue he raises is an important one: Is the point of undergraduate study to prepare students to become professional intellectuals? Or to put it another way, even if our aim is to teach students a particular form of writing (and not some neutral "standard"), is that form best described as "academic"? For some time now in composition, *academic* has served as the opposing term to words like *personal* or *expressive*. That is, if one does not ask students to write directly from experience but instead sets them to writing about books and ideas, then, according to common usage, their work is "academic."[9] But I'm not so sure about the usefulness of the term, which at best tends to suggest a stylistic distance or formality and at worst to serve as a shorthand for pretension and bad writing. And I don't think that the sort of writing I usually imagine myself as teaching toward is in any strict sense *academic* (although it is not simply personal either). That is, while I almost always ask undergraduates to write on texts and ideas, I rarely ask them to do the sort of reading through the relevant academic literature that I would routinely require of graduate students (who *are* training to become professional intellectuals), and I don't spend much time on issues of citation, documentation, and the like.[10] (I rarely even teach anything like the "research paper.") I'm more interested in having students read the work of others closely and aggressively, and to use their reading in thinking and writing about issues that concern them. I would like my students to begin to think of themselves as critics and intellectuals. But that is not at all the same as preparing them to become academics.

I think this is more than a fussing over terms. In his 1994 "Travels to the Hearts of the Forest: Dilettantes, Professionals, and Knowledge," Kurt Spellmeyer shows how academics routinely lay claim to expertise by denigrating the knowledge of nonspecialists or amateurs (a kind of sinister version of the critical move defined by David Bartholomae in "Inventing the University"). By way of example, Spellmeyer shows how university ethnographers and art historians labored to assert the authority of their own systematized and restricted bodies of knowledge over the more idiosyncratic works of "mere" travel writers and connoisseurs. But he might just as easily have chosen to talk about how academic literary scholars have over the years differentiated themselves from mere reviewers or how a newly disciplined generation of composition scholars now seek to distinguish themselves from mere classroom practitioners. With Spellmeyer, I believe we need to be wary of an increasingly narrow professionalization of knowledge — and thus that we should resist equating the "critical" with the "academic."

In making this distinction I also think of books like Peter Medway's 1980 *Finding a Language*, in which he reports on his attempts to do something more than simply pass time as the teacher of a set of working-class British youths near the end of their formal schooling, none of whom were likely to go on to university and all of whom had resisted most other attempts to interest them in their course work. Medway had these students define an issue that mattered to them in their lives outside of school (jobs, politics, sports, and so on), and then had them spend the rest of the term reading and writing about it. There's little about the course, as thoughtful as it is, that would be likely to startle an informed American teacher of basic writing; in fact, it seems very much like the sort of course described in *Facts, Artifacts*. But that's precisely my point. Medway's aim was not to help his students enter the academy (there was little realistic hope of doing so for all but one or two of them); his goal was to have them reflect critically on the world they were part of right then. Freed from having to prepare his students to write according to the formal standards of an academy they would never enter, Medway was able instead to think about how to engage their intellectual curiosity and urge them toward a self-reflectiveness.

Of course Medway was only freed from such expectations by working in a culture that is more stratified by social class than ours. His students had little prospect of moving out of the circumstances that they were born into, whatever they did in school. But the promise of America is to be able to do just that — and education has long been advertised as one way of doing it. Underneath all the worries about correctness in writing, then, there is hope — that getting it right will mean getting ahead (or at least allow the chance of getting ahead). But there is fear, too: What is the point of having a standard that includes everyone, a marker that fails to separate? Language is not only a means of communicating but a form of identification, a badge that seems to define its wearer and yet, paradoxically, can be changed. It is the fear and hope of such change that so powerfully charges the debate on error.

Notes

1. *College English* published sharply critical responses to Rouse by Graff, Michael Allen, and William Lawlor, along with a counterstatement by Rouse, "Feeling Our Way Along." That none of Rouse's critics identified themselves with the field of composition studies points to the politically charged quality of the debate about error.

2. City College's experiment with open admissions sparked a remarkable number of accounts from its faculty, both advocates and opponents, radi-

cals and conservatives. Sidney Hook (*Out of Step*) and Irving Howe (*A Margin of Hope*), for instance, have interesting things to say in their memoirs about the struggles of the 1970s at City. And there have also been a number of accounts by people involved in some way with the teaching of English or basic writing, although this did not always mitigate the sententiousness of their prose — as is shown in the titles of Geoffrey Wagner's *The End of Education* and Theodore Gross's *Academic Turmoil*. And for a quick overview of the events of the 1970s at City, see James Traub's *City on a Hill*.

3. Shaughnessy's career has perhaps been documented more thoroughly than any other recent figure in composition studies. Janet Emig briefly traced her work in an obituary appearing in the February 1979 issue of *CCC*, and a series of writers — including E. D. Hirsch, Benjamin DeMott, John Lyons, Richard Hogart, and Sarah D'Eloia — commented on her work in a special issue, "Towards a Literate Democracy," of the *Journal of Basic Writing* in 1980, and then the same journal published still more reminiscences of Shaughnessy in 1994. John Lyons has a detailed and affectionate, although not uncritical, biographical essay on Shaughnessy in Brereton's *Traditions of Inquiry*. And, more recently, James Traub writes respectfully of Shaughnessy in a book, *City on a Hill*, that is more often quite critical of the open admissions experiment at City College.

4. In "Politics," Rouse points to how Shaughnessy's first example of a basic writer in action shows "his desperate effort to find *something* to say about the assigned topic" given him by his teacher, as he changes his position on the prompt no less than four times in an attempt to get his essay started (2). Similarly, in an article written some ten years later on "Redefining the Legacy of Mina Shaughnessy," Min-Zhan Lu analyzes the writings of a student whom Shaughnessy singles out for praise, pointing out that while the student does indeed seem to grow stylistically more fluent, the political positions she expresses in her successive writings also seem to shift significantly — although this attracts no comment from Shaughnessy.

5. There is a gendered subtext here as well that I can only begin to hint at: The Greek view of *arete* is closely connected with manliness, valor (the word is etymologically related to *Ares*, the god of war). It is thus peculiarly suggestive (even if also coincidental) that Rose should begin to form his notion of teaching toward "habits of mind" while working with a set of war veterans, and certainly the kind of teaching that he, David Bartholomae, and others have been associated with has strong masculinist overtones. ("Reading involves a fair measure of push and shove" is the first sentence of the introduction to Bartholomae and Petrosky's *Ways of Reading*.) On the other hand, the sort of "fussbudget" course that Rose wants to avoid, and that Shaughnessy provides with her emphasis on form and correctness, has a stereotypically feminine and nurturing (or perhaps schoolmarmish) quality. James Catano offers an interesting look into this issue in his 1990 article on "The Rhetoric of Masculinity."

6. A 1994 poll of parents of public school students, for instance, found them strongly suspicious of "new methods of teaching composition" and desirous for a return to "the basics" (Johnson and Immerwahr); more sustained outsider criticisms of progressive language teaching have also appeared in magazines like *The New Republic* (Traub) and *The Atlantic Monthly* (Levine).

7. The first and still most ringing statement of this professional consensus came from Braddock, Lloyd-Jones, and Schoer in their 1963 *Research on Written Composition*: "In view of the widespread agreement of research studies based upon many types of students and teachers, the conclusion can be stated in strong and unqualified terms: the teaching of grammar has a negligible or, because it usually displaces some instruction and practice in composition, even a harmful effect on improvement in writing" (37–38). In 1985, Patrick Hartwell revisited the research on the effectiveness of explicit teaching of rules of correctness and once again concluded (along with virtually everyone he cites) that such teaching has little usefulness and thus that we ought to "move on to more interesting areas of inquiry" ("Grammar, Grammars, and the Teaching of Grammar" 127).

8. Some of the practical difficulties of teaching and learning proofreading are hinted at by the very number of people who have written on its complexities. The first issue of the *Journal of Basic Writing*, founded and edited by Mina Shaughnessy in 1975, was devoted entirely to the topic of error and included pieces by Sarah D'Eloia, Isabella Halstead, and Valerie Krishna. The 1980s saw more work on the subject from David Bartholomae ("Study of Error"), Mary Epes, Glynda Hull, and Elaine Lees; more recently, Bruce Horner ("Editing") and Min-Zhan Lu ("Professing") have written on the problematic relations between "error" and "style."

9. This standoff between the "academic" and the "personal" gets played out in a 1995 *CCC* interchange between David Bartholomae ("Writing with Teachers") and Peter Elbow ("Being a Writer vs. Being an Academic") — although, tellingly, when pushed, Bartholomae ends up defending not "academic" writing but something he calls *criticism*. Kurt Spellmeyer offers a powerful reading of this exchange, which began as a series of talks at CCCC, in the last chapter of *Common Ground*.

10. We do sometimes talk, though, about the rhetorical and stylistic uses of footnotes.

Works Cited

Bartholomae, David. "Inventing the University." *When a Writer Can't Write: Studies in Writer's Block and Other Composing-Process Problems.* Ed. Mike Rose. New York: Guilford, 1985. 134–65.

———. "A Reply to Stephen North." *Pre/Text* 11 (1990): 122–30.

———. "The Study of Error." *CCC* 31 (1980): 253–69.

———. "Writing with Teachers: A Conversation with Peter Elbow." *CCC* 46 (1995): 62–71, 84–87.

Bartholomae, David, and Anthony Petrosky. *Facts, Artifacts, and Counterfacts: Theory and Method for a Reading and Writing Course.* Upper Montclair, NJ: Boynton, 1986.

———. *Ways of Reading: An Anthology for Writers.* 2nd ed. Boston: Bedford, 1990.

"The Basic Issues in the Teaching of English." *PMLA* 74.4 (1959): 1–19.

Britton, James. "The Distinction between Participant and Spectator Role Language in Research and Practice." *Research in the Teaching of English* 18 (1984): 320–31.

———. *Language and Learning.* Harmondsworth: Penguin, 1970.

———. "Response to Working Party Paper No. 1. — What Is English?" *Working Papers of the Dartmouth Seminar.* ERIC, 1966. ED 082 201.

———. "The Spectator as Theorist: A Reply." *English Education* 21 (1989): 53–60.

Britton, James, Tony Burgess, Nancy Martin, Alex McLeod, and Harold Rosen. *The Development of Writing Abilities (11–18)*. London: Macmillan, 1975.

Coles, William E., Jr. *Composing: Writing as a Self-Creating Process*. Rochelle Park, NJ: Hayden, 1974.

———. "Literacy for the Eighties: An Alternative to Losing." *Literacy for Life: The Demand for Reading and Writing*. Ed. Richard W. Bailey and Robin Melanie Fosheim. New York: MLA, 1983. 248–62.

———. *The Plural I*. New York: Holt, 1978.

———. *Seeing through Writing*. New York: Harper, 1988.

———. *Teaching Composing*. Rochelle Park, NJ: Hayden, 1974.

———. "An Unpetty Pace." *CCC* 23 (1972): 378–82.

Coles, William E., Jr., and James Vopat. *What Makes Writing Good? A Multiperspective*. Lexington, MA: Heath, 1985.

Dixon, John. "Conference Report: The Dartmouth Seminar." *Harvard Educational Review* 39 (1969): 366–72.

———. *Growth through English: A Record Based on the Dartmouth Seminar 1966*. Reading, England: NATE, 1967.

———. *Growth through English (Set in the Perspective of the Seventies)*. 3rd ed. London: NATE, 1974.

Elbow, Peter. "Being a Writer vs. Being an Academic: A Conflict in Goals." *CCC* 46 (1995): 72–83, 87–92.

———. "Forward: About Personal Expressive Academic Writing." *Pre/Text* 11 (1990): 7–20.

———. "The Pleasures of Voice in the Literary Essay: Explorations in the Prose of Gretel Ehrlich and Richard Selzer." *Literary Nonfiction: Theory, Criticism, Pedagogy*. Ed. Chris Anderson. Carbondale, IL: Southern Illinois UP, 1989. 211–34.

———. "Reflections on Academic Discourse: How It Relates to Freshmen and Colleagues." *College English* 53 (February 1991): 135–55.

———. *Writing without Teachers*. New York: Oxford UP, 1973.

———. *Writing with Power: Techniques for Mastering the Writing Process*. New York: Oxford UP, 1981.

Graff, Gerald. "The Politics of Composition: A Reply to John Rouse." *College English* 41 (1980): 851–56.

———. *Professing Literature: An Institutional History*. Chicago: U of Chicago P, 1987.

Hairston, Maxine. "Breaking Our Bonds and Reaffirming Our Connections." *CCC* 36 (1985): 272–82.

———. "Not All Errors Are Created Equal: Nonacademic Readers in the Professions Respond to Lapses in Usage." *College English* 43 (1981): 794–806.

———. "The Winds of Change: Thomas Kuhn and the Revolution in the Teaching of Writing." *CCC* 33 (1982): 76–88.

Holbrook, David. *English for Meaning*. New York: Taylor, 1979.

———. *English for the Rejected*. London: Cambridge UP, 1964.

Horner, Bruce. "Mapping Errors and Expectations for Basic Writing: From 'Frontier Field' to 'Border Country.'" *English Education* 26 (1994): 29–51.

———. "Rethinking the 'Sociality' of Error: Teaching Editing as Negotiation." *Rhetoric Review* 11 (1992): 172–99.

Kiniry, Malcolm, and Mike Rose. *Critical Strategies for Academic Writing*. Boston: Bedford, 1990.

Lu, Min-Zhan. "Conflict and Struggle: The Enemies or Preconditions of Basic Writing?" *College English* 54 (1992): 887–913.

———. "Professing Multiculturalism: The Politics of Style in the Contact Zone." *CCC* 45 (1994): 305–21.

———. "Redefining the Legacy of Mina Shaughnessy: A Critique of the Politics of Linguistic Innocence." *Journal of Basic Writing* 10 (1991): 26–40.

Medway, Peter. *Finding a Language: Autonomy and Learning in School.* London: Writers and Readers, 1980.

Moffett, James. *Coming on Center: English Education in Evolution.* Montclair, NJ: Boynton/Cook, 1981.

———. "Liberating Inner Speech." *CCC* 36 (1985): 304–08.

———. *Storm in the Mountains: A Case Study of Censorship, Conflict, and Consciousness.* Carbondale, IL: Southern Illinois UP, 1988.

———. *A Student-Centered Language Arts Curriculum, K–12.* Boston: Houghton, 1968.

———. *Teaching the Universe of Discourse.* Boston: Houghton, 1968.

———. "Writing, Inner Speech, and Meditation." *Coming on Center* 133–81.

Moffett, James, and Kenneth R. McElheny. *Points of View: An Anthology of Short Stories.* New York: Mentor, 1966.

Olson, Gary A. "Social Construction and Composition Theory: A Conversation with Richard Rorty." *Journal of Advanced Composition* 9 (1989): 1–9.

Rose, Mike. *Lives on the Boundary.* New York: Free Press, 1989.

Rosen, Jay. "Making Journalism More Public." *Communication* 12 (1991): 267–84.

Rouse, John. "Feeling Our Way Along." *College English* 41 (1980): 868–75.

———. "The Politics of Composition." *College English* 41 (1979): 1–12.

Shaughnessy, Mina. "The English Professor's Malady." *Journal of Basic Writing* 3.1 (1980): 91–97.

———. *Errors and Expectations: A Guide for the Teacher of Basic Writing.* New York: Oxford UP, 1977.

Smitherman, Geneva. *Talkin and Testifyin: The Language of Black America.* Detroit: Wayne State UP, 1977.

Spellmeyer, Kurt. *Common Ground: Dialogue, Understanding, and the Teaching of Composition.* New York: Prentice Hall, 1993.

———. "Foucault and the Freshman Writer: Considering the Self in Discourse." *College English* 51 (1989): 715–29.

———. "Travels to the Hearts of the Forest: Dilettantes, Professionals, and Knowledge." *College English* 56 (1994): 788–809.

Trillin, Calvin. *Runestruck.* Boston: Little, Brown, 1977.

Williams, Joseph. "The Phenomenology of Error." *CCC* 32 (1981): 152–68.

Harris's Insights as a Resource for Your Teaching

1. Think about conversations you've had about grammar with students, colleagues, and acquaintances. Did they address the sorts of polarities that Harris discusses? Did they reflect the larger politics that interest him? If not, what aspects of the issue has Harris neglected, and how might you use his thinking to address these hidden problems?

2. What do you think of Harris's suggestion that a principal goal of the classroom must be to honor the students' search for a certain kind of identity and sense of authority and credibility? Do you think that this goal might conflict with other agendas? With what specific issues might this goal be in conflict?

Harris's Insights as a Resource for Your Writing Classroom

1. Ask your students to record their initial ideas of, or associations with, grammar. Next, outline Harris's basic principles for students. Ask your students if they had ever thought of grammar not as a fixed standard, but in terms of having social and cultural ramifications, and have them read the powerful last two lines of the article, which identify grammar as a hot-button issue:

   > Language is not only a means of communicating but a form of identification, a badge that seems to define its wearer and yet, paradoxically, can be changed. It is the fear and hope of such change that so powerfully charges the debate on error.

   Have their perceptions of grammar changed after reflecting on these issues? How? How is this awareness important or relevant to their own lives and learning?

2. Outline the basic principles of the Graff-Rouse debate for your students and ask them which position they support, and why. List specific points of support on the board during the ensuing discussion. Consider having students use these points as a basis for developing a paper topic.

Grammar, Grammars, and the Teaching of Grammar

Patrick Hartwell

First published in College English *(1985), this classic essay confronts the enormous complexity of a central "hot-button" issue in our field — the question of error — and negotiates a rich middle ground between those who reject all grammar instruction and those who would organize their classrooms around it. Patrick Hartwell begins by offering five different definitions of grammar; in doing so, he eliminates the confusion generated by competing senses of the term. These five different grammars range from the basic linguistic programming that is an intrinsic feature of human beings, like the opposable thumb, up through the sort of grammar that he calls "metalinguistic," a kind of context-sensitive sophistica-*

tion about style that one develops after years of careful reflection. By setting forth these different definitions of grammar, Hartwell provides us with a clear way of dealing with this delicate subject.

For me the grammar issue was settled at least twenty years ago with the conclusion offered by Richard Braddock, Richard Lloyd-Jones, and Lowell Schoer in 1963.

> In view of the widespread agreement of research studies based upon many types of students and teachers, the conclusion can be stated in strong and unqualified terms: the teaching of formal grammar has a negligible or, because it usually displaces some instruction and practice in composition, even a harmful effect on improvement in writing.[1]

Indeed, I would agree with Janet Emig that the grammar issue is a prime example of "magical thinking": the assumption that students will learn only what we teach and only because we teach.[2]

But the grammar issue, as we will see, is a complicated one. And, perhaps surprisingly, it remains controversial, with the regular appearance of papers defending the teaching of formal grammar or attacking it.[3] Thus Janice Neuleib, writing on "The Relation of Formal Grammar to Composition" in *College Composition and Communication* (23 [1977], 247–250), is tempted "to sputter on paper" at reading the quotation above (p. 248), and Martha Kolln, writing in the same journal three years later ("Closing the Books on Alchemy," *CCC*, 32 [1981], 139–151), labels people like me "alchemists" for our perverse beliefs. Neuleib reviews five experimental studies, most of them concluding that formal grammar instruction has no effect on the quality of students' writing nor on their ability to avoid error. Yet she renders in effect a Scots verdict of "Not proven" and calls for more research on the issue. Similarly, Kolln reviews six experimental studies that arrive at similar conclusions, only one of them overlapping with the studies cited by Neuleib. She calls for more careful definition of the word *grammar* — her definition being "the internalized system that native speakers of a language share" (p. 140) — and she concludes with a stirring call to place grammar instruction at the center of the composition curriculum: "our goal should be to help students understand the system they know unconsciously as native speakers, to teach them the necessary categories and labels that will enable them to think about and talk about their language" (p. 150). Certainly our textbooks and our pedagogies — though they vary widely in what they see as "necessary categories and labels" — continue to emphasize mastery of formal grammar, and popular discussions of a presumed literacy crisis are almost unanimous in their call for a renewed emphasis on the teaching of formal grammar, seen as basic for success in writing.[4]

An Instructive Example

It is worth noting at the outset that both sides in this dispute — the grammarians and the anti-grammarians — articulate the issue in the same positivistic terms: What does experimental research tell us about the value of teaching formal grammar? But seventy-five years of experimental research has for all practical purposes told us nothing. The two sides are unable to agree on how to interpret such research. Studies are interpreted in terms of one's prior assumptions about the value of teaching grammar: their results seem not to change those assumptions. Thus the basis of the discussion, a basis shared by Kolln and Neuleib and by Braddock and his colleagues — "what does educational research tell us?" — seems designed to perpetuate, not to resolve, the issue. A single example will be instructive. In 1976 and then at greater length in 1979, W. B. Elley, I. H. Barham, H. Lamb, and M. Wyllie reported on a three-year experiment in New Zealand, comparing the relative effectiveness at the high school level of instruction in transformational grammar, instruction in traditional grammar, and no grammar instruction.[5] They concluded that the formal study of grammar, whether transformational or traditional, improved neither writing quality nor control over surface correctness.

> After two years, no differences were detected in writing performance or language competence; after three years small differences appeared in some minor conventions favoring the TG [transformational grammar] group, but these were more than offset by the less positive attitudes they showed towards their English studies. (p. 18)

Anthony Petrosky, in a review of research ("Grammar Instruction: What We Know," *English Journal,* 66, No. 9 [1977], 86–88), agreed with this conclusion, finding the study to be carefully designed, "representative of the best kind of educational research" (p. 86), its validity "unquestionable" (p. 88). Yet Janice Neuleib in her essay found the same conclusions to be "startling" and questioned whether the findings could be generalized beyond the target population, New Zealand high school students. Martha Kolln, when her attention is drawn to the study ("Reply to Ron Shook," *CCC,* 32 [1981], 139–151), thinks the whole experiment "suspicious." And John Mellon has been willing to use the study to defend the teaching of grammar; the study of Elley and his colleagues, he has argued, shows that teaching grammar does no harm.[6]

It would seem unlikely, therefore, that further experimental research, in and of itself, will resolve the grammar issue. Any experimental design can be nitpicked, any experimental population can be criticized, and any experimental conclusion can be questioned or, more often, ignored. In fact, it may well be that the grammar question is not open to resolution by experimental research, that, as Noam Chomsky has argued in *Reflections on Language* (New York: Pantheon, 1975), criticizing the trivialization of human learning by behavioral psychologists, the issue is simply misdefined.

There will be "good experiments" only in domains that lie outside the organism's cognitive capacity. For example, there will be no "good experiments" in the study of human learning.

This discipline . . . will, of necessity, avoid those domains in which an organism is specially designed to acquire rich cognitive structures that enter into its life in an intimate fashion. The discipline will be of virtually no intellectual interest, it seems to me, since it is restricting itself in principle to those questions that are guaranteed to tell us little about the nature of organisms. (p. 36)

Asking the Right Questions

As a result, though I will look briefly at the tradition of experimental research, my primary goal in this essay is to articulate the grammar issue in different and, I would hope, more productive terms. Specifically, I want to ask four questions:

1. Why is the grammar issue so important? Why has it been the dominant focus of composition research for the last seventy-five years?

2. What definitions of the word *grammar* are needed to articulate the grammar issue intelligibly?

3. What do findings in cognate disciplines suggest about the value of formal grammar instruction?

4. What is our theory of language, and what does it predict about the value of formal grammar instruction? (This question — "what does our theory of language predict?" — seems a much more powerful question than "what does educational research tell us?")

In exploring these questions I will attempt to be fully explicit about issues, terms, and assumptions. I hope that both proponents and opponents of formal grammar instruction would agree that these are useful as shared points of reference: care in definition, full examination of the evidence, reference to relevant work in cognate disciplines, and explicit analysis of the theoretical bases of the issue.

But even with that gesture of harmony it will be difficult to articulate the issue in a balanced way, one that will be acceptable to both sides. After all, we are dealing with a professional dispute in which one side accuses the other of "magical thinking," and in turn that side responds by charging the other as "alchemists." Thus we might suspect that the grammar issue is itself embedded in larger models of the transmission of literacy, part of quite different assumptions about the teaching of composition.

Those of us who dismiss the teaching of formal grammar have a model of composition instruction that makes the grammar issue "uninteresting" in a scientific sense. Our model predicts a rich and complex

interaction of learner and environment in mastering literacy, an interaction that has little to do with sequences of skills instruction as such.
Those who defend the teaching of grammar tend to have a model of
composition instruction that is rigidly skills-centered and rigidly sequential: The formal teaching of grammar, as the first step in that sequence, is the cornerstone or linchpin. Grammar teaching is thus su-
premely interesting, naturally a dominant focus for educational
research. The controversy over the value of grammar instruction, then,
is inseparable from two other issues: the issues of sequence in the teaching of composition and of the role of the composition teacher. Consider,
for example, the force of these two issues in Janice Neuleib's conclusion: After calling for yet more experimental research on the value of
teaching grammar, she ends with an absolute (and unsupported) claim
about sequences and teacher roles in composition.

> We do know, however, that some things must be taught at different
> levels. Insistence on adherence to usage norms by composition teachers
> does improve usage. Students can learn to organize their papers if
> teachers do not accept papers that are disorganized. Perhaps composi-
> tion teachers can teach those two abilities before they begin the more
> difficult tasks of developing syntactic sophistication and a winning
> style. ("The Relation of Formal Grammar to Composition," p. 250)

(One might want to ask, in passing, whether "usage norms" exist in the
monolithic fashion the phrase suggests and whether refusing to accept
disorganized papers is our best available pedagogy for teaching arrangement.)[7]
   But I want to focus on the notion of sequence that makes the grammar issue so important: first grammar, then usage, then some absolute
model of organization, all controlled by the teacher at the center of the
learning process, with other matters, those of rhetorical weight — "syntactic sophistication and a winning style" — pushed off to the future. It
is not surprising that we call each other names: Those of us who question the value of teaching grammar are in fact shaking the whole elaborate edifice of traditional composition instruction.

The Five Meanings of "Grammar"

Given its centrality to a well-established way of teaching composition,
I need to go about the business of defining grammar rather carefully,
particularly in view of Kolln's criticism of the lack of care in earlier
discussions. Therefore I will build upon a seminal discussion of the
word *grammar* offered a generation ago, in 1954, by W. Nelson Francis,
often excerpted as "The Three Meanings of Grammar."[8] It is worth reprinting at length, if only to re-establish it as a reference point for
future discussions.

> The first thing we mean by "grammar" is "the set of formal patterns
> in which the words of a language are arranged in order to convey larger

meanings." It is not necessary that we be able to discuss these patterns self-consciously in order to be able to use them. In fact, all speakers of a language above the age of five or six know how to use its complex forms of organization with considerable skill; in this sense of the word — call it "Grammar 1" — they are thoroughly familiar with its grammar.

The second meaning of "grammar" — call it "Grammar 2" — is "the branch of linguistic science which is concerned with the description, analysis, and formulization of formal language patterns." Just as gravity was in full operation before Newton's apple fell, so grammar in the first sense was in full operation before anyone formulated the first rule that began the history of grammar as a study.

The third sense in which people use the word "grammar" is "linguistic etiquette." This we may call "Grammar 3." The word in this sense is often coupled with a derogatory adjective: we say that the expression "he ain't here" is "bad grammar." . . .

As has already been suggested, much confusion arises from mixing these meanings. One hears a good deal of criticism of teachers of English couched in such terms as "they don't teach grammar any more." Criticism of this sort is based on the wholly unproven assumption that teaching Grammar 2 will improve the student's proficiency in Grammar 1 or improve his manners in Grammar 3. Actually, the form of Grammar 2 which is usually taught is a very inaccurate and misleading analysis of the facts of Grammar 1; and it therefore is of highly questionable value in improving a person's ability to handle the structural patterns of his language. (pp. 300–301)

Francis' Grammar 3 is, of course, not grammar at all, but usage. One would like to assume that Joseph Williams' recent discussion of usage ("The Phenomenology of Error," *CCC,* 32 [1981], 152–168), along with his references, has placed those shibboleths in a proper perspective. But I doubt it, and I suspect that popular discussions of the grammar issue will be as flawed by the intrusion of usage issues as past discussions have been. At any rate I will make only passing reference to Grammar 3 — usage — naïvely assuming that this issue has been discussed elsewhere and that my readers are familiar with those discussions.

We need also to make further discriminations about Francis' Grammar 2, given that the purpose of his 1954 article was to substitute for one form of Grammar 2, that "inaccurate and misleading" form "which is usually taught," another form, that of American structuralist grammar. Here we can make use of a still earlier discussion, one going back to the days when *PMLA* was willing to publish articles on rhetoric and linguistics, to a 1927 article by Charles Carpenter Fries, "The Rules of the Common School Grammars" (42 [1927], 221–237). Fries there distinguished between the scientific tradition of language study (to which we will now delimit Francis' Grammar 2, scientific grammar) and the separate tradition of "the common school grammars," developed unscientifically, largely based on two inadequate principles — appeals to "logical principles," like "two negatives make a positive," and analogy to Latin grammar; thus, Charlton Laird's characterization, "the grammar of Latin, ingeniously warped to suggest English" (*Language in America*

[New York: World, 1970], p. 294). There is, of course, a direct link between the "common school grammars" that Fries criticized in 1927 and the grammar-based texts of today, and thus it seems wise, as Karl W. Dykema suggests ("Where Our Grammar Came From," *CE*, 22 [1961], 455–465), to separate Grammar 2, "scientific grammar," from Grammar 4, "school grammar," the latter meaning, quite literally, "the grammars used in the schools."

Further, since Martha Kolln points to the adaptation of Christensen's sentence rhetoric in a recent sentence-combining text as an example of the proper emphasis on "grammar" ("Closing the Books on Alchemy," p. 140), it is worth separating out, as still another meaning of *grammar,* Grammar 5, "stylistic grammar," defined as "grammatical terms used in the interest of teaching prose style." And, since stylistic grammars abound, with widely variant terms and emphases, we might appropriately speak parenthetically of specific forms of Grammar 5 — Grammar 5 (Lanham); Grammar 5 (Strunk and White); Grammar 5 (Williams, *Style*); even Grammar 5 (Christensen, as adapted by Daiker, Kerek, and Morenberg).[9]

The Grammar in Our Heads

With these definitions in mind, let us return to Francis' Grammar 1, admirably defined by Kolln as "the internalized system of rules that speakers of a language share" ("Closing the Books on Alchemy," p. 140), or, to put it more simply, the grammar in our heads. Three features of Grammar 1 need to be stressed: first, its special status as an "internalized system of rules," as tacit and unconscious knowledge; second, the abstract, even counterintuitive, nature of these rules, insofar as we are able to approximate them indirectly as Grammar 2 statements; and third, the way in which the form of one's Grammar 1 seems profoundly affected by the acquisition of literacy. This sort of review is designed to firm up our theory of language, so that we can ask what it predicts about the value of teaching formal grammar.

A simple thought experiment will isolate the special status of Grammar 1 knowledge. I have asked members of a number of different groups — from sixth graders to college freshmen to high-school teachers — to give me the rule for ordering adjectives of nationality, age, and number in English. The response is always the same: "We don't know the rule." Yet when I ask these groups to perform an active language task, they show productive control over the rule they have denied knowing. I ask them to arrange the following words in a natural order:

French   the   young   girls   four

I have never seen a native speaker of English who did not immediately produce the natural order, "the four young French girls." The rule is that in English the order of adjectives is first, number, second, age, and third, nationality. Native speakers can create analogous phrases using the rule — "the seventy-three aged Scandinavian lechers"; and the drive for meaning is so great that they will create contexts to make sense out of violations of the rule, as in foregrounding for emphasis: "I want to talk to the French four young girls." (I immediately envision a large room, perhaps a banquet hall, filled with tables at which are seated groups of four young girls, each group of a different nationality.) So Grammar 1 is eminently usable knowledge — the way we make our life through language — but it is not accessible knowledge; in a profound sense, we do not know that we have it. Thus neurolinguist Z. N. Pylyshyn speaks of Grammar 1 as "autonomous," separate from common-sense reasoning, and as "cognitively impenetrable," not available for direct examination.[10] In philosophy and linguistics, the distinction is made between formal, conscious, "knowing about" knowledge (like Grammar 2 knowledge) and tacit, unconscious, "knowing how" knowledge (like Grammar 1 knowledge). The importance of this distinction for the teaching of composition — it provides a powerful theoretical justification for mistrusting the ability of Grammar 2 (or Grammar 4) knowledge to affect Grammar 1 performance — was pointed out in this journal by Martin Steinmann, Jr., in 1966 ("Rhetorical Research," *CE*, 27 [1966], 278–285).

Further, the more we learn about Grammar 1 — and most linguists would agree that we know surprisingly little about it — the more abstract and implicit it seems. This abstractness can be illustrated with an experiment, devised by Lise Menn and reported by Morris Halle,[11] about our rule for forming plurals in speech. It is obvious that we do indeed have a "rule" for forming plurals, for we do not memorize the plural of each noun separately. You will demonstrate productive control over that rule by forming the spoken plurals of the nonsense words below:

thole   flitch   plast

Halle offers two ways of formalizing a Grammar 2 equivalent of this Grammar 1 ability. One form of the rule is the following, stated in terms of speech sounds:

a.   If the noun ends in /s z š ž č ǰ/, add /ɨ/;
b.   otherwise, if the noun ends in /p t k f θ/, add /s/;
c.   otherwise, add /z/.

This rule comes close to what we literate adults consider to be an adequate rule for plurals in writing, like the rules, for example, taken from a recent "common school grammar," Eric Gould's *Reading into Writing: A Rhetoric, Reader, and Handbook* (Boston: Houghton Mifflin, 1983):

Plurals can be tricky. If you are unsure of a plural, then check it in the dictionary.
The general rules are:
Add *s* to the singular: *girls, tables*
Add *es* to nouns ending in *ch, sh, x* or *s; churches, boxes, wishes*
Add *es* to nouns ending in *y* and preceded by a vowel once you have changed *y* to *i: monies, companies.* (p. 666)

(But note the persistent inadequacy of such Grammar 4 rules: here, as I read it, the rule is inadequate to explain the plurals of *ray* and *tray,* even to explain the collective noun *monies,* not a plural at all, formed from the mass noun *money* and offered as an example.) A second form of the rule would make use of much more abstract entities, sound features:

    a. If the noun ends with a sound that is [coronal, strident], add /ɨ/;
    b. otherwise, if the noun ends with a sound that is [non-voiced], add /s/;
    c. otherwise, add /z/.

(The notion of "sound features" is itself rather abstract, perhaps new to readers not trained in linguistics. But such readers should be able to recognize that the spoken plurals of *lip* and *duck,* the sound [s], differ from the spoken plurals of *sea* and *gnu,* the sound [z], only in that the sounds of the latter are "voiced" — one's vocal cords vibrate — while the sounds of the former are "non-voiced.")

To test the psychologically operative rule, the Grammar 1 rule, native speakers of English were asked to form the plural of the last name of the composer Johann Sebastian *Bach,* a sound [x], unique in American (though not in Scottish) English. If speakers follow the first rule above, using word endings, they would reject (a) and (b), then apply (c), producing the plural as */baxz/,* with word-final /z/. (If writers were to follow the rule of the common school grammar, they would produce the written plural *Baches,* apparently, given the form of the rule, on analogy with *churches.)* If speakers follow the second rule, they would have to analyze the sound [x] as [non-labial, non-coronal, dorsal, non-voiced, and non-strident], producing the plural as */baxs/,* with word-final /s/. Native speakers of American English overwhelmingly produce the plural as */baxs/.* They use knowledge that Halle characterizes as "unlearned and untaught" (p. 140).

Now such a conclusion is counterintuitive — certainly it departs maximally from Grammar 4 rules for forming plurals. It seems that native speakers of English behave as if they have productive control, as Grammar 1 knowledge, of abstract sound features (± coronal, ± strident, and so on) which are available as conscious, Grammar 2 knowledge only to trained linguists — and, indeed, formally available only within the last hundred years or so. ("Behave as if," in that last sentence, is a necessary hedge, to underscore the difficulty of "knowing about" Grammar 1.)

Moreover, as the example of plural rules suggests, the form of the Grammar 1 in the heads of literate adults seems profoundly affected by the acquisition of literacy. Obviously, literate adults have access to different morphological codes: the abstract print -*s* underlying the predictable /s/ and /z/ plurals, the abstract print -*ed* underlying the spoken past tense markers /t/, as in "walked," /əd/, as in "surrounded," /d/, as in "scored," and the symbol /Ø/ for no surface realization, as in the relaxed standard pronunciation of "I walked to the store." Literate adults also have access to distinctions preserved only in the code of print (for example, the distinction between "a good sailer" and "a good sailor" that Mark Aranoff points out in "An English Spelling Convention," *Linguistic Inquiry,* 9 [1978], 299–303). More significantly, Irene Moscowitz speculates that the ability of third graders to form abstract nouns on analogy with pairs like *divine: :divinity* and *serene: :serenity,* where the spoken vowel changes but the spelling preserves meaning, is a factor of knowing how to read. Carol Chomsky finds a three-stage developmental sequence in the grammatical performance of seven-year-olds, related to measures of kind and variety of reading; and Rita S. Brause finds a nine-stage developmental sequence in the ability to understand semantic ambiguity, extending from fourth graders to graduate students.[12] John Mills and Gordon Hemsley find that level of education, and presumably level of literacy, influence judgments of grammaticality, concluding that literacy changes the deep structure of one's internal grammar; Jean Whyte finds that oral language functions develop differently in readers and non-readers; José Morais, Jésus Alegria, and Paul Bertelson find that illiterate adults are unable to add or delete sounds at the beginning of nonsense words, suggesting that awareness of speech as a series of phonemes is provided by learning to read an alphabetic code. Two experiments — one conducted by Charles A. Ferguson, the other by Mary E. Hamilton and David Barton — find that adults' ability to recognize segmentation in speech is related to degree of literacy, not to amount of schooling or general ability.[13]

It is worth noting that none of these investigators would suggest that the developmental sequences they have uncovered be isolated and taught as discrete skills. They are natural concomitants of literacy, and they seem best characterized not as isolated rules but as developing schemata, broad strategies for approaching written language.

Grammar 2

We can, of course, attempt to approximate the rules or schemata of Grammar 1 by writing fully explicit descriptions that model the competence of a native speaker. Such rules, like the rules for pluralizing nouns or ordering adjectives discussed above, are the goal of the science of linguistics, that is, Grammar 2. There are a number of scientific grammars — an older structuralist model and several versions within a generative-transformational paradigm, not to mention isolated schools like tagmemic grammar, Montague grammar, and the like. In fact, we cannot think of Grammar 2 as a stable entity, for its form changes with each new issue of each linguistics journal, as new "rules of grammar" are proposed and debated. Thus Grammar 2, though of great theoretical interest to the composition teacher, is of little practical use in the classroom, as Constance Weaver has pointed out (*Grammar for Teachers* [Urbana, Ill.: NCTE, 1979], pp. 3–6). Indeed Grammar 2 is a scientific model of Grammar 1, not a description of it, so that questions of psychological reality, while important, are less important than other, more theoretical factors, such as the elegance of formulation or the global power of rules. We might, for example, wish to replace the rule for ordering adjectives of age, number, and nationality cited above with a more general rule — what linguists call a "fuzzy" rule — that adjectives in English are ordered by their abstract quality of "nouniness": adjectives that are very much like nouns, like French or Scandinavian, come physically closer to nouns than do adjectives that are less "nouny," like four or aged. But our motivation for accepting the broader rule would be its global power, not its psychological reality.[14]

I try to consider a hostile reader, one committed to the teaching of grammar, and I try to think of ways to hammer in the central point of this distinction, that the rules of Grammar 2 are simply unconnected to productive control over Grammar 1. I can argue from authority: Noam Chomsky has touched on this point whenever he has concerned himself with the implications of linguistics for language teaching, and years ago transformationalist Mark Lester stated unequivocally, "there simply appears to be no correlation between a writer's study of language and his ability to write."[15] I can cite analogies offered by others: Francis Christensen's analogy in an essay originally published in 1962 that formal grammar study would be "to invite a centipede to attend to the sequence of his legs in motion,"[16] or James Britton's analogy, offered informally after a conference presentation, that grammar study would be like forcing starving people to master the use of a knife and fork before allowing them to eat. I can offer analogies of my own, contemplating the wisdom of asking a pool player to master the physics of momentum before taking up a cue or of making a prospective driver get a degree in automotive engineering before engaging the clutch. I consider a hypothetical argument, that if Grammar 2 knowledge affected Grammar 1 performance, then linguists would be our best writers. (I can certify that they are, on the whole, not.) Such a position, after all, is only in accord with other domains of science: the formula for catching a fly ball in baseball ("Playing It by Ear," *Scientific American,* 248, No. 4 [1983], 76) is of such complexity that it is beyond my understanding — and, I would suspect, that of many workaday centerfielders. But perhaps I can best hammer in this claim — that Grammar 2 knowledge has no effect on Grammar 1 performance — by offering a demonstration.

The diagram [above] is an attempt by Thomas N. Huckin and Leslie A. Olsen (*English for Science and Technology* [New York: McGraw-Hill,

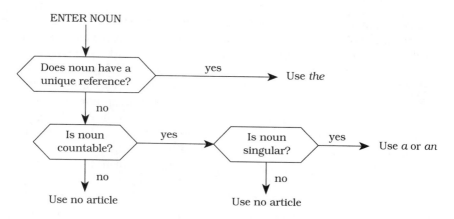

1983]) to offer, for students of English as a second language, a fully explicit formulation of what is, for native speakers, a trivial rule of the language — the choice of definite article, indefinite article, or no definite article. There are obvious limits to such a formulation, for article choice in English is less a matter of rule than of idiom ("I went to college" versus "I went to a university" versus British "I went to university"), real-world knowledge (using indefinite "I went into a house" instantiates definite "I looked at the ceiling," and indefinite "I visited a university" instantiates definite "I talked with the professors"), and stylistic choice (the last sentence above might alternatively end with "the choice of the definite article, the indefinite article, or no article"). Huckin and Olsen invite non-native speakers to use the rule consciously to justify article choice in technical prose, such as the passage below from P. F. Brandwein (*Matter: An Earth Science* [New York: Harcourt Brace Jovanovich, 1975]). I invite you to spend a couple of minutes doing the same thing, with the understanding that this exercise is a test case: You are using a very explicit rule to justify a fairly straightforward issue of grammatical choice.

> Imagine a cannon on top of _____ highest mountain on earth. It is firing _____ cannonballs horizontally. _____ first cannonball fired follows its path. As _____ cannonball moves, _____ gravity pulls it down, and it soon hits _____ ground. Now _____ velocity with which each succeeding cannonball is fired is increased. Thus, _____ cannonball goes farther each time. Cannonball 2 goes farther than _____ cannonball 1 although each is being pulled by _____ gravity toward the earth all _____ time. _____ last cannonball is fired with such tremendous velocity that it goes completely around _____ earth. It returns to _____ mountaintop and continues around the earth again and again. _____ cannonball's inertia causes it to continue in motion indefinitely in _____ orbit around earth. In such a situation, we could consider _____ cannonball to be _____ artificial satellite, just like _____ weather satellites launched by _____ U.S. Weather Service. (p. 209)

Most native speakers of English who have attempted this exercise report a great deal of frustration, a curious sense of working against, rather than with, the rule. The rule, however valuable it may be for non-native speakers, is, for the most part, simply unusable for native speakers of the language.

Cognate Areas of Research

We can corroborate this demonstration by turning to research in two cognate areas, studies of the induction of rules of artificial languages and studies of the role of formal rules in second language acquisition. Psychologists have studied the ability of subjects to learn artificial languages, usually constructed of nonsense syllables or letter strings. Such languages can be described by phrase structure rules:

$$S \Rightarrow VX$$
$$X \Rightarrow MX$$

More clearly, they can be presented as flow diagrams, as below:

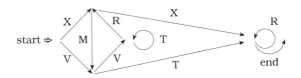

This diagram produces "sentences" like the following:

VVTRXRR.	XMVTTRX.	XXRR.
XMVRMT.	VVTTRMT.	XMTRRR.

The following "sentences" would be "ungrammatical" in this language:

*VMXTT.	*RTXVVT.	*TRVXXVVM.

Arthur S. Reber, in a classic 1967 experiment, demonstrated that mere exposure to grammatical sentences produced tacit learning: subjects who copied several grammatical sentences performed far above chance in judging the grammaticality of other letter strings. Further experiments have shown that providing subjects with formal rules — giving them the flow diagram above, for example — remarkably degrades performance: subjects given the "rules of the language" do much less well in acquiring the rules than do subjects not given the rules. Indeed, even telling subjects that they are to induce the rules of an artificial language degrades performance. Such laboratory experiments are admittedly contrived, but they confirm predictions that our theory of language would make about the value of formal rules in language learning.[17]

The thrust of recent research in second language learning similarly works to constrain the value of formal grammar rules. The most explicit statement of the value of formal rules is that of Stephen D. Krashen's monitor model.[18] Krashen divides second language mastery into *acquisition* — tacit, informal mastery, akin to first language acquisition — and formal learning — conscious application of Grammar 2 rules, which he calls "monitoring" output. In another essay Krashen uses his model to predict a highly individual use of the monitor and a highly constrained role for formal rules:

> Some adults (and very few children) are able to use conscious rules to increase the grammatical accuracy of their output, and even for these people, very strict conditions need to be met before the conscious grammar can be applied.[19]

In *Principles and Practice in Second Language Acquisition* (New York: Pergamon, 1982) Krashen outlines these conditions by means of a series of concentric circles, beginning with a large circle denoting the rules of English and a smaller circle denoting the subset of those rules described by formal linguists (adding that most linguists would protest that the size of this circle is much too large):

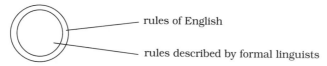

Krashen then adds smaller circles, as shown below — a subset of the rules described by formal linguists that would be known to applied linguists, a subset of those rules that would be available to the best teachers, and then a subset of those rules that teachers might choose to present to second language learners:

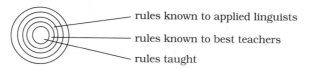

Of course, as Krashen notes, not all the rules taught will be learned, and not all those learned will be available, as what he calls "mental baggage" (p. 94), for conscious use.

An experiment by Ellen Bialystock, asking English speakers learning French to judge the grammaticality of taped sentences, complicates this issue, for reaction time data suggest that learners first make an intuitive judgment of grammaticality, using implicit or Grammar 1 knowledge, and only then search for formal explanations, using explicit or Grammar 2 knowledge.[20] This distinction would suggest that Grammar 2 knowledge is of use to second language learners only after the principle has already been mastered as tacit Grammar 1 knowledge.

In the terms of Krashen's model, learning never becomes acquisition (*Principles,* p. 86).

An ingenious experiment by Herbert W. Seliger complicates the issue yet further ("On the Nature and Function of Language Rules in Language Learning," *TESOL Quarterly,* 13 [1979], 359–369). Seliger asked native and non-native speakers of English to orally identify pictures of objects (e.g., "an apple," "a pear," "a book," "an umbrella"), noting whether they used the correct form of the indefinite articles *a* and *an.* He then asked each speaker to state the rule for choosing between *a* and *an.* He found no correlation between the ability to state the rule and the ability to apply it correctly, either with native or non-native speakers. Indeed, three of four adult non-native speakers in his sample produced a correct form of the rule, but they did not apply it in speaking. A strong conclusion from this experiment would be that formal rules of grammar seem to have no value whatsoever. Seliger, however, suggests a more paradoxical interpretation. Rules are of no use, he agrees, but some people think they are, and for these people, assuming that they have internalized the rules, even inadequate rules are of heuristic value, for they allow them to access the internal rules they actually use.

The Incantations of the "Common School Grammars"

Such a paradox may explain the fascination we have as teachers with "rules of grammar" of the Grammar 4 variety, the "rules" of the "common school grammars." Again and again such rules are inadequate to the facts of written language; you will recall that we have known this since Francis' 1927 study. R. Scott Baldwin and James M. Coady, studying how readers respond to punctuation signals ("Psycholinguistic Approaches to a Theory of Punctuation," *Journal of Reading Behavior,* 10 [1978], 363–383), conclude that conventional rules of punctuation are "a complete sham" (p. 375). My own favorite is the Grammar 4 rule for showing possession, always expressed in terms of adding -*'s* or -*s'* to nouns, while our internal grammar, if you think about it, adds possession to noun phrases, albeit under severe stylistic constraints: "the horses of the Queen of England" are "the Queen of England's horses" and "the feathers of the duck over there" are "the duck over there's feathers." Suzette Haden Elgin refers to the "rules" of Grammar 4 as "incantations" (*Never Mind the Trees,* p. 9: see note 3).

It may simply be that as hyperliterate adults we are conscious of "using rules" when we are in fact doing something else, something far more complex, accessing tacit heuristics honed by print literacy itself. We can clarify this notion by reaching for an acronym coined by technical writers to explain the readability of complex prose — COIK: "clear only if known." The rules of Grammar 4 — no, we can at this point be more honest — the incantations of Grammar 4 are COIK. If you know how to signal possession in the code of print, then the advice to add -*'s* to nouns makes perfect sense, just as the collective noun *monies* is a fine example of changing -*y* to -*i* and adding -*es* to form the plural. But if you have not grasped, tacitly, the abstract representation of possession in print, such incantations can only be opaque.

Worse yet, the advice given in "the common school grammars" is unconnected with anything remotely resembling literate adult behavior. Consider, as an example, the rule for not writing a sentence fragment as the rule is described in the best-selling college grammar text, John C. Hodges and Mary S. Whitten's *Harbrace College Handbook,* 9th ed. (New York: Harcourt Brace Jovanovich, 1982). In order to get to the advice, "as a rule, do not write a sentence fragment" (p. 25), the student must master the following learning tasks:

Recognizing verbs.

Recognizing subjects and verbs.

Recognizing all parts of speech. (*Harbrace* lists eight.)

Recognizing phrases and subordinate clauses. (*Harbrace* lists six types of phrases, and it offers incomplete lists of eight relative pronouns and eighteen subordinating conjunctions.)

Recognizing main clauses and types of sentences.

These learning tasks completed, the student is given the rule above, offered a page of exceptions, and then given the following advice (or is it an incantation?):

> Before handing in a composition, . . . proofread each word group written as a sentence. Test each one for completeness. First, be sure that it has at least one subject and one predicate. Next, be sure that the word group is not a dependent clause beginning with a subordinating conjunction or a relative clause. (p. 27)

The school grammar approach defines a sentence fragment as a conceptual error — as not having conscious knowledge of the school grammar definition of *sentence.* It demands heavy emphasis on rote memory, and it asks students to behave in ways patently removed from the behaviors of mature writers. (I have never in my life tested a sentence for completeness, and I am a better writer — and probably a better person — as a consequence.) It may be, of course, that some developing writers, at some points in their development, may benefit from such advice — or, more to the point, may think that they benefit — but, as Thomas Friedman points out in "Teaching Error, Nurturing Confusion" (*CE,* 45 [1983], 390–399), our theory of language tells us that such advice is, at the best, COIK. As the Maine joke has it, about a tourist asking directions from a farmer, "you can't get there from here."

Redefining Error

In the specific case of sentence fragments, Mina P. Shaughnessy (*Errors and Expectations* [New York: Oxford University Press, 1977]) argues that such errors are not conceptual failures at all, but performance errors — mistakes in punctuation. Muriel Harris' error counts support this view ("Mending the Fragmented Free Modifier," *CCC,* 32 [1981], 175–182). Case studies show example after example of errors that occur *because* of instruction — one thinks, for example, of David Bartholomae's student explaining that he added an *-s* to *children* "because it's a plural" ("The Study of Error," *CCC,* 31 [1980], 262). Surveys, such as that by Muriel Harris ("Contradictory Perceptions of the Rules of Writing," *CCC,* 30 [1979], 218–220), and our own observations suggest that students consistently misunderstand such Grammar 4 explanations (COIK, you will recall). For example, from Patrick Hartwell and Robert H. Bentley and from Mike Rose, we have two separate anecdotal accounts of students, cited for punctuating a *because*-clause as a sentence, who have decided to avoid using *because.* More generally, Collette A. Daiute's analysis of errors made by college students shows that errors tend to appear at clause boundaries, suggesting short-term memory load and not conceptual deficiency as a cause of error.[21]

Thus, if we think seriously about error and its relationship to the worship of formal grammar study, we need to attempt some massive dislocation of our traditional thinking, to shuck off our hyperliterate perception of the value of formal rules, and to regain the confidence in the tacit power of unconscious knowledge that our theory of language gives us. Most students, reading their writing aloud, will correct in essence all errors of spelling, grammar, and, by intonation, punctuation, but usually without noticing that what they read departs from what they wrote.[22] And Richard H. Haswell ("Minimal Marking," *CE,* 45 [1983], 600–604) notes that his students correct 61.1 percent of their errors when they are identified with a simple mark in the margin rather than by error type. Such findings suggest that we need to redefine error, to see it not as a cognitive or linguistic problem, a problem of not knowing a "rule of grammar" (whatever that may mean), but rather, following the insight of Robert J. Bracewell ("Writing as a Cognitive Activity," *Visible Language,* 14 [1980], 400–422), as a problem of metacognition and metalinguistic awareness, a matter of accessing knowledges that, to be of any use, learners must have already internalized by means of exposure to the code. (Usage issues — Grammar 3 — probably represent a different order of problem. Both Joseph Emonds and Jeffrey Jochnowitz establish that the usage issues we worry most about are linguistically unnatural, departures from the grammar in our heads.)[23]

The notion of metalinguistic awareness seems crucial. The sentence below, created by Douglas R. Hofstadter ("Metamagical Themas," *Scientific American,* 235, No. 1 [1981], 22–32), is offered to clarify that notion; you are invited to examine it for a moment or two before continuing.

Their is four errors in this sentence. Can you find them?

Three errors announce themselves plainly enough, the misspellings of *there* and *sentence* and the use of *is* instead of *are*. (And, just to illustrate the perils of hyperliteracy, let it be noted that, through three years of drafts, I referred to the choice of *is* and *are* as a matter of "subject-verb agreement.") The fourth error resists detection, until one assesses the truth value of the sentence itself — the fourth error is that there are not four errors, only three. Such a sentence (Hofstadter calls it a "self-referencing sentence") asks you to look at it in two ways, simultaneously as statement and as linguistic artifact — in other words, to exercise metalinguistic awareness.

A broad range of cross-cultural studies suggest that metalinguistic awareness is a defining feature of print literacy. Thus Sylvia Scribner and Michael Cole, working with the triliterate Vai of Liberia (variously literate in English, through schooling; in Arabic, for religious purposes; and in an indigenous Vai script, used for personal affairs), find that metalinguistic awareness, broadly conceived, is the only cognitive skill underlying each of the three literacies. The one statistically significant skill shared by literate Vai was the recognition of word boundaries. Moreover, literate Vai tended to answer "yes" when asked (in Vai). "Can you call the sun the moon and the moon the sun?" while illiterate Vai tended to have grave doubts about such metalinguistic play. And in the United States Henry and Lila R. Gleitman report quite different responses by clerical workers and Ph.D. candidates asked to interpret nonsense compounds like "house-bird glass": clerical workers focused on meaning and plausibility (for example, "a house-bird made of glass"), while Ph.D. candidates focused on syntax (for example, "a very small drinking cup for canaries" or "a glass that protects house-birds").[24] More general research findings suggest a clear relationship between measures of metalinguistic awareness and measures of literacy level.[25] William Labov, speculating on literacy acquisition in inner-city ghettoes, contrasts "stimulus-bound" and "language-bound" individuals, suggesting that the latter seem to master literacy more easily.[26] The analysis here suggests that the causal relationship works the other way, that it is the mastery of written language that increases one's awareness of language as language.

This analysis has two implications. First, it makes the question of socially nonstandard dialects, always implicit in discussions of teaching formal grammar, into a non-issue.[27] Native speakers of English, regardless of dialect, show tacit mastery of the conventions of Standard English, and that mastery seems to transfer into abstract orthographic knowledge through interaction with print.[28] Developing writers show the same patterning of errors, regardless of dialect.[29] Studies of reading and of writing suggest that surface features of spoken dialect are simply irrelevant to mastering print literacy.[30] Print is a complex cultural code — or better yet, a system of code — and my bet is that, regardless of instruction, one masters those codes from the top down, from pragmatic questions of voice, tone, audience, register, and rhetorical strategy, not from the bottom up, from grammar to usage to fixed forms of organization.

Second, this analysis forces us to posit multiple literacies, used for multiple purposes, rather than a single static literacy, engraved in "rules of grammar." These multiple literacies are evident in cross-cultural studies.[31] They are equally evident when we inquire into the uses of literacy in American communities.[32] Further, given that students, at all levels, show widely variant interactions with print literacy, there would seem to be little to do with grammar — with Grammar 2 or with Grammar 4 — that we could isolate as a basis for formal instruction.[33]

Grammar 5: Stylistic Grammar

Similarly, when we turn to Grammar 5, "grammatical terms used in the interest of teaching prose style," so central to Martha Kolln's argument for teaching formal grammar, we find that the grammar issue is simply beside the point. There are two fully articulated positions about "stylistic grammar," which I will label "romantic" and "classic," following Richard Lloyd-Jones and Richard E. Young.[34] The romantic position is that stylistic grammars, though perhaps useful for teachers, have little place in the teaching of composition, for students must struggle with and through language toward meaning. This position rests on a theory of language ultimately philosophical rather than linguistic (witness, for example, the contempt for linguists in Ann Berthoff's *The Making of Meaning: Metaphors, Models, and Maxims for Writing Teachers* [Montclair, N.J.: Boynton/Cook, 1981]); it is articulated as a theory of style by Donald A. Murray and, on somewhat different grounds (that stylistic grammars encourage overuse of the monitor), by Ian Pringle. The classic position, on the other hand, is that we can find ways to offer developing writers helpful suggestions about prose style, suggestions such as Francis Christensen's emphasis on the cumulative sentence, developed by observing the practice of skilled writers, and Joseph Williams' advice about predication, developed by psycholinguistic studies of comprehension.[35] James A. Berlin's recent survey of composition theory (*CE*, 45 [1982], 765–777) probably understates the gulf between these two positions and the radically different conceptions of language that underlie them, but it does establish that they share an overriding assumption in common: that one learns to control the language of print by manipulating language in meaningful contexts, not by learning about language in isolation, as by the study of formal grammar. Thus even classic theorists, who choose to present a vocabulary of style to students, do so only as a vehicle for encouraging productive control of communicative structures.

We might put the matter in the following terms. Writers need to develop skills at two levels. One, broadly rhetorical, involves communication in meaningful contexts (the strategies, registers, and procedures of discourse across a range of modes, audiences, contexts, and purposes).

The other, broadly metalinguistic rather than linguistic, involves active manipulation of language with conscious attention to surface form. This second level may be developed tacitly, as a natural adjunct to developing rhetorical competencies — I take this to be the position of romantic theorists. It may be developed formally, by manipulating language for stylistic effect, and such manipulation may involve, for pedagogical continuity, a vocabulary of style. But it is primarily developed by any kind of language activity that enhances the awareness of language as language.[36] David T. Hakes, summarizing the research on metalinguistic awareness, notes how far we are from understanding this process:

> the optimal conditions for becoming metalinguistically competent involve growing up in a literate environment with adult models who are themselves metalinguistically competent and who foster the growth of that competence in a variety of ways as yet little understood. ("The Development of Metalinguistic Abilities," p. 205: see note 25)

Such a model places language, at all levels, at the center of the curriculum, but not as "necessary categories and labels" (Kolln, "Closing the Books on Alchemy," p. 150), but as literal stuff, verbal clay, to be molded and probed, shaped and reshaped, and, above all, enjoyed.

The Tradition of Experimental Research

Thus, when we turn back to experimental research on the value of formal grammar instruction, we do so with firm predictions given us by our theory of language. Our theory would predict that formal grammar instruction, whether instruction in scientific grammar or instruction in "the common school grammar," would have little to do with control over surface correctness nor with quality of writing. It would predict that any form of active involvement with language would be preferable to instruction in rules or definitions (or incantations). In essence, this is what the research tells us. In 1893, the Committee of Ten (*Report of the Committee of Ten on Secondary School Studies* [Washington, D.C.: U.S. Government Printing Office, 1893]) put grammar at the center of the English curriculum, and its report established the rigidly sequential mode of instruction common for the last century. But the committee explicitly noted that grammar instruction did not aid correctness, arguing instead that it improved the ability to think logically (an argument developed from the role of the "grammarian" in the classical rhetorical tradition, essentially a teacher of literature — see, for example, the etymology of *grammar* in the *Oxford English Dictionary*).

But Franklin S. Hoyt, in a 1906 experiment, found no relationship between the study of grammar and the ability to think logically; his research led him to conclude what I am constrained to argue more than seventy-five years later, that there is no "relationship between a knowledge of technical grammar and the ability to use English and to interpret language" ("The Place of Grammar in the Elementary Curriculum," *Teachers College Record,* 7 [1906], 483–484). Later studies, through the 1920s, focused on the relationship of knowledge of grammar and ability to recognize error; experiments reported by James Boraas in 1917 and by William Asker in 1923 are typical of those that reported no correlation. In the 1930s, with the development of the functional grammar movement, it was common to compare the study of formal grammar with one form or another of active manipulation of language; experiments by I. O. Ash in 1935 and Ellen Frogner in 1939 are typical of studies showing the superiority of active involvement with language.[37] In a 1959 article, "Grammar in Language Teaching" (*Elementary English,* 36 [1959], 412–421), John J. DeBoer noted the consistency of these findings.

> The impressive fact is . . . that in all these studies, carried out in places and at times far removed from each other, often by highly experienced and disinterested investigators, the results have been consistently negative so far as the value of grammar in the improvement of language expression is concerned. (p. 417)

In 1960 Ingrid M. Strom, reviewing more than fifty experimental studies, came to a similarly strong and unqualified conclusion:

> direct methods of instruction, focusing on writing activities and the structuring of ideas, are more efficient in teaching sentence structure, usage, punctuation, and other related factors than are such methods as nomenclature drill, diagramming, and rote memorization of grammatical rules.[38]

In 1963 two research reviews appeared, one by Braddock, Lloyd-Jones, and Schorer, cited at the beginning of this paper, and one by Henry C. Meckel, whose conclusions, though more guarded, are in essential agreement.[39] In 1969 J. Stephen Sherwin devoted one-fourth of his *Four Problems in Teaching English: A Critique of Research* (Scranton, Penn.: International Textbook, 1969) to the grammar issue, concluding that "instruction in formal grammar is an ineffective way to help students achieve proficiency in writing" (p. 135). Some early experiments in sentence combining, such as those by Donald R. Bateman and Frank J. Zidonnis and by John C. Mellon, showed improvement in measures of syntactic complexity with instruction in transformational grammar keyed to sentence combining practice. But a later study by Frank O'Hare achieved the same gains with no grammar instruction, suggesting to Sandra L. Stotsky and to Richard Van de Veghe that active manipulation of language, not the grammar unit, explained the earlier results.[40] More recent summaries of research — by Elizabeth I. Haynes, Hillary Taylor Holbrook, and Marcia Farr Whiteman — support similar conclusions. Indirect evidence for this position is provided by surveys reported by Betty Bamberg in 1978 and 1981, showing that time spent in grammar instruction in high school is the least important factor, of eight factors examined, in separating regular from remedial writers at the college level.[41]

More generally, Patrick Scott and Bruce Castner, in "Reference Sources for Composition Research: A Practical Survey" (*CE*, 45 [1983], 756–768), note that much current research is not informed by an awareness of the past. Put simply, we are constrained to reinvent the wheel. My concern here has been with a far more serious problem: that too often the wheel we reinvent is square.

It is, after all, a question of power. Janet Emig, developing a consensus from composition research, and Aaron S. Carton and Lawrence V. Castiglione, developing the implications of language theory for education, come to the same conclusion: that the thrust of current research and theory is to take power from the teacher and to give that power to the learner.[42] At no point in the English curriculum is the question of power more blatantly posed than in the issue of formal grammar instruction. It is time that we, as teachers, formulate theories of language and literacy and let those theories guide our teaching, and it is time that we, as researchers, move on to more interesting areas of inquiry.

Notes

1. *Research in Written Composition* (Urbana, Ill.: National Council of Teachers of English, 1963), pp. 37–38.

2. "Non-magical Thinking: Presenting Writing Developmentally in Schools," in *Writing Process, Development and Communication,* Vol. II of *Writing: The Nature, Development and Teaching of Written Communication,* ed. Charles H. Frederiksen and Joseph F. Dominic (Hillsdale, N.J.: Lawrence Erlbaum, 1980), pp. 21–30.

3. For arguments in favor of formal grammar teaching, see Patrick F. Basset, "Grammar — Can We Afford Not to Teach It?" *NASSP Bulletin,* 64, No. 10 (1980), 55–63; Mary Epes et al., "The COMP-LAB Project: Assessing the Effectiveness of a Laboratory-Centered Basic Writing Course on the College Level" (Jamaica, N.Y.: York College, CUNY, 1979) ERIC 194 908; June B. Evans, "The Analogous Ounce: The Analgesic for Relief," *English Journal,* 70, No. 2 (1981), 38–39; Sydney Greenbaum, "What Is Grammar and Why Teach It?" (a paper presented at the meeting of the National Council of Teachers of English, Boston, Nov. 1982) ERIC 222 917; Marjorie Smelstor, *A Guide to the Role of Grammar in Teaching Writing* (Madison: University of Wisconsin School of Education, 1978) ERIC 176 323; and A. M. Tibbetts, *Working Papers: A Teacher's Observations on Composition* (Glenview, Ill.: Scott, Foresman, 1982).

   For attacks on formal grammar teaching, see Harvey A. Daniels, *Famous Last Words: The American Language Crisis Reconsidered* (Carbondale: Southern Illinois University Press, 1983); Suzette Haden Elgin, *Never Mind the Trees: What the English Teacher Really Needs to Know about Linguistics* (Berkeley: University of California College of Education, Bay Area Writing Project Occasional Paper No. 2, 1980) ERIC 198 536; Mike Rose, "Remedial Writing Courses: A Critique and a Proposal," *College English,* 45 (1983), 109–128; and Ron Shook, Response to Martha Kolln, *College Composition and Communication,* 34 (1983), 491–495.

4. See, for example, Clifton Fadiman and James Howard, *Empty Pages: A Search for Writing Competence in School and Society* (Belmont, Cal.: Fearon Pitman, 1979); Edwin Newman, *A Civil Tongue* (Indianapolis, Ind.: Bobbs-Merrill, 1976); and *Strictly Speaking* (New York: Warner Books, 1974); John Simons, *Paradigms Lost* (New York: Clarkson N. Potter, 1980); A. M. Tibbetts and Charlene Tibbetts, *What's Happening to American English?* (New York: Scribner's, 1978); and "Why Johnny Can't Write," *Newsweek,* 8 Dec. 1975, pp. 58–63.

5. "The Role of Grammar in a Secondary School English Curriculum," *Research in the Teaching of English,* 10 (1976), 5–21; *The Role of Grammar in a Secondary School Curriculum* (Wellington: New Zealand Council of Teachers of English, 1979).

6. "A Taxonomy of Compositional Competencies," in *Perspectives on Literacy,* ed. Richard Beach and P. David Pearson (Minneapolis: University of Minnesota College of Education, 1979), pp. 247–272.

7. On usage norms, see Edward Finegan, *Attitudes toward English Usage: The History of a War of Words* (New York: Teachers College Press, 1980), and Jim Quinn, *American Tongue in Cheek: A Populist Guide to Language* (New York: Pantheon, 1980); on arrangement, see Patrick Hartwell, "Teaching Arrangement: A Pedagogy," *CE,* 40 (1979), 548–554.

8. "Revolution in Grammar," *Quarterly Journal of Speech,* 40 (1954), 299–312.

9. Richard A. Lanham, *Revising Prose* (New York: Scribner's, 1979); William Strunk and E. B. White, *The Elements of Style,* 3rd ed. (New York: Macmillan, 1979); Joseph Williams, *Style: Ten Lessons in Clarity and Grace* (Glenview, Ill.: Scott, Foresman, 1981); Christensen, "A Generative Rhetoric of the Sentence," *CCC,* 14 (1963), 155–161; Donald A. Daiker, Andrew Kerek, and Max Morenberg, *The Writer's Options: Combining to Composing,* 2nd ed. (New York: Harper & Row, 1982).

10. "A Psychological Approach," in *Psychobiology of Language,* ed. M. Studdert-Kennedy (Cambridge, Mass.: MIT Press, 1983), pp. 16–19. See also Noam Chomsky, "Language and Unconscious Knowledge," in *Psychoanalysis and Language: Psychiatry and the Humanities,* Vol. III, ed. Joseph H. Smith (New Haven, Conn.: Yale University Press, 1978), pp. 3–44.

11. Morris Halle, "Knowledge Unlearned and Untaught: What Speakers Know about the Sounds of Their Language," in *Linguistic Theory and Psychological Reality,* ed. Halle, Joan Bresnan, and George A. Miller (Cambridge, Mass.: MIT Press, 1978), pp. 135–140.

12. Moscowitz, "On the Status of Vowel Shift in English," in *Cognitive Development and the Acquisition of Language,* ed. T. E. Moore (New York: Academic Press, 1973), pp. 223–260; Chomsky, "Stages in Language Development and Reading Exposure," *Harvard Educational Review,* 42 (1972), 1–33; and Brause, "Developmental Aspects of the Ability to Understand Semantic Ambiguity, with Implications for Teachers," *RTE,* 11 (1977), 39–48.

13. Mills and Hemsley, "The Effect of Levels of Education on Judgments of Grammatical Acceptability," *Language and Speech,* 19 (1976), 324–342; Whyte, "Levels of Language Competence and Reading Ability: An Exploratory Investigation," *Journal of Research in Reading,* 5 (1982), 123–132;

Morais et al., "Does Awareness of Speech as a Series of Phones Arise Spontaneously?" *Cognition,* 7 (1979), 323–331; Ferguson, *Cognitive Effects of Literacy: Linguistic Awareness in Adult Non-readers* (Washington, D.C.: National Institute of Education Final Report, 1981) ERIC 222 857; Hamilton and Barton, "A Word Is a Word: Metalinguistic Skills in Adults of Varying Literacy Levels" (Stanford, Cal.: Stanford University Department of Linguistics, 1980) ERIC 222 859.

14. On the question of the psychological reality of Grammar 2 descriptions, see Maria Black and Shulamith Chiat, "Psycholinguistics without 'Psychological Reality,'" *Linguistics,* 19 (1981), 37–61; Joan Bresnan, ed., *The Mental Representation of Grammatical Relations* (Cambridge, Mass.: MIT Press, 1982); and Michael H. Long, "Inside the 'Black Box': Methodological Issues in Classroom Research on Language Learning," *Language Learning,* 30 (1980), 1–42.

15. Chomsky, "The Current Scene in Linguistics," *College English,* 27 (1966), 587–595; and "Linguistic Theory," in *Language Teaching: Broader Contexts,* ed. Robert C. Meade, Jr. (New York: Modern Language Association, 1966), pp. 43–49; Mark Lester, "The Value of Transformational Grammar in Teaching Composition," *CCC,* 16 (1967), 228.

16. Christensen, "Between Two Worlds," in *Notes toward a New Rhetoric: Nine Essays for Teachers,* rev. ed., ed. Bonniejean Christensen (New York: Harper & Row, 1978), pp. 1–22.

17. Reber, "Implicit Learning of Artificial Grammars," *Journal of Verbal Learning and Verbal Behavior,* 6 (1967), 855–863; "Implicit Learning of Synthetic Languages: The Role of Instructional Set," *Journal of Experimental Psychology: Human Learning and Memory,* 2 (1976), 889–894, and Reber, Saul M. Kassin, Selma Lewis, and Gary Cantor, "On the Relationship Between Implicit and Explicit Modes in the Learning of a Complex Rule Structure," *Journal of Experimental Psychology: Human Learning and Memory,* 6 (1980), 492–502.

18. "Individual Variation in the Use of the Monitor," in *Principles of Second Language Learning,* ed. W. Richie (New York: Academic Press, 1978), pp. 175–185.

19. "Applications of Psycholinguistic Research to the Classroom," in *Practical Applications of Research in Foreign Language Teaching,* ed. D. J. James (Lincolnwood, Ill.: National Textbook, 1983), p. 61.

20. "Some Evidence for the Integrity and Interaction of Two Knowledge Sources," in *New Dimensions in Second Language Acquisition Research,* ed. Roger W. Andersen (Rowley, Mass.: Newbury House, 1981), pp. 62–74.

21. Hartwell and Bentley, *Some Suggestions for Using Open to Language: A New College Rhetoric* (New York: Oxford University Press, 1982), p. 73; Rose, *Writer's Block: The Cognitive Dimension* (Carbondale: Southern Illinois University Press, 1983), p. 99; Daiute, "Psycholinguistic Foundations of the Writing Process," *RTE,* 15 (1981), 5–22.

22. See Bartholomae, "The Study of Error"; Patrick Hartwell, "The Writing Center and the Paradoxes of Written-Down Speech," in *Writing Centers: Theory and Administration,* ed. Gary Olson (Urbana, Ill.: NCTE, 1984), pp. 48–61; and Sondra Perl, "A Look at Basic Writers in the Process of Composing," in *Basic Writing: A Collection of Essays for Teachers, Researchers, and Administrators* (Urbana, Ill.: NCTE, 1980), pp. 13–32.

23. Emonds, *Adjacency in Grammar: The Theory of Language-Particular Rules* (New York: Academic, 1983); and Jochnowitz, "Everybody Likes Pizza, Doesn't He or She?" *American Speech,* 57 (1982), 198–203.

24. Scribner and Cole, *Psychology of Literacy* (Cambridge, Mass.: Harvard University Press, 1981); Gleitman and Gleitman, "Language Use and Language Judgment," in *Individual Differences in Language Ability and Language Behavior*, ed. Charles J. Fillmore, Daniel Kemper, and William S.-Y. Wang (New York: Academic Press, 1979), pp. 103–126.

25. There are several recent reviews of this developing body of research in psychology and child development: Irene Athey, "Language Development Factors Related to Reading Development," *Journal of Educational Research*, 76 (1983), 197–203; James Flood and Paula Menyuk, "Metalinguistic Development and Reading/Writing Achievement," *Claremont Reading Conference Yearbook*, 46 (1982), 122–132; and the following four essays: David T. Hakes, "The Development of Metalinguistic Abilities: What Develops?" pp. 162–210; Stan A. Kuczaj II and Brooke Harbaugh, "What Children Think about the Speaking Capabilities of Other Persons and Things," pp. 211–227; Karen Saywitz and Louise Cherry Wilkinson, "Age-Related Differences in Metalinguistic Awareness," pp. 229–250; and Harriet Salatas Waters and Virginia S. Tinsley, "The Development of Verbal Self-Regulation: Relationships between Language, Cognition, and Behavior," pp. 251–277; all in *Language, Thought, and Culture*, Vol. II of *Language Development*, ed. Stan Kuczaj, Jr. (Hillsdale, N.J.: Lawrence Erlbaum, 1982). See also Joanne R. Nurss, "Research in Review: Linguistic Awareness and Learning to Read," *Young Children*, 35, No. 3 (1980), 57–66.

26. "Competing Value Systems in Inner City Schools," in *Children In and Out of School: Ethnography and Education*, ed. Perry Gilmore and Allan A. Glatthorn (Washington, D.C.: Center for Applied Linguistics, 1982), pp. 148–171; and "Locating the Frontier between Social and Psychological Factors in Linguistic Structure," in *Individual Differences in Language Ability and Language Behavior*, ed. Fillmore, Kemper, and Wang, pp. 327–340.

27. See, for example, Thomas Farrell, "IQ and Standard English," *CCC*, 34 (1983), 470–484; and the responses by Karen L. Greenberg and Patrick Hartwell, *CCC*, 35 (1984): 455–478.

28. Jane W. Torrey, "Teaching Standard English to Speakers of Other Dialects," in *Applications of Linguistics: Selected Papers of the Second International Conference of Applied Linguistics*, ed. G. E. Perren and J. L. M. Trim (Cambridge, Mass.: Cambridge University Press, 1971), pp. 423–428; James W. Beers and Edmund H. Henderson, "A Study of the Developing Orthographic Concepts among First Graders," *RTE*, 11 (1977), 133–148.

29. See the error counts of Samuel A. Kirschner and G. Howard Poteet, "Non-Standard English Usage in the Writing of Black, White, and Hispanic Remedial English Students in an Urban Community College," *RTE*, 7 (1973), 351–355; and Marilyn Sternglass, "Close Similarities in Dialect Features of Black and White College Students in Remedial Composition Classes," *TESOL Quarterly*, 8 (1974), 271–283.

30. For reading, see the massive study by Kenneth S. Goodman and Yetta M. Goodman, *Reading of American Children Whose Language Is a Stable Rural Dialect of English or a Language Other than English* (Washington, D.C.: National Institute of Education Final Report, 1978) ERIC 175 754; and the overview by Rudine Sims, "Dialect and Reading: Toward Redefining the Issues," in *Reader Meets Author/Bridging the Gap: A Psycholinguistic and Sociolinguistic Approach*, ed. Judith A. Langer and M. Tricia Smith-Burke (Newark, Del.: International Reading Association, 1982), pp. 222–

232. For writing, see Patrick Hartwell, "Dialect Interference in Writing: A Critical View," *RTE,* 14 (1980), 101–118; and the anthology edited by Barry M. Kroll and Roberta J. Vann, *Exploring Speaking-Writing Relationships: Connections and Contrasts* (Urbana, Ill.: NCTE, 1981).

31. See, for example, Eric A. Havelock, *The Literary Revolution in Greece and Its Cultural Consequences* (Princeton, N.J.: Princeton University Press, 1982); Lesley Milroy on literacy in Dublin, *Language and Social Networks* (Oxford: Basil Blackwell, 1980); Ron Scollon and Suzanne B. K. Scollon on literacy in central Alaska, *Interethnic Communication: An Athabascan Case* (Austin, Tex.: Southwest Educational Development Laboratory Working Papers in Sociolinguistics, No. 59, 1979) ERIC 175 276; and Scribner and Cole on literacy in Liberia, *Psychology of Literacy* (see note 24).

32. See, for example, the anthology edited by Deborah Tannen, *Spoken and Written Language: Exploring Orality and Literacy* (Norwood, N.J.: Ablex, 1982); and Shirley Brice Heath's continuing work: "Protean Shapes in Literacy Events: Ever-Shifting Oral and Literate Traditions," in *Spoken and Written Language,* pp. 91–117; *Ways with Words: Language, Life and Work in Communities and Classrooms* (New York: Cambridge University Press, 1983); and "What No Bedtime Story Means," *Language in Society,* 11 (1982), 49–76.

33. For studies at the elementary level, see Dell H. Hymes et al., eds., *Ethnographic Monitoring of Children's Acquisition of Reading/Language Arts Skills In and Out of the Classroom* (Washington, D.C.: National Institute of Education Final Report, 1981) ERIC 208 096. For studies at the secondary level, see James L. Collins and Michael M. Williamson, "Spoken Language and Semantic Abbreviation in Writing," *RTE,* 15 (1981), 23–36. And for studies at the college level, see Patrick Hartwell and Gene LoPresti, "Sentence Combining as Kid-Watching," in *Sentence Combining: Toward a Rhetorical Perspective,* ed. Donald A. Daiker, Andrew Kerek, and Max Morenberg (Carbondale: Southern Illinois University Press, 1984).

34. Lloyd-Jones, "Romantic Revels — I Am Not You," *CCC,* 23 (1972), 251–271; and Young, "Concepts of Art and the Teaching of Writing," in *The Rhetorical Tradition and Modern Writing,* ed. James J. Murphy (New York: Modern Language Association, 1982), pp. 130–141.

35. For the romantic position, see Ann E. Berthoff, "Tolstoy, Vygotsky, and the Making of Meaning," *CCC,* 29 (1978), 249–255; Kenneth Dowst, "The Epistemic Approach," in *Eight Approaches to Teaching Composition,* ed. Timothy Donovan and Ben G. McClellan (Urbana, Ill.: NCTE, 1980), pp. 65–85; Peter Elbow, "The Challenge for Sentence Combining"; and Donald Murray, "Following Language toward Meaning," both in *Sentence Combining: Toward a Rhetorical Perspective* (Carbondale: Southern Illinois University Press, 1984); and Ian Pringle, "Why Teach Style? A Review-Essay," *CCC,* 34 (1983), 91–98.

   For the classic position, see Christensen's "A Generative Rhetoric of the Sentence"; and Joseph Williams' "Defining Complexity," *CE,* 41 (1979), 595–609; and his *Style: Ten Lessons in Clarity and Grace* (see note 9).

36. Courtney B. Cazden and David K. Dickinson, "Language and Education: Standardization versus Cultural Pluralism," in *Language in the USA,* ed. Charles A. Ferguson and Shirley Brice Heath (New York: Cambridge University Press, 1981), pp. 446–468; and Carol Chomsky, "Developing Facility with Language Structure," in *Discovering Language with Children,* ed. Gay Su Pinnell (Urbana, Ill.: NCTE, 1980), pp. 56–59.

37. Boraas, "Formal English Grammar and the Practical Mastery of English." Diss. University of Illinois, 1917; Asker, "Does Knowledge of Grammar Function?" *School and Society,* 17 (27 January 1923), 109–111; Ash, "An Experimental Evaluation of the Stylistic Approach in Teaching Composition in the Junior High School," *Journal of Experimental Education,* 4 (1935), 54–62; and Frogner, "A Study of the Relative Efficacy of a Grammatical and a Thought Approach to the Improvement of Sentence Structure in Grades Nine and Eleven," *School Review,* 47 (1939), 663–675.

38. "Research on Grammar and Usage and Its Implications for Teaching Writing," *Bulletin of the School of Education,* Indiana University, 36 (1960), pp. 13–14.

39. Meckel, "Research on Teaching Composition and Literature," in *Handbook of Research on Teaching,* ed. N. L. Gage (Chicago: Rand McNally, 1963), pp. 966–1006.

40. Bateman and Zidonis, *The Effect of a Study of Transformational Grammar on the Writing of Ninth and Tenth Graders* (Urbana, Ill.: NCTE, 1966); Mellon, *Transformational Sentence Combining: A Method for Enhancing the Development of Fluency in English Composition* (Urbana, Ill.: NCTE, 1969); O'Hare, *Sentence-Combining: Improving Student Writing without Formal Grammar Instruction* (Urbana, Ill.: NCTE, 1971); Stotsky, "Sentence-Combining as a Curricular Activity: Its Effect on Written Language Development," *RTE,* 9 (1975), 30–72; and Van de Veghe, "Research in Written Composition: Fifteen Years of Investigation," ERIC 157 095.

41. Haynes, "Using Research in Preparing to Teach Writing," *English Journal,* 69, No. 1 (1978), 82–88; Holbrook, "ERIC/RCS Report: Whither (Wither) Grammar," *Language Arts,* 60 (1983), 259–263; Whiteman, "What We Can Learn from Writing Research," *Theory into Practice,* 19 (1980), 150–156; Bamberg, "Composition in the Secondary English Curriculum: Some Current Trends and Directions for the Eighties," *RTE,* 15 (1981), 257–266; and "Composition Instruction Does Make a Difference: A Comparison of the High School Preparation of College Freshmen in Regular and Remedial English Classes," *RTE,* 12 (1978), 47–59.

42. Emig, "Inquiry Paradigms and Writing," *CCC,* 33 (1982), 64–75; Carton and Castiglione, "Educational Linguistics: Defining the Domain," in *Psycholinguistic Research: Implications and Applications,* ed. Doris Aaronson and Robert W. Rieber (Hillsdale, N.J.: Lawrence Erlbaum, 1979), pp. 497–520.

Hartwell's Insights as a Resource for Your Teaching

1. Make a list of the different ways in which you might "teach grammar," and then try to identify the assumptions that underlie each one. Which methods are most appropriate, given Hartwell's argument? Which are the least appropriate?

2. Hartwell's "Grammar 5" is clearly the sort of grammar and usage that we want our students to master. What types of difficulties might you expect to encounter in striving to teach this approach? How would you prepare for these?

Hartwell's Insights as a Resource for Your Writing Classroom

1. Briefly outline for your students Hartwell's five different types of grammar. Ask them to describe what specific components they think might constitute the all-important "Grammar 5."

2. Ask your students to describe their chief concerns about grammar. Challenge them to address these concerns by following Hartwell's ideas about formal grammar instruction and considering specific methods to engage active language involvement.

Issues in Writing Pedagogy: Institutional Politics and the Other

C heck the table of contents of journals like *Rhetoric Review*, *Journal of Teaching Writing*, or *College English*; scan a program of the Conference on College Composition and Communication; subscribe to a composition listserv; browse in the "new acquisitions" section of your library; or pick up the weekly *Chronicle of Higher Education*. You will find vigorous discussion of multiple issues that influence and grow out of the teaching of writing at the college level. Of the many issues that challenge and encourage teachers of writing, one continues to dominate much of our focus: How might writing teachers acknowledge the diversity of our students' experience? Answers to this question can lead us down a variety of paths, and the readings in Chapter 4 are portals to the many subtopics within the larger discussion of diversity. Each reading provides both an entry to the discussion and reading paths to follow when you decide to broaden and deepen your engagement.

Paradigms of writing, language acquisition, and reading as recursive processes have led to recognition of and respect for the individual engaged in learning. This recognition and respect has in turn informed the discussion, research, and practice in many areas: admissions policies; the teaching of writing, English as a second language, and composition as cultural critique; collaborative learning; whole-language learning; the "feminization" of composition; and assessment. There is also greater awareness of multicultural perspectives on writing, reading, and the gaining of wisdom.

Nouns such as *literacy, diversity, feminism, multiculturalism, social construction, negotiation, discourse communities,* and *postmodernism* resonate in our professional conversations. We hear national, state, local, and institutional mandates for increasing and enhancing literacy, for acknowledging and respecting diversity, and for broadening our awareness of and inquiry into the multiple perspectives, issues, and cultures (ethnic, regional, social, political, gender-linked, religious, and so on) that make up the mosaic of "America" and of the world community. The selections in this chapter can help bring us to a more concrete understanding of how these often vaguely defined issues impact teaching and learning in our classrooms.

The community of writers with whom we work brings together individuals who have traditionally been welcomed to and included in knowledge communities and individuals who have been excluded. We teach these students in times of vigorous debate about how education could and should serve all these learners. The task is daunting and exciting. Look to the Annotated Bibliography for more readings to guide you in reflecting on your practices within this environment.

Tutoring ESL Students: Issues and Options

Muriel Harris and Tony Silva

Muriel Harris, a writing center administrator and theorist, and Tony Silva, an English as a Second Language specialist, wrote this piece for colleagues who train tutors to work with ESL writers. However, the essay, which appeared in College Composition and Communication *(1993), also provides composition teachers a clear overview of issues and practical teaching strategies for working with ESL writers. The questions that nag new peer tutors and their responses to texts written by ESL students differ only by degree of apprehension from the questions and reading responses of writing teachers. The "tutorial principles" cited are also standard teaching practices of writing instructors. The recommended readings are useful additions to the professional library of a writing instructor. Use this essay as a jumping-in point for thinking about, and planning to work with, students who compose in English as their second — or third or fourth — language.*

For students whose first language is not English, the writing classroom cannot provide all the instructional assistance that is needed to become proficient writers. For a variety of reasons, these students need the kind of individualized attention that tutors offer, instruction that casts no aspersions on the adequacy of the classroom or the ability of the student. We should recognize that along with different linguistic backgrounds, ESL students have a diversity of concerns that can only be dealt with in the one-to-one setting where the focus of attention is on that particular student and his or her questions, concerns, cultural presuppositions, writing processes, language learning experiences, and conceptions of what writing in English is all about. Typically, the tutorial assistance available for these students is provided by writing centers, and much of the personal help available there is precisely the same as for any native speaker of English: The goal of tutors who work in the center is to attend to the individual concerns of every writer who walks in the door — writing process questions, reader feedback, planning conversations, and so on. But also typically, tutors, who bring to their work a background of experience and knowledge in interacting effectively with native speakers of English, are not adequately equipped to deal with some additional concerns of non-native speakers of English — the unfamiliar grammatical errors, the sometimes bewilderingly different rhetorical patterns and conventions of other languages, and the expectations that accompany ESL writers when they come to the writing center. Tutors can be reduced to stunned silence when they try to explain why "I have many homeworks to completed" is wrong or why we say "on Monday" but "in June."

Tutors need some perspective on rhetorical approaches other than those they expect to find, such as a direct statement of the topic or discourse with a linear development. When tutors find, instead, an implicitly stated point or when they become lost in a long, seemingly meandering introduction or digressions that appear irrelevant, they flounder, not recognizing that implicitness and digressions may be acceptable rhetorical strategies in the writing of some other cultures. Because the need to learn more about how to work with ESL writers in tutorials is immediate and real, one of the authors of this essay, a writing center director, asked the other author, the coordinator of ESL writing courses at our university, for help. The conversations that ensued are summarized here in terms of the questions that guided our discussion of various issues and options, and our hope is that our exchanges will be of interest to others who train tutors to work with ESL students. We also hope that composition teachers looking for guidance when conferencing with ESL students will find useful suggestions for their own interactions with these students.

Plunging In: How Do We Prioritize among Errors?

In the peer tutor training course in our writing center, peer tutors are especially eager to meet and work with ESL students, but their initial contacts can be somewhat frightening because some unfamiliar concerns crop up. To the untrained tutor's eye what is most immediately noticeable is that a draft written by an ESL student looks so different. Vocabulary choices might be confusing, familiar elements of essays are missing, and sentences exhibit a variety of errors — some we can categorize, some we cannot. Tutors' first concern is often a matter of wanting some guidance about where to plunge in. Where should they start? New tutors who have not yet completely internalized the concept of the tutorial as focusing only on one or two concerns think initially it is their responsibility to help the writer fix everything in the draft in front of them. As tutors learn the pedagogy of the tutorial, they become more comfortable with selecting something to work on for that session, but they still need suggestions for a hierarchy and some sense of what is most important.

When tutors ask how to prioritize among errors, they should be encouraged to begin by looking for what has been done well in the paper, acknowledge that, and go from there. Such a suggestion fits in well with the tutorial principle of beginning all interaction with writers on a positive note and reminds us that ESL writers should not be separated out as different or unlike other students in this regard. And tutors should also be encouraged to let their students know that errors are a natural part of language learning and that most readers will be interested primarily in what writers have to say. So tutors need to distinguish between errors that will interfere with the intended reader's understanding of the text (global errors) and those that will not (local errors) and to give priority to the former. To illustrate for tutors this notion of global vs. local errors at the sentence level, the following example can help. Suppose an ESL student, attempting to describe some classmates as uninspired by a particular lecture, wrote: "Those students are boring" instead of "Those students are bored." This would constitute a global error. On the other hand, a construction such as "Those student are bored" would represent a local error.

Using Research: How Helpful Is It to Look for Patterns?

With our heightened awareness of multiculturalism, we are also more aware of cultural preferences that are reflected in writing, such as the often-cited Asian preference for indirection. The question in working one-to-one with ESL students is how helpful such generalizations really are. Work in contrastive rhetoric would seem to be particularly valuable because it describes patterns of rhetorical preferences in other cultures, patterns which may explain the seemingly inappropriate rhetorical strategies used by ESL students. But to what degree is such knowledge useful? To what extent should we help tutors become aware of such differences? On the one hand, there is a danger that they can begin to use general patterns as givens, expecting all speakers of other languages to fit the models they have learned. On the other hand, without any knowledge of cultural preferences tutors are likely to see differences as weaknesses and to assume that the ESL student needs basic writing help. For example, instead of introducing the American intolerance of digression as culturally appropriate for American discourse, a tutor might treat an ESL student purposefully using digression as an inadequate writer who has problems with organization. If the tutor assumes that student is deficient, the tutor's tendency might be to work on outlining and to leave aside any rationale for why digressions should be avoided. Tutors need to introduce preferences and conventions of American discourse for what they are — alternate conventions and preferences.

However, to consider the extent to which such knowledge is helpful, we have to begin with some background information. The study of first-language transfer at or below the sentence level, typically referred to as "contrastive analysis" (see Brown 153–63 for a concise summary of this work), and the study of differences in rhetorical preferences among various cultures, usually termed "contrastive rhetoric" (see, for example, Grabe and Kaplan; Leki), have given us useful insights into how the writing of ESL students may differ from accepted standards of American discourse. The question of the transfer of first-language (L1) linguistic and rhetorical patterns to second-language (L2) writing has been a central and contentious issue in ESL studies since the beginning of work in this area. In the early days it was believed that L1 transfer (then called interference) was the primary if not exclusive cause of L2 problems. Therefore, it was felt that if one could catalog the differences between a student's L1 and L2, one could anticipate — and thus be prepared to deal with — any problems that student might encounter in the L2. However, research showed that this was not the case. There were many problems that could not be accounted for by L1 interference. Other factors, such as cognitive development, prior language and/or writing instruction, and experience were also implicated. Today, it is generally believed that transfer can be positive or negative and that it is only one of the potential causes of L2 writing problems. Thus we have to approach the question of the use of such knowledge with some hedging. On one hand, being cognizant of typical problems associated with particular groups of ESL students can be helpful — especially if tutors work largely with one or two particular groups. At the very least, this would make tutors very familiar with these problems and perhaps enhance their ability to deal with them. However, tutors need to keep two things in mind: (1) not all members of a particular group may manifest all of the problems or cultural preferences associated with that group; and (2) not all problems will be a result of transfer of L1 patterns.

A related issue is that of culturally conditioned patterns of behavior, some articulated, some not. In the Writing Lab's tutor-training course, we dip into Edward Hall's work to help tutors-to-be become aware of the variety of human behaviors which are conditioned, consciously or unconsciously, by one's culture. Since some of these behaviors can impede communication in a tutorial, it's important to recognize that such differences occur. A few favorite topics among the tutors-in-training are their reactions to the preference for or avoidance of eye contact, the differences among cultures in regard to the amount of space that people expect to maintain between themselves and others, the acceptability of touching between strangers, and so on. The cautionary advice about not doing too much large-scale or whole-group predicting is worth recalling here, but we also have to be aware that we might make unconscious judgments about others based on our expectations about such behaviors. In addition, we have to deal with different cultural assumptions about time, keeping appointments vs.

showing up (if at all) much later, and so on. Understanding and accommodating cultural differences is, to a great extent, what ESL instruction is all about. This is especially true when working with students who are very new to and not very cognizant of the workings of American culture.

Recognizing Differences: How Do We Distinguish Language Learning from Writing Process Needs?

There is a tendency to think about ESL students as if they're all alike when obviously they're not. And in writing centers our focus is on working with individual differences of all kinds. So when the tutor and student negotiate the agenda of what they'll work on, the tutor has to do some assessment about a variety of things, including some sense of what skills the student has or doesn't have — not an easy matter when it might be that the writer's low level of language proficiency, not weak writing skills, is causing the problem. For example, does the thin, undeveloped two-paragraph essay an ESL student brings in indicate the need to talk about how to develop topics or is the student's lack of language proficiency in English keeping her from expressing a rich internal sense of what she wants to write about? As tutors we know that our conversation would take on a somewhat different emphasis depending on our analysis of the situation. The question then becomes one of how to decide whether the student needs help with language or with writing processes.

While the distinction between language proficiency and writing ability is not clear cut, it is crucial to make such a distinction in order to understand and address a given ESL writer's problems (see Barbara Kroll's "The Rhetoric and Syntax Split" for an excellent discussion of this issue). In some cases, a very low level of English proficiency will prevent a student from producing any kind of coherent prose. For such a student some basic language instruction, preceding or accompanying writing instruction, would be indicated. Then there is the student with enough English proficiency to make it unclear whether problems result primarily from rhetorical or linguistic difficulties or from both. There are a number of ways tutors can proceed when trying to ascertain the cause of the problem — assuming they will see the student more than once. They can try to locate the student's results on general English proficiency tests or tests of English writing ability. They can consult with an ESL professional. They can analyze some samples of the student's writing and make a judgment of their own. They can ask the student's opinion about what the basic difficulty is.

Exploring Writing Process Differences: Do ESL Writers Compose Differently?

A rather small but growing body of research, reviewed and synthesized by Silva, compares the composing of ESL and native English-speaking (NES) writers. The findings of this research suggest that while the composing processes of these two groups are similar in their broad outlines, that is, for both groups writing is a recursive activity involving planning, writing, and revising, there are some salient and important differences. The findings (and these should be seen as very tentative) suggest that adult ESL writers plan less, write with more difficulty (primarily due to a lack of lexical resources), reread what they have written less, and exhibit less facility in revising by ear, that is, in an intuitive manner — on the basis of what "sounds" right, than their NES peers. One implication that can be drawn from this research is that those who deal with ESL writers might find it helpful to stretch out the composing process: (1) to include more work on planning — to generate ideas, text structure, and language — so as to make the actual writing more manageable; (2) to have their ESL students write in stages, e.g., focusing on content and organization in one draft and focusing on linguistic concerns in another subsequent draft; and (3) to separate their treatments of revising (rhetorical) and editing (linguistic) and provide realistic strategies for each, strategies that do not rely on intuitions ESL writers may not have.

Confronting Error: Does It Help to Categorize Sentence-Level Concerns?

When working on grammar with native speakers, tutors categorize types of error so that they can address seemingly disparate problems by focusing on a larger language principle at work. While it's useful to know how to do this so that one can figure out what the problem is and explain it in an effective way to the student, such categorization in the writing of ESL students is often difficult. To do such categorizing well, tutors may need to take a course in the grammar of modern English. Or maybe a short in-service seminar or self-study would do the trick. In any case, a merely intuitive understanding of how English works would not be sufficient for helping ESL writers — who do not share the tutor's native speaker intuitions and who often need explicit explanations. We should also remember that the "rules" of English vary in terms of level of usefulness. Most don't work all the time; some have as many exceptions as cases covered by the rule. So knowing the rules can help tutors a lot; but they can't count on the rules solving their problems in every case. Such advice should make tutors feel more comfortable with their role as writing collaborators rather than as grammarians whose function it is to spout rules. Tutors are there to help with the whole spectrum of writing processes, not to be talking grammar handbooks.

Although tutors do not work primarily on grammar and mechanics, some ESL writers — especially those whose first acquaintance with English was as a foreign language taught in classrooms in other countries — have a tendency to want to know rules. For example, in a tutorial with a native speaker of English or a student born in the United

States who spoke another language before entering school, the student might ask "Is this sentence OK?" or "How do I fix this sentence?" But an ESL student who comes to the United States after studying English as a foreign language in another country is more likely to ask "Why is this wrong?" Such students seem to have a strong inclination toward organizing their knowledge of English by rules. Though things are changing, many foreign language classes (and this includes foreign language classes in the United States) privilege the learning of grammatical rules, of learning about the language as an object, and neglect the learning of how to actually communicate, orally or in writing, in the foreign language. Certainly, this can make learners very rule-oriented in their outlook. However, there is something else that may also contribute to an ESL student's seeming preoccupation with rules. It's necessary to keep in mind that non-native speakers of a language (especially ones with lower levels of second language proficiency) simply don't have the intuitions about the language that native speakers do; that is, it is harder for them to recognize when something "sounds good." Therefore, in lieu of these intuitions, these students will have to rely on explicit rules to a certain extent.

Adjusting Expectations: How Do We Withstand the Pressure to Correct Every Error?

ESL writers often come to the writing center seeking an editor, someone who will mark and correct their errors and help them fix the paper. On one hand, as tutors we are collaborators who listen to the student's concerns when setting the tutorial agenda. On the other hand, as tutors we also want to begin with rhetorical concerns before looking at sentence-level matters. This causes delicate negotiating between tutor and student when these differing preferences for the agenda collide. But tutors should be firm about dealing with rhetorical matters before linguistic ones (recognizing that sometimes this distinction is hard to make), a sequence as beneficial for ESL writers as it is for native speakers. Tutors should remind ESL writers that their linguistic options may be determined to a large degree by the rhetorical requirements of their papers and that, correlatively, it doesn't make sense to focus initially on grammatical or mechanical problems which may disappear as a result of rhetorically based revisions.

A related problem is that when ESL students are particularly insistent on having tutors correct all grammatical errors in a paper, tutors are at a loss to explain in meaningful ways why this is not productive. Resisting such pressure is very difficult, especially when ESL students are writing papers for other courses where they think the paper should be "correct." One way to address this is for tutors to adjust expectations. Tutors need to tell ESL writers that it is unrealistic for them to expect to be able to write like native speakers of English — especially when it comes to the small but persistent problems like articles and prepositions. Tutors can explain that even non-native speakers of English who live in an English-speaking area for many years and write regularly in English maintain a written accent. It might help to compare this to a foreign accent in pronunciation and to remind ESL students that most native speakers (their professors included) will probably not penalize them much or at all for minor problems in their writing. It also helps to remind such students to focus on substance and not worry so much about style. But there are faculty who do have unrealistic demands about the level of correctness, who expect non-native speakers of English to write error-free prose — not to have a written accent, so to speak. If an ESL student's teacher has such unrealistic expectations, then the student is justified in seeking out editing help, and a native English-speaking colleague, friend, or tutor is justified in providing such help.

Another way that tutors can deal with students' insistence on having all errors corrected is to explain the role of a tutor. ESL students need to know that tutors are expected to help them with strategies that will make them effective, independent writers. We need to explicitly state that tutors are supposed to be educators, not personal editors. This problem is often a result of a mismatch between the assumptions and expectations of tutors and students, though tutors do tend to hang on to their kind-hearted desire to help the student turn in a good paper. Writing center specialists endlessly quote Steve North's now famous one-liner that the tutor's job "is to produce better writers, not better writing" (438). But we still suffer pangs when the student leaves with less than an "A" paper in hand. Offering editorial services is not a learning experience — except for the editor, of course — and tutors need to resist their impulse to help as much as ESL students need to resist their desire to have every grammatical error corrected.

Setting Goals: What Can We Accomplish?

Since second-language learning is typically a long, slow process, tutors have to confront the realities of the time constraints they face in tutorials. Sometimes tutors meet briefly with ESL writers who are about to hand in a paper, sometimes tutors may have a few more leisurely tutorials with the same student, and sometimes tutors are able to meet over a more extended period of time, including sessions when the student is not working on a particular paper. The question then becomes one of deciding what can reasonably be done in the varying situations tutors find themselves in. In terms of last-minute encounters, a tutor can't do much with a paper that is about to be handed in — except act as a proofreader or offer moral support. And neither of these has much instructional value in the long run. However, dealing with an early or intermediate draft of a paper at one or more short sessions can be very useful if tutors can resist trying to deal with all of a draft's problems at once. It is more realistic and more useful to focus on one or two salient difficulties, the things that strike the tutor as most problematic for the reader. To do more would probably overload and frustrate the student and wind up being counterproductive. Going this slowly will probably not result in great improvements in a particular paper, but is more likely to facilitate real learning and writing improvement over time.

When tutors are able to meet with ESL students over a period of time and meet when the student is not working on a particular paper, there are several kinds of tutorial activities that might be useful in helping the student build language proficiency. To begin this sequence, a tutor should first look at one or more samples of the student's writing to get a feel for what linguistic features need to be addressed and in what order (global first, local later). Then, always working with a text the student has written previously or writes in the tutorial, the tutor can help the student identify and remedy errors or help the student generate lexical and/or syntactic options that would improve the student's text. This sort of procedure would help with building language proficiency and might also help the student develop effective personalized strategies for generating language, revising, and editing. Such an approach also harmonizes with the writing center philosophy that what we do particularly well in the tutorial setting is to help writers develop strategies individually matched to their own preferences and differences. Because the tutorial is also especially well suited to working through writing processes, to engaging in various processes such as planning, organizing, revising, and editing with the writer, working through various texts the ESL writer is drafting and revising is easily accomplished in a one-to-one setting.

Resisting the Urge to "Tell": How Do We Stop Supplying All the Answers?

Since writing center pedagogy has given high priority to working collaboratively and interactively, a major goal of a tutor is to help students find their own solutions. Tutors thus don't see themselves as "instructors" who "tell" things. Yet the ESL student cannot easily come to some of the realizations that native speakers can as a result of tutorial questioning and collaboration. To confound the problem even more, while the tutor is uncomfortable straying from the role of collaborator, ESL writers are likely to find such a situation strange or uncomfortable when they come from cultures/educational systems where teachers are expected to be "tellers," where those who don't "tell" are seen as poor teachers, or where such casual interaction with relative strangers is seen as odd or inappropriate. This means that tutors cannot assume that a pattern of interaction that is common and accepted in their culture will be familiar or comfortable for their ESL students. Therefore, tutors might find it useful to make sure that they and their ESL students understand each other's goals and expectations vis-à-vis their tutoring sessions.

In terms of the tutor's role, there may have to be adjustments in their pedagogical orientation. Tutors who work with ESL students may have to be "tellers" to some extent because they will probably need to provide cultural, rhetorical, and/or linguistic information which native speakers intuitively possess and which ESL students do not have, but need to have to complete their writing assignments effectively. That is, regardless of their level of skill in collaboration or interpersonal interaction, tutors will not be able to elicit knowledge from ESL students if the students don't have that knowledge in the first place. This is not to suggest that "telling" should become a tutor's primary style of interacting with ESL writers; they should use it when they feel it would be necessary or appropriate, just as they assume the role of informant occasionally when working with native speakers of English. Tutors can also make minor accommodations in their tutoring style when working with ESL writers. For example, with non-native students who are used to hearing directive statements from teachers, Judith Kilborn has suggested that where it is appropriate, tutors modify the normal mode of asking questions so that instead of asking "Why . . ." or "How . . . ," tutors can, for example, say, "Please explain. . . ." An answer to a relatively open-ended request for explanation might be more useful and enlightening for both the ESL student and the tutor.

Making Hierarchies: What Aspects of Grammar Are Most Important?

Although tutorials should begin with discussions of larger rhetorical concerns, at some point ESL students will want help with grammatical correctness. When tutors do confront working with grammar, problems with verb endings and tenses, prepositions, and deleted articles often are the most noticeable. But are these the most useful things to start with? One way to define the most important areas is functionally; that is, the ones most important to address are those that most interfere with the reader's understanding of what the writer wants to say (global errors) regardless of their structural characteristics. Research suggests that ESL writers most commonly make the following errors:

Verbs

> Inflectional morphology (agreement with nouns in person, number, etc.)
>
> Verbal forms (participials, infinitives, gerunds)
>
> Verb complementation (the types of clauses or constructions that must follow a particular verb)

Nouns

> Inflection (especially in terms of singular/plural and count/ mass distinctions)

Derivation (deriving nouns from other parts of speech, e.g., *quick — quickness,* which often seems quite arbitrary to non-native speakers)

Articles (related to problems in classifying nouns)

Use of wrong article

Missing article

Use of an article when none is necessary or appropriate

Prepositions (primarily a result of limited lexical resources)

Knowing which one goes with a particular noun, verb, adjective, or adverb

These four error types account for most of the errors made by ESL writers with a fairly high level of English proficiency; ESL writers with lower levels of proficiency may also exhibit more problems with basic sentence, clause, and phrase structure — which (when combined with vocabulary limitations) result in writing that is very difficult to decipher. Article problems can be important, too; that is, they can seriously obscure meaning in some contexts. But they generally do not cause readers any serious difficulties, and because they are so hard to eradicate, they should not be a high priority for tutors. It might help both tutors and ESL writers to think of article problems in writing as akin to a slight foreign accent in writing — something that doesn't pose serious difficulties and disappears only gradually — if at all.

When working with the complicated matter of articles and prepositions and non-rule-governed matters such as idioms, tutors need some new pedagogies as well as guidance for explaining topics not normally discussed in grammar handbooks. But, while we can develop an explanation of article use in English, such an explanation will not be simple by any means. It would involve making sequential decisions about the noun phrase that an article modifies — common or proper, count or non-count, singular or plural, definite or indefinite. Then, of course, there are the several classes of special cases and the many outright exceptions to the rules (Ann Raimes's *Grammar Troublespots* is helpful here; see 85–92). ESL writers could understand such explanations — but it's not clear that this understanding would translate into greatly improved performance in making correct article decisions while actually writing. Article use can improve gradually with increased exposure to English, but it's not realistic to expect that an ESL writer will ever use articles like a native speaker does. ESL students should be encouraged to do the best they can and then get a native speaker to proofread their work — if proofreading is absolutely necessary. As for preposition problems, they are lexical rather than grammatical problems. We either know the correct preposition in a given context or we don't — there are really no rules we can appeal to. Therefore, ESL writers need to learn prepositions the same way they learn other vocabulary items — through study or exposure to the language. Idioms are also a lexical rather than a grammatical matter. Second language learners usually have a keen interest in idiomatic expressions and are eager to learn and use them. Tutors can capitalize on this interest by providing students with idiomatic options for words and expressions they have used in their text. Both tutor and student might find this a useful and enjoyable activity. One proviso: When introducing an idiom, tutors need to also supply information about the appropriate context for the use of that idiom in order to avoid putting the student in a potentially embarrassing situation.

Encouraging Proofreading: What Strategies Work Well?

With native English speakers we are often successful in helping them learn to edit for correctness by reading aloud, something some ESL students can also learn how to do. Some are able to find their own mistakes, even add omitted articles, and it really works. But for other ESL students, this doesn't seem to be an effective strategy. ESL writers who can't successfully edit "by ear" aren't proficient enough in English to have a "feel" for what is correct and what isn't. It follows that those with higher levels of proficiency will have more success with reading aloud, but even the most proficient aren't likely to display native-speaker-like intuitions. Therefore, some recourse to more mechanical rule-based proofreading strategies or to outside help, such as a native speaker reader, will probably be necessary.

Adding Resources: What Are Useful Readings for Tutors?

Since many tutors and directors would like to better prepare themselves to work with ESL students but have limited time to spend, we will limit our suggestions for further reading to a small fraction of the abundant literature produced in recent years on ESL writing and ESL writers. The resources described in this section were chosen on the basis of their timeliness, breadth, and accessibility.

The first resources are book-length treatments of issues in ESL writing and writing instruction. One is Ilona Leki's, *Understanding ESL Writers: A Guide for Teachers*. This introductory book addresses the history of ESL writing instruction, relevant models of second language acquisition, differences between basic writers and ESL writers, personal characteristics of ESL writers, ESL writers' expectations, writing behaviors, and composing processes, contrastive rhetoric, common sentence-level errors, and responding to ESL writing. The second is Joy M. Reid's *Teaching ESL Writing*. This work deals with the special problems and concerns that distinguish first and second language writing instruction, addressing in particular the variables of language and cultural background, prior education, gender, age, and language proficiency. Reid also provides an overview of different ESL composition teaching methodologies and offers specific information on developing curricula, syllabi, and lesson plans for basic, intermediate, and advanced ESL writing classes. Also useful are two collections covering a broad range of issues in ESL writing. The first is Barbara Kroll's *Second Language Writing: Research Insights for the Classroom,* which contains thirteen papers in two major sections. The papers in the first section address theories of L2 writing and provide overviews of research in a number of basic areas of ESL composition. The second section is comprised of reports of empirical research on current issues in L2 writing instruction. The second collection, Donna M. Johnson and Duane H. Roen's *Richness in Writing: Empowering ESL Students,* includes eighteen papers in three sections which deal respectively with contexts for ESL writing, specific rhetorical concerns of L2 writers, and cultural issues in the writing of ESL students.

Two additional resources are the *Journal of Second Language Writing,* a scholarly journal which publishes reports of research and discussions of issues in second and foreign language writing and writing instruction, and *Resources for CCCC Members Who Want to Learn about Writing in English as a Second Language,* a fact sheet of information about professional organizations, conferences, publications, and educational and employment opportunities for those interested in working with ESL writers. (For a copy of the *Resources* fact sheet, write to Tony Silva, CCCC Committee on ESL, Department of English, Heavilon Hall, Purdue University, West Lafayette, Indiana 47907-1356.)

Conclusion

ESL instructors and writing center people need to keep interacting with and learning from each other. We each have insights, methods, research, and experiences to share. For those of us in writing centers, it's useful to know that writing center tutors can draw on both research and language teaching approaches used in ESL classrooms. Writing center directors can share with ESL teachers one-to-one pedagogies that work in the writing center as well as our perceptions of how individual differences interact with various classroom pedagogies on different students. We can also share our awareness of the kinds of questions students really ask, our first-hand observations of how students cope with writing assignments and teacher responses, and our encounters with non-native differences that interfere with learning how to write in American classrooms. Such information can only serve to illuminate the work of ESL teachers. Similarly, insights from ESL writing theory, research, and practice can help writing centers, and mainstream composition in general, to deal effectively with their increasingly multilingual and multicultural student populations.

Works Cited

Brown, H. Douglas. *Principles of Language Learning and Teaching.* 2nd ed. Englewood Cliffs: Prentice, 1987.

CCCC Committee on ESL. *Resources for CCCC Members Who Want to Learn about Writing in English as a Second Language (ESL).* Urbana: NCTE, 1992.

Grabe, William, and Robert B. Kaplan. "Writing in a Second Language: Contrastive Rhetoric." *Richness in Writing: Empowering ESL Students.* Ed. Donna Johnson and Duane Roen. New York: Longman, 1989. 263–83.

Hall, Edward. *The Silent Language.* New York: Doubleday, 1959.

Johnson, Donna M., and Duane H. Roen, eds. *Richness in Writing: Empowering ESL Students.* New York: Longman, 1989.

Kilborn, Judith. "Tutoring ESL Students: Addressing Differences in Cultural Schemata and Rhetorical Patterns in Reading and Writing." Minnesota, TESOL Conference. St. Paul, 2 May 1992.

Kroll, Barbara. "The Rhetoric and Syntax Split: Designing a Curriculum for ESL Students." *Journal of Basic Writing* 9 (Spring 1990): 40–45.

———, ed. *Second Language Writing: Research Insights for the Classroom.* New York: Cambridge UP, 1990.

Leki, Ilona. "Twenty-Five Years of Contrastive Rhetoric: Text Analysis and Writing Pedagogies." *TESOL Quarterly* 25 (Spring 1991): 123–43.

———. *Understanding ESL Writers: A Guide for Teachers.* Portsmouth: Boynton, 1992.

North, Stephen. "The Idea of a Writing Center." *College English* 46 (Sep. 1984): 433–46.

Raimes, Ann. *Grammar Troublespots: An Editing Guide for Students.* 2nd ed. New York: St. Martin's, 1992.

Reid, Joy M. *Teaching ESL Writing.* Englewood Cliffs: Regents, 1993.

Silva, Tony. "Differences in ESL and Native Speaker Writing." *Writing in Multicultural Settings.* Ed. Johnnella Butler, Juan Guerra, and Carol Severino. New York: MLA, 1997.

Harris and Silva's Insights as a Resource for Your Teaching

1. Harris and Silva's advice that ESL tutors distinguish global errors from local errors is also a rule of thumb for writing teachers. Have you worked with ESL students who seem to have a product-centered introduction to writing in English and assume "correctness" will be your first criterion for evaluation? How might you emphasize in your comments on drafts or in your conferences with ESL writers that your first concern is with the message and that you will focus primarily on errors that impede you in understanding what the writer wants to say? You might remind students that, as they revise for ideas and structure, some of their global errors will disappear. Remind them to separate revising (rhetorical concerns) from editing (linguistic concerns).

2. In the conclusion of their article, Harris and Silva stress the need for interaction between ESL instructors and writing center tutors and administrators. If you work with ESL writers in your classroom, meet with some tutors or faculty from the writing center to share insights and experiences. What successful writing center strategies might work well in the classroom? In turn, what insights from your research or classroom practice might help the writing center more effectively work with non-native speakers?

Harris and Silva's Insights as a Resource for Your Writing Classroom

1. Early in the semester, invite all your students to write you letters describing their histories as writers and scholars and detailing anything you need to know about them to work with them as writers. In conferences with individual writers, use your reading of and response to an early writing assignment, journal entries, and the letter to initiate a conversation about the ESL student's writing experiences and about his or her confidence and fluency in spoken and written English. Anticipate that some ESL students — perhaps because of their fluency level or lack of proficiency with basic communication skills in English or perhaps because of cultural communication patterns — will need to become comfortable with one-to-one conferences. They may not articulate their concerns and questions clearly in a first conference or may send verbal and nonverbal messages that they comprehend what you say when in fact they don't. Anticipate that some students will be silent in classroom discussions because they fear speaking incorrectly or they lack cognitive readiness.

2. Collaborative activities are high-risk experiences for some ESL students and familiar experiences for others. To introduce small-group discussions or projects and peer critique, ask class members to write a three-minute letter about their expectations for and fears about working collaboratively. Merge the letters and make a handout for large-group discussion. Ask the class to agree on some shared responsibilities for collaborative activities. On self-assessment protocols afterward, ask students to evaluate how well these responsibilities were met. (Return the letter and protocols and ask students to keep them to use in conferences when they assess their work in groups later in the semester.)

Dispositions toward Language: Teacher Constructs of Knowledge and the Ann Arbor Black English Case

Arnetha Ball and Ted Lardner

In this essay examining the questions of "Black English" in the writing classroom, Arnetha Ball and Ted Lardner consider the ways in which we define knowledge in the field of composition and how these different concepts of knowledge carry implicit patterns of emotional response to the all-important differences (social, linguistic) that distinguish our students from each other. Technical knowledge and knowledge-as-lore both obscure the crucial question of the teacher's affective relation to student diversity, which is the decisive factor in whether many students learn to write. This essay confronts the often shielded yet very real issue of institutional racism — the "subtle, unconscious manifestations" of internalized bias and prejudice that persist as insidious factors in our educational systems. First published in 1997 in College Composition and Communication, *the essay was awarded the journal's Braddock Award for best CCC article of the year.*

> So here's our hypothesis: what students learn about writing depends more than anything else on the context in which they write. . . . And if the linguists are right that the social context is the driving force behind literacy acquisition, then *the social context of your English/language-arts classroom is the most powerful and important variable you can experiment with.* More important than what textbook or speller or dictionary to use; more important than what kinds of assignments to give; more important than how to set up cumulative writing folders; more important than the criteria by which you assign kids to peer response groups; more important than "teaching Graves" versus teaching Calkins or Hillocks. More important than anything.
>
> — Steven Zemelman and Harvey Daniels (50–51)

Because composition has been organized as a field in terms of the classroom, the production, transmission, and assimilation of teacher knowledge continues to be a significant theoretical and practical concern. As John Schilb has recently pointed out, though many writing instructors attempt to separate pedagogy from theory, the "field identifies itself with pedagogy" (*Between* 30). In developing its discussion of pedagogical theory (as distinct from rhetorical theory), scholarship in composition studies has generated what we call constructs of teacher knowledge. In this essay we address competing constructs of teacher knowledge, analyzing them from a perspective which takes racially informed language attitudes and their effects on teaching and learning in culturally diverse classrooms as its central concern. In developing this analysis, our point of departure is the 1979 Ann Arbor "Black English" court case. This case focused on the language barriers created by teachers' unconscious negative attitudes toward students' uses of African American English and the negative effect these attitudes had on student learning.

In our reading, the Ann Arbor case is significant for composition studies for two reasons. First, it stands as a legal intervention into the educational process, disrupting business as usual by holding the school system responsible for the educational underachievement of Black students. It associated low educational achievement not with shortcomings within learners, but with inadequate, ineffective curricular and pedagogical routines. Second, in the Ann Arbor case the court held the school district and teachers responsible for rethinking pedagogy and curriculum in light of extant information about African American English. In so doing, it raised then and continues now to pose the question of how educators accomplish the necessary but complicated task of assimilating new knowledge about race and language in order to translate that knowledge into classroom practice. We believe that barriers similar to those identified in Ann Arbor still affect teaching and learning in many secondary-level and college writing classrooms. Similarly, the complex issues surrounding teacher education and changing teachers' attitudes and behaviors in the classroom remain to be explored in the scholarly dialogue of our field.

We begin here with a summary of the Ann Arbor case, highlighting its focus on teacher attitudes and the consequent issue of teacher knowledge and practice. Next, we argue that three distinct constructs of teacher knowledge are evident in writing studies today, each of which is differentially linked to the issue of race reflected in language attitudes raised in the Ann Arbor case. We conclude with some implications for composition as a field, arguing in particular that pedagogical theory in composition needs to more adequately address questions of language diversity and race in order to affect the climate in the writing classroom.

Background: The Court Decision

In 1979, a Federal District Court handed down a decision in favor of eleven African American children, residents of a scatter-site low-income housing project and students at Martin Luther King Jr. Elementary School, holding the Ann Arbor School District Board responsible for failing to adequately prepare the King School teachers to teach children whose home language was African American English. The case drew national and international attention to the role of language variation in the education of Black children. Stating that a major goal of a school system is to teach reading, writing, speaking, and understanding standard English (Memorandum 1391), Judge Charles Joiner wrote that "when teachers fail to take into account the home language" (1380) of their students, "some children will turn off and not learn" (1381). Challenging a pedagogical ethos grounded in the presumption of universalities, Judge Joiner observed that the teachers involved in the case all testified that they treated the plaintiff students just as they treated other students. However, in so doing they may have created a barrier to learning (1379). In the Ann Arbor case, the Court ruled that the teachers' unconscious but evident attitudes toward the African American English used by the plaintiff children constituted a language barrier that impeded the students' educational progress (1381).

Like the recent Oakland School Board resolution on Ebonics, the Ann Arbor case stirred controversy. As in Oakland, the controversy was in part a result of inaccurate reporting in the media, some of which represented the Court as requiring teachers to teach African American English (see Smitherman, "What"). However, outside of the public furor and of much more substantive import, in ordering the defendant school board to invest time and money in a staff development program for King School teachers, the Court in the Ann Arbor case disrupted the institutional status quo by holding the school district accountable for the inadequate educational progress of the Black children involved. From this perspective, the Ann Arbor case can be viewed as a turning point in the history of educational justice for African American children, and the Court's Memorandum Opinion and Order signals this recognition:

> The problem posed by this case is one which the evidence indicates has been compounded by efforts on the part of society to fully integrate blacks into the mainstream of society by relying solely on simplistic devices such as scatter housing and busing of students. Full integration and equal opportunity require much more and one of the matters requiring more attention is the teaching of the young blacks to read standard English. (1381)

As much as the Court's decision can be viewed as an answer to "a cry for judicial help in opening the doors to the establishment" (1381), it must also be recognized that the overriding theme of the Court's ruling was to uphold existing linguistic, educational, and social arrangements. Many educators have viewed the Ann Arbor decision as a step forward on the same road leading from the *Brown v. Topeka* decision in 1954. Keith Gilyard, for example, calls the Ann Arbor decision a precedent-setting case which ought to have an officially established place within the educational environment (10). But while it is important to note such celebrating of the Ann Arbor case, it is also important to note that the elements of the decision which directly address language barriers and African American English have yet to be cited as a precedent in other cases aimed at school policy. Furthermore, the Court's final Memorandum Opinion and Order explicitly and unequivocally positions African American English in a subordinate relationship to the mainstream:

> Black English is not a language used by the mainstream of society —
> black or white. It is not an acceptable method of communication in the

educational world, in the commercial community, in the community of the arts and science, or among professionals. (1378)

The Michigan Legal Services attorneys who mounted the case for the plaintiff children in Ann Arbor drew on the testimony of experts in sociolinguistics and education in order to establish two key propositions: that African American English is a rule-governed language system, and that the teachers' failure to recognize this linguistic fact led to negative attitudes toward the children who spoke it, that, in effect, their attitudes constituted a language barrier impeding students' educational progress. Establishing the first proposition, the expert testimony addressed the second by asserting that communicative interference can derive from either structural mismatches among dialects or from nonstructural phenomena. Nonstructural interference phenomena refers to differing attitudes and conflicting values about speech systems and the individuals who use them. Experts testified that negative linguistic attitudes shaped the institutional policies and practices that hindered the education of African American English speaking children. Then as now, research on language attitudes consistently indicates that teachers believe African American English speaking children are "nonverbal" and possess limited vocabularies. Speakers of African American English are often perceived to be slow learners or uneducable; their speech is often considered to be unsystematic and in need of constant correction and improvement.

In the Ann Arbor case, the Court identified teachers' language attitudes as a significant impediment to children's learning. Because the children failed to develop reading skills, they were thereby impeded from full participation in the educational program at King School. The Court enumerated multiple potential causes (absences from class, classroom misbehavior, learning disabilities, and emotional impairment and lack of reading role models [1391]) for their difficulties, but focused on one:

> Research indicates that the black dialect or vernacular used at home by black students in general makes it more difficult for such children to read because teachers' unconscious but evident attitudes toward the home language causes a psychological barrier to learning by the student. (1381)

The Court called for the Ann Arbor School District Board to develop a program to (1) help the teachers understand the problem, (2) provide them with knowledge about the children's use of African American English, and (3) suggest ways and means of using that knowledge in teaching the students to read (1381). In a court-ordered, twenty-hour inservice program for the King School teachers, experts in reading and sociolinguistics furnished teachers with information on these topics. In spite of the wealth of information delivered to teachers, however, the school district's report of the results of this inservice program concludes that though teacher respondents "felt positively about all substantive issues, they were somewhat less positive about their understanding of the pedagogical issues" (Howard 17).

The nonstructural barriers resulting from negative attitudes were the focus of the Ann Arbor case, and they remain to challenge successful practice and our students' educational progress today. Survey results reported by Balester suggest that this was as true in 1992 as it was in 1979, the year of the Ann Arbor trial, or in the late sixties when scholarship in applied linguistics first took direct aim at many teachers' traditional, prescriptivist orientations. In 1994, Bowie and Bond found that teachers still continue to exhibit negative attitudes toward African American English, often stating that African American English has a faulty grammar system and that children who speak African American English are less capable than children who speak standard English.

Constructs of Teacher Knowledge

It is clear that the outcome of the Ann Arbor case left many questions unanswered, including the most pressing question of how teachers are to respond to the linguistic and cultural diversity of their students. At the heart of the Ann Arbor decision was the recognition of the need for teachers to become sensitive to students' uses of African American English, to move into a way of being in the classroom which is responsive to and informed by recognition of racial and linguistic difference. However, the unresolved pedagogical issues reflected in the King School teachers' responses to their inservice program remain at the center of our reading of the Ann Arbor case in relation to composition studies: How do teachers learn and transform new knowledge into classroom practice? We argue that three competing constructs of teacher knowledge offer divergent ways of responding to this question. The three constructs we wish to describe are the *teacher as technician, teacher knowledge as lore,* and *teacher efficacy.* We distinguish these constructs from one another in terms of their approaches to the underlying issue of racially informed language attitudes: How do they situate teachers in relation to confronting race as an element in classroom climate? How do they bring to the surface for teachers the awareness of unconscious negative language attitudes? How do they dispose teachers to be able to reflect on and move forward into alternative classroom practices?

Teacher as Technician

The teacher as technician is clearly the operative construct evident in the Ann Arbor case. This construct was a necessary feature of the "objectivist rhetoric" which made up the expert testimony in the trial, which was the dominant rhetoric in the Court's Memorandum Opinion and Order, and which continues to be the undergirding rhetoric of current scholarship on African American English in sociolinguistics, education, and literacy studies. Cy Knoblauch has identified "objectivist rhetoric" as empirical discourse which portrays knowledge as derived from unbiased observation and rigorous argumentative procedure. Because of this, the objectivist paradigm has served as a corrective to superstitions, emotional excesses, and prejudices (130). The Ann Arbor case demonstrates just this corrective potential.

One feature of objectivist rhetoric is its organization of knowledge in linear, cause-and-effect terms. A second feature, evident in the discourse of the case, is the trope of application. The Court acknowledged the necessary contributions of the King School teachers' "skill and empathy" (1391) to classroom success. But the chief significance of the trial lies in the way in which it focused on the need for teachers to apply in practice the findings of modern sociolinguistic scholarship. The process and outcome of the case reflects a technical construct of teacher knowledge in that it subordinates teachers' own reflective resources ("skill and empathy") to disciplinary (sociolinguistic) expertise. The case inscribes teachers as needy recipients of already-formed information which would, it was presumed, ameliorate their attitudes and which would (somehow) be translated into new, more effective writing strategies.

The Final Evaluation of the results of the Ann Arbor inservice program stated that a great deal of information was available regarding such topics as the history and structure of African American English and the effect of teacher attitudes on student learning. But there was evidently little if any attention given at the time to the process of applying this knowledge in practice. Its application was apparently presumed to be automatic. Thomas Pietras, the Language Arts Coordinator for the Ann Arbor School District at the time of the King School trial, wrote that disseminating information to teachers about African American English "assumes that teacher knowledge will result in success in language arts" for speakers of African American English (qtd. in Howard et al. 59), but the results of the questionnaire that teachers filled out subsequent to the inservice speak to the disconnection between knowledge and application. The Final Evaluation distinguishes "substantive" issues from "pedagogical" issues, and the content of the inservice program itself virtually ignored questions of pedagogy, assuming perhaps that providing teachers with knowledge would lead by itself to improved student performance. How that improved student performance was (or is) to be achieved was never addressed; the teacher as technician construct doesn't ask that question, because it tends to bypass altogether the responsive decision-making that teachers must engage in.

The objectivist rhetoric exemplified in the Ann Arbor case in the testimony of experts served to move the Court to intervene in an ingrained, discriminatory institutional practice at King School. When William Labov, one of the leading expert witnesses to testify in Ann Arbor, wrote about the case saying that "negative attitudes can be changed by providing people with scientific evidence" (32), he expressed perfectly the objectivist view in which science serves as a corrective to prejudice. It also reflects a view of teachers as technicians and of pedagogy as the transparent process of translating "substantive" information in the classroom. Unfortunately, as the King School teachers' own evaluation of their training session indicates, introducing sociolinguistic information seems not to have led them to recognize avenues toward more effective classroom practice. Describing the limitations of objectivist rhetoric and the construct of teacher as technician we argue it entails, Knoblauch suggests that educators may speak of "advances" in "our knowledge of the processes of human learning, including the development of literacy" (130), and may thereby evince "a willingness to ground instruction in what we can observe about those processes" (130). However, Knoblauch goes on, "teachers and researchers accept the least advantageous assumptions of a positivist outlook . . . when they encourage [for example] the new knowledge of linguistics . . . to dictate instructional and learning agendas" (131). The practical (non-) consequences of this acceptance of a "positivist outlook" are evident in the King School teachers' responses. As much as they may have wished for it to be so, they seemed to recognize no clear way in which linguistic or sociolinguistic knowledge could "dictate" teaching and learning processes.

Teacher Knowledge as Lore

Such an impasse is perhaps what composition theorists who talk about teacher knowledge as lore might have predicted. Lore is a postmodern, "postdisciplinary" construct that rejects objectivist, linear, cause-and-effect discourse in favor of complex, multifaceted, and improvisational ways of understanding pedagogical interactions to explain how teachers know what to do.

We identify postdisciplinary views of teacher knowledge as lore with work which has emerged in composition in the last ten years — subsequent, that is, to the Ann Arbor case. Variously formulated by scholars ranging from Stephen North to Louise Wetherbee Phelps and Patricia Harkin, this work has complicated the idea of disciplinary knowledge governing a teacher's practice in the classroom. In Harkin's formulation, lore is identified with teachers' informed intuitions about what works in the classroom. At the center of her discussion is the example of Mina Shaughnessy's *Errors and Expectations*. Harkin identifies Shaughnessy's book as exemplary of lore, and goes on to illustrate the disciplinary critique of lore by reference to critiques of Shaughnessy's work. Harkin writes that critics of teacher knowledge as lore see a danger in teachers who "are willfully ignorant of disciplinary knowledge," and who

> think they should be free . . . to ignore [for example] modern linguistic scholarship, free to invent their own programs as they go along . . . free

> to ignore evidence or theory, free to rely on their own insight, free, that is, to ignore facts. (130)

Harkin's reply is to turn aside the ethical implications (teachers ignore facts) and to deconstruct the idea of "facts" in itself: "Facts are only facts in the discipline which constitutes them," she asserts (130). Going on, she argues that because the complex scene of teaching cannot be reduced to the linear causality which disciplinary knowledge demands, teachers cannot be expected to obey disciplinary imperatives. Lore, with its improvisational logic, is the more appropriate interpretive framework with which to think about teaching, to think about how we know what to do in the classroom. The construct of teacher knowledge as lore thus turns us in the right direction as it asks directly about the process of discovery, application, and transformation of teacher knowledge in the classroom. Privileging teachers' direct experiences and reflective practice, lore draws our attention to the moment-to-moment process of observing, interpreting, and decision making that is characteristic of engaged teaching.

However, what the construct of teacher knowledge as lore works to resist — the apparent necessity for teachers to attune their practice to, for example, modern linguistic scholarship — lies at the heart of the Ann Arbor case and the intervention it represented into a discriminatory status quo. One unintended effect, then, of the construct of lore, of relying on teachers' informed intuitions, is to displace a direct confrontation with race as it may be manifested in students' strategic uses of African American English. In its effort to disrupt the disciplinary encroachment of, for example, sociolinguistics (we find Harkin's selection of "linguistics" as evidence quite telling), "postdisciplinary" theory substitutes for one problematic construct, the teacher as technician, an equally problematic construct of teacher knowledge as lore produced through "a process of informed intuition" when "practitioners do what works" (Harkin 134). In Ann Arbor, it took two years of legal action to force the school district to acknowledge that whatever its teachers' intuitions were, what was supposed to be working didn't work for a significant number of African American children. The case highlighted facts about language variation, race, language attitudes, and school performance which teachers ultimately were not free to ignore. Another effect of the postmodern construct of lore might thus be to undermine the strategic uses to which the objectivist discourses of the social sciences have been put. Since *Brown v. Topeka*, these discourses have been a chief weapon in the fight for educational justice for African American students. The familiar antifoundationalist critique that denies truth as a transcendent category could thus also deny access to the court of last appeal against racism in the quest for civil rights and educational equity. It is interesting to imagine but difficult to see how a postdisciplinary perspective might have carried the day in the Ann Arbor case.

The Ann Arbor case thus reveals possibilities and limitations of lore. We remain skeptical of the unintended effects of the antifoundationalism upon which lore is premised since this seems to rule out "appeals to truth, objectivity, ethics, and identity that social critics have traditionally made" (Schilb, "Cultural" 174). In terms of the issues of race and literacy highlighted by the Ann Arbor case and at play in composition classrooms today, postdisciplinarity and lore remain susceptible to such criticisms. Whereas scholars in other fields draw on postmodern theory to make race a prominent element in their analyses of cultural transactions (Cornel West, Patricia Williams), in many of composition's important discussions of postmodern theory, race is hardly mentioned. This is a striking oversight. What we are most concerned with, however, is to find ways to raise teachers' awareness of their own processes of pedagogical discovery and change, to help teachers recognize what their own habits of reflection make accessible to them, and what these habits of mind may leave out. The construct of lore moves us a long way toward the goal of seeing teachers' own reflective practice as the nexus of pedagogical theory. Our concern is that this construct does not put enough pressure on the question of "what works," thereby pushing teachers to confront the limitations of their practice — especially when for the majority of students everything seems to be running along smoothly, as was the case in Ann Arbor, where most of the students at King School were doing very well. In reference to issues of race which are raised in writing classes when students speak or draw on African American English in their writing, we see a need for teachers to avail themselves of facts which may seem external or peripheral to their experience of the classroom, but which may carry significance for some students. When lore does not confront practitioners with their own language biases, it works against change.

Teacher Efficacy

The third construct of teacher knowledge we wish to consider is teacher efficacy. It differs in one significant way from each of the first two constructs insofar as it draws attention to affect as an essential — perhaps the essential — component in teaching practice. In a field closely allied with composition, teacher educators such as Henry Giroux, Kenneth Zeichner, and Daniel Liston have offered a construct of teacher knowledge generated through reflective practice where teachers examine classroom routines in light of encompassing social and institutional pressures. We argue that the construct of teacher efficacy pushes beyond this enlarged view of reflective practice. By making affect a central issue in theorizing pedagogy, teacher efficacy moves closest to the largely unspoken dimensions of pedagogical experience when, let's say, white teachers in university writing courses attempt to mediate the discourse practices of African American English speaking students. Opening up these deeply felt but difficult to name dimensions of interaction, teacher efficacy speaks to the cumulative effect of teachers' knowledge and experience on their feelings about their students and their own ability to teach them.

This was what the Ann Arbor case was really about: the psychological barriers to learning that cause some students to dis-identify with school. Teacher efficacy as a construct of teacher knowledge places affect at the center and in so doing opens up and addresses questions of motivation and stance which are prior to and underlie curricular designs or pedagogical technique. When we speak of affect here, we refer to the emotional tone of classroom interactions. With reference to the Ann Arbor case, insofar as language variation is a factor in educational achievement, language as the medium of instruction is what counts. What is most relevant about Ann Arbor was how it drew attention to language as the medium of instruction and the interference generated by teachers' unconscious negative responses to their students' own language.

Defining affect in terms of "teachers' expectations, their empathy, and their own sense of self-efficacy" (370), Susan McLeod reminds us of the research which demonstrates the variable influence (positive or negative) of teacher affect on students' motivations for learning. Teacher efficacy refers to a teacher's beliefs about the power she or he has to produce a positive effect on students. McLeod points out that a teacher's emotional state or disposition forms one source of this sense of self-efficacy. Another source, and the most influential, is "the cultural beliefs that go to make up the macrosystem of American education," beliefs which inform teachers' common sense assumptions including "conceptions of the learner and the teacher and the role of education" (379). McLeod and others have shown that many variables contribute to teacher efficacy, including prior experience in multicultural settings, available resources, and teachers' visions of themselves as agents of social change. Teachers with high personal teaching efficacy believe that all students can be motivated and that it is their responsibility to explore with students the tasks that will hold their attention in the learning process. Valerie Pang and Velma Sablan propose that teacher efficacy is an especially important construct in the context of multicultural classrooms, and that teachers and teacher educators need to seriously examine what they believe about their ability to teach children from various cultural and linguistic backgrounds, particularly African American students. Pang and Sablan note that "when the overwhelming majority of the teaching force in this country is not from under-represented groups, the need to look at teacher misconceptions of African American culture, customs, history, and values is essential" (16).

Until the lawsuit, institutional custom invited the Ann Arbor School District to explain away African American student failure by attributing it to shortcomings in students rather than to shortcomings in the educational system or to the teachers' own lack of "skills or knowledge to help low achievers" (McLeod 380). Subsequent to the inservice program ordered by the Court, the King School teachers reflected low efficacy, that is, little confidence in their ability to adapt pedagogy to the various strengths and needs of speakers of African American English. Applied to the teaching of literacy that goes on in college writing courses, the question becomes, how do teachers become aware of unconscious negative attitudes (or even the dimly felt sense of unease resulting from lack of experience) they may bring with them to the learning environment? And, what steps can teachers take to communicate their sense of efficacy and high expectations to culturally diverse students?

Among the three constructs of teacher knowledge considered here, only that of teacher efficacy, grounded as it is in the consideration of affect in the classroom, makes these questions of felt sense, of emotional response, available for reflection. The Ann Arbor case focused on the language barrier which resulted from teachers' negative attitudes toward African American English. Racism — unconscious and institutional — was the clear subtext in the trial. Arthur Spears describes the problematic relationships among race, language variety, and school achievement. Citing dialect differences in other countries, Spears notes:

> Greater language differences are overcome elsewhere. Why can't they be overcome in American schools? The answer that comes through in a number of studies of the issue is that the real problems are attitudinal and social. All these problems can be related to the general problem of institutional racism . . . low teacher expectations and disrespect for the home language and culture of inner-city pupils. (53–54)

Though rarely acknowledged as such, racism in the sense reflected here still remains an issue in the current teaching of writing, surfacing in the classroom in a variety of often subtle, unconscious manifestations (see Delpit). Neither of the first two constructs of teacher knowledge described offer adequate approaches to this problem; neither offers a vocabulary within which to directly address teachers' affective responses — low expectations, disrespect — which are the chief means through which institutional racism is manifested. Neither the teacher as technician construct nor lore offers direct access to unconscious negative racial stereotypes as a central issue in pedagogical theory. Our conclusion is that while unconscious attitudes are indeed, as Labov points out, partly a problem of (lack of) knowledge per se, they are more urgently a matter of feeling, the affective domain of racialized classroom experience which neither the technician model nor lore explicitly engages.

Implications for Practice

The question remains, however: If our goal is to move urban youth in cities like Cleveland or Detroit into academic discourse communities, what stands in the way of that happening? In working toward building a sense of efficacy we need to give particular attention to staff development and writing programs in which teachers re-envision their capacity to function as catalysts of positive growth and development in students. In part, this improved sense of efficacy stems from an improved teacher knowledge base concerning the linguistic practices of diverse students. This can be accomplished by reviewing the literature diligently developed over the past four decades to provide a more complex, more complete linguistic profile of African American linguistic behavior. Characteristic features, discourse patterns, and rhetorical modes in African American English had been identified in the literature prior to the Ann Arbor case (Abrahams; Labov; Smitherman, *Talkin*). Research published since the conclusion of the case in 1979 has shed more light on distinctive discourse patterns and rhetorical modes. Much of this work has generated new knowledge of organizational patterns in the oral and written expository language of African American English speakers (Ball, "Expository"), the subtle ways that academically successful students strategically use African American English in their writing (Ball, "Cultural"), and on the assessment of writing produced by African American English speakers (Richardson). Research investigating the teaching practices of exemplary African American teachers working in community-based organizations has shown that these teachers build on the language practices of their African American students. They work explicitly to make students metacognitively aware of their oral and written uses of African American English and of alternative ways of expressing their ideas in academic and in technical, workplace English (Ball, Broussard, and Dinkins; Morgan; Ball, "Community").

Becoming informed about cultural discourse patterns and rhetorical modes is a significant resource that successful teachers can build on. Most interesting, however, is the impact of an awareness of cultural differences in discourse patterns on classroom interactions. The presence of varied patterns of discourse in classrooms can impact instruction in positive as well as in negative ways (Foster, "Effective"). Speech behavior is central to a full understanding of how a community expresses its realities, and research on teacher efficacy suggests that effective teachers develop strong human bonds with their students, have high expectations, focus on the total child, and are able to use communication styles familiar to their students. Exemplary African American teachers in community-based organizations are able to draw, to varying degrees, on primarily the rhetorical modes and discourse-level strategies of African American English in shaping interactive discourse as the medium of instruction with their students (Ball, Broussard, Dinkins; Foster "Educating"). Their practice in this regard stands as a model for other teachers to reflect on as they consider expanding their own pedagogical repertoires. We are not advocating that all teachers need to learn and teach Black English. We are arguing that the practices of exemplary African American teachers show us ways of focusing on participation patterns in interactive discourse as the medium of instruction in order to raise the awareness of teachers of the possible links between their own styles of communication and their students' responsiveness in classroom exchanges. Having high expectations and good intentions is not enough; these intentions and expectations need to be evident to students in observable or, we might say, audible behaviors in the classroom.

But as important as this knowledge base may be, it will not in and of itself activate teachers to change their practice. The cognitive internalization of information is not enough to increase teacher efficacy. The Ann Arbor case suggests that the key to effective uses of language diversity in the classroom relates fundamentally to teachers' dispositions toward literacy — that is, depends upon teachers' affective stance toward themselves, their work environment, and especially their culturally diverse students. More current research seems to confirm this. Addressing disposition as the most important variable, we have begun to push beyond internalization of knowledge about African American English in the teacher-education programs we are involved in. In doing so, we have found ourselves observing the ways preservice teachers encounter and contextualize the pedagogical ramifications of language diversity. Our observations suggest that preservice teachers who attempt to address the complex issues relating to this topic may do so by examining personal experiences of crossing borders from one speech community to another. Given these observations, we have begun to consider occasions for knowledge-making that appear in "extra-professional" sites where teachers become aware of their own culturally influenced dispositions toward literacy. We have begun to explore ways of talking that help teachers connect to parts of their experience that conventional academic, theoretical frameworks seem to silence.

Implications for Pedagogical Theory

In 1991 Ann Dyson and Sarah Freedman challenged writing and composition professionals to take significant and positive steps toward building a more powerful theoretical framework for writing research and instruction by expanding our framework to

> include more analytic attention to how the complex of sociocultural experiences enter into literacy learning experiences that have roots in social class, ethnicity, language background, family, neighborhood, and gender. Without serious attention to the unfolding of this wider cultural frame in literacy learning, our vision of the whole remains partially obscured. (4)

This call addresses the ways we construct theory in our field, how we represent the relationships among literacy processes, pedagogy, interactions within the classroom, and cultural expectations which embed our institutions. The first two constructs — teacher as technician and teacher knowledge as lore — share a *curricular* view of the theory-practice relationship. Both of these views are consistent with extent models of pedagogical theory offered in composition studies (Brannon; Fulkerson). Each of the first two constructs we consider here analyzes the decisions teachers make in terms of the propositions of theory: a view of the writing process, the development of writing ability, the goal of writing and teaching, the ways knowledge is constructed. Each locates teacher authority within professional discourse, and assigns teachers a stable, centered, and professional subjectivity which is monologic, perhaps ungendered, and more to our point, unmarked by race. Both constructs are therefore, for teachers and the profession alike, discourses of control.

The third construct, teacher efficacy, reconfigures the representation of pedagogical theory. In particular, instead of seeing writing pedagogy as determined by a general theory of writing (in whatever versions this general theory might appear), the alternative we propose would place the teacher, the student, and the site of literacy instruction at the center, each exerting its influence on the others, each influencing an orientation toward the activity of the course, each in relationships with the others which are at best dialogical and, as some scholars have pointed out, often contradictory and conflictual (Lu). The construct of teacher efficacy does not subordinate pedagogy to a teacher's "substantive" knowledge, nor does it place teacher knowledge in dialogue with its situation, as the postdisciplinary view would have it. The construct of efficacy locates pedagogical theory in relation to three intersecting points of view: the institutional context of the writing course, the teacher's sense of herself as an actor within that institutional site, and the dialogizing, ambivalent, often resistant perspectives of students. The virtue of this model of pedagogical theory in composition is that by drawing attention to the "complex sociocultural experiences of literacy learning" Dyson and Freedman refer to, it sharpens the kinds of questions practitioners may ask about what works in and what works on the activity sponsored by the writing classroom.

Changing Dispositions

Disposition has two meanings which offer complementary views of the challenges surrounding literacy education in multicultural classrooms. The first meaning is "one's customary manner or emotional response; temperament." In its response to Oakland's Ebonics resolution, the American public's customary manner of emotional response toward African American English became front-page public news. The second meaning of disposition is "the power to control, direct, or dispose." These two meanings of disposition frame the interrelated issues surrounding the Ebonics controversy and the Ann Arbor "Black English" case, and the significance each holds for the field of composition. On the one hand, the Ann Arbor case came to focus on the language barrier which results from teachers' unconscious, negative attitudes toward African American English. On the other, ill-disposed toward their students' use of African American English, the Ann Arbor teachers expected less and their students not surprisingly lived down to these lowered expectations, evidence of the power of self-fulfilling prophecy.

More than twenty years ago, in response to the Ann Arbor case, the Black Caucus of NCTE and CCCC disseminated a carefully prepared "Commentary" regarding African American English. Recently reprinted in response to the Ebonics initiative, the purpose of the "Commentary" was to express the viewpoints of Black linguists and language arts educators on the topic. Briefly summarized, the "Commentary" asserts that the Black language system in and of itself is not a barrier to learning. The barrier is negative attitudes toward that language system, compounded by lack of information about the language system and inefficient techniques for teaching language skills, all of which is manifested in an unwillingness to adapt teaching styles to students' needs. Such barriers, in fact, reflect teachers', and the public's, dispositions toward literacy. In light of the public outcry over Ebonics, we ask: Have those dispositions changed today? The "Commentary" of the Black Caucus went on to say that the language of Black students is actually a strength on which teachers might draw in order to develop effective approaches to teaching. They concluded the statement with a call for thorough, unbiased research on the topic. However, based on the tone of the criticisms and emotional responses to the Ebonics issue, it became evident that society in general does not take such a detailed or objective view on the matter of the representations of diverse languages in the classroom.

After looking closely at the Ann Arbor case, it seems clear that for writing teachers today, many of the same barriers exist in the classroom that stood between the teachers at King School and their students. Because of cultural differences in patterns of language use, and because of differences in styles of interaction used to demonstrate knowledge, many students from diverse social and linguistic backgrounds are entering urban classrooms where teachers still have a difficult time recognizing and fully utilizing the wealth of language resources students use effectively outside school. These are resources that often go unrecognized and unrewarded within classroom settings. In spite of the considerable professional rhetoric over the past twenty years or so, recent research indicates that African Americans and other students of color are still faring very poorly in our nation's urban schools (Quality Education for Minorities Project). In light of the history of failure and miscommunication that marks the educational experiences of many African American English speakers, educators must continue to insist on seeking ways that the barriers created by diversity in language as the medium of instruction can become, instead, bridges between home language practices and academic registers teachers want students to learn. Making a significant place for affect within pedagogical theories is an important step toward this goal.

Acknowledgments

We would like to thank Ralph Stevens, Margaret Marshall, and Thomas Fox for their careful reading and suggestions on this article.

Works Cited

Abrahams, Roger. *Deep Down in the Jungle.* Chicago: Aldine, 1970.

Balester, Valerie. *Cultural Divide.* Portsmouth: Boynton, 1993.

Ball, Arnetha. "Community-Based Learning in Urban Settings as a Model for Educational Reform." *Applied Behavioral Science Review* 3 (1995): 127–46.

———. "Cultural Preference and the Expository Writing of African-American Adolescents." *Written Communication* 9 (1992): 501–32.

———. "Expository Writing Patterns of African-American Students." *English Journal* 85 (1996): 27–36.

Ball, Arnetha F., Kimberley C. Broussard, and Delvin M. Dinkins. "Investigating Interactive Discourse Patterns of African American Females in Community-Based Organizations." American Educational Research Association. New Orleans, 1994.

Bowie, R., and C. Bond. "Influencing Future Teachers' Attitudes toward Black English: Are We Making a Difference?" *Journal of Teacher Education* 45 (1994): 112–18.

Brannon, Lil. "Toward a Theory of Composition." *Perspectives on Research and Scholarship in Composition.* Ed. Ben McLelland and Timothy R. Donovan. New York: MLA, 1985. 6–25.

"Commentary." *Black Caucus Notes.* Urbana: NCTE. March, 1997.

Delpit, Lisa. "Education in a Multicultural Society: Our Future's Greatest Challenge." *Journal of Negro Education* 61 (1992): 237–49.

Dyson, A. H., and S. W. Freedman. *Critical Challenges for Research on Writing and Literacy: 1990–1995.* Technical Report No. 1–B. Berkeley, CA: Center for the Study of Writing, 1991.

Foster, Michelle. "Educating for Competence in Community and Culture: Exploring the Views of Exemplary African-American Teachers." *Urban Education* 27 (1993): 370–94.

———. "Effective Black Teachers: A Literature Review." *Teaching Diverse Populations Formulating a Knowledge Base.* Ed. Etta Hollins, Joyce King, and W. Hayman. Albany: State U of New York P, 1994. 225–42.

Fulkerson, Richard. "Composition Theory in the Eighties: Axiological Consensus and Paradigmatic Diversity." *CCC* 41 (1990): 409–29.

Gilyard, Keith. *Voices of the Self.* Detroit: Wayne State UP, 1992.

Giroux, Henry. *Teachers as Intellectuals toward a Critical Pedagogy of Learning.* New York: Bergin, 1988.

Harkin, Patricia. "The Postdisciplinary Politics of Lore." *Contending with Words.* Ed. Patricia Harkin and John Schilb. New York: MLA, 1991. 124–38.

Howard, Harry, Lee H. Hansen, and Thomas Pietras. *Final Evaluation: King Elementary School Vernacular Black English Inservice Program.* Ann Arbor: Ann Arbor Public Schools, 1980.

Knoblauch, C. H. "Rhetorical Constructions: Dialogue and Commitment." *College English* 50 (1988): 125–40.

Labov, William. "Recognizing Black English in the Classroom." *Black English Educational Equity and the Law.* Ed. John W. Chambers. Ann Arbor: Karoma, 1983. 29–55.

Lu, Min-zhan. "Conflict and Struggle: The Enemies or Preconditions of Basic Writing?" *College English* 54 (1992): 887–913.

McLeod, Susan H. "Pygmalion or Golem? Teacher Affect and Efficacy." *CCC* 46 (1995): 369–86.

Memorandum Opinion and Order. Martin Luther King Elementary School Children v. Ann Arbor School District Board. Civil Action No. 7–71861. 473 F. Supp. 1371 (1979).

Morgan, Marcyliena. "Indirectness and Interpretation in African American Women's Discourse." *Pragmatics* 1 (1991): 421–51.

North, Stephen. *The Making of Knowledge in Composition.* Portsmouth: Boynton, 1987.

Pang, Valerie O., and Velma Sablan. "Teacher Efficacy: Do Teachers Believe They Can Be Effective with African American Students?" San Francisco: American Educational Research Association, 1995.

Phelps, Louise Wetherbee. "Practical Wisdom and the Geography of Knowledge in Composition." *College English* 47 (1992): 338–56.

Quality Education for Minorities Project. *Education That Works: An Action Plan for the Education of Minorities.* Cambridge: MIT P, 1990.

Richardson, Elaine. *Where Did That Come From? Black Talk for Black Student Talking Texts.* MA Thesis. Cleveland State U, 1993.

Schilb, John. *Between the Lines: Relating Composition Theory and Literary Theory.* Portsmouth: Boynton, 1996.

———. "Cultural Studies, Postmodernism, and Composition." *Contending with Words.* Ed. Patricia Harkin and John Schilb. New York: MLA, 1991. 173–88.

Shaughnessy, Mina. *Errors and Expectations.* New York: Oxford UP, 1977.

Smitherman, Geneva. *Talkin and Testifyin.* Detroit: Wayne State UP, 1977.

———. "'What Go Round Come Round': *King* in Perspective." *Harvard Educational Review* 51 (1981): 40–56.

Spears, A. K., "Are Black and White Vernaculars Diverging?" *American Speech* 62 (1987): 48–55, 71–72.

West, Cornel. *Race Matters.* Boston: Beacon, 1993.

Williams, Patricia J. *The Alchemy of Race and Rights.* Cambridge, MA: Harvard UP, 1991.

Zeichner, Kenneth M. "Alternative Paradigms in Teacher Education." *Journal of Teacher Education* 34 (1983): 3–9.

Zeichner, Kenneth, and Daniel Liston. "Teaching Student Teachers to Reflect." *Harvard Educational Review* 57 (1987): 23–48.

Zemelman, Steven, and Harvey Daniels. *A Community of Writers.* Portsmouth: Boynton, 1988.

Ball and Lardner's Insights as a Resource for Your Teaching

1. Reflect on instances in which assumptions you have held or encountered have unconsciously affected your teaching. On what model are your expectations of student behavior and response based? How might your expectations or standards be culturally informed? Question your current practices to see whether your teaching values one pattern of cultural discourse over another. If so, what modifications will you need to make to adapt your teaching to various discourse styles?

2. Identify the particular features that distinguish what Ball and Lardner might call the affective atmosphere toward diversity at the institution where you teach. How might these impact the ways you address issues of race, diversity, and diverse literacy backgrounds with your class?

Ball and Lardner's Insights as a Resource for Your Writing Classroom

1. Ask students what associations come to mind from the phrase "mainstream American culture," and record examples on the board. How and why have they selected these examples? Challenge them to question their perceptions of "mainstream." On what have they based their ideas? Are their notions culturally founded? Do these notions exclude any societal groups?

2. Can students identify examples of institutional racism? What are the implications of this awareness for schools? For other institutions?

The Costs of Caring: "Femininism" and Contingent Women Workers in Composition Studies

Eileen E. Schell

In this selection from Feminism and Composition *(1998), Eileen Schell elaborates on a feminist discourse about teaching that is rooted in an explicitly "feminine" system of caring and nurturing rather than judging and criticizing, in connectedness and empathy rather than abstractions and edicts. This maternalistic mode, however, often conflicts with the desires of women to be taken seriously as teachers and intellectuals. Moreover, it directly corroborates the gender inequities that push women toward lower-paying and less secure jobs than their male colleagues. Women have less time to devote to scholarly activity and reflective inquiry into their practice. As a result, the body of knowledge generated about writing instruction is a distinctly masculine one.*

Lorie Goodman Batson contends that when we speak of women in composition studies — their varying interests, desires, motivations, and political affiliations —we often appeal to a common female identity that levels differences and creates alliances where there may be divergences (207–08). As identity categories become increasingly fragmented and contested in postmodern thought, it is important for feminists in composition "to begin challenging the privileging of singular political identities" (Wicke and Ferguson 7). Poststructuralist and postmodern critiques of identity politics necessitate that we reexamine previously unchallenged assumptions about women students and women teachers.

In particular, the argument that feminists in composition should favor what Elizabeth Flynn refers to as "femininist" principles or the "recuperation of those modes of thinking within the field that are compatible with a feminine epistemology" ("Studies" 143) needs to be reexamined. According to Flynn, a feminine epistemology is an approach to language study "characterized by modalities of relatedness and mutuality, indistinct boundaries, flexibility, and non-oppositional styles" (147). In this essay, I examine the limits of femininist thought; I critique arguments that advocate a feminist pedagogy based on an "ethic of care," which is a set of principles that Nel Noddings refers to as a reliance on an ethical subject's "feelings, needs, situational conditions," as a "personal ideal rather than universal ethical principles and their application" (96). It is my contention that femininist pedagogy, although compelling, may reinforce rather than critique or transform patriarchal structures by reinscribing what Magda Lewis calls the "woman as caretaker ideology," the "psychological investment women are required to make in the emotional well-being of men [and others] — an investment that goes well beyond the classroom into the private spaces of women's lives" (174). While I do not wish to discredit femininist pedagogy, I do wish to question the ways that an ethic of care may prevent feminists from addressing one of the most serious gender problems we face in composition studies: the relegating of women to contingent (part-time and non-tenure-track) writing instructorships.

"Femininism" in Composition Studies

Beginning in the latter half of the 1980s, femininists in composition have created a discourse on pedagogy that perpetuates feminine values and principles (Caywood and Overing; Phelps and Emig; Flynn, "Composing" and "Studies"; Frey, "Equity"; Rubin). In 1987, Cynthia Caywood and Gillian Overing coedited the anthology *Teaching Writing: Pedagogy, Gender, and Equity,* the first book-length work on feminist writing pedagogy. Drawing on the work of feminists Nancy Chodorow, Carol Gilligan, and Sara Ruddick, several volume contributors (Daumer and Runzo; Frey; Goulston; Stanger) advocate a pedagogical approach rooted in Nodding's ethic of care: a process of ethical decision making based on interrelationships and connectedness rather than on universalized and individualized rules and rights.[1] Weaving together strands of liberal and cultural feminisms, the editors contend that feminist pedagogy revalues the experience of women students and encourages individual voice and personal growth in the writing classroom (Caywood and Overing xi). In "Transforming the Composition Classroom," Elisabeth Daumer and Sandra Runzo urge feminist teachers to help their students "unearth" their authentic voices by encouraging them to "search out untraditional sources, often the forms of writing which have not been granted the status of literature because they are either personal (journals, letters, diaries) or community-based (Blues, spirituals, work songs)" (56). In this formulation, female students' subjectivities are represented as buried treasure, which must be brought to light with the assistance of the feminist teacher. Thus the theory of subjectivity in *Teaching Writing* is grounded in Enlightenment notions of the self-governing, autonomous individual.

Cultural feminism, as represented in *Teaching Writing,* entails a radical transformation of pedagogical relationships. "Cultural feminism," writes Linda Alcoff, "is the ideology of a female nature or female essence reappropriated by feminists themselves in an effort to revalidate undervalued female attributes" ("Feminism" 408). Following nineteenth-century ideals of femininity, cultural feminists argue that feminine values have been denigrated and superseded by masculine values such as aggressiveness, confrontation, control, competition, domination, and physical violence. To reverse the perpetuation of harmful masculine values, cultural feminists contend that all people — men and women alike — should emulate feminine values: nurturance, supportiveness, interdependence, and nondominance. In addition, cultural feminists deemphasize a model of communication based on argumentation and endorse a rhetoric of mediation, conciliation, and shared authority. Alcoff warns that, although many women have developed invaluable skills and abilities in response to patriarchal restrictions, feminists should be wary of advocating "the restrictive conditions that give rise to those attributes: forced parenting, lack of physical autonomy, dependency for survival on mediation skills" (414). Furthermore, Devoney Looser cautions that theories of gender identity that presume "a stable and/or recoverable homogenized" female subject "present costs that feminist compositionists may not be ready to pay" (55).

The happy marriage between cultural feminism and expressivist composition studies, however, is evident in many of the essays in *Teaching Writing.* As Wendy Goulston indicates, process theories of composing rely on qualities associated with a "female style" (25). In fact, Caywood and Overing locate their volume at the "recurrent intersection" between feminist theory and expressivist writing theory: the privileging of process over product; the encouragement of inner voice, exploratory or discovery writing; collaboration; and the decentering of teacherly authority (xii–xiii). Caywood and Overing find that "the process model, insofar as it facilitates and legitimizes the fullest expression of individual voice, is compatible with the feminist revisioning of hierarchy, if not essential to it" (xiv).

Unlike expressivist pedagogy, femininist pedagogy consciously embraces "maternal thinking," a term borrowed from Sara Ruddick's landmark essay "Maternal Thinking" (Daumer and Runzo 54). According to Ruddick, feminists should strive to bring the patterns of thinking characteristic of the social practices and intellectual capacities of the mother "in[to] the public realm, to make the preservation and growth of all children a work of public conscience and legislation" (361). In Ruddick's theory of ethics, maternal thinking is governed by three interests: preserving the life of the child, fostering the child's growth, and shaping an acceptable child (348–57). To accomplish these maternal interests, the mother must exercise a capacity for "attentive love," the supportive love and caring that allows a child to persevere and grow (357–58). Applied broadly to human relations, maternal thinking offers a radical alternative to a theory of ethics based on a concept of individual rights (see Perry).

Applied broadly to the feminist writing classroom, maternal thinking encourages writing teachers to create a supportive, nonhierarchical environment responsive to students' individual needs and cultural contexts (Daumer and Runzo 50). The maternal writing teacher "empowers and liberates students" by serving as a facilitator, a midwife to students' ideas; she individualizes her teaching by fostering "self-sponsored writing"; she decenters her authority by encouraging collaborative learning among peers (49). In "The Sexual Politics of the One-to-One Tutorial Approach," Carol Stanger borrows Gilligan's theory of women's moral development to argue for a model of collaborative learning that encourages students to build knowledge through consensus, not competition (41). In "Equity and Peace in the New Writing Classroom," Olivia Frey, like Stanger, endorses a "peaceful classroom" based on "understanding and cooperation," not on competition and aggression: "Group work and peer inquiry . . . discourage harmful confrontation since through cooperative learning students discover how to resolve conflict creatively and effectively" (100). Both Stanger and Frey eschew hierarchical forms of discourse in favor of discourses grounded in mediation and negotiation.

Overall, contributors to *Teaching Writing* suggest that a classroom based on an ethic of care can counteract patriarchal pedagogy's "emphasis on hierarchy, competition, and control" (Gore 70). They also appear to agree with the premise that feminists are better equipped to achieve a nonhierarchical and noncompetitive classroom because they possess the nurturing, maternal qualities to facilitate such a change (70). Yet will the maternal stance work for all women teachers and students, including those who are white and working-class, African American, Latina, or Asian? Caywood and Overing admit that their volume "may not meet some of the particular needs of minority students" (xv), implying that maternal teaching is best suited for white middle-class women. Although the volume omits the important perspectives of minority women and teachers, it nevertheless has served as the starting point for conversation about feminist pedagogy in composition studies (xv) and an inspiration for further feminist pedagogical models based on an ethic of care.

But what are the ethical, emotional, and material costs of a pedagogy based on an ethic of care? If teaching writing is considered women's work — underpaid and underrecognized — how might feminist pedagogy make it difficult for feminists in composition to address gender inequities in academic work, particularly the preponderance of women in part-time and non-tenure-track positions?

The Hidden Costs of an Ethic of Care

Ethnographic studies and surveys of feminist classrooms demonstrate that students, both male and female, expect their women teachers to act as nurturing mother figures (Friedman 205). There is often conflict between that expectation and the teacher's need to be taken seriously as a teacher and intellectual (205). Research on gender bias in student rating of women teachers, conducted by Diane Kierstead, Patti D'Agostino, and Heidi Dill, reveals that

> if female instructors want to obtain high student ratings, they must be not only highly competent with regard to factors directly related to teaching but also careful to act in accordance with traditional sex-role expectations. In particular . . . male and female instructors will earn equal student ratings for equal professional work only if the women also display stereotypically feminine behavior. (Kierstead et al. qtd. in Koblitz)

If a feminist teacher adopts a maternal stance, she may better conform to her students' expectations. But what if her pedagogy favors critical challenge and intellectual rigor, not overt encouragement and nurturance (Friedman 207)? Neal Koblitz reports that if women teachers give challenging assignments and exams and follow rigorous grading policies, students are more inclined to give them lower ratings. A study of teaching evaluations at the University of Dayton indicates that "college students of both sexes judged female authority figures who engaged in punitive behavior more harshly than they judged punitive males" (Elaine Martin qtd. in Koblitz).

The research that Koblitz cites shows that for women teachers caring is not merely a natural instinct or impulse, it is a socially and historically mandated behavior. "Caring," writes the feminist philosopher Joan C. Tronto, "may be a reflection of a survival mechanism for women or others who are dealing with oppressive conditions, rather than a quality of intrinsic value on its own" ("Women" 184). Women who do not occupy positions of power often adopt a posture of attentiveness or caring accompanied by "deferential mannerisms (e.g., differences in speech, smiling, other forms of body language, etc.)" as a way to appease and anticipate the needs of those in power (184).[2] Rather than view caring as solely a natural act, we can productively view it as a form of "emotional labor," a category that the feminist philosopher Sandra Bartky defines as the "emotional sustenance that women supply to others." It is the labor of "feeding egos" and "tending wounds": "The aim of this supporting and sustaining is to produce or to maintain in the one supported and sustained a conviction of the value and importance of his own chosen projects, hence of the value and importance of his own person" (102). Bartky characterizes emotional labor as a continuum occupied on the one end by commercial caregivers, who perform "perfunctory and routinized [caregiving] relationships," and on the other end by "sincere caregivers," who direct "wholehearted acceptance" and emotional support toward the objects of their caregiving (116).

Not surprisingly, academic women often feel compelled to direct their energy into caring labor: teaching, advising students, and performing lower-level administrative duties. As one tenured woman faculty member observes in Angela Simeone's study of academic women:

> I think the great trap of young women today is that there is a sort of subtle pressure to be compliant, to not assert themselves intellectually, to spend . . . more time with students than the men do, to be motherly and nurturing, to be on a million committees, not to be a power within the university but to just do the drudgery that has to be done, to be compliant in every way. And then they don't get tenure and they fail. They don't say no to these demands, and these demands are demands that are much more put on women. (36)

Many administrators and full-time faculty members believe that women make ideal candidates for teaching writing because the same qualities necessary for motherhood — patience, enthusiasm, and the ability to juggle multiple tasks — are qualities that effective writing teachers possess (Holbrook 207). The belief that women's essential nature is to marry and mother is reinforced consciously and unconsciously throughout the institutions of hegemonic culture: the schools, government, religion, and family life. These institutions — or ideological state apparatuses, to use Louis Althusser's term — structure the social relations that interpellate human subjects (81). Through sexual-role socialization in the family, schools, and churches, women learn to channel their energies into nurturing forms of labor: teaching, nursing, social work, and mothering.

This sexual division of labor charts a predetermined pattern for many women's lives, what Nadya Aisenberg and Mona Harrington call the "marriage plot": "The central tenet of the plot, of course, is that a proper goal is marriage, or, more generally, the woman's sphere is private and domestic. Her proper role within the sphere is to provide support for the male at the head of the household of which she forms a part" (6). The marriage plot carries over into the public sphere, where a woman's proper role "is still to be supportive — either to an employer . . . or in some cases to a cause" (6). The marriage plot requires that women's roles, even in academic work, be supportive and nurturing. Women should be satisfied and fulfilled by low-paying, low-status teaching jobs.

The marriage plot is particularly pervasive in composition studies, where a large group of contingent women workers "nurture" beginning writers for salaries that rival those of underpaid waitresses. Sue Ellen Holbrook's history "Women's Work: The Feminizing of Composition Studies" and Susan Miller's "The Feminization of Composition" and *Textual Carnivals* call attention to the prevalence of this caretaker ideology. Miller's metaphorical analysis of the hierarchical, gendered constructions of teaching illuminates how institutional scripts cast women teachers as nurturers (*Carnivals* 137), thus making it problematic for feminists to continue advocating nurturant behavior as a form of empowerment.

According to Judith Gappa and David Leslie, women make up only 27 percent of all full-time, tenure-track faculty members in American colleges and universities, yet they make up 67 percent of all part-time faculty members. In the humanities, 67 percent of part-time positions are filled by women, whereas 33 percent of full-time positions are filled by women (25; see also Burns 21). Bettina Huber reports that of a cohort of 1,674 women who received Ph.D.s in English between 1981 and 1986, 56 percent found tenure-track appointments by 1987, whereas of a cohort of 1,475 men, 77.8 percent did (62). Some women choose to teach part-time because it affords them the flexibility to raise a family or care for aging parents, to pursue a writing or artistic career, or to run a home business. Others are less than happy with their contingent status. Some women turn down full-time employment to avoid relocating a family or a partner already holding a full-time job. Others seek part-time work (often several part-time jobs pieced together) because they cannot find full-time work in an overcrowded job market.

Although conditions of employment vary, universities and colleges often hire contingent writing faculty members on a semester-to-semester basis through "informal interviewing and appointment procedures" and without the benefit of contractual job security (Wallace 11). Many administrators hire contingent faculty members a few weeks or even days before the semester begins, as soon as enrollment numbers materialize for first-year composition. When part-time faculty members are hired, their "research, creativity," or previous academic employment is often not valued (11). Once hired, these teachers may receive little or no training or work orientation. And the criteria for assessing their teaching are often ill-defined (13).

Keeping in mind these grim facts about the gendered nature of contingent writing instruction, we need to assess how theories of femininist pedagogy based on an ethic of care may reinforce the labor patterns that feminists critique. Socialist feminist analyses of women's work in nurturant occupations may help in that assessment.

Socialist Feminism and Sex-Affective Production

Like cultural feminists and liberal feminists, socialist feminists examine how patriarchal socioeconomic relations subordinate women's interests to the interests of men. Unlike cultural and liberal feminists, however, socialist feminists (Michele Barrett, Sandra Lee Bartky, Zillah Eisenstein, Ann Ferguson, Heidi Hartmann, Alison Jaggar) argue that sex, class, and racial oppression maintain the gendered division of labor. Moreover, socialist feminists critically examine women's labor, analyzing the costs and benefits of the ideology of nurturance. The socialist feminist philosopher Ann Ferguson has argued that contemporary American women, despite differences of race, class, and sexual orientation, have in common "a sex/class connection organized by the sexual division of unpaid labor in the family household as well as wage labor, the gender bias of the patriarchal state, the mass media and the public/private split of family household and economy" (8). Although Ferguson seemingly essentializes women's labor, she emphasizes that class identity highlights differences among women, since individual women belong to overlapping classes that are often in conflict with one another: family class, sex class (organized around the gendered division of labor), race class, and economic class (119). Within these different class positions, women are expected to engage in forms of labor that involve the function of caring or sex-affective production, "that human physical and social interaction which is common to human sexuality, parenting, kin and family relations, nurturance and social bonding" (7–8).

Sex-affective production is characterized by "unequal exchange," in which women often receive "less of the goods produced than men" although they work harder and spend more time producing those goods: "The relations between men and women can be considered exploitative because the men are able to appropriate more of women's labor time for their own uses and also receive more of the goods produced" (132). Since sex-affective modes of production are largely unpaid, underpaid, and underrecognized forms of labor — such as mothering, nursing, and teaching — they are essential to the successful functioning of a late-capitalist economy. Moreover, women's involvement in nurturant labor is made to seem natural by discourses on gender and work claiming that women choose "inferior work status" (Bergmann 23). The feminist economist Barbara Bergmann explains:

> If a person doing the [career] choosing is female, the person's choices are seen as powerfully conditioned by her "home responsibilities." This line of thinking leads to the view of women's inferior position in paid work as a benign and necessary adaptation to biological and social realities, and in no way due to biased and malign behavior on the part of employers. (23)

Maria Markus describes a "second tier" of work for women in the "less attractive, less creative, and usually less well-paid branches" of the professions. Women who end up in the second tier tend to be "'accused' of not 'planning their careers,' of not 'keeping their eyes open to the next step' but instead of burying themselves in the current tasks and awaiting 'natural justice' to reward them for working hard." Furthermore, women's lesser "agility" in professional careers includes their "lower mobility" as a result of family attachments and women's tendency to focus on human relations (105, 106).

In English studies, a second tier of work exists for women in the form of contingent writing instructorships, and such positions epitomize the paradox of sex-affective production. On the one hand, emotional rewards — a "psychic income"[3] — keep women invested in teaching; on the other hand, many contingent women writing instructors recount experiences of exploitation and express feelings of alienation. This paradox supports Bartky's claim that women may be epistemically and ethically disempowered by providing nurturance for others while they receive little compensation — emotional and material — in return (117). Women's so-called innate, instinctual desire to nurture and care for others brings them a psychic income — personal fulfillment and satisfaction — yet that psychic income is "the blood at the root" (A. Ferguson) of women's exploitation as underpaid workers.

To understand the costs as well as benefits of an ethic of care in feminist writing pedagogy, I conducted primary research on contingent women writing instructors' attitudes toward their work, exploring the contradictory forces that surround their involvement in writing instruction. My research reveals that a pedagogy based on an ethic of care is simultaneously empowering and disempowering: it offers psychic rewards while exacting a distinct emotional and material price from women workers.

Contingent Labor as Sex-Affective Production

In the fall of 1992 and spring of 1993, I interviewed a dozen lecturers (both full- and part-time) who held semester-to-semester teaching contracts in the first-year writing program at the University of Wisconsin, Milwaukee, where I worked as a teaching assistant and assistant writing program coordinator. The interviewees were white women ranging in ages from twenty-five to fifty-five; most had master's degrees in literature or education, and some had completed credits toward the doctoral degree. The women of ages twenty-five to thirty-five had five to seven years of teaching experience in community colleges or state universities; the women of ages thirty-five to fifty-five had taught for ten to fifteen years in community colleges, state universities, or public and private elementary and secondary schools. I conducted the interviews in an open-ended manner, allowing the responses to determine the order of the questions. Each interview lasted approximately ninety minutes and was taped and partially transcribed. To allow these women to speak candidly and without fear of institutional reprisal, I have omitted their identities. (I also surveyed essays and articles on women's experiences as part-time and non-tenure-track faculty members to broaden the perspective of my interview project. And as a former part-time faculty member, I drew on my own experiences.)

In the interviews, I investigated how contingent women faculty members describe the costs and benefits of their work, and I paid particular attention to their "workplace emotions," a term used by Carol Stearns and Peter Stearns, who research "emotionology," the history and sociology of the emotions (7–8). Stearns and Stearns define emotions as socially constructed, historically specific responses rather than as transhistorical and transcultural essences. In a separate essay, Peter Stearns describes how nineteenth-century industrialization brought technological displacement, inflation, management impersonality, white-middle-class downward mobility, and the increasing isolation of unskilled workers (149–50). In the early twentieth-century office, management began to suppress anger and impose a standard of surface friendliness, particularly among white-collar workers and those who worked "in a variety of service industries including the airlines and branches of social work" (156). Because of societal expectations and management policies that mandate friendliness and nurturant behavior, workers in caring professions increasingly experience emotions like anger, cynicism, and frustration in response to a loss of autonomy, increased work hierarchies, management domination and surveillance, job instability, lack of promotion, and specific forms of workplace discrimination.[4]

In my interviews with part-time women writing instructors, the concept of workplace emotion helped illuminate a split between the instructors' feelings about their classrooms and their feelings about the institutions that employed them. Both the interviewees and the writers of published narratives revealed that while they liked, even loved, to teach, they nearly all had negative feelings about their working conditions and their relation to the institution at large. In the classroom, they felt in control, valued, and alive; in the institution, they often felt invisible and alienated.

The separation between institutional space and classroom space mirrors the attitude that teaching is a private or individual activity and research a public activity. In an account of her experiences as a part-time writing instructor at the State University of New York, Stony Brook, Clare Frost characterizes this public-private split: "I may be a misfit in the academy but not in my classroom. For me it's not a job, it's a calling. The pain of being an adjunct is not inflicted in the classroom, but in the hallowed halls of academe. My struggle to be seen and heard in this discipline is also a struggle to have faith in myself and what I'm doing" (66).

In both the published narratives and the interviews I conducted, women writing instructors reported passionate feelings about teaching and described a sense of connection and satisfaction; they identified their teaching roles as supportive, nurturing, and facilitative. One interviewee characterized herself as a midwife: "I think they've got little baby writers in them that are going to be born. I'm helping the student who has had x number of bad encounters with writing give birth to that infant writer inside." Many of the interviewees remarked that they continue to endure exploitative working conditions because they enjoy teaching. Frost writes:

> I love the teaching of composition. I enjoy seeing my students use writing to tap into themselves, some for the first time in their lives. I glow when some of their final evaluations say that the course was better than they expected it or that their attitudes about writing have improved. For me, getting to know a new group of young people each semester and seeing what they can accomplish in a few short months is exhilarating. I don't find their writing boring, because I don't find them boring. (66)

One woman, in her late forties and with over ten years of teaching experience, argued that the students, not the institutional setting, offered her psychic rewards: "The students give a lot back to me. The institution doesn't give me much. I get a paycheck, I get an office, I get a nine-year-old computer. I don't get much support from the institution." The attachment to teaching is bittersweet because many contingent teachers are isolated from professional networks. Nancy Grimm, a formerly part-time writing teacher at Michigan Technological University, describes the unstable nature of part-time labor:

> For seven years I have taught part-time. I give conference presentations. I publish a little. I even direct the local site of the National Writing Project — one of the department's few graduate level offerings. But at this university I will never be full-time, and I will never be hired for more than a year at a time. My part-time teaching load fluctuates each year. More than once, I have made less money than I made the year before. My teaching load — and consequently my salary — depends on how many gaps the department has to fill. I am going nowhere, but to work effectively I can't let myself confront the issue too often. (14)

The key issue for contingent women faculty members who wish to participate in research and scholarship is "work time" — the way in which students and teachers circulate in the organizational structure of English (Watkins 4–6). In composition studies, the work time of intellectuals (specialists, practitioners) is directly affected by the research-teaching division, a split predicated on the difference between the creation of knowledge and the perpetuation of already existing knowledge or know-how. Teachers perpetuate what Antonio Gramsci has characterized as the "pre-existing traditional, accumulated intellectual wealth," whereas scholars create new forms of knowledge (307). Scholars, Evan Watkins writes, are classified as professionals "understood to work at the very frontiers of knowledge, at the edge of a 'heart of darkness' where expertise . . . [is] tested in the most demanding situations" (104).

Teaching writing, of course, resides on the low end of the research-teaching binary. Not only is writing instruction devalued, but it also requires substantial time and emotional energy from the teacher. The

CCCC "Statement on Principles and Standards for the Postsecondary Teaching of Writing" acknowledges that writing instruction is labor-intensive:

> The improvement of an individual student's writing requires persistent and frequent contact between teacher and student both inside and outside the classroom. It requires assigning far more papers than are usually assigned in other college classrooms; it requires reading them and commenting on them not simply to justify a grade, but to offer guidance and suggestions for improvement; and it requires spending a great deal of time with individual students, helping them not just to improve particular papers but to understand fundamental principles of effective writing that will enable them to continue learning throughout their lives. (335)

The labor-intensive nature of writing instruction makes it difficult for contingent faculty members in composition to take part in scholarly conversations. Mary Kupiec Cayton argues, "The material conditions of participating in the conversation that is academic scholarship include the ability to devote oneself to it wholeheartedly — at least at certain points in time." Borrowing Kenneth Burke's metaphor that scholarship resembles a parlor conversation, Cayton likens contingent faculty members to parlor maids who are busy "attending to the necessary chores that will free the guests for conversing." Because their teaching responsibilities — and often family responsibilities — remove them from the parlor conversation that is academic scholarship, contingent women faculty members often "play a supporting role rather than the role of the participant," and as a result they hear and understand less "of what is transpiring inside the parlor" (655). Frost attests to the difficult choices they must make regarding their work time:

> After family responsibilities and more than thirty hours a week spent directly on the teaching of three sections of composition, I have to think carefully and pragmatically about how I'm going to spend the precious remaining time. . . . For the sad truth is that even if I become more knowledgeable — read theorists, attend conferences, present papers, take additional courses — I will receive no additional institutional recognition of any sort. I will not receive a penny more in remuneration for the courses I currently teach, nor will I become eligible for a full-time position or additional employee benefits. In fact, no practical or professional benefit will result. (63–64)

One of the interviewees, an experienced instructor with a background in ESL and teaching experience at several institutions, commented that, while she felt the writing program administrator and his assistant valued and respected her work as a teacher, she was invisible to the rest of the university: "As far as the rest of the school goes, I don't even think they know who I am. I'm just someone filling a hole, and they don't know about my experiences, they don't know about my ideas,

I know they don't know who I am, they don't care who I am, they just want someone in there teaching classes."

She referred to herself as an interchangeable part, "not even a person — just a cog" in the university machine. Another interviewee described the university as a machine that consumes human labor: "A friend of mine once said the institution wants to chew you up and when they're done with you, they'll spit you out." She commented on her expendability: "You know there will be five more people standing in line to do what I do, and they'll love doing what they're doing just like I love doing what I'm doing."

For those interviewees who had been working for many years as contingent writing instructors, the overwhelming response to their professional situation was a growing and hardening cynicism. One woman stated that she had learned not to expect any rewards or recognition from the university: "I think I'm just very hard-nosed and resigned. I just say 'I like my job, I'm good at my job,' but I don't have any expectations. I don't expect any recognition. I'm just jaded and sort of hardened to anything like that." As Cynthia Tuell relates, contingent faculty members are like handmaids:

> We clean up the comma splices. We organize the discourse of our students as though straightening a closet. When it's straight the "regular" professors teaching "regular" courses don't have to pick through the clutter and can quickly find the suit that suits them. When we can't manage to scrub them clean, we are called on to flunk out the great unwashed before they sully the orderly classrooms of the upper divisions. As handmaids, we are replaceable and interchangeable. . . . As handmaids, we serve the needs of our masters, not the vision we may have of ourselves, of our work, or of our students. (126)

For many women, the cycle of contingent teaching constitutes a form of exploitation sweetened by emotional or psychic rewards.

Although teaching composition has been thought of as women's work for the past seventy years, we have only begun to question the larger socioeconomic structures that channel women into contingent work.[5] As feminists in composition studies, we need to understand how femininist arguments for an ethic of care may reinforce the cycle of sex-affective production, in which women work hard but appropriate few professional rewards for themselves. By studying women's work narratives, we can gain alternative visions of our disciplinary realities and begin to rethink fundamental assumptions about our disciplinary identities and the structure of academic work. Ultimately, we can work on multiple levels — national and local — to organize coalitions that improve the working conditions of our colleagues who are non-tenure-track writing instructors.

Addressing Professional Inequities

Although we — feminist teachers and intellectuals — may exercise an ethic of care in our writing classrooms, we may fail to exhibit an analogous ethic in our relations with non-tenure-track faculty members. Unlike Susan Miller's "sad women in the basement" (*Carnivals* 121), some of us work on the first floors of English departments, where we serve as writing program administrators and as directors of writing centers, writing-across-the-curriculum programs, and graduate programs in rhetoric and composition. Many of us train and supervise graduate teaching assistants and serve as dissertation advisers, holding power and prestige unimaginable to women writing teachers of previous generations.

But our privilege does not mean that we are exempt from the threat of sexual discrimination and sexual harassment. Some of us on the tenure track feel exploited and underappreciated; some of us have been denied tenure and feel that our work in writing pedagogy and rhetorical theory has been undervalued; some of us have been pushed into administering writing programs as untenured assistant professors and must fight to maintain time for our scholarly work. Our experiences resonate with those of the women scholars who pioneered composition studies and who tell us of the great personal and professional price they paid to achieve professional recognition in a fledgling subdiscipline (see Crowley).

Empowered financially and professionally yet subject to sexual discrimination and sexual harassment, women academics occupy contradictory roles (see Luke and Gore, "Women"). Evelyn Fox Keller and Helene Moglen find that academic women, because of their historically marginal positions in higher education, "continue to feel the oppression of past struggles and the ongoing burdens of tokenism" (26). Uncomfortable with newly won power and embattled by the criticisms of hostile colleagues, they may not realize the privileges or advantages they do have (28). Nor are they "immune to the problem of competition"; in an economy of scarce resources, where "influence and power are by definition in limited supply," women must compete with one another for positions, committee and teaching assignments, teaching awards, and book contracts (22). Academic women also directly and indirectly benefit from the exploitation of other women's labor, particularly the labor of non-tenure-track faculty members. Even as I write this essay, I am benefiting from the exploitation of contingent faculty members at my institution. My research load — and the research load of three dozen other tenure-track faculty members — is made possible by the labor of approximately forty part-time and full-time non-tenure-track writing faculty members, two-thirds of whom are women. I call attention to this issue to illustrate the deep contradictions — tensions and discontinuities — of academic life. While many of us work to alleviate inequities in our classrooms, we are nevertheless complicit in gendered inequities that are often invisible or appear natural to us.

Feminist research in composition studies, however, can serve as a site for exposing, questioning, and changing academic hierarchies that are considered natural. The continuing presence of women in contingent writing instructorships can become a site of activism for feminists in composition.

I am not alone in calling for better working conditions for contingent writing instructors. The CCCC has addressed the problem of contingent labor through its 1989 "Statement of Principles and Standards for Postsecondary Writing Instruction." Adapted from the 1986 "Wyoming Conference Resolution" — a grass-roots petition calling for improvements in the working conditions for exploited writing faculty members — the CCCC statement is "based on the assumption that the responsibility for the academy's most serious mission, helping students to develop their critical powers as readers and writers, should be vested in tenure-line faculty" (330).[6]

Although the statement acknowledges that "most teachers of writing are women and that many more of them are people of color than are tenure-line faculty" (CCCC Committee 336), it does not address the specific barriers to success women face in academic work: racial and sexual discrimination, sexual harassment, and the gendered division of labor.[7] Neither the "Wyoming Conference Resolution" nor the CCCC statement deals with the larger social and economic structures that channel women into contingent labor. The problem of contingent labor in composition studies is not just a professional issue that we can correct by eliminating contingent positions and hiring more full-time faculty members; it is a gender issue, and thus a feminist issue, tied to larger systems of exploitation. To ignore this problem is to ignore one of the largest gender inequities in English studies.

Feminists in composition must find ways to alleviate this problem through collective action. Two groups in the CCCC, the Committee on the Status of Women in the Profession and the Coalition of Women Scholars in the History of Rhetoric and Composition, offer sites for promoting the professional development and equitable treatment of women faculty members in composition. In addition, the yearly CCCC feminist workshop offers a forum for women to meet and discuss feminist research, pedagogy, and professional issues. At the 1995 CCCC feminist workshop, Women in the Academy: Can a Feminist Agenda Transform the Illusion of Equity into Reality?, presenters spoke about family and partner choices, part-time labor, administrative work, ageism, sexual orientation, race, ethnicity, and class issues. Workshop leaders Jody Millward and Susan Hahn distributed a mission statement entitled "Other Choices, Other Voices: Solutions to Gender Issues" and proposed that the CCCC, NCTE, American Association of University Women, and MLA conduct an investigative survey of the employment, underemployment, and professional choices of women in ESL, essential skills, and composition. They urged the organizations to establish an ethical code of hiring that would consider the traditional practice of hiring from the outside rather than promoting from within; the high teaching load and lack of institutional support for nonliterary fields; the overreliance of institutions on temporary contracts and part-time positions; recommendations for health and retirement benefits; recommendations for flexible careers, including job sharing, part-time tenure, and flexibility of tenure deadlines; maternal-leave policies and spousal hiring; the establishment and enforcement of sexual harassment policies; the enforcement of policies to prohibit discrimination based on ethnicity, age, marital status, sexual orientation, and number of children. In addition, members of the workshop drafted a statement on affirmative action to be presented to the CCCC Executive Committee.

Efforts to combat the problem of gender and contingent labor on a national level emphasize consciousness-raising and general organizing strategies, but local organizing may be a better way to change specific institutional climates. On university campuses across the country, faculty women's coalitions have offered many academic women the opportunity to act collectively and speak out against sex discrimination, sexual harassment, and the general exploitation of women faculty members.[8] For instance, on nonunionized campuses a local departmental or university-wide women's coalition could conduct a study of the working conditions of non-tenure-track women faculty members across campus, offering both a statistical analysis and testimonial accounts of hiring practices, salaries, evaluation procedures, contract renewal, fringe benefits, and professional development opportunities. Armed with such a report and a comparative analysis of working conditions at peer institutions, a women's coalition could influence departmental and university administrators to improve the working conditions, salary, benefits, and professional development opportunities for non-tenure-track women. Moreover, faculty women's coalitions provide psychological support for women, a designated space for women to meet and receive professional advice and mentoring (for coalition models see Childers et al.).

A major obstacle confronting women's coalition building is the meritocracy ideal — the individualist "work hard and you will succeed" mentality that fails to acknowledge power relations and hierarchies among women. Many powerful women faculty members see their achievements as individual efforts and hesitate to help other women, particularly non-tenure-track faculty members. Bernice Johnson Reagon characterizes the problem: "Sometimes you get comfortable in your little barred room and you decide you in fact are going to live there and carry out all of your stuff in there. And you gonna take care of everything that needs to be taken care of in the barred room" (358). For women the academy can operate as a barred room where a few enter while others are left outside. As we feminists in composition studies gain intellectual capital and institutional clout, we must not merely advance our individual careers and unquestioningly perpetuate the hierarchies and inequities of disciplinary culture; we must find ways to critique and transform the inequitable labor situation for non-tenure-track women faculty members, many of whom are our former students. While working at the material level — in local university and college settings and through professional organizations — we also need to reassess the theories that guide our feminist practices. Although femininist writing pedagogy deserves recognition and praise, we must ask if an ethic of care will enable us to improve and transform the working conditions and material realities of writing teachers. We need models of feminist thought that reassess rather than reinscribe the costs and benefits of the ideology of nurturance. Socialist feminist analyses enable us to see the costs of nurturant labor and help us make self-conscious choices about our investment in femininist pedagogies. Without acknowledging differences among women, the costs of maternal pedagogy, and the gendered constructions of teaching, theories of femininist pedagogy may reinscribe the woman-teacher-as-caretaker ideology, a time-honored role that has often limited and circumscribed women's mobility and creativity.

Acknowledgment

I thank Lynn Worsham for the term "contingent workers" and for her intellectual guidance in the formulation of this essay.

Notes

1. See Mary Field Belenky, Blythe McVicker Clinchy, Nancy Rule Goldberger, and Jill Mattuck Tarule's description of a "caring" or "connected" pedagogy in chapter 10 of *Women's Ways of Knowing* ("Connected Teaching"). See also Noddings.
2. See also Tronto's analysis of an ethic of care in *Moral Boundaries*. For a general overview of the philosophical and political debates over an "ethic of care," see Larrabee.
3. "Psychic income" is a term used in economic theory to describe the non-monetary rewards of labor. For a feminist assessment of the psychic costs of a psychic income, see Gillam.
4. For an insightful discussion of pedagogy and schooling as a site for the education of emotion, see Worsham, "Emotion and Pedagogic Violence."
5. For an informative survey of the problem of part-time labor in composition studies, see Slevin. For general accounts of contingent academic employment across the disciplines, see Emily Abel; Gappa and Leslie; Leslie, Kellams, and Gunne; Tuckman and Tuckman; Tuckman, Vogler, and Caldwell.
6. The CCCC statement advises that no more than ten percent of a department's course sections be staffed by part-time faculty members (CCCC Executive Committee 333). The statement, however, has been criticized by part-time teachers who object to the recommendation that departments transform part-time lines into tenure-track positions and impose "severe limits on the ratio of part-time to full-time faculty" (333). Part-time faculty teachers accused the statement of favoring research faculty members and discrediting practitioners, "those whose expertise has developed outside the typical, traditional scholarly track" (Gunner, "Fate" 117). They argue that

the Wyoming resolution has been transformed from an argument for improved working conditions for contingent faculty members to an argument for hiring Ph.D.s in rhetoric and composition. But neither side has fully examined the implications of the relation between gender and part-time status, and this is where feminists can make an important intervention.

7. Regardless of my criticisms of the CCCC "Statement," I would like to acknowledge the important work of Sharon Crowley, James Slevin, and other former members of the CCCC Committee on Professional Standards who have brought the issue of non-tenure-track labor to the attention of tenured faculty and administrators.

8. Faculty members who wish to address the problem of gender and part-time labor should consult the professional statements about reasonable contingent working conditions: Modern Language Association; AAUP Committee; AAUP Subcommittee; CCCC Executive Committee; CCCC Committee; Robertson, Crowley, and Lentricchia (on the "Wyoming Conference Resolution"); Wyche-Smith and Rose (on the "Wyoming Conference Resolution"). General guides to improving the working conditions of part-time faculty members through organizing efforts can be found in Gappa; Gappa and Leslie; Tuckman and Biles; Wallace. Journals and newsletters devoted exclusively to contingent instructors and the improvement of their working conditions are the *Adjunct Advocate, Professing: An Organ for Those Who Teach Undergraduates,* and *Forum: The Newsletter of the Part-Time Faculty Forum for the CCCC.* Helpful general guides to organizing women's coalitions are Bannerji et al.; DeSole and Hoffmann.

Works Cited

Aisenberg, Nadya, and Mona Harrington. *Women of Academe: Outsiders in the Sacred Grove.* Amherst: U of Massachusetts P, 1988.

Alcoff, Linda. "Cultural Feminism versus Post-structuralism: The Identity Crisis in Feminist Theory." *Signs: Journal of Women in Culture and Society* (1988): 405–36.

Althusser, Louis. "Ideology and Ideological State Apparatuses." *Contemporary Critical Theory.* Ed. Dan Latimer. San Diego: Harcourt, 1989. 61–102.

Bannerji, Himani. *Thinking Through: Essays on Feminism, Marxism, and Anti-racism.* Toronto: Women's Press, 1995.

Bartky, Sandra Lee. *Femininity and Domination: Studies in the Phenomenology of Oppression.* New York: Routledge, 1990.

Batson, Lorie Goodman. "Defining Ourselves as Women (in the Profession)." *Pre/Text: A Journal of Rhetorical Theory* (1988): 207–09.

Bergmann, Barbara R. "Feminism and Economics." *Academe* (Sept.-Oct. 1983): 22–25.

Burns, Margie. "Service Courses: Doing Women a Disservice." *Academe* (May-June 1983): 18–21.

Cayton, Mary Kupiec. "Writing as Outsiders: Academic Discourse and Marginalized Faculty." *College English* 53 (1991): 647–60.

Caywood, Cynthia L., and Gillian R. Overing. Introduction. *Teaching Writing.* Ed. Caywood and Overing. Albany: State U of New York P, 1987. xi–xvi.

Childers, Karen, et al. "A Network of One's Own." DeSole and Hoffmann 117–227.

Crowley, Sharon. "Three Heroines: An Oral History." *Pre/Text: A Journal of Rhetorical Theory* (1988): 202–06.

Daumer, Elisabeth, and Sandra Runzo. "Transforming the Composition Classroom." Caywood and Overing, *Teaching Writing* 45–62.

DeSole, Gloria, and Leonore Hoffmann, eds. *Rocking the Boat: Academic Women and Academic Processes.* New York: MLA, 1981.

Ferguson, Ann. *Blood at the Root: Motherhood, Sexuality, and Male Dominance.* London: Pandora, 1989.

Flynn, Elizabeth A. "Composing as a Woman." *College Composition and Communication* 39 (1988): 423–35.

Fontaine, Sheryl I., and Susan Hunter. *Writing Ourselves into the Story: Unheard Voices from Composition Studies.* Carbondale: Southern Illinois UP, 1993.

Friedman, Susan Stanford. "Authority in the Feminist Classroom: A Contradiction in Terms." *Gendered Subjects: The Dynamics of Feminist Teaching.* Ed. Margo Culley and Catherine Portugues. New York: Routledge, 1985. 203–08.

Frost, Clare. "Looking for a Gate in the Fence." Fontaine and Hunter 59–69.

Frey, Olivia. "Equity and Peace in the New Writing Class." Caywood and Overing 93–106.

Frye, Marilyn. "On Being White: Thinking toward a Feminist Understanding of Race and Race Supremacy." *The Politics of Reality.* Freedom: Crossing, 1983. 110–27.

Gappa, Judith, and David Leslie. *The Invisible Faculty: Improving the Status of Part-Timers in Higher Education.* San Francisco: Jossey-Bass, 1993.

Gore, Jennifer M. *The Struggle for Pedagogies: Critical and Feminist Discourses as Regimes of Truth.* New York: Routledge, 1993.

Goulston, Wendy. "Women Writing." Caywood and Overing. *Teaching Writing* 19–30.

Gramsci, Antonio. *An Antonio Gramsci Reader: Selected Writings*, 1916–1935. Ed. David Forgacs. New York: Schocken, 1988.

Grimm, Nancy. Account. "The Part-Time Problem: Four Voices." By Elizabeth A. Flynn, John F. Flynn, Nancy Grimm, and Ted Lockhart. *Academe* (Jan.–Feb. 1986): 14–15.

Holbrook, Sue Ellen. "Women's Work: The Feminizing of Composition Studies." *Rhetorical Review* 9 (1991): 201–29.

Huber, Bettina. "Women in the Modern Languages, 1970–90." *Profession* 90. New York: MLA, 1990. 58–73.

Keller, Evelyn Fox, and Helene Moglen. "Competition: A Problem for Academic Women." Miner and Longino 21–37.

Koblitz, Neal. "Bias and Other Factors in Student Ratings." *Chronicle of Higher Education* 1 Sept. 1993: B3.

Lewis, Magda. "Interrupting Patriarchy: Politics, Resistance, and Transformation in the Feminist Classroom." Luke and Gore, 167–91.

Looser, Devoney. "Composing as an 'Essentialist'? New Directions for Feminist Composition Theories." *Rhetoric Review* 12 (1993): 54–69.

Luke, Carmen, and Jennifer Gore, eds. "Women in the Academy: Strategy, Struggle, and Survival." *Feminisms and Critical Pedagogy.* New York: Routledge, 1992.

Markus, Maria. "Women, Success, and Civil Society: Submission to, or Subversion of, the Achievement Principle." *Feminism as Critique: Essays on the Politics of Gender in Late-Capitalist Societies.* Ed. Seyla Benhabib and Drucilla Cornell. Cambridge: Blackwell, 1987. 96–109.

Miller, Susan. "The Feminization of Composition." Bullock and Trimbur 39–53.

————. *Textual Carnivals.* Carbondale: Southern Illinois UP, 1991.

Miner, Valerie, and Helen E. Longino, eds. *Competition, a Feminist Taboo?* New York: Feminist P at City U of New York, 1987.

Noddings, Nel. *Caring: A Feminine Approach to Ethics and Moral Education.* Berkeley: U of California P, 1984.

Perry, William G. *Forms of Intellectual and Ethical Development in the College Years.* New York: Holt, Rinehart, 1970.

Phelps, Louise Wetherbee. "A Constrained Vision of the Writing Classroom." *Profession* 93. New York: MLA, 1993. 46–54.

Reagon, Bernice Johnson. "Coalition Politics: Turning the Century." B. Smith, *Girls* 356–68.

Rubin, Donnalee. *Gender Influences: Reading Student Texts.* Carbondale: Southern Illinois UP, 1993.

Simeone, Angela. *Academic Women: Working towards Equality.* Boston: Bergin, 1987.

Smith, Barbara, ed. *Home Girls: A Black Feminist Anthology.* New Brunswick, N.J.: Rutgers UP, 2000.

Stanger, Carol. "The Sexual Politics of the One-to-One Tutorial Approach and Collaborative Learning." Caywood and Overing, *Teaching Writing* 31–44.

Stearns, Carol Zisowitz, and Peter N. Stearns. Introduction. *Emotion and Social Change: Toward a New Psychohistory.* Ed. Stearns and Stearns. New York: Homes, 1988. 1–21.

Tronto, Joan C. *Moral Boundaries: A Political Argument for an Ethic of Care.* New York: Routledge, 1993.

————. "Women and Caring." *Women and Values,* Third ed. Ed. Pearsall. Belmont, Cal.: Wadsworth, 1999.

Tuckman, H. P., and G. E. Biles. *Part-time Faculty Personnel Management Policies.* New York: MacMillan, 1986.

Tuell, Cynthia. "Composition Teaching as 'Women's Work': Daughters, Handmaids, Whores, and Mothers." Fontaine and Hunter 123–39.

Wallace, M. Elizabeth. "Who Are These Part-Time Faculty Anyway?" *Part Time Academic Employment in the Humanities.* Ed. Wallace. New York: MLA, 1984. 3–29.

Watkins, Evan. *Work Time: English Departments and Circulation of Cultural Value.* Stanford: Stanford UP, 1989.

Wicke, Jennifer, and Margaret Ferguson. "Introduction: Feminism and Postmodernism; or The Way We Live Now." *Feminism and Postmodernism.* Ed. Wicke and Ferguson. Durham: Duke UP, 1994. 10–33.

Schell's Insights as a Resource for Your Teaching

1. In your journal, consider how sexual-identity politics inform your own classroom practice. Reflect on the tension between a "maternalistic" process and its masculine opposite. Which process predominates in your classroom? Which do the students seem to solicit? Which does your institution solicit? How do these solicitations work out in your day-to-day practice?

2. Schell suggests that there is a strong, though incomplete, link between what James A. Berlin (p. 19) calls the expressivist

approach and Schell's description of maternalistic processes. How might you modify Schell's claims about the particular ideologies that inform the gender dynamics of the composition classroom?

Schell's Insights as a Resource for Your Writing Classroom

1. Discuss with your students gender stereotypes that surround the study of literate practices. Broadly speaking, girls are supposed to be good at English, whereas boys are supposed to be good at science — and yet the standard conception of the great writer is typically male. Have them explore these stereotypes, and use Schell's arguments to organize questions for students.

2. Ask your students to write in their journals and then discuss in small groups their understanding of the role of writing instruction within the larger curriculum of their school. Ask them to consider the importance of writing with respect to their chances of success or failure in the world. What role does writing play in one's career? How significant is one's gender? How important is writing within the curriculum of your school? Do gender dynamics govern writing instruction? Are there inequities to discuss?

Becoming a Writerly Self: College Writers Engaging Black Feminist Essays

Juanita Rodgers Comfort

This article, from a 2000 issue of College Composition and Communication, *describes a method for enabling student writers to connect their personal and social identities in ways that will enhance their writing while avoiding the "self-indulgence" teachers typically fear when introducing the personal into writing. Juanita Rodgers Comfort argues, "Writing instruction should enable students to recognize the writerly self as a* persuasive instrument *that can be strategically deployed and to learn to make effective use of their own multiple locations to take personal stands on public issues that transcend the confessional." Black feminist writers, she feels, have mastered this effective juxtaposition with essays that go beyond the mere narrative while still invoking the self, and thus serve as excellent models of* authoritative *and* contextualized *writing.*

My work requires me to think about how free I can be as an African-American woman writer in my genderized, sexualized, wholly racialized world. To think about (and wrestle with) the full implications of my situation leads me to consider what happens when other writers work

in a highly and historically racialized society. For them, as for me, imagining is not merely looking or looking at; nor is it taking oneself intact into the other. It is for the purposes of the work, *becoming.*
— Toni Morrison, *Playing in the Dark*

Whenever I tell people that I am studying the rhetoric of contemporary black feminist essayists, I'm inevitably asked why rhetoricians should pay attention to the writings of African American women. I'm asked to account for what makes their discursive situations "noteworthy"; after all, my questioners reason, isn't the struggle for personal power, for voice, for credibility, shared by *all* writers? Then why focus on *black women's writing*, specifically — what can *they* show *us*? This question always echoes in my ears for days after each encounter with it. Despite my sense that most of the time it is asked out of intellectual curiosity and in a spirit of goodwill, it has always felt like a trick question to me, designed to somehow betray me as an academic "outsider," to put me in my place and, perhaps, out of the business of locating black women's voices more centrally within the discipline. I've always managed to give what I hoped was an acceptably distanced, "scholarly" response (one that I always hope does not saddle me with the burden of defending my well-considered standpoint as a black feminist rhetorician or the contributions of African American women's writing to "mainstream" scholarly projects):

> I study these works *as I think any rhetorician would*, in order to gain more insight into the challenges faced by all speakers and writers in negotiating an influential ethos for themselves. I examine the writing of African American women, specifically, because *their* texts document the authoritative spaces *they* have created for *themselves* within and against particular configurations of social, cultural, political, and economic power. This work represents *one scholarly direction to take among many*, but it is of vital importance because it contributes to *a useful culturally grounded theory* of rhetorical power.

This answer, for the most part, has satisfied my interlocutors. But I am usually left wondering how my answer, in positioning my black female self as critically distant from the issues involved, removes me from my own work and somehow impoverishes the meaning of that work. As I reread this answer, I see that several strategies of disengagement are apparent (and in fact work to negate the "I" that I have used twice): I locate myself in a mainstream — "as any rhetorician would" — that historically has been populated by white men. I exclude myself from the world of African American writers, obscuring the fact that I happen to be one, eschewing the self-inclusive pronouns "our," "we," and "ourselves" in favor of their self-excluding counterparts "their," "they," and "themselves." I assign myself almost anonymous status among a cohort of scholars. I choose to reduce my conclusions to the neutral terms of "*a* (generic) theory" instead of the "*my* (personally located) theory." And I choose not to articulate at all what is perhaps the most important part of my answer: *I'm doing this work because what "I" (a black woman who is also, ostensibly, an academic "insider") have to say about the African American women's discursive practices contributes to making those practices matter.*

I invoke this brief self-analysis to frame my vision of how literary essays by black feminist writers can be used by college writers at both the first-year and advanced levels to gain valuable insight into writing as a self-defining activity. Displayed through features comprising specific texts as well as through a rhetor's general reputation (whether that rhetor is a professional or student writer), her image in the minds of her audiences can be one of the most powerful influences on their judgments of her work. The enfranchisement of African American women as makers of knowledge in situations where forces work toward muting or silencing us may very well hinge on the task of distinguishing ourselves to audiences (for whom white male perspectives are the norm) specifically as black and female in our grounding assumptions, strategies of argument, and writing style, while simultaneously eliciting from those audiences a favorable impression of our perceived characters. Like all rhetors (student writers included), black feminist essayists must invent effective ways to answer readers' fundamental question: Who is this person and why should I believe what she says?

Cornel West's description of the struggle of the black diaspora to obtain and maintain status and credibility within a Eurocentric (masculinist) cultural framework invokes for me a similar struggle engaged in by student writers within the cultural framework of the academy. West analyzes the problematic of *invisibility* and *namelessness*, enacted by cultural authorities, which "promoted Black inferiority and constituted the European background against which Black diaspora struggles for identity, dignity . . . and material resources took place" (102). Perhaps because of my own search for a writerly self that is at once influential in the academic arena, representative of the places I come from outside the academy, and comfortable as a self-image, questions about the writerly self condition everything I write. Over the ten years that I have been teaching composition and rhetoric courses, I've observed that my most insightful students have generally sought to use their writing assignments as tools to help themselves mature as thinking individuals and become more powerful as social beings. Through their writerly eyes, I've come to see that successful college writing demands, and ultimately achieves, something more personally enriching than merely "inventing the university," as David Bartholomae would say. The most successful student writers in my experience learn how to move beyond merely imitating the prose styles and interpretive schemes of disciplinary discourses. They animate those discourses by inventing complex and versatile writerly selves who are able to place their extra-academic worlds into a carefully constructed relationship with those discourse communities.

Universities are, of course, part of the genderized, racialized society that Morrison speaks of. A genderized, racialized society is one in which the statuses and roles of the people in its institutions (educational, military, economic, governmental . . .) and communities (neighborhood, social, religious . . .) — and even the very structures of those institutions and communities — are influenced, even dictated on some level, by gender and race. Racial and gender groups, of course, must be understood not merely in terms of differential physical attributes, but also in terms of discursive habits and social practices, along with perceptions of intelligence, morality, values, and so forth that are typically associated with those attributes, habits, and practices.

The discourses of the university are heavily invested with markers of white race, male gender, and middle and upper socioeconomic classes. As an African American woman who studies and teaches rhetoric and composition at a university, I am keenly aware of the ways in which language constructs the person who knows as much as it defines what one knows. And I am unwilling to pretend that disciplinary discourses are value-neutral enclaves where race, gender, class, spirituality, and other cultural issues don't matter. And so, echoing Morrison, I think it's important for rhetoricians and composition specialists to ask important questions about what happens when *student writers* of any gender or any race work in a genderized, racialized society. If imagining, through composing, is something more significant to students than exercises in critical detachment, and if we do not expect them to remain essentially unchanged by their encounters with the ideas they write about, then composing text must be for the purposes of these students' education, *becoming* insurgent intellectuals (to use a term coined by West and bell hooks) who are personally invested in the world of ideas.

The rhetorical implications of writing one's way toward becoming in a racialized society came into particular focus for me last year, after teaching a graduate seminar on contemporary African American women essayists. The course employed methods of rhetorical criticism to draw insights from literary essays by black feminist writers June Jordan, Alice Walker, bell hooks, Nikki Giovanni, and Pearl Cleage. As I led the class of nine students through the semester (seven black women and two white women, along with several others who sat in on occasional sessions), we all felt strongly attracted to — and sometimes troubled by — the range of essayistic voices that were speaking to us. We raised numerous questions and engaged in more than a few debates about merits of the essayists' personal approaches to public issues. Class discussions defined spaces where issues of identity, location, and meaning emerged from a wide range of experiences with work, family, community, spirituality, and often, the academy. Our encounters with the diversity of these essayists' world views certainly complicated the taken-for-granted, almost stereotypical notions of "black" and "female" identity that were initially prevalent in the class. Regardless of the direction of our critiques, however, none of us doubted the powerful *presence* of these women in their works. As we moved through our reading list, it became increasingly evident to us that who these writers portray themselves to be as African American women had great bearing on their ability to entice us to entertain their positions, share their social agenda, or accept their conclusions. And their self-portrayals as distinctively raced and gendered beings posed a challenge to my students, both black and white, to reconsider what they themselves were about.

An extended example underscores this point. One of my students, a middle-aged white woman, whom I'll call Eleanor, was deeply troubled by the way June Jordan's essay "Requiem for the Champ" (which we read from her collection, *Technical Difficulties*) seemed to defend the aberrant personal behavior of heavyweight boxer Mike Tyson. On the day students presented proposals for their semester projects, Eleanor told the class that because she had always felt connected to Jordan, a renowned poet and political activist, as a "feminist thinker," she could not comprehend why the essayist would stoop to dignify Tyson with what she called an apology, and so she was planning to write a paper arguing for her misgivings. I don't think she realized it at the time she developed her proposal, but Eleanor was beginning an important journey toward a racialized consciousness made possible by Jordan's writing self.

Let me give some background about the essay. In "Requiem," Jordan outlines the horrific conditions of poverty and oppression under which Mike Tyson learned the life rules that have governed his personal behavior as an adult. In keeping with the theme identified by the subtitle of *Technical Difficulties* — "African-American Notes on the State of the Union" — she asks of readers to consider the attitudes of politicians, military personnel, filmmakers, recording artists, and others who authorize, carry out, and applaud both acts of violence and the objectification of women (226). She indicts those who might share responsibility for maintaining the kind of social order that could dehumanize not only Tyson, but even someone as apparently different from him as Jordan herself. It is upon this point that she makes a crucial connection between herself and Tyson, designed to disrupt readers' easy categorizations of either one of them.

The message in Jordan's essay is especially powerful because of its "self-disclosures" — bits of information about herself that Jordan endows with salience, places in specific locations in the essay, packages with other images, flags as revelatory, and connects to the essay's central message. Rhetorically, self-disclosures foreground the embodied nature of the self, which, through selective, insightful sharing, can build connections between writers and readers that authorize the writer to make claims and ensure the acceptability of those claims.

Jordan opens the essay with an assertion of physical proximity to Tyson:

> Mike Tyson comes from Brooklyn. And so do I. Where he grew up was about a twenty-minute bus ride from my house. (221)

Then, she confesses that it took her most of her own life to learn the social lessons that Tyson apparently had not, emphasizing that she was, *for most of her life*, very much like Tyson is now:

> *Mike Tyson comes from Brooklyn. And so do I.* In the big picture of America, I never had much going for me. And he had less. *I only learned, last year*, that I can stop whatever violence starts with me. *I only learned, last year*, that love is infinitely more interesting, and more exciting, and more powerful, than really winning or really losing a fight. *I only learned, last year*, that all war leads to death and that all love leads you away from death. (223, italics mine)

It is difficult to overlook that in the middle of this passage, Jordan speaks words that could easily have come from Tyson (which I indicate here in boldface):

> *I am more than twice Mike Tyson's age. And I'm not stupid. Or slow.* **But I'm Black. And I come from Brooklyn. And I grew up fighting. And I grew up and I got out of Brooklyn because I got pretty good at fighting. And winning.** Or else, intimidating my would-be adversaries with my fists, my feet, and my mouth. And I never wanted to fight. *I never wanted anybody to hit me. And I never wanted to hit anybody.* But the bell would ring at the end of another dumb day in school and I'd head out with dread and a nervous sweat because I knew some jackass more or less my age and more or less my height would be waiting for me because she or he had nothing better to do than to wait for me and hope to kick my butt or tear up my books or break my pencils or pull hair out of my head. (223, italics mine)

Then a little later in the essay, she identifies herself with Tyson again, and this time the connection moves beyond Tyson to identify Jordan with African Americans generally:

> *I'm Black. Mike Tyson is Black.* And neither one of us was ever supposed to win anything more than a fight between the two of us. And if you check out the mass-media material on "*us*," and if you check out the emergency-room reports on "*us*," you might well believe we're losing the fight to be more than our enemies have decreed. . . . (224, italics mine)

These passages illustrate two ways that self-disclosures function as a persuasive element. First, as a matter of strategy, Jordan provides specially chosen personal information in order to place herself directly — almost physically — between her readers and Mike Tyson. For the space of reading this essay, Jordan insists that readers perceive of her and Tyson not separately, but together, and as explicitly raced beings. The physical identification becomes a point of *stasis:* If Jordan is so much like Tyson, then we should either dislike Jordan as much as we dislike Tyson, or (the preferred reading) translate our respect for Jordan into a greater valuing of Tyson.

Second, the psychological power of Jordan's disclosures relies on her readers' sense that a defining relationship is taking place between the essayist and her subject. I'm drawn to Sharon Crowley's explanation for this phenomenon, that the writing subject is enmeshed in multiple relations, but when writing, the "writer becomes audience" as well (34). So, in the process of working through the problems posed by assuming a personal association with Tyson, Jordan constructs a self who speaks back to her from the pages of her work-in-progress. Having written part of Tyson's life into her own, and then reading reflexively what she has written from the subject position she created for herself, Jordan presumably has on some level become self-identified as "June Jordan, sister of Mike Tyson." So, in a sense, this is a "real" June Jordan who speaks to readers, not a mechanistically crafted persona. And as readers become familiar with the person in the essay who asserts a similar background to Tyson's but demonstrates a decidedly different outcome, Jordan can hope that readers will better understand her stance on the fallen Tyson and why a requiem for him might be justified.

These effects of self-disclosure can shed light on the challenge that Eleanor was faced with. Until she encountered "Requiem," she seems to have been comfortable in a relationship with the essayist that foregrounded gender solidarity over race division. As long as race can be ignored, the two of them can be kindred spirits. "Although I can't share her experience as a black person," Eleanor could reason, "I can certainly share her experiences as a woman, and I can feel good about that." The feminist values that she believed she already shared with Jordan should have precluded either of them from having sympathies for people like Tyson. But the Tyson/Jordan connection in "Requiem," in both its textual strategy and psychological implications, confounded her: How is it possible that Jordan and Tyson can co-exist on the same moral or intellectual plane?

As the essay unfolds, Tyson's rape conviction and its underpinnings of misogyny and violence, about which Eleanor expected Jordan to have an overriding outrage, seem far less of an issue for the essayist than the implications of their shared oppression as black people. Even though Jordan clearly states at one point that she *does not* condone Tyson's behavior, the essay's rhetoric of black identification seems to counter that disclaimer. Eleanor witnesses her woman-to-woman connection with Jordan disrupted by Jordan's identification as a *black* woman, something that Eleanor herself can never be. Therefore, Eleanor must decide how to establish a new relationship with the person that Jordan becomes in the essay, so that she can begin to understand Jordan's message.

As I read Eleanor's semester-project essay, "Down for the Count: The Selection of Metaphor in 'Requiem for the Champ,'" I saw that Jordan's self-disclosures had inspired Eleanor to measure herself against the emergent image of Jordan and to decide what it meant for her to identify with a feminist thinker who claimed the violent sensibility of a Mike Tyson. Her essay dealt with the challenge to her own self-identity by emulating Jordan's strategy of self-disclosure. Her struggle to accomplish this illustrates a theory of modern rhetoric that is, in the words of Michael Halloran, "distinguished by its emphasis on the responsibility of speakers to articulate their own worlds, and thereby their own selves" (342–43). "It is no longer valid," asserts Halloran, "to assume that speaker and audience live in the same world and to study the techniques by which the speaker moves his audience to act or think in a particular way. One must turn instead to the more fundamental problem of why the gap between the speaker's and audience's worlds is so broad and how one might bridge it smoothly" (336). Jordan forces Eleanor to take on the responsibility of first acknowledging and then attempting to bridge the racial gap between their feminist worlds.

Eleanor uses Jordan's self-representational strategies to help her interrogate Jordan's position, placing herself between her own readers (her classmates and me) and the June Jordan and Mike Tyson who are the joint subjects of her essay.

Eleanor opens her essay with a disclosure about her eyesight that becomes a metaphor for her struggle to gain insight into Jordan's message:

> The truth is that at age fifty-three, I see less clearly than I did at thirty-three. I now wear glasses most of the time so that my field of vision will not be so limited and the words on the page in front of me will be large enough for me to see without hyper-extending my arms. So you see, I have done my best to correct my vision. . . . so why am I having so much trouble "seeing" what June Jordan wants me to see? For the life of me, I just can't go along with her *apologia* for the troubled life of Mike Tyson, former heavyweight champion and lost soul. Or at least what I see as her defense of the fallen champ.

She answers her own question in a way that discloses her status as a white person:

> . . . but perhaps I am constitutionally incapable of seeing or hearing what you **are** saying. Perhaps it is, as my African American classmates suggest, the myopia that accompanies white skin. This is my limitation, my visual impairment.

And later, responding to, and echoing Jordan's disclosures about encountering the war-like devastation of the neighborhood where Tyson grew up, Eleanor offers her own growing-up story:

> I've never been to Brooklyn and I have not seen war up close and personal. I've never been in combat nor did I grow up in a war zone. I have only seen TV wars. I have not known the ugliness of racism and poverty, and I grew up in a neighborhood where you could buy tulips and ribbons for a girl.[1] . . . And mostly, *I have never been seen as "other"* the way Mike Tyson and June Jordan have. Maybe this is why I cannot see her point; but I can see that she has one. (my emphasis)

Jordan's assertion of a shared identity with Tyson became the catalyst for Eleanor to confront her feminist perspective *with her own whiteness*. I am defining "whiteness" here as a cultural construction of individual and group identity that is associated with the images of race that underpin the structure of our society. The cultural construction of whiteness may be one possible answer to bell hooks' question, "from what political perspective do we dream, look, create, and take action?" (4). In a culturally pluralistic society like America, whiteness does not exist in isolation from non-white cultural constructions such as "blackness"; it must exist in juxtaposition against those other constructions. Whiteness has been a locus of (often abusive) power and privilege for those in society who can claim it and a source of subjugation for those who cannot. Certainly, part of the advantage vested in whiteness lies in its ability to mask its own power and privilege — to render them normative, even invisible, in the minds of most whites, in order to maintain the framework of white supremacy. This dynamic is often painfully visible to those who cannot claim the power and privilege of whiteness.

What June Jordan's essay did for Eleanor, I think, was to force upon her a representation of whiteness that could only be conveyed from the vantage point of Jordan's blackness. The essay's intention and effect were to make uncomfortably visible the taken-for-granted privilege of whiteness, along with its potential to dominate the non-white. It disallowed Eleanor's attempt to claim a "sameness" of perspective with Jordan based on gender solidarity. She responded in her course paper with a set of personal disclosures that certainly cannot be dismissed as merely confessional or self-indulgent, but are in fact essential to the problem of race that Jordan has challenged her to resolve.

The kind of critical engagement exhibited by Eleanor and her classmates at the graduate level has led me to envision the *undergraduate* composition classroom as a place where students can learn strategies for expressing themselves meaningfully within the context of academic discourse. Because first-year and advanced composition courses are a large part of my teaching load, the essayist course enabled me to view authorship issues in student writing in a more focused way. I was particularly able to see that the experiences of my master's-level students, reflected in their class discussions and course papers, displayed important similarities to those of my undergraduate writers. They both seemed to share a strong desire to call upon the resources of their personal lives in order to make sense of their subject matter and to negotiate their stances relative to the conventional demands of academic discourse. While the writing of my master's students was somewhat more proficient, in a technical sense, than that of my undergraduates, the ability to effectively integrate personal stances into academically oriented discussions seemed about the same at both levels.

I further saw that the range of experiences that my undergraduate students — white and non-white, female and male — bring to their classrooms resonates strongly with experiences asserted in the black feminist essays from the seminar. Significant parallels exist between the lives of my students and those of the essayists, in their relationships with spouses/lovers, in their child-rearing responsibilities, in their religious and political affiliations, in their work situations, and in the depth of their community involvement. These students have taken on numerous sophisticated roles, such as parents of children with disabilities, litigants in major lawsuits, career military members, entrepreneurs and businesspeople, and caregivers for relatives with disabilities and catastrophic illnesses. Many of the social, political, and humanistic issues that they expressed a personal stake in resolving in their course papers were the same issues raised by the essayists that my graduate students studied. So whenever I was able to suggest the idea of infusing their school papers with personal stances (using excerpts from essayists to illustrate self-disclosure techniques), my writing students were as attentive as my seminar students. And anxious as well, since few of them felt that they had been given meaningful opportunities to express personal standpoints, and fewer still had been given explicit instruction in how to do so effectively.

What is most memorable about both the professional essayists and my students is what I believe most college writers can be convinced of — that, as Halloran asserts, "the rigor and passion with which they *disclose their world* to the audience, is their *ethos*" (343). Yet I am aware that many composition teachers have considerable difficulty in granting their student writers that *ethos*. Even while assigning compositions they call "essays," these teachers have largely denied to academic writing the essay's invitation to *explicit* personal engagement with its subject matter, viewing most attempts to assert such a personal relationship as incompatible with the critical detachment valued in much disciplinary discourse. I've heard teachers routinely insinuate, and sometimes even state outright, the criticism that Kurt Spellmeyer has described, that students are no more than incomplete knowers whose "right to speak must be learned — or perhaps more accurately, earned — through what is essentially the effacement of subjectivity" (265).

Anxiety over the disclosure of personal information has occasionally been expressed in our professional journals. In a *College English* article, for example, Gordon Harvey suggests that the overt "personal" gesture is often construed by academic readers as irrelevant, inconsequential, and counterproductive. He tries to resolve some of that anxiety by considering ways in which academic writing can be "*informed* by personal experience without injecting personal *information*" (649). Such a dance around the embodied self may well be based on an assumption that one's subjectivity is an element separate from the world being written about, and — especially when expressed through personal disclosures — somehow interferes with clear, logical, critical thinking. However, I am concerned that this attitude can hinder efforts of student writers to integrate disciplinary knowledge with other aspects of their lives, in order to define themselves as distinctive intellectual agents in academic and professional situations and thereby locate meaningful vantage points from which to interpret and apply the information they are learning. Such wholesale dismissal of college students' capability to assert credible knowledge created through placing one's knowledge about a subject within the framework of one's life experiences, which is reflected in the rather cynical teacherly question, "What do *students* know?" perverts the powerfully heuristic question, *Que sais je?* — what do *I* know? — that has driven the development of the essay genre from the time of Montaigne.

Harvey seems to reduce the territory of personal disclosure, advocated mainly by feminist theorists and scholars of the familiar essay, to narrative and autobiography motivated by a desire to make the public voice of academic discourse more connected with lived experience and empathetic to others, less abstract, and less competitive. In Harvey's view, the impulse toward personal disclosure, so defined, often produces bad writing by both college students and professional academic writers. He cites, in particular, the difficulty of contextualizing close analysis of primary texts with personal report; the analytical and the personal (which he admits is an arbitrary distinction), when treated as separate entities, are much like oil and water for most of his student writers.

> The students devote their energy to finding whatever personal connections they can, not to wrestling the issues out of the text or finding things to say besides summaries and platitudes. For students who can't yet manage an extended development of an idea in a "linear" fashion, the invitation to jump back and forth is added disincentive to extending thinking. The textual and the personal sections, sometimes jarringly different in style, are only very roughly stitched together — prompting one teacher I know to call these "Frankenstein" papers. But the assignment also provides an excuse to avoid even the more basic work of focusing closely and describing accurately. The picture given of the text in these essays is distorted, reductive, fudged to fit. (645)

Key for me in this statement is that students are often, at least implicitly, invited to invoke the personal, but not given any explicit rhetorical insight regarding its effective use. Jumping back and forth between personal and analytical is, as even Harvey later acknowledges, arbitrary. That the personal can be analytical, that the analytical can be usefully located from a personal vantage point, seems impossible not only for the student writer to manage but for the teacher to work from as well.

The idea that the essay might be faulted for being "personal" in the ways advanced by Harvey might be attributed, at least in part, to critics' reliance on the notion that identities are the private property of the individuals — as Celia Kitzinger asserts, "freely created products of introspection or the unproblematic reflections of the private sanctum of the 'inner self'" (82). The questionable relevance of the "personal" may stem from viewing the essay's subjectivity as an element separate from the world being written about that can cloud or detract from that world. From this perspective, the "personal" gesture is often construed as irrelevant, inconsequential, and counterproductive, as Harvey suggests. However, looking at the personal dimension from the perspective of black feminist writers, for example, can show how subjectivity is indeed inseparable from the world of ideas — from their interpretation and analysis — and thus essential for ideas to be properly developed by writers and understood by readers.

The problems that Harvey has encountered in many student compositions certainly should not be discounted. Engaging the overt personal gesture is indeed a strategy mishandled in much student writing. Many would agree, I think, that we would like students to go beyond writing that is personal, as Wendell Harris would say, "merely by virtue of narrating a personal experience" (941). Harvey does have an answer, in terms of his concept of "presence" that incorporates, among other things, a sense of motive or why a text needs writing; a development that allows the writer to explore and shape a topic as ideas dictate rather than as a thesis-plus-three ideas formula; use of details such as original metaphors, non-academic analogies; opening up larger questions and issues; and elaborating on reasons for judgments (651–53).

However, I disagree with Harvey's attempt to render *embodied* writers invisible — particularly student writers who, in his eyes, merely "drag in their personal experiences" or allow personal narrative to "infiltrate" traditional academic analysis. I am convinced that significant problems arise with student writing precisely when they have not defined and located themselves as effectively self-authorized knowers for their evaluative audiences. The problem I identify in much personal writing by students is a lack of skill in articulating a self that genuinely contributes to the rhetorical power of their compositions. But identifying a student's lack of skill in this area does not invalidate the *concept* of personal engagement of his or her subject matter as a potentially powerful strategy, which is what I believe happens too often. Dismissing the self-disclosure strategies themselves because students have not yet mastered those strategies seems senseless if the strategies are not being taught to them in the first place. The problematic *ethos* of student writers, which often seems to trigger their instructors' denial of their right to ask (heuristically) and then answer the question "what do I know" from all of their intellectual resources, strongly resonates with the struggle of many African American women writers to do the same. It is this connection between these two groups that allows me, as a composition instructor, to investigate how black feminist essayists attempt to solve the problematic, described by Cornel West, of "present[ing] themselves to themselves and others as complex human beings" (102), and to investigate what students might learn from studying their essays.

Pamela Klass Mittlefehldt's work provides considerable insight on issues involved in the construction of self-identity that black feminist writers typically bring to the essay form. For Mittlefehldt, the essay's focus on the author's voice, the visible process of contemplation, its grounding in particular experience, the reconsideration of and resistance to the orthodox, "make it a useful genre for Black feminists who are writing to change their worlds" (198). The essay's rhetorical edge, rather than the dispassionate contemplation that has characterized Western male essay traditions, is the attraction for black feminist writers. Essays by black feminist writers deal with the dynamic of social identity in provocative ways. Mittlefehldt explains that in the essay, "the author matters intensely. When that author is a black woman, the voice that comes through is one of radical import, for it is a voice that has been traditionally obliterated in Western thought and literature" (198). Having moved from the margins and established a space for their voices by virtue of their success as writers, black women find the essay to be an important space for continually re-forming, re-visioning, and renegotiating personal identity in light of the past and ongoing experiences that shape their lives.

In fact, it becomes even more important for these essayists to allow readers to enter their lives, after they have become more centrally located. Kevin Murray states: "Whereas social identity is a problem for marginal individuals . . . personal identity becomes difficult for people who have achieved a successful moral career to the point where it is hard to distinguish oneself from the official social order" (181). In ways not unlike black women in American society at large, college students constitute a social and cultural category within an institutional hierarchy that includes professors, administrators, support staff, and other members of the college/university community. In light of the diversity of our student populations (in terms of race, ethnicity, class, age, gender/sexual orientation, literacies, and so forth), it is all the more striking that college students, like members of other hierarchies in our society, are subject to the same kinds of invisibility and namelessness.

Black feminist essays teach many possibilities for negotiating self-identity and promoting *ethos* given *the multiple locations from which the authors speak as African American women* (gendered, cultural, economic, generational, spiritual). It is the skillful interweaving of those locations into the subject matter under discussion that allows African American women writers to claim authoritative voices. Two concepts related to this notion of *ethos* are of great import for writing instruction. The first, as expressed by Patricia Hill Collins, concerns the development of an "ethic of personal accountability," wherein individuals place themselves in positions of direct responsibility for their own knowledge claims. For Collins and other black feminist theorists,

> Assessments of an individual's knowledge claims simultaneously evaluate an individual's character, values, and ethics. African Americans reject the Eurocentric, masculinist belief that probing into an individual's personal viewpoint is outside the boundaries of discussion. Rather, all views expressed and actions taken are thought to derive

from a central set of core beliefs that cannot be other than personal. . . .
Knowledge claims made by individuals respected for their moral and
ethical connections to their ideas will carry more weight than those
offered by less respected figures. (218)

The second concept is a suggestion that black women's essays can
in fact model for student writers those strategies that would enable
them to create a distinctive place for themselves in a given discourse
community. Mittlefehldt asserts that black women's essays

. . . are a resistance, a refusal to be silenced, a refusal to be *said*. By
telling the stories of their own and other Black women's lives, [the
essays] counter the attempts to erase and deny the experiences of Black
women in American culture. At the same time, they also challenge the
seductive ease of connection by engaging in dialectic tensions of difference. (199)

These two concepts contribute to an understanding of the strategic
nature of the essay as a means of knowledge-making grounded in the
creation and manifestation of a writerly self. Writing instruction should
enable students to recognize the writerly self as a *persuasive instrument* that can be strategically deployed and to learn to make effective
use of their own multiple locations to take personal stands on public
issues *that transcend the confessional*. A large part of what writing
does for people is to help with their personal growth; as writers develop and then read their own work, they place themselves in subject
positions relative to their texts and adapt to the role they have laid out
for themselves in relation to the subject under discussion. Every text
that is produced (in college or elsewhere) contributes to this re-visioning of the self that has been constructed for the writer and includes
that self in the social dynamic that is writing. As Stuart Hall asserts:

we . . . occupy our identities very retrospectively: having produced them,
we then know who we are. We say, "Oh that's where I am in relation to
this argument and for these reasons." So, it's exactly the reverse of what
I think is the common sense way of understanding it, which is that we
already know our "self" and then put it out there. Rather, having put it
into play in language, we *then* discover what we are. I think that only
then do we make an investment in it, saying, "Yes, I like that position, I
am that sort of person, I'm willing to occupy that position." (qtd. in Drew
173)

This reciprocal movement between writer and text, I believe, must
be as much a part of a writing student's rhetorical education as the
movement between writer and reader. Since every text represents a
cultural position, drawing texts by African American women into writing instruction may serve to make student writers more keenly aware
of how their own (and other) texts are constructing them, so that they
can exercise greater influence over the Eurocentric masculinist van-

tage point that has been promoted as objectivity, even though it reinscribes Eurocentric masculinist scientistic vision and values.

Judicious use of these essays may also avoid another significant danger, articulated in Gesa Kirsch and Joy Ritchie's critique of the essay's invitation to the personal. They charge that the essayistic writing that has become popular in feminist scholarship offers essentialist renderings of a confessional voice leading to more master narratives (8). A sophisticated understanding of self-disclosure as rhetorical strategy can, I believe, be a way out of such a trap. According to Mittlefehldt, "The self that is constructed in [black feminist] essays emerges from the complexity of each writer's personal experiences as a Black woman. It is strikingly apparent that for these women, that self is multi-voiced and in constant dialogue with others" (201). The multi-layered voice of the writing self that speaks in the essays offers new angles of vision, unique juxtapositions of understanding and accountability. There is a passionate sense of connection in these writings, a clear impression that these words are directed towards others and that they invite response. The self that emerges here is one "grounded in a community. . . . It includes a spectrum of relationships, including ancestors, family, Black women, Black people, women, all living beings" (201–02).

The way a writer uses language to describe, report, narrate, or argue actually shapes a particular self-image both for the writer and the readers. This "rhetorical identity" — the presence invested in the text, developed by the writer to accomplish particular persuasive effects in the minds of readers, not only contributes to the writer's authority/ credibility but also helps build a mutual relationship to readers as fellow scholars. Effective rhetorical identity defines a textual voice that is at once distinctive and strongly resonant with readers. My essayist course afforded my students a measure of comfort and a greater sense of strategy in developing their own ideas, which I think can be transferred effectively to the undergraduate writing classroom. The results in my courses, in terms of the rhetorical impact of the writing produced, validated for me the claims of Kurt Spellmeyer, W. Ross Winterowd, William Zieger, and other composition scholars, summarized by Janis Forman, that critical reading of and writing essays in composition classes "open up for students ways of knowing that are too often underrepresented in the curriculum — a willingness to value ambiguity, to invent, to suspend closure, to situate the self in multiple and complex ways through discourse" (5).

What do writing teachers need to consider in helping student writers to develop a more sophisticated approach to personal disclosure, with help from black feminist essayists? One approach would be to consider how these essayists can increase our sensitivity to the situational factors that generate a writer's *ethos*, to compare the constraints of school writing with those traditionally imposed upon African American women writers, and ultimately to draw conclusions regarding the contribution of *ethos*, in turn, to the evolution of the essayist and the student writer alike as an intellectual, as a professional communicator, as an enlightened self.

Having seen personal power at work in the essays by black feminist writers that we studied, Eleanor and the other students in my essayist course managed to enhance the rhetorical force of their own writing. They were able to recognize more circumstances that invite writers to invoke personal statements, to use specific kinds of words, images, and signals that construct a personal perspective; to see how distinctions between spiritual and secular, or between blackness and whiteness, can be manipulated for various reasons; and to learn how these discursive actions taken by essayists make considerable difference in how readers think about a given topic. And sometimes, as happened with Eleanor, students followed up on their observations by taking the risk of asserting their writerly selves more explicitly in their papers. Reflecting on Eleanor's project and the rest of that semester's work, I have come to see that the questions and concerns — even complaints — raised in that class regarding self-portrayal and authorization to speak demand closer examination, not only in seminars on the essay, but also in first-year and advanced composition classes, as well as in writing-intensive courses across disciplines, where student writers are struggling for the kind of credibility born out of rhetorically meaningful self-representations, the kind of credibility that these essayists, at their best, were able to achieve.

One important goal of writing instruction, of course, is to help students become effective communicators in academic and professional situations, where the expectations of audiences constrain what and how something should be said. In a society that is so culturally diverse, technologically sophisticated, and hierarchically complex, finding a vantage point, a place to stand, and a locus of authority, respect, influence, and power cannot be ignored as a teachable subject in rhetoric and composition courses. What many student writers seem to long for, even without knowing exactly how to articulate it, is meaningful instruction in using writing to assess, define, and assert who they are becoming as knowing beings. I think these students would find black feminist essayists useful for their ability to reconcile social and personal identities and for directing those identities toward rhetorically useful ends.

Note

1. Here Eleanor is responding to the question posed by Jordan in describing Tyson's desolate environment: "In his neighborhood, where could you buy ribbons for a girl, or tulips?" (223).

Works Cited

Collins, Patricia Hill. *Black Feminist Thought: Knowledge, Consciousness, and the Politics of Empowerment.* New York: Routledge, 1990.

Crowley, Sharon. *A Teacher's Introduction to Deconstruction.* Urbana, IL: NCTE, 1989.

Drew, Julie. "Cultural Composition: Stuart Hall on Ethnicity and the Discursive Turn." *JAC* 18 (1998): 171–96.

Forman, Janis, ed. *What Do I Know: Reading, Writing, and Teaching the Essay.* Portsmouth, NH: Heinemann-Boynton/Cook, 1996.

Halloran, S. Michael. "On the End of Rhetoric, Classical and Modern." *Professing the New Rhetorics: A Sourcebook.* Eds. Theresa Enos and Stuart C. Brown. Englewood Cliffs, NJ: Blair/Prentice, 1994. 331–43.

Harris, Wendell. "Reflections on the Peculiar Status of the Personal Essay." *College English* 58 (1996): 934–53.

Harvey, Gordon. "Presence in the Essay." *College English* 56 (1994): 642–54.

hooks, bell. *Black Looks: Race and Representation.* Boston: South End, 1992.

Jordan, June. "Requiem for the Champ." *Technical Difficulties: African-American Notes on the State of the Union.* Ed. June Jordan. New York: Vintage/Random, 1994. 221–26.

Kirsch, Gesa E., and Joy S. Ritchie. "Beyond the Personal: Theorizing a Politics of Location in Composition Research." *College Composition and Communication* 46 (1995): 7–29.

Kitzinger, Celia. "Liberal Humanism as an Ideology of Social Control: The Regulation of Lesbian Identities." Shotter and Gergen 83–98.

Mittlefehldt, Pamela Klass. "A Weaponry of Choice: Black American Women Writers and the Essay." *Politics of the Essay: Feminist Perspectives.* Eds. Ruth-Ellen Boetcher Joeres and Elizabeth Mittman. Bloomington: Indiana UP, 1993. 196–208.

Morrison, Toni. *Playing in the Dark: Whiteness and the Literary Imagination.* Cambridge, MA: Harvard UP, 1992.

Murray, Kevin. "Construction of Identity in the Narratives of Romance and Comedy." Shotter and Gergen 177–205.

Shotter, John, and Kenneth J. Gergen. *Texts of Identity.* London: Sage, 1989.

Spellmeyer, Kurt. "A Common Ground: The Essay in the Academy." *College English* 51 (1989): 262–76.

West, Cornel. "The New Cultural Politics of Difference." *October* 53 (Summer 1990): 93–109.

Comfort's Insights as a Resource for Your Teaching

1. Comfort offers a pedagogy that tightly braids the personal and the political to improve student writing. How can you realistically ensure that in introducing the personal you do not invite the confessional? What other challenges do you anticipate this pedagogy presenting, and how would you meet them?

2. If you are to introduce this pedagogy or aspects of it, it is crucial to provide students with a variety of solid models to analyze. Discuss with your students how the writer juxtaposes the personal and the public. What other writers or essays would provide a solid model like June Jordan's?

Comfort's Insights as a Resource for Your Writing Classroom

1. Comfort's essay offers a powerful tool for teaching students about the bottomless complexity of the idea of "ethos" (the persona or worldview evinced by an author in his or her writing). Try using some of Comfort's ideas in a lesson or series of lessons on ethos.

2. Using essays that explicitly question the dominant culture provides an especially powerful means to enhance students' skills as critical thinkers. Consider how Comfort's use of the Jordan essay in her class might provide a model for your own attempts to enhance students' capacity for critique.

"So What Do We Do Now?" Necessary Directionality as the Writing Teacher's Response to Racist, Sexist, Homophobic Papers

David Rothgery

In this 1993 article from College Composition and Communication, *David Rothgery meditates on a quandary familiar to all teachers of writing or literature courses and particularly those who have learned to analyze texts rhetorically with the insights of contemporary theory. Contemporary "anti-foundational" theorists like Bakhtin and Derrida posit that humans cannot gain certainty about their existence, behavior, perspectives, or knowledge from universal principles or transcending truths. Any certainty about human experience comes from looking at the situation and examining the conditions of the historical moment, the institutional site, the power structure, the culture within which an event or phenomenon happens. Any "truth" is situational and judged as appropriate, functional, understandable, and reasonable within that situation; foundational moral certainty is illusive and moral pluralism is safe ground.*

When teachers read student or professional texts that seem to them morally reprehensible, analysis of "discursive formation" of the text seems insufficient. Rothgery finds no satisfaction in the suggestion that "usable" truths may exist even though transcendent truths do not. He believes there is a continuum by which teachers, learners, and other citizens can measure moral convictions and arrive at a "sense of a necessary direction — one of less cruelty to ourselves and the rest of humankind."

Then he waited, marshaling his thoughts and brooding over his still untested powers. For though he was master of the world, he was not quite sure what to do next.

But he would think of something. (221)

S o ends Arthur Clarke's classic *2001: A Space Odyssey,* and, as David Bowman contemplates with some dismay his seeming mastery of the universe, his unstated question is one the contemporary writing or literature teacher might well appropriate for his or her own contemporary pedagogical dilemma: So what do I do now with my students? It is the question a high-school English teacher once asked me as she read some Derrida and Nietzsche as part of a required Contemporary Theory and Pedagogy class I was teaching. Her pedagogical quandary was not an isolated one. I answered her with another question: "What if a student in your freshman writing class submits to you a rough draft of a paper which you consider to be racist — very racist? Would you, or should you, with that paper — or perhaps one that asserts that it is the duty of Christians to ferret out every gay and 'beat some sense into him' — mark it as any other paper?"

She seemed to squirm in her seat. She had, in fact, once gotten a racist paper, and her response had been unequivocal: she did not allow the paper and "sat the student down and set him right." Whatever truth there is to Foucault's assertion that each "society has its régime of truth, its 'general politics' of truth — i.e., the types of discourse which it accepts and makes function as true" ("Truth" 131), and whatever personal power agendas are working subtly at the heart of any particular discourse, still, to that teacher that morning, there were some things you could be *certain* about. In the case of a racist paper, some seemingly universal principle far beyond "political correctness," beyond situational truths, was at issue.

Still, as she struggled through some of the assigned readings for the course, it was clear she was having some difficulty reconciling her own moral fervor with what Bakhtin, Derrida, and other theorists of the "anti-foundational" persuasion were arguing: that the human condition does not permit certainty regarding any "Transcendent Truths" as our moral underpinnings, but rather some "truth" in a far less fundamental sense, no matter what we may "feel."

Patricia Bizzell, in restating the dilemma, points to a resolution which works for her and which has implications for any classroom teacher:

> We have not yet taken the next, crucially important step in our rhetorical turn. We have not yet acknowledged that if no unimpeachable authority and transcendent truth exist, this does not mean that no *respectable* authority and no *usable* truth exist. (665; emphasis added)

She implies that teachers must proceed by these "usable" truths and center pedagogical discussions not so much on how one piece of discourse can be made less value-laden, but rather on how all discourse *is* value-laden and therefore political. Dale Bauer, sensitive to a too "authoritative rhetoric" in the classroom, one necessarily tied to a "political position" (391), directs students' attention to "how signs can be manipulated" (391) so as to insure a "mastery that is not oppressive"

(395). On the surface, just as foundationalism in its search for the objective principle is an appealing way to go, so too the kind of anti-foundationalism represented by Bizzell and Bauer — with its recognition that we really can't be certain that any principle is "objective" beyond our saying it is — is appealing in a post-Nietzschean world wherein we have become acutely aware of the linguistic fictional nature of our "non-fictional truths" (consider, e.g., the Margaret Mead version of Samoa). It's all part of the same game. We knock out the big "T" (Truth or Transcendent Truth) but remain, nevertheless, committed to a "respectable authority," a "reasonable truth," an analysis of how power agendas "manipulate signs," and, while showing how our deep-seated aversions to racism, sexism, and homophobia can be subjected to the same process, we, nevertheless, push forward with our convictions. Surely we can and will do this. We will continue to evaluate student papers as to mechanics/usage, style, organization, thesis, and by way of thesis development we will surely "do in" our dangerously myopic, intellectually backward students with appropriately low grades. Our "situational truth" is, if not transcendently valid, certainly more valid than the kind of truth such students promote.

Something about this approach, however, smacks too much of "having our cake and eating it too": There are no Transcendent Truths, but rather "usable truths," which we, as teachers, will make serve as our moral underpinnings. I am uncomfortable. And if I refuse to buy off entirely on the anti-foundationalist argument, I do not believe that makes me a victim of wishful thinking, of a refusal to accept in some way the reality of our essential rhetoricity. Admittedly, the fundamental "situatedness" of the human condition does not allow for the certainty of Transcendent Principles emblazoned across the sky, but neither does it allow for the certainty of there *not* being universals which suggest a direction.

Again and again I have heard professors admit (not in these terms of course, for it is not quite academic to make such admissions) that pedagogical *practice* and contemporary *theory* have to be inconsistent. That is, if it is true we must now discard forever notions of universal principles, it is also true we cannot live (and teach) as though no universal principles underlie anything. In the classroom we encourage a healthy conviction because it leads to the purposefulness which, in turn, increases the probabilities for more creative and powerful rhetoric. This inconsistency is to me, though, as indefensible as an auto manufacturer's claim that it "builds the strongest car possible" when in fact it does not.

On the one hand, the teacher who received the racist paper could have evaluated the rough draft by way of the usual criteria: thesis or essential argument, validity and relevance of supporting evidence, logic and hierarchy of ideas. What better approach than letting the student demonstrate for himself or herself the untenable nature of racist arguments? Such an approach surely works with the arguments, untenable or not, set forth in any paper from "American Management Styles: Finest in the World" to "Survival of Our Wetlands: More Priority, Please."

After all, even with these papers we could argue that, in each case, something bordering on "fundamental" is at work: in the first paper, respect for the laborer perhaps; in the second, concern for our children's children. Still, teachers are not likely, with such papers, to react as our teacher did to the racist paper, which she regarded as a paper of an entirely different species. I suppose we could include in that extreme "different species" category (whether we ever receive them or not) papers which argue that we burn epileptics as devils, raze gay bars, lynch Blacks who dare to date White women, burn cats in satanic rites, or return women to their proper roles as child-rearers and sex toys.

My point in invoking these extreme examples is that, indeed, there is a *continuum,* a "more fundamental" at work, a sense of directionality. I take issue with those who believe we can buy into a universe of "situational ethics" or "usable" truths — that is, until we are willing to grant there is nothing to be gained in striving toward "fundamental" or "transcendent" principles which such papers violate in promoting cruel behavior towards humankind and the other creatures which populate the earth. Burning epileptics at the stake, abusing children, promoting by willful neglect the extinction of an animal species — such acts don't properly merit some gradation of ethical value relative to a particular culture or period of time.

Rarely do we come across extremely reprehensible papers — such as those which do openly promote cruel behavior. But our writing classes do become the setting for argument about capital punishment, euthanasia, abortion, women's rights. If we regard these discussions as having at most only "situational" weight — a "this time and place" payoff — then the dynamics of shared ideas is not allowed its proper role in the *necessary directionality* for the human condition and the condition of the planet we inhabit — that of alleviating suffering and cruelty, physical, mental, and spiritual — no matter which status the cosmic deities or demons accord such cruelty.

What is this "continuum," this "necessary directionality"? Consider the subject of racism. At one end of the continuum are non-racist papers arguing the merits of affirmative action, and at the other end are Skinhead-oriented papers arguing the supremacy of the White race. In between are many kinds of papers, such as one I once received which questioned why White students must be forced to mingle in small-group discussions with Hispanics and Blacks. Surely, for most teachers, something *more* fundamental is at stake in the Skinhead paper, and something *less* fundamental is at stake in the paper on classroom grouping. But this "more"/"less" continuum is, for the teacher, a different vision of ethics than "usable truth," which by its very nature admits of no true sense of continuum. My point is "more fundamental" and "usable" cannot inhabit the same world. At what point, for example, does the seemingly fundamental truth about cruelty and insensitivity to those of different color become the "usable" truth of arrangement of students within classroom groups or the "reasonable" and "situational ethic" of "Does Affirmative Action Succeed in Its Goals?"?

I am certainly *not* arguing that a teacher could not legitimately deal with papers presenting reprehensible ideas by way of the usual criteria of structure, logic, grammar, and style. The question I pose is this: Has contemporary theory, with its insights into the "situatedness" of our existence and perspectives, left us any sense of a valid — indeed, a *necessary,* "we-can-no-longer-go-back-to-that" — directionality by way of shared ideas? Can we indeed go back to treating women as objects, African Americans as possessions, homosexuals as freaks, epileptics as devils?

Stanley Fish argues, in *Doing What Comes Naturally,* that

> questions of fact, truth, correctness, validity, and clarity can neither be posed nor answered with reference to some extracontextual, ahistorical, nonsituational reality, or rule, or law, or value; rather, anti-foundationalism asserts, all these matters are intelligible and debatable only within the precincts of the contexts or situations or paradigms or communities that give them their local and changeable shape. (344)

Fish speaks only of what he can be certain. He cannot be certain of Transcendent Truths. Nor can we. But does this mean we cannot be committed to moving toward truths which are *so comprehensive* that their force cannot be ignored?

Necessary Direction away from cruelty is just such a truth. The question is not so much whether or not we must assign to these "truths" the status of "undeniable absolutes," but whether we must assign to them some essence which is *so fundamental,* so clearly pointing to a necessary direction, that *we must insist that, pedagogically, an unqualified moral conviction must assert itself.* As long as "better" is given its proper "transcendent" due, a true moral purpose remains, and a true moral conviction in the classroom can continue. The confrontation of values, of situational ethics, that defines any composition classroom dynamics is not a naive affective or fictional game that we as teachers must continue to play to produce what Stanley Fish calls the "small . . . yield" of a "few worn and familiar bromides" (355); on the contrary, it is a confrontation founded in our sense of a *necessary* direction — one of less cruelty to ourselves and the rest of humankind.

This is not a starry-eyed meliorism or naive social evolutionism. Surely we do need in our classrooms the kind of discursive analysis the anti-foundationalists call for. A deconstructionist reading of *Mein Kampf* could not have been all bad. But Fish and Bizzell leave us too precarious an anchoring. Without that sense of a *necessary direction,* hate crimes such as the burning of crosses will necessarily be prosecuted only as vandalism, and the Andersonville and Auschwitz behavior will be defended by way of "following orders." We have moved *beyond* that. Indeed, humankind's condition seems to be defined in great measure by "situatedness." But what is functional and reasonable for one time and place must always push against other times and places — other situations on a greater scale. Racist and sexist behavior of any sort that promotes unnecessary cruelty must never be afforded the justification a too-unexamined moral pluralism may allow.

Otherwise, the kind of phenomena I experienced in my Writing Theory class in the spring of 1992 will be the norm. We were discussing Michel Foucault's *The Archaeology of Knowledge.* I had written on the board the sentence "Saddam Hussein is a Hitler." On the one hand, I recognized, as did the students, that the politically "correct" position on this (or on Hussein and the Gulf War in general) would vary greatly from campus to campus. Furthermore, Fish's comment that anti-foundationalism's super-self-consciousness is not a way out, that

> any claim in which the notion of situatedness is said to be a lever that allows us to get a purchase on situations is finally a claim to have *escaped situatedness,* and is therefore nothing more or less than a reinvention of foundationalism by the very form of thought that has supposedly reduced it to ruins (348–49 emphasis added),

still seemed valid here. Thus, the immediate reaction to the "Saddam Hussein is a Hitler" sentence in my class of relatively sophisticated rhetorical-theory students was in line with Foucault (and Fish): that we had to look at who said it and other dimensions of the "enunciative modalities," what "institutional sites" were being represented, and so on. The students suggested several such "sites" each with its own particular "political" baggage, its own appropriation of the statement, and I put them on the board:

Bush   Hussein   *NY Times* Editors   Soldier's Mother

"SADDAM HUSSEIN IS A HITLER." — REALITY?

W.W. II Veteran   Berkeley Anti-War Activist   Kurds

Our "situating" of a bit of discourse was, for a while, only an *academic* exercise — much as composition classes, I fear, tend to be for anti-foundationalist teachers. But when we finished congratulating ourselves on the incisiveness of our dissection, I put the chalk down and took a different approach. "But what if Hussein really *is* a kind of Hitler?" I asked. "What of the *very real possibility* that Hussein was *greatly* responsible for the unnecessary and perhaps cruel deaths of thousands of Kurds? What then? That is, what do we do now beyond analyzing the 'discursive formation' of that sentence?"

The students were literally unable to speak for almost a minute. It had not occurred to any of the students, all of them very bright, that *even in the classroom* there are questions that require more than being asked — that must be *answered.* I was not asking my students to take arms against Hussein but to sort out for themselves the truths regarding the possibility of a very real atrocity.

The classroom may be a laboratory, but it is a laboratory for the world we live in. Analysis and determination of power zones is of course essential, and too little of that has been done in our classrooms in the past. But when the *only* result for the classroom of anti-foundationalist and post-modernist insights is a discursive analysis which takes on the character of some linguistic Rubic's Cube, then we have plunged into the same idiocy that allowed learning theory to transform classrooms into robotical M and M dispenser systems.

As writers and teachers of writing, we must continue to grope in the recognition that our moral convictions do not translate as self-contained situational ethics alone, that they will continue to be measured along greater and greater scales — scales so large we must of necessity grant *some* of them a "highest order" status. "Better" — though it may and will be misappropriated and misapplied by the inexperienced, the uneducated, the cowardly, the wicked — must continue to be an operational term. We must continue to act, to "do," to "write" not only *as though* our writing is just one more version of Foucault's "discursive formations," emanating from this "institutional site" or that, but indeed *because* some of our convictions *are* more true, *are* better — because we can now discard *forever* some situational ethics.

What is the "new pedagogy" for our composition classrooms? Can it reside in "style," in anti-foundationalist situational truths which do not even consider the possibility of necessary directions (i.e., directions defined by *what can no longer be acceptable*)? That is indeed a "small yield," and the resulting classroom environment will produce too many students with a "small yield" attitude about not only their papers but the convictions which underlie them. Whatever naiveté there may be in the persistent groping in the dark for "first" principles to understand our universe, the real force of the greatest literature, or of that "one in a hundred" student composition, lies in that *groping* beyond the imprisonment of our situatedness. And a pedagogy that chooses to ignore the moral sweat, if you will, does a disservice of the profoundest order to the appreciation of good writing, of great writing. Yes, the groping between student and teacher may clash, but in the areas of racism, sexism, homophobia, the clash should be loud and morally meaningful in recognition that Necessary Directionality remains a valid concept.

Works Cited

Bauer, Dale. "The Other 'F' Word: The Feminist in the Classroom." *College English* 52 (Apr. 1990): 385–96.

Bizzell, Patricia. "Beyond Anti-Foundationalism to Rhetorical Authority: Problems Defining Cultural Literacy." *College English* 52 (Oct. 1990): 661–75.

Clarke, Arthur C. *2001: A Space Odyssey.* New York: Signet, 1968.

Fish, Stanley. *Doing What Comes Naturally: Change, Rhetoric, and the Practice of Theory in Literary and Legal Studies.* Durham: Duke UP, 1989.

Foucault, Michel. *The Archaeology of Knowledge.* Trans. A. M. Sheridan Smith. New York: Pantheon, 1972.

———. "Truth and Power." *Power/Knowledge: Selected Interviews and Other Writings, 1972–77.* Trans. Colin Gordon, Leo Marshall, John Mepham, and Kate Soper. Ed. Colin Gordon. New York: Pantheon, 1980. 109–33.

Rothgery's Insights as a Resource for Your Teaching

1. Without a clear definition of *necessary directionality,* it can be difficult to distinguish what causes a personal reaction against the moral reasoning of a text. Whatever beliefs teachers hold about controversial issues such as abortion, capital punishment, or animal rights, censoring those issues as paper topics clearly denies students opportunities for discovering or defining their own beliefs and for learning how to present their beliefs to an audience that may disagree. Share Rothgery's essay with teaching colleagues and suggest a "brown bag" discussion. Ask colleagues how they work with texts and students to accommodate not only multiple perspectives but also shared convictions or perspectives "we cannot go back to."

2. Rothgery acknowledges that a teacher might evaluate reprehensible texts more rigorously than other texts, using only rhetorical analysis to define the quality of those papers. If you receive a text that repulses you, first draft a letter in which you describe all the strengths of the paper and any problems with it. Put the letter aside and ask three or four veteran instructors to read the text "holistically," citing strengths and weaknesses they find in the "discursive formation." Compare your letter with their feedback as a way to provide the student with a "fair" reading of the text. Then ask those colleagues how/if/why they would deal with what makes the essay reprehensible to you.

Rothgery's Insights as a Resource for Your Writing Classroom

1. Texts that are reprehensible to you will also disturb many of your students. Before you model peer criticism, bring in a text that triggers moral repulsion and pose the question, "If a peer wrote a text that was intentionally or unintentionally stepping beyond what you believe 'must not happen,' how would you help that writer understand your reaction?" Organize small groups of three or four and follow up with reports to the large group. Ask class members to identify common themes from the discussions and to write in their journals about those themes.

2. Swift's "A Modest Proposal" is "canonical" in composition texts partly because the satire deliberately triggers what to Swift was a "transcendent truth" and what Rothgery would describe as a "necessary directionality." Many students will not have read the satire and will be repulsed, sometimes missing the ironic juxtaposition of the two voices in the text. Organize a class discussion

of the text in terms of the traditional argument: demonstration of a problem, formal statement of solution, explanation of the solution, and refutation of alternative solutions. Use the board to outline the satire twice, side by side: first from the voice of the "modest proposal" and then from the covert voice of Swift as it undercuts and broadens the description of the problem and solutions. Expect that class members will be able to think about how Swift manipulated their early reactions (e.g., "This is sick").

The class conversation will come to focus on the proposer's criteria of evaluation ("fair, cheap, and easy") against the implied criteria of Swift. Assign follow-up journal entries, asking students to analyze the use of "fair, cheap, and easy" criteria in modern or contemporary world events and comment on the moral criteria that perhaps are used or could be used on a "larger scale" over time, across concepts of nation, race, gender, and so on.

Sponsors of Literacy

Deborah Brandt

Deborah Brandt's essay connects the idea of literacy as an individual development with the idea of literacy as an economic development by exploring how various agents enable, support, regulate, or suppress the development of literacy. In this essay, which first appeared in 1998 in College Composition and Communication, *Brandt reports on her findings from one hundred in-depth interviews with people around the country and concludes that we, as teachers of composition, are powerful enough to sponsor literacy on our own terms. We also, however, serve as "conflicted brokers between literacy's buyers and sellers," and Brandt emphasizes that we must sensitize ourselves to the ways patterns of sponsorship also follow patterns of social stratification.*

In his sweeping history of adult learning in the United States, Joseph Kett describes the intellectual atmosphere available to young apprentices who worked in the small, decentralized print shops of antebellum America. Because printers also were the solicitors and editors of what they published, their workshops served as lively incubators for literacy and political discourse. By the mid-nineteenth century, however, this learning space was disrupted when the invention of the steam press reorganized the economy of the print industry. Steam presses were so expensive that they required capital outlays beyond the means of many printers. As a result, print jobs were outsourced, the processes of editing and printing were split, and, in tight competition, print apprentices became low-paid mechanics with no more access to the multiskilled environment of the craftshop (Kett 67–70). While this shift in working conditions may be evidence of the deskilling of workers in-

duced by the Industrial Revolution (Nicholas and Nicholas), it also offers a site for reflecting upon the dynamic sources of literacy and literacy learning. The reading and writing skills of print apprentices in
this period were the achievements not simply of teachers and learners
nor of the discourse practices of the printer community. Rather, these
skills existed fragilely, contingently within an economic moment. The
pre-steam press economy enabled some of the most basic aspects of the
apprentices' literacy, especially their access to material production and
the public meaning or worth of their skills. Paradoxically, even as the
steam-powered penny press made print more accessible (by making
publishing more profitable), it brought an end to a particular form of
literacy sponsorship and a drop in literate potential.

The apprentices' experience invites rumination upon literacy learning and teaching today. Literacy looms as one of the great engines of
profit and competitive advantage in the twentieth century: a lubricant
for consumer desire; a means for integrating corporate markets; a foundation for the deployment of weapons and other technology; a raw
material in the mass production of information. As ordinary citizens
have been compelled into these economies, their reading and writing
skills have grown sharply more central to the everyday trade of information and goods as well as to the pursuit of education, employment,
civil rights, status. At the same time, people's literate skills have grown
vulnerable to unprecedented turbulence in their economic value, as
conditions, forms, and standards of literacy achievement seem to shift
with almost every new generation of learners. How are we to understand the vicissitudes of individual literacy development in relationship to the large-scale economic forces that set the routes and determine the wordly worth of that literacy?

The field of writing studies has had much to say about individual
literacy development. Especially in the last quarter of the twentieth
century, we have theorized, researched, critiqued, debated, and sometimes even managed to enhance the literate potentials of ordinary citizens as they have tried to cope with life as they find it. Less easily and
certainly less steadily have we been able to relate what we see, study,
and do to these larger contexts of profit making and competition. This
even as we recognize that the most pressing issues we deal with —
tightening associations between literate skill and social viability, the
breakneck pace of change in communications technology, persistent inequities in access and reward — all relate to structural conditions in
literacy's bigger picture. When economic forces are addressed in our
work, they appear primarily as generalities: contexts, determinants,
motivators, barriers, touchstones. But rarely are they systematically
related to the local conditions and embodied moments of literacy learning that occupy so many of us on a daily basis.[1]

This essay does not presume to overcome the analytical failure completely. But it does offer a conceptual approach that begins to connect
literacy as an individual development to literacy as an economic development, at least as the two have played out over the last ninety years

or so. The approach is through what I call sponsors of literacy. Sponsors, as I have come to think of them, are any agents, local or distant, concrete or abstract, who enable, support, teach, model, as well as recruit, regulate, suppress, or withhold literacy — and gain advantage by it in some way. Just as the ages of radio and television accustom us to having programs *brought* to us by various commercial sponsors, it is useful to think about who or what underwrites occasions of literacy learning and use. Although the interests of the sponsor and the sponsored do not have to converge (and, in fact, may conflict), sponsors nevertheless set the terms for access to literacy and wield powerful incentives for compliance and loyalty. Sponsors are a tangible reminder that literacy learning throughout history has always required permission, sanction, assistance, coercion, or, at minimum, contact with existing trade routes. Sponsors are delivery systems for the economies of literacy, the means by which these forces present themselves to — and through — individual learners. They also represent the causes into which people's literacy usually gets recruited.[2]

For the last five years I have been tracing sponsors of literacy across the twentieth century as they appear in the accounts of ordinary Americans recalling how they learned to write and read. The investigation is grounded in more than 100 in-depth interviews that I collected from a diverse group of people born roughly between 1900 and 1980. In the interviews, people explored in great detail their memories of learning to read and write across their lifetimes, focusing especially on the people, institutions, materials, and motivations involved in the process. The more I worked with these accounts, the more I came to realize that they were filled with references to sponsors, both explicit and latent, who appeared in formative roles at the scenes of literacy learning. Patterns of sponsorship became an illuminating site through which to track the different cultural attitudes people developed toward writing vs. reading as well as the ideological congestion faced by late-century literacy learners as their sponsors proliferated and diversified (see my essays on "Remembering Reading" and "Accumulating Literacy"). In this essay I set out a case for why the concept of sponsorship is so richly suggestive for exploring economies of literacy and their effects. Then, through use of extended case examples, I demonstrate the practical application of this approach for interpreting current conditions of literacy teaching and learning, including persistent stratification of opportunity and escalating standards for literacy achievement. A final section addresses implications for the teaching of writing.

Sponsorship

Intuitively, *sponsors* seemed a fitting term for the figures who turned up most typically in people's memories of literacy learning: older relatives, teachers, priests, supervisors, military officers, editors, influential authors. Sponsors, as we ordinarily think of them, are powerful figures who bankroll events or smooth the way of initiates. Usually richer, more knowledgeable, and more entrenched than the sponsored, sponsors nevertheless enter a reciprocal relationship with those they underwrite. They lend their resources or credibility to the sponsored but also stand to gain benefits from their success, whether by direct repayment or, indirectly, by credit of association. *Sponsors* also proved an appealing term in my analysis because of all the commercial references that appeared in these twentieth-century accounts — the magazines, peddled encyclopedias, essay contests, radio and television programs, toys, fan clubs, writing tools, and so on, from which so much experience with literacy was derived. As the twentieth century turned the abilities to read and write into widely exploitable resources, commercial sponsorship abounded.

In whatever form, sponsors deliver the ideological freight that must be borne for access to what they have. Of course, the sponsored can be oblivious to or innovative with this ideological burden. Like Little Leaguers who wear the logo of a local insurance agency on their uniforms, not out of a concern for enhancing the agency's image but as a means for getting to play ball, people throughout history have acquired literacy pragmatically under the banner of others' causes. In the days before free, public schooling in England, Protestant Sunday Schools warily offered basic reading instruction to working-class families as part of evangelical duty. To the horror of many in the church sponsorship, these families insistently, sometimes riotously demanded of their Sunday Schools more instruction, including in writing and math, because it provided means for upward mobility.[3] Through the sponsorship of Baptist and Methodist ministries, African Americans in slavery taught each other to understand the Bible in subversively liberatory ways. Under a conservative regime, they developed forms of critical literacy that sustained religious, educational, and political movements both before and after emancipation (Cornelius). Most of the time, however, literacy takes its shape from the interests of its sponsors. And, as we will see below, obligations toward one's sponsors run deep, affecting what, why, and how people write and read.

The concept of sponsors helps to explain, then, a range of human relationships and ideological pressures that turn up at the scenes of literacy learning — from benign sharing between adults and youths, to euphemized coercions in schools and workplaces, to the most notorious impositions and deprivations by church or state. It also is a concept useful for tracking literacy's material: the things that accompany writing and reading and the ways they are manufactured and distributed. Sponsorship as a sociological term is even more broadly suggestive for thinking about economies of literacy development. Studies of patronage in Europe and *compradrazgo* in the Americas show how patron-client relationships in the past grew up around the need to manage scarce resources and promote political stability (Bourne; Lynch; Horstman and Kurtz). Pragmatic, instrumental, ambivalent, patron-client relationships integrated otherwise antagonistic social classes into relationships of mutual, albeit unequal dependencies. Loaning land, money, protection, and other favors allowed the politically powerful to extend their influence and justify their exploitation of clients. Clients traded their labor and deference for access to opportunities for themselves or their children and for leverage needed to improve their social standing. Especially under conquest in Latin America, *compradrazgo* reintegrated native societies badly fragmented by the diseases and other disruptions that followed foreign invasions. At the same time, this system was susceptible to its own stresses, especially when patrons became clients themselves of still more centralized or distant overlords, with all the shifts in loyalty and perspective that entailed (Horstman and Kurtz 13–14).

In raising this association with formal systems of patronage, I do not wish to overlook the very different economic, political, and educational systems within which U.S. literacy has developed. But where we find the sponsoring of literacy, it will be useful to look for its function within larger political and economic arenas. Literacy, like land, is a valued commodity in this economy, a key resource in gaining profit and edge. This value helps to explain, of course, the lengths people will go to secure literacy for themselves or their children. But it also explains why the powerful work so persistently to conscript and ration the powers of literacy. The competition to harness literacy, to manage, measure, teach, and exploit it, has intensified throughout the century. It is vital to pay attention to this development because it largely sets the terms for individuals' encounters with literacy. This competition shapes the incentives and barriers (including uneven distributions of opportunity) that greet literacy learners in any particular time and place. It is this competition that has made access to the right kinds of literacy sponsors so crucial for political and economic well-being. And it also has spurred the rapid, complex changes that now make the pursuit of literacy feel so turbulent and precarious for so many.

In the next three sections, I trace the dynamics of literacy sponsorship through the life experiences of several individuals, showing how their opportunities for literacy learning emerge out of the jockeying and skirmishing for economic and political advantage going on among sponsors of literacy. Along the way, the analysis addresses three key issues: (1) how, despite ostensible democracy in educational chances, stratification of opportunity continues to organize access and reward in literacy learning; (2) how sponsors contribute to what is called "the literacy crisis," that is, the perceived gap between rising standards for achievement and people's ability to meet them; and (3) how encounters with literacy sponsors, especially as they are configured at the end of the twentieth century, can be sites for the innovative rerouting of resources into projects of self-development and social change.

Sponsorship and Access

A focus on sponsorship can force a more explicit and substantive link between literacy learning and systems of opportunity and access. A statistical correlation between high literacy achievement and high socioeconomic, majority-race status routinely shows up in results of national tests of reading and writing performance.[4] These findings capture yet, in their shorthand way, obscure the unequal conditions of literacy sponsorship that lie behind differential outcomes in academic performance. Throughout their lives, affluent people from high-caste racial groups have multiple and redundant contacts with powerful literacy sponsors as a routine part of their economic and political privileges. Poor people and those from low-caste racial groups have less consistent, less politically secured access to literacy sponsors — especially to the ones that can grease their way to academic and economic success. Differences in their performances are often attributed to family background (namely education and income of parents) or to particular norms and values operating within different ethnic groups or social classes. But in either case, much more is usually at work.

As a study in contrasts in sponsorship patterns and access to literacy, consider the parallel experiences of Raymond Branch and Dora Lopez, both of whom were born in 1969 and, as young children, moved with their parents to the same, mid-sized university town in the Midwest.[5] Both were still residing in this town at the time of our interviews in 1995. Raymond Branch, a European American, had been born in southern California, the son of a professor father and a real estate executive mother. He recalled that his first grade classroom in 1975 was hooked up to a mainframe computer at Stanford University and that, as a youngster, he enjoyed fooling around with computer programming in the company of "real users" at his father's science lab. This process was not interrupted much when, in the late 1970s, his family moved to the Midwest. Raymond received his first personal computer as a Christmas present from his parents when he was twelve years old, and a modem the year after that. In the 1980s, computer hardware and software stores began popping up within a bicycle-ride's distance from where he lived. The stores were serving the university community and, increasingly, the high-tech industries that were becoming established in that vicinity. As an adolescent, Raymond spent his summers roaming these stores, sampling new computer games, making contact with founders of some of the first electronic bulletin boards in the nation, and continuing, through reading and other informal means, to develop his programming techniques. At the time of our interview he had graduated from the local university and was a successful freelance writer of software and software documentation, with clients in both the private sector and the university community.

Dora Lopez, a Mexican American, was born in the same year as Raymond Branch, 1969, in a Texas border town, where her grandparents, who worked as farm laborers, lived most of the year. When Dora was still a baby her family moved to the same Midwest university town as had the family of Raymond Branch. Her father pursued an accounting degree at a local technical college and found work as a shipping and receiving clerk at the university. Her mother, who also attended technical college briefly, worked part-time in a bookstore. In the early 1970s, when the Lopez family made its move to the Midwest, the Mexican-American population in the university town was barely one percent. Dora recalled that the family had to drive seventy miles to a big city to find not only suitable groceries but also Spanish-language newspapers and magazines that carried information of concern and interest to them. (Only when reception was good could they catch Spanish-language radio programs coming from Chicago, 150 miles away.) During her adolescence, Dora Lopez undertook to teach herself how to read and write in Spanish, something, she said, that neither her brother nor her U.S.-born cousins knew how to do. Sometimes, with the help of her mother's employee discount at the bookstore, she sought out novels by South American and Mexican writers, and she practiced her written Spanish by corresponding with relatives in Colombia. She was exposed to computers for the first time at the age of thirteen when she worked as a teacher's aide in a federally funded summer school program for the children of migrant workers. The computers were being used to help the children to be brought up to grade level in their reading and writing skills. When Dora was admitted to the same university that Raymond Branch attended, her father bought her a used word processing machine that a student had advertised for sale on a bulletin board in the building where Mr. Lopez worked. At the time of our interview, Dora Lopez had transferred from the university to a technical college. She was working for a cleaning company, where she performed extra duties as a translator, communicating on her supervisor's behalf with the largely Latina cleaning staff. "I write in Spanish for him, what he needs to be translated, like job duties, what he expects them to do, and I write lists for him in English and Spanish," she explained.

In Raymond Branch's account of his early literacy learning we are able to see behind the scenes of his majority-race membership, male gender, and high-end socioeconomic family profile. There lies a thick and, to him, relatively accessible economy of institutional and commercial supports that cultivated and subsidized his acquisition of a powerful form of literacy. One might be tempted to say that Raymond Branch was born at the right time and lived in the right place — except that the experience of Dora Lopez troubles that thought. For Raymond Branch, a university town in the 1970s and 1980s provided an information-rich, resource-rich learning environment in which to pursue his literacy development, but for Dora Lopez, a female member of a culturally unsubsidized ethnic minority, the same town at the same time was information- and resource-poor. Interestingly, both young people were pursuing projects of self-initiated learning, Raymond Branch in computer programming and Dora Lopez in biliteracy. But she had to reach much further afield for the material and communicative systems needed to support her learning. Also, while Raymond Branch, as the son of an academic, was sponsored by some of the most powerful agents of the university (its laboratories, newest technologies, and most educated personnel), Dora Lopez was being sponsored by what her parents could pull from the peripheral service systems of the university (the mail room, the bookstore, the second-hand technology market). In these accounts we also can see how the development and eventual economic worth of Raymond Branch's literacy skills were underwritten by late-century transformations in communication technology that created a boomtown need for programmers and software writers. Dora Lopez's biliterate skills developed and paid off much further down the economic-reward ladder, in government-sponsored youth programs and commercial enterprises, that, in the 1990s, were absorbing surplus migrant workers into a low-wage, urban service economy.[6] Tracking patterns of literacy sponsorship, then, gets beyond SES shorthand to expose more fully how unequal literacy chances relate to systems of unequal subsidy and reward for literacy. These are the systems that deliver large-scale economic, historical, and political conditions to the scenes of small-scale literacy use and development.

This analysis of sponsorship forces us to consider not merely how one social group's literacy practices may differ from another's, but how everybody's literacy practices are operating in differential economies, which supply different access routes, different degrees of sponsoring power, and different scales of monetary worth to the practices in use. In fact, the interviews I conducted are filled with examples of how economic and political forces, some of them originating in quite distant corporate and government policies, affect people's day-to-day ability to seek out and practice literacy. As a telephone company employee, Janelle Hampton enjoyed a brief period in the early 1980s as a fraud investigator, pursuing inquiries and writing up reports of her efforts. But when the breakup of the telephone utility reorganized its workforce, the fraud division was moved two states away and she was returned to less interesting work as a data processor. When, as a seven-year-old in the mid-1970s, Yi Vong made his way with his family from Laos to rural Wisconsin as part of the first resettlement group of Hmong refugees after the Vietnam War, his school district — which had no ESL programming — placed him in a school for the blind and deaf, where he learned English on audio and visual language machines. When a meager retirement pension forced Peter Hardaway and his wife out of their house and into a trailer, the couple stopped receiving newspapers and magazines in order to avoid cluttering up the small space they had to share. An analysis of sponsorship systems of literacy would help educators everywhere to think through the effects that economic and political changes in their regions are having on various people's ability to write and read, their chances to sustain that ability, and their capacities to pass it along to others. Recession, relocation, immigration, technological change, government retreat all can — and do — condition the course by which literate potential develops.

Sponsorship and the Rise in Literacy Standards

As I have been attempting to argue, literacy as a resource becomes available to ordinary people largely through the mediations of more powerful sponsors. These sponsors are engaged in ceaseless processes of positioning and repositioning, seizing and relinquishing control over meanings and materials of literacy as part of their participation in economic and political competition. In the give and take of these struggles, forms of literacy and literacy learning take shape. This section examines more closely how forms of literacy are created out of competitions between institutions. It especially considers how this process relates to the rapid rise in literacy standards since World War II. Resnick and Resnick lay out the process by which the demand for literacy achievement has been escalating, from basic, largely rote competence to more complex analytical and interpretive skills. More and more people are now being expected to accomplish more and more things with reading and writing. As print and its spinoffs have entered virtually every sphere of life, people have grown increasingly dependent on their literacy skills for earning a living and exercising and protecting their civil rights. This section uses one extended case example to trace the role of institutional sponsorship in raising the literacy stakes. It also considers how one man used available forms of sponsorship to cope with this escalation in literacy demands.

The focus is on Dwayne Lowery, whose transition in the early 1970s from line worker in an automobile manufacturing plant to field representative for a major public employees union exemplified the major transition of the post–World War II economy — from a thing-making, thing-swapping society to an information-making, service-swapping society. In the process, Dwayne Lowery had to learn to read and write in ways that he had never done before. How his experiences with writing developed and how they were sponsored — and distressed — by institutional struggle will unfold in the following narrative.

A man of Eastern European ancestry, Dwayne Lowery was born in 1938 and raised in a semi-rural area in the upper Midwest, the third of five children of a rubber worker father and a homemaker mother. Lowery recalled how, in his childhood home, his father's feisty union publications and left-leaning newspapers and radio shows helped to create a political climate in his household. "I was sixteen years old before I knew that god-damn Republicans was two words," he said. Despite this influence, Lowery said he shunned politics and newspaper reading as a young person, except to read the sports page. A diffident student, he graduated near the bottom of his class from a small high school in 1956 and, after a stint in the Army, went to work on the assembly line of a major automobile manufacturer. In the late 1960s, bored with the repetition of spraying primer paint on the right door checks of 57 cars an hour, Lowery traded in his night shift at the auto plant for a day job reading water meters in a municipal utility department. It was at that time, Lowery recalled, that he rediscovered newspapers, reading them in the early morning in his department's break room. He said:

> At the time I guess I got a little more interested in the state of things within the state. I started to get a little political at that time and got a little more information about local people. So I would buy [a metropolitan paper] and I would read that paper in the morning. It was a pretty conservative paper but I got some information.

At about the same time Lowery became active in a rapidly growing public employees union, and, in the early 1970s, he applied for and received a union-sponsored grant that allowed him to take off four months of work and travel to Washington, D.C., for training in union activity. Here is his extended account of that experience:

> When I got to school, then there was a lot of reading. I often felt bad. If I had read more [as a high-school student] it wouldn't have been so tough. But they pumped a lot of stuff at us to read. We lived in a hotel and we had to some extent homework we had to do and reading we had to do and not make written reports but make some presentation on our part of it. What they were trying to teach us, I believe, was regulations, systems, laws. In case anything in court came up along the way, we would know that. We did a lot of work on organizing, you know, learning how to negotiate contracts, contractual language, how to write it. Gross National Product, how that affected the Consumer Price Index. It was pretty much a crash course. It was pretty much crammed in. And I'm not sure we were all that well prepared when we got done, but it was interesting.

After a hands-on experience organizing sanitation workers in the West, Lowery returned home and was offered a full-time job as a field staff representative for the union, handling worker grievances and contract negotiations for a large, active local near his state capital. His initial writing and rhetorical activities corresponded with the heady days of the early 1970s when the union was growing in strength and influence, reflecting in part the exponential expansion in information workers and service providers within all branches of government. With practice, Lowery said he became "good at talking," "good at presenting the union side," "good at slicing chunks off the employer's case." Lowery observed that, in those years, the elected officials with whom he was negotiating often lacked the sophistication of their Washington-trained union counterparts. "They were part-time people," he said. "And they didn't know how to calculate. We got things in contracts that didn't cost them much at the time but were going to cost them a ton down the road." In time, though, even small municipal and county governments responded to the public employees' growing power by hiring specialized attorneys to represent them in grievance and contract negotiations. "Pretty soon," Lowery observed, "ninety percent of the people I was dealing with across the table were attorneys."

This move brought dramatic changes in the writing practices of union reps, and, in Lowery's estimation, a simultaneous waning of the power of workers and the power of his own literacy. "It used to be we got our way through muscle or through political connections," he said. "Now we had to get it through legalistic stuff. It was no longer just sit down and talk about it. Can we make a deal?" Instead, all activity became rendered in writing: the exhibit, the brief, the transcript, the letter, the appeal. Because briefs took longer to write, the wheels of justice took longer to turn. Delays in grievance hearings became routine, as lawyers and union reps alike asked hearing judges for extensions on their briefs. Things went, in Lowery's words, "from quick, competent justice to expensive and long-term justice."

In the meantime, Lowery began spending up to seventy hours a week at work, sweating over the writing of briefs, which are typically fifteen- to thirty-page documents laying out precedents, arguments, and evidence for a grievant's case. These documents were being forced by the new political economy in which Lowery's union was operating. He explained:

> When employers were represented by an attorney, you were going to have a written brief because the attorney needs to get paid. Well, what do you think if you were a union grievant and the attorney says, well, I'm going to write a brief and Dwayne Lowery says, well, I'm not going to. Does the worker somehow feel that their representation is less now?

To keep up with the new demands, Lowery occasionally traveled to major cities for two- or three-day union-sponsored workshops on arbitration, new legislation, and communication skills. He also took short courses at a historic School for Workers at a nearby university. His writing instruction consisted mainly of reading the briefs of other field reps, especially those done by the college graduates who increasingly were being assigned to his district from union headquarters. Lowery said he kept a file drawer filled with other people's briefs from which he would borrow formats and phrasings. At the time of our interview in 1995, Dwayne Lowery had just taken an early and somewhat bitter retirement from the union, replaced by a recent graduate from a master's degree program in Industrial Relations. As a retiree, he was engaged in local Democratic party politics and was getting informal lessons in word processing at home from his wife.

Over a twenty-year period, Lowery's adult writing took its character from a particular juncture in labor relations, when even small units of government began wielding (and, as a consequence, began spreading) a "legalistic" form of literacy in order to restore political dominance over public workers. This struggle for dominance shaped the kinds of literacy skills required of Lowery, the kinds of genres he learned and used, and the kinds of literate identity he developed. Lowery's rank-and-file experience and his talent for representing that experience around a bargaining table became increasingly peripheral to his ability to prepare documents that could compete in kind with those written by his formally educated, professional adversaries. Face-to-face meetings became occasions mostly for a ritualistic exchange of texts, as arbitrators generally deferred decisions, reaching them in private, after solitary deliberation over complex sets of documents. What Dwayne Lowery was up against as a working adult in the second half of the twentieth century was more than just living through a rising standard in literacy expectations or a generalized growth in professionalization, specialization, or documentary power — although certainly all of those things are, generically, true. Rather, these developments should be seen more specifically, as outcomes of ongoing transformations in the history of literacy as it has been wielded as part of economic and political conflict. These transformations become the arenas in which new standards of literacy develop. And for Dwayne Lowery — as well as many like him over the last twenty-five years — these are the arenas in which the worth of existing literate skills become degraded. A consummate debater and deal maker, Lowery saw his value to the union bureaucracy subside, as power shifted to younger, university-trained staffers whose literacy credentials better matched the specialized forms of escalating pressure coming from the other side.

In the broadest sense, the sponsorship of Dwayne Lowery's literacy experiences lies deep within the historical conditions of industrial relations in the twentieth century and, more particularly, within the changing nature of work and labor struggle over the last several decades. Edward Stevens Jr. has observed the rise in this century of an "advanced contractarian society" (25) by which formal relationships of all kinds have come to rely on "a jungle of rules and regulations" (139). For labor, these conditions only intensified in the 1960s and 1970s when a flurry of federal and state civil rights legislation curtailed the previously unregulated hiring and firing power of management. These developments made the appeal to law as central as collective bargaining for extending employee rights (Heckscher 9). I mention this broader picture, first, because it relates to the forms of employer backlash that Lowery began experiencing by the early 1980s and, more important, because a history of unionism serves as a guide for a closer look at the sponsors of Lowery's literacy.

These resources begin with the influence of his father whose membership in the United Rubber Workers during the ideologically potent 1930s and 1940s grounded Lowery in class-conscious progressivism and its favorite literate form: the newspaper. On top of that, though, was a pragmatic philosophy of worker education that developed in the U.S. after the Depression as an anti-communist antidote to left-wing intellectual influences in unions. Lowery's parent union, in fact, had been a central force in refocusing worker education away from an earlier emphasis on broad critical study and toward discrete techniques for organizing and bargaining. Workers began to be trained in the discrete bodies of knowledge, written formats, and idioms associated with those strategies. Characteristic of this legacy, Lowery's crash course at the Washington-based training center in the early 1970s emphasized technical information, problem solving, and union-building skills and methods. The transformation in worker education from critical, humanistic study to problem-solving skills was also lived out at the school for workers where Lowery took short courses in the 1980s. Once a place where factory workers came to write and read about economics, sociology, and labor history, the school is now part of a university extension service offering workshops — often requested by management — on such topics as work restructuring, new technology, health and safety regulations, and joint labor-management cooperation.[7] Finally, in this inventory of Dwayne Lowery's literacy sponsors, we must add the latest incarnations shaping union practices: the attorneys and college-educated co-workers who carried into Lowery's workplace forms of legal discourse and "essayist literacy."[8]

What should we notice about this pattern of sponsorship? First, we can see from yet another angle how the course of an ordinary person's literacy learning — its occasions, materials, applications, potentials — follows the transformations going on within sponsoring institutions as those institutions fight for economic and ideological position. As a result of wins, losses, or compromises, institutions undergo change, affecting the kinds of literacy they promulgate and the status that such literacy has in the larger society. So where, how, why, and what Lowery practiced as a writer — and what he didn't practice — took shape as part of the post-industrial jockeying going on over the last thirty years by labor, government, and industry. Yet there is more to be seen in this inventory of literacy sponsors. It exposes the deeply textured history that lies within the literacy practices of institutions and within any individual's literacy experiences. Accumulated layers of sponsoring influences — in families, workplaces, schools, memory — carry forms of literacy that have been shaped out of ideological and economic struggles of the past. This history, on the one hand, is a sustaining resource in the quest for literacy. It enables an older generation to pass its literacy resources onto another. Lowery's exposure to his father's newspaper-reading and supper-table political talk kindled his adult passion for news, debate, and for language that rendered relief and justice. This history also helps to create infrastructures of opportunity. Lowery found crucial supports for extending his adult literacy in the educational networks that unions established during the first half of the twentieth century as they were consolidating into national powers. On the other hand, this layered history of sponsorship is also deeply conservative and can be maladaptive because it teaches forms of literacy that oftentimes are in the process of being overtaken by new political realities and by ascendent forms of literacy. The decision to focus worker education on practical strategies of recruiting and bargaining — devised in the thick of Cold War patriotism and galloping expansion in union memberships — became, by the Reagan years, a fertile ground for new forms of management aggression and cooptation.

It is actually this lag or gap in sponsoring forms that we call the rising standard of literacy. The pace of change and the place of literacy in economic competition have both intensified enormously in the last half of the twentieth century. It is as if the history of literacy is in fast forward. Where once the same sponsoring arrangements could maintain value across a generation or more, forms of literacy and their sponsors can now rise and recede many times within a single life span. Dwayne Lowery experienced profound changes in forms of union-based literacy not only between his father's time and his but between the time he joined the union and the time he left it, twenty-odd years later. This phenomenon is what makes today's literacy feel so advanced and, at the same time, so destabilized.

Sponsorship and Appropriation in Literacy Learning

We have seen how literacy sponsors affect literacy learning in two powerful ways. They help to organize and administer stratified systems of opportunity and access, and they raise the literacy stakes in struggles for competitive advantage. Sponsors enable and hinder literacy activity, often forcing the formation of new literacy requirements while decertifying older ones. A somewhat different dynamic of literacy sponsorship is treated here. It pertains to the potential of the sponsored to divert sponsors' resources toward ulterior projects, often projects of self-interest or self-development. Earlier I mentioned how Sunday School parishioners in England and African Americans in slavery appropriated church-sponsored literacy for economic and psychic survival. "Misappropriation" is always possible at the scene of literacy transmission, a reason for the tight ideological control that usually surrounds reading and writing instruction. The accounts that appear below are meant to shed light on the dynamics of appropriation, including the role of sponsoring agents in that process. They are also meant to suggest that diversionary tactics in literacy learning may be invited now by the sheer proliferation of literacy activity in contemporary life. The uses and networks of literacy crisscross through many domains, exposing people to multiple, often amalgamated sources of sponsoring powers, secular, religious, bureaucratic, commercial, technological. In other words, what is so destabilized about contemporary literacy today also makes it so available and potentially innovative, ripe for picking, one might say, for people suitably positioned. The rising level of schooling in the general population is also an inviting factor in this process. Almost everyone now has some sort of contact, for instance, with college-educated people, whose movements through workplaces, justice systems, social service organizations, houses of worship, local government, extended families, or circles of friends spread dominant forms of literacy (whether wanted or not, helpful or not) into public and private spheres. Another condition favorable for appropriation is the deep hybridity of literacy practices extant in many settings. As we saw in Dwayne Lowery's case, workplaces, schools, families bring together multiple strands of the history of literacy in complex and influential forms. We need models of literacy that more astutely account for these kinds of multiple contacts, both in and out of school and across a lifetime. Such models could begin to grasp the significance of re-appropriation, which, for a number of reasons, is becoming a key requirement for literacy learning at the end of the twentieth century.

The following discussion will consider two brief cases of literacy diversion. Both involve women working in subordinate positions as secretaries, in print-rich settings where better educated male supervisors were teaching them to read and write in certain ways to perform their clerical duties. However, as we will see shortly, strong loyalties outside the workplace prompted these two secretaries to lift these literate resources for use in other spheres. For one, Carol White, it was on behalf of her work as a Jehovah's Witness. For the other, Sarah Steele, it was on behalf of upward mobility for her lower middle-class family.

Before turning to their narratives, though, it will be wise to pay some attention to the economic moment in which they occur. Clerical work was the largest and fastest growing occupation for women in the twentieth century. Like so much employment for women, it offered a mix of gender-defined constraints as well as avenues for economic independence and mobility. As a new information economy created an acute need for typists, stenographers, bookkeepers, and other office workers, white, American-born women and, later, immigrant and minority women saw reason to pursue high school and business-college educations. Unlike male clerks of the nineteenth century, female secretaries in this century had little chance for advancement. However, office work represented a step up from the farm or the factory for women of the working class and served as a respectable occupation from which educated, middle-class women could await or avoid marriage (Anderson, Strom). In a study of clerical work through the first half of the twentieth century, Christine Anderson estimated that secretaries might encounter up to ninety-seven different genres in the course of doing dictation or transcription. They routinely had contact with an array of professionals, including lawyers, auditors, tax examiners, and other government overseers (52–53). By 1930, 30 percent of women office workers used machines other than typewriters (Anderson 76) and, in contemporary offices, clerical workers have often been the first employees to learn to operate CRTs and personal computers and to teach others how to use them. Overall, the daily duties of twentieth-century secretaries could serve handily as an index to the rise of complex administrative and accounting procedures, standardization of information, expanding communication, and developments in technological systems.

With that background, consider the experiences of Carol White and Sarah Steele. An Oneida, Carol White was born into a poor, single-parent household in 1940. She graduated from high school in 1960 and, between five maternity leaves and a divorce, worked continuously in a series of clerical positions in both the private and public sectors. One of her first secretarial jobs was with an urban firm that produced and disseminated Catholic missionary films. The vice-president with whom she worked most closely also spent much of his time producing a magazine for a national civic organization that he headed. She discussed how typing letters and magazine articles and occasionally proofreading for this man taught her rhetorical strategies in which she was keenly interested. She described the scene of transfer this way:

> [My boss] didn't just write to write. He wrote in a way to make his letters appealing. I would have to write what he was writing in this magazine too. I was completely enthralled. He would write about the people who were in this [organization] and the different works they were undertaking and people that died and people who were sick and about their personalities. And he wrote little anecdotes. Once in a while I made some suggestions too. He was a man who would listen to you.

The appealing and persuasive power of the anecdote became especially important to Carol White when she began doing door-to-door missionary work for the Jehovah's Witnesses, a pan-racial, millenialist religious faith. She now uses colorful anecdotes to prepare demonstrations that she performs with other women at weekly service meetings at their Kingdom Hall. These demonstrations, done in front of the congregation, take the form of skits designed to explore daily problems through Bible principles. Further, at the time of our interview, Carol White was working as a municipal revenue clerk and had recently enrolled in an on-the-job training seminar called Persuasive Communication, a two-day class offered free to public employees. Her motivation for taking the course stemmed from her desire to improve her evangelical work. She said she wanted to continue to develop speaking and writing skills that would be "appealing," "motivating," and "encouraging" to people she hoped to convert.

Sarah Steele, a woman of Welsh and German descent, was born in 1920 into a large, working-class family in a coal mining community in eastern Pennsylvania. In 1940, she graduated from a two-year commercial college. Married soon after, she worked as a secretary in a glass factory until becoming pregnant with the first of four children. In the 1960s, in part to help pay for her children's college educations, she returned to the labor force as a receptionist and bookkeeper in a law firm, where she stayed until her retirement in the late 1970s.

Sarah Steele described how, after joining the law firm, she began to model her household management on principles of budgeting that she was picking up from one of the attorneys with whom she worked most closely. "I learned cash flow from Mr. B_____," she said. "I would get all the bills and put a tape in the adding machine and he and I would sit down together to be sure there was going to be money ahead." She said that she began to replicate that process at home with household bills. "Before that," she observed, "I would just cook beans when I had to instead of meat." Sarah Steele also said she encountered the genre of the credit report during routine reading and typing on the job. She figured out what constituted a top rating, making sure her husband followed these steps in preparation for their financing a new car. She also remembered typing up documents connected to civil suits being brought against local businesses, teaching her, she said, which firms never to hire for home repairs. "It just changes the way you think," she observed about the reading and writing she did on her job. "You're not a pushover after you learn how business operates."

The dynamics of sponsorship alive in these narratives expose important elements of literacy appropriation, at least as it is practiced at the end of the twentieth century. In a pattern now familiar from the earlier sections, we see how opportunities for literacy learning — this time for diversions of resources — open up in the clash between long-standing, residual forms of sponsorship and the new: between the lingering presence of literacy's conservative history and its pressure for change. So, here, two women — one Native American and both working-class — filch contemporary literacy resources (public relations techniques and accounting practices) from more educated, higher-status men. The women are emboldened in these acts by ulterior identities beyond the workplace: Carol White with faith and Sarah Steele with family. These affiliations hark back to the first sponsoring arrangements through which American women were gradually allowed to acquire literacy and education. Duties associated with religious faith and child rearing helped literacy to become, in Gloria Main's words, "a permissible feminine activity" (579). Interestingly, these roles, deeply sanctioned within the history of women's literacy — and operating beneath the newer permissible feminine activity of clerical work — become grounds for covert, innovative appropriation even as they reinforce traditional female identities.

Just as multiple identities contribute to the ideologically hybrid character of these literacy formations, so do institutional and material conditions. Carol White's account speaks to such hybridity. The missionary film company with the civic club vice president is a residual site for two of literacy's oldest campaigns — Christian conversion and civic participation — enhanced here by twentieth-century advances in film and public relations techniques. This ideological reservoir proved a pleasing instructional site for Carol White, whose interests in literacy, throughout her life, have been primarily spiritual. So literacy appropriation draws upon, perhaps even depends upon, conservative forces in the history of literacy sponsorship that are always hovering at the scene of acts of learning. This history serves as both a sanctioning force and a reserve of ideological and material support.

At the same time, however, we see in these accounts how individual acts of appropriation can divert and subvert the course of literacy's history, how changes in individual literacy experiences relate to larger scale transformations. Carol White's redirection of personnel management techniques to the cause of the Jehovah's Witnesses is an almost ironic transformation in this regard. Once a principal sponsor in the initial spread of mass literacy, evangelism is here rejuvenated through late-literate corporate sciences of secular persuasion, fund-raising, and bureaucratic management that Carol White finds circulating in her contemporary workplaces. By the same token, through Sarah Steele, accounting practices associated with corporations are, in a sense, tracked into the house, rationalizing and standardizing even domestic practices. (Even though Sarah Steele did not own an adding machine, she penciled her budget figures onto adding-machine tape that she kept for that purpose.) Sarah Steele's act of appropriation in some sense explains how dominant forms of literacy migrate and penetrate into private spheres, including private consciousness. At the same time, though, she accomplishes a subversive diversion of literate power. Her efforts to move her family up in the middle class involved not merely contributing a second income but also, from her desk as a bookkeeper, reading her way into an understanding of middle-class economic power.

Teaching and the Dynamics of Sponsorship

It hardly seems necessary to point out to the readers of *CCC* that we haul a lot of freight for the opportunity to teach writing. Neither rich nor powerful enough to sponsor literacy on our own terms, we serve instead as conflicted brokers between literacy's buyers and sellers. At our most worthy, perhaps, we show the sellers how to beware and try to make sure these exchanges will be a little fairer, maybe, potentially, a little more mutually rewarding. This essay has offered a few working case studies that link patterns of sponsorship to processes of stratification, competition, and reappropriation. How much these dynamics can be generalized to classrooms is an ongoing empirical question.

I am sure that sponsors play even more influential roles at the scenes of literacy learning and use than this essay has explored. I have focused on some of the most tangible aspects — material supply, explicit teaching, institutional aegis. But the ideological pressure of sponsors affects many private aspects of writing processes as well as public aspects of finished texts. Where one's sponsors are multiple or even at odds, they can make writing maddening. Where they are absent, they make writing unlikely. Many of the cultural formations we associate with writing development — community practices, disciplinary traditions, technological potentials — can be appreciated as make-do responses to the economics of literacy, past and present. The history of literacy is a catalogue of obligatory relations. That this catalogue is so deeply conservative and, at the same time, so ruthlessly demanding of change is what fills contemporary literacy learning and teaching with their most paradoxical choices and outcomes.[9]

In bringing attention to economies of literacy learning I am not advocating that we prepare students more efficiently for the job markets they must enter. What I have tried to suggest is that as we assist and study individuals in pursuit of literacy, we also recognize how literacy is in pursuit of them. When this process stirs ambivalence, on their part or on ours, we need to be understanding.

Acknowledgments

This research was sponsored by the NCTE Research Foundation and the Center on English Learning and Achievement. The Center is supported by the U.S. Department of Education's Office of Educational Research and Improvement, whose views do not necessarily coincide with the author's. A version of this essay was given as a lecture in the Department of English, University of Louisville, in April 1997. Thanks to Anna Syvertsen and Julie Nelson for their help with archival research. Thanks too to colleagues who lent an ear along the way: Nelson Graff, Jonna Gjevre, Anne Gere, Kurt Spellmeyer, Tom Fox, and Bob Gundlach.

Notes

1. Three of the keenest and most eloquent observers of economic impacts on writing teaching and learning have been Lester Faigley, Susan Miller, and Kurt Spellmeyer.
2. My debt to the writings of Pierre Bourdieu will be evident throughout this essay. Here and throughout I invoke his expansive notion of "economy," which is not restricted to literal and ostensible systems of money making but to the many spheres where people labor, invest, and exploit energies — their own and others' — to maximize advantage. See Bourdieu and Wacquant, especially 117–20 and Bourdieu, Chapter 7.
3. Thomas Laqueur (124) provides a vivid account of a street demonstration in Bolton, England, in 1834 by a "pro-writing" faction of Sunday School students and their teachers. This faction demanded that writing instruction continue to be provided on Sundays, something that opponents of secular instruction on the Sabbath were trying to reverse.
4. See, for instance, National Assessments of Educational Progress in reading and writing (Applebee et al.; and "Looking").
5. All names used in this essay are pseudonyms.
6. I am not suggesting that literacy that does not "pay off" in terms of prestige or monetary reward is less valuable. Dora Lopez's ability to read and write in Spanish was a source of great strength and pride, especially when she was able to teach it to her young child. The resource of Spanish literacy carried much of what Bourdieu calls cultural capital in her social and family circles. But I want to point out here how people who labor equally to acquire literacy do so under systems of unequal subsidy and unequal reward.
7. For useful accounts of this period in union history, see Heckscher; Nelson.
8. Marcia Farr associates "essayist literacy" with written genres esteemed in the academy and noted for their explicitness, exactness, reliance on reasons and evidence, and impersonal voice.
9. Lawrence Cremin makes similar points about education in general in his essay "The Cacophony of Teaching." He suggests that complex economic and social changes since World War Two, including the popularization of

schooling and the penetration of mass media, have created "a far greater range and diversity of languages, competencies, values, personalities, and approaches to the world and to its educational opportunities" than at one time existed. The diversity most of interest to him (and me) resides not so much in the range of different ethnic groups there are in society but in the different cultural formulas by which people assemble their educational — or, I would say, literate — experience.

Works Cited

Anderson, Mary Christine. "Gender, Class, and Culture: Women Secretarial and Clerical Workers in the United States, 1925–1955." Diss. Ohio State U, 1986.

Applebee, Arthur N., Judith A. Langer, and Ida V. S. Mullis. *The Writing Report Card: Writing Achievement in American Schools.* Princeton: ETS, 1986.

Bourdieu, Pierre. *The Logic of Practice.* Trans. Richard Nice. Cambridge: Polity, 1990.

Bourdieu, Pierre, and Loic J. D. Wacquant. *An Invitation to Reflexive Sociology.* Chicago: Chicago UP, 1992.

Bourne, J. M. *Patronage and Society in Nineteenth-Century England.* London: Edward Arnold, 1986.

Brandt, Deborah. "Remembering Reading, Remembering Writing." *CCC* 45 (1994): 459–79.

———. "Accumulating Literacy: Writing and Learning to Write in the Twentieth Century." *College English* 57 (1995): 649–68.

Cornelius, Janet Duitsman. *"When I Can Read My Title Clear": Literacy, Slavery, and Religion in the Antebellum South.* Columbia: U of South Carolina, 1991.

Cremin, Lawrence. "The Cacophony of Teaching." *Popular Education and Its Discontents.* New York: Harper, 1990.

Faigley, Lester. "Veterans' Stories on the Porch." *History, Reflection and Narrative: The Professionalization of Composition, 1963–1983.* Eds. Beth Boehm, Debra Journet, and Mary Rosner. Norwood: Ablex, 1999.

Farr, Marcia. "Essayist Literacy and Other Verbal Performances." *Written Communication* 8 (1993): 4–38.

Heckscher, Charles C. *The New Unionism: Employee Involvement in the Changing Corporation.* New York: Basic, 1988.

Hortsman, Connie, and Donald V. Kurtz. *Compradrazgo in Post-Conquest Middle America.* Milwaukee: Milwaukee-UW Center for Latin America, 1978.

Kett, Joseph F. *The Pursuit of Knowledge under Difficulties: From Self-Improvement to Adult Education in America 1750–1990.* Stanford: Stanford UP, 1994.

Laqueur, Thomas. *Religion and Respectability: Sunday Schools and Working Class Culture 1780–1850.* New Haven: Yale UP, 1976.

Looking at How Well Our Students Read: The 1992 National Assessment of Educational Progress in Reading. Washington: U.S. Dept. of Education, Office of Educational Research and Improvement, Educational Resources Information Center, 1992.

Lynch, Joseph H. *Godparents and Kinship in Early Medieval Europe.* Princeton: Princeton UP, 1986.

Main, Gloria L. "An Inquiry into When and Why Women Learned to Write in Colonial New England." *Journal of Social History* 24 (1991): 579–89.

Miller, Susan. *Textual Carnivals: The Politics of Composition.* Carbondale: Southern Illinois UP, 1991.

Nelson, Daniel. *American Rubber Workers and Organized Labor, 1900–1941.* Princeton: Princeton UP, 1988.

Nicholas, Stephen J., and Jacqueline M. Nicholas. "Male Literacy, 'Deskilling,' and the Industrial Revolution." *Journal of Interdisciplinary History* 23 (1992): 1–18.

Resnick, Daniel P., and Lauren B. Resnick. "The Nature of Literacy: A Historical Explanation." *Harvard Educational Review* 47 (1977): 370–85.

Spellmeyer, Kurt. "After Theory: From Textuality to Attunement with the World." *College English* 58 (1996): 893–913.

Stevens, Jr., Edward. *Literacy, Law, and Social Order.* DeKalb: Northern Illinois UP, 1987.

Strom, Sharon Hartman. *Beyond the Typewriter: Gender, Class, and the Origins of Modern American Office Work, 1900–1930.* Urbana: U of Illinois P, 1992.

Brandt's Insights as a Resource for Your Teaching

1. Reflect on the patterns of sponsorship by which you came to reading and writing, and see if you can delineate points of contrast or overlap with those of your students.

2. How might you define your own mission in the classroom in terms of Brandt's idea of sponsorship?

Brandt's Insights as a Resource for Your Writing Classroom

1. Outline Brandt's idea of sponsorship for your students and ask them to identify the primary sponsor of their literacy. What do they make of the fact that their literacy was sponsored the way it was?

2. Ask your students to imagine how they might serve as a literacy sponsor in the future. How might they imagine this project? How will they inhabit that role? Why one way rather than another?

Annotated Bibliography

Research and reflection about writers, writing, and our practices of working with writers have proliferated over the last two decades. Ph.D. programs in rhetoric and composition theory have increased. You can find multiple resources to assist you as you teach yourself more about working with writers: Many sourcebooks and introductions to teaching writing are available; journals and NCTE (National Council of Teachers of English, <http://www.ncte.org>) anthologies offer additional theoretical and pedagogical perspectives on the range of topics addressed in this ancillary. Supplementing the works cited in the individual readings, this brief and selective bibliography offers you a starting point for broadening and deepening your thinking about writers and about ways to work with writers.

Entering the Field

Bruffee, Kenneth A. *A Short Course in Writing: Composition, Collaborative Learning, and Constructive Reading.* 4th ed. New York: Harper, 1993. This textbook with prompts for creative and transactional writing can be used in classrooms or by an individual for self-teaching. Bruffee's introduction offers a clear description of the relationships among writing, reading, teaching, and social construction as a needed direction in higher education.

Corbett, Edward P. J., Nancy Myers, and Gary Tate, eds. *The Writing Teacher's Sourcebook.* 4th ed. New York: Oxford UP, 2000. With each edition, the editing team adds new articles to a "canon" of essential discussions. These new articles extend theory and perspective or, as with readings about writers and computers, introduce the teaching strategies that had been considered on the "borders" or not central to teaching practice and have now become necessary strategies.

Ede, Lisa, ed. *On Writing Research: The Braddock Essays, 1975–1998.* Boston: Bedford/St. Martin's, 1999. This book collects nearly twenty-five years of articles that won composition's most prestigious award. It offers not only, then, the best composition scholarship of the last three decades, but a rich historical perspective on the ways the field's interests and methods have evolved.

Enos, Theresa, ed. *A Sourcebook for Basic Writing Teachers.* New York: Random House, 1987. Thirty-nine essays extend the discussion of basic writing. The collection focuses on the sociolinguistic dimensions of literacy and shows the range of contemporary research, theory, and practice, building on the foundation laid by Mina Shaughnessy in *Errors and Expectations.*

Goswami, Dixie, and Peter Stillman, ed. *Reclaiming the Classroom: Teacher Research as an Agency for Change*. Upper Montclair: Boynton-Cook, 1987. This book of essays describes reasons for and methods of conducting research in the classroom. Its scope is impressive, both in variety of research projects and methodologies and in discussions of the effects on instructors and students. The editor has pulled together important — and often original — essays by the leading teacher-scholars in composition and rhetoric.

Graves, Richard. *Rhetoric and Composition: A Sourcebook for Teachers and Writers*. 3rd ed. Portsmouth, NH: Boynton-Cook, 1990. Graves organized this sourcebook for writing teachers of all levels. The thirty-eight selections by well-known theorists and researchers document the energetic growth in the discipline of writing since 1963. Five chapters introduce the novice instructor to and update the veteran instructor about the growth and health of the scholarly discipline; practicing teachers' reports and "lore"; strategies to motivate student writers; questions about style; and "new perspectives, new horizons."

Irmscher, William F. *Teaching Expository Writing*. New York: Holt, 1979. The first text written for teachers of writing, this book poses the central questions every new teacher has. Irmscher writes from all the writer's resources: recall of his decades of teaching writing and his status as the "most senior" director of a composition program; humanistic observation of students as writers; conversation with writers and writing specialists; continuous reading in the discipline; and a lively imagination.

Lindemann, Erika. *A Rhetoric for Writing Teachers*. 3rd ed. New York: Oxford UP, 1995. Lindemann does not supplant Irmscher but enriches the reading about teaching writing. Her text reports both theory and practice.

Myers, Miles. *The Teacher-Researcher: How to Study Writing in the Classroom*. Urbana: NCTE, 1985. An introduction to classroom writing assessment and research into writing processes, this book reviews procedures for teacher research and theoretical frameworks. It shows teachers — from kindergarten through college — ways to study writing in the classroom using specific examples of research.

Pytlik, Betty, and Sarah Liggett, eds. *Preparing College Teachers of Writing: Histories, Theories, Programs, Practices*. New York: Oxford UP, 2002. This book assembles essays from nearly forty teachers from twenty-eight institutions to discuss what new teachers of writing at the college-level need to learn in order to teach well and what sorts of programs are most able to foster the intellectual and professional development of these teachers. It offers rich historical and theoretical contexts for thinking about teacher preparation, as well as insights into institutional, departmental, and programmatic structures, policies, and politics.

Roen, Duane, Veronica Pantoja, Lauren Yena, Susan K. Miller, and Eric Waggoner, eds. *Strategies for Teaching First-Year Composition*. Urbana: NCTE, 2002. An invaluable resource for thinking about the day-to-day workings of the classroom, this book offers several dozen short, practical essays on matters of immediate concern to beginning teachers. Many practical issues that are covered include constructing a syllabus or an assignment, situating the writing course in the context of the wider curriculum, and managing the classroom.

Shaughnessy, Mina P. *Errors and Expectations: A Guide for the Teacher of Basic Writing*. New York: Oxford UP, 1977. Shaughnessy was the first to demonstrate an understanding of the processes that "basic writers" experience.

This landmark study helps clarify the philosophy of teaching basic writers and design curriculum and classroom practice to assist these writers to develop into mature writers.

Villanueva, Victor, ed. *Cross Talk in Comp Theory: A Reader.* Urbana: NCTE, 1997. This massive collection of articles represents an overview of the last thirty years of composition theory, a veritable "who's who" of the emerging discipline and offers a kind of chronology of the field's major interests, as the editor puts it, from "process to cohesion to cognition to social construction to ideology." The book contains forty-one essays, including the major, historical statements by Janet Emig, James Berlin, Mike Rose, Mina Shaughnessy, and others.

Wiener, Harvey S. *The Writing Room: A Resource Book for Teachers of English.* New York: Oxford UP, 1981. Like Irmscher and Lindemann, Wiener offers advice about teaching writing from day one. His focus is the basic writing classroom and his discussion is informed — like Shaughnessy's — by his classroom experiences in an open-door writing program.

Teaching Writing: Key Concepts and Philosophies for Reflective Practice

Berthoff, Ann E. *Reclaiming the Imagination: Philosophical Perspectives for Writers and Teachers of Writing.* Upper Montclair: Boynton-Cook, 1984. Berthoff's theme of "reclaiming the imagination" reflects her philosophy and practice of encouraging writing as dialectical and reflective action.

Blitz, Michael, and C. Mark Hulbert. *Letters for the Living: Teaching Writing in a Violent Age.* Urbana: NCTE, 1998. By examining closely their students' accounts of life in New York City and in the mining and steel towns of western Pennsylvania, the authors argue that not only is violence a defining feature of many students' experience but that composition can be understood and even taught as an activity of peacemaking. The students in Blitz and Hulbert's classes wrote letters to each other about the diverse circumstances of their lives, and Blitz and Hulbert include this correspondence in the book and accompany it with their own e-mail correspondence to raise difficult questions about the stakes of our mission as teachers of writing.

Bruffee, Kenneth A. "Social Construction, Language, and the Authority of Knowledge: A Bibliographical Essay." *College English* 48 (Dec. 1986): 773–90. This introduction to social constructivist thought in literary criticism and history with its connections to composition studies lays out a foundation of a "social-epistemic" approach to teaching writing. Bruffee provides a bibliography to help other writing teachers explore these philosophical underpinnings.

Emig, Janet. "Writing as a Mode of Learning." *College Composition and Communication* 28.2 (May 1977): 122–27. Emig asserts a "first principle" that informs both contemporary practice in composition classrooms and writing-across-the-curriculum initiatives and programs.

Freire, Paulo. *Pedagogy of the Oppressed.* Trans. Myra Bergman Ramos. New York: Continuum, 2000. Among the most important books written about education in the twentieth century, this book sketches Freire's fundamental insights into the ways classrooms are configured either to alienate students and prepare them for lives of servitude in oppressive regimes or to liberate them through an ongoing practice of critical reflection, dialogue, collaboration, and what he calls "problem-posing." The pedagogy that Freire favors moves beyond the binary opposition of teacher versus student and encourages a more egalitarian dynamic in which everyone plays both roles.

Harris, Joseph. *A Teaching Subject: Composition Since 1966.* Upper Saddle River, NJ: Prentice Hall, 1997. This book is comprised of five elegant essays, each devoted to sorting out the recent history and the different meanings of a key term in the field of composition. The discussions of "Growth," "Voice," "Process," "Error," and "Community" offer one of the best introductions to the key debates within composition theory.

Hillocks, George, Jr. "What Works in Teaching Composition: A Meta-Analysis of Experimental Treatment Studies." *American Journal of Education* 93 (Nov. 1984): 133–70. Hillocks reviews experimental treatment studies of the teaching of composition over twenty years. While assessing effectiveness of different modes and focuses of instruction, he found that a writing-as-process focus within an "environmental mode" was more effective than other approaches to composition. His discussion of the implications of the research is especially useful.

Myers, Miles, and James Gray. *Theory and Practice in the Teaching of Composition.* Urbana: NCTE, 1983. The text has a double audience: It shows teachers how their strategies for teaching writing connect to and reflect an area of research, and it shows researchers that what teachers do intuitively can often be validated by research. The organization of readings by the teaching methods of processing, distancing, and modeling is especially useful.

North, Stephen. *The Making of Knowledge in Composition: Portrait of an Emerging Field.* Upper Montclair: Boynton-Cook, 1987. North discusses the place of "practitioner's lore" and the development of new research methodologies to study questions generated by reflection on the writing experiences of diverse students.

Raymond, James C. "What Good Is All This Heady, Esoteric Theory?" *Teaching English in the Two-Year College* (Feb. 1990): 11–15. Raymond answers this question (often posed by writing teachers who are busy with the daily tasks of working with writers). He "translates" poststructural theory into practical applications.

Smith, Frank. "Myths of Writing." *Language Arts* 58.7 (Oct. 1981): 792–98. Smith describes and clarifies twenty-one misconceptions that students, faculty, and the public hold about what writing is, how it is learned, and who can teach it.

Tate, Gary, Amy Rupiper, and Kurt Schick, eds. *A Guide to Composition Pedagogies.* New York: Oxford UP, 2001. This book surveys today's major approaches to the teaching of writing. Each chapter is devoted to a different approach and is written by a leading figure in the field. For example, Susan Jarratt discusses feminist approaches to teaching writing, and William Covino discusses rhetorical approaches. Other contributors include Chris Burnham on expressivism, Laura Julier on community-oriented pedagogy, and Susan McLeod on writing across the curriculum.

Thinking about the Writing Process

Generating a Draft

Fulwiler, Toby. *The Journal Book.* Portsmouth, NH: Boynton-Cook, 1987. Forty-two essays discuss the use of journals for discovery and invention in writing classrooms and in other disciplines across the curriculum.

Hilbert, Betsy S. "It Was a Dark and Nasty Night It Was a Dark and You Would Not Believe How Dark It Was a Hard Beginning." *College Composition and Communication* 43.1 (Feb. 1992): 75–80. Hilbert writes from lengthy experience as a writing instructor about beginning a new semester with new writers and predictable difficulties. The essay is tonic and a healthy reminder to us about staying focused on why we teach writing as we enter or return to the classroom.

Johnson, T. R. "School Sucks." *College Composition and Communication* 52.4 (June 2001): 620–50. This essay explores the sources, incarnations, and resistances to pedagogies that emphasize writing as a process. Occasioned by the recent epidemic of school shootings and the author's memory of violent schoolyard rhymes, the essay ranges from rhetoric's historical discussion of the pleasures of writing to composition's more recent interest in academic professionalism to Gilles Deleuze's theory of masochism to the problem of teaching and learning in a consumer culture.

Perl, Sondra. *Landmark Essays on Writing Process.* Davis, CA: Hermagoras, 1994. This volume collects more than a dozen essays as well as a bibliography for further study on the central, even founding insight of contemporary composition — that is, the idea that composing is a process. The book features work by the leading figures in the field, work that articulated, substantiated, and disseminated the crucial new pedagogy that began to capture the attention of many writing teachers in the 1970s and that continues to focus our field in primary, pervasive ways.

Rose, Mike, ed. *When a Writer Can't Write: Studies in Writer's Block and Other Composing-Process Problems.* New York: Guilford, 1985. Eleven essays identify and analyze cognitive and affective dimensions of writing apprehension. The range of discussion emphasizes the effects of the environment and writing situations on the writer: Novice writers, ESL writers, graduate students, and professional writers are all affected by writing apprehension at various times.

———. *Writer's Block: The Cognitive Dimension.* Carbondale: Southern Illinois UP, 1984. This landmark book researching and analyzing writer's block emphasizes that a variety of cognitive difficulties are behind the problem. Case studies and the report of research results offer useful insights about ways to teach writing that will enable writers to get beyond blocks.

Young, Richard, and Yameng Liu, eds. *Landmark Essays on Rhetorical Invention in Writing.* Davis, CA: Hermagoras, 1994. This book offers nineteen classic essays from figures including Wayne Booth, Kenneth Burke, Janet Emig, and Chaim Perelman.

Revising a Draft and Crafting Sentences

Faigley, Lester. "Names in Search of a Concept: Maturity, Fluency, Complexity, and Growth in Written Syntax." *CCC* 31 (Oct. 1980): 291–300. In this article, Faigley argues that sentence combining does not directly correlate with mature and fluent writing style. The relationship between writing fluency and syntactical maturity is more complex than previous research acknowledges.

Flower, Linda, John R. Hayes, Linda Carey, Karen Schriver, and James Stratman. "Detection, Diagnosis, and the Strategies of Revision." *College Composition and Communication* 37 (Feb. 1986): 16–55. This article, produced through collaborative research and writing, describes some of the important intellectual activities that underlie and affect the process of revision. The article presents a working model for revision, for identifying "problems," and for generating solutions.

Harris, Muriel. "Composing Behaviors of One- and Multi-Draft Writers." *College English* 51 (Feb. 1989): 174–91. This study of eight experienced writers who described themselves as one-draft or multidraft writers provides useful materials for individualizing the processes of rewriting for students.

Mlynarczyk, Rebecca Williams. "Finding Grandma's Words: A Case Study in the Art of Revising." *Journal of Basic Writing* 15 (Summer 1996): 3–22. This essay explores how one basic writer's habit of revising for surface features only changed once her teacher's comments shifted from an emphasis on "fixing" the paper to discussing the essay empathetically with the student.

Sommers, Nancy. "Between the Drafts." *College Composition and Communication* 43 (Nov. 1992): 23–31. Nancy Sommers models the use of personal narrative as another kind of "evidence" to support or argue points in academic writing. She suggests that we should encourage and help students to use personal narrative in academic writing when they can. Use of personal narrative along with the traditional sources is a recurring theme in discussions of assisting writers as they rethink purpose, readership, and identity during the process of revising and re-visioning text.

Sudol, Ronald A., ed. *Revising: New Essays for Teachers of Writing.* Urbana: NCTE, 1982. Useful essays describing both the practice and the theory of revising strategies and processes.

Teaching Critical Reading and Writing

Bartholomae, David, and Anthony Petrosky. *Facts, Artifacts, and Counterfacts: Theory and Method for a Reading and Writing Course.* Upper Montclair: Boynton-Cook, 1986. A thorough plan for teaching writing as wholly intertwined with the act of reading critically. This book sets forth a course that is perhaps the complete opposite of the current traditional emphasis on dry exercises as well as the romantic interest in unfettered self-expression. Instead, it locates writing in a rhetorical context comprised of the writing of others. The book is surely one of the most important contributions to the field of composition in the 1980s, and it is yet unsurpassed as a detailed model of how the most recent, major developments in composition theory can be articulated on a day-to-day basis in the classroom.

Berthoff, Ann. "Is Teaching Still Possible? Writing, Meaning, and Higher-Order Reasoning." *College English* 46.6 (Dec. 1984): 743–55. Berthoff surveys and evaluates models of cognitive development and their connections to positivist perspectives on language. She discusses alternative perspectives on language and learning that emphasize reading and writing as interpretation and as the making of meaning.

Elbow, Peter. "Teaching Thinking by Teaching Writing." *Change* 15.6 (Sept. 1983): 37–40. Elbow's argument that "first-order creative, intuitive thinking and second-order critical thinking" can and should be encouraged in writing instruction, could be used for writing-across-the-curriculum initiatives.

Flower, Linda, and John R. Hayes. "The Cognition of Discovery: Defining a Rhetorical Problem." *College Composition and Communication* 31.1 (Feb. 1980): 21–32. The researchers used protocol analysis to study the differences between writers engaged in problem-solving cognitive processes.

Karbach, Joan. "Using Toulmin's Model of Argumentation." *Journal of Teaching Writing* 6.1 (Spring 1987): 81–91. This article illustrates the use of Toulmin's three-part model of argumentation: data, warrant, and claim. While describing heuristic procedures, Karbach proposes this informal logic as a strategy for teaching inductive and deductive logic within any writing assignment.

Kneupper, Charles. "Argument: A Social Constructivist Perspective." *Journal of the American Forensic Association* 17.4 (Spring 1981): 183–89. A communication specialist analyzes argumentation theory from the perspective of social constructionism. He examines uses and connections between argument as structure and argument as process along with their social-epistemic implications.

Lunsford, Andrea. "Cognitive Development and the Basic Writer." *College English* 41 (Sept. 1979): 39–46. After reviewing theories of cognitive development, Lunsford demonstrates that many basic writers operate below the stage of forming concepts and have difficulty in "decentering." She recommends strategies and writing assignments to help basic writers practice and acquire more complex cognitive skills.

Shor, Ira. *Critical Teaching and Everyday Life.* Chicago: U Chicago P, 1987. Influenced by Paulo Freire's pedagogical theories, Shor emphasizes learning through dialogue. His analysis of education is inclusive: open admissions teaching of writing, traditional and nontraditional students and learning environments, elite and nonelite educational missions, and "liberatory" teaching modes that challenge social limits of thought and action and encourage cultural literacy. Cognitive skills are acquired and enhanced through collaborative problem solving and reflection leading to action.

Wink, Joan. *Critical Pedagogy: Notes from the Real World.* 2nd ed. New York: Longman, 2000. This analyzes the often-difficult rhetoric of critical pedagogy to push to new, deeper perspectives on the dynamics of the classroom and the community. The book is rooted in powerful, personal narratives and written in a lively, even informal voice. It brings otherwise abstract ideas to life and constantly tests those ideas against the author's own experience of many years in the classroom.

Teaching Writing with Computers and Teaching Visual Literacy

Blair, Kristine, and Pamela Takayoshi, eds. *Feminist Cyberscapes: Mapping Gendered Academic Spaces.* Stamford, CT: Ablex, 1999. This collection of essays explores varying contexts (virtual and physical, institutional and cultural) that shape electronic space for women. Although issues of gender and cyberspace have most often been relegated to the margins, the editors of this collection hope to bring into the mainstream of composition studies a rich array of concerns about the relationship between women and technology as a way of understanding women's participation in and resistance to systems of inequality. The contributors to the collection rely on materialist feminism, feminist critiques of technology design and its uses, and feminist pedagogy to examine computerized classrooms, Internet technologies (including e-mail, listservs, and MOOs), and professional development opportunities for women working in computers and composition.

Bolter, Jay David. *Writing Space: The Computer, Hypertext, and the History of Writing.* Hillsdale, NJ: Lawrence Erlbaum, 1991. This book offers a useful contextualization of computer-based writing in the larger history of writing itself, emphasizing the ways computers are at once rooted in familiar technologies and, at the same time, are able to destablize the power-relations and hierarchies that those old technologies support. Bolter provides a useful set of "first principles" for re-imagining rhetoric in the age of the electronic text.

Bruce, Bertram, Joy Kreeft Peyton, and Trent Batson, eds. *Network-Based Classrooms: Promises and Realities.* New York: Cambridge UP, 1993. The collaborative technology of "electronic networks for interaction" accommodates and prompts the social construction of knowledge. The collection ranges from descriptions of "how to" to "effects." Caveat: The rapid development and redesign of the technology and the advent of the World Wide Web may make the nuts and bolts obsolete, so focus on themes, issues, and significance to writing improvement.

Hassett, Michael, and Rachel W. Lott. "Seeing Student Texts." *Composition Studies* 28.1 (2000): 29–47. This article argues for increased attention to document design in composition courses. Centering their discussion on four types of design — intra-textual (fonts), inter-textual (headings), extra-textual (tables and charts), and supra-textual (table of contents) — Hassett and Lott offer a pedagogy that focuses students' attention on audience needs.

Hawisher, Gail E., and Charles Moran. "Electronic Mail and the Writing Instructor." *College English* 55.6 (Oct. 1993): 627–43. The writers describe advantages and effects of introducing electronic communication to a composition course. The essay gives practical advice to newcomers.

Hawisher, Gail E., and Cynthia L. Selfe, eds. *Passions, Pedagogies, and 21st Century Technologies.* Logan: Utah State UP; Urbana: NCTE, 1999. This anthology collects twenty-three essays from leaders in the field of computers and composition, including Charles Moran, Anne Frances Wysocki, Patricia Sullivan, and Lester Faigley. The selections in this collection cover such wide-ranging topics as technology and literacy, pedagogical matters, ethical and feminist concerns, and visual rhetoric.

Lanham, Richard. *The Electronic Word: Democracy, Technology, and the Arts.* Chicago: U of Chicago P, 1993. In a reader-based study, rhetorician Lanham analyzes the creative potential of electronic writing for coming closer to these long-standing goals: access, unfettered imagination, and effective communication. He views the electronic word as dramatically and healthily changing the construction and experience of "knowledge."

Responding to and Evaluating Student Writing

Anson, Chris, ed. *Writing and Response: Theory, Practice, and Research.* Urbana: NCTE, 1989. The essays include discussion of responding to student journal writing, responding via electronic media, and responding in conferences. Theoretical perspectives and instructional practice are intermixed.

Belanoff, Patricia, and Marcia Dickson, eds. *Portfolios: Process and Product.* Portsmouth, NH: Boynton-Cook, 1991. In the first comprehensive collection of writings on using portfolios for classroom and portfolio assessment, the editors called for "practitioners' lore" and research. This is the book to start with when considering use of writing portfolios.

Berthoff, Ann. *Forming, Thinking, Writing: The Composing Imagination.* 2nd ed. Portsmouth, NH: Boynton-Cook, 1988. Berthoff focuses on the reading-writing relationship within a course organized around the central task of teaching composition. Insights and practical suggestions abound.

Black, Laurel, Donald Daiker, Jeffrey Sommers, and Gail Stygall, eds. *New Directions in Portfolio Assessment: Reflective Practice, Critical Theory, and Large-Scale Scoring.* Portsmouth, NH: Boynton-Cook, 1994. This collection moves readers beyond the merely introductory discussion of portfolios to critical questions of practice and theory: How do changing notions of literacy intersect with the growing interest in portfolios? How can we apply the portfolio approach to large-scale projects of assessment, involving not simply individual classrooms, but whole programs and schools? How do gender and cultural expectations affect readers of portfolios? This collection addresses these and other challenging questions for the reader already versed in the basics of portfolio assessment.

Brooke, Robert E. *Writing and Sense of Self: Identity Negotiation in Writing Workshops.* Urbana: NCTE, 1991. Brooke describes the effects of responding in the context of writing through workshops: effects on the kinds of writing projects students risked and effects on their processes of negotiating identities as writers.

Cooper, Charles R., and Lee Odell, eds. *Evaluating Writing: Describing, Measuring, Judging.* Urbana: NCTE, 1977. With its comprehensive survey of ways teachers can describe writing and measure the growth of writing, this remains a useful sourcebook. The discussion of involving students in the evaluation of writing includes individual goal setting, self-evaluation, and peer evaluation. Multiple responses to multiple processes and features of the writing are implicitly recommended.

Flower, Linda, and Thomas Hucking. "Reading for Points and Purposes." *Journal of Advanced Composition* 11.2 (Fall 1991): 347–62. By researching how undergraduate and graduate students use point-driven or purpose-driven reading strategies, the authors conclude that readers who use a point-driven strategy tend to stay at a less complex level of interpretation.

Freire, Paulo. *Education for Critical Consciousness.* New York: Continuum, 2002. Freire's argument for educational reform focuses on the need for the development of "critical consciousness" in learners, who thus become the agents rather than the subjects of their education. Freire's focus is congenial with social-epistemic rhetoric and emphasizes the social construction of knowledge through collaborative work.

Hamp-Lyons, Liz, ed. *Assessing Second Language Writing in Academic Contexts.* Norwood, NJ: Ablex, 1991. Twenty-one essays examine the multiple issues of assessing second language writing. Many of the articles focus on assessment design and decision making that affect ESL writers in an assessment program, but the principles of good assessment practices for diverse populations are clearly defined.

Hillocks, George, Jr. "The Interaction of Instruction, Teacher Comment, and Revision in Teaching the Composing Process." *Research in the Teaching of English* 16 (Oct. 1982): 261–82. An early study of the effects of instructor response on student revision and attitudes toward writing. The article points out that helpful commentary or conference discussion promotes a writer's growth.

Huot, Brian, and Michael Williamson, eds. *Validating Holistic Scoring for Writing Assessment: Theoretical and Empirical Foundations.* Cresskill, NJ: Hampton, 1993. While research into composing processes and the cultural contexts that shape them have boomed in recent decades, inquiry into how we assess student writing has proceeded at the same pace. This collection takes up the issue of assessment from diverse angles: the history of holistic scoring, the question of reliability, placement exams, and ESL programs. An important, thorough, expansive set of essays on a much neglected composition issue with which every teacher must grapple.

Newkirk, Thomas, ed. *Only Connect: Uniting Reading and Writing.* Upper Montclair: Boynton-Cook, 1986. The fifteen articles in this collection by major scholars in the discipline of "English" explore the relationships of reading and literary study to composition.

Noguchi, Rei R. *Grammar and the Teaching of Writing: Limits and Possibilities.* Urbana: NCTE, 1991. Beginning with the shared conviction that grammar must be taught within the context and processes of drafting and revising, Noguchi helps writing teachers identify the sites where grammar and writing overlap and suggests productive ways to integrate grammar instruction with issues of meaning, organization, and style.

Odell, Lee. "Defining and Assessing Competence in Writing." *The Nature and Measurement of Competency in English.* Ed. Charles R. Cooper. Urbana: NCTE, 1981. Practical advice about clarifying what an instructor defines as writing competence along with descriptions of holistic and other assessment measures for both classroom and large-scale assessment.

Roseberry, Ann S., Linda Flower, Beth Warren, Betsy Bowen, Bertram Bruce, Margaret Kantz, and Ann M. Penrose. "The Problem-Solving Processes of Writers and Readers." *Collaboration through Writing and Reading: Exploring Possibilities.* Ed. Anne Haas Dyson. Urbana: NCTE, 1989. 136–64.

Welch, Nancy. "One Student's Many Voices: Reading, Writing, and Responding with Bakhtin." *Journal of Advanced Composition* 13.2 (Fall 1993): 493–502. Welch demonstrates a "Bakhtinian" reading of a student text to argue that teachers should respond to the many voices in a student text.

White, Edward M. *Assigning, Responding, Evaluating: A Writing Teacher's Guide.* 3rd ed. New York: Bedford/St. Martin's, 1998. For the "state of the art" in writing assessment, White surveys and evaluates the designs and applications of writing assessments and helps writing instructors use the information garnered through assessment to improve classroom instruction.

——. *Teaching and Assessing Writing.* San Francisco: Jossey-Bass, 1985. The publisher here is significant: In this first major discussion of the symbiosis of writing assessment and classroom teaching, the preeminent publisher of discourse in higher education agreed that this would be an important test. This should be the first book a new writing teacher uses to learn about contemporary research and practice in understanding, evaluating, and improving students' writing performance.

Yancey, Kathleen Blake, ed. *Portfolios in the Writing Classroom: An Introduction.* Urbana: NCTE, 1992. This collection focuses on the use of writing portfolios in secondary and higher education courses across the curriculum. The articles describe objectives and designs for the use of portfolios. This is a very useful introduction to the field.

Issues in Writing Pedagogy

Fostering Literacy

Brandt, Deborah. *Literacy as Involvement: The Acts of Writers, Readers, and Texts.* Carbondale: Southern Illinois UP, 1990. This book explores the ways literacy is commonly understood and criticizes, in particular, the dominant theory that becoming literate hinges on a withdrawal from the immediate social world. Brandt suggests that the move from oral to literate modes of action does not significantly reconfigure the fundamental terms of the interpretive dynamic — context, reference, and meaning.

Cushman, Ellen, Eugene R. Kintgen, Barry M. Kroll, and Mike Rose, eds. *Literacy: A Critical Sourcebook.* Boston: Bedford/St. Martin's, 2001. A useful overview of the contemporary discussion about literacy, this substantial volume of nearly forty lengthy essays considers the topic of literacy in terms of technology and knowledge, cultural history and community involvement, and politics and the workforce.

Dyson, Anne Haas, ed. *Collaboration through Writing and Reading: Exploring Possibilities.* Urbana: NCTE, 1989. The discussion of the interrelationships of reading, writing, and learning was first generated at a conference of researchers and theorists concerned with literacy teaching and training.

Heath, Shirley Brice. "An Annotated Bibliography on Multicultural Writing and Literacy Issues." *Quarterly of the National Writing Project and the Center for the Study of Writing and Literacy* 12.1 (Winter 1990): 22–24. This bibliography lists and annotates sixteen books and articles that focus on multicultural writing and literacy issues, including bilingual education, ESL, writing instruction, literacy, and multicultural education.

Many, Joyce. *Handbook of Instructional Practices for Literacy Teacher-Educators.* Mahweh, NJ: Lawrence Erlbaum, 2001. This book offers accounts by well-known literacy researchers of how they approach literacy instruction and what they have learned from their actual classroom experiences. Divided into specific areas within literary studies, this book offers a strong starting point for those interested in questions of literacy.

Fostering Diversity

Delpit, Lisa. *Other People's Children: Cultural Conflict in the Writing Classroom.* New York: New, 1995. This book develops a powerful, if counterintuitive argument: Much so-called "liberatory" pedagogy actually silences and marginalizes the very minority students it seeks to help. These nine essays explore the particular ways in which the expectations, hopes, and desires that minority students bring to the classroom can diametrically oppose the good intentions of their teachers.

Eichorn, Jill, Sara Farris, Karen Hayes, Adriana Hernandez, Susan C. Jarratt, Karen Powers-Stubbs, and Marian M. Schiachitano. "A Symposium on Feminist Experiences in the Composition Classroom." *College Composition and Communication* 43 (Oct. 1992): 297–332. In describing their experiences using feminist composition pedagogies, the writers illustrate ways of respecting diversity within a writing community.

Flynn, Elizabeth A. "Feminist Theories/Feminist Composition." *College English* 57.2 (Feb. 1995): 201–12. Flynn reviews four book-length studies in "feminist composition," connecting them to theoretical perspectives and demonstrating the vigorous dialogue from many directions that feminist pedagogues and theorists have engendered.

Herrington, Anne. "Basic Writing: Moving the Voices on the Margin to the Center." *Harvard Educational Review* 60.4 (Nov. 1990): 489–96. Herrington describes the redesign of a basic writing course to give voice to marginalized minority students. After a shift to reading works by mostly nonwhite authors, students were encouraged to reflect in writing on those readings and on their experiences of marginalization.

Rose, Mike. *Lives on the Boundary: The Struggles and Achievements of America's Underprepared*. New York: Free, 1989. Through personal narrative and incisive analysis, Rose describes the underclass of students representing diverse cultures and subcultures who are considered underachieving, remedial, or illiterate. Rose speculates about the nature of literacy and learning curricula that could empower these marginalized writers and learners.

Teaching ESL Students

Carson, Joan G., and Gayle L. Nelson. "Writing Groups: Cross-Cultural Issues." *Journal of Second Language Writing* 3.1 (1994): 17–30. Citing the dearth of research on communication assumptions and behaviors of Asian students in collaborative writing communities, Carson and Nelson call for additional studies of ways in which culturally specific beliefs and behaviors might affect cooperation and interaction in peer response groups and collaborative writing projects.

Connor, Ulla. *Contrastive Rhetoric: Cross Cultural Aspects of Second Language Acquisition*. New York: Cambridge UP, 1996. This excellent survey of the major theories and empirical studies of second-language acquisition pays particular attention to the way a student's first language interferes with the process of learning a second language. A powerful blend of work from a variety of fields, the book combines discourse theory, genre theory, applied and theoretical linguistics, as well as composition studies and rhetoric.

Kasper, Loretta, ed. *Content-Based College ESL Instruction*. Mahweh, NJ: Lawrence Erlbaum, 2000. This book is designed to train teachers in a particular approach to ESL students: pedagogy rooted in actual cultural contents. It offers clear descriptions of classroom practices, as well as for assessing student progress, and even delineates means for incorporating technology.

Leki, Ilona. *Understanding ESL Writers: A Guide for Teachers*. Portsmouth, NH: Boynton-Cook, 1992. This is an excellent handbook for learning about the concerns, expectations, and errors of ESL students. Written for the double audience of ESL instructors and writing teachers, it provides useful advice about responding to the texts of ESL writers.

Reid, Joy, and Barbara Kroll. "Designing and Assessing Effective Writing Assignments for NES and ESL Students." *Journal of Second Language Writing* 3.1 (1995): 17–41. Reid and Kroll emphasize the need to design fair writing assignments that encourage students to learn from writing experiences as they demonstrate what course material they know and understand. They analyze successful and flawed writing prompts and assignments from the perspective of ESL writers; the practical advice they offer is also pertinent to mainstream composition teaching.

Writing across the Curriculum

Anson, Chris, John Schwiebert, and Michael M. Williamson. *Writing across the Curriculum: An Annotated Bibliography*. Westport, CT: Greenwood, 1993. This very useful bibliography describes both scholarship in and pedagogic strategies for extending and using writing across the curriculum, whether the model is "writing as learning" or "writing in the discipline."

Bazerman, Charles, and David Russell, eds. *Landmark Essays on Writing across the Curriculum*. Davis, CA: Hermagoras, 1994. These thirteen essays represent key texts in the development of the writing-across-the-curriculum movement and offer a valuable historical and theoretical synopsis of the field. Included are classic works by Janet Emig, Greg Myers, Susan McLeod, and Toby Fulwiler.

Duke, Charles, and Rebecca Sanchez, eds. *Assessing Writing across the Curriculum.* Durham: Carolina Academic P, 2001. This book offers guidelines for effective assessment of student writing and tools to improve writing in diverse content areas. It also offers ways to rethink particular methods of instructing and grading and ways to craft assignments more effectively.

Fulwiler, Toby, and Art Young, eds. *Language Connections: Writing and Reading across the Curriculum.* Urbana: NCTE, 1982. This text, aimed at all college and university instructors, offers theoretical perspectives and practical activities to prompt writing as learning. The text encourages peer evaluation, conferences between instructors and students, and shared evaluation and includes a bibliography on cross-curricular language and learning.

About the Contributors

Chris M. Anson is a professor of English and director of the writing program at North Carolina State University. He has published twelve books and over sixty journal articles and book chapters and is on the editorial or readers' boards of ten journals, including *Writing Program Administration, College Composition and Communication, College English, Written Communication, Assessing Writing,* and *The Journal of Writing Assessment.* His most recent book, *The WAC Casebook: Scenes for Faculty Reflection and Program Development,* is an edited collection of scenarios for faculty development in writing across the curriculum. He is currently writing a book on the social construction of error.

Arnetha Ball is an associate professor in the School of Education at Stanford University. She has recently published essays in collections on Lev Vygotsky and writing assessment, as well as in *Journal of Narrative Inquiry.* She and Ted Lardner won the Braddock Award in 1998 for "Dispositions toward Language: Teacher Constructs of Knowledge and the Ann Arbor Black English Case." Ball continues to develop sociocultural and linguistic theory concerning the literacy patterns of marginalized English speakers, particularly in urban schools in the United States.

David Bartholomae chaired the Department of English at the University of Pittsburgh for several years. He has coauthored three books on writing, including *Ways of Reading: An Anthology for Writers* and *Facts, Artifacts, and Counterfacts,* the highly influential text on teaching developmental writing. He is also coeditor of the Pittsburgh Series on Composition, Literacy, and Culture and a former chair of the Conference on College Composition and Communication.

James A. Berlin's *Rhetoric and Reality: Writing Instruction in American Colleges, 1900–1985,* began to exert enormous influence on the field of composition studies immediately after it was published in 1987. *Rhetoric and Reality* was not only the first detailed and powerful study of how the field developed, but it also provided crucial support for what was then an exciting new turn in composition studies — the emergence of rhetorics informed by social-constructionist theory. In his teaching career, Berlin held positions such as director of freshman English at the University of Cincinnati and professor of English at Purdue University. A leading figure in the cultural studies movement in composition, Berlin was writing *Rhetorics, Poetics, and Cultures: Re-Figuring English Studies* when he died quite suddenly at what should have been the midpoint in a long career.

Ann E. Berthoff was among the first scholars to bring rigorous and wide-ranging philosophic depth to our thinking about writing instruction. The two books most compositionists associate with her are *Reclaiming the Imagination: Philosophical Perspectives for Writers and Teachers of Writing* and *The Making of Meaning: Metaphors, Models, and Maxims for Writing Teachers.* She taught at the University of Massachusetts, Boston.

Wayne C. Booth is a professor emeritus at the University of Chicago. His most well-known books include *A Rhetoric of Fiction* and *The Company We Keep: An Ethics of Fiction.* He is himself the subject of an increasing number of scholarly books, essays, and graduate seminars, for the depth and range of his work in rhetoric in the latter half of the twentieth century may ultimately draw comparison to that giant of the first half of the century, Kenneth Burke.

Deborah Brandt is a professor of English at the University of Wisconsin–Madison. Her most recent book is *Literacy in American Lives.* Her other works include *Literacy as Involvement* and scholarly articles in *College English, College Composition and Communication, Written Communication,* and *Harvard Educational Review.*

Francis Christensen was a professor of English at the University of Southern California. He began to publish essays about sentence-level pedagogy in the early 1960s, all of which are collected in *Notes Toward a New Rhetoric.* These essays have been widely discussed since his death in 1970, and, in 1978, Lester Faigley tested Christensen's ideas in formal, empirical studies. Faigley found that Christensen's program indeed produced student writing that was measurably more mature and received better ratings in blind, holistic scoring.

Juanita Rodgers Comfort is an assistant professor of English at West Chester University. Her work has appeared in *The WPA Journal, College Composition and Communication,* and in a number of collections, including *The Relevance of English: Teaching that Matters in Students' Lives, Beyond English, Inc.,* and *Contrastive Rhetoric Revisited and Redefined.*

Robert J. Connors was perhaps the most rigorous historian the field of rhetoric and composition has ever had. He won the Braddock Award in 1982 for his study of the rise and fall of the modes of discourse. He is also the author of *Composition-Rhetoric: Backgrounds, Theory, Pedagogy,* as well as numerous other works. From 1984 through 2000, he taught at the University of New Hampshire, where he served as a professor of English and director of the writing center. At the time of his death in a motorcycle accident in 2000, he was working on a book on the history of process-pedagogy.

Peter Elbow has been a central figure in the field of composition for more than three decades. His numerous books and articles most often focus on the phenomenology of invention, authorial voice, and teaching. His early books in the 1970s, *Writing Without Teachers* and *Writing with Power,* are landmarks of that period; his debates with David Bartholomae in the early to mid-1990s are arguably the focal point of the field in that phase of its development. Elbow is currently a professor emeritus at the University of Massachusetts, Amherst, though he has also taught at Massachusetts Institute of Technology, Evergreen College, and Stony Brook University of the State University of New York.

Paulo Freire, among the most influential educational theorists of the twentieth century, served as secretary of education for Sao Paulo, Brazil, and as educational advisor for the World Congress of Churches in Switzerland. He also taught at Harvard University as well as at universities in Chile and Brazil. His experiences in teaching literacy to underprivileged Brazilians helped shape his philosophy of liberatory education — a pedagogy that aims to empower students with the critical literacy needed to assess and transform the conditions in which they live. His most well-known book, *Pedagogy of the Oppressed,* is not only cited widely in the field of composition, but has also become a classic in all fields of education.

Diana George is a professor of English at Michigan Technological University. She is the author of *Kitchen Cooks, Plate Twirlers, and Troubadours: Writing Program Administrators Tell Their Stories.* Her scholarly articles on poverty, literacy, cultural studies, and communication studies have appeared in distinguished collections of essays and in many leading journals in composition studies.

Jeffrey T. Grabill is an associate professor in the Department of Writing, Rhetoric, and American Cultures at Michigan State University. In describing his research, Grabill says that he works "at the intersection of professional and technical writing, rhetorical theory, and literacy theory." His book *Community Literacy Programs and the Politics of Change* was published in 2001.

Joseph Harris is an associate professor of English and director of the Center for Teaching, Learning, and Writing at Duke University. He served as editor of *College Composition and Communication* from 1994 to 1999, and has authored three books: *A Teaching Subject: Composition since 1966; Rewriting: How to Do Things with Texts;* and *Media Journal: Reading and Writing about Popular Culture.*

Muriel Harris is a professor of English and director of the writing center at Purdue University. She has published several books and articles about writing and has edited the *Writing Lab Newsletter* since 1976, when she first established it. In 2000, she won the NCTE Exemplar Award. She has published numerous scholarly essays and book chapters.

Patrick Hartwell taught at Indiana University at Pennsylvania and was the author of a number of works on the teaching of writing, among them *Open to Language: A New College Rhetoric.* He was also known for his development of various games to generate and revise prose. He died in the spring of 2003.

Douglas D. Hesse is a professor of English at Illinois State University. His work on creative nonfiction has appeared in *College English* and a number of edited collections. He has also published several essays on writing program administration.

Mary E. Hocks is an assistant professor of English at Georgia State University, where she is director of the Writing across the Curriculum Program. She has edited a collection of essays titled *Eloquent Images: Writing Visually in New Media.*

Ted Lardner is an associate professor of English at Cleveland State University, where he also codirects the university's poetry center. He has written much on the connections between composition and creative writing, as well as about Native American literature and theater arts. He recently coauthored *Literacies Unleashed: Re-imagining the Possibilities for African-American Students in the Composition Classroom* with Arnetha Ball.

Sondra Perl is a professor of English at Lehman College of the City University of New York, as well as the founder of the New York City Writing Project and a Guggenheim Fellow. Her work on the composing processes of developmental college writers and the concept of the "felt sense" have long been benchmarks of composition studies.

Nedra Reynolds is an associate professor of English and director of the writing program at the University of Rhode Island. She is the author of *Geographies of Writing: Inhabiting Places and Encountering Difference,* as well as other works on portfolio assessment, feminism, and service-learning. She is a coeditor of *The Bedford Bibliography for Teachers of Writing.*

Mike Rose is a professor of social research methodology at UCLA. He has published numerous books and articles on teaching writing, most famously *Lives on the Boundary,* a critique of the American school system in which he argues against viewing underprepared students as "remedial" or "deficient." Rose has received awards from the National Academy of Education and the McDonnell Foundation. He has also won a Guggenheim Fellowship, the Grawemeyer Award in Education, and the Commonwealth Club of California Award for Literary Excellence in Non-Fiction.

David Rothgery teaches at Lane Community College in Eugene, Oregon. In addition to his work in composition, he is also a novelist. He has taught in Africa and the Far East, and he recently won his institution's award for outstanding teaching.

Eileen E. Schell is an associate professor in the writing program and the graduate director of Composition and Cultural Rhetoric at Syracuse University. With Patricia Stock, she won the Outstanding Book Award in 2003 at the Conference on College Composition and Communication for *Moving a Mountain: Transforming the Role of Contingent Faculty in Composition Studies and Higher Education.* She has published more than two dozen articles, book chapters, responses, and reviews in leading journals in the field. She is also the author of *Gypsy Academics and Mother-Teachers: Gender, Contingent Labor and Writing Instruction.*

Cynthia L. Selfe served as chair of the Humanities Department at Michigan Technological University and also as chair of the Conference on College Composition and Communication. She is the author of numerous works on literacy and technology. She is the first woman to win the EDUCOM medal and is the founding editor of *Computers and Composition: An International Journal for Teachers of Writing.*

Tony Silva is a professor of English and director of the ESL program at Purdue University. With Ilona Leki, he founded and edits *The Journal of Second Language Writing.* He has published widely on issues in ESL pedagogy.

Nancy Sommers is the director of the Expository Writing Program at Harvard University. She has won the highly prestigious Braddock Award twice (1983, 1993), and, most recently, she has developed a longitudinal study of the writing abilities of the Harvard class of 2001.

Kurt Spellmeyer is an associate professor of English and director of the writing program at Rutgers University. He has published numerous articles and three books, most recently *Arts of Living: Reinventing the Humanities for the Twenty-First Century.*

Nancy Welch is an associate professor of English at the University of Vermont. She has published scholarly work in *College English, College Composition and Communication,* and *JAC: A Journal of Composition Theory,* as well as fiction in *The Three Penny Review* and *Prairie Schooner.* She has also coedited *The Dissertation and the Discipline: Re-inventing Composition Studies.*

Robert P. Yagelksi is an associate professor of English at the State University of New York, Albany, where he directs the writing center. He specializes in issues of technology and literacy, and he is the author of *Literacy Matters: Writing and Reading the Social Self.*

Acknowledgments (continued from page iv)

Ann E. Berthoff, "Learning the Uses of Chaos" from *The Making of Meaning: Metaphors, Models, and Maxims for Writing Teachers*. Copyright © 1981 by Boynton/Cook Publishers, Inc. Reprinted with the permission of Boynton/Cook, a subsidiary of Reed Elsevier, Inc., Portsmouth, NH.

Wayne C. Booth, "The Rhetorical Stance" from *College Composition and Communication* (October 1963). Copyright ©1963 by the National Council of Teachers of English. Reprinted with permission.

Deborah Brandt, "Sponsors of Literacy" from *College Composition and Communication* 49:2 (1998). Copyright © 1998 by the National Council of Teachers of English. Reprinted with permission.

Francis Christensen, "A Generative Rhetoric of the Sentence" from *College Composition and Communication* 16 (October 1965): 144–56. Copyright © 1965 by the National Council of Teachers of English. Reprinted with permission.

Juanita Rodgers Comfort, "Becoming a Writerly Self: College Writers Engaging Black Feminist Essays" from *College Composition and Communication* 51:4 (June 2000). Copyright © 2000 by the National Council of Teachers of English. Reprinted with permission. Excerpts from Gordon Harvey, "Presence in the Essay" from *College English* 58 (1994). Copyright © 1994 by the National Council of Teachers of English. Reprinted with permission.

Robert J. Connors, "The Erasure of the Sentence" from *College Composition and Communication* 52:1 (2000): 96, 28. Copyright © 2000 by the National Council of Teachers of English. Reprinted with permission.

Peter Elbow, "Ranking, Evaluating, and Liking: Sorting Out Three Forms of Judgment" from *College English* 55:2 (February 1993). Copyright © 1993 by the National Council of Teachers of English. Reprinted with permission. "Closing My Eyes as I Speak: An Argument for Ignoring Audience" from *College English* (January 1987). Copyright © 1987 by the National Council of Teachers of English. Reprinted with permission.

Paulo Freire, "The 'Banking' Concept of Education" (Chapter 2) from *Pedagogy of the Oppressed*. Copyright © 1972 by Herder and Herder. Reprinted with the permission of The Continuum International Publishing Group.

Diana George, "From Analysis to Design: Visual Communication in the Teaching of Writing" from *College Composition and Communication* 54:1 (September 2002). Copyright © 2002 by the National Council of Teachers of English. Reprinted with permission.

Joseph Harris, "Error" from *A Teaching Subject: Composition Since 1966*. Copyright © 1997 by Joseph Harris. Reprinted with the permission of Pearson Education, Upper Saddle River, NJ. This piece contains an excerpt from Gary A. Olson, excerpts from "Social Construction and Composition Theory: A Conversation with Richard Rorty" from *Journal of Advanced Composition* 9 (1989). Reprinted with the permission of the author and the Association of Teachers of Advanced Composition.

Muriel Harris and Tony Silva, "Tutoring ESL Students: Issues and Options" from *College Composition and Communication* (December 1993). Copyright © 1993 by the National Council of Teachers of English. Reprinted with permission.

Patricia Hartwell, "Grammar, Grammars, and the Teaching of Grammar" from *College English* 47:2 (February 1985). Copyright © 1985 by the National Council of Teachers of English. Reprinted with permission. This selection contains an excerpt from W. Nelson Francis, excerpt from "Revolution in Grammar" from *Quarterly Journal of Speech* 40 (1954). Copyright © 1954. Reprinted with permission.

Douglas D. Hesse, "Portfolio Standards for English 101" from *Strategies for Teaching First-Year English*, edited by Duane Roen, Veronica Pantoja, Lauren Yena, Susan K. Miller, and Eric Waggoner. Copyright © 2002 by the National Council of Teachers of English. Reprinted with permission.

ESSENTIAL READINGS IN COMPARATIVE POLITICS

THIRD EDITION

ESSENTIAL READINGS IN COMPARATIVE POLITICS THIRD EDITION

EDITED BY

PATRICK H. O'NEIL AND RONALD ROGOWSKI

W. W. NORTON & COMPANY

New York • London

Copyright © 2010, 2006, 2004 by W. W. Norton & Company, Inc.
All rights reserved
Printed in the United States of America

Editor: Aaron Javsicas
Assistant editor: Carly Fraser
Production editor: Kate Feighery
Production manager, College: Eric Pier-Hocking
Composition: Matrix Publishing Services, Inc.
Manufacturing: Quebecor World—Fairfield division

Library of Congress Cataloging-in-Publication Data

Essential readings in comparative politics / edited by Patrick O'Neil and Ronald Rogowski.— 3rd ed.
    p. cm.
    Includes bibliographical references.

ISBN-978-0-393-93401-4 (pbk.)

    1. Comparative government. I. O'Neil, Patrick H., 1966– II. Rogowski, Ronald.

JF51.E77 2010
320.3—dc22

2009023585

W. W. Norton & Company, Inc., 500 Fifth Avenue, New York, N.Y. 10110
www.wwnorton.com

W. W. Norton & Company Ltd., Castle House,
75/76 Wells Street, London W1T 3QT

4 5 6 7 8 9 0

CONTENTS

v

10 POLITICAL VIOLENCE   441

11 GLOBALIZATION   508

CREDITS   534

PREFACE

One of the greatest problems in comparative politics is that it lacks an agreed upon core. While this problem can be found across political science as a whole, the study of comparative politics has been plagued by disagreements over what merits study and how to go about this study. Whereas the study of international relations (political relations between countries) draws upon a set of key ideas and scholarship, not until recently has there been some similar consensus within comparative politics. Even now, scholars vary widely in the questions, approaches, and evidence that they bring to bear. It was this very problem that led to the creation of the *Essentials* set of texts in comparative politics.

Bringing together the "essentials" of comparative politics in a volume of manageable dimensions presented us with a serious challenge, but also, in our view, an irresistible opportunity. Where textbooks inevitably only summarize the original literature, if they discuss it at all, we have long thought it crucial—not least in our own teaching—to expose our students to the key works and original ideas and to show how they fit together in a larger and more generous understanding of comparative politics. Thus when Ann Shin and Roby Harrington suggested, on behalf of Norton, that we collaborate on a set of original readings to complement *Essentials of Comparative Politics*, we quickly overcame our initial trepidation and took up the challenge.

The readings have been chosen and organized to serve a number of purposes. On most topics, we have combined one or more "classic" pieces—widely recognized as having shaped the present field—with more recent influential contributions. Other works provide valuable surveys of changes in the field over time. Where possible, we have juxtaposed contending views on a topic, giving readers the opportunity to weigh the merits of competing arguments. Finally, we have sought to include a number of shorter and contemporary pieces that help link theory to current political events and developments. The headnotes to each chapter explain more fully our rationale for including the readings we did. The chapters of this volume parallel those of *Essentials of Comparative Politics*, often tying directly to concepts addressed in that textbook. They are also meant to flesh out ideas and developments addressed in *Cases in Comparative Politics*.

The reader begins with an overview of some of the ideas and debates concerning the study of comparative politics itself. From there, we investigate the key concepts of the state and sovereignty, and how scholars have thought about its rise, fall, and failure. We then consider national and ethnic identities and their relationship to political stability and violent conflict. Our discussion of political economy helps trace the relationship between states, markets, and property, while the chapters on democratic and nondemocratic regimes consider how democracies emerge, the foundations of nondemocratic rule, and the prospects for democracy and democratization around the world. From here, we lay out readings on advanced, less-developed and newly industrializing, and communist and postcommunist countries, attempting to apply some of the ideas addressed in the chapters above in understanding these parts of the world. Finally, our sections on political violence and globalization consider how comparative politics investigates the causes and effects of revolution and terrorism, and the ways in which globalization may—or may not—shape the role and place of domestic and international politics in the future. Hopefully, this material will provide the reader a sense of the core issues and ideas within comparative political scholarship, and its relationship to real world issues. The readings also build upon and often reference each other, giving the reader a sense of how they are interconnected as a single body of scholarship. While comparative politics may be diverse and even fractious, the readings underscore the perennial questions and concepts that drive our teaching and research.

While this collection is addressed primarily to undergraduates who are deepening their knowledge of comparative politics, we intend it also as a contribution—and in our view a highly necessary one—to *intra*disciplinary professional dialogue. Far too many graduate students and practicing scholars, in our view, are forgetting or ignoring the impressive depth and breadth of comparative politics. We thus intend this volume as both an introduction and a remedy. Now in its third edition, we have refined and improved our selections, seeking to strike a balance between complexity and accessibility.

We owe deep and extensive thanks to the various individuals who contributed to this work. Ann Shin played a critical role in initiating this project, reviewing our choices and helping us maintain order in the face of constant changes, updates, and second thoughts. Aaron Javsicas has taken the lead on the third edition, helping us further refine the material. Our thanks, too, to those external reviewers who considered our selections and provided important suggestions on how the reader might be improved. Finally, thanks to all those students with whom we have shared these readings in the past. Their responses, tacit and explicit, greatly influenced our selections and rationale. We hope that this range of materials can serve comparative politics courses across a range of levels, and that students and faculty alike will find them both wide-ranging and compelling.

Patrick O'Neil
Ron Rogowski
May 2009

ESSENTIAL READINGS IN COMPARATIVE POLITICS THIRD EDITION

1 WHAT IS COMPARATIVE POLITICS?

The ancestry of comparative politics can be traced back to ancient Greece and Aristotle and to the classic social theorists of the Renaissance and Enlightenment. From its modern revival in the late nineteenth century until the mid-1950s, it was a predominantly legalistic, normative, and descriptive enterprise: it focused on legal texts; it argued about how institutions should *be, rather than analyzing their actual characteristics; and it described—often in numbing detail—how countries' institutions worked. However, there was almost no explicit comparison of countries' institutions, and political scientists demonstrated little interest in what we would now call the comparative method.*

All of this changed with stunning rapidity in the late 1950s and the 1960s, as leading comparativists rediscovered the "grand tradition" in social theory, particularly the works of Karl Marx and Max Weber. Also, through such works as Anthony Downs's An Economic Theory of Democracy, *political scientists discovered the possibilities of game-theoretic and economic approaches. What has come to be called the "rational-choice" perspective came in the 1980s and 1990s to underlie some of the most significant work in comparative politics.*

In a work that has already become a modern classic, Mark Lichbach and Alan Zuckerman (1997) give a brilliant capsule history of these developments and focus our attention on what they and many others regard as the three major theories that have emerged within the field of comparative politics: the cultural, the structural, and the rational-choice approaches. Lichbach and Zuckerman trace the intellectual antecedents of these approaches, examine the reasons for their ascendance, and address the research questions that each theory pushes to the fore.

Lichbach and Zuckerman also note that despite their disagreements, today's comparativists agree on the need for comparison and explanation. Most would also agree with the great sociologist Max Weber (1864–1920) that social-scientific explanation is best achieved by what we now call a model— *or, as Weber put it, a conjecture or hypothesis about people's behavior that (a) "makes sense" in terms of what we already know about how people think;*

(b) is "fertile," meaning that it logically implies predictions about behavior that we are not immediately studying; and (c) is "testable," particularly in a comparative setting.

One can also divide comparativists into those who emphasize area studies—*close knowledge of a country or region (the Middle East, Latin America, Africa, China, Nigeria)—and those who stress the "science" in "social science," seeking* general laws *of political behavior and institutions that would apply in all areas of the world. In Lichbach and Zuckerman's terms, almost all "culturalists" fall into the first category and almost all "rationalists" into the second, while "structuralists" divide between the two.*

In his 2004 essay, Francis Fukuyama argues strongly against the decline of area studies in recent decades. The ascendancy of rationalist and economistic work, he contends, has left us ill prepared to understand the world, particularly as previously neglected regions (the Middle East, Southeast Asia) and domains of knowledge (comparative religions, terrorism) have acquired increasing urgency.

Robert Bates, writing earlier (and, of course, before September 11, 2001), took a more measured view: while agreeing that area studies had lost resources and intellectual sway, Bates (1997) argued that the rational-choice perspective could give us deeper insights into culture and that a new generation of comparativists would need both *area studies* and *technical expertise (in a phrase, exotic languages plus cutting-edge econometrics). Perhaps more important, Bates recalled why area studies had declined in the first place: too many area-studies experts had signally failed to understand what was going on in the areas they knew best (few Sovietologists even vaguely foresaw the decline of the Soviet Union, even as later too many Middle East experts denigrated the possibility of Sunni-Shiite conflict); and, as previous dictatorships and planned economies shifted to more democratic and more market-oriented politics and policies, general expertise in voting, public opinion, and comparative institutions came to be more widely applied—and often to seem more important than area specialization.*

Closing the circle, King, Keohane, and Verba's textbook, Designing Social Inquiry *(1994), to which Bates refers, sought presciently (if not always successfully) to bridge the divide between "qualitative" and "quantitative," between "area-studies" and "scientific" work in comparative politics. The difference, they contended, was "stylistic," not fundamental. Whether one studied a few cases (or even just one) in depth, or many more on only a few dimensions, the same standards of scientific inference must (and, indeed, among practitioners usually did) apply. Exactly as Lichbach and Zuckerman (and, long before them, Weber) had argued, good comparative theory must be fertile, testable, and tentative, and must seek to simplify complexity. The crucial insights of "KKV" (as the text became known) bear repetition and internalization. More than just about any other single text, these insights help us to understand what we are all trying to do, and to achieve, in studying comparative politics.*

MARK I. LICHBACH AND
ALAN S. ZUCKERMAN

RESEARCH TRADITIONS AND THEORY IN COMPARATIVE POLITICS: AN INTRODUCTION

The Common Heritage of Comparative Politics

Comparativists inherit their dream of theorizing about politics from the founders of social theory. Their intellectual forebears represent the pantheon of Western thought. In the classic survey of the field's intellectual origins, Harry Eckstein (1963) highlights the past masters.

> Comparative politics . . . has a particular right to claim Aristotle as an ancestor because of the primacy that he assigned to politics among the sciences and because the problems he raised and the methods he used are similar to those still current in political studies (Eckstein 1963: 3).

Machiavelli and Montesquieu, Hobbes and Smith are the progenitors who lived during the Renaissance and the Enlightenment. The classic theorists of social science—Karl Marx, Max Weber, Emile Durkheim, Vilfredo Pareto, Gaetano Mosca, and Roberto Michels—established the field's research agenda, mode of analysis, and contrasting theoretical visions. Several seminal theorists of contemporary political science—Harry Eckstein, David Apter, Robert Dahl, Seymour Lipset, Karl Deutsch, Gabriel Almond, and Sidney Verba—drew on this heritage to rebuild and reinvigorate the field of comparative politics. A shared, grand intellectual vision motivates comparativists.

From *Comparative Politics: Rationality, Culture, and Structure* (New York: Cambridge University Press, 1997), pp. 3–8.

Comparativists want to understand the critical events of the day, a position that ensures that dreams of theory address the political world as it exists, not formal abstractions or utopias. Just as Marx and Weber responded to the fundamental transformations associated with the rise of capitalism, just as Marx developed a general strategy for a socialist revolution and Weber grappled with the theoretical and normative demands of the bureaucratic state, and just as Mosca, Pareto, and Michels strove to understand the possibilities and limits of democratic rule, students of comparative politics examine pressing questions in the context of their immediate political agenda. The contemporary study of comparative politics therefore blossomed in response to the political problems that followed World War II. New forms of conflict emerged: Communist threats; peasant rebellions and revolutions; social movements, urban riots, student upheavals, military coups, and national liberation struggles swept the world. Government decisions replaced markets as foci for economic development. New states followed the disintegration of colonial empires, and the worldwide movement toward democratic rule seemed to resume after the fascist tragedies. The challenges of the current era—domestic conflict, state-building, the political bases of economic growth, and democratization, to note but a few—stand at the center of today's research, indicating that the need to respond to contemporary issues guides the field.

Comparative politics therefore asserts an ambitious scope of inquiry. No political phenomenon is foreign to it; no level of analysis is irrelevant, and no time period beyond its reach. Civil war in Afghanistan; voting decisions in Britain; ethnic conflict in Quebec, Bosnia, and Burundi; policy interactions among the bureaucracies of the European Union in Brussels, government agencies in Rome, regional offices in Basilicata, and local powers in Potenza; the religious bases of political action in Iran, Israel, and the United States; the formation of democracies in Eastern Europe and the collapse of regimes in Africa; and global economic patterns are part of the array of contemporary issues that stand before the field. Questions about the origins of capitalism; the formation of European states; the rise of fascism and the collapse of interwar democracies; and the transition to independence after colonial rule are some of the themes of past eras that still command our attention.

Second, comparativists assert an ambitious intellectual vision in that they approach these substantive concerns with general questions in mind. Anyone who studies the politics of a particular country—whether Germany or Ghana, the United Arab Emirates or the United States of America—so as to address abstract issues, does comparative politics. Anyone who is interested in who comes to power, how, and why—the names, places, and dates of politics in any one place or other—in order to say something about the politics of succession or the determinants of vote choice, is a comparativist. In other words, students of comparative politics examine a case to reveal what it tells us about a larger set of political phenomena, or they relate the particulars of politics to more general theoretical ideas about politics.

Comparativists therefore insist that analysis requires explicit comparisons. Because events of global historical significance affect so many countries in so short a period of time, studies of single countries and abstract theorizing are woefully inadequate to capture epoch-shaping developments. More than three decades ago, when the founders of the contemporary field of comparative politics initiated the most recent effort to merge theory and data in the study of politics,

they therefore established another of the field's guiding principles: The proper study of politics requires systematic comparisons.[1]

Finally, comparativists assert a grand intellectual vision in that their generalizations are situated in the context of the Big Questions of social thought: Who rules? How are interests represented? Who wins and who loses? How is authority challenged? Why are some nations "developed"? These questions have produced much contemporary theorizing about the connections among social order, the state, civil society, and social change, especially in democracies. Comparativists engage the basic issues that inform social and political thought.

In sum, comparative politics follows the lead of the grand masters in their approach to substantive issues, to the scope of inquiry, to the nature of theory-building, and to the enduring problems of social thought. As comparativists address politically significant matters, explore a range of political phenomena, propose general explanatory propositions based on systematic evidence from multiple cases, and address Big Questions, they move along a path first marked by the founders of social science.

The Competing Traditions in Comparative Politics

In spite of this shared dream, long-standing disagreements separated the field's forebears and contrasting research schools characterize current efforts to build theories in comparative politics. When many of today's senior scholars were graduate students, their training included courses that compared psychological and culturalist approaches, institutional studies of political organizations, structural-functional and systems analyses, cybernetics and modes of information theory, pluralist, elitist, and Marxist analyses, modernization theory and its alternatives of dependency and world-systems theories, and rational choice theory, to name the most obvious. Most of these perspectives have disappeared and some have formed new combinations. Today, rational choice theories, culturalist approaches, and structural analyses stand as the principal competing theoretical schools in comparative politics. Rational choice theorists follow a path laid out by Hobbes, Smith, and Pareto; culturalists continue work begun by Montesquieu and developed by Weber and Mosca; and structuralists build on Marx's foundations and add to Weber's edifice. The themes and debates of contemporary comparative politics are therefore rooted in the enduring questions of social thought. They continue to lie at the center of work in all the social sciences.

Rationalists begin with assumptions about actors who act deliberately to maximize their advantage. This research school uses the power of mathematical reasoning to elaborate explanations with impressive scope. Analysis begins at the level of the individual and culminates in questions about collective actions, choices, and institutions. Following the path first charted by Downs (1957), Olson (1968), and Riker (1962), rational choice theory has spread to address diverse problems: from electoral choice to revolutionary movements, from coalitions to political economy, and from institution formation to state-building. Here, the clarity of mathematical reasoning takes pride of place; powerful abstract logics facilitate a shared understanding among the members of the research school.

As comparativists engage in fieldwork in diverse societies, they grapple with the need to understand varied ways of life, systems of meaning, and values. As students who cut their teeth on the abstractions of modernization and dependency theory encounter the realities of particular villages, political parties, and legislatures, they seek to ground their observations in the politics that is being analyzed. Following the lead of social and cultural anthropologists, many comparativists adhere to Geertz's (1973) admonition to provide "thick descriptions." Culturalists therefore provide nuanced and detailed readings of particular cases, frequently drawn from fieldwork, as they seek to understand the phenomena

being studied. This stance usually joins strong doubts about both the ability to generalize to abstract categories and the ability to provide explanations that apply to more than the case at hand.

Structuralists draw together long-standing interests in political and social institutions. Many emphasize the formal organizations of governments; some retain Marx's concern with class relations; some study political parties and interest groups; some combine these into analyses of how states and societies interact; and some emphasize the themes of political economy. Although these scholars display diverse patterns of reasoning, from mathematical models to verbal arguments, and many modes of organizing empirical evidence, they continue to follow Marx's and Weber's contention that theory and data guide social analysis.

* * * These research traditions take strong positions on the methodological issues that divide comparativists.[2] Rational choice theorists seek to maximize the ability to provide universal laws that may be used in nomothetic explanations. They consider problems of reliability—the concern with the evidence required to support generalizations from the particular to sets of cases—as a challenge to research design. Cultural interpreters maximize the importance of reliability as they describe the constellations of particular cases and minimize the value of generalist research expectations. They interpret particular events, decisions, and patterns, eschewing any need to tie explanations to general principles. Structural analysts who follow Marx offer universal theories that include causal accounts. At the same time, they struggle to tie reliable descriptions into powerful generalizations; they grapple self-consciously with the requirements of case selection and how best to move from the particular analysis to the set of cases about which they seek to theorize. Comparativists' long-standing debates over method thus reappear in the three research traditions.

However, * * * the dispute among the schools goes beyond the ideographic-nomothetic divide.

The traditions differ with respect to ontology: Rationalists study how actors employ reason to satisfy their interests, culturalists study rules that constitute individual and group identities, and structuralists explore relations among actors in an institutional context. Reasons, rules, and relations are the various starting points of inquiry. The traditions also differ with respect to explanatory strategy: Rationalists perform comparative static experiments, culturalists produce interpretive understandings, and structuralists study the historical dynamics of real social types. Positivism, interpretivism, and realism are the possible philosophies of social science.

Moreover, * * * no school displays a rigid and uniform orthodoxy. Rationalists debate the utility of relaxing the core assumption that defines individuals as maximizers of their self-interest. They differ as well over the proper form of explanation, some seeking covering laws and others proposing causal accounts, as they debate the necessity of transforming formal models into accounts of events. Continuing the debate initiated by Marx and Weber, structuralists differ over the ontological status of their concepts: Are social class, ethnicity, state, and other concepts that characterize this research school natural types? Are political processes best seen as determined and closed ended or probabilistic and open-ended processes? Structuralists differ as well over the utility of nomothetic and causal explanations. Culturalists disagree over the theoretical importance of generalizations drawn from their fieldwork. May one derive or test general propositions from the analysis of a particular village? Do public opinion surveys provide an adequate picture of people's goals, values, and identities? They differ over the nature of explanation in comparative politics as well. Some culturalists reject any form of covering law or causal accounts, offering only interpretations of political life in particular places; others move toward the mainstream of comparative politics, incorporating values and systems of meaning into theories that adhere to the standard forms of explanation. In short, as Lichbach makes clear in his essay, ideal-type rationalists, culturalists, and structuralists need to be identified so that we may recognize how practicing comparativists employ a battery of ideal-type strategies in their concrete empirical work.

Comparative politics is dominated today by rationalist, culturalist, and structuralist approaches. What explains the imperialist expansion of these schools and the disappearance of earlier approaches? [For one thing,] These schools share an ontological and epistemological symmetry. They offer—indeed force—choices along the same dimensions. Furthermore, at a more fundamental level, the themes of the research schools rest at the heart of the human sciences. Reason, rules, and relations are unique to social theory. Focusing on these themes sets research in the social sciences apart from the physical sciences, providing a fundamental basis on which to theorize about political phenomena. Rationalist, culturalist, and structuralist theories are thus embedded in strong research communities, scholarly traditions, and analytical languages.

NOTES

1. Classic works that appeared to herald the emergence of comparative politics as a subdiscipline of political science include Almond and Coleman (1960), Almond and Verba (1963), Beer and Ulam (1958), Dahl (1966; 1971), Eckstein and Apter (1963), Holt and Turner (1970), Huntington (1968), La Palombara and Weiner (1966), Lipset and Rokkan (1967), Moore (1966), Przeworski and Teune (1970); Pye and Verba (1965), Riker (1962), and Sartori (1970). At the same time, two journals, *Comparative Politics* and *Comparative Political Studies*, appeared, helping to institutionalize the subfield.

2. There is also a long-standing debate in comparative politics about methodology. As comparativists propose explanations that cover sets of cases, perhaps based on causal

accounts, they grapple with questions that relate to theory-building, concept formation, and case selection: How do concepts carry across cases? What is the value of treating concepts as variables that are measured by indicators? What is the proper use of case-specific information in theories that cover many cases? How does the choice of cases affect the general propositions offered? Are there requirements that define the number of cases that need to be included in an analysis? What is the relevance of single case studies to the development of theory? How can single case studies be used to speak to general sets of phenomena? Is it possible or desirable to include all relevant instances in the analysis? Is it possible to devise an adequate methodology that permits powerful generalizations based on the observation of a small number of cases? These questions raise problems of external validity, the ability to generalize beyond the case being observed.

Nearly thirty years ago, Sartori (1970) drew attention to fundamental questions of concept formation. At that same time, Lijphart (1971) and Przeworski and Teune (1970) initiated a controversy about the proper methodology of comparative research, in which Eckstein (1975), Ragin (1987), Ragin and Becker (1992), and Skocpol and Somers (1980) have offered significant alternative positions (see Collier 1993 for a review of this literature). Most recently, Collier and Mahon (1993), Collier (1993), and Sartori (1994) illustrate further developments concerning the proper formation of concepts, and King, Keohane, and Verba (1994; 1995) initiated a productive debate over issues of research design in comparative politics. On the latter, see especially Bartels (1995), Brady (1995), Caporaso (1995), Collier (1995), Laitin (1995), Mohr (1996), Rogowski (1995), and Tarrow (1995). There is a natural affinity between studies of research design and comparative method that is frequently overlooked. King, Keohane, and Verba (1994; 1995) argue that there is only one scientific method. Hence, their strictures resemble those proposed by Cook and Campbell (1979).

FRANCIS FUKUYAMA

HOW ACADEMIA FAILED THE NATION: THE DECLINE OF REGIONAL STUDIES

September 11, 2001, was a wake-up call—not just concerning the threat of terrorism, but also regarding the way we educate Americans about the outside world. This event brought home the degree to which events taking place in troubled, obscure places like Afghanistan could have major effects on the United States. It also showed us how poorly prepared we were in our knowledge of the Middle East, Islam and related issues to deal with the world we now face.

At the time of the attacks, the entire U.S. government could call on no more than two or three speakers of Pushto (the dominant language in Afghanistan); only a handful of U.S. diplomats know Arabic well enough to appear on al-Jazeera, the Arabic language channel famous for broadcasting videos of Osama bin Laden, without embarrassing themselves. U.S. forces inter-

From *Saisphere* (2004), pp. 6–9.

vened in Iraq without basic cultural literacy, a problem that consistently hampered our ability to collect intelligence on the growing insurgency there.

The scandal that the media has thus far failed to cover is the utter failure of the American academy to train adequate numbers of people with deep knowledge about the world outside the United States. This failure is linked to the decline of regional studies in American universities over the past generation and the misguided directions being taken by the social sciences in recent years, particularly political science and economics.

The story here is one of colonization of the study of politics by economics. Known as the "queen of the social sciences," economics is the only discipline that looks like a natural science. Economists are carefully trained to gather data and build causal models that can be rigorously tested empirically. The data that economists work from are quantitative from the start and can be analyzed with a powerful battery of statistical tools.

Economists' powerful methodology has been a source of envy and emulation on the part of other social scientists. The past two decades have seen the growth of what is known as "rational choice" political science, in which political scientists seek to model political behavior using the same mathematical tools (game theory, for the most part) used by economists. Economists tend to believe that regularities in human behavior are universal and invariant across different cultures and societies (for example, the law of supply and demand is the same in Japan and Botswana). Similarly, rational choice political science seeks to create broad, universally applicable laws of political behavior by generalizing across large numbers of countries rather than focusing intensively on the history and context of individual countries or regions.

As a result, regional studies fell seriously out of favor in the 1980s and 1990s. Foundations ceased to fund area studies programs, money for language training and fieldwork evaporated and require-

ments were changed from knowing languages and history to learning quantitative methods.

Regional studies requires a huge personal investment, not just in specialized training but also in having to live in a particular country and building up a network of contacts to keep one's knowledge fresh throughout a career. Given shifting incentives, it is not surprising that the best and brightest graduate students started shifting into more theoretical or functional types of political science. Area studies programs were closed or merged into other units; on the eve of the September 11 attacks, half of the top political science departments in the United States did not have a Middle East studies program.

It is certainly desirable for a social science to be rigorous, empirical and seek general rules of human behavior. But as Aristotle explained, it should not try to achieve a rigor that goes beyond what is possible given the limitations inherent in the subject matter. In fact, most of what is truly useful for policy is context-specific, culture-bound and non-generalizable. The typical article appearing today in a leading journal like the *American Political Science Review* contains a lot of complex-looking math, whose sole function is often to formalize a behavioral rule that everyone with common sense understands must be true. What is missing is any deep knowledge about the subtleties and nuances of how foreign societies work, knowledge that would help us better predict the behavior of political actors, friendly and hostile, in the broader world.

Examples abound. In trying to understand what kind of political actors might emerge in a post–Saddam Hussein Iraq, we don't need math or game theory; what we need is an up-to-date understanding of the ethnic, religious and tribal structure of the country, knowledge of who the figures of authority are in Iraqi Shiism, how they relate to their Iranian counterparts and how the tribes in the Sunni Triangle are intermarried with one another. Understanding bin Ladenism requires historical knowledge of the development in the 20th century of radical Islamism, from its roots in the Muslim Brotherhood in Egypt through the Iranian revolution to the Wahhabi imams, or religious leaders, in Saudi Arabia.

You cannot model European-American differences unless you understand them, which involves, of all things, actually talking to Europeans. Anyone who has thought about great historical events like the outbreak of World War I or the end of the Cold War recognizes the role of historical contingency, accident and personality in the way they eventually played out. If the German General von Kluck had been able to break through the French lines at the first battle of the Marne in September 1914, or if Soviet General Secretary Yuri Andropov had been in better health, the history of both the beginning and the end of the 20th century would have been written very differently.

Regional studies, of course, has its own limitations. Area specialists tend to become parochial and overspecialized; many draw unwarranted general conclusions from their own limited experience or else fail to see their own countries as instances of broader patterns of po-

litical behavior. The great sociologist and political scientist Seymour Martin Lipset was fond of saying that someone "who knows only one country knows no countries." Americans tend to be particularly guilty of this, believing that the way we organize our institutions constitutes a kind of norm for modern democracies. In fact, American institutions are quite exceptional among those of developed liberal democracies, and it is only through a broadening of one's horizons that one can come to understand how exceptional—for good and ill—America is.

* * * With the 9/11 attacks and the Iraq War, America has fallen into a deeply troubled relationship with the outside world. We cannot hope to navigate our way through the difficult policy choices in the years ahead unless we have leaders who understand how the world beyond our shores works and who are able to see the United States from the viewpoint of non-Americans. We cannot cooperate or spread our influence around the world unless we are able to train non-Americans to see things from our perspective or help them acquire the intellectual tools by which dispassionate analysis is made possible.

ROBERT H. BATES

AREA STUDIES AND THE DISCIPLINE: A USEFUL CONTROVERSY?*

When arguments become polarized, it often signals that divisions are falsely drawn. Such appears to be the case with this controversy. Why must one choose between area studies and the discipline? There are strong reasons for endorsing both. In this essay, I sketch the current debate and explore the ways in local knowledge can and is being incorporated into

From *PS: Political Science & Politics*, 30, no. 2 (June 1997), pp. 166–170.

general analytic frameworks. I conclude by stressing the work that lies ahead. In doing so, it should be stressed, I deal only with political science. The dynamics in other disciplines, I have found, differ greatly from those within our own (Bates et al. 1993).

Caricaturing the Present Divide

Within political science, area specialists are multidisciplinary by inclination and training. In addition to knowing the politics of a region or nation, they seek also to master its history, literature, and languages. They not only absorb the work of humanists but also that of other social scientists. Area specialists invoke the standard employed by the ethnographer: serious scholarship, they believe, must be based upon field research. The professional audience of area specialists consists of researchers from many disciplines, who have devoted their scholarly life to work on the region or nation.

Those who consider themselves "social scientists" seek to identify lawful regularities, which, by implication, must not be context-bound. Rather than seeking a deeper understanding of a particular area, social scientists strive to develop general theories and to identify, and test, hypotheses derived from them. Social scientists will attack with confidence political data extracted from any region of the world. They will approach electoral data from South Africa in the same manner as that from the United States and eagerly address cross-national data sets, thereby manifesting their rejection of the presumption that political regularities are area-bound. Social scientists do not seek to master the literature on a region but rather to master the literature of a discipline. The professional audience of social scientists consists of other scholars from their discipline who share similar theoretical concerns—and who draw their data from a variety of regions of the world.

Like all caricatures, these depictions distort in order to highlight important elements of reality. The implications of this reality have profoundly unsettled our discipline.

Most immediately, the shift from area studies to "social scientific" approaches has influenced graduate training. Graduate students, whose resources of time and money are necessarily limited, increasingly shift from the study of a region to instruction in theory and methods. When confronted by a choice between a course in African history or one in econometrics, given their constraints, many now choose the latter.

The shift from area specialization to "social science" also alters the balance of power within the academy. Political science departments have long resembled federations, with their faculty in comparative politics dwelling within semi-autonomous, area studies units. Possessing access to resources for seminars, administrative support, fellowships, research and travel independent of the department, the comparative politics faculty has had little reason to defer to the demands of department heads. The move toward a disciplinary-oriented view of comparative politics, and the declining resource base for area studies, has shifted the political center of gravity back to the chairs, who can now apply disciplinary criteria, rather than area knowledge, in evaluating and rewarding professional contributions.

Change in the notions of professional merit also alters the balance of power between generations. Old field hands are giving way to young technicians. It is those in the middle who are the most threatened. Like their elders, they have trained as area specialists; but they are being evaluated by a new set of standards—ones by which they compare unfavorably with younger scholars. The mid-career scholars now scramble to master the new vocabulary and techniques; and departments that once would have readily promoted them too often decide to refrain from doing so, in the expectation of later filling the slots from the best and brightest of the new generation.

The result of these changes is heightened tension within the field, as the controversy resonates with divisions between scholars of different generations, locations within the university, and stages in their careers.

Clearly, the causes of these tensions lie outside the academy: they lie in the rising concerns with government deficits and the end of the cold war. The one has led to reductions in spending for higher education; the other, to a lower priority on area training. For reasons I do not fully understand, rather than cushioning the impact of these changes, foundations have instead exacerbated them by moving in concert with the government. Resources for the study of foreign areas are therefore declining, and we in academics are being required to establish new priorities, as we adjust to tighter constraints.

Reacting to the New Realities

Many departments were once characterized by a core of technocrats, many of whom specialized in the study of American politics, and a congery of others, many of whom studied foreign political systems. Students of American politics viewed themselves as social scientists; but the political system on which they concentrated, they came to realize, was singularly devoid of variation. Even comparisons across states within the greater federation failed to provide insight into differences, say, between presidential and parliamentary systems, much less between polities in market as opposed to centrally planned economies. A vocal minority within American politics had long dismissed students of comparative politics as "mere area specialists;" [sic] but the more sophisticated increasingly realized that their hard won, cumulative, scientific knowledge about politics in the United States was itself area-bound. There therefore arose *among Americanists* a demand for *comparative* political research, and some of the most theoretically ambitious among them sought to escape the confines imposed by the American political system.

On the one hand, this trend creates allies for comparativists who seek to resist retrenchment; their knowledge of political variation has acquired greater significance. On the other, this trend will promote a transformation in the comparative study of politics; it will force those who have a command of local knowledge to enter into dialogue with those who seek to understand how institutional variation affects political outcomes or who see particular political systems as specific realizations of broader political processes.

Pressures from outside the discipline amplify these changes; they emerge from trends that have affected political systems throughout the world. Following the recession of the 1980s, authoritarian governments fell, and the collapse of communism in Eastern Europe further contributed to the spread of democracy. This change underscored the broader relevance of the Americanists' research into elections, legislatures and political parties. The spread of market forces and the liberalization of economic systems highlighted the broader significance of research conducted on the advanced industrial democracies as well. The impact of economic conditions upon voting, the politics of central banking, the effect of openness upon partisan cleavages and political institutions: long studies in the Western democracies, these subjects have recently become important, and researchable, in the formerly socialist systems in the North and in the developing nations of the South. As students of comparative politics have addressed them, they have come increasingly to share intellectual orientations, and a sense of necessary skills and training, with their more "social scientific" colleagues in the discipline.

The attention given to King, Keohane, and Verba's *Designing Social Inquiry* (1994) provides a measure of the impact of these trends. It suggests the urgency with which students of comparative politics feel a need for guidance, as they have sought ways to move from the in depth study of cases, typical of area studies, to sophisticated research designs, required for scientific inference.

Deeper Fusion

The field is thus undergoing significant changes, and the increased stringency of funding strengthens these trends. Less visible, but highly significant, forces run just below the surface and these too will shape the final outcome. Insofar as they do so, they may well define a new synthesis. I refer to a synthesis not only between area studies and the discipline but also between context-specific knowledge and formal theory, as developed in the study of choice.

Area studies emphasizes the importance of cultural distinctions. Cultures are distinguished by their institutions. Game theoretic techniques, established for the study of economic and political organizations, provide a source of formal tools for investigating such institutions. They show how institutions shape individual choices and collective outcomes, and therefore provide a framework for exploring the origins of political difference.

Cultures are also distinguished by their histories and beliefs. The theory of decisions with imperfect information, newly prominent in political science, can be used to explore the manner in which such differences arise and matter. Individuals with similar expectations, it shows, come to diverge in their beliefs if exposed to different data; persons can be shaped by their histories. Even if exposed to the same data, decision theory suggests, persons will revise their beliefs in different ways, if they bring different likelihood functions to bear upon observations. The theory of decisions thus yields insight into the way in which history and world views shape individual choices and therefore collective outcomes. The theory thus provides a framework for exploring cross-cultural differences.

The relationship between "local knowledge" and rational choice theory can be illustrated by Elizabeth Colson's well-known research into the Plateau Tonga of Zambia (1974). The lives of the Tonga, she reports, resemble the Rousseauian myth, with people residing in peaceful communities, sharing their belongings, and legislating wisely in village assemblies. But, Colson reports, the surface harmony disguises deep fears: of the greed and envy of neighbors, of their wrath, and of their desire and capacity to harm. While the lives of the Plateau Tonga may resemble the accounts of Rousseau, their beliefs, she finds, are

better captured in the writings of Hobbes. Colson resolves the paradoxical contrast between beliefs and behavior by arguing that it is the beliefs that support peaceful conduct: people scrupulously choose to act in ways that preserve the peace, she argues, for fear of the violence they would unleash should they impinge upon the interests of others.

Viewed in terms of game theory, Colson's argument represents a claim that behaving courteously constitutes an equilibrium strategy. The strategy is supported in equilibrium by beliefs as to the costs that would be incurred were people to stray from the equilibrium path. It would be easy to use the theory of games to specify the conditions under which the argument follows. More significantly, doing so would suggest additional insights into what must also necessarily be true for the argument to hold. Given that this is so, transforming the narrative into a rational choice account would generate additional testable implications (Ferejohn 1991). Some of these implications might be non-obvious; when this is the case formalization inspires new insights as well. Others might be crashingly obvious. But even jejune propositions, if deduced from a theory, are significant; for when they are tested, it is the theory from which they derive that is put at risk. Embedding narrative accounts in theories thus increases the opportunities for testing; it therefore increases our ability to judge the adequacy of an explanation.

By the same token, theory must be complemented by contextual knowledge. Consider the problem faced by an observer who encounters a person who is inflicting damage upon another. If a family head, he may be refusing a request for bride wealth; if a faction leader, he may be withholding patronage; if a mayor, she may be bringing the forces of the law to bear upon a rival political. Such actions inflict harm. But, in interpreting their political importance, the observer will need to know: Do they represent initial defections? Or do they represent punishments for an earlier defection? Without knowledge of the history, the investigator cannot determine the *significance* of these behaviors. The first history suggests that they should be analyzed as a political rupture; the second, that they should be treated as a punishment phase of a game—a phase that may in fact constitute a prelude to reconciliation. In the absence of local knowledge, the actions remain observationally equivalent; nothing in the theory alone suggests their strategic significance and thus their implications for subsequent interactions. Just as in the parable related by Geertz, a "wink" differs from a "twitch," so too does strategic behavior thus require interpretation. To be analyzed correctly, such behavior needs to be addressed by theory that is informed by empirical observation (1973).

To the degree that rational choice theory comes to occupy a central position within the discipline, then, the conflict between area studies and the "social scientific" core of political science will be misplaced. The approach provides explanations for difference; it requires knowledge of the difference for the construction and testing of its accounts. It provides a framework which transforms ethnography and narratives into theory-driven claims, amenable to refutation and it requires precisely targeted observations to establish the force of its arguments (Bates et al. 1998).

It is important to realize that the present debate has been energized by adjacent controversies. It echoes recent ideological struggles. The debate over area studies is often exacerbated by debates over the merits of the market, the state, or the impact of the West, with those who endorse area studies viewing those who use rational choice theory as being pro-market, anti-state, and given to applying historically contingent categories in a universalistic manner. And it resonates with earlier battles over the qualitative and quantitative, between numeracy and literacy, and between the humanities and the sciences. In other cultures, well-educated people are expected to excel at both; strength in the one need not imply weakness in the other. But the division remains powerful within our own cul-ture, particularly among academics, where it limits and impedes. It reinforces the foundations for the present debate between area studies and the discipline.

Not being hard-wired, the division between "the scientific" and "the humanistic" can be transcended. The issue is not whether to use the left side of the brain rather than the right. It is, rather, how to employ both. The combination of local knowledge and general modes of reasoning, of area studies and formal theory, represents a highly promising margin of our field. The blend will help to account for the power of forces that we know shape human behavior, in ways that we have hitherto been able to describe but not to explain. It is time to insist upon the pursuit of both rather than upon the necessity of choosing sides.

NOTE

*This article draws heavily on Robert H. Bates, "Area Studies and Political Science: Rupture and Possible Synthesis," *Africa Today,* Volume 44, No. 2 (1997), special issue on "The Future of Regional Studies." I wish also to thank Timothy Cotton and Peter Hall, and the junior fellows of Harvard Academy, especially Daniel Posner, for their tough criticisms. I have failed to incorporate many of their suggestions, and therefore must assume complete responsibility of the defects that remain.

REFERENCES

Bates, Robert H., Jean O'Barr, and V. S. Mudimbe. 1993. *Africa and the Disciplines*. Chicago: University of Chicago Press.

Bates, Robert H., Avner Greif, Margaret Levi, Jean-Laurent Rosenthal, and Barry Weingast. 1998. *Analytic Narratives*. Princeton: Princeton University Press.

Colson, Elizabeth. 1974. *Tradition and Contract*. Chicago: Aldine.

Ferejohn, John. 1991. "Rationality and Interpretation," in *The Economic Approach to Poli-*

tics, ed. Kristen Renwick Monroe. New York: Harper Collins.

Geertz, Clifford. 1973. *Interpretation of Cultures.* New York: Basic Books.

King, Gary, Robert Keohane, and Sydney Verba. 1994. *Designing Social Inquiry.* Princeton: Princeton University Press.

GARY KING, ROBERT O. KEOHANE, AND SIDNEY VERBA

THE *SCIENCE* IN SOCIAL SCIENCE

*   *   *

For several decades, political scientists have debated the merits of case studies versus statistical studies, area studies versus comparative studies, and "scientific" studies of politics using quantitative methods versus "historical" investigations relying on rich textual and contextual understanding. Some quantitative researchers believe that systematic statistical analysis is the only road to truth in the social sciences. Advocates of qualitative research vehemently disagree. This difference of opinion leads to lively debate; but unfortunately, it also bifurcates the social sciences into a quantitative-systematic-generalizing branch and a qualitative-humanistic-discursive branch. As the former becomes more and more sophisticated in the analysis of statistical data (and their work becomes less comprehensible to those who have not studied the techniques), the latter becomes more and more convinced of the irrelevance of such analyses to the seemingly nonreplicable and nongeneralizable events in which its practitioners are interested.

A major purpose of this book is to show that the differences between the quantitative and qualitative traditions are only stylistic and are methodologically and substantively unimportant. All good research can be understood—

From *Designing Social Inquiry: Scientific Interest in Qualitative Research* (Princeton: Princeton University Press, 1994), pp. 3–12.

indeed, is best understood—to derive from the same underlying logic of inference. Both quantitative and qualitative research can be systematic and scientific. Historical research can be analytical, seeking to evaluate alternative explanations through a process of valid causal inference. History, or historical sociology, is not incompatible with social science (Skocpol 1984: 374–86).

Breaking down these barriers requires that we begin by questioning the very concept of "qualitative" research. We have used the term in our title to signal our subject matter, not to imply that "qualitative" research is fundamentally different from "quantitative" research, except in style.

Most research does not fit clearly into one category or the other. The best often combines features of each. In the same research project, some data may be collected that is amenable to statistical analysis, while other equally significant information is not. Patterns and trends in social, political, or economic behavior are more readily subjected to quantitative analysis than is the flow of ideas among people or the difference made by exceptional individual leadership. If we are to understand the rapidly changing social world, we will need to include information that cannot be easily quantified as well as that which can. Furthermore, all social science requires comparison, which entails judgments of which phenomena are "more" or "less" alike in degree (i.e., quantitative differences) or in kind (i.e., qualitative differences).

* * * Neither quantitative nor qualitative research is superior to the other, regardless of the research problem being addressed. Since many subjects of interest to social scientists cannot be meaningfully formulated in ways that permit statistical testing of hypotheses with quantitative data, we do not wish to encourage the exclusive use of quantitative techniques. We are not trying to get all social scientists out of the library and into the computer center, or to replace idiosyncratic conversations with structured interviews. Rather, we argue that nonstatistical research will produce more reliable results if researchers pay attention to the rules of scientific inference—rules that are sometimes more clearly stated in the style of quantitative research. Precisely defined statistical methods that undergird quantitative research represent abstract formal models applicable to all kinds of research, even that for which variables cannot be measured quantitatively. The very abstract, and even unrealistic, nature of statistical models is what makes the rules of inference shine through so clearly.

The rules of inference that we discuss are not relevant to all issues that are of significance to social scientists. Many of the most important questions concerning political life—about such concepts as agency, obligation, legitimacy, citizenship, sovereignty, and the proper relationship between national societies and international politics—are philosophical rather than empirical. But the rules are relevant to all research where the goal is to learn facts about the real world. Indeed, the distinctive characteristic that sets social science apart from casual observation is that social science seeks to arrive at valid inferences by the systematic use of well-established procedures of inquiry. Our focus here on empirical research means that we sidestep many issues in the philosophy of social science as well as controversies about the role of postmodernism, the nature and existence of truth, relativism, and related subjects. We assume that it is possible to have some knowledge of the external world but that such knowledge is always uncertain.

Furthermore, nothing in our set of rules implies that we must run the perfect experiment (if such a thing existed) or collect all relevant data before we can make valid social scientific inferences. An important topic is worth studying even if very little information is available. The result of applying any research design in this situation will be relatively uncertain conclusions, but so long as we honestly report our uncertainty, this kind of study can be very useful. Limited information is often a necessary feature of social inquiry. Because the social world changes rapidly, analyses that help us understand those changes require that we describe them and seek to understand them contemporaneously, even when uncertainty about our conclusions is high. The urgency of a problem may be so great that data gathered by the most useful scientific methods might be obsolete before it can be accumulated. If a distraught person is running at us swinging an ax, administering a five-page questionnaire on psychopathy may not be the best strategy. Joseph Schumpeter once cited Albert Einstein, who said "as far as our propositions are certain, they do not say anything about reality, and as far as they do say anything about reality, they are not certain" (Schumpeter [1936] 1991:298–99). Yet even though certainty is unattainable, we can improve the reliability, validity, certainty, and honesty of our conclusions by paying attention to the rules of scientific inference. The social science we espouse seeks to make descriptive and causal inferences about the world. Those who do not share the assumptions of partial and imperfect knowability and the aspiration for descriptive and causal understanding will have to look elsewhere for inspiration or for paradigmatic battles in which to engage.***

1.1.2 Defining Scientific Research in the Social Sciences

Our definition of "scientific research" is an ideal to which any actual quantitative or qualitative research, even the most careful, is only an approximation. Yet, we need a definition of good research, for which we use the word "scientific" as our descriptor.[1] This word comes with many connotations that are unwarranted or inappropriate or downright incendiary for some qualitative researchers. Hence, we provide an explicit definition here. As should be clear, we do not regard quantitative research to be any more scientific than qualitative research. Good research, that is, scientific research, can be quantitative or qualitative in style. In design, however, scientific research has the following four characteristics:

1. **The goal is inference.** Scientific research is designed to make descriptive or explanatory *inferences* on the basis of empirical information about the world. Careful descriptions of specific phenomena are often indispensable to scientific research, but the accumulation of facts alone is not sufficient. Facts can be collected (by qualitative or quantitative researchers) more or less systematically, and the former is obviously better than the latter, but our particular definition of science requires the additional step of attempting to infer beyond the immediate data to something broader that is not directly observed. That something may involve *descriptive inference*—using observations from the world to learn about other unobserved facts. Or that something may involve *causal inference*—learning about causal effects from the data observed. The domain of inference can be restricted in space and time—voting behavior in American elections since 1960, social movements in Eastern Europe since 1989—or it can be extensive—human behavior since the invention of agriculture. In either case, the key distinguishing mark of scientific research is the goal of making inferences that go beyond the particular observations collected.

2. **The procedures are public.** Scientific research uses explicit, codified, and *public* methods to generate and analyze data whose

reliability can therefore be assessed. Much social research in the qualitative style follows fewer precise rules of research procedure or of inference. As Robert K. Merton ([1949] 1968:71–72) put it, "The sociological analysis of qualitative data often resides in a private world of penetrating but unfathomable insights and ineffable understandings. . . . [However,] science . . . is public, not private." Merton's statement is not true of all qualitative researchers (and it is unfortunately still true of some quantitative analysts), but many proceed as if they had no method—sometimes as if the use of explicit methods would diminish their creativity. Nevertheless they cannot help but use some method. Somehow they observe phenomena, ask questions, infer information about the world from these observations, and make inferences about cause and effect. If the method and logic of a researcher's observations and inferences are left implicit, the scholarly community has no way of judging the validity of what was done. We cannot evaluate the principles of selection that were used to record observations, the ways in which observations were processed, and the logic by which conclusions were drawn. We cannot learn from their methods or replicate their results. Such research is not a *public* act. Whether or not it makes good reading, it is not a contribution to social science.

All methods—whether explicit or not—have limitations. The advantage of explicitness is that those limitations can be understood and, if possible, addressed. In addition, the methods can be taught and shared. This process allows research results to be compared across separate researchers and research projects studies to be replicated, and scholars to learn.

3. **The conclusions are uncertain.** By definition, inference is an imperfect process. Its goal is to use quantitative or qualitative data to learn about the world that produced them. Reaching perfectly certain conclu-

sions from uncertain data is obviously impossible. Indeed, uncertainty is a central aspect of all research and all knowledge about the world. Without a reasonable estimate of uncertainty, a description of the real world or an inference about a causal effect in the real world is uninterpretable. A researcher who fails to face the issue of uncertainty directly is either asserting that he or she knows everything perfectly or that he or she has no idea how certain or uncertain the results are. Either way, inferences without uncertainty estimates are not science as we define it.

4. **The content is the method.** Finally, scientific research adheres to a set of rules of inference on which its validity depends. Explicating the most important rules is a major task of this book.[2] The content of "science" is primarily the methods and rules, not the subject matter, since we can use these methods to study virtually anything. This point was recognized over a century ago when Karl Pearson (1892: 16) explained that "the field of science is unlimited; its material is endless; every group of natural phenomena, every phase of social life, every stage of past or present development is material for science. The unity of all science consists alone in its method, not in its material."

These four features of science have a further implication: science at its best is a *social enterprise*. Every researcher or team of researchers labors under limitations of knowledge and insight, and mistakes are unavoidable, yet such errors will likely be pointed out by others. Understanding the social character of science can be liberating since it means that our work need not be beyond criticism to make an important contribution—whether to the description of a problem or its conceptualization, to theory or to the evaluation of theory. As long as our work explicitly addresses (or attempts to redirect) the concerns of the community of scholars and uses public methods to arrive at inferences that are consistent with rules of science and the information at our disposal, it is likely to make a contribution. And the contribution of even a minor article is greater than that of the "great work" that stays forever in a desk drawer or within the confines of a computer.

1.1.3 Science and Complexity

Social science constitutes an attempt to make sense of social situations that we perceive as more or less complex. We need to recognize, however, that what we perceive as complexity is not entirely inherent in phenomena: the world is not naturally divided into simple and complex sets of events. On the contrary, the perceived complexity of a situation depends in part on how well we can simplify reality, and our capacity to simplify depends on whether we can specify outcomes and explanatory variables in a coherent way. Having more observations may assist us in this process but is usually insufficient. Thus *"complexity" is partly conditional on the state of our theory.*

Scientific methods can be as valuable for intrinsically complex events as for simpler ones. Complexity is likely to make our inferences less certain but should *not* make them any less scientific. Uncertainty and limited data should not cause us to abandon scientific research. On the contrary: the biggest payoff for using the rules of scientific inference occurs precisely when data are limited, observation tools are flawed, measurements are unclear, and relationships are uncertain. With clear relationships and unambiguous data, method may be less important, since even partially flawed rules of inference may produce answers that are roughly correct.

Consider some complex, and in some sense unique, events with enormous ramifications. The collapse of the Roman Empire, the French Revolution, the American Civil War, World War I, the Holocaust, and the reunification of Germany in 1990 are all examples of such events. These events seem to be the result of complex interactions of many forces whose conjuncture appears crucial to the event having taken place. That is, independently caused sequences of events and forces converged at a given place and time, their interaction appearing to bring about the events being observed (Hirschman 1970). Furthermore, it is often difficult to believe that these events were inevitable products of large-scale historical forces: some seem to have depended, in part, on idiosyncracies of personalities, institutions, or social movements. Indeed, from the perspective of our theories, chance often seems to have played a role: factors outside the scope of the theory provided crucial links in the sequences of events.

One way to understand such events is by seeking generalizations: conceptualizing each case as a member of a *class of events* about which meaningful generalizations can be made. This method often works well for ordinary wars or revolutions, but some wars and revolutions, being much more extreme than others, are "outliers" in the statistical distribution. Furthermore, notable early wars or revolutions may exert such a strong impact on subsequent events of the same class—we think again of the French Revolution—that caution is necessary in comparing them with their successors, which may be to some extent the product of imitation. Expanding the class of events can be useful, but it is not always appropriate.

Another way of dealing scientifically with rare, large-scale events is to engage in counterfactual analysis: "the mental construction of a course of events which is altered through modifications in one or more 'conditions'" (Weber [1905] 1949:173). The application of this idea in a systematic, scientific way is illustrated in a particularly extreme example of a rare event from geology and evolutionary biology, both historically oriented natural sciences. Stephen J. Gould has suggested that one way to distinguish systematic features of evolution from stochastic, chance events may be to imagine what the world would be like if all conditions up to a specific point were fixed and then the rest of history were

rerun. He contends that if it were possible to "replay the tape of life," to let evolution occur again from the beginning, the world's organisms today would be a completely different (Gould 1989).

A unique event on which students of evolution have recently focused is the sudden extinction of the dinosaurs 65 million years ago. Gould (1989:318) says, "we must assume that consciousness would not have evolved on our planet if a cosmic catastrophe had not claimed the dinosaurs as victims." If this statement is true, the extinction of the dinosaurs was as important as any historical event for human beings; however, dinosaur extinction does not fall neatly into a class of events that could be studied in a systematic, comparative fashion through the application of general laws in a straightforward way.

Nevertheless, dinosaur extinction can be studied scientifically: alternative hypotheses can be developed and tested with respect to their observable implications. One hypothesis to account for dinosaur extinction, developed by Luis Alvarez and collaborators at Berkeley in the late 1970s (Alvarez 1990), posits a cosmic collision: a meteorite crashed into the earth at about 72,000 kilometers an hour, creating a blast greater than that from a full-scale nuclear war. If this hypothesis is correct, it would have the observable implication that iridium (an element common in meteorites but rare on earth) should be found in the particular layer of the earth's crust that corresponds to sediment laid down sixty-five million years ago; indeed, the discovery of iridium at predicted layers in the earth has been taken as partial confirming evidence for the theory. Although this is an unambiguously unique event, there are many other observable implications. For one example, it should be possible to find the meteorite's crater somewhere on Earth (and several candidates have already been found).[3]

The issue of the cause(s) of dinosaur extinction remains unresolved, although the controversy has generated much valuable research. For our purposes, the point of this example is that scientific generalizations are useful in studying even highly unusual events that do not fall into a large class of events. The Alvarez hypothesis cannot be tested with reference to a set of common events, but it does have observable implications for other phenomena that can be evaluated. We should note, however, that a hypothesis is not considered a reasonably certain explanation until it has been evaluated empirically and passed a number of demanding tests. At a minimum, its implications must be consistent with our knowledge of the external world; at best, it should predict what Imre Lakatos (1970) refers to as "new facts," that is, those formerly unobserved.

The point is that even apparently unique events such as dinosaur extinction can be studied scientifically if we pay attention to improving theory, data, and our use of the data. Improving our theory through conceptual clarification and specification of variables can generate more observable implications and even test causal theories of unique events such as dinosaur extinction. Improving our data allows us to observe more of these observable implications, and improving our use of data permits more of these implications to be extracted from existing data. That a set of events to be studied is highly complex does not render careful research design irrelevant. Whether we study many phenomena or few—or even one—the study will be improved if we collect data on as many observable implications of our theory as possible.

NOTES

1. We reject the concept, or at least the word, "quasi-experiment." Either a research design involves investigator control over the observations and values of the key causal variables (in which case it is an experiment) or it does not (in which case it is nonexperimental research). Both experimental and nonexperimental research have their advantages and drawbacks; one is not better in all research situations than the other.

2. Although we do cover the vast majority of the important rules of scientific inference,

they are not complete. Indeed, most philosophers agree that a complete, exhaustive inductive logic is impossible, even in principle.

3. However, an alternative hypothesis, that extinction was caused by volcanic eruptions, is also consistent with the presence of iridium, and seems more consistent than the meteorite hypothesis with the finding that all the species extinctions did not occur simultaneously.

REFERENCES

Alvarez, Walter, and Frank Asaro. 1990. "An Extraterrestrial Impact." *Scientific American* (October): 78–84.

Gould, Stephen J. 1989. *Wonderful Life: The Burgess Shale and the Nature of History*. New York: Norton.

Hirschmann, Albert O. 1970. "The Search for Paradigms as a Hindrance to Understanding." *World Politics* 22, no. 3 (April): 329–43.

Lakatos, Imre. 1970. "Falsification and the Methodology of Scientific Research Programs." In I. Lakatos and A. Musgrave, eds. *Criticism and the Growth of Knowledge*. Cambridge: Cambridge University Press.

Merton, Robert K. [1949] 1968. *Social Theory and Social Structure*. Reprint. New York: Free Press.

Schumpeter, Joseph A. [1936] 1991. "Can Capitalism Survive?" In Richard Swedberg, ed. *The Economics of Sociology and Capitalism*, Princeton: Princeton University Press.

Skocpol, Theda. 1984. "Emerging Agendas and Recurrent Strategies in Historical Sociology." In Theda Skocpol, ed. *Vision and Method in Historical Sociology*. New York: Cambridge University Press.

Weber, Max. [1905] 1949. "Critical Studies in the Logic of the Cultural Sciences." In Max Weber, ed. *The Methodology of the Social Sciences*. Translated and edited by Edward A. Shils and Henry A. Fluch. New York: Free Press.

2 THE STATE

At the center of most discussions of comparative politics lies the state, the organization that wields power over people and territory. In this section we will consider the ways in which we think about and measure the state, and how these have changed over time. A theoretical discussion of the state is complemented by more concrete discussions of the challenges that states confront in the current international system.

Max Weber is often cited as one of the forefathers of modern social science. In addition to political science, the fields of sociology and economics also owe a debt to Weber. Indeed, at the time of his writing, in the late nineteenth and early twentieth century, these fields were not clearly distinguished from one another. Politics as a Vocation *(1918) was a speech originally presented at Munich University, in which he sought to lay out some of the most basic ways in which he understood political power. Weber provides the modern definition of the state (a monopoly of force over territory) and from there outlines what he believes to be the central forms of political authority (traditional, charismatic, rational-legal). For Weber, the development of the modern state occurs alongside the growing domination of the bureaucracy and rational legal authority—politics as a profession, rather than a calling or an inherited role. Thus, charismatic or traditional leaders gave way to the modern professional state. In spite of the profound influence of Weber's work, by the mid-twentieth century, state-focused analysis began to lose favor, particularly in the United States. Swept up in the so-called behavioral revolution, political scientists began to concentrate more on societal factors, downplaying the degree to which the state itself was an important source of politics.*

However, over the past two decades, political scientists have returned their attention to the idea of state power and how the state's autonomy and capacity can shape such things as the emergence of democracy or economic progress (topics that we discuss in Chapters 4 and 5). Comparative politics has again become a much more state-focused field of study.

A wide range of contemporary scholars has refocused on the state as an important variable in comparative politics. Jeffery Herbst's "War and the State in Africa" (1990) draws on historical studies of state formation in Europe to consider whether we can expect a similar outcome in other parts of the world, such as Africa. In Europe, the author notes, interstate war was a critical component in the development of the modern state, helping to improve taxation, administration, and the development of symbols to establish national identity, a process that occurred over many centuries. In Africa, however, states have not formed out of a long process of warfare, but rather are the remnants of empires that once dominated the continent. These states are ill equipped to carry out most administrative tasks and lack the kind of national unity that can help build state legitimacy. There is a terrible irony, then: the absence of interstate war across Africa has left the continent with an array of weak states that cannot secure either prosperity or security. Indeed, one could go so far as to argue that the lack of war between states has resulted in horrific wars within them, such as the civil conflicts of Liberia or the genocide of Rwanda. Herbst is skeptical that peaceful state-building policies could serve as an alternative to war, and though he does not suggest that war between countries should be welcomed in Africa in order to build stronger states, it is hard not to draw such an uncomfortable conclusion. In the foreseeable future, the author anticipates an Africa of "permanently weak states."

In the years since Herbst's work was written, Africa and other parts of the world have seen the rise of something much worse than the weak states Herbst discusses. This is what is known as the "failed state." From the former Soviet Union to Latin America, Asia, and Africa, various countries have teetered on the edge or plunged into the abyss of state failure, where the most basic functions of the state—including the monopoly of force—have broken down, leading to civil conflict and anarchy. These have become a tremendous concern, not only because of the suffering that such state failures have caused, but also because of the fear that failed states often provide the perfect breeding ground for terrorism. Robert Rotberg considers this in "The New Nature of Nation-State Failure" (2002). Where states fail, we see greater civil conflict, weak infrastructure, inequality, corruption, and economic decline. As we learned from Herbst, it is very difficult to build a strong state, and for a failed state, this task is even more difficult. Policy makers, Rotberg argues, should take more care to identify and strengthen states in danger of collapse before they are beyond assistance and become an international threat.

Scholars are concerned about not only the power of the state, but also the state's future direction. In "Sovereignty" (2001), Stephen D. Krasner takes on many of the recent arguments that, in one way or another, suggest the decline of the state as a major political actor. In spite of such factors as globalization and political integration, the state is still very much alive and will continue to be the driving force in domestic and international politics. This is not to say, however, that the state itself may not change. In "The New Religious State" (1995), Mark Juergensmeyer addresses what he considers to be the most important challenge to modern states in the coming decades, specifically religious fundamentalism, which he refers to as "religious nationalism." Juergensmeyer notes that the rise of the modern state was driven in part by the rise of national identity and ideology, which made the state the sovereign authority and pushed religion out of public life. However, across the world, religion has reemerged as an ideology in its own right, and some fundamentalists assert that the state and faith should be merged into a single authority that recognizes only the sovereignty of God. What are the implications of this development for domestic and international politics? Would religious states inherently be hostile to democracies and other nonreligious states? These questions are largely academic now, but they may become critical as religion and politics continue to clash in future.

MAX WEBER

POLITICS AS A VOCATION

This lecture, which I give at your request, will necessarily disappoint you in a number of ways. You will naturally expect me to take a position on actual problems of the day. But that will be the case only in a purely formal way and toward the end, when I shall raise certain questions concerning the significance of political action in the whole way of life. In today's lecture, all questions that refer to what policy and what content one should give one's political activity must be eliminated. For such questions have nothing to do with the general question of what politics as a vocation means and what it can mean. Now to our subject matter.

What do we understand by politics? The concept is extremely broad and comprises any kind of *independent* leadership in action. One speaks of the currency policy of the banks, of the discounting policy of the Reichsbank, of the strike policy of a trade union; one may speak of the educational policy of a municipality or a township, of the policy of the president of a voluntary association, and, finally, even of the policy of a prudent wife who seeks to guide her husband. Tonight, our reflections are, of course, not based upon such a broad concept. We wish to understand by politics only the leadership, or the influencing of the leadership, of a *political* association, hence today, of a *state*.

But what is a "political" association from the sociological point of view? What is a "state"? Sociologically, the state cannot be defined in terms of its ends. There is scarcely any task that some political association has not taken in hand, and there is no task that one could say has always been exclusive and peculiar to those associations which are designated as political ones: today the state, or historically, those associations which have been the predecessors of the modern state. Ultimately, one can define the modern state sociologically only in terms of the specific means peculiar to it, as to every political association, namely, the use of physical force.

"Every state is founded on force," said Trotsky at Brest-Litovsk. That is indeed right. If no social institutions existed which knew the use of violence, then the concept of "state" would be eliminated, and a condition would emerge that could be designated as "anarchy," in the specific sense of this word. Of course, force is certainly not the

From H. H. Gerth and C. Wright Mills, eds., trans. *From Max Weber: Essays in Sociology* (New York: Galaxy, 1958), pp. 77–87.

normal or the only means of the state—nobody says that—but force is a means specific to the state. Today the relation between the state and violence is an especially intimate one. In the past, the most varied institutions—beginning with the sib—have known the use of physical force as quite normal. Today, however, we have to say that a state is a human community that (successfully) claims the *monopoly of the legitimate use of physical force* within a given territory. Note that "territory" is one of the characteristics of the state. Specifically, at the present time, the right to use physical force is ascribed to other institutions or to individuals only to the extent to which the state permits it. The state is considered the sole source of the "right" to use violence. Hence, "politics" for us means striving to share power or striving to influence the distribution of power, either among states or among groups within a state.

This corresponds essentially to ordinary usage. When a question is said to be a "political" question, when a cabinet minister or an official is said to be a "political" official, or when a decision is said to be "politically" determined, what is always meant is that interests in the distribution, maintenance, or transfer of power are decisive for answering the questions and determining the decision or the official's sphere of activity. He who is active in politics strives for power either as a means in serving other aims, ideal or egoistic, or as "power for power's sake," that is, in order to enjoy the prestige-feeling that power gives.

Like the political institutions historically preceding it, the state is a relation of men dominating men, a relation supported by means of legitimate (i.e. considered to be legitimate) violence. If the state is to exist, the dominated must obey the authority claimed by the powers that be. When and why do men obey? Upon what inner justifications and upon what external means does this domination rest?

To begin with, in principle, there are three inner justifications, hence basic *legitimations* of domination.

First, the authority of the "eternal yesterday," i.e. of the mores sanctified through the unimag-

inably ancient recognition and habitual orientation to conform. This is "traditional" domination exercised by the patriarch and the patrimonial prince of yore.

There is the authority of the extraordinary and personal *gift of grace* (charisma), the absolutely personal devotion and personal confidence in revelation, heroism, or other qualities of individual leadership. This is "charismatic" domination, as exercised by the prophet or—in the field of politics—by the elected war lord, the plebiscitarian ruler, the great demagogue, or the political party leader.

Finally, there is a domination by virtue of "legality," by virtue of the belief in the validity of legal statute and functional "competence" based on rationally created *rules*. In this case, obedience is expected in discharging statutory obligations. This is domination as exercised by the modern "servant of the state" and by all those bearers of power who in this respect resemble him.

It is understood that, in reality, obedience is determined by highly robust motives of fear and hope—fear of the vengeance of magical powers or of the power-holder, hope for reward in this world or in the beyond—and besides all this, by interests of the most varied sort. Of this we shall speak presently. However, in asking for the "legitimations" of this obedience, one meets with these three "pure" types: "traditional," "charismatic," and "legal."

These conceptions of legitimacy and their inner justifications are of very great significance for the structure of domination. To be sure, the pure types are rarely found in reality. But today we cannot deal with the highly complex variants, transitions, and combinations of these pure types, which problems belong to "political science." Here we are interested above all in the second of these types: domination by virtue of the devotion of those who obey the purely personal "charisma" of the "leader." For this is the root of the idea of a *calling* in its highest expression.

Devotion to the charisma of the prophet, or the leader in war, or to the great demagogue in the *ecclesia* or in parliament, means that the leader is personally recognized as the innerly "called" leader of men. Men do not obey him by virtue of tradition or statute, but because they believe in him. If he is more than a narrow and vain upstart of the moment, the leader lives for his cause and "strives for his work." The devotion of his disciples, his followers, his personal party friends is oriented to his person and to its qualities.

Charismatic leadership has emerged in all places and in all historical epochs. Most importantly in the past, it has emerged in the two figures of the magician and the prophet on the one hand, and in the elected war lord, the gang leader and *condotierre* on the other hand. *Political* leadership in the form of the free "demagogue" who grew from the soil of the city state is of greater concern to us; like the city state, the demagogue is peculiar to the Occident and especially to Mediterranean culture. Furthermore, political leadership in the form of the parliamentary "party leader" has grown on the soil of the constitutional state, which is also indigenous only to the Occident.

These politicians by virtue of a "calling," in the most genuine sense of the word, are of course nowhere the only decisive figures in the crosscurrents of the political struggle for power. The sort of auxiliary means that are at their disposal is also highly decisive. How do the politically dominant powers manage to maintain their domination? The question pertains to any kind of domination, hence also to political domination in all its forms, traditional as well as legal and charismatic.

Organized domination, which calls for continuous administration, requires that human conduct be conditioned to obedience towards those masters who claim to be the bearers of legitimate power. On the other hand, by virtue of this obedience, organized domination requires the control of those material goods which in a given case are necessary for the use of physical violence. Thus, organized domination requires control of the personal executive staff and the material implements of administration.

The administrative staff, which externally represents the organization of political domina-tion, is, of course, like any other organization, bound by obedience to the power-holder and not alone by the concept of legitimacy, of which we have just spoken. There are two other means, both of which appeal to personal interests: material reward and social honor. The fiefs of vassals, the prebends of patrimonial officials, the salaries of modern civil servants, the honor of knights, the privileges of estates, and the honor of the civil servant comprise their respective wages. The fear of losing them is the final and decisive basis for solidarity between the executive staff and the power-holder. There is honor and booty for the followers in war; for the demagogue's following, there are "spoils"—that is, exploitation of the dominated through the monopolization of office—and there are politically determined profits and premiums of vanity. All of these rewards are also derived from the domination exercised by a charismatic leader.

To maintain a dominion by force, certain material goods are required, just as with an economic organization. All states may be classified according to whether they rest on the principle that the staff of men themselves own the administrative means, or whether the staff is "separated" from these means of administration. This distinction holds in the same sense in which today we say that the salaried employee and the proletarian in the capitalistic enterprise are "separated" from the material means of production. The power-holder must be able to count on the obedience of the staff members, officials, or whoever else they may be. The administrative means may consist of money, building, war material, vehicles, horses, or whatnot. The question is whether or not the power-holder himself directs and organizes the administration while delegating executive power to personal servants, hired officials, or personal favorites and confidants, who are nonowners, i.e. who do not use the material means of administration in their own right but are directed by the lord. The distinction runs through all administrative organizations of the past.

These political associations in which the material means of administration are autonomously controlled, wholly or partly, by the dependent administrative staff may be called associations organized in "*estates*." The vassal in the feudal association, for instance, paid out of his own pocket for the administration and judicature of the district enfeoffed to him. He supplied his own equipment and provisions for war, and his subvassals did likewise. Of course, this had consequences for the lord's position of power, which only rested upon a relation of personal faith and upon the fact that the legitimacy of his possession of the fief and the social honor of the vassal were derived from the overlord.

However, everywhere, reaching back to the earliest political formations, we also find the lord himself directing the administration. He seeks to take the administration into his own hands by having men personally dependent upon him: slaves, household officials, attendants, personal "favorites," and prebendaries enfeoffed in kind or in money from his magazines. He seeks to defray the expenses from his own pocket, from the revenues of his patrimonium; and he seeks to create an army which is dependent upon him personally because it is equipped and provisioned out of his granaries, magazines, and armories. In the association of "estates," the lord rules with the aid of an autonomous "aristocracy" and hence shares his domination with it; the lord who personally administers is supported either by members of his household or by plebeians. These are propertyless strata having no social honor of their own; materially, they are completely chained to him and are not backed up by any competing power of their own. All forms of patriarchal and patrimonial domination, Sultanist despotism, and bureaucratic states belong to this latter type. The bureaucratic state order is especially important; in its most rational development, it is precisely characteristic of the modern state.

Everywhere the development of the modern state is initiated through the action of the prince. He paves the way for the expropriation of the autonomous and "private" bearers of executive power who stand beside him, of those who in their own right possess the means of administration, warfare, and financial organization, as well as politically usable goods of all sorts. The whole process is a complete parallel to the development of the capitalist enterprise through gradual expropriation of the independent producers. In the end, the modern state controls the total means of political organization, which actually come together under a single head. No single official personally owns the money he pays out, or the buildings, stores, tools, and war machines he controls. In the contemporary "state"—and this is essential for the concept of state—the "separation" of the administrative staff, of the administrative officials, and of the workers from the material means of administrative organization is completed. Here the most modern development begins, and we see with our own eyes the attempt to inaugurate the expropriation of this expropriator of the political means, and therewith of political power.

The revolution [of Germany, 1918] has accomplished, at least in so far as leaders have taken the place of the statutory authorities, this much: the leaders, through usurpation or election, have attained control over the political staff and the apparatus of material goods; and they deduce their legitimacy—no matter with what right—from the will of the governed. Whether the leaders, on the basis of this at least apparent success, can rightfully entertain the hope of also carrying through the expropriation within the capitalist enterprises is a different question. The direction of capitalist enterprises, despite far-reaching analogies, follows quite different laws than those of political administration.

Today we do not take a stand on this question. I state only the purely *conceptual* aspect for our consideration: the modern state is a compulsory association which organizes domination. It has been successful in seeking to monopolize the legitimate use of physical force as a means of domination within a territory. To this end the state has combined the material means of organization in the hands of its leaders, and it has expropriated all autonomous functionaries of estates who formerly controlled these means in their own right. The state has taken their positions and now stands in the top place.

During this process of political expropriation, which has occurred with varying success in all countries on earth, "professional politicians" in another sense have emerged. They arose first in the service of a prince. They have been men who, unlike the charismatic leader, have not wished to be lords themselves, but who have entered the *service* of political lords. In the struggle of expropriation, they placed themselves at the princes' disposal and by managing the princes' politics they earned, on the one hand, a living and, on the other hand, an ideal content of life. Again, it is *only* in the Occident that we find this kind of professional politician in the service of powers other than the princes. In the past, they have been the most important power instrument of the prince and his instrument of political expropriation.

Before discussing "professional politicians" in detail, let us clarify in all its aspects the state of affairs their existence presents. Politics, just as economic pursuits, may be a man's avocation or his vocation. One may engage in politics, and hence seek to influence the distribution of power within and between political structures, as an "occasional" politician. We are all "occasional" politicians when we cast our ballot or consummate a similar expression of intention, such as applauding or protesting in a "political" meeting, or delivering a "political" speech, etc. The whole relation of many people to politics is restricted to this. Politics as an avocation is today practiced by all those party agents and heads of voluntary political associations who, as a rule, are politically active only in case of need and for whom politics is, neither materially nor ideally, "their life" in the first place. The same holds for those members of state counsels and similar deliberative bodies that function only when summoned. It also holds for rather broad strata of our members of parliament who are politically active only during sessions. In the past, such strata were found especially among the estates. Proprietors of military implements in their own right, or proprietors of goods important for the administration, or proprietors of personal pre-

rogatives may be called "estates." A large portion of them were far from giving their lives wholly, or merely preferentially, or more than occasionally, to the service of politics. Rather, they exploited their prerogatives in the interest of gaining rent or even profits; and they became active in the service of political associations only when the overlord of their status-equals especially demanded it. It was not different in the case of some of the auxiliary forces which the prince drew into the struggle for the creation of a political organization to be exclusively at his disposal. This was the nature of the *Rate von Haus aus* [councilors] and, still further back, of a considerable part of the councilors assembling in the "Curia" and other deliberating bodies of the princes. But these merely occasional auxiliary forces engaging in politics on the side were naturally not sufficient for the prince. Of necessity, the prince sought to create a staff of helpers dedicated wholly and exclusively to serving him, hence making this their major vocation. The structure of the emerging dynastic political organization, and not only this but the whole articulation of the culture, depended to a considerable degree upon the question of where the prince recruited agents.

A staff was also necessary for those political associations whose members constituted themselves politically as (so-called) "free" communes under the complete abolition or the far-going restriction of princely power.

They were "free" not in the sense of freedom from domination by force, but in the sense that princely power legitimized by tradition (mostly religously sanctified) as the exclusive source of all authority was absent. These communities have their historical home in the Occident. Their nucleus was the city as a body politic, the form in which the city first emerged in the Mediterranean culture area. In all these cases, what did the politicians who made politics their major vocation look like?

There are two ways of making politics one's vocation: Either one lives "for" politics or one lives "off" politics. By no means is this contrast an exclusive one. The rule is, rather, that man does both, at least in thought, and certainly he also does both in practice. He who lives "for" politics makes politics his life, in an internal sense. Either he enjoys the naked possession of the power he exerts, or he nourishes his inner balance and self-feeling by the consciousness that his life has *meaning* in the service of a "cause." In this internal sense, every sincere man who lives for a cause also lives off this cause. The distinction hence refers to a much more substantial aspect of the matter, namely, to the economic. He who strives to make politics a permanent *source of income* lives "off" politics as a vocation, whereas he who does not do this lives "for" politics. Under the dominance of the private property order, some—if you wish—very trivial preconditions must exist in order for a person to be able to live "for" politics in this economic sense. Under normal conditions, the politician must be economically independent of the income politics can bring him. This means, quite simply, that the politician must be wealthy or must have a personal position in life which yields a sufficient income.

This is the case, at least in normal circumstances. The war lord's following is just as little concerned about the conditions of a normal economy as is the street crowd following of the revolutionary hero. Both live off booty, plunder, confiscations, contributions, and the imposition of worthless and compulsory means of tender, which in essence amounts to the same thing. But necessarily, these are extraordinary phenomena. In everyday economic life, only some wealth serves the purpose of making a man economically independent. Yet this alone does not suffice. The professional politician must also be economically "dispensable," that is, his income must not depend upon the fact that he constantly and personally places his ability and thinking entirely, or at least by far predominantly, in the service of economic acquisition. In the most unconditional way, the rentier is dispensable in this sense. Hence, he is a man who receives completely unearned income. He may

be the territorial lord of the past or the large landowner and aristocrat of the present who receives ground rent. In Antiquity and the Middle Ages they who received slave or serf rents or in modern times rents from shares or bonds or similar sources—these are rentiers.

Neither the worker nor—and this has to be noted well—the entrepreneur, especially the modern, large-scale entrepreneur, is economically dispensable in this sense. For it is precisely the entrepreneur who is tied to his enterprise and is therefore *not* dispensable. This holds for the entrepreneur in industry far more than for the entrepreneur in agriculture, considering the seasonal character of agriculture. In the main, it is very difficult for the entrepreneur to be represented in his enterprise by someone else, even temporarily. He is as little dispensable as is the medical doctor, and the more eminent and busy he is the less dispensable he is. For purely organizational reasons, it is easier for the lawyer to be dispensable; and therefore the lawyer has played an incomparably greater, and often even a dominant, role as a professional politician. We shall not continue in this classification; rather let us clarify some of its ramifications.

The leadership of a state or of a party by men who (in the economic sense of the word) live exclusively for politics and not off politics means necessarily a "plutocratic" recruitment of the leading political strata. To be sure, this does not mean that such plutocratic leadership signifies at the same time that the politically dominant strata will not also seek to live "off" politics, and hence that the dominant stratum will not usually exploit their political domination in their own economic interest. All that is unquestionable, of course. There has never been such a stratum that has not somehow lived "off" politics. Only this is meant: that the professional politician need not seek remuneration directly for his political work, whereas every politician without means must absolutely claim this. On the other hand, we do not mean to say that the propertyless politician will pursue private economic advantages through politics, exclusively, or even predominantly. Nor do we mean that he will not think, in the first place, of "the subject matter." Nothing would be more incorrect. According to all experience, a care for the economic "security" of his existence is consciously or unconsciously a cardinal point in the whole life orientation of the wealthy man. A quite reckless and unreserved political idealism is found if not exclusively at least predominantly among those strata who by virtue of their propertylessness stand entirely outside of the strata who are interested in maintaining the economic order of a given society. This holds especially for extraordinary and hence revolutionary epochs. A non-plutocratic recruitment of interested politicians, of leadership and following, is geared to the self-understood precondition that regular and reliable income will accrue to those who manage politics.

Either politics can be conducted "honorifically" and then, as one usually says, by "independent," that is, by wealthy, men, and especially by rentiers. Or, political leadership is made accessible to propertyless men who must then be rewarded. The professional politician who lives "off" politics may be a pure "prebendary" or a salaried "official." Then the politician receives either income from fees and perquisites for specific services—tips and bribes are only an irregular and formally illegal variant of this category of income—or a fixed income in kind, a money salary, or both. He may assume the character of an "entrepreneur," like the *condottiere* or the holder of a farmed-out or purchased office, or like the American boss who considers his costs a capital investment which he brings to fruition through exploitation of his influence. Again, he may receive a fixed wage, like a journalist, a party secretary, a modern cabinet minister, or a political official. Feudal fiefs, land grants, and prebends of all sorts have been typical, in the past. With the development of the money economy, perquisites and prebends especially are the typical rewards for the following of princes, victorious conquerors, or successful party chiefs. For loyal services today, party leaders give offices of all sorts—in parties, newspapers, co-operative societies, health insurance, municipalities, as well as in the state. *All* party struggles are struggles for the patronage of office, as well as struggles for objective goals.

JEFFREY HERBST

WAR AND THE STATE IN AFRICA

Most analyses assume that in Africa, as elsewhere, states will eventually become strong. But this may not be true in Africa, where states are developing in a fundamentally new environment. Lessons drawn from the case of Europe show that war is an important cause of state formation that is missing in Africa today.

From *International Security*, 14, no. 4. (Spring 1990), pp. 117–39.

The crucial role that war has played in the formation of European states has long been noted. Samuel P. Huntington argued that "war was the great stimulus to state building," and Charles Tilly went so far as to claim that "war made the state, and the state made war."[1] Similarly, two of the most successful states in the Third World today, South Korea and Taiwan, are largely "warfare" states that have been molded, in part, by the near constant threat of external aggression.

However, studies of political development and state consolidation in Africa and many other parts of the Third World have all but ignored the important role that war can play in political development.

The role of war has not been examined because the vast majority of states in Africa and elsewhere in the world gained independence without having to resort to combat and have not faced a security threat since independence.[2] Those scholars who have analyzed the military in the developing world have studied the armed forces' role in economic and political processes but have not examined the changes that war could potentially effect on a state.[3] Studying the military and studying warfare are not the same, especially in the area of state consolidation, because warfare has independent effects on economic policies, administrative structures, and the citizenry's relationship with the state that have very little to do with the military.[4] Finally, beyond the usual problem of trying to study the impact of a factor that is missing, there is a less excusable normative bias which has sometimes prevented students of politics from examining the effects of war. The question of whether it is only possible to create a nation out of "blood and iron" is apparently one that many analysts find too disturbing to examine.[5]

Comparison of the European case with that of Africa is therefore crucial to understanding whether the analogy holds. War in Europe played an important role in the consolidation of many now-developed states: war caused the state to become more efficient in revenue collection; it forced leaders to dramatically improve administrative capabilities; and it created a climate and important symbols around which a disparate population could unify. While there is little reason to believe that war would have exactly the same domestic effects in Africa today as it did in Europe several centuries ago, it is important to ask if developing countries can accomplish in times of peace what war enabled European countries to do. I conclude that they probably cannot because fundamental changes in economic structures and

societal beliefs are difficult, if not impossible, to bring about when countries are not being disrupted or under severe external threat.

The next section of this article outlines how war affected state formation in Europe, with particular attention to two crucial developments: the creation of centralized and efficient structures to collect taxes, and the development of nationalism. I then compare the European experience of state building through warfare to the relative peace that Africa has experienced since the 1960s. While African states have benefited from peace, their development has been stunted by the very problems that war helped European countries to solve. I then evaluate the possibilities that African states might develop strategies to solve these fundamental problems in times of peace. I conclude that some states will probably be unsuccessful in finding ways of building the state in times of peace and will therefore remain permanently weak. Accordingly, the international community will have to develop non-traditional policies for helping a new brand of states: those that will continue to exist but that will not develop. Other states, perceiving that peace locks them into a permanently weak position, may be tempted to use war as a means of resolving their otherwise intractable problems of state consolidation.

Effects of War on State Consolidation: The European Case

It is instructive to look at war's impact on European societies because, as will be noted below, war in Europe helped alleviate some of the problems that affect African countries today. At the most basic level, war in Europe acted as a filter whereby weak states were eliminated and political arrangements that were not viable either were reformed or disappeared. Weak states do exist in Europe today—Belgium is one example—but the near-constant threat of war did prompt most states to become stronger to survive. The contrast between this evolutionary development and the current situation in the Third

World, where even states that are largely dependent on foreign aid will continue to exist for the foreseeable future, is dramatic. It is, of course, important not to generalize too much because war had many different effects over time, and even in the same period states reacted in a variety of ways to external threats. However, war did affect the ability of European states to increase taxation and contributed to the forging of national identities in many countries. It is therefore important to examine the potential impact of external threat to better understand state consolidation in the Third World.

Taxes

Perhaps the most noticeable effect of war in European history was to cause the state to increase its ability to collect significantly more revenue with greater efficiency and less public resistance. Given the freedom of European states to attack each other, those states that could raise money quickly could successfully threaten their neighbors with a war that might lead to significant damage or even complete destruction. Richard Bean writes, "Once the power to tax had been successfully appropriated by any one sovereign, once he had used that power to bribe or coerce his nobility into acquiescence, that state could face all neighboring states with the choice of being conquered or of centralizing authority and raising taxes."[6] While success in war depends on many factors including technology, tactics, and morale of the troops, raising sufficient revenue was a necessary condition to prevent defeat. States that did not raise sufficient revenue for war perished. As Michael Mann notes, "A state that wished to survive had to increase its extractive capacity to pay for professional armies and/or navies. Those that did not would be crushed on the battlefield and absorbed into others—the fate of Poland, of Saxony, of Bavaria in [the seventeenth and eighteenth centuries]. No European states were continuously at peace. It is impossible to escape the conclusion that a peaceful state would have ceased to exist even more speedily

than the militarily inefficient actually did."[7]

War affects state finances for two reasons. First, it puts tremendous strains on leaders to find new and more regular sources of income. While rulers may recognize that their tax system is inadequate, a war may be the only thing that forces them to expend the necessary political capital and undertake the coercion required to gain more revenue. For instance, in Mann's study of taxation in England between 1688 and 1815, he finds that there were six major jumps in state revenue and that each corresponds with the beginning of a war.[8] The association between the need to fight and the need to collect revenue is perhaps clearest in Prussia, where the main tax collection agency was called the General War Commissariat.[9]

Second, citizens are much more likely to acquiesce to increased taxation when the nation is at war, because a threat to their survival will overwhelm other concerns they might have about increased taxation. In fact, taxation for a war can be thought of as a "lumpy" collective good: not only must the population pay to get the good, but it must also pay a considerable amount more than the current level of taxation, because a small increase in revenue is often not enough to meet the new security threat facing the state.[10] In this way, taxation for a war is like taxation for building a bridge: everyone must pay to build the bridge and a small increase in revenue will not be enough, because half a bridge, like fighting half a war, is useless.

Thus, war often causes a "ratchet effect" whereby revenue increases sharply when a nation is fighting but does not decline to the *ante bellum* level when hostilities have ceased.[11] Once governments have invested the sunken costs in expanding tax collection systems and routinized the collection of new sources of revenue, the marginal costs of continuing those structures are quite low and the resources they collect can be used for projects that will enhance the ruling group's support.

While it is not a universal rule, war in other societies at other times often played the same kind of role that war did in Europe. For instance, Joseph Smaldone writes in his study of the Sokoto Caliphate (in what is now Nigeria) between 1500 and 1800:

> War was the principal instrument for the establishment and extension of political authority over subject people and foreign territory, and for the organization, maintenance, and reinforcement of that authority. The demands of perennial war evoked institutions to subordinate the sectors of society crucial to the interests of these militarized polities. The permanent requirement to mobilize human and material resources for military purposes [i.e., taxation] intensified tendencies toward the monopolization of power and the elaboration of auxiliary institutions of social control.[12]

Similarly, the South Korean and Taiwanese states have been able to extract so many resources from their societies in part because the demands to be constantly vigilant provoked the state into developing efficient mechanisms for collecting resources and controlling dissident groups.[13] A highly extractive state also could cloak demands for greater resources in appeals for national unity in the face of a determined enemy.

Nationalism

War also had a major impact on the development of nationalism of Europe. Indeed, the presence of a palpable external threat may be the strongest way to generate a common association between the state and the population. External threats have such a powerful effect on nationalism because people realize in a profound manner that they are under threat because of who they are as a nation; they are forced to recognize that it is only as a nation that they can successfully defeat the threat. Anthony Giddens recounts the effects of World War I: "The War canalized the development of states' sovereignty, tying this to citizenship and to nationalism in such a profound way that any other scenario [of how the international system would be ordered] came to appear as little more than idle fantasy."[14] Similarly, Michael Howard notes the vis-

ceral impact of wars on the development of nationalism throughout Europe:

> Self-identification as a Nation implies almost by definition alienation from other communities, and the most memorable incidents in the group-memory consisted in conflict with and triumph over other communities. France *was* Marengo, Austerlitz and Jena: military triumph set the seal on the new-found national consciousness. Britain *was* Trafalgar—but it had been a nation for four hundred years, since those earlier battles Crecy and Agincourt. Russia *was* the triumph of 1812. Germany *was* Gravelotte and Sedan.[15]

In Europe there was an almost symbiotic relationship between the state's extractive capacity and nationalism: war increased both as the population was convinced by external threat that they should pay more to the state, and as, at the same time, the population united around common symbols and memories that were important components of nationalism. Fighting wars may be the only way whereby it is possible to have people pay more taxes and at the same time feel more closely associated with the state.

The Absence of Interstate War in the Modern Era

While trying to study the chaos caused by administrative disintegration, the forceful crushing of ethnic challenges, and large-scale human rights abuses, many scholars have generally assumed that poor countries today face even more external challenges than European states did in their formative periods.[16] In fact, since the end of the Second World War, very few Third World states have fought interstate wars of the type that affected the evolution of European states. The few Third World interstate wars that have occurred (e.g., India-Pakistan, Iran-Iraq, China-Vietnam) have obscured the fact that the vast majority of Third World states most of the time do not face significant external threats. States like Israel, South Korea, or Taiwan, where national survival has been a real consideration in national politics, are exceptional and even these countries have survived intact.

Even in Africa, the continent seemingly destined for war given the colonially-imposed boundaries and weak political authorities, there has not been one involuntary boundary change since the dawn of the independence era in the late 1950s, and very few countries face even the prospect of a conflict with their neighbors. Most of the conflicts in Africa that have occurred were not, as in Europe, wars of conquest that threatened the existence of other states, but conflicts over lesser issues that were resolved without threatening the existence of another state. For instance, Tanzania invaded Uganda in 1979 to overthrow Idi Amin, not to conquer Uganda. Similarly, the war in the Western Sahara is a colonial question, not a conflict between independent states. Even South Africa's destabilization efforts against its neighbors are primarily attempts to influence the policies of the majority-ruled countries, not to change the borders of the region. Lesotho or Swaziland would not exist today if South Africa had any real territorial ambitions. In the few conflicts that did have the potential to threaten fundamentally the existence of states—Somalia's attempt to invade Ethiopia in the 1970s and Libya's war against Chad in the 1970s and 1980s—the aggressor did not succeed.[17]

African states have seldom fought interstate wars and the continent has not witnessed significant boundary changes, because independent leaders have continued the system of boundary maintenance that the colonial powers first developed to regulate the scramble for Africa in the late 1800s.[18] African leaders recognized in the early 1960s that a potentially large number of groups would want to secede from the states they are presently in, to join others or create entirely new ones. In order to prevent the continent from being thrown into the chaos of large-scale boundary changes in which the stability and integrity of any state could be threatened, they created a system of explicit norms, propounded by the Organization of African Unity in 1963, which

declared any change in the inherited colonial boundaries to be illegitimate. Most of the continent has, accordingly, refused to recognize boundary changes (e.g., Biafra, Eritrea) even where the principle of self-determination might have led them to do so. This system has been successful in preserving African national boundaries and has so far deterred almost all countries from initiating the kind of conquest wars that were so common in European history. The system that maintained the inherited borders as inviolate was strengthened somewhat inadvertently, because two of the largest states on the continent (Nigeria and Zaire), which could conceivably have threatened their much smaller neighbors, faced significant secessionist threats (from the Ibo and Kataganese respectively) and therefore worked resolutely to strengthen the norm that the borders should not be changed.

The stability of new states, especially in Africa, is a remarkable development given that the vast majority of the over one hundred countries in the Third World that have gained their independence since 1945 are poor, have weak administrative structures, and consist of populations that are splintered along regional or ethnic lines. In other words, they are precisely the kind of states that before 1945 were routinely invaded and taken over by stronger states in their region or by external powers. Yet, very few states in the Third World, despite their evident military and political weaknesses, face any significant external threat.

In contrast, Tilly estimates, the "enormous majority" of states in Europe failed. Peace was the exception and long periods with no major fighting were almost unknown, as for centuries weak states were routinely defeated and populations regularly absorbed by foreign rulers.[19] The psychology of Europe in its formative centuries, where state survival was a very real issue of constant concern to leaders, is so different from the outlook facing Third World leaders today as to suggest that there has been a fundamental change in the survival prospects of weak states and that control of territory is no longer correlated with military power.[20]

Problems of State Consolidation in Africa

African states face numerous problems in their efforts to consolidate power. They are poor, short of trained manpower, and confront societies that are often fragmented and have little orientation to the state as a whole. Many other Third World nations face these same problems although they are often most extreme in Africa, given the poverty of the continent and the fragility of the states. Elites can come to power but, given the precariousness of control in countries where rules governing leadership and succession have not been institutionalized, they may be displaced. Once they lose power, or are prevented from gaining it, ambitious politicians have no other opportunity to accumulate wealth or power because the state controls the badges of status and many of the free-floating resources in the economy, such as they are.[21] Even when they do control the apex of the state, elites may feel that because of their country's vulnerability to exogenous shocks (e.g., sudden sharp drops in the price of their raw material exports) and the presence of sophisticated multinational enterprises and well-connected minority groups (e.g., Lebanese in West Africa, Indians in East Africa), they are not really in control of their own destiny and therefore are vulnerable. As a result of their gross insecurities, these "lame Leviathans"[22] try desperately to control ever-greater parts of society through outright ownership or regulation. However, since they are weak, their efforts are almost inevitably clumsy, heavy-handed, and authoritarian.

Therefore, although the average state in Africa compared to other states is small (as measured by government spending as a percentage of gross domestic product [GDP],[23] it appears to be too large because its clumsy extractive efforts cause so much damage compared to the benefits that it delivers. Thus arises the image of so many African states as "overdeveloped" or "swollen."[24] The problems confronted by states in Africa can be illustrated by comparing their experience with European states in two areas where war had a significant impact: the state's ability to extract resources through taxes, and the degree of nationalism in the countries south of the Sahara.

A classic example of how weak state power causes the state to institute desperate and self-defeating economic policies is in the area of government revenue. Government revenue poses a major problem for all African states and many others in the Third World. These states are desperately short of revenue to fund even minimal state services (e.g., pay nurses' salaries, buy books for schools, supply transport for agricultural extension services) that their populations have long been promised. In addition to these recurrent costs, Third World countries are in need of more extensive and more efficient tax systems because the process of development requires large expenditures on infrastructure to promote economic activity throughout the country and to handle the ramifications of development, especially the large expenses incurred by urbanizing countries.[25] W. Arthur Lewis estimates that the public sector in Third World countries should be spending on the order of 20 percent of GDP on services, exclusive of defense and debt repayment.[26] However, when defense (2.5 percent of GDP) and debt repayments (3.4 percent of GDP) are subtracted, the average African country spends only 15.7 percent of its GDP on all government functions.[27] While these figures are only rough estimates given the problems associated with African economic statistics, they do illustrate the extent of the fiscal crisis facing African states.

Due to the weakness of administrative and statistical structures in Africa, many governments rely on taxation of foreign trade, because imports and exports must physically pass through a relatively small number of border posts that can be easily manned. Thus, the average African state depends on revenue from tariffs for 20.5 percent of total revenue, compared to all developing countries which, on average, gain 12.9 percent of their revenue from tariffs, and industrialized countries where tariffs account for only 1.3 percent of total revenue.[28]

Unfortunately, funding the state through indirect taxes on foreign trade damages national economies because leaders are compelled to erect ever-greater administrative controls on imports. These tariffs promote corruption, smuggling and, most importantly, over-valued exchange rates, because governments grow to rely on administrative controls rather than the market to regulate imports. Overvalued exchange rates in turn lead to wide-spread damage within poorer economies as exporters are universally hurt, the population is encouraged to become dependent on imported food, and black markets quickly develop to take advantage of distorted prices.[29] Beyond the immediate damage caused by a tax system dependent on imports and exports, this *type* of tax system is particularly inappropriate for Third World countries. These countries need guarantees of slow and steady increases in government revenue above the rate of economic growth in order to accomplish the tasks crucial to development: build transport and communications systems, establish utilities, and create educational systems.[30]

Another major problem facing leaders in Africa is the absence of a strong popular identity with the state. The lack of a popular consensus over national purpose both aggravates the state's clumsy efforts to extract resources and is itself exacerbated by an insecure, authoritarian elite. Indeed, the picture of African societies widely accepted today is of populations trying desperately to escape the clutches of the state, rather than becoming more involved in it, and certainly not willing to pay more taxes to it.[31] Twenty-five years after "the nationalist period," there are few signs of nationalism in most African countries despite the now *pro forma* exhortations from propaganda organs to engage in state-building. Indeed, the majority of states still have difficulty

creating viable symbols to attract the loyalties of their citizens.

Not surprisingly, therefore, there are today very few attempts in African countries to forge a national consensus on major issues, much less a national identity. For instance, most formulas to decrease inter-ethnic tension concentrate only on ameliorating the negative aspects of ethnic conflict by accomodating it through decentralized government structures and preferential policies.[32] However, formulas such as federalism often are inappropriate in countries where national institutions are not strong. Federalist solutions broke down in Sudan and Uganda, among other places, because the incentives for leaders to attempt to gain total control were much greater than the barriers posed by recently adopted institutional arrangements.[33] Moreover, no matter how well accommodationist formulas of intra-societal conflict work, almost everyone in Africa and elsewhere in the Third World would agree that a more basic national loyalty by all societal groups would still be desirable. However, the means by which to induce a disparate society to identify more with the nation-state are unknown in Africa and few in the current era are even attempting to speculate on how to develop a national consensus.

Difficulties of State Consolidation without War

War in Europe played such an important role in the evolution of the state mechanism and society's relationship with the state because it is extraordinarily difficult, outside times of crisis, to reform elemental parts of the governmental system, such as the means of taxation, or to effect a real change in national identity. For instance, since taxes are so consequential to every business decision, the tax system over time reflects a large number of political bargains made by the state with different interest groups. Often governments find it too politically difficult to provide direct subsidies to those they want to favor, so the tax system is a convenient backdoor to aid politically important groups without incurring opprobrium. The political bargains that constitute the tax system develop a momentum of their own because individuals and businesses base their future economic decisions on the incentives and disincentives in the existing tax code. Indeed, Joseph Schumpeter called the fiscal system "a collection of hard, naked facts" and claimed that "the spirit of a people, its cultural level, its social structure, the deeds its policy may prepare—all this and more is written in its fiscal history, stripped of all phrases."[34]

Therefore, even minor changes such as alterations in the level of taxation or shifts in the tax burden, as the United States and most Western European countries have made in the last few years, engender tremendous political battles. Not only the previously favored political groups but all those that simply followed the signals sent out by government will forcefully oppose fiscal reform. Greater changes in the nature of the tax system are even more difficult. Edward Ames' and Richard Rapp's conclusion that tax systems "last until the end of the government that instituted them" and that tax systems in some European countries survived "almost intact" from the thirteenth and fourteenth centuries until the late eighteenth century may be an exaggeration, but their conclusions suggest just how much inertia a particular system for collecting government revenue can develop over time.[35] Other than war, no type of crisis demands that the state increase taxes with such forcefulness, and few other situations would impel citizens to accept those demands, or at least not resist them as strongly as they otherwise might have. It is therefore hard to counter Tilly's argument that "the formation of standing armies provided the largest single incentive to extraction and the largest single means of state coercion over the long run of European state-making."[36]

Domestic security threats, of the type African countries face so often, may force the state to increase revenue; however, these crises are almost never as grave as the type of external threat the European states had to confront, because they do not threaten the very existence of the state. In addition, domestic conflicts result in fragmentation and considerable hostility among different segments of the population. As a result, the state does not necessarily achieve the greater revenue efficiency gains engendered by an external crisis. Indeed, in a civil war—as in Nigeria in the late 1960s—parts of the state are fighting against each other, which hardly promotes efficiency in tax collection. Public acceptance of tax increases, a crucial factor in allowing European states to extract greater resources in times of war, will be a much more complicated issue in civil disputes. As Mann notes, "the growth of the modern state, as measured by finances, is explained primarily not in domestic terms but in terms of geopolitical relations of violence."[37]

The obstacles posed by large peasant populations, significant nonmonetarized sectors, and widespread poverty are, of course, important contributors to the revenue crisis of the African state. However, these problems do not fully explain why poor states do not extract greater resources from society in a manner that is less economically harmful. Factors such as political will, administrative ability, and the population's willingness to be taxed—issues that can be affected by the decisions of political leaders—are also crucial in understanding why states are unable to achieve their potential level of taxation in a benign manner.[38] For instance, Margaret Levi successfully shows that in such diverse cases as republican Rome, France and England in the Middle Ages, eighteenth-century Britain, and twentieth-century Australia, levels of taxation were affected primarily by political constraints faced by rulers, despite the fact that most of these economies also posed significant barriers to increased tax collection.[39]

Nor has there been any success in developing means to cause the population to identify more with the state, other than fighting a war. Nationalism, which was never nearly as strong or widespread (especially outside the major cities) in

Africa as many had thought, was palpable in the late colonial period because there was a "relevant other"—the colonialists—who could be easily identified as oppressors and around which a nominal national identity could be built.[40] However, since independence in most African countries, there has been no "relevant other" to oppose, so it has been extremely difficult to create nation-wide symbols of identity. There has therefore been no way of generating a national identity in Africa such as wars forged in Europe. Anthony Smith writes, "the central difficulty of 'nation-building' in much of Africa and Asia is the lack of any shared historical mythology and memory on which state elites can set about 'building' the nation. The 'nation' [is built up] from the central fund of culture and symbolism and mythology provided by shared historical experiences."[41] The result is the anomie in most African countries today.

It could be argued that the lack of nationalism simply reflects the fact that African countries are artificial groupings of disparate peoples and therefore are not really nation-states. However, no "natural" nation-states are mature at birth with populations that have readily agreed to a central identity. Rather, the goal of those who want to create the nation-state is to convince different groups that they do, in fact, share a common identity. This is why even in Europe, which today seems to have nation-states that are more "natural" than Africa's, war had such a crucial role to play in the forging of common identities.

Indeed, the symbiotic relationship that war fostered in Europe between tax collection and nationalism is absent in Africa, precisely because there is no external threat to encourage people to acquiesce in the state's demands, and no challenge that causes them to respond as a nation. Instead, the African state's clumsy efforts at greater extraction are met by popular withdrawal rather than by a populace united around a common identity.

Of course, not all wars led to the strengthening of administrative institutions and greater na-

tionalism. For example, Joseph Strayer notes that the Hundred Years War "was so exhausting for both sides that it discouraged the normal development of the apparatus of the state. There was a tendency to postpone structural reforms, to solve problems on an ad hoc basis rather than [to create] new agencies of government, to sacrifice efficiency for immediate results."[42] However, the Hundred Years War was exceptional because of its length and it therefore did not allow rulers to consolidate the gains usually achieved after facing a short period of external danger. Yet overall, the historical record suggests that war was highly efficient in promoting state consolidation in Europe, and that it would be much more difficult for states to accomplish the same tasks in peacetime.

Are There Peaceful Routes to State Consolidation?

Since African and other Third World countries need to transform important parts of their governmental systems, including their fiscal arrangements, and to promote nationalism, but do not have the traditional avenue of war to aid them, the immediate question is whether they can follow a path other than that adopted by Europe to consolidate state power and to develop new national identities to reduce the divisions between society and the state.

Once again it is interesting to focus on government revenue because the issue is so decisive in its own right and because tax systems are such a good reflection of the basic bargains in society. In an age with reduced levels of interstate war, African countries are faced with the problem of trying to increase the capacity of the state without being able to use wars to "ratchet up" the state's extractive ability. Given the evidence of European fiscal inertia, it is clear that it will be even more difficult to institute major reforms when states are operating in normal circumstances. The one clear chance African countries did have to institute major reforms was at independence, because at that moment political arrangements were in such flux that significant new initiatives could be undertaken. Indeed, some African countries (e.g., Mozambique, Angola) did make massive changes in their political economy (e.g., nationalization, collectivization); unfortunately, these particular reforms were economically ruinous because their socialist policies distorted economies even more than in most African countries. Once independence becomes the normal situation, as it has in African countries, it becomes extraordinarily difficult for leaders to make basic reforms of political arrangements, such as fiscal systems, which might hurt powerful groups. As Peter Bachrach and Morton Baratz noted in the context of American politics, dominant values, myths, rituals, and institutions quickly ossify so that crucial issues, such as fiscal reform, are not even on the agenda.[43] There appears to be no impetus from inside African countries to disrupt the current fiscal arrangements significantly. Indeed, much of the argument that there is currently a significant economic crisis in Africa, and that this crisis was caused by malfunctioning government policies, came from outside the continent.[44]

However, it could be argued that structural adjustment, pressed on African countries by the International Monetary Fund (IMF), the World Bank, and bilateral donors, could serve many state-making functions. As external actors dedicated to fundamental reforms of the economy and of the way the state operates, the IMF and other donors are not subject to the same rigidities that paralyze domestic reformers. The IMF and other actors who insist on fundamental reform could pressure African states for significant changes in their tax system. Demands from an external actor are similar to war, in that a leader can legitimately argue to its population that it has no choice in asking them to make very difficult sacrifices because it is under too much external pressure.

It would be a major mistake, however, to take too far the analogy between pressure from actors such as the IMF and the effects of war.

For instance, war produced such spectacular gains in governmental efficiency because the state itself felt threatened. The IMF, or any other actor, cannot produce that feeling; indeed, structural adjustment has been least successful when it has tried to address the issues of how the state itself operates in areas such as public enterprises or fiscal arrangements.[45] The cost to the state itself in failing to adopt a structural adjustment program can be severe, but falls far short of what war would threaten. The IMF will never cause a state to disappear. At worst, a state can simply opt for the high cost of breaking off relations with the IMF.

Nor does external pressure of the type the Fund exerts produce any change in national identity. While leaders can occasionally rally people against the external threat posed by "imperialists," these sentiments usually are not long-lasting because the population may be unable to distinguish between international actors supposedly draining away the nation's funds during a structural adjustment exercise, and those national leaders who led their country into such a spectacular economic debacle. While Europe's leaders in previous centuries hardly treated their populations well by modern standards, it was usually unambiguous that people would be better off if they won the war than if they lost.

The prospects of structural adjustment fostering some kind of nationalism based on resisting foreigners is also limited because the IMF is not really a "relevant other" to a largely peasant population, and cannot induce changes in national consciousness of the type that wars in Europe produced. Unlike a war where the entire population was threatened because of its national identity, structural adjustment will help certain groups unambiguously (e.g., peasants who grow export crops), clearly hurt some (e.g., the urban population dependent on imported food), and have ambiguous effects on many others. Further, the intensity in shared experience that a war generates simply cannot be replicated by, say, protracted negotiations over the IMF's Extended Fund Facility.

The Likelihood of War in Africa

If internal reform seems improbable and there is no other external threat that can perform quite the same role as war, the question becomes whether at some point in the future African leaders will begin to see war as a potential avenue for state-making. Some leaders may look to war simply because they are truly concerned about the fate of the nation and see no other option. Others may not be concerned particularly with nation-building, but may find that their countries have suffered economic decline for so long that the possibilities for their own personal enrichment have become severely limited, and therefore will seek to seize the assets of other countries. So far, the system that has preserved the continent's boundaries has not been significantly tested because most leaders considered it obvious that they were better off with their inherited boundaries than they would be in a chaotic war situation where sovereignty or considerable territory might be lost. However, especially in the context of decades of economic decline, it is possible that some African leaders may recalculate the benefits of a peace that locks them into perpetual weakness. Instead, they may try to increase their state's extractive ability and divert their citizens from inter-ethnic squabbles by seizing upon the multitude of provocations, always present, to provoke a fight with neighboring states. Paul Colinvaux presents the extreme case for the prospects of interstate war in Africa:

> Africa holds the greatest possibilities for the aspiring general. . . . That there will be battles between African nations as they build their African continent in a new image is as certain as anything in history. For each country there must come times when wealth, hopes, ambitions, and numbers all rise together. It then needs only access to high-quality weapons for an aggression to be an attractive undertaking.[46]

If significant interstate wars break out when provocations are small but elites realize what war could do for the state and the nation, it would not be a strikingly new development.

Rather, increased interstate warfare in Africa would simply be a return to the European norm. Whether war in Africa today would actually bring about the same kind of changes that it did in Europe centuries ago is unclear, but the possibility that leaders might become so desperate that they try in some fundamental way to alter the political rules under which their nations function should not be ignored.

Many are the possible provocations that could bring about significant interstate war in Africa. Certainly, there are plenty of border disputes and fragments of ethnic groups that need to be rescued from "foreign domination" to provide enough rationalization for hostile action against other African countries. Conflicts between language blocs (e.g., English versus French),[47] disputes over control of crucial rivers and railroads (especially given the number of land-locked countries), or the simple need to have more land for populations that double every twenty years provide many other potential reasons for war in Africa. More than a few African leaders might someday agree with Bismarck, a brilliant consolidator of a "new nation," on the only real way to unite a fragmented people:

> Prussia . . ., as a glance at the map will show, could no longer wear unaided on its long narrow figure the panoply which Germany required for its security; it must be equally distributed over all German peoples. We should get no nearer the goal by speeches, associations, decisions of majorities; we should be unable to avoid a serious contest, a contest which could only be settled by blood and iron.[48]

Although African countries had more or less equal defense capabilities at independence, the growing differential in force projection capabilities have led some to suggest that Africa will experience much greater resort to force in the future. Inventories of tanks and other armored vehicles as well as artillery, jet fighters, and naval craft have increased considerably throughout the continent. For instance, just in the period between 1966 and 1981, the number of countries in sub-Saharan Africa with tanks increased from two to eighteen, the number with field artillery went from seven to thirty-six, the number with light armor went from thirteen to thirty-six, and the number possessing jet aircraft went from six to twenty-one.[49] Countries such as Nigeria and Zaire have developed military capabilities that are far greater than their neighbors'. So far, the assurance of stability that is the central advantage of the current African state system has almost always been more attractive than whatever reasons African leaders may have had to begin conflict with their neighbors. However, as President Nyerere of Tanzania showed when he invaded Uganda to depose Idi Amin, even strong proponents of African norms can be driven to interstate conflict if they believe that the costs of not acting are high enough. In the future, African leaders may find that, despite all their efforts, economic reform cannot progress and they cannot get their citizenry to unite around national symbols; it is conceivable that then the deterrent value of the norms of sovereignty may seem much less powerful than they do now. If these norms no longer provided protection to a large number of states, they would lose all meaning throughout the African continent. While the timing of these wars is not predictable, it should be obvious that the incentives that African leaders have to incite wars for the purposes of state-making are significant and may become much stronger in the future when the futility of domestic reform during times of business as usual, that is, peace, becomes clear.

The Permanently Weak State: A New Development

Much of this discussion has focused on the potential opportunities for African states that, in a European-type state system, might have engaged in battle, won (or at least not lost too badly), and thereby used war in order to further state building. However, it should be recognized that another class of states in Africa is directly affected

by the current absence of war: those states that would have lost badly and would have been absorbed by the winners. These states range from those that are just geographic anachronisms left by colonialism (e.g., The Gambia, Djibouti), and very small states in the shadow of giants (e.g., Benin and Togo, close to Nigeria, or Rwanda and Burundi bordering Zaire), to those that simply lack significant resources for development or defense (e.g., Mali, Mauritania). In Europe during the formative centuries, disintegration of weak states like these was a regular occurrence. Weak states that were defeated then became the poorer regions of richer countries, but at least they had a chance to share in the revenue and resources of a viable state. Yet the absence of a truly competitive state system that penalizes military weakness means that even those states that have no other prospects than long-term dependence on international aid will survive in their crippled form for the foreseeable future. Perhaps the only task of state consolidation that these otherwise weak states can accomplish is to physically capture their populations within the stable boundaries of the African state system.[50]

The presence of permanently weak states that will not be eliminated is a new development in international relations and one that poses novel development challenges. All theoretical work on development so far, no matter what the ideological predisposition of the authors, has implicitly assumed that somehow the nation-states as they currently exist are viable arrangements for development, if only they follow the proper strategies and receive enough help from the international community. This assumption was appropriate for the European context where centuries of war had eliminated states that simply were not viable. However, for Africa, whose states have not been tested by an international system that severely punishes political weakness, there is little reason to believe that many of them will be able to have a favorable enough geographic position, control adequate natural resources, gain the support of a significant portion of their populations, and construct strong administrative structures to ever develop. In the long term, these states may disappear if interstate wars finally do break out in Africa.

In the meantime, what is to be done with states that exist but cannot develop? It is far too early to write off any state's prospects. We have been wrong about the development prospects of many states both in Africa (where scholars were too optimistic) and elsewhere in the world, such as East Asia.[51] It would also be morally unacceptable simply to allow these countries to gradually slide from the world's view into a twilight of perpetual poverty because nature and history have been unkind to them. However, thought must be given to nontraditional alternatives for aid to states that in previous times would simply have been defeated and absorbed by stronger neighbors in a war. For instance, the international community might consider rewarding those countries in the Third World that have taken in economic migrants from non-viable states.[52] The West could consider providing additional aid to those countries willing to engage in some kind of regional integration to mitigate the problems of unchanging boundaries, much as countries that have adopted more rational economic policies have attracted greater aid from donors. The world may simply have to recognize that a certain number of countries are locked into non-viable positions, and develop a long-term approach to their welfare rather than acting surprised every time the inevitable famine or ecological disaster occurs.

Conclusion

It is important not to glorify war. The wars that Europe went through caused immense suffering for generations and wholesale destruction of some societies. Yet it is undeniable that out of this destruction emerged stronger political arrangements and more unified populations. No one would advocate war as a solution to Africa's political and economic problems, where the costs of interstate war could be even higher than in Eu-

rope. It is doubtful that, if African countries do start fighting wars, they will undergo exactly the same processes of state consolidation that war engendered in Europe. However, it should be recognized that there is very little evidence that African countries, or many others in the Third World, will be able to find peaceful ways to strengthen the state and develop national identities. In particular, the prospects for states that will not disappear, but simply cannot develop, must be examined. At the same time, we must recognize the possibility that some African leaders in the future may come to believe that the costs of peace—limits on reform pos-sibilities and a fragmented population—are so high that war may not seem like such an undesirable alternative. If African leaders do indeed make this calculation, the suffering that Africa has seen in the last twenty-five years may only be a prelude to much more dangerous developments.

NOTES

1. Samuel P. Huntington, *Political Order in Changing Societies* (New Haven: Yale University Press, 1968), p. 123; and Charles Tilly, "Reflections on the History of European State-Making," in Charles Tilly, ed., *The Formation of National States in Western Europe* (Princeton: Princeton University Press, 1975), p. 42. An important recent addition to this literature is Brian M. Downing, "Constitutionalism, Warfare and Political Change in Early Modern Europe," *Theory and Society*, Vol. 17, No. 1 (January 1988), pp. 7–56. The general literature on warfare's effect on society is voluminous. An early work which concentrates on some of the themes examined here is Hans Delbrück, *History of the Art of War within the Framework of Political History*, Vol. III, trans. Walter J. Renfroe, Jr. (Westport, Conn.: Greenwood Press, 1982).

2. For instance, in Morris Janowitz's classic study of the military in the developing world, the political, social, and economic functions of the military are studied exten-

sively but the potential effects of war, or of peace, are not analyzed. Morris Janowitz, *The Military in the Political Development of New Nations: An Essay in Comparative Analysis* (Chicago: University of Chicago Press, 1964), p. 12.

3. The literature is reviewed by Henry Bienen, "Armed Forces and National Modernization: Continuing the Debate," *Comparative Politics*, Vol. 16, No. 1 (October 1983), pp. 1–16.

4. Gabriel Ardent, "Financial Policy and Economic Infrastructure of Modern States and Nations," in Tilly, *The Formation of National States*, p. 89.

5. A useful corrective to the conventional view is provided by John A. Hall, "War and the Rise of the West," in Colin Creighton and Martin Shaw, eds., *The Sociology of War and Peace* (London: Macmillan, 1987).

6. Richard Bean, "War and the Birth of the Nation State," *Journal of Economic History*, Vol. 33, No. 1 (March 1973), p. 220.

7. Michael Mann, "State and Society, 1130–1815: An Analysis of English State Finances," in Mann, *States, War and Capitalism: Studies in Political Sociology* (Oxford: Basil Blackwell, 1988), p. 109.

8. Michael Mann, *The Sources of Social Power* (Cambridge: Cambridge University Press, 1986), p. 486.

9. Michael Duffy, "The Military Revolution and the State, 1500–1800," in Michael Duffy, ed., *The Military Revolution and the State, 1500–1800*, Exeter Studies in History No. 1 (Exeter, U.K.: University of Exeter, 1980), p. 5.

10. "Lumpy" goods are products which are not useful if only part is purchased. Margaret Levi, *Of Rule and Revenue* (Berkeley: University of California Press, 1988), pp. 56–57.

11. Mann, *Sources of Social Power*, pp. 483–490.

12. Joseph P. Smaldone, *Warfare in the Sokoto Caliphate: Historical and Sociological Perspectives* (Cambridge: Cambridge University Press, 1977), p. 139. The same point is made by Richard L. Roberts in his *Warriors, Merchants, and Slaves: The State and the Economy in the Middle Niger Valley, 1700–1914* (Palo Alto: Stanford University Press, 1987), p. 20.

13. Joel S. Migdal, *Strong Societies and Weak States: State-Society Relations and State Capabilities in the Third World* (Princeton: Princeton University Press, 1988), p. 274.

14. Anthony Giddens, *The Nation-State and Violence*, vol. II of *A Contemporary Critique of Historical Materialism* (Berkeley: University of California Press, 1985), p. 235.

15. Michael Howard, *War and the Nation State* (Oxford: Clarendon Press, 1978), p. 9. Emphasis in the original.

16. See, for instance, Joseph LaPalombara, "Penetration: A Crisis of Governmental Capacity," in Leonard Binder, et al., *Crises and Sequences in Political Development* (Princeton: Princeton University Press, 1971), p. 222.

17. In 1977 Somalia, as part of its irredentist project to create "Greater Somalia," invaded Ethiopia in the hope of annexing the Ogaden; the Ethiopians, with significant help from the Soviet Union and Cuba, defeated Somalia in 1978. David D. Laitin and Said S. Samatar, *Somalia: Nation in Search of a State* (Boulder, Colo.: Westview, 1987), pp. 140–143. In 1973 Libyan forces invaded Chad by moving forces into the disputed Aozou strip. The Libyan military presence gradually expanded until a dramatic series of conflicts with the Chadian government (heavily supported by France and the United States) in 1987 forced the Libyans to agree to an end to hostilities. John Wright, *Libya, Chad and the Central Sahara* (London: Hurst, 1989), pp. 126–146.

18. This argument is developed in Jeffrey Herbst, "The Creation and Maintenance of National Boundaries in Africa," *International Organization*, Vol. 43, No. 4 (Fall 1989), pp. 673–692.

19. Tilly, "Reflections on the History of European State-Making," p. 38.

20. Ibid., p. 81.

21. Richard Hodder-Williams, *An Introduction*

to the Politics of Tropical Africa (London: Allen and Unwin, 1984), p. 95.

22. Thomas M. Callaghy, "The State and the Development of Capitalism in Africa: Theoretical, Historical, and Comparative Reflections," in Donald Rothchild and Naomi Chazan, eds., *The Precarious Balance: State and Society in Africa* (Boulder, Colo.: Westview, 1988), p. 82.

23. The share of total gross domestic product of sub-Saharan African states is smaller, at 21.6 percent, than the developing country average of 25.5 percent. (Both figures are from 1984.) International Monetary Fund (IMF), *Government Finance Statistics Yearbook 1988* (Washington, D.C.: IMF, 1988), p. 94.

24. See, for instance, Larry Diamond, "Class Formation in the Swollen African State," *The Journal of Modern African Studies*, Vol. 25, No. 4 (December 1987), pp. 592–596; and Nzongola-Ntalaja, "The Crisis of the State in Post-Colonial Africa," in Nzongola-Ntalaja, *Revolution and Counter-Revolution in Africa* (London: Zed Books, 1987), p. 85.

25. W. Arthur Lewis, *The Evolution of the International Economic Order* (Princeton: Princeton University Press, 1978), p. 39.

26. W. Arthur Lewis, *Development Planning: The Essentials of Economic Policy* (New York: Harper and Row, 1966), p. 115.

27. Calculated from IMF, *Government Finance Statistics Yearbook 1988*, pp. 58, 74, and 94.

28. Calculated from ibid., p. 54.

29. See World Bank, *Accelerated Development in Sub-Saharan Africa: An Agenda for Action* (Washington, D.C.: World Bank, 1981), pp. 24–30.

30. Alex Radian, *Resource Mobilization in Poor Countries: Implementing Tax Policies* (New Brunswick, NJ: Transaction Books, 1980), pp. 13–17.

31. See Rothchild and Chazan, *The Precarious Balance*.

32. See, for instance, Donald L. Horowitz, *Ethnic Groups in Conflict* (Berkeley: University of California Press, 1985), pp. 563–680.

33. Buganda had a degree of autonomy when Uganda gained independence and the Kabaka, the traditional ruler of the Buganda people, was the country's first president. However, this arrangement fell apart in 1966 when then Prime Minister Milton Obote overthrew the Kabaka and invaded Buganda. Crawford Young, *The Politics of Cultural Pluralism* (Madison: University of Wisconsin Press, 1976), pp. 149–156. In 1983, President Gaafar Mohamed Nimeiri of the Sudan effectively abrogated the Addis Ababa agreement which had given autonomy to Southern Sudan. The Sudan has been embroiled in a civil war ever since. Mansour Khalid, *Nimeiri and the Revolution of Dis-May* (London: KPI, 1985), pp. 234–240.

34. Joseph A. Schumpeter, "The Crisis of the Tax State," in Alan T. Peacock, et al., eds., *International Economic Papers*, No. 4 (London: Macmillan, 1954), pp. 6–7.

35. Edward Ames and Richard T. Rapp, "The Birth and Death of Taxes: A Hypothesis," *Journal of Economic History*, Vol. 37, No. 1 (March 1977), p. 177.

36. Tilly, "Reflections on the History of European State-Making," p. 73.

37. Mann, *Sources of Social Power*, p. 490.

38. Raja J. Chelliah, "Trends in Taxation in Developing Countries," *International Monetary Fund Staff Papers*, Vol. 18, No. 2 (July 1971), p. 312. On the possibility of changing fiscal arrangements in Africa, see Dennis Anderson, *The Public Revenue and Economic Policy in African Countries*, World Bank Discussion Paper No. 19 (Washington, D.C.: World Bank, 1987), pp. 14–15.

39. For instance, see Levi, *Of Rule and Revenue*, p. 105.

40. The importance of the "relevant other" concept in developing group cohesion is explored by Young, *The Politics of Cultural Pluralism*, p. 42.

41. Anthony D. Smith, "State-Making and Nation-Building," in John A. Hall, ed., *States*

in History (Oxford: Basil Blackwell, 1986), p. 258.

42. Joseph R. Strayer, *On the Medieval Origins of the Modern State* (Princeton: Princeton University Press, 1970), p. 60.

43. Peter Bachrach and Morton S. Baratz, "Two Faces of Power," *American Political Science Review*, Vol. 56, No. 4 (December 1962), p. 950.

44. For instance, the World Bank's report, *Accelerated Development in Sub-Saharan Africa*, was crucial in noting the dimensions of Africa's economic crisis; it set the agenda for reform of African economies.

45. Jeffrey Herbst, "Political Impediments to Economic Rationality: Why Zimbabwe Cannot Reform its Public Sector," *The Journal of Modern African Studies*, Vol. 27, No. 1 (March 1989), pp. 67–85.

46. Paul Colinvaux, *The Fates of Nations: A Biological Theory of History* (London: Penguin, 1980), pp. 219–220.

47. Ibid., p. 219.

48. Otto, Prince von Bismarck, *Bismarck, the Man and the Statesman: Being the Reflections and Reminiscences of Otto, Prince von Bismarck, Written and Dictated by Himself after his Retirement from Office*, translated under the supervision of A.J. Butler, Vol. I (New York: Harper and Brothers, 1899), p. 313.

49. William G. Thom, "Sub-Saharan Africa's Changing Military Capabilities," in Bruce E. Arlinghaus and Pauline H. Baker, eds., *African Armies: Evolution and Capabilities* (Boulder, Colo.: Westview, 1986), p. 101. See also Walter L. Barrows, "Changing Military Capabilities in Black Africa," in William Foltz and Henry Bienen, eds., *Arms and the African: Military Influence and Africa's International Relations* (New Haven: Yale University Press, 1985), p. 99 and p. 120; and Henry Bienen, "African Militaries as Foreign Policy Actors," *International Security*, Vol. 5, No. 2 (Fall 1980), p. 176.

50. See Jeffrey Herbst, "Migration, the Politics of Protest, and State Consolidation in Africa," *African Affairs*, Vol. 89, No. 355 (April 1990), pp. 183–203.

51. In the 1950s American administrations debated whether South Korea could achieve any increase in living standards and if American aid should be devoted to simply preventing the country from getting poorer. Clive Crook, "Trial and Error," *The Economist*, September 23, 1989, p. 4.

52. See Jeffrey Herbst, "Migration Helps Poorest of Poor," *Wall Street Journal*, June 15, 1988, p. 12.

ROBERT I. ROTBERG

THE NEW NATURE OF NATION-STATE FAILURE

Nation-states fail because they can no longer deliver positive political goods to their people. Their governments lose legitimacy and, in the eyes and hearts of a growing plurality of its citizens, the nation-state itself becomes illegitimate.

Only a handful of the world's 191 nation-states can now be categorized as failed, or collapsed, which is the end stage of failure. Several dozen more, however, are weak and serious candidates for failure. Because failed states are hospitable to and harbor nonstate actors—warlords and terrorists—understanding the dynamics of

From *The Washington Quarterly*, 25, no. 3 (Summer 2002), pp. 85–96.

nation-state failure is central to the war against terrorism. Strengthening weak nation-states in the developing world has consequently assumed new urgency.

Defining State Failure

Failed states are tense, deeply conflicted, dangerous, and bitterly contested by warring factions. In most failed states, government troops battle armed revolts led by one or more rivals. Official authorities in a failed state sometimes face two or more insurgencies, varieties of civil unrest, differing degrees of communal discontent, and a plethora of dissent directed at the state and at groups within the state.

The absolute intensity of violence does not define a failed state. Rather, it is the enduring character of that violence (as in Angola, Burundi, and Sudan), the direction of such violence against the existing government or regime, and the vigorous character of the political or geographical demands for shared power or autonomy that rationalize or justify that violence that identifies the failed state. Failure for a nation-state looms when violence cascades into all-out internal war, when standards of living massively deteriorate, when the infrastructure of ordinary life decays, and when the greed of rulers overwhelms their responsibilities to better their people and their surroundings.

The civil wars that characterize failed states usually stem from or have roots in ethnic, religious, linguistic, or other intercommunal enmity. The fear of "the other" that drives so much ethnic conflict may stimulate and fuel hostilities between ruling entities and subordinate and less-favored groups. Avarice also propels antagonism, especially when discoveries of new, frequently contested sources of resource wealth, such as petroleum deposits or diamond fields, encourage that greed.

There is no failed state without disharmonies between communities. Yet, the simple fact that many weak nation-states include haves and have-nots, and that some of the newer states contain a heterogeneous collection of ethnic, religious, and linguistic interests, is more a contributor to than a root cause of nation-state failure. In other words, state failure cannot be ascribed primarily to the inability to build nations from a congeries of ethnic groups. Nor should it be ascribed baldly to the oppression of minorities by a majority, although such brutalities are often a major ingredient of the impulse toward failure.

In contrast to strong states, failed states cannot control their borders. They lose authority over chunks of territory. Often, the expression of official power is limited to a capital city and one or more ethnically specific zones. Indeed, one measure of the extent of a state's failure is how much of the state's geographical expanse a government genuinely controls. How nominal is the central government's sway over rural towns, roads, and waterways? Who really rules upcountry, or in particular distant districts?

In most cases, driven by ethnic or other intercommunal hostility or by regime insecurity, failed states prey on their own citizens. As in Mobutu Sese Seko's Zaire or the Taliban's Afghanistan, ruling cadres increasingly oppress, extort, and harass the majority of their own compatriots while favoring a narrowly based elite. As in Zaire, Angola, Siaka Stevens's Sierra Leone, or Hassan al-Turabi's pre-2001 Sudan, patrimonial rule depends on a patronage-based system of extraction from ordinary citizens. The typical weak-state plunges toward failure when this kind of ruler-led oppression provokes a countervailing reaction on the part of resentful groups or newly emerged rebels.

Another indicator of state failure is the growth of criminal violence. As state authority weakens and fails, and as the state becomes criminal in its oppression of its citizens, so general lawlessness becomes more apparent. Gangs and criminal syndicates assume control over the streets of the cities. Arms and drug trafficking become more common. Ordinary police forces become paralyzed. Anarchy becomes more and more the norm. For protection, citizens naturally turn to warlords and other strong figures who express ethnic or clan solidarity, thus projecting strength at a time when all else, including the state itself, is crumbling.

Fewer and Fewer Political Goods

Nation-states exist to deliver political goods—security, education, health services, economic opportunity, environmental surveillance, a legal framework of order and a judicial system to administer it, and fundamental infrastructural requirements such as roads and communications facilities—to their citizens. Failed states honor these obligations in the breach. They increasingly forfeit their function as providers of political goods to warlords and other nonstate actors. In other words, a failed state is no longer able or willing to perform the job of a nation-state in the modern world.

Failed states are unable to provide security—the most central and foremost political good—across the whole of their domains. Citizens depend on states and central governments to secure their persons and free them from fear. Because a failing state is unable to establish an atmosphere of security nationwide and is often barely able to assert any kind of state power beyond a capital city, the failure of the state becomes obvious even before rebel groups and other contenders threaten the residents of central cities and overwhelm demoralized government contingents, as in contemporary Liberia and recent Sierra Leone.

Failed states contain weak or flawed institutions—that is, only the executive institution functions. If legislatures exist at all, they are rubber-stamp machines. Democratic debate is noticeably absent. The judiciary is derivative of the executive rather than being independent, and citizens know that they cannot rely on the court system for significant redress or remedy, especially against the state. The bureaucracy has long ago lost its sense of professional responsi-

bility and exists solely to carry out the orders of the executive and, in petty ways, to oppress citizens. The military is possibly the only institution with any remaining integrity, but the armed forces of failed states are often highly politicized, without the esprit that they once exhibited.

Deteriorating or destroyed infrastructures typify failed states. Metaphorically, the more potholes (or main roads turned to rutted tracks), the more likely a state will exemplify failure. As rulers siphon funds from the state, so fewer capital resources are available for road crews, and maintaining road or rail access to distant provinces becomes less and less of a priority. Even refurbishing basic navigational aids along arterial waterways, as in the Democratic Republic of the Congo (DRC), succumbs to neglect. Where the state still controls the landline telephone system, that form of political and economic good also betrays a lack of renewal, upkeep, investment, and bureaucratic interest. Less a metaphor than a daily reality is the index of failed connections, repeated required dialing, and interminable waits for repair or service. If state monopolies have permitted private entrepreneurs to erect cell telephone towers and offer mobile telephone service, cell telephones may already have rendered the government's landline monopoly obsolete. In a state without a government, such as Somalia, the overlapping system of privately provided cell telephone systems is effective.

In failed states, the effective educational and health systems have either been privatized (with a resulting hodgepodge of shady schools and medical clinics in the cities) or have slowly slumped to increasingly desperate levels of decrepitude. Teachers, physicians, nurses, and orderlies are paid late or not at all, and absenteeism rises. Textbooks and essential medicines become scarce. X-ray machines cannot be repaired. Reports to the relevant ministries go unanswered; and parents, students, and patients—especially rural ones—slowly realize that the state has abandoned them to the forces of nature and to their own devices. Sometimes, where a failed state is effectively split (Sudan), essential services are still provided to the favored half (northern Sudan) but not to the half engulfed by war. Most of the time, however, the weakened nation-state completely fails to perform. Literacy falls, infant mortality rises, the AIDS epidemic overwhelms any health infrastructure that exists, life expectancies plummet, and an already poor and neglected citizenry becomes even poorer and more immiserated.

Failed states provide unparalleled economic opportunity, but only for a privileged few. Those close to the ruler or the ruling oligarchy grow richer while their less-fortunate brethren starve. Immense profits can be made from currency speculation, arbitrage, and knowledge of regulatory advantages. But the privilege of making real money when everything else is deteriorating is confined to clients of the ruling elite or to especially favored external entrepreneurs. The responsibility of a nation-state to maximize the well-being and personal prosperity of all of its citizens is conspicuously absent, if it ever existed.

Corruption flourishes in failed states, often on an unusually destructive scale. Petty or lubricating corruption is widespread. Levels of venal corruption escalate, especially kickbacks on anything that can be put out to bid, including medical supplies, textbooks, bridges; unnecessarily wasteful construction projects solely for the rents they will generate; licenses for existing and nonexisting activities; the appropriating by the ruling class of all kinds of private entrepreneurial endeavors; and generalized extortion. Corrupt ruling elites invest their gains overseas, not at home. A few build numerous palaces or lavish residences with state funds. Military officers always benefit from these corrupt regimes and feed ravenously from the same illicit troughs as their civilian counterparts.

An indicator, but not a cause, of failure is declining real national and per capita levels of gross domestic product (GDP). The statistical foundations of most states in the developing world are shaky, most certainly, but failed states—even, or particularly, failed states with abundant natural resources—show overall worsening GDP figures, slim year-to-year growth rates, and greater disparities of income between the wealthiest and poorest fifths of the population. High official deficits (Zimbabwe's reached 30 percent of GDP in 2001) support lavish security spending and the siphoning of cash by elites. Inflation usually soars because the ruling elite raids the central bank and prints money. From the resulting economic insecurity, often engineered by rulers to maximize their own fortunes and their own political as well as economic power, entrepreneurs favored by the prevailing regime can reap great amounts of money. Smuggling becomes rife. When state failure becomes complete, the local currency falls out of favor, and some or several international currencies take its place. Money changers are everywhere, legal or not, and arbitrage becomes an everyday national pursuit.

Sometimes, especially if climatic disasters intervene, the economic chaos and generalized neglect that is endemic to failed states can lead to regular food scarcities and widespread hunger—even to episodes of starvation and resulting international humanitarian relief efforts. Natural calamities can overwhelm the resources even of nonfailed but weak states in the developing world. But when unscrupulous rulers and ruling elites have consciously sucked state competencies dry, unforeseen natural disasters or manmade wars can drive ignored populations over the edge of endurance into starvation. Once such populations have lost their subsistence plots or sources of income, they lose their homes, forfeit already weak support networks, and are forced into an endless cycle of migration and displacement. Failed states offer no safety nets, and the homeless and destitute become fodder for anyone who can provide food and a cause.

A nation-state also fails when it loses a basic legitimacy—when its nominal borders become irrelevant and when one or more groups seek autonomous control within one or more parts of the national territory or, sometimes, even across its borders. Once the state's capacity deteriorates and what little capacity still remains is devoted largely to the fortunes of a few or to a favored ethnicity or community, then there is every reason to expect less and less loyalty to the state on the part of the excluded and the disenfranchised. When the rulers are seen to be working for themselves and their kin, and not for the state, their legitimacy, and the state's legitimacy, plummets. The state increasingly is perceived as owned by an exclusive class or group, with all others pushed aside.

Citizens naturally become more and more conscious of the kinds of sectional or community loyalties that are their main recourse and their only source of security and economic opportunity. They transfer their allegiances to clan and group leaders, some of whom become warlords. These warlords or other local strongmen derive support from external and local supporters. In the wilder, more marginalized corners of failed states, terror can breed along with the prevailing anarchy that emerges from state breakdown and failure.

A collapsed state is an extreme version of a failed state. It has a total vacuum of authority. A collapsed state is a mere geographical expression, a black hole into which a failed polity has fallen. Dark energy exists, but the forces of entropy have overwhelmed the radiance that hitherto provided some semblance of order and other vital political goods to the inhabitants embraced by language affinities or borders. When a state such as Somalia collapses (or Lebanon and Afghanistan a decade ago and Sierra Leone in the late 1990s), substate actors take over. They control regions and subregions, build their own local security apparatuses, sanction markets or other trading arrangements, and even establish an attenuated form of international relations. By definition, they are illegitimate and unrecognized, but some may assume the trappings of a quasi-state, such as Somaliland in northern Somalia. Yet, within the collapsed state prevail disorder, anomic behavior, and the kinds of anarchic mentality and entrepreneurial pursuits—especially gun and drug running—that are compatible with networks of terror.

Contemporary State Failure

This decade's failed states are Afghanistan, Angola, Burundi, the DRC, Liberia, Sierra Leone, and Sudan. These seven states exemplify the criteria of state failure. Beyond those states is one collapsed state: Somalia. Each of these countries has typified state failure continuously since at least 1990, if not before. Lebanon was once a failed state. So were Bosnia, Tajikistan, and Nigeria. Many other modern states approach the brink of failure, some much more ominously than others. Others drift disastrously downward from weak to failing to failed.

Of particular interest is why and how states slip from endemic weakness (Haiti) toward failure, or not. The list of weak states is long, but only a few of those weak and badly governed states necessarily edge into failure. Why? Even the categorization of a state as failing—Colombia and Indonesia, among others—need not doom it unquestionably to full failure. Another critical question is, what does it take to drive a failing state into collapse? Why did Somalia not stop at failure rather than collapsing?

Not each of the classical failed and collapsed states fully fills all of the cells on the matrix of failure. To be termed a failure, however, a state certainly needs to demonstrate that it has met most of the explicit criteria. "Failure" is meant to describe a specific set of conditions and to exclude states that only meet a few of the criteria. In other words, how truly minimal are the roads, the schools, the hospitals, and the clinics? How far has GDP fallen and infant mortality risen? How far does the ambit of the central government reach? How little legitimacy remains? Most importantly, because civil conflict is decisive for state failure, can the state still provide security to its citizens and to what extent? Continuously? Only on good days and nights? Has the state lost control of large swaths of territory or only some provinces and regions?

Several test cases are interesting. Sri Lanka has been embroiled in a bitter and destructive civil war for 19 years. The rebel Liberation

Tigers of Tamil Eelam (LTTE), a Tamil separatist insurgency, has at times in the last decade
controlled as much as 15 percent of Sri Lanka's
total land mass. Additionally, with relative impunity, the LTTE has been able to assassinate
prime ministers, bomb presidents, kill off rival
Tamils, and last year even wreak destruction at
the nation's civil aviation terminal and main air
force base. But, as unable as the Sinhala-
dominated governments of Sri Lanka have been
to put down the LTTE rebellion, so the nation-
state has remained merely weak, never close to
failure. For 80 percent of Sri Lankans, the government performs reasonably well. Since the
early 1990s, too, Sri Lanka has exhibited robust
levels of economic performance. The authority
of successive governments, even before the recent ceasefire, extended securely to the Sinhala-
speaking 80 percent of the country, and the
regime recaptured some of the contested Tamil
areas. Before the truce, road maintenance, educational and medical services, and the other necessary political goods continued to be delivered
despite the civil war, to some limited degree even
into the war-torn parts of the country. For all of
these reasons, despite a consuming internal conflict founded on majority-minority discrimination and deprivation and on ethnic and religious
differences, Sri Lanka has successfully escaped
failure.

Indonesia is another example of weakness
avoiding failure despite widespread insecurity.
As the world's largest Muslim nation, its farflung
archipelago harbors the separatist wars of Aceh
in the west and Papua (Irian Jaya) in the east,
plus Muslim-Christian conflict in Ambon and
the Mulukus, Muslim-Christian hostility in Su-
lawesi, and ethnic xenophobic outbursts in West
Kalimantan. Given all of these conflictual situations, none of which have become less bitter
since the end of Suharto's dictatorship, suggesting that Indonesia is approaching failure is easy.
Yet, as one argument goes, only the insurgents
in Aceh and Papua want to secede from the
state; and, even in Aceh, official troops have the
upper hand. Elsewhere, hostilities are intercom-

munal and not directed against the government
or the state. Unlike the low-level war in Aceh,
they do not threaten the integrity and resources
of the state. Overall, most of Indonesia is still
secure and is "glued" together well by an abiding sense of nationalism. The government still
projects power and authority. Despite dangerous
economic and other vicissitudes in the post-
Suharto era, the state provides most of the
other necessary political goods and remains
legitimate. Indonesia need not be classified as
anything other than a weak state, but the government's performance and provision of security
should be monitored closely.

What about Colombia? An otherwise well-
endowed, prosperous, and stable state has the
second-highest murder rate per capita in the
world, its politicians and businessmen wear flak
jackets and travel with armed guards, and three
private armies control relatively large chunks of
its territory with impunity. The official defense
and political establishment has effectively ceded
authority in those zones to the insurgencies and
to drug traffickers. Again, why should Colombia
not be ranked as a failed state? Although it could
deteriorate into further failure, at present the
Colombian government still performs for the 70
percent of the nation that remains under official
authority. It provides political goods, even some
improving security, for the large part of the state
under official authority. When and if the government of Colombia can reassert itself into the disputed zones and further reduce drug trafficking,
the power of the state will grow and a weak, endangered state such as Colombia can move away
from possible failure toward the stronger side of
the equation.

Zimbabwe is an example of a once unquestionably strong African state—indeed, one of the
strongest—that has fallen rapidly through weakness to the very edge of failure. All that Zimbabwe
lacks in order to join the ranks of failed states is a
widespread internal insurgent movement directed
at the government, which could still emerge.
Meanwhile, per capita GDP has receded by 10
percent annually for two years. During the same

period, inflammation has galloped from 30 percent to 116 percent. The local currency has fallen against the U.S. dollar from 38:1 to 400:1. Foreign and domestic investment have largely ceased. Health and educational services are almost nonexistent and shrinking further. Road maintenance and telephone service are obviously suffering. Judicial independence survives, but barely, and not in critical political cases. The state has also been preying on its own citizens for at least two years. Corruption is blatant and very much dominated by the avaricious ruling elite. Zimbabwe is an example of a state that, like Sierra Leone and the DRC at earlier moments in history, has been driven into failure by human agency.

Indonesia, Colombia, Sri Lanka, and Zimbabwe are but four among a large number of nation-states (two dozen by a recent count) that contain serious elements of failure but will probably avoid failure, especially if they receive sufficient outside assistance. They belong to a category of state that is designated weak but that encompasses and spreads into the category of failing—the precursor to true failure. Haiti, Chad, and Kyrgyzstan, from three continents, are representative examples of perpetual weakness. Argentina has recently joined an analogous rank; Russia was once a candidate. Fiji, the Solomon Islands, Tajikistan, Lebanon, Nigeria, Niger, and Burkina Faso remain vulnerable to further deterioration. Even Kenya is a weak state with some potential for definitive failure if ethnic disparities and ambitions provoke civil strife.

The list of states in weakness is longer and hardly static. Some of the potentially stronger states move in and out of weakness and nearer or farther from failure. Others are foreordained weak. Particular decisions by ruling groups would be needed to destabilize members of this second group further and drive them into failure.

The Hand of Man

State failure is man-made, not merely accidental nor—fundamentally—caused geographically, en-

vironmentally, or externally. Leadership decisions and leadership failures have destroyed states and continue to weaken the fragile polities that operate on the cusp of failure. Mobutu's kleptocratic rule extracted the marrow of Zaire/DRC and left nothing for his national dependents. Much of the resource wealth of that vast country ended up in Mobutu's or his cronies' pockets. During four decades, hardly any money was devoted to uplifting the Congolese people, improving their welfare, building infrastructures, or even providing more than rudimentary security. Mobutu's government performed only for Mobutu, not for Zaire/DRC.

Likewise, oil-rich Angola continues to fail because of three decades of war, but also because President Eduardo dos Santos and his associates have refused to let the Angolan government deliver more than basic services within the large zone that they control. Stevens (1967–1985) decapitated the Sierra Leonean state in order to strengthen his own power amid growing chaos. Sierra Leone has not yet recovered from Stevens's depredations. Nor has Liberia been resuscitated in the aftermath of the slashing neglect and unabashed greed of Samuel Doe, Prince Johnson, and Charles Taylor. In Somalia, Mohammed Siad Barre arrogated more and more power and privilege to himself and his clan. Finally, nothing was left for the other pretenders to power. The Somali state was gutted, the abilities of the Somali government to provide political goods endlessly compromised, and the descent into failure and then full collapse followed.

President Robert Gabriel Mugabe has personally led Zimbabwe from strength to the precipice of failure. His high-handed and seriously corrupt rule bled the resources of the state into his own pocket, squandered foreign exchange, discouraged domestic and international investment, subverted the courts, and this year drove his country to the very brink of starvation. In Sri Lanka, Solomon and Sirimavo Bandaranaike, one after the other, drove the LTTE into reactive combat by abrogating minority rights and vitiating the social contract on which the country called Ceylon had been created. In Afghanistan, Gulbuddin Hakmatyar and Burrhan ul-Din Rabani tried to prevent Afghans other than their fellow Pushtun and Tajik nationals from sharing the perquisites of governance; their narrowly focused, self-enriching decisions enabled the Taliban to triumph and Afghanistan to become a safe harbor for terrorists.

Preventing State Failure

Strengthening weak states against failure is far easier than reviving them after they have definitively failed or collapsed. As the problem of contemporary Afghanistan shows, reconstruction is very long, very expensive, and hardly a smooth process. Creating security and a security force from scratch, amid bitter memories, is the immediate need. Then comes the re-creation of an administrative structure—primarily re-creating a bureaucracy and finding the funds with which to pay the erstwhile bureaucrats and policemen. A judicial method is required, which means the establishment or reestablishment of a legitimate legal code and system; the training of judges, prosecutors, and defenders (as attempted recently in East Timor); and the opening of courtrooms and offices. Restarting the schools, employing teachers, refurbishing and re-equipping hospitals, building roads, and even gathering statistics—all of these fundamental chores take time, large sums of money (especially in war-shattered Afghanistan), and meticulous oversight in postconflict nations with overstretched human resources. Elections need not be an early priority, but constitutions must be written eventually and elections held in order to encourage participatory democracy.

Strengthening states prone to failure before they fail is prudent policy and contributes significantly to world order and to minimizing combat, casualties, refugees, and displaced persons. Doing so is far less expensive than reconstructing states after failure. Strengthening weak states also has the potential to eliminate the authority and power vacuums within which terror thrives.

From a policy perspective, however, these are obvious nostrums. The mechanisms for amelioration are also more obvious than obscure. In order to encourage responsible leadership and good governance, financial assistance from international lending agencies and bilateral donors must be designed to reinforce positive leadership only. Outside support should be conditional on monetary and fiscal streamlining, renewed attention to good governance, reforms of land tenure systems, and strict adherence to the rule of law. External assistance to create in-country jobs by reducing external tariff barriers (e.g., on textiles) and by supporting vital foreign direct investment is critical. So is support for innovations that can reduce importation and exportation transport expenditures for the weak nations, improve telephone and power systems through privatization, open predominantly closed economies in general, create new incentives for agricultural productivity, and bolster existing security forces through training and equipment.

All these ingredients of a successful strengthening process are necessary. The developed world can apply tough love and assist the developing and more vulnerable world to help itself in many more similarly targeted ways. In addition to the significant amounts of cash (grants are preferred over loans) that must be transferred to help the poorer nations help themselves, however, the critical ingredient is sustained interest and sustained assistance over the very long run. Nothing enduring can be accomplished instantaneously. If the world order wants to dry up the reservoirs of terror, as well as do good more broadly, it must commit itself and its powers to a campaign of decades, not months. The refurbishment and revitalization of Afghanistan will take much more than the $4.7 billion pledged and the many years that Secretary of State Colin L. Powell has warned the U.S. people will be necessary to make Afghanistan a self-sufficient state. Strengthening Indonesia, for example, would

take a concerted effort for decades. So would strengthening any of the dangerous and needy candidates in Africa or in Central Asia.

Preventing state failure is imperative, difficult, and costly. Yet, doing so is profoundly in the interest not only of the inhabitants of the most deprived and ill-governed states of the world, but also of world peace.

Satisfying such lofty goals, however—making the world much safer by strengthening weak states against failure—is dependent on the political will of the wealthy big-power arbiters of world security. Perhaps the newly aroused awareness of the dangers of terror will embolden political will in the United States, Europe, and Japan. Otherwise, the common ingredients of zero-sum leadership; ethnic, linguistic, and religious antagonisms and fears; chauvinistic ambition; economic insufficiency; and inherited fragility will continue to propel nation-states from weakness toward failure. In turn, that failure will be costly in terms of humanitarian relief and postconflict reconstruction. Ethnic cleansing episodes will recur, as will famines, and in the thin and hospitable soils of newly failed and collapsed states, terrorist groups will take root.

STEPHEN D. KRASNER

SOVEREIGNTY

The idea of states as autonomous, independent entities is collapsing under the combined onslaught of monetary unions, CNN, the Internet, and nongovernmental organizations. But those who proclaim the death of sovereignty misread history. The nation-state has a keen instinct for survival and has so far adapted to new challenges—even the challenge of globalization.

The Sovereign State Is Just About Dead

Very Wrong

Sovereignty was never quite as vibrant as many contemporary observers suggest. The conventional norms of sovereignty have always been challenged. A few states, most notably the United States, have had autonomy, control, and recogni-

From *Foreign Policy* (January/February 2001), pp. 20–29.

tion for most of their existence, but most others have not. The politics of many weaker states have been persistently penetrated, and stronger nations have not been immune to external influence. China was occupied. The constitutional arrangements of Japan and Germany were directed by the United States after World War II. The United Kingdom, despite its rejection of the euro, is part of the European Union.

Even for weaker states—whose domestic structures have been influenced by outside actors, and whose leaders have very little control over transborder movements or even activities within their own country—sovereignty remains attractive. Although sovereignty might provide little more than international recognition, that recognition guarantees access to international organizations and sometimes to international finance. It offers status to individual leaders. While the great powers of Europe have eschewed many elements of sovereignty, the United States, China, and Japan have neither the interest nor the inclination to abandon their usually effective claims to domestic autonomy.

In various parts of the world, national borders still represent the fault lines of conflict, whether it is Israelis and Palestinians fighting over the status of Jerusalem, Indians and Pakistanis threatening to go nuclear over Kashmir, or Ethiopia and Eritrea clashing over disputed territories. Yet commentators nowadays are mostly concerned about the erosion of national borders as a consequence of globalization. Governments and activists alike complain that multilateral institutions such as the United Nations, the World Trade Organization, and the International Monetary Fund overstep their authority by promoting universal standards for everything from human rights and the environment to monetary policy and immigration. However, the most important impact of economic globalization and transnational norms will be to alter the scope of state authority rather than to generate some fundamentally new way to organize political life.

Sovereignty Means Final Authority

Not Anymore, If Ever

When philosophers Jean Bodin and Thomas Hobbes first elaborated the notion of sovereignty in the 16th and 17th centuries, they were concerned with establishing the legitimacy of a single hierarchy of domestic authority. Although Bodin and Hobbes accepted the existence of divine and natural law, they both (especially Hobbes) believed the word of the sovereign was law. Subjects had no right to revolt. Bodin and Hobbes realized that imbuing the sovereign with such overweening power invited tyranny, but they were predominately concerned with maintaining domestic order, without which they believed there could be no justice. Both were writing in a world riven by sectarian strife. Bodin was almost killed in religious riots in France in 1572. Hobbes published his seminal work, *Leviathan*, only a few years after parliament (composed of Britain's emerging wealthy middle class) had executed Charles I in a civil war that had sought to wrest state control from the monarchy.

This idea of supreme power was compelling, but irrelevant in practice. By the end of the 17th century, political authority in Britain was divided between king and parliament. In the United States, the Founding Fathers established a constitutional structure of checks and balances and multiple sovereignties distributed among local and national interests that were inconsistent with hierarchy and supremacy. The principles of justice, and especially order, so valued by Bodin and Hobbes, have best been provided by modern democratic states whose organizing principles are antithetical to the idea that sovereignty means uncontrolled domestic power.

If sovereignty does not mean a domestic order with a single hierarchy of authority, what does it mean? In the contemporary world, sovereignty primarily has been linked with the idea that states are autonomous and independent from each other. Within their own boundaries, the members of a polity are free to choose their own form of government. A necessary corollary of this claim is the principle of nonintervention: One state does not have a right to intervene in the internal affairs of another.

More recently, sovereignty has come to be associated with the idea of control over transborder movements. When contemporary observers assert that the sovereign state is just about dead, they do not mean that constitutional structures are about to disappear. Instead, they mean that technological change has made it very difficult, or perhaps impossible, for states to control movements across their borders of all kinds of material things (from coffee to cocaine) and not-so-material things (from Hollywood movies to capital flows).

Finally, sovereignty has meant that political authorities can enter into international agreements. They are free to endorse any contract they find attractive. Any treaty among states is legitimate provided that it has not been coerced.

The Peace of Westphalia Produced the Modern Sovereign State

No, It Came Later

Contemporary pundits often cite the 1648 Peace of Westphalia (actually two separate treaties, Münster and Osnabrück) as the political big bang that created the modern system of autonomous states. Westphalia—which ended the Thirty Years' War against the hegemonic power of the Holy Roman Empire—delegitimized the already waning transnational role of the Catholic Church and validated the idea that international relations should be driven by balance-of-power considerations rather than the ideals of Christendom. But Westphalia was first and foremost a new constitution for the Holy Roman Empire. The preexisting right of the principalities in the empire to make treaties was affirmed, but the Treaty of Münster stated that "such Alliances be not against the Emperor, and the Empire, nor against the Publick Peace, and this Treaty, and without prejudice to the Oath by which every one is bound to the Emperor and the Empire." The domestic political structures of the principalities remained embedded in the Holy Roman Empire. The Duke of Saxony, the Margrave of Brandenburg, the Count of Palatine, and the Duke of Bavaria were affirmed as electors who (along with the archbishops of Mainz, Trier, and Cologne) chose the emperor. They did not become or claim to be kings in their own right.

Perhaps most important, Westphalia established rules for religious tolerance in Germany. The treaties gave lip service to the principle (*cuius regio, eius religio*) that the prince could set the religion of this territory—and then went on to violate this very principle through many specific provisions. The signatories agreed that the religious rules already in effect would stay in place. Catholics and Protestants in German cities with mixed populations would share offices. Religious issues had to be settled by a majority of both Catholics and Protestants in the

diet and courts of the empire. None of the major political leaders in Europe endorsed religious toleration in principle, but they recognized that religious conflicts were so volatile that it was essential to contain rather than repress sectarian differences. All in all, Westphalia is a pretty medieval document, and its biggest explicit innovation—provisions that undermined the power of princes to control religious affairs within their territories—was antithetical to the ideas of national sovereignty that later became associated with the so-called Westphalian system.

Universal Human Rights Are an Unprecedented Challenge to Sovereignty

Wrong

The struggle to establish international rules that compel leaders to treat their subjects in a certain way has been going on for a long time. Over the centuries the emphasis has shifted from religious toleration, to minority rights (often focusing on specific ethnic groups in specific countries), to human rights (emphasizing rights enjoyed by all or broad classes of individuals). In a few instances states have voluntarily embraced international supervision, but generally the weak have acceded to the preferences of the strong: the Vienna settlement following the Napoleonic wars guaranteed religious toleration for Catholics in the Netherlands. All of the successor states of the Ottoman Empire, beginning with Greece in 1832 and ending with Albania in 1913, had to accept provisions for civic and political equality for religious minorities as a condition for international recognition. The peace settlements following World War I included extensive provisions for the protection of minorities. Poland, for instance, agreed to refrain from holding elections on Saturday because such balloting would have violated the Jewish Sabbath. Individuals could bring complaints against governments through a minority rights bureau established within the League of Nations.

But as the Holocaust tragically demonstrated, interwar efforts at international constraints on domestic practices failed dismally. After World War II, human, rather than minority, rights became the focus of attention. The United Nations Charter endorsed both human rights and the classic sovereignty principle of nonintervention. The 20-plus human rights accords that have been signed during the last half century cover a wide range of issues including genocide, torture, slavery, refugees, stateless persons, women's rights, racial discrimination, children's rights, and forced labor. These UN agreements, however, have few enforcement mechanisms, and even their provisions for reporting violations are often ineffective.

The tragic and bloody disintegration of Yugoslavia in the 1990s revived earlier concerns with ethnic rights. International recognition of the Yugoslav successor states was conditional upon their acceptance of constitutional provisions guaranteeing minority rights. The Dayton accords established externally controlled authority structures in Bosnia, including a Human Rights Commission (a majority of whose members were appointed by the Western European states). NATO created a de facto protectorate in Kosovo.

The motivations for such interventions—humanitarianism and security—have hardly changed. Indeed, the considerations that brought the great powers into the Balkans following the wars of the 1870s were hardly different from those that engaged NATO and Russia in the 1990s.

Globalization Undermines State Control

No

State control could never be taken for granted. Technological changes over the last 200 years have increased the flow of people, goods, capital, and ideas—but the problems posed by such movements are not new. In many ways, states are better able to respond now than they were in the past.

The impact of the global media on political authority (the so-called CNN effect) pales in comparison to the havoc that followed the invention of the printing press. Within a decade after Martin Luther purportedly nailed his 95 theses to the Wittenberg church door, his ideas had circulated throughout Europe. Some political leaders seized upon the principles of the Protestant Reformation as a way to legitimize secular political authority. No sovereign monarch could contain the spread of these concepts, and some lost not only their lands but also their heads. The sectarian controversies of the 16th and 17th centuries were perhaps more politically consequential than any subsequent transnational flow of ideas.

In some ways, international capital movements were more significant in earlier periods than they are now. During the 19th century, Latin American states (and to a lesser extent Canada, the United States, and Europe) were beset by boom-and-bust cycles associated with global financial crises. The Great Depression, which had a powerful effect on the domestic politics of all major states, was precipitated by an international collapse of credit. The Asian financial crisis of the late 1990s was not nearly as devastating. Indeed, the speed with which countries recovered from the Asian flu reflects how a better working knowledge of economic theories and more effective central banks have made it easier to states to secure the advantages (while at the same time minimizing the risks) of being enmeshed in global financial markets.

In addition to attempting to control the flows of capital and ideas, states have long struggled to manage the impact of international trade. The opening of long-distance trade for bulk commodities in the 19th century created fundamental cleavages in all of the major states. Depression and plummeting grain prices made it possible for German Chancellor Otto von Bismarck to prod the landholding aristocracy into a protectionist alliance with urban heavy industry (this coalition of "iron and rye" dominated German politics for decades). The tariff question was a basic divide in U.S. politics for much of the last half of the 19th and first half of the 20th centuries. But, despite growing levels of imports and exports since 1950, the political salience of trade has receded because national governments have developed social welfare strategies that cushion the impact of international competition, and workers with higher skill levels are better able to adjust to changing international conditions. It has become easier, not harder, for states to manage the flow of goods and services.

Globalization Is Changing the Scope of State Control

Yes

The reach of the state has increased in some areas but contracted in others. Rulers have recognized that their effective control can be enhanced by walking away from issues they cannot resolve. For instance, beginning with the Peace of Westphalia, leaders chose to surrender their control over religion because it proved too volatile. Keeping religion within the scope of state authority undermined, rather than strengthened, political stability.

Monetary policy is an area where state control expanded and then ultimately contracted. Before the 20th century, states had neither the administrative competence nor the inclination to conduct independent monetary policies. The mid-20th-century effort to control monetary affairs, which was associated with Keynesian economics, has now been reversed due to the magnitude of short-term capital flows and the inability of some states to control inflation. With the exception of Great Britain, the major European states have established a single monetary authority. Confronting recurrent hyperinflation,

Ecuador adopted the U.S. dollar as its currency in 2000.

Along with the erosion of national currencies, we now see the erosion of national citizenship—the notion that an individual should be a citizen of one and only one country, and that the state has exclusive claims to that person's loyalty. For many states, there is no longer a sharp distinction between citizens and noncitizens. Permanent residents, guest workers, refugees, and undocumented immigrants are entitled to some bundle of rights even if they cannot vote. The ease of travel and the desire of many countries to attract either capital or skilled workers have increased incentives to make citizenship a more flexible category.

Although government involvement in religion, monetary affairs, and claims to loyalty has declined, overall government activity, as reflected in taxation and government expenditures, has increased as a percentage of national income since the 1950s among the most economically advanced states. The extent of a country's social welfare programs tends to go hand in hand with its level of integration within the global economy. Crises of authority and control have been most pronounced in the states that have been the most isolated, with sub-Saharan Africa offering the largest number of unhappy examples.

NGOs Are Nibbling at National Sovereignty

To Some Extent

Transnational nongovernmental organizations (NGOs) have been around for quite a while, especially if you include corporations. In the 18th century, the East India Company possessed political power (and even an expeditionary military force) that rivaled many national governments. Throughout the 19th century, there were transnational movements to abolish slavery, promote the rights of women, and improve conditions for workers.

The number of transnational NGOs, however, has grown tremendously, from around 200 in 1909 to over 17,000 today. The availability of inexpensive and very fast communications technology has made it easier for such groups to organize and make an impact on public policy and international law—the international agreement banning land mines being a recent case in point. Such groups prompt questions about sovereignty because they appear to threaten the integrity of domestic decision making. Activists who lose on their home territory can pressure foreign governments, which may in turn influence decision makers in the activists' own nation.

But for all of the talk of growing NGO influence, their power to affect a country's domestic affairs has been limited when compared to governments, international organizations, and multinational corporations. The United Fruit Company had more influence in Central America in the early part of the 20th century than any NGO could hope to have anywhere in the contemporary world. The International Monetary Fund and other multilateral financial institutions now routinely negotiate conditionality agreements that involve not only specific economic targets but also domestic institutional changes, such as pledges to crack down on corruption and break up cartels.

Smaller, weaker states are the most frequent targets of external efforts to alter domestic institutions, but more powerful states are not immune. The openness of the U.S. political system means that not only NGOs but also foreign governments can play some role in political decisions. (The Mexican government, for instance, lobbied heavily for the passage of the North American Free Trade Agreement.) In fact, the permeability of the American polity makes the United States a less threatening partner; nations are more willing to sign on to U.S.-sponsored international arrangements because they have some confidence that they can play a role in U.S. decision making.

Sovereignty Blocks Conflict Resolution

Yes, Sometimes

Rulers as well as their constituents have some reasonably clear notion of what sovereignty means—exclusive control within a given territory—even if this norm has been challenged frequently by inconsistent principles (such as universal human rights) and violated in practice (the U.S.- and British-enforced no-fly zones over Iraq). In fact, the political importance of conventional sovereignty rules has made it harder to solve some problems. There is, for instance, no conventional sovereignty solution for Jerusalem, but it doesn't require much imagination to think of alternatives: divide the city into small pieces; divide the Temple Mount vertically with the Palestinians controlling the top and the Israelis the bottom; establish some kind of international authority; divide control over different issues (religious practices versus taxation, for instance) among different authorities. Any one of these solutions would be better for most Israelis and Palestinians than an ongoing stalemate, but political leaders on both sides have had trouble delivering a settlement because they are subject to attacks by counterelites who can wave the sovereignty flag.

Conventional rules have also been problematic for Tibet. Both the Chinese and the Tibetans might be better off if Tibet could regain some of the autonomy it had as a tributary state within the traditional Chinese empire. Tibet had extensive local control but symbolically (and sometimes through tribute payments) recognized the supremacy of the emperor. Today, few on either side would even know what a tributary state is, and even if the leaders of Tibet worked out some kind of settlement that would give their country more self-government, there would be no guarantee that they could gain the support of their own constituents.

If, however, leaders can reach mutual agreements, bring along their constituents, or are willing to use coercion, sovereignty rules can be violated in inventive ways. The Chinese, for instance, made Hong Kong a special administrative region after the transfer from British rule, allowed a foreign judge to sit on the Court of Final Appeal, and secured acceptance by other states not only for Hong Kong's participation in a number of international organizations but also for separate visa agreements and recognition of a distinct Hong Kong passport. All of these measures violate conventional sovereignty rules, since Hong Kong does not have juridical independence. Only by inventing a unique status for Hong Kong, which involved the acquiescence of other states, could China claim sovereignty while simultaneously preserving the confidence of the business community.

The European Union Is a New Model for Supranational Governance

Yes, But Only for the Europeans

The European Union (EU) really is a new thing, far more interesting in terms of sovereignty than Hong Kong. It is not a conventional international organization because its member states are now so intimately linked with one another that withdrawal is not a viable option. It is not likely to become a "United States of Europe"—a large federal state that might look something like the United States of America—because the interests, cultures, economies, and domestic institutional arrangements of its members are too diverse. Widening the EU to include the former communist states of Central Europe would further complicate any efforts to move toward a political organization that looks like a conventional sovereign state.

The EU is inconsistent with conventional sovereignty rules. Its member states have created supranational institutions (the European Court

of Justice, the European Commission, and the Council of Ministers) that can make decisions opposed by some member states. The rulings of the court have direct effect and supremacy within national judicial systems, even though these doctrines were never explicitly endorsed in any treaty. The European Monetary Union created a central bank that now controls monetary affairs for three of the union's four largest states. The Single European Act and the Maastricht Treaty provide for majority or qualified majority, but not unanimous, voting in some issue areas. In one sense, the European Union is a product of state sovereignty because it has been created through voluntary agreements among its member states. But, in another sense, it fundamentally contradicts conventional understandings of sovereignty because these same agreements have undermined the juridical autonomy of its individual members.

The European Union, however, is not a model that other parts of the world can imitate. The initial moves toward integration could not have taken place without the political and economic support of the United States, which was, in the early years of the Cold War, much more interested in creating a strong alliance that could effectively oppose the Soviet Union than it was in any potential European challenge to U.S. leadership. Germany, one of the largest states in the European Union, has been the most consistent supporter of an institutional structure that would limit Berlin's own freedom of action, a reflection of the lessons of two devastating wars and the attractiveness of a European identity for a country still grappling with the sins of the Nazi era. It is hard to imagine that other regional powers such as China, Japan, or Brazil, much less the United States, would have any interest in tying their own hands in similar ways. (Regional trading agreements such as Mercosur and NAFTA have very limited supranational provisions and show few signs of evolving into broader monetary or political unions.) The EU is a new and unique institutional structure, but it will coexist with, not displace, the sovereign-state model.

MARK JUERGENSMEYER

THE NEW RELIGIOUS STATE

One of the most interesting—some would say disturbing—features of the post–Cold War era is the resurgence of religious politics. It appears as a dark cloud over what many regard as the near-global victory of liberal democracy following the collapse of the Soviet Empire.[1] It fuels regional disputes in North Africa, the Middle East, and South Asia and may be leading toward what Samuel Huntington has apocalyptically called "the clash of civilizations."[2] It has led to some impressive gains: radical religious parties are now firmly established not only in Iran but in Algeria, Sudan, Egypt, India, Afghanistan, Pakistan, the incipient Palestine, and elsewhere in what was once called the Third World. Although it is tempting to dismiss the religious activists involved in these uprisings as "fundamentalists," their goals and their motivations are as political as they are religious. For this reason I prefer to call them "religious nationalists," implying that they are political actors striving for new forms of national order based on religious values.[3]

The question I will pursue in this essay is how religious nationalists conceive this relationship between religion and politics. In the past several years, I have examined various movements of religious nationalism, including Hindu and Sikh partisans in India, militant Buddhists in Sri Lanka and Mongolia, Christian activists in eastern Europe and Latin America, right-wing Jewish politicians in Israel, and Islamic activists in the Middle East and Central Asia. I have described some of these movements in other essays and in a recent book.[4] Therefore, I will not discuss these cases in depth here, but rather will explore an issue that I believe is central to virtually

all of these movements: their assumption that religion can replace liberal democracy in providing the ideological glue that holds a nation together and that it can provide the justification for a modern religious state.

In this essay I will first describe how traditional religion can play the same ideological role that secular nationalist theories play in providing a theoretical basis for a nation-state. Because of this ideological role, I will then show, religion and liberal democratic ideas are seen as competitive in both the West and the Third World. Finally, I will explore a kind of resolution of this competition: the rise of a potent new synthesis between the nation-state and religion.

The Confrontation of Two Ideologies of Order

One of the most striking features of religious nationalists' rhetoric is the way that it juxtaposes religion with western notions of national ideology. Secular nationalism is "a kind of religion," one of the leaders of the Iranian revolution proclaimed.[5] He and other religious nationalists regard secularism not only as a religion, but as one peculiar to the West.[6] They assume that secular nationalism responds to the same sorts of needs for collective identity, ultimate loyalty, and moral authority to which religion has traditionally responded. Some go further and state that the western form of secular nationalism is simply a cover for Christianity. For evidence, they offer the fact that the word "Christian" is used in the title of some political parties in Europe. But whether or not secular nationalism in the West is overtly labeled Christian, most religious activists

From *Comparative Politics* (July 1995), pp. 379–91. Some of the author's notes have been omitted.

see it as occupying the same place in human experience as Islam in Muslin societies, Buddhism in Theravada Buddhist societies, and Hinduism and Sikhism in Indian society. To these Muslims, Buddhists, Hindus, and Sikhs it is perfectly obvious; the West's secular nationalism competes in every way with religion as they know it.

Behind this charge is a certain vision of social reality, one that involves a series of concentric circles. The smallest are families and clans; then come ethnic groups and nations; the largest, and implicitly most important, are global civilizations. Among these civilizations are to be found Islam, Buddhism, and what some who hold this view call "Christendom" and others call "western civilization." Particular nations such as Germany, France, and the United States, in this conceptualization, stand as subsets of Christendom/western civilization; similarly, Egypt, Iran, Pakistan, and other nations are subsets of Islamic civilization.

Are they correct in this assessment, that the social functions of traditional religion and secular nationalism are so similar they both can be regarded as two aspects of a similar phenomenon? Huntington's recent essay seems to agree.[7] Earlier, Benedict Anderson suggested that religion and secular nationalism are both "imagined communities;" Ninian Smart regarded them both as "world-views."[8] In an interesting way, these scholars concur with religious nationalists' understanding of the social character of religion: like secular nationalism, religion has the ability to command communal loyalty and to legitimize authority. To this extent I agree with Anderson and Smart—and with many religious nationalists—that religion and secular nationalism are species of the same genus. I prefer to call this genus "ideologies of order."

My use of the word "ideology" should not be misconstrued as an effort to revive the meanings attached to it by Karl Marx or Karl Mannheim or by those identified with the "end of ideology" debate some years ago.[9] Rather, I use it in the original, late-eighteenth-century sense. At that time a group of French *idéologues*, as they called themselves, were attempting to build a science of ideas based on the theories of Francis Bacon, Thomas Hobbes, John Locke, and René Descartes that would be sufficiently comprehensive to replace religion. According to one of the *idéologues*, Destutt de Tracy, whose book *Elements of Ideology* introduced the term to the world, "logic" was to be the sole basis of "the moral and political sciences."[10] In proposing their own "science of ideas" as a replacement for religion, the *idéologues* were in fact putting what they called ideology and what we call religion on an equal plane. Perhaps Clifford Geertz, among modern users of the term, has come closest to its original meaning by speaking of ideology as a "cultural system."[11]

To make clear that I am referring to the original meaning of the term and not to "political ideology" in a narrow sense or to a Marxian or Mannheimian notion of ideology, I will refer to what I have in mind as "ideologies of order." Both religious and secular nationalistic frameworks of thought are ideologies of order in the following ways: they both conceive of the world around them as a coherent, manageable system; they both suggest that there are levels of meaning beneath the day-to-day world that explain things unseen; they both provide identity for and evoke loyalty from secular communities; and they both provide the authority that gives social and political order a reason for being. In doing so they define how an individual should properly act in the world, and they relate persons to the social whole.

I have defined both nationalism and religion in terms of order as well as ideology. For this definition there is ample precedent. Regarding nationalism, Karl Deutsch has pointed out the importance of orderly systems of communication in fostering a sense of nationalism. Ernest Gellner argues that the political and economic network of a nation-state requires a spirit of nationalism that draws upon a homogeneous culture, a unified pattern of communication, and a common system of education. Other social scientists have stressed the psychological aspect of national identity: the sense of historical location that is engendered when individuals feel they are a part of a larger, national history. But behind these notions of community are also images of order, for nationalism always involves the loyalty to an authority who, as Max Weber observed, holds a monopoly over the "legitimate use of physical force" in a given society.[12] Anthony Giddens describes nationalism as the "cultural sensibility of sovereignty," implying that the awareness of being subject to such an authority—an authority invested with the power of life and death—is what gives nationalism its potency.[13] It is not only an attachment to a spirit of social order but also an act of submission to an ordering agent.

Religion has also been defined in terms of order, albeit in a conceptual more than a political or social sense. Clifford Geertz, for example, sees religion as the effort to integrate messy everyday reality into a pattern of coherence that takes shape at a deeper level.[14] Robert Bellah also thinks of religion as an attempt to reach beyond ordinary phenomena in a "risk of faith" that allows people to act "in the face of uncertainty and unpredictability" on the basis of a higher order of reality.[15] Peter Berger specifies that such faith is an affirmation of the sacred, which acts as a doorway to a more certain kind of truth.[16] Louis Dupré prefers to avoid the term "sacred" but integrates elements of both Berger's and Bellah's definitions in his description of religion as "a commitment to the transcendent as to *another* reality."[17] In all of these cases there is a tension between this imperfect, disorderly world and a perfected, orderly one to be found at a higher, transcendent state or in a cumulative moment in time. As Durkheim, whose thought is fundamental to each of these thinkers, was adamant in observing, religion has a more encompassing force than can be suggested by any dichotomization of the sacred and the profane. To Durkheim, the religious point of view includes both the notion that there is such a dichotomy and the belief that the sacred side will always, ultimately, reign supreme.[18]

From this perspective, both religion and secular nationalism are about order. They are therefore potential rivals. Either could claim to be the guarantor of orderliness within a society; either could claim to be the ultimate authority for social order. Such claims carry with them an extraordinary degree of power, for contained within them is the right to give moral sanction for life and death decisions, including the right to kill. When either nationalism or religion assumes this role by itself, it reduces the other to a peripheral social role.

The rivalry has historical roots. Earlier in history it was often religion that denied moral authority to secular politicians, but in recent centuries, especially in the West, it has been the other way around. Political authorities now attempt to monopolize the authority to sanction violence. They asserted this authority long before the advent of the nation-state, but usually in collusion with religious authority, not in defiance of it. What is unusual about the modern period is how victorious the secular state has been in denying the right of religious authorities to be ultimate moral arbiters. In the modern state, the state alone is given the moral power to kill (albeit for limited purposes, military defense, police protection, and capital punishment). Yet all of the rest of the state's power to persuade and to shape the social order is derived from these fundamental powers. In Max Weber's view, the monopoly over legitimate violence in a society is the very definition of a state. But the secular state did not always enjoy a monopoly over this right, and in challenging its authority, today's religious activists, wherever they assert themselves around the world, reclaim the traditional right of religious authorities to say when violence is moral and when it is not.

Religious conflict is one indication of the power of religion to sanction killing. The parties in such an encounter may command a greater degree of loyalty than contestants in a purely political war. Their interests can subsume national interests. In some cases a religious battle may preface the attempt to establish a new religious state. It is interesting to note, in this regard, that the best known incidents of religious violence throughout the contemporary world have occurred in places where it is difficult to define or accept the idea of a nation-state. Palestine, the Punjab, and Sri Lanka are the most obvious examples, but the revolutions in Iran, Nicaragua, Afghanistan, Tajikistan, and the countries of eastern Europe also concern themselves with what the state should be like and what elements of society should lead it. In these instances, religion provides the basis for a new national consensus and a new kind of leadership.

Modern religious activists are thereby reasserting the role of religion in most traditional societies where religion, as Donald E. Smith puts it, "answers the question of political legitimacy."[19] In the modern West, this legitimacy is provided by nationalism, a secular nationalism. But even here, religion continues to wait in the wings, a potential challenge to the nationalism based on secular assumptions. Perhaps nothing indicates the continuing challenge of religion more than the persistence of religious politics in American society, including most recently the rise of politically active religious fundamentalists in the 1980s and the potency of the Christian right in the 1992 and 1994 national elections. Religion is ready to demonstrate that, like secular nationalism, it can provide a faith in the unitary nature of a society that will authenticate both political rebellion and political rule.

Competition between Religion and Secular Nationalism in the West

Putting aside the recent electoral victories of America's religious right, secular nationalism has largely been the victor in the competition between religion and secular nationalism that has been going on in the West for several centuries now. At one time, the medieval church possessed "many aspects of a state," as one historian put it, and it had commanded more political power "than most of its secular rivals."[20] Perhaps more important, religion provided the legitimacy on which the power of monarchy and civil order was based. By the mid-nineteenth century, however, the Christian church had ceased to have much influence on European or American politics. The church—the great medieval monument of Christendom with all its social and political panoply—had been replaced by churches, various denominations of Protestantism and a largely depoliticized version of Roman Catholicism. These churches functioned like religious clubs, voluntary associations for the spiritual edification of individuals in their leisure time, rarely cognizant of the social and political world around them.

Secular nationalism began to replace religion several centuries ago as the ideological agent of political legitimacy. But the form in which we know it today—as the ideological ally of the nation-state—did not appear in England and American until the eighteenth century. Only by then had the nation-state taken root deeply enough to nurture an ideological loyalty of its own, unassisted by religious or ethnic identifications, and only by then had the political and military apparatus of the nation-state expanded sufficiently to encompass a large geographic region. Prior to that time, as Giddens explains, "the administrative reach" of the political center was so limited that rulers did not govern in "the modern sense."[21] Until the advent of the nation-state, the authority of a political center did not systematically and equally cover an entire population, so that what appeared to be a single homogeneous polity was in fact a congeries of fiefdoms. The further one got from the center of power, the weaker was the grip of centralized political influence, until at the periphery whole sections of a country might exist as a political no man's land. Therefore, one should speak of countries prior to the modern nation-state as having frontiers rather than boundaries.

The changes of the late eighteenth and nineteenth centuries included the development of the technical ability to knit a country together through roads, rivers, and other means of transportation and communication, the economic ability to do so through an increasingly integrated market structure, an emerging world economic system which was based on the building blocks of nation-states, the development of mass education which socialized each generation of youth into a homogeneous society, and the emergence of parliamentary democracy as a system of representation and an expression of the will of people. The glue that held all these changes together was secular nationalism: the notion that individuals naturally associate with the people and place of their ancestral birth in an economic and political system identified with a nation-state. Secular nationalism was thought to be not only natural, but also universally applicable and morally right. Although it was regarded almost as a natural law, secular nationalism was ultimately viewed as an expression of neither god nor nature but of the will of a nation's citizens. The ideas of John Locke about the origins of a civil community and the "social contract" theories of Jean-Jacques Rousseau required very little commitment to religious belief. Although they allowed for a divine order that made the rights of humans possible, their ideas did not directly buttress the power of the church and its priestly administrators, and they had the effect of taking religion—at least church religion—out of public life.

At the same time religion was becoming less political, secular nationalism was becoming more religious. It became clothed in romantic and xenophobic images that would have startled its Enlightenment forbears. The French Revolution, the model for much of the nationalist fervor that developed in the nineteenth century, infused a religious zeal into revolutionary democracy, which took on the trappings of church religion in the priestly power meted out to its demagogic leaders and in the slavish devotion to what it called "the temple of reason." According to Alexis de Tocqueville, the French Revolution "assumed many of the aspects of a religious revolution."[22] The American Revolution also had a religious side: many of its leaders had been influenced by eighteenth-century Deism, a religion of science and natural law which was "devoted to exposing

[church] religion to the light of knowledge."[23] As in France, American nationalism developed its own religious characteristics, blending the ideals of secular nationalism and the symbols of Christianity into a "civil religion."

The nineteenth century fulfilled de Tocqueville's prophecy that the "strange religion" of secular nationalism would, "like Islam, overrun the whole world with its apostles, militants, and martyrs."[24] It was spread throughout the world with an almost missionary zeal and was shipped to the newly colonized areas of Asia, Africa, and Latin America as part of the ideological freight of colonialism. It became the ideological partner of what came to be known as "nation-building." As the colonial governments provided their colonies with the political and economic infrastructures to turn territories into nation-states, the ideology of secular nationalism emerged as a by-product of the colonial nation-building experience. As it had in the West in previous centuries, secular nationalism in the colonized countries in the nineteenth and twentieth centuries came to represent one side of a great encounter between two vastly different ways of perceiving the sociopolitical order and the relationship of the individual to the state: one informed by religion, the other by a notion of a secular compact.

In the mid-twentieth century, when the colonial powers retreated, they left behind the geographical boundaries they had drawn and the political institutions they had fashioned. Created as administrative units of the Ottoman, Hapsburg, French, and British empires, the borders of most Third World nations continued after independence, even if they failed to follow the natural divisions among ethnic and linguistic communities. By the second half of the twentieth century, it seemed as if the cultural goals of the colonial era had been reached: although the political ties were severed, the new nations retained all the accoutrements of westernized countries. The only substantial empire to remain virtually intact until 1990 was the Soviet Union. It was based on a different vision of political or-

der, of course, in which international socialism was supposed to replace a network of capitalist nations. Yet the perception of many members of the Soviet states was that their nations were not so much integral units in a new internationalism as they were colonies in a secular Russian version of imperialism. This perception became dramatically clear after the breakup of the Soviet Union and its sphere of influence in the early 1990s, when old ethnic and national loyalties sprang to the fore.

Competition between Religion and Secular Nationalism in the Third World

The new nations that emerged as the "Third World" in the middle of the twentieth century had to confront the same competition between religion and nationalism as the West has had to confront, but in a very short period of time, and they simultaneously had to contend with the political by-products of colonial rule. If accommodating religion was difficult for the West, efforts to bridle religion in the new nations were a thousand times more problematic. There, the political competition of religion was much more obvious. Given religious histories that were part of national heritages, religious institutions that were sometimes the nations' most effective systems of communication, and religious leaders who were often more devoted, efficient, and intelligent than government officials, religion could not be ignored. The attempts to accommodate it, however, have not always been successful. * * *

*   *   *

A New Synthesis: The Religious Nation-State

Religious activists are well aware that, if a nation starts with the premise of secular nationalism, religion is often made marginal to the political order. This marginality is especially onerous from many revolutionary religious perspectives, * * * because they regard the two ideologies as unequal: the religious one is far superior. Rather than to start with secular nationalism, they prefer to begin with religion.

The implication of this way of speaking is not that religion is antithetical to nationalism, but that religious rather than secular nationalism is the appropriate premise on which to build a nation, even a modern nation-state. In fact, virtually every reference to nationhood used by religious nationalists assumes that the modern nation-state is the only way in which a nation can be construed.

Although the link between religion and nationalism has historical precedents, the present attempt to forge an alliance between religion and the modern democratic nation-state is a new development in the history of nationalism, and it immediately raises the question whether it is possible: whether what we in the West think of as a modern nation—a unified, democratically controlled system of economic and political administration—can in fact be accommodated within religion. Many western observers would automatically answer no. Even as acute an interpreter of modern society as Giddens regarded most religious cultures as at best a syncreticism between "tribal cultures, on the one hand, and modern societies, on the other."[25]

Yet by Giddens' own definition of a modern nation-state, postrevolutionary Iran would qualify: the Islamic revolution in Iran has solidified not just a central power but a systematic control over the population that is more conducive to nationhood than the monarchical political order of the shah. A new national entity came into being that was quite different from both the polity under the old Muslim rulers and the nation the shah ineptly attempted to build. The shah dreamed of creating Ataturk's Turkey in Iran and bringing to his country what he perceived as the instant modernity brought to Turkey by Ataturk. Ironically, Khomeini—along with his integrative religious ideology and his grass-roots network of mullahs—ultimately accomplished the unity and national organization that the shah had sought.

A similar claim is made in India, where Hindu nationalists are emphatic on the point that "Hindutva," as they call Hindu national culture, is the defining characteristic of Indian nationalism. In Sri Lanka, according to one Sinhalese writer, "it is clear that the unifying, healing, progressive principle" that held together the entity known as Ceylon throughout the years has always been "the Buddhist faith."[26] The writer goes on to say that religion in Sri Lanka continues to provide the basis for a "liberating nationalism" and that Sinhalese Buddhism is "the only patriotism worthy of the name, worth fighting for or dying for."[27] Similar sentiments are echoed in movements of religious nationalism in Egypt, Israel, and elsewhere in the world.

In these efforts to accommodate modern politics, has religion compromised its purity? Some religious leaders think that it has. In favoring the nation-state over a particular religious congregation as its major community of reference, religion loses the exclusivity held by smaller, subnational religious communities, and the leaders of those communities lose some of their autonomy. Many religious leaders are therefore suspicious of religious nationalism. Among them are religious utopians who would rather build their own isolated political societies than to deal with the problems of a whole nation, religious liberals who are satisfied with the secular nation-state the way it is, and religious conservatives who would rather ignore politics altogether. Some Muslims have accused Khomeini of making Islam into a political ideology and reducing it to the terms of modern politics. Moreover, as Bernard Lewis claims, most Islamic rebellions are aimed in the opposite direction: to shed Islam of the alien idea of the nation-state.[28] Yet, even if that is their aim, one of the curious consequences of their way of thinking is the appropriation of many of the most salient elements of modern nationhood into an Islamic frame of reference. Rather than ridding Islam of the nation-state, they too have created a new synthesis.

Modern movements of religious nationalism, therefore, are subjects of controversy within both religious and secular circles. The marriage between religious faith and the nation-state is an interesting turn in modern history, frought with dangers, for even if it is possible, the radical accommodation of religion to nationalism may not necessarily be a good thing. A merger of the absolutism of nationalism with the absolutism of religion might create a rule so vaunted and potent that it might destroy itself and its neighbors as well. The actions of religious terrorists in the 1980s and early 1990s in South Asia and the Middle East warrant some of those fears. When a society's secular state and its religious community are both strong and respected, the power of life and death that is commanded by any single absolute authority—be it secular or religious—may be held tenuously in check. Without that balance, an absolute power of the worst sort could claim its most evil deeds to be legitimate moral duties. The revolutionary religious movements that have emerged in many parts of the world in the 1980s and 1990s exhibit some of those dangers—as well as many of the more hopeful aspects—of the religious nationalists' synthesis between the two great ideologies of order.

*   *   *

NOTES

1. For the optimistic point of view that liberal democracy has triumphed, see Francis Fukuyama, "The End of History," *The National Interest*, 16 (Summer 1989), 3–18: and *The End of History and the Last Man* (New York: The Free Press, 1992), pp. xi–xxiii.

2. Samuel P. Huntington, "The Clash of Civilizations?," *Foreign Affairs*, 72 (Summer 1993), 2–11: and "If Not Civilizations, What? Paradigms of the Post-Cold War World," *Foreign Affairs*, 72 (November–December 1993), 186–94.

3. See Mark Juergensmeyer, "Why Religious Nationalists Are Not Fundamentalists," *Religion*, 23 (Spring 1993).

4. See Mark Juergensmeyer, "The Logic of Religious Violence," in David C. Rapoport, ed., *Inside Terrorist Organizations* (London: Frank Cass, 1988), pp. 172–93: "What the Bhikkhu Said: Reflections on the Rise of Militant Religious Nationalism," *Religion*, 20 (1990), 53–75: and *The New Cold War? Religious Nationalism Confronts the Secular State* (Berkeley: University of California Press, 1993). Some of the book's arguments and revised segments from it have been incorporated into this essay.

5. Abolhassan Banisadr, *The Fundamental Principles and Precepts of Islamic Government* (Lexington: Mazda Publishers, 1981), p. 40.

6. Interview with Dr. Essem el Arian. Member of the National Assembly, Cairo, January 11, 1989; Sheik Ahmed Yassin, Gaza, January 14, 1989; and Bhikkhu Udawawala Chandrananda, Kandy, Sri Lanka, January 5, 1991.

7. Huntington, "Clash of Civilizations?"

8. Benedict Anderson, *Imagined Communities: Reflections on the Origin and Spread of Nationalism* (London: Verso, 1983); and Ninian Smart, *Worldviews: Crosscultural Explorations of Human Beliefs* (New York: Scribner's, 1983).

9. Karl Marx and Friedrich Engels, *The German Ideology* (New York: International Publishers, 1939); Karl Mannheim, *Ideology and Utopia* (New York: Harcourt, Brace and World, 1936); David Apter, ed., *Ideology and Discontent* (New York: The Free Press, 1964); and Chaim I. Waxman, ed., *The End of Ideology Debate* (New York: Simon and Schuster, 1964).

10. Destutt de Tracy, "Elements of Ideology", in Richard H. Cox. *Ideology, Politics, and Political Theory* (Belmont: Wadsworth Publishing Company, 1969), p. 17.

11. Clifford Geertz, "Ideology as a Cultural System," in Apter, ed.

12. Max Weber, "Politics as a Vocation," in Hans H. Gerth and C. Wright Mills, eds., *From Max Weber: Essays in Sociology* (New York: Oxford University Press, 1946), p. 78. Regarding the state's monopoly on violence, see John Breuilly, *Nationalism and the State* (Manchester: Manchester University Press, 1982); and Anthony D. Smith, *Theories of Nationalism* (London: Duckworth, 1971).

13. Anthony Giddens, *A Contemporary Critique of Historical Materialism, Volume Two: The Nation-State and Violence* (Berkeley: University of California Press, 1985), p. 219.

14. Clifford Geertz, "Religion as a Cultural System," reprinted in William A. Lessa and Evon Z. Vogt, eds., *Reader in Comparative Religion: An Anthropological Approach*, 3rd ed. (New York: Harper and Row, 1972), p. 168.

15. Robert Bellah, "Transcendence in Contemporary Piety," in Donald R. Cutler, *The Religious Situation: 1969* (Boston: Beacon Press, 1969), p. 907.

16. Peter Berger, *The Heretical Imperative* (New York: Doubleday, 1980), p. 38. See also Peter Berger, *Sacred Canopy: Elements of a Sociological Theory of Religion* (Garden City: Doubleday, 1967).

17. Louis Dupré, *Transcendent Selfhood: The Loss and Rediscovery of the Inner Life* (New York: Seabury Press, 1976), p. 26. For a discussion of Berger's and Dupré's definitions, see Mary Douglas, "The Effects of Modernization on Religious Change," *Daedalus*, 111 (Winter 1982), 1–19.

18. Émile Durkheim, *The Elementary Forms of the Religious Life* (London: George Allen and Unwin, 1976), pp. 38–39.

19. Donald E. Smith, ed., *Religion, Politics, and Social Change in the Third World: A Sourcebook* (New York: The Free Press, 1971), p. 11.

20. Joseph Strayer, *Medieval Statecraft and the Perspectives of History* (Princeton: Princeton University Press, 1971), p. 323.

21. Giddens, *Nation-State*, p. 4.

22. Alexis de Tocqueville, *The Old Regime and the French Revolution* (New York: Doubleday Anchor Books, 1955), p. 11. See also John McManners, *The French Revolution and the Church* (Westport: Greenwood Press, 1969).

23. Ernst Cassirer, *The Philosophy of the Enlightenment* (Boston: Beacon Press, 1955), p. 171. Among the devotees of Deism were Thomas Jefferson, Benjamin Franklin, and other founding fathers of America.

24. De Tocqueville, *The Old Regime*, p. 13.

25. Giddens, *The Nation-State*, p. 71.

26. D. C. Vejayavardhana, *The Revolt in the Temple: Composed to Commemorate 2,500 Years of the Land, the Race, and the Faith* (Colombo: Sinha Publications, 1953), reprinted in Smith, ed., *Religion, Politics and Social Change*, p. 105.

27. Vejayavardhana, *The Revolt in the Temple*, p. 105.

28. Bernard Lewis, *The Political Language of Islam* (Chicago: University of Chicago Press, 1988).

3 NATIONS AND SOCIETY

The readings presented in this chapter address three basic issues: nationalism, the role of ethnic conflict in civil war, and "civilizational" conflict.

Certainly until the sixteenth century, and plausibly even until the eighteenth century, there was no nationalism in the modern sense. People were loyal to a particular lord or locality, but not to a linguistically or ethnically defined nation, and no one was surprised that the typical state or empire embraced a large variety of languages and ethnicities. How, then, did modern nationalism become so powerful a force, and why are most states today "nation-states," that is, ones that have, or seek, national unity?

In his 1962 book The Age of Revolution: 1789–1848, *the eminent historian E. J. Hobsbawm wrote what many comparativists regard still as the most convincing account of how modern nationalisms arose, with clear implications for present-day ethnic conflicts around the globe. Hobsbawm's crucial insight—that nationalism is always linked to the rapid rise of an indigenous middle class and to the spread of literacy in the native language—remains valid today and has been stressed in analyses of (among many others) Québecois, Basque, Eritrean, and Kurdish nationalism. One should also remember, as Hobsbawm notes, that a sizeable proportion of the "national" languages claimed by such groups—among them Croatian, Romanian, Gaelic, Norwegian, Czech, and modern Hebrew—were as much invented (that is, constructed out of a welter of dialects or the imagined evolution of an ossified language) as revived.*

Ethnic divisions sometimes lead to violent conflict, inflicting heavy costs on societies both poor (Rwanda) and rich (Northern Ireland). In the 1990s, some economists held that economic fragmentation alone, at least in Africa, led directly to bad policies, weak trust, and continuing poverty. Violence, and particularly civil war, undoubtedly inhibited economic growth; but Paul Collier and other World Bank economists argued that most civil wars were a result of "greed" rather than "grievance": conflict was often all about, and fueled by, huge and readily marketable reserves of valuable natural resources (oil, diamonds, copper ore, mahogany). In 2003, the comparativists James Fearon and David Laitin went far toward settling these questions in a famous article (excerpted here) entitled "Ethnicity, Insurgency, and Civil War." They showed that ethnically diverse societies were no likelier than homogeneous ones to experience civil war; rather, the chief causes were poverty, political instability, and a terrain that favored insurgency.

Samuel P. Huntington, a renowned comparativist and development specialist, contended in a 1993 article (presented here in slightly abridged form) and a 1996 book that the twenty-first century would be characterized not by ethnic, ideological, or even international conflict, but by what he called a "conflict of civilizations." By "civilization" he meant something much broader than ethnicity, and he devoted considerable attention to what he foresaw as a likely violent conflict between Islam and the West. Understandably, his prognosis found great resonance after September 11, 2001, the terrorist attacks on London and Madrid, and the Paris riots by predominantly Muslim immigrants.

Among the sharpest rebuttals to Huntington's argument were those by the Nobel laureate Amartya Sen and the Middle East expert Fouad Ajami. In "The Summoning" (1993), included here, Ajami argued that Huntington had underestimated the power, throughout the Third World, of secularism and modernism. Calls for returns to "tradition," in Islamic societies or elsewhere, would remain (he predicted) largely a fringe phenomenon.

ERIC HOBSBAWM

NATIONALISM

Every people has its special mission, which will cooperate towards the fulfilment of the general mission of humanity. That mission constitutes its nationality. Nationality is sacred.

Act of Brotherhood *of Young Europe, 1834*

The day will come . . . when sublime Germania shall stand on the bronze pedestal of liberty and justice, bearing in one hand the torch of enlightenment, which shall throw the beam of civilization into the remotest corners of the earth, and in the other the arbiter's balance. The people will beg her to settle their disputes; those very people who now show us that

From *The Age of Revolution* (London: Weidenfeld & Nicholson, 1962), pp. 132–45. Some of the author's notes have been omitted.

might is right, and kick us with the jackboot of scornful contempt.

From Siebenpfeiffer's speech at the Hambach Festival, 1832

After 1830, as we have seen, the general movement in favour of revolution split. One product of this split deserves special attention: the self-consciously nationalist movements.

The movements which best symbolize this development are the 'Youth' movements founded or inspired by Giuseppe Mazzini shortly after the 1830 revolution: Young Italy, Young Poland, Young Switzerland, Young Germany, and Young France (1831–6) and the analogous Young Ireland of the 1840s, the ancestor of the only lasting and successful revolutionary organization on the model of the early nineteenth-century conspiratory brotherhoods, the Fenians or Irish Republican Brotherhood, better known through its executive arm of the Irish Republican Army. In themselves these movements were of no great importance; the mere presence of Mazzini would have been enough to ensure their total ineffectiveness. Symbolically they are of extreme importance, as is indicated by the adoption in subsequent nationalist movements of such labels as "Young Czechs" or "Young Turks." They mark the distintegration of the European revolutionary movement into national segments. Doubtless each of these segments had much the same political programme strategy, and tactics as the others, and even much the same flag—almost invariably a tricolour of some kind. Its members saw no contradiction between their own demands and those of other nations, and indeed envisaged a brotherhood of all, simultaneously liberating themselves. On the other hand each now tended to justify its primary concern with its own nation by adopting the role of a Messiah for all. Through Italy (according to Mazzini), through Poland (according to Mickiewicz), the suffering peoples of the world were to be led to freedom; an attitude readily adaptable to conservative or indeed imperialist policies, as witness the Russian Slavophils with their championship of Holy Russia, the Third Rome, and the Germans who were subsequently to tell the world at some length that it would be healed by the German spirit. Admittedly this ambiguity of nationalism went back to the French Revolution. But in those days there had been only *one* great and revolutionary nation and it made sense (as indeed it still did) to regard it as the headquarters of all revolutions, and the necessary prime mover in the liberation of the world. To look to Paris was rational; to look to a vague "Italy," "Poland," or "Germany" (represented in practice by a handful of conspirators and emigrés) made sense only for Italians, Poles, and Germans.

If the new nationalism had been confined only to the membership of the national-

revolutionary brotherhoods, it would not be worth much more attention. However, it also reflected much more powerful forces, which were emerging into political consciousness in the 1830s as the result of the double revolution. The most immediately powerful of these were the discontent of the lesser landowners or gentry and the emergence of a national middle and even lower-middle class in numerous countries, the spokesmen for both being largely professional intellectuals.

The revolutionary role of the lesser gentry is perhaps best illustrated in Poland and Hungary. There, on the whole, the large landed magnates had long found it possible and desirable to make terms with absolutism and foreign rule. The Hungarian magnates were in general Catholic and had long been accepted as pillars of Viennese court society; very few of them were to join the revolution of 1848. The memory of the old *Rzeczpospolita* made even Polish magnates nationally minded, but the most influential of their quasi-national parties, the Czartoryski connection, now operating from the luxurious emigration of the Hotel Lambert in Paris, had always favoured the alliance with Russia and continued to prefer diplomacy to revolt. Economically they were wealthy enough to afford what they needed, short of really titanic dissipation, and even to invest enough in the improvement of their estates to benefit from the economic expansion of the age, if they chose to. Count Széchenyi, one of the few moderate liberals from this class and a champion of economic improvement, gave a year's income for the new Hungarian Academy of Sciences—some 60,000 florins. There is no evidence that his standard of life suffered from such disinterested generosity. On the other hand the numerous gentlemen who had little but their birth to distinguish them from other impoverished farmers—one in eight of the Hungarian population claimed gentlemanly status—had neither the money to make their holdings profitable nor the inclination to compete with Germans and Jews for middle-class wealth. If they could not live decently on their rents, and a degenerate age deprived them of a soldier's chances, then they might, if not too ignorant, consider the law, administration, or some intellectual position, but no bourgeois activity. Such gentlemen had long been the stronghold of opposition to absolutism, foreigners, and magnate rule in their respective countries, sheltering (as in Hungary) behind the dual buttress of Calvinism and county organization. It was natural that their opposition, discontent, and aspiration for more jobs for local gentlemen should now fuse with nationalism.

The national business classes which emerged in this period were, paradoxically, a rather less nationalist element. Admittedly in disunited Germany and Italy the advantages of a large unified national market made sense. The author of *Deutschland über Alles* apostrophized

> Ham and scissors, boots and garters,
> Wool and soap and yarn and beer,

because they had achieved, what the spirit of nationality had been unable to, a genuine sense of national unity through customs union. However, there is little evidence that, say, the shippers of Genoa (who were later to provide much of the financial backing for Garibaldi) preferred the possibilities of a national Italian market to the larger prosperity of trading all over the Mediterranean. And in the large multinational empires the industrial or trading nuclei which grew up in particular provinces might grumble about discrimination, but at bottom clearly preferred the great markets open to them now to the little ones of future national independence. The Polish industrialists, with all Russia at their feet, took little part as yet in Polish nationalism. When Palacky claimed on behalf of the Czechs that "if Austria did not exist, it would have to be invented," he was not merely calling on the monarchy's support against the Germans, but also expressing the sound economic reasoning of the economically most advanced sector of a large and otherwise backward empire. Business interests were sometimes at the head of nationalism, as in Belgium, where a strong pioneer industrial community regarded itself, with doubtful reason, as disadvantaged under the rule of the powerful Dutch merchant community, to which it had been hitched in 1815. But this was an exceptional case.

The great proponents of middle-class nationalism at this stage were the lower and middle professional, administrative and intellectual strata, in other words the *educated* classes. (These are not, of course, distinct from the business classes, especially in backward countries where estate administrators, notaries, lawyers, and the like are among the key accumulators of rural wealth.) To be precise, the advance guard of middle-class nationalism fought its battle along the line which marked the educational progress of large numbers of "new men" into areas hitherto occupied by a small elite. The progress of schools and universities measures that of nationalism, just as schools and especially universities became its most conscious champions: the conflict of Germany and Denmark over Schleswig-Holstein in 1848 and again in 1864 was anticipated by the conflict of the universities of Kiel and Copenhagen on this issue in the middle 1840s.

The progress was striking, though the total number of the "educated" remained small. The number of pupils in the French state *lycées* doubled between 1809 and 1842, and increased with particular rapidity under the July monarchy, but even so in 1842 it was only just under 19,000. (The total of all children receiving secondary education then was about 70,000.) Russia, around 1850, had some 20,000 secondary pupils out of a total population of sixty-eight million. The number of university students was naturally even smaller, though it was rising. It is difficult to realize that the Prussian academic youth which was so stirred by the idea of liberation after 1806 consisted in 1805 of not much more than 1,500 young men all told; that the *Polytechnique*, the bane of the post-1815 Bourbons, trained a total of 1,581 young men in the entire period from 1815 to 1830, i.e., an annual intake of about one hundred. The revolutionary prominence of the students in the 1848 period makes us forget that in the whole continent of Europe, including the unrevolutionary British Isles, there were probably not more than 40,000 university students in all. Still their numbers rose. In Russia it rose from 1,700 in 1825 to 4,600 in 1848. And even if they did not, the transformation of society and the universities . . . gave them a new consciousness of themselves as a social group. Nobody remembers that in 1789 there were something like 6,000 students in the University of Paris, because they played no independent part in the Revolution. But by 1830 nobody could possibly overlook such a number of young academics.

Small elites can operate in foreign languages; once the cadre of the educated becomes large enough, the national language imposes itself (as witness the struggle for linguistic recognition in the Indian states since the 1940s). Hence the moment when textbooks or newspapers in the national language are first written, or when that language is first used for some official purpose, measures a crucial step in national evolution. The 1830s saw this step taken over large areas of Europe. Thus the first major Czech works on astronomy, chemistry, anthropology, mineralogy, and botany were written or completed in this decade; and so, in Rumania, were the first school textbooks substituting Rumanian for the previously current Greek. Hungarian was adopted instead of Latin as the official language of the Hungarian Diet in 1840, though Budapest University, controlled from Vienna, did not abandon Latin lectures until 1844. (However, the struggle for the use of Hungarian as an official language had gone on intermittently since 1790.) In Zagreb, Gai published his *Croatian Gazette* (later: *Illyrian National Gazette*) from 1835 in the first literary version of what had hitherto been merely a complex of dialects. In countries which had long possessed an official national language, the change cannot be so easily measured, though it is interesting that after 1830 the number of German books published in Germany (as against Latin and French titles) for the first time consistently exceeded 90 per cent; the number of

French ones after 1820 fell below 4 per cent.[1] More generally the expansion of publishing gives us a comparable indication. Thus in Germany the number of books published remained much the same in 1821 as in 1800—about 4,000 titles a year, but by 1841 it had risen to 12,000 titles.

Of course the great mass of Europeans, and of non-Europeans, remained uneducated. Indeed, with the exception of the Germans, the Dutch, Scandinavians, Swiss, and the citizens of the USA, no people can in 1840 be described as literate. Several can be described as totally illiterate, like the Southern Slavs, who had less than one-half per cent literacy in 1827 (even much later only one per cent of Dalmatian recruits to the Austrian army could read and write), or the Russians, who had two per cent (1840), and a great many as almost illiterate, like the Spaniards, the Portuguese (who appear to have had barely 8,000 children in all *at school* after the Peninsular War) and, except for the Lombards and Piedmontese, the Italians. Even Britain, France, and Belgium were 40 to 50 per cent illiterate in the 1840s. Illiteracy is no bar to political consciousness, but there is, in fact, no evidence that nationalism of the modern kind was a powerful mass force except in countries already transformed by the dual revolution: in France, in Britain, in the USA and—because it was an economic and political dependency of Britain—in Ireland.

To equate nationalism with the literate class is not to claim that the mass of, say, Russians, did not consider themselves "Russian" when confronted with somebody or something that was not. However, for the masses in general the test of nationality was still religion: the Spaniard was defined by being Catholic, the Russian by being Orthodox. However, though such confrontations were becoming rather more frequent, they were still rare, and certain kinds of national feeling, such as the Italian, were as yet wholly alien to the great mass of the people, which did not even speak the national literary language but mutually almost incomprehensible *patois*. Even in Germany patriotic mythology has greatly exaggerated the degree of national feeling against Napoleon. France was extremely popular in Western Germany, especially among soldiers, whom it employed freely. Populations attached to the Pope or the Emperor might express resentment against their enemies, who happened to be the French, but this hardly implied any feelings of national consciousness, let alone any desire for a national state. Moreover, the very fact that nationalism was represented by middle class and gentry was enough to make the poor man suspicious. The Polish radical-democratic revolutionaries tried earnestly—as did the more advanced of the South Italian Carbonari and other conspirators—to mobilize the peasantry even to the point of offering agrarian reform. Their failure was almost total. The Galician peasants in 1846 opposed the Polish revolutionaries even though these actually proclaimed the abolition of serfdom, preferring to massacre gentlemen and trust to the Emperor's officials.

The uprooting of peoples, which is perhaps the most important single phenomenon of the nineteenth century, was to break down this deep, age-old and localized traditionalism. Yet over most of the world up to the 1820s hardly anybody as yet migrated or emigrated, except under the compulsion of armies and hunger, or in the traditionally migratory groups such as the peasants from Central France who did seasonal building jobs in the north, or the travelling German artisans. Uprooting still meant, not the mild form of homesickness which was to become the characteristic psychological disease of the nineteenth century (reflected in innumerable sentimental popular songs), but the acute, killing *mal de pays* or *mal de cœur* which had first been clinically described by doctors among the old Swiss mercenaries in foreign lands. The conscription of the revolutionary wars revealed it, notably among the Bretons. The pull of the remote northern forests was so strong that it could lead an Estonian servant-girl to leave her excellent employers the Kügelgens in Saxony, where she was free, and return home to serfdom. Migration and emigration, of which the migration to the USA is the most convenient index, increased notably from the 1820s, though it did not reach anything like major proportions until the 1840s, when one and three-quarter millions crossed the North Atlantic (a little less than three times the figure for the 1830s). Even so, the only major migratory nation outside the British Isles was as yet the German, long used to sending its sons as peasant settlers to Eastern Europe and America, as travelling artisans across the continent and as mercenaries everywhere.

We can in fact speak of only one Western national movement organized in a coherent form before 1848 which was genuinely based on the masses, and even this enjoyed the immense advantage of identification with the strongest carrier of tradition, the Church. This was the Irish Repeal movement under Daniel O'Connell (1785–1847), a golden-voiced lawyer–demagogue of peasant stock, the first—and up to 1848 the only one—of those charismatic popular leaders who mark the awakening of political consciousness in hitherto backward masses. (The only comparable figures before 1848 were Feargus O'Connor (1794–1855), another Irishman, who symbolized Chartism in Britain, and perhaps Louis Kossuth (1802–1894), who may have acquired something of his subsequent mass prestige before the 1848 revolution, though in fact his reputation in the 1840s was made as a champion of the gentry, and his later canonization by nationalist historians makes it difficult to see his early career at all clearly.) O'Connell's Catholic Association, which won its mass support and the not wholly justified confidence of the clergy in the successful struggle for Catholic Emancipation (1829), was in no sense tied to the gentry, who were in any case Protestant and Anglo-Irish. It was a movement of peasants, and such elements of a native Irish lower-middle class as existed in that pauperized island. 'The Liberator' was borne into leadership by successive waves of a mass movement of agrarian revolt, the chief motive force of Irish politics throughout that appalling century. This was organized in secret terrorist societies which themselves helped to break down the parochialism of Irish life. However, his aim was neither revolution nor national independence, but a moderate middle-class Irish autonomy by agreement or negotiation with the British Whigs. He was, in fact, not a nationalist and still less a peasant revolutionary but a moderate middle-class autonomist. Indeed, the chief criticism which has been not unjustifiably raised against him by later Irish nationalists (much as the more radical Indian nationalists have criticized Gandhi, who occupied an analogous position in his country's history) was that he could have raised all Ireland against the British, and deliberately refused to do so. But this does not alter the fact that the movement he led was genuinely supported by the mass of the Irish nation.

II

Outside the zone of the modern bourgeois world there were, however, movements of popular revolt against alien rule (i.e., normally understood as meaning rule by a different religion rather than a different nationality) which sometimes appear to anticipate later national movements. Such were the rebellions against the Turkish Empire, against the Russians in the Caucasus, and the fight against the encroaching British raj in and on the confines of India. It is unwise to read too much modern nationalism into these, though in backward areas populated by armed and combative peasants and herdsmen, organized in clan groups and inspired by tribal chieftains, bandit-heroes, and prophets, resistance to the foreign (or better, the unbelieving) ruler could take the form of veritable people's wars quite unlike the elite nationalist movements in less Homeric countries. In fact, however, the resistance of Mahrattas (a feudal-military Hindu group) and Sikhs (a militant religious sect) to the British in 1803–18 and 1845–49 respectively have little connection with subsequent Indian nationalism and produced none of their own.[2] The Caucasian tribes, savage, heroic, and feud-ridden, found in the puritan Islamic sect of Muridism a temporary bond of unity against the invading Russians and in Shamyl (1797–1871) a leader of major stature; but there is not to this day a Caucasian nation, but merely a congeries of small mountain peoples in small Soviet republics. (The Georgians and Armenians, who have formed nations in the modern sense, were not involved in the Shamyl movement.) The Bedouin, swept by puritan religious sects like the Wahhabi in Arabia and the Senussi in what is today Libya, fought for the simple faith of Allah and the simple life of the herdsman and raider against the corruption of taxes, pashas, and cities; but what we know as Arab nationalism—a product of the twentieth century—has come out of the cities, not the nomadic encampments.

Even the rebellions against the Turks in the Balkans, especially among the rarely subdued mountain peoples of the south and west, should not be too readily interpreted in modern nationalist terms though the bards and braves of several—the two were often the same, as among the poet-warrior bishops of Montenegro—recalled the glories of quasi-national heroes like the Albanian Skanderbeg and the tragedies like the Serbian defeat at Kossovo in the remote battles against the Turks. Nothing was more natural than to revolt, where necessary or desirable, against a local administration of a weakening Turkish Empire. However, little but a common economic backwardness united what we now know as the Yugoslavs, even those in the Turkish Empire, and the very concept of Yugoslavia was the product of intellectuals in Austro-Hungary rather than of those who actually fought for liberty.[3] The Orthodox Montenegrins, never subdued, fought the Turks, but with equal zest they fought the unbelieving Catholic Albanians and the unbelieving, but solidly Slav, Moslem Bosnians. The Bosnians revolted against the Turks, whose religion many of them shared, with as much readiness as the Orthodox Serbs of the wooded Danube plain, and with more zest than the Orthodox "old Serbs" of the Albanian frontier-area. The first of the Balkan peoples to rise in the nineteenth century were the Serbs under a heroic pig-dealer and brigand Black George (1760–1817), but the initial phase of his rising (1804–7) did not even claim to be against Turkish rule, but on the contrary for the Sultan against the abuses of the local rulers. There is little in the early history of mountain rebellion in the Western Balkans to suggest that the local Serbs, Albanians, Greeks, and others would not in the early nineteenth century have been satisfied with the sort of non-national autonomous principality which a powerful satrap, Ali Pasha "the Lion of Jannina" (1741–1822), for a time set up in Epirus.

In one and only one case did the perennial fight of the shepherding clansmen and bandit-heroes against *any* real government fuse with the ideas of middle-class nationalism and the French Revolution: in the Greek struggle for independence (1821–30). Not unnaturally Greece therefore became the myth and inspiration of nationalists and liberals everywhere. For in Greece alone did an entire people rise against the oppressor in a manner which could be plausibly identified with the cause of the European left; and in turn the support of the European left, headed by the poet Byron who died there, was of very considerable help in the winning of Greek independence.

Most Greeks were much like the other forgotten warrior-peasantries and clans of the Balkan peninsula. A part, however, formed an international merchant and administrative class also settled in colonies or minority communities throughout the Turkish Empire and beyond, and the language and higher ranks of the entire Orthodox Church, to which most Balkan peoples belonged, were Greek, headed by the Greek Patriarch of Constantinople. Greek civil servants, transmuted into vassal princes, governed the Danubian principalities (the present Rumania). In a sense the entire educated and mercantile classes of the Balkans, the Black Sea area, and the Levant, whatever their national origins, were hellenized by the very nature of their activities. During the eighteenth century this hellenization proceeded more powerfully than before, largely

because of the marked economic expansion which also extended the range and contacts of the Greek diaspora. The new and thriving Black Sea grain trade took it into Italian, French, and British business centres and strengthened its links with Russia; the expansion of Balkan trade brought Greek or Grecized merchants into Central Europe. The first Greek language newspapers were published in Vienna (1784–1812). Periodic emigration and resettlement of peasant rebels further reinforced the exile communities. It was among this cosmopolitan diaspora that the ideas of the French Revolution—liberalism, nationalism, and the methods of political organization by masonic secret societies—took root. Rhigas (1760–98), the leader of an early obscure and possibly pan-Balkanist revolutionary movement, spoke French and adapted the *Marseillaise* to Hellenic conditions. The *Philiké Hetairía*, the secret patriotic society mainly responsible for the revolt of 1821, was founded in the great new Russian grain port of Odessa in 1814.

Their nationalism was to some extent comparable to the elite movements of the West. Nothing else explains the project of raising a rebellion for Greek independence in the Danube principalities under the leadership of local Greek magnates; for the only people who could be described as Greeks in these miserable serf-lands were lords, bishops, merchants, and intellectuals. Naturally enough that rising failed miserably (1821). Fortunately, however, the Hetairía had also set out to enrol the anarchy of local brigand-heroes, outlaws, and clan chieftains in the Greek mountains (especially in the Peloponnese), and with considerably greater success—at any rate after 1818—than the South Italian gentlemen Carbonari, who attempted a similar proselytization of their local banditti. It is doubtful whether anything like modern nationalism meant much to these "klephts," though many of them had their "clerks"—a respect for and interest in book-learning was a surviving relic of ancient Hellenism—who composed manifestoes in the Jacobin terminology. If they stood for anything it was for the age-old ethos of a peninsula in which the role of man was to become a hero, and the outlaw who took to the mountains to resist any government and to right the peasant's wrongs was the universal political ideal. To the rebellions of men like Kolokotrones, brigand and cattle-dealer, the nationalists of the Western type gave leadership and a pan-hellenic rather than a purely local scale. In turn they got from them that unique and awe-inspiring thing, the mass rising of an armed people.

The new Greek nationalism was enough to win independence, though the combination of middle-class leadership, klephtic disorganization, and great power intervention produced one of those petty caricatures of the Western liberal ideal which were to become so familiar in areas like Latin America. But it also had the paradoxical result of narrowing Hellenism to Hellas, and thus creating or intensifying the latent nationalism of the other Balkan peoples. While being Greek had been little more than the professional requirement of the literate Orthodox Balkan Christian, hellenization had made progress. Once it meant the political support for Hellas, it receded, even among the assimilated Balkan literate classes. In this sense Greek independence was the essential preliminary condition for the evolution of the other Balkan nationalisms.

Outside Europe it is difficult to speak of nationalism at all. The numerous Latin American republics which replaced the token Spanish and Portuguese Empires (to be accurate, Brazil became and remained an independent monarchy from 1816 to 1889), their frontiers often reflecting little more than the distribution of the estates of the grandees who had backed one rather than another of the local rebellions, began to acquire vested political interests and territorial aspirations. The original pan-American ideal of Simón Bolívar (1783–1830) of Venezuela and San Martín (1788–1850) of the Argentine was impossible to realize, though it has persisted as a powerful revolutionary current throughout all the areas united by the Spanish language, just as pan-Balkanism, the heir of Orthodox unity against Islam, persisted and may still persist to-day. The vast extent and variety of the continent, the existence of independent foci of rebellion in Mexico (which determined Central America), Venezuela, and Buenos Aires, and the special problem of the centre of Spanish colonialism in Peru, which was liberated from without, imposed automatic fragmentation. But the Latin American revolutions were the work of small groups of patricians, soldiers and gallicized *évolués*, leaving the mass of the Catholic poor-white population passive and the Indians indifferent or hostile. Only in Mexico was independence won by the initiative of a popular agrarian, i.e., Indian, movement marching under the banner of the Virgin of Guadalupe, and Mexico has consequently ever since followed a different and politically more advanced road from the remainder of continental Latin America. However, even among the tiny layer of the politically decisive Latin Americans it would be anachronistic in our period to speak of anything more than the embryo of Colombian, Venezuelan, Ecuadorian, etc. "national consciousness."

Something like a proto-nationalism, however, existed in various countries of Eastern Europe, but paradoxically it took the direction of conservatism rather than national rebellion. The Slavs were oppressed everywhere, except in Russia and in a few wild Balkan strongholds, but in their immediate perspective the oppressors were, as we have seen, not the absolute monarchs, but the German or Magyar landlords and urban exploiters. Nor did the nationalism of these allow any place for Slav national existence: even so radical a programme as that of the German United States proposed by the republicans and democrats of Baden (in South-west Germany) envisaged the inclusion of an Illyrian (i.e., Croat and Slovene) republic with its capital in Italian Trieste, a Moravian one with its capital in Olomouc, and a Bohemian one led by Prague. Hence the immediate hope of the Slav nationalists lay in the emperors of Austria and Russia. Various versions of Slav solidarity expressed the Russian orientation, and attracted Slav rebels—even the anti-Russian Poles—especially in times of defeat and hopelessness as after the failure of the risings in 1846. "Illyrianism" in Croatia and a moderate Czech nationalism expressed the Austrian trend, and both received deliberate support from the Habsburg rulers, two of whose leading ministers—Kolowrat and the chief of the police system, Sedlnitzky—were themselves Czechs. Croatian cultural aspirations were protected in the 1830s, and by 1840 Kolowrat actually proposed what was later to prove so useful in the 1848 revolution, the appointment of a Croat military *ban* as chief of Croatia, and with control over the military frontier with Hungary, as a counterweight to the obstreperous Magyars. To be a revolutionary in 1848 therefore came to be virtually identical with opposition to Slav national aspirations; and the tacit conflict between the "progressive" and the "reactionary" nations did much to doom the revolutions of 1848 to failure.

Nothing like nationalism is discoverable elsewhere, for the social conditions for it did not exist. In fact, if anything, the forces which were later to produce nationalism were at this stage opposed to the alliance of tradition, religion, and mass poverty which produced the most powerful resistance to the encroachment of Western conquerors and exploiters. The elements of a local bourgeoisie which grew up in Asian countries did so in the shelter of the foreign exploiters whose agents, intermediaries and dependants they largely were. The Parsee community of Bombay is an example. Even if the educated and "enlightened" Asian was not a *compradore* or a lesser official of some foreign ruler or firm (a situation not dissimilar to that of the Greek diaspora in Turkey), his first political task was to Westernize—i.e., to introduce the ideas of the French Revolution and of scientific and technical modernization among his people, against the united resistance of traditional rulers and traditional ruled (a situation not dissimilar to that of the gentlemen-Jacobins of Southern Italy). He was therefore doubly cut off from his people. Nationalist mythology has often obscured this divorce, partly by suppressing the link between

colonialism and the early native middle classes, partly lending to earlier anti-foreign resistance the colours of a later nationalist movement. But in Asia, in the Islamic countries, and even more in Africa, the junction between the *évolués* and nationalism, and between both and the masses, was not made until the twentieth century.

Nationalism in the East was thus the eventual product of Western influence and Western conquest. This link is perhaps most evident in the one plainly Oriental country in which the foundations of what was to become the first modern colonial nationalist movement[4] were laid: in Egypt. Napoleon's conquest introduced Western ideas, methods, and techniques, whose value an able and ambitious local soldier, Mohammed Ali (Mehemet Ali), soon recognized. Having seized power and virtual independence from Turkey in the confused period which followed the withdrawal of the French, and with French support, Mohammed Ali set out to establish an efficient and Westernizing despotism with foreign (mainly French) technical aid. European left-wingers in the 1820s and 30s hailed this enlightened autocrat, and put their services at his disposal, when reaction in their own countries looked too dispiriting. The extraordinary sect of the Saint-Simonians, equally suspended between the advocacy of socialism and of industrial development by investment bankers and engineers, temporarily gave him their collective aid and prepared his plans of economic development. * * * They thus also laid the foundation for the Suez Canal (built by the Saint-Simonian de Lesseps) and the fatal dependence of Egyptian rulers on vast loans negotiated by competing groups of European swindlers, which turned Egypt into a centre of imperialist rivalry and anti-imperialist rebellion later on. But Mohammed Ali was no more a nationalist than any other Oriental despot. His Westernization, not his or his people's aspirations, laid the foundations for later nationalism. If Egypt acquired the first nationalist movement in the Islamic world and Morocco one of the last, it was because Mohammed Ali (for perfectly comprehensible geopolitical reasons) was in the main paths of Westernization and the isolated self-sealed Sherifian Empire of the Moslem far west was not, and made no attempts to be. Nationalism, like so many other characteristics of the modern world, is the child of the dual revolution.

NOTES

1. In the early eighteenth century only about 60 per cent of all titles published in Germany were in the German language; since then the proportion had risen fairly steadily.
2. The Sikh movement has remained largely *suigeneris* to this day. The tradition of combative Hindu resistance in Maharashtra made that area an early centre of the Indian nationalism, and provided some of its earliest—and highly traditionalist—leaders, notably B. G. Tilak; but this was at best a regional, and far from dominant strain in the movement. Something like Mahratta nationalism may exist today, but its social basis is the resistance of large Mahratta working class and underprivileged lower-middle class to the economically and until recently linguistically dominant Gujeratis.
3. It is significant that the present Yugoslav regime has broken up what used to be classed as the Serb nation into the much more realistic sub-national republics and units of Serbia, Bosnia, Montenegro, Macedonia, and Kossovo-Metohidja. By the linguistic standards of nineteenth-century nationalism most of these belonged to a single "Serb" people, except the Macedonians, who are closer to the Bulgarians, and the Albanian minority in Kosmet. But in fact they have never developed a single Serb nationalism.
4. Other than the Irish.

JAMES D. FEARON AND DAVID D. LAITIN

ETHNICITY, INSURGENCY, AND CIVIL WAR

Between 1945 and 1999, about 3.33 million battle deaths occurred in the 25 interstate wars that killed at least 1,000 and had at least 100 dead on each side. These wars involved just 25 states that suffered casualties of at least 1,000 and had a median duration of not quite 3 months. In contrast, in the same period there were roughly 127 civil wars that killed at least 1,000, 25 of which were ongoing in 1999. A conservative estimate of the total dead as a direct result of these conflicts is 16.2 million, five times the interstate toll. These civil wars occurred in 73 states—more than a third of the United Nations system—and had a median duration of roughly six years.[1] The civil conflicts in this period surely produced refugee flows far greater than their death toll and far greater than the refugee flows associated with interstate wars since 1945. Cases such as Afghanistan, Somalia, and Lebanon testify to the economic devastation that civil wars can produce. By these crude measures, civil war has been a far greater scourge than interstate war in this period, though it has been studied far less.

What explains the recent prevalence of violent civil conflict around the world? Is it due to the end of the Cold War and associated changes in the international system, or is it the result of longer-term trends? Why have some countries

From *American Political Science Review*, 97, no. 1 (2003), pp. 75–90.

had civil wars while others have not? and Why did the wars break out when they did? We address these questions using data for the period 1945 to 1999 on the 161 countries that had a population of at least half a million in 1990.

The data cast doubt on three influential conventional wisdoms concerning political conflict before and after the Cold War. First, contrary to common opinion, the prevalence of civil war in the 1990s was *not* due to the end of the Cold War and associated changes in the international system. The current level of about one in six countries had already been reached prior to the breakup of the Soviet Union and resulted from a steady, gradual accumulation of civil conflicts that began immediately after World War II.

Second, is appears *not* to be true that a greater degree of ethnic or religious diversity— or indeed any particular cultural demography— by itself makes a country more prone to civil war. This finding runs contrary to a common view among journalists, policy makers, and academics, which holds "plural" societies to be especially conflict-prone due to ethnic or religious tensions and antagonisms.

Third, we find little evidence that one can predict where a civil war will break out by looking for where ethnic or other broad political grievances are strongest. Were this so, one would expect political democracies and states that observe civil liberties to be less civil war-prone than dictatorships. One would further anticipate that state discrimination against minority religions or languages would imply higher risks of civil war. We show that when comparing states at similar levels of per capita income, these expectations are not borne out.

The main factors determining both the secular trend and the cross-sectional variation in civil violence in this period are not ethnic or religious differences or broadly held grievances but, rather, conditions that favor *insurgency*. Insurgency is a technology of military conflict characterized by small, lightly armed bands practicing guerrilla warfare from rural base areas. As a form of warfare insurgency can be harnessed to diverse political agendas, motivations, and grievances. The concept is most closely associated with communist insurgency, but the methods have equally served Islamic fundamentalists, ethnic nationalists, or "rebels" who focus mainly on traffic in coca or diamonds.

We hypothesize that financially, organizationally, and politically weak central governments render insurgency more feasible and attractive due to weak local policing or inept and corrupt counterinsurgency practices. These often include a propensity for brutal and indiscriminate retaliation that helps drive noncombatant locals into rebel forces. Police and counterinsurgent weakness, we argue, is proxied by a low per capita income. Shocks to counterinsurgent capabilities can arise from political instability at the center or the sudden loss of a foreign patron. On the rebel side, insurgency is favored by rough terrain, rebels with local knowledge of the population superior to the government's, and a large population. All three aid rebels in hiding from superior government forces. Foreign base camps, financial support, and training also favor insurgency.

Our data show that measures of cultural diversity and grievances fail to postdict civil war onset, while measures of conditions that favor insurgency do fairly well. Surely ethnic antagonisms, nationalist sentiments, and grievances often motivate rebels and their supporters. But such broad factors are too common to distinguish the cases where civil war breaks out. Also, because insurgency can be successfully practiced by small numbers of rebels under the right conditions, civil war may require only a small number with intense grievances to get going.

Using data on about 45 civil wars since 1960, Collier and Hoeffler (1999, 2001) find similarly that measures of "objective grievance" fare worse as predictors than economic variables, which they initially interpreted as measures of rebel "greed" (i.e., economic motivation).[2] More recently, they argue that rebellion is better explained by "opportunity" than by grievance (cf. Eisinger 1973 and Tilly 1978) and that the main determinant of opportunity is the availability of finance and recruits for rebels. They proxy these with measures of primary commodity exports and rates of secondary-school enrollment for males. We agree that financing is one determinant of the viability of insurgency. We argue, however, that economic variables such as per capita income matter primarily because they proxy for state administrative, military, and police capabilities. We find no impact for primary commodity exports, and none for secondary schooling rates distinct from income. Our theoretical interpretation is more Hobbesian than economic. Where states are relatively weak and capricious, both fears and opportunities encourage the rise of would-be rulers who supply a rough local justice while arrogating the power to "tax" for themselves and, often, for a larger cause.

Civil War Since 1945

*   *   *

Trends over Time

Figure 1 shows the number of countries with ongoing civil wars by year from 1945 to 1999. Since the number of independent states grew sharply in this period, it also shows the proportion of countries with at least one ongoing war in each year.

The graph indicates that, contrary to popular belief, the prevalence of civil wars in the 1990s is *not* due to effects of the end of the Cold War. The 1999 level of 25 ongoing wars had already been reached by the mid 1980s. Conflicts associated with the Soviet collapse were partly responsible for the sharp increase in the early 1990s, but a marked *decline* has followed.[3]

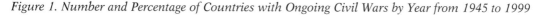

Figure 1. Number and Percentage of Countries with Ongoing Civil Wars by Year from 1945 to 1999

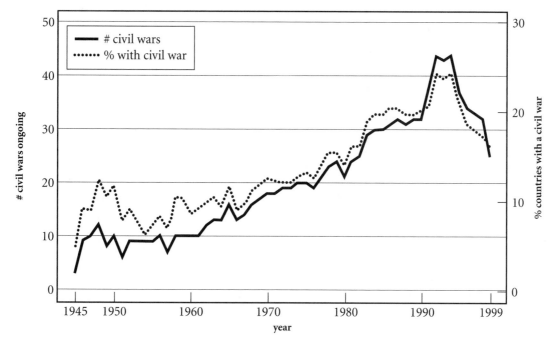

One might conjecture that more and more civil wars are breaking out over time, thus producing the secular increase. This is incorrect. The rate of outbreak is 2.31 per year since 1945, highly variable but showing no significant trend up or down. The secular increase stems from the fact that civil wars have ended at a rate of only about 1.85 per year. The result has been a steady, almost-linear accumulation of unresolved conflicts since 1945.

Put differently, states in the international system have been subject to a more or less constant risk of violent civil conflict over the period, but the conflicts they suffer have been difficult to end. The average duration of the civil wars in progress has increased steadily from two years in 1947 to about 15 years in 1999. From a policy perspective this suggests caution about seeing as a temporary "blip" the sorts of military and political problems Western foreign policy makers have faced recently in Kosovo, Macedonia, Bosnia, Somalia, Haiti, East Timor, Colombia, and elsewhere.

Ethnicity, Discrimination, and Grievances

During the Cold War, political scientists and sociologists often sought to trace rebellion to economic inequality (Muller 1985; Paige 1975; Russett 1964), to rapid economic growth said to destabilize traditional rural social systems (Huntington 1968; Scott 1976), or to frustrations arising from the failure to gain expected benefits of economic modernization (Gurr 1971). A few scholars argued that the real source of rebellion was often ethnic nationalism (Connor 1994), and a rich literature on the sources of nationalist mobilization developed in comparative politics (e.g., Anderson 1983, Deutsch 1953, and Gellner 1983). With the collapse of the Soviet Union and Yugoslavia, such culturalist perspectives became a dominant frame for interpreting inter- and intranational conflict (e.g., Huntington 1996).

*   *   *

Are More Diverse Countries Prone to Civil War?

Figure 2 shows how probabilities of civil war onset vary at different percentiles for country income (on the x axis, measured in lagged 1985 dollars) and ethnic homogeneity (on the y axis, measured by the population share of the largest ethnic group). The lines in the plot show the probability of war onset in the next five years for a country at the given level of income and ethnic homogeneity. For example, countries at the twentieth percentile in terms of the size of their largest ethnic group—thus quite ethnically *diverse*—but at the eightieth percentile on income have had about a 5% chance of civil war outbreak in the next five years. In contrast, countries at the eightieth percentile on ethnic homogeneity and at the twentieth percentile on income had a 15% chance of war in the next five years.[4]

Note that *for any level of ethnic diversity,* as one moves up the income scale (to the right in Figure 2), the odds of civil war decrease, by substantial factors in all cases and dramatically among the most homogeneous countries. The richest fifth is practically immune regardless of ethnic composition. In contrast, for given levels of country income, no consistent effect is associated with variation in ethnic homogeneity (i.e., moving up or down the figure). Among the poorest countries where we observe the highest rates of civil war, the data indicate a tendency for *more homogeneous* countries to be more civil war-prone. Among the richest countries there may be a weak tendency for the most homogeneous countries to have fewer civil wars, but the size of the effect, if any, is small.

The empirical pattern is thus inconsistent with *** the common expectation that ethnic diversity is a major and direct cause of civil violence. Nor is there strong evidence in favor of [the hypothesis that] ethnic strife [is] activated as modernization advances. Ethnic diversity

Figure 2. Probability of Civil War Onset per Five-Year Period

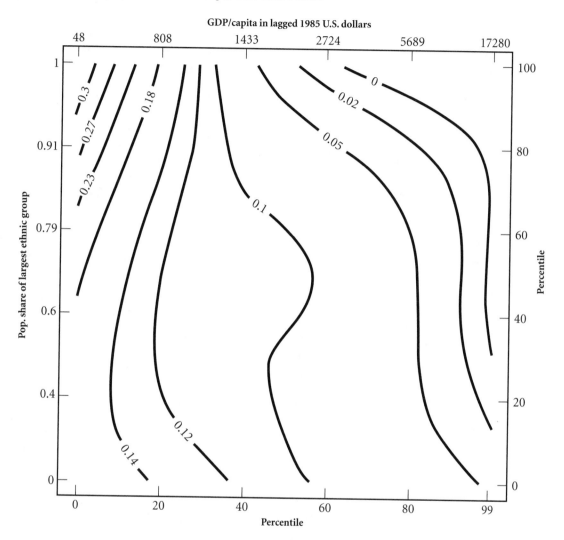

could still cause civil war *indirectly,* if it causes a low per capita income (Easterly and Levine 1997) or a weak state. But then the mechanisms that actually produce the violence would more likely be those of the insurgency perspective than the culturalist arguments.

*   *   *

Conclusion

The prevalence of internal war in the 1990s is mainly the result of an accumulation of protracted conflicts since the 1950s rather than a sudden change associated with a new, post–Cold War international system. Decolonization from the 1940s through the 1970s gave birth to a large number of financially, bureaucratically, and militarily weak states. These states have been at risk for civil violence for the whole period, almost entirely in the form of insurgency, or rural guerrilla warfare. Insurgency is a mode of military practice that can be harnessed to various political agendas, be it communism in Southeast Asia and Latin America, Islamic fundamentalism in Afghanistan, Algeria, or Kashmir, right-wing "reaction" in Nicaragua, or ethnic nationalism in a great many states. The conditions that favor insurgency—in particular, state weakness marked by poverty, a large population, and instability—are better predictors of which countries are at risk for civil war than are indicators of ethnic and religious diversity or measures of grievances such as economic inequality, lack of democracy or civil liberties, or state discrimination against minority religions or languages.

How could democracy and cultural or religious homogeneity fail to associate with civil peace across countries? Viewing "ethnic wars" as a species of insurgency may help explain this paradoxical result. If, under the right environmental conditions, just 500 to 2,000 active guerrillas can make for a long-running, destructive internal war, then the average level of grievance in a group may not matter that much. What matters is whether active rebels can hide from government forces and whether economic opportunities are so poor that the life of a rebel is attractive to 500 or 2,000 young men. Grievance may favor rebellion by leading nonactive rebels to help in hiding the active rebels. But all the guerrillas really need is superior local knowledge, which enables them to threaten reprisal for denunciation.

If our analysis is correct, then policy makers should not assume that civil wars and the "failed states" they sometimes produce are temporary phenomena of the immediate post–Cold War world. Nor should policy makers or academics infer that ethnic diversity is the root cause of civil conflict when they observe insurgents in a poor country who mobilize fighters along ethnic lines. Instead, the civil wars of the period have structural roots, in the combination of a simple,

robust military technology and decolonization, which created an international system numerically dominated by fragile states with limited administrative control of their peripheries.

Regarding policy implications, the spread of democracy and tolerance for ethnic and religious minorities should be major foreign policy goals because they are desirable for their own sake, but not with the expectation that they are "magic bullets" for the prevention or resolution of civil war. Sometimes recommended as a general international policy for resolving ethnic civil wars (e.g., Kaufmann 1996), ethnic partitions should be viewed as having large international implications and high costs. International support for partition would increase the expected benefits for rebels, who, we have argued, may be able to get a nasty civil war going on the basis of small numbers when the conditions for insurgency are right.

Policies to redress grievances, or, in the limit, partition, *could* be important to resolve ongoing conflicts. We cannot say on the basis of this research, which focused on civil war onset rather than termination. We find little evidence that civil war is predicted by large cultural divisions or broadly held grievances. But it seems quite clear that intense grievances *are produced by* civil war—indeed, this is often a central objective of rebel strategy. These could well pose obstacles to settlement.

Regarding prevention, our analysis suggests that while economic growth may correlate with fewer civil wars, the causal mechanism is more likely a well-financed and administratively competent government. In specific terms, international and nongovernmental organizations should develop programs that improve legal accountability within developing world militaries and police, and make aid to governments fighting civil wars conditional on the state observing counterinsurgency practices that do not help rebels recruit militias. Governments that follow horrible, war-perpetuating counterinsurgency practices or are so corrupt as to be helpless should be left on their own or, when there are major implications for regional stability or international terrorism, be viewed as candidates for "neotrusteeship" under the United Nations or regional military and political organizations such as NATO and the European Union. The latter system, which we already see operating, in effect, in Bosnia, Kosovo, and East Timor, should be rationalized so as to improve internal coordination among the many players involved in such operations.

NOTES

1. The interstate war data derive from Singer and Small 1994, updated to include the Kargil and Eritrean wars. The bases for the civil war estimates are discussed below.

2. There are 79 wars in their sample, but they lose about 34 due to missing values on explanatory variables, which are mainly economic. Standard economic data tend to be missing for countries that are poor and civil war-torn. This highly nonrandom listwise deletion may account for some of the differences between our results.

3. Gurr (2000) notes the late-1990s decline in ethic war and argues that the trend reflects improved management strategies by states and international organizations. The basic pattern in Figure 1 is not an artifact of the way we have coded "civil war"; it is observed in a broad range of other data sets on violent domestic conflict for this period (e.g., Gleditsch et al. 2002).

4. The figure was produced using R's locfit package, with a smoothing parameter of 0.9, and transforming annual probabilites of outbreak to five-year equivalents. The figure looks highly similar if we use other measures of ethnic diversity, such as fractionalization.

REFERENCES

Anderson, Benedict. 1983. *Imagined Communities.* London: Verso.

Collier, Paul, and Anke Hoeffler. 1999. "Justice Seeking and Loot-seeking in Civil War," World Bank. Typescript. http://econ .worldbank.org/programs/conflict/library (November 18, 2002).

Collier, Paul, and Anke Hoeffler. 2001. "Greed and Grievance in Civil War." World Bank. Typescript. http://econ.worldbank.org/programs/library (November 18, 2002).

Connor, Walker. 1994. *Ethnonationalism.* Princeton, NJ: Princeton University Press.

Deutsch, Karl W. 1953. *Nationalism and Social Communication.* Cambridge, MA: MIT Press.

Easterly, William, and Ross Levine. 1997. "Africa's Growth Tragedy: Policies and Ethnic Divisions." *Quarterly Journal of Economics* 112 (4): 1203–50.

Eisinger, Peter. 1973. "The Conditions of Protest Behavior in American Cities." *American Political Science Review* 67: 11–28.

Gellner, Ernest. 1983. *Nations and Nationalism.* Ithaca, NY: Cornell University Press.

Gleditsch, Nils, Havard Strand, Mikael Eriksson, Margareta Sollenberg, and Peter Wallensteen. 2002. "Armed Conflict 1946–2001: A New Dataset." *Journal of Peace Research* 39 (5): 615–37.

Gurr, Ted R. 1971. *Why Men Rebel.* Princeton, NJ: Princeton University Press.

Gurr, Ted R. 2000. *Peoples versus States.* Washington, DC: United States Institute of Peace Press.

Huntington, Samuel P. 1968. *Political Order in Changing Societies.* New Haven, CT: Yale University Press.

Huntington, Samuel P. 1996. *The Clash of Civilizations and the Remaking of World Order.* New York: Simon & Schuster.

Kaufmann, Chaim. 1996. "Possible and Impossible Solutions to Ethnic Civil Wars." *International Security* 20 (4): 136–75.

Muller, Edward N. 1985. "Income Inequality, Regime Repressiveness, and Political Violence." *American Sociological Review* 50: 47–61.

Paige, Jeffery M. 1975. *Agrarian Revolution.* New York: Free Press.

Russett, Bruce M. 1964. "Inequality and Instability." *World Politics* 16: 442–54.

Scott, James C. 1976. *The Moral Economy of the Peasant.* New Haven: Yale University Press.

Singer, J. David and Melvin H. Small. 1994. "Correlates of War Project: International and Civil War Data, 1816–1992." ICPSR 9905, April.

Tilly, Charles. 1978. *From Mobilization to Revolution.* Reading, MA: Addison-Wesley.

SAMUEL P. HUNTINGTON

THE CLASH OF CIVILIZATIONS?

The Next Pattern of Conflict

World politics is entering a new phase, and intellectuals have not hesitated to proliferate visions of what it will be—the end of history, the return of traditional rivalries between nation states, and the decline of the nation state from the conflicting pulls of tribalism and globalism, among others. Each of these visions catches aspects of the emerging reality. Yet they all miss a crucial, indeed a central, aspect of what global politics is likely to be in the coming years.

It is my hypothesis that the fundamental source of conflict in this new world will not be primarily ideological or primarily economic. The great divisions among humankind and the dominating source of conflict will be cultural. Nation states will remain the most powerful actors in world affairs, but the principal conflicts of global politics will occur between nations and groups of different civilizations. The clash of civilizations will dominate global politics. The fault lines between civilizations will be the battle lines of the future.

Conflict between civilizations will be the latest phase in the evolution of conflict in the modern world. For a century and a half after the emergence of the modern international system with the Peace of Westphalia, the conflicts of the

Western world were largely among princes—emperors, absolute monarchs and constitutional monarchs attempting to expand their bureaucracies, their armies, their mercantilist economic strength and, most important, the territory they ruled. In the process they created nation states, and beginning with the French Revolution the principal lines of conflict were between nations rather than princes. In 1793, as R. R. Palmer put it, "The wars of kings were over; the wars of peoples had begun." This nineteenth-century pattern lasted until the end of World War I. Then, as a result of the Russian Revolution and the reaction against it, the conflict of nations yielded to the conflict of ideologies, first among communism, fascism-Nazism and liberal democracy, and then between communism and liberal democracy. During the Cold War, this latter conflict became embodied in the struggle between the two superpowers, neither of which was a nation state in the classical European sense and each of which defined its identity in terms of its ideology.

These conflicts between princes, nation states and ideologies were primarily conflicts within Western civilization, "Western civil wars," as William Lind has labeled them. This was as true of the Cold War as it was of the world wars and the earlier wars of the seventeenth, eighteenth and nineteenth centuries. With the end of the Cold War, international politics moves out of its Western phase, and its center-piece becomes

From *Foreign Affairs,* 72, no. 3 (Summer 1993), pp. 22–49.

the interaction between the West and non-Western civilizations and among non-Western civilizations. In the politics of civilizations, the peoples and governments of non-Western civilizations no longer remain the objects of history as targets of Western colonialism but join the West as movers and shapers of history.

The Nature of Civilizations

During the Cold War the world was divided into the First, Second and Third Worlds. Those divisions are no longer relevant. It is far more meaningful now to group countries not in terms of their political or economic systems or in terms of their level of economic development but rather in terms of their culture and civilization.

What do we mean when we talk of a civilization? A civilization is a cultural entity. Villages, regions, ethnic groups, nationalities, religious groups, all have distinct cultures at different levels of cultural heterogeneity. The culture of a village in southern Italy may be different from that of a village in northern Italy, but both will share in a common Italian culture that distinguishes them from German villages. European communities, in turn, will share cultural features that distinguish them from Arab or Chinese communities. Arabs, Chinese and Westerners, however, are not part of any broader cultural entity. They constitute civilizations. A civilization is thus the highest cultural grouping of people and the broadest level of cultural identity people have short of that which distinguishes humans from other species. It is defined both by common objective elements, such as language, history, religion, customs, institutions, and by the subjective self-identification of people. People have levels of identity: a resident of Rome may define himself with varying degrees of intensity as a Roman, an Italian, a Catholic, a Christian, a European, a Westerner. The civilization to which he belongs is the broadest level of identification with which he intensely identifies. People can and do redefine their identities and, as a result, the composition and boundaries of civilizations change.

Civilizations may involve a large number of people, as with China ("a civilization pretending to be a state," as Lucian Pye put it), or a very small number of people, such as the Anglophone Caribbean. A civilization may include several nation states, as is the case with Western, Latin American and Arab civilizations, or only one, as is the case with Japanese civilization. Civilizations obviously blend and overlap, and may include subcivilizations. Western civilization has two major variants, European and North American, and Islam has its Arab, Turkic and Malay subdivisions. Civilizations are nonetheless meaningful entities, and while the lines between them are seldom sharp, they are real. Civilizations are dynamic; they rise and fall; they divide and merge. And, as any student of history knows, civilizations disappear and are buried in the sands of time.

Westerners tend to think of nation states as the principal actors in global affairs. They have been that, however, for only a few centuries. The broader reaches of human history have been the history of civilizations. In *A Study of History*, Arnold Toynbee identified 21 major civilizations; only six of them exist in the contemporary world.

Why Civilizations Will Clash

Civilization identity will be increasingly important in the future, and the world will be shaped in large measure by the interactions among seven or eight major civilizations. These include Western, Confucian, Japanese, Islamic, Hindu, Slavic-Orthodox, Latin American and possibly African civilization. The most important conflicts of the future will occur along the cultural fault lines separating these civilizations from one another.

Why will this be the case?

First, differences among civilizations are not only real; they are basic. Civilizations are differentiated from each other by history, language, culture, tradition and, most important, religion. The people of different civilizations have different views on the relations between God and man, the individual and the group, the citizen and the state, parents and children, husband and wife, as well as differing views of the relative importance of rights and responsibilities, liberty and authority, equality and hierarchy. These differences are the product of centuries. They will not soon disappear. They are far more fundamental than differences among political ideologies and political regimes. Differences do not necessarily mean conflict, and conflict does not necessarily, mean violence. Over the centuries, however, differences among civilizations have generated the most prolonged and the most violent conflicts.

Second, the world is becoming a smaller place. The interactions between peoples of different civilizations are increasing; these increasing interactions intensify civilization consciousness and awareness of differences between civilizations and commonalities within civilizations. North African immigration to France generates hostility among Frenchmen and at the same time increased receptivity to immigration by "good" European Catholic Poles. Americans react far more negatively to Japanese investment than to larger investments from Canada and European countries. Similarly, as Donald Horowitz has pointed out, "An Ibo may be . . . an Owerri Ibo or an Onitsha Ibo in what was the Eastern region of Nigeria. In Lagos, he is simply an Ibo. In London, he is a Nigerian. In New York, he is an African." The interactions among peoples of different civilizations enhance the civilization-consciousness of people that, in turn, invigorates differences and animosities stretching or thought to stretch back deep into history.

Third, the processes of economic modernization and social change throughout the world are separating people from longstanding local identities. They also weaken the nation state as a source of identity. In much of the world religion has moved in to fill this gap, often in the form of movements that are labeled "fundamentalist."

Such movements are found in Western Christianity, Judaism, Buddhism and Hinduism, as well as in Islam. In most countries and most religions the people active in fundamentalist movements are young, college-educated, middle-class technicians, professionals and business persons. The "unsecularization of the world," George Weigel has remarked, "is one of the dominant social facts of life in the late twentieth century." The revival of religion, "la revanche de Dieu," as Gilles Kepel labeled it, provides a basis for identity and commitment that transcends national boundaries and unites civilizations.

Fourth, the growth of civilization-consciousness is enhanced by the dual role of the West. On the one hand, the West is at a peak of power. At the same time, however, and perhaps as a result, a return to the roots phenomenon is occurring among non-Western civilizations. Increasingly one hears references to trends toward a turning inward and "Asianization" in Japan, the end of the Nehru legacy and the "Hinduization" of India, the failure of Western ideas of socialism and nationalism and hence "re-Islamization" of the Middle East, and now a debate over Westernization versus Russianization in Boris Yeltsin's country. A West at the peak of its power confronts non-Wests that increasingly have the desire, the will and the resources to shape the world in non-Western ways.

In the past, the elites of non-Western societies were usually the people who were most involved with the West, had been educated at Oxford, the Sorbonne or Sandhurst, and had absorbed Western attitudes and values. At the same time, the populace in non-Western countries often remained deeply imbued with the indigenous culture. Now, however, these relationships are being reversed. A de-Westernization and indigenization of elites is occurring in many non-Western countries at the same time that Western, usually American, cultures, styles and habits become more popular among the mass of the people.

Fifth, cultural characteristics and differences are less mutable and hence less easily compromised and resolved than political and economic ones. In the former Soviet Union, communists can become democrats, the rich can become poor and the poor rich, but Russians cannot become Estonians and Azeris cannot become Armenians. In class and ideological conflicts, the key question was "Which side are you on?" and people could and did choose sides and change sides. In conflicts between civilizations, the question is "What are you?" That is a given that cannot be changed. And as we know, from Bosnia to the Caucasus to the Sudan, the wrong answer to that question can mean a bullet in the head. Even more than ethnicity, religion discriminates sharply and exclusively among people. A person can be half-French and half-Arab and simultaneously even a citizen of two countries. It is more difficult to be half-Catholic and half-Muslim.

Finally, economic regionalism is increasing. The proportions of total trade that were intraregional rose between 1980 and 1989 from 51 percent to 59 percent in Europe, 33 percent to 37 percent in East Asia, and 32 percent to 36 percent in North America. The importance of regional economic blocs is likely to continue to increase in the future. On the one hand, successful economic regionalism will reinforce civilization-consciousness. On the other hand, economic regionalism may succeed only when it is rooted in a common civilization. The European Community rests on the shared foundation of European culture and Western Christianity. The success of the North American Free Trade Area depends on the convergence now underway of Mexican, Canadian and American cultures. Japan, in contrast, faces difficulties in creating a comparable economic entity in East Asia because Japan is a society and civilization unique to itself. However strong the trade and investment links Japan may develop with other East Asian countries, its cultural differences with those countries inhibit and perhaps preclude its promoting regional economic integration like that in Europe and North America.

Common culture, in contrast, is clearly facilitating the rapid expansion of the economic relations between the People's Republic of China and Hong Kong, Taiwan, Singapore and the overseas Chinese communities in other Asian countries. With the Cold War over, cultural commonalities increasingly overcome ideological differences, and mainland China and Taiwan move closer together. If cultural commonality is a prerequisite for economic integration, the principal East Asian economic bloc of the future is likely to be centered on China. This bloc is, in fact, already coming into existence. As Murray Weidenbaum has observed.

> Despite the current Japanese dominance of the region, the Chinese-based economy of Asia is rapidly emerging as a new epicenter for industry, commerce and finance. This strategic area contains substantial amounts of technology and manufacturing capability (Taiwan), outstanding entrepreneurial, marketing and services acumen (Hong Kong), a fine communications network (Singapore), a tremendous pool of financial capital (all three), and very large endowments of land, resources and labor (mainland China) . . . From Guangzhou to Singapore, from Kuala Lumpur to Manila, this influential network—often based on extensions of the traditional clans—has been described as the backbone of the East Asian economy.[1]

Culture and religion also form the basis of the Economic Cooperation Organization, which brings together ten non-Arab Muslim countries: Iran, Pakistan, Turkey, Azerbaijan, Kazakhstan, Kyrgyzstan, Turkmenistan, Tadjikistan, Uzbekistan and Afghanistan. One impetus to the revival and expansion of this organization, founded originally in the 1960 by Turkey, Pakistan and Iran, is the realization by the leaders of several of these countries that they had no chance of admission to the European Community. Similarly, Caricom, the Central American Common Market and Mercosur rest on common cultural foundations. Efforts to build a broader Caribbean-Central American economic entity bridging the Anglo-Latin divide, however, have to date failed.

As people define their identity in ethnic and religious terms, they are likely to see an "us" versus "them" relation existing between themselves and people of different ethnicity or religion. The end of ideologically defined states in Eastern Europe and the former Soviet Union permits traditional ethnic identities and animosities to come to the fore. Differences in culture and religion create differences over policy issues, ranging from human rights to immigration to trade and commerce to the environment. Geographical propinquity gives rise to conflicting territorial claims from Bosnia to Mindanao. Most important, the efforts of the West to promote its values of democracy and liberalism as universal values, to maintain its military predominance and to advance its economic interests engender countering responses from other civilizations. Decreasingly able to mobilize support and form coalitions on the basis of ideology, governments and groups will increasingly attempt to mobilize support by appealing to common religion and civilization identity.

The clash of civilizations thus occurs at two levels. At the micro-level, adjacent groups along the fault lines between civilizations struggle, often violently, over the control of territory and each other. At the macro-level, states from different civilizations compete for relative military and economic power, struggle over the control of international institutions and third parties, and competitively promote their particular political and religious values.

The Fault Lines between Civilizations

The fault lines between civilizations are replacing the political and ideological boundaries of the Cold War as the flash points for crisis and bloodshed. The Cold War began when the Iron Curtain divided Europe politically and ideologically. The Cold War ended with the end of the Iron Curtain. As the ideological division of Europe has disappeared, the cultural division of Europe between Western Christianity, on the one hand, and Orthodox Christianity and Islam,

on the other, has reemerged. The most significant dividing line in Europe, as William Wallace has suggested, may well be the eastern boundary of Western Christianity in the year 1500. This line runs along what are now the boundaries between Finland and Russia and between the Baltic states and Russia, cuts through Belarus and Ukraine separating the more Catholic western Ukraine from Orthodox eastern Ukraine, swings westward separating Transylvania from the rest of Romania, and then goes through Yugoslavia almost exactly along the line now separating Croatia and Slovenia from the rest of Yugoslavia. In the Balkans this line, of course, coincides with the historic boundary between the Hapsburg and Ottoman empires. The peoples to the north and west of this line are Protestant or Catholic; they shared the common experiences of European history—feudalism, the Renaissance, the Reformation, the Englightenment, the French Revolution, the Industrial Revolution; they are generally economically better off than the peoples to the east; and they may now look forward to increasing involvement in a common European economy and to the consolidation of democratic political systems. The peoples to the east and south of this line are Orthodox or Muslim; they historically belonged to the Ottoman or Tsarist empires and were only lightly touched by the shaping events in the rest of Europe; they are generally less advanced economically; they seem much less likely to develop stable democratic political systems. The Velvet Curtain of culture has replaced the Iron Curtain of ideology as the most significant dividing line in Europe. As the events in Yugoslavia show, it is not only a line of difference; it is also at times a line of bloody conflict.

Conflict along the fault line between Western and Islamic civilizations has been going on for 1,300 years. After the founding of Islam, the Arab and Moorish surge west and north only ended at Tours in 732. From the eleventh to the thirteenth century the Crusaders attempted with temporary success to bring Christianity and Christian rule to the Holy Land. From the fourteenth to the seventeenth century, the Ottoman Turks reversed the balance, extended their sway over the Middle East and the Balkans, captured Constantinople, and twice laid siege to Vienna. In the nineteenth and early twentieth centuries as Ottoman power declined Britain, France, and Italy established Western control over most of North Africa and the Middle East.

After World War II, the West, in turn, began to retreat; the colonial empires disappeared; first Arab nationalism and then Islamic fundamentalism manifested themselves; the West became heavily dependent on the Persian Gulf countries for its energy; the oil-rich Muslim countries became money-rich and, when they wished to, weapons-rich. Several wars occurred between Arabs and Israel (created by the West). France fought a bloody and ruthless war in Algeria for most of the 1950s; British and French forces invaded Egypt in 1956; American forces went into Lebanon in 1958; subsequently American forces returned to Lebanon, attacked Libya, and engaged in various military encounters with Iran; Arab and Islamic terrorists, supported by at least three Middle Eastern governments, employed the weapon of the weak and bombed Western planes and installations and seized Western hostages. This warfare between Arabs and the West culminated in 1990, when the United States sent a massive army to the Persian Gulf to defend some Arab countries against aggression by another. In its aftermath NATO planning is increasingly directed to potential threats and instability along its "southern tier."

This centuries-old military interaction between the West and Islam is unlikely to decline. It could become more virulent. The Gulf War left some Arabs feeling proud that Saddam Hussein had attacked Israel and stood up to the West. It also left many feeling humiliated and resentful of the West's military presence in the Persian Gulf, the West's overwhelming military dominance, and their apparent inability to shape their own destiny. Many Arab countries, in addition to the oil exporters, are reaching levels of economic and social development where autocratic forms

of government become inappropriate and efforts to introduce democracy become stronger. Some openings in Arab political systems have already occurred. The principal beneficiaries of these openings have been Islamist movements. In the Arab world, in short, Western democracy strengthens anti-Western political forces. This may be a passing phenomenon, but it surely complicates relations between Islamic countries and the West.

Those relations are also complicated by demography. The spectacular population growth in Arab countries, particularly in North Africa, has led to increased migration to Western Europe. The movement within Western Europe toward minimizing internal boundaries has sharpened political sensitivities with respect to this development. In Italy, France and Germany, racism is increasingly open, and political reactions and violence against Arab and Turkish migrants have become more intense and more widespread since 1990.

On both sides the interaction between Islam and the West is seen as a clash of civilizations. The West's "next confrontation," observes M. J. Akbar, an Indian Muslim author, "is definitely going to come from the Muslim world. It is in the sweep of the Islamic nations from the Maghreb to Pakistan that the struggle for a new world order will begin." Bernard Lewis comes to a similar conclusion:

> We are facing a mood and a movement far transcending the level of issues and policies and the governments that pursue them. This is no less than a clash of civilizations—the perhaps irrational but surely historic reaction of an ancient rival against our Judeo-Christian heritage, our secular present, and the worldwide expansion of both.[2]

Historically, the other great antagonistic interaction of Arab Islamic civilization has been with the pagan, animist, and now increasingly Christian black peoples to the south. In the past, this antagonism was epitomized in the image of Arab slave dealers and black slaves. It has been reflected in the ongoing civil war in the Sudan between Arabs and blacks, the fighting in Chad between Libyan-supported insurgents and the government, the tensions between Orthodox Christians and Muslims in the Horn of Africa, and the political conflicts, recurring riots and communal violence between Muslims and Christians in Nigeria. The modernization of Africa and the spread of Christianity are likely to enhance the probability of violence along this fault line. Symptomatic of the intensification of this conflict was Pope John Paul II's speech in Khartoum in February 1993 attacking the actions of the Sudan's Islamist government against the Christian minority there.

On the northern border of Islam, conflict has increasingly erupted between Orthodox and Muslim peoples, including the carnage of Bosnia and Sarajevo, the simmering violence between Serbs and Albanians, the tenuous relations between Bulgarians and their Turkish minority, the violence between Ossetians and Ingush, the unremitting slaughter of each other by Armenians and Azeris, the tense relations between Russians and Muslims in Central Asia, and the deployment of Russian troops to protect Russian interests in the Caucasus and Central Asia. Religion reinforces the revitalization of ethnic identities and restimulates Russian fears about the security of their southern borders. This concern is well captured by Archie Roosevelt:

> Much of Russian history concerns the struggle between the Slavs and the Turkic peoples on their borders, which dates back to the foundation of the Russian state more than a thousand years ago. In the Slavs' millennium-long confrontation with their eastern neighbors lies the key to an understanding not only of Russian history, but Russian character. To understand Russian realities today one has to have a concept of the great Turkic ethnic group that has preoccupied Russians through the centuries.[3]

The conflict of civilizations is deeply rooted elsewhere in Asia. The historic clash between Muslim and Hindu in the subcontinent manifests itself now not only in the rivalry between Pakistan and India but also in intensifying religious strife within India between increasingly militant Hindu groups and India's substantial Muslim minority. The destruction of the Ayodhya mosque in December 1992 brought to the fore the issue of whether India will remain a secular democratic state or become a Hindu one. In East Asia, China has outstanding territorial disputes with most of its neighbors. It has pursued a ruthless policy toward the Buddhist people of Tibet, and it is pursuing an increasingly ruthless policy toward its Turkic-Muslim minority. With the Cold War over, the underlying differences between China and the United States have reasserted themselves in areas such as human rights, trade and weapons proliferation. These differences are unlikely to moderate. A "new cold war," Deng Xaioping reportedly asserted in 1991, is under way between China and America.

The same phrase has been applied to the increasingly difficult relations between Japan and the United States. Here cultural difference exacerbates economic conflict. People on each side allege racism on the other, but at least on the American side the antipathies are not racial but cultural. The basic values, attitudes, behavioral patterns of the two societies could hardly be more different. The economic issues between the United States and Japan are no less serious than those between the United States and Europe, but they do not have the same political salience and emotional intensity because the differences between American culture and European culture are so much less than those between American civilization and Japanese civilization.

The interactions between civilizations vary greatly in the extent to which they are likely to be characterized by violence. Economic competition clearly predominates between the American and European subcivilizations of the West and between both of them and Japan. On the Eurasian continent, however, the proliferation of ethnic conflict, epitomized at the extreme in "ethnic cleansing," has not been totally random. It has been most frequent and most violent between groups belonging to different civilizations. In Eurasia the great historic fault lines between civilizations are once more aflame. This is particularly true along the boundaries of the crescent-shaped Islamic bloc of nations from the bulge of Africa to central Asia. Violence also occurs between Muslims, on the one hand, and Orthodox Serbs in the Balkans, Jews in Israel, Hindus in India, Buddhists in Burma and Catholics in the Philippines. Islam has bloody borders.

Civilization Rallying: The Kin-Country Syndrome

Groups or states belonging to one civilization that become involved in war with people from a different civilization naturally try to rally support from other members of their own civilization. As the post–Cold War world evolves, civilization commonality, what H. D. S. Greenway has termed the "kin-country" syndrome, is replacing political ideology and traditional balance-of-power considerations as the principal basis for cooperation and coalitions.

* * *

Civilization rallying to date has been limited, but it has been growing, and it clearly has the potential to spread much further. As the conflicts in the Persian Gulf, the Caucasus and Bosnia continued, the positions of nations and the cleavages between them increasingly were along civilizational lines. Populist politicians, religious leaders and the media have found it a potent means of arousing mass support and of pressuring hesitant governments. In the coming years, the local conflicts most likely to escalate into major wars will be those, as in Bosnia and the Caucasus, along the fault lines between civilizations. The next world war, if there is one, will be a war between civilizations.

The West Versus the Rest

The West is now at an extraordinary peak of power in relation to other civilizations. Its super-

power opponent has disappeared from the map. Military conflict among Western states is unthinkable, and Western military power is unrivaled. Apart from Japan, the West faces no economic challenge. It dominates international political and security institutions and with Japan international economic institutions. Global political and security issues are effectively settled by a directorate of the United States, Britain and France, world economic issues by a directorate of the United States, Germany and Japan, all of which maintain extraordinarily close relations with each other to the exclusion of lesser and largely non-Western countries. Decisions made at the U.N. Security Council or in the International Monetary Fund that reflect the interests of the West are presented to the world as reflecting the desires of the world community. The very phrase "the world community" has become the euphemistic collective noun (replacing "the Free World") to give global legitimacy to actions reflecting the interest of the United States and other Western powers.[4] Through the IMF and other international economic institutions, the West promotes its economic interests and imposes on other nations the economic policies it thinks appropriate. In any poll of non-Western peoples, the IMF undoubtedly would win the support of finance ministers and a few others, but get an overwhelmingly unfavorable rating from just about everyone else, who would agree with Georgy Arbatov's characterization of IMF officials as "neo-Bolsheviks who love expropriating other people's money, imposing undemocratic and alien rules of economic and political conduct and stifling economic freedom."

Western domination of the U.N. Security Council and its decisions, tempered only by occasional abstention by China, produced U.N. legitimation of the West's use of force to drive Iraq out of Kuwait and its elimination of Iraq's sophisticated weapons and capacity to produce such weapons. It also produced the quite unprecedented action by the United States, Britain and France in getting the Security Council to demand that Libya hand over the Pan Am 103 bombing suspects and then to impose sanctions when Libya refused. After defeating the largest Arab army, the West did not hesitate to throw its weight around in the Arab world. The West in effect is using international institutions, military power and economic resources to run the world in ways that will maintain Western predominance, protect Western interests and promote Western political and economic values.

That at least is the way in which non-Westerners see the new world, and there is a significant element of truth in their view. Differences in power and struggles for military, economic and institutional power are thus one source of conflict between the West and other civilizations. Differences in culture, that is basic values and beliefs, are a second source of conflict. V. S. Naipaul has argued that Western civilization is the "universal civilization" that "fits all men." At a superficial level much of Western culture has indeed permeated the rest of the world. At a more basic level, however, Western concepts differ fundamentally from those prevalent in other civilizations. Western ideas of individualism, liberalism, constitutionalism, human rights, equality, liberty, the rule of law, democracy, free markets, the separation of church and state, often have little resonance in Islamic, Confucian, Japanese, Hindu, Buddhist or Orthodox cultures. Western efforts to propagate such ideas produce instead a reaction against "human rights imperialism" and a reaffirmation of indigenous values, as can be seen in the support for religious fundamentalism by the younger generation in non-Western cultures. The very notion that there could be a "universal civilization" is a Western idea, directly at odds with the particularism of most Asian societies and their emphasis on what distinguishes one people from another. Indeed, the author of a review of 100 comparative studies of values in different societies concluded that "the values that are most important in the West are least important worldwide."[5] In the political realm, of course, these differences are most manifest in the efforts of the United States and other Western powers to induce other peoples to adopt Western ideas

concerning democracy and human rights. Modern democratic government originated in the West. When it has developed in non-Western societies it has usually been the product of Western colonialism or imposition.

The central axis of world politics in the future is likely to be, in Kishore Mahbubani's phrase, the conflict between "the West and the Rest" and the responses of non-Western civilizations to Western power and values.[6] Those responses generally take one or a combination of three forms. At one extreme, non-Western states can, like Burma and North Korea, attempt to pursue a course of isolation, to insulate their societies from penetration or "corruption" by the West, and, in effect, to opt out of participation in the Western-dominated global community. The costs of this course, however, are high, and few states have pursued it exclusively. A second alternative, the equivalent of "band-wagoning" in international relations theory, is to attempt to join the West and accept its values and institutions. The third alternative is to attempt to "balance" the West by developing economic and military power and cooperating with other non-Western societies against the West, while preserving indigenous values and institutions; in short, to modernize but not to Westernize.

The Torn Countries

In the future, as people differentiate themselves by civilization, countries with large numbers of peoples of different civilizations, such as the Soviet Union and Yugoslavia, are candidates for dismemberment. Some other countries have a fair degree of cultural homogeneity but are divided over whether their society belongs to one civilization or another. These are torn countries. Their leaders typically wish to pursue a band-wagoning strategy and to make their countries members of the West, but the history, culture and traditions of their countries are non-Western. The most obvious and prototypical torn country is Turkey. The late twentieth-century leaders of Turkey have followed in the

Attaturk tradition and defined Turkey as a modern, secular, Western nation state. They allied Turkey with the West in NATO and in the Gulf War; they applied for membership in the European Community. At the same time, however, elements in Turkish society have supported an Islamic revival and have argued that Turkey is basically a Middle Eastern Muslim society. In addition, while the elite of Turkey has defined Turkey as a Western society, the elite of the West refuses to accept Turkey as such. Turkey will not become a member of the European Community, and the real reason, as President Ozal said, "is that we are Muslim and they are Christian and they don't say that." Having rejected Mecca, and then being rejected by Brussels, where does Turkey look? Tashkent may be the answer. The end of the Soviet Union gives Turkey the opportunity to become the leader of a revived Turkic civilization involving seven countries from the borders of Greece to those of China. Encouraged by the West, Turkey is making strenuous efforts to carve out this new identity for itself.

During the past decade Mexico has assumed a position somewhat similar to that of Turkey. Just as Turkey abandoned its historic opposition to Europe and attempted to join Europe, Mexico has stopped defining itself by its opposition to the United States and is instead attempting to imitate the United States and to join it in the North American Free Trade Area. Mexican leaders are engaged in the great task of redefining Mexican identity and have introduced fundamental economic reforms that eventually will lead to fundamental political change. In 1991 a top adviser to President Carlos Salinas de Gortari described at length to me all the changes the Salinas government was making. When he finished, I remarked: "That's most impressive. It seems to me that basically you want to change Mexico from a Latin American country into a North American country." He looked at me with surprise and exclaimed: "Exactly! That's precisely what we are trying to do, but of course we could never say so publicly." As his remark indicates, in Mexico as in Turkey, significant elements in society resist the redefinition of their country's identity. In Turkey, European-oriented leaders have to make gestures to Islam (Ozal's pilgrimage to Mecca); so also Mexico's North American-oriented leaders have to make gestures to those who hold Mexico to be a Latin American country (Salinas' Ibero-American Guadalajara summit).

Historically Turkey has been the most profoundly torn country. For the United States, Mexico is the most immediate torn country. Globally the most important torn country is Russia. The question of whether Russia is part of the West or the leader of a distinct Slavic-Orthodox civilization has been a recurring one in Russian history. That issue was obscured by the communist victory in Russia, which imported a Western ideology, adapted it to Russian conditions and then challenged the West in the name of that ideology. The dominance of communism shut off the historic debate over Westernization versus Russification. With communism discredited Russians once again face that question.

* * *

To redefine its civilization identity, a torn country must meet three requirements. First, its political and economic elite has to be generally supportive of and enthusiastic about this move. Second, its public has to be willing to acquiesce in the redefinition. Third, the dominant groups in the recipient civilization have to be willing to embrace the convert. All three requirements in large part exist with respect to Mexico. The first two in large part exist with respect to Turkey. It is not clear that any of them exist with respect to Russia's joining the West. The conflict between liberal democracy and Marxism-Leninism was between ideologies which, despite their major differences, ostensibly shared ultimate goals of freedom, equality and prosperity. A traditional, authoritarian, nationalist Russia could have quite different goals. A Western democrat could carry on an intellectual debate with a Soviet Marxist. It would be virtually impossible for him to do that with a Russian traditionalist. If, as the Russians stop behaving like Marxists, they reject liberal democracy and begin behaving like Russians but not like Westerners, the relations between Russia and the West could again become distant and conflictual.[7]

The Confucian-Islamic Connection

The obstacles to non-Western countries joining the West vary considerably. They are least for Latin American and East European countries. They are greater for the Orthodox countries of the former Soviet Union. They are still greater for Muslim, Confucian, Hindu and Buddhist societies. Japan has established a unique position for itself as an associate member of the West: it is in the West in some respects but clearly not of the West in important dimensions. Those countries that for reason of culture and power do not wish to, or cannot, join the West compete with the West by developing their own economic, military and political power. They do this by promoting their internal development and by cooperating with other non-Western countries. The most prominent form of this cooperation is the Confucian-Islamic connection that has emerged to challenge Western interests, values and power.

Almost without exception, Western countries are reducing their military power; * * * so also is Russia. China, North Korea and several Middle Eastern states, however, are significantly expanding their military capabilities. They are doing this by the import of arms from Western and non-Western sources and by the development of indigenous arms industries. * * *

The non-Western nations * * * also have absorbed, to the full, the truth of the response of the Indian defense minister when asked what lesson he learned from the Gulf War: "Don't fight the United States unless you have nuclear weapons." Nuclear weapons, chemical weapons and missiles are viewed, probably erroneously, as the potential equalizer of superior Western conventional power. China, of course, already has nuclear weapons; Pakistan and India have the capability to deploy them. North Korea, Iran, Iraq, Libya and Algeria appear to be attempting to acquire them. A top Iranian official has declared that all Muslim states should acquire nuclear weapons, and in 1988 the president of Iran reportedly issued a directive calling for development of "offensive and defensive chemical, biological and radiological weapons."

Centrally important to the development of counter-West military capabilities is the sustained expansion of China's military power and its means to create military power. Buoyed by spectacular economic development, China is rapidly increasing its military spending and vigorously moving forward with the modernization of its armed forces. It is purchasing weapons from the former Soviet states; it is developing long-range missiles.

*   *   *

A Confucian-Islamic military connection has thus come into being, designed to promote acquisition by its members of the weapons and weapons technologies needed to counter the military power of the West. It may or may not last. At present, however, it is, as Dave McCurdy has said, "a renegades' mutual support pact, run by the proliferators and their backers." A new form of arms competition is thus occuring between Islamic-Confucian states and the West. In an old-fashioned arms race, each side developed its own arms to balance or to achieve superiority against the other side. In this new form of arms competition, one side is developing its arms and the other side is attempting not to balance but to limit and prevent that arms build-up while at the same time reducing its own military capabilities.

Implications for the West

This article does not argue that civilization identities will replace all other identities, that nation states will disappear, that each civilization will become a single coherent political entity, that groups within a civilization will not conflict with and even fight each other. This paper does set forth the hypotheses that differences between civilizations are real and important; civilization-consciousness is increasing; conflict between civ-ilizations will supplant ideological and other forms of conflict as the dominant global form of conflict; international relations, historically a game played out within Western civilization, will increasingly be de-Westernized and become a game in which non-Western civilizations are ac-tors and not simply objects; successful political, security and economic international institutions are more likely to develop within civilizations than across civilizations; conflicts between groups in different civilizations will be more fre-quent, more sustained and more violent than conflicts between groups in the same civiliza-tion; violent conflicts between groups in differ-ent civilizations are the most likely and most dangerous source of escalation that could lead to global wars; the paramount axis of world politics will be the relations between "the West and the Rest"; the elites in some torn non-Western coun-tries will try to make their countries part of the West, but in most cases face major obstacles to accomplishing this; a central focus of conflict for the immediate future will be between the West and several Islamic-Confucian states.

This is not to advocate the desirability of conflicts between civilizations. It is to set forth descriptive hypotheses as to what the future may be like. If these are plausible hypotheses, how-ever, it is necessary to consider their implica-tions for Western policy. These implications should be divided between short-term advantage and long-term accommodation. In the short term it is clearly in the interest of the West to promote greater cooperation and unity within its own civilization, particularly between its Euro-pean and North American components; to incor-porate into the West societies in Eastern Europe and Latin America whose cultures are close to those of the West; to promote and maintain co-operative relations with Russia and Japan; to prevent escalation of local inter-civilization con-flicts into major inter-civilization wars; to limit the expansion of the military strength of Con-fucian and Islamic states; to moderate the re-duction of Western military capabilities and maintain military superiority in East and South-west Asia; to exploit differences and conflicts among Confucian and Islamic states; to support in other civilizations groups sympathetic to Western values and interests; to strengthen in-ternational institutions that reflect and legiti-mate Western interests and values and to promote the involvement of non-Western states in those institutions.

In the longer term other measures would be called for. Western civilization is both Western and modern. Non-Western civilizations have at-tempted to become modern without becoming Western. To date only Japan has fully succeeded in this quest. Non-Western civilizations will con-tinue to attempt to acquire the wealth, technol-ogy, skills, machines and weapons that are part of being modern. They will also attempt to rec-oncile this modernity with their traditional cul-ture and values. Their economic and military strength relative to the West will increase. Hence the West will increasingly have to accommodate these non-Western modern civilizations whose power approaches that of the West but whose values and interests differ significantly from those of the West. This will require the West to maintain the economic and military power nec-essary to protect its interests in relation to these civilizations. It will also, however, require the West to develop a more profound understanding of the basic religious and philosophical assump-tions underlying other civilizations and the ways in which people in those civilizations see their interests. It will require an effort to identify ele-ments of commonality between Western and other civilizations. For the relevant future, there will be no universal civilization, but instead a world of different civilizations, each of which will have to learn to coexist with the others.

NOTES

1. Murray Weidenbaum, *Greater China: The Next Economic Superpower?*, St. Louis: Washington University Center for the Study

of American Business, Contemporary Issues, Series 57, February 1993, pp. 2–3.

2. Bernard Lewis, "The Roots of Muslim Rage," *The Atlantic Monthly*, vol. 266, September 1990, p. 60; *Time*, June 15, 1992, pp. 24–28.

3. Archie Roosevelt, *For Lust of Knowing*, Boston: Little, Brown, 1988, pp. 332–333.

4. Almost invariably Western leaders claim they are acting on behalf of "the world community." One minor lapse occurred during the run-up to the Gulf War. In an interview on "Good Morning America," Dec. 21, 1990, British Prime Minister John Major referred to the actions "the West" was taking against Saddam Hussein. He quickly corrected himself and subsequently referred to "the world community." He was, however, right when he erred.

5. Harry C. Triandis, *The New York Times*, December 25, 1990, p. 41, and "Cross-Cultural Studies of Individualism and Collectivism,"

Nebraska Symposium on Motivation, vol. 37, 1989, pp. 41–133.

6. Kishore Mahbubani, "The West and the Rest," *The National Interest*, Summer 1992, pp. 3–13.

7. Owen Harries has pointed out that Australia is trying (unwisely in his view) to become a torn country in reverse. Although it has been a full member not only of the West but also of the ABCA military and intelligence core of the West, its current leaders are in effect proposing that it defect from the West, redefine itself as an Asian country and cultivate close ties with its neighbors. Australia's future, they argue, is with the dynamic economies of East Asia. But, as I have suggested, close economic cooperation normally requires a common cultural base. In addition, none of the three conditions necessary for a torn country to join another civilization is likely to exist in Australia's case.

FOUAD AJAMI

THE SUMMONING: "BUT THEY SAID, 'WE WILL NOT HEARKEN,'" JEREMIAH 6: 17.

In Joseph Conrad's *Youth*, a novella published at the turn of the century, Marlowe, the narrator, remembers when he first encountered "the East":

> And then, before I could open my lips, the East spoke to me, but it was in a Western voice. A torrent of words was poured into the enigmatical, the fateful silence; outlandish, angry words mixed with words and even whole sentences of good English, less strange but even more surprising. The voice

From *Foreign Affairs*, 72, no. 4 (September/October 1993), pp. 2–9.

swore and cursed violently; it riddled the solemn peace of the bay by a volley of abuse. It began by calling me Pig, and from that went crescendo into unmentionable adjectives—in English.

The young Marlowe knew that even the most remote civilization had been made and remade by the West, and taught new ways.

Not so Samuel P. Huntington. In a curious essay, "The Clash of Civilizations," Huntington has found his civilizations whole and intact, watertight under an eternal sky. Buried alive, as it were, during the years of the Cold War, these civilizations (Islamic, Slavic-Orthodox, Western, Confucian, Japanese, Hindu, etc.) rose as soon as the stone was rolled off, dusted themselves off, and proceeded to claim the loyalty of their adherents. For this student of history and culture, civilizations have always seemed messy creatures. Furrows run across whole civilizations, across individuals themselves—that was modernity's verdict. But Huntington looks past all that. The crooked and meandering alleyways of the world are straightened out. With a sharp pencil and a steady hand Huntington marks out where one civilization ends and the wilderness of "the other" begins.

More surprising still is Huntington's attitude toward states, and their place in his scheme of things. From one of the most influential and brilliant students of the state and its national interest there now comes an essay that misses the slyness of states, the unsentimental and cold-blooded nature of so much of what they do as they pick their way through chaos. Despite the obligatory passage that states will remain "the most powerful actors in world affairs," states are written off, their place given over to clash civilizations. In Huntington's words, "The next world war, if there is one, will be a war between civilizations."

The Power of Modernity

Huntington's meditation is occasioned by his concern about the state of the West, its power and the terms of its engagement with "the rest."[1] "He who gives, dominates," the great historian Fernand Braudel observed of the traffic of civilizations. In making itself over the centuries, the West helped make the others as well. We have come to the end of this trail, Huntington is sure. He is impressed by the "de-Westernization" of societies, their "indigenization" and apparent willingness to go their own way. In his view of things such phenomena as the "Hinduization" of India and Islamic fundamentalism are ascen-

dant. To these detours into "tradition" Huntington has assigned great force and power.

But Huntington is wrong. He has underestimated the tenacity of modernity and secularism in places that acquired these ways against great odds, always perilously close to the abyss, the darkness never far. India will not become a Hindu state. The inheritance of Indian secularism will hold. The vast middle class will defend it, keep the order intact to maintain India's—and its own—place in the modern world of nations. There exists in that anarchic polity an instinctive dread of playing with fires that might consume it. Hindu chauvinism may coarsen the public life of the country, but the state and the middle class that sustains it know that a detour into religious fanaticism is a fling with ruin. A resourceful middle class partakes of global culture and norms. A century has passed since the Indian bourgeoisie, through its political vehicle the Indian National Congress, set out to claim for itself and India a place among nations. Out of that long struggle to overturn British rule and the parallel struggle against "communalism," the advocates of the national idea built a large and durable state. They will not cede all this for a political kingdom of Hindu purity.

We have been hearing from the traditionalists, but we should not exaggerate their power, for traditions are often most insistent and loud when they rupture, when people no longer really believe and when age-old customs lose their ability to keep men and women at home. The phenomenon we have dubbed as Islamic fundamentalism is less a sign of resurgence than of panic and bewilderment and guilt that the border with "the other" has been crossed. Those young urban poor, half-educated in the cities of the Arab world, and their Sorbonne-educated lay preachers, can they be evidence of a genuine return to tradition? They crash Europe's and America's gates in search of liberty and work, and they rail against the sins of the West. It is easy to understand Huntington's frustration with his kind of complexity, with the strange mixture of attraction and repulsion that the West breeds, and his need to simplify matters, to mark out the borders of civilizations.

Tradition-mongering is no proof, though, that these civilizations outside the West are intact, or that their thrashing about is an indication of their vitality, or that they present a conventional threat of arms. Even so thorough and far-reaching an attack against Western hegemony as Iran's theocratic revolution could yet fail to wean that society from the culture of the West. That country's cruel revolution was born of the realization of the "armed Imam" that his people were being seduced by America's ways. The gates had been thrown wide open in the 1970s, and the high walls Ayatollah Khomeini built around his polity were a response to that culture seduction. Swamped, Iran was "rescued" by men claiming authenticity as their banner. One extreme led to another.

"We prayed for the rain of mercy and received floods," was the way Mehdi Bazargan, the decent modernist who was Khomeini's first prime minister, put it. But the millennium has been brought down to earth, and the dream of a pan-Islamic revolt in Iran's image has vanished into the wind. The terror and the shabbiness have caught up with the utopia. Sudan could emulate the Iranian "revolutionary example." But this will only mean the further pauperization and ruin of a desperate land. There is no rehabilitation of the Iranian example.

A battle rages in Algeria, a society of the Mediterranean, close to Europe—a wine-producing country for that matter—and in Egypt between the secular powers that be and an Islamic alternative. But we should not rush to print with obituaries of these states. In Algeria the nomenklatura of the National Liberation Front failed and triggered a revolt of the young, the underclass and the excluded. The revolt raised an Islamic banner. Caught between a regime they despised and a reign of virtue they feared, the professionals and the women and the modernists of the middle class threw their support to the forces of "order." They hailed the army's crackdown on the Islamicists; they al-

lowed the interruption of a democratic process sure to bring the Islamicists to power; they accepted the "liberties" protected by the repression, the devil you know rather than the one you don't.

The Algerian themes repeat in the Egyptian case, although Egypt's dilemma over its Islamicist opposition is not as acute. The Islamicists continue to hound the state, but they cannot bring it down. There is no likelihood that the Egyptian state—now riddled with enough complacency and corruption to try the celebrated patience and good humor of the Egyptians—will go under. This is an old and skeptical country. It knows better than to trust its fate to enforcers of radical religious dogma. These are not deep and secure structures of order that the national middle classes have put in place. But they will not be blown away overnight.

Nor will Turkey lose its way, turn its back on Europe and chase after some imperial temptation in the scorched domains of Central Asia. Huntington sells that country's modernity and secularism short when he writes that the Turks—rejecting Mecca and rejected by Brussels—are likely to head to Tashkent in search of a Pan-Turkic role. There is no journey to that imperial past. Ataturk severed that link with fury, pointed his country westward, embraced the civilization of Europe and did it without qualms or second thoughts. It is on Frankfurt and Bonn—and Washington—not on Baku and Tashkent that the attention of the Turks is fixed. The inheritors of Ataturk's legacy are too shrewd to go chasing after imperial glory, gathering about them the scattered domains of the Turkish peoples. After their European possessions were lost, the Turks clung to Thrace and to all that this link to Europe represents.

Huntington would have nations battle for civilizational ties and fidelities when they would rather scramble for their market shares, learn how to compete in a merciless world economy, provide jobs, move out of poverty. For their part, the "management gurus" and those who believe that the interests have vanquished the passions in today's world tell us that men want Sony, not soil.[2] There is a good deal of truth in what they say, a terrible exhaustion with utopias, a reluctance to set out on expeditions of principle or belief. It is hard to think of Russia, ravaged as it is by inflation, taking up the grand cause of a "second Byzantium," the bearer of the Orthodox-Slavic torch.

And where is the Confucian world Huntington speaks of? In the busy and booming lands of the Pacific Rim, so much of politics and ideology has been sublimated into finance that the nations of East Asia have turned into veritable workshops. The civilization of Cathay is dead; the Indonesian archipelago is deaf to the call of the religious radicals in Tehran as it tries to catch up with Malaysia and Singapore. A different wind blows in the lands of the Pacific. In that world economics, not politics, is in command. The world is far less antiseptic than Lee Kuan Yew, the sage of Singapore, would want it to be. A nemesis could lie in wait for all the prosperity that the 1980s brought to the Pacific. But the lands of the Pacific Rim—protected, to be sure, by an American security umbrella—are not ready for a great falling out among the nations. And were troubles to visit that world they would erupt within its boundaries, not across civilizational lines.

The things and ways that the West took to "the rest"—those whole sentences of good English that Marlowe heard a century ago—have become the ways of the world. The secular idea, the state system and the balance of power, pop culture jumping tariff walls and barriers, the state as an instrument of welfare, all these have been internalized in the remotest places. We have stirred up the very storms into which we now ride.

The Weakness of Tradition

Nations "cheat": they juggle identities and interests. Their ways meander. One would think that the traffic of arms from North Korea and China

to Libya and Iran and Syria shows this—that states will consort with any civilization, however alien, as long as the price is right and the goods are ready. Huntington turns this routine act of selfishness into a sinister "Confucian-Islamic connection." There are better explanations: the commerce of renegades, plain piracy, an "underground economy" that picks up the slack left by the great arms suppliers (the United States, Russia, Britain and France).

Contrast the way Huntington sees things with Braudel's depiction of the traffic between Christendom and Islam across the Mediterranean in the sixteenth century—and this was in a religious age, after the fall of Constantinople to the Turks and of Granada to the Spanish: "Men passed to and fro, indifferent to frontiers, states and creeds. They were more aware of the necessities for shipping and trade, the hazards of war and piracy, the opportunities for complicity or betrayal provided by circumstances."[3]

Those kinds of "complicities" and ambiguities are missing in Huntington's analysis. Civilizations are crammed into the nooks and crannies—and checkpoints—of the Balkans. Huntington goes where only the brave would venture, into that belt of mixed populations stretching from the Adriatic to the Baltic. Countless nationalisms make their home there, all aggrieved, all possessed of memories of a fabled past and equally ready for the demagogues vowing to straighten a messy map. In the thicket of these pan-movements he finds the line that marked "the eastern boundary of Western Christianity in the year 1500." The scramble for turf between Croatian nationalism and its Serbian counterpart, their "joint venture" in carving up Bosnia, are made into a fight of the inheritors of Rome, Byzantium and Islam.

But why should we fall for this kind of determinism? "An outsider who travels the highway between Zagreb and Belgrade is struck not by the decisive historical fault line which falls across the lush Slavonian plain but by the opposite. Serbs and Croats speak the same language, give or take a few hundred words, have shared the same village way of life for centuries."[4] The cruel genius of Slobodan Milosevic and Franjo Tudjman, men on horseback familiar in lands and situations of distress, was to make their bids for power into grand civilizational undertakings—the ramparts of the Enlightenment defended against Islam or, in Tudjman's case, against the heirs of the Slavic-Orthodox faith. Differences had to be magnified. Once Tito, an equal opportunity oppressor, had passed from the scene, the balancing act among the nationalities was bound to come apart. Serbia had had a measure of hegemony in the old system. But of the world that loomed over the horizon—privatization and economic reform—the Serbs were less confident. The citizens of Sarajevo and the Croats and the Slovenes had a head start on the rural Serbs. And so the Serbs hacked at the new order of things with desperate abandon.

Some Muslim volunteers came to Bosnia, driven by faith and zeal. Huntington sees in these few stragglers the sweeping power of "civilizational rallying," proof of the hold of what he calls the "kin-country syndrome." This is delusion. No Muslim cavalry was ever going to ride to the rescue. The Iranians may have railed about holy warfare, but the Chetniks went on with their work. The work of order and mercy would have had to be done by the United States if the cruel utopia of the Serbs was to be contested.

It should have taken no powers of prophecy to foretell where the fight in the Balkans would end. The abandonment of Bosnia was of a piece with the ways of the world. No one wanted to die for Srebrenica. The Europeans averted their gaze, as has been their habit. The Americans hesitated for a moment as the urge to stay out of the Balkans did battle with the scenes of horror. Then "prudence" won out. Milosevic and Tudjman may need civilizational legends, but there is no need to invest their projects of conquest with this kind of meaning.

In his urge to find that relentless war across Islam's "bloody borders," Huntington buys Saddam Hussein's interpretation of the Gulf War. It

was, for Saddam and Huntington, a civilizational battle. But the Gulf War's verdict was entirely different. For if there was a campaign that laid bare the interests of states, the lengths to which they will go to restore a tolerable balance of power in a place that matters, this was it. A local despot had risen close to the wealth of the Persian Gulf, and a Great Power from afar had come to the rescue. The posse assembled by the Americans had Saudi, Turkish, Egyptian, Syrian, French, British and other riders.

True enough, when Saddam Hussein's dream of hegemony was shattered, the avowed secularist who had devastated the *ulama,* the men of religion in his country, fell back on Ayatollah Khomeini's language of fire and brimstone and borrowed the symbolism and battle cry of his old Iranian nemesis. But few, if any, were fooled by this sudden conversion to the faith. They knew the predator for what he was: he had a Christian foreign minister (Tariq Aziz); he had warred against the Iranian revolution for nearly a decade and had prided himself on the secularism of his regime. Prudent men of the social and political order, the *ulama* got out of the way and gave their state the room it needed to check the predator at the Saudi/Kuwaiti border.[5] They knew this was one of those moments when purity bows to necessity. Ten days after Saddam swept into Kuwait, Saudi Arabia's most authoritative religious body, the Council of Higher Ulama, issued a *fatwa,* or a ruling opinion, supporting the presence of Arab and Islamic and "other friendly forces." All means of defense, the ulama ruled, were legitimate to guarantee the people "the safety of their religion, their wealth, and their honor and their blood, to protect what they enjoy of safety and stability." At some remove, in Egypt, that country's leading religious figure, the Shaykh of Al Ashar, Shaykh Jadd al Haqq, denounced Saddam as a tyrant and brushed aside his Islamic pretensions as a cover for tyranny.

Nor can the chief Iranian religious leader Ayatollah Ali Khamenei's rhetoric against the Americans during the Gulf War be taken as evidence of Iran's disposition toward that campaign. Crafty men, Iran's rulers sat out that war. They stood to emerge as the principal beneficiaries of Iraq's defeat. The American-led campaign against Iraq held out the promise of tilting the regional balance in their favor. No tears were shed in Iran for what befell Saddam Hussein's regime.

It is the mixed gift of living in hard places that men and women know how to distinguish between what they hear and what there is: no illusions were thus entertained in vast stretches of the Arab Muslim world about Saddam, or about the campaign to thwart him for that matter. The fight in the gulf was seen for what it was: a bid for primacy met by an imperial expedition that laid it to waste. A circle was closed in the gulf: where once the order in the region "east of Suez" had been the work of the British, it was now provided by Pax Americana. The new power standing sentry in the gulf belonged to the civilization of the West, as did the prior one. But the American presence had the anxious consent of the Arab lands of the Persian Gulf. The stranger coming in to check the kinsmen.

The world of Islam divides and subdivides. The battle lines in the Caucasus, too, are not coextensive with civilizational fault lines. The lines follow the interests of states. Where Huntington sees a civilizational duel between Armenia and Azerbaijan, the Iranian state has cast religious zeal and fidelity to the wind. Indeed, in that battle the Iranians have tilted toward Christian Armenia.

The Writ of States

We have been delivered into a new world, to be sure. But it is not a world where the writ of civilizations runs. Civilizations and civilizational fidelities remain. There is to them as astonishing measure of permanence. But let us be clear: civilizations do not control states, states control civilizations. States avert their gaze from blood ties when they need to; they see brotherhood and faith and kin when it is in their interest to do so.

We remain in a world of self-help. The solitude of states continues; the disorder in the contemporary world has rendered that solitude more pronounced. No way has yet been found to reconcile France to Pax Americana's hegemony, or to convince it to trust its security or cede its judgment to the preeminent Western power. And no Azeri has come up with a way that lands of Islam could be rallied to the fight over Nagorno Karabakh. The sky has not fallen in Kuala Lumpur or in Tunis over the setbacks of Azerbaijan in its fight with Armenia.

The lesson bequeathed us by Thucydides in his celebrated dialogue between the Melians and the Athenians remains. The Melians, it will be recalled, were a colony of the Lacedaemonians. Besieged by Athens, they held out and were sure that the Lacedaemonians were "bound, if only for very shame, to come to the aid of their kindred." The Melians never wavered in their confidence in their "civilizational" allies: "Our common blood insures our fidelity."[6] We know what became of the Melians. Their allies did not turn up, their island was sacked, their world laid to waste.

NOTES

1. The West itself is unexamined in Huntington's essay. No fissures run through it. No multiculturalists are heard from. It is orderly within its ramparts. What doubts Huntington has about the will within the walls, he has kept within himself. He has assumed that his call to unity will be answered, for outside flutter the banners of the Saracens and the Confucians.
2. Kenichi Ohmae, "Global Consumers Want Sony, Not Soil," *New Perspectives Quarterly,* Fall 1991.
3. Fernand Braudel, *The Mediterranean and the Mediterranean World in the Age of Philip II,* Vol. II, New York: Harper & Row, 1976, p. 759.

4. Michael Ignatieff, "The Balkan Tragedy," *New York Review of Books*, May 13, 1993.

5. Huntington quotes one Safar al Hawali, a religious radical at Umm al Qura University in Mecca, to the effect that the campaign against Iraq was another Western campaign against Islam. But this can't do as evidence. Safar al Hawali was a crank. Among the *ulama* class and the religious scholars in Saudi Arabia he was, for all practical purposes, a loner.

6. Thucydides, *The Peloponnesian War*, New York: The Modern American Library, 1951, pp. 334–335.

4 POLITICAL ECONOMY

The field of political economy, the concept of laissez-faire *economic liberalism, and the modern discipline of economics are all generally considered to have originated with Adam Smith's* Wealth of Nations, *published in 1776. Many of Smith's most important ideas, particularly the division and specialization of labor, were already familiar to literate Europeans from earlier works, including Bernard Mandeville's witty and enduring poem* Fable of the Bees, *first published in 1705, and the French* Encyclopédie *of the 1750s. But it was Smith who, through plain examples and seemingly irrefutable logic, convinced three generations of European and American elites that free markets and minimal government would maximize economic growth. The excerpts from* The Wealth of Nations *included here encapsulate Smith's arguments on the division of labor, the self-regulating nature of capitalism (the "invisible hand"), the advantages of free trade, and the importance of limited but effective government.*

Perhaps the most fundamental, and certainly the most counterintuitive, argument in political economy is that free international trade *benefits all countries, and perhaps particularly poorer countries.[1] Virtually every serious student of political economy today, as well as political theorists and practitioners of almost all ideological persuasions—liberals, conservatives, social democrats, most Marxists[2]— from poor and rich countries alike, believe in free trade and expanding world markets. (Mercantilists of course do not accept free trade, but the long stagnation of the Japanese economy has cast mercantilism into almost as much disrepute as Communism.)*

Why is the intellectual case for free trade so strong? Smith's argument had seemed to depend on differences between countries in absolute *advantage (i.e., that a product could be produced in one country with fewer hours of labor than in another.) But what if a country were at absolute disadvantage in every product? The great early economist David Ricardo argued, with what most still consider to be airtight logic, that free trade would benefit all countries as long as there were differences in* relative *advantage. In the brief excerpt from Ricardo's* Principles of Political Economy *(1817) presented here,*

Ricardo argues that even if one country (in his example, England) is at an absolute disadvantage in producing both wine and cloth (i.e., more hours of labor are required to produce each product in England than in Portugal), it still has comparative *advantage in one, and will benefit from trading freely with an absolutely advantaged country (in this case, Portugal). Ricardo's insights have been complemented, but in part called into question, by some recent work (notably that of the new Nobel laureate Paul Krugman). In "Beyond Belief" (2007), Clive Crook, a regular columnist for the* Financial Times *and earlier chief economics commentator for* The Economist *magazine, offers a vigorous rebuttal to the new doubts.*

If the classical laissez-faire endorsement of free trade remains almost universally accepted, another major tenet—that of the minimalist state—does not. In the classical analyses of Adam Smith, of most nineteenth-century thinkers, and even of Libertarians today, government taxation and expenditure always entail "deadweight costs," and are justified only to provide collective goods that voluntary or market-based action would undersupply: defense against foreign enemies, enforcement of contracts, roads and harbors, public education.³ Yet in modern times government expenditures in advanced economies have grown enormously, apparently at little cost to growth or productivity (see more in Chapter 7); and efforts to establish flourishing free-market economies in post-Communist and developing countries have frequently failed, not least because of deficient or perverse government institutions.

So how important are institutions, what kinds matter most, and why do so many countries seem to end up with too few or too poor institutions? In a pathbreaking 1991 article, the economic historian and Nobel laureate Douglass North brought history and logic to bear on these questions: What institutions are most essential to make markets work? Why do they sometimes fail to develop? And to what extent can that failure be reversed? North contended that "path dependence," including a country's colonial experience (e.g., the seemingly clear difference between former Spanish and former English colonies in North America), played a large role.

Some critics held that geography mattered more than institutions: a tropical climate, or long distance from major ports and trade routes, would inhibit development no matter how good institutions were. But in fundamental papers by Daron Acemoglu, Simon Johnson, and James Robinson in 2001 and 2002 (summarized here in Acemoglu's "Root Causes"), the geographical argument was refuted and the sources of institutional difference were clarified (2003). Precisely the regions of the world that were now poorest, they demonstrated, were often richest around 1500, when the European wave of colonization began. Because Europeans sought to plunder those regions, they established predatory institutions (rapacious governments, insecure property rights) that have often survived down to the present day. When Europeans colonized originally poorer and less densely settled regions (Australia, North America), and especially where the climate was more favorable to European survival, they could augment wealth only by attracting settlers, minimizing the burdens of government, and establishing clear property rights. The result had been a "reversal of fortune," in which originally poor regions wound up with good institutions, rapid economic growth, and ultimate wealth, while originally rich regions inherited bad institutions that made them poor.

NOTES

1. This is not the same thing as saying that every *person* benefits in every country. When the United States trades with China, skilled U.S. workers gain but unskilled U.S. workers lose; while in China unskilled workers benefit but skilled workers lose. Yet the gains of skilled U.S. workers far outweigh our unskilled workers' loss, just as the gains of unskilled Chinese workers far exceed the losses to skilled Chinese workers.
2. Karl Marx was as avid a supporter of free trade as Adam Smith had been, and every early Marxist party in Europe was free-trading. Social Democrats today, in all developed countries, are among the strongest supporters of trade expansion. Communist regimes of course walled themselves off from world markets; but in this, as in almost all else, they were diametrically opposed to original Marxism.
3. Even Adam Smith endorsed educational expenditures, since the social return (the overall productivity gain to the economy from a person who acquires greater skills) exceeds the private return (the increase in the educated person's earnings), meaning that voluntary action will always undersupply education.

ADAM SMITH

AN INQUIRY INTO THE NATURE AND CAUSES OF THE WEALTH OF NATIONS

Of the Division of Labour[1]

The greatest improvement[2] in the productive powers of labour, and the greater part of the skill, dexterity, and judgment with which it is any where directed, or applied, seem to have been the effects of the division of labour.

From Edwin Cannan, ed., Adam Smith, *An Inquiry into the Nature and Causes of the Wealth of Nations* (Chicago: The University of Chicago Press, 1976. Originally published in 1776.) Book I, pp. 7–19, Book IV, pp. 474–81, 208–9. Some notes have been omitted; those that follow are Cannan's.

The effects of the division of labour, in the general business of society, will be more easily understood, by considering in what manner it operates in some particular manufactures.

*   *   *

To take an example, therefore,[3] from a very trifling manufacture; but one in which the division of labour has been very often taken notice of, the trade of the pin-maker; a workman not educated to this business (which the division of labour has rendered a distinct trade),[4] nor acquainted with the use of the machinery employed in it (to the invention of which the same division of labour has probably given occasion), could scarce, perhaps, with his utmost industry, make one pin in a day, and certainly could not make twenty. But in the way in which this business is now carried on, not only the whole work is a peculiar trade, but it is divided into a number of branches, of which the greater part are likewise peculiar trades. One man draws out the wire, another straights it, a third cuts it, a fourth points it, a fifth grinds it at the top for receiving the head; to make the head requires two or three distinct operations; to put it on, is a peculiar business, to whiten the pins is another; it is even a trade by itself to put them into the paper; and the important business of making a pin is, in this manner, divided into about eighteen distinct operations, which, in some manufactories, are all performed by distinct hands, though in others the same man will sometimes perform two or three of them.[5] I have seen a small manufactory of this kind where ten men only were employed, and where some of them consequently performed two or three distinct operations. But though they were very poor, and therefore but indifferently accomodated with the necessary machinery, they could, when they exerted themselves, make among them about twelve pounds of pins in a day. There are in a pound upwards of four thousand pins of a middling size. Those ten persons, therefore, could make among them upwards of forty-eight thousand pins in a day. Each person, therefore, making a tenth part of forty-eight thousand pins, might be considered as making four thousand eight hundred pins in a day. But if they had all wrought separately and independently, and without any of them having been educated to this peculiar business, they certainly could not each of them have made twenty, perhaps not one pin in a day; that is, certainly, not the two hundred and fortieth, perhaps not the four thousand eight hundredth part of what they are at present capable of performing, in consequence of a proper division and combination of their different operations.

In every other art and manufacture, the effects of the division of labour are similar to what they are in this very trifling one; though, in many of them, the labour can neither be so much subdivided, nor reduced to so great a simplicity of operation. The division of labour, however, so far as it can be introduced, occasions, in every art, a proportionable increase of the productive powers of labour. The separation of different trades and employments from one another, seems to have taken place, in consequence of this advantage. This separation too is generally carried furthest in those countries which enjoy the highest degree of industry and improvement; what is the work of one man in a rude state of society, being generally that of several in an improved one.

*   *   *

This great increase of the quantity of work which, in consequence of the division of labour, the same number of people are capable of performing,[6] is owing to three different circumstances; first to the increase of dexterity in every particular workman; secondly, to the saving of the time which is commonly lost in passing from one species of work to another; and lastly, to the invention of a great number of machines which facilitate and abridge labour, and enable one man to do the work of many.[7]

*   *   *

It is the great multiplication of the productions of all the different arts, in consequence of the division of labour, which occasions, in a well-governed society, that universal opulence which extends itself to the lowest ranks of the people. Every workman has a great quantity of his own work to dispose of beyond what he himself has occasion for; and every other workman being exactly in the same situation, he is enabled to exchange a great quantity of his own goods for a great quantity, or, what comes to the same thing, for the price of a great quantity of theirs. He supplies them abundantly with what they have occasion for, and they accommodate him as amply with what he has occasion for, and a general plenty diffuses itself through all the different ranks of the society.

*   *   *

Of the Principle which gives Occasion to the Division of Labour

This division of labour, from which so many advantages are derived, is not originally the effect of any human wisdom, which foresees and intends that general opulence to which it gives occasion.[8] It is the necessary, though very slow and gradual, consequence of a certain propensity in human nature which has in view no such extensive utility; the propensity to truck, barter, and exchange one thing for another.

* * * [T]his propensity * * * is common to all men, and to be found in no other race of animals, which seem to know neither this nor any other species of contracts. * * *

Nobody ever saw a dog make a fair and deliberate exchange of one bone for another with another dog.[9] Nobody ever saw one animal by its gestures and natural cries signify to another, this is mine, that yours; I am willing to give this for that.

*   *   *

But man has almost constant occasion for the help of his brethren, and it is in vain for him to expect it from their benevolence only. He will be more likely to prevail if he can interest their self-love in his favour, and show them that it is for their own advantage to do for him what he requires of them. Whoever offers to another a bargain of any kind, proposes to do this. Give me that which I want, and you shall have this which you want, is the meaning of every such offer; and it is in this manner that we obtain from one another the far greater part of those good offices which we stand in need of. It is not from the benevolence of the butcher, the brewer, or the baker, that we expect our dinner, but from their regard to their own interest. We address ourselves, not to their humanity but to their self-love, and never talk to them of our own necessities but of their advantages. Nobody but a beggar chuses to depend chiefly upon the benevolence of his fellow-citizens.

*   *   *

As it is by treaty, by barter, and by purchase, that we obtain from one another the greater part of those mutual good offices which we stand in need of, so it is this same trucking disposition which originally gives occasion to the division of labour. In a tribe of hunters or shepherds a particular person makes bows and arrows, for example, with more readiness and dexterity than any other. He frequently exchanges them for cattle or for venison with his companions; and he finds at last that he can in this manner get more cattle and venison, than if he himself went to the field to catch them. From a regard to his own interest, therefore, the making of bows and arrows grows to be his chief business, and he becomes a sort of armourer. Another excels in making the frames and covers of their little huts or moveable houses. He is accustomed to be of use in this way to his neighbours, who reward him in the same manner with cattle and with venison, till at last he finds it his interest to dedicate himself entirely to this employment, and to become a sort of house-carpenter. In the same manner a third becomes a smith or a brazier; a fourth a tanner or dresser of hides or skins, the principal part of the clothing of savages. And thus the certainty of being able to exchange all that surplus part of the produce of his own labour, which is over and above his own consumption, for such parts of the produce of other men's labour as he may have occasion for, encourages every man to apply himself to a particular occupation, and to cultivate and bring to perfection whatever talent or genius he may possess for that particular species of business.[10]

*   *   *

Of Restraints upon the Importation from Foreign Countries of such Goods as can be Produced at Home

*   *   *

No regulation of commerce can increase the quantity of industry in any society beyond what its capital can maintain. It can only divert a part of it into a direction into which it might not otherwise have gone; and it is by no means certain that this artificial direction is likely to be more advantageous to the society than that into which it would have gone of its own accord.

Every individual is continually exerting himself to find out the most advantageous employment for whatever capital he can command. It is his own advantage, indeed, and not that of the society which he has in view. But the study of his own advantage naturally, or rather necessarily leads him to prefer that employment which is most advantageous to the society.

*   *   *

. . . [E]very individual . . . necessarily endeavours so to direct that industry, that its produce may be of the greatest possible value.

The produce of industry is what it adds to the subject or materials upon which it is employed. In proportion as the value of this produce is great or small, so will likewise be the profits of the employer. But it is only for the sake of profit that any man employs a capital in the support of industry; and he will always, therefore, endeavour to employ it in the support of that industry of which the produce is likely to be of the greatest value, or to exchange for the greatest quantity either of money or of other goods.

But the annual revenue of every society is always precisely equal to the exchangeable value of the whole annual produce of its industry, or rather is precisely the same thing with that exchangeable value. As every individual, therefore, endeavours as much as he can both to employ his capital in the support of domestic industry, and so to direct that industry that its produce may be of the greatest value; every individual necessarily labours to render the annual revenue of the society as great as he can. He generally, indeed, neither intends to promote the public interest, nor knows how much he is promoting it. By preferring the support of domestic to that of foreign industry, he intends only his own security; and by directing that industry in such a manner as its produce may be of the greatest value, he intends only his own gain, and he is in this, as in many other cases, led by an invisible hand to promote an end which was no part of his intention. Nor is it always the worse for the society that it was no part of it. By pursuing his own interest he frequently promotes that of the society more effectually than when he really intends to promote it. I have never known much good done by those who affected to trade for the public good. It is an affectation, indeed, not very common among merchants, and very few words need be employed in dissuading them from it.

What is the species of domestic industry which his capital can employ, and of which the produce is likely to be of the greatest value, every individual, it is evident, can, in his local situation, judge much better than any statesman or lawgiver can do for him. The statesman, who should attempt to direct private people in what manner they ought to employ their capitals, would not only load himself with a most unnecessary attention, but assume an authority which could safely be trusted, not only to no single person, but to no council or senate whatever, and which would no-where be so dangerous as in the hands of a man who had folly and presumption enough to fancy himself fit to exercise it.

To give the monopoly of the home-market to the produce of domestic industry, in any particular art or manufacture, is in some measure to direct private people in what manner they ought to employ their capitals, and must, in almost all cases, be either a useless or a hurtful regulation.

If the produce of domestic can be brought there as cheap as that of foreign industry, the regulation is evidently useless. If it cannot, it must generally be hurtful. It is the maxim of every prudent master of a family, never to attempt to make at home what it will cost him more to make than to buy. The taylor does not attempt to make his own shoes, but buys them of the shoemaker. The shoemaker does not attempt to make his own clothes, but employs a taylor. The farmer attempts to make neither the one nor the other, but employs those different artificers. All of them find it for their interest to employ their whole industry in a way in which they have some advantage over their neighbours, and to purchase with a part of its produce, or what is the same thing, with the price of a part of it, whatever else they have occasion for.

What is prudence in the conduct of every private family, can scarce be folly in that of a great kingdom. If a foreign country can supply us with a commodity cheaper than we ourselves can make it, better buy it of them with some part of the produce of our own industry, employed in a way in which we have some advantage. The general industry of the country, being always in proportion to the capital which employs it, will not thereby be diminished, no more than that of the above-mentioned artificers; but only left to find out the way in which it can be employed with the greatest advantage. It is certainly not employed to the greatest advantage, when it is thus directed towards an object which it can buy cheaper than it can make. The value of its annual produce is certainly more or less diminished, when it is thus turned away from producing commodities evidently of more value than the commodity which it is directed to produce. According to the supposition, that commodity could be purchased from foreign countries cheaper than it can be made at home. It could, therefore, have been purchased with a part only of the commodities, or what is the same thing, with a part only of the price of the commodities, which the industry employed by an equal capital would have produced at home, had it been left to follow its natural course. The indus-

try of the country, therefore, is thus turned away from a more, to a less advantageous employment, and the exchangeable value of its annual produce, instead of being increased, according to the intention of the lawgiver, must necessarily be diminished by every such regulation.

*   *   *

The natural advantages which one country has over another in producing particular commodities are sometimes so great, that it is acknowledged by all the world to be in vain to struggle with them. By means of glasses, hotbeds, and hotwalls, very good grapes can be raised in Scotland, and very good wine too can be made of them at about thirty times the expence for which at least equally good can be brought from foreign countries. Would it be a reasonable law to prohibit the importation of all foreign wines, merely to encourage the making of claret and burgundy in Scotland? But if there would be a manifest absurdity in turning towards any employment, thirty times more of the capital and industry of the country, than would be necessary to purchase from foreign countries an equal quantity of the commodities wanted, there must be an absurdity, though not altogether so glaring, yet exactly of the same kind, in turning towards any such employment a thirtieth, or even a three hundredth part more of either. Whether the advantages which one country has over another, be natural or acquired, is in this respect of no consequence. As long as the one country has those advantages, and the other wants them, it will always be more advantageous for the latter, rather to buy of the former than to make. It is an acquired advantage only, which one artificer has over his neighbour, who exercises another trade; and yet they both find it more advantageous to buy of one another, than to make what does not belong to their particular trades.

*   *   *

All systems either of preference or of restraint, therefore, being thus completely taken away, the obvious and simple system of natural liberty establishes itself of its own accord. Every man, as long as he does not violate the laws of justice, is left perfectly free to pursue his own interest his own way, and to bring both his industry and capital into competition with those of any other man, or order of men. The sovereign is completely discharged from a duty, in the attempting to perform which he must always be exposed to innumerable delusions, and for the proper performance of which no human wisdom or knowledge could ever be sufficient; the duty of superintending the industry of private people, and of directing it towards the employments most suitable to the interest of the society. According to the system of natural liberty, the sovereign has only three duties to attend to; three duties of great importance, indeed, but plain and intelligible to common understandings: first, the duty of protecting the society from the violence and invasion of other independent societies; secondly, the duty of protecting, as far as possible, every member of the society from the injustice or oppression of every other member of it, or the duty of establishing an exact administration of justice; and, thirdly, the duty of erecting and maintaining certain public works and certain public institutions, which it can never be for the interest of any individual, or small number of individuals, to erect and maintain; because the profit could never repay the expence to any individual or small number of individuals, though it may frequently do much more than repay it to a great society.

The proper performance of those several duties of the sovereign necessarily supposes a certain expence; and this expence again necessarily requires a certain revenue to support it.

* * *

NOTES

1. This phrase, if used at all before this time, was not a familiar one. Its presence here is probably due to a passage in Mandeville, *Fable of the Bees*, pt. ii. (1729), dial. vi., p. 335: 'CLEO. . . . When once men come to be governed by written laws, all the rest comes on apace . . . No number of men, when once they enjoy quiet, and no man needs to fear his neighbour, will be long without learning to divide and subdivide their labour. HOR. I don't understand you. CLEO. Man, as I have hinted before, naturally loves to imitate what he sees others do, which is the reason that savage people all do the same thing: this hinders them from meliorating their condition, though they are always wishing for it: but if one will wholly apply himself to the making of bows and arrows, whilst another provides food, a third builds huts, a fourth makes garments, and a fifth utensils, they not only become useful to one another, but the callings and employments themselves will, in the same number of years, receive much greater improvements, than if all had been promiscuously followed by every one of the five. HOR. I believe you are perfectly right there; and the truth of what you say is in nothing so conspicuous as it is in watch-making, which is come to a higher degree of perfection than it would have been arrived at yet, if the whole had always remained the employment of one person; and I am persuaded that even the plenty we have of clocks and watches, as well as the exactness and beauty they may be made of, are chiefly owing to the division that has been made of that art into many branches.' The index contains, 'Labour, The usefulness of dividing and subdividing it'. Joseph Harris, *Essay upon Money and Coins*, 1757, pt. i., § 12, treats of the 'usefulness of distinct trades,' or 'the advantages accruing to mankind from their betaking themselves severally to different occupations,' but does not use the phrase 'division of labour'.

2. Ed. 1 reads 'improvements'.

3. Another and perhaps more important reason for taking an example like that which follows is the possibility of exhibiting the ad-

vantage, of division of labour in statistical form.

4. This parenthesis would alone be sufficient to show that those are wrong who believe Smith did not include the separation of employments in 'division of labour'.

5. In Adam Smith's *Lectures*, p. 164, the business is, as here, divided into eighteen operations. This number is doubtless taken from the *Encyclopédie*, tom. v. (published in 1755), *s.v.* Épingle. The article is ascribed to M. Delaire, 'qui décrivait la fabrication de l'épingle dans les ateliers même des ouvriers,' p. 807. In some factories the division was carried further. E. Chambers, *Cyclopædia*, vol. ii., 2nd ed., 1738, and 4th ed., 1741, *s.v.* Pin, makes the number of separate operations twenty-five.

6. Ed. 1 places 'in consequence of the division of labour' here instead of in the line above.

7. 'Pour la célérité du travail et la perfection de l'ouvrage, elles dépendent entièrement de la multitude des ouvriers rassemblés. Lorsqu'une manufacture est nombreuse, chaque opération occupe un homme différent. Tel ouvrier ne fait et ne fera de sa vie qu'une seule et unique chose; tel autre une autre chose: d'où il arrive que chacune s'exécute bien et promptement, et que l'ouvrage le mieux fait est encore celui qu'on a à meilleur marché. D'ailleurs le goût et la façon se perfectionment nécessairement en-

tre un grand nombre d'ouvriers, parce qu'il est difficile qu'il ne s'en rencontre quelques-uns capables de réfléchir, de combiner, et de trouver enfin le seul moyen qui puisse les mettre audessus de leurs semblables; le moyen ou d'épargner la matière, oud'allonger le temps, ou de surfaire l'industrie, soit par une machine nouvelle, soit par une manœuvre plus commode.'— *Encyclopédie*, tom i. (1751), p. 717, *s.v.* Art. All three advantages mentioned in the text above are included here.

8. *I.e.*, it is not the effect of any conscious regulation by the state or society, like the 'law of Sesostris,' that every man should follow the employment of his father, referred to in the corresponding passage in *Lectures*, p. 168. The denial that it is the effect of individual wisdom recognising the advantage of exercising special natural talents comes lower down, p. 19.

9. It is by no means clear what object there could be in exchanging one bone for another.

10. This is apparently directed against Harris, *Money and Coins*, pt. i., § II, and is in accordance with the view of Hume, who asks readers to 'consider how nearly equal all men are in their bodily force, and even in their mental powers and faculties, ere cultivated by education'.—'Of the Original Contract,' in *Essays, Moral and Political*, 1748, p. 291.

DAVID RICARDO

ON FOREIGN TRADE

Under a system of perfectly free commerce, each country naturally devotes its capital and labour to such employments as are most beneficial to each. This pursuit of individual advantage is admirably connected with the universal good of the whole. By stimulating industry, by regarding ingenuity, and by using most efficaciously the peculiar powers bestowed by nature, it distributes labour most effectively and most economically: while, by increasing the general mass of productions, it diffuses general benefit, and binds together by one common tie of interest and intercourse, the universal society of nations throughout the civilized world. It is this principle which determines that wine shall be made in France and Portugal, that corn shall be grown in America and Poland, and that hardware and other goods shall be manufactured in England.

In one and the same country, profits are, generally speaking, always on the same level; or differ only as the employment of capital may be more or less secure and agreeable. It is not so between different countries. If the profits of capital employed in Yorkshire, should exceed those of capital employed in London, capital would speedily move from London to Yorkshire, and an equality of profits would be effected; but if in consequence of the diminished rate of production in the lands of England, from the increase of capital and population, wages should rise, and profits fall, it would not follow that capital and population would necessarily move from England to Holland, or Spain, or Russia, where profits might be higher.

From *Principles of Political Economy and Taxation* (London: J. Murray, 1817).

If Portugal had no commercial connexion with other countries, instead of employing a great part of her capital and industry in the production of wines, with which she purchases for her own use the cloth and hardware of other countries, she would be obliged to devote a part of that capital to the manufacture of those commodities, which she would thus obtain probably inferior in quality as well as quantity.

The quantity of wine which she shall give in exchange for the cloth of England, is not determined by the respective quantities of labour devoted to the production of each, as it would be, if both commodities were manufactured in England, or both in Portugal.

England may be so circumstanced, that to produce the cloth may require the labour of 100 men for one year; and if she attempted to make the wine, it might require the labour of 120 men for the same time. England would therefore find it her interest to import wine, and to purchase it by the exportation of cloth.

To produce the wine in Portugal, might require only the labour of 80 men for one year, and to produce the cloth in the same country, might require the labour of 90 men for the same time. It would therefore be advantageous for her to export wine in exchange for cloth. This exchange might even take place, notwithstanding that the commodity imported by Portugal could be produced there with less labour than in England. Though she could make the cloth with the labour of 90 men, she would import it from a country where it required the labour of 100 men to produce it, because it would be advantageous to her rather to employ her capital in the production of wine, for which she would obtain more cloth from England, than she could produce by diverting a portion of her capital from the cultivation of vines to the manufacture of cloth.

Thus England would give the produce of the labour of 100 men, for the produce of the labour of 80. Such an exchange could not take place between the individuals of the same country. The labour of 100 Englishmen cannot be given for that of 80 Englishmen, but the produce of the labour of 100 Englishmen may be given for the produce of the labour of 80 Portuguese, 60 Russians, or 120 East Indians. The difference in this respect, between a single country and many, is easily accounted for, by considering the difficulty with which capital moves from one country to another, to seek a more profitable employment, and the activity with which it invariably passes from one province to another in the same country.

CLIVE CROOK

BEYOND BELIEF

Paul Samuelson, an undisputed titan of 20th-century economics, was once challenged by the mathematician Stanislaw Ulam to name a single proposition in all social science that was both true and nontrivial. It took a while, but Samuelson finally thought of a good answer: the principle of comparative advantage. This classical theory was true, Samuelson explained, as a matter of mathematical deduction, and its nontriviality was "attested by the thousands of important and intelligent men who have never been able to grasp the doctrine for themselves or to believe it after it was explained to them."

The doctrine in question, devised by David Ricardo in 1817, makes a strong claim about the gains that accrue from trade. It would be difficult to exaggerate the centrality of the idea in modern economics. For nearly 200 years, the principle of comparative advantage, and the ideas about economic policy that flowed from it, divided the world into two camps: those with basic economic literacy, and the rest. Understand-

ing this idea, and advocating it to the world, was part of what it meant to be an economist—especially an American economist.

Lately things have changed. Some of America's most eminent economists, including Samuelson himself, have edged away from that earlier consensus. Their support for liberal trade is far more tepid and tentative than before. The shift is both momentous and disturbing. Just why it happened is a mystery.

To understand this issue, one must first understand what the principle of comparative advantage does *not* say. Intuitively, trade between two countries will make both better off so long as each is especially good at making something different from the other. They should specialize and trade to maximize this absolute advantage—as Adam Smith had earlier advocated in *The Wealth of Nations*. Ricardo's idea was subtler—and remarkable. He showed that there are mutual gains from trade even when one country is better at producing everything. All that matters is that its margin of superior efficiency is greater for some products than for others. The two

From *The Atlantic Monthly* (October 2007).

countries should still specialize, even on the basis of this comparative advantage—if England is slightly worse than France at making wool, and much worse at making wine, it should specialize in wool and trade. However unproductive a country may be, even if it is uncompetitive across the board, it gains from trade.

The proof is a few lines of math, as anyone with an hour or two's training in economics will know. Nearly everybody else, as Samuelson said, finds the idea difficult to believe. People sometimes think they believe it when they don't. The term *comparative advantage* is widely used, to be sure, but *absolute advantage* is what the politician or pundit usually has in mind. If I may speak for those with an hour or two's training, we used to find this confusion quite gratifying. "What happens if a country has no comparative advantage in anything?" people would ask, gravely. How we laughed.

Ricardo's theory did not cover every circumstance. Exceptions to its general rule (potential benefits from protecting "infant industries," for instance) were recognized long ago. Nor did the theory claim that everyone gains; only that gains exceed losses. Nonetheless, the idea and the literature that grew up around it created a strong presumption that free trade was best. Exceptions were narrow and often exotic. The case for liberal trade commanded close to universal agreement among America's leading economists.

Astonishingly, Samuelson himself struck the heaviest new blow against the discipline's confidence on the issue. In 2004, aged 89, he roused himself to a burst of indignation, in the pages of the American Economic Association's *Journal of Economic Perspectives*, at conventional defenses of globalization. They were simplistic, he later told *The New York Times*. Under certain circumstances, he pointed out, the losses from trade could exceed the benefits, not just for particular industries but for the economy as a whole. *BusinessWeek* said Samuelson and others were "beginning to question the basic tenets of free-trade theory. . . . Is it possible that David Ricardo's

economic analysis doesn't work for the 21st century?" Trade skeptics were exultant. Vindication from on high!

Since then, mainstream economists' disenchantment with the old near-certainties has continued to build, and at a gathering rate. Top-tier orthodox economists such as William Baumol, Alan Blinder, Paul Krugman, and Brad De-Long—invariably prefacing the point with the words "Although I'm no protectionist"—have expressed new fears about what imports and offshoring are doing to living standards. Lawrence Summers, Bill Clinton's treasury secretary from 1999 to 2001 (and before that a revered mainstream scholar), is the most surprising new doubter. In a July *Financial Times* forum, he wrote, "It is not even altogether clear that [globalization] benefits America in the aggregate."

Why has this happened? What has changed? I wish I could tell you. No new theoretical insight has emerged to challenge the old pro-trade presumption. Samuelson's 2004 article was mistaken for that in some quarters, but was actually a muddled combination of erroneous new theory on offshoring and uncontested old theory about monopoly power in global markets. The novel part was conclusively rubbished by Columbia's Arvind Panagariya, who showed that Samuelson had got his offshoring model plain wrong. So far, anyway, nobody has explained why offshoring needs a new theory; it is just another kind of trade. The old part—the idea that the United States might see its income fall if trade drives down the prices of its exports—was already encompassed by the earlier consensus.

Jagdish Bhagwati, a preeminent trade scholar, also of Columbia, helped to theorize this danger in the 1950s. As he explained, "immiserizing" trade can arise only under quite unusual circumstances. The principal benefit to a country from openness to trade is cheaper imports. In the ordinary case, additional imports may put some domestic producers out of business, but the displaced capital and labor get applied to more efficient new uses, so the economy as a whole still gains. Suppose, however, that the country had previously been collecting some monopoly profits on its exports. If new trade drives up its production of those goods, their price might fall—and in theory, they could fall by enough to outweigh the gains from cheaper imports. In practical terms, this is an unimportant exception. Bhagwati himself remains a trenchant defender of liberal trade.

"When the facts change, I change my mind," said John Maynard Keynes. "What do you do, sir?" Theory aside, the past decade has supplied a lot of new facts—not least, rising inequality and a protracted stagnation of middle-class earnings. It seems natural to blame the quickening pace of globalization for this. Again, however, no careful examination of the new facts on earnings shows trade or offshoring to be more than minor culprits. When you look closely, the shifts in earnings and the shifts in trade fail to marry up: The periods when imports have risen most rapidly are not the periods when wage pressures have been most intense. Studies suggest that labor-saving technology is a much more powerful force. No empirical work even comes close to supporting the claim that globalization is failing to benefit America in the aggregate. Countless studies have shown, and continue to show, the benefits of trade. Yes, some industries have shrunk or disappeared because of trade, and their workers have suffered the consequences; the pace of this change has probably quickened lately; better policies to insure and compensate the victims are surely called for. But to say this is very different from supposing that open markets hurt the United States as a whole.

The new trade doubters, as their disclaimers insist, are not yet trade-policy revisionists. For the moment they would mostly agree that a presumption in favor of open markets is best—but a weaker presumption than before, to be expressed more tentatively. Militant support for free trade, they seem to feel, will offend opinion at a time when so many are experiencing economic stress. The way to maintain open markets is a softer sell—one that acknowledges, and even seems to validate, popular fears that trade is to blame. But this posture is surely unwise. The doubters are influential, especially in Democratic politics, and their seeming conversion is itself altering the political climate. Would the campaign positions of the leading Democratic contenders for the presidency—so different from Bill Clinton's position on the issue—be so hostile to trade otherwise? Ideas do matter, and for the first time, America's leading orthodox economists are failing to speak with one voice in defense of liberal trade.

Samuelson once regarded the principle of comparative advantage—the modern theory of the gains from trade—as nontrivial. I would go a little further and say it was the greatest gift that economic wisdom ever bestowed on humankind. In a way that Samuelson did not envisage, the doubts that he and others have expressed threaten to make that idea trivial after all—dismissed as nothing more than an arresting curiosity, apt to be oversimplified by blinkered pro-trade types, with no real policy content and no claim on politicians' attention. What a tragedy that would be. And not just because economics would no longer have an answer to Stanislaw Ulam's question.

DOUGLASS C. NORTH

INSTITUTIONS

Institutions are the humanly devised constraints that structure political, economic and social interaction. They consist of both informal constraints (sanctions, taboos, customs, traditions, and codes of conduct), and formal rules (constitutions, laws, property rights). Throughout history, institutions have been devised by human beings to create order and reduce uncertainty in exchange. Together with the standard constraints of economics they define the choice set and therefore determine transaction and production costs and hence the profitability and feasibility of engaging in economic activity. They evolve incrementally, connecting the past with the present and the future; history in consequence is largely a story of institutional evolution in which the historical performance of economies can only be understood as a part of a sequential story. Institutions provide the incentive structure of an economy; as that structure evolves, it shapes the direction of economic change towards growth, stagnation, or decline. In this essay I intend to elaborate on the role of institutions in the performance of economies and illustrate my analysis from economic history.

What makes it necessary to constrain human interaction with institutions? The issue can be most succinctly summarized in a game theoretic context. Wealth-maximizing individuals will usually find it worthwhile to cooperate with other players when the play is repeated, when they possess complete information about the other player's past performance, and when there are small numbers of players. But turn the game upside down. Cooperation is difficult to sustain when the game is not repeated (or there is an endgame), when information on the other play-

From *Journal of Economic Perspectives*, 5, no. 1 (Winter 1991), pp. 97–112.

ers is lacking, and when there are large numbers of players.

These polar extremes reflect contrasting economic settings in real life. There are many examples of simple exchange institutions that permit low cost transacting under the former conditions. But institutions that permit low cost transacting and producing in a world of specialization and division of labor require solving the problems of human cooperation under the latter conditions.

It takes resources to define and enforce exchange agreements. Even if everyone had the same objective function (like maximizing the firm's profits), transacting would take substantial resources; but in the context of individual wealth-maximizing behavior and asymmetric information about the valuable attributes of what is being exchanged (or the performance of agents), transaction costs are a critical determinant of economic performance. Institutions and the effectiveness of enforcement (together with the technology employed) determine the cost of transacting. Effective institutions raise the benefits of cooperative solutions or the costs of defection, to use game theoretic terms. In transaction cost terms, institutions reduce transaction and production costs per exchange so that the potential gains from trade are realizeable. Both political and economic institutions are essential parts of an effective institutional matrix.

The major focus of the literature on institutions and transaction costs has been on institutions as efficient solutions to problems of organization in a competitive framework (Williamson, 1975; 1985). Thus market exchange, franchising, or vertical integration are conceived in this literature as efficient solutions to the complex problems confronting entrepreneurs under various competitive conditions. Valuable as this work has been, such an approach assumes away the central concern of this essay: to explain the varied performance of economies both over time and in the current world.

How does an economy achieve the efficient, competitive markets assumed in the foregoing approach? The formal economic constraints or property rights are specified and enforced by political institutions, and the literature simply takes those as a given. But economic history is overwhelmingly a story of economies that failed to produce a set of economic rules of the game (with enforcement) that induce sustained economic growth. The central issue of economic history and of economic development is to account for the evolution of political and economic institutions that create an economic environment that induces increasing productivity.

Institutions to Capture the Gains from Trade

Many readers will be at least somewhat familiar with the idea of economic history over time as a series of staged stories. The earliest economies are thought of as local exchange within a village (or even within a simple hunting and gathering society). Gradually, trade expands beyond the village: first to the region, perhaps as a bazaar-like economy; then to longer distances, through particular caravan or shipping routes; and eventually to much of the world. At each stage, the economy involves increasing specialization and division of labor and continuously more productive technology. This story of gradual evolution from local autarky to specialization and division of labor was derived from the German historical school. However, there is no implication in this paper that the real historical evolution of economies necessarily paralleled the sequence of stages of exchange described here.[1]

I begin with local exchange within the village or even the simple exchange of hunting and gathering societies (in which women gathered and men hunted). Specialization in this world is rudimentary and self-sufficiency characterizes

most individual households. Small-scale village trade exists within a "dense" social network of informal constraints that facilitates local exchange, and the costs of transacting in this context are low. (Although the basic societal costs of tribal and village organization may be high, they will not be reflected in additional costs in the process of transacting.) People have an intimate understanding of each other, and the threat of violence is a continuous force for preserving order because of its implications for other members of society.[2]

As trade expands beyond a single village, however, the possibilities for conflict over the exchange grow. The size of the market grows and transaction costs increase sharply because the dense social network is replaced; hence, more resources must be devoted to measurement and enforcement. In the absence of a state that enforced contracts, religious precepts usually imposed standards of conduct on the players. Needless to say, their effectiveness in lowering the costs of transacting varied widely, depending on the degree to which these precepts were held to be binding.

The development of long-distance trade, perhaps through caravans or lengthy ship voyages, requires a sharp break in the characteristics of an economic structure. It entails substantial specialization in exchange by individuals whose livelihood is confined to trading and the development of trading centers, which may be temporary gathering places (as were the early fairs in Europe) or more permanent towns or cities. Some economies of scale—for example, in plantation agriculture—are characteristic of this world. Geographic specialization begins to emerge as a major characteristic and some occupational specialization is occurring as well.

The growth of long distance trade poses two distinct transaction cost problems. One is a classical problem of agency, which historically was met by use of kin in long-distance trade. That is, a sedentary merchant would send a relative with the cargo to negotiate sale and to obtain a return cargo. The costliness of measuring performance, the strength of kinship ties, and the price of "defection" all determined the outcome of such agreements. As the size and volume of trade grew, agency problems became an increasingly major dilemma.[3] A second problem consisted of contract negotiation and enforcement in alien parts of the world, where there is no easily available way to achieve agreement and enforce contracts. Enforcement means not only such enforcement of agreements but also protection of the goods and services en route from pirates, brigands, and so on.

The problems of enforcement en route were met by armed forces protecting the ship or caravan or by the payment of tolls or protection money to local coercive groups. Negotiation and enforcement in alien parts of the world entailed typically the development of standardized weights and measures, units of account, a medium of exchange, notaries, consuls, merchant law courts, and enclaves of foreign merchants protected by foreign princes in return for revenue. By lowering information costs and providing incentives for contract fulfillment this complex of institutions, organizations, and instruments made possible transacting and engaging in long-distance trade. A mixture of voluntary and semi-coercive bodies, or at least bodies that effectively could cause ostracism of merchants that didn't live up to agreements, enabled long-distance trade to occur.[4]

This expansion of the market entails more specialized producers. Economies of scale result in the beginnings of hierarchical producing organizations, with full-time workers working either in a central place or in a sequential production process. Towns and some central cities are emerging, and occupational distribution of the population now shows, in addition, a substantial increase in the proportion of the labor force engaged in manufacturing and in services, although the traditional preponderance in agriculture continues. These evolving stages also reflect a significant shift towards urbanization of the society.

Such societies need effective, impersonal contract enforcement, because personal ties, vol-

untaristic constraints, and ostracism are no longer effective as more complex and impersonal forms of exchange emerge. It is not that these personal and social alternatives are unimportant; they are still significant even in today's interdependent world. But in the absence of effective impersonal contracting, the gains from "defection" are great enough to forestall the development of complex exchange. Two illustrations deal with the creation of a capital market and with the interplay between institutions and the technology employed.

A capital market entails security of property rights over time and will simply not evolve where political rulers can arbitrarily seize assets or radically alter their value. Establishing a credible commitment to secure property rights over time requires either a ruler who exercises forebearance and restraint in using coercive force, or the shackling of the ruler's power to prevent arbitrary seizure of assets. The first alternative was seldom successful for very long in the face of the ubiquitous fiscal crises of rulers (largely as a consequence of repeated warfare). The latter entailed a fundamental restructuring of the polity such as occurred in England as a result of the Glorious Revolution of 1688, which resulted in parliamentary supremacy over the crown.[5]

The technology associated with the growth of manufacturing entailed increased fixed capital in plant and equipment, uninterrupted production, a disciplined labor force, and a developed transport network; in short, it required effective factor and product markets. Undergirding such markets are secure property rights, which entail a polity and judicial system to permit low costs contracting, flexible laws permitting a wide latitude of organizational structures, and the creation of complex governance structures to limit the problems of agency in hierarchical organizations.[6]

In the last stage, the one we observe in modern western societies, specialization has increased, agriculture requires a small percentage of the labor force, and markets have become nationwide and worldwide. Economies of scale imply large-scale organization, not only in manufacturing but also in agriculture. Everyone lives by undertaking a specialized function and relying on the vast network of interconnected parts to provide the multitude of goods and services necessary to them. The occupational distribution of the labor force shifts gradually from dominance by manufacturing to dominance, eventually, by what are characterized as services. Society is overwhelmingly urban.

In this final stage, specialization requires increasing percentages of the resources of the society to be engaged in transacting, so that the transaction sector rises to be a large percentage of gross national product. This is so because specialization in trade, finance, banking, insurance, as well as the simple coordination of economic activity, involves an increasing proportion of the labor force.[7] Of necessity, therefore, highly specialized forms of transaction organizations emerge. International specialization and division of labor requires institutions and organizations to safeguard property rights across international boundaries so that capital markets (as well as other kinds of exchange) can take place with credible commitment on the part of the players.

These very schematic stages appear to merge one into another in a smooth story of evolving cooperation. But do they? Does any necessary connection move the players from less complicated to more complicated forms of exchange? At stake in this evolution is not only whether information costs and economies of scale together with the development of improved enforcement of contracts will permit and indeed encourage more complicated forms of exchange, but also whether organizations have the incentive to acquire knowledge and information that will induce them to evolve in more socially productive directions.

In fact, throughout history, there is no necessary reason for this development to occur. Indeed, most of the early forms of organization that I have mentioned in these sections still exist today in parts of the world. There still exist primitive tribal societies; the Suq (bazaar

economies engaged in regional trade) still flourishes in many parts of the world; and while the caravan trade has disappeared, its demise (as well as the gradual undermining of the other two forms of "primitive" exchange) has reflected external forces rather than internal evolution. In contrast, the development of European long-distance trade initiated a sequential development of more complex forms of organization.

The remainder of this paper will examine first some seemingly primitive forms of exchange that failed to evolve and then the institutional evolution that occurred in early modern Europe. The concluding section of the paper will attempt to enunciate why some societies and exchange institutions evolve and others do not, and to apply that framework in the context of economic development in the western hemisphere during the 18th and 19th centuries.

When Institutions Do Not Evolve

In every system of exchange, economic actors have an incentive to invest their time, resources, and energy in knowledge and skills that will improve their material status. But in some primitive institutional settings, the kind of knowledge and skills that will pay off will not result in institutional evolution towards more productive economies. To illustrate this argument, I consider three primitive types of exchange—tribal society, a regional economy with bazaar trading, and the long-distance caravan trade—that are unlikely to evolve from within.

As noted earlier, exchange in a tribal society relies on a dense social network. Elizabeth Colson (1974, p. 59) describes the network this way:

> The communities in which all these people live were governed by a delicate balance of power, always endangered and never to be taken for granted: each person was constantly involved in securing his own position in situations where he had to show his good intentions. Usages and customs appear to be flexible and fluid given that judgement on whether or not someone has done

rightly varies from case to case. . . . But this is be-cause it is the individual who is being judged and not the crime. Under these conditions, a flouting of generally accepted standards is tantamount to a claim to illegitimate power and becomes part of the evidence against one.

The implication of Colson's analysis as well as that of Richard Posner in his account of primitive institutions (1980) is that deviance and innovation are viewed as threats to group survival.

A second form of exchange that has existed for thousands of years, and still exists today in North Africa and the Middle East is that of the Suq, where widespread and relatively impersonal exchange and relatively high costs of transacting exist.[8] The basic characteristics are a multiplicity of small-scale enterprises with as much as 40 to 50 percent of the town's labor force engaged in this exchange process; low fixed costs in terms of rent and machinery; a very finely drawn division of labor; an enormous number of small transactions, each more or less independent of the next; face to face contacts; and goods and services that are not homogeneous.

There are no institutions devoted to assembling and distributing market information; that is, no price quotations, production reports, employment agencies, consumer guides, and so on. Systems of weights and measures are intricate and incompletely standardized. Exchange skills are very elaborately developed, and are the primary determinant of who prospers in the bazaar and who does not. Haggling over terms with respect to any aspect or condition of exchange is pervasive, strenuous, and unremitting. Buying and selling are virtually undifferentiated, essentially a single activity; trading involves a continual search for specific partners, not the mere offers of goods to the general public. Regulation of disputes involves testimony by reliable witnesses to factual matters, not the weighting of competing, juridical principles. Governmental controls over marketplace activity are marginal, decentralized, and mostly rhetorical.

To summarize, the central features of the Suq are (1) high measurement costs; (2) continu-ous effort at clientization (the development of repeat-exchange relationships with other partners, however imperfect); and (3) intensive bargaining at every margin. In essence, the name of the game is to raise the costs of transacting to the other party to exchange. One makes money by having better information than one's adversary.

It is easy to understand why innovation would be seen to threaten survival in a tribal society but harder to understand why these "inefficient" forms of bargaining would continue in the Suq. One would anticipate, in the societies with which we are familiar, that voluntary organizations would evolve to insure against the hazards and uncertainties of such information asymmetries. But that is precisely the issue. What is missing in the Suq are the fundamental underpinnings of institutions that would make such voluntary organizations viable and profitable. These include an effective legal structure and court system to enforce contracts which in turn depend on the development of political institutions that will create such a framework. In their absence there is no incentive to alter the system.

The third form of exchange, caravan trade, illustrates the informal constraints that made trade possible in a world where protection was essential and no organized state existed. Clifford Geertz (1979, p. 137) provides a description of the caravan trades in Morocco at the turn of the century:

> In the narrow sense, a zettata (from the Berber TAZETTAT, 'a small piece of cloth') is a passage toll, a sum paid to a local power . . . for protection when crossing localities where he is such a power. But in fact it is, or more properly was, rather more than a mere payment. It was part of a whole complex of moral rituals, customs with the force of law and the weight of sanctity—centering around the guest-host, client-patron, petitioner-petitioned, exile-protector, suppliant-divinity relations—all of which are somehow of a package in rural Morocco. Entering the tribal world physically, the outreaching trader (or at least his agents) had also to enter it culturally.
>
> Despite the vast variety of particular forms through which they manifest themselves, the char-

acteristics of protection in the Berber societies of the High and Middle Atlas are clear and constant. Protection is personal, unqualified, explicit, and conceived of as the dressing of one man in the reputation of another. The reputation may be political, moral, spiritual, or even idiosyncratic, or, often enough, all four at once. But the essential transaction is that a man who counts 'stands up and says' (*quam wa qal*, as the classical tag has it) to those to whom he counts: 'this man is mine; harm him and you insult me; insult me and you will answer for it.' Benediction (the famous *baraka*), hospitality, sanctuary, and safe passage are alike in this: they rest on the perhaps somewhat paradoxical notion that though personal identity is radically individual in both its roots and its expressions, it is not incapable of being stamped onto the self of someone else.

While tribal chieftains found it profitable to protect merchant caravans they had neither the military muscle nor the political structure to extend, develop, and enforce more permanent property rights.

Institutional Evolution in Early Modern Europe

In contrast to many primitive systems of exchange, long distance trade in early modern Europe from the 11th to the 16th centuries was a story of sequentially more complex organization that eventually led to the rise of the western world. Let me first briefly describe the innovations and then explore some of their underlying sources.[9]

Innovations that lowered transaction costs consisted of organizational changes, instruments, and specific techniques and enforcement characteristics that lowered the costs of engaging in exchange over long distances. These innovations occurred at three cost margins: (1) those that increased the mobility of capital, (2) those that lowered information costs, and (3) those that spread risk. Obviously, the categories are overlapping, but they provide a useful way to distinguish cost-reducing features of transacting.

All of these innovations had their origins in earlier times; most of them were borrowed from medieval Italian city states or Islam or Byzantium and then elaborated upon.

Among the innovations that enhanced the mobility of capital were the techniques and methods evolved to evade usury laws. The variety of ingenious ways by which interest was disguised in loan contracts ranged from "penalties for late payment," to exchange rate manipulation (Lopez and Raymond, 1955, p. 163), to the early form of the mortgage; but all increased the costs of contracting. The costliness of usury laws was not only that they made the writing of contracts to disguise interests complex and cumbersome, but also that enforceability of such contracts became more problematic. As the demand for capital increased and evasion became more general, usury laws gradually broke down and rates of interest were permitted. In consequence, the costs of writing contracts and the costs of enforcing them declined.

A second innovation that improved the mobility of capital, and the one that has received the most attention, was the evolution of the bill of exchange (a dated order to pay, say 120 days after issuance, conventionally drawn by a seller against a purchaser of goods delivered) and particularly the development of techniques and instruments that allowed for its negotiability as well as for the development of discounting methods. Negotiability and discounting in turn depended on the creation of institutions that would permit their use and the development of centers where such events could occur: first in fairs, such as the Champagne fairs that played such a prominent part in economic exchange in 12th and 13th century Europe; then through banks; and finally through financial houses that could specialize in discounting. These developments were a function not only of specific institutions but also of the scale of economic activity. Increasing volume obviously made such institutional developments possible. In addition to the economies of scale necessary for the development of the bills of exchange, improved enforceability of contracts was critical, and the interrelationship between the development of accounting and auditing methods and their use as evidence in the collection of debts and in the enforcement of contracts was an important part of this process (Yamey, 1949; Watts and Zimmerman, 1983).

Still a third innovation affecting the mobility of capital arose from the problems associated with maintaining control of agents involved in long distance trade. The traditional resolution of this problem in medieval and early modern times was the use of kinship and family ties to bind agents to principals. However, as the size and scope of merchant trading empires grew, the extension of discretionary behavior to others than kin of the principal required the development of more elaborate accounting procedures for monitoring the behavior of agents.

The major developments in the area of information costs were the printing of prices of various commodities, as well as the printing of manuals that provided information on weights, measures, customs, brokerage fees, postal systems, and, particularly, the complex exchange rates between monies in Europe and the trading world. Obviously these developments were primarily a function of the volume of international trade and therefore a consequence of economies of scale.

The final innovation was the transformation of uncertainty into risk. By uncertainty, I mean here a condition wherein one cannot ascertain the probability of an event and therefore cannot arrive at a way of insuring against such an occurrence. Risk, on the other hand, implies the ability to make an actuarial determination of the likelihood of an event and hence insure against such an outcome. In the modern world, insurance and portfolio diversification are methods for converting uncertainty into risks and thereby reducing, through the provision of a hedge against variability, the costs of transacting. In the medieval and early modern world, precisely the same conversion occurred. For example, marine insurance evolved from sporadic individual contracts covering partial payments for losses to contracts issued by specialized firms. As De Roover (1945, p. 198) described:

> By the fifteenth century marine insurance was established on a secure basis. The wording of the policies had already become stereotyped and changed very little during the next three or four hundred years. . . . In the sixteenth century it was already current practice to use printed forms provided with a few blank spaces for the name of the ship, the name of the master, the amount of the insurance, the premium, and a few other items that were apt to change from one contract to another.

Another example of the development of actuarial, ascertainable risk was the business organization that spread risk through either portfolio diversification or institutions that permitted a large number of investors to engage in risky activities. For example, the commenda was a contract employed in long distance trade between a sedentary partner and an active partner who accompanied the goods. It evolved from its Jewish, Byzantine, and Muslim origins (Udovitch, 1962) through its use at the hands of Italians to the English Regulated Company and finally the Joint Stock Company, thus providing an evolutionary story of the institutionalization of risk.

These specific innovations and particular institutional instruments evolved from interplay between two fundamental economic forces: the economies of scale associated with a growing volume of trade, and the development of improved mechanisms to enforce contracts at lower costs. The causation ran both ways. That is, the increasing volume of long distance trade raised the rate of return to merchants of devising effective mechanisms for enforcing contracts. In turn, the development of such mechanisms lowered the costs of contracting and made trade more profitable, thereby increasing its volume.

The process of developing new enforcement mechanisms was a long one. While a variety of courts handled commercial disputes, it is the development of enforcement mechanisms by merchants themselves that is significant. Enforceability appears to have had its beginnings in the development of internal codes of conduct in fraternal orders of guild merchants; those who did not live up to them were threatened with ostracism. A further step was the evolution of mercantile law. Merchants carried with them in long distance trade mercantile codes of conduct, so that Pisan laws passed into the sea codes of Marseilles; Oleron and Lubeck gave laws to the north of Europe, Barcelona to the south of Europe; and from Italy came the legal principle of insurance and bills of exchange (Mitchell, 1969, p. 156).

The development of more sophisticated accounting methods and of notarial records provided evidence for ascertaining facts in disputes. The gradual blending of the voluntaristic structure of enforcement of contracts via internal merchant organizations with enforcement by the state is an important part of the story of increasing the enforceability of contracts. The long evolution of merchant law from its voluntary beginnings and the differences in resolutions that it had with both the common and Roman law are a part of the story.

The state was a major player in this whole process, and there was continuous interplay between the state's fiscal needs and its credibility in its relationships with merchants and the citizenry in general. In particular, the evolution of capital markets was critically influenced by the policies of the state, since to the extent the state was bound by commitments that it would not confiscate assets or use its coercive power to increase uncertainty in exchange, it made possible the evolution of financial institutions and the creation of more efficient capital markets. The shackling of arbitrary behavior of rulers and the development of impersonal rules that successfully bound both the state and voluntary organizations were a key part of this whole process. The development of an institutional process by which government debt could be circulated, become a part of a regular capital market, and be funded by regular sources of taxation was also a key part (Tracy, 1985; North and Weingast, 1989).

It was in the Netherlands, Amsterdam specifically, that these diverse innovations and institutions were combined to create the predecessor of the efficient modern set of markets that make possible the growth of exchange and commerce. An open immigration policy attracted businessmen. Efficient methods of financing long distance trade were developed, as were capital markets and discounting methods in financial houses that lowered the costs of underwriting this trade. The development of techniques for spreading risk and transforming uncertainty into actuarial, ascertainable risks as well as the creation of large scale markets that allowed for lowering the costs of information, and the development of negotiable government indebtedness all were a part of this story (Barbour, 1949).

Contrasting Stories of Stability and Change

These contrasting stories of stability and change go to the heart of the puzzle of accounting for changes in the human economic condition. In the former cases, maximizing activity by the actors will not induce increments to knowledge and skills which will modify the institutional framework to induce greater productivity; in the latter case, evolution is a consistent story of incremental change induced by the private gains to be realized by productivity-raising organizational institutional changes.

What distinguished the institutional context of western Europe from the other illustrations? The traditional answer of economic historians has been competition among the fragmented European political units accentuated by changing military technology which forced rulers to seek more revenue (by making bargains with constituents) in order to survive (North and Thomas, 1973; Jones, 1981; Rosenberg and Birdzell, 1986). That is surely part of the answer; political competition for survival in early modern Europe was certainly more acute than in other parts of the world. But it is only a partial answer. Why the contrasting results within western Europe? Why did Spain, the great power of

16th century Europe, decline while the Netherlands and England developed?

To begin to get an answer (and it is only a beginning), we need to dig deeper into two key (and related) parts of the puzzle: the relationship between the basic institutional framework, the consequent organizational structure, and institutional change; and the path dependent nature of economic change that is a consequence of the increasing returns characteristic of an institutional framework.

In the institutional accounts given earlier, the direction and form of economic activity by individuals and organizations reflected the opportunities thrown up by the basic institutional framework of customs, religious precepts, and formal rules (and the effectiveness of enforcement). Whether we examine the organization of trade in the Suq or that in the Champagne Fairs, in each case the trader was constrained by the institutional framework, as well as the traditional constraints common to economic theory.

In each case the trader would invest in acquiring knowledge and skills to increase his wealth. But in the former case, improved knowledge and skills meant getting better information on opportunities and having greater bargaining skills than other traders, since profitable opportunities came from being better informed and being a more skilled bargainer than other traders. Neither activity induced alteration in the basic institutional framework. On the other hand, while a merchant at a medieval European fair would certainly gain from acquiring such information and skills, he would gain also from devising ways to bond fellow merchants, to establish merchant courts, to induce princes to protect goods from brigandage in return for revenue, to devise ways to discount bills of exchange. His investment in knowledge and skills would gradually and incrementally alter the basic institutional framework.

Note that the institutional evolution entailed not only voluntary organizations that expanded trade and made exchange more productive, but also the development of the state to take over protection and enforcement of property rights as impersonal exchange made contract enforcement increasingly costly for voluntary organizations which lacked effective coercive power. Another essential part of the institutional evolution entails a shackling of the arbitrary behavior of the state over economic activity.

Path dependence is more than the incremental process of institutional evolution in which yesterday's institutional framework provides the opportunity set for today's organizations and individual entrepreneurs (political or economic). The institutional matrix consists of an interdependent web of institutions and consequent political and economic organizations that are characterized by massive increasing returns.[10] That is, the organizations owe their existence to the opportunities provided by the institutional framework. Network externalities arise because of the initial setup costs (like the de novo creation of the U.S. Constitution in 1787), the learning effects described above, coordination effects via contracts with other organizations, and adaptive expectations arising from the prevalence of contracting based on the existing institutions.

When economies do evolve, therefore, nothing about that process assures economic growth. It has commonly been the case that the incentive structure provided by the basic institutional framework creates opportunities for the consequent organizations to evolve, but the direction of their development has not been to promote productivity-raising activities. Rather, private profitability has been enhanced by creating monopolies, by restricting entry and factor mobility, and by political organizations that established property rights that redistributed rather than increased income.

The contrasting histories of the Netherlands and England on the one hand and Spain on the other hand reflected the differing opportunity sets of the actors in each case. To appreciate the pervasive influence of path dependence, let us extend the historical account of Spain and England to the economic history of the New World and the striking contrast in the history of the areas north and south of the Rio Grande River.

In the case of North America, the English colonies were formed in the century when the struggle between Parliament and the Crown was coming to a head. Religious and political diversity in the mother country was paralleled in the colonies. The general development in the direction of local political control and the growth of assemblies was unambiguous. Similarly, the colonist carried over free and common socage tenure of land (fee simple ownership rights) and secure property rights in other factor and product markets.

The French and Indian War from 1755–63 is a familiar breaking point in American history. British efforts to impose a very modest tax on colonial subjects, as well as curb westward migration, produced a violent reaction that led via a series of steps, by individuals and organizations, to the Revolution, the Declaration of Independence, the Articles of Confederation, the Northwest Ordinance, and the Constitution, a sequence of institutional expressions that formed a consistent evolutionary pattern despite the precariousness of the process. While the American Revolution created the United States, post-revolutionary history is only intelligible in terms of the continuity of informal and formal institutional constraints carried over from before the Revolution and incrementally modified (Hughes, 1989).

Now turn to the Spanish (and Portuguese) case in Latin America. In the case of the Spanish Indies, conquest came at the precise time that the influence of the Castilian Cortes (parliament) was declining and the monarchy of Castile, which was the seat of power of Spain, was firmly establishing centralized bureaucratic control over Spain and the Spanish Indies.[11] The conquerors imposed a uniform religion and a uniform bureaucratic administration on an already existing agricultural society. The bureaucracy detailed every aspect of political and economic policy. There were recurrent crises over the problem of agency. Wealth-maximizing behavior by organizations and entrepreneurs (political and economic) entailed getting control of, or influence over, the bureaucratic machinery. While the nineteenth century Wars of Independence in Latin America turned out to be a struggle for control of the bureaucracy and consequent policy as between local colonial control and imperial control, nevertheless the struggle was imbued with the ideological overtones that stemmed from the American and French revolutions. Independence brought U.S.-inspired constitutions, but the results were radically different. In contrast to those of the United States, Latin American federal schemes and efforts at decentralization had one thing in common after the Revolutions. None worked. The gradual country-by-country reversion to centralized bureaucratic control characterized Latin America in the 19th century.[12]

The divergent paths established by England and Spain in the New World have not converged despite the mediating factors of common ideological influences. In the former, an institutional framework has evolved that permits complex impersonal exchange necessary to political stability as well as to capture the potential economic benefits of modern technology. In the latter, "personalistic" relationships are still the key to much of the political and economic exchange. They are the consequence of an evolving institutional framework that has produced erratic economic growth in Latin America, but neither political nor economic stability, nor realization of the potential of modern technology.

The foregoing comparative sketch probably raises more questions than it answers about institutions and the role that they play in the performance of economies. Under what conditions does a path get reversed, like the revival of Spain in modern times? What is it about informal constraints that gives them such a pervasive influence upon the long-run character of economies? What is the relationship between formal and informal constraints? How does an economy develop the informal constraints that make individuals constrain their behavior so that they make political and judicial systems effective forces for third party enforcement? Clearly we have a long way to go for complete answers, but the modern study of institutions offers the promise of dramatic new understanding of economic performance and economic change.

NOTES

1. In an article written many years ago (North, 1955), I pointed out that many regional economies evolved from the very beginning as export economies and built their development around the export sector. This is in comparison and in contrast to the old stage theory of history derived from the German historical school, in which the evolution was always from local autarky to gradual evolution of specialization and division of labor. It is this last pattern that is described here, even though it may not characterize the particular evolution that in fact has occurred.

2. For an excellent summary of the anthropological literature dealing with trade in tribal societies, see Elizabeth Colson (1974).

3. Jewish traders in the Mediterranean in the 11th century "solved" the agency problem as a result of close community relationships amongst themselves that lowered information costs and enabled them to act as a group to ostracize and retaliate against agents who violated their commercial code. See Avner Greif (1989).

4. Philip Curtin's *Cross Cultural Trade in World History* (1984) summarizes a good deal of the literature, but is short on analysis and examination of the mechanisms essential to the structure of such trade. The Cambridge Economic History, Volume III (1966), has more useful details on the organization of such trade.

5. North and Weingast (1989) provide a history and analysis of the political institutions of 17th century England leading up to the Revolution of 1688 and of the consequences for the development of the English capital market.

6. See North (1981), particularly chapter 13, and Chandler (1977). Joseph Stiglitz's (1989) essay, "Markets, Market Failures, and Development," details some of the theoretical issues.

7. The transaction sector (that proportion of transaction costs going through the market and therefore measureable) of the U.S. economy was 25 percent of GNP in 1870 and 45 percent of GNP in 1970 (Wallis and North, 1986).

8. There is an extensive literature on the Suq. A sophisticated analysis (on which I have relied) focused on the Suq in Sefrou, Morocco is contained in Geertz, Geertz, and Rosen (1979).

9. For a much more detailed description and analysis of the evolution of European trade see Tracy (forthcoming), particularly Volume II. For a game theoretic analysis of one aspect of this trade revival see Milgrom, North and Weingast (1990).

10. The concept of path dependence was developed by Brian Arthur (1988, 1989) and Paul David (1985) to explore the path of technological change. I believe the concept has equal explanatory power in helping us understand institutional change. In both cases increasing returns are the key to path dependence, but in the case of institutional change the process is more complex because of the key role of political organizations in the process.

11. The subsequent history of Spanish rise and decline is summarized in North and Thomas (1973).

12. For a summary account of the Latin American experience, see Veliz (1980) or Glade (1969).

REFERENCES

Arthur, W. Brian, "Self-Reinforcing Mechanisms in Economics." In Anderson, Phillip W., Kenneth J. Arrow, and David Pines, eds., *The*

Economy as an Evolving Complex System. Reading, MA: Addison-Wesley, 1988.

Arthur, W. Brian, "Competing Technologies, Increasing Returns, and Lock-In by Historical Events," *Economic Journal*, 1989, 99, 116–31.

Barbour, Violet, "Capitalism in Amsterdam in the Seventeenth Century," *Johns Hopkins University Studies in Historical and Political Science*, Volume LXVIII. Baltimore: The Johns Hopkins University Press, 1949.

The Cambridge Economic History. Cambridge: Cambridge University Press, 1966.

Chandler, Alfred, *The Visible Hand.* Cambridge: The Belknap Press, 1977.

Colson, Elizabeth, *Tradition and Contract: The Problem of Order.* Chicago: Adeline Publishing, 1974.

Curtin, Philip D., *Cross-Cultural Trade in World History.* Cambridge: Cambridge University Press, 1984.

David, Paul, "Clio and the Economics of QWERTY," *American Economic Review.* 1985, 75, 332–37.

De Roover, F. E., "Early Examples of Marine Insurance," *Journal of Economic History*, November 1945, 5, 172–200.

Geertz, C., H. Geertz, and L. Rosen, *Meaning and Order in Moroccan Society.* Cambridge: Cambridge University Press, 1979.

Glade, W. P., *The Latin American Economies: A Study of Their Institutional Evolution.* New York: American Book, 1969.

Greif, Avner, "Reputation and Economic Institutions in Medieval Trade: Evidences from the Geniza Documents," *Journal of Economic History*, 1989.

Hughes, J. R. T., "A World Elsewhere: The Importance of Starting English." In Thompson, F. M. L., ed., *Essays in Honor of H. J. Ha-bakkuk.* Oxford: Oxford University Press, 1989.

Jones, E. L., *The European Miracle: Environments, Economies, and Geopolitics in the History of Europe and Asia.* Cambridge: Cambridge University Press, 1981.

Kalt, J. P. and M. A. Zupan, "Capture and Ideology in the Economic Theory of Politics,"
American Economic Review, 1984, 74, 279–300.

Lopez, Robert S., and Irving W. Raymond, *Medieval Trade in the Mediterranean World.* New York: Columbia University Press, 1955.

Milgrom, P. R., D. C. North, and B. R. Weingast, "The Role of Institutions in the Revival of Trade: The Medieval Law Merchant," *Economics and Politics*, March 1990, II.

Mitchell, William, *An Essay on the Early History of the Law Merchant.* New York: Burt Franklin Press, 1969.

Nelson, Douglas, and Eugene Silberberg, "Ideology and Legislator Shirking," *Economic Inquiry*, January 1987, 25, 15–25.

North, Douglass C., "Location Theory and Regional Economic Growth," *Journal of Political Economy*, June 1955, LXIII, 243–258.

North, Douglass C., *Structure and Change in Economic History.* New York: Norton, 1981.

North, Douglass C., and Robert Thomas, *The Rise of the Western World: A New Economic History.* Cambridge: Cambridge University Press, 1973.

North, Douglass C., and Barry R. Weingast, "The Evolution of Institutions Governing Public Choice in 17th Century England," *Journal of Economic History*, November 1989, 5, 172–200.

Posner, Richard, "A Theory of Primitive Society, with Special Reference to the Law," *Journal of Law and Economics*, April 1980, XXIII, 1–54.

Rosenberg, Nathan, and L. E. Bridzell, *How the West Grew Rich: The Economic Transformation of the Industrial World.* New York: Basic Books, 1986.

Stiglitz, Joseph, "Markets, Market Failures, and Development," *American Economic Review*, 1989, 79, 197–203.

Tracy, James, *A Financial Revolution in the Hapsburg Netherlands: Renters and Rentiers in the Country of Holland, 1515–1565.* Berkeley: University of California Press, 1985.

Tracy, James, *The Rise of Merchant Empires.* Cambridge: Cambridge University Press, 1990.

Udovitch, Abraham, "At the Origins of the Western Commenda: Islam, Israel, Byzanteum?" *Speculum*, April 1962, *XXXVII*, 198–207.

Veliz, C., *The Centralist Tradition of Latin America*. Princeton: Princeton University Press, 1980.

Wallis, John J., and Douglass C. North, "Measuring the Transaction Sector in the American Economy, 1870–1970." In Engermann, Stanley, and Robert Gallman, eds., *Income and Wealth: Long-Term Factors in American Economic Growth*. Chicago: University of Chicago Press, 1986.

Watts, R., and J. Zimmerman, "Agency Problems, Auditing, and the Theory of the Firm: Some Evidence," *Journal of Law and Economics*, October 1983, *XXVI*, 613–633.

Williamson, Oliver E., *Markets and Hierarchies: Analysis and Antitrust Implications*. New York: Free Press, 1975.

Williamson, Oliver E., *The Economic Institutions of Capitalism*. New York: Free Press, 1985.

Yaney, B. S., "Scientific Bookkeeping and the Rise of Capitalism," *Economic History Review*, Second Series, 1949, *II*, 99–113.

DARON ACEMOGLU

ROOT CAUSES: A HISTORICAL APPROACH TO ASSESSING THE ROLE OF INSTITUTIONS IN ECONOMIC DEVELOPMENT

Tremendous differences in incomes and standards of living exist today between the rich and the poor countries of the world. Average per capita income in sub-Saharan Africa, for example, is less than one-twentieth that in the United States. Explanations for why the economic fortunes of countries have diverged so much abound. Poor countries, such as those in sub-Saharan Africa, Central America, or South Asia, often lack functioning markets, their populations are poorly educated, and their machinery and technology are outdated or nonexistent. But these are only *proximate* causes of poverty, begging the question of why these places don't have better markets, better human capital, more investments, and better machinery and technology. There must be some *fundamental* causes leading to these outcomes, and via these channels, to dire poverty.

The two main candidates to explain the fundamental causes of differences in prosperity between countries are geography and institutions. The *geography hypothesis*, which has a large following both in the popular imagination and in academia, maintains that the geography, climate, and ecology of a society shape both its technology and the incentives of its inhabitants. It emphasizes forces of nature as a primary factor in the poverty of nations. The alternative, the *institutions hypothesis*, is about human influences. According to this view, some societies have good institutions that encourage investment in machinery, human capital, and better technologies, and, consequently, these countries achieve economic prosperity.

Good institutions have three key characteristics: enforcement of property rights for a broad cross section of society, so that a variety of individuals have incentives to invest and take part in economic life; constraints on the actions of elites, politicians, and other powerful groups, so that these people cannot expropriate the in-

From *Finance & Development* (June 2003), pp. 27–30.

comes and investments of others or create a highly uneven playing field; and some degree of equal opportunity for broad segments of society, so that individuals can make investments, especially in human capital, and participate in productive economic activities. These good institutions contrast with conditions in many societies of the world, throughout history and today, where the rule of law is applied selectively; property rights are nonexistent for the vast majority of the population; the elites have unlimited political and economic power, and only a small fraction of citizens have access to education, credit, and production opportunities.

Geography's Influence

If you want to believe that geography is the key, look at a world map. Locate the poorest places in the world where per capita incomes are less than one-twentieth those in the United States. You will find almost all of them close to the equator, in very hot regions that experience periodic torrential rains and where, by definition, tropical diseases are widespread.

However, this evidence does not establish that geography is a primary influence on prosperity. It is true there is a *correlation* between geography and prosperity. But correlation does not prove causation. Most important, there are often omitted factors driving the associations we observe in the data.

Similarly, if you look around the world, you'll see that almost no wealthy country achieves this position without institutions protecting the property rights of investors and imposing some control over the government and elites. Once again, however, this correlation between institutions and economic development could reflect omitted factors or reverse causality.

To make progress in understanding the relative roles of geographic and institutional factors, we need to find a source of exogenous variation in institutions—in other words, a natural experi-

ment where institutions change for reasons unrelated to potential omitted factors (and geographic factors remain constant, as they almost always do).

The colonization of much of the globe by Europeans starting in the fifteenth century provides such a natural experiment. The colonization experience transformed the institutions in many lands conquered or controlled by Europeans but, by and large, had no effect on their geographies. Therefore, if geography is the key factor determining the economic potential of an area or a country, the places that were rich before the arrival of the Europeans should have remained rich after the colonization experience and, in fact, should still be rich today. In other words, since the key determinant of prosperity remains the same, we should see a high degree of persistence in economic outcomes. If, on the other hand, it is institutions that are central, then those places where good institutions were introduced or developed should be richer than those in which Europeans introduced or maintained extractive institutions to plunder resources or exploit the non-European population.

Historical evidence suggests that Europeans indeed pursued very different colonization strategies, with very different associated institutions, in various colonies. At one extreme, Europeans set up exclusively extractive institutions, exemplified by the Belgian colonization of the Congo, slave plantations in the Caribbean, and forced labor systems in the mines of Central America. These institutions neither protected the property rights of regular citizens nor constrained the power of elites. At the other extreme, Europeans founded a number of colonies where they created settler societies, replicating—and often improving—the European form of institutions protecting private property. Primary examples of this mode of colonization include Australia, Canada, New Zealand, and the United States. The settlers in these societies also managed to place significant constraints on elites and politicians, even if they had to fight to achieve this objective.

Shifting prosperity

Countries that were rich in 1500 are among the less-well-off societies today.

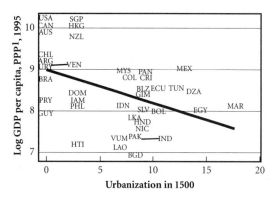

Urbanization in 1500

Source: Author.
Note: ARG = Argentina,   AUS = Ausralia,   BGD = Bangladesh,   BLZ = Belize,   BOL = Bolivia,   BRA = Brazil,   CAN = Canada,   CHL = Chile,   COL = Colombia,   CRI = Costa Rica,   DOM = Dominican Republic, DZA = Albania,   ECU = Ecuador,   EGY = Egypt, GTM = Guatemala, GUY = Guyana, HKG = Hong Kong SAR, HND = Honduras, HTI = Haiti, IDN = Idonesia, IND = India, LAO = Lao People's Democratic Republic, LKA = Sri Lanka, MAR = Morocco, MEX = Mexico, MYS = Malaysia, NIC = Nicaragua, NZL = New Zealand, PAK = Pakistan, PAN = Panama,   PER = Peru,   PHL = Philippines, PRY = Paraguay, SGP = Singapore, SLV = El Salvador, TUN = Tunisia, URY = Uruguay, USA = United States, VEN = Venezuela, VNM = Vietnam
[1]Purchasing power parity.

Reversal of Fortune

So what happened to economic development after colonization? Did places that were rich before colonization remain rich, as suggested by the geography hypothesis? Or did economic fortunes change systematically as a result of the changes in institutions?

The historical evidence shows no evidence of the persistence suggested by the geography hypothesis. On the contrary, there is a remarkable *reversal of fortune* in economic prosperity. Societies like the Mughals in India and the Aztecs and the Incas in America that were among the richest civilizations in 1500 are among the poorer societies of today. In contrast, countries occupying the territories of the less developed civilizations in North America, New Zealand, and Australia are now much *richer* than those in the lands of the Mughals, the Aztecs, and the Incas. Moreover, the reversal of fortune is not confined to this comparison. Using various proxies for prosperity before modern times, we can show that the reversal is a much more widespread phenomenon. For example, before industrialization, only relatively developed societies could sustain significant urbanization, so urbanization rates are a relatively good proxy for prosperity before European colonization. The chart here shows a strong negative relationship between urbanization rates in 1500 and income per capita today. That is, the former European colonies that are relatively rich today are those that were poor before the Europeans arrived.

This reversal is prima facie evidence against the most standard versions of the geography hypothesis discussed above: it cannot be that the climate, ecology, or disease environments of the tropical areas have condemned these countries to poverty today, because these same areas with the same climate, ecology, and disease environment were richer than the temperate areas 500 years ago. Although it is possible that the reversal may be related to geographic factors whose effects on economic prosperity vary over time— for example, certain characteristics that first cause prosperity then condemn nations to poverty—there is no evidence of any such factor or any support for sophisticated geography hypotheses of this sort.

Is the reversal of fortune consistent with the institutions hypothesis? The answer is yes. In fact, once we look at the variation in colonization strategies, we see that the reversal of fortune is exactly what the institutions hypothesis predicts. European colonialism made Europeans the most politically powerful group, with the capability to influence institutions more than any indigenous group was able to at the time. In places where Europeans did not settle and cared little about aggregate output and the welfare of the population, in places where there was a large population that could be coerced and employed cheaply in mines or in agriculture or simply taxed, in places where there were resources to be extracted, Europeans pursued the strategy of setting up extractive institutions or taking over existing extractive institutions and hierarchical structures. In those colonies, there were no constraints on the power of the elites (which were typically the Europeans themselves and their allies) and no civil or property rights for the majority of the population; in fact, many of them were forced into labor or enslaved. Contrasting with this pattern, in colonies where there was little to be extracted, where most of the land was empty, where the disease environment was favorable, Europeans settled in large numbers and developed laws and institutions to ensure that they themselves were protected, in both their political and their economic lives. In these colonies, the institutions were therefore much more conducive to investment and economic growth.

This evidence does not mean that geography does not matter at all, however. Which places were rich and which were poor before Europeans arrived might have been determined by geographic factors. These geographic factors also likely influenced the institutions that Europeans introduced. For example, the climate and soil quality in the Caribbean made it productive to grow sugar there, encouraging the development of a plantation system based on slavery. What the evidence shows instead is that geography neither condemns a nation to poverty nor guarantees its economic success. If you want to understand why a country is poor today, you have to look at its institutions rather than its geography.

No Natural Gravitation

If institutions are so important for economic prosperity, why do some societies choose or end up with bad institutions? Moreover, why do these bad institutions persist long after their disastrous consequences are apparent? Is it an accident of history or the result of misconceptions or mistakes by societies or their policymakers? Recent empirical and theoretical research suggests that the answer is no: there are no compelling reasons to think that societies will naturally gravitate toward good institutions. Institutions not only affect the economic prospects of nations but are also central to the distribution of income among individuals and groups in society—in other words, institutions not only affect the size of the social pie, but also how it is distributed.

This perspective implies that a potential change from dysfunctional and bad institutions toward better ones that will increase the size of the social pie may nonetheless be blocked when such a change significantly reduces the slice that powerful groups receive from the pie and when they cannot be credibly compensated for this loss. That there is no natural gravitation toward good institutions is illustrated by the attitudes of the landed elites and the emperors in Austria-Hungary and in Russia during the nineteenth century. These elite groups blocked industrialization and even the introduction of railways and protected the old regime because they realized capitalist growth and industrialization would reduce their power and their privileges.

Similarly, European colonists did not set up institutions to benefit society as a whole. They chose good institutions when it was in their interests to do so, when they would be the ones living under the umbrella of these institutions, as in much of the New World. In contrast, they introduced or maintained existing extractive institutions when it was in their interest to extract resources from the non-European populations of the colonies, as in much of Africa, Central America, the Caribbean, and South Asia. Furthermore, these extractive institutions showed no sign of evolving into better institutions, either under European control or once these colonies gained independence. In almost all cases, we can link the persistence of extractive institutions to the fact that, even after independence, the elites in these societies had a lot to lose from institutional reform. Their political power and claim to economic rents rested on the existing extractive institutions, as best illustrated by the Caribbean plantation owners whose wealth directly depended on slavery and extractive institutions. Any reform of the system, however beneficial for the country as a whole, would be a direct threat to the owners.

European colonialism is only one part of the story of the institutions of the former colonies, and many countries that never experienced European colonialism nonetheless suffer from institutional problems (while certain other former European colonies have arguably some of the best institutions in the world today). Nevertheless, the perspective developed in this article applies to these cases as well: institutional problems are important in a variety of instances, and, in most of these, the source of institutional problems and the difficulty of institutional reform lie in the fact that any major change creates winners and losers, and the potential losers are often powerful enough to resist change.

The persistence of institutions and potential resistance to reform do not mean that institutions are unchanging. There is often significant institutional evolution, and even highly dysfunctional institutions can be successfully transformed. For example, Botswana managed to build a functioning democracy after its independence from Britain and become the fastest-growing country in the world. Institutional change will happen either when groups that favor change become powerful enough to impose it on the potential losers, or when societies can strike a bargain with potential losers so as to credibly compensate them after the change takes place or, perhaps, shield them from the most adverse consequences of these changes. Recognizing the importance of institutions in economic development and the often formidable barriers to beneficial institutional reform is the first step toward significant progress in jump-starting rapid growth in many areas of the world today.

5 DEMOCRATIC REGIMES

If democracy is something positive to be strived for, how does it come about and what are its necessary components? The readings in this section try to address these questions by considering the origins and institutions of democracy as well as the dangers that democracy faces. Much of this work has emerged in the past fifteen years, following the end of the Cold War and the subsequent wave of democratization throughout much of the world.

Fareed Zakaria's "Brief History of Human Liberty" (2003) builds on our earlier discussion of the state in Chapter 2 to help us understand why modern democracy first emerged in Europe. With the collapse of the Roman Empire, Europe broke into an enormous number of rival political units, leading to diversity, competition, and interstate conflict that would help forge the modern state. These early states were often highly decentralized, leaving power in the hands of a local elite that could check a monarch's ability to gather absolute power. At the same time, the early division of church and state also weakened the ability of any leader to claim both spiritual and earthly authority, something reinforced by the Protestant Reformation. This decentralization of power allowed for greater individual liberties, helping to foster both capitalist development and the idea of democratic control. In the end, Zakaria concludes that democracy requires the development of the entrenched habits of liberty—individual rights supported by the rule of law—something not easily or intentionally created. His comments in many ways reflect Diamond's discussion of hybrid regimes in Chapter 6.

While Zakaria focuses on the origins of democracy, other scholars are concerned with how its institutions are actually constructed, and to what effect. In their widely cited work "What Democracy Is . . . and Is Not" (1991), Schmitter and Karl provide an overview of some of the most important elements, among them government accountability, public competition, and the mechanisms of elections and majority rule. Democracy is not just a set of mechanisms, however; it is also a set of agreed-upon principles promising that the members of the democracy will abide by the competitive outcome. But beyond these basic elements there is a wide array of democratic types,

*differing in such areas as how majorities are structured, the nature of execu-
tive power, the kinds of checks and balances that will be used to stabilize
power, or the way power is decentralized. There is no one necessary mix for
democracy, and how these institutions are combined or modified depends on
the historical circumstances and the contemporary challenges of the country
in question.*

*However, some scholars do believe that certain kinds of democratic com-
binations are more stable or responsive than others. Lijphart (1996) investigates two of the most important differences among democracies: presidential
versus parliamentary rule, and proportional representation (PR) versus plurality (also known as single-member district or first past the post) elections.
Presidentialism and plurality elections promote majoritarian or a "winner
take all" form of government; proportional representation tends to generate
more consensus in politics. Is one a better form than the other? Lijphart concludes that the parliamentary-PR system is superior to the presidential-
plurality system found in the United States in terms of minority rights,
participation, and economic equality. So, how democracies are constructed
can have a distinct impact on the kinds of policies and outcomes they
produce.*

*Finally, we turn to a consideration of social capital and participation. The
concept of social capital has become widely discussed in political science and
policy circles, due largely to the work of Robert Putnam and his 2000 book,*
Bowling Alone. *Drawing from research conducted in both the United States
and Italy (which appeared in an earlier work entitled* Making Democracy
Work*), Putnam has described the notion of social capital as networks and
"norms of reciprocity" that make people active participants in democratic life.
Where social capital is strong, Putnam argues, democracy is sustained by this
web of interconnections that promotes civic life. In the United States (and
perhaps elsewhere), however, civic organization is declining, leading to a
weakened democracy that is disconnected from the public. Yet while Putnam
lauds social capital and laments the decline of civic life, others are less convinced. In his recent work "The Myth of the Rational Voter" (2006), Bryan Caplan takes on the idea that as a whole, participation in politics is a good idea.
An economist, Caplan challenges the assumption in economics that voters are
essentially rational; poorly informed and often driven by emotion, voters
choose bad policies, particularly in the area of economics. What then to do?
Caplan argues that voters cannot be expected to become better informed or rational, and calls on elites to guide the public toward sounder policies—a call,
in a way, to the republics of the past.*

FAREED ZAKARIA

A BRIEF HISTORY OF HUMAN LIBERTY

It all started when Constantine decided to move. In A.D. 324 the leader of the greatest empire in the world went east, shifting his capital from Rome to Byzantium, the old Greek colony, at the mouth of the Black Sea, which he promptly renamed Constantinople. Why abandon Rome, the storied seat of the empire? Constantine explained that he did it "on command of God." You can't really argue with that kind of logic, though vanity and ambition surely played some part as well. Constantine desperately wanted to leave behind a grand legacy and, short of winning a war, what better way to do so than to build a new capital city? The move was also politically smart. Constantinople was closer to the great cultural and economic centers of the day, such as Athens, Thessalonika, and Antioch. (Rome in those days was considered a backwater.) And Constantinople was a more strategic point from which to defend the empire against its enemies, mainly Germanic tribes and Persian armies. In the fourth century, the pivots of history lay in the east.

Emperors don't travel light, and Constantine was no exception. He shifted not just the capital but tens of thousands of its inhabitants and commandeered immense quantities of food and wine from Egypt, Asia Minor, and Syria to feed his people. He sent his minions across the empire to bring art for the "new Rome." Such was the pillage that the historian Jacob Burckhardt described it as "the most disgraceful and extensive thefts of art in all history . . . committed for the purpose of decorating [Constantinople]."[1] Senators and other notables were given every inducement to move; exact replicas of their homes were waiting for them in the new city. But although he took most of his court, Constantine left one person behind: the bishop of Rome. This historic separation between church and state was to have fateful, and beneficial, consequences for humankind.

Although the bishop of Rome had nominal seniority—because the first holder of that office, Peter, was the senior apostle of Christ—Christianity had survived by becoming a decentralized religion, comprising a collection of self-governing churches. But Rome was now distant from the imperial capital. Other important priests, such as the bishop of Byzantium and those of nearby Antioch, Jerusalem, and Alexandria, now lived in the shadow of the emperor and quickly became appendages of state authority. But, far from palace power and intrigue, the Roman church flourished, asserting an independence that eventually allowed it to claim the mantle of spiritual leadership of the Christian peoples. As a result of this separation, the great English classical scholar Ernest Barker observed, the East (Byzantium) fell under the control of the state and the West (Rome) came under the sovereignty of religion. It would be more accurate to say that in the West sovereignty was contested; for 1,500 years after Constantine's move, European history was marked by continual strife between church and state. From the sparks of those struggles came the first fires of human liberty.

Liberty, Old and New

Obviously it is an oversimplification to pick a single event to mark the beginnings of a complex historical phenomenon—in this case, the development of human liberty—but stories have to

From *The Future of Freedom* (New York: W. W. Norton, 2003), pp. 29–58. Some of the author's notes have been omitted.

start somewhere. And the rise of the Christian Church is, in my view, the first important source of liberty in the West—and hence the world. It highlights the central theme of this chapter, which is that liberty came to the West centuries before democracy. Liberty led to democracy and not the other way around. It also highlights a paradox that runs through this account: whatever the deeper structural causes, liberty in the West was born of a series of power struggles. The consequences of these struggles—between church and state, lord and king, Protestant and Catholic, business and the state—embedded themselves in the fabric of Western life, producing greater and greater pressures for individual liberty, particularly in England and, by extension, in the United States.

Some might contest this emphasis on the Christian Church, pointing fondly to ancient Greece as the seedbed of liberty. They will think of Pericles' famous funeral oration, delivered in 431 B.C., which conjured a stirring vision of the Athens of his day, dedicated to freedom, democracy, and equality. For much of the nineteenth century British and German university curricula assumed that the greatest flowering of human achievement took place in the city-states of Greece around the fifth century B.C. (The study of ancient Greece and Rome at Oxford and Cambridge is still colloquially called "Greats.") But the Victorian obsession with Greece was part fantasy. Ancient Greece was an extraordinary culture, fertile in philosophy, science, and literature. It was the birthplace of democracy and some of its associated ideas, but these were practiced in only a few, small city-states for at most a hundred years and died with the Macedonian conquest of Athens in 338 B.C. Over a millennium later, Greece's experiment became an inspiration for democrats, but in the intervening centuries, it left no tangible or institutional influences on politics in Europe.

More to the point, Greece was not the birthplace of liberty as we understand it today. Liberty in the modern world is first and foremost the freedom of the individual from arbitrary authority, which has meant, for most of history, from the brute power of the state. It implies certain basic human rights: freedom of expression, of association, and of worship, and rights of due process. But ancient liberty, as the enlightenment philosopher Benjamin Constant explained, meant something different: that everyone (actually, every male citizen) had the right to participate in the governance of the community. Usually all citizens served in the legislature or, if this was impractical, legislators were chosen by lottery, as with American juries today. The people's assemblies of ancient Greece had unlimited powers. An individual's rights were neither sacred in theory nor protected in fact. Greek democracy often meant, in Constant's phrase, "the subjection of the individual to the authority of the community."[2] Recall that in the fourth century B.C. in Athens, where Greek democracy is said to have found its truest expression, the popular assembly—by democratic vote—put to death the greatest philosopher of the age because of his teachings. The execution of Socrates was democratic but not liberal.

If the Greek roots of Western liberty are often overstated, the Roman ones are neglected. When Herodotus wrote that the Greeks were "a free people" he meant that they were not slaves under foreign conquest or domination—an idea we would today call "national independence" or "self-determination." (By this definition, the North Koreans today are a free people.) The Romans emphasized a different aspect of freedom: that all citizens were to be treated equally under the law. This conception of freedom is much closer to the modern Western one, and the Latin word for it, *libertas*, is the root of ours. Whereas Greece gave the world philosophy, literature, poetry, and art, Rome gave us the beginnings of limited government and the rule of law. The Roman Republic, with its divided government (three branches), election of officials to limited terms, and emphasis on equality under law has been a model for governments ever since, most consciously in the founding of the American Republic. To this day Roman political concepts and terms endure throughout the Western world: senate, republic, constitution, prefecture. Western law is so filled with Roman legacies that until the early twentieth century, lawyers had to be well versed in Latin. Most of the world's laws of contract, property, liability, defamation, inheritance, and estate and rules of procedure and evidence are variations on Roman themes. For Herbert Asquith, the gifted amateur classicist who became prime minister of the United Kingdom, Rome's greatest gift to the ages was that "she founded, developed and systematized the jurisprudence of the world."[3]

The gaping hole in Roman law, however, was that as a practical matter, it didn't apply to the ruling class, particularly as the republic degenerated into a monarchy by the first century. Emperors such as Nero, Vitellius, and Galba routinely sentenced people to death without trial, pillaged private homes and temples, and raped and murdered their subjects. Caligula famously had his horse appointed senator, an act that probably violated the implicit, if not explicit, rules of that once-august body. Traditions of law that had been built carefully during Rome's republican years crumbled in the decadence of empire. The lesson of Rome's fall is that, for the rule of law to endure, you need more than the good intentions of the rulers, for they may change (both the intentions and the rulers). You need institutions within society whose strength is independent of the state. The West found such a countervailing force in the Catholic Church.

The Paradox of Catholicism

Rome's most concrete legacy has been the Roman Catholic Church, which the English philosopher Thomas Hobbes called "the ghost of the deceased Roman Empire sitting crowned upon [its] grave."[4] The culture of Rome became the culture of Catholicism. Through the church were transmitted countless traditions and ideas—and, of course, Latin which gave educated people all over Europe a common language and thus strengthened their sense of being a single community. To this day the ideas and structure of the Catholic Church—its universalism, its hierarchy, its codes and laws—bear a strong resemblance to those of the Roman Empire.

The Catholic Church might seem an odd place to begin the story of liberty. As an institution it has not stood for freedom of thought or even, until recently, diversity of belief. In fact, during the Middle Ages, as it grew powerful, it became increasingly intolerant and oppressive, emphasizing dogma and unquestioning obedience and using rather nasty means to squash dissent (recall the Spanish Inquisition). To this day, its structure remains hierarchical and autocratic. The church never saw itself as furthering individual liberty. But from the start it tenaciously opposed the power of the state and thus placed limits on monarchs' rule. It controlled crucial social institutions such as marriage and birth and death rites. Church properties and priests were not subject to taxation—hardly a small matter since at its height the church owned one-third of the land in Europe. The Catholic Church was the first major institution in history that was independent of temporal authority and willing to challenge it. By doing this it cracked the edifice of state power, and in nooks and crannies individual liberty began to grow.

The struggles between church and state began just over fifty years after Constantine's move. One of Constantine's successors, the emperor Theodosius, while in a nasty dispute with the Thessalonians, a Greek tribe, invited the whole tribe to Milan—and orchestrated a blood-curdling massacre of his guests: men, women, and children. The archbishop of Milan, a pious priest named Ambrose, was appalled and publicly refused to give the emperor Holy Communion. Theodosius protested, resorting to a biblical defense. He was guilty of homicide, he explained, but wasn't one of the Bible's heroic kings, David, guilty not just of homicide but of adultery as well? The archbishop was unyielding, thundering back, in the English historian

Edward Gibbon's famous account, "You have imitated David in his crime, imitate then his repentance."[5] To the utter amazement of all, for the next eight months the emperor, the most powerful man in the world, periodically dressed like a beggar (as David had in the biblical tale) and stood outside the cathedral at Milan to ask forgiveness of the archbishop.

As the Roman Empire crumbled in the East, the bishop of Rome's authority and independence grew. He became first among the princes of the church, called "Il Papa," the holy father. In 800, Pope Leo III was forced to crown the Frankish ruler Charlemagne as Roman emperor. But in doing so, Leo began the tradition of "investiture," whereby the church had to bless a new king and thus give legitimacy to his reign. By the twelfth century, the pope's power had grown, and he had become a pivotal player in Europe's complex political games. The papacy had power, legitimacy, money, and even armies. It won another great symbolic battle against Holy Roman Emperor Henry IV, who in 1077 challenged—unsuccessfully—Pope Gregory VII's expansion of the power of investiture. Having lost the struggle, Henry, so the legend goes, was forced to stand barefoot in the snow at Canossa to seek forgiveness from the holy father. Whether or not that tale is true, by the twelfth century the pope had clearly become, in power and pomp, a match for any of Europe's kings, and the Vatican had come to rival the grandest courts on the continent.

The Geography of Freedom

The church gained power in the West for a simple reason: after the decline of the Roman Empire, it never again faced a single emperor of Europe. Instead, the Catholic Church was able to play one European prince against another, becoming the vital "swing vote" in the power struggles of the day. Had one monarch emerged across the continent, he could have crushed the church's independence, turning it into a handmaiden of state

power. That is what happened to the Greek Orthodox Church and later the Russian Orthodox Church (and, for that matter, to most religions around the world). But no ruler ever conquered all of Europe, or even the greater part of it. Over the millennia only a few tried—Charlemagne, Charles V, Napoleon, Kaiser Wilhelm, and Hitler. All were thwarted, most fairly quickly.

What explains this? Probably mountains and rivers. Europe is riven with barriers that divide its highlands into river valleys bordered by mountain ranges. Its rivers flow into sheltered, navigable bays along the long, indented Mediterranean coastline—all of which means that small regions could subsist, indeed thrive, on their own. Hence Europe's long history of many independent countries. They are hard to conquer, easy to cultivate, and their rivers and seas provide ready trade routes. Asia, by contrast, is full of vast flatlands—the steppes in Russia, the plains in China—through which armies could march unhindered. Not surprisingly, these areas were ruled for millennia by centralized empires.

Europe's topography made possible the rise of communities of varying sizes—city-states, duchies, republics, nations, and empires. In 1500 Europe had within it more than 500 states, many no larger than a city. This variety had two wondrous effects. First, it allowed for diversity. People, ideas, art, and even technologies that were unwelcome or unnoticed in one area would often thrive in another. Second, diversity fueled constant competition between states, producing innovation and efficiency in political organization, military technology, and economic policy. Successful practices were copied; losing ways were cast aside. Europe's spectacular economic and political success—what the economic historian Eric Jones has termed "the European miracle"—might well be the result of its odd geography.[6]

Lords and Kings

Geography and history combined to help shape Europe's political structure. The crumbling of the Roman Empire and the backwardness of the German tribes that destroyed it resulted in decentralized authority across the continent; no ruler had the administrative capacity to rule a far-flung kingdom comprising so many independent tribes. By contrast, in their heyday, Ming and Manchu China, Mughal India, and the Ottoman Empire controlled vast lands and diverse peoples. But in Europe local landlords and chieftains governed their territories and developed close ties with their tenants. This became the distinctive feature of European feudalism—that its great landowning classes were independent. From the Middle Ages until the seventeenth century, European sovereigns were distant creatures who ruled their kingdoms mostly in name. The king of France, for example, was considered only a duke in Brittany and had limited authority in that region for hundreds of years. In practice if monarchs wanted to do anything—start a war, build a fort—they had to borrow and bargain for money and troops from local chieftains, who became earls, viscounts, and dukes in the process.

Thus Europe's landed elite became an aristocracy with power, money, and legitimacy—a far cry from the groveling and dependent courtier-nobles in other parts of the world. This near-equal relationship between lords and kings deeply influenced the course of liberty. As Guido de Ruggiero, the great historian of liberalism, wrote, "Without the effective resistance of particular privileged classes, the monarchy would have created nothing but a people of slaves."[7] In fact monarchs did just that in much of the rest of the world. In Europe, on the other hand, as the Middle Ages progressed, the aristocracy demanded that kings guarantee them certain rights that even the crown could not violate. They also established representative bodies—parliaments, estates general, diets—to give permanent voice to their claims. In these medieval bargains lie the foundations of what we today call "the rule of law." Building on Roman traditions, these rights were secured and strengthened by the power of the nobility. Like the clash between

church and state, the conflict between the aristocracy and the monarchy is the second great power struggle of European history that helped provide, again unintentionally, the raw materials of freedom.

The English aristocracy was the most independent in Europe. Lords lived on their estates, governing and protecting their tenants. In return, they extracted taxes, which kept them both powerful and rich. It was, in one scholar's phrase, "a working aristocracy": it maintained its position not through elaborate courtly rituals but by taking part in politics and government at all levels.[8] England's kings, who consolidated their power earlier than did most of their counterparts on the continent, recognized that their rule depended on co-opting the aristocracy—or at least some part of it. When monarchs pushed their luck they triggered a baronial backlash. Henry II, crowned king in 1154, extended his rule across the country, sending judges to distant places to enforce royal decrees. He sought to unify the country and create a common, imperial law. To do this he had to strip the medieval aristocracy of its powers and special privileges. His plan worked but only up to a point. Soon the nobility rose up in arms—literally—and after forty years of conflict, Henry's son, King John, was forced to sign a truce in 1215 in a field near Windsor Castle. That document, Magna Carta, was regarded at the time as a charter of baronial privilege, detailing the rights of feudal lords. It also had provisions guaranteeing the freedom of the church and local autonomy for towns. It came out (in vague terms) against the oppression of any of the king's subjects. Over time the document was interpreted more broadly by English judges, turning it into a quasi constitution that enshrined certain individual rights. But even in its day, Magna Carta was significant, being the first written limitation on royal authority in Europe. As such, the historian Paul Johnson noted, it is "justly classified as the first of the English Statutes of the Realm, from which English, and thus American, liberties can be said to flow."[9]

Rome versus Reform

After church versus state and king versus lord, the next great power struggle, between Catholics and Protestants, was to prove the longest and bloodiest, and once again it had accidental but revolutionary implications for freedom. Its improbable instigator was a devout German monk who lived in a small backwater town called Wittenberg. It was the early sixteenth century, and across Europe there was already great dissatisfaction with the papacy, which had become extraordinarily powerful and corrupt. Rome's most scandalous practice was the widespread sale of indulgences: papal certificates absolving the buyer of sins, even those not yet committed. The money financed the church's never-ending extravagance, which even by the glittering standards of the Baroque era was stunning. Its newest project was the largest, grandest cathedral ever known to man—St. Peter's in Rome. Even today, when one walks through the acres of marble in the Vatican, gazing at gilt, jewels, tapestries, and frescos from wall to wall and floor to ceiling, it is easy to imagine the pious rage of Martin Luther.

There had been calls for reform before Luther—Erasmus, for one, had urged a simpler, stripped down form of worship—but none had frontally challenged the authority of the church. Luther did so in ninety-five tightly reasoned theses, which he famously nailed to the door of the Castle Church in Wittenberg on the morning of October 31, 1517. Luther may have had right on his side, but he also had luck. His heresy came at an opportune moment in the history of technology. By the time the Catholic Church reacted and responded to his action, strictly forbidding the dissemination of his ideas, the new printing presses had already circulated Luther's document all over Europe. The Reformation had begun. One hundred and fifty bloody years later, almost half of Europe was Protestant.

Were Martin Luther to see Protestantism today, with its easygoing doctrines that tolerate much and require little, he would probably be horrified. Luther was not a liberal. On the contrary, he had accused the Vatican of being too lax in its approach to religion. In many ways he was what we would today call a fundamentalist, demanding a more literal interpretation of the Bible. Luther's criticisms of the papacy were quite similar to those made today by Islamic fundamentalists about the corrupt, extravagant regimes of the Middle East that have veered from the true, devout path. Luther was attacking the pope from the conservative end of the theological spectrum. In fact some have said that the clash between Catholicism and Protestantism illustrates the old maxim that religious freedom is the product of two equally pernicious fanaticisms, each canceling the other out.

Most of the sects that sprang up as a consequence of the Reformation were even more puritanical than Lutheranism. The most influential of them was a particularly dour creed, Calvinism, which posited the wretched depravity of man and the poor chances of salvation for all but a few, already chosen by God. But the various Protestant sects converged in rejecting the authority of the papacy and, by implication, all religious hierarchy. They were part of a common struggle against authority and, although they didn't know it at the time, part of the broader story of liberty.

For all their squabbles, these small Protestant sects in northern Europe opened up the possibility of a personal path to truth, unmediated by priests. To the extent that they imagined any clergy at all, it was to be elected by a self-governing congregation. Often minority sects within a larger community, they fought for the rights of all minorities to believe and worship as they chose. Together, they opened up the space for religious freedom in the Western world. They helped shape modern ideas about not only freedom of conscience and of speech but also critical scientific inquiry, first of religious texts such as the Bible, then of all received wisdom. Science, after all, is a constant process of challenging authority and contesting dogma. In that sense modern science owes an unusual debt to sixteenth-century religious zealots.

The more immediate, political effect of Protestantism was to give kings and princes an excuse to wrest power away from the increasingly arrogant Vatican, something they were looking to do anyway. The first major assault took place not in support of Protestant ideals but for the less-exalted reason that a restless monarch wanted an heir. Henry VIII of England asked Pope Clement VII to annul his marriage to Catherine of Aragon because she had not produced an heir to the throne. (Not for lack of effort: in eight years she had given birth to one daughter and five infants who had died, and had miscarried twice.) The pope refused and King Henry broke with the Vatican, proclaiming himself head of the Church of England. Henry had no doctrinal dispute with the Catholic Church. In fact he had defended the pope against Luther in an essay, for which the Vatican honored him as "Defender of the Faith," a title his successor, strangely, bears to this day. The newly independent Anglican Church was thus Catholic in doctrine—except for the small matter of the pope.

The English break was the first and most prominent of a series of religious revolts and wars against the Vatican involving virtually every state in Europe and lasting almost 150 years after Luther's act of defiance. The wars resulting from the Reformation came to an end in 1648. The Peace of Westphalia, as it was called, ended the Thirty Years' War among the Germans and rendered unto Caesar that which was Caesar's—plus a good bit of that which used to be God's (actually, the pope's). It revived a 1555 idea—*cuius regio eius religio* (whoever's domain, his religion prevails)—that princes could choose their state religions, and it explicitly permitted religious toleration and migration. The year 1648 is not a clean point of separation between church and state, but it does symbolize an important shift in Western history. Westphalia laid to rest the idea that Europe was one great Christian community—"Christendom"—governed spiritually by the Catholic Church and temporally by the holy Roman emperor. The future belonged to the state.

The Enlightened State

By the seventeenth century, the real challenge to princely power came not from religion but from local authorities: the princes, dukes, barons, and counts. But over the course of this century the prince would best his rivals. He strengthened his court and created a central government—a state—that dwarfed its local rivals. The state triumphed for several reasons: technological shifts, heightened military competition, the stirrings of nationalism, and the ability to centralize tax collection. One consequence, however, is worth noting. The strengthening of the state was not good for liberty. As the power of monarchs grew, they shut down most of the medieval parliaments, estates, assemblies, and diets. When France's Estates General were summoned in the spring of 1789—on the eve of the revolution—it was their first assembly in 175 years! The newly powerful royals also began abolishing the multilayered system of aristocratic privileges, regional traditions, and guild protections in favor of a uniform legal code, administered by the monarch. The important exception was the English Parliament, which actually gained the upper hand in its struggle with the monarchy after the Glorious Revolution of 1688.[10]

On the face of it the weakening of the aristocracy might seem a victory for equality under law, and it was presented as such at the time. As Enlightenment ideas swept through seventeenth century Europe, philosophers such as Voltaire and Diderot fantasized about the "rationalization" and "modernization" of government. But in practice these trends meant more power for the central government and the evisceration of local and regional authority. "Enlightened absolu-tism," as it was later called, had some progressive elements about it. Rulers such as Frederick II of Prussia, Catherine II of Russia, and Joseph II of Austria tolerated religious dissent, enacted legal reforms, and lavished money and attention on artists, musicians, and writers (which might help explain the good press they received). But the shift in power weakened the only groups in society capable of checking royal authority and excess. Liberty now depended on the largesse of the ruler. When under pressure from abroad or at home, even the most benign monarch—and his not-so-benign successors—abandoned liberalization and squashed dissent. By the end of the eighteenth century, with war, revolution, and domestic rebellion disturbing the tranquility of Europe, enlightened absolutism became more absolutist than enlightened.

The monarchy reached its apogee in France under Louis XIV. Feudalism in France had always been different from that in England. Sandwiched between hostile neighbors, France was perpetually mobilizing for war, which kept its central government strong. (Louis XIV was at war for thirty of his fifty-four years of rule.) The monarchy exploited these geopolitical realities to keep the nobles distant from their power base, which was their land. Building on the foundation laid by the brilliant Cardinal Richelieu, Louis XIV edged nobles out of local administration and put in their place his own regional officials. He also downgraded regional councils and assemblies. Louis was called the "Sun King" not because of his gilded possessions, as is often thought, but because of his preeminent position in the country. All other forces paled in comparison. Louis XIV brought France's aristocrats to Paris permanently, luring them with the most glittering court in Europe. His purpose was to weaken them. The legendary excess of the French monarchy—the ceaseless games, balls, hunts, and court rituals, the wonder of Versailles—was at one level a clever political device to keep the lords in a gilded cage. Behind the sumptuous silks and powdered wigs, the French aristocracy was becoming powerless and dependent.[11]

The French Revolution (1789) changed much in the country, but not these centripetal tendencies. Indeed, the revolution only centralized the country further. In contrast to England's Glorious Revolution (1688), which had strengthened the landed aristocracy, the French Revolution destroyed it. It also crippled the church and weakened local lords, parishes, and banks. As the great nineteenth century scholar-politician Lord Acton observed, the revolution was not so much about the limitation of central power as about the abrogation of all other powers that got in the way. The French, he noted, borrowed from Americans "their theory of revolution not their theory of government—their cutting but not their sewing." Popular sovereignty took on all the glory and unchecked power of royal sovereignty. "The people" were supreme, and they proclaimed their goals to be *liberté, égalité, fraternité*. Once dependent on royal largesse, liberty now depended on the whims of "the citizens," represented of course by the leaders of the revolution.

But there was another model of liberty and it took a Frenchman to see it. Montesquieu—actually Charles-Louis de Secondat, baron de La Brède et de Montesquieu—like many Enlightenment liberals in the eighteenth century admired England for its government. But Montesquieu went further, identifying the genius of the English system: that it guaranteed liberty in fact rather than proclaiming it in theory. Because government was divided between the king, aristocrats (House of Lords), and commoners (House of Commons), no one branch could grow too strong. This "separation of powers" ensured that civil liberties would be secure and religious dissent tolerated. Montesquieu did not put blind faith in the mechanics of government and constitutions; his major work was titled, after all, *The Spirit of the Laws*.

In fact, over the centuries, the British monarch's powers had been so whittled away that by the late eighteenth century, Britain, although formally a monarchy, was really an aristocratic republic, ruled by its landed elite. Montesquieu's flattering interpretation strongly influenced the British themselves. The preeminent English jurist of the era, William Blackstone, used

Montesquieu's ideas when writing his commentaries on English law. The American political philosopher Judith Shklar pointed out that during the founding of the American Republic "Montesquieu was an oracle." James Madison, Thomas Jefferson, John Adams, and others consciously tried to apply his principles in creating a new political system. He was quoted by them more than any modern author (only the Bible trumped him). His appeal was so widespread, noted Shklar, that "both those who supported the new constitution and those who opposed it relied heavily on Montesquieu for their arguments."[12]

The Consequences of Capitalism

By the eighteenth century, Britain's unusual political culture gained a final, crucial source of strength: capitalism. If the struggles between church and state, lords and kings, and Catholics and Protestants cracked open the door for individual liberty, capitalism blew the walls down. Nothing has shaped the modern world more powerfully than capitalism, destroying as it has millennia-old patterns of economic, social, and political life. Over the centuries it has destroyed feudalism and monarchism with their emphasis on bloodlines and birth. It has created an independent class of businesspeople who owe little to the state and who are now the dominant force in every advanced society in the world. It has made change and dynamism—rather than order and tradition—the governing philosophy of the modern age. Capitalism created a new world, utterly different from the one that had existed for millennia. And it took root most firmly in England.

It started elsewhere. By the fourteenth century, trade and commerce, frozen during much of the Middle Ages, was once again thriving in parts of Europe. A revolution in agricultural technology was producing surpluses of grain, which had to be sold or bartered. Market towns and port cities—Antwerp, Brussels, Venice, Genoa—became centers of economic activity.

Double-entry bookkeeping, the introduction of Arabic numerals, and the rise of banking turned money-making from an amateur affair into a systematic business. Soon the commercial impulse spread inland from the port cities, mostly in the Low Countries and later in England, where it was applied to all kinds of agriculture, crafts, manufacturing, and services. Why capitalism spread to these areas first is still debated, but most economic historians agree that a competent state that protected private property was an important factor. Where capitalism succeeded it was "in the main due to the type of property rights created," write the leading historians on the subject, Douglass North and Robert Thomas.[13] By the sixteenth century a consensus was developing across Europe that "Property belongs to the family, sovereignty to the prince and his magistrates." A fifteenth-century jurist in Spain had explained, "To the king is confided solely the administration of the kingdom and not dominion over things."[14] Only in England, however, was a king (Charles I) actually executed, in large part for levying arbitrary taxes.

The systematic protection of property rights transformed societies. It meant that the complex web of feudal customs and privileges—all of which were obstacles to using property efficiently—could be eliminated. The English landed elite took a leading role in modernizing agriculture. Through the enclosures system, a brutal process of asserting their rights over the pastures and commons of their estates, they forced the peasants and farmers who had lived off these lands into more specialized and efficient labors. The pastures were then used for grazing sheep, to service the highly profitable wool trade. By adapting to the ongoing capitalist revolution, the English landed classes secured their power but also helped modernize their society. The French aristocrats, in contrast, were absentee landlords who did little to make their properties more productive and yet continued to extract hefty feudal dues from their tenants. Like many continental aristocracies, they disdained commerce.

Beyond enterprising nobles, capitalism also created a new group of wealthy and powerful men who owed their riches not to land grants from the crown but to independent economic activity. Ranging from minor aristocrats to enterprising peasants, these English "yeomen" were, in the words of one historian, "a group of ambitious, aggressive small capitalists."[15] They were the first members of the bourgeoisie, the industrious property-owning class that Karl Marx defined as "the owners of the means of production of a society and employer of its laborers." Marx accurately recognized that this class was the vanguard of political liberalization in Europe. Since its members benefited greatly from capitalism, the rule of law, free markets, and the rise of professionalism and meritocracy, they supported gradual reforms that furthered these trends. In a now-legendary work of social science, the Harvard scholar Barrington Moore, Jr., studied the pathways to democracy and dictatorship around the world and presented his central conclusion in four words: "No bourgeoisie, no democracy."[16]

British politics was revolutionized as entrepreneurial activity became the principal means of social advancement. The House of Commons, which had wrested power from the king in the seventeenth century and ran the country, now swelled with newly rich merchants and traders. The number of titled nobles in Britain was always tiny: fewer than 200 by the end of the eighteenth century.[17] But beneath them lay a broad class, often called the "English gentry." The gentry usually had some connection to the aristocracy and often took on responsibilities in local government, but it ultimately drew its prestige and power from business, professional work, or efficient farming. Many of these men entered public life, and with a healthy distance from the old order, pushed for progressive reforms such as free trade, free markets, individual rights, and freedom of religion.

The three most powerful British prime ministers of the nineteenth century—Robert Peel, William Gladstone, and Benjamin Disraeli—all came from the ranks of the gentry. This newly powerful class adopted many of the traits of the aristocracy—manor houses, morning coats, hunting parties—but it was more fluid. "Gentlemen" were widely respected and, even more than lords, became the trendsetters of their society. Indeed, by the eighteenth century, the English gentleman became an almost mythic figure toward which society aspired. A nurse is said to have asked King James I to make her son a gentleman. The monarch replied, "A gentleman I could never make him, though I could make him a lord." A visiting Frenchman ridiculed the tendency of the English aristocracy to ape the gentry: "At London, masters dress like their valets and duchesses copy after their chambermaids."[18] Today the English gentleman is remembered mostly as a dandy, whose aesthetic sensibility is marketed worldwide by Ralph Lauren. But his origins are intimately connected with the birth of English liberty.

Anglo-America

Despite the rise of capitalism, limited government, property rights, and constitutionalism across much of Europe by the eighteenth century, England was seen as unique. It was wealthier, more innovative, freer, and more stable than any society on the continent. As Guido de Ruggiero noted, "The liberties of the individual, especially security of person and property, were solidly assured. Administration was decentralized and autonomous. The judiciary bodies were wholly independent of the central government. The prerogatives of the crown were closely restricted. . . . [P]olitical power was concentrated in the hands of Parliament. What similar spectacle could the continent offer?" Many observers at the time drew similar conclusions, praising England's constitution and national character. Some focused more specifically on economics. For Voltaire, "commerce which has enriched the citizens of England has helped make them free

. . . that liberty has in turn expanded commerce." Rather than cultivating the decadent pleasures of its nobility, the observant French clergyman Abbe Coyer remarked, the English government had helped "the honest middle class, that precious portion of nations."[19] Free markets helped enrich the middle class, which then furthered the cause of liberty. It seemed a virtuous circle.

The lands most like England were its colonies in America. The colonists had established governments that closely resembled those they had left behind in Tudor England. In 1776, when they rebelled against George III, the colonists couched their revolution as a call for the return of their rights as Englishmen. As they saw it, their long-established liberties had been usurped by a tyrannical monarch, forcing them to declare independence. In some ways it was a replay of England's own Glorious Revolution, in which Parliament rebelled against an arbitrary monarch whose chief sin was also to have raised taxes without the consent of the governed—or rather, the taxed. The winners in both 1688 and 1776 were the progressive, modernizing, and commercially minded elites. (The losers, in addition to the king, were the old Tories, who remained loyal to the crown both in seventeenth-century England and eighteenth-century America.)

But if England was exceptional, America was a special case of a special case. It was England without feudalism. Of course America had rich, landed families, but they were not titled, had no birth-rights, and were not endowed with political power comparable to that of the members of the House of Lords. To understand eighteenth-century America, the historian Richard Hofstadter wrote, one had to imagine that unique possibility, "a middle class world."[20] Aristocratic elements in the economy and society, though present, rarely dominated. In the North, they began to wane by the close of the eighteenth century. The historian Gordon Wood noted, "In the 1780s we can actually sense the shift from a premodern society to a modern one where business

interests and consumer tastes of ordinary people were coming to dominate." The American Revolution, which produced, in Wood's words, "an explosion of entrepreneurial power," widened the gulf between America and Europe.[21] America was now openly bourgeois and proud of it. Days after arriving in the United States in 1831, Tocqueville noted in his diary that in America "the whole society seems to have melted into a middle class."

The American path to liberal democracy was exceptional. Most countries don't begin their national experience as a new society without a feudal past. Free of hundreds of years of monarchy and aristocracy, Americans needed neither a powerful central government nor a violent social revolution to overthrow the old order. In Europe liberals feared state power but also fantasized about it. They sought to limit it yet needed it to modernize their societies. "The great advantage of the Americans," Tocqueville observed famously, "is that they have arrived at a state of democracy without having to endure a democratic revolution. . . . [T]hey are born equal without having to become equal."

By the early nineteenth century in the United Kingdom and the United States, for the most part, individual liberty flourished and equality under law ruled. But neither country was a democracy. Before the Reform Act of 1832, 1.8 percent of the adult population of the United Kingdom was eligible to vote. After the law that figure rose to 2.7 percent. After further widening of the franchise in 1867, 6.4 percent could vote, and after 1884, 12.1 percent.[22] Only in 1930, once women were fully enfranchised, did the United Kingdom meet today's standard for being democratic: universal adult suffrage. Yet it was widely considered the model of a constitutional liberal state—one that protected liberty and was governed by law.

The United States was more democratic than the United Kingdom, but not by as much as people think. For its first few decades, only white male property owners were eligible to vote—a system quite similar to that in the country whose rule it had just thrown off. In 1824—48 years after independence—only 5 percent of adult Americans cast a ballot in the presidential election. That number rose dramatically as the Jacksonian revolution spread and property qualifications were mostly eliminated. But not until the eve of the Civil War could it even be said that every white man in the United States had the right to vote. Blacks were enfranchised in theory in 1870, but in fact not until a century later in the South. Women got the vote in 1920. Despite this lack of democracy, for most of the nineteenth century, the United States and its system of laws and rights were the envy of the world. And with time, constitutional liberalism led to democracy, which led to further liberty, and so it went.

The rest of Europe followed a more complex path to liberal democracy than did the United Kingdom and the United States, but it eventually got there. What happened in Britain and America slowly and (mostly) peacefully happened on the continent in a jerky and bloody fashion (as will be discussed in the next chapter). Still, most became liberal democracies by the late 1940s and almost all the rest have done so since 1989, with consolidation taking place fast and firmly. The reason is clear: all Western countries shared a history that, for all its variations, featured the building of a constitutional liberal tradition. The English case is what scholars call the "ideal type," which makes it useful to highlight. But by the eighteenth century, even the most retrograde European power was a liberal regime when compared with its counterparts in Asia or Africa. Citizens had explicit rights and powers that no non-Western subject could imagine. Monarchs were restrained by law and tradition. A civil society of private enterprise, churches, universities, guilds, and associations flourished without much interference from the state. Private property was protected and free enterprise flowered. Often these freedoms were stronger in theory than in practice, and frequently they were subject to abuse by autocratic monarchs. But compared with the rest of the world the West was truly the land of liberty.

Culture as Destiny

This brief history of liberty might seem a discouraging guide. It suggests that any country hoping to become a liberal democracy should probably relocate to the West. And without a doubt, being part of the Western world—even if on the periphery—is a political advantage. Of all the countries that gained independence after the Soviet empire collapsed, those that have shared what one might call "the Western experience"—the old lands of the Austrian and German empires—have done best at liberal democracy. The line that separated Western and Eastern Christendom in 1500 today divides successful liberal regimes from unsuccessful, illiberal ones. Poland, Hungary, and the Czech Republic, which were most securely a part of Europe, are furthest along in consolidating their democracies; the Baltic states are next in line. Even in the Balkans, Slovenia and Croatia, which fall on the western side of that East-West line, are doing well while Serbia and Albania (on the east) are having a far more troubled transition.

Does this mean that culture is destiny? This powerful argument has been made by distinguished scholars from Max Weber to Samuel Huntington. It is currently a trendy idea. From business consultants to military strategists, people today talk about culture as the easy explanation to most puzzles. Why did the U.S. economy boom over the last two decades? It's obvious: our unique entrepreneurial culture. Why is Russia unable to adapt to capitalism? Also obvious: it has a feudal, antimarket culture. Why is Africa mired in poverty? And why is the Arab world breeding terrorists? Again, culture.

But these answers are too simple. After all, American culture also produced stagflation and the Great Depression. And the once-feudal cultures of Japan and Germany seem to have adapted to capitalism well, having become the second- and third-richest countries in the world, respectively. A single country can succeed and fail at different times, sometimes just a few decades apart, which would suggest that something other than its culture—which is relatively unchanging—is at work.

Singapore's brilliant patriarch Lee Kuan Yew once explained to me that if you want to see how culture works, compare the performance of German workers and Zambian workers anywhere in the world. You will quickly come to the conclusion that there is something very different in the two cultures that explains the results. Scholars make similar arguments: in his interesting work *Tribes*, Joel Kotkin argues that if you want to succeed economically in the modern world, the key is simple—be Jewish, be Indian, but above all, be Chinese.

Lee and Kotkin are obviously correct in their observation that certain groups—Chinese, Indians, Jews—do superbly in all sorts of settings. (In fact I find this variant of the culture theory particularly appealing, since I am of Indian origin.) But if being Indian is a key to economic success, what explains the dismal performance of the Indian economy over the first four decades after its independence in 1947—or, for that matter, for hundreds of years before that? Growing up in India I certainly did not think of Indians as economically successful. In fact I recall the day a legendary member of the Indian parliament, Piloo Mody, posed the following question to Indira Gandhi during the prime minister's "question hour" in New Delhi: "Can the prime minister explain why Indians seem to thrive economically under every government in the world except hers?"

Similar questions might be asked of China, another country that did miserably in economic terms for hundreds of years until two decades ago. If all you need are the Chinese, China has billions of them. As for Jews, although they have thrived in many places, the one country where they are a majority, Israel, was also an economic mess until recently. Interestingly, the economic fortunes of all three countries (India, China, Israel) improved markedly around the 1980s. But this was not because they got themselves new cultures, but because their governments changed specific policies and created a more market-friendly system. China is today growing faster than India, but that has more to do with the fact that China is reforming its economy more extensively than India is, than with any supposed superiority of the Confucian ethic over the Hindu mind-set.

It is odd that Lee Kuan Yew is such a fierce proponent of cultural arguments. Singapore is culturally not very different from its neighbor Malaysia. It is more Chinese and less Malay but compared to the rest of the world, the two countries share much in common. But much more than its neighbors, Singapore has had an effective government that has pursued wise economic policies. That surely, more than innate cultural differences, explains its success. The key to Singapore's success, in other words, is Lee Kuan Yew, not Confucius. The point is not that culture is unimportant; on the contrary it matters greatly. It represents the historical experience of a people, is embedded in their institutions, and shapes their attitudes and expectations about the world. But culture can change. German culture in 1939 was very different from what it became in 1959, just twenty years later. Europe, once the heartland of hypernationalism, is now postnationalist, its states willing to cede power to supranational bodies in ways that Americans can hardly imagine. The United States was once an isolationist republic with a deep suspicion of standing armies. Today it is a hegemon with garrisons around the world. The Chinese were once backward peasants; now they are smart merchants. Economic crises, war, political leadership—all these things change culture.

A hundred years ago, when East Asia seemed immutably poor, many scholars—most famously Max Weber—argued that Confucian-based cultures discouraged all the attributes necessary for success in capitalism.[23] A decade ago, when East Asia was booming, scholars had turned this explanation on its head, arguing that Confucianism actually emphasized the traits essential for economic dynamism. Today the wheel has turned again and many see in "Asian values" all the ingredients of crony capitalism. In his study Weber linked northern Europe's economic success to its "Protestant ethic" and predicted that the Catholic south would stay poor. In fact, Italy and France have grown faster than Protestant Europe over the last half-century. One may use the stereotype of shifty Latins and a *mañana* work ethic to explain the poor performance of some countries, but then how does one explain Chile? Its economy is doing as well as that of the strongest of the Asian "tigers." Its success is often attributed to another set of Latin values: strong families, religious values, and determination.

In truth we cannot find a simple answer to why certain societies succeed at certain times. When a society does succeed it often seems inevitable in retrospect. So we examine successful societies and search within their cultures for the seeds of success. But cultures are complex; one finds in them what one wants. If one wants to find cultural traits of hard work and thrift within East Asia, they are there. If you want instead to find a tendency toward blind obedience and nepotism, these too exist. Look hard enough and you will find all these traits in most cultures.

Culture is important. It can be a spur or a drag, delaying or speeding up change. It can get codified in institutions and practices, which are often the real barriers to success. Indian culture may or may not hurt its chances for economic growth, but Indian bureaucracy certainly does. The West's real advantage is that its history led to the creation of institutions and practices that, although in no sense bound up with Western genes, are hard to replicate from scratch in other societies. But it can be done.

The East Asian Model

Looking at the many non-Western transitions to liberal democracy over the last three decades one can see that the countries that have moved furthest toward liberal democracy followed a version of the European pattern: capitalism and the rule of law first, and then democracy. South Korea, Taiwan, Thailand, and Malaysia were all governed for decades by military juntas or single-party systems. These regimes liberalized the economy, the legal system, and rights of worship and travel, and then, decades later, held free elections. They achieved, perhaps accidentally, the two essential attributes of good government that James Madison outlined in the Federalist Papers. First, a government must be able to control the governed, then it must be able to control itself. Order plus liberty. These two forces will, in the long run, produce legitimate government, prosperity, and liberal democracy. Of course, it's easier said than done.

In the 1950s and 1960s, most Western intellectuals scorned East Asia's regimes as reactionary, embracing instead popular leaders in Asia and Africa who were holding elections and declaring their faith in the people—for example in Ghana, Tanzania, and Kenya. Most of these countries degenerated into dictatorships while East Asia moved in precisely the opposite direction. It should surely puzzle these scholars and intellectuals that the best-consolidated democracies in Latin America and East Asia—Chile, South Korea, and Taiwan—were for a long while ruled by military juntas. In East Asia, as in western Europe, liberalizing autocracies laid the groundwork for stable liberal democracies.

In almost every case the dictatorships opened the economy slowly and partially, but this process made the government more and more liberal. "An unmistakable feature in East Asia since World War II," wrote a leading scholar of East Asia, Minxin Pei,

> is the gradual process of authoritarian institutionalization. . . . At the center of this process was the slow emergence of modern political institutions exercising formal and informal constraining power through dominant parties, bureaucracies, semi-open electoral procedures, and a legal system that steadily acquired a measure of autonomy. The process had two beneficial outcomes—a higher level of stability and security of property rights (due to increasing constraints placed on rulers by the power of market forces and new political norms)."[24]

East Asia is still rife with corruption, nepotism, and voter fraud—but so were most Western democracies, even fifty years ago. Elections in Taiwan today are not perfect but they are probably more free and fair than those in the American South in the 1950s (or Chicago in the 1960s). Large conglomerates (*chaebols*) have improper influence in South Korean politics today, but so did their equivalents in Europe and the United States a century ago. The railroads, steel companies, shipbuilders, and great financiers of the past were probably more powerful than any East Asian tycoon today. They dominated America during its late-nineteenth-century Gilded Age. (Can you even name the political contemporaries of J. P. Morgan, E. H. Harriman, and John D. Rockefeller?) One cannot judge new democracies by standards that most Western countries would have flunked even thirty years ago. East Asia today is a mixture of liberalism, oligarchy, democracy, capitalism, and corruption—much like the West in, say, 1900. But most of East Asia's countries are considerably more liberal and democratic than the vast majority of other non-Western countries.

An even more striking proof that a constitutional liberal past can produce a liberal democratic present was identified by the late political scientist Myron Weiner in 1983. He pointed out that, as of then, "every single country in the Third World that emerged from colonial rule since the Second World War with a population of at least one million (and almost all the smaller colonies as well) with a continuous democratic experience is a former British colony."[25] British rule meant not democracy—colonialism is almost by definition undemocratic—but limited constitutional liberalism and capitalism. There are now other Third World democracies but Weiner's general point still holds. To say this is not to defend colonialism. Having grown up in a postcolonial country I do not need to be reminded of the institutionalized racism and the abuse of power that was part of the imperial legacy. But it is an undeniable fact that the British Empire left behind a legacy of law and

capitalism that has helped strengthen the forces of liberal democracy in many of its former colonies—though not all. France, by contrast, encouraged little constitutionalism or free markets in its occupied lands, but it did enfranchise some of its colonial populations in northern Africa. Early democratization in all those cases led to tyranny.

The Western path has led to liberal democracy far from the Western world. But the sequence and timing of democratization matter. Most Third World countries that proclaimed themselves democracies immediately after their independence, while they were poor and unstable, became dictatorships within a decade. As Giovanni Sartori, Columbia University's great scholar of democracy, noted about the path from constitutional liberalism to democracy, "the itinerary is not reversible." Even European deviations from the Anglo-American pattern—constitutionalism and capitalism first, only then democracy—were far less successful in producing liberal democracy. To see the complications produced by premature democratization, we could return to the heart of Europe—back in time to the early twentieth century.

NOTES

1. Jacob Burckhardt, *The Age of Constantine the Great*, tr. Moses Hadas (Berkeley: University of California Press, 1983), 351.
2. Benjamin Constant, "The Liberty of the Ancients Compared with That of the Moderns" (1819), in *Benjamin Constant: Political Writings*, Biancamaria Fontana, ed. (New York: Cambridge University Press, 1988).
3. Herbert Asquith, "Introduction," in Ernest Barker, *The Legacy of Rome* (Oxford, Clarendon Press, 1923), vii.
4. Quoted in David Gress, *From Plato to NATO: The Idea of the West and Its Opponents* (New York: Free Press, 1998), 125. I am particularly indebted to this fascinating and impor-

tant book for its discussion of Rome and the Catholic Church.

5. Edward Gibbon, *The Decline and Fall of the Roman Empire*, vol. 3, chapter 27, part 4. Again, thanks to David Gress for this story and source.

6. E. L. Jones, *The European Miracle: Environments, Economies, and Geopolitics in the History of Europe and Asia* (New York: Cambridge University Press, 1981). This is a wonderfully broad and suggestive book, but Jones places greater weight on culture than I do.

7. Guido de Ruggiero, *The History of European Liberalism* (Oxford: Oxford University Press, 1927). A wonderful book that deserves to be a classic.

8. Daniel A. Baugh, ed., *Aristocratic Government and Society in Eighteenth Century England* (New York: New Viewpoints, 1975).

9. Paul Johnson, "Laying Down the Law," *Wall Street Journal*, March 10, 1999.

10. In the historian J. H. Plumb's words, "the Revolution of 1688 was a monument raised by the gentry to its own sense of independence." J. H. Plumb, *The Growth of Political Stability in England, 1675–1725* (London: Macmillan, 1967), 29–30.

11. Jacques Barzun, *From Dawn to Decadence: 1500 to the Present* (New York: HarperCollins, 2000), 287–89.

12. Judith Shklar, *Montesquien* (New York: Oxford University Press, 1987), 121.

13. Douglass North and Robert Thomas, *The Rise of the Western World: A New Economic History* (Cambridge: Cambridge University Press, 1973), x.

14. Richard Pipes, *Property and Freedom* (New York: Knopf, 1999), 111.

15. Mildred Campbell, *The English Yeomen under Elizabeth and the Early Stuarts* (New York: A. M. Kelley, 1968), cited in Barrington Moore, *Social Origins of Dictatorship and Democracy: Lord and Peasant in the Making of the Modern World* (Boston: Beacon Press, 1966).

16. Moore, *Social Origins*, 418. The original says "bourgeois" not "bourgeoisie," but it is often quoted as the latter, which is what I have done.

17. J. M. Roberts, *The Penguin History of the World* (New York: Penguin, 1997), 553.

18. E. J. Hobsbawm, *Industry and Empire* (New York: Penguin, 1969), 26.

19. Hobsbawm, *Industry*, 48.

20. Richard Hofstadter, *America at 1750: A Social Portrait* (New York: Knopf, 1971), 131.

21. Gordon Wood, *The Radicalism of the American Revolution* (New York: Random House, 1993), 348.

22. Voting percentages calculated using B. R. Mitchell, *Abstract of British Historical Statistics* (Cambridge: Cambridge University Press, 1962); The Great Britain Historical G.I.S., University of Essex, available at www.geog.port.ac.uk/gbhgis/db; and E. J. Evans, *The Forging of the Modern Industrial State: Early Industrial Britain, 1783–1870* (New York: Longman, 1983). Also see Gertrude Himmelfarb, "The Politics of Democracy: The English Reform Act of 1867," *Journal of British Studies* 6 (1966).

23. Max Weber, *The Protestant Ethic and the Spirit of Capitalism* (New York: Scribner's, 1958).

24. Minxin Pei, "Constructing the Political Foundations for Rapid Economic Growth," in Henry Rowen, ed., *Behind East Asia's Growth: The Political and Social Foundations of an Economic Miracle* (London: Routledge, 1997), 39–59.

25. Myron Weiner, "Empirical Democratic Theory," in Myron Weiner and Ergun Ozbudun, eds., *Competitive Elections in Developing Countries* (Durham, N.C.: Duke University Press, 1987), 20.

PHILIPPE C. SCHMITTER AND
TERRY LYNN KARL

WHAT DEMOCRACY IS . . . AND IS NOT

For some time, the word democracy has been circulating as a debased currency in the political marketplace. Politicians with a wide range of convictions and practices strove to appropriate the label and attach it to their actions. Scholars, conversely, hesitated to use it—without adding qualifying adjectives—because of the ambiguity that surrounds it. The distinguished American political theorist Robert Dahl even tried to introduce a new term, "polyarchy," in its stead in the (vain) hope of gaining a greater measure of conceptual precision. But for better or worse, we are "stuck" with democracy as the catchword of contemporary political discourse. It is the word that resonates in people's minds and springs from their lips as they struggle for freedom and a better way of life; it is the word whose meaning we must discern if it is to be of any use in guiding political analysis and practice.

The wave of transitions away from autocratic rule that began with Portugal's "Revolution of the Carnations" in 1974 and seems to have crested with the collapse of communist regimes across Eastern Europe in 1989 has produced a welcome convergence toward [a] common definition of democracy.[1] Everywhere there has been a silent abandonment of dubious adjectives like "popular," "guided," "bourgeois," and "formal" to modify "democracy." At the same time, a remarkable consensus has emerged concerning the minimal conditions that polities must meet in order to merit the prestigious appellation of "democratic." Moreover, a number of international organizations now monitor how well these standards are met; indeed, some countries even consider them when formulating foreign policy.[2]

From *Journal of Democracy* (Summer 1991), pp. 67–73.

What Democracy Is

Let us begin by broadly defining democracy and the generic *concepts* that distinguish it as a unique system for organizing relations between rulers and the ruled. We will then briefly review *procedures*, the rules and arrangements that are needed if democracy is to endure. Finally, we will discuss two operative *principles* that make democracy work. They are not expressly included among the generic concepts or formal procedures, but the prospect for democracy is grim if their underlying conditioning effects are not present.

One of the major themes of this essay is that democracy does not consist of a single unique set of institutions. There are many types of democracy, and their diverse practices produce a similarly varied set of effects. The specific form democracy takes is contingent upon a country's socioeconomic conditions as well as its entrenched state structures and policy practices.

Modern political democracy is a system of governance in which rulers are held accountable for their actions in the public realm by citizens, acting indirectly through the competition and cooperation of their elected representatives.[3]

A *regime or system of governance* is an ensemble of patterns that determines the methods of access to the principal public offices; the characteristics of the actors admitted to or excluded from such access; the strategies that actors may use to gain access; and the rules that are followed in the making of publicly binding decisions. To work properly, the ensemble must be institutionalized—that is to say, the various patterns must be habitually known, practiced, and accepted by most, if not all, actors. Increasingly, the preferred mechanism of institutionalization is a written body of laws undergirded by a written constitution, though many enduring political norms can have an informal, prudential, or traditional basis.[4]

For the sake of economy and comparison, these forms, characteristics, and rules are usually bundled together and given a generic label. Democratic is one; others are autocratic, authoritarian, despotic, dictatorial, tyrannical, totalitarian, absolutist, traditional, monarchic, obligarchic, plutocratic, aristocratic, and sultanistic.[5] Each of these regime forms may in turn be broken down into subtypes.

Like all regimes, democracies depend upon the presence of *rulers*, persons who occupy specialized authority roles and can give legitimate commands to others. What distinguishes democratic rulers from nondemocratic ones are the norms that condition how the former come to power and the practices that hold them accountable for their actions.

The *public realm* encompasses the making of collective norms and choices that are binding on the society and backed by state coercion. Its content can vary a great deal across democracies, depending upon preexisting distinctions between the public and the private, state and society, legitimate coercion and voluntary exchange, and collective needs and individual preferences. The liberal conception of democracy advocates circumscribing the public realm as narrowly as possible, while the socialist or social-democratic approach would extend that realm through regulation, subsidization, and, in some cases, collective ownership of property. Neither is intrinsically more democratic than the other—just *differently* democratic. This implies that measures aimed at "developing the private sector" are no more democratic than those aimed at "developing the public sector." Both, if carried to extremes, could undermine the practice of democracy, the former by destroying the basis for satisfying collective needs and exercising legitimate authority; the latter by destroying the

basis for satisfying individual preferences and controlling illegitimate government actions. Differences of opinion over the optimal mix of the two provide much of the substantive content of political conflict within established democracies.

Citizens are the most distinctive element in democracies. All regimes have rulers and a public realm, but only to the extent that they are democratic do they have citizens. Historically, severe restrictions on citizenship were imposed in most emerging or partial democracies according to criteria of age, gender, class, race, literacy, property ownership, tax-paying status, and so on. Only a small part of the total population was eligible to vote or run for office. Only restricted social categories were allowed to form, join, or support political associations. After protracted struggle—in some cases involving violent domestic upheaval or international war—most of these restrictions were lifted. Today, the criteria for inclusion are fairly standard. All native-born adults are eligible, although somewhat higher age limits may still be imposed upon candidates for certain offices. Unlike the early American and European democracies of the nineteenth century, none of the recent democracies in southern Europe, Latin America, Asia, or Eastern Europe has even attempted to impose formal restrictions on the franchise or eligibility to office. When it comes to informal restrictions on the effective exercise of citizenship rights, however, the story can be quite different. This explains the central importance (discussed below) of procedures.

Competition has not always been considered an essential defining condition of democracy. "Classic" democracies presumed decision making based on direct participation leading to consensus. The assembled citizenry was expected to agree on a common course of action after listening to the alternatives and weighing their respective merits and demerits. A tradition of hostility to "faction," and "particular interests" persists in democratic thought, but at least since *The Federalist Papers* it has become widely accepted that competition among factions is a necessary evil in democracies that operate on a more-than-local scale. Since, as James Madison argued, "the latent causes of faction are sown into the nature of man," and the possible remedies for "the mischief of faction" are worse than the disease, the best course is to recognize them and to attempt to control their effects.[6] Yet while democrats may agree on the inevitability of factions, they tend to disagree about the best forms and rules for governing factional competition. Indeed, differences over the preferred modes and boundaries of competition contribute most to distinguishing one subtype of democracy from another.

The most popular definition of democracy equates it with regular *elections*, fairly conducted and honestly counted. Some even consider the mere fact of elections—even ones from which specific parties or candidates are excluded, or in which substantial portions of the population cannot freely participate—as a sufficient condition for the existence of democracy. This fallacy has been called "electoralism" or "the faith that merely holding elections will channel political action into peaceful contests among elites and accord public legitimacy to the winners"—no matter how they are conducted or what else constrains those who win them.[7] However central to democracy, elections occur intermittently and only allow citizens to choose between the highly aggregated alternatives offered by political parties, which can, especially in the early stages of a democratic transition, proliferate in a bewildering variety. During the intervals between elections, citizens can seek to influence public policy through a wide variety of other intermediaries: interest associations, social movements, locality groupings, clientelistic arrangements, and so forth. *Modern democracy, in other words, offers a variety of competitive processes and channels for the expression of interests and values—associational as well as partisan, functional as well as territorial, collective as well as individual. All are integral to its practice.*

Another commonly accepted image of democracy identifies it with *majority rule.* Any governing body that makes decisions by combining the votes of more than half of those eligible and present is said to be democratic, whether that majority emerges within an electorate, a parliament, a committee, a city council, or a party caucus. For exceptional purposes (e.g., amending the constitution or expelling a member), "qualified majorities" of more than 50 percent may be required, but few would deny that democracy must involve some means of aggregating the equal preferences of individuals.

A problem arises, however, when *numbers* meet *intensities*. What happens when a properly assembled majority (especially a stable, self-perpetuating one) regularly makes decisions that harm some minority (especially a threatened cultural or ethnic group)? In these circumstances, successful democracies tend to qualify the central principle of majority rule in order to protect minority rights. Such qualifications can take the form of constitutional provisions that place certain matters beyond the reach of majorities (bills of rights); requirements for concurrent majorities in several different constituencies (confederalism); guarantees securing the autonomy of local or regional governments against the demands of the central authority (federalism); grand coalition governments that incorporate all parties (consociationalism); or the negotiation of social pacts between major social groups like business and labor (neocorporatism). The most common and effective way of protecting minorities, however, lies in the everyday operation of interest associations and social movements. These reflect (some would say, amplify) the different intensities of preference that exist in the population and bring them to bear on democratically elected decision makers. Another way of putting this intrinsic tension between numbers and intensities would be to say that "in modern democracies, votes may be counted, but influences alone are weighted."

Cooperation has always been a central feature of democracy. Actors must voluntarily make collective decisions binding on the polity as a whole. They must cooperate in order to compete. They must be capable of acting collectively through parties, associations, and movements in order to select candidates, articulate preferences, petition authorities, and influence policies.

But democracy's freedoms should also encourage citizens to deliberate among themselves, to discover their common needs, and to resolve their differences without relying on some supreme central authority. Classical democracy emphasized these qualities, and they are by no means extinct, despite repeated efforts by contemporary theorists to stress the analogy with behavior in the economic marketplace and to reduce all of democracy's operations to competitive interest maximization. Alexis de Tocqueville best described the importance of independent groups for democracy in his *Democracy in America*, a work which remains a major source of inspiration for all those who persist in viewing democracy as something more than a struggle for election and re-election among competing candidates.[8]

In contemporary political discourse, this phenomenon of cooperation and deliberation via autonomous group activity goes under the rubric of "civil society." The diverse units of social identity and interest, by remaining independent of the state (and perhaps even of parties), not only can restrain the arbitrary actions of rulers, but can also contribute to forming better citizens who are more aware of the preferences of others, more self-confident in their actions, and more civic-minded in their willingness to sacrifice for the common good. At its best, civil society provides an intermediate layer of governance between the individual and the state that is capable of resolving conflicts and controlling the behavior of members without public coercion. Rather than overloading decision makers with increased demands and making the system ungovernable,[9] a viable civil society can mitigate conflicts and improve the quality of citizenship—without relying exclusively on the privatism of the marketplace.

Representatives—whether directly or indirectly elected—do most of the real work in modern democracies. Most are professional politicians who orient their careers around the desire to fill key offices. It is doubtful that any democracy could survive without such people. The central question, therefore, is not whether or not there will be a political elite or even a professional political class, but how these representatives are chosen and then held accountable for their actions.

As noted above, there are many channels of representation in modern democracy. The electoral one, based on territorial constituencies, is the most visible and public. It culminates in a parliament or a presidency that is periodically accountable to the citizenry as a whole. Yet the sheer growth of government (in large part as a byproduct of popular demand) has increased the number, variety, and power of agencies charged with making public decisions and not subject to elections. Around these agencies there has developed a vast apparatus of specialized representation based largely on functional interests, not territorial constituencies. These interest associations, and not political parties, have become the primary expression of civil society in most stable democracies, supplemented by the more sporadic interventions of social movements.

The new and fragile democracies that have sprung up since 1974 must live in "compressed time." They will not resemble the European democracies of the nineteenth and early twentieth centuries, and they cannot expect to acquire the multiple channels of representation in gradual historical progression as did most of their predecessors. A bewildering array of parties, interests, and movements will all simultaneously seek political influence in them, creating challenges to the polity that did not exist in earlier processes of democratization.

Procedures That Make Democracy Possible

The defining components of democracy are necessarily abstract, and may give rise to a considerable variety of institutions and subtypes of democracy. For democracy to thrive, however, specific procedural norms must be followed and civic rights must be respected. Any polity that fails to impose such restrictions upon itself, that fails to follow the "rule of law" with regard to its own procedures, should not be considered democratic. These procedures alone do not define democracy, but their presence is indispensable to its persistence. In essence, they are necessary but not sufficient conditions for its existence.

Robert Dahl has offered the most generally accepted listing of what he terms the "procedural minimal" conditions that must be present for modern political democracy (or as he puts it, "polyarchy") to exist:

1. Control over government decisions about policy is constitutionally vested in elected officials.
2. Elected officials are chosen in frequent and fairly conducted elections in which coercion is comparatively uncommon.
3. Practically all adults have the right to vote in the election of officials.
4. Practically all adults have the right to run for elective offices.
5. Citizens have a right to express themselves without the danger of severe punishment on political matters broadly defined. . . .
6. Citizens have a right to seek out alternative sources of information. Moreover, alternative sources of information exist and are protected by law.
7. . . . Citizens also have the right to form relatively independent associations or organizations, including independent political parties and interest groups.[10]

These seven conditions seem to capture the essence of procedural democracy for many theorists, but we propose to add two others. The first might be thought of as a further refinement of item (1), while the second might be called an implicit prior condition to all seven of the above.

1. Popularly elected officials must be able to exercise their constitutional powers without being subjected to overriding (albeit informal) opposition from unelected officials. Democracy is in jeopardy if military officers, entrenched civil servants, or state managers retain the capacity to act independently of elected civilians or even veto decisions made by the people's representatives. Without this additional caveat, the militarized polities of contemporary Central America, where civilian control over the military does not exist, might be classified by many scholars as democracies, just as they have been (with the exception of Sandinista Nicaragua) by U.S. policy makers. The caveat thus guards against what we earlier called "electoralism"—the tendency to focus on the holding of elections while ignoring other political realities.
2. The polity must be self-governing; it must be able to act independently of constraints imposed by some other overarching political system. Dahl and other contemporary democratic theorists probably took this condition for granted since they referred to formally sovereign nation-states. However, with the development of blocs, alliances, spheres of influence, and a variety of "neocolonial" arrangements, the question of autonomy has been a salient one. Is a system really democratic if its elected officials are unable to make binding decisions without the approval of actors outside their territorial domain? This is significant even if the outsiders are relatively free to alter or even end the encompassing arrangement (as in Puerto Rico), but it becomes especially critical if neither condition [pertains] (as in the Baltic states).

Principles That Make Democracy Feasible

Lists of component processes and procedural norms help us to specify what democracy is, but they do not tell us much about how it actually functions. The simplest answer is "by the consent of the people"; the more complex one is "by the contingent consent of politicians acting under conditions of bounded uncertainty."

In a democracy, representatives must at least informally agree that those who win greater electoral support or influence over policy will not use their temporary superiority to bar the losers from taking office or exerting influence in the future, and that in exchange for this opportunity to keep competing for power and place, momentary losers will respect the winners' right to make binding decisions. Citizens are expected to obey the decisions ensuing from such a process of competition, provided its outcome remains contingent upon their collective preferences as expressed through fair and regular elections or open and repeated negotiations.

The challenge is not so much to find a set of goals that command widespread consensus as to find a set of rules that embody contingent consent. The precise shape of this "democratic bargain," to use Dahl's expression,[11] can vary a good deal from society to society. It depends on social cleavages and such subjective factors as mutual trust, the standard of fairness, and the willingness to compromise. It may even be compatible with a great deal of dissensus on substantive policy issues.

All democracies involve a degree of uncertainty about who will be elected and what policies they will pursue. Even in those polities where one party persists in winning elections or one policy is consistently implemented, the possibility of change through independent collective action still exists, as in Italy, Japan, and the Scandinavian social democracies. If it does not, the system is not democratic, as in Mexico, Senegal, or Indonesia.

But the uncertainty embedded in the core of all democracies is bounded. Not just any actor can get into the competition and raise any issue he or she pleases—there are previously established rules that must be respected. Not just any policy can be adopted—there are conditions that

must be met. Democracy institutionalizes "normal," limited political uncertainty. These boundaries vary from country to country. Constitutional guarantees of property, privacy, expression, and other rights are a part of this, but the most effective boundaries are generated by competition among interest groups and cooperation within civil society. Whatever the rhetoric (and some polities appear to offer their citizens more dramatic alternatives than others), once the rules of contingent consent have been agreed upon, the actual variation is likely to stay within a predictable and generally accepted range.

This emphasis on operative guidelines contrasts with a highly persistent, but misleading theme in recent literature on democracy—namely, the emphasis upon "civic culture." The principles we have suggested here rest on rules of prudence, not on deeply ingrained habits of tolerance, moderation, mutual respect, fair play, readiness to compromise, or trust in public authorities. Waiting for such habits to sink deep and lasting roots implies a very slow process of regime consolidation—one that takes generations—and it would probably condemn most contemporary experiences *ex hypothesi* to failure. Our assertion is that contingent consent and bounded uncertainty can emerge from the interaction between antagonistic and mutually suspicious actors and that the far more benevolent and ingrained norms of a civic culture are better thought of as a *product* and not a producer of democracy.

How Democracies Differ

Several concepts have been deliberately excluded from our generic definition of democracy, despite the fact that they have been frequently associated with it in both everyday practice and scholarly work. They are, nevertheless, especially important when it comes to distinguishing subtypes of democracy. Since no single set of actual institutions, practices, or values embodies democracy, polities moving away from authoritarian rule can mix different components to produce different democracies. It is important to recognize that these do not define points along a single continuum of improving performance, but a matrix of potential combinations that are *differently* democratic.

1. *Consensus*: All citizens may not agree on the substantive goals of political action or on the role of the state (although if they did, it would certainly make governing democracies much easier).
2. *Participation*: All citizens may not take an active and equal part in politics, although it must be legally possible for them to do so.
3. *Access*: Rulers may not weigh equally the preferences of all who come before them, although citizenship implies that individuals and groups should have an equal opportunity to express their preferences if they choose to do so.
4. *Responsiveness*: Rulers may not always follow the course of action preferred by the citizenry. But when they deviate from such a policy, say on grounds of "reason of state" or "overriding national interest," they must ultimately be held accountable for their actions through regular and fair processes.
5. *Majority rule*: Positions may not be allocated or rules may not be decided solely on the basis of assembling the most votes, although deviations from this principle usually must be explicitly defended and previously approved.
6. *Parliamentary sovereignty*: The legislature may not be the only body that can make rules or even the one with final authority in deciding which laws are binding, although where executive, judicial, or other public bodies make that ultimate choice, they too must be accountable for their actions.
7. *Party government*: Rulers may not be nominated, promoted, and disciplined in their activities by well-organized and program-matically coherent political parties, although where they are not, it may prove more difficult to form an effective government.
8. *Pluralism*: The political process may not be based on a multiplicity of overlapping, voluntaristic, and autonomous private groups. However, where there are monopolies of representation, hierarchies of association, and obligatory memberships, it is likely that the interests involved will be more closely linked to the state and the separation between the public and private spheres of action will be much less distinct.
9. *Federalism*: The territorial division of authority may not involve multiple levels and local autonomies, least of all ones enshrined in a constitutional document, although some dispersal of power across territorial and/or functional units is characteristic of all democracies.
10. *Presidentialism*: The chief executive officer may not be a single person and he or she may not be directly elected by the citizenry as a whole, although some concentration of authority is present in all democracies, even if it is exercised collectively and only held indirectly accountable to the electorate.
11. *Checks and Balances*: It is not necessary that the different branches of government be systematically pitted against one another, although governments by assembly, by executive concentrations, by judicial command, or even by dictatorial fiat (as in time of war) must be ultimately accountable to the citizenry as a whole.

While each of the above has been named as an essential component of democracy, they should instead be seen either as indicators of this or that type of democracy, or else as useful standards for evaluating the performance of particular regimes. To include them as part of the generic definition of democracy itself would be to mistake the American polity for the universal model of democratic governance. Indeed, the parliamentary, consociational, unitary, corporatist, and concentrated arrangements of continental Europe may have some unique virtues for guiding polities through the uncertain transition from autocratic to democratic rule.[12]

What Democracy Is Not

We have attempted to convey the general meaning of modern democracy without identifying it with some particular set of rules and institutions or restricting it to some specific culture or level of development. We have also argued that it cannot be reduced to the regular holding of elections or equated with a particular notion of the role of the state, but we have not said much more about what democracy is not or about what democracy may not be capable of producing.

There is an understandable temptation to load too many expectations on this concept and to imagine that by attaining democracy, a society will have resolved all of its political, social, economic, administrative, and cultural problems. Unfortunately, "all good things do not necessarily go together."

First, democracies are not necessarily more efficient economically than other forms of government. Their rates of aggregate growth, savings, and investment may be no better than those of nondemocracies. This is especially likely during the transition, when propertied groups and administrative elites may respond to real or imagined threats to the "rights" they enjoyed under authoritarian rule by initiating capital flight, disinvestment, or sabotage. In time, depending upon the type of democracy, benevolent long-term effects upon income distribution, aggregate demand, education, productivity, and creativity may eventually combine to improve economic and social performance, but it is certainly too much to expect that these improvements will occur immediately—much less that they will be defining characteristics of democratization.

Second, democracies are not necessarily more efficient administratively. Their capacity to make decisions may even be slower than that of the regimes they replace, if only because more actors must be consulted. The costs of getting things done may be higher, if only because "payoffs" have to be made to a wider and more resourceful set of clients (although one should never underestimate the degree of corruption to be found within autocracies). Popular satisfaction with the new democratic government's performance may not even seem greater, if only because necessary compromises often please no one completely, and because the losers are free to complain.

Third, democracies are not likely to appear more orderly, consensual, stable, or governable than the autocracies they replace. This is partly a byproduct of democratic freedom of expression, but it is also a reflection of the likelihood of continuing disagreement over new rules and institutions. These products of imposition or compromise are often initially quite ambiguous in nature and uncertain in effect until actors have learned how to use them. What is more, they come in the aftermath of serious struggles motivated by high ideals. Groups and individuals with recently acquired autonomy will test certain rules, protest against the actions of certain institutions, and insist on renegotiating their part of the bargain. Thus the presence of antisystem parties should be neither surprising nor seen as a failure of democratic consolidation. What counts is whether such parties are willing, however reluctantly, to play by the general rules of bounded uncertainty and contingent consent.

Governability is a challenge for all regimes, not just democratic ones. Given the political exhaustion and loss of legitimacy that have befallen autocracies from sultanistic Paraguay to totalitarian Albania, it may seem that only democracies can now be expected to govern effectively and legitimately. Experience has shown, however, that democracies too can lose the ability to govern. Mass publics can become disenchanted with their performance. Even more threatening is the temptation for leaders to fiddle with procedures and ultimately undermine the principles of contingent consent and bounded uncertainty. Perhaps the most critical moment comes once the politicians begin to settle into the more predictable roles and relations of a consolidated democracy. Many will find their expectations frustrated; some will discover that the new rules of competition put them at a disadvantage; a few may even feel that their vital interests are threatened by popular majorities.

Finally, democracies will have more open societies and polities than the autocracies they replace, but not necessarily more open economies. Many of today's most successful and well-established democracies have historically resorted to protectionism and closed borders, and have relied extensively upon public institutions to promote economic development. While the long-term compatibility between democracy and capitalism does not seem to be in doubt, despite their continuous tension, it is not clear whether the promotion of such liberal economic goals as the right of individuals to own property and retain profits, the clearing function of markets, the private settlement of disputes, the freedom to produce without government regulation, or the privatization of state-owned enterprises necessarily furthers the consolidation of democracy. After all, democracies do need to levy taxes and regulate certain transactions, especially where private monopolies and oligopolies exist. Citizens or their representatives may decide that it is desirable to protect the rights of collectivities from encroachment by individuals, especially propertied ones, and they may choose to set aside certain forms of property for public or cooperative ownership. In short, notions of economic liberty that are currently put forward in neoliberal economic models are not synonymous with political freedom—and may even impede it.

Democratization will not necessarily bring in its wake economic growth, social peace, administrative efficiency, political harmony, free markets, or "the end of ideology." Least of all will it bring about "the end of history." No doubt some of these qualities could make the consolidation of democracy easier, but they are neither prerequisites for it nor immediate products of it. Instead, what we should be hoping for is the emergence of political institutions that can peacefully compete to form governments and influence public policy, that can channel social and economic conflicts through regular procedures, and that have sufficient linkages to civil society to represent their constituencies and commit them to collective courses of action. Some types of democracies, especially in developing countries, have been unable to fulfill this promise, perhaps due to the circumstances of their transition from authoritarian rule.[13] The democratic wager is that such a regime, once established, will not only persist by reproducing itself within its initial confining conditions, but will eventually expand beyond them.[14] Unlike authoritarian regimes, democracies have the capacity to modify their rules and institutions consensually in response to changing circumstances. They may not immediately produce all the goods mentioned above, but they stand a better chance of eventually doing so than do autocracies.

NOTES

1. For a comparative analysis of the recent regime changes in southern Europe and Latin America, see Guillermo O'Donnell, Philippe C. Schmitter, and Laurence Whitehead, eds., *Transitions from Authoritarian Rule*, 4 vols. (Baltimore: Johns Hopkins University Press, 1986). For another compilation that adopts a more structural approach see Larry Diamond, Juan Linz, and Seymour Martin Lipset, eds., *Democracy in Developing Countries*, vols. 2, 3, and 4 (Boulder, Colo.: Lynne Rienner, 1989).

2. Numerous attempts have been made to codify and quantify the existence of democracy across political systems. The best known is probably Freedom House's *Freedom in the*

World: Political Rights and Civil Liberties, published since 1973 by Greenwood Press and since 1988 by University Press of America. Also see Charles Humana, *World Human Rights Guide* (New York: Facts on File, 1986).

3. The definition most commonly used by American social scientists is that of Joseph Schumpeter: "that institutional arrangement for arriving at political decisions in which individuals acquire the power to decide by means of a competitive struggle for the people's vote." *Capitalism, Socialism, and Democracy* (London: George Allen and Unwin, 1943), 269. We accept certain aspects of the classical procedural approach to modern democracy, but differ primarily in our emphasis on the accountability of rulers to citizens and the relevance of mechanisms of competition other than elections.

4. Not only do some countries practice a stable form of democracy without a formal constitution (e.g., Great Britain and Israel), but even more countries have constitutions and legal codes that offer no guarantee of reliable practice. On paper, Stalin's 1936 constitution for the USSR was a virtual model of democratic rights and entitlements.

5. For the most valiant attempt to make some sense out of this thicket of distinctions, see Juan Linz, "Totalitarian and Authoritarian Regimes" in *Handbook of Political Science*, eds. Fred I. Greenstein and Nelson W. Polsby (Reading, Mass.: Addison Wesley, 1975), 175–411.

6. "Publius" (Alexander Hamilton, John Jay, and James Madison), *The Federalist Papers* (New York: Anchor Books, 1961). The quote is from Number 10.

7. See Terry Karl, "Imposing Consent? Electoralism versus Democratization in El Salvador," in *Elections and Democratization in Latin America, 1980–1985*, eds. Paul Drake and Eduardo Silva (San Diego: Center for Iberian and Latin American Studies, Center for US/Mexican Studies, University of California, San Diego, 1986), 9–36.

8. Alexis de Tocqueville, *Democracy in America*, 2 vols. (New York: Vintage Books, 1945).

9. This fear of overloaded government and the imminent collapse of democracy is well reflected in the work of Samuel P. Huntington during the 1970s. See especially Michel Crozier, Samuel P. Huntington, and Joji Watanuki, *The Crisis of Democracy* (New York: New York University Press, 1975). For Huntington's (revised) thoughts about the prospects for democracy, see his "Will More Countries Become Democratic?," *Political Science Quarterly* 99 (Summer 1984): 193–218.

10. Robert Dahl, *Dilemmas of Pluralist Democracy* (New Haven: Yale University Press, 1982), 11.

11. Robert Dahl, *After the Revolution: Authority in a Good Society* (New Haven: Yale University Press, 1970).

12. See Juan Linz, "The Perils of Presidentialism," *Journal of Democracy* 1 (Winter 1990): 51–69, and the ensuing discussion by Donald Horowitz, Seymour Martin Lipset, and Juan Linz in *Journal of Democracy* 1 (Fall 1990): 73–91.

13. Terry Lynn Karl, "Dilemmas of Democratization in Latin America" *Comparative Politics* 23 (October 1990): 1–23.

14. Otto Kirchheimer, "Confining Conditions and Revolutionary Breakthroughs," *American Political Science Review* 59 (1965): 964–974.

AREND LIJPHART

CONSTITUTIONAL CHOICES FOR NEW DEMOCRACIES

Two fundamental choices that confront architects of new democratic constitutions are those between plurality elections and proportional representation (PR) and between parliamentary and presidential forms of government. The merits of presidentialism and parliamentarism were extensively debated by Juan J. Linz, Seymour Martin Lipset, and Donald L. Horowitz in the Fall 1990 issue of the *Journal of Democracy*.[1] I strongly concur with Horowitz's contention that the electoral system is an equally vital element in democratic constitutional design, and therefore that it is of crucial importance to evaluate these two sets of choices in relation with each other. Such an analysis, as I will try to show, indicates that the combination of parliamentarism with proportional representation should be an especially attractive one to newly democratic and democratizing countries.

The comparative study of democracies has shown that the type of electoral system is significantly related to the development of a country's party system, its type of executive (one-party vs. coalition cabinets), and the relationship between its executive and legislature. Countries that use the plurality method of election (almost always applied, at the national level, in single-member districts) are likely to have two-party systems, one-party governments, and executives that are dominant in relation to their legislatures. These are the main characteristics of the Westminster or *majoritarian* model of democracy, in which power is concentrated in the hands of the majority party. Conversely, PR is likely to be associated with multiparty systems, coalition governments (including, in many cases, broad and inclusive

From Larry Diamond and Marc F. Plattner, eds., *The Global Resurgence of Democracy* (Baltimore: Johns Hopkins University Press, 1996), pp. 162–74.

coalitions), and more equal executive-legislative power relations. These latter characteristics typify the *consensus* model of democracy, which, instead of relying on pure and concentrated majority rule, tries to limit, divide, separate, and share power in a variety of ways.[2]

Three further points should be made about these two sets of related traits. First, the relationships are mutual. For instance, plurality elections favor the maintenance of a two-party system; but an existing two-party system also favors the maintenance of plurality, which gives the two principal parties great advantages that they are unlikely to abandon. Second, if democratic political engineers desire to promote either the majoritarian cluster of characteristics (plurality, a two-party system, and a dominant, one-party cabinet) or the consensus cluster (PR, multipartism, coalition government, and a stronger legislature), the most practical way to do so is by choosing the appropriate electoral system. Giovanni Sartori has aptly called electoral systems "the most specific manipulative instrument of politics."[3] Third, important variations exist among PR systems. Without going into all the technical details, a useful distinction can be made between *extreme* PR, which poses few barriers to small parties, and *moderate* PR. The latter limits the influence of minor parties through such means as applying PR in small districts instead of large districts or nationwide balloting, and requiring parties to receive a minimum percentage of the vote in order to gain representation, such as the 5-percent threshold in Germany. The Dutch, Israeli, and Italian systems exemplify extreme PR and the German and Swedish systems, moderate PR.

The second basic constitutional choice, between parliamentary and presidential forms of government, also affects the majoritarian or consensus character of the political system. Presidentialism yields majoritarian effects on the party system and on the type of executive, but a consensus effect on executive-legislative relations. By formally separating the executive and legislative powers, presidential systems generally promote a rough executive-legislative balance of power. On the other hand, presidentialism tends to foster a two-party system, as the presidency is the biggest political prize to be won, and only the largest parties have a chance to win it. This advantage for the big parties often carries over into legislative elections as well (especially if presidential and legislative elections are held simultaneously), even if the legislative elections are conducted under PR rules. Presidentialism usually produces cabinets composed solely of members of the governing party. In fact, presidential systems concentrate executive power to an even greater degree than does a one-party parliamentary cabinet—not just in a single *party* but in a single *person*.

Explaining Past Choices

My aim is not simply to describe alternative democratic systems and their majoritarian or consensus characteristics, but also to make some practical recommendations for democratic constitutional engineers. What are the main advantages and disadvantages of plurality and PR and of presidentialism and parliamentarism? One way to approach this question is to investigate why contemporary democracies made the constitutional choices they did.

Figure 1 illustrates the four combinations of basic characteristics and the countries and regions where they prevail. The purest examples of the combination of presidentialism and plurality are the United States and democracies heavily influenced by the United States, such as the Philippines and Puerto Rico. Latin American countries have overwhelmingly opted for presidential-PR systems. Parliamentary-plurality

systems exist in the United Kingdom and many former British colonies, including India, Malaysia, Jamaica, and the countries of the so-called Old Commonwealth (Canada, Australia, and New Zealand). Finally, parliamentary-PR systems are concentrated in Western Europe. Clearly, the overall pattern is to a large extent determined by geographic, cultural, and colonial factors—a point to which I shall return shortly.

Very few contemporary democracies cannot be accommodated by this classification. The major exceptions are democracies that fall in between the pure presidential and pure parliamentary types (France and Switzerland), and those that use electoral methods other than pure PR or plurality (Ireland, Japan, and, again, France).[4]

Two important factors influenced the adoption of PR in continental Europe. One was the problem of ethnic and religious minorities; PR was designed to provide minority representation and thereby to counteract potential threats to national unity and political stability. "It was no accident," Stein Rokkan writes, "that the earliest moves toward proportional representation (PR) came in the ethnically most heterogeneous countries." The second factor was the dynamic of the democratization process. PR was adopted "through a convergence of pressures from below and from above. The rising working class

Figure 1—Four Basic Types of Democracy

	Presidential	Parliamentary
Plurality Elections	United States Philippines	United Kingdom Old Commonwealth India Malaysia Jamaica
Proportional Representation	Latin America	Western Europe

wanted to lower the thresholds of representation in order to gain access to the legislatures, and the most threatened of the old-established parties demanded PR to protect their position against the new waves of mobilized voters created by universal suffrage."[5] Both factors are relevant for contemporary constitution making, especially for the many countries where there are deep ethnic cleavages or where new democratic forces need to be reconciled with the old antidemocratic groups.

The process of democratization also originally determined whether parliamentary or presidential institutions were adopted. As Douglas V. Verney has pointed out, there were two basic ways in which monarchical power could be democratized: by taking away most of the monarch's personal political prerogatives and making his cabinet responsible to the popularly elected legislature, thus creating a parliamentary system; or by removing the hereditary monarch and substituting a new, democratically elected "monarch," thus creating a presidential system.[6]

Other historical causes have been voluntary imitations of successful democracies and the dominant influence of colonial powers. As Figure 1 shows very clearly, Britain's influence as an imperial power has been enormously important. The U.S. presidential model was widely imitated in Latin America in the nineteenth century. And early in the twentieth century, PR spread quickly in continental Europe and Latin America, not only for reasons of partisan accommodation and minority protection, but also because it was widely perceived to be the most democratic method of election and hence the "wave of the democratic future."

This sentiment in favor of PR raises the controversial question of the *quality* of democracy achieved in the four alternative systems. The term "quality" refers to the degree to which a system meets such democratic norms as representativeness, accountability, equality, and participation. The claims and counterclaims are too well-known to require lengthy treatment here,

but it is worth emphasizing that the differences between the opposing camps are not as great as is often supposed. First of all, PR and plurality advocates disagree not so much about the respective effects of the two electoral methods as about the weight to be attached to these effects. Both sides agree that PR yields greater proportionality and minority representation and that plurality promotes two-party systems and one-party executives. Partisans disagree on which of these results is preferable, with the plurality side claiming that only in two-party systems can clear accountability for government policy be achieved.

In addition, both sides argue about the *effectiveness* of the two systems. Proportionalists value minority representation not just for its democratic quality but also for its ability to maintain unity and peace in divided societies. Similarly, proponents of plurality favor one-party cabinets not just because of their democratic accountability but also because of the firm leadership and effective policy making that they allegedly provide. There also appears to be a slight difference in the relative emphasis that the two sides place on quality and effectiveness. Proportionalists tend to attach greater importance to the *representativeness* of government, while plurality advocates view the *capacity to govern* as the more vital consideration.

Finally, while the debate between presidentialists and parliamentarists has not been as fierce, it clearly parallels the debate over electoral systems. Once again, the claims and counterclaims revolve around both quality and effectiveness. Presidentialists regard the direct popular election of the chief executive as a dem-ocratic asset, while parliamentarists think of the concentration of executive power in the hands of a single official as less than optimally democratic. But here the question of effectiveness has been the more seriously debated issue, with the president's strong and effective leadership role being emphasized by one side and the danger of executive-legislative conflict and stalemate by the other.

Evaluating Democratic Performance

How can the actual performance of the different types of democracies be evaluated? It is extremely difficult to find quantifiable measures of democratic performance, and therefore political scientists have rarely attempted a systematic assessment. The major exception is G. Bingham Powell's pioneering study evaluating the capacity of various democracies to maintain public order (as measured by the incidence of riots and deaths from political violence) and their levels of citizen participation (as measured by electoral turnout).[7] Following Powell's example, I will examine these and other aspects of democratic performance, including democratic representation and responsiveness, economic equality, and macroeconomic management.

Due to the difficulty of finding reliable data outside the OECD countries to measure such aspects of performance, I have limited the analysis to the advanced industrial democracies. In any event, the Latin American democracies, given their lower levels of economic development, cannot be considered comparable cases. This means that one of the four basic alternatives—the presidential-PR form of democracy prevalent only in Latin America—must be omitted from our analysis.

Although this limitation is unfortunate, few observers would seriously argue that a strong case can be made for this particular type of democracy. With the clear exception of Costa Rica and the partial exceptions of Venezuela and Colombia, the political stability and economic performance of Latin American democracies have been far from satisfactory. As Juan Linz has argued, Latin American presidential systems have been particularly prone to executive-legislative deadlock and ineffective leadership.[8] Moreover, Scott Mainwaring has shown persuasively that this problem becomes especially serious when presidents do not have majority support in their legislatures.[9] Thus the Latin

American model of presidentialism combined with PR legislative elections remains a particularly unattractive option.

The other three alternatives—presidential-plurality, parliamentary-plurality, and parliamentary-PR systems—are all represented among the firmly established Western democracies. I focus on the 14 cases that unambiguously fit these three categories. The United States is the one example of presidentialism combined with plurality. There are four cases of parliamentarism-plurality (Australia, Canada, New Zealand, and the United Kingdom), and nine democracies of the parliamentary-PR type (Austria, Belgium, Denmark, Finland, Germany, Italy, the Netherlands, Norway, and Sweden). Seven long-term, stable democracies are excluded from the analysis either because they do not fit comfortably into any one of the three categories (France, Ireland, Japan, and Switzerland), or because they are too vulnerable to external factors (Israel, Iceland, and Luxembourg).

Since a major purpose of PR is to facilitate minority representation, one would expect the PR systems to outperform plurality systems in this respect. There is little doubt that this is indeed the case. For instance, where ethnic minorities have formed ethnic political parties, as in Belgium and Finland, PR has enabled them to gain virtually perfect proportional representation. Because there are so many different kinds of ethnic and religious minorities in the democracies under analysis, it is difficult to measure systematically the *degree* to which PR succeeds in providing more representatives for minorities than does plurality. It is possible, however, to compare the representation of women—a minority in political rather than strictly numerical terms—systematically across countries. The first column of Table 1 shows the percentages of female members in the lower (or only) houses of the national legislatures in these 14 democracies during the early 1980s. The 16.4-percent average for the parliamentary-PR systems is about four times higher than the 4.1 percent for the United States or the 4.0-percent average for the

Table 1. Women's Legislative Representation, Innovative Family Policy, Voting Turnout, Income Inequality, and the Dahl Rating of Democratic Quality

	Women's Repr. 1980–82	Family Policy 1976–80	Voting Turnout 1971–80	Income Top 20% 1985	Dahl Rating 1969
Pres.-Plurality (N=1)	4.1	3.00	54.2%	39.9%	3.0
Parl.-Plurality (N=4)	4.0	2.50	75.3	42.9	4.8
Parl.-PR (N=9)	16.4	7.89	84.5	39.0	2.2

Note: The one presidential-plurality democracy is the United States; the four parliamentary-plurality democracies are Australia, Canada, New Zealand, and the United Kingdom; and the nine parliamentary-PR democracies are Austria, Belgium, Denmark, Finland, Germany, Italy, the Netherlands, Norway, and Sweden.

Sources: Based on Wilma Rule, "Electoral Systems, Contextual Factors and Women's Opportunity for Election to Parliament in Twenty-Three Democracies," *Western Political Quarterly* 40 (September 1987): 483; Harold L. Wilensky, "Common Problems, Divergent Policies: An 18-Nation Study of Family Policy," *Public Affairs Report* 31 (May 1990): 2; personal communication by Harold L. Wilensky to the author, dated 18 October 1990; Robert W. Jackman, "Political Institutions and Voter Turnout in the Industrial Democracies," *American Political Science Review* 81 (June 1987): 420; World Bank, *World Development Report 1989* (New York: Oxford University Press, 1989), 223; Robert A. Dahl, *Polyarchy: Participation and Opposition* (New Haven: Yale University Press, 1971), 232.

parliamentary-plurality countries. To be sure, the higher social standing of women in the four Nordic countries accounts for part of the difference, but the average of 9.4 percent in the five other parliamentary-PR countries remains more than twice as high as in the plurality countries.

Does higher representation of women result in the advancement of their interests? Harold L. Wilensky's careful rating of democracies with regard to the innovativeness and expansiveness of their family policies—a matter of special concern to women—indicates that it does.[10] On a 13-point scale (from a maximum of 12 to a minimum of 0), the scores of these countries range from 11 to 1. The differences among the three groups (as shown in the second column of Table 1) are striking: the PR countries have an average score of 7.89, whereas the parliamentary-plurality countries have an average of just 2.50, and the U.S. only a slightly higher score of 3.00. Here again, the Nordic countries have the highest scores, but the 6.80 average of the non-Nordic PR countries is still well above that of the plurality countries.

The last three columns of Table 1 show indicators of democratic quality. The third column lists the most reliable figures on electoral participation (in the 1970s); countries with compulsory voting (Australia, Belgium, and Italy) are not included in the averages. Compared with the extremely low voter turnout of 54.2 percent in the United States, the parliamentary-plurality systems perform a great deal better (about 75 percent). But the average in the parliamentary-PR systems is still higher, at slightly above 84 percent. Since the maximum turnout that is realistically attainable is around 90 percent (as indicated by the turnouts in countries with compulsory voting), the difference between 75 and 84 percent is particularly striking.

Another democratic goal is political equality, which is more likely to prevail in the absence of great economic inequalities. The fourth column of Table 1 presents the World Bank's percentages of total income earned by the top 20 percent of households in the mid-1980s.[11] They show a slightly less unequal distribution of income in the parliamentary-PR than in the parliamentary-plurality systems, with the United States in an intermediate position.

Finally, the fifth column reports Robert A. Dahl's ranking of democracies according to ten indicators of democratic quality, such as free-dom of the press, freedom of association, com-petitive party systems, strong parties and interest groups, and effective legislatures.[12] The stable democracies range from a highest rating of 1 to a low of 6. There is a slight pro-PR bias in Dahl's ranking (he includes a number-of-parties variable that rates multiparty systems some-what higher than two-party systems), but even when we discount this bias we find striking dif-ferences between the parliamentary-PR and parliamentary-plurality countries: six of the for-mer are given the highest score, whereas most of the latter receive the next to lowest score of 5.

No such clear differences are apparent when we examine the effect of the type of democracy on the maintenance of public order and peace. Parliamentary-plurality systems had the lowest incidence of riots during the period 1948–77, but the highest incidence of political deaths; the lat-ter figure, however, derives almost entirely from the high number of political deaths in the United Kingdom, principally as a result of the Northern Ireland problem. A more elaborate statistical analysis shows that societal division is a much more important factor than type of democracy in explaining variation in the incidence of politi-cal riots and deaths in the 13 parliamentary countries.[13]

A major argument in favor of plurality sys-tems has been that they favor "strong" one-party governments that can pursue "effective" public policies. One key area of government activity in which this pattern should manifest itself is the management of the economy. Thus advocates of plurality systems received a rude shock in 1987 when the average per capita GDP in Italy (a PR and multiparty democracy with notoriously un-cohesive and unstable governments) surpassed that of the United Kingdom, typically regarded as the very model of strong and effective govern-ment. If Italy had discovered large amounts of oil in the Mediterranean, we would undoubtedly explain its superior economic performance in terms of this fortuitous factor. But it was not Italy but Britain that discovered the oil!

Economic success is obviously not solely de-termined by government policy. When we exam-ine economic performance over a long period of time, however, the effects of external influences are minimized, especially if we focus on coun-tries with similar levels of economic develop-ment. Table 2 presents OECD figures from the 1960s through the 1980s for the three most important aspects of macroeconomic perfor-mance—average annual economic growth, infla-tion, and unemployment rates.

Although Italy's economic growth has indeed been better than that of Britain, the parliamentary-plurality and parliamentary-PR countries as groups do not differ much from each other or from the United States. The slightly higher growth rates in the parliamentary-PR sys-tems cannot be considered significant. With re-gard to inflation, the United States has the best record, followed by the parliamentary-PR sys-tems. The most sizable differences appear in un-employment levels; here the parliamentary-PR

Table 2. Economic Growth, Inflation, and Unemployment (in percent)

	Economic Growth 1961–88	Inflation 1961–88	Unemployment 1965–88
Pres.-Plurality (N=1)	3.3	5.1	6.1
Parl.-Plurality (N=4)	3.4	7.5	6.1
Parl.-PR (N=9)	3.5	6.3	4.4

Sources: *OECD Economic Outlook*, No. 26 (December 1979), 131; No. 30 (December 1981), 131, 140, 142; No. 46 (December 1989), 166, 176, 182.

countries perform significantly better than the plurality countries.[14] Comparing the parliamentary-plurality and parliamentary-PR countries on all three indicators, we find that the performance of the latter is uniformly better.

Lessons for Developing Countries

Political scientists tend to think that plurality systems such as the United Kingdom and the United States are superior with regard to democratic quality and governmental effectiveness—a tendency best explained by the fact that political science has always been an Anglo-American-oriented discipline. This prevailing opinion is largely contradicted, however, by the empirical evidence presented above. Wherever significant differences appear, the parliamentary-PR systems almost invariably post the best records, particularly with respect to representation, protection of minority interests, voter participation, and control of unemployment.

This finding contains an important lesson for democratic constitutional engineers: the parliamentary-PR option is one that should be given serious consideration. Yet a word of caution is also in order, since parliamentary-PR democracies differ greatly among themselves. Moderate PR and moderate multipartism, as in Germany and Sweden, offer more attractive models than the extreme PR and multiparty systems of Italy and the Netherlands. As previously noted, though, even Italy has a respectable record of democratic performance.

But are these conclusions relevant to newly democratic and democratizing countries in Asia, Africa, Latin America, and Eastern Europe, which are trying to make democracy work in the face of economic underdevelopment and ethnic divisions? Do not these difficult conditions require strong executive leadership in the form of a powerful president or a Westminster-style, dominant one-party cabinet?

With regard to the problem of deep ethnic cleavages, these doubts can be easily laid to rest.

Divided societies, both in the West and elsewhere, need peaceful coexistence among the contending ethnic groups. This requires conciliation and compromise, goals that in turn require the greatest possible inclusion of representatives of these groups in the decision-making process. Such power sharing can be arranged much more easily in parliamentary and PR systems than in presidential and plurality systems. A president almost inevitably belongs to one ethnic group, and hence presidential systems are particularly inimical to ethnic power sharing. And while Westminster-style parliamentary systems feature collegial cabinets, these tend not to be ethnically inclusive, particularly when there is a majority ethnic group. It is significant that the British government, in spite of its strong majoritarian traditions, recognized the need for consensus and power sharing in religiously and ethnically divided Northern Ireland. Since 1973, British policy has been to try to solve the Northern Ireland problem by means of PR elections and an inclusive coalition government.

As Horowitz has pointed out, it may be possible to alleviate the problems of presidentialism by requiring that a president be elected with a stated minimum of support from different groups, as in Nigeria.[15] But this is a palliative that cannot compare with the advantages of a truly collective and inclusive executive. Similarly, the example of Malaysia shows that a parliamentary system can have a broad multiparty and multiethnic coalition cabinet in spite of plurality elections, but this requires elaborate preelection pacts among the parties. These exceptions prove the rule: the ethnic power sharing that has been attainable in Nigeria and Malaysia only on a limited basis and through very special arrangements is a natural and straightforward result of parliamentary-PR forms of democracy.

PR and Economic Policy Making

The question of which form of democracy is most conducive to economic development is more difficult to answer. We simply do not have enough cases of durable Third World democracies representing the different systems (not to mention the lack of reliable economic data) to make an unequivocal evaluation. However, the conventional wisdom that economic development requires the unified and decisive leadership of a strong president or a Westminster-style dominant cabinet is highly suspect. First of all, if an inclusive executive that must do more bargaining and conciliation were less effective at economic policy making than a dominant and exclusive executive, then presumably an authoritarian government free of legislative interference or internal dissent would be optimal. This reasoning—a frequent excuse for the overthrow of democratic governments in the Third World in the 1960s and 1970s—has now been thoroughly discredited. To be sure, we do have a few examples of economic miracles wrought by authoritarian regimes, such as those in South Korea or Taiwan, but these are more than counterbalanced by the sorry economic records of just about all the nondemocratic governments in Africa, Latin America, and Eastern Europe.

Second, many British scholars, notably the eminent political scientist S.E. Finer, have come to the conclusion that economic development requires not so much a *strong* hand as a *steady* one. Reflecting on the poor economic performance of post–World War II Britain, they have argued that each of the governing parties indeed provided reasonably strong leadership in economic policy making but that alternations in governments were too "absolute and abrupt," occurring "between two sharply polarized parties each eager to repeal a large amount of its predecessor's legislation." What is needed, they argue, is "greater stability and continuity" and "greater moderation in policy," which could be provided by a shift to PR and to coalition governments much more likely to be centrist in orientation.[16] This argument would appear to be equally applicable both to developed and developing countries.

Third, the case for strong presidential or Westminster-style governments is most com-

pelling where rapid decision making is essential. This means that in foreign and defense policy parliamentary-PR systems may be at a disadvantage. But in economic policy making speed is not particularly important—quick decisions are not necessarily wise ones.

Why then do we persist in distrusting the economic effectiveness of democratic systems that engage in broad consultation and bargaining aimed at a high degree of consensus? One reason is that multiparty and coalition governments *seem* to be messy, quarrelsome, and inefficient in contrast to the clear authority of strong presidents and strong one-party cabinets. But we should not let ourselves be deceived by these superficial appearances. A closer look at presidential systems reveals that the most successful cases—such as the United States, Costa Rica, and pre-1970 Chile—are at least equally quarrelsome and, in fact, are prone to paralysis and deadlock rather than steady and effective economic policy making. In any case, the argument should not be about governmental aesthetics but about actual performance. The undeniable elegance of the Westminster model is not a valid reason for adopting it.

The widespread skepticism about the economic capability of parliamentary-PR systems stems from confusing governmental strength with effectiveness. In the short run, one-party cabinets or presidents may well be able to formulate economic policy with greater ease and speed. In the long run, however, policies supported by a broad consensus are more likely to be successfully carried out and to remain on course than policies imposed by a "strong" government against the wishes of important interest groups.

To sum up, the parliamentary-PR form of democracy is clearly better than the major alternatives in accommodating ethnic differences, and it has a slight edge in economic policy making as well. The argument that considerations of governmental effectiveness mandate the rejection of parliamentary-PR democracy for developing countries is simply not tenable. Constitution makers in new democracies would do themselves and their countries a great disservice by ignoring this attractive democratic model.

NOTES

1. Donald L. Horowitz, "Comparing Democratic Systems," Seymour Martin Lipset, "The Centrality of Political Culture," and Juan J. Linz, "The Virtues of Parliamentarism," *Journal of Democracy* 1 (Fall 1990): 73–91. A third set of important decisions concerns institutional arrangements that are related to the difference between federal and unitary forms of government: the degree of government centralization, unicameralism or bicameralism, rules for constitutional amendment, and judicial review. Empirical analysis shows that these factors tend to be related: federal countries are more likely to be decentralized, to have significant bicameralism, and to have "rigid" constitutions that are difficult to amend and protected by judicial review.

2. For a fuller discussion of the differences between majoritarian and consensus government, see Arend Lijphart, *Democracies: Patterns of Majoritarian and Consensus Government in Twenty-One Countries* (New Haven: Yale University Press, 1984).

3. Giovanni Sartori, "Political Development and Political Engineering," in *Public Policy* vol. 17, eds. John D. Montgomery and Alfred O. Hirschman (Cambridge: Harvard University Press, 1968), 273.

4. The first scholar to emphasize the close connection between culture and these constitutional arrangements was G. Bingham Powell, Jr. in his *Contemporary Democracies Participation, Stability, and Violence* (Cambridge: Harvard University Press, 1982), 67. In my previous writings, I have sometimes classified Finland as a presidential or semi-presidential system, but I now agree with Powell (pp. 56–57) that, although the di-

rectly elected Finnish president has special authority in foreign policy, Finland operates like a parliamentary system in most other respects. Among the exceptions, Ireland is a doubtful case; I regard its system of the single transferable vote as mainly a PR method, but other authors have classified it as a plurality system. And I include Australia in the parliamentary-plurality group, because its alternative-vote system, while not identical with plurality, operates in a similar fashion.

5. Stein Rokkan, *Citizens, Elections, Parties: Approaches to the Comparative Study of the Processes of Development* (Oslo: Universitetsforlaget, 1970), 157.

6. Douglas V. Verney, *The Analysis of Political Systems* (London: Routledge and Kegan Paul, 1959), 18–23, 42–43.

7. Powell, op. cit., esp. 12–29 and 111–74.

8. Juan J. Linz, "The Perils of Presidentialism," *Journal of Democracy* 1 (Winter 1990), 51–69.

9. Scott Mainwaring, "Presidentialism in Latin America," *Latin American Research Review* 25 (1990), 167–70.

10. Wilensky's ratings are based on a five-point scale (from 4 to 0) "for each of three policy clusters: existence and length of maternity and parental leave, paid and unpaid; availability and accessibility of public daycare programs and government effort to expand daycare; and flexibility of retirement systems. They measure government action to assure care of children and maximize choices in balancing work and family demands for everyone." See Harold L. Wilensky, "Common Problems, Divergent Policies: An 18-Nation Study of Family Policy," *Public Affairs Report* 31 (May 1990), 2.

11. Because of missing data, Austria is not included in the parliamentary-PR average.

12. Robert A. Dahl, *Polyarchy: Participation and Opposition* (New Haven: Yale University Press, 1971), 231–45.

13. This multiple-correlation analysis shows that societal division, as measured by the de-

gree of organizational exclusiveness of ethnic and religious groups, explains 33 percent
of the variance in riots and 25 percent of the
variance in political deaths. The additional
explanation by type of democracy is only 2
percent for riots (with plurality countries
slightly more orderly) and 13 percent for
deaths (with the PR countries slightly more
peaceful).

14. Comparable unemployment data for Austria, Denmark, and New Zealand are not
available, and these countries are therefore
not included in the unemployment figures in
Table 2.

15. Horowitz, op. cit., 76–77.

16. S.E. Finer, "Adversary Politics and Electoral
Reform," in *Adversary Politics and Electoral
Reform*, ed. S.E. Finer (London: Anthony
Wigram, 1975), 30–31.

ROBERT D. PUTNAM

TUNING IN, TUNING OUT: THE STRANGE DISAPPEARANCE OF SOCIAL CAPITAL IN AMERICA

It is a daunting honor to deliver the inaugural
Pool Lecture. Ithiel de Sola Pool was a
brilliant, broad-gauged scholar whose interests ranged from the Nazi elite to direct satellite
broadcasting, from the first rigorous computer
simulation of electoral behavior to the development of network theory, from which he invented "small world" research. He helped found
the field of political communications. A graduate of the University of Chicago's political science department during its classic golden age,
and first chair of the MIT political science department, Pool must also have been a remarkable teacher, for his students continue to
contribute to our understanding of technology,
communications, and political behavior. When
I accepted this honor, I did not guess how close
my own inquiry would lead me to Pool's own
professional turf. I shall return to the contem-

porary relevance of Pool's insights at the conclusion of this talk.

For the last year or so, I have been wrestling
with a difficult mystery. It is, if I am right, a puzzle of some importance to the future of American
democracy. It is a classic brain-teaser, with a cor-
pus delicti, a crime scene strewn with clues, and
many potential suspects. As in all good detective
stories, however, some plausible miscreants turn
out to have impeccable alibis, and some important clues hint at portentous developments that
occurred long before the curtain rose. Moreover,
like Agatha Christie's *Murder on the Orient Express*, this crime may have had more than one
perpetrator, so that we shall need to sort out
ringleaders from accomplices. Finally, I need to
make clear at the outset that I am not yet sure
that I have solved the mystery. In that sense, this
lecture represents work-in-progress. I have a
prime suspect that I am prepared to indict, but
the evidence is not yet strong enough to convict,
so I invite your help in sifting clues.

From *PS: Political Science & Politics* (December 1995),
pp. 664–83.

Theories and Measures of Social Capital

Allow me to set the scene by saying a word or two about my own recent work.[1] Several years ago I conducted research on the arcane topic of local government in Italy (Putnam 1993). That study concluded that the performance of government and other social institutions is powerfully influenced by citizen engagement in community affairs, or what (following Coleman 1990) I termed *social capital*. I am now seeking to apply that set of ideas and insights to the urgent problems of contemporary American public life.

By "social capital," I mean features of social life—networks, norms, and trust—that enable participants to act together more effectively to pursue shared objectives. Whether or not their shared goals are praiseworthy is, of course, entirely another matter. To the extent that the norms, networks, and trust link substantial sectors of the community and span underlying social cleavages—to the extent that the social capital is of a "bridging" sort—then the enhanced cooperation is likely to serve broader interests and to be widely welcomed. On the other hand, groups like the Michigan militia or youth gangs also embody a kind of social capital, for these networks and norms, too, enable members to cooperate more effectively, albeit to the detriment of the wider community.

Social capital, in short, refers to social connections and the attendant norms and trust. Who benefits from these connections, norms, and trust—the individual, the wider community, or some faction within the community—must be

Figure 1—Membership Trends (1974–1994) by Type of Group (education controlled)

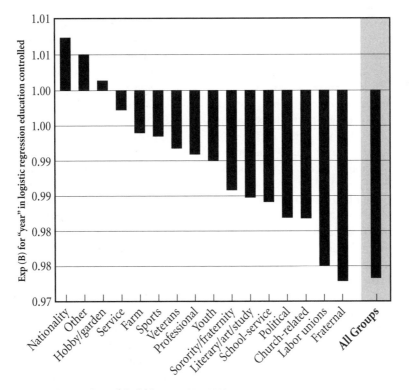

Source: General Social Survey, 1974–1994

determined empirically, not definitionally.[2] Sorting out the multiple effects of different forms of social capital is clearly a crucial task, although it is not one that I can address here. For present purposes, I am concerned with forms of social capital that, generally speaking, serve civic ends.

Social capital in this sense is closely related to political participation in the conventional sense, but these terms are not synonymous. Political participation refers to our relations with political institutions. Social capital refers to our relations with one another. Sending a check to a PAC is an act of political participation, but it does not embody or create social capital. Bowling in a league or having coffee with a friend embodies and creates social capital, though these are not acts of political participation. (A grassroots political movement or a traditional urban machine is a social capital-intensive form of political participation.) I use the term "civic engagement" to refer to people's connections with the life of their communities, not merely with politics. Civic engagement is correlated with political participation in a narrower sense, but whether they move in lock-step is an empirical question, not a logical certitude. Some forms of individualized political participation, such as check-writing, for example, might be rising at the same time that social connectedness was on the wane. Similarly, although social trust—trust in other people—and political trust—trust in political authorities—might be empirically related, they are logically quite distinct. I might well trust my neighbors without trusting city hall, or vice versa.

The theory of social capital presumes that, generally speaking, the more we connect with other people, the more we trust them, and vice versa. At least in the contexts I have so far explored, this presumption generally turns out to be true: social trust and civic engagement are strongly correlated. That is, with or without controls for education, age, income, race, gender, and so on, people who join are people who trust.[3] Moreover, this is true across different countries, and across different states in the

United States, as well as across individuals, and it is true of all sorts of groups.[4] Sorting out which way causation flows—whether joining causes trusting or trusting causes joining—is complicated both theoretically and methodologically, although John Brehm and Wendy Rahn (1995) report evidence that the causation flows mainly from joining to trusting. Be that as it may, civic connections and social trust move together. Which way are they moving?

Bowling Alone: Trends in Civic Engagement

Evidence from a number of independent sources strongly suggests that America's stock of social capital has been shrinking for more than a quarter century.

- Membership records of such diverse organizations as the PTA, the Elks club, the League of Women Voters, the Red Cross, labor unions, and even bowling leagues show that participation in many conventional voluntary associations has declined by roughly 25% to 50% over the last two to three decades (Putnam 1995, 1996).
- Surveys of the time budgets of average Americans in 1965, 1975, and 1985, in which national samples of men and women recorded every single activity undertaken during the course of a day, imply that the time we spend on informal socializing and visiting is down (perhaps by one quarter) since 1965, and that the time we devote to clubs and organizations is down even more sharply (probably by roughly half) over this period.[5]
- While Americans' interest in politics has been stable or even growing over the last three decades, and some forms of participation that require moving a pen, such as signing petitions and writing checks, have increased significantly, many measures of collective participation have fallen sharply

(Rosenstone and Hansen 1993; Putnam 1996), including attending a rally or speech (off 36% between 1973 and 1993), attending a meeting on town or school affairs (off 39%), or working for a political party (off 56%).

- Evidence from the General Social Survey demonstrates, at all levels of education and among both men and women, a drop of roughly one-quarter in group membership since 1974 and a drop of roughly one-third in social trust since 1972.[6] Moreover, as Figure 1 illustrates, slumping membership has afflicted all sorts of groups, from sports clubs and professional associations to literary discussion groups and labor unions.[7] Only nationality groups, hobby and garden clubs, and the catch-all category of "other" seem to have resisted the ebbing tide. Furthermore, Gallup polls report that church attendance fell by roughly 15% during the 1960s and has remained at that lower level ever since, while data from the National Opinion Research Center suggest that the decline continued during the 1970s and 1980s and by now amounts to roughly 30% (Putnam 1996).

Each of these approaches to the problem of measuring trends in civic engagement has advantages and drawbacks. Membership records offer long-term coverage and reasonable precision, but they may underrepresent newer, more vibrant organizations. Time budgets capture real investments of time and energy in both formal and informal settings, not merely nominal membership, but the available data are episodic and drawn from relatively small samples that are not entirely comparable across time. Surveys are more comprehensive in their coverage of various types of groups, but (apart from church attendance) comparable trend data are available only since the mid-1970s, a decade or more after the putative downturn began, so they may understate the full decline. No single source is perfect for testing the hypothesized decline in social con-

nectedness, although the consistency across different measuring rods is striking.

A fuller audit of American social capital would need to account for apparent countertrends.[8] Some observers believe, for example, that support groups and neighborhood watch groups are proliferating, and few deny that the last several decades have witnessed explosive growth in interest groups represented in Washington. The growth of "mailing list" organizations, like the American Association of Retired People or the Sierra Club, although highly significant in political (and commercial) terms, is not really a counter-example to the supposed decline in social connectedness, however, since these are not really associations in which members meet one another. Their members' ties are to common symbols and ideologies, but not to each other. These organizations are sufficiently different from classical "secondary" associations as to deserve a new rubric—perhaps "tertiary" associations. Similarly, although most secondary associations are not-for-profit, most prominent nonprofits (from Harvard University to the Metropolitan Opera) are bureaucracies, not secondary associations, so the growth of the "Third Sector" is not tantamount to a growth in social connectedness. With due regard to various kinds of counter-evidence, I believe that the weight of the available evidence confirms that Americans today are significantly less engaged with their communities than was true a generation ago.

Of course, lots of civic activity is still visible in our communities. American civil society is not moribund. Indeed, evidence suggests that America still outranks many other countries in the degree of our community involvement and social trust (Putnam 1996). But if we compare ourselves, not with other countries but with our parents, the best available evidence suggests that we are less connected with one another.

This prologue poses a number of important questions that merit further debate:

- Is it true that America's stock of social capital has diminished?

- Does it matter?
- What can we do about it?

The answer to the first two questions is, I believe, "yes," but I cannot address them further in this setting. Answering the third question—which ultimately concerns me most—depends, at least in part, on first understanding the *causes* of the strange malady afflicting American civic life. This is the mystery I seek to unravel here: Why, beginning in the 1960s and accelerating in the 1970s and 1980s, did the fabric of American community life begin to fray? Why are more Americans bowling alone?

Explaining the Erosion of Social Capital

Many possible answers have been suggested for this puzzle:

- Busyness and time pressure
- Economic hard times (or, according to alternative theories, material affluence)
- Residential mobility
- Suburbanization
- The movement of women into the paid labor force and the stresses of two-career families
- Disruption of marriage and family ties
- Changes in the structure of the American economy, such as the rise of chain stores, branch firms, and the service sector
- The Sixties (most of which actually happened in the Seventies), including
  —Vietnam, Watergate, and disillusion with public life
  —The cultural revolt against authority (sex, drugs, and so on)
- Growth of the welfare state
- The civil rights revolution
- Television, the electronic revolution, and other technological changes

Most respectable mystery writers would hesitate to tally up this many plausible suspects, no matter how energetic the fictional detective. I am not yet in a position to address all these theories—certainly not in any definitive form—but we must begin to winnow the list. To be sure, a social trend as pervasive as the one we are investigating probably has multiple causes, so our task is to assess the relative importance of such factors as these.

A solution, even a partial one, to our mystery must pass several tests.

Is the proposed explanatory factor correlated with trust and civic engagement? If not, it is difficult to see why that factor should even be placed in the lineup. For example, many women have entered the paid labor force during the period in question, but if working women turned out to be more engaged in community life than housewives, it would be harder to attribute the downturn in community organizations to the rise of two-career families.

Is the correlation spurious? If parents, for example, were more likely to be joiners than childless people, that might be an important clue. However, if the correlation between parental status and civic engagement turned out to be entirely spurious, due to the effects of (say) age, we would have to remove the declining birth rate from our list of suspects.

Is the proposed explanatory factor changing in the relevant way? Suppose, for instance, that people who often move have shallower community roots. That could be an important part of the answer to our mystery *only if* residential mobility itself had risen during this period.

Is the proposed explanatory factor vulnerable to the claim that it might be the result *of civic disengagement, not the cause?* For example, even if newspaper readership were closely correlated with civic engagement across individuals and across time, we would need to weigh the possibility that reduced newspaper circulation is the result (not the cause) of disengagement.

Against that set of benchmarks, let us consider various potential influences on social capital formation.

Education

Human capital and social capital are closely related, for education has a very powerful effect on trust and associational membership, as well as many other forms of social and political participation. Education is by far the strongest correlate that I have discovered of civic engagement in all its forms, including social trust and membership in many different types of groups.[9] In fact, as Figure 2 illustrates, the relationship between education and civic engagement is a curvilinear one of increasing returns. The last two years of college make twice as much difference to trust and group membership as the first two years of high school. The four years of education between 14 and 18 total years have *ten times more impact* on trust and membership than the first four years of formal education. The same basic pattern applies to both

men and women, and to all races and generations. Education, in short, is an extremely powerful predictor of civic engagement.

Sorting out just why education has such a massive effect on social connectedness would require a book, not a mere lecture.[10] Education is in part a proxy for social class and economic differences, but when income, social status, and education are used together to predict trust and group membership, education continues to be the primary influence. (Income and satisfaction with one's personal financial situation both have a significant independent effect.) In short, highly educated people are much more likely to be joiners and trusters, partly because they are better off economically, but mostly because of the skills, resources, and inclinations that were imparted to them at home and in school.

It is widely recognized that Americans today are better educated than our parents and

Figure 2—Social Trust and Group Membership by Years of Education

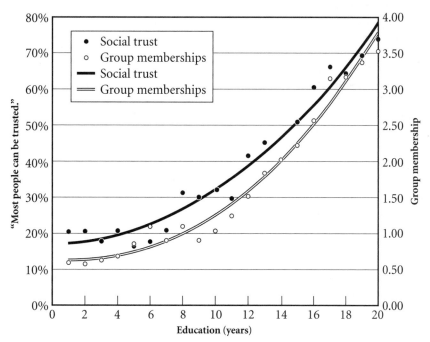

Source: General Social Survey, 1972–1994

grandparents. It is less often appreciated how massively and rapidly this trend has transformed the educational composition of the adult population during just the last two decades. Since 1972, the proportion of all adults with fewer than 12 years of education has been cut in half, falling from 40% to 18%, while the proportion with more than 12 years has nearly doubled, rising from 28% to 50%, as the generation of Americans educated around the turn of this century (most of whom did not finish high school) passed from the scene and were replaced by the baby boomers and their successors (most of whom attended college).

Thus, education boosts civic engagement sharply, and educational levels have risen massively. Unfortunately, these two undeniable facts only deepen our central mystery. By itself, the rise in educational levels should have *increased* social capital during the last 20 years by 15–20%, even assuming that the effects of education were merely linear. (Taking account of the curvilinear effect in Figure 1, the rise in trusting and joining should have been even greater, as Americans moved up the accelerating curve.) By contrast, however, the actual GSS figures show a net *decline* since the early 1970s of roughly the same magnitude (trust by about 20–25%, memberships by about 15–20%). The relative declines in social capital are similar *within* each educational category—roughly 25% in group memberships and roughly 30% in social trust since the early 1970s, and probably even more since the early 1960s.

Thus, this first investigative foray leaves us more mystified than before. We may nevertheless draw two useful conclusions from these findings, one methodological and one substantive:

1. Since education has such a powerful effect on civic engagement and social trust, we need to take account of educational differences in our exploration of other possible factors, in order to be sure that we do not confuse the consequences of education with the possible effects of other variables.[11]

2. Whatever forces lie behind the slump in civic engagement and social trust, those forces have affected all levels in American society.[12] Social capital has eroded among the one in every twelve Americans who have enjoyed the advantages (material and intellectual) of graduate study; it has eroded among the one in every eight Americans who did not even make it into high school; and it has eroded among all the strata in between. The mysterious disengagement of the last quarter century seems to have afflicted all echelons of our society.

Pressures of Time and Money

Americans certainly *feel* busier now than a generation ago: the proportion of us who report feeling "always rushed" jumped by half between the mid-1960s and the mid-1990s (Robinson and Godbey 1995). Probably the most obvious suspect behind our tendency to drop out of community affairs is pervasive busyness. And lurking nearby in the shadows are those endemic economic pressures so much discussed nowadays —job insecurity and declining real wages, especially among the lower two-thirds of the income distribution.

Yet, however culpable busyness and economic insecurity may appear at first glance, it is hard to find any incriminating evidence. In fact, the balance of the evidence argues that pressures of time and money are apparently *not* important contributors to the puzzle we seek to solve.

In the first place, time budget studies do *not* confirm the thesis that Americans are, on average, working longer than a generation ago. On the contrary, Robinson and Godbey (1995) report a five-hour per week *gain* in free time for the average American between 1965 and 1985, due partly to reduced time spent on housework and partly to earlier retirement. Their claim that Americans have more leisure time now than several decades ago is, to be sure, contested by other observers. Schor (1991), for example, reports evidence that our work hours are lengthening, especially for women. Whatever the resolution of that controversy, however, the thesis that attributes civic disengagement to longer workdays is rendered much less plausible by looking at the correlation between work hours, on the one hand, and social trust and group membership, on the other.

The available evidence strongly suggests that, in fact, long hours on the job are *not* associated with lessened involvement in civic life or reduced social trust. Quite the reverse: results from the General Social Survey show that employed people belong to somewhat *more* groups than those outside the paid labor force. Even more striking is the fact that among workers, longer hours are linked to *more* civic engagement, not less.[13] This surprising discovery is fully consistent with evidence from the time budget studies. Robinson (1990a) reports that, unsurprisingly, people who spend more time at work do feel more rushed, and these harried souls do spend less time eating, sleeping, reading books, engaging in hobbies, and just doing nothing. Compared to the rest of the population, they also spend a lot less time watching television— almost 30% less. However, they do *not* spend less time on organizational activity. In short, those who work longer forego *Nightline*, but not the Kiwanis club, *ER*, but not the Red Cross.

I do not conclude from the positive correlation between group membership and work hours that working longer actually *causes* greater civic involvement—there are too many uncontrolled variables here for that—but merely that hard work does not *prevent* civic engagement. Moreover, the nationwide falloff in joining and trusting is perfectly mirrored among full-time workers, among part-time workers, and among those outside the paid labor force. So if people are dropping out of community life, long hours do not seem to be the reason.

If time pressure is not the culprit we seek, how about financial pressures? It is true that people with lower incomes and those who feel financially strapped are less engaged in community

life and less trusting than those who are better off, even holding education constant. On the other hand, the downtrends in social trust and civic engagement are entirely visible at all levels in the income hierarchy, with no sign whatever that they are concentrated among those who have borne the brunt of the economic distress of the last two decades. Quite the contrary, the declines in engagement and trust are actually somewhat greater among the more affluent segments of the American public than among the poor and middle-income wage-earners. Furthermore, controlling for both real income and financial satisfaction does little to attenuate the fall in civic engagement and social trust. In short, neither objective nor subjective economic well-being has inoculated Americans against the virus of civic disengagement; if anything, affluence has slightly exacerbated the problem.

I cannot absolutely rule out the possibility that some part of the erosion of social capital in recent years might be linked to a more generalized sense of economic insecurity that may have affected all Americans, nor do I argue that economic distress *never* causes disengagement. Studies of the unemployed during and after the Great Depression (Jahoda, Lazarsfeld, and Zeisel 1933; Ginzberg 1943; Wilcock and Franke 1963) have described a tendency for them to disengage from community life. However, the basic patterns in the contemporary evidence are inconsistent with any simple economic explanation for our central puzzle. Pressures of time and money may be a part of the backdrop, but neither can be a principal culprit.[14]

Mobility and Suburbanization

Many studies have found that residential stability and such related phenomena as homeownership are associated with greater civic engagement. At an earlier stage in this investigation (Putnam 1995, 30), I observed that "mobility, like frequent repotting of plants, tends to disrupt root systems, and it takes time for an uprooted individual to

put down new roots." I must now report, however, that further inquiry fully exonerates residential mobility from any responsibility for our
fading civic engagement. Data from the U.S. Bureau of the Census 1995 (and earlier years) show
that rates of residential mobility have been remarkably constant over the last half century. In
fact, to the extent that there has been any change
at all, both long-distance and short-distance mobility have *declined* over the last five decades.
During the 1950s, 20% of Americans changed
residence each year and 6.9% annually moved
across county borders; during the 1990s, the
comparable figures are 17% and 6.6%. Americans, in short, are today slightly *more* rooted res-
identially than a generation ago. If the verdict on
the economic distress interpretation had to be
nuanced, the verdict on mobility is unequivocal.
This theory is simply wrong.

But if moving itself has not eroded our social
capital, what about the possibility that we have
moved to places—especially the suburbs—that
are less congenial to social connectedness? To
test this theory, we must first examine the correlation between place of residence and social capital. In fact, social connectedness does differ by
community type, but the differences turn out to
be modest and in directions that are inconsistent
with the theory.

Controlling for such demographic characteristics as education, age, income, work status,
and race, citizens of the nation's 12 largest metropolitan areas (particularly their central cities,
but also their suburbs) are roughly 10% less
trusting and report 10–20% fewer group memberships than residents of other cities and towns
(and their suburbs). Meanwhile, residents of
very small towns and rural areas are (in accord
with some hoary stereotypes) slightly more trusting and civically engaged than other Americans.
Unsurprisingly, the prominence of different
types of groups does vary significantly by location: major cities have more political and nationality clubs; smaller cities more fraternal, service,
hobby, veterans, and church groups; and rural
areas more agricultural organizations. But over-

all rates of associational memberships are not
very different.

Moreover, this pallid pattern cannot account
for our central puzzle. In the first place, there is
virtually no correlation between gains in population and losses in social capital, either across
states or across localities of different sizes. Even
taking into account the educational and social
backgrounds of those who have moved there, the
suburbs have faintly higher levels of trust and
civic engagement than their respective central
cities, a fact that *ceteris paribus* should have produced growth, not decay, in social capital over
the last generation. The central point, however,
is that the downtrends in trusting and joining
are virtually identically everywhere—in cities,
big and small, in suburbs, in small towns, and in
the countryside.

There are, of course, suburbs and suburbs.
Evanston is not Levittown is not Sun City. The
evidence available does not allow us to determine
whether different types of suburban living have
different effects on civic connections and social
trust. However, these data do rule out the thesis
that suburbanization per se has caused the erosion of America's social capital. In this respect,
size of place is like mobility—a cross-sectional
correlate that cannot explain our trend. Both
where we live and how long we've lived there
matter for social capital, but neither explains
why it is eroding everywhere.

The Changing Role of Women

Most of our mothers were housewives, and most
of them invested heavily in social capital formation—a jargony way of referring to untold, unpaid
hours in church suppers, PTA meetings, neighborhood coffee klatches, and visits to friends and
relatives. The movement of women out of the
home and into the paid labor force is probably the
most portentous social change of the last half century. However welcome and overdue the feminist
revolution may be, it is hard to believe that it has
had no impact on social connectedness. Could

this be the primary reason for the decline of social capital over the last generation?

Some patterns in the available survey evidence seem to support this claim. All things considered, women belong to somewhat fewer voluntary associations than men (Edwards, Edwards, and Watts 1984 and the sources cited there; more recent GSS data confirm this finding). On the other hand, time budget studies suggest that women spend more time on those groups and more time in informal social connecting than men (Robinson and Godbey 1995). Although the absolute declines in joining and trusting are approximately equivalent among men and women, the relative declines are somewhat greater among women. Controlling for education, memberships among men have declined at a rate of about 10–15% a decade, compared to about 20–25% a decade for women. The time budget data, too, strongly suggest that the decline in organizational involvement in recent years is concentrated among women. These sorts of facts, coupled with the obvious transformation in the professional role of women over this same period, led me in previous work to suppose that the emergence of two-career families might be the most important single factor in the erosion of social capital.

As we saw earlier, however, work status itself seems to have little net impact on group membership or on trust. Housewives belong to different types of groups than do working women (more PTAs, for example, and fewer professional associations), but in the aggregate working women are actually members of slightly more voluntary associations.[15] Moreover, the overall declines in civic engagement are somewhat greater among housewives than among employed women. Comparison of time budget data between 1965 and 1985 (Robinson and Godbey 1995) seems to show that employed women as a group are actually spending more time on organizations than before, while nonemployed women are spending less. This same study suggests that the major decline in informal socializing since 1965 has also been concentrated among nonemployed women. The central fact, of course, is that the overall trends are down for all categories of women (and for men, too—even bachelors), but the figures suggest that women who work full-time actually may have been more resistant to the slump than those who do not.

Thus, although women appear to have borne a disproportionate share of the decline in civic engagement over the last two decades, it is not easy to find any micro-level data that tie that fact directly to their entry into the labor force. It is hard to control for selection bias in these data, of course, because women who have chosen to enter the workforce doubtless differ in many respects from women who have chosen to stay home. Perhaps one reason that community involvement appears to be rising among working women and declining among housewives is that precisely the sort of women who, in an earlier era, were most involved with their communities have been disproportionately likely to enter the workforce, thus simultaneously lowering the average level of civic engagement among the remaining homemakers and raising the average among women in the workplace. Obviously, we have not been running a great national controlled experiment on the effects of work on women's civic engagement, and in any event the patterns in the data are not entirely clear. Contrary to my own earlier speculations, however, I can find little evidence to support the hypothesis that the movement of women into the workplace over the last generation has played a major role in the reduction of social connectedness and civic engagement. On the other hand, I have no clear alternative explanation for the fact that the relative declines are greater among women than among men. Since this evidence is at best circumstantial, perhaps the best interim judgment here is the famous Scots verdict: not proven.

Marriage and Family

Another widely discussed social trend that more or less coincides with the downturn in civic engagement is the breakdown of the traditional family unit—mom, dad, and the kids. Since the family itself is, by some accounts, a key form of social capital, perhaps its eclipse is part of the explanation for the reduction in joining and trusting in the wider community. What does the evidence show?

First of all, evidence of the loosening of family bonds is unequivocal. In addition to the century-long increase in divorce rates (which accelerated in the mid-1960s to the mid-1970s and then leveled off), and the more recent increase in single-parent families, the incidence of one-person households has more than doubled since 1950, in part because of the rising number of widows living alone (Caplow, Bahr, Modell, and Chadwick 1991, 47, 106, 113). The net effect of all these changes, as reflected in the General Social Survey, is that the proportion of all American adults who are currently unmarried climbed from 28% in 1974 to 48% in 1994.

Second, married men and women do rank somewhat higher on both our measures of social capital. That is, controlling for education, age, race, and so on, single people—both men and women, divorced, separated, and never-married—are significantly less trusting and less engaged civically than married people.[16] Roughly speaking, married men and women are about a third more trusting and belong to about 15–25% more groups than comparable single men and women. (Widows and widowers are more like married people than single people in this comparison.)

In short, successful marriage (especially if the family unit includes children) is statistically associated with greater social trust and civic engagement. Thus, some part of the decline in both trust and membership is tied to the decline in marriage. To be sure, the direction of causality behind this correlation may be complicated, since it is conceivable that loners and paranoids are harder to live with. If so, divorce may in some degree be the consequence, not the cause, of lower social capital. Probably the most reasonable summary of these arrays of data, how-

ever, is that the decline in successful marriage is a significant, though modest part of the reason for declining trust and lower group membership. On the other hand, changes in family structure cannot be a major part of our story, since the overall declines in joining and trusting are substantial even among the happily married. My own verdict (based in part on additional evidence to be introduced later) is that the disintegration of marriage is probably an accessory to the crime, but not the major villain of the piece.

The Rise of the Welfare State

Circumstantial evidence, particularly the timing of the downturn in social connectedness, has suggested to some observers (for example, Fukuyama 1995, 313–314) that an important cause—perhaps even *the* cause—of civic disengagement is big goverment and the growth of the welfare state. By "crowding out" private initiative, it is argued, state intervention has subverted civil society. This is a much larger topic than I can address in detail here, but a word or two may be appropriate.

On the one hand, some government policies have almost certainly had the effect of destroying social capital. For example, the so-called "slum clearance" policies of the 1950s and 1960s replaced physical capital, but destroyed social capital, by disrupting existing community ties. It is also conceivable that certain social expenditures and tax policies may have created disincentives for civic-minded philanthropy. On the other hand, it is much harder to see which government policies might be responsible for the decline in bowling leagues and literary clubs.

One empirical approach to this issue is to examine differences in civic engagement and public policy across different political jurisdictions to see whether swollen government leads to shriveled social capital. Among the U.S. states, however, differences in social capital appear essentially uncorrelated with various measures of welfare spending or government size.[17] Citizens in free-spending states are no less trusting or engaged than citizens in frugal ones. Cross-national comparison can also shed light on this question. Among 19 OECD countries for which data on social trust and group membership are available from the 1990–1991 World Values Survey, these indicators of social capital are, if anything, *positively* correlated with the size of the state.[18] This simple bivariate analysis, of course, cannot tell us whether social connectedness encourages welfare spending, whether the welfare state fosters civic engagement, or whether both are the result of some other unmeasured factor(s). Sorting out the underlying causal connections would require much more thorough analysis. However, even this simple finding is not easily reconciled with the notion that big government undermines social capital.

Race and the Civil Rights Revolution

Race is such an absolutely fundamental feature of American social history that nearly every other feature of our society is connected to it in some way. Thus, it seems intuitively plausible that race might somehow have played a role in the erosion of social capital over the last generation. In fact, some observers (both black and white) have noted that the decline in social connectedness and social trust began just after the greatest successes of the civil rights revolution of the 1960s. To some, that coincidence has suggested the possibility of a kind of sociological "white flight," as legal desegregation of civic life led whites to withdraw from community associations.

Like the theory about the welfare state, this racial interpretation of the destruction of social capital is highly controversial and can hardly be settled within the compass of these brief remarks. Nevertheless, the basic facts are these.

First, racial differences in associational membership are not large. At least until the 1980s, controlling for educational and income differences, blacks actually belonged to more associations on average than whites, essentially because they were more likely than comparably situated whites to belong to religious and ethnic organizations and no less likely to belong to any other type of group.[19] On the other hand, racial differences in social trust are very large indeed, even taking into account differences in education, income, and so on. On average, during the 1972–94 period, controlling for educational differences, about 17% of blacks endorsed the view that "most people can be trusted," as compared to about 45% of whites, and about 27% of respondents of other races.[20] These racial differences in social trust, of course, reflect not collective paranoia, but real experiences over many generations.

Second, the erosion of social capital has affected all races. In fact, during the 1980s the downturns in both joining and trusting were even greater among blacks (and other racial minorities) than among the white majority. This fact is inconsistent with the thesis that "white flight" is a significant cause of civic disengagement, since black Americans have been dropping out of religious and civic organizations at least as rapidly as white Americans. Even more important, the pace of disengagement among whites has been uncorrelated with racial intolerance or support for segregation. Avowedly racist or segregationist whites have been no quicker to drop out of community organizations during this period than more tolerant whites. Figure 3 presents illustrative evidence, its three parallel slopes showing that the decline in group membership is essentially identical among whites who favor segregation, whites who oppose it, and blacks.[21]

This evidence is far from conclusive, of course, but it does shift the burden of proof onto those who believe that racism is a primary explanation for growing civic disengagement over the last quarter century, however virulent racism continues to be in American society.[22] This evidence also suggests that reversing the civil rights gains of the last 30 years would do nothing to reverse the social capital losses.

Figure 3—Group Membership by Race and Racism, 1974–1994 (education controlled)

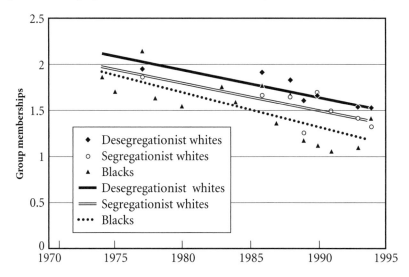

Source: General Social Survey, 1972–1994
Equal weighting of three educational categories.
White segregationism measured by support for racial segregation in social club.

Generational Effects

Our efforts thus far to localize the sources of civic disengagement have been singularly unfruitful. The downtrends are uniform across the major categories of American society—among men and among women; in central cities, in suburbs, and in small towns; among the wealthy, the poor, and the middle class; among blacks, whites, and other ethnic groups; in the North, in the South, on both coasts and in the heartland. One notable exception to this uniformity, however, involves age. In all our statistical analyses, age is second only to education as a predictor of all forms of civic engagement and trust. Older people belong to more organizations than young people, and they are less misanthropic. Older Americans also vote more often and read newspapers more frequently, two other forms of civic engagement closely correlated with joining and trusting.

Figure 4 shows the basic pattern—civic involvement appears to rise more or less steadily from early adulthood toward a plateau in middle

age, from which it declines only late in life. This humpback pattern, familiar from many analyses of social participation, including time-budget studies (Robinson and Godbey 1995), seems naturally to represent the arc of life's engagements. Most observers have interpreted this pattern as a life cycle phenomenon, and so, at first, did I.

Evidence from the General Social Survey (GSS) enables us to follow individual cohorts as they age. If the rising lines in Figure 4 represent deepening civic engagement with age, then we should be able to track this same deepening engagement as we follow, for example, the first of the baby boomers—born in 1947—as they aged from 25 in 1972 (the first year of the GSS) to 47 in 1994 (the latest year available). Startlingly, however, such an analysis, repeated for successive birth cohorts, produces virtually no evidence of such life cycle changes in civic engagement. In fact, as various generations moved through the period between 1972 and 1994, their levels of trust and membership more often fell than rose, reflecting a more or less simultaneous decline in civic engagement among young and old alike,

Figure 4—Civic Engagement by Age (education controlled)

Source: General Social Survey, 1972–1994
Respondents aged 21–89. Three-year moving averages.
Equal weighting of three educational categories.

particularly during the second half of the 1980s. But that downtrend obviously cannot explain why, throughout the period, older Americans were always more trusting and engaged. In fact, the only reliable life cycle effect visible in these data is a withdrawal from civic engagement very late in life, as we move through our 80s.

The central paradox posed by these patterns is this: Older people are consistently more engaged and trusting than younger people, yet we do not become more engaged and trusting as we age. What's going on here?

Time and age are notoriously ambiguous in their effects on social behavior. Social scientists have learned to distinguish three contrasting phenomena:

1. *Life-cycle effects* represent differences attributable to stage of life. In this case individu-

als change as they age, but since the effects of aging are, in the aggregate, neatly balanced by the "demographic metabolism" of births and deaths, life cycle effects produce no aggregate change. Everyone's close-focus eyesight worsens as we age, but the aggregate demand for reading glasses changes little.

2. *Period effects* affect all people who live through a given era, regardless of their age.[23] Period effects can produce both individual and aggregate change, often quickly and enduringly, without any age-related differences. The sharp drop in trust in government between 1965 and 1975, for example, was almost entirely this sort of period effect, as Americans of all ages changed their minds about their leaders' trustworthiness. Similarly, as just noted, a modest portion of the

decline in social capital during the 1980s appears to be a period effect.

3. *Generational effects*, as described in Karl Mannheim's classic essay on "The Problem of Generations," represent the fact that "[i]ndividuals who belong to the same generation, who share the same year of birth, are endowed, to that extent, with a common location in the historical dimension of the social process" (Mannheim 1952, 290). Like life cycle effects (and unlike typical period effects), generational effects show up as disparities among age groups at a single point in time, but like period effects (and unlike life cycle effects) generational effects produce real social change, as successive generations, enduringly "imprinted" with divergent outlooks, enter and leave the population. In pure generational effects, no individual ever changes, but society does.

At least since the landmark essay by Converse (1976), social scientists have recognized that to sort out life cycle, period, and generational effects requires sensitivity to a priori plausibility, "side knowledge," and parsimony, not merely good data and sophisticated math. In effect, cohort analysis inevitably involves more unknowns than equations. With some common sense, some knowledge of history, and some use of Ockham's razor, however, it is possible to exclude some alternatives and focus on more plausible interpretations.

Returning to our conundrum, how could older people today be more engaged and trusting, if they did not become more engaged and trusting as they aged? The key to this paradox, as David Butler and Donald Stokes (1974) observed in another context, is to ask, not *how old people are*, but *when they were young*. Figure 5 addresses this reformulated question, displaying various measures of civic engagement according to the respondents' year of birth.[24] (Figure 5 includes data on voting from the National Election Studies, since Miller 1992 and Miller and Shanks 1995 have drawn on that data to demonstrate

powerful generational effects on turnout, and it is instructive to see how parallel are the patterns that they discovered for voting turnout and the patterns for civic engagement that concern us here.[25] The figure also includes data on social trust from the National Election Studies, which will prove useful in parsing generational, life cycle, and period interpretations.)

The Long Civic Generation

In effect, Figure 5 lines up Americans from left to right according to their date of birth, beginning with those born in the last third of the nineteenth century and continuing across to the generation of their great-grandchildren, born in the last third of the twentieth century. As we begin moving along this queue from left to right—from those raised around the turn of the century to those raised during the Roaring Twenties, and so on—we find relatively high and unevenly rising levels of civic engagement and social trust. Then rather abruptly, however, we encounter signs of reduced community involvement, starting with men and women born in the early 1930s. Remarkably, this downward trend in joining, trusting, voting, and newspaper reading continues almost uninterruptedly for nearly 40 years. The trajectories for the various different indicators of civic engagement are strikingly parallel: each shows a high, sometimes rising plateau for people born and raised during the first third of the century; each shows a turning point in the cohorts born around 1930; and each then shows a more or less constant decline down to the cohorts born during the 1960s.[26]

By any standard, these intergenerational differences are extraordinary. Compare, for example, the generation born in the early 1920s with the generation of their grandchildren born in the late 1960s. Controlling for educational disparities, members of the generation born in the 1920s belong to almost twice as many civic associations as those born in the late 1960s (roughly 1.9 memberships per capita, compared to roughly

Figure 5—Social Capital and Civic Engagement by Generation (education controlled)

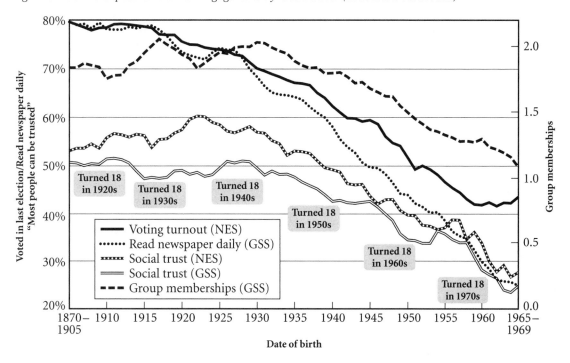

Source: General Social Survey (GSS), 1972–1994, and National Election Studies (NES), 1952–1992
Respondents aged 25–80. Five-year moving averages.
Equal weighting of three educational categories.

1.1 memberships per capita). The grandparents are more than twice as likely to trust other people (50–60%, compared with 25% for the grandchildren). They vote at nearly double the rate of the most recent cohorts (roughly 75% compared with 40–45%), and they read newspapers almost three times as often (70–80% read a paper daily compared with 25–30%). And bear in mind that we have found no evidence that the youngest generation will come to match their grandparents' higher levels of civic engagement as they grow older.

Thus, read not as life cycle effects, but rather as generational effects, the age-related patterns in our data suggest a radically different interpretation of our basic puzzle. Deciphered with this key, Figure 5 depicts a long "civic" generation, born roughly between 1910 and 1940, a broad group of people substantially more engaged in community affairs and substantially more trusting than those younger than they.[27] The culminating point of this civic generation is the cohort born in 1925–1930, who attended grade school during the Great Depression, spent World War II in high school (or on the battle field), first voted in 1948 or 1952, set up housekeeping in the 1950s, and watched their first television when they were in the late twenties. Since national surveying began, this cohort has been exceptionally civic: voting more, joining more, reading newspapers more, trusting more. As the distinguished sociologist Charles Tilly (born in 1928) said in commenting on an early version of this essay, "we are the last suckers."

To help in interpreting the historical contexts within which these successive generations of Americans matured, Figure 5 also indicates the decade within which each cohort came of age.

Thus, we can see that each generation who reached adulthood since the 1940s has been less engaged in community affairs than its immediate predecessor.

Further confirmation of this *generational* interpretation comes from a comparison of the two parallel lines that chart responses to an identical question about social trust, posed first in the National Election Studies (mainly between 1964 and 1976) and then in the General Social Survey between 1972 and 1994.[28] If the greater trust expressed by Americans born earlier in the century represented a *life cycle* effect, then the graph from the GSS surveys (conducted when these cohorts were, on average, 10 years older) should have been some distance *above* the NES line. In fact, the GSS line lies about 5–10% *below* the NES line. That downward shift almost surely represents a *period* effect that depressed social trust among all cohorts during the 1980s.[29] That downward period effect, however, is substantially more modest than the large generational differences already noted.

In short, the most parsimonious interpretation of the age-related differences in civic engagement is that they represent a powerful reduction in civic engagement among Americans who came of age in the decades after World War II, as well as some modest additional disengagement that affected all cohorts during the 1980s. These patterns hint that being raised after World War II was a quite different experience from being raised before that watershed. It is as though the postwar generations were exposed to some mysterious X-ray that permanently and increasingly rendered them less likely to connect with the community. Whatever that force might have been, *it*—rather than anything that happened during the 1970s and 1980s—accounts for most of the civic disengagement that lies at the core of our mystery.

But if this reinterpretation of our puzzle is correct, why did it take so long for the effects of that mysterious X-ray to become manifest? If the underlying causes of civic disengagement can be traced to the 1940s and 1950s, why did the effects become conspicuous in PTA meetings and

Masonic lodges, in the volunteer lists of the Red Cross and the Boy Scouts, and in polling stations and church pews and bowling alleys across the land only during the 1960s, 1970s, and 1980s?

The visible effects of this generational disengagement were delayed for several decades by two important factors:

1. The postwar boom in college enrollments boosted massive numbers of Americans up the sloping curve of civic engagement traced in Figure 2. Miller and Shanks (1995) observe that the postwar expansion of educational opportunities "forestalled a cataclysmic drop" in voting turnout, and it had a similar delaying effect on civic disengagement more generally.

2. The full effects of generational developments generally appear several decades after their onset, because it takes that long for a given generation to become numerically dominant in the adult population. Only after the mid-1960s did significant numbers of the "post-civic generation" reach adulthood, supplanting older, more civic cohorts. Figure 6 illustrates this generational accounting. The long civic generation (born between 1910 and 1940) reached its zenith in 1960, when it comprised 62% of those who chose between John Kennedy and Richard Nixon. By the time that Bill Clinton was elected president in 1992, that cohort's share in the electorate had been cut precisely in half. Conversely, over the last two decades (from 1974 to 1994) boomers and X-ers (that is, Americans born after 1946) have grown as a fraction of the adult population from 24% to 60%.

In short, the very decades that have seen a national deterioration in social capital are the same decades during which the numerical dominance of a trusting and civic generation has been replaced by the dominion of "post-civic" cohorts. Moreover, although the long civic generation has enjoyed unprecedented life expectancy, allowing its members to contribute more than their share to American social capital in recent decades,

Figure 6—The Rise and Decline of a "Civic" Generation

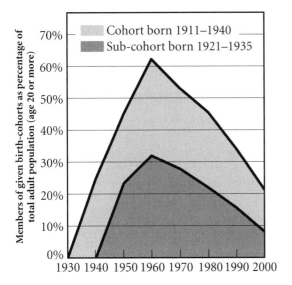

Source: Calculated from U.S. Census Bureau, current population reports.

they are now passing from the scene. Even the youngest members of that generation will reach retirement age within the next few years. Thus, a generational analysis leads almost inevitably to the conclusion that the national slump in trust and engagement is likely to continue, regardless of whether the more modest "period effect" depression of the 1980s continues.

More than two decades ago, just as the first signs of disengagement were beginning to appear in American politics, Ithiel de Sola Pool (1973, 818–21) observed that the central issue would be—it was then too soon to judge, as he rightly noted—whether the development represented a temporary change in the weather or a more enduring change in the climate. It now appears that much of the change whose initial signs he spotted did in fact reflect a climatic shift. Moreover, just as the erosion of the ozone layer was detected only many years after the proliferation of the chlorofluorocarbons that caused it, so too the erosion of America's social capital became visible only several decades after the un-

derlying process had begun. Like Minerva's owl that flies at dusk, we come to appreciate how important the long civic generation has been to American community life just as its members are retiring. Unless America experiences a dramatic upward boost in civic engagement (a favorable "period effect") in the next few years, Americans in 2010 will join, trust, and vote even less than we do today.

The Puzzle Reformulated

To say that civic disengagement in contemporary America is in large measure generational merely reformulates our central puzzle. We now know that much of the cause of our lonely bowling probably dates to the 1940s and 1950s, rather than to the 1960s and 1970s. What could have been the mysterious anti-civic "X-ray" that affected Americans who came of age after World War II and whose effects progressively deepened at least into the 1970s?[30]

A number of superficially plausible candidates fail to fit the timing required by this new formulation of our mystery.

- Family instability seems to have an ironclad alibi for what we have now identified as the critical period, for the generational decline in civic engagement began with the children of the maritally stable 1940s and 1950s.[31] The divorce rate in America actually fell after 1945, and the sharpest jump in the divorce rate did not occur until the 1970s, long after the cohorts who show the sharpest declines in civic engagement and social trust had left home. Similarly, working mothers are exonerated by this re-specification of our problem, for the plunge in civicness among children of the 1940s, 1950s, and 1960s happened while mom was still at home.

- Our new formulation of the puzzle opens the possibility that the *Zeitgeist* of national unity and patriotism that culminated in 1945 might have reinforced civic-mindedness. On the other hand, it is hard to assign any consistent role to the Cold War and the Bomb, since the anti-civic trend appears to have deepened steadily from the 1940s to the 1970s, in no obvious harmony with the rhythms of world affairs. Nor is it easy to construct an interpretation of Figure 5 in which the cultural vicissitudes of "the Sixties" could play a significant role.

- Neither economic adversity nor affluence can easily be tied to the generational decline in civic engagement, since the slump seems to have affected in equal measure those who came of age in the placid Fifties, the booming Sixties, and the busted Seventies.

I have discovered only one prominent suspect against whom circumstantial evidence can be mounted, and in this case, it turns out, some directly incriminating evidence has also turned up. This is not the occasion to lay out the full case for the prosecution, nor to review rebuttal evidence for the defense. However, I want to illustrate the sort of evidence that justifies indictment. The culprit is television.

First, the timing fits. The long civic generation was the last cohort of Americans to grow up without television, for television flashed into American society like lightning in the 1950s. In 1950 barely 10% of American homes had television sets, but by 1959 90% did, probably the fastest diffusion of a technological innovation ever recorded. The reverberations from this lightning bolt continued for decades, as viewing hours per capita grew by 17–20% during the 1960s and by an additional 7–8% during the 1970s. In the early years, TV watching was concentrated among the less educated sectors of the population, but during the 1970s the viewing time of the more educated sectors of the population began to converge upward. Television viewing increases with age, particularly upon retirement, but each generation since the introduction of television has begun its life cycle at a higher starting point. By 1995, viewing per TV household was more than 50% higher than it had been in the 1950s.[32]

Most studies estimate that the average American now watches roughly four hours per day.[33] Robinson (1990b), using the more conservative time-budget technique for determining how people allocate their time, offers an estimate closer to three hours per day, but concludes that as a primary activity, television absorbs 40% of the average American's free time, an increase of about one-third since 1965. Moreover, multiple sets have proliferated: by the late 1980s, three quarters of all U.S. homes had more than one set (Comstock 1989), and these numbers too are rising steadily, allowing ever more private viewing. In short, as Robinson and Godbey 1995 conclude, "television is the 800-pound gorilla of leisure time." This massive change in the way Americans spend our days and nights occurred precisely during the years of generational civic disengagement.

Evidence of a link between the arrival of television and the erosion of social connections is, however, not merely circumstantial. The links between civic engagement and television viewing can instructively be compared with the links between civic engagement and newspaper reading. The basic contrast is straightforward: newspaper reading is associated with high social capital, TV viewing with low social capital.

Controlling for education, income, age, race, place of residence, work status, and gender, TV viewing is strongly and negatively related to social trust and group membership, whereas the same correlations with newspaper reading are positive. Figure 7 shows that within every educational category, heavy readers are avid joiners, whereas Figure 8 shows that heavy viewers are more likely to be loners.[34] Viewing and reading are themselves uncorrelated—some people do lots of both, some do little of either—but Figure 9 shows that (controlling for education, as always) "pure readers" (that is, people who watch less TV than average and read more newspapers than average) belong to 76% more civic organizations than "pure viewers." Precisely the same pattern applies to other indicators of civic engagement, including social trust and voting

Figure 7—Group Membership by Newspaper Readership and Education

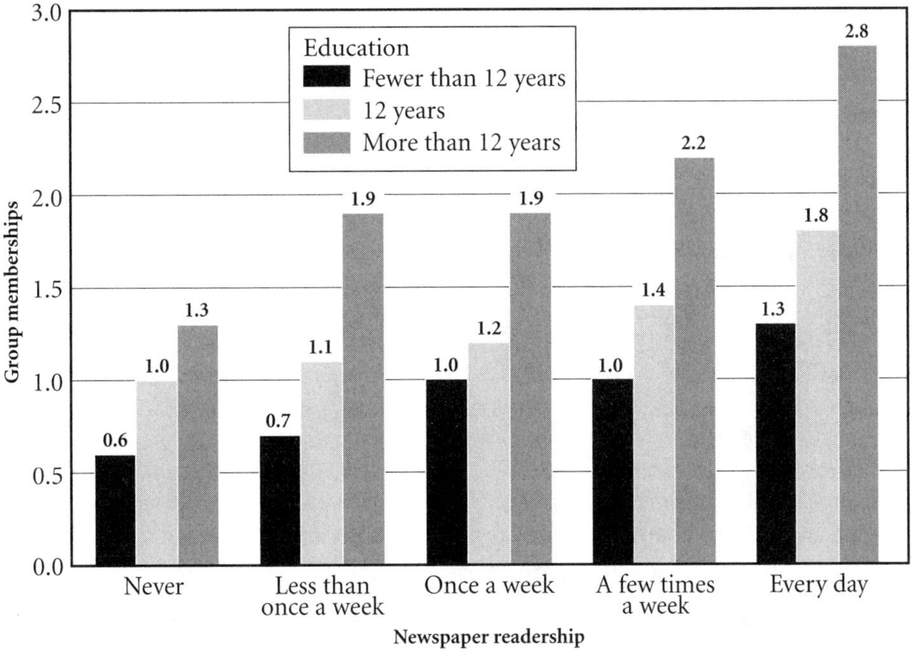

Source: General Social Survey, 1974–1994

turnout. "Pure readers," for example, are 55% more trusting than "pure viewers."[35]

In other words, each hour spent viewing television is associated with less social trust and less group membership, while each hour reading a newspaper is associated with more. An increase in television viewing of the magnitude that the United States has experienced in the last four decades might directly account for as much as one-quarter to one-half of the total drop in social capital, even without taking into account, for example, the indirect effects of television viewing on newspaper readership or the cumulative effects of "life-time" viewing hours.[36]

How might television destroy social capital?

- *Time displacement.* Even though there are only 24 hours in everyone's day, most forms of social and media participation are positively correlated. People who listen to lots of classical music are more likely, not less

likely, than others to attend Cubs games. Television is the principal exception to this generalization—the only leisure activity that seems to inhibit participation outside the home. TV watching comes at expense of nearly every social activity outside the home, especially social gatherings and informal conversations (Comstock et al 1978; Comstock 1989; Bower 1985; and Robinson and Godbey 1995). TV viewers are homebodies.

Most studies that report a negative correlation between television watching and community involvement (including my Figure 7) are ambiguous with respect to causality, because they merely compare different individuals at a single time. However, one important quasi-experimental study of the introduction of television in three Canadian towns (Williams 1986) found the same pattern at the aggregate level across time: a major effect of television's arrival was the

Figure 8—Group Membership by Television Viewing and Education

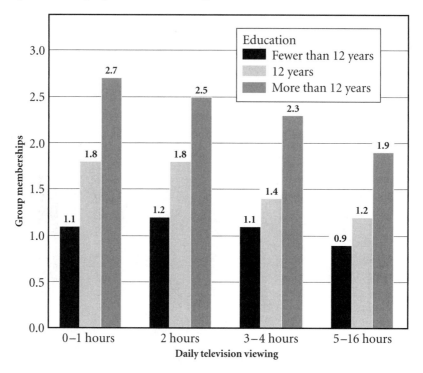

Source: General Social Survey, 1974–1994

reduction in participation in social, recreational, and community activities among people of all ages. In short, television is privatizing our leisure time.

- *Effects on the outlooks of viewers.* An impressive body of literature, gathered under the rubric of the "mean world effect," suggests that heavy watchers of TV are unusually skeptical about the benevolence of other people—overestimating crime rates, for example. This body of literature has generated much debate about the underlying causal patterns, with skeptics suggesting that misanthropy may foster couch-potato behavior rather than the reverse. While awaiting better experimental evidence, however, a reasonable interim judgment is that heavy television watching may well increase pessimism about human nature (Gerbner et al 1980; Dobb and MacDonald 1979; Hirsch 1980;

Hughes 1980; and Comstock 1989, 265–69). Perhaps, too, as social critics have long argued, both the medium and the message have more basic effects on our ways of interacting with the world and with one another. Television may induce passivity, as Postman (1985) has claimed, and it may even change our fundamental physical and social perceptions, as Meyrowitz (1985) has suggested.

- *Effects on children.* TV occupies an extraordinary part of children's lives—consuming about 40 hours per week on average. Viewing is especially high among pre-adolescents, but it remains high among younger adolescents: time-budget studies (Carnegie Council on Adolescent Development 1993, 5, citing Timmer et al. 1985) suggest that among youngsters aged 9–14 television consumes as much time as *all other discretionary activities combined*, including playing, hobbies, clubs, out-

Figure 9—Group Membership by Media Usage (education controlled)

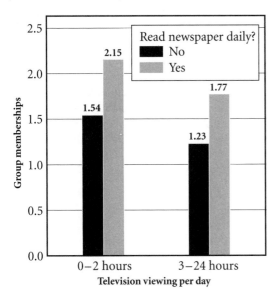

Source: General Social Survey, 1974–1994
Entries based on three equally weighted educational categories.

door activities, informal visiting, and just hanging out. The effects of television on childhood socialization have, of course, been hotly debated for more than three decades. The most reasonable conclusion from a welter of sometimes conflicting results appears to be that heavy television watching probably increases aggressiveness (although perhaps not actual violence), that it probably reduces school achievement, and that it is statistically associated with "psychosocial malfunctioning," although how much of this effect is self-selection and how much causal remains much debated (Condry, 1993). The evidence is, as I have said, not yet enough to convict, but the defense has a lot of explaining to do.

Conclusion

Ithiel de Sola Pool's posthumous book, *Technologies Without Borders* (1990), is a prescient work,

astonishingly relevant to our current national debates about the complicated links among technology, public policy, and culture. Pool defended what he called "soft technological determinism." Revolutions in communications technologies have profoundly affected social life and culture, as the printing press helped bring on the Reformation. Pool concluded that the electronic revolution in communications technology, whose outlines he traced well before most of us were even aware of the impending changes, was the first major technological advance in centuries that would have a profoundly decentralizing and fragmenting effect on society and culture.

Pool hoped that the result might be "community without contiguity." As a classic liberal, he welcomed the benefits of technological change for individual freedom, and, in part, I share that enthusiasm. Those of us who bemoan the decline of community in contemporary America need to be sensitive to the liberating gains achieved during the same decades. We need to avoid an uncritical nostalgia for the Fifties. On the other hand, some of the same freedom-friendly technologies whose rise Pool predicted may indeed be undermining our connections with one another and with our communities. I suspect that Pool would have been open to that argument, too, for one of Pool's most talented protégés, Samuel Popkin (1991, 226–31) has argued that the rise of television and the correlative decline of social interaction have impaired American political discourse. The last line in Pool's last book (1990, 262) is this: "We may suspect that [the technological trends that we can anticipate] will promote individualism and will make it harder, not easier, to govern and organize a coherent society."

Pool's technological determinism was "soft" precisely because he recognized that social values can condition the effects of technology. In the end this perspective invites us not merely to consider how technology is privatizing our lives—if, as it seems to me, it is—but to ask whether we entirely like the result, and if not, what we might do about it. But that is a topic for another day.

NOTES

1. I wish to thank several researchers for sharing valuable unpublished work on related themes: John Brehm and Wendy Rahn (1995); Warren Miller and Merrill Shanks (1995), John Robinson and Geoffrey Godbey (1995); and Eric Uslaner (1995). Professor Uslaner was generous in helping track down some elusive data and commenting on an earlier draft. I also wish to thank a fine team of research assistants, including Jay Braatz, Maryann Barakso, Karen Ferree, Archon Fung, Louise Kennedy, Jeff Kling, Kimberly Lochner, Karen Rothkin, and Mark Warren. Support for the research project from which this study derives has been provided by the Aspen Institute, Carnegie Corporation, the Ford, Kovler, Norman, and Rockefeller foundations, and Harvard University.

2. In this respect I deviate slightly from James Coleman's "functional" definition of social capital. See Coleman (1990): 300–21.

3. The results reported in this paragraph and throughout the paper, unless otherwise indicated, are derived from the General Social Survey. These exceptionally useful data derive from a series of scientific surveys of the adult American population, conducted nearly every year since 1972 by the National Opinion Research Center, under the direction of James A. Davis and Tom W. Smith. The cumulative sample size is approximately 32,000, although the questions on trust and group membership that are at the focus of our inquiry have not been asked of all respondents in all years. Our measure of trust derives from this question: "Generally speaking, would you say that most people can be trusted, or that you can't be too careful in dealing with people": for this question, N = 22390. For evidence confirming the power of this simple measure of social trust, see Uslaner (1995). Our measure of group membership derives from this question: "Now we would like to know something about the groups or organizations to which individuals belong. Here is a list of various organizations. Could you tell me whether or not you are a member of each type?" The list includes fraternal groups, service clubs, veterans' groups, political clubs, labor unions, sports groups, youth groups, school service groups, hobby or garden clubs, social fraternities or sororities, nationality groups, farm organizations, literary, arts, discussion or study groups, professional or academic societies, church-affiliated groups, and any other groups. For this question, N = 19326. Neither of these questions, of course, is a perfect measure of social capital. In particular, our measure of multiple memberships refers not to total groups, but to total *types* of groups. On the other hand, "noise" in data generally depresses observed correlations below the "true" value, so our findings are more likely to understate than to exaggerate patterns in the "real world."

4. Across the 35 countries for which data are available from the World Values Survey (1990–91), the correlation between the average number of associational memberships and endorsement of the view that "most people can be trusted" is r .65. Across the 42 states for which adequate samples are available in the General Social Survey (1972–1994), the comparable correlation is r .71. Across individuals in the General Social Survey (1972–1994), controlling for education, race, and age, social trust is significantly and separately correlated with membership in political clubs, literary groups, sports clubs, hobby and garden clubs, youth groups, school service groups, and other associations. The correlation with social trust is insignificant only for veterans' groups, labor unions, and nationality groups.

5. The 1965 sample, which was limited to non-retired residents of cities between 30,000 and 280,000 population, was not precisely equivalent to the later national samples, so

appropriate adjustments need to be made to ensure comparability. For the 1965–1975 comparison, see Robinson (1981, 125). For the 1975–1985 comparison (but apparently without adjustment for the 1965 sampling peculiarities), see Cutler (1990). Somewhat smaller declines are reported in Robinson and Godbey (1995), although it is unclear whether they correct for the sampling differences. Additional work to refine these cross-time comparisons is required and is currently underway.

6. Trust in political authorities—and indeed in many social institutions—has also declined sharply over the last three decades, but that is conceptually a distinct trend. As we shall see later, the etiology of the slump in social trust is quite different from the etiology of the decline in political trust.

7. For reasons explained below, Figure 1 reports trends for membership in various types of groups, *controlling for* the respondent's education level.

8. Some commentaries on "Bowling Alone" have been careless, however, in reporting apparent membership growth. *The Economist* (1995, 22), for example, celebrated a recent rebound in total membership in parent-teacher organizations, without acknowledging that this rebound is almost entirely attributable to the growing number of children. The fraction of parents who belong to PTAs has regained virtually none of the 50% fall that this metric registered between 1960 and 1975. Despite talk about the growth of "support groups," another oft-cited counterexample. I know of no statistical substantiation for this claim. One might even ask whether the vaunted rise in neighborhood watch groups might not represent only a partial, artificial replacement for the vanished social capital of traditional neighborhoods—a kind of sociological Astroturf, suitable only where you can't grow the real thing. See also Glenn (1987, S124) for survey evidence of "an increased tendency for individuals to withdraw allegiance from . . . anything outside of themselves."

9. The only exceptions are farm groups, labor unions, and veterans' organizations, whose members have slightly less formal education than the average American. Interestingly, sports clubs are *not* an exception; college graduates are nearly three times more likely to belong to a sports group than are high school drop-outs. Education is uncorrelated with church attendance, but positively correlated with membership in church-related groups.

10. For a thorough recent investigation of the role of education in accounting for differences in political participation, see Verba, Schlozman, and Brady (1995).

11. As a practical matter, all subsequent statistical presentations here implement this precept by equally weighing respondents from three broad educational categories—those with fewer than 12 years formal schooling, those with exactly 12 years, and those with more than 12 years. Conveniently, this categorization happens to slice the 1972–1994 GSS sample into nearly equal thirds. The use of more sophisticated mathematical techniques to control for educational differences would alter none of the central conclusions of this essay.

12. The downturns in both joining and trusting seem to be somewhat greater among Americans on the middle rungs of the educational ladder—high school graduates and college dropouts—than among those at the very top and bottom of the educational hierarchy, but the differences are not great, and the trends are statistically significant at all levels.

13. This is true with or without controls for education and year of survey. The patterns among men and women on this score are not identical, for women who work part-time appear to be somewhat more civically engaged and socially trusting than either those who work full-time or those who do not work outside the home at all. Whatever

we make of this intriguing anomaly, which apparently does not appear in the time budget data (Robinson and Godbey 1995) and which has no counterpart in the male half of the population, it cannot account for our basic puzzle, since female part-time workers constitute a relatively small fraction of the American population, and the fraction is growing, not declining. Between the first half of the 1970s and the first half of the 1990s, according to the GSS data, the fraction of the total adult population constituted by female part-time workers rose from about 8% to about 10%.

14. Evidence on generational differences presented below reinforces this conclusion.

15. Robinson and Godbey (1995); however, report that nonemployed women still spend more time on activity in voluntary associations than their employed counterparts.

16. Multivariate analysis hints that one major reason why divorce lowers connectedness is that it lowers family income, which in turn reduces civic engagement.

17. I have set aside this issue for fuller treatment in later work. However, I note for the record that (1) state-level differences in social trust and group membership are substantial, closely intercorrelated and reasonably stable, at least over the period from the 1970s to the 1990s, and (2) those differences are surprisingly closely correlated (R^2 = .52) with the measure of "state political culture" invented by Elazar (1966), and refined by Sharkansky (1969), based on descriptive accounts of state politics during the 1950s and traceable in turn to patterns of immigration during the nineteenth century and before.

18. Public expenditure as a percentage of GDP in 1989 is correlated r − .29 with 1990–1991 trust and r − .48 with 1990–1991 associational memberships.

19. For broadly similar conclusions, see Verba, Schlozman, and Brady (1995, 241–47) and the sources cited there.

20. As elsewhere in this essay, "controlling for educational differences" here means averaging the average scores for respondents with fewer than 12 years of schooling, with exactly 12 years, and with more than 12 years, respectively.

21. White support for segregation in Figure 3 is measured by responses to this question in the General Social Survey: "If you and your friends belonged to a social club that would not let Blacks join, would you try to change the rules so that Blacks could join?" Essentially identical results obtain if we measure white racism instead by support for antimiscegenation laws or for residential segregation.

22. As we shall see in a moment, much civic disengagement actually appears to be generational, affecting people born after 1930, but not those born before. If this phenomenon represented white flight from integrated community life after the civil rights revolution, it is difficult to see why the trend should be so much more marked among those who came of age in the more tolerant 1960s and 1970s, and hardly visible at all among those who came of age in the first half of the century, when American society was objectively more segregated and subjectively more racist.

23. Period effects that affect only people of a specific age shade into generational effects, which is why Converse, when summarizing these age-related effects, refers to "two-and-a-half" types, rather than the conventional three types.

24. To exclude the life cycle effects in the last years of life, Figure 5 excludes respondents over 80. To avoid well-known problems in reliably sampling young adults, as discussed by Converse (1976), Figure 5 also excludes respondents aged under 25. To offset the relatively small year-by-year samples and to control for educational differences, Figure 5 charts five-year moving averages across the

three educational categories used in this essay.

25. I learned of the Miller/Shanks argument only after discovering generational differences in civic engagement in the General Social Survey data, but their findings and mine are strikingly consistent.

26. Too few respondents born in the late nineteenth century appear in surveys conducted in the 1970s and 1980s for us to discern differences among successive birth cohorts with great reliability. However, those scant data (not broken out in Figure 5) suggest that the turn of the century might have been an era of rising civic engagement. Similarly, too few respondents born after 1970 have yet appeared in national surveys for us to be confident about their distinctive generational profile, although the slender results so far seem to suggest that the 40-year generational plunge in civic engagement might be bottoming out. However, even if this turns out to be true, it will be several decades before that development could arrest the aggregate drop in civic engagement, for reasons subsequently explained in the text.

27. Members of the 1910–1940 generation also seem more civic than their elders, at least to judge by the outlooks of the relatively few men and women born in the late nineteenth century who appeared in our samples.

28. The question on social trust appeared biennially in the NES from 1964 to 1976 and then reappeared in 1992. I have included the 1992 NES interviews in the analysis in order to obtain estimates for cohorts too young to have appeared in the earlier surveys.

29. Additional analysis of indicators of civic engagement in the GSS, not reported in detail here, confirms this downward shift during the 1980s.

30. I record here one theory attributed variously to Robert Salisbury (1985), Gerald Gamm, and Simon and Garfunkel. Devotees of our national pastime will recall that Joe DiMag-gio signed with the Yankees in 1936, just as the last of the long civic generation was beginning to follow the game, and he turned center field over to Mickey Mantle in 1951, just as the last of "the suckers" reached legal maturity. Almost simultaneously, the Braves, the Athletics, the Browns, the Senators, the Dodgers, and the Giants deserted cities that had been their homes since the late nineteenth century. By the time Mantle in turn left the Yankees in 1968, much of the damage to civic loyalty had been done. This interpretation explains why Mrs. Robinson's plaintive query that year about Joltin' Joe's whereabouts evoked such widespread emotion. A deconstructionist analysis of social capital's decline would highlight the final haunting lamentation, "our nation turns its *lonely* eyes to you" [emphasis added].

31. This exoneration applies to the possible effects of divorce on children, not to its effects on the couple themselves, as discussed earlier in this essay.

32. For introductions to the massive literature on the sociology of television, see Bower (1985), Comstock et al. (1978), Comstock (1989), and Grabner (1993). The figures on viewing hours in the text are from Bower (1985, 33) and *Public Perspective* (1995, 47). Cohort differences are reported in Bower 1985, 46.

33. This figure excludes periods in which television is merely playing in the background. Comstock (1989, 17) reports that "on any fall day in the late 1980s, the set in the average television owning household was on for about eight hours.")

34. In fact, multiple regression analysis, predicting civic engagement from television viewing and education, suggests that heavy TV watching is one important reason *why* less educated people are less engaged in the life of their communities. Controlling for differential TV exposure significantly reduces the correlation between education and engagement.

35. Controlling for education, 45% of respondents who watch TV two hours or less a day and read newspapers daily say that "most people can be trusted," as compared to 29% of respondents who watch TV three hours or more a day and do not read a newspaper daily.

36. Newspaper circulation (per household) has dropped by more than half since its peak in 1947. To be sure, it is not clear which way the tie between newspaper reading and civic involvement works, since disengagement might itself dampen one's interest in community news. But the two trends are clearly linked.

REFERENCES

Bower, Robert T. 1985. *The Changing Television Audience in America*. New York: Columbia University Press.

Brehm, John, and Wendy Rahn. 1995. "An Audit of the Deficit in Social Capital." Durham, NC: Duke University. Unpublished manuscript.

Butler, David, and Donald Stokes. 1974. *Political Change in Britain: The Evolution of Electoral Choice*, 2nd ed. New York: St. Martin's.

Caplow, Theodore, Howard M. Bahr, John Modell, and Bruce A. Chadwick. 1991. *Recent Social Trends in the United States: 1960–1990*. Montreal: McGill-Queen's University Press.

Carnegie Council on Adolescent Development. 1993. *A Matter of Time: Risk and Opportunity in the Nonschool Hours: Executive Summary*. New York: Carnegie Corporation of New York.

Coleman, James. 1990. *Foundations of Social Theory*. Cambridge, MA: Harvard University Press.

Comstock, George, Steven Chaffee, Natan Katzman, Maxwell McCombs, and Donald Roberts. 1978. *Television and Human Behavior*. New York: Columbia University Press.

Comstock, George. 1989. *The Evolution of American Television*. Newbury Park, CA: Sage.

Condry, John. 1993. "Thief of Time, Unfaithful Servant: Television and the American Child," *Daedalus* 122 (Winter): 259–78.

Converse, Philip E. 1976. *The Dynamics of Party Support: Cohort-Analyzing Party Identification*. Beverly Hills, CA: Sage.

Cutler, Blaine. 1990. "Where Does the Free Time Go?" *American Demographics* (November): 36–39.

Davis, James Allan, and Tom W. Smith. *General Social Surveys. 1972–1994*. [machine readable data file]. Principal Investigator, James A. Davis; Director and Co-Principal Investigator, Tom W. Smith. NORC⋅ ed. Chicago: National Opinion Research Center, producer, 1994; Storrs, CT: The Roper Center for Public Opinion Research, University of Connecticut, distributor.

Dobb, Anthony N., and Glenn F. Macdonald. 1979. "Television Viewing and Fear of Victimization: Is the Relationship Causal?" *Journal of Personality and Social Psychology* 37: 170–79.

The Economist. 1995. "The Solitary Bowler." 334 (18 February): 21–22.

Edwards, Patricia Klobus, John N. Edwards, and Ann DeWitt Watts, "Women, Work, and Social Participation." *Journal of Voluntary Action Research* 13 (January–March, 1984), 7–22.

Elazar, Daniel J. 1966. *American Federalism: A View from the States*. New York: Crowell.

Fukuyama, Francis. 1995. *Trust: The Social Virtues and the Creation of Prosperity*. New York: The Free Press.

Gerbner, George, Larry Gross, Michael Morgan, and Nancy Signorielli. 1980. "The 'Mainstreaming' of America: Violence Profile No. 11," *Journal of Communication* 30 (Summer): 10–29.

Ginzberg, Eli. *The Unemployed*. 1943. New York: Harper and Brothers.

Glenn, Norval D. 1987. "Social Trends in the United States: Evidence from Sample

Surveys." *Public Opinion Quarterly* 51: S109–S126.

Grabner, Doris A. 1993. *Mass Media and American Politics*. Washington, D.C.: CQ Press.

Hirsch, Paul M. 1980. "The 'Scary World' of the Nonviewer and Other Anomalies: A Re-analysis of Gerbner et al.'s Findings on Cultivation Analysis, Part I," *Communication Research* 7 (October): 403–56.

Hughes, Michael. 1980. "The Fruits of Cultivation Analysis: A Re-examination of the Effects of Television Watching on Fear of Victimization, Alienation, and the Approval of Violence." *Public Opinion Quarterly* 44: 287–303.

Jahoda, Marie, Paul Lazarsfeld, and Hans Zeisel. 1933. *Marienthal*. Chicago: Aldine-Atherton.

Mannheim, Karl. 1952. "The Problem of Generations." In *Essays on the Sociology of Knowledge*, ed. Paul Kecsckemeti. New York: Oxford University Press: 276–322.

Meyrowitz, Joshua. 1985. *No Sense of Place: The Impact of Electronic Media on Social Behavior*. New York: Oxford University Press.

Miller, Warren E. 1992. "The Puzzle Transformed: Explaining Declining Turnout." *Political Behavior* 14: 1–43.

Miller, Warren E., and J. Merrill Shanks. 1995. *The American Voter Reconsidered*. Tempe, AZ: Arizona State University. Unpublished manuscript.

Pool, Ithiel de Sola. 1973. "Public Opinion." In *Handbook of Communication*, ed. Ithiel de Sola Pool et al. Chicago: Rand McNally: 779–835.

Pool, Ithiel de Sola. 1990. *Technologies Without Boundaries: On Telecommunications in a Global Age*. Cambridge, MA: Harvard University Press.

Popkin, Samuel L. 1991. *The Reasoning Voter*. Chicago: University of Chicago Press.

Postman, Neil. 1985. *Amusing Ourselves to Death: Public Discourse in the Age of Show Business*. New York: Viking-Penguin Books.

Public Perspective. 1995. "People, Opinion, and Polls: American Popular Culture." 6 (August/September): 37–48.

Putnam, Robert D. 1993. *Making Democracy Work: Civic Traditions in Modern Italy*. Princeton, NJ: Princeton University Press.

Putnam, Robert D. 1995. "Bowling Alone, Revisited," *The Responsive Community* (Spring): 18–33.

Putnam, Robert D. 1996. "Bowling Alone: Democracy in America at the End of the Twentieth Century," forthcoming in a collective volume edited by Axel Hadenius. New York: Cambridge University Press.

Robinson, John. 1981. "Television and Leisure Time: A New Scenario," *Journal of Communication* 31 (Winter): 120–30.

Robinson, John. 1990a. "The Time Squeeze." *American Demographics* (February).

Robinson, John. 1990b. "I Love My TV." *American Demographics* (September): 24–27.

Robinson, John, and Geoffrey Godbey, 1995. *Time for Life*. College Park, MD: University of Maryland. Unpublished manuscript.

Rosenstone, Steven J., and John Mark Hansen. 1993. *Mobilization, Participation, and Democracy in America*. New York: Macmillan.

Salisbury, Robert H. 1985. "Blame Dismal World Conditions on . . . Baseball. *Miami Herald* (May 18): 27A.

Schor, Juliet. 1991. *The Overworked American*. New York: Basic Books.

Sharkansky, Ira. 1969. "The Utility of Elazar's Political Culture." *Polity* 2: 66–83.

Timmer, S. G., J. Eccles, and I. O'Brien. 1985. "How Children Use Time." In *Time, Goods, and Well-Being*, ed. F. T. Juster and F. B. Stafford. Ann Arbor, MI: University of Michigan, Institute for Social Research.

U.S. Bureau of the Census. 1995 (and earlier years). *Current Population Reports*. Washington, D.C.

Uslaner, Eric M. 1995. "Faith, Hope, and Charity: Social Capital, Trust, and Collective Action." College Park, MD: University of Maryland. Unpublished manuscript.

Verba, Sidney, Kay Lehman Schlozman, and
Henry E. Brady. 1995. *Voice and Equality:
Civic Volunteerism in American Politics*. Cambridge, MA: Harvard University Press.

Wilcock, Richard, and Walter H. Franke. 1963.
Unwanted Workers. New York: Free Press of
Glencoe.

Williams, Tannis Macbeth, ed. 1986. *The Impact
of Television: A Natural Experiment in Three
Communities*. New York: Academic Press.

BRYAN CAPLAN

THE MYTH OF THE RATIONAL VOTER

November 6th, 2006

There's an election tomorrow. Do voters know what they're doing? According to the typical economist—and many political scientists—the answer is "No, but it doesn't matter." How could it not matter? The main argument is that the public's errors cancel out.[1] For example, some people underestimate the benefits of immigration, and others overestimate the benefits. But as long as the average voter's belief is true, politicians win by promoting immigration policies based on the facts.

This story is clearly comforting, but is it correct? Are the average voter's beliefs true? In *The Myth of the Rational Voter*, my forthcoming book with Princeton University Press, I review a large body of evidence and conclude that the answer is definitely no. Like moths to the flame, voters gravitate to the same mistakes. They do not cancel each other out; they compound.

In my book, and in this essay, I focus on the public's mistaken beliefs about economics. Partly, this is because I am an economist, but mainly it is because economics is such a clear example of a subject that is politically important ("It's the economy, stupid,") yet poorly understood. I suspect that the public's errors extend

far beyond economics. There is convincing evidence that the public holds systematically biased beliefs about toxicology and cancer.[2] In foreign policy, similarly, we have the "rally round the flag" effect, the public's tendency to support wars as soon as they have been declared. But even if the average voter perfectly understood every non-economic subject, misconceptions about economics by themselves would pose a serious problem for democracy.

Identifying Misconceptions

Suppose that one scholar maintains that the average voter's belief about X is true, and another denies it. For their debate to make sense, both sides have to claim knowledge about (a) what the average voter believes, and (b) which belief is true. How can we get to the bottom of this sort of dispute?

It is fairly easy to figure out what the average voter believes. High-quality surveys abound. The hard thing is figuring out how to "grade" the beliefs of the average voter—to find a yardstick against which the beliefs can be measured.

The most straightforward is to compare voter beliefs to known fact. We can ask voters to tell us the fraction of the federal budget that goes to foreign aid, and compare their average

From *Cato Unbound*, November 6, 2006, www.cato-unbound.org.

answer to the actual number. Studies that use this approach find that the average voter has some truly bizarre beliefs. The National Survey of Public Knowledge of Welfare Reform and the Federal Budget finds, for example, that 41% of Americans believe that foreign aid is one of the two biggest areas in the federal budget—versus 14% for Social Security.

The main drawback of this approach is that many interesting questions are too complex to resolve with an almanac. But there is another mirror to hold up to public opinion. We can track down people who are usually likely to know the right answer, see what they think, then check whether the public agrees. Who might these unusually-likely-to-know people be? The most obvious candidates are experts.[3]

To see if the average voter's beliefs about the economic effects of immigration are right, for example, you can ask the general public and professional economists, and see if, on average, they agree. Is this an infallable test? No; experts have been wrong before. But it is hard to get around the strong presumption that if experts and laymen disagree, the experts are probably right, and the laymen are probably wrong. More importantly, if you have some specific reason to doubt the objectivity of the experts, you can control for it. If you think that economists' high income biases their beliefs, for example, you can check whether laymen and experts agree after statistically adjusting for income.

This was precisely the approach that I used to analyze the best available data set on economic beliefs, the Survey of Americans and Economists on the Economy. The overarching finding: Economists and the public hold radically different beliefs about the economy.[4] Compared to the experts, laymen are much more skeptical of markets, especially international and labor markets, and much more pessimistic about the past, present, and future of the economy. When laymen see business conspiracies, economists see supply-and-demand. When laymen see ruinous competition from foreigners, economists see the wonder of comparative advantage. When laymen see dangerous downsizing, economists see wealth-enhancing reallocation of labor. When laymen see decline, economists see progress.[5]

While critics of the economics profession like to attribute these patterns to economists' affluence, job security, and/or right-wing ideology, the facts are not with them. Controlling for income, income growth, job security, gender, and race only mildly reduces the size of the lay-expert belief gap. And, since the typical economist is actually a moderate Democrat, controlling for party identification and ideology makes the lay-expert belief gap get a little bigger. Economists think that markets work well not because of their extreme right-wing ideology, but despite their mild left-wing ideology.

From one perspective, we should have expected these findings all along. From the time of Adam Smith, if not earlier, economists have complained that economic policy was based on misconceptions, and tried to make a difference by correcting their students' prejudices against markets, international trade, and so on. Economists preserve this tradition to this day when they teach undergraduates, write for popular audiences, or talk amongst themselves. In recent decades, however, economic research has built on the contrary assumption that the beliefs of the average voter are true. What is surprising about my results is that I race long-standing economic tradition against recent economic research, and the traditional view wins.[6]

What Misconceptions Do

Political scientists have often criticized economists for assuming that voters are selfish. The data—along with personal experience—have convinced me that the political scientists are right—no matter how much you know about a voter's material interests, it is hard to predict how he is going to vote.[7] In contrast, if you know what a voter thinks is best for society, you can count on him to support it.

Before we can infer that the policies that are best for society will actually prevail, however, we have to add the very assumption I am challenging: that the beliefs of the average voter are true. If his beliefs are false, his good intentions lead him to support policies that are less than optimal, and possibly just plain bad.[8]

Consider the case of immigration policy. Economists are vastly more optimistic about its economic effects than the general public. The Survey of Americans and Economists on the Economy asks respondents to say whether "too many immigrants" is a major, minor, or non-reason why the economy is not doing better than it is. 47% of non-economists think it is a major reason; 80% of economists think it is not a reason at all. Economists have many reasons for their contrarian position: they know that specialization and trade enrich Americans and immigrants alike; there is little evidence that immigration noticeably reduces even the wages of low-skilled Americans; and, since immigrants are largely young males, and most government programs support the old, women, and children, immigrants wind up paying more in taxes than they take in benefits.[9]

Given what the average voter thinks about the effects of immigration, it is easy to understand why virtually every survey finds that a solid majority of Americans wants to reduce immigration, and almost no one wants to increase immigration. Unfortunately for both Americans and potential immigrants, there is ample reason to believe that the average voter is mistaken. If policy were based on the facts, we would be debating how much to increase immigration, rather than trying to "get tough" on immigrants who are already here.

Needless to say, I do not expect any prominent politicians to read this and publicly change their position on immigration. Democracy is a popularity contest. If the average voter believes that less immigration is best for society, democracy rewards politicians who oppose immigration. This does not necessarily mean that elected officials cynically pander to the prejudices of the public. Our leaders might have gotten to the top of the political game because they sincerely share popular prejudices. Regardless of what is going on in politicians' hearts and minds, though, we can expect democracy to listen to the average voter, even when he is wrong. The empirical evidence indicates that he often is.

How Misconceptions Are Possible

Most of the economic misconceptions that we see today were already well-known in the time of Adam Smith. How can the public keep making costly policy mistakes, year after year, century after century?

Public choice economists are used to blaming what they call "rational ignorance." In elections with millions of voters, the personal benefits of learning more about policy are negligible, because one vote is so unlikely to change the outcome. So why bother learning?

In my book, however, I argue that rational ignorance has been oversold. Rational ignorance cannot explain why people gravitate toward false beliefs, rather than simply being agnostic. Neither can it explain why people who have barely scratched the surface of a subject are so confident in their judgments—and even get angry when you contradict them. Why, to return to the case of immigration, do people leap to the conclusion that immigration is disastrous, and have trouble holding a civil conversation with someone who disagrees?

My view is that these are symptoms not of ignorance, but of irrationality. In politics as in religion, some beliefs are more emotionally appealing than others. For example, it feels a lot better to blame sneaky foreigners for our economic problems than it does to blame ourselves. This creates a temptation to relax normal intellectual standards and insulate cherished beliefs from criticism—in short, to be irrational.

But why are there are some areas—like politics and religion—where irrationality seems especially pronounced? My answer is that irrationality, like ignorance, is sensitive to price, and false beliefs about politics and religion are cheap.[10] If you underestimate the costs of excessive drinking, you can ruin your life. In contrast, if you underestimate the benefits of immigration, or the evidence in favor of the theory of evolution, what happens to you? In all probability, the same thing that would have happened to you if you knew the whole truth.

In a sense, then, there is a method to the average voter's madness. Even when his views are completely wrong, he gets the psychological benefit of emotionally appealing political beliefs at a bargain price. No wonder he buys in bulk.

What's Wrong With Democracy— and What's Better

Unfortunately, the social cost of irrationality can be high even though it is individually beneficial. If one person pollutes the air, we barely notice; but if millions of people pollute the air, life can be very unpleasant indeed. Similarly, if one person holds irrational views about immigration, we barely notice; but if millions of people share these irrational views, socially harmful policies prevail by popular demand.

When individual choices in markets have harmful social side effects, most people want to do something to about it. In the case of pollution, for example, economists usually want to tax emissions, and noneconomists want to set emission standards. Few people just shrug their shoulders and say, "The solution to the problems of markets is more markets."

When individual choices in democracy have harmful social side effects, however, many people really do just shrug their shoulders and say, "The solution to the problems of democracy is more democracy." If they wish to sound more hard-headed, they may instead quote Churchill: "[D]emocracy is the worst form of government, except all those other forms that have been tried from time to time."[11]

On reflection, though, quoting Churchill in the face of democratic failure makes about as much sense as seeing rampant air pollution, and saying, "The free market is the worst form of economic organization, except all the others." One can criticize markets or democracy—and propose remedies—without advocating socialism or dictatorship. Democracy, like the free market, can be limited, regulated, or overruled.

So what remedies for voter irrationality would I propose? Above all, relying less on democracy and more on private choice and free markets.[12] By and large, we don't even ask voters whether we should allow unpopular speech or religion, and this "elitist" practice has saved us a world of trouble. Why not take more issues off the agenda? Even if the free market does a mediocre job, the relevant question is not whether smart, well-meaning regulation would be better. The relevant question is whether the kind of regulation that appeals to the majority would be better.

Another way to deal with voter irrationality is institutional reform. Imagine, for example, if the Council of Economic Advisers, in the spirit of the Supreme Court, had the power to invalidate legislation as "uneconomical." Similarly, since the data show that well-educated voters hold more sensible policy views,[13] we could emulate pre-1949 Great Britain by giving college graduates an extra vote.[14]

I suspect that these—and other!—eccentric institutional reforms would be helpful if tried. Unfortunately, there is a catch-22: The majority is unlikely to vote to reduce the power of the majority. Still, milder versions of these reforms might slip through the cracks. The public has largely ceded control of monetary policy to professional economists; perhaps the public would be willing to defer to expert judgment on some other areas as well. In a similar vein, although the majority is unlikely to approve plural votes for college graduates, it does allow the well-educated to exert extra influence by virtue of their higher turnout rate. It might be politically possible to further increase the de facto influence of educated voters by spending less money to increase turnout.

In the end, though, the catch-22 means that institutional reform is unlikely to be a very effective check on voter irrationality. What else is there? Even in the most democratic countries, political actors have a degree of slack or "wiggle room." It is usually possible for officials to deviate moderately from voter preferences without being removed from power. And to be blunt, if the average voter holds irrational beliefs that lead him to support bad policies, using political slack to mitigate the damage seems like the right thing to do. If the average voter is wrong about immigration, and you have the political slack to push through an amnesty, go for it.

The Supreme Court may be the best example of a political body with a lot of slack. Justices serve for life, and it takes a constitutional amendment to overturn their decisions. This suggests—and history confirms—that they have significant power to improve upon democratic outcomes. If the Court has the chance to rule on the constitutionality of legislation inspired by anti-market misconceptions, why not overturn it for violating due process, or the Ninth Amendment, or the Tenth Amendment?[15] This was the essence of so-called "Lochner era jurisprudence." Given what we know about the public's economic biases, however, I think we owe those stodgy old judges an apology.

Of course, I do not expect the Supreme Court to revive Lochner anytime soon. At least as far as economics is concerned, the current justices basically accept the idea that they should defer to majoritarian wisdom. And obviously, they are not alone. The prevailing view even among the well-educated is that it is unseemly to question the competence of the average voter. Many elites go further by praising the insight of the average voter, no matter how silly his views seem.

As long as elites persist in unmerited deference to and flattery of the majority, containing the dangers of voter irrationality will be very hard. Someone has to tell the emperor when he is naked. He may not listen, but if no one speaks up, he will almost surely continue embarrassing himself and traumatizing spectators.

My final remedy for voter irrationality, then, is for people who know more than the average voter to stop being so modest. When experts and those who heed them address a broader audience—in the media, in their writings, or in a classroom—they need to focus on the questions where experts and the public disagree, and clearly explain why the experts are right and the public is wrong. Thus, when economists get the public's ear, they should not bore them with the details of national income statistics, or quibble with each other about marginal issues. They should challenge the public's misconceptions about markets, foreigners, saving labor, and progress.

But if the public is as irrational as I say, will this work? It might. Irrationality does not rule out persuasion, but it does change what people find persuasive. If people accept beliefs, in part, because they feel good, it is important to wrap your message in the right emotional packaging. "I'm right, you're wrong, change," falls flat. But in my experience, "I'm right, the people outside this classroom are wrong, and you don't want to be like them, do you?" is fairly persuasive. Frederic Bastiat, arguably the greatest economic educator in history, should be our role model. Who else could make a critique of popular economic prejudices not just charming, but funny?

Conclusion

I suspect that many readers will just view me as "tone-deaf" to democracy. Whether or not the people know what they are doing, don't they have a right to choose?

I can understand when people make this argument about self-regarding choice. Even if an individual does not know his own best interest, I normally think that he should be free to make his own mistakes. The problem with irrational voting, unfortunately, is that people who do it are not "just hurting themselves." If the average voter is irrational, we all have to live with the consequences.

Every parent eventually asks his child, "If all your friends jumped off the Brooklyn Bridge, would you?" I have an even more loaded question for those who refuse to second-guess the wisdom of the average voter: "If the majority said we all had to jump off the Brooklyn Bridge, would you push people who refused to jump?"

NOTES

1. See e.g. Wittman, Donald. 1995. *The Myth of Democratic Failure: Why Political Institutions Are Efficient.* Chicago: University of Chicago Press; Persson, Torsten, and Guideo Tabellini. 2000. *Political Economics: Explaining Economic Policy.* Cambridge: MIT Press; Drazen, Allan. 2000. *Political Economy in Macroeconomics.* Princeton, NJ: Princeton University Press; and Page, Benjamin, and Robert Shapiro. 1992. *The Rational Public: Fifty Years of Trends in Americans' Policy Preferences.* Chicago: University of Chicago Press.

2. See Kraus, Nancy, Torbjörn Malmfors, and Paul Slovic. 1992. "Intuitive Toxicology: Expert and Lay Judgments of Chemical Risks." *Risk Analysis* 12(2): 215–32; and Lichter, S. Robert, and Stanley Rothman. 1999. *Environmental Cancer—A Political Disease?* New Haven, CT: Yale University Press.

3. Another possibility is to compare the views of laymen who score well on tests of political knowledge to those of demographically similar laymen who score poorly. This is the standard approach in the political science literature on "enlightened preferences." The findings of this literature are quite compatible with my own; for a comprehensive survey, see Althaus, Scott. 2003. *Collective Preferences in Democratic Politics: Opinion Surveys and the Will of the People.* Cambridge: Cambridge University Press.

4. See here for a readable overview. For more academic treatments, see e.g. Caplan, Bryan. 2002. "Systematically Biased Beliefs About Economics: Robust Evidence of Judgemental Anomalies from the Survey of Americans and Economists on the Economy." *Economic Journal* 112(479): 433–58; Caplan, Bryan. 2002. "Sociotropes, Systematic Bias, and Political Failure: Reflections on the Survey of Americans and Economists on the Economy." *Social Science Quarterly* 83(2): 416–35; and Caplan, Bryan. 2001. "What Makes People Think Like Economists? Evidence on Economic Cognition from the Survey of Americans and Economists on the Economy." *Journal of Law and Economics* 44(2): 395–426.

5. How can these patterns be so clear-cut, given economists' legendary tendency to disagree with each other? The answer, quite simply, is that there is much more consensus than meets the eye. Popular culture creates a false impression because it is more entertaining to watch experts debate than it is to watch them agree; and in any case, once economists reach a common understanding, they move on to new topics.

6. For a two-round debate between myself and a leading defender of the rationality of the average voter, see [www.econjournalwatch.org/pdf/CaplanCommentApril2005.pdf] and [www.econjournalwatch.org/pdf/WittmanReplyApril2005.pdf].

7. For overviews, see Sears, David, and Carolyn Funk. 1990. "Self-Interest in Americans' Political Opinions." In Mansbridge, Jane, ed. 1990. *Beyond Self-Interest.* Chicago: University of Chicago Press: 147–70; Citrin, Jack, and Donald Green. 1990. "The Self-Interest Motive in American Public Opinion." *Research in Micropolitics* 3:1–28; and Caplan, Bryan. 2001. "Libertarianism Against Economism: How Economists Misunderstand Voters and Why Libertarians Should Care." *Independent Review* 5(4): 539–63.

8. For further discussion, see Caplan, Bryan. 2003. "The Logic of Collective Belief." *Rationality and Society* 15(2): 218–42; and Caplan, Bryan. 2001. "Rational Irrationality and the

Microfoundations of Political Failure." *Public Choice* 107(3/4): 311–31.

9. On the fiscal effects of immigration, see Lee, Ronald, and Timothy Miller. 2000. "Immigration, Social Security, and Broader Fiscal Impacts." *American Economic Review* 90(2): 350–4; and Simon, Julian. 1999. *The Economic Consequences of Immigration*. Ann Arbor, MI: University of Michigan Press.

10. For further discussion, see Caplan, Bryan. 2001. "Rational Ignorance versus Rational Irrationality." *Kyklos* 54(1): 3–26.

11. Eigen, Lewis, and Jonathan Siegel, eds. 1993. *The Macmillan Dictionary of Political Quotations*. New York: Macmillan Publishing Co.: 109.

12. Commentator Ian Shapiro has repeatedly denied that this is a coherent option. See Shapiro, Ian, and Casiano Hacker-Cordón. 1999. "Reconsidering Democracy's Value." In Shapiro, Ian, and Casiano Hacker-Cordón, eds. *Democracy's Value*. Cambridge: Cambridge University Press: 1–19; Shapiro, Ian. 1999. *Democratic Justice*. New Haven, CT: Yale University Press; and Shapiro, Ian. 1996. *Democracy's Place*. Ithaca, NY: Cornell University Press. I critique Shapiro's arguments at length in my forthcoming book. If he would like to pursue this issue, I would be happy to do so during the discussion phase.

13. In "What Makes People Think Like Economists?," I estimate that each step of education as a 1–7 scale has 9.3% as much effect on economic beliefs as a Ph.D. in economics.

14. As Speck explains, "[G]raduates had been able to vote for candidates in twelve universities in addition to those in their own constituencies, and businessmen with premises in a constituency other than their own domicile could vote in both." (Speck, W.A. 1993. *A Concise History of Britain, 1707–1975*. Cambridge: Cambridge University Press: 175).

15. See e.g. Barnett, Randy. 2004. *Restoring the Lost Constitution: The Presumption of Liberty*. Princeton, NJ: Princeton University Press; and Macedo, Stephen. 1987. *The New Right v. the Constitution*. Washington, DC: Cato Institute.

6 NONDEMOCRATIC REGIMES

When we think about different kinds of regimes around the world, we tend to think only in terms of democracy or authoritarianism. In democratic societies, authoritarianism is often viewed almost as a temporary aberration until a subject people are able to throw off their fetters and join the free world. As such, it might seem less important to understand the complexities of authoritarianism than concentrate on how countries make the transition from there to democracy. But authoritarianism is a much more diverse and entrenched form of politics. Remember that it is democracy that is the newcomer to political life, having been established relatively recently in human history, and that less than half of the world's population currently lives in fully free countries.

Juan Linz and Alfred Stepan's chapter on nondemocratic regimes (1996) is in many ways a culmination of research these two scholars have been conducting since the 1960s. For them, to understand how countries become democratic, it is important to understand their nondemocratic form. Linz and Stepan lay out a comprehensive analysis of the difference between totalitarianism and authoritarianism, and how each has an impact on the most basic facets of nondemocratic rule. Why does this matter? Put simply, Linz and Stepan argue that the type of authoritarian or totalitarian regime strongly affects how and if democracy will take its place. The institutions of nondemocratic rule will shape the path open to democracy in the future. This kind of analysis, sometimes called "path dependent," has grown in recent years in the study of comparative politics and is consistent with a greater focus on institutions as actors in their own right.

These issues are brought together in Fareed Zakaria's piece on democracy and the Middle East (2004). As Zakaria notes, it is not poverty that is the source of nondemocratic forces in the Middle East, but rather the maldistribution of wealth, fostered in part by natural resources or foreign aid. The absence of a strong middle class and democratic institutions left a void that religion in part filled, as a critique against the ruling authorities and the injustices of domestic and international politics. Here too, as in our previous readings, Zakaria stresses the need for economic reform as a prerequisite for *political reform. As long as there is little opportunity for the middle class, nondemocratic ideologies and regimes will hold sway.*

Larry Diamond, another prominent scholar of authoritarianism and democracy, takes this study a step further in his discussion (2008) of what he calls the "democratic rollback." After recent waves of democratization around the world, there has been a move backward in many countries, resulting in a number of illiberal and in some cases unstable regimes. Diamond goes so far as to label these "predatory states" that exist largely to concentrate power to the benefit of a handful of elites. Diamond suggests that the international community has an important role to play in keeping illiberalism in check, making foreign aid contingent on state reform, and supporting civic actors in these countries. Too often, he argues, the international community is indiscriminate in its support for nondemocratic regimes, or takes the presence of elections as evidence of democracy when true participation is stifled.

Such reforms, however, face some significant hurdles. As Diamond notes, in some cases nondemocratic regimes are a function of what has become known as the "resource curse." In Weinthal and Luong's "Combatting the Resource Curse" (2008), the authors explain the paradox that a country rich in resources can wind up both undemocratic and poor. It is commonly argued that democracy emerges when those who rule are compelled to share their power with a rising middle class. The state exchanges political power (representation) for economic resources (taxes). But in countries where significant wealth lies in the ground, the equation changes. Those in power can rely on oil or mineral wealth to support themselves and buy off or suppress the public. Natural resource wealth also tends to "crowd out" private business, leading to a smaller middle class that might demand greater participation. Here again, the international community can play a role in helping to move natural resources out of state hands. But this is only part of the solution, and a challenging one at that.

JUAN J. LINZ AND ALFRED STEPAN

MODERN NONDEMOCRATIC REGIMES

Democratic transition and consolidation involve the movement from a nondemocratic to a democratic regime. However, specific polities may vary immensely in the *paths* available for transition and the unfinished *tasks* the new democracy must face before it is consoli-

dated. Our central endeavor in the next two chapters is to show how and why much—though of course not all—of such variation can be explained by prior regime type.

For over a quarter of a century the dominant conceptual framework among analysts interested in classifying the different political systems in the world has been the tripartite distinction between democratic, authoritarian, and totalitarian regimes. New paradigms emerge because they help analysts see commonalities and implications they had previously overlooked. When Juan Linz wrote his 1964 article "An Authoritarian Regime: Spain," he wanted to call attention to the fact that between what then were seen as the two major stable political poles—the democratic pole and the totalitarian pole—there existed a form of polity that had its own internal logic and was a steady regime type. Though this type was nondemocratic, Linz argued that it was fundamentally different from a totalitarian regime on four key dimensions—pluralism, ideology, leadership, and mobilization. This was of course what he termed an *authoritarian regime*. He defined them as: "political systems with limited, not responsible, political pluralism, without elaborate and guiding ideology, but with distinctive mentalities, without extensive nor intensive political mobilization, except at some points in their development, and in which a leader or occasionally a small group exercises power within formally ill-defined limits but actually quite predictable ones."[1]

In the 1960s, as analysts attempted to construct categories with which to compare and contrast all the systems in the world, the authoritarian category proved useful. As the new paradigm took hold among comparativists, two somewhat surprising conclusions emerged. First, it became increasingly apparent that more regimes were "authoritarian" than were "totalitarian" or "democratic" combined. Authoritarian regimes were thus the modal category of regime type in the modern world. Second, authoritarian regimes were not necessarily in transition to a different type of regime. As Linz's studies of Spain in the 1950s and early 1960s showed, the

From *Problems of Democratic Transition and Consolidation: Southern Europe, South America, and Post-Communist Europe* (Baltimore: Johns Hopkins University Press, 1996), pp. 38–54. Some of the authors' notes have been omitted.

four distinctive dimensions of an authoritarian regime—limited pluralism, mentality, somewhat constrained leadership, and weak mobilization—could cohere for a long period as a reinforcing and integrated system that was relatively stable.

Typologies rise or fall according to their analytic usefulness to researchers. In our judgment, the existing tripartite regime classification has not only become less useful to democratic theorists and practitioners than it once was, it has also become an obstacle. Part of the case for typology change proceeds from the implications of the empirical universe we need to analyze. Very roughly, if we were looking at the world of the mid-1980s, how many countries could conceivably be called "democracies" of ten years' duration? And how many countries were very close to the totalitarian pole for that entire period?

Answers have, of course, an inherently subjective dimension, particularly as regards the evaluation of the evidence used to classify countries along the different criteria used in the typology. Fortunately, however, two independently organized studies attempt to measure most of the countries in the world as to their political rights and civil liberties. The criteria used in the studies are explicit, and there is a very high degree of agreement in the results. If we use these studies and the traditional tripartite regime type distinction, it turns out that more than 90 percent of modern nondemocratic regimes would have to share the same typological space—"authoritarian."[2] Obviously, with so many heterogenous countries sharing the same typological "starting place," this typology of regime type cannot tell us much about the extremely significant range of variation in possible transition paths and consolidation tasks that we believe in fact exists. Our purpose in the rest of this chapter is to reformulate the tripartite paradigm of regime type so as to make it more helpful in the analysis of *transition paths* and *consolidation tasks*. We propose therefore a revised typology, consisting of "democratic," "authoritarian," "totalitarian," "post-totalitarian," and "sultanistic" regimes.

Democracy

To start with the democratic type of regime, there are of course significant variations within democracy. However, we believe that such important categories as "consociational democracy" and "majoritarian democracy" are subtypes of democracy and not different regime types. Democracy as a regime type seems to us to be of sufficient value to be retained and not to need further elaboration at this point in the book.

Totalitarianism

We also believe that the concept of a totalitarian regime as an ideal type, with some close historical approximations, has enduring value. If a regime has eliminated almost all pre-existing political, economic, and social pluralism, has a unified, articulated, guiding, utopian ideology, has intensive and extensive mobilization, and has a leadership that rules, often charismatically, with undefined limits and great unpredictability and vulnerability for elites and nonelites alike, then it seems to us that it still makes historical and conceptual sense to call this a regime with strong totalitarian tendencies.

If we accept the continued conceptual utility of the democratic and totalitarian regime types, the area in which further typological revision is needed concerns the regimes that are clearly neither democratic nor totalitarian. By the early 1980s, the number of countries that were clearly totalitarian or were attempting to create such regimes had in fact been declining for some time. As many Soviet-type regimes began to change after Stalin's death in 1953, they no longer conformed to the totalitarian model, as research showed. This change created conceptual confusion. Some scholars argued that the totalitarian category itself was wrong. Others wanted to call post-Stalinist regimes authoritarian. Neither of these approaches seems to us fully satisfactory. Empirically, of course, most of the Soviet-type systems in the 1980s were not totalitarian. However, the "Soviet type" regimes, with the exception of Poland * * *, could not be understood in their distinctiveness by including them in the category of an authoritarian regime.

The literature on Soviet-type regimes correctly drew attention to regime characteristics that were no longer totalitarian and opened up promising new studies of policy-making. One of these perspectives was "institutional pluralism." However, in our judgment, to call these post-Stalinist polities *pluralistic* missed some extremely important features that could hardly be called pluralistic. Pluralist democratic theory, especially the "group theory" variant explored by such writers as Arthur Bentley and David Truman, starts with *individuals in civil society* who enter into numerous freely formed interest groups that are relatively autonomous and often criss-crossing. The many groups in civil society attempt to aggregate their interests and compete against each other in political society to influence state policies. However, the "institutional pluralism" that some writers discerned in the Soviet Union was radically different, in that almost all the pluralistic conflict occurred in *regime-created organizations within the party-state* itself. Conceptually, therefore, this form of competition and conflict is actually closer to what political theorists call *bureaucratic politics* than it is to *pluralistic politics*.

Rather than forcing these Soviet-type regimes into the existing typology of totalitarian, authoritarian, and democratic regimes, we believe we should expand that typology by explicating a distinctive regime type that we will call *post-totalitarian*.[3] Methodologically, we believe this category is justified because on each of the four dimensions of regime type—pluralism, ideology, leadership, and mobilization—there can be a post-totalitarian ideal type that is different from a totalitarian, authoritarian, or democratic ideal type. Later in this chapter we will also rearticulate the argument for considering sultanism as a separate ideal-type regime.

To state our argument in bold terms, we first present a schematic presentation of how the five ideal-type regimes we propose—democratic, totalitarian, post-totalitarian, authoritarian, and sultanistic—differ from each other on each one of the four constituent characteristics of regime type (table 1). In the following chapter we make explicit what we believe are the implications of each regime type for democratic transition paths and the tasks of democratic consolidation.

Post-Totalitarianism

Our task here is to explore how, on each of the four dimensions of regime type, post-totalitarianism is different from totalitarianism, as well as different from authoritarianism. Where appropriate we will also call attention to some under-theorized characteristics of both totalitarian and post-totalitarian regimes that produce dynamic pressures for out-of-type change. We do not subscribe to the view that either type is static.

Post-totalitarianism, as table 1 implies, can encompass a continuum varying from "early post-totalitarianism," to "frozen post-totalitarianism," to "mature post-totalitarianism." Early post-totalitarianism is very close to the totalitarian ideal type but differs from it on at least one key dimension, normally some constraints on the leader. There can be frozen post-totalitarianism in which, despite the persistent tolerance of some civil society critics of the regime, almost all the other control mechanisms of the party-state stay in place for a long period and do not evolve (e.g., Czechoslovakia, from 1977 to 1989). Or there can be mature post-totalitarianism in which there has been significant change in all the dimensions of the post-totalitarian regime except that politically the leading role of the official party is still sacrosanct (e.g., Hungary from 1982 to 1988, which eventually evolved by late 1988 very close to an out-of-type change).

Concerning *pluralism*, the defining characteristic of totalitarianism is that there is no political, economic, or social pluralism in the polity and that pre-existing sources of pluralism have been uprooted or systematically repressed. In an authoritarian regime there is some limited political pluralism and often quite extensive economic and social pluralism. In an authoritarian regime, many of the manifestations of the limited political pluralism and the more extensive social and economic pluralism predate the authoritarian regime. How does pluralism in post-totalitarian regimes contrast with the near absence of pluralism in totalitarian regimes and the limited pluralism of authoritarian regimes?

In mature post-totalitarianism, there is a much more important and complex play of institutional pluralism within the state than in totalitarianism. Also, in contrast to totalitarianism, post-totalitarianism normally has a much more significant degree of social pluralism, and in mature post-totalitarianism there is often discussion of a "second culture" or a "parallel culture." Evidence of this is found in such things as a robust underground *samizdat* literature with multi-issue journals of the sort not possible under totalitarianism.[4] This growing pluralism is simultaneously a dynamic source of vulnerability for the post-totalitarian regime and a dynamic source of strength for an emerging democratic opposition. For example, this "second culture" can be sufficiently powerful that, even though leaders of the second culture will frequently be imprisoned, in a mature post-totalitarian regime opposition leaders can generate substantial followings and create enduring oppositional organizations in civil society. At moments of crisis, therefore, a mature post-totalitarian regime can have a cadre of a democratic opposition based in civil society with much greater potential to form a democratic political opposition than would be available in a totalitarian regime. A mature post-totalitarian regime can also feature the coexistence of a state-planned economy with extensive partial market

Table 1. *Major Modern Regime Ideal Types and Their Defining Characteristics*

Characteristic	Democracy	Authoritarianism	Totalitarianism	Post-totalitarianism	Sultanism
Pluralism	Responsible political pluralism reinforced by extensive areas of pluralist autonomy in economy, society, and internal life of organizations. Legally protected pluralism consistent with "societal corporatism" but not "state corporatism."	Political system with limited, not responsible political pluralism. Often quite extensive social and economic pluralism. In authoritarian regimes most of pluralism had roots in society before the establishment of the regime. Often some space for semiopposition.	No significant economic, social, or political pluralism. Official party has *de jure* and *de facto* monopoly of power. Party has eliminated almost all pretotalitarian pluralism. No space for second economy or parallel society.	Limited, but not responsible social, economic, and institutional pluralism. Almost no political pluralism because party still formally has monopoly of power. May have "second economy," but state still the overwhelming presence. Most manifestations of pluralism in "flattened polity" grew out of tolerated state structures or dissident groups consciously formed in opposition to totalitarian regime. In mature post-totalitarianism opposition often creates "second culture" or "parallel society."	Economic and social pluralism does not disappear but is subject to unpredictable and despotic intervention. No group or individual in civil society, political society, or the state is free from sultan's exercise of despotic power. No rule of law. Low institutionalization. High fusion of private and public.
Ideology	Extensive intellectual commitment to citizenship and procedural rules of contestation. Not teleological. Respect for rights of minorities, state of law, and value of individualism.	Political system without elaborate and guiding ideology but with distinctive mentalities.	Elaborate and guiding ideology that articulates a reachable utopia. Leaders, individuals, and groups derive most of their sense of mission, legitimation, and often specific policies from their commitment to some holistic conception of humanity and society.	Guiding ideology still officially exists and is part of the social reality. But weakened commitment to or faith in utopia. Shift of emphasis from ideology to programmatic consensus that presumably is based on rational decision-making and limited debate without too much reference to ideology.	Highly arbitrary manipulation of symbols. Extreme glorification of ruler. No elaborate or guiding ideology or even distinctive mentalities outside of despotic personalism. No attempt to justify major initiatives on the basis of ideology. Pseudo-ideology not believed by staff, subjects, or outside world.
Mobilization	Participation via autonomously generated organization of civil society and competing parties of political society guaranteed by a system of law. Value is on low regime mobilization but high citizen participation. Diffuse effort by regime to induce good citizenship and patriotism. Toleration of peaceful and orderly opposition.	Political system without extensive or intensive political mobilization except at some points in their development.	Extensive mobilization into a vast array of regime-created obligatory organizations. Emphasis on activism of cadres and militants. Effort at mobilization of enthusiasm. Private life is decried.	Progressive loss of interest by leaders and nonleaders involved in organizing mobilization. Routine mobilization of population within state-sponsored organizations to achieve a minimum degree of conformity and compliance. Many "cadres" and "militants" are mere careerists and opportunists. Boredom, withdrawal, and ultimately privatization of population's values become an accepted fact.	Low but occasional manipulative mobilization of a ceremonial type by coercive or clientelistic methods without permanent organization. Periodic mobilization of parastate groups who use violence against groups targeted by sultan.

(continued)

Table 1. (continued)

Characteristic	Democracy	Authoritarianism	Totalitarianism	Post-totalitarianism	Sultanism
Leadership	Top leadership produced by free elections and must be exercised within constitutional limits and state of law. Leadership must be periodically subjected to and produced by free elections.	Political system in which a leader or occasionally a small group exercises power within formally ill-defined but actually quite predictable norms. Effort at cooptation of old elite groups. Some autonomy in state careers and in military.	Totalitarian leadership rules with undefined limits and great unpredictability for members and nonmembers. Often charismatic. Recruitment to top leadership highly dependent on success and commitment in party organization.	Growing emphasis by post-totalitarian political elite on personal security. Checks on top leadership via party structures, procedures, and "internal democracy." Top leaders are seldom charismatic. Recruitment to top leadership restricted to official party but less dependent upon building a career within party's organization. Top leaders can come from party technocrats in state apparatus.	Highly personalistic and arbitrary. No rational-legal constraints. Strong dynastic tendency. No autonomy in state careers. Leader unencumbered by ideology. Compliance to leaders based on intense fear and personal rewards. Staff of leader drawn from members of his family, friends, business associates, or men directly involved in use of violence to sustain the regime. Staff's position derives from their purely personal submission to the ruler.

experiments in the state sector that can generate a "red bourgeoisie" of state sector managers and a growing but subordinate private sector, especially in agriculture, commerce and services.

However, in a post-totalitarian regime this social and economic pluralism is different in degree and kind from that found in an authoritarian regime. It is different in degree because there is normally more social and economic pluralism in an authoritarian regime (in particular there is normally a more autonomous private sector, somewhat greater religious freedom, and a greater amount of above-ground cultural production). The difference in kind is typologically even more important. In a post-totalitarian society, the historical reference both for the power holders of the regime and the opposition is the previous totalitarian regime. By definition, the existence of a previous totalitarian regime means that most of the pre-existing sources of responsible and organized pluralism have been eliminated or repressed and a totalitarian order has been established. There is therefore an active effort at "detotalitarianization" on the part of oppositional currents in civil society. Much of the

emotional and organizational drive of the opposition in civil society is thus consciously crafted to forge alternatives to the political, economic, and social structures created by the totalitarian regime, structures that still play a major role in the post-totalitarian society. Much of the second culture therefore is not traditional in form but is found in new movements that arise out of the totalitarian experience. There can also be a state-led detotalitarianization in which the regime itself begins to eliminate some of the most extreme features of the monist experience. Thus, if there is growing "institutional pluralism," or a growing respect for procedure and law, or a newly tolerated private sector, it should be understood as a kind of pluralism that emerges *out of* the previous totalitarian regime.

However, it is typologically and politically important to stress that there are significant limits to pluralism in post-totalitarian societies. In contrast to an authoritarian regime, there is *no* limited and relatively autonomous pluralism in the explicitly political realm. The official party in all post-totalitarian regimes is still legally accorded the leading role in the polity. The institutional pluralism of a post-totalitarian regime should not be confused with political pluralism; rather, institutional pluralism is exercised within the party-state or within the newly tolerated second economy or parallel culture. The pluralism of the parallel culture or the second culture should be seen as a *social* pluralism that may have political implications. But we must insist that the party and the regime leaders in post-totalitarian regimes, unless they experience out-of-type change, accord *no* legitimacy or responsibility to nonofficial political pluralism.[5] Even the formal pluralism of satellite parties becomes politically relevant only in the final stages of the regime after the transition is in progress.

When we turn to the dimension of *leadership*, we also see central tendencies that distinguish totalitarian from authoritarian leadership. Totalitarian leadership is unconstrained by laws and procedures and is often charismatic. The leadership can come from the revolutionary party or movement, but members of this core are as vulnerable to the sharp policy and ideological changes enunciated by the leader (even more so in terms of the possibility of losing their lives) as the rest of the population. By contrast, in the Linzian scheme, authoritarian leadership is characterized by a political system in which a leader or occasionally a small group exercises power within formally ill-defined but actually quite predictable norms. There are often extensive efforts to co-opt old elite groups into leadership roles, and there is some autonomy in state careers and in the military.

As in a totalitarian regime, post-totalitarian leadership is still exclusively restricted to the revolutionary party or movement. However, in contrast to a totalitarian regime, post-totalitarian leaders tend to be more bureaucratic and state technocratic than charismatic. The central core of a post-totalitarian regime normally strives successfully to enhance its security and lessen its fear by reducing the range of arbitrary discretion allowed to the top leadership.

In contrast to those who say that the totalitarian regime concept is static, we believe that, when an opportunity presents itself (such as the death of the maximum leader), the top elite's desire to reduce the future leader's absolute discretion is predictably a dynamic source of pressure for out-of-type regime change from totalitarianism to post-totalitarianism. The post-totalitarian leadership is thus typologically closer in this respect to authoritarian leadership, in that the leader rules within unspecified but in reality reasonably predictable limits. However, the leadership in these two regime types still differs fundamentally. Post-totalitarian leadership is exclusively recruited from party members who develop their careers in the party organization itself, the bureaucracy, or the technocratic apparatus of the state. They all are thus recruited from the structures created by the regime. In sharp contrast, in most authoritarian regimes, the norm is for the regime to co-opt much of the leadership from groups that have some power, presence, and legitimacy that does not derive directly from the regime itself. Indeed, the authoritarian regime has often been captured by powerful fragments of the pre-existing society. In some authoritarian regimes, even access to top positions can be established not by political loyalties as much as by some degree of professional and technical expertise and some degree of competition through examinations that are open to the society as a whole. In mature post-totalitarian regimes, technical competence becomes increasingly important, but we should remember that the original access to professional training was controlled by political criteria. Also, the competences that are accepted or recognized in post-totalitarian systems are technical or managerial but do not include skills developed in a broader range of fields such as the law, religious organizations, or independent business or labor.

The limited party-bureaucratic-technocratic pluralism under post-totalitarianism does not give the regime the flexibility for change within the regime that co-optation of nonregime elites can give to many authoritarian regimes. The desire to resist the personalized leadership of the

First Secretary–ideologue can be a source of change from totalitarian to post-totalitarian, but it can also lead eventually to the oligarchic leadership of aging men supported by the nomenklatura. Attempts at rejuvenation at the top by including or co-opting new men and women from the outside are normally very limited. In extreme cases (i.e., the GDR and post-1968 Czechoslovakia), frozen post-totalitarianism shows geriatric tendencies. Under crisis circumstances, the inability to renovate leadership, not so paradoxically, is a potential source of dynamic change in that a frozen post-totalitarian regime, with its old and narrow leadership base, has a very limited capacity to negotiate. Such a leadership structure, if it is not able to repress opponents in a crisis, is particularly vulnerable to *collapse*. One of the reasons why midlevel cadres in the once all-powerful coercive apparatus might, in time of crisis, let the regime collapse rather than fire upon the democratic opposition has to do with the role of ideology in post-totalitarianism.

The contrast between the role of *ideology* in a totalitarian system and in a post-totalitarian system is sharp, but it is more one of behavior and belief than one of official canon. In the area of ideology, the dynamic potential for change from a totalitarian to a post-totalitarian regime, both on the part of the cadres and on the part of the society, is the growing empirical disjunction between official ideological claims and reality. This disjunction produces lessened ideological commitment on the part of the cadres and growing criticism of the regime by groups in civil society. In fact, many of the new critics in civil society emerge out of the ranks of former true believers, who argue that the regime does not—or, worse, cannot—advance its own goals. The pressures created by this tension between doctrine and reality often contributes to an out-of-type shift from a totalitarian regime effort to mobilize enthusiasm to a post-totalitarian effort to maintain acquiescence. In the post-totalitarian phase, the elaborate and guiding ideology created under the totalitarian regime still exists as the official

state canon, but among many leaders there is a weakened commitment to and faith in utopia. Among much of the population, the official canon is seen as an obligatory ritual, and among groups in the "parallel society" or "second culture," there is constant reference to the first culture as a "living lie." This is another source of weakness, of the "hollowing out" of the post-totalitarian regime's apparent strength.

The role of ideology in a post-totalitarian regime is thus diminished from its role under totalitarianism, but it is still quite different from the role of ideology in an authoritarian regime. Most authoritarian regimes have diffuse non-democratic mentalities, but they do not have highly articulated ideologies concerning the leading role of the party, interest groups, religion, and many other aspects of civil society, political society, the economy, and the state that still exist in a regime we would call post-totalitarian. Therefore, a fundamental contrast between a post-totalitarian and authoritarian regime is that in a post-totalitarian regime there is an important ideological legacy that cannot be ignored and that cannot be questioned officially. The state-sanctioned ideology has a *social presence* in the organizational life of the post-totalitarian polity. Whether it expresses itself in the extensive array of state-sponsored organizations or in the domain of incipient but still officially controlled organizations, ideology is part of the social reality of a post-totalitarian regime to a greater degree than in most authoritarian regimes.

The relative de-ideologization of post-totalitarian regimes and the weakening of the belief in utopia as a foundation of legitimacy mean that, as in many authoritarian regimes, there is a growing effort in a post-totalitarian polity to legitimate the regime on the basis of performance criteria. The gap between the original utopian elements of the ideology and the increasing legitimation efforts on the basis of efficacy, particularly when the latter fails, is one of the sources of weakness in post-totalitarian regimes. Since democracies base their claim to obedience on the procedural foundations of democratic citizenship, as well as performance, they have a layer of insulation against weak performance not available to most post-totalitarian or authoritarian regimes. The weakening of utopian ideology that is a characteristic of post-totalitarianism thus opens up a new dynamic of regime vulnerabilities—or, from the perspective of democratic transition, new opportunities—that can be exploited by the democratic opposition. For example, the discrepancy between the constant reiteration of the importance of ideology and the ideology's growing irrelevance to policymaking or, worse, its transparent contradiction with social reality contribute to undermining the commitment and faith of the middle and lower cadres in the regime. Such a situation can help contribute to the rapid collapse of the regime if midlevel functionaries of the coercive apparatus have grave doubts about their right to shoot citizens who are protesting against the regime and its ideology, as we shall see when we discuss events in 1989 in East Germany and Czechoslovakia.

The final typological difference we need to explore concerns *mobilization*. Most authoritarian regimes never develop complex, all-inclusive networks of association whose purpose is the mobilization of the population. They may have brief periods of intensive mobilization, but these are normally less intensive than in a totalitarian regime and less extensive than in a post-totalitarian regime. In totalitarian regimes, however, there is extensive and intensive mobilization of society into a vast array of regime-created organizations and activities. Because utopian goals are intrinsic to the regime, there is a great effort to mobilize enthusiasm to activate cadres, and most leaders emerge out of these cadres. In the totalitarian system, "privatized" bourgeois individuals at home with their family and friends and enjoying life in the small circle of their own choosing are decried.

In post-totalitarian regimes, the extensive array of institutions of regime-created mobilization

vehicles still dominate associational life. However, they have lost their intensity. Membership is still generalized and obligatory but tends to generate more boredom than enthusiasm. State-technocratic employment is an alternative to cadre activism as a successful career path, as long as there is "correct" participation in official organizations. Instead of the mobilization of enthusiasm that can be so functional in a totalitarian regime, the networks of ritualized mobilization in a post-totalitarian regime can produce a "cost" of time away from technocratic tasks for professionals and a cost of boredom and flight into private life by many other people. When there is no structural crisis and especially when there is no perception of an available alternative, such privatization is not necessarily a problem for a post-totalitarian regime. Thus, Kadar's famous saying, "Those who are not against us are for us," is a saying that is conceivable only in a post-totalitarian regime, not in a totalitarian one. However, if the performance of a post-totalitarian as opposed to a totalitarian regime is so poor that the personal rewards of private life are eroded, then privatization and apathy may contribute to a new dynamic—especially if alternatives are seen as possible—of crises of "exit," "voice," and "loyalty."[6]

Let us conclude our discussion of post-totalitarianism with a summary of its political and ideological weaknesses. We do this to help enrich the discussion of why these regimes collapsed so rapidly once entered into prolonged stagnation and the USSR withdrew its extensive coercive support. Indeed in chapter 17, "Varieties of Post-totalitarian Regimes," we develop a theoretical and empirical argument about why frozen post-totalitarian regimes are more vulnerable to collapse than are authoritarian or totalitarian regimes.

Totalitarianism, democracy, and even many authoritarian regimes begin with "genetic" legitimacy among their core supporters, given the historical circumstances that led to the establishment of these regimes. By contrast, post-totalitarianism regimes do not have such a founding genetic legitimacy because they emerge out of the routinization, decay, or elite fears of the totalitarian regime. Post-totalitarian regimes, because of coercive resources they inherit and the related weaknesses of organized opposition, can give the appearance of as much or more stability than authoritarian regimes; if external support is withdrawn, however, their inner loss of purpose and commitment make them vulnerable to collapse.

Post-totalitarian politics was a result in part of the moving away from Stalinism, but also of social changes in Communist societies. Post-totalitarian regimes did away with the worst aspects of repression but at the same time maintained most mechanisms of control. Although less bloody than under Stalinism, the presence of security services—like the Stasi in the GDR—sometimes became more pervasive. Post-totalitarianism could have led to moderate reforms in the economy, like those discussed at the time of the Prague Spring, but the Brezhnev restoration stopped dynamic adaptation in the USSR and in most other Soviet-type systems, except for Hungary and Poland.

Post-totalitarianism had probably less legitimacy for the ruling elites and above all the middle-level cadres than had a more totalitarian system. The loss of the utopian component of the ideology and the greater reliance on performance (which after some initial success did not continue) left the regimes vulnerable and ultimately made the use of massive repression less justifiable. Passive compliance and careerism opened the door to withdrawal into private life, weakening the regime so that the opposition could ultimately force it to negotiate or to collapse when it could not rely on coercion.

The weakness of post-totalitarian regimes has not yet been fully analyzed and explained but probably can be understood only by keeping in mind the enormous hopes and energies initially associated with Marxism-Leninism that in the past explained the emergence of totalitarianism and its appeal.[7] Many distinguished and influential Western intellectuals admired or excused Leninism and in the 1930s even Stalinism, but few Western intellectuals on the left could muster enthusiasm for post-totalitarianism in the USSR or even for perestroika and glasnost.

As we shall see in part 4, the emergence and evolution of post-totalitarianism can be the result of three distinct but often interconnected processes: (1) deliberate policies of the rulers to soften or reform the totalitarian system (detotalitarianism by choice), (2) the internal "hollowing out" of the totalitarian regimes' structures and an internal erosion of the cadres' ideological belief in the system (detotalitarianism by decay), and (3) the creation of social, cultural, and even economic spaces that resist or escape totalitarian control (detotalitarianism by societal conquest).

"Sultanism"

A large group of polities, such as Haiti under the Duvaliers, the Dominican Republic under Trujillo, the Central African Republic under Bokassa, the Philippines under Marcos, Iran under the Shah, Romania under Ceauşescu, and North Korea under Kim Il Sung, have had strong tendencies toward an extreme form of patrimonialism that Weber called *sultanism*. For Weber,

> *patrimonialism* and, in the extreme case, *sultanism* tend to arise whenever traditional domination develops an administration and a military force which are purely personal instruments of the master. . . . Where domination . . . operates primarily on the basis of discretion, it will be called *sultanism* . . . The non-traditional element is not, however, rationalized in impersonal terms, but consists only in the extreme development of the ruler's discretion. It is this which distinguishes it from every form of rational authority.[8]

Weber did not intend the word *sultanism* to imply religious claims to obedience. In fact, under Ottoman rule, the ruler held two distinct offices and titles, that of sultan and that of caliph.

Initially, the Ottoman ruler was a sultan, and only after the conquest of Damascus did he assume the title of caliph, which entailed religious authority. After the defeat of Turkey in World War I and the proclamation of the republic, the former ruler lost his title of sultan but retained his religious title of caliph until Atatürk eventually forced him to relinquish even that title. Our point is that the secular and religious dimensions of his authority were conceptually and historically distinguished. Furthermore, the term *sultan* should not be analytically bound to the Middle East. Just as there are mandarins in New Delhi and Paris as well as in Peking and there is a macho style of politics in the Pentagon as well as in Buenos Aires, there are sultanistic rulers in Africa and the Caribbean as well as in the Middle East. What we do want the term *sultanism* to connote is a generic style of domination and regime rulership that is, as Weber says, an extreme form of patrimonialism. In sultanism, the private and the public are fused, there is a strong tendency toward familial power and dynastic succession, there is no distinction between a state career and personal service to the ruler, there is a lack of rationalized impersonal ideology, economic success depends on a personal relationship to the ruler, and, most of all, the ruler acts only according to his own unchecked discretion, with no larger, impersonal goals.

Table 1 gives substantial details on what a sultanistic type is in relation to pluralism, ideology, mobilization, and leadership. In this section we attempt to highlight differences between sultanism, totalitarianism, and authoritarianism because, while we believe they are distinct ideal types, in any concrete case a specific polity could have a mix of some sultanistic and some authoritarian tendencies (a combination that might open up a variety of transition options) or a mix of sultanistic and totalitarian tendencies (a combination that would tend to eliminate numerous transition options).

In his long essay, "Totalitarian and Authoritarian Regimes," Juan Linz discussed the special features that make sultanism a distinctive type of nondemocratic regime.[9] Since the sultanistic regime type has not been widely accepted in the literature, we believe it will be useful for us to highlight systematically its distinctive qualities so as to make more clear the implications of this type of regime for the patterns of democratic resistance and the problems of democratic consolidation.

In sultanism, there is a high fusion by the ruler of the private and the public. The sultanistic polity becomes the personal domain of the sultan. In this domain there is no rule of law and there is low institutionalization. In sultanism there may be extensive social and economic pluralism, but almost never political pluralism, because political power is so directly related to the ruler's person. However, the essential reality in a sultanistic regime is that all individuals, groups, and institutions are permanently subject to the unpredictable and despotic intervention of the sultan, and thus all pluralism is precarious.

In authoritarianism there may or may not be a rule of law, space for a semi-opposition, or space for regime moderates who might establish links with opposition moderates, and there are normally extensive social and economic activities that function within a secure framework of relative autonomy. Under sultanism, however, there is no rule of law, no space for a semiopposition, no space for regime moderates who might negotiate with democratic moderates, and no sphere of the economy or civil society that is not subject to the despotic exercise of the sultan's will. As we demonstrate in the next chapter, this critical difference between pluralism in authoritarian and sultanistic regimes has immense implications for the types of transition that are *available* in an authoritarian regime but *unavailable* in a sultanistic regime.

There is also a sharp contrast in the function and consequences of ideology between totalitarian and sultanistic regimes. In a totalitarian regime not only is there an elaborate and guiding ideology, but ideology has the function of legitimating the regime, and rulers are often somewhat constrained by their own value system and ideology. They or their followers, or both, believe in that ideology as a point of reference and justification for their actions. In contrast, a sultanistic ruler characteristically has no elaborate and guiding ideology. There may be highly personalistic statements with pretensions of being an ideology, often named after the sultan, but this ideology is elaborated after the ruler has assumed power, is subject to extreme manipulation, and, most importantly, is not believed to be constraining on the ruler and is relevant only as long as he practices it. Thus, there could be questions raised as to whether Stalin's practices and statements were consistent with Marxism-Leninism, but there would be no reason for anyone to debate whether Trujillo's statements were consistent with Trujilloism. The contrast between authoritarian and sultanistic regimes is less stark over ideology; however, the distinctive mentalities that are a part of most authoritarian alliances are normally more constraining on rulers than is the sultan's idiosyncratic and personal ideology.

The extensive and intensive mobilization that is a feature of totalitarianism is seldom found in a sultanistic regime because of its low degree of institutionalization and its low commitment to an overarching ideology. The low degree of organization means that any mobilization that does occur is uneven and sporadic. Probably the biggest difference between sultanistic mobilization and authoritarian mobilization is the tendency within sultanism (most dramatic in the case of the Duvalier's Tonton Macoutes in Haiti) to use para-state groups linked to the sultan to wield violence and terror against anyone who opposes the ruler's will. These para-state groups are not modern bureaucracies with generalized norms and procedures; rather, they are direct extensions of the sultan's will. They have no significant institutional autonomy. As Weber stressed, they are purely "personal treatments of the master."

Finally, how does leadership differ in sultanism, totalitarianism, and authoritarianism?

The essence of sultanism is *unrestrained personal rulership*. This personal rulership is, as we have seen, unconstrained by ideology, rational-legal norms, or any balance of power. "Support is based not on a coincidence of interest between preexisting privileged social groups and the ruler but on interests created by his rule, rewards he offers for loyalty, and the fear of his vengeance."[10]

In one key respect leadership under sultanism and totalitarianism is similar. In both regimes the leader rules with undefined limits on his power and there is great unpredictability for elites and nonelites alike. In this respect, a Stalin and a Somoza are alike. However, there are important differences. The elaborate ideology, with its sense of nonpersonal and public mission, is meant to play an important legitimating function in totalitarian regimes. The ideological pronouncements of a totalitarian leader are taken seriously not only by his followers and cadres, but also by the society and intellectuals, including—in the cases of Leninism, Stalinism, and Marxism (and even fascism)—by intellectuals outside the state in which the leader exercises control. This places a degree of organizational, social, and ideological constraint on totalitarian leadership that is not present in sultanistic leadership. Most importantly, the intense degree to which rulership is personal in sultanism makes the *dynastic* dimension of rulership normatively acceptable and empirically common, whereas the public claims of totalitarianism make dynastic ambition, if not unprecedented, at least aberrant.

The leadership dimension shows an even stronger contrast between authoritarianism and sultanism. As Linz stated in his discussion of authoritarianism, leadership is exercised in an authoritarian regime "with formally ill-defined but actually quite predictable" norms.[11] In most authoritarian regimes some bureaucratic entities play an important part. These bureaucratic entities often retain or generate their own norms, which imply that there are procedural and normative limits on what leaders can ask them to do in their capacity as, for example, military officers, judges, tax officials, or police officers. However, a sultanistic leader simply "demands unconditional administrative compliance, for the official's loyalty to his office is not an impersonal commitment to impersonal tasks that define the extent and content of his office, but rather a servant's loyalty based on a strictly personal relationship to the ruler and an obligation that in principle permits no limitation."[12]

We have now spelled our the central tendencies of five ideal-type regimes in the modern world, four of which are nondemocratic. We are ready for the next step, which is to explore why and how the *type* of prior nondemocratic regime has an important effect on the democratic transition paths available and the tasks to be addressed before democracy can be consolidated.

NOTES

1. Juan J. Linz, "An Authoritarian Regime: The Case of Spain," in Erik Allardt and Yrjö Littunen, eds., *Cleavages, Ideologies and Party Systems* (Helsinki: Transactions of the Westermarck Society, 1964), 291–342. Reprinted in Erik Allardt and Stein Rokkan, eds., *Mass Politics: Studies in Political Sociology* (New York: Free Press, 1970). The definition is found on 255.

2. We arrive at this conclusion in the following fashion. The annual survey coordinated by Raymond D. Gastil employs a 7-point scale of the political rights and civil liberties dimensions of democracy. With the help of a panel of scholars, Gastil, from 1978 to 1987, classified annually 167 countries on this scale. For our purposes if we call the universe of democracies those countries that from 1978 to 1987 never received a score of lower than 2 on the Gastil scale for political rights and 3 for civil liberty, we come up with 42 countries. This is very close to the number of countries that Coppedge and Reinicke classify as "full polyarchies" in their independent study of the year 1985. Since our interest is in how countries become democracies we will exclude those 42 countries from our universe of analysis. This would leave us with 125 countries in the universe we want to explore.

If we then decide to call long-standing "totalitarian" regimes those regimes that received the lowest possible score on political rights and civil liberties on the Gastil scale for each year in the 1978–1987 period, we would have a total of nine countries that fall into the totalitarian classification. Thus, if one used the traditional typology, the Gastil scale would imply that 116 of 125 countries, or 92.8 percent of the universe under analysis, would have to be placed in the same typological space. See Gastil, *Freedom in the World*, 54–65.

3. Juan Linz, in his "Totalitarian and Authoritarian Regimes," in Fred I. Greenstein and Nelson W. Polsby, eds., *Handbook of Political Science* (Reading, Mass.: Addison-Wesley Publishing Co., 1975), 3:175–411, analyzed what he called "post-totalitarian authoritarian regimes," see 336–50. Here, with our focus on the available paths to democratic transition and the tasks of democratic consolidation, it seems to both of us that it is more useful to treat post-totalitarian regimes not as a subtype of authoritarianism, but as an ideal type in its own right.

4. For example, in mature post-totalitarian Hungary the most influential *samizdat* publication, *Beszélő*, from 1982 to 1989, was issued as a quarterly with publication runs of 20,000. Information supplied to Alfred Stepan by the publisher and editorial board member, Miklós Haraszti. Budapest, August 1994.

5. Hungary in 1988–89 represents a mature post-totalitarian regime which, by engaging in extensive detotalitarianization and by increasingly recognizing the legitimacy of other parties, had experienced significant

out-of-type changes even before the Communist Party lost power. See chapter 17.

6. The reference, of course, is to Albert Hirschman, *Exit, Voice and Loyalty* (Cambridge: Harvard University Press, 1970), 59. For a fascinating discussion of this dynamic in relation to the collapse of the GDR, see Hirschman, "Exit, Voice and the Fate of the German Democratic Republic: An Essay on Conceptual History," *World Politics* 45:2 (January 1993): 173–202.

7. On the ideological and moral attractiveness of revolutionary Marxist-Leninism as a total system and the "vacuum" left in the wake of

its collapse, see Ernest Gellner, "Homeland of the Unrevolution," *Daedalus* (Summer 1993): 141–54.

8. Max Weber, *Economy and Society: An Outline of Interpretive Sociology*, ed. Guenther Roth and Claus Wittich (Berkeley: University of California Press, 1978), 1:231, 232. Italics in the original.

9. Linz, "*Totalitarian and Authoritarian Regimes*," 259–63.

10. Ibid., 260.

11. Ibid., 255.

12. Ibid., 260.

FAREED ZAKARIA

ISLAM, DEMOCRACY, AND CONSTITUTIONAL LIBERALISM

It is always the same splendid setting, and the same sad story. A senior U.S. diplomat enters one of the grand presidential palaces in Heliopolis, the neighborhood of Cairo from which President Hosni Mubarak rules over Egypt. He walks through halls of marble, through rooms filled with gilded furniture—all a bad imitation of imperial French style that has been jokingly called "Louis Farouk" (after the last king of Egypt). Passing layers of security guards, he arrives at a formal drawing room where he is received with great courtesy by the Egyptian president. The two talk amiably about U.S.-Egyptian relations, regional affairs, and the state of the peace process between Israel and the Palestinians. Then the American gently raises the issue of human rights and suggests that Egypt's government might ease up on political dissent, allow more press freedoms, and stop

jailing intellectuals. Mubarak tenses up and snaps, "If I were to do what you ask, Islamic fundamentalists will take over Egypt. Is that what you want?" The conversation moves back to the latest twist in the peace process.

Over the years, Americans and Arabs have had many such exchanges. When President Clinton urged Palestinian leader Yasser Arafat to agree to the Camp David peace plan that had been negotiated in July 2001, Arafat reportedly responded with words to this effect: "If I do what you want, Hamas will be in power tomorrow." The Saudi monarchy's most articulate spokesman, Prince Bandar bin Sultan, often reminds American officials that if they press his government too hard, the likely alternative to the regime is not Jeffersonian democracy but a Taliban-style theocracy.

The worst part of it is, they may be right. The Arab rulers of the Middle East are autocratic, corrupt, and heavy-handed. But they are still more liberal, tolerant, and pluralistic than those who would likely replace them. Elections in

From *Political Science Quarterly*, 119, no. 1 (2004), pp. 1–20.

many Arab countries would produce politicians who espouse views that are closer to those of Osama bin Laden than those of Jordan's liberal monarch, King Abdullah. Last year, the emir of Kuwait, with American encouragement, proposed giving women the vote. But the democratically elected Kuwaiti parliament—filled with Islamic fundamentalists—roundly rejected the initiative. Saudi crown prince Abdullah tried something much less dramatic when he proposed that women in Saudi Arabia be allowed to drive. (They are currently forbidden to do so, which means that Saudi Arabia has had to import half a million chauffeurs from places like India and the Philippines.) But the religious conservatives mobilized popular opposition and forced him to back down.

A similar dynamic is evident elsewhere in the Arab world. In Oman, Qatar, Bahrain, Jordan, and Morocco, on virtually every political issue, the monarchs are more liberal than the societies over which they reign. Even in the Palestinian territories, where secular nationalists like Arafat and his Palestine Liberation Organization have long been the most popular political force, militant and religious groups such as Hamas and Islamic Jihad are gaining strength, especially among the young. And although they speak the language of elections, many of the Islamic parties have been withering in their contempt for democracy, which they see as a Western form of government. They would happily come to power through an election, but then would set up their own theocratic rule. It would be one man, one vote, one time.

Compare, for example, the wildly opposite reactions of state and society to the November 2001 videotape of a gloating bin Laden found by U.S. armed forces in an al-Qaeda hideout in Kabul. On tape, bin Laden shows an intimate knowledge of the September 11 attacks and delights in the loss of life they caused. Most of the region's governments quickly noted that the tape seemed genuine and proved bin Laden's guilt. Prince Bandar issued a statement: "The tape displays the cruel and inhumane face of a murder-ous criminal who has no respect for the sanctity of human life or the principles of his faith." Abdul Latif Arabiat, head of Jordan's Islamic party, the Islamic Action Front, asked "Do Americans really think the world is that stupid that they would believe that this tape is evidence?"

In most societies, dissidents force their country to take a hard look at its own failings. In the Middle East, those who advocate democracy are the first to seek refuge in fantasy, denial, and delusion. The region is awash in conspiracy theories, such as those claiming that the Israeli intelligence service, Mossad, was actually behind the World Trade Center attacks. In a CNN poll conducted across nine Muslim countries in February 2002, 61 percent of those polled said that they did not believe that Arabs were responsible for the September 11 attacks. Al-Jazeera, the first independent satellite television station in the region, which has an enormous pan-Arab audience, is populist and modern. Many of its anchors are women. It broadcasts news that the official media routinely censor. And yet it fills its airwaves with crude appeals to Arab nationalism, anti-Americanism, anti-Semitism, and religious fundamentalism.

The Arab world today is trapped between autocratic states and illiberal societies, neither of them fertile ground for liberal democracy. The dangerous dynamic between these two forces has produced a political climate filled with religious extremism and violence. As the state becomes more repressive, opposition within society grows more pernicious, goading the state into further repression. It is the reverse of the historical process in the Western world, where liberalism produced democracy and democracy fueled liberalism. The Arab path has instead produced dictatorship, which has bred terrorism. But terrorism is only the most noted manifestation of this dysfunction, social stagnation, and intellectual bankruptcy.

The Middle East today stands in stark contrast to the rest of the world, where freedom and democracy have been gaining ground over the past two decades. In its 2002 survey, Freedom

House finds that 75 percent of the world's countries are currently "free" or "partly free." Only 28 percent of the Middle Eastern countries could be so described, a percentage that has fallen during the last twenty years. By comparison, more than 60 percent of African countries today are classified as free or partly free.

Since September 11, the political dysfunctions of the Arab world have suddenly presented themselves on the West's doorstep. In the back of everyone's mind—and in the front of many—is the question why. Why is this region the political basket case of the world? Why is it the great holdout, the straggler in the march of modern societies?

Islam's Wide World

Bin Laden has an answer. For him the problem with Arab regimes is that they are insufficiently Islamic. Only by returning to Islam, he tells his followers, will Muslims achieve justice. Democracy, for bin Laden, is a Western invention. Its emphasis on freedom and tolerance produces social decay and licentiousness. Bin Laden and those like him seek the overthrow of the regimes of the Arab world—perhaps of the whole Muslim world—and their replacement by polities founded on strict Islamic principles, ruled by Islamic law (*sharia*) and based on the early Caliphate (the seventh-century Islamic kingdom of Arabia). Their more recent role model was the Taliban regime in Afghanistan.

There are those in the West who agree with bin Laden that Islam is the key to understanding the Middle East's turmoil. Preachers such as Pat Robertson and Jerry Falwell and writers such a Paul Johnson and William Lind have made the case that Islam is a religion of repression and backwardness. More serious scholars have argued—far more insightfully—that the problem is more complex: for fundamentalist Muslims, Islam is considered a template of all life, including politics. But classical Islam, developed in the seventh and eighth centuries, contains few of the

ideas that we associate with democracy today. Elie Kedourie, an eminent student of Arab politics, wrote, "The idea of representation, of elections, of popular suffrage, of political institutions being regulated by laws laid down by a parliamentary assembly, of these laws being guarded and upheld by an independent judiciary, the ideas of the secularity of state . . . all these are profoundly alien to the Muslim political tradition."[1]

Certainly the Koranic model of leadership is authoritarian. The Muslim holy book is bursting with examples of the just king, the pious ruler, the wise arbiter. But the Bible has its authoritarian tendencies as well. The kings of the Old Testament were hardly democrats. The biblical Solomon, held up as the wisest man of all, was, after all, an absolute monarch. The Bible also contains passages that seem to justify slavery and the subjugation of women. The truth is that little is to be gained by searching in the Koran for clues to Islam's true nature. The Koran is a vast book, filled with poetry and contradictions—much like the Bible and the Torah. All three books praise kings, as do most religious texts. As for mixing spiritual and temporal authority, Catholic popes combined religious and political power for centuries in a way that no Muslim ruler has ever been able to achieve. Judaism has had much less involvement with political power because, until Israel's founding, Jews were a minority elsewhere in the modern world. Yet, the word "theocracy" was coined by Josephus to describe the political views of ancient Jews.[2] The founding religious texts of all faiths were, for the most part, written in another age, one filled with monarchs, feudalism, war, and insecurity. They bear the stamp of their times.

Still, Western scholars of the nineteenth and early twentieth centuries often argued that Islam encourages authoritarianism. This assertion was probably influenced by their view of the Ottoman Empire, a community of several hundred million Muslims laboring docilely under the sultan in distant Constantinople, singing hosannas to him before Friday prayers. But most of the

world at the time was quite similar in its deference to political authority. In Russia, the czar
was considered almost a god. In Japan, the emperor was a god. On the whole, Asian empires
were more despotic than Western ones, but Islamic rule was no more autocratic than were
Chinese, Japanese, or Russian versions.

Indeed, if any intrinsic aspect of Islam is
worth noting, it is not its devotion to authority,
but the opposite: Islam has an antiauthoritarian
streak that is evident in every Muslim land today. It originates, probably, in several *hadith*—
sayings of the Prophet Mohammed—in which
obedience to the ruler is incumbent on the Muslim only so far as the ruler's commands are in
keeping with God's law.[3] If the ruler asks you to
violate the faith, all bets are off. ("If he is ordered to do a sinful act, a Muslim should neither
listen to [his leader] nor should he obey his order."[4]) Religions are vague, of course. This
means that they are easy to follow—you can interpret their prescriptions as you like. But it also
means that it is easy to slip up—there is always
some injunction you are violating. But Islam
has no religious establishment—no popes or
bishops—that can declare by fiat which is the
correct interpretation. As a result, the decision to
oppose the state on the grounds that it is insufficiently Islamic can be exercised by anyone who
wishes to do so. This much Islam shares with
Protestantism. Just as a Protestant with just a little training—Jerry Falwell, Pat Robertson—can
declare himself a religious leader, so also can
any Muslim opine on issues of faith. In a religion
without an official clergy, bin Laden has as
much—or as little—authority to issue *fatwas* (religious orders) as does a Pakistani taxi driver in
New York City. The problem, in other words, is
the absence of religious authority in Islam, not
its dominance.

Consider the source of the current chaos in
Arab land. In Egypt, Saudi Arabia, Algeria, and
elsewhere, Islamist[5] groups wage bloody campaigns against states that they accuse of betray-
ing Islam. Bin Laden and his deputy, the
Egyptian Ayman Zawahiri, both laymen, began

their careers by fighting their own governments
because of policies they deemed un-Islamic (for
Zawahiri, it was Egyptian president Anwar Sadat's 1978 peace treaty with Israel; for bin
Laden, it was King Fahd's decision to allow
American troops on Saudi soil in 1991). In his
1996 declaration of jihad, bin Laden declared
that the Saudi government had left the fold of Islam, and so it was permissible to take up arms
against it: "The regime betrayed the *ummah*
(community of believers) and joined the *kufr*
(unbelievers), assisting and helping them against
the Muslims." Bin Laden called for rebellion
against rulers, and many responded to his
call. The rulers of the Middle East probably wish
that Muslims were more submissive toward
authority.

There is also the question of timing: if Islam
is the problem, then why is this conflict taking
place now? Why did Islamic fundamentalism
take off only after the 1979 Iranian revolution?
Islam and the West have coexisted for fourteen
centuries. There have been periods of war but
many more periods of peace. Many scholars
have pointed out that, until the 1940s, minorities, and particularly Jews, were persecuted less
under Muslim rule than under any other majority religion. That is why the Middle East was for
centuries home to many minorities. It is commonly noted that a million Jews left or were ex-
pelled from Arab countries after the creation of
Israel in 1948. No one asks why so many were
living in Arab countries in the first place.

The trouble with thundering declarations
about "Islam's nature" is that Islam, like any religion, is not what books make it but what people
make it. Forget the rantings of the fundamentalists, who are a minority. Most Muslims' daily
lives do not confirm the idea of a faith that is intrinsically anti-Western or antimodern. The
most populous Muslim country in the world, Indonesia, has had secular government since its independence in 1949, with a religious opposition
that is tiny (although now growing). As for Islam's compatibility with capitalism, Indonesia
was until recently the World Bank's model Third

World country, having liberalized its economy and grown at 7 percent a year for almost three decades. It has now embraced democracy (still a fragile experiment) and has elected a woman as its president. After Indonesia, the three largest Muslim populations in the world are in Pakistan, Bangladesh, and India (India's Muslims number more than 120 million). Not only have these countries had much experience with democracy, all three have elected women as prime ministers, and they did so well before most Western countries. So although some aspects of Islam are incompatible with women's rights, the reality on the ground is sometimes quite different. And South Asia is not an anomaly with regard to Islamic women. In Afghanistan, before its twenty-year descent into chaos and tyranny, 40 percent of all doctors were women and Kabul was one of the most liberated cities for women in all of Asia. Although bin Laden may have embraced the Taliban's version of Islam, most Afghans did not—as was confirmed by the sight of men in post-Taliban Kabul and Mazar-e-Sharif lining up to watch movies, listen to music, dance, shave, and fly kites.

The real problem lies not in the Muslim world but in the Middle East. When you get to this region, you see in lurid color all the dysfunctions that people conjure up when they think of Islam today. In Iran,[6] Egypt, Syria, Iraq, the West Bank, the Gaza Strip, and the Persian Gulf states, dictatorships pose in various stripes and liberal democracy appears far from reach. The allure of Islamic fundamentalism seems strong, whether spoke of urgently behind closed doors or declared in fiery sermons in mosques. This is the land of flag burners, fiery mullahs, and suicide bombers. American went to war in Afghanistan, but not a single Afghan was linked to any terrorist attack against Americans. Afghanistan was the campground from which an Arab army was battling America.

The Arab world is an important part of the world of Islam—its heartland. But it is only one part and, in numerical terms, a small one. Of the 1.2 billion Muslims in the world, only 260 mil-

lion live in Arabia. People in the West often use the term "Islamic," "Middle Eastern," and "Arab" interchangeably. But they do not mean the same thing.

The Arab Mind

Today, characterizations of "the Oriental" have about them the whiff of illegitimacy, reminders of the days when ideas such as phrenology passed for science. (And if "Orientals" are to include the Chinese and the Indians—as they did then—then what to make of the stunning success of these groups at science, math, and other such manifestations of rationality?) But things have moved from one extreme to the other. Those who have resorted to such cultural stereotypes, the "Orientalists," have been succeeded by a new generation of politically correct scholars who will not dare to ask why it is that Arab countries seem to be stuck in a social and political milieu very different from that of the rest of the world. Nor is there any self-criticism in this world. Most Arab writers are more concerned with defending their national honor against the pronouncements of dead Orientalists than with trying to understand the predicament of the Arab world.

The reality is impossible to deny. Of the twenty-two members of the Arab League, not one is an electoral democracy, whereas 63 percent of all the [countries] in the world are. And although some—Jordan, Morocco—have, in some senses, liberal authoritarian regimes, most do not. The region's recent history is bleak. Its last five decades are littered with examples of Arab crowds hailing one dictator after another as a savior. Gamal Abdel Nasser in Egypt, Mu'ammer Qaddafi in Libya, and Saddam Hussein in Iraq all have been the recipients of the heartfelt adulation of the Arab masses.

The few Arab scholars who venture into the cultural field point out that Arab social structure is deeply authoritarian. The Egyptian-born scholar Bahgat Korany writes that "Arab political discourse [is] littered with descriptions of the enlightened dictator, the heroic leader, the exceptional Za'im, the revered head of family."[7] The Lebanese scholar Halim Barakat suggests that the same patriarchal relations and values that prevail in the Arab family seem also to prevail at work, at school, and in religious, political, and social organizations. In all of these, a father figure rules over others, monopolizing authority, expecting strict obedience, and showing little tolerance of dissent. Projecting a paternal image, those in positions of responsibility (as rulers, leaders, teachers, employers, or supervisors) securely occupy the top of the pyramid of authority. Once in this position, the patriarch cannot be dethroned except by someone who is equally patriarchal.[8]

The Failure of Politics

It is difficult to conjure up the excitement in the world in the late 1950s as Nasser consolidated power in Egypt. For decades Arabs had been ruled by colonial governors and decadent kings. Now they were achieving their dreams of independence, and Nasser was their new savior, a modern man for the postwar era. He had been born under British rule, in Alexandria, a cosmopolitan city that was more Mediterranean than Arab. His formative years had been spent in the army, the most Westernized segment of Egyptian society. With his tailored suits and fashionable dark glasses, he cut a daring figure on the world stage. "The Lion of Egypt" spoke for all the Arab world.

Nasser believed that Arab politics needed to be fired by ideas such as self-determination, socialism, and Arab unity. These were modern notions; they were also Western ones. Like many Third World leaders of the time, Nasser was a devoted reader of the British *New Statesman*. His "national charter" of 1962 reads as if it had been written by left-wing intellectuals in Paris or London. Even his most passionately pursued goal, pan-Arabism, was European inspired. It was a version of the nationalism that had united first Italy and then Germany in 1870—the idea that those who spoke one language should be one nation.

Before wealth fattened the Gulf states into golden geese, Egypt was the leader of the Middle East. Thus, Nasser's vision became the region's. Every regime, from the Baathists and generals in Syria and Iraq to the conservative monarchies of the Gulf, spoke in similar terms and tones. They were not simply aping Nasser. The Arab world desperately wanted to become modern, and it saw modernity in an embrace of Western ideas, even if it went hand in hand with a defiance of Western power.

The colonial era of the late nineteenth and early twentieth centuries raised hopes of British friendship that were to be disappointed, but still Arab elites remained fascinated with the West. Future kings and generals attended Victoria College in Alexandria, learning the speech and manners of British gentlemen. Many then went to Oxford, Cambridge, or Sandhurst—a tradition that is still maintained by Jordan's royal family, although now they go to American schools. After World War I, a new liberal age flickered briefly in the Arab world, as ideas about opening politics and society gained currency in places like Egypt, Lebanon, Iraq, and Syria. But the liberal critics of kings and aristocrats were swept away along with those old regimes. A more modern, coarser ideology of military republicanism, state socialism, and Arab nationalism came into vogue. These ideas, however, were still basically Western; the Baathists and Nasserites all wore suits and wanted to modernize their countries.

The new politics and politics of the Arab world went nowhere. For all their energy Arab regimes chose bad ideas and implemented them in worse ways. Socialism produced bureaucracy and stagnation. Rather than adjusting to the failures of central planning, the economies never really moved on. Instead of moving toward democracy, the republics calcified into dictatorships. Third World "nonalignment" became pro-Soviet propaganda. Arab unity cracked and crumbled as countries discovered their own national interests and opportunities. An Arab "Cold War" developed between the countries led by pro-Western kings (the Gulf states, Jordan) and those ruled by revolutionary generals (Syria, Iraq). Worst of all, Israel dealt the Arabs a series of humiliating defeats on the battlefield. Their swift, stunning defeat in 1967 was in some ways the turning point, revealing that behind the rhetoric and bombast lay societies that were failing. When Saddam invaded Kuwait in 1990, he destroyed the last remnants of the pan-Arab idea.

By the late 1980s, while the rest of the world was watching old regimes from Moscow to Prague to Seoul to Johannesburg crack, the Arabs were stuck with their corrupt dictators and aging kings. Regimes that might have seemed promising in the 1960s were now exposed as tired kleptocracies, deeply unpopular and thoroughly illegitimate. In an almost unthinkable reversal of a global pattern, almost every Arab country today is less free than it was forty years ago. There are few places in the world about which one can say that.

The Failure of Economics

At almost every meeting or seminar on terrorism organized by think tanks and universities since September 11, 2001, whenever someone wanted to sound thoughtful and serious, he would say in measured tones, "We must fight not just terrorism but also the roots of terrorism." This platitude has been invariably followed by a suggestion for a new Marshall Plan to eradicate poverty in the Muslim world. Who can be opposed to eradicating poverty? But the problem with this diagnosis is that it overlooks an inconvenient fact: the al-Qaeda terrorist network is not made up of the poor and dispossessed.

This is obviously true at the top; bin Laden was born into a family worth more than $5 billion. But it is also true of many of his key associates, such as his deputy, Zawahiri, a former

surgeon in Cairo who came from the highest ranks of Egyptian society. His father was a distinguished professor at Cairo University, his grandfather the chief imam of Al Azhar (the most important center of mainstream Islam in the Arab world), and his uncle the first secretary general of the Arab League. Mohammed Atta, the pilot of the first plane to hit the World Trade Center, came from a modern—and moderate—Egyptian family. His father was a lawyer. He had two sisters, a professor and a doctor. Atta himself studied in Hamburg, as had several of the other terrorists. Even the lower-level al-Qaeda recruits appear to have been educated, middle-class men. In this sense, John Walker Lindh, the California kid who dropped out of American life and tuned into the Taliban, was not that different from many of his fellow fundamentalists. In fact, with his high school diploma against their engineering degrees, one could say that he was distinctly undereducated by comparison.

In fact, the breeding grounds of terror have been places that have seen the greatest influx of wealth over the last thirty years. Of the nineteen hijackers, fifteen were from Saudi Arabia, the world's largest petroleum exporter. It is unlikely that poverty was at the heart of their anger. Even Egypt—the other greater feeder country for al Qaeda—is not really a poor country by international standards. Its per capita income, $3,690, places it in the middle rank of nations, and it has been growing at a decent 5 percent for the last decade. That may not be enough when you take population growth into account—its population growth has been about 3 percent—but many countries around the world are doing far worse. Yet, they have not spawned hordes of men who are willing to drive planes into Manhattan skyscrapers. If poverty were the source of terror, the recruits should have come from sub-Saharan Africa or South Asia, not the Middle East.

There is, however, a powerful economic dimension to the crisis in the Arab world. The problem is wealth, not poverty. Regimes that get rich through natural resources tend never to develop, modernize, or gain legitimacy. The Arab world is the poster child for this theory of trust-fund states. And this is true not only for the big oil producers. Consider Egypt, which is a small but significant exporter of oil and gas. It also earns $2 billion a year in transit fees paid by ships crossing the Suez Canal, and gets another $2.2 billion a year in aid from the United States. In addition, it gets large sums in remittances—money sent home—from Egyptians who work in the Gulf states. All told, it gets a hefty percentage of its GDP from unearned income. Or consider Jordan, a progressive state that is liberalizing; it gets $1 billion a year in aid from the United States. Although that may seem to be a small figure, keep in mind that Jordan's GDP is only $17 billion. Almost 6 percent of its annual income is foreign aid from one country.

Easy money means little economic or political modernization. The unearned income relieves the government of the need to tax its people—and in return provide something to them in the form of accountability, transparency, even representation.[9] History shows that a government's need to tax its people forces it to become more responsive and representative of its people. Middle Eastern regimes ask little of their people and, in return, give little to them. Another bad effect of natural-resource-derived wealth is that it makes the government rich enough to become repressive. There is always money enough for the police and the army. Saudi Arabia, for example, spends 13 percent of its GDP on the military, as does Oman. Kuwait spends around 8 percent. Various estimates of Iraqi military spending before the Gulf War have put its military spending at somewhere between 25 and 40 percent of annual GDP, an unusually high rate no doubt sustained, in part, by the Iran-Iraq War, but also by the massive internal intelligence network maintained by Saddam Hussein and his Baath Party.

For years, many in the oil-rich states argued that their enormous wealth would bring modernization. They pointed to the impressive appetites of Saudis and Kuwaitis for things Western, from McDonald's hamburgers to Rolex watches to Cadillac limousines. But importing Western goods is easy; importing the inner stuffing of modern society—a free market, political parties, accountability, the rule of law—is difficult and even dangerous for the ruling elites. The Gulf states, for example, have gotten a bastardized version of modernization, with the goods and even the workers imported from abroad. Little of their modernness is home-grown; if the oil evaporated tomorrow, these states would have little to show for decades of wealth except, perhaps, an overdeveloped capacity for leisure.

Fear of Westernization

There is a sense of pride and fall at the heart of the Arab problem. It makes economic advance impossible and political progress fraught with difficulty. America thinks of modernity as all good—and it has been almost all good for America. But for the Arab world, modernity has been one failure after another. Each path followed—socialism, secularism, nationalism—has turned into a dead end. People often wonder why the Arab countries will not try secularism. In fact, for most of the last century, most of them did. Now Arabs associate the failure of their governments with the failure of secularism and of the Western path. The Arab world is disillusioned with the West when it should be disillusioned with its on leaders.

The new, accelerated globalization that flourished in the 1990s has hit the Arab world in a strange way. Its societies are open enough to be disrupted by modernity, but not so open that they can ride the wave. Arabs see the television shows, eat the fast foods, and drink the sodas, but they do not see genuine liberalization in their societies, with ordinary opportunities and dynamism—just the same elites controlling things. Globalization in the Arab world is the critic's caricature of globalization, a slew of Western products and billboards with little else. For the elites in Arab societies, it means more things to buy. But for some of them, it is also an unsettling phenomenon that threatens their comfortable base of power.

This mixture of fascination and repulsion with the West—with modernity—has utterly disoriented the Arab world. Young men, often better educated than their parents, leave their traditional villages to find work. They arrive in the noisy, crowded cities of Cairo, Beirut, or Damascus, or go to work in the oil states. (Almost 10 percent of Egypt's working population has worked in the Gulf states at some point.) In their new world, they see great disparities in wealth and the disorienting effects of modernity; most unsettlingly, they see women, unveiled and in public places, taking buses, eating in cafes, and working alongside them. They come face to face with the contradictions of modern life, seeking the wealth of the new world but the tradition and certainty of the old.

The Rise of Religion

Nasser was a reasonably devout Muslim, but he had no interest in mixing religion with politics, which struck him as moving backward. This became painfully apparent to the small Islamic parties that supported Nasser's rise to power. The most important one, the Muslim Brotherhood, began opposing him vigorously, often violently, by the early 1950s. Nasser cracked down on it ferociously, imprisoning more than a thousand of its leaders and executing six of them in 1954. One of those jailed was Sayyid Qutb, a frail man with a fiery pen, who wrote a book in prison called *Signposts on the Road*, which in some ways marked the beginning of modern political Islam or what is often called Islamic fundamentalism.[10]

In his book, Qutb condemned Nasser as an impious Muslim and his regime as un-Islamic. Indeed, he went on, almost every modern Arab regime was similarly flawed. Qutb envisioned a better, more virtuous polity based on strict Islamic principles, a core goal of orthodox Muslims since the 1880s.[11] As the regimes of the

Middle East grew more distant, oppressive, and hollow in the decades following Nasser, fundamentalism's appeal grew. It flourished because the Muslim Brotherhood and organizations like it at least tried to give people a sense of meaning and purpose in a changing world, something no leader in the Middle East tried to do. In his seminal work, *The Arab Predicament*, which best explains the fracture of Arab political culture, Fouad Ajami explains, "The fundamentalist call has resonance because it invited men to participate . . . [in] contrast to a political culture that reduces citizens to spectators and asks them to leave things to their rulers. At a time when the future is uncertain, it connects them to a tradition that reduces bewilderment." Fundamentalism gave Arabs who were dissatisfied with their lot a powerful language of opposition.

On that score, Islam had little competition. The Arab world is a political desert with no real political parties, no free press, and few pathways for dissent. As a result, the mosque became the place to discuss politics. As the only place that cannot be banned in Muslim societies, it is where all the hate and opposition toward the regimes collected and grew. The language of opposition became, in these lands, the language of religion. This combination of religion and politics has proven to be combustible. Religion, at least the religion of the Abrahamic traditions (Judaism, Christianity, and Islam), stresses moral absolutes. But politics is all about compromise. The result has been a ruthless, winner-take-all attitude toward political life.

Islamic fundamentalism got a tremendous boost in 1979 when Ayatollah Ruhollah Khomeini toppled the staunchly pro-American shah of Iran. The Iranian Revolution demonstrated that a powerful ruler could be taken on by groups within the society. It also revealed how, in a developing society, even seemingly benign forces of progress—for example, education—can add to the turmoil. Until the 1970s most Muslims in the Middle East were illiterate and lived in villages and towns. They practiced a kind of village Islam that had adapted itself to local cultures and to normal human desires. Pluralistic and tolerant, these villages often worshipped saints, went to shrines, sang religious hymns, and cherished art—all technically disallowed in Islam. By the 1970s, however, these societies were being urbanized. People had begun moving out of the villages to search for jobs in towns and cities. Their religious experience was no longer rooted in a specific place with local customs and traditions. At the same time, they were learning to read, and they discovered that a new Islam was being preached by a new generation of writers, preachers, and teachers. This was an abstract faith not rooted in historical experience but literal and puritanical—the Islam of the high church as opposed to the Islam of the street fair.

In Iran, Ayatollah Khomeini used a powerful technology—the audiocassette. Even when he was exiled in Paris in the 1970s, his sermons were distributed throughout Iran and became the vehicle of opposition to the shah's repressive regime. But they also taught people a new, angry, austere Islam in which the West is evil, America is the "Great Satan," and the unbeliever is to be fought. Khomeini was not alone in using the language of Islam as a political tool. Intellectuals, disillusioned by the half-baked or overly rapid modernization that was throwing their world into turmoil, were writing books against "Westoxification" and calling the modern Iranian man—half Western, half Eastern—"rootless." Fashionable intellectuals, often writing from the comfort of London or Paris, would criticize American secularism and consumerism and endorse an Islamic alternative. As theories like these spread across the Arab world, they appealed not to the poorest of the poor, for whom Westernization was magical, since it meant food and medicine; rather, they appealed to the educated hordes entering the cities of the Middle East or seeking education and jobs in the West. They were disoriented and ready to be taught that their disorientation would be solved by recourse to a new, true Islam.

In the Sunni world, the rise of Islamic fundamentalism was shaped and quickened by the fact that Islam is a highly egalitarian religion. This for most of its history has proved an empowering call for people who felt powerless. But it also means that no Muslim really has the authority to question whether someone is a "proper Muslim." In the Middle ages, there was an informal understanding that a trained scholarly-clerical community, the *ulama*, had the authority to pronounce on such matters.[12] But fundamentalist thinkers, from Pakistani Maulana Maududi and Qutb to their followers, have muscled in on that territory. They loudly and continuously pronounce judgment as to whether people are "good Muslims." In effect, they excommunicate those whose Islam does not match their own. This process has terrified the Muslim world. Leaders dare not take on the rising tide of Islamists. Intellectual and social elites, widely discredited by their slavish support of the official government line, are also scared to speak out against a genuinely free-thinking clergy. As a result, moderate Muslims are loath to criticize or debunk the fanaticism of the fundamentalists. Some worry, like the moderates in Northern Ireland, about their safety if they speak their mind. Even as venerated a figure as Naguib Mahfouz was stabbed in Egypt for his mildly critical comments about the Islamists.

Nowhere is this more true than in the moderate monarchies of the Persian Gulf, particularly Saudi Arabia. The Saudi regime has played a dangerous game: it has tried to deflect attention away from its spotty economic and political record by allowing free reign to its most extreme clerics, hoping to gain legitimacy by association. Saudi Arabia's educational system is run by medieval-minded religious bureaucrats. Over the past three decades, the Saudis—mostly through private trusts—have funded religious schools (*madrasas*) and centers that spread Wahhabism (a rigid, desert variant of Islam that is the template for most Islamic fundamentalists) around the world. In the past thirty years, Saudi-funded *madrasas* have churned out tens of thousands of half-educated, fanatical Muslims who view the modern world and non-Muslims with great suspicion. American in this world-view is almost always uniquely evil.

This exported fundamentalism has infected not just other Arab societies but countries outside the Arab world. It often carries with it a distinctly parochial Arab political program. Thus, Indonesian Muslims, who twenty years ago did not know where Palestine was, are today militant in their support of its cause. The Arab influence extends even into the realm of architecture. In its buildings, the Islamic world has always mixed Arab influences with local ones—Hindu, Javan, Russian. But local cultures are now being ignored in places such as Indonesia and Malaysia because they are seen as insufficiently Islamic (meaning Arab).

Pakistan has had a particularly bad experience with exported fundamentalism. During the eleven-year reign of General Zia ul-Haq (1977–1988), the dictator decided that he needed allies, since he had squashed political dissent and opposition parties. He found them in the local fundamentalists, who became his political allies. With the aid of Saudi financiers and functionaries, he set up scores of *madrasas* throughout the country. The Afghan war attracted religious zealots, eager to fight godless communism. These "jihadis" came mostly from Arabia. Without Saudi money and men, the Taliban would not have existed, nor would Pakistan have become the hotbed of fundamentalism that it is today. Zia's embrace of Islam brought him a kind of legitimacy, but it has eroded the social fabric of Pakistan. The country is now full of armed radicals, who first supported the Taliban, then joined in the struggle of Kashmir, and are now trying to undermine the secular regime of General Pervez Musharraf. They have infected the legal and political system with medieval ideas of blasphemy, the subordinate role of women, and the evils of modern banking.

Pakistan is not alone. A similar process has been at work in countries as diverse as Yemen, Indonesia, and the Philippines. During the 1980s and 1990s, a kind of competition emerged between Iran and Saudi Arabia, the two most religious states in the Middle East, to see who would be the greater religious power in the Islamic World. As a result, what were once small, extreme strains of Islam, limited to parts of the Middle East, have taken root around the world—in the globalization of radical Islam.

The Road to Democracy

For the most part, the task of reform in the Middle East must fall to the peoples of the region. No one can make democracy, liberalism, or secularism take root in these societies without their own search, efforts, and achievements. But the Western world in general, and the United States in particular, can help enormously. The United States is the dominant power in the Middle East; every country views its relations with Washington as the most critical tie they have. Oil, strategic ties, and the unique U.S. relationship with Israel ensure American involvement. Washington will continue to aid the Egyptian regime, protect the Saudi monarchy, and broker negotiations between Israel and the Palestinians. The question really is, should it not ask for something in return? By not pushing these regimes, the United States would be making a conscious decision to let things stay as they are—to opt for stability. This is a worthwhile goal, except that the current situation in the Middle East is highly unstable. Even if viewed from a strategic perspective, it is in America's immediate security interests to try to make the regimes of the Middle East less prone to breeding fanatical and terrorist opposition movements.

As a start, the West must recognize that it does not seek democracy in the Middle East—at least not yet. We seek first conditional liberalism, which is very different. Clarifying our immediate goals will actually make them more easily attainable. The regimes in the Middle East will be delighted to learn that we will not try to force them to hold elections tomorrow. They will be less pleased to know that we will continually press them on a whole array of other issues. The Saudi monarchy must do more to end its governmental and nongovernmental support for extreme Islam, which is now the kingdom's second largest export to the rest of the world. If this offends advocates of pure free speech, so be it. It must rein in its religious and educational leaders and force them to stop flirting with fanaticism. In Egypt, we must ask President Mubarak to insist that the state-owned press drop its anti-American and anti-Semitic rants and begin opening itself up to other voices in the country. Some of these voices will be worse than those we hear now, but some will be better. Most important, people in these countries will begin to speak about what truly concerns them—not only the status of Jerusalem or American policies in the Gulf, but also the regimes they live under and the politics they confront.

Israel has become the great excuse for much of the Arab world, the way for regimes to deflect attention from their own failures. Other countries have foreign policy disagreements with one another—think of China and Japan—but they do not have the sometimes poisonous quality of the Israeli-Arab divide. Israel's occupation of the West Bank and Gaza Strip has turned into the great cause of the Arab world. But even if fomented by cynical Arab rulers, this cause is now a reality that cannot be ignored. There is a new Arab street in the Middle East, built on Al-Jazeera and Internet chat sites. And the talk is all about the plight of the Palestinians. If unaddressed, this issue will only grow in importance, infecting America's relations with the entire Muslim world and ensuring permanent insecurity for Israel. The United States should maintain its unyielding support for the security of Israel. But it should also do what is in the best interest of itself, Israel, and the Palestinians, which is to press hard to broker a settlement that provides Israel and the Palestinians a viable state. Peace between the Israelis and Palestinians will not solve the problem of Arab dysfunction, but it would ease some of the tensions between the Arab world and the West.

The more lasting solution is economic and political reform. Economic reforms must come first, for they are fundamental. Even though the problems facing the Middle East are not purely economic, their solution may lie in economics. Moving toward capitalism, as we have seen, is the surest path to creating a limited, accountable state and a genuine middle class. And just as in Spain, Portugal, Chile, Taiwan, South Korea, and Mexico, economic reform means the beginnings of a genuine rule of law (capitalism needs contracts), openness to the world, access to information, and, perhaps most important, the development of a business class. If you talk with Arab businessman and women, they want the old system to change. They have a stake in openness, in rules, and in stability. They want their societies to modernize and move forward rather than stay trapped in factionalism and war. Instead of the romance of ideology, they seek the reality of material progress. In the Middle East today, there are too many people consumed by political dreams and too few interested in practical plans.

There is a dominant business class in the Middle East, but it owes its position to oil or to connections to the ruling families.[13] Its wealth is that of feudalism, not capitalism, and its political effects remain feudal as well. A genuinely entrepreneurial business class would be the single most important force for change in the Middle East, pulling along all others in its wake. If culture matters, this is one place it would help. Arab culture for thousands of years has been full of traders, merchants, and businessmen. The bazaar is probably the oldest institution in the Middle East. And Islam has been historically highly receptive to business—Mohammed himself was a businessman. Ultimately, the battle for reform is one that Middle Easterners will have to fight, which is why there needs to be some group within these societies that advocates and benefits from economic and political reform.

This is not as fantastic an idea as it might sound. Already stirrings of genuine economic activity can be seen in parts of the Middle East. Jordan has become a member of the World Trade Organization (WTO), signed a free-trade pact with the United States, privatized key industries, and even encouraged cross-border business ventures with Israel. Saudi Arabia is seeking WTO membership. Egypt has made some small progress on the road to reform. Among the oil-rich countries, Bahrain and the United Arab Emirates are trying to wean themselves of their dependence on oil. Dubai, part of the United Arab Emirates, has already gotten oil down to merely 8 percent of its GDP and has publicly announced its intention of becoming a trading and banking center—the "Singapore of the Middle East." (It would do well to emulate Singapore's tolerance of its ethnic and religious minorities.) Even Saudi Arabia recognizes that its oil economy can provide only one job for every three of its young men coming into the work force. In Algeria, President Abdelaziz Bouteflika desperately wants foreign investment to repair his tattered economy.

If we could choose one place to press hardest to reform, it should be Egypt. Although Jordan has a more progressive ruler, and Saudi Arabia is more critical because of its oil, Egypt is the intellectual soul of the Arab world. If Egypt were to progress economically and politically, it would demonstrate more powerfully than any essay or speech that Islam is compatible with modernity, and that Arabs can thrive in today's world. In East Asia, Japan's economic success proved a powerful example that others in the region looked to and followed. The Middle East needs one such homegrown success story.

There is another possible candidate for the role: Iraq. Before it became a playpen for Saddam's megalomania, Iraq was one of the most advanced, literate, and secular countries in the region. It has oil, but more importantly, it has water. Iraq is the land of one of the oldest river-valley civilizations in the world. Its capital, Baghdad, is home to one of the wonders of the ancient world, the Hanging Gardens of Babylon, and has been an important city for thousands of years. Iraq in the 1950s was a country with a highly developed civil society, with engineers, doctors, and architects, many of whom were women. Now that Saddam has been dislodged, the United States must engage in a serious long-term project of nation building, because Iraq could well become the first major Arab country to combine Arab culture with economic dynamism, religious tolerance, liberal politics, and a modern outlook on the world. And success is infectious.

The Importance of Constitutionalism

Spreading democracy is tough. But that does not mean that the West—in particular the United States—should stop trying to assist the forces of liberal democracy. Nor does it imply accepting blindly authoritarian regimes as the least bad alternative. It does, however, suggest the need for a certain sophistication. The haste to press countries into elections over the last decade has been, in many cases, counterproductive. In countries such as Bosnia, which went to the polls within a year of the Dayton peace accords, elections only made more powerful precisely the kinds of ugly ethnic forces that have made it more difficult to build genuine liberal democracy there. The ethnic thugs stayed in power and kept the courts packed and the police well fed. The old system has stayed in place, delaying real change for years, perhaps decades. In East Timor and Afghanistan, a longer period of state-building has proved useful. In general, a five-year period of transition, political reform, and institutional development should precede national multiparty elections. In a country with strong regional, ethnic, or religious divisions—like Iraq—this is crucial. It ensures that elections are held after civic institutions, courts, political parties, and the economy have all begun to function. As with everything in life, timing matters.

Although it is easy to impose elections on a country, it is more difficult to push constitutional liberalism on a society. The process of genuine liberalization and democratization, in which an election is only one step, is gradual and long term. Recognizing this, governments and nongovernmental organizations are increasingly promoting an array of measures designed to bolster constitutional liberalism in developing countries. The National Endowment for Democracy promotes free markets, independent labor movements, and political parties. The U.S. Agency for International Development funds independent judiciaries. In the end, however, elections trump everything. If a country holds elections, Washington and the world will tolerate a great deal from the resulting government, as they did with Russia's Boris Yeltsin, Kyrgyzstan's Askar Akayev, and Argentina's Carlos Menem. In an age of images and symbols, elections are easy to capture on film. But how to do you televise the rule of law? Yet, there is life after elections, especially for the people who live there.

Conversely, the absence of free and fair elections should be viewed as one flaw, not the definition of tyranny. Elections are an important virtue of governance, but they are not the only virtue. It is more important that governments be judged by yardsticks related to constitutional liberalism. Economic, civil, and religious liberties are at the core of human autonomy and dignity. If a government with limited democracy steadily expands these freedoms, it should not be branded a dictatorship. Despite the limited political choice they offer, countries such as Singapore, Malaysia, Jordan, and Morocco provide a better environment for the life, liberty, and happiness of citizens than do the dictatorships in Iraq and Libya or the illiberal democracies of Venezuela, Russia, or Ghana. And the pressures of global capitalism can push the process of liberalization forward, as they have in China. Markets and morals can work together.

The most difficult task economically is reforming the trust-fund states. It has proved nearly impossible to wean them of their easy money. In 2002, the World Bank began experimenting with a potentially pathbreaking model in the central African country of Chad. Chad has major oil fields, but foreign companies were wary of major investments to extract and transport the oil because of the country's history of political instability. The World Bank agreed to step in, bless the project, and loan the government money to partner with a multinational consortium—led by ExxonMobil—to get the oil flowing. But it also put in place certain conditions. Chad's parliament had to pass a law guaranteeing that 80 percent of the oil revenues would be spent on health, education, and rural infrastructure, 5 percent would be spent on locals near the oil fields, and 10 percent would be put into an escrow account for future generations. That leaves the government 5 percent to spend as it wishes. To ensure that the system works in practice as well as in theory, the bank required that all oil revenues be deposited in an offshore account that is managed by an independent oversight committee (made up of some of Chad's leading citizens). It is too soon to tell if this model works, but if it does, it could be copied elsewhere. Even in countries that do not need the World Bank's help, it could have a demonstration effect. The Chad model provides a method by which natural-resource revenues can become a blessing for countries rather than the curse they currently are.

Finally, we need to revive constitutionalism. One effect of the overemphasis of pure democracy is that little effort is given to creating imaginative constitutions for transitional countries. Constitutionalism, as it was understood by its greatest eighteenth-century exponents, such as Montesquieu and Madison, is a complicated system of checks and balances designed to prevent the accumulation of power and the abuse of office. This is accomplished not by simply writing up a list of rights but by constructing a system in which government will not violate those rights. Various groups must be included and empowered because, as Madison explained, "ambition must be made to counteract ambition."

Constitutions were also meant to tame the passions of the public, creating not simply democratic but also deliberative government. The South African constitution is an example of an unusually crafted, somewhat undemocratic structure. It secures power for minorities, both those regionally based, such as the Zulus, and those that are dispersed, such as the whites. In doing so it has increased the country's chances of success as a democracy, despite its poverty and harrowing social catastrophes.

Unfortunately, the rich variety of unelected bodies, indirect voting, federal arrangements, and checks and balances that characterized so many of the formal and informal constitutions of Europe are now regarded with suspicion. What could be called the Weimar syndrome—named after Germany's beautifully constructed constitution, which nevertheless failed to avert fascism—has made people regard constitutions as simply paperwork that cannot make much difference (as if any political system in Germany would have easily weathered military defeat, social revolution, the Great Depression, and hyperinflation). Procedures that inhibit direct democracy are seen as inauthentic, muzzling the voice of the people. Today, around the world, we see variations on the same majoritarian theme. But the trouble with these winner-take-all systems is that, in most democratizing countries, the winner really does take all.

Of course, cultures vary, and different societies will require different frameworks of government. This is a plea not for the wholesale adoption of any one model of government but rather for a more variegated conception of liberal democracy, one that emphasizes both words in that phrase. Genuine democracy is a fragile system that balances not just these two but other forces—what Tocqueville called "intermediate associations"—to create, in the end, a majestic clockwork. Understanding this system requires an intellectual task of recovering the constitutional liberal tradition, central to Western experience and to the development of good government throughout the world.

This recovery will be incomplete if we limit it in our minds to what is happening in faraway countries that are troubled and poor and utterly different from the prosperous, democratic West. Democracy is a work in progress, abroad as well as at home. The tension between democracy and liberalism is one that flourished in the West's own past. In a very different form, it still exists and is growing in the Western world. It is most widely prevalent in one country in particular: the United States of America.

NOTES

1. Elie Kedourie, *Democracy and Arab Political Culture* (Washington, DC: Washington Institute for Near East Studies, 1992), 5.
2. Bernard Lewis, *What Went Wrong: Western Impact and Middle Eastern Response* (Oxford: Oxford University Press, 2002), 97.
3. The *hadith* are often more important than the Koran because they tell Muslims how to implement the sometimes general Koranic injunctions. For example, the Koran commands Muslims to pray, but it does not tell them how to pray; this is found in the *hadith*. (There are, of course, many *hadith*, many of dubious authenticity, and sometimes they contradict each other.)
4. *Sahih Muslim*, book 20, *hadith* 4533.
5. "Islamist" refers to people, like bin Laden, who want to use Islam as a political ideology, setting up an Islamic state that follows Islamic law strictly. I use this term interchangeably with the more commonly used "Islamic fundamentalist," although many scholars prefer the former.
6. I often lump Iran together with Arab countries. It is technically not one of them; Iranians speak Farsi, not Arabic. But Iran's Islamic Revolution of 1979 gave an enormous fillip to the broader fundamentalist

movement and, for now, has dulled the age-old divide between the two largest sects of Islam, Sunni (mostly Arabs) and Shia (mostly Iranians).

7. Bahgat Korany, "Arab Democratization: A Poor Cousin?" *PS: Political Science and Politics* 27, no. 3 (September 1994), 511.

8. Halim Barakat, *The Arab World: Society, Culture, and State* (Berkeley: University of California Press, 1993), 23.

9. John Waterbury has demonstrated that, far from being undertaxed, the Middle East is the "most heavily taxed of the developing regions." Using World Bank data from 1975 to 1985, Waterbury showed that "tax revenues as a proportion of GNP averaged 25 percent for Middle Eastern states while Latin America averaged 12 percent. This reflects not merely the effect of the preponderant weight of captive petroleum corporations in several Middle Eastern countries, which can be easily and heavily taxed. On average, 19 percent of overall tax revenues in the Middle East came from corporate profits tax, while the corresponding figure for Africa was 20 percent, for Asia 19 percent, and for Latin America 10 percent." But Waterbury errs by neglecting to disaggregate Arab states by type and amount of unearned income. If he had done so, he would have found that the oil-producing states—such as Saudi Arabia and Kuwait—levy few or no taxes, whereas the larger non–oil-producing states such as Egypt and Syria do levy substantial direct and indirect taxes. Although the unearned income that non–oil-producing states receive is significant, it is not enough to live on.

Most of the unearned income in such states goes straight to the military. So the absence of demands for democracy in the Middle East can be chalked up to two separate factors: mass bribery in the really rich states and mass repression in the poorer ones. But both are courtesy of income that flows into the governments' coffers and requires very little real economic activity.

10. In many ways, the original fundamentalist was Qutb's contemporary, the Pakistani scholar Abul Ala Maududi. Qutb was an admirer of Maududi and translated his writings into Arabic. But it is Qutb who is read throughout the Islamic world today.

11. Maududi argued that the colonial powers could be viewed in the same manner as the pagan tribes at the dawn of Islam. Just as the pagans were fought and resisted by the Prophet, so too should a jihad be waged by Muslims against their colonial oppressors. Qutb adopted Maududi's reasoning and extended it to propose jihad against irreligious Muslim governments. Sayyid Qutb, *Milestones* (Indianapolis: American Trust Publications, 1990). The best introduction to Qutb is Gilles Kepel, *Muslim Extremism in Egypt: The Prophet and Pharaoh* (Berkeley: University of California Press, 1985).

12. On the power of the medieval *ulama*, see Richard W. Bulliet, *Islam: The View from the Edge* (New York: Columbia University Press, 1994).

13. There are some exceptions to this rule in Gulf states such as Dubai, Bahrain, and even Saudi Arabia.

LARRY DIAMOND

THE DEMOCRATIC ROLLBACK: THE RESURGENCE OF THE PREDATORY STATE

Since 1974, more than 90 countries have made transitions to democracy, and by the turn of the century approximately 60 percent of the world's independent states were democratic. The democratization of Mexico and Indonesia in the late 1990s and the more recent "color revolutions" in Georgia and Ukraine formed the crest of a tidal wave of democratic transitions. Even in the Arab world, the trend is visible: in 2005, democratic forces in Lebanon rose up to peacefully drive out Syrian troops and Iraqis voted in multiparty parliamentary elections from the first time in nearly half a century.

But celebrations of democracy's triumph are premature. In a few short years, the democratic wave has been slowed by a powerful authoritarian undertow, and the world has slipped into a democratic recession. Democracy has recently been overthrown or gradually stifled in a number of key states, including Nigeria, Russia, Thailand, Venezuela, and, most recently, Bangladesh and the Philippines. In December 2007, electoral fraud in Kenya delivered another abrupt and violent setback. At the same time, most newcomers to the democratic club (and some long-standing members) have performed poorly. Even in many of the countries seen as success stories, such as Chile, Ghana, Poland, and South Africa, there are serious problems of governance and deep pockets of disaffection. In South Asia, where democracy once predominated, India is now surrounded by politically unstable, undemocratic states. And aspirations for democratic progress have been thwarted everywhere in the Arab world (except Morocco), whether by terrorism and political and religious violence (as in Iraq), externally manipulated societal divisions (as in Lebanon), or authoritarian regimes themselves (as in Egypt, Jordan, and some of the Persian Gulf monarchies, such as Bahrain).

Before democracy can spread further, it must take deeper root where it has already sprouted. It is a basic principle of any military or geopolitical campaign that at some point an advancing force must consolidate its gains before it conquers more territory. Emerging democracies must demonstrate that they can solve their governance problems and meet their citizens' expectations for freedom, justice, a better life, and a fairer society. If democracies do not more effectively contain crime and corruption, generate economic growth, relieve economic inequality, and secure freedom and the rule of law, people will eventually lose faith and turn to authoritarian alternatives. Struggling democracies must be consolidated so that all levels of society become enduringly committed to democracy as the best form of government and to their country's constitutional norms and constraints. Western policymaker can assist in this process by demanding more than superficial electoral democracy. By holding governments accountable and making foreign aid contingent on good governance, donors can help reverse the democratic recession.

Beyond the Façade

Western policymakers and analysts have failed to acknowledge the scope of the democratic recession for several reasons. First, global assessments by the Bush administration and by respected independent organizations such as

From *Foreign Affairs*, 87, no. 2 (March/April 2008), pp. 36–48.

Freedom House tend to cite the overall number of democracies and aggregate trends while neglecting the size and strategic importance of the countries involved. With some prominent exceptions (such as Indonesia, Mexico, and Ukraine), the democratic gains of the past decade have come primarily in smaller and weaker states. In large, strategically important countries, such as Nigeria and Russia, the expansion of executive power, the intimidation of the opposition, and the rigging of the electoral process have extinguished even the most basic form of electoral democracy. In Venezuela, President Hugo Chávez narrowly lost a December 2 [2007] referendum that would have given him virtually unlimited power, but he still does not allow the sort of free and fair political process that could turn him out of office.

Despite two decades of political scientists warning of "the fallacy of electoralism," the United States and many of its democratic allies have remained far too comfortable with this superficial form of democracy. Assessments often fail to apply exacting standards when it comes to defining what constitutes a democracy and what is necessary to sustain it. Western leaders (particularly European ones) have too frequently blessed fraudulent or unfair elections and have been too reluctant to criticize more subtle degradations of democracy. They tend to speak out only when democratic norms are violated by unfriendly governments (as in Russia and Venezuela or in Bolivia) and soft-pedal abuses when allies (such as Ethiopia, Iraq, or Pakistan) are involved.

Elsewhere in the developing and postcommunist worlds, democracy has been a superficial phenomenon, blighted by multiple forms of bad governance: abusive police and security forces, domineering local oligarchies, incompetent and indifferent state bureaucracies, corrupt and inaccessible judiciaries, and venal ruling elites who are contemptuous of the rule of law and accountable to no one but themselves. Many people in these countries—especially the poor—are thus citizens only in name and have few meaningful channels of political participation. There are elections, but they are contests between corrupt, clientelistic parties. There are parliaments and local governments, but they do not represent broad constituencies. There are constitutions, but not constitutionalism.

As a result, disillusioned and disenfranchised voters have embraced authoritarian strongmen (such as Vladimir Putin in Russia) or demagogic populists (such as Chávez in Venezuela). Many observers fear that Evo Morales in Bolivia and Rafael Correa in Ecuador may be headed down the same road as Chávez. In Thailand, voters (especially in the countryside) have turned repeatedly to a softer autocrat by electing Thaksin Shinawatra, whom the military overthrew in September 2006 only to see his party reemerge triumphant in the December 2007 elections. All of these cases of democratic distress reflect a common challenge: for democratic structures to endure—and to be worthy of endurance—they must listen to their citizens' voices, engage their participation, tolerate their protests, protect their freedoms, and respond to their needs.

For a country to be a democracy, it must have more than regular, multiparty elections under a civilian constitutional order. Even significant opposition in presidential elections and opposition party members in the legislature are not enough to move beyond electoral authoritarianism. Elections are only democratic if they are truly free and fair. This requires the freedom to advocate, associate, contest, and campaign. It also requires a fair and neutral electoral administration, a widely credible system of dispute resolution, balanced access to mass media, and independent vote monitoring. By a strict application of these standards, a number of countries typically counted as democracies today—including Georgia, Mozambique, the Philippines, and Senegal—may have slipped below the threshold. Alarmingly, a January 2008 Freedom House survey found that for the first time since 1994, freedom around the world had suffered a net decline in two successive years. The ratio of the number of countries whose scores had improved to the number whose scores had declined—a key indicator—was the worst since the fall of the Berlin Wall.

Where democracy survives, it often labors under serious difficulties. In most regions, majorities support democracy as the best form of government in principle, but substantial minorities are willing to entertain an authoritarian option. Furthermore, in much of the democratic world, citizens lack any confidence that politicians, political parties, or government officials are serving anyone other than themselves. According to surveys by Latinobarómetro (a Santiago-based corporation conducting public opinion surveys throughout Latin America), only one-fifth of the Latin American population trusts political parties, one-quarter trusts legislatures, and merely one-third has faith in the judiciary. According to similar surveys conducted by the Scotland-based New Democracies Barometer, the figures are even worse in the new democracies of eastern Europe.

Public confidence in many civilian constitutional regimes has been declining. The Asian Barometer (which conducts public opinion surveys throughout Asia) found that the percentage of Filipinos who believe democracy is always the best form of government dropped from 64 percent to 51 percent between 2001 and 2005. At the same time, satisfaction with democracy fell from 54 percent to 39 percent, and the share of the Filipino population willing to reject the option of an authoritarian "strong leader" declined from 70 percent to 59 percent. The Afrobarometer (which conducts similar surveys in African countries) uncovered even sharper decreases in Nigerians' public confidence in democracy between 2000 and 2005 and also found that the proportion of the Nigerian public that felt the government was working to control corruption dropped from 64 percent to 36 percent. This is no surprise: during this period, President Olusegun Obasanjo saw many of his laudable economic reforms overshadowed or undone by continuing massive corruption, by his obsessive bid to remove a constitutional term limit on his presidency, and by the gross rigging of the 2007

elections on behalf of his ruling party.

Electoral fraud and endemic corruption have once again ravaged a promising democratic experiment. If Nigeria reverts to military rule, descends into political chaos, or collapses, it will deal a harsh blow to democratic hopes across Africa. Indeed, the many African countries that remain blatantly authoritarian will never liberalize if the continent's new and partial democracies cannot make democracy work.

It's the Government, Stupid

It is often assumed that economic growth—or the free-market economy, as Michael Mandelbaum recently argued in these pages—is the key to creating and consolidating democracy. Certainly, the viability of democracy does hinge to some significant degree on economic development and open markets. But in most of the world's poor countries, the "economy first" advocates have the causal chain backward. Without significant improvements in governance, economic growth will not take off or be sustainable. Without legal and political institutions to control corruption, punish cheating, and ensure a level economic and political playing field, pro-growth policies will be ineffective and their economic benefits will be overshadowed or erased.

Kenya is a tragic case in point. In the last five years, under President Mwai Kibaki's leadership, it has made significant economic progress for the first time in many years, achieving a record five percent annual growth rate and establishing free universal primary education. But much of this progress has since unraveled amid the paroxysms of ethnic violence that greeted allegations of fraud following the December 27, 2007, presidential election. President Kibaki did not fail on the economic policy front, nor did his country lack international tourism and development aid (apart from a brief suspension of World Bank assistance in 2006 due to reports of egregious graft). Rather, he failed politically by condoning massive corruption, ethnic favoritism, and electoral malpractice—a poisonous mix that has brought a promising new democracy to the brink of chaos.

In the coming decade, the fate of democracy will be determined not by the scope of its expansion to the remaining dictatorships of the world but rather by the performance of at-risk democracies such as Kenya. A list of such democracies would encompass more than 50 states, including most countries in Latin America and the Caribbean, four of the eight democracies in Asia, all of the post-Soviet democracies that do not belong to the European Union, and virtually all of the democracies in Africa. The most urgent task of the next decade is to shore up democracy in these countries.

At-risk democracies are almost universally plagued by poor governance. Some appear so trapped in patterns of corrupt and abusive rule that it is hard to see how they can survive as democracies without significant reform. The problem in these states is that bad governance is not an aberration or an illness to be cured. It is, as the economists Douglass North, John Wallis, and Barry Weingast have argued, a natural condition. For thousands of years, the natural tendency of elites everywhere has been to monopolize power rather than to restrain it— through the development of transparent laws, strong institutions, and market competition. And once they have succeeded in restricting political access, these elites use their consolidated power to limit economic competition so as to generate profits that benefit them rather than society at large. The result is a predatory state.

In such states, the behavior of elites is cynical and opportunistic. If there are competitive elections, they become a bloody zero-sum struggle in which everything is at stake and no one can afford to lose. Ordinary people are not truly citizens but clients of powerful local bosses, who are themselves the clients of still more powerful patrons. Stark inequalities in power and status create vertical chains of dependency, secured by patronage, coercion, and demagogic electoral appeals to ethnic pride and prejudice. Public policies and programs do not really matter, since rulers have few intentions of delivering on them anyway. Officials feed on the state, and the powerful prey on the weak. The purpose of government is not to generate public goods, such as roads, schools, clinics, and sewer systems. Instead, it is to produce private goods for officials, their families, and their cronies. In such a system, as Robert Putnam wrote in his classic *Making Democracy Work*, "corruption is widely regarded as the norm," political participation is mobilized from above, civic engagement is meager, compromise is scarce, and "nearly everyone feels powerless, exploited, and unhappy." Predatory states cannot sustain democracy, for sustainable democracy requires constitutionalism, compromise, and a respect for law. Nor can they generate sustainable economic growth, for that requires actors with financial capital to invest in productive activity.

The most egregious predatory states produce predatory societies. People do not get rich through productive activity and honest risk taking; they get rich by manipulating power and privilege, by stealing from the state, extracting from the weak, and shirking the law. Political actors in predatory societies use any means necessary and break any rules possible in their quest for power and wealth. Politicians bribe election officials, attack opposition campaigners, and assassinate rival candidates. Presidents silence dissent with threats, detentions, show trials, and murder. Government ministers worry first about the money they can collect and only second about whether government contracts serve the public good. Military officers buy weapons on the basis of how large a kickback they can pocket. In such societies, the line between the police and the criminals is thin. The police do not enforce the law, judges do not decide the law, customs officials do not inspect goods, manufacturers do not produce, bankers do not invest, and borrowers do not repay. Every transaction is manipulated to someone's immediate advantage.

By contrast, sustainable democracy and development require active "civic communities," in which citizens trust one another and interact as political equals. In sustainable democracies, institutions of good governance—such as impartial judicial systems and vigorous audit agencies—induce, enforce, and reward civic behavior. The tendency toward corrupt governance and the monopoly of power is checked by the rule of law (both culturally and institutionally) and a resourceful civil society. As Putnam argues, people in such societies by and large obey the law, pay their taxes, behave ethically, and serve the public good not simply because they are public-spirited but because they believe others will, too—and because they know that there are penalties for failing to do so.

Escaping the Predators

For democracy to triumph, the natural predatory tendencies of rulers must be restrained by rigorous rules and impartial institutions. Some fundamental innovations are necessary to transform closed, predatory societies into open, democratic ones. Proponents of democracy both within troubled countries and in the international community must understand the problem and pursue the necessary reforms if they hope to restore the forward momentum of democracy in the world. Citizens must build links across ethnic and regional divides to challenge elitist hierarchies and rule by strongmen. This requires dense, vigorous civil societies, with independent organizations, mass media, and think tanks, as well as other networks that can foster civic norms, pursue the public interest, raise citizen consciousness, break the bonds of clientelism, scrutinize government conduct, and lobby for good-governance reforms.

States must also build effective institutions in order to constrain the nearly unlimited discretion that predatory rulers enjoy, subject those rulers' decisions and transactions to public scrutiny, and hold them accountable before the law. This requires both vertical and horizontal accountability. The premier example of vertical accountability is a genuinely democratic election. But ensuring democratic elections requires a truly independent electoral administration capable of conducting all the necessary tasks—from registering voters to counting votes—with strict integrity and neutrality. Other effective forms of vertical accountability include public hearings, citizen audits, the regulation of campaign finance, and a freedom-of-information act.

Horizontal accountability invests some agencies of the state with the power and responsibility to monitor the conduct of their counterparts. No institution is more important than a counter-corruption commission, which should collect regular declarations of assets from all significant elected and appointed officials. To be effective, such commissions need legal authority, professional staffs, vigorous leadership, and the resources to check the veracity of financial declarations, probe allegations of wrongdoing, impose civil penalties, and bring criminal charges against violators. Their work must be reinforced by ombudsmen; public audits of all major government agencies and ministries; parliamentary oversight committees to investigate evidence of waste, fraud, and abuse by executive agencies; and competent independent judiciaries capable of penalizing bribery and embezzlement. In at-risk democracies, these institutions often exist but do not function well (or at all)—largely because they are not meant to. Typically, they either limp along, starved of resources and bereft of morale and serious leadership, or become instruments of the ruling party and investigate only its political opponents. Counter-corruption agencies cannot make a difference unless they are independent of the government actors they are supposed to monitor, restrain, and punish.

Poorly performing democracies need better, stronger, and more democratic institutions—political parties, parliaments, and local governments—linking citizens to one another and to the political process. In shallow democracies, these institutions do not generate much citizen participation (beyond occasional voting) because the political systems are so elite-dominated, corrupt, and unresponsive. Reform requires the internal democratization of political parties through the improvement of their transparency and accessibility and the strengthening of other representative bodies.

It is not only the regulatory and participatory institutions of government that need strengthening. Effective democracy also requires improving the technical skills, resources, professional standards, and organizational efficiency of the state. Such improvements allow the government to maintain security, manage the economy, develop infrastructure, settle disputes, and deliver services such as health care, education, and clean water. Just as corruption erodes the basic functions of government, a feeble state drives people toward informal and corrupt networks to get things done.

Finally, reforms must generate a more open market economy in which it is possible to accumulate wealth through honest effort and initiative in the private sector—with the state playing a limited role. The wider the scope of state control over economic life, the greater the possibility of graft by abusive and predatory elites. Reducing administrative barriers to doing business and implementing corporate-responsibility initiatives can address the supply side of the corruption problem. Strong guarantees of property rights, including the ability of owners of small farms and informal-sector workers to obtain titles to their land and business property, can provide the foundation for a broader institutional landscape that limits government corruption.

The most urgent imperative is to restructure and empower the institutions of accountability and bolster the rule of law. Changing the way government works means changing the way politics and society work, and that, in turn, requires sustained attention to how public officials utilize their offices. This is the fundamental challenge that all at-risk democracies face.

Aiding the Democratic Revival

The current situation may seem discouraging, but there is hope. Even in very poor nations drowning in corruption and clientelism, citizens have repeatedly used the democratic process to try to replace predatory governments. Connected by grass-roots movements, community radio stations, cell phones, civic organizations, and the Internet, citizens are rising up as never before to challenge corruption, defend the electoral process, and demand better governance. The most important challenge now for the United States and other international actors is to stand with them.

The leverage needed to bring about radical change will never exist unless the politicians and officials who sit atop the structures of predation come to realize that they have no choice but to reform. In the early 1990s, many African regimes moved toward free elections when a combination of internal and external pressure left them no choice: they were running out of money and could not pay their soldiers and civil servants. Now, with the momentum going against democracy, a resurgent and oil-rich Russia flexing its muscles, and China emerging as a major aid donor in the rest of Asia and Africa, it will be more difficult to encourage reforms. Forcing change that leads to better governance will require serious resolve and close coordination among the established bilateral and multilateral donors.

The key is the principle of conditionality (or selectivity), which lies at the core of the Millennium Challenge Account—one of the Bush administration's least heralded but most important foreign policy innovations. Under the program, states qualify for generous new aid payments by competing on the basis of three broad criteria: whether they rule justly, whether they invest in basic health care and education, and whether they promote economic freedom. The instrument of aid selectivity is showing promise as a tool that civil-society actors in predatory states can use to campaign for governance reforms and as an incentive for corrupt governments in need of more aid to reform their ways.

The international donor community's habit of keeping afloat predatory and other troubled states (in some cases covering up to half of their recurrent government expenditures) must end. The overriding purpose of foreign assistance must be genuine development, not the assuaging of Western guilt or the care and feeding of the massive network of career professionals, non-profit organizations, and private-sector companies that constitute the global aid industry. It is time to start listening to the growing chorus of activists and organizations in developing countries that are imploring the West to please stop "helping" them with indiscriminate aid that only serves to entrench corrupt elites and practices. To be sure, it will be an uphill struggle to get international donors, and especially institutions such as the World Bank, to refocus their aid strategies on good-governance goals. Still, the reality of the link between development and decent governance—in particular the control of corrup-

tion—is gradually taking hold in foreign-aid circles, and the civil societies of developing countries are emerging as some of the most compelling and legitimate advocates of this concept.

Now, as democratic setbacks multiply, is the moment for a new strategy. Without a clear understanding of the fundamental problem—bad governance—and the necessary institutional responses, more democratic breakdowns are likely. Without a resolute and relentless international campaign to rein in corruption and improve the quality of governance in at-risk democracies, the current democratic recession could lead to a global democratic depression. Such a development would be enormously costly to human freedom and dangerous for U.S. national security. Public opinion surveys continue to show that majorities in every region of the world believe democracy is the best form of government. The urgent imperative is to demonstrate, through the effective functioning of democracies worldwide, that it really is.

ERIKA WEINTHAL AND
PAULINE JONES LUONG

COMBATING THE RESOURCE CURSE: AN ALTERNATIVE SOLUTION TO MANAGING MINERAL WEALTH

The race to find new sources of petroleum has been ongoing since commercially viable oil was discovered in Titusville, Pennsylvania in 1859. Almost a century and a half later,

From *Perspectives on Politics*, 4, no. 1 (March 2008), pp. 35–53.

the discovery of new oil wealth in several parts of the world, including Azerbaijan, Kazakhstan, East Timor, Chad, and Sudan has muffled increasingly popular cries that world oil production would ultimately peak by the middle of this decade.[1]

For most industrial countries heavily dependent upon fossil fuels for economic growth, these new petroleum sources were a welcome blessing that could delay an impending global energy shortage. Europe's reliance upon imported oil and gas is expected to increase dramatically over the next few decades, especially as oil production in the North Sea declines from approximately seven million barrels per day to less than four million barrels per day by 2020.[2] Similarly, the United States has become increasingly dependent upon foreign petroleum supplies since 1998 when petroleum imports surpassed the 50 percent barrier for the first time.[3] These new petroleum discoveries are even more vital for meeting the rising energy demand in the world's fastest growing economies of developing Asia including China and India.[4]

For the countries where these discoveries were made, however, new concerns arose over whether they could avoid the curse associated with mineral wealth. Countless studies document the correlation between abundant mineral resources (for example, oil, gas, diamonds, copper, and gold) and a series of negative economic and political outcomes, including poor economic performance and authoritarian regimes, across the developing world.[5] There are also numerous empirical examples of countries that have squandered their mineral wealth and actually made their citizens worse off. Nigeria (the world's seventh largest oil producer) provides a notorious one. Its government has accrued $350 billion in oil revenues since independence, and yet its economy has shrunk; in purchasing power parity (PPP) terms, Nigeria's per capita GDP was $1,113 in 1970 but only $1,084 in 2000, and during this same period, its poverty rate, "measured as the share of the population subsisting on less than US$1 per day increased from close to 36 percent to just under 70 percent."[6] Thus, despite its vast oil wealth, Nigeria is among the 15 poorest nations in the world.

The disappointing experience of mineral-rich countries has generated a large body of scholarship aimed at explaining this empirical correlation and a list of prescriptions for combating the resource curse. The most popular solutions emphasize macroeconomic policies, economic diversification, natural resource funds, transparency and accountability, and direct distribution as mechanisms for managing mineral wealth wisely. While many mineral-rich countries in the developing world have implemented one or more of these solutions, their success has been limited to only a few exceptional cases (for example, Botswana, Chile, and Malaysia). We contend that this is because these solutions either presuppose strong state institutions, which are widely absent in the developing world, or assume state ownership over mineral wealth and thus the need for external actors to constrain the state.

Despite the emerging consensus that robust political institutions are the determining factor in successful efforts to disrupt the link between mineral wealth and the aforementioned negative outcomes, we know little about how to build such institutions. We suggest one possible way— domestic private ownership. Domestic private ownership is rarely discussed in the literature and, when discussed, it often is maligned. Our research indicates, however, that it would foster institutions that more effectively constrain state leaders, encourage them to invest in institution building, and enable them to respond more successfully to commodity booms and busts.

The Paradox of Mineral Wealth

The central paradox that has inspired innumerable studies of mineral-rich countries in the developing world is that, since the 1970s, they have consistently underperformed their mineral-poor counterparts on a variety of economic and political indicators, including economic performance, good governance, income equality, and democracy.

It has been well established that—controlling for income—the more intense a country's reliance on mineral exports (measured as a percentage of GDP) during this time period, the more slowly its economy grew.[7] From 1960 to 1990, GDP per capita in mineral-rich countries increased 1.7 percent compared to 2.5–3.5 percent in mineral-poor countries; similarly, from 1970–1993, mineral-rich countries grew by only 0.8 percent PCGDP compared to 2.1–3.7 percent in mineral-poor countries.[8] A prominent illustration of this surprising result are the "tigers" in mineral-poor East Asia (Hong Kong, Korea, Singapore and Taiwan), whose economies maintained phenomenal growth rates from the early 1960s to the 1990s while the economies of mineral-rich Latin America stagnated or declined.[9] Also during this period (roughly 1965–1998), members of the Organization of Petroleum Exporting Countries (OPEC) experienced nearly universally low or negative annual growth rates.[10]

Mineral exporters were also more likely to incur greater debt, even as world prices soared, and thus forced to commit a significant percentage of their shrinking GDP to debt servicing.[11] The World Bank classifies 12 of the world's most mineral-dependent countries and six of the world's most oil-dependent countries as "highly indebted poor countries."[12] Six out of the top 10 most indebted countries in Africa are major fuel exporters.[13] Outside Africa, similar patterns emerge; although Ecuador is one of the smallest countries in South America, in 2002 it ranked seventh in the region for external indebtedness—just below Brazil, Argentina, and Venezuela—and had the highest debt per capita.[14]

Related to these economic problems is the consistent finding that mineral wealth is strongly correlated with poor governance and high levels of corruption—all the more so if the primary commodity is oil.[15] Mineral exporters in the developing world find themselves ranked at the bottom of the list among countries included in both the World Bank Governance Research Indicators[16] and the Transparency International's Corruption Perception Index (CPI).[17]

Mineral-exporting states also fare much worse when it comes to standards of living and the condition of the poor. Citizens living in such countries are subjected to high levels of poverty, child mortality, and income inequality.[18]

Finally, mineral-dependent countries tend to have authoritarian regimes. Several studies exploring this relationship have found that mineral wealth not only impedes democratic transitions but also prevents the consolidation of democracies,[19] and conversely, promotes the consolidation of authoritarian regimes.[20] Oil wealth in particular has been identified as inhibiting democratization, especially in oil-poor and low-income countries—thus indicating that even a little "oil *does* hurt democracy."[21] Of the 20 major oil exporters in 2000, only Mexico and Venezuela—both of which have previously experienced long periods of dictatorship—could be classified as democracies.

That mineral-abundant countries in the developing world are more prone to poor economic performance, unbalanced growth, corruption, income inequality, and authoritarian regimes is certainly alarming, especially given the initial optimism about their future prospects. In the 1950s and 1960s many development economists argued that these countries would grow much faster than their resource-poor counterparts precisely because their mineral wealth would provide them with the necessary capital to industrialize and diversify their exports.[22] Economic growth, in turn, was widely believed to promote the degree of social change and income equality necessary for democratization.[23] What is even more striking, then, is that by the 1990s a scholarly consensus emerged that these countries' vast wealth is the root cause of their severe political and economic problems—often referred to as the "resource curse."

These scholars emphasize two main aspects of the resource curse: first, the economic consequences that rapid booms and the volatility of commodity markets have for sustained growth; and second, the negative impact that reliance on external rents has on governance, state capacity, and democracy, which is exacerbated by boom and bust cycles. We review these briefly below.

Windfalls and Economic Growth

The most prevalent cause attributed to poor rates of economic growth in mineral-rich countries is Dutch Disease—a term originally coined to refer to the short-lived problems that the Netherlands faced when it discovered huge gas reserves off its northern coast in 1959. Yet, the direct effects of export booms—whether due to a rapid rise in exports or commodity prices—is a common source of economic stagnation across mineral-rich states. Simply put, these windfalls lead to an appreciation of the real exchange rate (that is, the rate of exchange between currencies adjusted for inflation) by shifting production inputs (capital and labor) to the booming mineral sector and non-tradable sector (that is, retail trade, services, and construction), thereby reducing the competitiveness of the non-booming exports sectors (for example, agriculture and manufacturing) and hence precipitating their collapse. The shift into the non-tradable sector accelerates domestic inflation, which is responsible for the rise in the real exchange rate.

These short-term macro-adjustment problems result in long-term effects on growth by reducing the country's economic diversity and increasing its reliance on exports from its natural resource sector. Equatorial Guinea—one of Africa's newest oil producers—is illustrative of how fast Dutch Disease effects can transform the domestic economy: cocoa and coffee have declined from approximately 60 percent of GDP in 1991 to less than 9 percent of GDP in 2001.[24]

The decline of the manufacturing sector also retards economic growth by decreasing both the demand for and supply of skilled labor, which in turn, affects the level of income inequality and educational opportunities.[25] A number of recent studies have found, for example, that school enrollment at all levels and public expenditures on education relative to national income are inversely related to natural resource abundance.

The phenomenon of Dutch Disease, however, is not the only mechanism whereby economic growth is negatively affected by windfalls. Perhaps equally important are the incentives that windfalls create for unproductive investments, rent-seeking, and corruption.

First, the export boom exerts pressure on governments to share increased revenues with the public, often by investing in unproductive public work projects that are motivated by politics rather than profit (that is, "white elephants") or subsidizing food, fuel, failing industries and even government jobs. There is no shortage of prominent examples, such as the Ajaokuta steel mill that Nigeria built in the 1970s to appease the Yoruba region, which "has absorbed over US$3 billion,"[26] and yet, "has still not produced a commercial ton of steel."[27] In addition to squandering the proceeds from their most precious commodities on failed investment programs, countries also suffer from spiraling inflation, the collapse of private savings and investment, and economic stagnation.

Second, many argue that because windfall rents are concentrated and easily obtained, they exert pressure to engage in rent-seeking and corruption—both of which harm economic growth. Windfalls can shift the focus to competition over rents, leading to a "feeding frenzy"[28] and thereby distract both individuals and governments from long-term developmental goals. For example, in the late 1960s and early 1970s Indonesia's state oil company, Pertamina, accrued large windfalls that generated rent-seeking opportunities for actors closely tied to the state; these mineral rents became a source of patronage for the Indonesian military.[29] The long-term effects on Indonesia's economy are evident in the lack of foreign investment in new energy projects over the last decade and its unique distinction of becoming OPEC's first member to import oil in 2004.[30]

Validity and Economic Growth

Another chief concern is the effect that the extreme volatility of commodities, also known as "boom and bust" cycles, can have on economic growth. Although market volatility is a problem for all exporters of primary commodities, it especially plagues oil exporters because the economic importance of oil makes this particular commodity both a valuable and an attractive political weapon.

The economic impact includes, first and foremost, unpredictable revenue streams because widely fluctuating export revenues lead to fluctuating levels in overall government revenues.[31] These "frequent upward or downward adjustments of fiscal expenditures are costly" because they simultaneously discourage private investment and wreak havoc on the government's budget, thereby impeding its ability to sustain investment and public goods provision.[32] Moreover, once expenditures become entrenched, it is harder for governments to make budget cuts; rather than reversing their spending patterns during busts, they often opt to borrow, and hence, incur huge debt burdens.[33]

Excessive borrowing also occurs during booms. Many countries have followed the ill-advised strategy of "borrow[ing] on the strength of their booms."[34] For example, although it experienced "only a small oil windfall in 1979–81," Mexico "borrowed abroad against future oil earnings to boost expenditures by a further 1.8 percent of non-oil GDP."[35] In fact, oil exporters "built up more debt during the 1970s"—that is, as oil revenues were rising the fastest.[36]

Political Consequences of Reliance on External Rents

The main political consequences of relying on external rents[37] are weakly institutionalized states and skewed state-societal relations. Relying on an external source of revenue fosters weakly institutionalized states because the ease of financing state expenditures provides no incentives for government officials to build strong institutions. More specifically, countries rich in minerals, particularly petroleum, fail to develop a robust central bureaucracy because their ability to rely on an external revenue source engenders rigid and myopic decision making. This includes, most importantly, the failure to build a viable tax regime because rulers do not feel compelled to extract revenue from domestic sources to fill their coffers.

In short, mineral-rich states inevitably become rentier states. Rentier states seek to exert social and political control over their populations by creating and maintaining economic dependencies through their sole authority to allocate and redistribute income obtained from natural resource rents. This has three critical implications for state-societal relations.

First, the freedom to rely on external rather than internal sources of income both enfeebles the state and impairs the development of societal opposition because it reduces both the need for leaders to be accountable to the public and popular demands for representation. Indeed, the lack of a viable tax regime has been consistently identified with not only impeding broad economic growth but also undermining state capacity and democratization.

Second, rentier states bolster their autonomy from societal forces by exploiting their fiscal independence to engage in discretionary spending. Large sums of money are spent on sustaining patronage networks and/or providing huge subsidies to the population to garner social and political support, rather than on developing institutionalized mechanisms of responsiveness. The Kuwaiti government, for example, employed 75 percent of the workforce in 1975, but most were "underqualified and underutilized."[38] In short, these states are characterized by the "progressive substitution of public spending for statecraft."[39]

Third, rentier states are subject to state capture and high levels of corruption. While the majority of the population is effectively disenfranchised, those who run the natural resource sector are able to exert disproportionate influence over government policies. There are primarily two reasons for this. First, the highly concentrated nature of the mineral sector enables the small number of firms that occupy it to form a united front to pressure the state. Second, the sheer economic impact of the mineral sector fosters a tendency for the state to conflate this sector's interest with its own.[40] The Gulf states, where the oil sector and the ruling families are nearly indistinguishable, represent the most extreme illustration.[41] As a result, both sides have a vested interest in nontransparent transactions, thereby ensuring state autonomy vis-à-vis the broader population and enabling those with access to mineral rents (first and foremost, government officials) to enrich themselves at society's expense.

The cumulative impact of external rent reliance, therefore, is not just weakly institutionalized states and skewed state-societal relations but also corrupt, authoritarian regimes. With unfettered access to huge rents, incumbents have such a disproportionate advantage over their opponents so that they can remain in office almost indefinitely. These regimes also sustain themselves by simultaneously creating a strong deterrent to popular mobilization—either because they successfully preempt social discontent with populist policies or because they possess effective internal security forces. The result is that only very few developing countries, such as the Republic of Congo and Venezuela, have been able to channel their oil wealth into creating the socioeconomic and political conditions conducive to democratic transition.

Boom and bust cycles also play a role by aggravating the effects of external rents reliance. Booms exacerbate both state spending and rent-seeking behavior, thus reinforcing the dynamic of weakly institutionalized states and corrupt, authoritarian regimes.[42] They also further enfeeble the state by actually creating a disincentive for state leaders to build strong institutions that might interfere with their ability to allocate rents to supporters.[43] Weakly institutionalized states, in turn, are unable to respond to busts, either because their bureaucracies are too centralized and bloated to adjust, sectoral interests have

captured the policy-making process, or some combination.[44] * * *

The Missing Link: Private Ownership and State Capacity

In sum, these existing solutions have largely failed because making the state a better "manager" of its mineral wealth requires institutions that promote transparency, accountability, and oversight—that is, institutions that are widely absent in developing countries.[45] In contrast, we propose a solution that deliberately addresses the core problem of weak institutions—private domestic ownership.

Robust institutions are the product of both supply and demand; governments must have an incentive to supply them and societal actors must have both the interest and ability to make a credible demand for them. In the majority of mineral-rich states in the developing world, however, neither condition is met. State ownership in particular creates a distinctive for supplying institutions that would limit the government's fiscal independence or discretionary decision-making power. It also undermines the development of societal actors that are either powerful enough to challenge the state or have a keen interest in limiting its power. Not surprisingly, then, the vast majority of mineral-rich countries exercised state ownership over their mineral reserves from the late 1960s to the early 1990s—the very historical time period on which most of the literature on the resource curse focuses.***

By taking resource rents out of the state's direct control, privatization to domestic owners simultaneously fosters the conditions under which governments have an incentive to build strong fiscal and regulatory institutions and creates a new set of societal actors with the potential to demand these institutions. Because these private owners benefit directly from the production and export of the country's mineral reserves, they have a vested interest in securing both their property rights and a stable revenue stream as well as the means to bring state actors to the bargaining table. At the same time, because the state has less control over how these resources are extracted and utilized, it is more likely to invest in institution building that enables it to extract revenue from private owners, regulate the private sector, and generate other sources of revenue outside the natural resource sector. Thus, privatization to domestic actors offers an alternative path out of the "resource curse" because it creates an incentive for both state and societal actors to bargain over and eventually establish the formal rules of the game.

Russia provides a powerful illustration of this proposition. In the mid-1990s, Russia began privatizing its oil sector to domestic investors but retained state control over the gas sector.[46] Since then, the degree of reform and economic promise in these two leading sectors has diverged significantly. By the end of 1990s, the majority of the oil industry was privatized to multiple owners, substantially deregulated, and had undergone significant internal restructuring. Under private ownership, the Russian oil industry has successfully expanded production and seen its net profits jump to $25 billion in 2003.[47] In addition, the domestic owners that emerged from this process have increasingly pressured the Russian government not only to support greater liberalization within the energy sector itself, but also to develop institutions outside the energy sector to promote greater transparency and fiscal stability. The gas sector, in contrast, continues to be dominated by the primarily state-owned monopoly Gazprom, which has resisted any structural reform, amassed substantial foreign debt, and remained chronically undercapitalized, translating into direct losses to the Russian economy and indirect losses to the institutional capacity of the Russian state.

Why Ownership Matters

Why should we expect state and private ownership to result in such distinct institutional outcomes? In short, because they foster a very different relationship between the main actors they generate. While both sets of actors under state ownership (that is, state elites and bureaucrats) and private ownership (that is, state elites and domestic owners) are *relatively* symmetrical in their ability to exert influence over the other, the boundaries between them are blurred and clear, respectively. These boundaries, in turn, promote very different incentives for institution building because they impose very different transaction and monitoring costs for the actors involved.

Under state ownership, the boundary between the main actors—state elites and bureaucrats—is blurred because there is no clearly identifiable principal. Rather, the population as a whole is the nominal principal whose interests are ostensibly served by a multitude of agents. At the same time, because the control structure is not clearly defined and there are no objective criteria for determining managerial performance, these agents often act like principals such that administrative tasks and political goals also become blurred. The relative power between state elites and bureaucrats is symmetrical because both have direct access to the proceeds from mineral exploitation. They also both have exclusive access to information about the income—as well as the misdeeds—of the other.

In the case of the Russian gas sector, for example, it is difficult to distinguish the management from the government. For most of the 1990s, Gazprom's president and board of directors not only controlled their own shares but also were entrusted with the government's shares. Thus, they openly ran the company as if they owned it. Then, as now, the Gazprom CEO is a presidential appointee and Gazprom's managers and government representatives form a majority on the board of directors. As a result, some have suggested that it has been hard to determine where "Gazprom ends and the Russian state begins."[48]

Blurred boundaries reduce transaction and monitoring costs by making revenue readily available to multiple principals, all of whom are charged with managing this revenue but none of whom can benefit directly when it is generated efficiently. In most developing countries, for example, petroleum resources are managed through a state oil company. Bureaucrats are assigned to run the company on behalf of the state, with the understanding that the company—and most importantly, its income—ultimately falls under the jurisdiction of the state elites.[49] These bureaucrats not only have a greater opportunity to steal from the company but also a greater incentive to do so because, as de facto government employees, they are not compensated for performance. Because they have no direct claim to the residual (or profits), they also have a greater incentive to operate the company without regard for profitability.[50] This is reinforced by soft budget constraints—that is, continued access to state revenue, regardless of whether or not the company is profitable.

As a result, state elites and bureaucrats share incentives for building or sustaining weak institutions. Both prefer greater discretionary power, and thus, institutions that are unlikely to constrain their behavior in any meaningful or predictable way. Neither side has an incentive to support the development of institutions that foster internal and external oversight mechanisms, increase transparency, or impose hard budget constraints. Rather, because both sides have direct access to the proceeds from the exploitation of the energy sector, they prefer greater discretionary power and informal agreements over the allocation and use of these proceeds. This encourages a form of implicit bargaining whereby each side tacitly agrees to either undermine existing institutions that might pose a treat to their discretionary authority, for example, by increasing transparency and accountability, or to maintain the status quo, and thus neglect institution building altogether. These tendencies are likely to be exacerbated, moreover, by an exogenous shock or economic crisis because time horizons shorten and opportunities for rent-seeking expand.

The blurred boundary between the state and Gazprom, for example, has benefited both sides.

On the one hand, it has empowered the gas sector to operate with very little internal or external scrutiny over its transactions. For example, during most of the 1990s, the Russian Audit Chamber did not demand an official audit of Gazprom's finances. This lack of oversight is evident in Gazprom's notorious mismanagement of investment funds and arbitrary transfer of assets to board members and relatives during Boris Yeltsin's presidency. Gazprom's integrated structure also provides the company with a relatively costless and effortless way of hiding its profits, and thus lining its managers' pockets.

On the other hand, this blurred boundary has enabled the Russian government to utilize its leverage as the ultimate owner to fulfill its domestic fiscal and spending requirements. Gazprom remains subjected to price controls and delivery requirements for nonpaying domestic customers, which account for a large portion of its implicit tax burden. As a result, Gazprom is forced to sell most of the gas it produces (70 percent) on the domestic market for approximately 15 percent of the price it would receive on the global market. Combined with the high rate of tariff arrears in Russia among industrial and household consumers alike, therefore, it is not surprising that Gazprom operates at a loss. Nonetheless, the government has refused to lower Gazprom's explicit tax burden, contributing further to its well-earned position as Russia's largest taxpayer. Gazprom's explicit tax burden has actually increased following the August 1998 financial crisis and the adoption of a new tax code in 2000–2001. Meanwhile, its implicit tax burden has also steadily increased as government officials utilize Gazprom's budget for social and political goals such as financing election campaigns.

Yet, the long-term costs of weak fiscal, regulatory, and supervisory institutions outweigh the short-term benefits to each side. In sum, the blurred boundary has created and reinforced an informal agreement whereby Gazprom's managers accept a high tax burden in exchange for the ability to line their own pockets and the government accepts less transparency and accountability for virtually unlimited access to Gazprom's coffers. This has resulted in a net economic loss for both Gazprom as a company and the Russian economy as a whole. "Years of asset stripping and lack of transparency," for example, are responsible for Gazprom's gross undercapitalization.

Under private domestic ownership, in contrast, the boundary between the main actors—state elites and domestic owners—is clear because there is a clearly identifiable principle. Because the control structure is clearly defined and there are objective criteria for evaluating managerial performance, agents do not conflate administrative tasks with political goals. Rather, they are punished and rewarded based on their ability, for example, to maximize efficiency, increase profits and market capitalization, and expanded market share. Their relative power is symmetrical because each has an independent source of authority over the other. Domestic owners possess the rights to revenue from mineral exploitation, and thus, are a critical source of tax revenue for the state. State elites possess the authority to revoke property rights and reduce revenue streams through demanding excessive taxation. In short, they need each other not just to survive, but also to thrive.

Clear boundaries increase transaction and monitoring costs by simultaneously making it more difficult for state elites to extract revenue and for private owners to hide their income. During Yeltsin's presidency (1991–98), for example, the government was forced to either confiscate revenue from the oil companies or to engage in continuous bargaining over revenue burdens. Also during this period, the Russian oil companies (hereafter, ROCs) devised several legal and semi-legal schemes to reduce their profitability on paper that eventually proved too costly—not only because it required expending effort and finances on nonproductive activities but also because it earned them a lower stock market valuation.

Clear boundaries also make it less rational to steal. Unlike state companies, in private compa-

nies managers are compensated based on performance and the owners have a direct claim to profits, and thus, both owners and managers are primarily concerned with profitability. Owners—including shareholders with a minority stake (that is, 25 percent of the shares)[51]—also have a vested interest in ensuring that both their managers and employees do not steal or otherwise jeopardize the company's financial health. When these minority shareholders are multinational corporations (MNCs), moreover, they can also provide further defense against state predation because they carry the added weight of access to capital, international arbitration, and foreign governments to both deter and challenge such practices.

Nor can private companies necessarily rely on the state to bail them out if they are operating at a loss. Hard budget constraints and the fear of bankruptcy thus reinforce the desire of owners and managers to run the company efficiently. As a result, they are unlikely to invest in unproductive public work projects or provide subsidies—tasks that a government often demands of state-owned companies to promote its own social and political objectives.

High transaction and monitoring costs, therefore, promote mutual incentives for building stable, effective, and far-reaching institutions—that is, strong institutions. Both state elites and private actors, for example, prefer a tax regime that is stable, so as to ensure fiscal predictability, and one that is broad-based, so as to decrease the state's fiscal reliance on the mineral sector. Both also prefer regulatory institutions that will effectively monitor companies' profits and employees. The main actors' interests concerning institution building thus converge. Yet, their preferences over the exact content of these institutions (for example, tax rates, number of audits, and so forth) will vary based on their specific interests. Combined with the fact that their relative power is symmetrical (that is, neither can impose their preferred outcome on the other), this variation in preferences over content encourages these two sets of actors to engage in explicit bargaining to formulate strong institutions. The mutual desire for formal guarantees is likely to be reinforced, moreover, by an exogenous shock or economic crisis because both actors will feel vulnerable and their continued survival will depend more acutely on the actions of the other.

The mutual desire for fiscal predictability following the August 1998 financial crisis, for example, provided the impetus for the Russian government and private domestic oil companies to negotiate a broad-based tax code that was enacted between 1999–2002.[52] By most accounts, this new tax code exceeds Western standards— not only because it sets lower tax rates than the OECD recommends but also because it is much simpler and clearer than the previous one. Most important, the new tax code has resulted in an increase in the contribution of the personal income tax to the budget.[53] Foreign and domestic financial and political analysts alike have also praised the new tax code for the inclusive nature of tax benefits, and thus, its potentially positive impact on the Russian economy as a whole. The increased tax collection rates since the new code was put into effect support this optimism. In 2004 alone, for example, Russia's federal budget recorded a 17.7 percent increase in tax revenue.[54]

The financial crisis also motivated the ROCs to alter significantly their prior behavior and to design forward-looking development strategies.[55] Whereas governments across mineral-rich countries in which the oil sector is under state ownership commonly respond to economic crises linked to sharp declines in the market price of petroleum (or commodity "busts") by increasing production to make up for budgetary shortfalls, thereby lowering their profits, and/or by borrowing against future expected revenues,[56] the ROCs did neither. Nor did they pool their lobbying efforts or resources to seek state protection or "capture" the policy process, as Michael Shafer[57] and others would have predicted.[58] Rather, the ROCs consciously and successfully adjusted to the current bust and prepared for future booms by concentrating their efforts on cleaning up

their internal operations so as to get their finances in order and finding ways to increase both production and profits over the long-term.

A central component of this adjustment strategy consisted of building foreign partnerships through attracting minority shareholders from abroad and/or bringing in foreign management.[59] This has had several undeniably positive effects on the development of the Russian oil industry. First, the ROCs' desire to attract foreign capital, and consequently to increase share prices, bolstered their commitment to greater transparency and corporate governance. Indeed, hiring foreign managers was a conscious attempt to signal this commitment to shareholders, as well as the Russian government. Second, bringing foreign expertise and capital directly into their respective enterprises enabled the ROCs to invest in new technology to increase production by tapping into old (brown) wells—a strategy that was both technologically impossible and highly unpopular among *neftyaniki* (oilmen) during the late Soviet period. Several of the ROC representatives and foreign investors we interviewed commented that Soviet-trained oilmen viewed this practice as "unmanly," preferring to open up new wells when oil did not easily flow from existing ones. Some of the ROCs also viewed foreign expertise and capital as a means to realize their ambitions to build new pipelines that would open up new markets—especially China—and provide an alternative to government-controlled pipelines as a prelude to investment in exploring and developing new wells. Finally, many ROCs deliberately sought foreign partnerships in order to simultaneously expand their operations at home—in particular to the Northern Territories where exploration requires both more capital and advanced technology—and abroad so as to reduce their future dependence on domestic reserves. By 2001, for example, Lukoil had already teamed up with Conoco International to explore oil in Russia's Timan-Pechora region[60] and had approximately 40 percent of its operations in foreign markets.[61]

Thus while some Western analysts have criticized the ROCs failure to invest in exploration, and hence, the development of new oil wells,[62] these efforts suggest a different picture. Combined, they indicate a strategy that is aimed not only at long-term investment but also at securing multiple sources of oil and access to new markets. On the one hand, these analysts and others have downplayed the ROCs attempts to explore new fields in the Far East, for which present production-sharing agreement (PSA) legislation privileges foreign investors.[63] On the other, they have overlooked the fact that the ROCs eventually want to be able to compete on the same playing field as other multinational oil companies, which requires looking beyond domestic production and existing markets.

Conclusion

In a recent op-ed, Joseph Stiglitz writes, "Abundant natural resources can and should be a blessing, not a curse. We know what must be done. What is missing is the political will to make it so."[64] Scholars and policy makers alike have become increasingly convinced that it is possible to combat the resource curse through a broad array of policies that include natural resource funds, economic diversification, transparency and accountability, and direct distribution. These solutions, however, rely on a degree of institutional capacity that is widely absent in mineral-rich countries, and thus they are prone to suffer from the aforementioned negative economic, political, and social outcomes.

In contrast, we offer a solution that directly addresses the pervasive problem of weak institutions in mineral-rich states—privatization to domestic owners. By taking resource rents out of the state's direct control, domestic privatization simultaneously fosters the conditions under which governments have an incentive to build strong fiscal and regulatory institutions and creates a new set of societal actors with the potential to demand these institutions.

Domestic privatization, however, is not a short-term remedy for institutional weakness. Building institutions is a lengthy process, involving numerous conflicts between the government and domestic capitalists over their respective roles in the economy and the rules that define them. This process is also a highly political one and, as such, is often mired in the political priorities of the moment, which can temporarily derail economic ones.

Russia again serves to illustrate. In June 2003 various agencies within the Russian government launched an increasingly fierce assault against Yukos, which had become the largest and most profitable ROC by 2002 owing to the aforementioned strategic changes.[65] This assault culminated in the arrest of Yukos's former CEO, Mikhail Khodorkovsky, and the forced sale of its most valuable subsidiary and covetable asset— Yuganskneftegaz[66]—on December 19, 2004, to cover unsubstantiated tax claims exceeding the company's revenue. Yet, while many analysts have interpreted the government's assault against Yukos as the death knell of private ownership in the oil sector, and thus, a calculated move toward regaining control over the country's most important economic assets, the overwhelming evidence indicates that the primary motivation was political and personal.[67]

First, Khodorkovsky openly flaunted his economic success—most notably through arranging the first shipments of Russian crude oil to the United States in the summer of 2002 and financially sponsoring opposition parties in the 2003 parliamentary elections—and used it to launch his own political career, suggesting that he would run for president in 2008. The state prosecutor's recent decision in March 2005 not to demand additional jail terms for Khodorkovsky and Platon Lebedev, Yukos's second largest shareholder, for their role in the illegal purchase of shares in *Apatit*, a fertilizer company, in 1994 has reinforced the political nature of government's case, given that in addition to alleged tax fraud, this was the main reason underlying their arrest.[68]

Second, the assault on Yukos has thus far been unique, both in form and content. It has not amounted to the renationalization of the oil sector, but rather, the *partial* dismantling of Yukos. As of the spring of 2005, no concrete action had been taken against Yukos's other subsidiaries, Tomskneft and Samaraneftegaz. If Yukos managers to retain these two subsidiaries, it would still be a major contender in the Russian oil industry.[69] At the same time, other ROCs—particularly those with a formidable MNC partner[70]—have escaped the degree of government predation that Yukos has experienced. While minority foreign ownership, perhaps because it only constituted 10 percent of the shares, did not prevent the government's assault against Yukos, minority shareholders in both this company and its single largest domestic investor, Menatep Bank, played a key role in foiling the Russian government's plan to buy Yugaskneftegaz outright via Gazprom's winning bid and seem to have stalled any further legal action against the company.[71]

Finally, the government has remained committed to private ownership and securing property rights, as evidenced by its decision to sell its remaining shares in Lukoil in 2004[72] and Putin's recent initiative to provide legal protection for the various "insider privatizations" that occurred in the mid-1990s by reducing the statute of limitations on them from 10 years to three years.[73] That this commitment is credible is evidenced by the fact that, despite the assault against Yukos, other ROCs have continued to increase their domestic investments.[74]

Domestic privatization is also not universally applicable. Like any policy prescription, the domestic context can be more or less conducive to its feasibility. First, state leaders are more likely to privatize their mineral sector where they are both able to rely on an alternative source of export revenue in the short-term and feel threatened by the emergence of a rival political cleavage.[75] Transferring ownership of these resources from the state to private domestic actors thus becomes a way to bolster existing supporters and/or appease emerging rivals without the immediate need for attracting foreign capital. When privatization occurs in this manner, moreover, it is more likely to lead to the establishment of clear boundaries between those who own the resource (that is, domestic capitalists) and those who regulate it (that is, the state). Second, domestic privatization is more likely to succeed where domestic entrepreneurs have an interest in developing the mineral sector, as is clearly the case in Russia today as well as the United States in the late 1800s and Romania during the interwar period.[76]

While Stiglitz and others tend to view the problem of mineral wealth as a matter of political will alone, our research suggests that this approach fails to take the broader picture into account. Political will, like institutional capacity, is the product of incentives. Thus, even though domestic privatization can be a highly contentious process, it remains the only solution that can generate the incentives for governments in mineral-rich countries to both acquire the will and build the capacity to manage their resources effectively. Precisely because domestic capitalists own its mineral resources, rather than the state, Russia has the potential to build a brighter future than its mineral-rich counterparts in the developing world. International actors and organizations would therefore be well advised to advocate privatization to domestic owners as another possible solution for combating the resource curse, especially for new producers of mineral wealth like Azerbaijan, Kazakhstan, East Timor, Chad, and Sudan. With time and international support, they can pursue domestic privatization as a strategy and thereby create the necessary institutions to turn their mineral wealth into a blessing rather than a curse.

NOTES

1. See, for example, Deffeyes 2003, Campbell 1997.
2. Gault 2002.
3. Klare 2004.

4. U.S. Department of Energy, Energy Information Administration (DoE/EIA) 2004.

5. Davis 1995 is the only exception.

6. Sala-i-Martin and Subramanian 2003, 3.

7. See, for example, Auty 1993, Auty and Gelb 2001, Sachs and Warner 1995.

8. Auty and Mikesell 1998.

9. See, for example, Wade 1990, World Bank 1993.

10. World Bank 2001.

11. See, for example, Lewis 1984, Philip 1994.

12. World Bank 2004.

13. CIA 2003, World Bank 2004.

14. CIA 2003.

15. See, for example, Gylfason 2001, Leite and Weidmann 1999.

16. This includes six indicators (Voice and Accountability, Political Stability and Lack of Violence, Government Effectiveness, Regulatory Quality, Rule of Law, and Control of Corruption) "based on 25 separate data sources at 18 different organizations, including the World Bank itself, Gallup International, the Economist Intelligence Unit, IMD, DRI/McGraw-Hill, Columbia University, Freedom House, Afrobarometer, Latinobarometro, the World Economic Forum, and Reporters Without Borders." World Bank 2003. Data available at http://www.worldbank.org/wbi/governance/data.html.

17. World Bank 2002, Transparency International 2004. CPI ranks countries according to the degree to which corruption is perceived to exist among public officials and politicians, ranging between 10 (highly clean) and 0 (highly corrupt). For more information, see http://www.transparency.org/surveys/index.html#cpi.

18. See, for example, Ross 2001b.

19. See, for example, Jensen and Wantchekon 2004.

20. See, for example, Wantchekon 1999, Smith 2004.

21. Ross 2001a, 356. Herb 2005, in contrast, argues that the negative effects of oil rents on democracy have been overestimated.

22. See, for example, Baldwin 1966, Hirschman 1958.

23. See, for example, Lipset 1960, Deutsch 1961.

24. Gary and Karl 2003, 41.

25. See, for example, Sachs and Warner 1995.

26. Ascher 1999, 179.

27. Sala-I-Martin and Subramanian 2003, 13.

28. Lane and Tornell 1997.

29. Ascher 1999, 62.

30. Bradsher 2005.

31. Mikesell 1997.

32. Katz et al. 2004, 9–10.

33. Katz et al. 2004, 10, McMahon 1997.

34. Sarraf and Jiwanji 2001, 7.

35. Gelb 1985, 76.

36. Philip 1994, 12.

37. A rent is "a return in excess of a resource owner's opportunity costs: (Tollison 1982, 575); in the case of mineral-exporting countries, these returns are thus generated from foreign sources.

38. Crystal 1989, 434.

39. Karl 1997, 16.

40. Shafer 1994.

41. Crystal 1989.

42. Karl 1997, 139.

43. Ascher 1999, Ross 2001a.

44. Karl 1997, Shafer 1994, Chaudhry 1989.

45. It is worth mentioning here that our portrayal of effective state institutions differs from the large and distinguished literature on the "developmental state." The latter focuses on the need for a competent state bureaucracy for promoting industrialization and export-led growth. See, for example, Wade 1990, Evans 1995, Kohli 2004.

46. Comparing the oil and gas sector within Russia (as opposed to oil sectors in two different countries) also allows us to control for national level variation, and thus to isolate ownership structure as the key explanatory variable.

47. *Russia Journal,* May 19, 2004.

48. Rutland 1997, 8.

49. This is not the case where state oil companies are effectively monitored by a third

party, such as the parliament or an independent regulatory agency, as is the case with Statoil in Norway. These institutions tend to either not exist or be ineffective, however, in developing countries.

50. On "residual claimant" theory, see Alchian and Demsetz 1972.

51. The 25 percent threshold is crucial because it allows them to block any major decision, such as the transfer of assets.

52. See Jones Luong and Weinthal 2004 for details.

53. Aslund 2001, 22.

54. *Russia Journal*, January 25, 2005.

55. Authors' interviews with representatives from both Russian and foreign oil and gas companies, Russian government officials, and Russian and foreign financial and energy experts, Moscow, September 2001 and July 2002.

56. It is interesting to note that many scholars attribute this common failure to respond to busts to *weak institutions* in resource-rich states. See, for example, Chaudhry 1989 and Shafer 1994.

57. Shafer, 1994.

58. See Jones Luong and Weinthal 2004 for details. Although they have similar interests, as direct competitors and possibly intense rivals, private owners are unlikely to rely on collusion to exert influence. In attempting to work together in order to pressure the government for favorable policies, therefore, even a small number of actors face a considerable collective action problem—particularly in a fluid context such as Russia. See, for example, Olson 1982.

59. Authors' interviews (op. cit.).

60. Authors' interview with Eric Bell, President, Conoco International Petroleum Company, Moscow, September 20, 2001.

61. Author's interview with Konstantin Reznikov, Alfa Bank, Senior Oil and Gas Analyst, Moscow, September 19, 2001.

62. See, for example, Dienes 2004, Hill 2004.

63. Authors' interviews (op. cit.).

64. Stiglitz 2004.

65. See Weinthal and Jones Luong forthcoming for details.

66. Yuganskneftegaz accounts for two-thirds of Yukos's and approximately 11 percent of Russia's total oil production.

67. Indeed, our comprehensive survey of the Russian language press from June 2003 to August 2004, which we do not have the space to present here, indicates that this is the consensus among Russian analysts.

68. In his decision, the state prosecutor cited the 100-year statute of limitations. Faulconbridge 2005.

69. Korchagina 2004.

70. This is true, for example, of the ROC Tyumenskaia Neftianaia Kompaaniia (TNK), which partnered with British Petroleum in 2003.

71. The fear of a lengthy (and high-profile) legal battle propelled a consortium of international banks to withdraw their financial support for Gazprom's bid and the Russian government to come up with an elaborate scheme to find another Kremlin-friendly buyer. See, for example, Belton 2004.

72. *Radio Free Europe/Radio Liberty (RFE/RL)*; back issues can be accessed at http://search.rferl.org/. September 29, 2004.

73. Granville and Lissovolik 2005. Russia's "insider privatization" refers to its controversial privatization program in the 1990s that allowed those with close ties to the Kremlin to gain control over the state's most important strategic resources.

74. *Moscow Times*, April 7, 2005.

75. See Jones Luong and Weinthal 2001 for details.

76. In contrast, domestic capitalists in Colombia refused the government's offer to take on the development of oilfields (Kline 1995). In Venezuela they quickly sold off their oil fields to foreign companies in order to pursue other economic interests (Lieuwen 1954).

REFERENCES

Alchian, Arman A., and Harold Demsetz. 1972. Production, information costs, and economic organization. *American Economic Review* 62 (5): 777–95.

Ascher, William. 1999. *Why governments waste natural resources: Policy failures in developing countries.* Baltimore: Johns Hopkins University Press.

Aslund, Anders. 2001. Russia. *Foreign Policy.* July/August: 20–25.

Auty, Richard M., and Raymond F. Mikesell. 1998. *Sustainable development in mineral economies.* Oxford: Clarendon Press.

Baldwin, Robert E. 1966. *Economic development and export growth.* Berkeley: University of California Press.

Belton, Catherine. 2004. Yukos accused of "filthy theft." *Moscow Times,* December 14.

Bradsher, Keith. 2005. Oil wealth wasting away in Indonesia. *New York Times,* March 19.

Campbell, Colin J. 1997. *The coming oil crisis.* Essex, UK: Multi-Science Publishing.

Central Intelligence Agency (CIA). 2003. *World Factbook 2003.* Washington, DC: Central Intelligence Agency.

Chaudhry, Kiren Aziz. 1989. The price of wealth: Business and state in labor remittance and oil economies. *International Organization* 43 (1): 101–45.

Crystal, Jill. 1989. Coalitions in oil monarchies: Kuwait and Qatar. *Comparative Politics* 21 (4): 427–43.

Davis, Graham. 1995. Learning to love the Dutch disease: Evidence from the mineral economies. *World Development* 23 (10): 1765–79.

Deffeyes, Kenneth S. 2003. *Hubbert's peak: The impending world oil shortage.* Princeton: Princeton University Press.

Deutsch, Karl W. 1961. Social mobilization and political development. *American Political Science Review* 55 (3): 493–514.

Dienes, Leslie. 2004. Observations on the problematic potential of Russian oil and the complexities of Siberia. *Eurasian Geography and Economics* 45 (5): 319–45.

Evans, Peter. 1995. *Embedded autonomy: State and industrial transformation.* Princeton: Princeton University Press.

Faulconbridge, Guy. 2005. Prosecutors go for the full 10 years. *Moscow Times,* March 30.

Friends of the Earth. 2002. Oil funds: Answer to the paradox of plenty? November.

Gary, Ian, and Terry Karl. 2003. *Bottom of the barrel: Africa's oil boom and the poor.* Catholic Relief Services.

Gault, John. 2002. The European Union: Energy security and the periphery. *Occasional Paper Series, No. 40.* Geneva Centre for Security Policy. http://www.gcsp.ch/e/publications/Other-pubs/Occ-papers/2002/40-Gault.pdf

Gelb, Alan H. 1985. Adjustment to windfall gains: A comparative study of oil-exporting countries. In *Natural resources and the macroeconomy,* eds. J. Peter Neary and Sweder van Wijnbergen, 54–95. Cambridge: MIT Press.

Gelb, Alan H., and Associates. 1988. *Oil windfalls: Blessing or curse?* New York: Oxford University Press.

Granville, Christopher, and Yaroslav Lissovolik. 2005. Dusting off a difficult amnesty. *Moscow Times,* March 30.

Gylfason, Thorvaldur. 2001. Nature, power, and growth. *Journal of Political Economy* 48 (5): 558–88.

Herb, Michael. 2005. No representation without taxation? Rents, development, and democracy. *Comparative Politics* 37 (3): 297–317.

Hill, Fiona. 2004. *Energy empire: Oil, gas, and Russia's revival.* London: Foreign Policy Centre.

Hirschman, Albert O. 1958. *The strategy of economic development.* New Haven: Yale University Press.

Jensen, Nathan, and Leonard Wantchekon. 2004. Resource wealth and political regimes in Africa. *Comparative Political Studies* 37 (7): 816–41.

Jones Luong, Pauline, and Erika Weinthal. 2001. Prelude to the resource curse: Explaining oil and gas development strategies in the Soviet successor states and beyond. *Comparative Political Studies* 34 (4): 367–99.

Karl, Terry Lynn. 1987. Petroleum and political pacts: The transition to democracy in Venezuela. *Latin American Research Review* 22 (1): 63–94.

Karl, Terry Lynn. 1997. *The paradox of plenty: Oil booms and petro-states.* Berkeley: University of California Press.

Katz, Menachem, Ulrich Bartsch, Harinder Malothra, and Milan Cuc. 2004. *Lifting the oil curse: Improving petroleum revenue management in Sub-Saharan Africa.* Washington, DC: IMF.

Klare, Michael T. 2004. *Blood and oil: The dangers and consequences of America's growing dependency on imported petroleum.* New York: Metropolitan Books.

Kline, Harvey. 1995. *Colombia democracy under assault.* Boulder: Westview Press.

Kohli, Atul. 2004. *State-directed development: Political power and industrialization in the global periphery.* Cambridge: Cambridge University Press.

Korchagina, Valeria. 2004. Kagalovsky makes new Yukos offer. *Moscow Times,* December 15.

Lane, Philip R., and Aaron Tornell. 1997. Voracity and growth. *Discussion Paper 1807.* Harvard Institute of Economic Research, Harvard University, Cambridge, MA.

Leite, Carlos, and Jens Weidmann. 1999. Does mother nature corrupt? Natural resources, corruption, and economic growth. *IMF Working Paper 99/85.*

Lewis, Stephen R. 1984. Development problems of the mineral-rich countries. In *Economic structure and performance,* eds. Moshe Syrquin, Lance Taylor, and Larry E. Westphal, 157–77. New York: Academic Press.

Lieuwen, Edwin. 1954. *Petroleum in Venezuela: A history.* Berkeley: University of California Press.

Lipset, Seymour Martin. 1960. *Political man: The social bases of politics.* Garden City, NY: Doubleday.

McMahon, Gary. 1997. The natural resource curse: Myth or reality? Mimeo, World Bank Institute.

Mikesell, Raymond F. 1997. Explaining the resource curse, with specific reference to mineral exporting countries. *Resources Policy* 23 (4): 191–99.

Olson, Mancur. 1982. *The rise and decline of nations: Economic growth, stagflation, and social rigidities.* New Haven: Yale University Press.

Philip, George. 1994. *The political economy of international oil.* Edinburgh: Edinburgh University Press.

Ross, Michael L. 2001a. Does oil hinder democracy? *World Politics* 53 (3): 325–61.

———. 2001b. *Extractive sectors and the poor: An Oxfam America report.* Boston, MA: Oxfam America.

Rutland, Peter. 1997. Lost opportunities: Energy and politics in Russia. *NBR Analysis* 8 (5).

Sachs, Jeffrey D., and Andrew M. Warner. 1995. Natural resource abundance and economic growth. *NBER Working Paper 5398.*

Sala-i-Martin, Xavier, and Arvind Subramanian. 2003. Addressing the natural resource curse: An illustration from Nigeria. *IMF Working Paper WP/03/139.*

Sarraf, Maria, and Moortaza Jiwanji. 2001. Beating the resource curse: The case of Botswana. *Environmental Economics Series, Paper 83,* World Bank.

Shafer, D. Michael. 1994. *Winners and losers: How sectors shape the developmental prospects of states.* Ithaca: Cornell University Press.

Shleifer, Andrei, and Robert Vishny. 1994. Politicians and firms. *Quarterly Journal of Economics* 109 (4): 995–1025.

Smith, Benjamin. 2004. Oil wealth and regime survival in the developing world, 1960–1999. *American Journal of Political Science* 48 (2): 232–46.

Stiglitz, Joseph. 2004. We can now cure Dutch disease. *The Guardian,* August 18.

Tollison, Robert D. 1982. Rent-seeking: A survey. *Kyklos* 35: 575–602.

U.S. Department of Energy, Energy Information Administration (DoE/EIA). 2004. *International energy outlook 2004.* Washington, DC: DoE/EIA. http://www.eia.doe.gov/oiaf/ieo/index.html.

Wade, Robert. 1990. *Governing the market: Economic theory and the role of government in East Asia industrialization.* Princeton: Princeton University Press.

Wantchekon, Leonard. 1999. Why do resource dependent countries have authoritarian governments? *Leitner Working Paper 1999–11.* New Haven: Yale Center for International and Area Studies.

Weinthal, Erika, and Pauline Jones Luong. 2001. Energy wealth and tax reform in Russia and Kazakhstan. *Resources Policy* 27 (4): 215–23.

———. Forthcoming. The paradox of energy sector reform in Russia. In *The state after communism: Governance in the new Russia,* eds. Timothy Colton and Stephen Holmes.

World Bank. 1993. *The East Asian miracle: Economic growth and public policy.* Washington, DC: World Bank Group and Oxford University Press.

———. 2001. *World development indicators 2000.* Washington, DC: World Bank.

———. 2002. *Worldwide governance research indicators dataset 2002.* Washington, DC: World Bank.

———. 2003. Measuring the quality of governance. *Development News,* July 14.

———. 2004. *World development indicators 2003.* Washington, DC: World Bank.

7 ADVANCED DEMOCRACIES

This chapter explores some of the aspects and challenges of advanced democracies, *countries that have stable democratic regimes, a high level of economic development, and extensive civil rights and liberties. It focuses specifically on three questions:*

1. *What enables advanced democracies to emerge and thrive?*
2. *How do institutional differences among advanced democracies affect their politics and policy?*
3. *Can advanced democracies continue to promote equality—for example, through generous welfare states—in the twenty-first century?*

By most measures the northern states of the United States were the first "advanced democracy." Universal male suffrage—albeit almost always restricted to white males—had been achieved by the 1830s in almost all U.S. states (in Britain, even the 1832 Reform Act extended the franchise to only about one in five adult males), institutionalization was advanced, and per capita income (according to the economic historian Angus Maddison) already exceeded that of contemporary France. The liberal French nobleman, intellectual, and politician Alexis de Tocqueville visited the United States in 1831 and set out to explain to his European compatriots why and how American democracy worked. He came to two firm conclusions, well set out in his own Introduction to his 1835 classic, Democracy in America: *(a) social equality led inevitably to democracy, and (b) equality, at least in Europe and America, was everywhere increasing.*

Tocqueville saw economic growth and prosperity as but one of the causes of social equalization, and thus of democracy. The sociologist and political scientist Seymour Martin Lipset, in his classic Political Man *(1960), first perceived what is now taken as a commonplace: that while other factors still matter, richer countries are highly likely to be both more equal and more democratic. Wealth alone, through a series of processes that Lipset explored, leads normally to democracy. (In the readings for Chapter 9 we shall see an important modification of Lipset's thesis.)*

As discussed in Chapter 5, democracies divide between "majoritarian" and "proportional" (PR) electoral systems. Advanced democracies also differ on this dimension: the United States, the United Kingdom, Canada, Australia, France, and Japan are majoritarian (or mostly so), whereas most of the other advanced democracies (including virtually all of the smaller ones) use PR. An interesting sidelight is that several of the advanced democracies have recently changed their electoral systems: France used PR for one election in 1986, then reverted to a majoritarian system; in the early 1990s Italy and Japan changed from mostly proportional systems to mostly majoritarian ones, while at almost the same time New Zealand replaced a "first-past-the-post" majoritarian system with PR; and Italy has since shifted back to a mostly PR system.

What are countries actually choosing when they adopt (or retain) one electoral system or another? As was emphasized in Chapter 5, a majoritarian system normally (as in the United States) allows only two major parties to survive, whereas PR encourages a multiplicity of parties. This regularity is so powerful and has such strong causal properties that it is called, after its discoverer, Duverger's Law—one of the very few causal laws in political science. Duverger's original (1951) explanation of it has never really been surpassed, and its essence is presented here. Note particularly how Duverger shows that, in a majoritarian system, the rise of a new "third" party (e.g., Labour in the UK between 1900 and 1930) normally dooms the old "second" party (in this case, the Liberals) to insignificance, and how the introduction of PR has often "rescued" the declining second party from that fate.

Since Duverger, PR has been shown in numerous studies to have one other very important effect, this time on policy: PR is associated with much higher levels of welfare spending, greater redistribution of income, and hence greater equality. But why? Perhaps voters in PR countries just happen to prefer higher levels of welfare spending. As early as 2002, the comparativist Bingham Powell showed that this was unlikely to be true: rather, given identical voter preferences, majoritarian systems were likely to produce more right-wing (i.e., less redistributionist) policies, whereas paradoxically PR would more reliably produce the policy that voters (or, more precisely, the median voter) actually wanted. In a yet more fundamental contribution, reproduced here in abridged form, Torben Iversen and David Soskice (2006) advanced powerful logic and evidence about how exactly this result came about: given identical voter preferences, a PR system was far likelier to produce a "center-left" coalition, a majoritarian one a "center-right" government, with the latter adopting far less redistributionist policies and lower levels of welfare expenditure. As they note, fully three-quarters of the governments chosen under PR systems in the postwar period have been center-left, whereas three-quarters of those elected under majoritarian systems have been center-right.

But can generous welfare states survive in an increasingly competitive global economy (see also Chapter 11)? Although the conventional wisdom holds that they cannot because the high taxes that fund their outlays make their products to expensive to compete, the 2001 article from The Economist, *"Is Government Disappearing?" contends that "big government" is far from*

*being doomed—not least because, precisely in the most trade-exposed soci-
eties, citizens come to want greater welfare spending, as insurance against
"market shocks."*

*A deeper reason why welfare states work, and may even make their soci-
eties more competitive, is suggested in by Margarita Estévez-Abe and her
coauthors in their contribution to the seminal volume on* Varieties of Capitalism *(2001). Many of the most globally competitive economies, they suggest,
depend on high-quality, specialized production that requires well-trained
workers with firm- or sector-specific skills. Workers will only invest in acquiring those skills, they contend, if generous policies of social insurance buffer
them against transient market downturns or permanent obsolescence. Hence
generous welfare states (e.g., Sweden) tend to have workers with highly specialized skills, whereas less generous ones (e.g., the United States) have work-
forces with more general and transferable skills. As logical side effects, they
show, the generous welfare states are economically more equal and encourage
greater achievement by less talented youth; paradoxically, the less redistributionist countries encourage greater gender equality.*

ALEXIS DE TOCQUEVILLE

AUTHOR'S INTRODUCTION

Among the novel objects that attracted my
attention during my stay in the United
States, nothing struck me more forcibly
than the general equality of condition among the
people. I readily discovered the prodigious influence that this primary fact exercises on the
whole course of society; it gives a peculiar direction to public opinion and a peculiar tenor to the
laws; it imparts new maxims to the governing
authorities and peculiar habits to the governed.

I soon perceived that the influence of this fact
extends far beyond the political character and the

laws of the country, and that it has no less effect
on civil society than on the government; it creates
opinions, gives birth to new sentiments, founds
novel customs, and modifies whatever it does not
produce. The more I advanced in the study of
American society, the more I perceived that this
equality of condition is the fundamental fact
from which all others seem to be derived and the
central point at which all my observations constantly terminated.

I then turned my thoughts to our own hemisphere, and thought that I discerned there something analogous to the spectacle which the New
World presented to me. I observed that equality
of condition, though it has not there reached the
extreme limit which it seems to have attained in

From *Democracy in America* (New York: A. A. Knopf,
1945), pp. 3–16. Author's notes have been omitted.

the United States, is constantly approaching it; and that the democracy which governs the American communities appears to be rapidly rising into power in Europe.

Hence I conceived the idea of the book that is now before the reader.

It is evident to all alike that a great democratic revolution is going on among us, but all do not look at it in the same light. To some it appears to be novel but accidental, and, as such, they hope it may still be checked; to others it seems irresistible, because it is the most uniform, the most ancient, and the most permanent tendency that is to be found in history.

I look back for a moment on the situation of France seven hundred years ago, when the territory was divided among a small number of families, who were the owners of the soil and the rulers of the inhabitants; the right of governing descended with the family inheritance from generation to generation; force was the only means by which man could act on man; and landed property was the sole source of power.

Soon, however, the political power of the clergy was founded and began to increase: the clergy opened their ranks to all classes, to the poor and the rich, the commoner and the noble; through the church, equality penetrated into the government, and he who as a serf must have vegetated in perpetual bondage took his place as a priest in the midst of nobles, and not infrequently above the heads of kings.

The different relations of men with one another became more complicated and numerous as society gradually became more stable and civilized. Hence the want of civil laws was felt; and the ministers of law soon rose from the obscurity of the tribunals and their dusty chambers to appear at the court of the monarch, by the side of the feudal barons clothed in their ermine and their mail.

While the kings were ruining themselves by their great enterprises, and the nobles exhausting their resources by private wars, the lower orders were enriching themselves by commerce. The influence of money began to be perceptible in state affairs. The transactions of business opened a new road to power, and the financier rose to a station of political influence in which he was at once flattered and despised.

Gradually enlightenment spread, a reawakening of taste for literature and the arts became evident; intellect and will contributed to success; knowledge became an attribute of government, intelligence a social force; the educated man took part in affairs of state.

The value attached to high birth declined just as fast as new avenues to power were discovered. In the eleventh century, nobility was beyond all price; in the thirteenth, it might be purchased. Nobility was first conferred by gift in 1270, and equality was thus introduced into the government by the aristocracy itself.

In the course of these seven hundred years it sometimes happened that the nobles, in order to resist the authority of the crown or to diminish the power of their rivals, granted some political power to the common people. Or, more frequently, the king permitted the lower orders to have a share in the government, with the intention of limiting the power of the aristocracy.

In France the kings have always been the most active and the most constant of levelers. When they were strong and ambitious, they spared no pains to raise the people to the level of the nobles; when they were temperate and feeble, they allowed the people to rise above themselves. Some assisted democracy by their talents, others by their vices. Louis XI and Louis XIV reduced all ranks beneath the throne to the same degree of subjection; and finally Louis XV descended, himself and all his court, into the dust.

As soon as land began to be held on any other than a feudal tenure, and personal property could in its turn confer influence and power, every discovery in the arts, every improvement in commerce of manufactures, created so many new elements of equality among men. Henceforward every new invention, every new want which it occasioned, and every new desire which craved satisfaction were steps towards a general leveling. The taste for luxury, the love of war, the rule of fashion, and the most superficial as well as the deepest passions of the human heart seemed to cooperate to enrich the poor and to impoverish the rich.

From the time when the exercise of the intellect became a source of strength and of wealth, we see that every addition to science, every fresh truth, and every new idea became a germ of power placed within the reach of the people. Poetry, eloquence, and memory, the graces of the mind, the fire of imagination, depth of thought, and all the gifts which Heaven scatters at a venture turned to the advantage of democracy; and even when they were in the possession of its adversaries, they still served its cause by throwing into bold relief the natural greatness of man. Its conquests spread, therefore, with those of civilization and knowledge; and literature became an arsenal open to all, where the poor and the weak daily resorted for arms.

In running over the pages of our history, we shall scarcely find a single great event of the last seven hundred years that has not promoted equality of condition.

The Crusades and the English wars decimated the nobles and divided their possessions: the municipal corporations introduced democratic liberty into the bosom of feudal monarchy; the invention of firearms equalized the vassal and the noble on the field of battle; the art of printing opened the same resources to the minds of all classes; the post brought knowledge alike to the door of the cottage and to the gate of the palace; and Protestantism proclaimed that all men are equally able to find the road to heaven. The discovery of America opened a thousand new paths to fortune and led obscure adventures to wealth and power.

If, beginning with the eleventh century, we examine what has happened in France from one half-century to another, we shall not fail to perceive that at the end of each of these periods a twofold revolution has taken place in the state of society. The noble has gone down the social ladder, and the commoner has gone up; the one descends as the other rises. Every half-century

brings them nearer to each other, and they will soon meet.

Nor is this peculiar to France. Wherever we look, we perceive the same revolution going on throughout the Christian world.

The various occurrences of national existence have everywhere turned to the advantage of democracy: all men have aided it by their exertions, both those who have intentionally labored in its cause and those who have served it unwittingly; those who have fought for it and even those who have declared themselves its opponents have all been driven along in the same direction, have all labored to one end; some unknowingly and some despite themselves, all have been blind instruments in the hands of God.

The gradual development of the principle of equality is, therefore, a providential fact. It has all the chief characteristics of such a fact: it is universal, it is lasting, it constantly eludes all human interference, and all events as well as all men contribute to its progress.

Would it, then, be wise to imagine that a social movement the causes of which lie so far back can be checked by the efforts of one generation? Can it be believed that the democracy which has overthrown the feudal system and vanquished kings will retreat before tradesmen and capitalists? Will it stop now that it has grown so strong and its adversaries so weak?

Whither, then, are we tending? No one can say, for terms of comparison already fail us. There is greater equality of condition in Christian countries at the present day than there has been at any previous time, in any part of the world, so that the magnitude of what already has been done prevents us from foreseeing what is yet to be accomplished.

The whole book that is here offered to the public has been written under the influence of a kind of religious awe produced in the author's mind by the view of that irresistible revolution which has advanced for centuries in spite of every obstacle and which is still advancing in the midst of the ruins it has caused.

It is not necessary that God himself should

speak in order that we may discover the unquestionable signs of his will. It is enough to ascertain what is the habitual course of nature and the constant tendency of events. I know, without special revelation, that the planets move in the orbits traced by the Creator's hand.

If the men of our time should be convinced, by attentive observation and sincere reflection, that the gradual and progressive development of social equality is at once the past and the future of their history, this discovery alone would confer upon the change the sacred character of a divine decree. To attempt to check democracy would be in that case to resist the will of God; and the nations would then be constrained to make the best of the social lot awarded to them by Providence.

The Christian nations of our day seem to me to present a most alarming spectacle; the movement which impels them is already so strong that it cannot be stopped, but it is not yet so rapid that it cannot be guided. Their fate is still in their own hands; but very soon they may lose control.

The first of the duties that are at this time imposed upon those who direct our affairs is to educate democracy, to reawaken, if possible, its religious beliefs; to purify its morals; to mold its actions; to substitute a knowledge of statecraft for its inexperience, and an awareness of its true interest for its blind instincts, to adapt its government to time and place, and to modify it according to men and to conditions. A new science of politics is needed for a new world.

This, however, is what we think of least; placed in the middle of a rapid stream, we obstinately fix our eyes on the ruins that may still be descried upon the shore we have left, while the current hurries us away and drags us backward towards the abyss.

In no country in Europe has the great social revolution that I have just described made such rapid progress as in France; but it has always advanced without guidance. The heads of the state have made no preparation for it, and it has advanced without their consent or without their knowledge. The most powerful, the most intelligent, and the most moral classes of the nation have never attempted to control it in order to guide it. Democracy has consequently been abandoned to its wild instincts, and it has grown up like those children who have no parental guidance, who receive their education in the public streets, and who are acquainted only with the vices and wretchedness of society. Its existence was seemingly unknown when suddenly it acquired supreme power. All then servilely submitted to its caprices; it was worshipped as the idol of strength; and when afterwards it was enfeebled by its own excesses, the legislator conceived the rash project of destroying it, instead of instructing it and correcting its vices. No attempt was made to fit it to govern, but all were bent on excluding it from the government.

The result has been that the democratic revolution has taken place in the body of society without that concomitant change in the laws, ideas, customs, and morals which was necessary to render such a revolution beneficial. Thus we have a democracy without anything to lessen its vices and bring out its natural advantages; and although we already perceive the evils it brings, we are ignorant of the benefits it may confer.

While the power of the crown, supported by the aristocracy, peaceably governed the nations of Europe, society, in the midst of its wretchedness, had several sources of happiness which can now scarcely be conceived or appreciated. The power of a few of his subjects was an insurmountable barrier to the tyranny of the prince; and the monarch, who felt the almost divine character which he enjoyed in the eyes of the multitude, derived a motive for the just use of his power from the respect which he inspired. The nobles, placed high as they were above the people, could take that calm and benevolent interest in their fate which the shepherd feels towards his flock; and without acknowledging the poor as their equals, they watched over the destiny of those whose welfare Providence had entrusted to their care. The people, never having conceived the idea of a social condition different from their own, and never expecting to become equal to their leaders, received benefits from them without discussing their rights. They became attached to them when they were clement and just and submitted to their exactions without resistance or servility, as to the inevitable visitations of the Deity. Custom and usage, moreover, had established certain limits to oppression and founded a sort of law in the very midst of violence.

As the noble never suspected that anyone would attempt to deprive him of the privileges which he believed to be legitimate, and as the serf looked upon his own inferiority as a consequence of the immutable order of nature, it is easy to imagine that some mutual exchange of goodwill took place between two classes so differently endowed by fate. Inequality and wretchedness were then to be found in society, but the souls of neither rank of men were degraded.

Men are not corrupted by the exercise of power or debased by the habit of obedience, but by the exercise of a power which they believe to be illegitimate, and by obedience to a rule which they consider to be usurped and oppressive.

On the one side were wealth, strength, and leisure, accompanied by the pursuit of luxury, the refinements of taste, the pleasures of wit, and the cultivation of the arts; on the other were labor, clownishness, and ignorance. But in the midst of this coarse and ignorant multitude it was not uncommon to meet with energetic passions, generous sentiments, profound religious convictions, and wild virtues.

The social state thus organized might boast of its stability, its power, and, above all, its glory.

But the scene is now changed. Gradually the distinctions of rank are done away with; the barriers that once severed mankind are falling; property is divided, power is shared by many, the light of intelligence spreads, and the capacities of all classes tend towards equality. Society becomes democratic, and the empire of democracy is slowly and peaceably introduced into institutions and customs.

I can conceive of a society in which all men would feel an equal love and respect for the laws of which they consider themselves the authors; in which the authority of the government would be respected as necessary, and not divine; and in which the loyalty of the subject to the chief magistrate would not be a passion, but a quiet and rational persuasion. With every individual in the possession of rights which he is sure to retain, a kind of manly confidence and reciprocal courtesy would arise between all classes, removed alike from pride and servility. The people, well acquainted with their own true interests, would understand that, in order to profit from the advantages of the state, it is necessary to satisfy its requirements. The voluntary association of the citizens might then take the place of the individual authority of the nobles, and the community would be protected from tyranny and license.

I admit that, in a democratic state thus constituted, society would not be stationary. But the impulses of the social body might there be regulated and made progressive. If there were less splendor than in an aristocracy, misery would also be less prevalent; the pleasures of enjoyment might be less excessive, but those of comfort would be more general; the sciences might be less perfectly cultivated, but ignorance would be less common; the ardor of the feelings would be constrained, and the habits of the nation softened; there would be more vices and fewer crimes.

In the absence of enthusiasm and ardent faith, great sacrifices may be obtained from the members of a commonwealth by an appeal to their understanding and their experience; each individual will feel the same necessity of union with his fellows to protect his own weakness; and as he knows that he can obtain their help only on condition of helping them, he will readily perceive that his personal interest is identified with the interests of the whole community. The nation, taken as a whole, will be less brilliant, less glorious, and perhaps less strong; but the majority of the citizens will enjoy a greater degree of prosperity, and the people will remain peaceable, not because they despair of a change for the better, but because they are conscious that they are well off already.

If all the consequences of this state of things were not good or useful, society would at least have appropriated all such as were useful and good; and having once and forever renounced the social advantages of aristocracy, mankind would enter into possession of all the benefits that democracy can offer.

But here it may be asked what we have adopted in the place of those institutions, those ideas, and those customs of our forefathers which we have abandoned.

The spell of royalty is broken, but it has not been succeeded by the majesty of the laws. The people have learned to despise all authority, but they still fear it; and fear now extorts more than was formerly paid from reverence and love.

I perceive that we have destroyed those individual powers which were able, single-handed, to cope with tyranny; but it is the government alone that has inherited all the privileges of which families, guilds, and individuals have been deprived; to the power of a small number of persons, which if it was sometimes oppressive was often conservative, has succeeded the weakness of the whole community.

The division of property has lessened the distance which separated the rich from the poor; but it would seem that, the nearer they draw to each other, the greater is their mutual hatred and the more vehement the envy and the dread with which they resist each other's claims to power; the idea of right does not exist for either party, and force affords to both the only argument for the present and the only guarantee for the future.

The poor man retains the prejudices of his forefathers without their faith, and their ignorance without their virtues; he has adopted the doctrine of self-interest as the rule of his actions without understanding the science that puts it to use; and his selfishness is no less blind than was formerly his devotion to others.

If society is tranquil, it is not because it is conscious of its strength and its well-being, but because it fears its weakness and its infirmities; a single effort may cost it its life. Everybody feels the evil, but no one has courage or energy enough to seek the cure. The desires, the repinings, the sorrows, and the joys of the present time lead to nothing visible or permanent, like the passions of old men, which terminate in impotence.

We have, then, abandoned whatever advantages the old state of things afforded, without receiving any compensation from our present condition; we have destroyed an aristocracy, and we seem inclined to survey its ruins with complacency and to accept them.

The phenomena which the intellectual world presents are not less deplorable. The democracy of France, hampered in its course or abandoned to its lawless passions, has overthrown whatever crossed its path and has shaken all that it has not destroyed. Its empire has not been gradually introduced or peaceably established, but it has constantly advanced in the midst of the disorders and the agitations of a conflict. In the heat of the struggle each partisan is hurried beyond the natural limits of his opinions by the doctrines and the excesses of his opponents, until he loses sight of the end of his exertions, and holds forth in a way which does not correspond to his real sentiments or secret instincts. Hence arises the strange confusion that we are compelled to witness.

I can recall nothing in history more worthy of sorrow and pity than the scenes which are passing before our eyes. It is as if the natural bond that unites the opinions of man to his tastes, and his actions to his principles, was now broken; the harmony that has always been observed between the feelings and the ideas of mankind appears to be dissolved and all the laws of moral analogy to be abolished.

Zealous Christians are still found among us, whose minds are nurtured on the thoughts that pertain to a future life, and who readily espouse the cause of human liberty as the source of all moral greatness. Christianity, which has de-clared that all men are equal in the sight of God, will not refuse to acknowledge that all citizens are equal in the eye of the law. But, by a strange coincidence of events, religion has been for a time entangled with those institutions which democracy destroys; and it is not infrequently brought to reject the equality which it loves, and to curse as a foe that cause of liberty whose ef-forts it might hallow by its alliance.

By the side of these religious men I discern others whose thoughts are turned to earth rather than to heaven. These are the partisans of lib-erty, not only as the source of the noblest virtues, but more especially as the root of all solid advan-tages; and they sincerely desire to secure its au-thority, and to impart its blessings to mankind. It is natural that they should hasten to invoke the assistance of religion, for they must know that liberty cannot be established without moral-ity, nor morality without faith. But they have seen religion in the ranks of their adversaries, and they inquire no further; some of them attack it openly, and the rest are afraid to defend it.

In former ages slavery was advocated by the venal and slavish-minded, while the independent and the warm-hearted were struggling without hope to save the liberties of mankind. But men of high and generous character are now to be met with, whose opinions are directly at vari-ance with their inclinations, and who praise that servility and meanness which they have them-selves never known. Others, on the contrary, speak of liberty as if they were able to feel its sanctity and its majesty, and loudly claim for hu-manity those rights which they have always re-fused to acknowledge.

There are virtuous and peaceful individuals whose pure morality, quiet habits, opulence, and talents fit them to be the leaders of their fellow men. Their love of country is sincere, and they are ready to make the greatest sacrifices for its welfare. But civilization often finds them among its opponents; they confound its abuses with its benefits, and the idea of evil is inseparable in their minds from that of novelty.

Near these I find others whose object is to materialize mankind, to hit upon what is expedi-ent without heeding what is just, to acquire knowledge without faith, and prosperity apart from virtue; claiming to be the champions of modern civilization, they place themselves arro-gantly at its head, usurping a place which is abandoned to them, and of which they are wholly unworthy.

Where are we, then?

The religionists are the enemies of liberty, and the friends of liberty attack religion; the high-minded and the noble advocate bondage, and the meanest and most servile preach inde-pendence; honest and enlightened citizens are opposed to all progress, while men without patriotism and without principle put them-selves forward as the apostles of civilization and intelligence.

Has such been the fate of the centuries which have preceded our own? and has man always in-habited a world like the present, where all things are not in their proper relationships, where virtue is without genius, and genius without honor; where the love of order is confused with a taste for oppression, and the holy cult of freedom with a contempt of law; where the light thrown by conscience on human actions is dim, and where nothing seems to be any longer forbidden or al-lowed, honorable or shameful, false or true?

I cannot believe that the Creator made man to leave him in an endless struggle with the in-tellectual wretchedness that surrounds us. God destines a calmer and a more certain future to the communities of Europe. I am ignorant of his designs, but I shall not cease to believe in them because I cannot fathom them, and I had rather mistrust my own capacity than his justice.

There is one country in the world where the great social revolution that I am speaking of seems to have nearly reached its natural limits. It has been effected with ease and simplicity; say rather that this country is reaping the fruits of the democratic revolution which we are un-dergoing, without having had the revolution itself.

The emigrants who colonized the shores of America in the beginning of the seventeenth century somehow separated the democratic principle from all the principles that it had to contend with in the old communities of Europe, and transplanted it alone to the New World. It has there been able to spread in perfect freedom and peaceably to determine the character of the laws by influencing the manners of the country.

It appears to me beyond a doubt that, sooner or later, we shall arrive, like the Americans, at an almost complete equality of condition. But I do not conclude from this that we shall ever be necessarily led to draw the same political consequences which the Americans have derived from a similar social organization. I am far from supposing that they have chosen the only form of government which a democracy may adopt; but as the generating cause of laws and manners in the two countries is the same, it is of immense interest for us to know what it has produced in each of them.

It is not, then, merely to satisfy a curiosity, however legitimate, that I have examined America; my wish has been to find there instruction by which we may ourselves profit. Whoever should imagine that I have intended to write a panegyric would be strangely mistaken, and on reading this book he will perceive that such was not my design; nor has it been my object to advocate any form of government in particular, for I am of the opinion that absolute perfection is rarely to be found in any system of laws. I have not even pretended to judge whether the social revolution, which I believe to be irresistible, is advantageous or prejudicial to mankind. I have acknowledged this revolution as a fact already accomplished, or on the eve of its accomplishment; and I have selected the nation, from among those which have undergone it, in which its development has been the most peaceful and the most complete, in order to discern its natural consequences and to find out, if possible, the means of rendering it profitable to mankind. I confess that in America I saw more than America; I sought there the image of democracy itself, with its inclinations, its char-

acter, its prejudices, and its passions, in order to learn what we have to fear or to hope from its progress.

In the first part of this work I have attempted to show the distinction that democracy, dedicated to its inclinations and tendencies and abandoned almost without restraint to its instincts, gave to the laws the course it impressed on the government, and in general the control which it exercised over affairs of state. I have sought to discover the evils and the advantages which it brings. I have examined the safeguards used by the Americans to direct it, as well as those that they have not adopted, and I have undertaken to point out the factors which enable it to govern society.

My object was to portray, in a second part, the influence which the equality of conditions and democratic government in America exercised on civil society, on habits, ideas, and customs; but I grew less enthusiastic about carrying out this plan. Before I could have completed the task which I set for myself, my work would have become purposeless. Someone else would before long set forth to the public the principal traits of the American character and, delicately cloaking a serious picture, lend to the truth a charm which I should not have been able to equal.

I do not know whether I have succeeded in making known what I saw in America, but I am certain that such has been my sincere desire, and that I have never, knowingly, molded facts to ideas, instead of ideas to facts.

Whenever a point could be established by the aid of written documents, I have had recourse to the original text, and to the most authentic and reputable works. I have cited my authorities in the notes, and anyone may verify them. Whenever opinions, political customs, or remarks on the manners of the country were concerned, I have endeavored to consult the most informed men I met with. If the point in question was important or doubtful, I was not satisfied with one witness, but I formed my opinion on the evidence of several witnesses. Here the reader must necessarily rely upon my word. I could frequently have cited names which either are known to him or deserve to be so in support of my assertions; but I have carefully abstained from this practice. A stranger frequently hears important truths at the fireside of his host, which the latter would perhaps conceal from the ear of friendship; he consoles himself with his guest for the silence to which he is restricted, and the shortness of the traveler's stay takes away all fear of an indiscretion. I carefully noted every conversation of this nature as soon as it occurred, but these notes will never leave my writing-case. I had rather injure the success of my statements than add my name to the list of those strangers who repay generous hospitality they have received by subsequent chagrin and annoyance.

*   *   *

SEYMOUR MARTIN LIPSET

ECONOMIC DEVELOPMENT AND DEMOCRACY

*   *   *

Economic Development in Europe and the Americas

Perhaps the most common generalization linking political systems to other aspects of society has been that democracy is related to the state of economic development. The more well-to-do a nation, the greater the chances that it will sustain democracy. From Aristotle down to the present, men have argued that only in a wealthy society in which relatively few citizens lived at the level of real poverty could there be a situation in which the mass of the population intelligently participate in politics and develop the self-restraint necessary to avoid succumbing to the appeals of irresponsible demagogues. A society divided between a large impoverished mass and a small favored elite results either in oli-

garchy (dictatorial rule of the small upper stratum) or in tyranny (popular-based dictatorship). To give these two political forms modern labels, tyranny's face today is communism or Peronism; while oligarchy appears in the traditionalist dictatorships found in parts of Latin America, Thailand, Spain, or Portugal.

To test this hypothesis concretely, I have used various indices of economic development—wealth, industrialization, urbanization, and education—and computed averages (means) for the countries which have been classified as more or less democratic in the Anglo-Saxon world and Europe, and in Latin America.

In each case, the average wealth, degree of industrialization and urbanization, and level of education is much higher for the more democratic countries, as the data in Table I indicate. If I had combined Latin America and Europe in one table, the differences would have been even greater.

The main indices of *wealth* used are per capita income, number of persons per motor vehicle and thousands of persons per physician, and the number of radios, telephones, and news-

From *Political Man* (Garden City, N.Y.: Doubleday, 1960), pp. 31–51. Some of the author's notes have been omitted.

Table 1. A Comparison of European, English-speaking, and Latin-American Countries, Divided into Two Groups, "More Democratic" and "Less Democratic," by Indices of Wealth, Industrialization, Education, and Urbanization

A. Indices of Wealth

Means	Per Capita Income	Thousands of Persons per Doctor	Persons per Motor Vehicle
European and English-speaking Stable Democracies	U.S.$ 695	.86	17
European and English-speaking Unstable Democracies and Dictatorships	308	1.4	143
Latin-American Democracies and Unstable Dictatorships	171	2.1	99
Latin-American Stable Dictatorships	119	4.4	274

Ranges			
European Stable Democracies	420–1,453	.7–1.2	3–62
European Dictatorships	128–482	.6–4	10–538
Latin-American Democracies	112–346	.8–3.3	31–174
Latin-American Stable Dictatorships	40–331	1.0–10.8	38–428

Means	Telephones per 1,000 Persons	Radios per 1,000 Persons	Newspaper Copies per 1,000 Persons
European and English-speaking Stable Democracies	205	350	341
European and English-speaking Unstable Democracies and Dictatorships	58	160	167
Latin-American Democracies and Unstable Dictatorships	25	85	102
Latin-American Stable Dictatorships	10	43	43

Ranges			
European Stable Democracies	43–400	160–995	242–570
European Dictatorships	7–196	42–307	46–390
Latin-Amercian Democracies	12–58	38–148	51–233
Latin-American Stable Dictatorships	1–24	4–154	4–111

Table 1. A Comparison of European, English-speaking, and Latin-American Countries, Divided into Two Groups, "More Democratic" and "Less Democratic," by Indices of Wealth, Industrialization, Education, and Urbanization (cont.)

1B. Indices of Industrialization

Means	Percentage of Males in Agriculture	Per Capita Energy Consumed
European Stable Democracies	21	3.6
European Dictatorships	41	1.4
Latin-American Democracies	52	.6
Latin-American Stable Dictatorships	67	.25
Ranges		
European Stable Democracies	6–46	1.4–7.8
European Dictatorships	16–60	.27–3.2
Latin-American Democracies	30–63	.30–0.9
Latin-American Stable Dictatorships	46–87	.02–1.27

1C. Indices of Education

Means	Percentage Literate	Primary Education Enrollment per 1,000 Persons	Post-Primary Enrollment per 1,000 Persons	Higher Education Enrollment per 1,000 Persons
European Stable Democracies	96	134	44	4.2
European Dictatorships	85	121	22	3.5
Latin-American Democracies	74	101	13	2.0
Latin-American Dictatorships	46	72	8	1.3
Ranges				
European Stable Democracies	95–100	96–179	19–83	1.7–17.83
European Dictatorships	55–98	61–165	8–37	1.6–6.1
Latin-American Democracies	48–87	75–137	7–27	.7–4.6
Latin-American Dictatorshps	11–76	11–149	3–24	.2–3.1

1D. Indices in Urbanization

Means	*Per Cent in Cities over 20,000*	*Per Cent in Cities over 100,000*	*Per Cent in Metropolitan Areas*
European Stable Democracies	43	28	38
European Dictatorships	24	16	23
Latin-American Democracies	28	22	26
Latin-American Stable Dictatorships	17	12	15
Ranges			
European Stable Democracies	28–54	17–51	22–56
European Dictatorships	12–44	6–33	7–49
Latin-American Democracies	11–48	13–37	17–44
Latin-American Stable Dictatorships	5–36	4–22	7–26

papers per thousand persons. The differences are striking on every score (See Table I). In the more democratic European countries, there are 17 persons per motor vehicle compared to 143 for the less democratic. In the less dictatorial Latin-American countries there are 99 persons per motor vehicle versus 274 for the more dictatorial.[1] Income differences for the groups are also sharp, dropping from an average per capita income of $695 for the more democratic countries of Europe to $308 for the less democratic; the corresponding difference for Latin America is from $171 to $119. The ranges are equally consistent, with the lowest per capita income in each group falling in the "less democratic" category, and the highest in the "more democratic."

Industrialization, to which indices of wealth are of course clearly related, is measured by the percentage of employed males in agriculture and the per capita commercially produced "energy" being used in the country (measured in terms of tons of coal per person per year). Both of these show equally consistent results. The average percentage of employed males working in agricul-

ture and related occupations was 21 in the "more democratic" European countries and 41 in the "less democratic"; 52 in the "less dictatorial" Latin-American countries and 67 in the "more dictatorial." The differences in per capita energy employed are equally large.

The degree of *urbanization* is also related to the existence of democracy.[2] Three different indices of urbanization are available from data compiled by International Urban Research (Berkeley, California): the percentage of the population in communities of 20,000 and over, the percentage in communities of 100,000 and over, and the percentage residing in standard metropolitan areas. On all three of these indices the more democratic countries score higher than the less democratic for both of the areas under investigation.

Many people have suggested that the higher the *education* level of a nation's population, the better the chances for democracy, and the comparative data available support this proposition. The "more democratic" countries of Europe are almost entirely literate: the lowest has a rate of 96 percent; while the "less democratic" nations have an average rate of 85 per cent. In Latin America the difference is between an average rate of 74 per cent for the "less dictatorial" countries and 46 per cent for the "more dictatorial."[3] The educational enrollment per thousand total population at three different levels—primary, post-primary, and higher educational—is equally consistently related to the degree of democracy. The tremendous disparity is shown by the extreme cases of Haiti and the United States. Haiti has fewer children (11 per thousand) attending school in the primary grades than the United States has attending colleges (almost 18 per thousand).

The relationship between education and democracy is worth more extensive treatment since an entire philosophy of government has seen increased education as the basic requirement of democracy.[4] As James Bryce wrote, with special reference to South America, "education, if it does not make men good citizens, makes it at least easier for them to become so."[5] Education presumably broadens man's outlook, enables him to understand the need for norms of tolerance, restrains him from adhering to extremist doctrines, and increases his capacity to make rational electoral choices.

The evidence on the contribution of education to democracy is even more direct and strong on the level of individual behavior *within* countries than it is in cross-national correlations. Data gathered by public opinion research agencies which have questioned people in different countries about their beliefs on tolerance for the opposition, their attitudes toward ethnic or racial minorities, and their feelings for multiparty as against one-party systems have showed that the most important single factor differentiating those giving democratic responses from the others has been education. The higher one's education, the more likely one is to believe in democratic values and support democratic practices.[6] All the relevant studies indicate that education is more significant than either income or occupation.

These findings should lead us to anticipate a far higher correlation between national levels of education and political practice than we in fact find. Germany and France have been among the best educated nations of Europe, but this by itself did not stabilize their democracies.[7] It may be, however, that their educational level has served to inhibit other anti-democratic forces.

If we cannot say that a "high" level of education is a *sufficient* condition for democracy, the available evidence suggests that it comes close to being a *necessary* one. In Latin America, where widespread illiteracy still exists, only one of all the nations in which more than half the population is illiterate—Brazil—can be included in the "more democratic" group.

Lebanon, the one member of the Arab League which has maintained democratic institutions since World War II, is also by far the best educated (over 80 per cent literacy). East of the Arab world, only two states, the Philippines and Japan, have since 1945 maintained democratic regimes without the presence of large anti-democratic parties. And these two countries, although lower than most European states in per capita income, are among the world's leaders in educational attainment. The Philippines actually rank second to the United States in the proportion of people attending high schools and universities, and Japan has a higher educational level than any European nation.[8]

Although the evidence has been presented separately, all the various aspects of economic development—industrialization, urbanization, wealth, and education—are so closely interrelated as to form one major factor which has the political correlate of democracy.[9] A recent study of the Middle East further substantiates this. In 1951–52, a survey of Turkey, Lebanon, Egypt, Syria, Jordan, and Iran, conducted by Daniel Lerner and the Bureau of Applied Social Research, found a close connection between urbanization, literacy, voting rates, media consumption and production, and education.[10] Simple and multiple correlations between the four basic variables were computed for all countries for which United Nations statistic were available (in this case 54) with the following results:[11]

Dependent Variable	Multiple Correlation Coefficient
Urbanization	.61
Literacy	.91
Media Participation	.84
Political Participation	.82

In the Middle East, Turkey and Lebanon score higher on most of these indices than do the other four countries analyzed, and Daniel Lerner, in reporting on the study, points out that the "great post-war events in Egypt, Syria, Jordan and Iran have been the violent struggles for the control of power—struggles notably absent in Turkey and Lebanon [until very recently] where the control of power has been decided by elections."[12]

Lerner further points out the effect of disproportionate development, in one area or another, for over-all stability, and the need for co-ordinated changes in all of these variables. Comparing urbanization and literacy in Egypt and Turkey, he concludes that although Egypt is far more urbanized than Turkey, it is not really "modernized," and does not even have an adequate base for modernization, because literacy has not kept pace. In Turkey, all of the several indices of modernization have kept pace with each other, with rising voting participation (36 per cent in 1950), balanced by rising literacy, urbanization, etc. In Egypt, the cities are full of "homeless illiterates," who provide a ready audience for political mobilization in support of extremist ideologies. On Lerner's scale, Egypt should be twice as literate as Turkey, since it is twice as urbanized. The fact that it is only half as literate explains, for Lerner, the "imbalances" which "tend to become circular and to accelerate social disorganization," political as well as economic.[13]

Lerner introduces one important theoretical addition—the suggestion that these key variables in the modernization process may be viewed as historical phases, with democracy part of later developments, the "crowning institution of the participant society" (one of his terms for a mod-

ern industrial society). His view on the relations between these variables, seen as stages, is worth quoting at some length:

> The secular evolution of a participant society appears to involve a regular sequence of three phases. Urbanization comes first, for cities alone have developed the complex of skills and resources which characterize the modern industrial economy. Within this urban matrix develop both of the attributes which distinguish the next two phases—literacy and media growth. There is a close reciprocal relationship between these, for the literate develop the media which in turn spread literacy. But, literacy performs the key function in the second phase. The capacity to read, at first acquired by relatively few people, equips them to perform the varied tasks required in the modernizing society. Not until the third phase, when the elaborate technology of industrial development is fairly well advanced, does a society begin to produce newspapers, radio networks, and motion pictures on a massive scale. This, in turn, accelerates the spread of literacy. Out of this interaction develop those institutions of participation (e.g., voting) which we find in all advanced modern societies.[14]

Lerner's thesis, that these elements of modernization are functionally interdependent, is by no means established by his data. But the material presented in this chapter offers an opportunity for research along these lines. Deviant cases, such as Egypt, where "lagging" literacy is associated with serious strains and potential upheaval, may also be found in Europe and Latin America, and their analysis—a task not attempted here—will further clarify the basic dynamics of modernization and the problem of social stability in the midst of institutional change.

Economic Development and the Class Struggle

Economic development, producing increased income, greater economic security, and widespread higher education, largely determines the form of the "class struggle," by permitting those in the lower strata to develop longer time perspectives and more complex and gradualist views of politics. A belief in secular reformist gradualism can be the ideology of only a relatively well-to-do lower class. Striking evidence for this thesis may be found in the relationship between the patterns of working-class political action in different countries and the national income, a correlation that is almost startling in view of the many other cultural, historical, and juridical factors which affect the political life of nations.

In the two wealthiest countries, the United States and Canada, not only are communist parties almost nonexistent but socialist parties have never been able to establish themselves as major forces. Among the eight next wealthiest countries—New Zealand, Switzerland, Sweden, United Kingdom, Denmark, Australia, Norway, Belgium, Luxembourg and Netherlands—all of whom had a per capita income of over $500 a year in 1949 (the last year for which standardized United Nations statistics exist), moderate socialism predominates as the form of leftist politics. In none of these countries did the Communists secure more than 7 per cent of the vote, and the actual Communist party average among them has been about 4 per cent. In the eight European countries which were below the $500 per capita income mark in 1949—France, Iceland, Czechoslovakia, Finland, West Germany, Hungary, Italy, and Austria—and which have had at least one postwar democratic election in which both communist and noncommunist parties could compete, the Communist party has had more than 16 per cent of the vote in six, and an over-all average of more than 20 per cent in the eight countries as a group. The two low-income countries in which the Communists are weak—Germany and Austria—have both had direct experience with Soviet occupation.[15]

Leftist extremism has also dominated working-class politics in two other European nations which belong to the under $500 per capita income group—Spain and Greece. In Spain before Franco, anarchism and left socialism were much stronger than moderate socialism; while in Greece, whose per capita income in 1949 was only $128, the Communists have always been much stronger than the socialists, and fellow-traveling parties have secured a large vote in recent years.

The inverse relationship between national economic development as reflected by per capita income and the strength of Communists and other extremist groups among Western nations is seemingly stronger than the correlations between other national variables like ethnic or religious factors.[16] Two of the poorer nations with large Communist movements—Iceland and Finland—are Scandinavian and Lutheran. Among the Catholic nations of Europe, all the poor ones except Austria have large Communist or anarchist movements. The two wealthiest Catholic democracies—Belgium and Luxembourg—have few Communists. Though the French and Italian cantons of Switzerland are strongly affected by the cultural life of France and Italy, there are almost no Communists among the workers in these cantons, living in the wealthiest country in Europe.

The relation between low per capita wealth and the precipitation of sufficient discontent to provide the social basis for political extremism is supported by a recent comparative polling survey of the attitudes of citizens of nine countries. Among these countries, feelings of personal security correlated with per capita income (.45) and with per capita food supply (.55). If satisfaction with one's country, as measured by responses to the question, "Which country in the world gives you the best chance of living the kind of life you would like to live?" is used as an index of the amount of discontent in a nation, then the relationship with economic wealth is even higher. The study reports a rank order correlation of .74 between per capita income and the degree of satisfaction with one's own country.[17]

This does not mean that economic hardship or poverty *per se* is the main cause of radicalism. There is much evidence to sustain the argument that stable poverty in a situation in which individuals are not exposed to the possibilities of change breeds, if anything, conservatism.[18] Individuals whose experience limits their significant communications and interaction to others on the same level as themselves will, other conditions being equal, be more conservative than people who may be better off but who have been exposed to the possibilities of securing a better way of life.[19] The dynamic in the situation would seem to be exposure to the possibility of a better way of life rather than poverty as such. As Karl Marx put it in a perceptive passage: "A house may be large or small; as long as the surrounding houses are equally small it satisfies all social demands for a dwelling. But if a palace arises beside the little house, the little house shrinks into a hut."[20]

With the growth of modern means of communication and transportation both within and among countries, it seems increasingly likely that the groups in the population that are poverty-stricken but are isolated from knowledge of better ways of life or unaware of the possibilities for improvement in their condition are becoming rarer and rarer, particularly in the urban areas of the Western world. One may expect to find such stable poverty only in tradition-dominated societies.

Since position in a stratification system is always relative and gratification or deprivation is experienced in terms of being better or worse off than other people, it is not surprising that the lower classes in all countries, regardless of the wealth of the country, show various signs of resentment against the existing distribution of rewards by supporting political parties and other organizations which advocate some form of redistribution.[21] The fact that the form which these political parties take in poorer countries is more extremist and radical than it is in wealthier ones is probably more related to the greater degree of inequality in such countries than to the fact that their poor are actually poorer in absolute terms. A comparative study of wealth distribution by the United Nations "suggest[s] that the richest fraction of the population (the richest 10th, 5th, etc.) generally receive[s] a greater pro-

portion of the total income in the less developed than in the more developed countries."[22] The gap between the income of professional and semi-professional personnel on the one hand and ordinary workers on the other is much wider in the poorer than in the wealthier countries. Among manual workers, "there seems to be a greater wage discrepancy between skilled and unskilled workers in the less developed countries. In contrast the leveling process, in several of the developed countries at least, has been facilitated by the over-all increase of national income . . . not so much by reduction of the income of the relatively rich as by the faster growth of the incomes of the relatively poor."[23]

The distribution of consumption goods also tends to become more equitable as the size of national income increases. The wealthier a country, the larger the proportion of its population which owns automobiles, telephones, bathtubs, refrigerating equipment, and so forth. Where there is a dearth of goods, the sharing of such goods must inevitably be less equitable than in a country in which there is relative abundance. For example, the number of people who can afford automobiles, washing machines, decent housing, telephones, good clothes, or have their children complete high school or go to college still represents only a small minority of the population in many European countries. The great national wealth of the United States or Canada, or even to a lesser extent the Australasian Dominions or Sweden, means that there is relatively little difference between the standards of living of adjacent social classes, and that even classes which are far apart in the social structure will enjoy more nearly similar consumption patterns than will comparable classes in Southern Europe. To a Southern European, and to an even greater extent to the inhabitant of one of the "underdeveloped" countries, social stratification is characterized by a much greater distinction in ways of life, with little overlap in the goods the various strata own or can afford to purchase. It may be suggested, therefore, that the wealthier a country, the less is status inferiority experienced as a major source of deprivation.

Increased wealth and education also serve democracy by increasing the lower classes' exposure to cross-pressures which reduce their commitment to given ideologies and make them less receptive to extremist ones. The operation of this process will be discussed in more detail in the next chapter, but it means involving those strata in an integrated national culture as distinct from an isolated lower-class one.

Marx believed that the proletariat was a revolutionary force because it had nothing to lose but its chains and could win the whole world. But Tocqueville, analyzing the reasons why the lower strata in America supported the system, paraphrased and transposed Marx before Marx ever made his analysis by pointing out that "only those who have nothing to lose ever revolt."[24]

Increased wealth also affects the political role of the middle class by changing the shape of the stratification structure from an elongated pyramid, with a large lower-class base, to a diamond with a growing middle class. A large middle class tempers conflict by rewarding moderate and democratic parties and penalizing extremist groups.

The political values and style of the upper class, too, are related to national income. The poorer a country and the lower the absolute standard of living of the lower classes, the greater the pressure on the upper strata to treat the lower as vulgar, innately inferior, a lower caste beyond the pale of human society. The sharp difference in the style of living between those at the top and those at the bottom makes this psychologically necessary. Consequently, the upper strata in such a situation tend to regard political rights for the lower strata, particularly the right to share power, as essentially absurd and immoral. The upper strata not only resist democracy themselves; their often arrogant political behavior serves to intensify extremist reactions on the part of the lower classes.

The general income level of a nation also affects its receptivity to democratic norms. If there is enough wealth in the country so that it does not make too much difference whether some redistribution takes place, it is easier to accept the idea that it does not matter greatly which side is in power. But if loss of office means serious losses for major power groups, they will seek to retain or secure office by any means available. A certain amount of national wealth is likewise necessary to ensure a competent civil service. The poorer the country, the greater the emphasis on nepotism—support of kin and friends. And this in turn reduces the opportunity to develop the efficient bureaucracy which a modern democratic state requires.[25]

Intermediary organizations which act as sources of countervailing power seem to be similarly associated with national wealth. Tocqueville and other exponents of what has come to be known as the theory of the "mass society"[26] have argued that a country without a multitude of organizations relatively independent of the central state power has a high dictatorial as well as revolutionary potential. Such organizations serve a number of functions: they inhibit the state or any single source of private power from dominating all political resources; they are a source of new opinions; they can be the means of communicating ideas, particularly opposition ideas, to a large section of the citizenry; they train men in political skills and so help to increase the level of interest and participation in politics. Although there are no reliable data on the relationship between national patterns of voluntary organization and national political systems, evidence from studies of individual behavior demonstrates that, regardless of other factors, men who belong to associations are more likely than others to give the democratic answer to questions concerning tolerance and party systems, to vote, or to participate actively in politics. Since the more well-to-do and better educated a man is, the more likely he is to belong to voluntary organizations, the propensity to form such groups seems to be a function of level of income and opportunities for leisure within given nations.[27]

The Politics of Rapid Economic Development

The association between economic development and democracy has led many Western statesmen and political commentators to conclude that the basic political problem of our day is produced by the pressure for rapid industrialization. If only the underdeveloped nations can be successfully started on the road to high productivity, the assumption runs, we can defeat the major threat to newly established democracies, their domestic Communists. In a curious way, this view marks the victory of economic determinism or vulgar Marxism within democratic political thought. Unfortunately for this theory, political extremism based on the lower classes, communism in particular, is not to be found only in low-income countries but also in newly industrializing nations. This correlation is not, of course, a recent phenomenon. In 1884, Engels noted that explicitly socialist labor movements had developed in Europe during periods of rapid industrial growth, and that these movements declined sharply during later periods of slower change.

The pattern of leftist politics in northern Europe in the first half of the twentieth century in countries whose socialist and trade-union movements are now relatively moderate and conservative illustrates this point. Wherever industrialization occurred *rapidly*, introducing sharp *discontinuities* between the pre-industrial and industrial situation, more rather than less extremist working-class movements emerged. In Scandinavia, for example, the variations among the socialist movements of Denmark, Sweden, and Norway can be accounted for in large measure by the different timing and pace of industrialization, as the economist Walter Galenson has pointed out.[28] The Danish Social Democratic movement and trade-unions have always been in the reformist, moderate, and relatively non-Marxist wing of the international labor movement. In Denmark, industralization developed as a slow and gradual process. The rate of urban

growth was also moderate, which had a good effect on urban working-class housing conditions. The slow growth of industry meant that a large proportion of Danish workers all during the period of industrialization were men who had been employed in industry for a long time, and, consequently, newcomers who had been pulled up from rural areas and who might have supplied the basis for extremist factions were always in a minority. The left-wing groups which gained some support in Denmark were based on the rapidly expanding industries.

In Sweden, on the other hand, manufacturing industry grew very rapidly from 1900 to 1914. This caused a sudden growth in the number of unskilled workers, largely recruited from rural areas, and the expansion of industrial rather than craft unions. Paralleling these developments in industry, a left-wing movement arose within the trade-unions and the Social Democratic party which opposed the moderate policies that both had developed before the great industrial expansion. A strong anarcho-syndicalist movement also emerged in this period. Here again, these aggressive left-wing movements were based on the rapidly expanding industries.[29]

Norway, the last of the three Scandinavian countries to industrialize, had an even more rapid rate of growth. As a result of the emergence of hydroelectric power, the growth of an electrochemical industry, and the need for continued construction, Norway's industrial workers doubled between 1905 and 1920. And as in Sweden, this increase in the labor force meant that the traditional moderate craft-union movement was swamped by unskilled and semiskilled workers, most of whom were young migrants from rural areas. A left wing emerged within the Federation of Labor and the Labor party, capturing control of both in the latter stages of World War I. It should be noted that Norway was the only Western European country which was still in its phase of rapid industrialization when the Comintern was founded, and its Labor party was the only one which went over almost intact to the Communists.

In Germany before World War I, a revolutionary Marxist left wing, in large measure derived from workers in the rapidly growing industries, retained considerable support within the Social Democratic party, while the more moderate sections of the party were based on the more stable established industries.[30]

The most significant illustration of the relationship between rapid industrialization and working-class extremism is the Russian Revolution. In Czarist Russia, the industrial population jumped from 16 million in 1897 to 26 million in 1913.[31] Trotsky in his *History of the Russian Revolution* has shown how an increase in the strike rate and in union militancy paralleled the growth of industry. It is probably not coincidental that two nations in Europe in which the revolutionary left gained control of the dominant section of the labor movement before 1920—Russia and Norway—were also countries in which the processes of rapid capital accumulation and basic industrialization were still going on.[32]

The revolutionary socialist movements which arise in response to strains created by rapid industrialization decline, as Engels put it, wherever "the transition to large-scale industry is more or less completed . . . [and] the conditions in which the proletariat is placed become stable."[33] Such countries are, of course, precisely the industrialized nations where Marxism and revolutionary socialism exist today only as sectarian dogmas. In those nations of Europe where industrialization never occurred, or where it failed to build an economy of efficient large-scale industry with a high level of productivity and a constant increase in mass-consumption patterns, the conditions for the creation or perpetuation of extremist labor politics also exist.

A different type of extremism, based on the small entrepreneurial classes (both urban and rural), has emerged in the less developed and often culturally backward sectors of more industrialized societies. The social base of classic fascism seems to arise from the ever present vulnerability of part of the middle class, particularly small businessmen and farm owners, to large-scale capitalism and a powerful labor movement. Chapter 5 analyzes this reaction in detail as it is manifest in a number of countries.

It is obvious that the conditions related to stable democracy discussed here are most readily found in the countries of northwest Europe and their English-speaking offspring in America and Australasia; and it has been suggested, by Weber among others, that a historically unique concatenation of elements produced both democracy and capitalism in this area. Capitalist economic development, the basic argument runs, had its greatest opportunity in a Protestant society and created the burgher class whose existence was both a catalyst and a necessary condition for democracy. Protestantism's emphasis on individual responsibility furthered the emergence of democratic values in these countries and resulted in an alignment between the burghers and the throne which preserved the monarchy and extended the acceptance of democracy among the conservative strata. Men may question whether any aspect of this interrelated cluster of economic development, Protestantism, monarchy, gradual political change, legitimacy, and democracy is primary, but the fact remains that the cluster does not hang together.

NOTES

1. It must be remembered that these figures are means, compiled from census figures for the various countries. The data vary widely in accuracy, and there is no way of measuring the validity of compound calculated figures such as those presented here. The consistent direction of all these differences, and their large magnitude, is the main indication of validity.

2. Urbanization has often been linked to democracy by political theorists. Harold J. Laski asserted that "organized democracy is

the product of urban life," and that it was natural therefore that it should have "made its first effective appearance" in the Greek city states, limited as was their definition of "citizen." See his article "Democracy" in the *Encyclopedia of the Social Sciences* (New York: Macmillan, 1937), Vol. V, pp. 76–85. Max Weber held that the city, as a certain type of political community, is a peculiarly Western phenomenon, and traced the emergence of the notion of "citizenship" from social developments closely related to urbanization. For a partial statement of his point of view, see the chapter on "Citizenship" in *General Economic History* (Glencoe: The Free Press, 1950), pp. 315–38.

3. The pattern indicated by a comparison of the averages for each group of countries is sustained by the ranges (the high and low extremes) for each index. Most of the ranges overlap; that is, some countries which are in the "less democratic" category are higher on any given index than some which are "more democratic." It is noteworthy that in both Europe and Latin America, the nations which are lowest on any of the indices presented in the table are also in the "less democratic" category. Conversely, almost all countries which rank at the top of any of the indices are in the "more democratic" class.

4. See John Dewey, *Democracy and Education* (New York: Macmillan, 1916).

5. James Bryce, *South America: Observations and Impressions* (New York: Macmillan, 1912), p. 546.

6. See G. H. Smith, "Liberalism and Level of Information," *Journal of Educational Psychology*, 39 (1948), pp. 65–82; Martin A. Trow, *Right Wing Radicalism and Political Intolerance* (Ph.D. thesis, Department of Sociology, Columbia University, 1957), p. 17; Samuel A. Stouffer, *Communism, Conformity, and Civil Liberties* (New York: Doubleday & Co., Inc., 1955); Kotaro Kido and Masataka Sugi, "A Report of Research on Social Stratification and Mobility in Tokyo"

(III), *Japanese Sociological Review*, 4 (1954), pp. 74–100.

7. Dewey has suggested that the character of the educational system will influence its effect on democracy, and this may shed some light on the sources of instability in Germany. The purpose of German education, according to Dewey, writing in 1916, was one of "disciplinary training rather than of personal development." The main aim was to produce "absorption of the aims and meaning of existing institutions," and "thoroughgoing subordination" to them. See John Dewey, *op. cit.*, pp. 108–10.

8. Ceylon, which shares the distinction with the Philippines and Japan of being the only democratic countries in South and Far East Asia in which the communists are unimportant electorally, also shares with them the distinction of being the only countries in this area in which a *majority* of the population is literate. It should be noted, however, that Ceylon does have a fairly large Trotskyist party, now the official opposition, and while its educational level is high for Asia, it is much lower than either Japan or the Philippines.

9. This statement is a "statistical" statement, which necessarily means that there will be many exceptions to the correlation. Thus we know that poorer people are more likely to vote for the Democratic or Labor parties in the U.S. and England. The fact that a large minority of the lower strata vote for the more conservative party in these countries does not challenge the proposition that stratification position is a main determinant of party choice.

10. The study is reported in Daniel Lerner's *The Passing of Traditional Society* (Glencoe: The Free Press, 1958). These correlations are derived from census data; the main sections of the survey dealt with reactions to and opinions about the mass media, with inferences as to the personality types appropriate to modern and to traditional society.

11. *Ibid.*, p. 63. The index of political participation was the per cent voting in the last five elections. These results cannot be considered as independent verification of the relationships presented in this paper, since the data and variables are basically the same, but the identical results using three entirely different methods, the phi coefficient, multiple correlations, and means and ranges, show decisively that the relationships cannot be attributed to artifacts of the computations. It should also be noted that the three analyses were made without knowledge of each other.

12. *Ibid.*, pp. 84–85.

13. *Ibid.*, pp. 87–89. Other theories of underdeveloped areas have also stressed the circular character of the forces sustaining a given level of economic and social development, and in a sense this paper may be regarded as an effort to extend the analysis of the complex of institutions constituting a "modernized" society to the political sphere.

14. Lerner, *op. cit.*, p. 60.

15. It should be noted that before 1933–34, Germany had one of the largest Communist parties in Europe; while the Socialist party of Austria was the most left-wing and Marxist European party in the Socialist International.

16. The relationship expressed above can be presented in another way. The seven European countries in which Communist or fellow-traveling parties have secured large votes in free elections had an average per capita income in 1949 of $330. The ten European countries in which the Communists have been a failure electorally had an average per capita income of $585.

17. William Buchanan and Hadley Cantril, *How Nations See Each Other* (Urbana: University of Illinois Press, 1953), p. 35.

18. See Emile Durkheim, *Suicide: A Study in Sociology* (Glencoe: The Free Press, 1951), pp. 253–54; see also Daniel Bell, "The Theory of Mass Society," *Commentary*, 22 (1956), p. 80.

19. There is also a considerable body of evidence which indicates that those occupations which are economically vulnerable and those workers who have experienced unemployment are prone to be more leftist in their outlook.

20. Karl Marx, "Wage-Labor and Capital," in *Selected Works*, Vol. I (New York: International Publishers, 1933), pp. 268–69. "Social tensions are an expression of unfulfilled expectations," Daniel Bell, *op. cit.*, p. 80.

21. A summary of the findings of election studies in many countries shows that, with few exceptions, there is a strong relationship between lower social position and support of "leftist" politics. There are, of course, many other characteristics which are also related to left voting, some of which are found among relatively well paid but socially isolated groups. Among the population as a whole, men are much more likely to vote for the left than women, while members of minority religious and ethnic groups also display a leftist tendency.

22. *United Nations Preliminary Report on the World Social Situation* (New York: 1952), pp. 132–33. Gunnar Myrdal, the Swedish economist, has recently pointed out: "It is, indeed, a regular occurrence endowed almost with the dignity of an economic law that the poorer the country, the greater the difference between poor and rich." *An International Economy* (New York: Harper & Bros., 1956), p. 133.

23. *United Nations Preliminary Report . . . , ibid.* A recently completed comparison of income distribution in the United States and a number of western European countries concludes that "there has not been any great difference" in patterns of income distribution among these countries. These findings of Robert Solow appear to contradict those reported above from the U.N. Statistics Office, although the latter are dealing primarily with differences between industrialized and underdeveloped nations. In any case, it

should be noted that Solow agrees that the relative position of the lower strata in a poor as compared with a wealthy country is quite different. As he states, "in comparing Europe and America, one may ask whether it makes sense to talk about relative income inequality independently of the absolute level of income. An income four times another income has different content according as the lower income means malnutrition on the one hand or provides some surplus on the other." Robert M. Solow, *A Survey of Income Inequality Since the War* (Stanford: Center for Advanced Study in the Behavioral Sciences, 1958, mimeographed), pp. 41–44, 78.

24. Alexis de Tocqueville, *Democracy in America*, Vol. I (New York: Alfred A. Knopf, Vintage ed., 1945), p. 258.

25. For a discussion of this problem in a new state, see David Apter, *The Gold Coast in Transition* (Princeton: Princeton University Press, 1955), esp. Chaps. 9 and 13. Apter shows the importance of efficient bureaucracy, and the acceptance of bureaucratic values and behavior patterns for the existence of a democratic political order.

26. See Emil Lederer, *The State of the Masses* (New York: Norton, 1940); Hannah Arendt, *Origins of Totalitarianism* (New York: Harcourt, Brace & Co., 1951); Max Horkheimer, *Eclipse of Reason* (New York: Oxford University Press, 1947); Karl Mannheim, *Man and Society in an Age of Reconstruction* (New York: Harcourt, Brace & Co., 1940); Philip Selznick, *The Organizational Weapon* (New York: McGraw-Hill Book Co., 1952); José Ortega y Gasset, *The Revolt of the Masses* (New York: Norton, 1932); William Kornhauser, *The Politics of Mass Society* (Glencoe: The Free Press, 1959).

27. See Edward Banfield, *The Moral Basis of a Backward Society* (Glencoe: The Free Press, 1958), for an excellent description of the way in which abysmal poverty serves to reduce community organization in southern Italy. The data which do exist from polling surveys

conducted in the United States, Germany, France, Great Britain, and Sweden show that somewhere between 40 and 50 per cent of the adults in these countries belong to voluntary associations, without lower rates of membership for the less stable democracies, France and Germany, than among the more stable ones, the United States, Great Britain, and Sweden. These results seemingly challenge the general proposition, although no definite conclusion can be made, since most of the studies employed noncomparable categories. This point bears further research in many countries.

28. See Walter Galenson, *The Danish System of Labor Relations* (Cambridge: Harvard University Press, 1952); see also Galenson, "Scandinavia," in Galenson, ed., *Comparative Labor Movements* (New York: Prentice-Hall, 1952), esp. pp. 105–20.

29. See Rudolf Heberle, *Zur Geschichte der Arbeiter-bewegung in Schweden*, Vol. 39 of *Probleme der Weltwirtschaft* (Jena: Gustav Fischer, 1925).

30. See Ossip Flechtheim, *Die KPD in der Weimarer Republik* (Offenbach am Main: Bollwerk-Verlag Karl Drott, 1948), pp. 213–14; see also Rose Laub Coser, *An Analysis of the Early German Socialist Movement* (unpublished M.A. thesis, Department of Sociology, Columbia University, 1951).

31. Colin Clark, *The Conditions of Economic Progress* (London: Macmillan, 1952), p. 421.

32. The Communists also controlled the Greek trade-unions and Socialist Labor party. The Greek case while fitting this pattern is not completely comparable, since no real pre-Communist labor movement existed and a pro-Bolshevik movement arose from a combination of the discontents of workers in the war-created new industry and the enthusiasm occasioned by the Russian Revolution.

33. Friedrich Engels, "Letter to Karl Kautsky," Nov. 8, 1884, in Karl Marx and Friedrich Engels, *Correspondence 1846–1895* (New York: International Publishers, 1946), p. 422;

see also Val R. Lorwin, "Working-class Politics and Economic Development in Western Europe," *American Historical Review*, 63 (1958), pp. 338–51; for an excellent discus-sion of the effects of rapid industrialization on politics, see also Reinhold Niebuhr, *The Irony of American History* (New York: Charles Scribner's Sons, 1952), pp. 112–18.

MAURICE DUVERGER

THE NUMBER OF PARTIES

*   *   *

Only individual investigation of the circum-stances in each country can determine the real origins of the two-party system. The in-fluence of such national factors is certainly very considerable; but we must not in their *favour* un-derestimate the importance of one general factor of a technical kind, the electoral system. Its effect can be expressed in the following formula: *the simple-majority single-ballot system favours the two-party system.* Of all the hypotheses that have been de-fined in this book, this approaches the most nearly perhaps to a true sociological law. An almost com-plete correlation is observable between the simple-majority single-ballot system and the two-party system: dualist countries use the simple-majority vote and simple-majority vote countries are dualist. The exceptions are very rare and can generally be explained as the result of special conditions.

We must give a few details about this coexis-tence of the simple-majority and the two-party systems. First let us cite the example of Great Britain and the Dominions: the simple-majority system with a single ballot is in operation in all; the two-party system operates in all, with a Conservative-Labour antagonism tending to re-place the Conservative-Liberal antagonism. It

From *Political Parties: Their Organization and Activity in the Modern State* (New York: Wiley, 1954), pp. 217–28.

will be seen later that Canada, which appears to present an exception, in fact conforms to the general rule.[1] Although it is more recent and more restricted in time the case of Turkey is per-haps more impressive. In this country, which had been subjected for twenty years to the rule of a single party, divergent tendencies were man-ifest as early as 1946; the secession of the Na-tionalist party, which broke away from the opposition Democratic party in 1948, might have been expected to give rise to a multi-party sys-tem. On the contrary, at the 1950 elections the simple-majority single-ballot system, based on the British pattern (and intensified by list-voting), gave birth to a two-party system: of 487 deputies in the Great National Assembly only ten (i.e. 2.07%) did not belong to one or other of the two major parties, Democrats and Popular Re-publicans. Nine were Independents and one be-longed to the Nationalist party. In the United States the traditional two-party system also co-exists with the simple-majority single-ballot sys-tem. The American electoral system is, of course, very special, and the present-day development of primaries introduces into it a kind of double poll, but the attempt sometimes made to identify this technique with the "second ballot" is quite mistaken. The nomination of candidates by an internal vote inside each party is quite a differ-ent thing from the real election. The fact that the nomination is open makes no difference: the pri-

Fig. 1. Disparity between percentage of votes and percentage of seats in Great Britain.

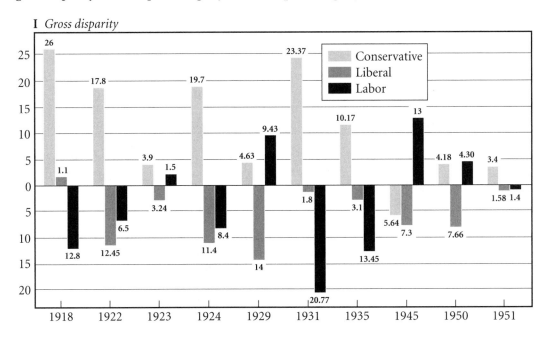

I *Gross disparity*

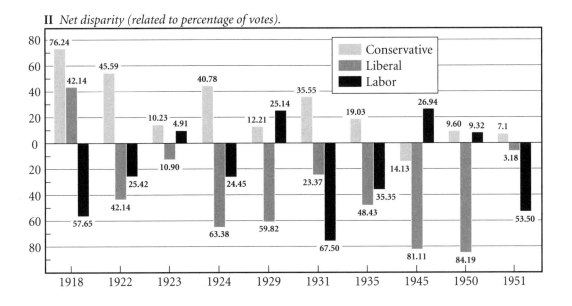

II *Net disparity (related to percentage of votes).*

maries are a feature of party organization and not of the electoral system.

The American procedure corresponds to the usual machinery of the simple-majority single-ballot system. The absence of a second ballot and of further polls, particularly in the presidential election, constitutes in fact one of the historical reasons for the emergence and the maintenance of the two-party system. In the few local elections in which proportional representation has from time to time been tried it shattered the two-party system: for example in New York between 1936 and 1947, where there were represented on the City Council 5 parties in 1937 (13 Democrats, 3 Republicans, 5 American Labor, 3 City Fusionists, 2 dissident Democrats), 6 parties in 1941 (by the addition of 1 Communist), and 7 parties in 1947 (as a result of an internal split in the American Labor party supported by the Garment Trade Unions).

*   *   *

Elimination [of third parties] is itself the result of two factors working together: a mechanical and a psychological factor. The mechanical factor consists in the "under-representation" of the third, i.e. the weakest party, its percentage of seats being inferior to its percentage of the poll. Of course in a simple-majority system with two parties the vanquished is always under-represented by comparison with the victor, as we shall see below, but in cases where there is a third party it is under-represented to an even greater extent than the less favoured of the other two. The example of Britain is very striking: before 1922, the Labour party was under-represented by comparison with the Liberal party; thereafter the converse regularly occurred (with the one exception of 1931, which can be explained by the serious internal crisis in the Labour party and the crushing victory of the Conservatives); in this way the third party finds the electoral system mechanically unfair to it (Fig. 1). So long as a new party which aims at

Fig. 2. Elimination of Liberal Party in Great Britain

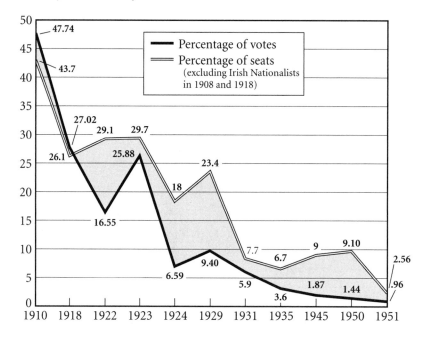

competing with the two old parties still remains weak the system works against it, raising a barrier against its progress. If, however, it succeeds in outstripping one of its forerunners, then the latter takes its place as third party and the process of elimination is transferred.

The psychological factor is ambiguous in the same way. In cases where there are three parties operating under the simple-majority single-ballot system the electors soon realize that their votes are wasted if they continue to give them to the third party: whence their natural tendency to transfer their vote to the less evil of its two adversaries in order to prevent the success of the greater evil. This "polarization" effect works to the detriment of a new party so long as it is the weakest party but is turned against the less favoured of its older rivals as soon as the new party outstrips it. It operates in fact in the same way as "under-representation." The reversal of the two effects does not always occur at the

same moment, under-representation generally being the earlier, for a certain lapse of time is required before the electors become aware of the decline of a party and transfer their votes to another. The natural consequence is a fairly long period of confusion during which the hesitation of the electors combines with the transposition of the "under-representation" effect to give an entirely false picture of the balance of power amongst the parties: England experienced such drawbacks between 1923 and 1935. The impulse of the electoral system towards the creation of bipartism is therefore only a long-term effect.

The simple-majority single-ballot system appears then to be capable of maintaining an established dualism in spite of schisms in old parties and the birth of new parties. For a new party to succeed in establishing itself firmly it must have at its disposal strong backing locally or great and powerful organization nationally. In the first case, moreover, it will remain circum-

Fig. 3. "Rescue" of Belgian Liberal Party by P.R.
(No. of seats in Chamber of Deputies.)

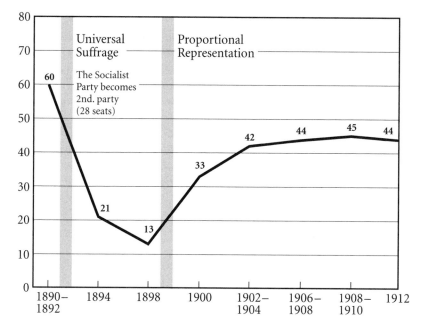

scribed within the geographical area of its origin and will only emerge from it slowly and painfully, as the example of Canada demonstrates. Only in the second case can it hope for a speedy development which will raise it to the position of second party, in which it will be favoured by the polarization and under-representation effects. Here perhaps we touch upon one of the deep-seated reasons which have led all Anglo-Saxon Socialist parties to organize themselves on a Trade Union basis; it alone could put at their disposal sufficient strength for the "take-off," small parties being eliminated or driven back into the field of local campaigns. The simple-majority system seems equally capable of re-establishing dualism when it has been destroyed by the appearance of a third party. The comparison between Great Britain and Belgium offers a striking contrast: in both countries a traditional two-party system was broken up at the beginning of the century by the emergence of Socialism. Fifty years later the majority system restored bipartism in Great Britain by the elimination of the Liberals (Fig. 2), whereas in Belgium proportional representation saved the Liberal party and later made possible the birth of the Communist party, without counting a few other parties between the wars (Fig. 3).

Can we go further and say that the simple-majority system is capable of producing bipartism in countries where it has never existed? If they already show a fairly clear tendency towards two parties, the answer would unquestionably be in the affirmative. The establishment of the simple-majority single-ballot system in Western Germany would undoubtedly have the effect of gradually destroying the small and medium-sized parties, leaving the Socialists and Christian Dem-

ocrats face to face; there is undoubtedly no country in which the technical conditions more nearly approach those required for the establishment of a parliamentary system after the British pattern. In Italy an electoral reform of the same kind would have the same results—with the sole difference that the Communists would be one of the two parties, which would greatly imperil the future of the democratic system. However, the brutal application of the single-ballot system in a country in which multipartism has taken deep root, as in France, would not produce the same results, except after a very long delay. The electoral system works in the direction of bipartism; it does not necessarily and absolutely lead to it in spite of all obstacles. The basic tendency combines with many others which attenuate it, check it, or arrest it. With these reserves we can nevertheless consider that dualism of parties is the "brazen law" (as Marx would have said) of the simple-majority single-ballot electoral system.

*   *   *

NOTES

1. Australia too offers an exception since the development of the *Country party*. But the system of preferential voting in operation there profoundly modifies the machinery of the simple-majority poll and makes it more like a two-ballot system by allowing a regrouping of the scattered votes. It is moreover a striking fact that the appearance of the Country party coincided with the introduction of the preferential vote.

TORBEN IVERSEN AND DAVID SOSKICE

ELECTORAL INSTITUTIONS AND THE POLITICS OF COALITIONS: WHY SOME DEMOCRACIES REDISTRIBUTE MORE THAN OTHERS

Why do some countries redistribute more than others? Most work on the politics of redistribution starts from the premise that democratic institutions empower those who stand to benefit from redistribution. The basic logic is succinctly captured in the Meltzer–Richard (1981) model, where the voter with the median income is also the decisive voter. With a typical right-skewed distribution of income, the median voter will push for redistributive spending up to the point where the benefit of such spending to the median voter is outweighed by the efficiency costs of distortionary taxation.

This argument implies that redistribution is much greater in democracies than in nondemocracies (at least of the right-authoritarian variety), and that, among the latter, inegalitarian societies redistribute more than egalitarian ones. There is some evidence to support the first implication, although it is disputed (see Ross 2005), but most of the variance in redistribution is probably within the same regime type. According to data from the Luxembourg Income Study, for example, the reduction in the poverty rate in United States as a result of taxation and transfers was 13% in 1994, whereas the comparable figure for Sweden was 82% (the poverty rate is the percentage of households below 50% of the median income). To explain this variance, we have to look at political and economic differences among democracies, but the second implication—that inegalitarian societies redistribute more—turns out to be of little help. In fact the empirical relationship between inequality and redistribution is the opposite of the predicted one (see Bénabou 1996; Moene and Wallerstein 2001; Perotti 1996). Sweden not only redistributes more than the United States, but also is a much more egalitarian society. So the explanation for why some democracies redistribute more than others would seem to lie more or less wholly outside the standard framework in political economy to explain democratic redistribution.

One possibility is that the power of the working class and left political parties varies across countries (see, e.g., Korpi 1983, 1989; Hicks and Swank 1992; Huber and Stephens 2001). Because it is plausible that redistribution is a function of government policies, and such policies reflect the preferences of those who govern, looking for differences in government partisanship is a promising avenue. Furthermore, if left governments not only redistribute more but also reduce inequality of earnings by, say, investing heavily in public education, partisanship may also explain why equality and redistribution tend to co-vary. Indeed, there is much evidence to the effect that government partisanship helps explain cross-national differences in redistribution (Boix 1998; Bradley et al. 2003; Kwon and Pontusson 2003), and our finding corroborate this evidence. But it raises another puzzle: why are some democracies dominated by left governments, whereas others are dominated by right governments?

Although government partisanship is often assumed to reflect the level of working-class mobilization, we argue that it is in fact mainly determined by differences in coalitional dynamics

From *American Political Science Review*, 100, no. 2 (May 2006), pp. 165–181.

associated with particular electoral systems. Table 1 shows the strong empirical relationship using a new dataset on parties and legislatures (see Cusack and Engelhardt 2002; Cusack and Fuchs 2002). The figures are the total number of years with right and left governments in 17 advanced democracies between 1945 and 1998, organized by type of electoral system. Mirroring a similar finding by Powell (2002), about three fourths of governments in majoritarian systems were center-*right*, whereas three fourths of governments under PR were center-*left* (excluding here "pure" center governments). The numbers in parentheses convey a sense of the evidence at the level of countries, classifying countries according to whether they have an overweight (more than 50%) of center-left or center-right governments during the 1945–98 period. We discuss the data (and the one outlier) in detail next.

Our explanation for the association of Table 1 builds on an emerging literature on the effects of electoral formulae on economic policies and outcomes (see, e.g., Persson and Tabellini 1999, 2000, 2003; Rogowski and Kayser 2002; Austen-Smith 2000). In particular, we argue that the electoral formula affects coalition behavior and leads to systematic differences in the partisan composition of governments—hence, to different distributive outcomes. The model we propose assumes that parties represent classes, or coalition of classes, and that it is difficult for parties to commit credibly to electoral platforms that deviate from the preferences of their constituents. We also make a critical departure from standard models based on Meltzer–Richard (1981) by allowing taxes and transfers to vary across classes, thereby transforming redistributive politics into a multidimensional game. In particular, we move away from a simple rich-poor model to one in which the middle class will fear taxation by the poor, even as it faces an incentive to ally with the poor to take from the rich. The only constraint is that the rich cannot "soak" the middle class and poor under democracy—a condition that can be justified on empirical, normative, and institutional grounds.

Based on these very general assumptions we show that in a two-party majoritarian system the center-right party is more likely to win government power, and redistribute less, than in a multiparty PR system where the center party is more likely to ally with parties to its left. The intuition is that in a majoritarian system where parties cannot fully commit, the median voter faces low taxes if a center-right party deviates to the right if elected, but faces high taxes and redistribution to low-income groups if a center-left party in government deviates to the left. With PR, on the other hand, the middle-class party has an incentive to form a coalition with the left party because they can together "exploit" the rich. No such exploitation of the poor is feasible under realistic assumptions. Remarkably, therefore, the same set of assumptions about redistributive

Table 1. Electoral System and the Number of Years With Left and Right Governments (1945–98)

		Government Partisanship		Proportion of Right Governments
		Left	Right	
Electoral system	Proportional	342 (8)	120 (1)	0.26
	Majoritarian	86 (0)	256 (8)	0.75

Note: Excludes centrist governments (see text for details).

policies leads to opposite predictions about government partisanship depending on the electoral system. We test the model on postwar data for redistribution and government partisanship for advanced democracies since the Second World War.

The Evidence

We test our argument in two parts. In the first part, we use partisanship and electoral system as explanatory variables to account for differences in the level of redistribution. In the second part, we use partisanship as the dependent variable, testing the proposition that the electoral system shapes coalition behavior and therefore the composition of governments.

Data

We base our analysis of redistribution on the Luxembourg Income Study (LIS), which has been compiling a large database on pre- and post-tax and transfer income inequality during the past three decades. The LIS data used for this study cover 14 countries from the late 1960s (the first observation is 1967) to the late 1990s (the last observation is 1997). All 14 countries have been democracies since the Second World War. There are a total of 61 observations, with the number of observations for each country ranging from 2 to 7. About one fifth of the observations are from the 1970s and late 1960s, about 40% from the 1980s, and the remainder from the 1990s. The data are based on separate national surveys, but considerable effort has gone into harmonizing (or "Lissifying") them to ensure comparability across countries and time. The LIS data are widely considered to be of high quality and the best available for the purposes of studying distribution and redistribution (see Brady 2003; OECD 1995).

As noted previously, we use the data specifically to explore the determinants of redistribution as measured by the percentage reduction in

the gini coefficient from before to after taxes and transfers. The gini coefficient is perhaps the best summary measure of inequality, and varies from 0 (when there is a perfectly even distribution of income) to 1 (when all income goes to the top decile). Using an adjusted version of the LIS data—constructed by Huber, Stephens, and their associates (Bradley et al. 2003)[1]—we include only working age families, primarily because generous public pension systems (especially in Scandinavia) discourage private savings and therefore exaggerate the degree of redistribution among older people. Furthermore, because data are only available at the household level, income is adjusted for household size using a standard square root divisor (see OECD 1995).

On the independent side, the key variables for explaining redistribution are government partisanship and electoral system. The first is an index of the partisan left-right "center of gravity" of the cabinet based on (1) the average of three expert classifications of government parties' placement on a left-right scale, weighted by (2) their decimal share of cabinet portfolios. The index goes from left to right and is standardized to vary between 0 and 1. The measure was conceived by Gross and Sigelman (1984) and has been applied to OECD countries by Cusack in a new comprehensive data set on parties and partisanship (see Cusack and Fuchs 2002 and Cusack and Engelhardt 2002 for details). The expert codings are from Castles and Mair (1984), Laver and Hunt (1992), and Huber and Inglehart (1995).

One issue raised by this measure is how we can be sure that partisan effects are due to differences in "who governs" as opposed to differences in voter preferences. Our argument is that the electoral system affects the party composition of governments, and hence government policies—*not* that electorates in different countries want different governments and policies (although that might of course also be the case). One way of making sure is to use the difference between the ideological center of gravity of the government and the ideological position of the median voter. Because the position of each party represented in the legislature is known, we can use the position of the party with the median legislator as a proxy for the median voter preference. Hence, we also test our model using this relative center of gravity measure. In cases with single-party majority governments (such as the current British Labour government)—where the government party controls the median legislator by definition—we use the *mean* position of the legislative parties weighted by the parties' seat shares (so that the Labour government would be recorded as being left of center).[2]

Turning to measurement of electoral system, the theoretical distinction between majoritarian two-party systems and proportional multiparty systems is roughly matched by differences in actual electoral systems (see Table 2). With the partial exception of Austria (because of the strong position of the two main parties), all PR systems tend to have multiple parties and coalition governments, whereas the non-PR systems have few parties and frequent single-party majority governments (although Australia and Ireland *have* experienced several instances of coalition governments).[3] This is indicated in the

Table 2. Key Indicators of Party and Electoral Systems

	Electoral System	Effective Number of Legislative Parties	Proportionality of Electoral System
Majoritarian			
Australia	Majority[a]	2.5	0.19
Canada	SMP	2.2	0.13
France	Runoff[b]	3.8	0.16
Ireland	STV[c]	2.8	0.70
Japan	SNTV[d]	2.7	0.61
New Zealand	SMP	2.0	0.00
UK	SMP	2.1	0.16
USA	SMP	1.9	0.39
Average		2.5	*0.30*
Proportional			
Austria	PR	2.4	0.89
Belgium	PR	5.2	0.86
Denmark	PR	4.4	0.96
Finland	PR	5.1	0.87
Germany	PR	2.6	0.91
Italy	PR	4.0	0.91
Netherlands	PR	4.6	1.00
Norway	PR	3.3	0.76
Sweden	PR	3.3	0.90
Average		3.9	*0.90*

a. The use of the single transferable vote in single-member constituencies makes the Australian electoral system a majority rather than plurality system.

b. The two-round runoff system has been in place for most of the postwar period with short interruptions of PR (1945 until early 1950s and 1986–88).

c. The Irish single transferable vote system (STV) is unique. Although sometimes classified as a PR system, the low constituency size (five or less) and the strong centripetal incentives for parties in the system makes it similar to a median-voter-dominated SMP system.

d. The single nontransferable voting (SNTV) in Japan (until 1994) deviates from SMP in that more than one candidate is elected from each district, but small district size and nontransferability make it clearly distinct from PR list systems.

third column of Table 2 using Laasko and Taagepera's (1979) measure of the effective number of parties in parliament.[4] France is somewhat of an outlier among the majoritarian cases, but the second round of voting in the French runoff system usually involves candidates from only two parties.

The division of countries into two electoral systems is bolstered by the quantitative proportionality measure in the last column. This is a composite index based on Lijphart's measure of the effective threshold of representation and Gallagher's measure of the disproportionality between votes and seats (data are from Lijphart 1994). Note that the index is consistent with the division into a majoritarian and a proportional group: there are no cases that should be "switched" based on their value on the index. All our results go through if we use this index instead of the PR-majoritarian dichotomy.

We also controlled for variables that are commonly assumed to affect redistribution and/or partisanship. These variables, with definitions, sources, as well as a short discussion of causal logic, are listed next.

PRETAX AND TRANSFER INEQUALITY

This variable is included to capture the Meltzer-Richard logic that more inequality leads to more redistribution. It is measured as the earnings of a worker in the 90th percentile of the earnings distribution as a share of the earnings of the worker with a median income. We are using earnings data, despite their limitations, because the Meltzer-Richard model applies to individuals, not households. The data is from OECD's wage dispersion data set (unpublished electronic data).

CONSTITUTIONAL VETO POINTS

Composite measure of federalism, presidentialism, bicameralism, and the frequency of referenda, based on Huber, Ragin, and Stephens (1993). The more independent decision nodes,

the more veto points. The left in countries with many veto points may have found it harder to overcome opposition to redistributive spending.

UNIONIZATION

According to power resource theory, high union density should lead to more political pressure for redistribution and a stronger left, whereas simultaneously reducing primary income inequality. The data are from Visser (1989, 1996).

VOTER TURNOUT

Lijphart (1997) argues that there is much evidence to the effect that voter nonturnout is concentrated among the poor. Higher turnout may therefore be associated with less redistribution. The turnout data are from annual records in Mackie and Rose (1991) and in International Institute for Democracy and Electoral Assistance (1997).

UNEMPLOYMENT

Because the unemployed receive no wage income, they are typically poor in the absence of transfers. Because all countries have public unemployment insurance, higher unemployment will therefore "automatically" be linked to more redistribution. We use standardized rates from OECD, *Labour Force Statistics* (Paris: OECD, various years).

REAL PER CAPITA INCOME

This is a standard control to capture "Wagner's Law," which says that demand for social insurance is income elastic. The data are expressed in constant 1985 dollars and are from the World Bank's Global Development Network Growth Database (http://www.worldbank.org/research/growth/GDNdata.htm)—itself based on Penn World Table 5.6, Global Development Finance and World Development Indicators.

FEMALE LABOR FORCE PARTICIPATION

Women's participation in the labor market is likely to affect redistributive spending because it entitles some women to benefits (unemployment insurance, health insurance, etc.) for which they would otherwise be ineligible. Because women tend to be lower paid it may also increase support for the left and for redistributive policies. The measure is female labor force participation as a percentage of the working age population and is taken from OECD, *Labour Force Statistics*, Paris: OECD, various years.

*   *   *

Findings

REDISTRIBUTION

We begin our presentation with the results from estimating a simple baseline model with economic variables only (column 1 in Table 3). As expected, female labor force participation and unemployment are associated with more redistribution. Contrary to Wagner's Law, higher per capita income slightly reduces redistribution, although the result is not statistically significant across model specifications.

As in other studies, we also find that inequality of pretax and transfer earnings has a *negative* effect on redistribution, contrary to the Meltzer-Richard model expectation. This negative effect is statistically significant at a .01 level, and the substantive impact is strong: a 1 SD increase in inequality is associated with a .3 standard deviation reduction in redistribution.

Yet the effect of inequality *reverses* (though the positive effect is not significant) when we include controls for the political-institutional variables (columns 2–4). One likely reason for this change is that left governments, as well as strong unions and PR, not only cause an increase in redistribution but also reduce inequality. Ansell (2005), for example, has found strong evidence that left governments spend more on primary

education, which is likely to increase the equality of the wage structure. If so, excluding partisanship produces an omitted variable bias on the coefficient for inequality.

The most important result in Table 3 is that right partisanship has a strong and statistically significant negative effect on redistribution, regardless of whether we use the absolute (column 2) or the relative (column 3) measure of partisanship. A 1 SD shift to the right reduces redistribution by about 1/3 SD. This confirms previous research, especially that of Bradley et al. (2003), and it adds the finding that partisanship matters *even* when measured relative to the ideological center of the legislature. This is important to our story because it implies that political parties, and the coalitions they form, matter for redistribution—not just differences in the preferences of electorates.

The results also suggest that multiple veto points, as expected, reduce redistribution, and that PR has a direct (positive) effect on redistribution. The latter effect holds regardless of which measure of electoral system in Table 2 that we use. Our model suggests one possible reason for this because if the probability of left deviation from a median voter platform is not too high, center-left governments will always redistribute more to the poor under PR than under majoritarian rules. To test this, we ran the same model using the percentage reduction in the poverty rate instead of reduction in the gini coefficient as the dependent variable. Consistent with this proposition it turns out that whereas the effect of partisanship is about the same, the direct effect of PR is notably stronger.[5]

There may also be effects of electoral systems that we have not modeled. Persson and Tabellini (2003), for example, have argued that single member plurality systems incentivize politicians to target spending on geographically concentrated constituencies, whereas PR, with ideally only one electoral district, encourages politicians to spend more on universalistic benefit programs. Because universalistic programs are likely to be more redistributive than geographi-

Table 3. Regression Results for Reduction in Inequality (Standard Errors in Parentheses)

	(1)	(2)	(3)
Inequality	−16.75***	13.17	12.48
	(5.68)	(9.36)	(8.96)
Political–institutional variables			
Government partisanship (right)	—	−2.38***	—
		(0.73)	
Government partisanship relative to	—	—	−2.93***
median legislator			(0.75)
Voter turnout	—	0.01	−0.06
		(0.10)	(0.10)
Unionization	—	0.16*	0.15*
		(0.09)	(0.09)
Number of veto points	—	−1.57**	−1.79***
		(0.62)	(0.59)
Electoral system (PR)	—	5.00**	4.44**
Controls		(2.15)	(2.06)
Per capita income	−0.001***	−0.001	−0.001
	(0.00)	(0.00)	(0.000)
Female labor force	0.73***	0.36	0.45***
participation	(0.11)	(0.20)	(0.20)
Unemployment	0.81***	0.99***	1.08***
	(0.27)	(0.27)	(0.26)
ρ	.4	.7	.7
R-squared	0.648	0.746	0.765
N	47	47	47

Note: *Significance levels*: *** < .01; ** < .05; * < .10 (two-tailed tests). All independent variables are measures of the cumulative effect of these variables between observations on the dependent variable. See regression equation and text for details.

cally targeted programs, this would mean that PR has a direct effect on redistribution. But our focus is on the effect of electoral system on partisanship, to which we now turn.

PARTISANSHIP

Whereas both government partisanship and electoral system are important in explaining redistribution, partisanship itself is shaped by the distinct coalitional politics associated with different electoral systems. A key implication of our argument is that center-left governments tend to dominate over long periods of time under PR, whereas center-right governments tend to dominate under majoritarian institutions. Although

the electoral system has a direct effect on redistribution, we argue that partisanship is one of the key mechanisms through which it exerts an effect on redistribution. * * *

Conclusion

The details of actual tax-and-spend policies for the purpose of redistribution are complex, but the explanation for redistribution in advanced democracies is arguably fairly simple. We propose here that to a very considerable extent, redistribution is the result of electoral systems and the class coalitions they engender. The contribution of this paper is to provide a very general model that explains the electoral system effect, and to empirically test this model.

To explain redistributive policies under democracy, it is essential to understand that policies are multidimensional and that groups have to form partisan coalitions to govern. Both features of redistributive politics are assumed away in standard political economy models that follow the setup in Meltzer and Richard (1981). In our model, by contrast, there is nothing that prevents the poor from taking from the middle class, or the middle class taking from the rich. This means that the middle class, which tends to decide who governs, has an incentive to ally with the poor to exploit the rich, but also an incentive to support the rich to avoid being exploited by the poor. In a majoritarian two-party system, the latter motive dominates because the middle-class cannot be sure that the poor will not set policies in a center-left leadership party. In a PR system with three representative parties, on the other hand, the first motive dominates because the middle-class party *can* make sure that a coalition with the left party will not deviate from pursuing their common interest in taxing and redistributing from the rich. The center-right governments therefore tend to dominate in majoritarian systems, whereas the center-left governments tend to dominate in PR systems.

NOTES

1. We are grateful to the authors for letting us use their data.
2. We did the same in a small number of cases where the government position is equivalent to the median legislator, but where it is not a single-party majority government.
3. Ireland is perhaps the most ambiguous case, but it is not part of the redistribution regression, and the results for partisanship are not sensitive to the particular electoral system measure we use or whether Ireland is included or excluded.

4. The effective number of parties is defined as one divided by the sum of the square root of the shares of seats held by different parties (or one divided by the Hilferding index).
5. The effect of going from a majoritarian system to a PR system is to increase redistribution to the poor by .7 SD whereas the effect on the gini coefficient is .5 SD.

REFERENCES

Ansell, Ben. 2005. "From the Ballot to the Blackboard? Partisan and Institutional Effects on Human Capital Policy in the OECD. Department of Government." Harvard University. Typescript.

Austen-Smith, David. 2000. "Redistributing Income Under Proportional Representation." *Journal of Political Economy* 108 (6): 1235–69.

Bénabou, Roland. 1996. "Inequality and Growth." In *National Bureau of Economic Research Macro Annual*, ed. Ben S. Bernanke and Julio J. Rotemberg, Cambridge: MIT Press, Vol. 11, pp. 11–74.

Boix, Carles. 1998. *Political Parties, Growth and Equality*. New York: Cambridge University Press.

Bradley David, Evelyne Huber, Stephanie Moller, François Nielsen, and John Stephens. 2003. "Distribution and Redistribution in Postindustrial Democracies." *World Politics* 55 (2): 193–228.

Brady, David. 2003. "Rethinking the Sociological Measure of Poverty." *Social Forces* 81 (3): 715–52.

Castles, Francis, and Peter Mair. 1984. "Left-Right Political Scales: Some Expert Judgments." *European Journal of Political Research* 12: 73–88.

Cusack, Thomas R., and Lutz Engelhardt. 2002. "The PGL File Collection: File Structures and Procedures." Wissenschaftszentrum Berlin für Sozialforschung.

Cusack, Thomas R., and Susanne Fuchs. 2002. "Documentation Notes for Parties, Governments, and Legislatures Data Set." Wissenschaftszentrum Berlin für Sozialforschung.

Gross, Donald A., and Lee Sigelman. 1984. "Comparing Party Systems: A Multidimensional Approach." *Comparative Politics* 16: 463–79.

Hicks, Alexander, and Duane Swank. 1992. "Politics, Institutions, and Welfare Spending in Industrialized Democracies, 1960–82." *American Political Science Review* 86 (3): 649–74.

Huber, Evelyne, Charles Ragin, and John Stephens. 1993. "Social Democracy, Christian Democracy, Constitutional Structure and the Welfare State." *American Journal of Sociology* 99 (3): 711–49.

Huber, Evelyne, and John D. Stephens. 2001. *Development and Crisis of the Welfare State: Parties and Policies in Global Markets*. Chicago: University of Chicago Press.

Huber, John D., and Ronald Inglehart. 1995. "Expert Interpretations of Party Space and Party Locations in 42 Societies." *Party Politics* 1: 73–111.

International Institute for Democracy and Electoral Assistance. 1997. *Voter Turnout from 1945 to 1997: A Global Report on Political Participation*. Stockholm: IDEA Information Services.

Korpi, Walter. 1983. *The Democratic Class Struggle*. London: Routledge & Kegan Paul.

Korpi, Walter. 1989. "Power, Politics and State Autonomy in the Development of Social Citizenship—Social Rights During Sickness in 18 OECD Countries Since 1930." *American Sociological Review* 54 (3): 309–28.

Kwon, Hyeok Yong, and Jonas Pontusson. 2003. "The Zone of Partisanship, Parties, Unions and Welfare Spending on OECD Countries, 1962–99." Unpublished Manuscript, Department of Political Science, Cornell University.

Laasko, Markku, and Rein Taagepera. 1979. "Effective Number of Parties: A Measure with Applications to Western Europe." *Comparative Political Studies* 12 (3): 3–27.

Laver, Michael, and W. Ben Hunt. 1992. *Policy and Party Competition*. New York: Routledge.

Lijphart, Arend. 1994. *Electoral Systems and Party Systems: A Study of Twenty-Seven Democracies, 1945–90*. New York: Oxford University Press.

Lijphart, Arend. 1997. "Unequal Participation: Democracy's Unresolved Dilemma." *American Political Science Review* 91: 1–14.

Mackie, Thomas T., and Richard Rose. 1991. *The International Almanac of Electoral History*, 3rd edition. London: Macmillan.

Meltzer, Allan H., and Scott F. Richard. 1981. "A Rational Theory of the Size of Government." *Journal of Political Economy* 89: 914–27.

Moene, Karl Ove, and Michael Wallerstein. 2001. "Inequality, Social Insurance and Redistribution." *American Political Science Review* 95 (4): 859–74.

OECD. 1995. "Income Distribution in OECD Countries: Evidence from the Luxembourg Income Study." *Social Policy Studies* No. 18.

Perotti, Roberto. 1996. "Growth, Income Distribution and Democracy: What the Data Say." *Journal of Economic Growth* 1 (2): 149–87.

Persson, Torsten, and Guido Tabellini. 1999. "The Size and Scope of Government: Comparative Politics with Rational Politicians." *European Economic Review* 43: 699–735.

Persson, Torsten, and Guido Tabellini. 2000. *Political Economics: Explaining Economic Policy*. Cambridge: MIT Press.

Persson, Torsten, and Guido Tabellini. 2003. *The Economic Effects of Constitutions*. MIT Press.

Powell, Bingham. 2002. "PR, the Median Voter, and Economic Policy: An Exploration." Paper presented at the 2002 Meetings of the American Political Science Association, Boston.

Rogowski, Ronald, and Mark Andreas Kayser. 2002. "Majoritarian Electoral Systems and Consumer Power: Price-level Evidence from the OECD Countries." *American Journal of Political Science* 46 (3): 526–39.

Ross, Michael. 2005. "Does Democracy Reduce Infant Mortality?" Paper presented in Workshop on Democratic Institutions and Economic Performance. Duke University. April 1–2, 2005.

Visser, Jelle. 1989. *European Trade Unions in*

Figures. Deventer/Netherlands: Kluwer Law and Taxation Publishers.

Visser, Jelle. 1996. "Unionization Trends Revisited." Mimeo. University of Amsterdam.

THE ECONOMIST

IS GOVERNMENT DISAPPEARING?

Not As Quickly As One Might Wish

Economists are often accused of greeting some item of news with the observation, "That may be so in practice, but is it true in theory?" Sceptics too seem much more interested in superficially plausible theories about the diminishing power of the state than in the plain facts.

In practice, though perhaps not in theory, governments around the world on average are now collecting slightly more in taxes—not just in absolute terms, but as a proportion of their bigger economies—than they did ten years ago. This is true of the G7 countries, and of the smaller OECD economies as well (see chart 1). The depredations of rampant capitalists on the overall ability of governments to gather income and do good works are therefore invisible. These findings are so strange in theory that many economic analysts have decided not to believe them.

Tax burdens vary a lot from country to country—something else which is wrong in theory. Despite the variations, governments in all the advanced economies are well provided for. The United States is invoked by some European anti-globalists as the land of naked capitalism, the nadir of "private affluence and public squalor" to

Chart 1   *Onward and Upward*
General Government Receipts, % of GDP

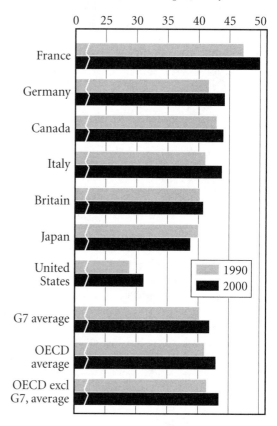

From *The Economist* (September 27, 2001), pp. 14–18.

Source: OECD

which other countries are being driven down. Well, its government collected a little over 30% of GDP in taxes last year: an average of some $30,000 per household, adding up to roughly $3 trillion. This is a somewhat larger figure than the national income of Germany, and it goes a long way if spent wisely.

At the other extreme is Sweden, despite its celebrated taxpayer revolt of the early 1990s. Last year its taxes came to 57% of GDP, a savage reduction of three percentage points since 1990. Next comes Denmark, on 53%, fractionally higher than in 1990. And here's a funny thing. Sweden and Denmark are among the most open economies in the world, far more open than the United States. Denmark's ratio of imports to national income is 33%, compared with America's 14%. And in common with other advanced economies, neither of these Scandinavian countries has capital controls to keep investment penned in.

Harvard's Dani Rodrik, one of the more careful and persuasive globalisation sceptics, has written: "Globalisation has made it exceedingly difficult for government to provide social insurance . . . At present, international economic integration is taking place against the background of receding governments and diminished social obligations. The welfare state has been under attack for two decades." Sweden, admittedly, is reeling, its government now able to collect only 57% of GDP in tax. But plucky Denmark is resisting these attacks well, and so is most of the rest of Europe.

Money Isn't Everything

Even if taxes were falling precipitously, it would be absurd to claim, as many globalisation sceptics do, that companies are nowadays more powerful than governments. It is routine to be told, as in *The Silent Takeover*, a new book by a Cambridge University academic, Noreena Hertz, things like this: "51 of the 100 biggest economies in the world are now corporations." Quite what

that implies is never explained: readers are invited to draw their own conclusion about the relative power of governments and companies.

Before you even think about whether it makes sense to weigh corporate power against state power, you can see that this particular comparison, which measures the size of companies by their sales, is bogus. National income is a measure of value added. It cannot be compared with a company's sales (equal to value added plus the cost of inputs). But even if that tiresome, endlessly repeated error were corrected, there would be no sense in comparing companies with governments in terms of their power over people.

The power of even the biggest companies is nothing compared with that of governments—no matter how small or poor the country concerned. The value added of Microsoft is a little over $20 billion a year, about the same as the national income of Uruguay. Does this make it remotely plausible that Bill Gates has more sway over the people of Uruguay than their government does? Or take Luxembourg—another small economy with, presumably, a correspondingly feeble state. Can Microsoft tax the citizens of Luxembourg (whose government collected 45% of GDP from them last year), conscript them if it has a mind to, arrest and imprison them for behaviour it disapproves of, or deploy physical force against them at will? No, not even using Windows XP.

But those are specious comparisons, you might reply. Of course Bill Gates is less powerful than the government of Uruguay in Uruguay, but Mr. Gates exercises his power, such as it is, globally. Well then, where, exactly, is Mr. Gates supposed to be as powerful in relation to the government as the alarming comparison between value added and national income implies? And if Bill Gates does not have this enormous power in any particular country or countries, he does not have it at all. In other words, the power that Mr. Gates exercises globally is over Microsoft. Every government he ever meets is more powerful than he is in relation to its own citizens.

In a war between two countries, national income is relevant as a measure of available resources. If companies raised armies and fought wars, their wealth would count for something. But they don't, and couldn't: they lack the power. Big companies do have political influence. They have the money to lobby politicians and, in many countries, to corrupt them. Even so, the idea that companies have powers over citizens remotely as great as those of governments—no matter how big the company, no matter how small or poor the country—is fatuous. Yet it is never so much as questioned by anti-globalists.

Any power to tax, however limited, gives a country more political clout than Microsoft or General Electric could dream of. But how can a small, exceptionally open economy such as Denmark manage to collect more than 50% of GDP in taxes, in utter defiance of the logic of global capitalism? The answer seems inescapable: Denmark no longer exists, and questions are starting to be asked about the existence of many other European countries. At least, that is how it looks in theory; in practice, the theory needs to be looked at again.

The Limits of Government

The alleged squeeze on government arises from the fact that, in a world of integrated economies, again in Mr. Rodrik's words, "owners of capital, highly skilled workers, and many professionals . . . are free to take their resources where they are most in demand." The people Mr. Rodrik refers to have high incomes. Through the taxes they pay, they make an indispensable contribution to the public finances. If economic integration allows capital and skills to migrate to low-tax jurisdictions, the tax base will shrink. Governments will find themselves unable to finance social programmes, safety nets or redistribution of income. Anticipating this flight of capital and skills, governments have to cut taxes and dismantle the welfare state before the migration gets under way. Markets triumph over democracy.

That is the theory. Experience largely refutes it, but it is not entirely wrong. In a variety of ways, economic integration does put limits on what governments can do. However, some of those constraints are eminently desirable. Integration makes it harder to be a tyrant. Governments have been known to oppress their subjects. Oppression is more difficult with open borders: people can leave and take their savings with them. In such cases, global markets are plainly an ally of human rights.

The affinity of totalitarianism and economic isolation was obvious in the case of the Soviet Union and communist Eastern Europe; it is still plain today in the case of North Korea, say. But democracies are capable of oppression too. It would therefore be wrong to conclude that integration is undesirable merely because it limits the power of government, even if the government concerned is democratic. One needs to recognise that some constraints on democracy are desirable, and then to ask whether the constraints imposed by markets are too tight.

These issues are rarely, if ever, addressed by the critics of globalisation: it is simpler to deplore the notion of "profits before people." The sceptics either insist, or regard it as too obvious even to mention, that the will of the people, democratically expressed, must always prevail. This is amazingly naive. Even the most elementary account of democracy recognises the need for checks and balances, including curbs on the majoritarian "will of the people." Failing those, democracies are capable of tyranny over minorities.

The sceptics are terribly keen on "the people." Yet the idea that citizens are not individuals with different goals and preferences, but an undifferentiated body with agreed common interests, defined in opposition to other monolithic interests such as "business" or "foreigners," is not just shallow populism, it is proto-fascism. It is self-contradictory, as well. The sceptics would not hesitate to call for "the people" to be overruled if, for instance, they voted for policies that violated human rights, or speeded the extermination of endangered species, or offended against other values the sceptics regard as more fundamental than honouring the will of the majority.

The possibility that people might leave is not the only curb that economic integration puts on government. The global flow of information, a by-product of the integration of markets, also works to that effect. It lets attention be drawn to abuses of all kinds: of people especially, but also of the environment or of other things that the sceptics want to protect. Undeniably, it also fosters a broader kind of policy competition among governments. This works not through the sort of mechanical market arbitrage that would drive down taxes regardless of what citizens might want, but through informing voters about alternatives, thus making them more demanding.

The fashion for economic liberalisation in recent years owes something to the remarkable success of the American economy during the 1990s: a success which, thanks to globalisation, has been seen and reflected upon all over the world. Growing knowledge about the West helped precipitate the liberation of Eastern Europe. But information of this kind need not always favour the market. For instance, the failure of the American government to extend adequate health care to all its citizens has been noticed as well, and voters in countries with universal publicly financed healthcare systems do not, on the whole, want to copy this particular model. The global flow of knowledge creates, among other things, better-informed voters, and therefore acts as a curb on government power. This does nothing but good.

The anti-globalists themselves, somewhat self-contradictorily, use the information-spreading aspect of globalisation to great effect. Organising a worldwide protest movement would be much harder without the World Wide Web, but the web itself is merely one dimension of globalisation. The economic integration that sceptics disapprove of is in many ways necessary for effective resistance to the more specific things they object to—not all of which, by any means, are themselves the products of globalisation.

Still, all this is to acknowledge that economic integration does limit the power of government, including democratic government. The question is whether it limits it too much, or in undesirable ways. So far as far public spending is concerned, the answer seems clear. Given that even in conditions of economic integration people are willing to tolerate tax burdens approaching 60% of GDP, and that tax burdens of between 40% and 55% of GDP are routine in industrial economies other than the United States, the limits are plainly not that tight. These figures say that democracy has plenty of room for manoeuvre.

The Mystery of the Missing Tax Cut

One puzzle remains: why are taxes not coming down? There are several answers. One is that international integration is far from complete, and is likely to remain so. Technology has caused distance to shrink, but not to disappear. National borders still matter as well, even more than mere distance, and far more than all the interest in globalisation might lead you to expect. For all but the smallest economies, trade and investment are still disproportionately intranational rather than international. Especially in the developed world, borders still count not so much because of overt protectionist barriers, but because countries remain jurisdictionally and administratively distinct. This is not likely to change in the foreseeable future.

For instance, if a supplier defaults on a contract to sell you something, it is much easier to get legal redress if your seller is in the same country (and subject to the same legal authority) than it would be if you had to sue in a foreign court. Because of these difficulties in contracting, trading across borders still calls for much more trust between buyers and sellers than trading within borders—so much so as to rule out many transactions. This remains true even in systems such as the European Union's, where heroic efforts have been made to overcome inadvertent obstacles to trade, suggesting that they will prove even more durable everywhere else.

You would expect the international mobility of capital to be especially high, given that the costs of physically transporting the stuff are virtually zero, yet it is surprising just how relatively immobile even capital remains. In the aggregate, the flow of capital into or out of any given country can be thought of as balancing that country's saving and investment. If the country invests more than it saves (that is, if it runs a current-account deficit), capital flows in; if it saves more than it invests (a current-account surplus), the country must lend capital to the rest of the world. Perfect capital mobility would imply that, country by country, national saving and investment would move freely in relation to each other. Very large inflows or outflows of capital in relation to national income would be the order of the day. In fact they are not. Nowadays, a surplus or deficit of just a few percentage points of GDP is regarded as big.

Still, capital is much more mobile than labour—and mobile enough, to be sure, to have given rise to some tax competition among governments. So far this competition has affected the structure of tax codes rather than overall tax burdens; total yields have been unaffected. In an effort to attract inflows of capital, and especially inflows of foreign direct investment, governments have been lowering their tax rates for corporate income and raising them for personal income, or relying more on a variety of indirect taxes, or both (see chart 2). But it is easy to exaggerate the extent even of this structural shift, never mind the effect on total taxation. This is because taxes on corporate income were small to begin with, so not much was at stake. In fact, heavy reliance on corporate taxes is bad policy even in a closed economy. Indeed, in a closed economy, you can make a respectable case on efficiency grounds for excluding corporate income from taxes altogether.

Taxes on company profits, the argument goes, are taxes on shareholders' income—ultimately, that is, taxes on a particular category of personal income. In the end, although it is politically convenient to pretend otherwise, "the people" pay all the taxes: companies are mere intermediaries.

There is no reason to tax the income people receive as shareholders any differently from the income they receive as owners of bank deposits or as workers. In a closed economy, you might as well abolish the corporate-income tax and instead tax profits when they turn up as dividends in the incomes of individual taxpayers: it is simpler, and it is less likely to affect investment decisions in unintended ways.

In an open economy, however, company ownership is to some extent in the hand of foreigners, not just the citizens of the country where the company is based. This makes it more tempting to tax corporate income, because this allows the government to bring foreigners within the scope of its tax base. Seen this way, it is odd to blame globalisation for downward pressure on corporate-tax rates. Were it not for globalisation, there would be no reason to have corporate

Chart 2   ***Count the Ways***
OECD Tax Mix, % of GDP

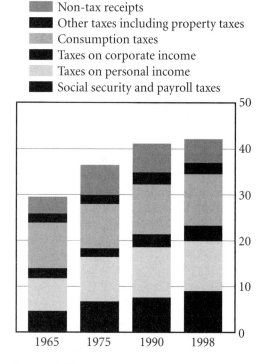

Non-tax receipts
Other taxes including property taxes
Consumption taxes
Taxes on corporate income
Taxes on personal income
Social security and payroll taxes

Source: OECD

taxes in the first place. But it is true that once you are collecting corporate taxes, greater capital mobility limits your take. Economic integration rationalises, and at the same time limits, reliance on corporate-income taxes. The issue is subtler than it seems.

Staying Put

But what matters far more than corporate tax policy is that most people, skilled as well as unskilled, are reluctant to move abroad. Since workers tend to stay put, governments can tax them at surprisingly high rates without provoking flight. In all but extreme cases, the democratic constraint (the need to secure a broad measure of popular support for tax increases) binds governments long before the economic constraint imposed by international integration (the risk that groups facing very high taxes will leave). In the case of taxes on profits, it is true that the economic constraint will bind before the democratic one, and that globalisation serves to tighten the economic constraint further—but this does not matter. There is no need for high taxes on profits if people are willing to hand over 50% or more of what they produce in the form of taxes on income and consumption.

To simple-minded believers in the most desiccated branch of neoclassical economics, all this may seem surprising. Their theories regard people as "rational economic men," narrow utility-maximisers with no ties to family, place or culture. Presumably, these ciphers would shop around for low-tax jurisdictions. Oddly, the same benighted view of human nature must be shared by many globalisation sceptics—otherwise, why would they fear taxpayer flight on a scale sufficient to abolish the European welfare state? But in real life, it is better to take a fuller, broader view of the human condition. Since people seem to choose to be tied down, indeed to relish it, governments, within broad limits, can carry on taxing them regardless of globalisation. If it seems prudent to cut taxes on profits in order to attract inflows of foreign investment, no problem. Taxes on people will still be sufficient to finance generous public spending of every kind.

Be Very Afraid

Many anti-globalists have strangely little confidence in the merits of the policies they are anxious to sustain. Fearing what may be lost if globalisation continues uncurbed, Mr. Rodrik writes:

> If it was the 19th century that unleashed capitalism in its full force, it was the 20th century that tamed it and boosted its productivity by supplying the institutional underpinnings of market-based economies. Central banks to regulate credit and the supply of liquidity, fiscal policies to stabilise aggregate demand, antitrust and regulatory authorities to combat fraud and anti-competitive behaviour, social insurance to reduce lifetime risk, political democracy to make the above institutions accountable to the citizenry—these were all innovations that firmly took root in today's rich countries only during the second half of the 20th century. That the second half of the century was also a period of unprecedented prosperity for Western Europe, the United States, Japan and some other parts of East Asia is no coincidence. These institutional innovations greatly enhanced the efficiency and legitimacy of markets and in turn drew strength from the material advancement unleashed by market forces . . . The dilemma that we face as we enter the 21st century is that markets are striving to become global while the institutions needed to support them remain by and large national . . . The desire by producers and investors to go global weakens the institutional base of national economies.

The argument, presumably, is that international capital will flow away from countries with the high public spending and taxes that these highly developed institutions involve. One answer is that international investment, as already noted, is much less important in most countries than domestic investment. But a more fundamental question is this: why should foreign capital flow away from countries that have equipped themselves with these institutions, if, as Mr. Rodrik emphasises, those arrangements have "boosted . . . productivity" and "greatly enhanced the efficiency . . . of markets"—so much so that the most ambitious period of national institution-building was also a time of growing and "unprecedented" prosperity for the nations that joined in?

If public spending boosts productivity, then competition among governments for inward investment is likely to favour more public spending (and the taxes needed to pay for it), not less. Suppose, as seems plausible, that public spending on education raises productivity by increasing the supply of skilled workers. Then you would expect international investment to be drawn to countries that invest heavily in top-quality schools and universities. Suppose, as may also be true, that public spending on social programmes such as health and welfare raises productivity, by producing a healthier and more contented workforce, with better labour relations and greater labour mobility. If so, again international capital will be drawn to countries that spend money on those things. Globalisation, surely, will not frown on policies whose net effect is to foster productivity and efficiency.

But what about policies that do not serve those goals? Many would argue, for instance, that welfare policies, especially if too generous, encourage idleness and reduce economy-wide productivity. Suppose that is true. Also suppose that, knowing it to be true, most people want such policies anyway. You might feel that they are entitled to that opinion, and in a democracy they are entitled to get their way. Another example might be policies to limit working hours. Suppose that they reduce productivity, but that people vote for them anyway. Must globalisation overrule democracy?

Globalisation v. Democracy

The answer even in this case is no—and to see why is to understand why so many of the fears about globalisation and democracy are groundless. Policies that reduce productivity do, in the

first instance, cut a country's feasible standard of living, narrowly defined in terms of GDP per head. But what happens after that? If a country that is open to international trade and capital flows adopts some such policies, perhaps on the ground that they will raise living standards according to some broader definition, wages and profits will fall relative to what they would otherwise have been. Next, investment will fall and the capital stock will shrink, again compared with what they would otherwise have been. This will continue until the scarcity of capital drives the rate of profit back up, at the margin, to the rate prevailing in the global capital market.

All this time the economy will grow more slowly than if the policies had not been followed. Once the economy has adjusted, however, it remains as "competitive" as it was at the outset: lower wages have restored labour costs per unit of output, and a smaller stock of capital has restored the return on capital. The economy has grown more slowly for a spell. It is less prosperous than it would have been. But in due course, once wages and profits have adjusted, the economy will again be as attractive, or unattractive, to foreign investors as it was at the outset. The government's adoption of policies that compromise efficiency is not punished by excommunication from the global economy, or with an accelerating spiral of decline; the only penalty is compromised efficiency and lower measured incomes, which is what the country chose in the first place.

Would the economy have fared any better without globalisation? Had it been closed to international flows of goods and capital, could it have adopted those productivity-cutting policies and paid no price at all? The answer is no. Even in a closed economy, policies that reduce productivity would cause wages and profits to fall, as in the open-economy case. The return on capital would be lower, so saving and investment would decline, relative to what they would have been (there would be no cross-border capital flows in this case, so saving and investment must always be equal). The capital stock would shrink and growth would be held back until the scarcity of capital drove the return back up. As in the open-economy case, the result would be a spell of slower growth and a standard of living permanently lower than it would otherwise have been.

The main difference is probably that in the closed-economy case, the losses would be subtracted from an economy that is already very much poorer than its open-economy counterpart, because it is closed. Conceivably, this would make further losses politically easier to sustain. But that is the most you can say in defence of the view that globalisation forbids social policies which jeopardise productivity. "Stay poor, because once you start to get rich you may find that you like it." Not exactly compelling, is it?

You might well conclude from all this that globalisation, if anything, will lead to higher rather than lower social spending. As argued earlier, globalisation raises aggregate incomes but at the same time increases economic insecurity for certain groups. Both of these consequences tend to raise social spending. Generous social spending is a "superior good": as countries grow richer, they want to spend more of their incomes on it, and can afford to. At the same time, quite separately, greater economic insecurity directly spurs demand for social spending.

Given that globalisation increases the demand for social spending; given that it does not rule out any decision to increase such spending which harms productivity, any more than a closed economy would; given that increases in social spending which raise productivity will be rewarded with inflows of capital; given all this, should globalisation and the generous social spending that democracies favour not go hand in hand? They should, and indeed rising social spending alongside faster, deeper globalisation is exactly what the figures for the past several decades show.

Governments in rich countries need to look again at their social policies, partly to make sure that temporary and longer-term losers from globalisation, and from economic growth in general, get well-designed help. But there is no reason whatever to fear that globalisation makes social policies more difficult to finance. In the end, by raising incomes in the aggregate, it makes them easier to finance. It creates additional economic resources, which democracies can use as they see fit.

MARGARITA ESTÉVEZ-ABE, TORBEN IVERSEN, AND DAVID SOSKICE

SOCIAL PROTECTION AND THE FORMATION OF SKILLS: A REINTERPRETATION OF THE WELFARE STATE

Introduction

Social protection rescues the market from itself by preventing market failures. More specifically, * * * social protection * * *

From Peter A. Hall and David Soskice, eds., *Varieties of Capitalism: The Institutional Foundations of Comparative Advantage* (New York: Oxford University Press, 2001), pp. 145–183.

[helps] economic actors overcome market failures in skill formation. We show, in this chapter, that different types of social protection are complementary to different skill equilibria. * * *

Young people are less likely to invest in specific skills if the risk of loss of employment opportunities that require those specific skills is high. Employers who rely on specific skills to compete effectively in international markets therefore need to institutionalize some sort of guarantee to insure workers against potential risks. Without implicit agreements for long-term employment and real wage stability, their specific skills will be under-supplied. Employers' promises are not, however, sufficiently credible by themselves. This is why social protection as governmental policy becomes critical. * * *

Institutional differences that safeguard returns on specific skills explain why workers and employers invest more in specific skills. The absence of such institutions, in countries such as the USA and UK, gives workers a strong incentive to invest in transferable skills. In such an environment, it then also makes more economic sense for firms to pursue product market strategies that use these transferable skills intensely. * * *

The model of micro-level links between skills and social protection we develop in this chapter has important policy implications. First, our model predicts what types of political alliance are likely to emerge in support of a particular type of social protection. For example, in economies where companies engage in product market strategies that require a combination of firm- and industry-specific skills, and where a large number of workers invest in such skills, a strong alliance between skilled workers and their employers in favor of social protection advantageous to them is likely to emerge—even if this means reducing job opportunities for low-skilled workers. By contrast, where business has no common interest in the promotion of specific skills, it will have no interest in defending * * * social protection. Second, we show that different systems of social protection have deeper ramifications for inequality than commonly assumed. Some skill equilibria—sustained by different systems of social protection—produce more inequalities based on the academic background of workers, while others produce more inequalities based on gender.

* * *

Product Market Strategies, Skill Types, and The Welfare State

* * *

Skills and Product Market Strategies

[We distinguish] three types of skills associated with different product market strategies: (i) firm-specific skills; (ii) industry-specific skills; and (iii) general skills.[1] These skills differ significantly in terms of their asset specificity (i.e. portability). Firm-specific skills are acquired through on-the-job training, and are least portable. They are valuable to the employer who carried out the training but not to other employers. Industry-specific skills are acquired through apprenticeship and vocational schools. These skills, especially when authoritatively certified, are recognized by any employer within a specific trade. General skills, recognized by all employers, carry a value that is independent of the type of firm or industry. Of course, any actual production system will involve all three types of skills to some degree. Nonetheless, we can characterize distinctive product market strategies based upon the "skill profile" they require.

* * * [M]ass production of standardized goods does not require a highly trained workforce. Production work is broken into a narrow range of standardized tasks that only require semi-skilled workers. Traditional US manufacturing industries such as automobile and other consumer durables fall into this category. There is, however, a variant of mass production called diversified mass production (DMP). The DMP strategy, in contrast, aims at producing a varied range of products in large volumes. Japanese auto-makers and domestic electronic appliances industry are good examples. This production strategy depends on workers capable of performing a wide range of tasks to enable frequent product changes in the line (Koike 1981). Workers are also expected to solve problems that

emerge in the production line themselves to minimize downtime (Shibata 1999). The tasks these workers perform involve high levels of knowledge about their company products and machineries in use, and hence are highly firm-specific.

There are product market strategies that do not mass produce. One strategy is a high-quality product niche market strategy. It requires a highly trained workforce with industry-specific craft skills. The prototype of this production strategy does not involve any scale merit, and the process tends to involve highly craft-intensive workshops. Custom-made clothing, jewelry, and fine porcelain may be examples of such production. Another strategy is a hybrid. It pursues high-quality product lines, but takes the production out of small-scale craft shops in order to increase the volume of production. Streeck (1992b) calls this diversified quality production. This production strategy requires firm-specific skills in addition to high levels of craft skills. Germany is a prototype of this type of production.

All the above strategies require firm-specific and industry-specific skills to varying degrees. It is important, however, to note that relative abundance of high levels of general skills (i.e. university and postgraduate qualifications) brings comparative advantages in radical product innovation. Let us take the example of the USA to illustrate this point. For example, start-up software companies in the USA take advantage of a highly flexible labor market with university-educated people combining excellent general skills with valuable knowledge about the industry acquired from switching from one job to another. Another example would be American financial institutions, which have taken advantage of an abundant supply of math Ph.D.s to develop new products such as derivatives. Complex systems development (for e-commerce, for example), biotechnology, segments of the telecommunications industry, and advanced consulting services are other examples that fall into this class of industries.

The Welfare-Skill Formation Nexus

We make the three following assumptions about workers' economic behavior:

(i) *People calculate overall return to their educational/training investment before deciding to commit themselves. (The investment cost of further training and education can be conceptualized in terms of wages forgone during the period of training and education, in addition to any tuition or training fees incurred.)*

(ii) *People choose to invest in those skills that generate higher expected returns, provided that the riskiness of the investments is identical.*

(iii) Ceteris paribus, *people refrain from investing in skills that have more uncertain future returns (i.e. people are risk averse).*

From these assumptions, it follows that a rational worker must consider three factors in making skill investment decisions: (i) the initial cost of acquiring the skills as, for instance, when a worker receives a reduced wage during the period of training; (ii) the future wage premium of specific skills; and (iii) the risks of losing the current job and the associated wage premium.

The core skills required by an industry are critical for this analysis because they vary in the degree to which they expose workers to the risk of future income losses. Highly portable skills are less risky than highly specific skills because in the former case the market value of the skill is not tied to a particular firm or industry. Faced with future job insecurity, a rational worker will not invest his or her time and money in skills that have no remunerative value outside the firm or industry. In other words, in the absence of institutional interventions into workers' payoff structure, general rather than asset-specific skill acquisition represents the utility-maximizing strategy.

Let us now examine what types of institutions are necessary in order to protect investments in asset-specific skills. We can distinguish three different types of protection, which might be called *employment protection, unemployment protection,* and *wage protection. Employment protection* refers to institutionalized employment security. The higher the employment protection, the less likely that a worker will be laid off even during economic downturns. *Unemployment protection* means protection from income reduction due to unemployment, and can thus reduce the uncertainty over the wage level throughout one's career. *Wage protection,* finally, is an institutional mechanism that protects wage levels from market fluctuations. In this section, we first contrast the significance of *employment protection* and *unemployment protection* for firm-specific and industry-specific skills. We will discuss wage protection in a separate section, because it is generally not considered to be part of the welfare system.

Firm-specific skills are, *ex hypothesi,* worthless outside that specific firm, and they therefore require a high level of *employment protection* in order to convince workers to invest in such skills (Aoki 1988). Since workers will only be paid the value of their non-firm-specific skills in the external market, the greater their investment in specific skills the greater the discrepancy between current wages and the wages they could fetch in the external market. In order to invest heavily in firm-specific skills, workers therefore need assurances that they can remain in the company for a long enough period to reap the returns on such investments (see Lazear and Freeman 1996; Osterman 1987; Schettkat 1993). If not, the expenditures of training must be commensurably lower, and/or the premium on future wages higher. In either case, the cost of training for the firm goes up, and it will offer less training.

Because rational workers weigh higher expected income later in their career against the risks of losing their current job, the only way to encourage workers to carry a substantial part of the costs of firm-specific training is to increase job security and/or reduce the insecurity of job loss. Hence we can interpret institutionalized lifetime employment, or subsidies to keep redundant workers within the firm, as safeguarding mechanisms for firm-specific skill investment.

*   *   *

For firms pursuing product market strategies which depend heavily on firm- and industry-specific skills, promise of employment and unemployment security can thus provide a cost-effective path to improving the firms' competitive position in international markets (cf. Ohashi and Tachibanaki 1998; Koike 1994). Contrary to conventional neoclassical theory, which sees efforts to increase protection against job loss as an interference with the efficient operation of labor markets, measures to reduce future uncertainty over employment status—hence uncertainty over future wage premiums—can significantly improve firms' cost effectiveness (Schettkat 1993). And the more successful these firms are, the greater their demand for specific skills. We are in a specific skills equilibrium.

If there is little protection built into either the employment or the unemployment system, the best insurance against labor market risks for the worker is to invest in general, or portable, skills that are highly valued in the external labor market. If general skills are what firms need for pursuing their product market strategies successfully, low employment protection can thus give these firms a competitive edge. Indeed, if most firms are pursuing general skills strategies, then higher protection will undermine workers' incentives to invest in these skills, *without* significantly increasing their appropriation of specific skills (because there is little demand for

Fig. 1   Social Protection and Predicted Skill Profiles

| | | Employment protection | |
		Low	High
Unemployment protection	High	Industry-specific skills Example: Denmark	Industry-specific, firm-specific skill mix Example: Germany
	Low	General skills Example: United States	Firm-specific skills Example: Japan

such skills). In this general skills equilibrium the neoclassical efficiency argument for little protection is more valid.[2]

The predictions of the argument are summarized in Fig. 1, which identifies the four main welfare production regimes and gives an empirical example of each (discussed below).

＊　　＊　　＊

Self-Reinforcing Inequalities and Political Preferences

So far the discussion has focused on the efficiency aspects of social protection. In this section we extend the core argument to unravel two sets of previously neglected logics by which welfare production regimes perpetuate inequalities. First, we point out that general skill systems are more likely to create a "poverty trap." Second, we cast light upon the gender inequality consequences of different product market strategies. Finally, we discuss how these distributive implications of different welfare state regimes are reproduced and perpetuated through distinct patterns of political support for social protection.

Distribution, Poverty Traps, and Product Market Strategies

Our argument has far-reaching implications for equality and labor market stratification, some of which are poorly understood in the existing welfare state literature. Product market strategies that rely on high levels of industry-specific and firm-specific skills are likely to create more egalitarian societies than product market strategies based on general skills. They therefore help us understand large and persistent cross-national differences in the distribution of wages and incomes. The existing literature can only account for these differences in so far as they are caused by redistributive state policies. This is far too narrow an approach. We contend that most inequalities result from particular welfare production regimes (i.e., combinations of product market strategies, skill profiles, and the political-institutional framework that supports them).

The basic logic of our argument is straightforward. We argue that different skill systems and accompanying training systems have important economic implications for those who are academically weak and strong respectively. For the bottom one third, or so, of the academic ability distribution, a highly developed vocational training system offers the best opportunities for students to acquire skills that are valued by employers. When entry into vocational training is competitive, these students have an incentive to be as good as they can academically in order to get into the best training programs with the most promising career prospects (Soskice 1994). Therefore, countries with well-developed (and competitive) vocational training systems provide a stable economic future even to those students who are not academically strong. General education systems, in contrast, offer these students relatively few opportunities for improving their labor market value outside of the school system. As a result, there are fewer incentives for them to work hard inside the school system.

In firm-specific skill-training systems, employers develop strong stakes in overseeing the quality of potential employees (i.e. trainees) and developing clear job entry patterns.[3] Since employers are committed to make significant initial human capital investment in new job entrants, they will be interested in monitoring the quality of the pool of the new school leavers. As a result, they are likely to establish a working relationship with various schools for systematic hiring of new school leavers. Since employers in a firm-specific skill system carry out initial job training, new school graduates have a chance of building careers as skilled workers. This gives young schoolgoers a strong incentive to work hard in school. The "from-school-to-work" transition is likely to be more institutionalized (Dore and Sako 1989). Similarly, in the case of industry-specific skills where employers are involved, employers take an interest in ensuring the quality of vocational training and the certification of skills (Finegold and Soskice 1988). In these systems, education-work transition is also relatively institutionalized (Ni Cheallaigh 1995; Blossfeld and Mayer 1988).

In general skill regimes, in contrast, the "from-school-to-work" transition is less institutionalized (see Allmendinger 1989). Hiring is more flexible. Employers hire new job entrants with different educational backgrounds. Promotion and opportunities for further skill training are themselves contingent upon the job performance of the worker. There is not so much initial human capital investment by employers as there is in firm-specific skill systems. Because of the absence of a clear vocational track, systems based on general skills therefore tend to disadvantage those who are not academically inclined. Regardless of the presence or absence of vocational schools and apprenticeship programs, for employers who emphasize general skills a certificate from a vocational school does not add much value to the worker. Potential workers therefore have to demonstrate their competence in terms of general scholarly achievement, and getting a tertiary degree becomes an essential component. Because there is a hierarchy of post-secondary schools, if the student thinks there is a possibility of making it into the tertiary educational system, he or she has a strong incentive to work hard. For those who are not academically inclined, by contrast, the system produces the unintended consequence of undermining the incentive to work hard in school. In the absence of a specialized vocational track, unless a student believes that he or she can make the cut into college, there is not much gained by being a good student.

In short, in general skill systems, since the completion of elementary and secondary school does not qualify them for a vocational certificate that leads to secure jobs, academically weak students face lower returns from their educational investment. Since the opportunity for vocational training—both on the job and off the job—for these students will remain low, it creates an im-

poverished labor pool. In contrast, at the top end of the ability distribution, a general education system offers the largest returns to those with advanced graduate and postgraduate degrees. These returns tend to be more modest in specific skills systems because a large number of companies depend more on industry-specific and firm-specific skills than professional degrees or broad academic qualifications. General skill systems, therefore, reward those students who are academically talented in terms of labor market entry. Distribution of academic aptitude thus translates into distribution of skills, and consequently into a very skewed distribution of earnings. As a consequence, academically weak students in general skill regimes are worse off than their counterparts elsewhere: they are more likely to be trapped in low-paid unskilled jobs.

Gender Equality and Skill Types

Compared to men, women face an additional set of issues when making skill investment choices (see Estévez-Abe 1999). In addition to the probability of layoff, women have to take into consideration the likelihood of career interruption due to their role as mothers (see Daly 1994; Rubery et al. 1996). For a woman to invest in specific skills, she has to be assured that potential career interruptions will not (i) lead to dismissal; or (ii) reduce her wage level in the long run. A high probability of dismissal reduces the incentives to acquire firm-specific skills. A high probability of reduction in wages after becoming a mother—because of time off due to childbirth and -rearing—reduces the incentives to invest in either firm-specific or industry-specific skills.

For women, therefore, employment protection necessarily involves two factors in addition to the employment and unemployment protection discussed earlier. These two factors are (i) protection against dismissal, such as maternity, parental, and family leave policies; and (ii) income maintenance during leaves and guarantees of reinstatement to the same job at the same wage level upon return to work.

As for industry-specific skill investments, leave programs and generous income maintenance during the leave function in the same way as unemployment protection for male skilled workers. A higher wage replacement ratio thus encourages specific skill investment. Firm-specific and industry-specific skills again require slightly different institutional guarantees. While income maintenance during leave is sufficient for industry-specific skills, firm-specific skill investment by women faces another issue. In firm-specific skill regimes, reinstatement to the original job after the leave means that women fall behind their male cohort in skill formation and promotion. This means that despite generous income replacement during the leave, time off due to childbirth and -rearing reduces women's overall earnings. The very fact that the child-rearing years for women coincide with the critical early years of employment compounds the problem. Therefore, for women to invest in firm-specific skills, affordable childcare is more important than a family leave policy. In short, compared to men, it takes more institutional support to encourage women to make specific skill investments. This means that employers' incentives differ significantly from the earlier descriptions of employment and unemployment protection. From the employers' perspective, it costs more to provide incentives for women to invest in specific skills than it does for men (Spencer 1973). Not only do additional income maintenance and childcare create a greater financial burden, but they come with the organizational cost of hiring replacement workers during regular workers' maternal and childcare leaves. And not only is it expensive to hire highly skilled workers as replacement workers, but it is also very difficult to seek those skills in the external labor market—especially in the case of firm-specific skills.

Given these additional financial and organizational costs, employers are unlikely to support family leave or childcare programs except under two circumstances: (i) when someone other than the employer covers the program expenses; or

(ii) when there is an acute shortage of men willing to invest in the skills they need.

From a woman's perspective, this means that it does not pay to invest in skills for which there is an abundant supply of males. Even if a woman invests to acquire a specific skill, as far as there is an abundant supply of male skilled workers, her skill investment will not be protected to the same degree as men's. Given this situation, women are more likely than men to invest in general skills. Furthermore, even women who are willing to invest in skill training will rationally choose trades and professions where there are few men. Hence a vicious cycle of occupational segregation of women arises. In countries where there is an established vocational training system, women's enrollment choices will reflect women's tendency to avoid "male jobs."

In short, product market strategies that rely on firm-specific and industry-specific skills are more gender segregating than product market strategies based on general skills. As we argued, general skills provide more flexibility without penalizing career interruptions, precisely because they do not require any external guarantee and reinforcement. We can thus predict that economies with a large presence of companies with specific skill strategies demonstrate high occupational gender segregation, while general skill systems are more gender neutral.

*   *   *

Comparative Patterns

Our argument implies a tight coupling between employment protection, unemployment protection, and skill formation. The dominant mode of firm structure, as well as circumstances in the historical development of different welfare production regimes, have led some countries to emphasize *employment protection* over *unemployment protection,* or vice versa. As we noted in the theoretical discussion, political opposition to strong *employment protection* legislation will be greater in countries with a high proportion of small firms.

The predictions of our model are summarized in Fig. 1.

When *neither* employment *nor* unemployment protection is high, workers have a strong incentive to protect themselves against labor market insecurities by investing heavily in highly portable skills. Since workers are reluctant to take on specific skills in this scenario—or at least unlikely to share much of the cost of training such skills—firms have an incentive to use technologies that rely least on specific skills. This, in turn, increases demand for general skills, and availability of general skill jobs makes general education more attractive for workers, thus creating a self-reinforcing dynamic. In this case we expect skill profiles to be heavily tilted toward general and broad occupational skills, with a weak or absent vocational training system.

When employment and unemployment protection are both high, on the other hand, workers will find it more attractive to invest in firm- and industry-specific skills. In turn, this makes it more cost-efficient for firms to engage in production that require large inputs of labor with specific skills. As firms specialize in this type of production, the job market for general skills shrinks. Note here that a standard trade argument supports the idea of self-reinforcing dynamics in both types of systems: institutional comparative advantage makes an intensive use of relatively more abundant skills an efficient production strategy. Yet, not all countries necessarily conform to these two ideal types. Where companies can offer very high levels of job protection and a large and attractive internal labor market, firm-specific skill formation can flourish in the absence of strong unemployment protection (represented by the south-east corner of Fig. 1). If career opportunities are extensive within the firm, and if the firm makes credible commitments to job security, the external labor market will be small and workers will have an incentive to take advantage of internal career opportunities by investing in company-specific skills. This,

essentially, is the Japanese situation (see Aoki 1988; Koike 1981). In most other cases, firms neither have the size nor the resources and institutional capacity to commit credibly to lifetime employment. It is for this reason that we would *ordinarily* expect the development of firm-specific skills to be coupled with generous protection against unemployment.

On the flip side of the Japanese system, we find welfare production regimes with extensive unemployment protection, but low or only modest employment protection. Especially in economies dominated by small firms, with small internal labor markets and little organizational capacity to adapt to business cycles, employment protection is a costly and unattractive option for employers. Denmark is an archetypal example of an economy with a small-firm industrial structure. Yet, generous unemployment protection for skilled workers is still a requisite for workers to invest in industry-specific skills in these cases, much the same way as employment protection is a requisite for investment in firm-specific skills. In effect, unemployment protection increases employment security *within the industry* as opposed to security within a particular firm. At a high level of abstraction, therefore, the *industry* in a country with high unemployment and low employment protection becomes functionally equivalent to the *firm* in a country with low unemployment and high employment protection.

*   *   *

Putting the Pieces Together

Fig. 2 plots the eighteen OECD countries on the employment and unemployment protection indexes [that we have adopted]. Countries are distributed along a primary axis, corresponding to the south-west–north-east diagonal in Fig. 2, with some countries further divided along a secondary axis, corresponding to the north-west–south-east diagonal in Fig. 2. The main axis separates countries into two distinct welfare

Fig. 2 Social Protection and Skill Profiles

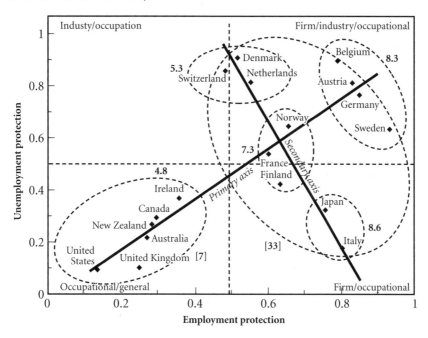

Source: OECD, *Database on Unemployment Benefit Entitlements and Replacement Rates* (undated); Huber, Ragin, Stephens (1997); OECD Economic Outlook (Paris: OECD, various years); OECD, *Labour Force Statistics* (Paris: OECD, various years); European Commission, *Unemployment in Europe* (various years); and national sources; Income Data Services, *Industrial Relations and Collective Bargaining*. London, Institute of Personnel and Development, 1996.

production regimes: one combining weak employment and unemployment protection with a general skills profile, represented by the Anglo-Saxon countries and Ireland; and one combining high protection on at least one of the two social protection dimensions with firm- and/or industry-specific skills, represented by the continental European countries and Japan. The secondary axis divides the latter group into one with greater emphasis on employment protection and the creation of firm-specific skills, exemplified primarily by Japan and Italy,[4] and one with greater emphasis on unemployment protection and the production of industry-specific skills, exemplified by Denmark, the Netherlands, and Switzerland.

The data on skills * * * have been summarized in the form of averages for each cluster of countries (only tenure rates are relevant for the division along the secondary axis). The high protection countries are also those with the most developed vocational training systems, and tenure rates decline with employment protection. Clearly, the empirical patterns we observe correspond rather closely to our main theoretical thesis, namely that skill formation is closely linked to social protection.

The coupling of social protection and skill systems helps us understand the product market strategies of companies and the creation of comparative advantages in the global economy. Thus, where there is a large pool of workers with advanced and highly portable skills, and where social protection is low, companies enjoy considerable flexibility in attracting new workers, laying off old ones, or starting new production lines. This flexibility allows for high responsiveness to new business opportunities, and facilitates the use of rapid product innovation strategies. In economies with a combination of firm- and industry-specific skills, such strategies are hampered by the difficulty of quickly adapting skills to new types of production, and by restrictions in the ability of firms to hire and fire workers. On the other hand, these welfare-production regimes advantage companies that seek to develop deep competencies within established technologies, and to continuously upgrade and diversify existing product lines ("diversified quality production" in the terminology of Streeck 1991).

There is considerable case-oriented research to support these propositions (see especially Soskice 1999 and Hollingsworth and Boyer 1997), and they can be bolstered by quantitative evidence constructed by Thomas Cusack from US Patent Office data. Broken into thirty technology classes, Cusack counted the number of references to scientific articles for patents in each technology class and country, and then divided this number by the world number of scientific citations per technology class.[5] The idea is that the number of scientific citations, as opposed to citations to previous patents and non-scientific sources, is a good proxy for the extent to which national firms are engaged in radical innovation strategies. The results are shown in the first column of Table 1, with countries ranked by the average ratio of scientific citations for patents secured by national firms. As it turns out, the Anglo-Saxon countries and Ireland all have ratios that are significantly higher than in the specific skills countries of continental Europe and Japan. Precisely as we would expect.

At the low-tech end of product markets, we have to rely on a different type of data to detect cross-national differences. In column (2) of Table 1 we used the proportion of the working-age population employed in private social and personal services as a proxy. As argued by Esping-Andersen (1990: ch. 8) and Iversen and

Table 1 Scientific Citation Rates and Low-Wage Service Employment in Eighteen OECD Countries

	(1)	(2)
	Scientific citation ratio[a]	Private service employment[b]
Ireland	1.514	—
United States	1.310	23
New Zealand	1.267	—
Canada	1.032	20
United Kingdom	0.837	16
Australia	0.804	26
Sweden	0.757	14
The Netherlands	0.754	14
Norway	0.690	17
Switzerland	0.639	—
France	0.601	11
Belgium	0.598	13
Germany	0.592	14
Japan	0.586	—
Austria	0.575	—
Finland	0.552	11
Denmark	0.536	11
Italy	0.491	9

a. The average number of scientific citations per patent by national firms in each of 30 technology classes as a proportion of the average number of citations in each class for the entire world.
b. The number of people employed in wholesale, retail trade, restaurants and hotels, and in community, social and personal services, 1982–91 as a percentage of the working-age population.
Source: Col. 1: United States Patent Office Data. Col. 2: OECD (1996).

Wren (1998), firms that rely heavily on low-skilled and low-paid labor for profitability tend to be concentrated in these industries. Although we only have data for a subset of countries, the numbers display a rather clear cross-national pattern. Producers of standardized and low-productivity services thrive in general skills countries such as Australia and the United States because they can hire from a large pool of unskilled workers who are afforded much job protection and whose wages are held down by low unemployment protection. By contrast, firms trying to compete in this space in specific skills countries such as Germany and Sweden are inhibited by higher labor costs and lower flexibility in hiring and firing. These differences have magnified during the 1980s and 1990s, and Britain is now closer to the mean for the general skills countries.

In an open international trading system, differences in product market strategies will tend to be perpetuated, which in turn feed back into organized support for existing social protection regimes. Contrary to the popular notion of a "race to the bottom" in social policies, differences across countries persist and are even attenuated through open trade. Correspondingly, from the 1970s to the 1980s and 1990s, unemployment benefits remained stable or rose in most continental European countries, but they were cut in Ireland and all the Anglo-Saxo countries with the exception of Australia.[6] Moreover, whereas labor markets have become even more deregulated in the latter countries, employment protection has remained high in the former. Although some countries have seen a notable relaxation in the protection of temporary employment, there is no reduction in the level of protection for regular employment (*OECD Employment Outlook* 1999). This evidence, and the theoretical explanation we provide for it, seriously challenge the notion, popular in much of the economic literature, that social protection is simply inefficient forms of labor market "rigidities." Social protection can provide important competitive advantages. By the same token we question the prevalent approach in the sociological and political science literature, which understands social protection solely in terms of its redistributive effects.

Implications for Labor Market Stratification

That said, we are not implying that welfare production regimes are irrelevant for distributive outcomes. To the contrary, our argument has important implications for equality and labor market stratification, and it helps account for the political divisions over the welfare state. Partly these effects are direct consequences of particular product market strategies and their associated skill profiles; partly they reflect the effects of the collective wage-bargaining system that is itself an important component of the wage protection system.

With respect to wage protection, the most important issue is what we have previously referred to as wage protection for the unemployed. Such protection implies that workers with similar skills are paid the same amount across firms and industries, and in practice this is accomplished through collective wage-bargaining at the industry level or at higher levels. It is striking, though not surprising, that all countries with a strong emphasis on industry-specific skills have developed effective wage coordination at the industry level. Conversely, general skills countries, and countries with a strong emphasis on firm-specific skills (Japan in particular), lack such coordination.

Very extensive evidence has now been accumulated that demonstrates the importance of the structure of the wage-bargaining system for the wage structure (see especially Rowthorn 1992; Wallerstein 1999; and Rueda and Pontusson 2000), but we believe the skill system is equally important. Fig. 3, which uses the incidence of vocational training as the indicator for skill system, clearly shows the empirical association between skills and earnings equality, and there is a good reason. Because specific skills systems generate high demand for workers with good vocational training, young people who are not academically inclined have career opportunities that are largely missing in general skills systems. Whereas a large proportion of early school leavers in the former acquire valuable skills through the vocational training system, in the latter most early school leavers end up as low-paid unskilled workers for most or all of their working lives.

Fig. 3 Vocational Training and Wage Inequality

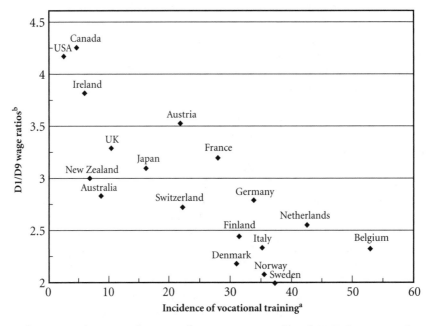

a) The share of an age cohort in either secondary or post-secondary (ISCED5) vocational training. *Source:* UNESCO (1999).

b) The earnings of worker in the top decile of the earnings distribution relative to a worker in the bottom decile of the earnings distribution. *Source:* OECD, *Electronic Data Base on Wage Dispersion.* Undated.

Sources: D1/D9 wage ratios: UNESCO (1999). Incidence of vocational training: OECD, *Electronic Data Based on Wage Dispersion* (undated).

In combination, the wage-bargaining system —i.e. whether it is industry coordinated or not— and the skill system—i.e. whether it is specific skills or general skills biased—provides a powerful explanation of earnings inequality as we have illustrated in Fig. 4. The figure shows earnings and income inequality for each combination of bargaining and skill system. The big drop in earnings equality occurs as we move from specific skills systems with industry-coordinated bargaining to general skills systems where industry-coordinated wage-bargaining is lacking. By themselves this pair of dichotomous variables account for nearly 70 per cent of the cross-national variance in income inequality.[7] Yet, despite their importance for explaining inequality, neither vari-

able is accorded much attention in the established welfare state literature, notwithstanding the focus on distribution in this literature. In our theoretical framework, on the other hand, they are integral parts of the story, even though we have focused on micro mechanisms that emphasize the importance of efficiency.

The hypothesized relationship between product market strategies, skill composition, and equality points to another, and quite different, source of evidence: academic test scores. Because specific skills systems create strong incentives among young schoolgoers to do as well as they can in school in order to get the best vocational training spots, whereas those at the bottom of the academic ability distribution in

Fig. 4 Skills, the Bargaining System, and Equality[a]

Wage–bargaining system

	Industry coordinated	Not industry coordinated
Biased towards specific skills	.49 (.34) (N=9)[b]	.34 (.28) (N=3)[c]
Biased towards specific skills		.29 (.23) (N=6)[d]

Skills system

[a]Numbers are D9/D1 earnings ratios based on gross earnings (including all employer contributions for pensions, social security etc.) of a worker at the bottom decile of the earnings distribution relative to the worker at the top decile. Figures are averages for the period 1977-1993. Numbers in parentheses are D9/D1 income ratios based on disposable income of a person at the bottom decile of the earnings distribution relative to a person at the top decile. Most figures are from the early 1990s, with a few from the 1980s.

[b]Austria, Belgium, Denmark, Finland, Germany, Netherlands, Norway, Sweden, Switzerland

[c]France, Italy, Japan

[d]Australia, Canada, Ireland, New Zealand, UK, US

Sources: Skills: see Table 1. Bargaining system: see Iversen (1999a: ch. 3). Inequality measures: see *OECD Employment Outlook* (1991, 1996); Gottschalk and Smeeding (2000: fig. 2).

general skills systems have few such incentives, we should expect the number of early school leavers who fail internationally standardized tests to be higher in general skills countries than in specific skills countries.

Although the data are limited in coverage, this is in fact what we observe (see Fig. 5). Whereas the percentage failing the test varies between 15 and 22 per cent in the Anglo-Saxon countries, it is only between 8 and 14 in the countries emphasizing more specific skills for which we have data. Although these differences could be due to the overall quality of the educational system, it is not the case that the Anglo-Saxon countries spend less money on primary

education, and there is no systematic difference in average scorers. This points to the importance of incentives outside the school system, which vary systematically according to the dominant product market strategies of firms and their associated demand for particular skills.

But general skills systems are not necessarily bad for all types of inequality. They perform better in terms of gender equality at work (Estévez-Abe 1999). When we compare degrees of occupational segregation, specific skills systems fare worse than general skills systems. Specific skills systems segregate women into "female occupations" such as low-rank clerical and service jobs. Table 2 shows the occupational breakdown of women employed expressed in terms of a percentage of women over total workforce within the same category. While the data are not conclusive, it nonetheless shows that countries (see Germany and Sweden in Table 2) that adopt high-quality product market strategies—thus dependent on high industry-specific skills—employ women for production jobs to a lesser degree. The USA, the archetypal general skills system, shows significantly higher ratios of women in technical and managerial positions when compared to specific skills systems. Our findings support Esping-Andersen's argument about the US employment system being more gender equal than that found in Germany and Sweden (Esping-Andersen 1999). Our explanation, however, differs from his.

Conclusion

Protection of employment and income is widely seen in the welfare state literature as reducing workers' dependence on the market and employers ("decommodification" in Esping-Andersen's terminology). In turn, this is argued to reflect a particular balance of power between labor and capital. We reject both theses. Although strong

Table 2 Share of Women by Occupation (%)[a]

	(1) Professional, technical, and related workers	(2) Administrative and managerial workers	(3) Clerical and related workers	(4) Sales workers	(5) Service workers	(6) Production and related workers
USA (1989)	22	26	70	33	30	30
Japan (1988)	10	7	58	11	40	39[b]
Germany (1986)	15	11	59	52	67	21
The Netherlands (1993)	14	0	55	32	45	12
Sweden (1989)	15		57	25	72	24
Australia (1987)	8	18	20	43	76	31

a. Percentages represent the ratio of women over the total of men and women employed within each occupational category.
b. The female ratio for occupational category (6) in Japan is exceptionally high due to a demographically shrinking pool of young male workers (Estévez-Abe 1999).
Source: ILO (1989–90).

Fig. 5 The Failure of Early School Leavers to Pass Standardized Tests in Eleven OECD Countries

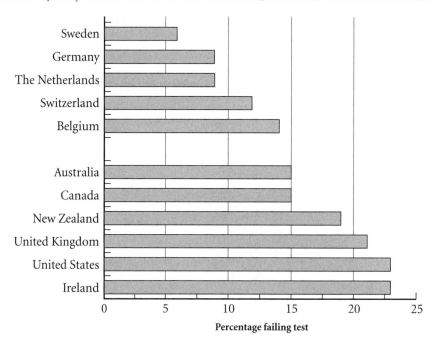

Source: OECD (2000).

unions and left governments undoubtedly affect distributive outcomes, we have argued that employment and income protection can be seen as efforts to *increase* workers' dependence on particular employers, as well as their exposure to labor market risks. Moreover, social protection often stems from the strength rather than the weakness of employers.

The key to our argument is the link between social protection and the level and composition of skills. In a modern economy, skills are essential for firms to compete in international markets, and depending on the particular product market strategy of firms, they rely on a workforce with a certain combination of firm-specific, industry-specific, and general skills. To be cost-effective firms need workers who are willing to make personal investments in these skills. And if firms want to be competitive in product markets that require an abundance of specific skills, workers must be willing to acquire these skills at the cost of increasing their dependence on a particular employer or group of employers. Because investment in specific skills increases workers' exposure to risks, only by insuring against such risks can firms satisfy their need for specific skills.

The particular combination of employment protection and unemployment protection determines the profile of skills that is likely to emerge in an economy. Thus employment protection increases the propensity of workers to invest in firm-specific skills, whereas unemployment protection facilitates investment in industry-specific skills. The absence of both gives people strong incentives to invest in general skills. These predictors are borne out by the comparative data, which show that most countries combine either low protection with general skills, or high protection with specific skills.

Two factors contribute to the distinctiveness and resilience of particular welfare production regimes. The first is that such regimes tend to be reinforced by institutions—collective wage-bargaining systems, business organizations, employee representation, and financial systems—

that facilitate the credible commitment of actors to particular strategies, such as wage restraint and long-term employment, that are necessary to sustain cooperation in the provision of specific skills. The second is that those workers and employers who are being most advantaged by these institutional complementaries also tend to be in strong political positions, in terms of both economic clout and sheer numbers. For example, the more a welfare production system emphasizes the creation of specific skills, the more likely it is that the median voter will be someone with considerable investments in specific skills, and the more likely it is that employers' interest organizations will be dominated by firms pursuing specific skills strategies. Both will contribute to perpetuating institutions and policies that advantage firms and workers with heavy investments in specific skills.

Our argument has broader implications for our understanding of the welfare state that reach well beyond the immediate effects of employment and income protection. In particular, earnings dispersion, by far the most important determinant of the overall distribution of income, is closely related to particular skill systems as well as the wage-bargaining institutions that tend to go with these systems. Similarly, the combination of particular product market strategies and skills has distinct effects on the career opportunities of particular groups, especially women. Thus, our theory implies that gender-based segmentation of the labor market varies systematically across welfare production systems.

*　　*　　*

NOTES

1. Our framework builds upon Gary Becker's distinction between general and specific skills (1964: ch. 3). In Becker's definition, firm-specific training increases productivity only in the firm where training takes place.

General training, in contrast, raises productivity equally in all firms. In an analogous manner, industry-specific training can be defined as training that raises productivity in all firms in the industry, but not in other industries. Firm-, industry-, and general skills are skills acquired through firm-specific, industry-specific, and general training.

2. Since the general skills are portable, there is no risk associated with separation from current employer. See Gary Becker (1964). This does not mean that high turnover in countries with more general skills does not produce negative welfare consequences from the economy-wide efficiency perspective. For an interesting elaboration on this issue, see Chang and Wang (1995).

3. It is worth noting that monitoring the quality of the general education system becomes important where a lot of human capital investment takes place beyond the general education system, because poor general education increases the cost of training workers in industry-specific and firm-specific skills.

4. Although the position of Italy is probably exaggerated by the failure to account for semi-public unemployment insurance arrangements, as noted above.

5. The data are coded into references to previous patents and others, where many of the latter are references to scientific articles. To get a good estimate for the number of scientific articles in the "other" category, the proportion of scientific references to other references was calculated for a random sample (6,000) for each country and technology class. These factors were then used to correct the overall dataset so as to get a better measure of scientific citations.

6. Based on gross unemployment replacement rates published in OECD's *Database on Unemployment Benefit Entitlements and Replacement Rates* (undated).

7. The estimated regression equation is:

Income equality = 0.23 + 0.048 × Specific skills + 0.055 × Industry coordination, where $R^2 = 0.69$

REFERENCES

Allmendinger, Jutta. 1989. 'Educational Systems and Labor Market Outcomes.' *European Sociological Review* 5 (3): 231–50.

Aoki, Masahiko. 1988. *Information, Incentives and Bargaining in the Japanese Economy.* Cambridge: Cambridge University Press.

Becker, Gary. 1964. *Human Capital: A Theoretical and Empirical Analysis, with Special Reference to Education.* New York: Columbia University Press.

Blossfeld, Hans-Peter, and Karl Ulrich Mayer. 1988. 'Labor Market Segmentation in the Federal Republic of Germany: An Empirical Study of Segmentation Theories from a Life Course Perspective.' *European Sociologic Review* 4 (2): 123–40.

Daly, Mary. 1994. 'A Matter of Dependency? The Gender Dimension of British Income-Maintenance Provision.' *Sociology* 28 (3): 779–97.

Dore, Ronald. and Mari Sako. 1989. *How the Japanese Learn to Work.* London: Routledge.

Esping-Andersen, Gøsta. 1990. *Three Worlds of Welfare Capitalism.* Princeton: Princeton University Press.

——— 1999. *Social Foundations of Postindustrial Economies.* Oxford: Oxford University Press.

Estévez-Abe, Margarita. 1999. 'Comparative Political Economy of Female Labor Force Participation.' Paper presented at the meeting of the American Political Science Association, Atlanta, 2–5 September.

Finegold, David, and David Soskice. 1988. 'The Failure of Training in Britain: Analysis and Prescription.' *Oxford Review of Economic Policy* 4 (3): 21–53.

Gottschalk, Peter, and T. M. Smeeding. 2000. 'Empirical Evidence on Income Inequality in Industrialized Countries.' In *The Handbook of*

Income Distribution, ed. A. B. Atkinson and F. Bourguignon. London: North Holland Press.

Hollingsworth, J. Rogers and Robert Boyers, eds. 1997. *Contemporary Capitalism: The Embeddedness of Institutions.* Cambridge: Cambridge University Press.

Huber, Evelyne, John D. Stephens, Charles Ragin, and John Stephens. 1993. 'Social Democracy, Christian Democracy, Constitutional Structure and the Welfare State.' *American Journal of Sociology* 99 (3): 711–49.

ILO. 1989–90. *Yearbook of Labour Statistics.* Geneva: ILO.

Income Data Services. 1996. *Industrial Relations and Collective Bargaining.* London: Institute of Personnel and Development.

Iversen, Torben. 1999. *Contested Economic Institutions: The Politics of Macroeconomics and Wage Bargaining in Advanced Democracies.* New York: Cambridge University Press.

———— and Anne Wren. 1998. 'Equality, Employment, and Budgetary Restraint: The Trilemma of the Service Economy.' *World Politics* 50 (July): 507–46.

Koike, Kazuo. 1981. *Nihon no Jukuren: Sugureta Jinzai Keisei Shisutemu* [Skills in Japan: An Effective Human Capital Formation System]. Tokyo: Yuhikaku.

————. 1994. 'Learning and Incentive Systems in Japanese Industry.' In *The Japanese Firm,* ed. Masahiko Aoki and Ronald Dore. Oxford: Clarendon Press: 41–65.

Lazear, Edward, and Richard Freeman. 1996. 'Relational Investing: The Workers' Perspective.' NBER Working Paper 5346.

Ni Cheallaigh, Martina. 1995. *Apprenticeship in the EU Member States: A Comparison.* Berlin: European Center for the Development of Vocational Training.

OECD. 1991. 'Unemployment Benefit Rules and Labour Market Policy.' *OECD Employment Outlook.* Paris: OECD: 199–236.

————. 1996. *OECD International Sectoral Data Base.* Paris: OECD.

————. 1999. *OECD Education Database.* Paris: OECD.

————. *OECD Employment Outlook.* Paris: OECD (various years).

————. *Labour Force Statistics.* Paris: OECD (various years).

Ohashi, Isao, and Toshiaki Tachibanaki, eds. 1998. *Internal Labor Markets, Incentives and Employment.* New York: St Martin's Press.

Osterman, Peter. 1987. 'Choice of Employment Systems in Internal Labour Markets.' *Industrial Relations* 26 (1): 46–67.

Rowthorn, Robert. 1992. 'Corporatism and Labour Market Performance.' In *Social Corporatism: A Superior Economic System?,* ed. Jukka Pekkarinen, Matti Pohjola, and Bob Rowthorn. Oxford: Clarendon Press: 44–81.

Rubery, Jill, Colette Fagan, and Friederike Maier. 1996. 'Occupational Segregation, Discrimination and Equal Opportunity.' In *International Handbook of Labour Market Policy and Evaluation,* ed. Gunther Schmid, Jacqueline O'Reilly, and Klaus Schomann. Cheltenham: Edward Elgar: 431–61.

Rueda, David, and Jonas Pontusson. 2000. 'Wage Inequality and Varieties of Capitalism.' *World Politics* 52 (April): 350–83.

Schettkat, Ronald. 1993. 'Compensating Differentials? Wage Differentials and Employment Stability in the US and German Economies.' *Journal of Economic Issues* 27 (1): 153–70.

Shibata, Hiromichi. 1999. 'Comparison of American and Japanese Work Practices: Skill Formation, Communications and Conflict Resolution.' *Industrial Relations* 38 (2): 192–214.

Soskice, David. 1994. 'Reconciling Markets and Institutions: The German Apprenticeship System.' In *Training and the Private Sector: International Comparisons,* ed. Lisa M. Lynch. Chicago: Chicago University Press: 25–60.

———— 1999. 'Divergent Production Regimes: Coordinated and Uncoordinated Market Economies in the 1980s and 1990s.' In *Conti-*

nuity and Change in Contemporary Capitalism, ed. Herbert Kitschelt et al. Cambridge: Cambridge University Press: 101–34.

Spencer, Michael. 1973. 'Job Market Signaling.' *Quarterly Journal of Economics* 87 (3): 355–74.

Streeck, Wolfgang. 1991. 'On the Institutional Conditions of Diversified Quality Production.' In *Beyond Keynesianism: The Socioeconomics of Production and Full Employment,* ed. Egon Matzner and Wolfgang Streeck. Aldershot: Elgar: 21–61.

———. 1992. *Social Institutions and Economic Performance: Studies on Industrial Relations in Advanced European Capitalist Countries.* London: Sage.

UNESCO. 1999. *UNESCO Statistical Yearbook.* New York: UNESCO.

Wallerstein, Michael. 1999. 'Wage-Setting Institutions and Pay Inequality in Advanced Industrial Societies.' *American Journal of Political Science* 43 (3): 649–80.

8 COMMUNISM AND POSTCOMMUNISM

This section traces the concept of communism, its limitations, collapse, and future prospects. We begin with the most commonly read work of Karl Marx and Friedrich Engels, Manifesto of the Communist Party *(1848), where they lay out their understanding of human history and its dynamics, and the inevitability of the communist revolution to come. For Marx and Engels, economic relations are the driving force of all human relations, and it is these changes in economic relations that drive history. History is a succession of revolutions by those who are exploited against those who exploit them. At the midpoint of the nineteenth century, with the Industrial Revolution just under way, the authors predicted that the limitations of capitalism would soon bring about its overthrow and replacement by a system in which resources and wealth were equally shared. Marx and Engels thus combined research with activism, and their ideas would go on to spark communist movements across the globe, and revolutions in such places as Russia and China.*

But communism in practice was more challenging than Marx or Engels anticipated. The idea of eliminating private property and market forces led to an economy administered by the state and backed by authoritarian rule. In addition to denying democratic freedoms, communism also grew increasingly unable to provide material needs and economic growth. By the 1980s, attempts to reform this ossified structure in the Soviet Union and Eastern Europe quickly led to its undoing.

Why did communism in Eastern Europe fall apart, and what explains the differences from country to country and region to region? Scholars have been grappling with these puzzles for the past twenty years. Valerie Bunce's "Rethinking Recent Democratization" (2003) draws on these cases as well as earlier examples of political transition in southern Europe and Latin America to deepen our understanding of successful political change. Historical factors, popular mobilization, nationalism, the role of the military, and the degree of uncertainty about the prospects for change all contributed to different paths away from communism, allowing some countries to break decisively from the past while other transitions were much more constrained. Bunce reminds us that there is no uniform path of political transitions, and that the constraints and opportunities that might exist in one region (such as Latin America or southern Europe) may be quite different from those that exist in another.

In a more recent and novel argument, Keith Darden and Anna Grzymala-Busse (2006) add an additional variable to Bunce's discussion: literacy. In their view, the various explanations that Bunce laid out, such as culture, history and geography, fail to take into account the importance of mass schooling across these countries, which was less uniform than we might imagine. In many places, mass school and literacy predated communism by several decades, whereas in other countries it spread only under communism and even then was not complete or comprehensive. Why should this matter? According to the authors, the legacy of schooling before communism helped generate a national identity that would survive and eventually become an ideological alternative to communism. In contrast, where schooling prior to communism was limited, education and modernization were largely associated with the Soviet era, making it more difficult for opponents of communism to articulate an alternative. These historical differences continue to shape how these now postcommunist states still view themselves and their relationship toward democracy and capitalism.

These discussions take us in turn to considering where postcommunist states are bound in the future. Michael McFaul, who has been an adviser to President Barack Obama, writes in "Transitions from Postcommunism" (2005) about the prospects for change in those postcommunist countries that abandoned communism but did not embrace democracy. Since 2000, there has been a notable push toward greater democracy in several important countries in postcommunist Europe, most notably Ukraine. What are we to make of this change? In contrast to our gloomier assumptions that illiberal regimes seem particularly adept at coopting and controlling the public, in postcommunist Europe the presence of nongovernmental organizations and somewhat open media, among other factors, helped bring down those in power. Not all of this change has been promising. Ukraine's democratization has been dragged down in political polarization; the democratic government of Georgia went to war with Russia. That said, McFaul reminds us that the transition from communism is far from over, and that the simple collapse of the communist idea does not lead to democracy by default.

This lesson is particularly important with regard to Russia and China. In the former, early and chaotic democratization has given way under Putin's centralization of power, such that it is even difficult to speak of this as an illiberal regime. China, too, has abandoned communism in all but name, relying on rapid economic growth and nationalism as sources of legitimacy. For Azar Gat (2007), the rise of Russia and China as major world powers has brought a new era of international relations akin to the 1930s. Postcommunist, authoritarian and capitalist, Russia and China will be a major challenge to liberal democracy in the coming decades, as Germany and Japan were in the interwar period—an alternative to the assumption that capitalism and liberal democracy must go hand in hand.

Since Gat wrote this article, the downturn of the global economy has only raised additional questions. Will global economic recession only further weaken liberal democracies? Or will Russia and China, both highly dependent on international trade, find that their rising status in the global order (and their authoritarian regimes) are open to challenge?

KARL MARX AND FRIEDRICH ENGELS

MANIFESTO OF THE COMMUNIST PARTY

A spectre is haunting Europe—the spectre of communism. All the powers of old Europe have entered into a holy alliance to exorcise this spectre: Pope and Tsar, Metternich and Guizot, French Radicals and German police-spies.

Where is the party in opposition that has not been decried as communistic by its opponents in power? Where is the opposition that has not hurled back the branding reproach of communism, against the more advanced opposition parties, as well as against its reactionary adversaries?

Two things result from this fact:

I. Communism is already acknowledged by all European powers to be itself a power.
II. It is high time that Communists should openly, in the face of the whole world, publish their views, their aims, their tendencies, and meet this nursery tale of the spectre of communism with a manifesto of the party itself.

To this end, Communists of various nationalities have assembled in London and sketched the following manifesto, to be published in the English, French, German, Italian, Flemish and Danish languages.

From *Selected Works in Three Volumes*, Vol. 1 (Moscow, USSR: Progress Publishers, 1969), pp. 98–137.

I—Bourgeois and Proletarians

The history of all hitherto existing society is the history of class struggles.

Freeman and slave, patrician and plebian, lord and serf, guild-master and journeyman, in a word, oppressor and oppressed, stood in constant opposition to one another, carried on an uninterrupted, now hidden, now open fight, a fight that each time ended, either in a revolutionary reconstitution of society at large, or in the common ruin of the contending classes.

In the earlier epochs of history, we find almost everywhere a complicated arrangement of society into various orders, a manifold gradation of social rank. In ancient Rome we have patricians, knights, plebians, slaves; in the Middle Ages, feudal lords, vassals, guild-masters, journeymen, apprentices, serfs; in almost all of these classes, again, subordinate gradations.

The modern bourgeois society that has sprouted from the ruins of feudal society has not done away with class antagonisms. It has but established new classes, new conditions of oppression, new forms of struggle in place of the old ones.

Our epoch, the epoch of the bourgeoisie, possesses, however, this distinct feature: it has simplified class antagonisms. Society as a whole is more and more splitting up into two great hostile camps, into two great classes directly facing each other—bourgeoisie and proletariat.

From the serfs of the Middle Ages sprang the chartered burghers of the earliest towns. From these burgesses the first elements of the bourgeoisie were developed.

The discovery of America, the rounding of the Cape, opened up fresh ground for the rising bourgeoisie. The East-Indian and Chinese markets, the colonisation of America, trade with the colonies, the increase in the means of exchange and in commodities generally, gave to commerce, to navigation, to industry, an impulse never before known, and thereby, to the revolutionary element in the tottering feudal society, a rapid development.

The feudal system of industry, in which industrial production was monopolized by closed guilds, now no longer suffices for the growing wants of the new markets. The manufacturing system took its place. The guild-masters were pushed aside by the manufacturing middle class; division of labor between the different corporate guilds vanished in the face of division of labor in each single workshop.

Meantime, the markets kept ever growing, the demand ever rising. Even manufacturers no longer sufficed. Thereupon, steam and machinery revolutionized industrial production. The place of manufacture was taken by the giant, MODERN INDUSTRY; the place of the industrial middle class by industrial millionaires, the leaders of the whole industrial armies, the modern bourgeois.

Modern industry has established the world market, for which the discovery of America paved the way. This market has given an immense development to commerce, to navigation, to communication by land. This development has, in turn, reacted on the extension of industry; and in proportion as industry, commerce, navigation, railways extended, in the same proportion the bourgeoisie developed, increased its capital, and pushed into the background every class handed down from the Middle Ages.

We see, therefore, how the modern bourgeoisie is itself the product of a long course of development, of a series of revolutions in the modes of production and of exchange.

Each step in the development of the bourgeoisie was accompanied by a corresponding political advance in that class. An oppressed class under the sway of the feudal nobility, an armed and self-governing association of medieval commune: here independent urban republic (as in Italy and Germany); there taxable "third estate" of the monarchy (as in France); afterward, in the period of manufacturing proper, serving either the semi-feudal or the absolute monarchy as a counterpoise against the nobility, and, in fact, cornerstone of the great monarchies in general— the bourgeoisie has at last, since the establishment of Modern Industry and of the world market, conquered for itself, in the modern representative state, exclusive political sway. The executive of the modern state is but a committee for managing the common affairs of the whole bourgeoisie.

The bourgeoisie, historically, has played a most revolutionary part.

The bourgeoisie, wherever it has got the upper hand, has put an end to all feudal, patriarchal, idyllic relations. It has pitilessly torn asunder the motley feudal ties that bound man to his "natural superiors," and has left no other nexus between people than naked self-interest, than callous "cash payment." It has drowned out the most heavenly ecstacies of religious fervor, of chivalrous enthusiasm, of philistine sentimentalism, in the icy water of egotistical calculation. It has resolved personal worth into exchange value, and in place of the numberless indefeasible chartered freedoms, has set up that single, unconscionable freedom—Free Trade. In one word, for exploitation, veiled by religious and political illusions, it has substituted naked, shameless, direct, brutal exploitation.

The bourgeoisie has stripped of its halo every occupation hitherto honored and looked up to with reverent awe. It has converted the physician, the lawyer, the priest, the poet, the man of science, into its paid wage laborers.

The bourgeoisie has torn away from the family its sentimental veil, and has reduced the family relation into a mere money relation.

The bourgeoisie has disclosed how it came to pass that the brutal display of vigor in the Middle Ages, which reactionaries so much admire, found its fitting complement in the most slothful indolence. It has been the first to show what man's activity can bring about. It has accomplished wonders far surpassing Egyptian pyramids, Roman aqueducts, and Gothic cathedrals; it has conducted expeditions that put in the shade all former exoduses of nations and crusades.

The bourgeoisie cannot exist without constantly revolutionizing the instruments of production, and thereby the relations of production, and with them the whole relations of society. Conservation of the old modes of production in unaltered form, was, on the contrary, the first condition of existence for all earlier industrial classes. Constant revolutionizing of production, uninterrupted disturbance of all social conditions, everlasting uncertainty and agitation distinguish the bourgeois epoch from all earlier ones. All fixed, fast frozen relations, with their train of ancient and venerable prejudices and opinions, are swept away, all new-formed ones become antiquated before they can ossify. All that is solid melts into air, all that is holy is profaned, and man is at last compelled to face with sober senses his real condition of life and his relations with his kind.

The need of a constantly expanding market for its products chases the bourgeoisie over the entire surface of the globe. It must nestle everywhere, settle everywhere, establish connections everywhere.

The bourgeoisie has, through its exploitation of the world market, given a cosmopolitan character to production and consumption in every country. To the great chagrin of reactionaries, it has drawn from under the feet of industry the national ground on which it stood. All old-established national industries have been destroyed or are daily being destroyed. They are dislodged by new industries, whose introduction becomes a life and death question for all civilized nations, by industries that no longer work up indigenous raw material, but raw material drawn from the remotest zones; industries whose products are consumed, not only at home, but in every quarter of the globe. In place of the old wants, satisfied by the production of the country, we find new wants, requiring for their satisfaction the products of distant lands and climes. In place of the old local and national seclusion and self-sufficiency, we have intercourse in every direction, universal interdependence of nations. And as in material, so also in intellectual production. The intellectual creations of individual nations become common property. National one-sidedness and narrow-mindedness become more and more impossible, and from the numerous national and local literatures, there arises a world literature.

The bourgeoisie, by the rapid improvement of all instruments of production, by the immensely facilitated means of communication, draws all, even the most barbarian, nations into civilization. The cheap prices of commodities are the heavy artillery with which it forces the barbarians' intensely obstinate hatred of foreigners to capitulate. It compels all nations, on pain of extinction, to adopt the bourgeois mode of production; it compels them to introduce what it calls civilization into their midst, i.e., to become bourgeois themselves. In one word, it creates a world after its own image.

The bourgeoisie has subjected the country to the rule of the towns. It has created enormous cities, has greatly increased the urban population as compared with the rural, and has thus rescued a considerable part of the population from the idiocy of rural life. Just as it has made the country dependent on the towns, so it has made barbarian and semi-barbarian countries dependent on the civilized ones, nations of peasants on nations of bourgeois, the East on the West.

The bourgeoisie keeps more and more doing away with the scattered state of the population, of the means of production, and of property. It has agglomerated population, centralized the means of production, and has concentrated property in a few hands. The necessary consequence of this was political centralization. Independent, or but loosely connected provinces, with separate interests, laws, governments, and systems of taxation, became lumped together into one nation, with one government, one code of laws, one national class interest, one frontier, and one customs tariff.

The bourgeoisie, during its rule of scarce one hundred years, has created more massive and more colossal productive forces than have all preceding generations together. Subjection of nature's forces to man, machinery, application of chemistry to industry and agriculture, steam navigation, railways, electric telegraphs, clearing of whole continents for cultivation, canalization or rivers, whole populations conjured out of the ground—what earlier century had even a presentiment that such productive forces slumbered in the lap of social labor?

We see then: the means of production and of exchange, on whose foundation the bourgeoisie built itself up, were generated in feudal society. At a certain stage in the development of these means of production and of exchange, the conditions under which feudal society produced and exchanged, the feudal organization of agriculture and manufacturing industry, in one word, the feudal relations of property became no longer compatible with the already developed productive forces; they became so many fetters. They had to be burst asunder; they were burst asunder.

Into their place stepped free competition, accompanied by a social and political constitution adapted in it, and the economic and political sway of the bourgeois class.

A similar movement is going on before our own eyes. Modern bourgeois society, with its relations of production, of exchange and of property, a society that has conjured up such gigantic means of production and of exchange, is like the sorcerer who is no longer able to control the powers of the nether world whom he has called up by his spells. For many a decade past, the history of industry and commerce is but the history of the revolt of modern productive forces against modern conditions of production, against the property relations that are the conditions for the existence of the bourgeois and of its rule. It is enough to mention the commercial crises that, by their periodical return, put the existence of the entire bourgeois society on its trial, each time more threateningly. In these crises, a great part not only of the existing products, but also of the previously created productive forces, are periodically destroyed. In these crises, there breaks out an epidemic that, in all earlier epochs, would have seemed an absurdity—the epidemic of over-production. Society suddenly finds itself put back into a state of momentary barbarism; it appears as if a famine, a universal war of devastation, had cut off the supply of every means of subsistence; industry and commerce seem to be destroyed. And why? Because there is too much civilization, too much means of subsistence, too much industry, too much commerce. The productive forces at the disposal of society no longer tend to further the development of the conditions of bourgeois property; on the contrary, they have become too powerful for these conditions, by which they are fettered, and so soon as they overcome these fetters, they bring disorder into the whole of bourgeois society, endanger the existence of bourgeois property. The conditions of bourgeois society are too narrow to comprise the wealth created by them. And how does the bourgeoisie get over these crises? On the one hand, by enforced destruction of a mass of productive forces; on the other, by the conquest of new markets, and by the more thorough exploitation of the old ones. That is to say, by paving the way for more extensive and more destructive crises, and by diminishing the means whereby crises are prevented.

The weapons with which the bourgeoisie felled feudalism to the ground are now turned against the bourgeoisie itself.

But not only has the bourgeoisie forged the weapons that bring death to itself; it has also called into existence the men who are to wield those weapons—the modern working class—the proletarians.

In proportion as the bourgeoisie, i.e., capital, is developed, in the same proportion is the proletariat, the modern working class, developed—a class of laborers, who live only so long as they find work, and who find work only so long as their labor increases capital. These laborers, who must sell themselves piecemeal, are a commodity, like every other article of commerce, and are consequently exposed to all the vicissitudes of competition, to all the fluctuations of the market.

Owing to the extensive use of machinery, and to the division of labor, the work of the proletarians has lost all individual character, and, consequently, all charm for the workman. He becomes an appendage of the machine, and it is only the most simple, most monotonous, and most easily acquired knack, that is required of him. Hence, the cost of production of a workman is restricted, almost entirely, to the means of subsistence that he requires for maintenance, and for the propagation of his race. But the price of a commodity, and therefore also of labor, is equal to its cost of production. In proportion, therefore, as the repulsiveness of the work increases, the wage decreases. What is more, in proportion as the use of machinery and division of labor increases, in the same proportion the burden of toil also increases, whether by prolongation of the working hours, by the increase of the work exacted in a given time, or by increased speed of machinery, etc.

Modern Industry has converted the little workshop of the patriarchal master into the great factory of the industrial capitalist. Masses of laborers, crowded into the factory, are organized like soldiers. As privates of the industrial army, they are placed under the command of a perfect hierarchy of officers and sergeants. Not only are they slaves of the bourgeois class, and of the bourgeois state; they are daily and hourly enslaved by the machine, by the overlooker, and, above all, in the individual bourgeois manufacturer himself. The more openly this despotism proclaims gain to be its end and aim, the more petty, the more hateful and the more embittering it is.

The less the skill and exertion of strength implied in manual labor, in other words, the more modern industry becomes developed, the more is the labor of men superseded by that of women. Differences of age and sex have no longer any distinctive social validity for the working class. All are instruments of labor, more or less expensive to use, according to their age and sex.

No sooner is the exploitation of the laborer by the manufacturer, so far at an end, that he receives his wages in cash, than he is set upon by the other portion of the bourgeoisie, the landlord, the shopkeeper, the pawnbroker, etc.

The lower strata of the middle class—the small tradespeople, shopkeepers, and retired tradesmen generally, the handicraftsmen and peasants—all these sink gradually into the proletariat, partly because their diminutive capital does not suffice for the scale on which Modern Industry is carried on, and is swamped in the competition with the large capitalists, partly because their specialized skill is rendered worthless by new methods of production. Thus, the proletariat is recruited from all classes of the population.

The proletariat goes through various stages of development. With its birth begins its struggle with the bourgeoisie. At first, the contest is carried on by individual laborers, then by the work of people of a factory, then by the operative of one trade, in one locality, against the individual bourgeois who directly exploits them. They direct their attacks not against the bourgeois condition of production, but against the instruments of production themselves; they destroy imported wares that compete with their labor, they smash to pieces machinery, they set factories ablaze, they seek to restore by force the vanished status of the workman of the Middle Ages.

At this stage, the laborers still form an incoherent mass scattered over the whole country, and broken up by their mutual competition. If anywhere they unite to form more compact bodies, this is not yet the consequence of their own active union, but of the union of the bourgeoisie, which class, in order to attain its own political ends, is compelled to set the whole proletariat in motion, and is moreover yet, for a time, able to do so. At this stage, therefore, the proletarians do not fight their enemies, but the enemies of their enemies, the remnants of absolute monarchy, the landowners, the non-industrial bourgeois, the petty bourgeois. Thus, the whole historical movement is concentrated in the hands of the bourgeoisie; every victory so obtained is a victory for the bourgeoisie.

But with the development of industry, the proletariat not only increases in number; it becomes concentrated in greater masses, its strength grows, and it feels that strength more. The various interests and conditions of life within the ranks of the proletariat are more and more equalized, in proportion as machinery obliterates all distinctions of labor, and nearly everywhere reduces wages to the same low level. The growing competition among the bourgeois, and the resulting commercial crises, make the wages of the workers ever more fluctuating. The increasing improvement of machinery, ever more rapidly developing, makes their livelihood more and more precarious; the collisions between individual workmen and individual bourgeois take more and more the character of collisions between two classes. Thereupon, the workers begin to form combinations (trade unions) against the bourgeois; they club together in order to keep up the rate of wages; they found permanent associations in order to make provision beforehand for these occasional revolts. Here and there, the contest breaks out into riots.

Now and then the workers are victorious, but only for a time. The real fruit of their battles lie not in the immediate result, but in the ever expanding union of the workers. This union is helped on by the improved means of communication that are created by Modern Industry, and that place the workers of different localities in contact with one another. It was just this contact that was needed to centralize the numerous local struggles, all of the same character, into one national struggle between classes. But every class struggle is a political struggle. And that union, to attain which the burghers of the Middle Ages, with their miserable highways, required centuries, the modern proletarian, thanks to railways, achieve in a few years.

This organization of the proletarians into a class, and, consequently, into a political party, is continually being upset again by the competition between the workers themselves. But it ever rises up again, stronger, firmer, mightier. It compels legislative recognition of particular interests of the workers, by taking advantage of the divisions among the bourgeoisie itself. Thus, the Ten-Hours Bill in England was carried.

Altogether, collisions between the classes of the old society further in many ways the course of development of the proletariat. The bourgeoisie finds itself involved in a constant battle. At first with the aristocracy; later on, with those portions of the bourgeoisie itself, whose interests have become antagonistic to the progress of industry; at all time with the bourgeoisie of foreign countries. In all these battles, it sees itself compelled to appeal to the proletariat, to ask for help, and thus to drag it into the political arena. The bourgeoisie itself, therefore, supplies the proletariat with its own elements of political and general education, in other words, it furnishes the proletariat with weapons for fighting the bourgeoisie.

Further, as we have already seen, entire sections of the ruling class are, by the advance of industry, precipitated into the proletariat, or are at least threatened in their conditions of existence. These also supply the proletariat with fresh elements of enlightenment and progress.

Finally, in times when the class struggle nears the decisive hour, the progress of dissolution going on within the ruling class, in fact within the whole range of old society, assumes such a violent, glaring character, that a small section of the ruling class cuts itself adrift, and joins the revolutionary class, the class that holds the future in its hands. Just as, therefore, at an earlier period, a section of the nobility went over to the bourgeoisie, so now a portion of the bourgeoisie goes over to the proletariat, and in particular, a portion of the bourgeois ideologists, who have raised themselves to the level of comprehending theoretically the historical movement as a whole.

Of all the classes that stand face to face with the bourgeoisie today, the proletariat alone is a genuinely revolutionary class. The other classes decay and finally disappear in the face of Modern Industry; the proletariat is its special and essential product.

The lower middle class, the small manufacturer, the shopkeeper, the artisan, the peasant, all these fight against the bourgeoisie, to save from extinction their existence as fractions of the middle class. They are therefore not revolutionary, but conservative. Nay, more, they are reactionary, for they try to roll back the wheel of history. If, by chance, they are revolutionary, they are only so in view of their impending transfer into the proletariat; they thus defend not their present, but their future interests; they desert their own standpoint to place themselves at that of the proletariat.

The "dangerous class," the social scum, that passively rotting mass thrown off by the lowest layers of the old society, may, here and there, be swept into the movement by a proletarian revolution; its conditions of life, however, prepare it far more for the part of a bribed tool of reactionary intrigue.

In the condition of the proletariat, those of old society at large are already virtually swamped. The proletarian is without property; his relation to his wife and children has no longer anything in common with the bourgeois family relations; modern industry labor, modern subjection to capital, the same in England as in France, in America as in Germany, has stripped him of every trace of national character. Law,

morality, religion, are to him so many bourgeois prejudices, behind which lurk in ambush just as many bourgeois interests.

All the preceding classes that got the upper hand sought to fortify their already acquired status by subjecting society at large to their conditions of appropriation. The proletarians cannot become masters of the productive forces of society, except by abolishing their own previous mode of appropriation, and thereby also every other previous mode of appropriation. They have nothing of their own to secure and to fortify; their mission is to destroy all previous securities for, and insurances of, individual property.

All previous historical movements were movements of minorities, or in the interest of minorities. The proletarian movement is the self-conscious, independent movement of the immense majority, in the interest of the immense majority. The proletariat, the lowest stratum of our present society, cannot stir, cannot raise itself up, without the whole superincumbent strata of official society being sprung into the air.

Though not in substance, yet in form, the struggle of the proletariat with the bourgeoisie is at first a national struggle. The proletariat of each country must, of course, first of all settle matters with its own bourgeoisie.

In depicting the most general phases of the development of the proletariat, we traced the more or less veiled civil war, raging within existing society, up to the point where that war breaks out into open revolution, and where the violent overthrow of the bourgeoisie lays the foundation for the sway of the proletariat.

Hitherto, every form of society has been based, as we have already seen, on the antagonism of oppressing and oppressed classes. But in order to oppress a class, certain conditions must be assured to it under which it can, at least, continue its slavish existence. The serf, in the period of serfdom, raised himself to membership in the commune, just as the petty bourgeois, under the yoke of the feudal absolutism, managed to develop into a bourgeois. The modern laborer, on the contrary, instead of rising with the process of industry, sinks deeper and deeper below the conditions of existence of his own class. He becomes a pauper, and pauperism develops more rapidly than population and wealth. And here it becomes evident that the bourgeoisie is unfit any longer to be the ruling class in society, and to impose its conditions of existence upon society as an overriding law. It is unfit to rule because it is incompetent to assure an existence to its slave within his slavery, because it cannot help letting him sink into such a state, that it has to feed him, instead of being fed by him. Society can no longer live under this bourgeoisie, in other words, its existence is no longer compatible with society.

The essential conditions for the existence and for the sway of the bourgeois class is the formation and augmentation of capital; the condition for capital is wage labor. Wage labor rests exclusively on competition between the laborers. The advance of industry, whose involuntary promoter is the bourgeoisie, replaces the isolation of the laborers, due to competition, by the revolutionary combination, due to association. The development of Modern Industry, therefore, cuts from under its feet the very foundation on which the bourgeoisie produces and appropriates products. What the bourgeoisie therefore produces, above all, are its own grave-diggers. Its fall and the victory of the proletariat are equally inevitable.

II—Proletarians and Communists

In what relation do the Communists stand to the proletarians as a whole? The Communists do not form a separate party opposed to the other working-class parties.

They have no interests separate and apart from those of the proletariat as a whole.

They do not set up any sectarian principles of their own, by which to shape and mold the proletarian movement.

The Communists are distinguished from the other working-class parties by this only:

1. In the national struggles of the proletarians of the different countries, they point out and bring to the front the common interests of the entire proletariat, independently of all nationality.
2. In the various stages of development which the struggle of the working class against the bourgeoisie has to pass through, they always and everywhere represent the interests of the movement as a whole.

The Communists, therefore, are on the one hand practically, the most advanced and resolute section of the working-class parties of every country, that section which pushes forward all others; on the other hand, theoretically, they have over the great mass of the proletariat the advantage of clearly understanding the lines of march, the conditions, and the ultimate general results of the proletarian movement.

The immediate aim of the Communists is the same as that of all other proletarian parties: Formation of the proletariat into a class, overthrow of the bourgeois supremacy, conquest of political power by the proletariat.

The theoretical conclusions of the Communists are in no way based on ideas or principles that have been invented, or discovered, by this or that would-be universal reformer.

They merely express, in general terms, actual relations springing from an existing class struggle, from a historical movement going on under our very eyes. The abolition of existing property relations is not at all a distinctive feature of communism.

All property relations in the past have continually been subject to historical change consequent upon the change in historical conditions.

The French Revolution, for example, abolished feudal property in favor of bourgeois property.

The distinguishing feature of communism is not the abolition of property generally, but the abolition of bourgeois property. But modern bourgeois private property is the final and most complete expression of the system of producing and appropriating products that is based on class antagonisms, on the exploitation of the many by the few.

In this sense, the theory of the Communists may be summed up in the single sentence: Abolition of private property.

We Communists have been reproached with the desire of abolishing the right of personally acquiring property as the fruit of a man's own labor, which property is alleged to be the groundwork of all personal freedom, activity and independence.

Hard-won, self-acquired, self-earned property! Do you mean the property of petty artisan and of the small peasant, a form of property that preceded the bourgeois form? There is no need to abolish that; the development of industry has to a great extent already destroyed it, and is still destroying it daily.

Or do you mean the modern bourgeois private property?

But does wage labor create any property for the laborer? Not a bit. It creates capital, i.e., that kind of property which exploits wage labor, and which cannot increase except upon conditions of begetting a new supply of wage labor for fresh exploitation. Property, in its present form, is based on the antagonism of capital and wage labor. Let us examine both sides of this antagonism.

To be a capitalist, is to have not only a purely personal, but a social STATUS in production. Capital is a collective product, and only by the united action of many members, nay, in the last resort, only by the united action of all members of society, can it be set in motion.

Capital is therefore not only personal; it is a social power.

When, therefore, capital is converted into common property, into the property of all members of society, personal property is not thereby transformed into social property. It is only the social character of the property that is changed. It loses its class character.

Let us now take wage labor.

The average price of wage labor is the minimum wage, i.e., that quantum of the means of subsistence which is absolutely requisite to keep the laborer in bare existence as a laborer. What, therefore, the wage laborer appropriates by means of his labor merely suffices to prolong and reproduce a bare existence. We by no means intend to abolish this personal appropriation of the products of labor, an appropriation that is made for the maintenance and reproduction of human life, and that leaves no surplus wherewith to command the labor of others. All that we want to do away with is the miserable character of this appropriation, under which the laborer lives merely to increase capital, and is allowed to live only in so far as the interest of the ruling class requires it.

In bourgeois society, living labor is but a means to increase accumulated labor. In communist society, accumulated labor is but a means to widen, to enrich, to promote the existence of the laborer.

In bourgeois society, therefore, the past dominates the present; in communist society, the present dominates the past. In bourgeois society, capital is independent and has individuality, while the living person is dependent and has no individuality.

And the abolition of this state of things is called by the bourgeois, abolition of individuality and freedom! And rightly so. The abolition of bourgeois individuality, bourgeois independence, and bourgeois freedom is undoubtedly aimed at.

By freedom is meant, under the present bourgeois conditions of production, free trade, free selling and buying.

But if selling and buying disappears, free selling and buying disappears also. This talk about free selling and buying, and all the other "brave words" of our bourgeois about freedom in general, have a meaning, if any, only in contrast with restricted selling and buying, with the fettered traders of the Middle Ages, but have no meaning when opposed to the communist abolition of buying and selling, or the bourgeois conditions of production, and of the bourgeoisie itself.

You are horrified at our intending to do away with private property. But in your existing society, private property is already done away with for nine-tenths of the population; its existence for the few is solely due to its non-existence in the hands of those nine-tenths. You reproach us, therefore, with intending to do away with a form of property, the necessary condition for whose existence is the non-existence of any property for the immense majority of society.

In one word, you reproach us with intending to do away with your property. Precisely so; that is just what we intend.

From the moment when labor can no longer be converted into capital, money, or rent, into a social power capable of being monopolized, i.e., from the moment when individual property can no longer be transformed into bourgeois property, into capital, from that moment, you say, individuality vanishes.

You must, therefore, confess that by "individual" you mean no other person than the bourgeois, than the middle-class owner of property. This person must, indeed, be swept out of the way, and made impossible.

Communism deprives no man of the power to appropriate the products of society; all that it does is to deprive him of the power to subjugate the labor of others by means of such appropriations.

It has been objected that upon the abolition of private property, all work will cease, and universal laziness will overtake us.

According to this, bourgeois society ought long ago to have gone to the dogs through sheer idleness; for those who acquire anything, do not work. The whole of this objection is but another expression of the tautology: There can no longer be any wage labor when there is no longer any capital.

All objections urged against the communistic mode of producing and appropriating material products, have, in the same way, been urged against the communistic mode of producing and appropriating intellectual products. Just as to the bourgeois, the disappearance of class property is the disappearance of production itself, so the disappearance of class culture is to him identical with the disappearance of all culture.

That culture, the loss of which he laments, is, for the enormous majority, a mere training to act as a machine.

But don't wrangle with us so long as you apply, to our intended abolition of bourgeois property, the standard of your bourgeois notions of freedom, culture, law, etc. Your very ideas are but the outgrowth of the conditions of your bourgeois production and bourgeois property, just as your jurisprudence is but the will of your class made into a law for all, a will whose essential character and direction are determined by the economical conditions of existence of your class.

The selfish misconception that induces you to transform into eternal laws of nature and of reason the social forms stringing from your present mode of production and form of property—historical relations that rise and disappear in the progress of production—this misconception you share with every ruling class that has preceded you. What you see clearly in the case of ancient property, what you admit in the case of feudal property, you are of course forbidden to admit in the case of your own bourgeois form of property.

Abolition of the family! Even the most radical flare up at this infamous proposal of the Communists.

On what foundation is the present family, the bourgeois family, based? On capital, on private gain. In its completely developed form, this family exists only among the bourgeoisie. But this state of things finds its complement in the practical absence of the family among proletarians, and in public prostitution.

The bourgeois family will vanish as a matter of course when its complement vanishes, and both will vanish with the vanishing of capital.

Do you charge us with wanting to stop the exploitation of children by their parents? To this crime we plead guilty.

But, you say, we destroy the most hallowed of relations, when we replace home education by social.

And your education! Is not that also social, and determined by the social conditions under which you educate, by the intervention direct or indirect, of society, by means of schools, etc.? The Communists have not intended the intervention of society in education; they do but seek to alter the character of that intervention, and to rescue education from the influence of the ruling class.

The bourgeois claptrap about the family and education, about the hallowed correlation of parents and child, becomes all the more disgusting, the more, by the action of Modern Industry, all the family ties among the proletarians are torn asunder, and their children transformed into simple articles of commerce and instruments of labor.

But you Communists would introduce community of women, screams the bourgeoisie in chorus.

The bourgeois sees his wife a mere instrument of production. He hears that the instruments of production are to be exploited in common, and, naturally, can come to no other conclusion that the lot of being common to all will likewise fall to the women.

He has not even a suspicion that the real point aimed at is to do away with the status of women as mere instruments of production.

For the rest, nothing is more ridiculous than the virtuous indignation of our bourgeois at the community of women which, they pretend, is to be openly and officially established by the Communists. The Communists have no need to introduce free love; it has existed almost from time immemorial.

Our bourgeois, not content with having wives and daughters of their proletarians at their disposal, not to speak of common prostitutes, take the greatest pleasure in seducing each other's wives. (Ah, those were the days!)

Bourgeois marriage is, in reality, a system of wives in common and thus, at the most, what the Communists might possibly be reproached with is that they desire to introduce, in substitution for a hypocritically concealed, an openly legalized system of free love. For the rest, it is self-evident that the abolition of the present system of production must bring with it the abolition of free love springing from that system, i.e., of prostitution both public and private.

The Communists are further reproached with desiring to abolish countries and nationality.

The workers have no country. We cannot take from them what they have not got. Since the proletariat must first of all acquire political supremacy, must rise to be the leading class of the nation, must constitute itself *the* nation, it is, so far, itself national, though not in the bourgeois sense of the word.

National differences and antagonism between peoples are daily more and more vanishing, owing to the development of the bourgeoisie, to freedom of commerce, to the world market, to uniformity in the mode of production and in the conditions of life corresponding thereto.

The supremacy of the proletariat will cause them to vanish still faster. United action of the leading civilized countries at least is one of the first conditions for the emancipation of the proletariat.

In proportion as the exploitation of one individual by another will also be put an end to, the exploitation of one nation by another will also be put an end to. In proportion as the antagonism between classes within the nation vanishes, the hostility of one nation to another will come to an end.

The charges against communism made from a religious, a philosophical and, generally, from an ideological standpoint, are not deserving of serious examination.

Does it require deep intuition to comprehend that man's ideas, views, and conception, in one word, man's consciousness, changes with every change in the conditions of his material existence, in his social relations and in his social life?

What else does the history of ideas prove, than that intellectual production changes its character in proportion as material production is changed? The ruling ideas of each age have ever been the ideas of its ruling class.

When people speak of the ideas that revolutionize society, they do but express that fact that within the old society the elements of a new one have been created, and that the dissolution of the old ideas keeps even pace with the dissolution of the old conditions of existence.

When the ancient world was in its last throes, the ancient religions were overcome by Christianity. When Christian ideas succumbed in the eighteenth century to rationalist ideas, feudal society fought its death battle with the then revolutionary bourgeoisie. The ideas of religious liberty and freedom of conscience merely gave expression to the sway of free competition within the domain of knowledge.

"Undoubtedly," it will be said, "religious, moral, philosophical, and juridicial ideas have been modified in the course of historical development. But religion, morality, philosophy, political science, and law, constantly survived this change."

"There are, besides, eternal truths, such as Freedom, Justice, etc., that are common to all states of society. But communism abolishes eternal truths, it abolishes all religion, and all morality, instead of constituting them on a new basis; it therefore acts in contradiction to all past historical experience."

What does this accusation reduce itself to? The history of all past society has consisted in the development of class antagonisms, antagonisms that assumed different forms at different epochs.

But whatever form they may have taken, one fact is common to all past ages, viz., the exploitation of one part of society by the other. No wonder, then, that the social consciousness of past ages, despite all the multiplicity and variety it displays, moves within certain common forms, or general ideas, which cannot completely vanish except with the total disappearance of class antagonisms.

The communist revolution is the most radical rupture with traditional relations; no wonder that its development involved the most radical rupture with traditional ideas.

But let us have done with the bourgeois objections to communism.

We have seen above that the first step in the revolution by the working class is to raise the proletariat to the position of ruling class to win the battle of democracy.

The proletariat will use its political supremacy to wrest, by degree, all capital from the bourgeoisie, to centralize all instruments of production in the hands of the state, i.e., of the proletariat organized as the ruling class; and to increase the total productive forces as rapidly as possible.

Of course, in the beginning, this cannot be effected except by means of despotic inroads on the rights of property, and on the conditions of bourgeois production; by means of measures, therefore, which appear economically insufficient and untenable, but which, in the course of the movement, outstrip themselves, necessitate further inroads upon the old social order, and are unavoidable as a means of entirely revolutionizing the mode of production.

These measures will, of course, be different in different countries.

Nevertheless, in most advanced countries, the following will be pretty generally applicable.

1. Abolition of property in land and application of all rents of land to public purposes.
2. A heavy progressive or graduated income tax.
3. Abolition of all rights of inheritance.
4. Confiscation of the property of all emigrants and rebels.
5. Centralization of credit in the banks of the state, by means of a national bank with state capital and an exclusive monopoly.
6. Centralization of the means of communication and transport in the hands of the state.
7. Extension of factories and instruments of production owned by the state; the bringing into cultivation of waste lands, and the improvement of the soil generally in accordance with a common plan.
8. Equal obligation of all to work. Establishment of industrial armies, especially for agriculture.

9. Combination of agriculture with manufacturing industries; gradual abolition of all the distinction between town and country by a more equable distribution of the populace over the country.

10. Free education for all children in public schools. Abolition of children's factory labor in its present form. Combination of education with industrial production, etc.

When, in the course of development, class distinctions have disappeared, and all production has been concentrated in the hands of a vast association of the whole nation, the public power will lose its political character. Political power, properly so called, is merely the organized power of one class for oppressing another. If the proletariat during its contest with the bourgeoisie is compelled, by the force of circumstances, to organize itself as a class; if, by means of a revolution, it makes itself the ruling class, and, as such, sweeps away by force the old conditions of production, then it will, along with these conditions, have swept away the conditions for the existence of class antagonisms and of classes generally, and will thereby have abolished its own supremacy as a class.

In place of the old bourgeois society, with its classes and class antagonisms, we shall have an association in which the free development of each is the condition for the free development of all.

*   *   *

IV—Position of the Communists in Relation to the Various Existing Opposition Parties

Section II has made clear the relations of the Communists to the existing working-class parties, such as the Chartists in England and the Agrarian Reformers in America.

The Communists fight for the attainment of the immediate aims, for the enforcement of the momentary interests of the working class; but in the movement of the present, they also represent and take care of the future of that movement. In France, the Communists ally with the Social Democrats against the conservative and radical bourgeoisie, reserving, however, the right to take up a critical position in regard to phases and illusions traditionally handed down from the Great Revolution.

In Switzerland, they support the Radicals, without losing sight of the fact that this party consists of antagonistic elements, partly of Democratic Socialists, in the French sense, partly of radical bourgeois.

In Poland, they support the party that insists on an agrarian revolution as the prime condition for national emancipation, that party which fomented the insurrection of Krakow in 1846.

In Germany, they fight with the bourgeoisie whenever it acts in a revolutionary way, against the absolute monarchy, the feudal squirearchy, and the petty-bourgeoisie.

But they never cease, for a single instant, to instill into the working class the clearest possible recognition of the hostile antagonism between bourgeoisie and proletariat, in order that the German workers may straightway use, as so many weapons against the bourgeoisie, the social and political conditions that the bourgeoisie must necessarily introduce along with its supremacy, and in order that, after the fall of the reactionary classes in Germany, the fight against the bourgeoisie itself may immediately begin.

The Communists turn their attention chiefly to Germany, because that country is on the eve of a bourgeois revolution that is bound to be carried out under more advanced conditions of European civilization and with a much more developed proletariat than that of England was in the seventeenth, and France in the eighteenth century, and because the bourgeois revolution in Germany will be but the prelude to an immediately following proletarian revolution.

In short, the Communists everywhere support every revolutionary movement against the existing social and political order of things.

In all these movements, they bring to the front, as the leading question in each, the property question, no matter what its degree of development at the time.

Finally, they labor everywhere for the union and agreement of the democratic parties of all countries.

The Communists disdain to conceal their views and aims. They openly declare that their ends can be attained only by the forcible overthrow of all existing social conditions. Let the ruling classes tremble at a communist revolution. The proletarians have nothing to lose but their chains. They have a world to win.

Proletarians of all countries, unite!

VALERIE BUNCE

RETHINKING RECENT DEMOCRATIZATION: LESSONS FROM THE POST-COMMUNIST EXPERIENCE

Recent Democratization

Our understanding of recent democratization—of such issues as the origins and the consolidation of new democracies—has been heavily influenced by the experiences of Latin America and southern Europe. This is not surprising. The third wave of democratization, as Samuel Huntington termed it, began in southern Europe and then moved quickly to Latin America. Moreover, given the political oscillations of the region they study, specialists in Latin American politics were unusually well positioned to address questions of regime transition. Finally, combining the experiences of these two regions offered a comparative advantage. They contained a large number of countries, virtually all of which had redemocratized over the course of a decade and a half; they shared some commonalities in terms of history and culture; and yet they varied with respect to the timing and mode of transition. It is pre-

From *World Politics*, 55 (January 2003), pp. 167–92. Some of the author's notes have been omitted.

cisely such a mix of similarities and differences that makes for instructive comparison.

The breakdown of state socialism in the Soviet Union and Eastern Europe between 1989 and 1991 and the subsequent rise of new regimes and new states throughout this region provide us with an opportunity to broaden the discussion of recent democratization. By broadening, I refer, most obviously, to the geography of the conversation. If recent democratization is, indeed, a global process, then the terrain of these studies should better reflect that fact. Moreover, only by expanding the geographical horizons can we know whether our conceit as social scientists—that is, our presumption of generalizability—is well founded.

There are, in addition, three other aspects of broadening. One is the familiar argument, central to the ideology of pluralism, that more voices are preferable to fewer in producing quality outcomes. This is particularly important in comparative politics, given the correlation between geographical and intellectual boundaries. As we all know, the concepts used, the questions asked, and the theories evaluated all tend to take on a regional cast.

Just as familiar is a second consideration. Stepping outside our familiar terrain often alerts us to new factors and new relationships—more generally, new thinking, to borrow from Gorbachev. As already suggested, this is not just a matter of reaping intellectual benefits from liberalization of trade among scholarly cultures. This is also a function of the new issues that additional cases often introduce. For example, with the rise of new states and new economic and political regimes in the former communist world came heightened sensitivity among scholars to a series of previously overlooked concerns. These include the impact of economic regime transition on the democratic project; the critical distinction between founding genuinely new democracies (as in most postcommunist states) versus redemocratization (as with much of Latin America and southern Europe); the impact of identity politics and the state on democratization; the consequences for democratic politics of deficiencies in civil and political society; and the role of international institutions in founding, sustaining, and/or undermining new democracies.

A final benefit of broadening is methodological. The most illuminating comparisons are those that restrain the universe of causes while expanding the range of results. In the case of comparative democratization, while Latin America and southern Europe go far in meeting the first condition, they are less helpful on the second—though recent threats to democracy in, say, Peru, Venezuela, Colombia, and perhaps Argentina have provided greater variation in dependent variables. By contrast, the postcommunist region of East-Central Europe and the former Soviet Union is unusually useful on both counts, given, for example, similarities in institutional legacies and in both the timing and the agenda of transformation alongside the sheer diversity of the region's economic and political pathways—what Charles King has aptly termed the "mercurial dependent variables" of postcommunism.[1]

The appeal of this region as an ideal laboratory for comparative inquiry has not been lost on analysts. There are thus a number of studies that use cases from the postcommunist area to address such questions as why democracies either do or do not arise and why some of the new democracies succeed, whereas others break down; whether variations in economic performance reflect historical or more recent influences and geographical, economic, or political factors; and why transitions to democracy are sometimes accompanied by nationalist protests, why some states dissolve in reaction to these protests, and why state dissolution is either violent or peaceful.

Comparing New Democracies

This article aims to use the postcommunist experience in East-Central Europe and the former Soviet Union—twenty-seven cases in all—to rethink our understanding of recent democratization. It does so by conducting a conversation between two bodies of research: (1) studies of Latin America and southern Europe, which collectively have constituted the reigning wisdom in the field, and (2) research on postcommunist politics. The discussion will focus on two relationships central to discussions in the field— between transitional politics and subsequent regime trajectories and between the consolidation and the sustainability of democracy. We will see that the postcommunist experience challenges the way both issues have been understood.

In particular, I argue the following. First, the degree of uncertainty in democratic transitions varies considerably. This in turn affects the strategies of transition and their payoffs. Second, mass mobilization can contribute to both the founding and the consolidation of democracy. Third, under certain conditions the democratic project is furthered by transitions that involve both nationalist protest and changes in state boundaries. Fourth, while rapid progress in democratic consolidation improves the prospects for democratic survival in the future, it does not follow that unconsolidated democracies are necessarily less sustainable. Indeed, compromising democracy (and the state) may *contribute* to democratic survival. Finally, while comparisons among new democracies can identify the optimal *conditions* for democratization, they may have less to say about optimal *strategies* for democratization.

Transitions to Democracy: Assumptions and Arguments

The analysis of recent democratization has been premised on some core assumptions about transitions from dictatorship to democracy—with the transitional period understood as beginning with an evident weakening of authoritarian rule and ending with the first competitive elections. These assumptions include the following: (1) that immediate influences are more important than historical considerations in shaping transitional dynamics; (2) that transitions are inherently quite uncertain; (3) that the central dynamic in a transition is bargaining between authoritarian leaders and leaders of the democratic opposition, with outcomes a function of their relative power; and (4) that the key issues on the table during the transition are breaking with authoritarian rule, building democratic institutions, and eliciting the cooperation of authoritarians.[2]

These assumptions, coupled with comparative studies of Latin America and southern Europe, have produced several generalizations about what constitutes the ideal approach to transition. First, as Dankwart Rustow argued more than thirty years ago, successful democratization seems to require at the very least a prior settlement of the national and state questions.[3] Second, bargaining about the rules of the transition and the new political order should be limited to a small group of authoritarian elites and representatives of the democratic opposition. Finally, given the uncertainty of transitions, it is useful to forge compromises that promote political stability during the construction of a democratic order. In practice, this means pacting; reducing the range of issues on the bargaining table (for example, avoiding reforms of the state and, if possible, major and inherently destabilizing economic reforms); demobilizing publics (which also limits the issues on the table, while depriving the authoritarians of a rationale for sabotaging democratization); forming interim governments with leaders agreeable to both sides; giving the military some room for political maneuver in the constitution; and holding a competitive election that produces a government broadly representative of both authoritarians and democrats.

Mass Mobilization

The postcommunist experience seems to challenge many of these assumptions about transitional strategies. Let us begin by addressing the role of mass publics in the transition. It is widely agreed among specialists and confirmed by the rankings over time by Freedom House that the most successful transitions to democracy in the postcommunist region have been in the Czech Republic, Estonia, Hungary, Latvia, Lithuania, Poland, and Slovenia. The transition to democracy in every one of these cases, except Hungary, began with mass protests.[4] Moreover, if we restrict our focus to those countries that show significant improvement in their democratic performance over time, or Bulgaria and Romania, we see the same pattern: mass mobilization at the beginning of the transition.

Why was mass mobilization so often helpful to the democratic transition in the postcommunist context? The answer is that political protests performed a number of valuable functions. They signaled the breakdown of the authoritarian order; created a widespread sense that there were alternatives to that order; pushed authoritarian leaders (and sometimes even leaders of the opposition, as with Walesa in Poland) to the bargaining table; created (and sometimes restored) a large opposition united by its rejection of the incumbent regime; and gave opposition leaders a resource advantage when bargaining with authoritarian elites. Finally, mass mobilization created a mandate for radical change that subsequently translated into a large victory for the democratic forces in the first competitive elections and, following that, led to the introduction of far-reaching economic and political reforms.

Uncertainty

If we accept that mass mobilization during the transition can further the democratic project, then we necessarily confront additional challenges to the received wisdom about recent democratization. First, it can be argued that in many cases such mobilization in the postcommunist region reduced the uncertainty of the transition—by providing a clear reading of mass sentiments, by strengthening the bargaining power of opposition leaders, and by forcing the communists to give up their defense of the old order, either stepping aside quickly (as in Czechoslovakia) or, when thinking prospectively, joining the movement for democracy (as in Poland, Slovenia, and the Baltic states).[5] At the same time, mass mobilization promised—and delivered—a popular mandate for democracy in the first competitive elections.

Most of the transitions to democracy in the postcommunist world were, of course, highly uncertain. This is evidenced by the fact that the first competitive election in most of the countries in the region led to a communist victory. Indeed, the larger the victory, the more likely that authoritarian rule continued. Moreover, even ten years after the transition began, only one-third of the postcommunist regimes were ranked fully free. Although this is the highest number since state socialism fell, it is a percentage much lower than what one finds at a comparable point in the Latin American and southern

European transitions. When combined with the earlier observations, these patterns suggest that the uncertainty surrounding postcommunist political trajectories varied significantly.[6] In some cases, a democratic outcome was relatively predictable; in most others, the political options after communism were far more open-ended.

Strategic Implications of Uncertainty

The existence of a more certain political environment in some countries calls into question both the necessity and the logic, outlined earlier, of safeguarding the new democracy by forging compromises between authoritarians and democrats. It is precisely the absence of pressure to do so in the Polish, the Czech, and the other highly successful transitions that explains another contrast between the "East" and the "South." It is true that many of the most successful transitions in the postcommunist area included pacting (though rarely as elaborate as the Spanish experience) and that some also evidenced for a brief time broadly representative interim governments. It is also true, however, that the transitions in the postcommunist region that combined pacting with demobilized publics—or what has been asserted to be the preferred approach in the South—were precisely the transitions that were most likely to continue authoritarian rule in the postcommunist region. Moreover, the other compromises that were deemed so beneficial for the southern European and Latin American transitions were rejected by opposition leaders in Poland, Hungary, Slovenia, and the like. Instead, they were strongly positioned to favor an immediate and sharp break with the authoritarian past. Thus, in every highly successful case of democratization in the region, the military was excluded from political influence from the start; the first elections involved a radical break with the political leadership of the past; and major changes in the economy were introduced quickly. Just as important was the commitment in each of these cases to reforming the state, including in most of them its very boundaries. For the Czech Republic, Hungary, Poland, Slovenia, and the Baltic states, then, the agenda of transition was unusually ambitious.

Postcommunist transition dynamics therefore ask us to amend the familiar formulation drawn from the South. It was precisely because mass mobilization was so threatening to authoritarians that leaders of the opposition in some of these countries were free to carry out radical political and economic reforms. Put differently: because of popular mobilization or, in the Hungarian case, reform communism and collaboration between democrats and authoritarians, opposition leaders in what became the most sustainable and full-scale democracies in the East could proceed quickly in breaking with authoritarian rule and building democratic (and, for that matter, capitalist) institutions without worrying as much as their counterparts elsewhere about appeasing authoritarian interests.

This, in turn, altered the strategies of transition and their payoffs. While bridging between the old and the new order constituted by all accounts the most successful approach to democratization in Latin America and southern Europe, the most successful strategy in the postcommunist region was the opposite—severing ties.

The Role of the Military

Also contributing to these interregional contrasts in the optimal strategies of transition was the very different role of the military in Latin America and southern Europe, on the one hand, and in the communist area, on the other hand. Specialists in the South have argued with essentially one voice that the biggest threat to democracy today, as in the past, is the military. One has only to recall, for example, the long history of military interventions in Latin American politics, most of which termi-

nated democracy (though some of them oversaw a return to democratic governance, as also occurred in unusually circuitous fashion, in the Portuguese transition). There is, in addition, the attempted military coup d'état in Spain in 1982. Indeed, precisely because of its long importance in politics, the military has been awarded remarkable powers in many Latin American constitutions, their democratic claims notwithstanding. When combined, these examples carry an obvious message: the military in these contexts can make or break regimes. It is precisely this capacity that contributed to the uncertainty of the transitions in the South and that necessitated compromises with authoritarian forces.

In much of the postcommunist world, by contrast, there is a long tradition of civilian control over the military—a tradition that goes far back in Russian history and that, following the Bolshevik Revolution and the demilitarization after the Civil War, was maintained at home and then after World War II was projected outward to the members of the Soviet bloc. Civil-military relations, in short, constituted one area where the authoritarian past proved to be beneficial, rather than a burden, for democratization after state socialism.

With the military less threatening in the postcommunist context and with mass publics in some cases mobilized in support of democracy, authoritarian elites in the postcommunist region were indeed under siege. This was particularly the case in East-Central Europe, where domestic control over the military (and the secret police)—except in Yugoslavia, Romania, and Albania—had been ceded to the Soviet Union after 1968. All this left the opposition in what came to be the most successful democracies in the region with unusual freedom of maneuver—a freedom enhanced by public support in the streets. As a result, both the effects of mass mobilization *and* the most successful strategies of transition were different in the postcommunist context from what they had been in Latin America and southern Europe.

Nationalist Mobilization

The analysis thus far has sidestepped an issue of considerable importance in the transitions from state socialism: the distinction between protests against the regime and protests against the state. Here, the postcommunist region exhibits another surprising pattern. While popular protest in both the Czech lands and Poland targeted the regime, the Baltic and Slovene demonstrations are better understood as both liberal and nationalist. In the latter cases, then, nationalism supported democratic governance, even when nationalist concerns grew out of and were in part responsible for the disintegration of a state.

There also seems to be another positive linkage between nationalist mobilization and successful, sustained democratization. The republics that made up the Soviet Union, Yugoslavia, and Czechoslovakia varied considerably from each other with respect to whether publics protested, whether the opposition was strong and united, and whether publics, the opposition, and, indeed, even the communists were committed to democratization. With the breakup of these three ethnofederal states along republican lines, those republics with the best conditions for democratic governance were liberated from a political and economic context that made such an outcome unlikely, if not impossible. Thus, not just Slovenia and the Baltic republics, but also Macedonia, Moldova, Russia, and Ukraine were better positioned to pursue a democratic course following state disintegration.

How can we reconcile these observations with the familiar argument that nationalist mobilization poses a threat to democracy on the grounds that the logics of state building and democratization are contradictory? This argument, moreover, has empirical support in the post-communist world, given the deleterious effects of nationalism on political developments after state socialism in Bosnia, Croatia, Georgia, Serbia and Montenegro (and Kosovo), and Slovakia. In each of these cases the nationalist movement excluded minorities residing within the republic; transformed some communists into nationalists, who then used nationalism to maintain authoritarian control; and constructed illiberal successor regimes while deconstructing successor states. What explains these divergent consequences of nationalism?

When nationalism enters the discussion, parsimonious arguments often give way to thick explanations. In this instance, however, there seems to be a relatively simple distinction: *when* nationalist demonstrations began in the republics. Late nationalist mobilization—or nationalist demonstrations that first appeared when the communist regime and state were disintegrating—is associated in virtually every instance with a rapid transition to democracy and progress since that time in building a stable—or at least increasingly stable—democratic order. This describes, in particular, not just the cases of Estonia, Latvia, Lithuania, and Slovenia, but also the far more flawed, but nonetheless durable democracies of Moldova, Russia, and Ukraine.

By contrast, nationalist demonstrations that first occurred before the regime and state began to unravel are associated with very different political pathways after state socialism—either democratic breakdown or a delayed transition to democracy. There were five republics and one autonomous province that experienced such demonstrations by their titular nation during the 1970s or at the beginning of the 1980s: Armenia, Croatia, Georgia, Kosovo, Slovakia, and, to a more limited extent, Serbia. In every one of these cases the subsequent transition to democracy was undermined, as was the successor state in most cases.

Why is timing so important? The key seems to be differences in regime context. In the "early" cases, nationalist mobilization arose in response to two conditions: a strong sense of identity on the part of members and especially the self-appointed leaders of the republic's titular nation (reflecting earlier developments, such as the experience of statehood prior to communist party rule) coupled with republican political dynamics that featured domination by the titular nation along with significant autonomy from the center. Once demonstrations began, three developments followed: minorities within these republics (except homogeneous Armenia) defended themselves from titular domination by building countermovements while allying with the center; the center, fearing that nationalist protests would spread and thereby challenge both the regime and the state, suppressed the titular national protesters, purged the republican party, and empowered minorities as a counterweight to the titular nation; and the republican party fissured in the face of irreconcilable demands from local nationalists versus central communists.

As a result, by the time state socialism began to dissolve, the stage was already set for an unusually problematic transition to both democratic rule and independent statehood. Two insurmountable divides were in place. The first was between nationalists, who dominated the political scene, and liberals, who had been demobilized. The second was between leaders of the majority nation and leaders of minority communities. The national identities of these groups were well defined and exclusivist, and their competing identities were joined with competing interests, political alliances, and preferences for the future. Moreover, the communist leaders of these republics, facing the loss of both their institutional and their ideological bases for ruling, did not have the option their Slovenian counterparts had, of defecting to an opposition that embraced both independent statehood and liberal democracy. Instead, they could either become nationalists or, if adopting a liberal position, face political marginalization.

By contrast, when nationalist mobilization began only later, in response to the weakening of the regime and the state, all these conditions were absent—or at least less well defined. This meant that the majority and the minorities were free to coalesce around the issues of republican sovereignty and liberal democracy. Thus, in these contexts a liberal agenda combined with a nationalist agenda; and not only opposition forces but even many communists embraced that agenda.

We can now conclude our discussion of transitions in the South versus the East. The experiences of the latter region suggest the following, all running counter to the received wisdom about Latin America and southern Europe. First, historical factors are critical in shaping the resources and especially the preferences of elites during the transition, as well as, more generally, transition trajectories. Second, one proximate and positive influence, lying outside the high politics of the transition, is mass mobilization. Third, transitions seem to vary in their degree of uncertainty, and this affects what constitutes the most successful path. In the postcommunist world, where some transitions were less uncertain, the most successful approach was one that moved quickly on both political and economic fronts. Fourth, democratization can be successful when it is combined with nationalist mobilization and the founding of a new state. This is particularly so when such mobilization first begins with the weakening of the state and the regime.

Finally, if we divide the transitions in the postcommunist world into two types—where nationalist mobilization was present and where it was not—we find two simple stories. One has already been noted—the consequences for democratization of timing—when nationalist mobilization begins. The second story describes the remaining countries in the region. Here, the key issue appears to be the strength of the opposition, as indicated by their competitiveness in the first election. Put succinctly, the better their electoral performance, the more successful the transition to democracy.

*   *   *

Conclusions

Research on democratization, particularly the founding and performance of new democracies, is largely a literature about the choices political leaders have made and the consequences of those choices. It is also largely a literature based on the return to democracy in Latin America and southern Europe. The purpose of this article has been both to question and to complicate the focus on elites and the generalizations that have been made about transitions to democracy, democratic consolidation, and democratic sustainability. I have done so by adding an additional region to the empirical equation—the twenty-seven countries that make up the Eurasian postcommunist region.

Several conclusions emerged. First, transitions to democracy seem to vary considerably with respect to the uncertainty surrounding the process. This variance in turn affects the strategies of transition and their payoffs. In the postcommunist region it was widely assumed that the uncertainty surrounding these transitions was unusually high, given, for example, the absence in most cases of a democratic past together, the extraordinary economic and political penetration of state socialism, and the seeming tensions among democratization, state building, the construction of a capitalist economy, and the radically changed relationship of the state to the international system. It turns out, however, that for a number of countries in the region the transition to democracy was in fact not so uncertain, for two reasons. First, the military was eliminated from the transition. Second, there was present a powerful opposition that gained strength from popular mobilization against the regime (often also against the state) (as with the Baltic, Slovenian, Czech, and Polish cases) and/or reform communists who collaborated with an opposition committed to democracy (as with the Baltic countries, Slovenia, Poland, and Hungary).

Because uncertainty was lower, moreover, the transition in all of these cases produced a sharp break with the state socialist past—for example, through founding elections that gave the opposition a large mandate, rapid progress in constructing democratic institutions, quick introduction of far-reaching economic reforms, and, in most of the cases, the construction of a new state. By contrast, transition was far more uncertain where the military was engaged in the transition, where mass mobilization focused on leaving the state but not building democracy, and/or where the communists were able to command considerable support in the first election. As a result, the break with the authoritarian past was less definitive—in terms of both political leadership and public policy.

These contrasts have several implications. One is that, while the most successful transitions in the South involved bridging, the most successful transitions in the East involved breakage. Indeed, it is precisely the bridging approach in the East that produced the most fragile democracies. The other is that the contrast between bridging and breakage—and the costs and benefits of each approach—in large measure reflected differences in uncertainty.

Another conclusion is that mass mobilization can play a very positive role in the transition, as it did, for example, in the Baltic, Polish, Czech, and Slovenian cases and, most recently, in Serbia and Montenegro. This is largely because mass mobilization can reduce uncertainty, thereby influencing the preferences of the communists, as well as the division of power between them and the opposition.

Nationalist mobilization and the disintegration of the state can also influence the democratic project. Whether this occurs seems to reflect a key distinction: whether such protests first arose when the regime and state were unraveling or whether the demonstrations at that time were the culmination of a longer history of such protests. In the first case, which describes Slovenia, the Baltic countries, Russia, Ukraine, and Moldova, the transition produced sustainable democratic orders, albeit of varying quality. By contrast, in every transition where nationalist protest had a longer lineage, both the old and the new state, as well as the democratic project, experienced continuing contestation.

This leads to another conclusion. If we divide the twenty-seven cases into two groups—where the transition was accompanied by significant nationalist mobilization and where it was not—we find two sets of stories. As already noted, the first story is about the timing of nationalist mobilization. In the second group, the key issue is the strength of the opposition, which is indicated, for example, by the outcome of the first election.

This brings us to our final set of arguments. It is true, when adding the amendments already discussed, that political leaders—their preferences, their power, and their actions—are critical to the founding and the sustainability of democracy. However, it does not then follow that leaders in different countries have the same menu from which to choose; that similar choices in different contexts necessarily have the same consequences; that there are, as a result, optimal choices that are generally applicable; or that compromising the democratic project and the state during and after the transition necessarily reduces the sustainability of democracy. There are two basic distinctions here: between conditions and strategies and between the consolidation of democracy and sustaining it.

In the first distinction, the key point is that some transitions are more constrained—or more uncertain—than others, and it is precisely the degree of uncertainty that defines both the strategies available to political leaders and the consequences of those strategies. Thus, "easy" transitions feature very different matrices of choices and payoffs than do "hard" transitions. In the postcommunist world there were transitions, as noted above, where the opposition was powerful and the authoritarians either marginalized or collaborative and where, as a result, there could be a radical break with the past. These transitions then produced a quick consolidation of both democracy and capitalism and, when accompanied by state disintegration, even the state. They also set the standard for what constituted the ideal approach—in economics, as well as in politics.

Most transitions in the postcommunist world did not fall into this category, however. Instead, uncertainty was higher, and the best result was a compromised democracy, capitalism, and state. Nonetheless, this did not necessarily mean that leaders in these contexts adopted the wrong strategies. Rather, they merely faced the "wrong" conditions. Moreover, if they had pretended otherwise and opted for breaking over bridging, thereby emulating their more successful counterparts, they might very well have ended up with no state, democracy, or capitalism. Thus, strategies and their particular payoffs are defined by contexts, not by other cases—unless those cases have similar contexts.

This leads, in turn, to the relationship between the consolidation and sustainability of democracy. It is certainly true that consolidated democracies are very likely to sustain themselves. But it does not follow that unconsolidated democracies are necessarily less sustainable or that policies and behaviors that compromise the consolidation of democracy necessarily detract from its sustainability. Indeed, as the Russian case suggests, it may be precisely the limits to democracy, as well as to the state and capitalism, and the policies that contributed to those limits that sustain all three.

We are now in a position to address some issues of broader concern. First, as this article reinforces, the cases chosen do indeed seem to determine the conclusions drawn. This is particularly the case, one can argue, when case selection reduces variation in dependent variables. Moreover, case selection also seems to shape assumptions and therefore analytical approaches. Second, as noted in the introduction, it can be costly to restrict our regional reach. As we have discovered, expanding regional horizons can introduce new variables and new issues, while challenging common assumptions, approaches, and arguments. However, given the repeated contrasts between the South and the East that emerged in this article, an obvious question presents itself: do these contrasts mean that political dynamics are regionally defined?

It is tempting to concur with this statement. After all, for the postcommunist cases in particular, the notion of regional effects is logical—

given, for instance, the structural similarities forged by the political economy of state socialism and the Soviet bloc; the common origins of all the new states as a result of disintegration of the ethnofederal states in the region along republican lines; and the similarities in the timing as well as the key players involved in the transition to democracy. However, I would nonetheless argue against the notion that political dynamics respond to regional effects.

First and most obviously, a major rationale for analyzing the postcommunist cases is their extraordinary variability, not their similarities. Indeed, it is ironic that the variable practices of authoritarianism in Latin America and southern Europe and the variable timing of their transitions to democracy seem to have produced less variation in transition dynamics and in the quality and sustainability of the democratic project than we see in the postcommunist context. Second, like urban-rural distinctions and even some nongeographical cleavages, such as gender and class, that analysts habitually employ, region only begs the question about the factors actually at work. As Adam Przeworski and Henry Teune argued more than thirty years ago: the purpose of comparative analysis is to replace place-names with variables.[7] Indeed, this is precisely what this article has attempted to do by framing the discussion in terms of variations (1) in the timing of nationalist mobilization, (2) in the historical role of the military in politics, (3) in the strength of the opposition, (4) in the uncertainty built into the transition, and (5) in the range of policy options available to political leaders and their payoffs.

Thus, region is merely a summary of factors that have taken on geographical form. For this reason and because regions can provide not just new factors and variation in those factors, cross-regional studies can be quite helpful in contesting or complicating those assumptions and arguments that were derived from the analysis of one or several similar regions.[8] This is particularly the case when regions are very different from one another in culture, historical development, and relationship to the international system; when they add new causal considerations to the analysis; when they vary the timing of the political dynamics of interest; and when they evidence considerable variation in dependent variables. It is precisely for these reasons—and not because region itself matters—that it is advisable where possible to expand our geographical horizons. This is particularly the case for democratization, given its global reach.

NOTES

1. Charles King, "Post-Postcommunism: Transition, Comparison, and the End of 'Eastern Europe,'" *World Politics* 53 (October 2000). On the divergent political and economic dynamics of the postcommunist region, see Valerie Bunce, "The Political Economy of Postsocialism," *Slavic Review* 58 (Winter 1999); www.freedomhouse.org/ratings/index; Karen Dawisha, "Post-Communism's Troubled Steps toward Democracy: An Aggregate Analysis of Progress in the Twenty-seven New States" (Manuscript, Center for the Study of Post-Communist Societies, University of Maryland, September 1997).

2. Guillermo O'Donnell, Philippe C. Schmitter, and Laurence Whitehead, eds. *Transitions from Authoritarian Rule: Comparative Perspectives* (Baltimore: Johns Hopkins University Press, 1986); Terry Lynn Karl, "Dilemmas of Democratization in Latin America," *Comparative Politics* 23 (Spring 1990); Guiseppe Di Palma, *To Craft Democracy* (Berkeley: University of California Press, 1990).

3. Dankwart A. Rustow, "Transitions to Democracy: Toward a Dynamic Model," *Comparative Politics* 2 (April 1970).

4. In Hungary mass mobilization was understood to be politically risky (and turned out ultimately to be unnecessary), given the brutal suppression of the Hungarian Revolution in 1956, on the one hand, and the willingness of the reform communists, even before

the roundtable, to jump on the democratic bandwagon, on the other hand. See Patrick H. O'Neil, "Revolution from Within: Institutional Analysis, Transitions from Authoritarianism, and the Case of Hungary," *World Politics* 48 (July 1996).

5. See Anna M. Grzymala-Busse, *Redeeming the Communist Past: The Regeneration of Communist Parties in East-Central Europe* (Cambridge: Cambridge University Press, 2002).

6. Because Poland was the first country in the region to break with communist party rule,

its transition was somewhat more uncertain. Given the character of the Soviet bloc, however, developments in Poland during the first half of 1989 lowered the risks of transition for other members of the bloc.

7. Adam Przeworski and Henry Teune, *The Logic of Social Inquiry* (New York: John Wiley, 1970).

8. See, for example, Doug McAdam, Sidney Tarrow, and Charles Tilly, *Dynamics of Contention* (Cambridge: Cambridge University Press, 2001).

KEITH DARDEN AND
ANNA GRZYMALA-BUSSE

THE GREAT DIVIDE: LITERACY, NATIONALISM, AND THE COMMUNIST COLLAPSE

I. Introduction

Why do some governing parties, closely associated with a collapsed authoritarian regime, nonetheless retain power and continue to govern? This paradoxical outcome occurred in 45 percent of countries of the former Soviet Union and its satellites. In some of these countries the first free elections returned the Communist Party to rule, while in others unreconstructed communists retained power and free elections were never held. In the remaining 55 percent, however, communist parties lost the first free elections and exited power completely.

In this article, we seek to explain these patterns of communist exit, which has spawned

From *World Politics*, 59 (October 2006), pp. 83–115. Some of the author's notes have been omitted.

both empirical and theoretical controversies. The communist exit in the first free elections has been strongly correlated with subsequent democratic consolidation, successful economic reforms, and patterns of political party competition.[1] Communist persistence, by contrast, resulted in "democracy with adjectives": (1) quasi-democratic systems that hold elections but do not foster competition or representation and (2) the rise of antireform coalitions that extract private benefits from the state and sabotage reforms.[2]

At the same time, considerable criticism of the communist exit as an *explanation* for subsequent trajectories has emerged. First, Herbert Kitschelt, in particular, has charged that accounts focusing on the communist exit as a main explanatory variable suffer from excessive causal proximity, leading to an explanation that "yields little insight into the causal genealogy of a phenomenon."[3] His critique begs a significant question: if the communist exit is so highly correlated with favorable outcomes, how do we account for the exit? Second, the *mechanisms* of this influence on economic and democratic outcomes have been difficult to pinpoint. Does the communist exit act as an independent causal factor that eliminates a source of antireformist sentiment and thus promotes greater elite consensus? Is it a simple symptom of deeper readiness for democracy and the free market or a necessary but not sufficient condition for subsequent reforms? Third, there has been little explanation of the reasons behind the communist exit, or how those reasons might themselves relate to postcollapse outcomes. This shortcoming has led to the criticism that, much as with the communist collapse itself, political science has focused on the wrong set of explanatory factors and mechanisms. One striking omission, for example, is a theory of one-party rule and the factors that could sustain its efficacy and even its legitimacy.[4]

The critical question underlying all these controversies is why communist rule ended in such divergent outcomes. Why, that is, was there communist exit from power in some countries but not in others? We argue that the ultimate roots of the explanation lie in precommunist schooling, which fomented and fostered nationalist ideas that led to the delegitimation of communist rule. The exit itself was the culmination of decades of nursed nationalist grievances, invidious comparisons, and carefully sustained mass hostility to the communist project as a foreign and inferior imposition. Section II reviews and tests the competing explanations. Section III examines the patterns of schooling. Section IV presents an alternative model that establishes a causal chain linking the introduction of mass schooling, subsequent ideas about the nation and its legitimate authority, the rise of anticommunist opposition, and the communist exit. As a result, some countries were much less hospitable to communism, more likely to kindle an opposi-

tion, and more likely to promote the kind of communist party that could and would leave. Section V concludes.

II. Existing Explanations of the Communist Exit

The literature on both the collapse of the communist regimes and the transitions that followed provides us with several competing explanations for the variation in the communist exit. These locate the forces behind the communist exit along a temporal continuum that begins with long-standing structural forces, such a geography, moves through the legacies of the precommunist era, and ends with the immediate causes of the communist collapse, such as the strength of the anticommunist opposition.

One prominent explanation for postcommunist trajectories focuses on *structural factors,* the favorable geopolitical settings that placed some of these countries in the Western Christian orbit, with its Enlightenment tradition, potential for trade, and diffusion of democratic ideas. One manifestation of this influence is the remarkable correlation that exists between proximity to the West (defined as the geographic distance between state capitals and either Vienna or Berlin) and the favorable configuration of communist exit, democratic reforms, and market liberalization, as Kopstein and Reilly 2000 demonstrate.[5] Such settings allowed for the favorable influence of international organizations, "not so much of actual EU or NATO membership as of *anticipated* membership. These divergent, externally induced incentives are part of what accounts for differences in institutional reform, state behavior, and popular discourse in the countries of postcommunist Europe."[6] After all, the nearest neighbors were also the objects of the most intense focus of the EU and other West European initiatives, and communism may have appeared less desirable if one's neighboring noncommunist points of reference were Germany and

Austria rather than Afghanistan and Iran. Geographic proximity had also earlier fostered a sense of "belonging" to Europe.

A second influential approach examines the *legacies of precommunist development* and the ways in which the political experience of the interwar era shaped the politics of the communist years and beyond.[7] In the classic "modernization" account, wealth, industrialization prior to statehood, and overall levels of economic development are critical to the development of democracy and to the maintenance of regime stability.[8] Considerable disparities persisted here in the communist era. Even though East Central Europe has been characterized as a backward periphery relative to Western Europe,[9] its development levels were always higher than in Central Asia, for example. The communist exit, therefore, could be a function of precommunist economic development and, more broadly, of modernization.

In a similar account, the length of the prewar democratic experience and the political configurations that dominated it translate into distinct communist regime types. The resulting typology of communist regimes comprises bureaucratic-authoritarian, national-accommodative, and patrimonial systems.[10] The first type, built on interwar working-class parties and a preexisting professional bureaucracy, results in a configuration of weak communist insiders, unable to forestall their own replacement during the communist collapse. At the opposite end of the spectrum, patrimonial communism, built on authoritarian regimes and nonprofessional bureaucracies, privileges the communist insiders and allows them to hold on to political and economic power. One prediction is that the longer the democratic and legal-rational experience prior to the onset of communism, the greater the likelihood of a communist exit.

Finally, the most temporally immediate explanation for the communist exit is the *strength of the anticommunist opposition* in the waning years of the communist regimes. As several scholars of regime transitions have noted, the strength of the opposition (and its constituent radicals and moderates) affects not only the likelihood of negotiations with an authoritarian government but also its outcome.[11] The more powerful the opposition, the more likely is communist exit. Conversely, as Andrew Janos argued, "because it was rooted in the communalism and paternalism of Byzantine Orthodoxy, communism resonated far more positively in the Orthodox societies of the southeast, than in the legalistic, contrast societies of the northwest tier."[12] The implication here is that cultural receptiveness to communism underlies the patterns we observe and either promotes the rise of the opposition or sustains communist rule.[13]

While all of these explanations offer compelling accounts, they face two challenges. First, many of the accounts tend to rely on powerful correlations, rather than on clearly specified mechanisms by which the legacies of the past, for example, translate into outcomes decades later. Second, these accounts tend to address national-level variation: therefore, they cannot as easily explain the differences among the countries emerging from the former Soviet Union or the intranational diversity in support of the communist party. Yet these are as intriguing and as potentially important for theory building as are their national-level counterparts. As several scholars have noted, pockets of subnational authoritarianism can coexist with democratic national governments,[14] producing very divergent regimes within the same nation-state.

More specific problems arise with the individual explanations. One complication with an emphasis on geographic factors is that some countries were considerably more pro-West than their geographic location would seem to suggest: Estonia, Latvia, and Lithuania are all farther from Western capitals than Belarus, for example. Nor can geography explain the differences in *achieving* a "return to the West." How, that is, did geographic or cultural affinities translate into domestic political action. Moreover, the mechanisms of the affinity for Europe remain underspecified. Integration into specific regional and international organizations is an unlikely candidate: neither the EU nor NATO offered any serious prospects for membership until many years *after* the communist exit and the initial democratic and market reforms.[15] In East Central Europe, when even the most ardent reformists spoke of a "return to Europe," they were referring to a normalcy defined by the lack of Soviet imperial interference and not to anticipated membership in specific international structures. Further, these sentiments did not break cleanly along geographic lines. Thus, European Serbians kept their communist party in power, while non-European Georgians rapidly dispensed with theirs. The desire to "join the West" or "return to Europe" was a significant motive and clustered geographically, but its roots do not lie in location alone. We thus need a better account of the mechanism underlying the desire to "return to Europe."

The mechanisms by which precommunist bureaucratic development and regime types translate into the communist exit are similarly underspecified. Temporal distance should not be conflated with causal depth. What, for example, are the causal links between a professional interwar bureaucracy and the weakness of communist insiders at the time of the communist collapse? There is little question that the precommunist development of a rational bureaucracy and direct rule distinguishes the communist and postcommunist development of many Central European countries from that of Central Asian states, where the Soviet Union was the first to bring any bureaucracy to nomadic societies. However, it is not clear why these differences would lead to the rejection of communist parties. Indeed, one could easily argue that the superior bureaucracy made communism more rational, efficient, and competent and that its bureaucratic legacy should have bolstered rather than undermined the legitimacy of communism. Moreover, having the right bureaucratic legacy was not a necessary condition; otherwise patrimonial Moldova, Armenia, and

Georgia would have kept their communist parties in power.

The strength of the anticommunist opposition movement as an explanatory variable explains both too much and too little. On the one hand, it is so strongly correlated with the communist exit that the possibility the two are part of the same phenomenon cannot be discounted. Once again, if we take warnings of excessive causal proximity seriously, we ought to beware of positing such powerful causal relationships between events that are so temporally close together. On the other hand, this explanation requires that we identify the determinants of a strong opposition: what are they, and do they explain the communist exit as well?[16]

A better, alternative explanation of the communist exit is therefore needed, one that accounts both for the immediate impetus for the exit and for its facilitating conditions. It should also provide a mechanism through which the communist exit becomes feasible and likely. If we turn to the precommunist past, we need to specify precisely which factors and processes made some societies less hospitable to communism on both the individual and the collective level, more likely to foment opposition, and more likely to foster the kind of ruling party that could and would leave power. A country's location and "neighborhood" by itself is unlikely to influence either the popular opposition or the legitimacy of communist rule. Prewar democratic statehood is a more likely candidate, since it may very well engender memories of noncommunist governance and the subsequent identification of communism as an "abnormal" form of governance. Finally, the development of anticommunist opposition itself needs explaining, since it is analytically and empirically so close to the communist exit.

One of the most striking aspects of the anticommunist opposition was its fusion with nationalism. Opposition movements claimed to be rescuing the nation from the grasp of an alien, imposed, and illegitimate communist regime. As Valerie Bunce argues, "The diffusion of the national idea served as the mechanism for opposition elites to confront imperial domination by seeking states and regimes of their own making."[17] Yet if nationalism drives the opposition to communism, this begs the questions of how and why these mass sentiments varied across the region and of which mechanisms link those beliefs—largely historical in origin—to contemporary events.

Although the development of nationalism has been linked to many tools of the modern state, the clearest mechanism for the transmission of a shared national identity and history is education.[18] Although education is typically seen as part of a bundle of developments—urbanization, industrialization, income growth—due to the legacy of modernization theory,[19] the role of education is causally and empirically distinct. Schooling provides the one clear channel for the *deliberate and systematic* inculcation of a set of values.[20] And the critical aspect of mass literacy is its timing: the national ideas instilled in a

population during the *first round of mass schooling* —when a community first shifts from an oral to a literature mass culture—are durable, and the first schooled generation will transmit those values in ways that previous or subsequent cohorts do not, as we will see.[21]

We therefore focus on a historical legacy that predates not only communism but also, in several cases, nation-states; the legacy includes the timing of mass schooling and the nature of its national content. The communist exit could not have occurred without mass opposition to the regime—and that opposition in turn rested on notions of statehood and legitimate governance first inculcated by mass schooling. Attaining literacy under a noncommunist regime led to the transmission of a national identity separate from, and often directly opposed to, the communist regimes. Precommunist schooling thus lowers the magnitude of support for the communist party and increases the likelihood that widespread opposition to the communist party will

Figure 1 Precommunist Schooling and Share of Seats to Noncommunist Parties in the First Free Postcommunist Elections

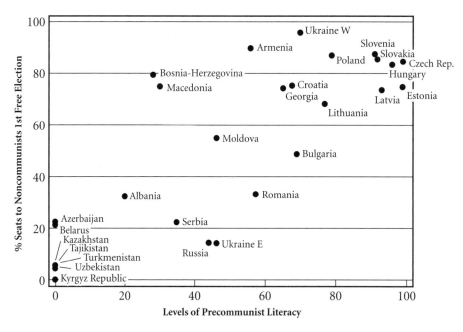

arise. We therefore hypothesize that *the communist exit is more likely to occur where literacy preceded the onset of communism.****

The findings support the claim that where precommunist schooling was firmly established and literacy was widespread, the populations were more likely to vote the communists out of power at the first available opportunity. As shown in the simple scatterplot of Figure 1, there is a clear linear relationship between the percentage of the population that was literate at the onset of communism and the defeat of the communists in the first free elections. In all countries with high levels of precommunist literacy, the communists were soundly defeated in the first free elections.

*   *   *

III. Correlating Mass Schooling and the Communist Exit

What, then, were the patterns of mass schooling? To measure the extent to which the population has been schooled, our primary measure is the literacy rate, because by the turn of the twentieth century, virtually all education was taking place in schools. Typically, a literate citizen would have spent at least four years in school and been exposed to the standard history, literature, geography, and music curricula that shaped common national identities and political loyalties. The illiterate peasantry or herdsmen, by contrast, were typically fragmented into "islands of local customs and relationships, festivity and folklore, which were set apart from the rest of society by dialect and tradition, as well as by the limits on scale which oral communication inevitably imposes."[22] The rate of literacy thus marks the extent of schooling and the degree to which a standardized "high culture" and written history had become a common culture that was shared on a mass scale.

With respect to precommunist literacy and culture, postcommunist countries fall into three basic categories. In the first group are those with highly schooled populations and substantial national content in the schooling curriculum at the onset of the communist period: the Czech Republic, Estonia, Hungary, Latvia, Slovakia, Slovenia, Poland, Lithuania, Croatia, Romania, and the Western Ukrainian region of Galicia. All of these countries/regions had achieved over 70 percent literacy before communism. Most of these areas had already sustained universal primary education for several generations prior to communism and typically also had high rates of secondary education and well-established institutions of higher education.

The precommunist schooling in these countries was infused with national content.[23] In the Habsburg provinces that became Hungary, the Czech Republic, Poland, Croatia, Slovakia, Slovenia, Romania, and Ukrainian Galicia this nationalist content was, in part, the legacy of a long-standing Habsburg policy of divide and rule—national antagonisms were cultivated in an effort to prevent challenges to the monarchy from coalescing. In the nineteenth century Vienna used school curricula to cultivate a new Ukrainian identity in Galicia to counter the active nationalism of the Poles and potential irredentism of the Russians, and similarly assisted the national development of the Romanians, Croats, and Slovaks to undermine the growing influence of Hungarian nobles (the Hungarians, in response, cultivated Serbian identity to divide the Serbo-Croats).[24] Subsequently, the progressive decentralization of Habsburg control over educational content also created opportunities for new nationalist elites, particularly in Hungary, the Czech lands, and Poland, to build support for their claims to independent statehood. Even Croatia, the least educated of these countries, had crossed a 50 percent threshold of literacy by 1910, and its educational system had substantial national content. Thus, even under imperial rule, the curriculum had national content and stressed the cultivation of distinctive identities.

During the interwar period, these governments and the three Baltic states were using nationalist school curricula to build loyalty to the new states and to legitimate their territorial claims. Hungary, Romania, Bulgaria, the three Baltic states, and (by the 1930s) Poland created centralized, standardized school curricula and teacher training with a strong focus on nationalizing and homogenizing their populations. In the Czech and Slovak territories, the vast majority of schools cultivated the identity of the titular nationality of their respective provinces: schooling was decentralized, so the curriculum was often decided at the level of the school.[25]

Elsewhere, in Transcarpathia, there was no consistent policy to introduce national content in education, and a mix of Russophile Russian émigrés, Rusynophile intellectuals, and Ukranian nationalists from neighboring Galicia provided the limited education that the province had achieved by 1938, when it was occupied by Hungary.[26] Yugoslavia's educational apparatus was so poorly funded that prior teachers, curricula, and many texts remained in place through the interwar years.[27] This meant that regions with strong school systems and a history of education (Slovenia, Croatia, and Vojvodina) typically retained their literacy levels, whereas the less educated regions showed only marginal advancement.[28] In all these cases, the explicit purpose of the mass education of the peasantry was to infuse them with new forms of national loyalty believed to be necessary to secure loyal bureaucrats, loyal soldiers, and loyal citizens.[29]

At the other end of the spectrum falls the second cluster of countries, those with little or no exposure to literate culture prior to communism. Albania, Azerbaijan, the five countries of Soviet Central Asia, Bosnia-Herzegovina, and Macedonia each had no more than 30 percent literacy when the communists took power. Prior to communism, these regions had little or no schooling and were marked by high levels of cultural heterogeneity and fragmented, localized identities and political loyalties attributed to traditional societies.[30]

The few literate residents were either national minorities or imperial administrators. In Azerbaijan and Central Asia those who could read and write were typically Russians or other nontitular nationalists. Of the non-Slavic populations of these regions, none but the Uzbeks had achieved even 5 percent literacy by 1920, when the Soviet Union began its literacy campaigns and conducted its first census in the region. In the tsarist empire, the limited schooling in Azerbaijan and Central Asia was almost exclusively in Russian and the cheap, popular reading materials of the time (*lubok*) were entirely Russocentric.[31] Aside from a handful of Jadidist (pan-Turkic nationalistic) intellectuals, the schooling and educational life of the region were entirely lacking in "national" content that would link the local cultures of the region to a claim to legitimate rule or sovereign rights. As late as 1909 Albania did not have even a single teacher training school and the Albanian language had no standard alphabet.[32] Even by the end of the interwar period, Albania had achieved only a meager 20 percent literacy rate and this training was almost entirely of a religious nature. The schooling that these regions eventually received would be under communist control.

In the remaining cases mass education was in the process of being established or varied considerably within the country, having been complete in some regions but hardly begun in others. In Romania, for example, an overall literacy rate of 57.1 percent in 1930 masked difference between Transylvania, with nearly full literacy and strong national content as in other Habsburg communities, and Bessarabia, where only 38 percent of the population could read and write. Serbia, similarly, had nearly full literacy in Vojvodina and in areas around Belgrade but exceptionally low rates of literacy in Kosovo, confirming "that the Serbian national program was not complete."[33]

Russia, Ukraine, Belarus, and the interwar Moldovan ASSR (current Transdniestria) had all achieved moderate rates of literacy, and the youngest generation would have had nearly universal coverage in most of these provinces.[34] These populations were schooled to believe, however, that they were part of a broader Russian nation, with a common past in Kievan Rus, comprising the Great Russians, the Lesser Russians (Ukrainians), and the White Russians (Belorussians).[35] Hence, while the Slavic populations of Belarus and Ukraine had achieved moderate rates of schooling prior to communism, the schooling was Russian in language and focused on broader Russian and Orthodox unity.

Of the cases where mass schooling was initiated but full literacy was not yet attained prior to the communist period, the most interesting are Armenia and Georgia, where the content of schooling was nationalist, despite the fact that the main educational push was carried out when these territories were under Soviet control. Following the Bolshevik Revolution, Georgia and Armenia formed a separate independent Transcaucasian Confederation with Azerbaijan that lasted until 1920–21. During this brief time, both republics set up national primary school systems, with nationalist texts and teacher training.[36] The Soviet government, according to Martin, following the annexation "boasted that Soviet power had deepened the national work begun"[37] by precommunist nation-building governments. Teachers and curricula were retained, and by the time that the "Great Retreat" from this policy began in 1933 and especially by the "Great Purge" of 1937,[38] the populations of these territories were already schooled in an alternative pre-Soviet national curriculum. Thus, even according to the 1939 census, ethnic Georgians made up 72.2 percent of the teachers in the republic and 73.6 percent of the professors and researchers even though they were only 61.4 percent of the population of the republic.[39] Similarly, ethnic Armenians constituted 84.2 percent of teachers and 88.5 percent of professors and researchers in the Armenian SSR, both in excess of their 82.8 percent share of the population as a whole.[40]

More important than the raw percentage of titulars, however, is the fact that the titular nationality had been educated in a fundamentally different in Georgia and Armenia than it had been elsewhere in the USSR prior to World War II. As a result, even though Georgia and Armenia

had literacy of less than 50 percent upon their incorporation into the USSR, these two countries preserved their pre-Soviet nationalist school curricula and teaching cadre into the early 1930s, when the population as a whole achieved nearly full literacy.

Section IV. From Schooling to Anticommunism

The processes linking mass schooling to broad-based nationalism unfolded via three mechanisms. First, schools brought mass literacy. Literacy meant that face-to-face communication was no longer required for the easy dissemination of ideas across time and space. It also dramatically increased a society's capacity to record and convey history, literature, and myth; the amount that could reliably be stored in books and accessed from them was much greater than what could be retained in memory.[41] Mass literacy allowed the social communication among strangers that Deutsch, Anderson, and others have identified as a precondition of nationalism.[42] Education thus increased society's "carrying capacity" for transmitting, replicating, and sustaining nationalist ideas.

Second, and more important, mass schooling used the curriculum to convey nationalist ideas. Most schools in the late nineteenth and early twentieth century purveyed nationalist *content* in the basic subjects of literature, history, geography, and music and thereby inculcated a sense of patriotism in the children. As a result, the rise of nationalism in most European cases can be traced directly to changes in the education and socialization of the young and to the simultaneous introduction of nationalist content into school curricula. Prior to the development of mass schooling, education and socialization consisted of children imitating the rituals, mores, habits, skills, and beliefs of their parents or elders. This form of informal education was inherently conservative. Culture was predominantly learned—or replicated—through observation and experience. Nationalism, however, was a novel idea that could not be conveyed well through such traditional channels. It was not a set of ideas prevalent among the previous generation; and as an abstract, imaginary bond among a community of strangers, nationalism could not be learned through experience. It could, however, be learned in school. As the reading of school texts replaced the observation of experience as the primary form of instruction, children came to think and categorize the world more in terms of the general and the abstract than in terms of the practical categories based on experience. The nation and their place in it was one of the abstract categories that children acquired in school.

Third, this content was monitored and purveyed by a broad, national-institutional apparatus devoted to indoctrinating the younger generation in a common set of ideas. In each community a bounded, controlled setting was established. It was in this environment—the school—that a majority of children spent much of their waking life over a period of many years. Authority over the dissemination of ideas in this setting was strictly controlled by a teaching staff. The staff, in turn, was under the control of the state, educated in its central institutions, and teaching from a generally standardized curriculum. This curriculum and the broad nationwide educational apparatus that disseminated it conveyed a consistent national culture over an enormous territorial domain, typically within a single generation.

In short, mass schooling explains a critical element in the supply of nationalist ideas. A considerable institutional apparatus is required to convey an abstract, shared idea like common nationhood to masses of people who have little or no face-to-face interaction with one another. The rise of formal schooling accomplished this (1) by bringing a shift from oral, informal socialization to general training based on the written word and school texts, (2) by introducing nationalist content into school curricula, and (3) by disseminating this nationalist cultural message through titular-language teachers and standardized statewide institutions.

The mass schooling received by this first literate generation was critical, in that it "immunized" that generation against subsequent attempts to inculcate the populace with different notions of nation, such as those found under communist education. Once established, these ideas were sustained despite border shifts, the decimation of wars, and the migrations of populations. Thus, Germans living in Poland or in Czechoslovakia saw themselves as distinctly German. And Poles forced to migrate to the Soviet Union or the "Volga Germans" maintained their respective identities.

As a result, ideas initially introduced through schooling came to be instilled in the popular culture and eventually accepted as commonplace truths. Unlike previous modes of ideational transmission such as church organizations, which rested on the authority of trained elites with cloistered knowledge, mass schooling embedded ideas in the community at large, making all members "authorities."[43] Schooling carried ideas directly into the household, and any schoolchild could replicate the history of the nation, could sing the national songs, recite the national poets, and explain the significance of dates and symbols of national importance. A society transformed by literacy was particularly suited to the rigors of underground subversion, solidarity, and perseverance. These identities were also robust to the enormous upheavals of war, genocide, and population transfers that surrounded World War II: the national identities were instilled in families and thus survived with family units as they were transferred and resettled hundreds of miles away. (Ironically, the increased population homogenity in Poland, Czechoslovakia, and Hungary that followed World War II also meant greater homogeneity of anticommunist sentiment.)

Two caveats are important here. First, mass schooling and literacy were not *necessary* conditions for the spread of nationalism—nationalist ideas could also be conveyed through church pulpits or other forms of mass oral communication, if not as effectively or irreversibly. Second, schooling alone was not *sufficient* to foment nationalism; it had to be schooling with nationalist content. Nineteenth-century schooling included new subjects such as geography and history that served to inculcate ideas of nation and nationalism. Earlier, Protestant Reformers and Jesuit Counter-Reformers had employed schools in a battle for the minds of children in the seventeenth century, but such schooling resulted in strong attachments to a sectarian catechism rather than to different national identities.[44] Nationalism and schooling become causally linked only when a nationalist curriculum was introduced in the nineteenth century. It was at that time that literacy began to spread to the populations of eastern Europe and parts of what would become the USSR. Hence, in the precommunist cases that we examine here, nationalism accompanied the rise of the school.

From Nations to Values

Notions of a shared national identity then provided standards for what would constitute legitimate rule—governments consonant with national values that advance shared understandings of economic and political development. Both potential counterelites and citizens used three criteria in evaluating the legitimacy of communism. First, was communism a domestic development or was it the imposition of an occupying force? Second, was its sponsor, the Soviet Union, a historical enemy or a more friendly power? Third, and most important, did communism represent a political, cultural, and economic advancement for the nation, or was it an antimodern step backward? Put differently, was communism in keeping with religious, cultural, and economic national expectations?

Where national schooling existed prior to communist rule, these questions were answered in the negative. The communist regime was perceived to be an alien, inferior imposition by a suspect regional superpower. This is not to say that some local elites were not fervent communists who played a key role in establishing com-

munist rule or that the values of socialism, such as guaranteed employment, social security, and egalitarians, were rejected. But as both historical accounts and communist-era public opinion polls show, the communist regimes were not seen as legitimate. Instead, communist parties first battled popular resistance in establishing their rule and then battled apathy once it was established, while the plurality of society looked back with nostalgia to the precommunist era.

Thus, after World War II, the Communist Party experienced success in free elections only in Czechoslovakia, where a strong local tradition of social democracy had existed prior to the war.[45] This was largely the result both of a moderation in communist appeals and of the uncertain status of the newly regained Sudetenland.[46] As soon as the communists began the move to consolidate their power, however, they met with protest and criticism. In Slovakia the communists lost the 1946 elections by a wide margin. In Poland and in Hungary communism arrived with Soviet tanks, was imposed with the clear support of the Soviet Union and its occupying forces, and was never approved electorally. Even in Yugoslavia, where communism was "homegrown," it support was not ensured.

Russia and then the Soviet Union were seen as enemies of both the nation and the national idea. This notion stemmed both from the wartime experiences of Soviet occupation (and in the case of Poland, the refusal to aid the anti-Nazi uprisings) and from the prewar teaching of history. The partial exceptions here are Bulgaria and to some extent Serbia: where nationalist schooling also included a heavily pro-Russian and then a pro-Soviet component, largely due to Russia's role in the liberation of these areas from Ottoman rule.

For countries that had tasted independent economic and cultural development in the interwar period, communism represented a step back from modernity and from national values. It was secular, whereas many of the national ideas of Poland, Hungary, Croatia, and Slovakia were closely aligned with the Catholic church. It was nominally antinationalist and cosmopolitan at a time when local national sentiments were intense. Finally, it entailed an industrial production profile that ignored local comparative advantages and pushed both standards of living and gross national products below prewar levels. For the petite bourgeoisie of Czechoslovakia, Slovenia, and Hungary, nationalization of property and the perception that economic policy now favored Soviet interests represented an economic disaster.

These standards for what would constitute legitimate rule arose from a set of shared expectations about who would best serve national interests and about what constituted the bundle of cultural and economic goods, civic rights, and political responsibilities such a government ought to provide for its citizens. The existence of these standards then led to two sets of comparisons made throughout the communist era: with noncommunist neighbors and with the counterfactual for the communist countries—the imagined trajectories of development had communism not been imposed. As a result, where Central Asian republics saw development and enormous advances in the rights of women, economic growth, industrialization, and the building of national infrastructure, many of their East Central European counterparts saw a massive slide backward into oppression, economic stagnation, nationalization of markets, and national underdevelopment. In Poland the constant standard of reference was *przedwojenny*, or "prewar," an adjective used to describe lost excellence in everything from buildings to scouting associations to fruit preserves. In Hungary, Czechoslovakia, and Poland, scholars covertly calculated the economic costs of belonging to the Soviet sphere of influence and of having to engage in forced trade with the Soviet bloc on unfavorable terms, while their Slovenian and Croatian counterparts estimated the costs of subsidizing other republics in the Yugoslav federation. The comparisons were not favorable. Even as these societies became more industrialized and urbanized under communism, for example, relative incomes did not increase. While East Central Eu-

ropean incomes per capita averaged 37 percent of West European per capita incomes in the prewar 1930s, this proportion dropped slightly to an average of 35 percent by the 1970s and 1980s.[47] Even where material conditions improved under communism, as Slovakia and Western Ukraine, the hostility to communism continued unabated.

At the same time, as Bunce and Kopstein and Reilly point out, geographic proximity meant constant and invidious comparisons to neighboring countries. For Czechs, Slovaks, Slovenians, and Hungarians, the proximity of Austria (and their shared historical past) was one benchmark against which their countries could be measured—and their postwar development was found to be wanting. The availability of Austrian and German media broadcasts in the border regions only accentuated the shortcomings of the socialist system. For Estonians and Latvians, Finland provided the comparison. Romanian intellectuals looked to France, whereas for Polish dissidents, Scandinavia provided an alternative model.[48] As a result, even though communism produced a massive economic and societal transformation with some positive effects, particularly in developing rural areas, such achievements were discounted in comparison with the counterfactual of noncommunist statehood and the ready comparisons with the West. As one observer noted, the prevailing sentiment was that "if not for communism, we would have been like the West."[49]

The same dynamics appear in those nations of the former Soviet Union that had received mass schooling prior to the advent of communism. In Georgia communism was seen as alien and violently imposed during the Bolshevik annexation of the Transcarpathian republic in 1921 and the repression of the Georgian uprising in 1924. In the 1920s and 1930s senior Soviet officials (including Stalin himself) recognized that Georgians refused to accept the legitimacy of Soviet communism, especially in Western Georgia.[50] A detailed ethnographic account from the 1970s from the Abari and Likheti regions found that even rural residents romanticized their precommunist past, schooled their children at home in precommunist national myths, and viewed Russian and Soviet culture as inferior.[51] Sentiments in Armenia tended to be more pro-Russian, because in precommunist Armenian myth, Russians were depicted as providing Armenians with a haven from their historical oppressors, the Turks.

In Estonia, Latvia, Lithuania, and the areas of Ukraine that had national schooling prior to their incorporation into the USSR, anti-Russian sentiments were—and remain—pervasive. Even though the USSR brought industrialization and electrification to rural areas, communism never achieved broad popular support; indeed, it was seen as undermining the more progressive European character of these regions. And nationalist views were expressed in underground publications despite the ruthless suppression of any public expression of anticommunist sentiment. In Ukraine these regions had considerably higher levels of arrests of nationalist dissidents in the 1960s and 1970s.[52] And as in Georgia, a parallel underground culture existed alongside official Soviet life that consisted of anticommunist histories, literature, and songs. Significant religious or national holidays were celebrated privately and the underground culture was passed on in private gatherings of family and friends. Communism was seen as forcibly imposed by Russian (or "Muscovite" in the Ukrainian case) occupation, and the horrors of Soviet annexation in 1939 and then 1944 were recounted to show the nonindigenous, ethnically Russian (or Jewish) nature of communist rule. Local communists were viewed as collaborators with an occupying power. Only anticommunist activities were considered patriotic and loyal.

By contrast, in Central Asia and Azerbaijan the comparisons with both the pre-Soviet past and the noncommunist neighboring states were highly favorable. Communism, closely linked to the Soviet Union, was identified with enlightenment and progress, rather than with forced imposition. Communism was credited with bringing electrification, industry, schooling and high culture, and all forms of modern life to the region. It was associated in particular with the liberation of women from the oppression of traditional life. In Central Asia primary identification appears to have been with the communist-era administrative units (oblasts), rather than with clans, tribes, or any real or imagined precommunist community.[53] The precommunist past was seen in the late 1980s and the 1990s largely as it had been depicted in Soviet accounts, as a world of ignorance, superstition, and poverty.[54] Even as specific policies from Moscow could be subject to criticism, the general assessment was that Soviet rule had brought dramatic improvement to the lives of Central Asians. Russians and their cultural impact on the region were viewed in a very positive light.[55]

For the Central Asian states, comparisons with their neighbors confirmed their favorable view of the impact of communism. Today, Afghanistan and Pakistan still represent examples of life without communism. Afghanistan under the Taliban fit precisely the Soviet stereotype of precommunist life. Only neighboring China is viewed in a favorable light, but as a communist country the Chinese example simply reinforces the general view equating communism with the forces of enlightenment and modernity in the region. Indeed, it is typically viewed as the counterfactual "path not taken," that is, what life might be like had communism not ended with the USSR.

In areas of Ukraine, Belarus, and Moldova schooled by the Soviets—much like Central Asia—pro-Russian sentiments predominated and continue to predominate. Consistent with Soviet ideology, communism is associated with technology, industry, and progress. Even in the areas of Ukraine hit hardest by the famine during collectivization, communism is credited with bringing the mechanization of agriculture, literacy, and progress. Indeed, surveys indicate that these areas are the most staunchly pro-Russian and most nostalgic for the Soviet system.[56] Communism was also viewed as an indigenous movement in these regions, with local communist

heroes lionized and considered to be true patri-
ots. While Ukrainians and Belarussians see
themselves as having a distinct identity and culture, this culture is viewed as closely related and
equal to or inferior to the literature and art of
the broader Russian community. The collective
effort to defend the Soviet Union from Nazi aggression is considered the major patriotic
achievement of the local populations and the
Communist Party, especially in Belarus. Communist partisans and Red Army soldiers were
viewed as defenders of the motherland, not as an
occupying force.[57]

From Comparisons to Opposition

These widespread comparisons meant that the
appeals of nationalist opposition elites would
find different levels of resonance among the populace. Across the communist world, elite groups
were opposed to communist rule, criticizing it
on nationalist and cultural grounds. However,
whether or not such critiques would find broad
popular support depended on extant national
sentiment and identity. Where nationalist
schooling existed, anticommunist opposition
resonated with popularly held notions of communism as an alien and antimodern imposition.
Such opposition took the form of highly organized mass movements, such as Solidarity in
Poland in 1980 (with over ten million members,
or one-third of the adult population) or the
smaller but similarly recognizable opposition
groups in Hungary. In Slovenia a nationalist
communist leader, Milan Kučan, assumed power
in 1986 and led the republic to greater independence from the Yugoslav federation, culminating
in the 1990 elections of DEMOS, a six-party opposition coalition that had arisen in the late 1980s.

The anticommunist opposition, whether organized or still inchoate, made explicit references to
the prewar past. Prewar national holidays, such
as August 17 (the anniversary of the Battle of
Vistula during the Bolshevik War) or May 3 (the
1792 constitution) were occasions for Poles to fly
the Polish flag on their houses and balconies.[58]

March 15, the anniversary of the 1848 revolution
in Hungary, was similarly celebrated with
marches and slogans, many of which took on an
anticommunist cast. In 1989, when the opposition's demonstration was five times larger than
the Hungarian communists' official observance,
the holiday confirmed the public rejection of the
communist regime.[59]

Where the communist regime had been
more repressive but schooling had inculcated
nationalist identities, the opposition consisted
of ad hoc coalitions of mass movements uniting
behind elites in the last days of the communist
regime. Thus, in Czechoslovakia, mass opposition groups, Public against Violence and Civic
Forum, arose only in the days and weeks before
the communist collapse. The Czechoslovak case
also shows that the communists may be forced
to exit in face of popular hostility, even where
no entrenched organization of dissent exists.
The ultimate cause for the communist exit is the
popular sentiment engendered by nationalist
schooling and the comparisons it breeds, rather
than the power of elite organization itself. Conversely, Communist Party strategies may shape
the *form* of the protests, but they do not determine the party's legitimacy or the extent of its
delegitimation.

Once communism began to collapse, these
forces revived prewar democratic parties (the
Polish PPS, Czech Social Democrats, Hungarian
Smallholders'), resuscitated prewar party
acronyms (the Polish BBWR), and adopted historical institutional solutions (parliamentary systems or prewar constitutions, which were
initially adopted wholesale by the new postcommunist governments in the Baltic Republics).
The essence of the opposition project was encap-
sulated in the slogan of a "Return to Europe," as
the motivation for the enormous project of democratization, market reforms, and social transformation that followed.[60] This is not to say the
prewar period was idolized without reservations
or without awareness of its obvious flaws: but
much of the opposition saw the communist collapse and the possibility of establishing new do-

mestic forms of rule as a return to "normalcy," the natural state of these nations.[61]

In the former Soviet Union internal variation corresponds precisely to precommunist nationalist schooling. Popular anticommunist opposition movements appeared in the three Baltic states, Moldova, Georgia, and Western Ukraine and amassed demonstrations of over one hundred thousand people, in many cases already as early as 1988.[62] In each of these cases the movement organizers laid out an explicit nationalist agenda that drew on banned precommunist flags and symbols (the flags of the interwar period in the Baltics, the blue-and-yellow flag and trident in Western Ukraine, the Georgian flag from 1918, and the flag and symbols of interwar Romania in Moldova). The largest protests typically took place on dates of symbolic significance in the precommunist national calendar, such as dates of independence. One of the first large-scale demonstrations, for example, held on May 28, 1988, in Armenia by the Association for National Self-Determination, marked the sixtieth anniversary of precommunist Armenia's date of independence in 1918.[63] Consistent with our claims, Karklins argues that such "calendar demonstrations," as they were called in the Baltics, rested on a shared cultural knowledge that "facilitated mobilization by reducing the need for formal communication."[64] Banned precommunist anthems, nationalist songs, or songs from the wartime anticommunist partisans—known to all—were also used to mobilize mass protests.[65] The movements also demanded revision of communist historical narratives (surrounding the Molotov-Ribbentrop pact in the Baltic case) and the protection of important national or religious sites (the Davitgaredzha monastery in Georgia).[66] In each of these countries, anticommunist opposition was broad based, took the form of a nationalist movement, and drew on precommunist myths, symbols, and rituals.

These movements channeled directly into political organizations that defeated the Communist Party in the first set of free elections in 1990.

In Georgia nationalist organizations such as the Chavchavadze society coalesced into the Free Georgia movement, led by the nationalist dissident Zviad Gamsakhurdia. The movement drew explicitly on Georgia's heroic pre-Soviet past (Chavchavadze was a prominent nineteenth-century nationalist writer). Gamsakhurdia's nationalist agenda decried mixed marriages and even Soviet industrial advancements such as the "building of gigantic hydro-electric power stations and enterprises" as "a manifestation of an ecological war against Georgia and in the end its aim was the genocide of its people," and it attacked the importation of Soviet engineers to run the factories as part of a plan for the forced assimilation of Georgia.[67]

In Armenia the nationalist movement to unite the Nagorno-Karabakh region of Azerbaijan with Armenia repeatedly drew crowds in the tens of thousands to the streets in the late 1990s. The de facto leader of the Karabakh committee, Levon Ter-Petrosian, a nationalist linguist born outside the USSR, drew on historical myths of a greater Armenia to legitimate claims to Karabakh. With the first free elections in 1990, Ter-Petrosian and the Karabakh committee rode to power easily and Ter-Petrosian became head of state. In all three Baltic states the national movements rapidly developed political organizations with broad popular appeal (ENIP, the Estonian Popular Front, and the defection of a proindependence group from the ECP in Estonia, Sajudis in Lithuania, and the Latvian Popular Front). Each of these swept the communists from power in the Supreme Soviet elections in 1990. In Ukraine, despite considerable repression from the hard-line communist leadership in Kiev, massive nationalist demonstrations in the provincial capitals of Galicia (Lvov, Ivano-Frankovsk, Ternopol) led to the formation of Rukh, which took control of these local governments in the 1990 elections and took all of the elected seats from these regions to the Supreme Soviet elections of 1990s.[68] In other Ukrainian provinces the Communist Party safely and comfortably held on to power, even in Transcarpathia, which had also been incorporated into the USSR after World War II. It was only in those Ukrainian provinces that had precommunist national schooling that the communists were voted out of power. What was true for Ukraine was true for the Soviet Union as a whole: where mass schooling was introduced under communism, the communists held on to power in the elections of 1990.

Where no nationalist schooling took place, there was no pool of national sentiment from which elites opposing the communist regimes could draw. Even where prominent opposition figures existed, such as Mihai Botez, Doina Cornea, and Mircea Dinescu in Romania, they were unable to foment the kind of mass opposition to communist rule that was the immediate cause of the communist collapse. Without the groundswell of demands for their exit, Romanian communists were able to hold on to power as their counterpart regimes fell. Their internal coup of 1989 kept them in power until the 1996 first free elections, which forced them out. Similarly, the communists in Albania held on to power through the elections of April 1991 with over 56 percent of the vote, leaving office only in May 1992.

Bulgaria appears at first to be an exception to the correlation between nationalist schooling and the communist exit: despite the introduction of Bulgarian national schooling (albeit one that was strongly pre-Russian and pro-Soviet, given the Russian liberation of Bulgaria in 1905), the Communist Party formed the government after the first free elections in 1990, with 47 percent of the vote.[69] It is important to note, however, that the combined anticommunist opposition actually won more votes, with 50 percent: the Union of Democratic Forces, the main opposition movement, received 36 percent of the vote, the Bulgarian National People's Union (a throwback to prewar agrarian parties) received 8 percent, and the Turkish minority opposition party, 6 percent.

In short, nationalist schooling produced shared expectations and standards for a legitimate government. It sustained both anticommu-

nist sentiment throughout the postwar era and the opposition that arose (and organized where the communist regime made it possible). The overwhelming and shared desirability of a "return to normalcy" produced an elite consensus about the need for a new and noncommunist regime, even if, as the cases of Slovakia, Croatia, Georgia, and Armenia show, elite commitments to democracy itself were far shakier. As Valerie Bunce points out, nationalism is "wanton" and can coexist with both democratic and authoritarian regimes. It is the *content* of nationalism, not its advocacy of uniting political and administrative units, that determines whether it serves as a force for consolidating democracy or for undermining liberal rule.[70]

V. Conclusion

To lengthen and deepen the causal chain behind the patterns of communist exit from power, we argued that precommunist nationalist schooling produced the shared memories and standards that made popular acceptance of communist rule unlikely. Constant comparisons to both the prewar era of independence and to neighboring noncommunist countries meant that where nationalist schooling existed, such comparisons would strengthen anticommunist convictions. As a result, decades of these comparisons under communism led to the rise of widespread opposition to communist rule (whether highly organized or not). In a much shorter causal link, this opposition then led to the communist exit, both because communist rule had been discredited and because the opposition provided a salient and far more legitimate governing alternative. By contrast, where schooling was introduced under communism, no such invidious comparisons were made. Rather, the shared understanding was that communist rule brought modernity and its attendant advancements.

The communist exit pinpoints which factors identified by earlier modernization analyses changed popular values and expectations regarding good governance. While education, economic development, and urbanization were bundled together by these earlier analyses, we show that it was mass schooling—and the national content it transmitted—that influenced the degree to which communist rule was viewed as legitimate (or not) and the subsequent mobilization against it. Other factors may correlate with each other, but they do not explain the developments in the communist world or the eventual trajectories of its collapse.

The timing and content of schooling explain more variation than do the alternative models, while also complementing them. The account presented here elaborates the underlying mechanisms of geographic proximity and prewar legacies and shows why the anticommunist opposition arose in the first place. The key to these extensions and to the causal chain behind the communist exit is the reincorporation of the microfoundations of individual and societal behavior: the shared understandings, expectations, and standards for legitimate government. These notions are why anticommunism was equated with nationalism (even if not always with democracy). National identities may have also helped to propel these countries through the troughs of painful market reforms and confusing political change, generating popular acceptance of the sacrifices necessary. This, then, may be one way in which "culture matters"—not as a structural predisposition for particular behaviors or as an affinity for specific institutional solutions but as a historically created set of widely shared standards for government origin, legitimacy, and performance.

NOTES

1. M. Steven Fish, "The Determinants of Economic Reform in the Post-Communist World," *East European Politics and Societies* 12 (Winter 1998); Valerie Bunce, "The Political Economy of Postsocialism," *Slavic Review* 58 (Winter 1999); Herbert Kitschelt,

"Accounting for Postcommunist Regime Diversity: What Counts as a Good Cause?" in Grzegorz Ekiert and Stephen Hanson, eds., *Capitalism and Democracy in Central and Eastern Europe* (Cambridge: Cambridge University Press, 2003).

2. Steven Levitsky and Lucan Way, "The Rise of Competitive Authoritarianism," *Journal of Democracy* 13 (April 2002); Joel S. Hellman, "Winner Takes All: The Politics of Partial Reform in Postcommunist Transitions," *World Politics* 50 (January 1998).

3. Kitschelt (fn. 1).

4. Stathis Kalyvas, "The Decay and Breakdown of Communist One-Party Regimes," *Annual Review of Political Science* 2 (1999); Timur Kuran, "Now out of Never: The Element of Surprise in the East European Revolution of 1989," *World Politics* 44 (October 1991).

5. Jeffrey S. Kopstein and David A. Reilly, "Geographic Diffusion and the Transformation of the Postcommunist World," *World Politics* 53 (October 2000); Anna Grzymala-Busse and Pauline Jones Luong, "Reconceptualizing the State: Lessons from Post-Communism," *Politics and Society* 30 (December 2002).

6. Kopstein and Reilly (fn. 5), 25.

7. George Schöpflin, *Politics in Eastern Europe* (Oxford: Blackwell, 1993); Grzegorz Ekiert, "Democratic Processes in East Central Europe: A Theoretical Reconsideration," *British Journal of Political Science* 21, no. 3 (1991); Ken Jowitt, *A New World Disorder* (Berkeley: University of California Press, 1991); Ekiert and Hanson (fn. 1); Beverly Crawford and Arend Lijphart, "Enduring Political and Economic Change in Post-Communist Eastern Europe: Old Legacies, New Institutions, Hegemons, Norms and International Pressures," *Comparative Political Studies* 28, no. 2 (1995).

8. Seymour Martin Lipset, *Political Man: The Social Basis of Politics* (New York: Doubleday and Company, 1960); Daniel Lerner, *The Passing of Traditional Society: Modernizing*

the Middle East (Glencoe, Ill.: Free Press, 1958); Alexander Inkeles, *Becoming Modern: Individual Change in Six Developing Countries* (Cambridge: Harvard University Press, 1969); Karl W. Deutsch, "Social Mobilization and Political Development," *American Political Science Review* 55 (September 1961); see also Adam Przeworski, Michael E. Alvarez, Jose Antonio Cheibub, and Fernando Limongi, *Democracy and Development: Political Institutions and Well-being in the World, 1950–1990* (New York: Cambridge University Press, 2000).

9. Andrew C. Janos, *East Central Europe in the Modern World: The Politics of the Borderlands from Pre- to Postcommunism* (Stanford, Calif.: Stanford University Press, 2000).

10. Herbert Kitschelt, Zdenka Mansfeldová, Radosław Markowski, and Gábor Tóka, *Post-Communist Party Systems* (Cambridge: Cambridge University Press, 1999).

11. Samuel Huntington, *The Third Wave* (Norman: University of Oklahoma Press, 1991); Laszlo Bruszt and David Stark, "Remaking the Political Field in Hungary," *Journal of International Affairs* 46 (Summer 1992). For the negotiations, see Jon Elster, ed. *Round Table Talks and the Breakdown of Communism* (Chicago: University of Chicago Press, 1997). See also Pauline Jones Luong, *Institutional Change and Political Continuity in Post-Soviet Central Asia* (Cambridge: Cambridge University Press, 2002); John Ishiyama, "Transitional Electoral Systems in Post-communist Eastern Europe," *Political Science Quarterly* 112 (Spring 1997); Thomas Remington and Steven Smith, "Institutional Design, Uncertainty, and Path Dependency during Transition," *American Journal of Political Science* 40 (October 1996); Patrick O'Neil, "Presidential Power in Post-communist Europe: The Hungarian Case in Comparative Perspective," *Journal of Communist Studies* 9 (September 1993); Timothy Frye, "A Politics of Institutional Choice: Post-communist Presidencies," *Comparative Political Studies* 30 (October 1997).

12. Janos (fn. 9), 326.

13. An excellent analysis of these arguments is in Grigore Pop-Eleches, "Which Past Matters? Communist and Pre-Communist Legacies and Post-Communist Regime Change" (Paper presented at the annual meeting of the American Political Science Association, Washington, D.C., September 1–4, 2005).

14. Richard Snyder, "After the State Withdraws: Neoliberalism and Subnational Authoritarian Regimes in Mexico," in W. Cornelius, T. Eisenstadt, and J. Hindley, eds., *Subnational Politics and Democratization in Mexico* (La Jolla: Center for U.S.-Mexican Studies, University of California, San Diego, 1999); Levitsky and Way (fn. 2); Robert Mickey, "Paths out of Dixie: The Democratization of Authoritarian Enclaves in America's Deep South, 1944–1972" (Book manuscript, Department of Political Science, University of Michigan, 2006).

15. Thus, the EU was content to conduct bilateral agreements with postcommunist countries; membership as a feasible option did not even enter the discussion until 1995 and the Bosnia conflict.

16. Bunce (fn. 1) and Janos (fn. 12) identified the rise of the opposition with prior statehood and the linking of the state project with liberalism.

17. Bunce, "The National Idea: Imperial Legacies and Post-Communist Pathways in Eastern Europe," *East European Politics and Societies* 19 (Summer 2005).

18. Ernest Gellner, *Nations and Nationalism* (Ithaca, N.Y.: Cornell University Press, 1983); E. J. Hobsbawm, *Nations and Nationalism since 1780* (New York: Cambridge University Press, 1990), chap. 3; Barry Posen, "Nationalism, the Mass Army and Military Power," *International Security* 18 (Autumn 1993).

19. Deutsch (fn. 8); Lipset (fn. 8); Inkeles (fn. 8); Lerner (fn. 8).

20. Sylvia Scribner and Michael Cole, "Cognitive Consequences of Formal and Informal Education," *Science* 182 (November 9, 1973).

21. Keith Darden, "Mass Schooling and the For-mation of Enduring National Loyalties" (Book manuscript, Department of Political Science, Yale University, 2007).

22. James Sheehan, "What Is German History? Reflections on the Role of the Nation in German History and Historiography," *Journal of Modern History* 53 (March 1981), 8.

23. For a useful contemporary overview of these cases published under the auspices of the League of Nations, see Jonathan French Scott, *The Menace of Nationalism in Education* (London: G. Allen and Unwin, 1926). On the general development of history and social studies in education, which at the time was highly infused with national and racial categories, see Aaron Benavot, Yun-Kying Cha, David Kamens, John W. Meyer, and Suk-Ying Yong, "Knowledge for the Masses: World Models and National Curricula, 1920–1986," *American Sociological Review* 56 (February 1991).

24. Robert A. Kann, *The Multinational Empire: Nationalism and Reform in the Habsburg Monarchy, 1848–1918* (New York: Octagon Books, 1970); Charles Jelavich, *South Slav Nationalism: Textbooks and Yugoslav Union before 1914* (Columbia: Ohio State University Press, 1980), 18–20; Paul Robert Magocsi, *A History of Ukraine* (Seattle: University of Washington Press, 1996), 407–15.

25. Magocsi (fn. 24), 168.

26. Ibid., 177.

27. Jelavich (fn. 24).

28. In fact the slight improvement in literacy rates for Yugoslavia as a whole is probably attributable to the death of an older generation of illiterates rather than any significant improvements in education.

29. Hobsbawm (fn. 18), chap. 3; Posen (fn. 18).

30. Robert J. Kaiser, *The Geography of Nationalism in Russia and USSR* (Princeton: Princeton University Press, 1994), 44; Nicholas Vakar, *Belorussia: The Making of a Nation* (Cambridge: Harvard University Press, 1956); Loring Danforth, *The Macedonian Conflict*

(Princeton: Princeton Unviersity Press, 1995).

31. Kaiser (fn. 30), 67; Ben Eklof, *Russian Peasant Schools: Officialdom, Village Culture, and Popular Pedagogy, 1861–1914* (Berkeley: University of California Press, 1986).

32. Barbara Jelavich, *History of the Balkans* (Cambridge: Cambridge University Press, 1983), 88.

33. Jelavich (fn. 24), 16.

34. Jews, who were nearly all annihilated in the territory of Ukraine and Belarus during the Second World War and thus could have little effect on postcommunist trajectories, would have inflated the precommunist literacy statistics of these regions somewhat.

35. Eklof (fn. 31).

36. On Georgia, see Wladimir Woytinsky, *La Démocratie géorgienne* (Paris: Librairie Alcan Lévy, 1921), 266–70; and Karl Kautsky, *Georgia: A Social-Democratic Peasant Republic*, trans. H. J. Stenning (London: International Bookshops, 1921).

37. Terry Martin, *The Affirmative Action Empire: Nations and Nationalism in the Soviet Union, 1923–1939* (Ithaca, N.Y.: London: Cornell University Press, 2001), 15.

38. It was a purge that, in Georgia, largely targeted teachers and the intelligentsia. Tamara Dragadze, *Rural Families in Soviet Georgia* (New York: Routledge, 1988), 185.

39. *USSR Census of 1939: Aggregate Statistics from the USSR Census of 1939* (Computer file, Toronto, University of Toronto, Centre for Research in East European Studies), Robert E. Johnson, producer (Toronto: University of Toronto, Data Library Service [distributor], 1995), table 63b.

40. Ibid., table 66b.

41. Jack Goody, *The Power of the Written Tradition* (Washington, D.C.: Smithsonian Institution Press, 2000), 27.

42. Karl W. Deutsch, *Nationalism and Social Communication* (Cambridge: MIT Press, 1953), 87, 101; Benedict Anderson, *Imagined Communities* (New York: Verso, 1991), 44–46.

43. Gellner (fn. 18), 32.

44. C. John Sommerville, *The Discovery of Child-*

hood in Puritan England (Athens: University of Georgia Perss, 1992), chap. 9.

45. The Communist Party won 38 percent in the Czech lands but far less in Slovakia.

46. The Red Army and Soviet presence were seen as the main guarantee of border integrity in the Sudetenland.

47. Figures calculated from Janos (fn. 9), 349.

48. A 1970s joke plaintively asked, "Why did the Black Madonna fight back the Swedish onslaught? We could have been Sweden . . ."

49. Adam Przeworski, *Sustainable Democracy* (New York: Cambridge University Press, 1995), 3.

50. Tamara Dragadze, *Rural Families in Soviet Georgia* (New York: Routledge, 1988).

51. Ibid., 183–84.

52. Kenneth C. Farmer, *Ukrainian Nationalism in the Post-Stalin Era: Myth, Symbols and Ideology in Soviet Nationalities Policy* (Boston: Martinus Nijhoff, 1980), 176–79.

53. See Jones Luong (fn. 11), chap. 3.

54. The same depictions of the positive impact of communist rule depicted in the 1920s propaganda film *Three Songs for Lenin* (Dziga Vertov) were repeated in many conversations with Central Asian respondents in the mid-1990s.

55. According to State Department surveys conducted through the 1990s, the share of respondents with a "favorable" opinion of Russia in 1994 was 74 percent in Azerbaijan, 78 percent in Kazakhstan, 86 percent in Uzbekistan, 83 percent in Kyrgyzstan, 90 percent in Armenia (up from 43 percent in 1992), but only 36 percent in Georgia. See Regina Faranda, "Ties That Bind, Opinions That Divide" (Manuscript, U.S. State Department Opinion Surveys, 2001); see also David D. Laitin, *Identity in Formation: The Russian-Speaking Nationality in Estonia and Bashkortostan* (Glasgow: Centre for the Study of Public Policy, University of Strathclyde, 1995).

56. In 1994, 81 percent of respondents in Ukraine and 88 percent in Belarus took a fa-

vorable view of Russia, and these figures were consistent throughout the 1990s. Only 27 percent of respondents in Western Ukraine viewed Russia as an ally; Faranda (fn. 55), 44.

57. Andrew Wilson, *Ukrainian Nationalism in the 1990s: A Minority Faith* (New York: Cambridge University Press, 1997); Karel C. Berkhoff, *Harvest of Despair: Life and Death in Ukraine under Nazi Rule* (Cambridge: Harvard University Press, 2004), 206–13.

58. See Jan Kubik, *The Power of Symbols against the Symbols of Power* (Pittsburgh: Pennsylvania State University Press, 1994); Janine Wedel, *The Private Poland* (New York: Facts on File Publications, 1986).

59. Rudolf Tőkés, *Hungary's Negotiated Revolution* (Cambridge: Cambridge University Press, 1986), 318.

60. Even the 1989 slogan for Kučan's extremely liberal Slovene communists was "Europe Now!"

61. See Padraic Kenney, *A Carnival of Revolution* (Princeton: Princeton University Press, 2002).

62. As these movements and the manner in which they drew on precommunist national symbols and dates of significance to mobilize the population are demonstrated in detail by Beissinger, we will give only a brief overview here. See Mark R. Beissinger, *Nationalist Mobilization and the Collapse of the Soviet State* (Cambridge: Cambridge University Press 2002), chap. 4.

63. Beissinger (fn. 62), 187.

64. Rasma Karklins, *Ethnopolitics and Transition to Democracy: The Collapse of the USSR in Latvia* (Washington, D.C.: Woodrow Wilson Center Press, 1994), 94–95, cited in Beissinger (fn. 62), 169.

65. In Estonia, for example, the "singing revolution" replicated the national singing festivals of the late nineteenth century, singing precommunist songs and mobilizing as much as a third of the population into demonstrations calling for independence; Beissinger

(fn. 62), 172. Robert Person, "Resisting Hegemony: Transformations in Estonian Identity under Soviet Rule" (Manuscript, Yale University, 2005).

66. Beissinger (fn. 62), 180.

67. Zviad Gamsakhurdia, "Open Letter to Eduard Shevardnadze," translated from the Russian by the Zviad Gamsakhurdia Society in the Netherlands, April 19, 1992.

68. Beissinger (fn. 62), 194–98; Wilson (fn. 57).

69. They then exited office after their government collapsed in November 1991.

70. See Milada Anna Vachudová and Timothy Snyder, "Are Transitions Transitory? Two Models of Political Change in East Central Europe since 1989," *East European Politics and Societies* 11 (Winter 1997).

MICHAEL MCFAUL

TRANSITIONS FROM POSTCOMMUNISM

The collapse of communism did not lead smoothly or quickly to the consolidation of liberal democracy in Europe and the former Soviet Union.[1] At the time of regime change, from 1989 into the first few years of the 1990s, popular democratic movements in the three Baltic states, Hungary, Poland, Slovenia, eastern Germany, and western Czechoslovakia translated initial electoral victories into consolidated liberal democracy. These quick and successful democratic breakthroughs were the exception, however. Bulgaria, Croatia, Romania, and eastern Czechoslovakia (after 1992 known simply as Slovakia) failed to consolidate liberal democracy soon after communism collapsed. Yet in time, the gravitational force of the European Union did much to draw these countries onto a democratic path.

Farther from Western Europe, however, there was no such strong prodemocratic pull. Full-blown dictatorships entrenched themselves early across most of Central Asia and, after its 1994 presidential election, in Belarus. Semi-autocracies and partial democracies spread across the rest of the ex-Soviet states, including Russia. By the end of the 1990s, further democratic gains in the region seemed unlikely.

Starting in the year 2000, however, democracy gained new dynamism in the region in unexpected ways and places. In October of that year, Serbian democratic forces ousted dictator Slobodan Milošević. Three years later, Georgia's far less odious but still semi-autocratic president Eduard Shevardnadze fell before a mobilization of democratic forces. The following year, in a similar drama but on a much grander stage, Ukrainian democrats toppled the handpicked successor of corrupt outgoing president Leonid Kuchma.[2]

The Serbian, Georgian, and Ukrainian cases of democratic breakthrough resemble one another—and differ from other democratic transitions or revolutions—in four critical respects. First, in all three cases, the spark for regime change was a fraudulent national election, not a war, an economic crisis, a split between ruling elites, an external shock or international factor, or the death of a dictator. Second, the democratic challenges deployed extraconstitutional means solely to defend the existing, democratic constitution rather than to achieve a fundamen-

From *Journal of Democracy*, 16, no. 3 (July 2005), pp. 5–19.

tal rewriting of the rules of the political game. Third, each country for a time witnessed challengers and incumbents making competing and simultaneous claims to hold sovereign authority —one of the hallmarks of a revolutionary situation.[3] Fourth, all of these revolutionary situations ended without mass violence. The challengers often consciously embraced nonviolence on principle, using occasionally extraconstitutional but almost always peaceful tactics. The failing incumbents do seem to have tried coercive methods including assaults on journalists and opposition candidates and the closing of media outlets. But no incumbents dared to call on military or other state-security forces to repress protest.

Another remarkable thing about these democratic breakthroughs is how few analysts predicted them. To many it seemed a miracle that Serbian democratic forces could overcome a decade of disunity in order first to beat Milošević in a presidential election on 24 September 2000, and then to galvanize hundreds of thousands of citizens to demand that the actual election result be honored when it became clear that Milošević was trying to falsify it. Similarly dramatic events unfolded in Georgia after Shevardnadze tried to steal the November 2003 parliamentary elections, leading to his resignation as president and a landslide victory for opposition leader Mikheil Saakashvili in a hastily scheduled January 2004 balloting. While many anticipated controversy over Ukraine's autumn 2004 presidential election, most observers still expect that Kuchma would find a way to make his chosen successor, Prime Minister Viktor Yanukovich, Ukraine's next president. Not even opposition leaders predicted the scale and duration of the street protests, which would break out after the government tried to claim that Yanukovich had won the November runoff against Viktor Yushchenko of the prodemocratic "Our Ukraine" coalition.[4]

Identifying the common factors that contributed to success in these cases may be our best method of predicting future democratic breakthroughs not only in this region but perhaps in others as well. Deploying John Stuart Mill's "method of similarity"—which holds that in order to be considered necessary to the causation of a certain effect, a variable must be present be in every case—we can assemble a list of commonalities that unite Serbia in 2000, Georgia in 2003, and Ukraine in 2004 as cases of successful democratic breakthrough.

The factors for success include 1) a semiautocratic rather than fully autocratic regime; 2) an unpopular incumbent; 3) a united and organized opposition; 4) an ability quickly to drive home the point that voting results were falsified, 5) enough independent media to inform citizens about the falsified vote, 6) a political opposition capable of mobilizing tens of thousands or more demonstrators to protest electoral fraud, and 7) divisions among the regime's coercive forces. We should also note that these cases were not wholly independent from one another, and indeed were most likely linked by demonstration effects. Moreover, identifying the commonalities may also help us to isolate other factors often regarded as vital to success that were not present in all these cases.

A Semi-autocratic Regime

All autocratic regimes are vulnerable to collapse at some point. But which kinds of autocracies are more vulnerable than others? Some observers posit that semi-autocratic or "competitive authoritarian" regimes are more open to democratization than full-blown dictatorships, while others argue that semi-autocracies or partial democracies can actually do more to block genuine democratization by deflecting societal pressures for change.[5]

In this second wave of democratization in the postcommunist world, every incumbent regime was some form of competitive autocracy or partial democracy, in which formal democratic procedures—elections especially—were never suspended.[6] This particular regime type in turn allowed pockets of pluralism and opposition within the state, which proved critical to democratic breakthrough.

Even Milošević, the communist-turned-ultra-nationalist provocateur who won election to first the Serbian and later the Yugoslav federal presidency while pursuing policies of ethnic cleansing and aggression, never set up a full-blown dictatorship. He harassed opposition movements but never outlawed them. He occasionally shut down independent media outlets, and ordered the assassination of outspoken journalists, but he also allowed critical outlets such as the B-92 radio station to reopen. He let human rights organizations continue their work, and while he tampered with the results of elections, he never banned them altogether. Parliamentary elections helped to sustain opposition leaders and parties, even if they enjoyed no real power. More importantly, local elections allowed the democratic movement to gain footholds in more than a dozen regional parliaments as well as the Belgrade mayor's office in 1996 and 1997 (though only after more than three months of protests to force Milošević to honor the results). With control of these regional governments also came control over regional media outlets, a vital resource in Milošević's ouster in 2000.

In Georgia, Shevardnadze early in his rule created conditions for democratic institutions and actors to emerge, including Georgia's most popular television station, Rustavi-2. Although he tried to become more authoritarian as time wore on, his achievements fell far short of his ambitions. Attempts at monitoring and curtailing the activities of civil society and the media had limited effects or even backfired. Shevardnadze's state lacked the resources to be more effectively harsher, and the president himself often seemed irresolute about repression, perhaps because so many of his leading critics had at one time been part of his own camp.

Kuchma came to power in Ukraine through a competitive 1994 election, in which he had proclaimed it as his goal to move forward with the consolidation of democracy. Instead he eventually tried to build a "managed democracy"—combining formal democratic practices with informal control of all political institutions—similar to President Vladimir Putin's in Russia. But Kuchma never enjoyed anything like Putin's popularity, and many of his clumsy and brutal attempts to squelch critics served to mobilize even greater opposition. The "Ukraine Without Kuchma" campaign from December 2000 to March 2001 and the results of the March 2002 parliamentary elections demonstrated that Ukrainian society was active and politically sophisticated. The success of "Our Ukraine" in the 2002 voting gave it a foothold within state institutions. Kuchma never quite rallied all of Ukraine's economic elites behind his rule, and the fall of 2004 found them still divided.

An Unpopular Incumbent

A second necessary condition for democratic breakthrough in all of these countries was the falling popularity of the incumbent leader. This factor may seem obvious, but it is also a feature that distinguishes these cases from countries such as Russia, where President Putin is still popular, or countries like Mexico during the heyday of semi-authoritarian rule, when the ruling party could manufacture electoral victories without major voter fraud. In Serbia, polls put Milošević's popularity at less than 30 percent by the summer of 2000.[7] In Georgia, 82 percent of respondents were saying as early as 2001 that the country was going in the wrong direction, up from 51 percent the year before.[8] Kuchma's approval ratings plummeted during his last year in office.

The causes of presidential unpopularity differ from case to case and can be difficult to trace within each one. Milošević had won a number of free and fair elections and persistently sought mandates from the voters. He himself had changed the Yugoslav constitution to set up his campaign for direct election to the federal presidency in September 2000. Yet several military defeats, culminating with capitulation to the 1999 NATO air campaign, and years of economic decline severely undermined his support.

Shevardnadze too was popular at first. Yet he failed to set Georgia's economy on a sound course even as Rustavi-2 and other independent media sources began exposing the growing corruption of his government and made honesty in public life a major issue in the 2003 parliamentary elections. Shevardnadze also suffered for having failed to win or satisfactorily resolve wars or territorial disputes in the troubled regions of Abkhazia, South Ossetia, and Ajaria.

In 1994 and again in 1999, Kuchma won a presidential election judged relatively free and fair by regional standards. During his second term, economic growth began after a decade of contraction, roaring to a record 12 percent in 2004. Yet severe corruption made him unpopular. Typifying the rot was Kuchma's apparent complicity—illustrated by leaked audiotapes—in the 2000 abduction and assassination of Web-based investigative reporter Georgi Gongadze. More than any other event, Gongadze's murder exposed the illegitimacy of Kuchma and his allies.

A United Opposition

A united opposition—or at least the perception of one—is a third factor that appears crucial for democratic breakthrough, although the extent of unity varies widely enough across the cases that one may question its necessity as a factor. In Serbia and Ukraine, unity before the election was critical to success; in Georgia, less so. This may have been because the former countries had presidential elections, while Georgia held parliamentary balloting. In each case, however, a viable alternative to the incumbent leader seemed critical.

Throughout the 1990s, personality clashes had plagued the Serbian democratic movement and tarnished its reputation. In January 2000, Serbia's democrats agreed to set aside their differences to create a united front, the Democratic

Opposition of Serbia (DOS). Most importantly, DOS settled behind one presidential candidate, Vojislav Koštunica, for the September 2000 presidential election. At the time, Koštunica headed the relatively small Democratic Party of Serbia and had only modest fame. Yet polls showed that Koštunica's newness, coupled with his brand of moderate nationalism, made him the ideal opposition candidate. Support began to gel behind him firmly and broadly enough to make him seem the potent challenger for whom so many Serbian voters had been longing.

Ukrainian democrats also created the perception of unity in the runup to the 2004 presidential election. For much of the previous decade, Ukraine's democratic forces had remained divided and disorganized. The crafting of opposition unity was complicated by the presence of strong and legitimate Socialist Party, which made cooperation with liberals difficult. Nor, for many years, was there a single, charismatic leader of the opposition who stood out as an obvious first among equals. Ironically, Kuchma helped to create such a leader when he dismissed Viktor Yushchenko as his prime minister in 2001.

While known more as a technocrat than a politician, Yushchenko had overseen economic growth and otherwise done well in office, making him a dangerous opponent to the party of power. His new "Our Ukraine" bloc captured a quarter of the popular vote in the 2002 parliamentary elections, causing other contenders for the role of opposition standard-bearer to step aside in advance of the 2004 presidential balloting.

Facing legislative elections under a system of proportional representation, the Georgian opposition had little reason to unite before polling day. Saakashvili's National Movement was one of three serious opposition blocs, and gained only a fifth of the popular vote. But in the 37-year-old Saakashvili, a U.S.-trained lawyer and former justice minister, the transformative moment of the postelectoral protests against Shevardnadze's chicanery found a revolutionary leader. Saakashvili gave fiery speeches, mobilized popular protest, and took bold decisions. His thin ties to the old regime (he had quit the cabinet in protest) helped him. His decision to lead unarmed protestors to storm into the parliament chamber and interrupt a Shevardnadze speech was a more radical and less constitutional step than anything that the Serbian or Ukrainian democrats did or would later do. It was also tactically risky: Had part of the Georgian democratic opposition refused to go along, Shevardnadze might have been tempted to fight harder to stay in power.

Independent Electoral-Monitoring Capabilities

A fourth condition critical to democratic breakthrough in Serbia, Georgia, and Ukraine was the ability of NGOs to provide an accurate and independent tally of the actual vote quickly after polls had closed. In Serbia, the Center for Free Elections and Democracy (CeSID) provided the critical data exposing voter fraud in the first round of the presidential election in September 2000. Exit polls were illegal in 2000, so CeSID conducted a parallel vote tabulation, a technique now used in many transitional democracies that CeSID founders originally observed in Bulgaria.[9] They posted their representatives at 7,000 polling sites, which allowed them to produce a remarkably sophisticated estimation of the actual vote. On election night, DOS officials announced the results of their own parallel vote tabulation, but did so knowing that their results corresponded with CeSID results. CeSID, in other words, provided the legitimacy for the claim of falsification. CeSID's figures also supported Koštunica's claim that he had won more than 50 percent in the first round and therefore did not need to stand in a second round.

In Georgia as well, independent electoral monitoring was crucial. Buoyed by international funding, Georgian NGOs and survey firms carried out the country's first-ever exit polls and parallel vote count. All told, around 20,000 voters across 500 precincts were questioned, while about 8,000 foreign and domestic monitors observed the voting.[10] The results from the exit polling and the parallel count were remarkably similar and strikingly at odds with official tallies. Observation teams documented instances of vote fraud.

In Ukraine, the Committee of Ukrainian Voters (CVU) played the central role in monitoring all rounds of the 2004 presidential vote. CVU also conducted a parallel vote tabulation. A consortium of polling firms coordinated by the Ukrainian NGO "Democratic Initiatives" did exit polls, though so too did firms associated closely with the Kuchma regime. Unlike their Georgian counterparts, the Ukrainian organizations had years of experience. Yet they also had to contend with a far more sophisticated vote manipulator using novel tactics. Kuchma and his allies falsified the vote at the level of precinct, and not between the precinct level and higher levels of counting, where fraud traditionally occurs.[11] A parallel vote tabulation attempts to expose fraud by sampling the actual vote count at the precinct level. But if the precinct numbers are already phony, then a parallel count will also reflect the result of the falsified vote, an outcome that the CVU had to face. Second, Kuchma's government muddied the results of the exit polls by compelling two of the consortium partners to use a method in the second round different from the method used by the other two polling firms more closely tied to the opposition.[12] After the second round of the presidential vote, therefore, two different exit polls were released with different results.

Where quantitative or large-scale methods for exposing fraud failed, however, finer-grained or qualitative methods came to the rescue. Individual election monitors affiliated with Ukrainian NGOs and international organizations reported hundreds upon hundreds of specific irregularities. At the same time, the turnout levels that the government was claiming in some regions of the east (a pro-Kuchma bastion) were so absurdly high that analysts knew they had to be false. The combination of systematically reported irregularities with ridiculous turnout claims gave a few members of the Central Election Commission the courage to refuse to certify the final count, sending the issue to the Supreme Court.[13] The Court, deliberating amid the grand peaceful protests of late November and December 2004, then used the evidence of fraud that the CVU and other NGOs had gathered as grounds for overturning the official results and ordering a rerun of the second round, which Yushchenko won decisively.

A Modicum of Independent Media

A fifth critical element in Serbia, Georgia, and Ukraine was the presence of independent media able to relay news about the falsified vote and to publicize mounting popular protests. For years, such media outlets and brave individual journalists had been reporting the misdeeds of semiautocratic incumbents. At the moment of breakthrough, autonomous media remained vital in triggering change despite the incumbents' last-ditch efforts to hang on to power.

In Serbia, several important independent media outlets contributed to the decline of Milošević's popularity. The B-92 radio station had offered unsparing professional coverage of Milošević and his regime since 1989.[14] B-92 cofounder Goran Matić also played an instrumental role in establishing a regional radio and television network to distribute independent news broadcasts. The ANEM network, a media cluster consisting of a news agency, several independent dailies and weeklies, and a television station, helped to give Serbians news from outside state-dominated channels. Critical coverage of Milošević's wars, his economic policies, and his government's violent arrests and abuses of young protestors helped to undermine his support within the population. In September 2000, independent media coverage of official vote fraud brought outraged Serbians into the streets. At the time, Milošević had closed B-92, but ANEM and Radio Index in Belgrade ensured that there was no letup in coverage. Without these media outlets, popular mobilization would have been much harder.

In Georgia, too, independent media were key. Shevardnadze's second term had seen him take a pounding from the serious, corruption-exposing "60 Minutes" show on Rustavi-2, while the cartoon satire "Dardubala" skewered him with tongue in cheek. During the late fall of 2003, Rustavi-2 and some smaller media outlets broadcast the exit-poll and parallel-count results endlessly, right next to the official results released by the Georgian Central Electoral Commission. Unlike the opposition media in Serbia or Ukraine, Rustavi-2 had become the most watched television network in Georgia even before the controversial election. Once people took to the streets, Rustavi-2's cameras showed them all. Networks once loyal to Shevardnadze followed suit, and even more Georgians came out to speak their minds once it became clear that the government would not use force.

While Ukraine's democratic opposition had access to fewer traditional sources of independent media and found all their major broadcast channels owned or controlled by oligarchs loyal to Kuchma and Yanukovich, Ukrainians made up for this with their slightly richer country's higher level of Internet connectivity. Indeed, the Orange Revolution (so called after the party color of "Our Ukraine") may have been the first in history to be organized largely online.

Gongadze's own Web-based publication, *Ukrainskaya Pravda*, had carried on despite his murder and remained a critical (in both senses) source of news and analysis about the Kuchma regime. By the end of the Orange Revolution, this Internet publication was the most widely read news source of any kind in Ukraine. During the critical hours and days after the second-round vote, *Ukrainskaya Pravda* displayed the results of exit polling, detailed news about other allegations of fraud, and provided all sorts of logistical information to protestors. Text messaging via cell phones or handheld digital devices was a great tool for spreading information among the large crowds of outdoor protestors in Kyiv and its tent city.

The comparatively old-fashioned technology of television also played a role in the Orange Revolution's success. Realizing that national television access was going to be a problem, the wealthy Yushchenko supporter Viktor Poroshenko bought a small station in 2003 that he then renamed Channel 5. Amazingly, the authorities let the sale go through. They would have cause to rue this when Channel 5 began running round-the-clock coverage of the protest in downtown Kyiv after the false official results came out. As Ukrainians witnessed the peaceful, even festive mood of the crowd, more came out to join the 11-day demonstration. By the fourth day, the staffs at most other proregime stations had joined forces with the street demonstrators. So in Ukraine as in Georgia, television proved a major headache for the fraudulent incumbents.

Mobilizing the Masses

A sixth critical factor for democratic breakthrough in Serbia, Georgia, and Ukraine was the opposition's capacity to mobilize significant numbers of protestors to challenge the falsified electoral results. In all three cases, newly formed student groups—Otpor in Serbia, Kmara in Georgia, and Pora in Ukraine—provided logistical support and in the case of Ukraine, the first wave of protestors. Beyond that early boost, all of these student groups worked together with both the main opposition parties and other NGOs in helping to mobilize the giant demonstrations (in Serbia and Ukraine the crowds topped a million) that forced the election violators of the old administration to leave office.

In Serbia, the opposition had planned for street-level activism well in advance. A broad coalition of Otpor, DOS, regional government heads, union leaders, and civil society organizers coordinated efforts that culminated in the million-strong 5 October 2000 march on Belgrade. As columns of protesters neared the capi-

tal, they met police barricades, but not one seriously tried to stop the caravans. The sheer scale of the unarmed demonstration (the total population of Serbia is about ten million) overwhelmed any thought of resistance. Within hours, the opposition had seized the parliament building, police headquarters, and the national television station. The next day, Milošević resigned.

In contrast to their Serbian predecessors, Georgia's protestors seemed less organized and were smaller in number (in population terms, Georgia is about half Serbia's size, and about eleven times smaller than Ukraine). But by Georgians standards, the mobilization was coordinated, well organized and massive, involving not only citizens of Tbilisi, but people from all parts of the country. The student group Kmara, modeled after Serbia's Otpor, took the lead.[15] Kmara was new, and so had not paved the way for protest as Otpor had, but once the vote was stolen, Kmara played a more central role than had its Serbian counterpart in mobilizing street protests. Saakashvili became the voice and face of the opposition. He used his boldness and speaking skills to coordinate a new United Opposition coalition joining the three opposition parties with Kmara and other civil society organizations. Eventually, the protests in Tbilisi reached that unspecifiable tipping point where anyone could see that suppression would mean mass casualties, an outcome that no powerholder—including Shevardnadze—deemed acceptable.

Compared to their counterparts in Serbia and Ukraine, Georgia's demonstrators (or at least their leaders) were more radical in both their demands and their actions. In Serbia, protestors took to the streets to press the government to recognize the results of the presidential election. In Georgia, Saakashvili called for and succeeded in obtaining not only recognition of the actual parliamentary election results, but Shevardnadze's ouster, even though the Georgian president was not standing for reelection at the time. The demand was unconstitutional. Like Serbian democrats, but in contrast to the Ukrainian demonstration, Georgia's protestors initiated physical contact with the authorities by storming into parliament.

In Kyiv on the day after Yanukovich's fraudulent runoff "victory," Pora and "Our Ukraine" set up hundreds of tents near Independence Square, where "Our Ukraine" activists and legislators were erecting a large stage. Truckloads of tents, styrofoam mats, and food soon appeared. But these were logistics for tens of thousands, not the more than one million people who would eventually turn out. As the numbers rose, organizers succeeded in keeping people fed, clean, calm, and warm in the dead of a Ukrainian winter only because thousands of small businesspeople lent aid and because the city government of Kyiv (the city was a Yushchenko bastion) was supportive. In fact, support from city hall was critical not only in Kyiv, but also Belgrade and Tbilisi, and may even constitute another necessary condition for success.

Splits Among the "Guys With Guns"

A seventh and final necessary condition for success is a split among the "guys with guns," meaning the state's military, police, and security forces. A segment of these must distance itself far enough from the incumbents to show that the option of violent repression is risky if not untenable. In all three cases such a split developed, though its size as well as the threat of violence varied from case to case.

In Serbia, Milošević called upon local police to undertake increasingly violent actions against young Otpor protestors. Many police officials disliked such orders. As demonstrations grew in size and intensity throughout 2000, many in the security ministries came to suspect that Milošević would soon be finished. The size of the fresh protests that broke out after Milošević falsified the presidential vote convinced many police and intelligence officials that violent repression was no longer an option. On the eve of the giant march on the capital in early October, the major opposition politician Zoran Djindjić convinced the Yugoslav army's

chief of staff to have his troops stand down the next day. This helped greatly in preventing bloodshed during the October 5 march, since some demonstrators had come to Belgrade armed and ready to fight.

The Georgian opposition began courting the security ministries well before the 2003 election. Once demonstrators took to the streets, some key officials either openly deserted Shevardnadze or made it clear that they would refuse to order units under their command to arrest, much less to shoot, peaceful protestors. When an elite Interior Ministry paramilitary unit went over to the side of the protestors, other formations followed. Memories of the heroism that Georgian police had shown in trying to protect civilians from attacks by Soviet security troops during a 1989 rally in Tbilisi also played a huge role in stimulating defections and keeping the 2003 response peaceful.

Compared to his counterparts in Serbia and Ukraine, Shevardnadze had a more legitimate reason to use force against the rebellious opposition. They, after all, stormed the parliament and then demanded his resignation, not simply the recognition of the results of the parliamentary election. Shevardnadze, however, refrained from trying to use force. He may have realized that finding reliable forces to carry out such an order would be no sure thing, but also may have had sincere qualms. Then too, Shevardnadze enjoys a positive reputation in the West by dint of his role in winding down the Cold War as Mikhail Gorbachev's foreign minister, and no doubt felt reluctant to mar that good name with the blood of civilians.

In Ukraine, the contacts that opposition leaders made with the security *apparat* also helped to close the door to violent repression.[16] On the streets, where protestors and soldiers were close together for days, Pora's humorous tone (as well as the number of young female demonstrators who took positions on the front line, eye-to-eye with the soldiers guarding government buildings) defused tensions. As in Georgia, several police and intelligence units made clear that the "guys with guns" could not be trusted to carry out a repressive order.

As laudable as some of the defections may have been, it is wise not to overidealize the attitude of the security forces in these situations. More than their good will, what kept violence at bay was the sheer size of the crowds. Smaller, less organized protests would have been tempting targets for aggressive police action. Ten thousand people can be dispersed with tear gas and armored cars. A crowd of one million cannot be.

Unessential Factors

Highlighting these seven factors implicitly suggests that other factors were not as important. For instance, the state of the economy or level of economic development did not play a uniform causal role in these cases of democratic breakthrough. Students of modernization have identified a long-term positive correlation between rising wealth in a country and the emergence of a middle class and democratization.[17] But while Ukraine has a growing middle class and a recent history of robust growth, the same cannot be said of Serbia or Georgia. Those latter two countries, indeed, had been living through periods of economic trauma and hardship that served to undermine Milošević and Shevardnadze, but in neither case was an economic meltdown the trigger for transition. Instead, it was a purely political factor—vote fraud—that set things off.

While all three countries had some recent history of ethnic tensions or troubles up to and including outright warfare, neither a full resolution of all border disputes nor clear stipulation of who "belonged" in the polity formed a precondition for democratic breakthrough.

Splits between hard-liners and soft-liners among the semi-authoritarian incumbents also figured little as tactical triggers for democratizing change. In part this may be because such splits had taken place years before, so that the oppositions in these three cases were denominated not by dissidents or civil society leaders, but by former reformists within the regime. Koštunica had sat in parliament, Saakashvili had been recruited for government service by Shevardnadze, and Yushchenko had been Kuchma's premier.

The relationships between the incumbents and the West in these cases do not fit into a single clear pattern. Milošević obviously had the worst such relationship: After he had refused to accept NATO peacekeeping plans for Kosovo, NATO warplanes had bombed Serbia for almost the entire spring of the year before his ouster (the effect of the air war on democratization is still a hotly debated topic among Serbian democrats and students of Serbian politics generally).[18] Shevardnadze, by contrast, enjoyed much better ties with Western leaders, but this good standing did not help him keep power. Kuchma's cordial but strained relations with the West may have pushed him at the margin to do the right thing and relinquish the succession rather than try to force his handpicked successor on a country that had elected someone else.

Western democracy-assistance programs played a visible role in all three cases. Saying which instance of aid helped, hurt, or made no difference to democratic breakthrough is a complex subject well beyond the scope of this essay. It seems safe to say that foreign aid played no independent role in any of these breakthroughs (and rarely does), but contributed to the drama by increasing or decreasing the relative value of each of the seven factors outlined above. With the possible exception of election monitoring, each factor would still have been present had no Western assistance been forthcoming.

Another possible factor, the quality of the positive appeals or platforms worked out by the opposition in each country, also appears fairly insignificant. In every case, the heart of the matter was getting rid of unpopular and deeply dishonest incumbents, not backing some specific new set of policies or reforms. Even the role that democratic ideas played in mobilizing first voters and then protestors is not uniform across these cases. Rather, all three successful movements constructed compelling ideologies of op-position, whose main message was a cry of "Enough!" hurled in the face of the incumbent powerholders.

Even the pivotal role of the opposition leader is not easy to discern in all three cases. After the breakthrough, it seems as if no other leader could have united the opposition and toppled the regime. But this "fact" only seems obvious after success. Immediately after victory in 2000, Koštunica looked like the only moderate nationalist who could have defeated Milošević in a free and fair election, yet Koštunica's limited skills as a politician have since diminished his heroic status. The diabolical tactics of the Kuchma regime, including most obviously the poisoning of Yushchenko, transformed Yushchenko into an indispensable hero of the Orange Revolution. Yet just months before victory, several leaders within the Ukrainian democratic movement questioned whether he had the political and campaigning skills needed to win. In Georgia, Saakashvili became essential and one-of-a-kind only after he ordered the storming of the parliament and Shevardnadze's ouster. Had the opposition maintained more modest objectives—a new parliamentary vote or the recognition of the actual results of the vote already held—Saakashvili's place in Georgian history could have evolved into a very different narrative. Whether leaders seize greatness or have it thrust upon them by circumstance is not a question that these cases will settle.

In seeking to learn lessons from these democratic breakthroughs, it is important to realize that the list of necessary conditions is long. (It is bad social science to have seven independent variables to explain three outcomes!) The presence of only a few of these factors is unlikely to generate the same outcome. A more popular or more clever and ruthless autocrat might have been able to outmaneuver the democratic opposition. A less-organized electoral-monitoring effort in any of these three countries might not have been able to convince people to take to the streets. Smaller numbers of protestors in the streets might have led to outcomes that looked more like Tiananmen Square in 1989 than the big and peaceful wins for democratization that actually happened. The stars must really be aligned to produce such dramatic events.

Democratic breakthroughs are a start, but in and of themselves they cannot ensure success in consolidating democracy. In Serbia, Georgia, and Ukraine, we have seen an antidemocratic status quo knocked off its pins and a stalled democratic transition get a new lease on life. But renewed democratic stagnation and even reversal remain possible.

Moreover, each case played out in a different way that has consequences (social scientists call this "path dependency"). In Serbia, the 4 October 2000 deal that prevented shooting also allowed top security officials from the Milošević administration to stay in power. The very general who negotiated with Djindjić appears to have ordered his murder three years later. Corrupt officials entrenched within the interior and intelligence ministries still threaten the deepening of Serbian democracy—a problematic legacy of October 2000.[19]

Georgia's breakthrough was not pacted or negotiated. Rather, one side seized power, which was both good and bad. In the plus column, Saakashvili owed no favors and could clean house, which to his credit he has tried to do. In the minus column, the lack of constraints faced by a man who seized power in what was very like a coup and then had it ratified by 96 percent of his country's voters makes some worried that he too might one day turn to autocratic methods.[20] To date, these predictions have all proved premature: Saakashvili is still a force for democratic consolidation. But critics recall that Shevardnadze, after all, became president under somewhat similar circumstances and appeared, at least comparatively, as a liberalizing figure. Georgia has yet to see executive authority change hands through an elective and rule-based process.

By contrast, Ukraine's leaders eventually did agree to negotiate, with the assistance of international mediators, a pacted arrangement by which Kuchma and his side allowed the second round of the presidential election to be rerun and Yushchenko and his side agreed to changes in the constitution, giving the parliament and prime minister more powers and the president fewer. At the time of these roundtable talks, some leaders of Ukraine's opposition wanted to end discussions, follow the example of the Rose Revolution, and simply seize power.[21] Yushchenko, however, rejected these calls for storming government building three times, and insisted instead on the negotiated path. Yushchenko's decision will constrain his presidential powers in the short run, but in the long run may help to consolidate democratic practices of compromise and checks and balances between branches of government. If so, he may prove the most visionary of the three anti-authoritarian leaders.

NOTES

The author would like to thank David Abesadze, Valerie Bunce, Daniel Calingaert, Taras Kuzio, Ryan Podolsky, Matthew Spence, and Cory Welt for comments on earlier drafts of this article.

1. On why, see Valerie Bunce, "The Political Economy of Postsocialism," *Slavic Review* 58 (Winter 1999): 756–93; M. Steven Fish, "The Determinants of Economic Reform in the Post-Communist World," *East European Politics and Societies* 12 (Winter 1998): 31–78; and Michael McFaul, "The Fourth Wave of Democracy and Dictatorship: Noncooperative Transitions in the Postcommunist World," *World Politics* 54 (January 2002): 212–44.

2. In early 2005, Kyrgyzstan's semi-autocratic president Askar Akayev also suffered an ouster at least in part due to the factors described in this essay, but the nature of the events remains too murky—and their implications for democracy too uncertain—to be included in this analysis at this time.

3. Charles Tilly, *From Mobilization to Revolution* (New York: McGraw-Hill, 1978), 191.

4. Author's interview with Taras Stetskiv ("Our Ukraine" leader and one of the central organizers of the protest at Kyiv's Independence Square after 22 November 2004), Kyiv, 10 March 2005.

5. Daniel Brumberg, "Liberalization versus Democracy," in Thomas Carothers and Marina Ottoway, eds., *Uncharted Journey: Promoting Democracy in the Middle East* (Washington: Carnegie Endowment for International Peace, 2004), 15–36.

6. On this regime type, see Larry Diamond, "Thinking about Hybrid Regimes," *Journal of Democracy* 13 (April 2002): 21–35; and Steven Levitsky and Lucan Way, "The Rise of Competitive Authoritarianism," *Journal of Democracy* 13 (April 2002): 51–65.

7. Zeljko Cvijanović, "Belgrade Opposition Upbeat," Institute for War and Peace Reporting, 28 July 2000.

8. Richard Dobson, U.S. Department of State, "Georgians Fast Losing Faith in Shevardnadze and Their Democracy," M-238-01, 3 December 2001, 1.

9. Author's interviews with CeSID officials Zoran Lucić and Marko Blagojević, Belgrade, 13 January 2005.

10. Author's interview with Anna Tarkhnishuili (director of the Business and Consulting Company, one of the three firms involved in the exit poll), Tbilisi, 14 October 2004.

11. Author's interview with Ihor Popov (chairman of the Committee of Ukrainian Voters), Kyiv, 10 March 2005.

12. Author's interview with Ilko Kuecheriv (president of Democratic Initiatives and organizer of the exit-poll consortium), Kyiv, 10 March 2005.

13. Author's interview with CEC member Roman Knyazevich, Kyiv, 12 March 2005.

14. On B-92's history, see Matthew Collin, *Guerrilla Radio: Rock 'n' Roll Radio and Serbia's Underground Resistance* (New York: Nation, 2001).

15. On the Serbia connections, see interview with David Zurabishvili (former head of the Liberty Institute), in Zurab Karumidze and James Wertsch, eds., *Enough! The Rose Revolution in the Republic of Georgia 2003* (New York: Nova Science, 2004), 61–68; and Peter Baker, "Tbilisi's 'Revolution of Roses' Mentored by Serbian Activists," *Washington Post,* 25 November 2003, A22.

16. C. J. Chivers, "How Top Spies in Ukraine Changed the Nation's Path," *New York Times,* 17 January 2005, A1.

17. Seymour Martin Lipset, *Political Man: The Social Basis of Politics* (Garden City, N.Y.: Doubleday, 1960).

18. Author's interviews with several democratic activists involved in the anti-Milošević campaign in 2000. Polls show that Milošević benefited in the short run from the bombing campaign, although, ironically, this spike in popularity might have caused him to miscalculate his chances of winning a direct election.

19. Helsinki Committee for Human Rights in Serbia, *Human Rights and Accountability: Serbia 2003* (Belgrade: Helsinki Committee for Human Rights in Serbia, 2004), 163–66.

20. Author's interviews with several Georgian NGO leaders, Tbilisi, 12–14 October 2004.

21. Author's interview with Pora leader Vladislav Kaskiv, Kyiv, 9 March 2005.

AZAR GAT

THE RETURN OF AUTHORITARIAN GREAT POWERS

The End of the End of History

Today's global liberal democratic order faces two challenges. The first is radical Islam—and it is the lesser of the two challenges. Although the proponents of radical Islam find liberal democracy repugnant, and the movement is often described as the new fascist threat, the societies from which it arises are generally poor and stagnant. They represent no viable alternative to modernity and pose no significant military threat to the developed world. It is mainly the potential use of weapons of mass destruction—particularly by nonstate actors—that makes militant Islam a menace.

The second, and more significant, challenge emanates from the rise of nondemocratic great powers: the West's old Cold War rivals China and Russia, now operating under authoritarian capitalist, rather than communist, regimes. Authoritarian capitalist great powers played a leading role in the international system up until 1945. They have been absent since then. But today, they seem poised for a comeback.

Capitalism's ascendancy appears to be deeply entrenched, but the current predominance of democracy could be far less secure. Capitalism has expanded relentlessly since early modernity, its lower-priced goods and superior economic power eroding and transforming all other socioeconomic regimes, a process most memorably described by Karl Marx in *The Communist Manifesto*. Contrary to Marx's expectations, capitalism had the same effect on communism, eventually "burying" it without the proverbial shot being fired. The triumph of the market, precipitating and reinforced by the industrial-technological revolution, led to the rise of the middle class, intensive urbanization, the spread of education, the emergence of mass

From *Foreign Affairs,* 86, no. 4 (July/August 2007), pp. 59–69.

society, and ever greater affluence. In the post–Cold War era (just as in the nineteenth century and the 1950s and 1960s), it is widely believed that liberal democracy naturally emerged from these developments, a view famously espoused by Francis Fukuyama. Today, more than half of the world's states have elected governments, and close to half have sufficiently entrenched liberal rights to be considered fully free.

But the reasons for the triumph of democracy, especially over its nondemocratic capitalist rivals of the two world wars, Germany and Japan, were more contingent than is usually assumed. Authoritarian capitalist states, today exemplified by China and Russia, may represent a viable alternative path to modernity, which in turn suggests that there is nothing inevitable about liberal democracy's ultimate victory—or future dominance.

Chronicle of a Defeat Not Foretold

The liberal democratic camp defeated its authoritarian, fascist, and communist rivals alike in all of the three major great-power struggles of the twentieth century—the two world wars and the Cold War. In trying to determine exactly what accounted for this decisive outcome, it is tempting to trace it to the special traits and intrinsic advantages of liberal democracy.

One possible advantage is democracies' international conduct. Perhaps they more than compensate for carrying a lighter stick abroad with a greater ability to elicit international cooperation through the bonds and discipline of the global market system. This explanation is probably correct for the Cold War, when a greatly expanded global economy was dominated by the democratic powers, but it does not apply to the two world wars. Nor is it true that liberal democracies succeed because they always cling together. Again, this was true, at least as a contributing factor, during the Cold War, when the democratic capitalist camp kept its unity, whereas growing antagonism between the Soviet Union and China pulled the communist bloc apart. During World

War I, however, the ideological divide between the two sides was much less clear. The Anglo-French alliance was far from preordained; it was above all a function of balance-of-power calculations rather than liberal cooperation. At the close of the nineteenth century, power politics had brought the United Kingdom and France, bitterly antagonistic countries, to the brink of war and prompted the United Kingdom to actively seek an alliance with Germany. Liberal Italy's break from the Triple Alliance and joining of the Entente, despite its rivalry with France, was a function of the Anglo-French alliance, as Italy's peninsular location made it hazardous for the country to be on a side opposed to the leading maritime power of the time, the United Kingdom. Similarly, during World War II, France was quickly defeated and taken out of the Allies' side (which was to include nondemocratic Soviet Russia), whereas the right-wing totalitarian powers fought on the same side. Studies of democracies' alliance behavior suggest that democratic regimes show no greater tendency to stick together than other types of regimes.

Nor did the totalitarian capitalist regimes lose World War II because their democratic opponents held a moral high ground that inspired greater exertion from their people, as the historian Richard Overy and others have claimed. During the 1930s and early 1940s, fascism and Nazism were exciting new ideologies that generated massive popular enthusiasm, whereas democracy stood on the ideological defensive, appearing old and dispirited. If anything, the fascist regimes proved more inspiring in wartime than their democratic adversaries, and the battlefield performance of their militaries is widely judged to have been superior.

Liberal democracy's supposedly inherent economic advantage is also far less clear than is often assumed. All of the belligerents in the twentieth century's great struggles proved highly effective in producing for war. During World War I, semiautocratic Germany committed its resources as effectively as its democratic rivals did. After early victories in World War II, Nazi Germany's economic mobilization and military production proved lax during the critical years 1940–42. Well positioned at the time to fundamentally alter the global balance of power by destroying the Soviet Union and straddling all of continental Europe, Germany failed because its armed forces were meagerly supplied for the task. The reasons for this deficiency remain a matter of historical debate, but one of the problems was the existence of competing centers of authority in the Nazi system, in which Hitler's "divide and rule" tactics and party functionaries' jealous guarding of their assigned domains had a chaotic effect. Furthermore, from the fall of France in June 1940 to the German setback before Moscow in December 1941, there was a widespread feeling in Germany that the war had practically been won. All the same, from 1942 onward (by which time [it] was too late), Germany greatly intensified its economic mobilization and caught up with and even surpassed the liberal democracies in terms of the share of GDP devoted to the war (although its production volume remained much lower than that of the massive U.S. economy). Likewise, levels of economic mobilization in imperial Japan and the Soviet Union exceeded those of the United States and the United Kingdom thanks to ruthless efforts.

Only during the Cold War did the Soviet command economy exhibit deepening structural weaknesses—weaknesses that were directly responsible for the Soviet Union's downfall. The Soviet system had successfully generated the early and intermediate stages of industrialization (albeit at a frightful human cost) and excelled at the regimentalized techniques of mass production during World War II. It also kept abreast militarily during the Cold War. But because of the system's rigidity and lack of incentives, it proved ill equipped to cope with the advanced stages of development and the demands of the information age and globalization.

There is no reason, however, to suppose that the totalitarian capitalist regimes of Nazi Germany and imperial Japan would have proved inferior economically to the democracies had they survived. The inefficiencies that favoritism and unaccountability typically create in such regimes might have been offset by higher levels of social discipline. Because of their more efficient capitalist economies, the right-wing totalitarian powers could have constituted a more viable challenge to the liberal democracies than the Soviet Union did; Nazi Germany was judged to be such a challenge by the Allied powers before and during World War II. The liberal democracies did not possess an inherent advantage over Germany in terms of economic and technological development, as they did in relation to their other great-power rivals.

So why did the democracies win the great struggles of the twentieth century? The reasons are different for each type of adversary. They defeated their nondemocratic capitalist adversaries, Germany and Japan, in war because Germany and Japan were medium-sized countries with limited resource bases and they came up against the far superior—but hardly preordained—economic and military coalition of the democratic powers and Russia or the Soviet Union. The defeat of communism, however, had much more to do with structural factors. The capitalist camp—which after 1945 expanded to include most of the developed world—possessed much greater economic power than the communist bloc, and the inherent inefficiency of the communist economies prevented them from fully exploiting their vast resources and catching up to the West. Together, the Soviet Union and China were larger and thus had the potential to be more powerful than the democratic capitalist camp. Ultimately, they failed because their economic systems limited them, whereas the nondemocratic capitalist powers, Germany and Japan, were defeated because they were too small. Contingency played a decisive role in tipping the balance against the nondemocratic capitalist powers and in favor of the democracies.

American Exception

The most decisive element of contingency was the United States. After all, it was little more than a chance of history that the scion of Anglo-Saxon liberalism would sprout on the other side of the Atlantic, institutionalize its heritage with independence, expand across one of the most habitable and thinly populated territories in the world, feed off of massive immigration from Europe, and so create on a continental scale what was—and still is—by far the world's largest concentration of economic and military might. A liberal regime and other structural traits had to do with the United States' economic success, and even with its size, because of its attractiveness to immigrants. But the United States would scarcely have achieved such greatness had it not been located in a particularly advantageous and vast ecological-geographic niche, as the counterexamples of Canada, Australia, and New Zealand demonstrate. And location, of course, although crucial, was but one necessary condition among many for bringing about the giant and, indeed, United States as the paramount political fact of the twentieth century. Contingency was at least as responsible as liberalism for the United States' emergence in the New World and, hence, for its later ability to rescue the Old World.

Throughout the twentieth century, the United States' power consistently surpassed that of the next two strongest states combined, and this decisively tilted the global balance of power in favor of whichever side Washington was on. If any factor gave the liberal democracies their edge, it was above all the existence of the United States rather than any inherent advantage. In fact, had it not been for the United States, liberal democracy may well have lost the great struggles of the twentieth century. This is a sobering thought that is often overlooked in studies of the spread of democracy in the twentieth century, and it makes the world today appear much more contingent and tenuous than linear theories of development suggest. If it were not for the U.S. factor, the judgment of later generations on liberal democracy would probably have echoed the negative verdict on democracy's performance, issued by the fourth-century-BC Greeks, in the wake of Athens' defeat in the Peloponnesian War.

The New Second World

But the audit of war is, of course, not the only one that societies—democratic and nondemocratic—undergo. One must ask how the totalitarian capitalist powers would have developed had they not been defeated by war. Would they, with time and further development, have shed their former identity and embraced liberal democracy, as the former communist regimes of eastern Europe eventually did? Was the capitalist industrial state of imperial Germany before World War I ultimately moving toward increasing parliamentary control and democratization? Or would it have developed into an authoritarian oligarchic regime, dominated by an alliance between the officialdom, the armed forces, and industry, as imperial Japan did (in spite of the latter's liberal interlude in the 1920s)? Liberalization seems even more doubtful in the case of Nazi Germany had it survived, let alone triumphed. Because all these major historical experiments were cut short by war, the answers to these questions remain a matter of speculation. But perhaps the peacetime record of other authoritarian capitalist regimes since 1945 can offer a clue.

Studies that cover this period show that democracies generally outdo other systems economically. Authoritarian capitalist regimes are at least as successful—if not more so—in the early stages of development, but they tend to democratize after crossing a certain threshold of economic and social development. This seems to have been a recurring pattern in East Asia, southern Europe, and Latin America. The attempt to draw conclusions about development patterns from these findings, however, may be misleading, because the sample set itself may be polluted. Since 1945, the enormous gravitational pull exerted by the United States and the liberal hegemony has bent patterns of development worldwide.

Because the totalitarian capitalist great powers, Germany and Japan, were crushed in war, and these countries were subsequently threatened by Soviet power, they lent themselves to a sweeping restructuring and democratization. Consequently, smaller countries that chose capitalism over communism had no rival political and economic model to emulate and no powerful international players to turn to other than the liberal democratic camp. These small and medium-sized countries' eventual democratization probably had as much to do with the overwhelming influence of the Western liberal hegemony as with internal processes. Presently, Singapore is the only example of a country with a truly developed economy that still maintains a semiauthoritarian regime, and even it is likely to change under the influence of the liberal order within which it operates. But are Singapore-like great powers that prove resistant to the influence of this order possible?

The question is made relevant by the recent emergence of nondemocratic giants, above all formerly communist and booming authoritarian capitalist China. Russia, too, is retreating from its postcommunist liberalism and assuming an increasingly authoritarian character as its economic clout grows. Some believe that these countries could ultimately become liberal democracies through a combination of internal development, increasing affluence, and outside influence. Alternatively, they may have enough weight to create a new nondemocratic but economically advanced Second World. They could establish a powerful authoritarian capitalist order that allies political elites, industrialists, and the military; that is nationalist in orientation; and that participates in the global economy on its own terms, as imperial Germany and imperial Japan did.

It is widely contended that economic and social development creates pressures for democratization that an authoritarian state structure cannot contain. There is also the view that "closed societies" may be able to excel in mass manufacturing but not in the advanced stages of the information economy. The jury on these issues is still out, because the data set is incomplete. Imperial and Nazi Germany stood at the forefront of the advanced scientific and manufacturing economies of their times, but some would argue that their success no longer applies because the information economy is much more diversified. Nondemocratic Singapore has a highly successful information economy, but Singapore is a city-state, not a big country. It will take a long time before China reaches the stage when the possibility of an authoritarian state with an advanced capitalist economy can be tested. All that can be said at the moment is that there is nothing in the historical record to suggest that a transition to democracy by today's authoritarian capitalist powers is inevitable, whereas there is a great deal to suggest that such powers have far greater economic and military potential than their communist predecessors did.

China and Russia represent a return of economically successful authoritarian capitalist powers, which have been absent since the defeat of Germany and Japan in 1945, but they are much larger than the latter two countries ever were. Although Germany was only a medium-sized country uncomfortably squeezed at the center of Europe, it twice nearly broke out of its confines to become a true world power on account of its economic and military might. In 1941, Japan was still behind the leading great powers in terms of economic development, but its growth rate since 1913 had been the highest in the world. Ultimately, however, both Germany and Japan were too small—in terms of population, resources, and potential—to take on the United States. Present-day China, on the other hand, is the largest player in the international system in terms of population and is experiencing spectacular economic growth. By shifting from communism to capitalism, China has switched to a far more efficient brand of authoritarianism. As China rapidly narrows the economic gap with the developed world, the possibility looms that it will become a true authoritarian superpower.

Even in its current bastions in the West, the liberal political and economic consensus is vulnerable to unforeseen developments, such as a crushing economic crisis that could disrupt the global trading system or a resurgence of ethnic strife in a Europe increasingly troubled by immigration and ethnic minorities. Were the West to be hit by such upheavals, support for liberal democracy in Asia, Latin America, and Africa—where adherence to that model is more recent, incomplete, and insecure—could be shaken. A successful nondemocratic Second World could then be regarded by many as an attractive alternative to liberal democracy.

Making the World Safe for Democracy

Although the rise of authoritarian capitalist great powers would not necessarily lead to a nondemocratic hegemony or a war, it might imply that the near-total dominance of liberal democracy since the Soviet Union's collapse will be short-lived and that a universal "democratic peace" is still far off. The new authoritarian capitalist powers could become as deeply integrated into the world economy as imperial Germany and imperial Japan were and not choose to pursue autarky, as Nazi Germany and the communist bloc did. A great-power China may also be less revisionist than the territorially confined Germany and Japan were (although Russia, which is still reeling from having lost an empire, is more likely to tend toward revisionism). Still, Beijing, Moscow, and their future followers might well be on antagonistic terms with the democratic countries, with all the potential for suspension, insecurity, and conflict that this entails—while holding considerably more power than any of the democratics' past rivals ever did.

So does the greater power potential of authoritarian capitalism mean that the transformation of the former communist great powers may ultimately prove to have been a negative development for global democracy? It is too early to tell. Economically, the liberalization of the former communist countries has given the global economy a tremendous boost, and there may be more in store. But the possibility of a move toward protectionism by them in the future also needs to be taken into account—and assiduously avoided. It was, after all, the prospect of growing protectionism in the world economy at the turn of the twentieth century and the protectionist bent of the 1930s that helped radicalize the nondemocratic capitalist powers of the time and precipitate both world wars.

On the positive side for the democracies, the collapse of the Soviet Union and its empire stripped Moscow of about half the resources it commanded during the Cold War, with eastern Europe absorbed by a greatly expanded democratic Europe. This is perhaps the most significant change in the global balance of power since the forced postwar democratic reorientation of Germany and Japan under U.S. tutelage. Moreover, China may still eventually democratize, and Russia could reverse its drift away from democracy. If China and Russia do not become democratic, it will be critical that India remain so, both because of its vital role in balancing China and because of the model that it represents for other developing countries.

But the most important factor remains the United States. For all the criticism leveled against it, the United States—and its alliance with Europe—stands as the single most important hope for the future of liberal democracy. Despite its problems and weaknesses, the United States still commands a global position of strength and is likely to retain it even as the authoritarian capitalist powers grow. Not only are its GDP and productivity growth rate the highest in the developed world, but as an immigrant country with about one-fourth the population density of both the European Union and China and one-tenth of that of Japan and India, the United States still has considerable potential to grow—both economically and in terms of population—whereas those others are all experiencing aging and, ultimately, shrinking populations. China's economic growth rate is among the highest in the world, and given the country's huge population and still low levels of development, such growth harbors the most radical potential for change in global power relations. But even if China's superior growth rate persists and its GDP surpasses that of the United States by the 2020s, as is often forecast, China will still have just over one-third of the United States' wealth per capita and, hence, considerably less economic and military power. Closing that far more challenging gap with the developed world would take several more decades. Furthermore, GDP alone is known to be a poor measure of a country's power, and evoking it to celebrate China's ascendancy is highly misleading. As it was during the twentieth century, the U.S. factor remains the greatest guarantee that liberal democracy will not be thrown on the defensive and relegated to a vulnerable position on the periphery of the international system.

9 LESS-DEVELOPED AND NEWLY INDUSTRIALIZING COUNTRIES

Few people in any developed country can imagine the grinding burden of poverty, and the horrible moral dilemmas it brings, in the typical "less-developed" country. Do famine-stricken parents, themselves the only support for several children, feed themselves or their children first? Do they sell or abandon some children to keep the others alive? We recoil at even contemplating such choices. William Easterly, a World Development Bank economist, confronts us directly with such images in the opening chapter of his important book, The Elusive Quest for Growth *(2001).*

The intellectual puzzle of Third World poverty is that, according to all our standard economic models, it should not persist. Investment in poor countries should earn much higher returns than in rich ones—a phenomenon known technically as "declining marginal productivity of capital"—and hence investment rates and economic growth should also be much higher. This standard result of economic theory is usually called the theory of convergence, *and it holds that initially poor countries should grow so much faster than rich ones that their growth rates (and, allowing for random variation, their levels of wealth) should very quickly "converge" on those of rich countries. In a sentence, all poor countries should be duplicating the experience of the Asian "tigers." Korea, Taiwan, and China should be the rule, not the exception. More shockingly perhaps, rapid growth and rapid convergence should occur especially where poorer countries are open to foreign investment (since foreign investors will want those higher returns) and even more under imperialism (since it opens countries to foreign investment and guarantees foreign investors' property rights).*

It seems at first self-evident that nothing like this has happened in the real world, and Lant Pritchett, a development economist at the World Bank, argues forcefully in his influential article "Divergence, Big-Time" (1997) that virtually all of the predictions of convergence theory have been wrong over the last century and more: countries have diverged, not converged, in their rates of growth and levels of wealth. But this turns out to be true only if we weight all countries, big and small, equally. As Branko Milanovic, the lead economist in the World Bank's research department, shows in his 2005 book Worlds Apart *(from which we include a short excerpt here), population-weighted between-nation inequality has been trending almost uniformly downward since the 1960s. This is due chiefly to the very rapid economic growth of China, and to a lesser extent India, both with huge populations. Thus, convergence has been happening, in one important sense, at the world level; but this does not resolve the mystery of why so many smaller nations have remained impoverished.*

The region that has failed most signally to grow is sub-Saharan Africa. Indeed, a significant number of African countries are poorer today than they were at independence. Thus, Paul Collier (another World Bank economist) and Jan Willem Gunning (an Oxford University economist who specializes in Africa) ask simply, "Why Has Africa Grown Slowly?" and weigh the major competing explanations: "policy" versus "destiny," and external versus internal factors (1999). They conclude that mostly "policy"—rather than the longer-term factors emphasized by such scholars as Acemoglu (see Chapter 4)—is to blame: in the past, external policies (e.g., of richer and more powerful countries), and, more recently, internal policies.

How does democracy relate to economic growth, and to government policy generally? Most rich countries are democratic, and most democracies are rich; but is a democratic government likelier to adopt pro-growth policies? Some have argued that less-developed countries will actually grow more quickly under "enlightened" dictatorships. Robert Barro (1994) and Adam Przeworski and his associates (2000) address this question and find at best a weak link: while wealth makes countries democratic, democracy normally does not make them rich; but neither does democracy inhibit growth. Przeworski and his associates do however find another important effect of democracy: under democratic governments, workers receive a much higher share of what society produces. Others have argued convincingly for a related effect: democracies spend far more on the kinds of "public goods" that matter to average citizens—above all education and public health—while dictatorships spend more on "rents" (corrupt and noncorrupt prerequisites of office) for the rulers themselves and for their cronies. This effect emerges even in the relatively short run: spending on public goods rises dramatically in the first few years after a dictatorship yields to a democracy.[1]

Does it matter, then, if a less-developed country is a democracy? In the short term, democracy will not cause growth (but neither will it hinder it). In the longer term, many now argue, democracies' higher rate of investment in "human capital" (i.e., in education) will provide the basis for higher growth. And in the meantime, democracies certainly provide more to average citizens, both in wages and in public goods.

NOTE

1. See, in particular, David A. Lake and Matthew A. Baum, "The Invisible Hand of Democracy," from *Comparative Political Studies* 34 (2001), pp. 587–621, and David A. Brown and Wendy Hunter, "Democracy and Human Capital Formation," from *Comparative Political Studies* 37 (2004), pp. 842–64.

WILLIAM EASTERLY

TO HELP THE POOR

When I see another child eating, I watch him,
and if he doesn't give me something I think
I'm going to die of hunger.
          —*A ten-year-old child in Gabon, 1997*

I am in Lahore, a city of 6 million people in Pakistan, on a World Bank trip as I write this chapter. Last weekend I went with a guide to the village of Gulvera, not far outside Lahore. We entered the village on an impossibly narrow paved road, which the driver drove at top speed except on the frequent occasions that cattle were crossing the road. We continued as the road turned into a dirt track, where there was barely enough space between the village houses for the car. Then the road seemed to dead-end. But although I could not detect any road, the guide pointed out to the driver how he could make a sharp right across an open field, then regain a sort of a road—flat dirt anyway. I hated to think what would happen to these dirt roads in rainy season.

The "road" brought us to the community center for the village, where a number of young and old men were hanging out (no women, on which more in a moment). The village smelled of manure. The men were expecting us and were extremely hospitable, welcoming us in to the brick-and-mortar community center, everyone grasping each of our right hands with their two hands and seating us on some rattan benches. They provided pillows for us to lean on or with which to otherwise make ourselves comfortable. They served us a drink of lassi, a sort of yogurt-milk mixture. The lassi pitcher was thickly covered with flies, but I drank my lassi anyway.

The men said that during the week, they worked all day in the fields, then came to the

From *The Elusive Quest for Growth: Economists' Adventures and Misadventures in the Tropics* (Cambridge, Mass.: MIT Press, 2001), pp. 5–19. Author's notes have been omitted.

community center in the evenings to play cards and talk. The women couldn't come, they said, because they still had work to do in the evenings. Flocks of flies hummed everywhere, and some of the men had open sores on their legs. There was one youngish but dignified man nicknamed Deenu to whom everyone seemed to defer. Most of the men were barefoot, wearing long dusty robes. A crowd of children hung around the entrance watching us—only boys, no girls.

I asked Deenu what the main problems of Gulvera village were. Deenu said they were glad to have gotten electricity just six months before. Imagine getting electricity after generations spent in darkness. They were glad to have a boys' elementary school. However, they still lacked many things: a girls' elementary school, a doctor, drainage or sewerage (everything was dumped into a pool of rancid water outside the community center), telephone connections, paved roads. The poor sanitary conditions and lack of access to medical care in villages like Gulvera may help explain why a hundred out of every thousand babies die before their first birthday in Pakistan.

I asked Deenu if we could see a house. He walked with us over to his brother's house. It was an adobe-walled dirt-floor compound, which had two small rooms where they lived, stalls for the cattle, an outside dung-fired oven built into a wall, piles of cattle dung stacked up to dry, and a hand pump hooked up to a well. Children were everywhere, including a few girls finally, staring curiously at us. Deenu said his brother had seven children. Deenu himself had six brothers and seven sisters. The brothers all lived in the village; the sisters had married into other villages. The women in the household hung back near the two small rooms. We were not introduced to them.

Women's rights have not yet come to rural Pakistan, a fact reflected in some grim statistics: there are 108 men for every 100 women in Pakistan. In rich countries, women slightly outnumber men because of their greater longevity. In Pakistan, there are what Nobel Prize winner Amartya Sen called "missing women," reflecting some combination of discrimination against girls in nutrition, medical care, or even female infanticide. Oppression of women sometimes takes an even more violent turn. There was a story in the Lahore newspaper of a brother who had killed his sister to preserve the family honor; he had suspected her of an illicit affair.

Violence in the countryside is widespread in Pakistan, despite the peaceful appearance of Gulvera. Another story in the Lahore paper described a village feud in which one family killed seven members of another family. Bandits and kidnappers prey on travelers in parts of the countryside in Pakistan.

We walked back to the community center, passing a group of boys playing a game, where they threw four walnuts on the ground and then tried to hit one of the walnuts with another one. Deenu asked us if we would like to stay for lunch, but we politely declined (I didn't want to take any of their scarce food), said our good-byes, and drove away. One of the villagers rode away with us, just to have an adventure. He told us that they had arranged for two cooks to prepare our lunch. I felt bad about having declined the lunch invitation.

We drove across the fields to where four brothers had grouped their compounds into a sort of a village and went through the same routine: the men greeting us warmly with two hands and seating us on rattan benches outside. No women were to be seen. The children were even more numerous and uninhibited than in Gulvera; they were mostly boys but this time also a few girls. They crowded around us watching everything we did, frequently breaking into laughter at some unknown faux pas by one of us. The men served us some very good milky sweet tea. I saw a woman peeking out from inside the house, but when I looked in her direction, she pulled back out of sight.

We walked into one of the brothers' compounds. Many women stood at the doors into their rooms, hanging back but watching us. The men showed us a churn that they used to make butter and yogurt. One of the men tried to show us how to use it, but he himself didn't know; this was woman's work. The children nearly passed out from laughing. The men brought us some butter to taste. They said they melted the butter to make ghee—clarified butter—which was an important ingredient in their cooking. They said if you ate a lot of ghee, it made you stronger. Then they gave us some ghee to taste. Most of their food seemed to consist of dairy products.

I asked what problems they faced. They had gotten electricity just one month before. They otherwise had the same unfulfilled needs as Gulvera: no telephone, no running water, no doctor, no sewerage, no roads. This was only a kilometer off the main road just outside Lahore, so we weren't in the middle of nowhere. They were poor, but these were relatively well-off villagers compared to more remote villages in Pakistan. The road leading to their minivillage was a half-lane track constructed of bricks that they had made themselves.

The majority of people in Pakistan are poor: 85 percent live on less than two dollars a day and 31 percent live in extreme poverty at less than one dollar a day. The majority of the world's people live in poor nations like Pakistan, where people live in isolated poverty even close to a major city. The majority of the world's people live in poor nations where women are oppressed, far too many babies die, and far too many people don't have enough to eat. We care about economic growth for the poor nations because it makes the lives of poor people like those in Gulvera better. Economic growth frees the poor from hunger and disease. Economy-wide GDP growth per capita translates into rising incomes for the poorest of the poor, lifting them out of poverty.

The Deaths of the Innocents

The typical rate of infant mortality in the richest fifth of countries is 4 out of every 1,000 births; in the poorest fifth of countries, it is 200 out of every 1,000 births. Parents in the poorest countries are fifty times more likely than in the richest countries to know grief rather than joy from the birth of a child. Researchers have found that a 10 percent decrease in income is associated with about a 6 percent higher infant mortality rate.

The higher rates of babies dying in the poorest countries reflect in part the higher rates of communicable and often easily preventable diseases such as tuberculosis, syphillis, diarrhea, polio, measles, tetanus, meningitis, hepatitis, sleeping sickness, schistosomiasis, river blindness, leprosy, trachoma, intestinal worms, and lower respiratory infections. At low incomes, disease is more dangerous because of lower medical knowledge, lower nutrition, and lower access to medical care.

Two million children die every year of dehydration from diarrhea. Another 2 million children die annually from pertussis, polio, diphtheria, tetanus, and measles.

Three million children die annually from bacterial pneumonia. Overcrowding of housing and indoor wood or cigarette smoke make pneumonia among children more likely. Malnourished children are also more likely to develop pneumonia than well-fed children. Bacterial pneumonia can be cured by a five-day course of antibiotics, like cotrimoxazole, that costs about twenty-five cents.

Between 170 million and 400 million children annually are infected with intestinal parasites like hookworm and roundworm, which impair cognition and cause anemia and failure to thrive.

Deficiency of iodine causes goiters—swelling of the thyroid gland at the throat—and lowered mental capacity. About 120,000 children born each year suffer from mental retardation and physical paralysis caused by iodine deficiency. About 10 percent of the world's population, adults and children both, suffer from goiter.

Vitamin A deficiency causes blindness in about half a million children and contributes to the deaths of about 8 million children each year. It is not independent of the other diseases dis-

cussed here; it makes death more likely from diarrhea, measles, and pneumonia.

Medicines that would alleviate these diseases are sometimes surprisingly inexpensive, a fact that UNICEF often uses to dramatize the depths of poverty of these suffering people. Oral rehydration therapy, at a cost of less than ten cents for each dose, can alleviate dehydration. Vaccination against pertussis, polio, diphtheria, measles, and tetanus costs about fifteen dollars per child. Vitamin A can be added to diets through processing of salt or sugar or administered directly through vitamin A capsules every six months. Vitamin A capsules cost about two cents each. Iodizing salt supplies, which costs about five cents per affected person per year, alleviates iodine deficiency. Intestinal parasites can be cured with inexpensive drugs like albendazole and praziquantel.

Wealthier and Healthier

Lant Pritchett, from Harvard's Kennedy School of Government, and Larry Summers, the former U.S. secretary of the treasury, found a strong association between economic growth and changes in infant mortality. They pointed out that a third factor that was unchanging over time for each country, like "culture" or "institutions," could not be explaining the simultaneous change in income and change in infant mortality. Going further, they argued that the rise in income was causing the fall in mortality rather than the other way around. They used a statistical argument that we will see more of later in this book. They observed some income increases that were probably unrelated to mortality, like income increases due to rises in a country's export prices. They traced through the effect of such an income increase, finding that it still did result in a fall in infant mortality. If an income increase that has nothing to do with mortality changes is still associated with a fall in mortality, this suggests that income increases are causing reduced mortality.

Pritchett and Summers's findings, if we can take them literally, imply huge effects of income growth on the death of children. The deaths of about half a million children in 1990 would have been averted if Africa's growth in the 1980s had been 1.5 percentage points higher.

The Poorest of the Poor

The statistics presented so far are national averages. Behind the averages of even the poorest nation, there is still regional variation. Mali is one of the poorest nations on earth. The countryside along the Niger River around the city of Tombouctou (Timbuktu) is one of the poorest regions in Mali and thus one of the poorest places on earth. At the time of a survey in 1987, over a third of the children under age five had had diarrhea in the preceding two weeks. Very few of them were on simple and cheap oral rehydration therapy. None had been vaccinated for diphtheria, pertussis, or typhoid. Forty-one percent of children born do not live to the age of five, three times the mortality rate in the capital of Bamako and one of the highest child mortality rates ever recorded.

As in Tomboctou, there are some regions or peoples at the very bottom of the economic pyramid, despised even by other poor. "In Egypt they were *madfoun*—the buried or buried alive; in Ghana, *ohiabrubro*—the miserably poor, with no work, sick with no one to care for them; in Indonesia, *endek arak tadah*; in Brazil, *miseraveis*—the deprived; in Russia, *bomzhi*—the homeless; in Bangladesh *ghrino gorib*—the despised/hated poor." In Zambia the *balandana sana* or *bapina* were described in these terms: "Lack food, eat once or twice; poor hygiene, flies fall over them, cannot afford school and health costs, lead miserable lives, poor dirty clothing, poor sanitation, access to water, look like made people, live on vegetables and sweet potatoes." In Malawi, the bottom poor were *osaukitsitsa*, "mainly households headed by the aged, the sick, disabled, orphans and widows." Some were described as *onyentchera*, "the stunted poor, with thin bodies, short stature and thin hairs, bodies that did not

shine even after bathing, and who experience frequent illnesses and a severe lack of food."

Eating

High mortality in the poorest countries also reflects the continuing problem of hunger. Daily calorie intake is one-third lower in the poorest fifth of countries than in the richest fifth.

A quarter of the poorest countries had famines in the past three decades; none of the richest countries faced a famine. In the poorest nations like Burundi, Madagascar, and Uganda, nearly half of all children under the age of three are abnormally short because of nutritional deficiency.

An Indian family housed in a thatched hut seldom "could have two square meals a day. The lunch would be finished munching some sugarcane. Once in a while they would taste 'sattu' (made of flour), pulses [dried beans], potatoes etc. but for occasions only."

In Malawi, the poorest families "stay without food for 2–3 days or even the whole week . . . and may simply cook vegetables for a meal . . . some households literally eat bitter maize bran (*gaga/ deya owawa*) and *gmelina* sawdust mixed with a little maize flour especially during the hunger months of January and February."

Oppression of the Poor

Poor societies sometimes have some form of debt bondage. To take one example, observers of India report "a vicious cycle of indebtedness in which a debtor may work in a moneylender's house as a servant, on his farm as a laborer. . . . The debt may accumulate substantially due to high interest rates, absence due to illness, and expenses incurred for food or accommodations."

Ethnic minorities are particularly prone to oppression. In Pakistan in 1993, the Bengali community of Rehmanabad in Karachi "had been subject to evictions and bulldozing, and on returning to the settlement and constructing temporary housing of reeds and sacks, have faced on-going harassment by land speculators, the police and political movements."

Poor children are particularly vulnerable to oppression. Forty-two percent of children aged ten to fourteen are workers in the poorest countries. Less than 2 percent of children aged ten to fourteen are workers in the richest countries. Although most countries have laws forbidding child labor, the U.S. State Department classifies many countries as not enforcing these laws. Eighty-eight percent of the poorest countries are in this no-enforcement category; none of the richest countries is. For example, we have this story of Pachawak in western Orissa state in India: "Pachawak dropped out of class 3 when one day his teacher caned him severely. Since then he has been working as child labor with a number of rich households. Pachawak's father owns 1.5 acres of land and works as a laborer. His younger brother of 11-years-old also became a bonded laborer when the family had to take a loan for the marriage of the eldest son. The system is closely linked to credit, as many families take loans from landlords, who in lieu of that obligation keep the children as 'kuthia.' Pachawak worked as a cattle grazer from 6 A.M. to 6 P.M. and got paid two to four sacks of paddy a year, two meals a day, and one lungi [wrap-around clothing]."

One particularly unsavory kind of child labor is prostitution. In Benin, for example, "the girls have no choice but to prostitute themselves, starting at 14, even at 12. They do it for 50 francs, or just for dinner."

Another occupation in which children work in poor countries is particularly dangerous: war. As many as 200,000 child soldiers from the ages of six to sixteen fought wars in poor countries like Myanmar, Angola, Somalia, Liberia, Uganda, and Mozambique.

Women are also vulnerable to oppression in poor countries. Over four-fifths of the richest fifth of countries have social and economic equality for women most of the time, according to the *World Human Rights Guide* by Charles Humana. None of the poorest fifth of countries has social and economic equality for women. In Cameroon, "Women in some regions require a husband's, father's, or brother's permission to go out. In addition, a woman's husband or brother has access to her bank accounts, but not vice versa." A 1997 survey in Jamaica found that "in all communities, wife-beating was perceived as a common experience in daily life." In Georgia in the Caucasus, "women confessed that frequent household arguments resulted in being beaten." In Uganda in 1998, when women were asked, "What kind of work do men in your area do?" they laughed and said, "Eat and sleep then wake up and go drinking again."

Growth and Poverty

My World Bank colleagues Martin Ravallion and Shaohua Chen collected data on spells of economic growth and changes in poverty covering the years 1981 to 1999. They get their data from national surveys of household income or expenditure. They require that the methodology of the survey be unchanged over the period that they are examining so as to exclude spurious changes due to changing definitions. They found 154 periods of change in 65 developing countries with data that met this requirement.

Ravallion and Chen defined poverty as an absolute concept within each country: the poor were defined as the part of the population that had incomes below $1 a day at the beginning of each period they were examining. Ravallion and Chen keep this poverty line fixed within each country during the period they analyze. So the question was, How did aggregate economic growth change the share of people below this poverty line?

The answer was quite clear: fast growth went with fast poverty reduction, and overall economic contraction went with increased poverty. Here I summarize Ravallion and Chen's data by dividing the number of episodes into four equally sized groups from the fastest growing to the fastest declining. I compare the change in

	Percentage change in average incomes per year	Percent change in poverty rate per year
Strong contraction	−9.8	23.9
Moderate contraction	−1.9	1.5
Moderate expansion	1.6	−0.6
Strong expansion	8.2	−6.1

poverty in countries with the fastest growth to the poverty change in countries with the fastest decline [see table above].

The increases in poverty were extremely acute in the economies with severe economic declines—most of them in Eastern Europe and Central Asia. These were economies that declined with the death of the old communist system and kept declining while awaiting the birth of a new system. Several of these poverty-increasing declines also occurred in Africa. Poverty shot up during severe recessions in Zambia, Mali, and Côte d'Ivoire, for example.

Countries with positive income growth had a decline in the proportion of people below the poverty line. The fastest average growth was associated with the fastest poverty reductions. Growth was reaching the poor in Indonesia, for example, which had average income growth of 76 percent from 1984 to 1996. The proportion of Indonesians beneath the poverty line in 1993 was one-quarter of what it was in 1984. (A bad reversal came with Indonesia's crisis over 1997–1999, with average income falling by 12 percent and the poverty rate shooting up 65 percent, again confirming that income and poverty move together.)

All of this in retrospect seems unsurprising. For poverty to get worse with economic growth, the distribution of income would have to get much more unequal as incomes increased. There is no evidence for such disastrous deteriorations in income inequality as income rises. In Ravallion and Chen's data set, for example, measures of inequality show no tendency to get either better or worse with economic growth. If the degree of inequality stays about the same, then income of the poor and the rich must be rising together or falling together.

This is indeed what my World Bank colleagues David Dollar and Aart Kraay have found. A 1 percent increase in average income of the society translates one for one into a 1 percent increase in the incomes of the poorest 20 percent of the population. Again using statistical techniques to isolate direction of causation, they found that an additional one percentage point per capita growth *causes* a 1 percent rise in the poor's incomes.

There are two ways the poor could become better off: income could be redistributed from the rich to the poor, and the income of both the poor and the rich could rise with overall economic growth. Ravallion and Chen's and Dollar and Kraay's findings suggest that on average, growth has been much more of a lifesaver to the poor than redistribution.

To Begin the Quest

The improvement in hunger, mortality, and poverty as GDP per capita rises over time motivates us on our quest for growth. Poverty is not just low GDP; it is dying babies, starving children, and oppression of women and the downtrodden. The well-being of the next generation in poor countries depends on whether our quest to make poor countries rich is successful. I think again back to the woman I saw peering out at me from a house in a village in Pakistan. To that unknown woman I dedicate the elusive quest for growth as we economists, from rich countries and from poor countries, trek the tropics trying to make poor countries rich.

*   *   *

LANT PRITCHETT

DIVERGENCE, BIG TIME

Divergence in relative productivity levels and living standards is the dominant feature of modern economic history. In the last century, incomes in the "less developed" (or euphemistically, the "developing") countries have fallen far behind those in the "developed" countries, both proportionately and absolutely. I estimate that from 1870 to 1990 the ratio of per capita incomes between the richest and the poorest countries increased by roughly a factor of five and that the difference in income between the richest country and all others has increased by an order of magnitude.[1] This divergence is the result of the very different patterns in the long-run economic performance of two sets of countries.

One set of countries—call them the "developed" or the "advanced capitalist" (Maddison, 1995) or the "high income OECD" (World Bank, 1995)—is easily, if awkwardly, identified as European countries and their offshoots plus Japan. Since 1870, the long-run growth rates of these countries have been rapid (by previous historical standards), their growth rates have been remarkably similar, and the poorer members of the group grew sufficiently faster to produce considerable convergence in absolute income levels. The other set of countries, called the "developing" or "less developed" or "nonindustrialized," can be easily, if still awkwardly, defined only as "the other set of countries," as they have nothing else in common. The growth rates of this set of countries have been, on average, slower than the richer countries, producing divergence in relative incomes. But amongst this set of countries there have been strikingly different patterns of growth: both across countries, with some converging rapidly on the leaders while others stag-

nate; and over time, with a mixed record of take-offs, stalls and nose dives.

The next section of this paper documents the pattern of income growth and convergence within the set of developed economies. This discussion is greatly aided by the existence of data, whose lack makes the discussion in the next section of the growth rates for the developing countries tricky, but as I argue, not impossible. Finally, I offer some implications for historical growth rates in developing countries and some thoughts on the process of convergence.

Convergence in Growth Rates of Developed Countries

Some aspects of modern historical growth apply principally, if not exclusively, to the "advanced capitalist" countries. By "modern," I mean the period since 1870. To be honest, the date is chosen primarily because there are nearly complete national income accounts data for all of the now-developed economies since 1870. Maddison (1983, 1991, 1995) has assembled estimates from various national and academic sources and has pieced them together into time series that are comparable across countries. An argument can be made that 1870 marks a plausible date for a modern economic period in any case, as it is near an important transition in several countries: for example, the end of the U.S. Civil War in 1865; the Franco-Prussian War in 1870–71, immediately followed by the unification of Germany; and Japan's Meiji Restoration in 1868. Perhaps not coincidentally, Rostow (1990) dates the beginning of the "drive to technological maturity" of the United States, France and Germany to around that date, although he argues that this stage began earlier in Great Britain.[2]

From *Journal of Economic Perspectives*, 11, no. 3 (Summer 1997), pp. 3–17.

Table 1 displays the historical data for 17 presently high-income industrialized countries, which Maddison (1995) defines as the "advanced capitalist" countries. The first column of Table 1 shows the per capita level of income for each country in 1870, expressed in 1985 dollars. The last three columns of Table 1 show the average per annum growth rate of real per capita income in these countries over three time periods: 1870–1960, 1960–1980 and 1980–1994. These dates are not meant to date any explicit shifts in growth rates, but they do capture the fact that there was a golden period of growth that began some time after World War II and ended sometime before the 1980s.

Three facts jump out from Table 1. First, there is strong convergence in per capita incomes within this set of countries. For example, the poorest six countries in 1870 had five of the six fastest national growth rates for the time period 1870–1960; conversely, the richest five countries in 1870 recorded the five slowest growth rates from 1870 to 1960.[3] As is well known, this convergence has not happened at a uniform rate. There is as much convergence in the 34 years between 1960 and 1994 as in the 90 years from 1870 to 1960. Even within this earlier period, there are periods of stronger convergence pre-1914 and weaker convergence from 1914 to 1950.

Table 1. Average Per Annum Growth Rates of GDP Per Capita in the Presently High-Income Industrialized Countries, 1870–1989

Country	Level in 1870 (1985 P$)	Per annum growth rates		
		1870–1960	1960–80	1980–94
Average	1757	1.54	3.19	1.51
Std dev. of growth rates		.33	1.1	.51
Australia	3192	.90	2.43	1.22
Great Britain	2740	1.08	2.02	1.31
New Zealand	2615	1.24	1.39	1.28
Belgium	2216	1.05	3.70	1.52
Netherlands	2216	1.25	2.90	1.29
USA	2063	1.70	2.48	1.52
Switzerland	1823	1.94	2.07	.84
Denmark	1618	1.66	2.77	1.99
Germany	1606	1.66	3.03	1.56
Austria	1574	1.40	3.81	1.58
France	1560	1.56	3.53	1.31
Sweden	1397	1.85	2.74	.81
Canada	1360	1.85	3.32	.86
Italy	1231	1.54	4.16	1.62
Norway	1094	1.81	3.78	2.08
Finland	929	1.91	3.77	1.09
Japan	622	1.86	6.28	2.87

Source: Maddison (1995).
Notes: Data is adjusted from 1990 to 1985 P$ by the U.S. GDP deflator, by a method described later in this article. Per annum growth rates are calculated using endpoints.

Second, even though the poorer countries grew faster than the richer countries did, the narrow range of the growth rates over the 1870–1960 period is striking. The United States, the richest country in 1960, had grown at 1.7 percent per annum since 1870, while the overall average was 1.54. Only one country, Australia, grew either a half a percentage point higher or lower than the average, and the standard deviation of the growth rates was only .33. Evans (1994) formally tests the hypothesis that growth rates among 13 European and offshoot countries (not Japan) were equal, and he is unable to reject it at standard levels of statistical significance.

Third, while the long run hides substantial variations, at least since 1870 there has been no obvious acceleration of overall growth rates over time. As Charles Jones (1995) has pointed out, there is remarkable stability in the growth rates in the United States. For instance, if I predict per capita income in the United States in 1994 based only on a simple time trend regression of (natural log) GDP per capita estimated with data from 1870 to 1929, this prediction made for 65 years ahead is off by only 10 percent.[4] Although this predictive accuracy is not true for every country, it is true that the average growth rate of these 17 countries in the most recent period between 1980 and 1994 is almost exactly the same as that of the 1870–1960 period. However, this long-run stability does mask modest swings in the growth rates over time, as growth was considerably more rapid in the period between 1950 to 1980, especially outside the United States, than either in earlier periods or since 1980.

These three facts are true of the sample of countries that Maddison defines as the "advanced capitalist" countries. However, the discussion of convergence and long-run growth has always been plagued by the fact that the sample of countries for which historical economic data exists (and has been assembled into convenient and comparable format) is severely nonrepresentative. Among a sample of now "advanced capi-

talist" countries something like convergence (or at least nondivergence) is almost tautological, a point made early on by De Long (1988). Defining the set of countries as those that are the richest *now* almost guarantees the finding of historical convergence, as either countries are rich now and were rich historically, in which case they all have had roughly the same growth rate (like nearly all of Europe) or countries are rich now and were poor historically (like Japan) and hence grew faster and show convergence. However, examples of divergence, like countries that grew much more slowly and went from relative riches to poverty (like Argentina) or countries that were poor and grew so slowly as to become relatively poorer (like India), are not included in the samples of "now developed" countries that tend to find convergence.

Calculating a Lower Bound for Per Capita GDP

This selectivity problem raises a difficult issue in trying to estimate the possible magnitude of convergence or divergence of the incomes since 1870. There is no historical data for many of the less developed economies, and what data does exist has enormous problems with comparability and reliability. One alternative to searching for historical data is simply to place a reasonable lower bound on what GDP per capita could have been in 1870 in any country. Using this lower bound and estimates of recent incomes, one can draw reliable conclusions about the historical growth rates and divergence in cross-national distribution of income levels.

There is little doubt life was nasty, brutish and short in many countries in 1870. But even deprivation has its limit, and some per capita incomes must imply standards of living that are unsustainably and implausibly low. After making conservative use of a wide variety of different methods and approaches, I conclude that $250 (expressed in 1985 purchasing power equivalents) is the lowest GDP per capita could have been in 1870. This figure can be defended on three grounds: first, no one has ever observed consistently lower living standards at any time or place in history; second, this level is well below extreme poverty lines actually set in impoverished countries and is inconsistent with plausible levels of nutritional intake; and third, at a lower standard of living the population would be too unhealthy to expand.

Before delving into these comparisons and calculations, it is important to stress that using the purchasing power adjustments for exchange rates has an especially important effect in poor countries. While tradable goods will have generally the same prices across countries because of arbitrage, nontradable goods are typically much cheaper in poorer countries because of their lower income levels. If one applies market exchange rates to convert incomes in these economies to U.S. dollars, one is typically far understating the "true" income level, because nontradable goods can be bought much more cheaply than market exchange rates will imply. There have been several large projects, especially the UN International Comparisons Project and the Penn World Tables, that through the collection of data on the prices of comparable baskets of goods in all countries attempt to express different countries' GDP in terms of a currency that represents an equivalent purchasing power over a basket of goods. Since this adjustment is so large and of such quantitative significance, I will denote figures that have been adjusted in this way by P\$. By my own rough estimates, a country with a per capita GDP level of \$70 in U.S. dollars, measured in market exchange rates, will have a per capita GDP of P\$250.

The first criteria for a reasonable lower bound on GDP per capita is that it be a lower bound on measured GDP per capita, either of the poorest countries in the recent past or of any country in the distant past. The lowest five-year average level of per capita GDP reported for any country in the Penn World Tables (Mark 5) is P\$275 for Ethiopia in 1961–65; the next lowest is P\$278 for Uganda in 1978–1982. The countries

with the lowest level of GDP per capita ever observed, even for a single year, are P\$260 for Tanzania in 1961, P\$299 for Burundi in 1965 and P\$220 for Uganda in 1981 (in the middle of a civil war). Maddison (1991) gives estimates of GDP per capita of some less developed countries as early as 1820: P\$531 for India, P\$523 for China and P\$614 for Indonesia. His earliest estimates for Africa begin in 1913: P\$508 for Egypt and P\$648 for Ghana. Maddison also offers increasingly speculative estimates for western European countries going back much further in time; for example, he estimates that per capita GDPs in the Netherlands and the United Kingdom in 1700 were P\$1515 and P\$992, respectively, and ventures to guess that the average per capita GNP in western Europe was P\$400 in 1400. Kuznet's (1971) guess of the trough of the average per capita GDP of European countries in 900 is around P\$400.[5] On this score, P\$250 is a pretty safe bet.

A complementary set of calculations to justify a lower bound are based on "subsistence" income. While "subsistence" as a concept is out of favor, and rightfully so for many purposes, it is sufficiently robust for the task at hand. There are three related calculations: poverty lines, average caloric intakes and the cost of subsistence. Ravallion, Datt and van de Walle (1991) argue that the lowest defensible poverty line based on achieving minimally adequate consumption expenditures is P\$252 per person per year. If we assume that personal consumption expenditures are 75 percent of GDP (the average for countries with GDP per capita less than P\$400) and that mean income is 1.3 times the median, then even to achieve median income at the lowest possible poverty line requires a per capita income of \$437.[6]

As an alternative way of considering subsistence GDP per capita, begin with the finding that estimated average intake per person per day consistent with working productively is between 2,000 to 2,400 calories.[7] Now, consider two calculations. The first is that, based on a cross-sectional regression using data on incomes from the Penn World Tables and average caloric intake data from the FAO, the predicted caloric consumption at P$250 is around 1,600.[8] The five lowest levels of caloric availability ever recorded in the FAO data for various countries—1,610 calories/person during a famine in Somalia in 1975; 1,550 calories/person during a famine in Ethiopia in 1985; 1,443 calories/person in Chad in 1984; 1,586 calories/person in China in 1961 during the famines and disruption associated with the Cultural Revolution; and 1,584 calories/person in Mozambique in 1987—reveal that nearly all of the episodes of average daily caloric consumption below 1,600 are associated with nasty episodes of natural and/or man-made catastrophe. A second use of caloric requirements is to calculate the subsistence income as the cost of meeting caloric requirements. Bairoch (1993) reports the results of the physiological minimum food intake at $291 (at market exchange rates) in 1985 prices. These calculations based on subsistence intake of food again suggest P$250 is a safe lower bound.

That life expectancy is lower and infant mortality higher in poorer countries is well documented, and this relation can also help establish a lower bound on income (Pritchett and Summers, 1996). According to demographers, an under-five infant mortality rate of less than 600 per 1000 is necessary for a stable population (Hill, 1995). Using a regression based on Maddison's (1991) historical per capita income estimates and infant mortality data from historical sources for 22 countries, I predict that infant mortality in 1870 for a country with income of P$250 would have been 765 per 1000.[9] Although the rate of natural increase of population back in 1870 is subject to great uncertainty, it is typically estimated to be between .25 and 1 percent annually in that period, which is again inconsistent with income levels as low as P$250.[10]

Divergence, Big Time

If you accept: a) the current estimates of relative incomes across nations; b) the estimates of the historical growth rates of the now-rich nations; and c) that even in the poorest economies incomes were not below P$250 at any point—then you cannot escape the conclusion that the last 150 years have seen divergence, big time. The logic is straightforward and is well illustrated by Figure 1. If there had been no divergence, then we could extrapolate backward from present income of the poorer countries to past income assuming they grew at least as fast as the United States. However, this would imply that many poor countries must have had incomes below P$100 in 1870. Since this cannot be true, there must have been divergence. Or equivalently, per capita income in the United States, the world's richest industrial country, grew about four-fold from 1870 to 1960. Thus, any country whose income was not fourfold higher in 1960 than it was in 1870 grew more slowly than the United States. Since 42 of the 125 countries in the Penn World Tables with data for 1960 have levels of per capita incomes below $1,000 (that is, less than four times $250), there must have been substantial divergence between the top and bottom. The figure of P$250 is not meant to be precise or literal and the conclusion of massive divergence is robust to any plausible assumption about a lower bound.

Consider some illustrative calculations of the divergence in per capita incomes in Table 2. I scale incomes back from 1960 such that the poorest country in 1960 just reaches the lower bound by 1870, the leader in 1960 (the United States) reaches its actual 1870 value, and all relative rankings between the poorest country and the United States are preserved.[11] The first row shows the actual path of the U.S. economy. The second row gives the level of the poorest economy in 1870, which is P$250 by assumption, and then the poorest economies in 1960 and 1990 taken from the Penn World Tables. By division, the third row then shows that the ratio of the top to the bottom income countries has increased from 8.7 in 1870 to 38 by 1960 and to 45 by 1990. If instead one takes the 17 richest countries (those shown in Table 1) and applies the

Figure 1
Simulation of Divergence of Per Capita GDP, 1870–1985
(showing only selected countries)

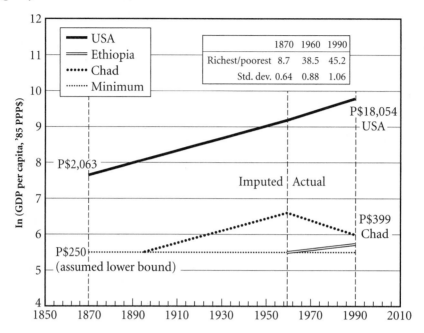

Table 2. Estimates of the Divergence of Per Capita Incomes Since 1870

	1870	*1960*	*1990*
USA (*P*$)	2063	9895	18054
Poorest (*P*$)	250	257	399
	(assumption)	(Ethiopia)	(Chad)
Ratio of GDP per capita of richest to poorest country	8.7	38.5	45.2
Average of seventeen "advanced capitalist" countries from Maddison (1995)	1757	6689	14845
Average LDCs from PWT5.6 for 1960, 1990 (imputed for 1870)	740	1579	3296
Average "advanced capitalist" to average of all other countries	2.4	4.2	4.5
Standard deviation of natural log of per capita incomes	.51	.88	1.06
Standard deviation of per capita incomes	*P*$459	*P*$2112	*P*$3988
Average absolute income deficit from the leader	*P*$1286	*P*$7650	*P*$12662

Notes: The estimates in the columns for 1870 are based on backcasting GDP per capita for each country using the methods described in the text assuming a minimum of *P*$250. If instead of that method, incomes in 1870 are backcast with truncation at *P*$250, the 1870 standard deviation is .64 (as reported in Figure 1).

Table 3. Mean Per Annum Growth Rates of GDP Per Capita

	1870–1960	1960–1979	1980–1994
Advanced capitalist countries (17)	1.5	3.2	1.5
	(.33)	(1.1)	(.51)
Less developed countries (28)	1.2	2.5	.34
	(.88)	(1.7)	(3.0)
Individual countries:			
India	.31	1.22	3.07
China	.58	2.58	6.45
Korea (1900)	.71	5.9	7.7
Brazil	1.28	4.13	−.54
Argentina (1900)	1.17	1.99	.11
Egypt (1900)	.56	3.73	2.21

Source: Calculations based on data from Maddison (1995).

same procedure, their average per capita income is shown in the fourth row. The average for all less developed economies appearing in the Penn World Tables for 1960 and 1990 is given in the fifth row; the figure for 1870 is calculated by the "backcasting" imputation process for historical incomes described above. By division, the sixth row shows that the ratio of income of the richest to all other countries has almost doubled from 2.4 in 1870 to 4.6 by 1990.

The magnitude of the change in the absolute gaps in per capita incomes between rich and poor is staggering. From 1870 to 1990, the average absolute gap in incomes of all countries from the leader had grown by an order of magnitude, from $1,286 to $12,662, as shown in the last row of Table 2.[12]

While the growth experience of all countries is equally interesting, some are more equally interesting than others. China and India account for more than a third of the world's population. For the conclusion of divergence presented here, however, a focus on India and China does not change the historical story. One can estimate their growth rates either by assuming that they were at $250 in 1870 and then calculating their growth rate in per capita GDP to reach the levels given by the Penn World Tables in 1960 (India, $766; China, $567), or by using Maddison's his-

torical estimates, which are shown in Table 3, India's growth rate is a fifth and China's a third of the average for developed economies. Either way, India's and China's incomes diverged significantly relative to the leaders between 1870 and 1960.

The idea that there is some lower bound to GDP per capita and that the lower bound has implications for long-run growth rates (and hence divergence) will not come as news either to economic historians or to recent thinkers in the area of economic growth (Lucas, 1996). Kuznets (1966, 1971) pointed out that since the now-industrialized countries have risen from very low levels of output to their presently high levels, and that their previously very low levels of output were only consistent with a very slow rate of growth historically, growth rates obviously accelerated at some point. Moreover, one suspects that many of the estimates of income into the far distant past cited above rely on exactly this kind of counterfactual logic.

Considering Alternate Sources of Historical Data

Although there is not a great deal of historical evidence on GDP estimates in the very long-run for the less developed countries, what there is confirms the finding of massive divergence. Maddison (1995) reports time series data on GDP per capita incomes for 56 countries. These include his 17 "advanced capitalist" countries (presented in Table 1), five "southern" European countries, seven eastern European countries and 28 countries typically classified as "less developed" from Asia (11), Africa (10) and Latin America (7). This data is clearly nonrepresentative of the poorest countries (although it does include India and China), and the data for Africa is very sparse until 1960. Even so, the figures in Table 3 show substantially lower growth for the less developed countries than for the developed countries. If one assumes that the ratio of incomes between the "advanced capitalist" countries and less developed countries was 2.4 in 1870, then the .35 percentage point differential would have produced a rich-poor gap of 3.7 in 1994, similar to the projected increase in the gap to 4.5 in Table 2.

Others have argued that incomes of the developing relative to the developed world were even higher in the past. Hanson (1988, 1991) argues that adjustments of comparisons from official exchange rates to purchasing power equivalents imply that developing countries were considerably richer historically than previously believed. Bairoch (1993) argues that there was almost no gap between the now-developed countries and the developing countries as late as 1800. As a result, his estimate of the growth rate of the "developed" world is 1.5 percent between 1870 and 1960 as opposed to .5 percent for the "developing" world, which implies even larger divergence in per capita incomes than the lower bound assumptions reported above.

Poverty Traps, Takeoffs and Convergence

The data on growth in less developed countries show a variety of experiences, but divergence is not a thing of the past. Some countries are "catching up" with very explosive but sustained bursts of growth, some countries continue to experience slower growth than the richest countries, and others have recently taken nosedives.

Let's set the standard for explosive growth in per capita GDP at a sustained rate of 4.2 percent; this is the fastest a country could have possibly grown from 1870 to 1960, as at this rate a country would have gone from the lower bound in 1870 to the U.S. level in 1960. Of the 108 developing countries for which there are available data in the Penn World Tables, 11 grew faster than 4.2 per annum over the 1960–1990 period. Prominent among these are east Asian economies like Korea (6.9 percent annual growth rate in per capita GDP from 1960–1992), Taiwan (6.3 percent annual growth) and Indonesia (4.4 percent). These countries are growing at an historically unprecedented pace. However, many countries that were poor in 1960 continued to stagnate. Sixteen developing countries had *negative* growth over the 1960–1990 period, including Mozambique (–2.2 percent per annum) and Guyana (–.7 percent per annum). Another 28 nations, more than a quarter of the total number of countries for which the Penn World Tables offers data, had growth rates of per capita GDP less than .5 percent per annum from 1960 to 1990 (for example, Peru with .1 percent); and 40 developing nations, more than a third of the sample, had growth rates less than 1 percent per annum.[13]

Moreover, as Ben-David and Papell (1995) emphasize, many developing countries have seen their economies go into not just a slowdown, but a "meltdown." If we calculate the growth rates in the Penn World Tables and allow the data to dictate one break in the growth rate over the whole 1960–1990 period, then of the 103 developing countries, 81 have seen a deceleration of growth over the period, and the average deceleration is over 3 percentage points. From 1980–1994, growth in per capita GDP averaged 1.5 percent in the advanced countries and .34 percent in the less developed countries. There has been no acceleration of growth in most poor countries, either absolutely or relatively, and there is no obvious reversal in divergence.

These facts about growth in less developed countries highlight its enormous variability and volatility. The range of annual growth rates in per capita GDP across less developed economies from 1960 to 1990 is from –2.7 percent to positive 6.9 percent.

Taken together, these findings imply that almost nothing that is true about the growth rates of advanced countries is true of the developing countries, either individually or on average. The growth rates for developed economies show convergence, but the growth rates between developed and developing economies show considerable divergence. The growth rates of developed countries are bunched in a narrow group, while the growth rates of less developed countries are all over with some in explosive growth and others in implosive decline.

Conclusion

For modern economists, Gerschenkron (1962) popularized the idea of an "advantage to backwardness," which allows countries behind the technological frontier to experience episodes of rapid growth driven by rapid productivity catch-up.[14] Such rapid gains in productivity are certainly a possibility, and there have been episodes of individual countries with very rapid growth. Moreover, there are examples of convergence in incomes amongst regions. However, the prevalence of absolute divergence implies that while there may be a potential advantage to backwardness, the cases in which backward countries, and especially the most backward of countries, actually gain significantly on the leader are historically rare. In poor countries there are clearly forces that create the potential for explosive growth, such as those witnessed in some countries in east Asia. But there are also strong forces for stagnation: a quarter of the 60 countries with

initial per capita GDP of less than $1000 in 1960 have had growth rates less than zero, and a third have had growth rates less than .05 percent. There are also forces for "implosive" decline, such as that witnessed in some countries in which the fabric of civic society appears to have disintegrated altogether, a point often ignored or acknowledged offhand as these countries fail to gather plausible economic statistics and thus drop out of our samples altogether. Backwardness seems to carry severe disadvantages. For economists and social scientists, a coherent model of how to overcome these disadvantages is a pressing challenge.

But this challenge is almost certainly not the same as deriving a single "growth theory." Any theory that seeks to unify the world's experience with economic growth and development must address at least four distinct questions: What accounts for continued per capita growth and technological progress of those leading countries at the frontier? What accounts for the few countries that are able to initiate and sustain periods of rapid growth in which they gain significantly on the leaders? What accounts for why some countries fade and lose the momentum of rapid growth? What accounts for why some countries remain in low growth for very long periods?

Theorizing about economic growth and its relation to policy needs to tackle these four important and distinct questions. While it is conceivable that there is an all-purpose universal theory and set of policies that would be good for promoting economic growth, it seems much more plausible that the appropriate growth policy will differ according to the situation. Are we asking about more rapid growth in a mature and stable economic leader like the United States or Germany or Japan? About a booming rapidly industrializing economy trying to prevent stalling on a plateau, like Korea, Indonesia, or Chile? About a once rapidly growing and at least semi-industrialized country trying to initiate another episode of rapid growth, like Brazil or Mexico or the Philippines? About a country still trying to escape a poverty trap into sustained growth, like Tanzania or Myanmar or Haiti? Discussion of the theory and policy of economic growth seems at times remarkably insensitive to these distinctions.

NOTES

1. To put it another way, the standard deviation of (natural log) GDP per capita across all countries has increased between 60 percent and 100 percent since 1870, in spite of the convergence amongst the richest.

2. For an alternative view, Maddison (1991) argues the period 1820–1870 was similar economically to the 1870–1913 period.

3. The typical measure of income dispersion, the standard deviation of (natural log) incomes, fell from .41 in 1870 to .27 in 1960 to only .11 in 1994.

4. Jones (1995) uses this basic fact of the constancy of growth to good effect in creating a compelling argument that the steadiness of U.S. growth implies that endogenous growth models that make growth a function of non-stationary variables, such as the level of R&D spending or the level of education of the labor force, are likely incorrect as they imply an accelerating growth rate (unless several variables working in opposite directions just happen to offset each other). These issues are also discussed in his paper in this issue.

5. More specifically, Kuznets estimated that the level was about $160, if measured in 1985 U.S. dollars. However, remember from the earlier discussion that a conversion at market exchange rates—which is what Kuznets was using—is far less than an estimate based on purchasing power parity exchange rates. If we use a multiple of 2.5, which is a conservative estimate of the difference between the two, Kuznets's estimate in purchasing power equivalent terms would be equal to a per capita GDP of $400 in 1985

U.S. dollars, converted at the purchasing power equivalent rate.

6. High poverty rates, meaning that many people live below these poverty lines, are not inconsistent with thinking of these poverty lines as not far above our lower bound, because many individuals can be in poverty, but not very far below the line. For instance, in South Asia in 1990, where 33 percent of the population was living in "extreme absolute poverty," only about 10 percent of the population would be living at less than $172 (my estimates from extrapolations of cumulative distributions reported in Chen, Datt and Ravallion, 1993).

7. The two figures are based on different assumptions about the weight of adult men and women, the mean temperature and the demographic structure. The low figure is about as low as one can go because it is based on a very young population, 39 percent under 15 (the young need fewer calories), a physically small population (men's average weight of only 110 pounds and women of 88), and a temperature of 25° C (FAO, 1957). The baseline figure, although based on demographic structure, usually works out to be closer to 2,400 (FAO, 1974).

8. The regression is a simple log-log of caloric intake and income in 1960 (the log-log is for simplicity even though this might not be the best predictor of the level). The regression is

in (average caloric intake) = 6.37 + .183*ln(GDP per capita),
$$(59.3)\ (12.56).$$

with t-statistics in parentheses, $N = 113$, and R-squared = .554.

9. The regression is estimated with country fixed effects:

ln(IMR) = – .59 In(GDP per capita) _ .013*Trend _ 002*Trend*(1 if.1960)
$$(23.7) \qquad\qquad (32.4) \qquad (14.23)$$

$N = 1994$ and t-statistics are in parenthesis. The prediction used the average country constant of 9.91.

10. Livi-Basci (1992) reports estimates of population growth in Africa between 1850 and 1900 to be .87 percent, and .93 percent between 1900 and 1950, while growth for Asia is estimated to be .27 1850 to 1900, and .61 1900 to 1950. Clark (1977) estimates the population growth rates between 1850 and 1900 to be .43 percent in Africa and India and lower, .33 percent, in China.

11. The growth rate of the poorest country was imposed to reach P250$ at exactly 1870, and the rate of the United States was used for the growth at the top. Then each country's growth rate was assumed to be a weighted average of those two rates, where the weights depended on the scaled distance from the bottom country in the beginning period of the imputation, 1960. This technique "smushes" the distribution back into the smaller range between the top and bottom while maintaining all cross country rankings. The formula for estimating the log of GDP per capita (GDPPC) in the ith country in 1870 was

$$GDPPC_i^{1870} = GDPPC_i^{1960} * (1/w_i)$$

where the scaling weight w_i was

$$w_i = (1 - \alpha_i) * \min (GDPPC^{1960})/P\$250 + \alpha_i * GDPPC_{USA}^{1960}/GDPPC_{USA}^{1970},$$

and where α_i is defined by

$$\alpha_i = (GDPPC_i^{1960} - \min (GDPPC^{1960}))/(GDPPC_{USA}^{1960} - \min (GDPPC^{1960})).$$

12. In terms of standard deviations, the method described in the text implies that the standard deviation of the national log of per capita GDP has more than doubled from 1870 to 1990, rising from .51 in 1870 to .88 in 1960 to 1.06 by 1990. In dollar terms, the standard deviation of per capita incomes rose from $459 in 1870 to $2,112 in 1960 in 1960 to $3,988 in 1990 (again, all figures expressed in 1985 dollars, converted at purchasing power equivalent exchange rates).

13. The division into developed and developing is made here by treating all 22 high-income members of the OECD as "developed" and all others as "developing."

14. I say "for modern economists," since according to Rostow (1993), David Hume more than 200 years ago argued that the accumulated technological advances in the leading countries would give the followers an advantage.

REFERENCES

Bairoch, Paul, *Economics and World History: Myths and Paradoxes*. Chicago: University of Chicago Press, 1993.

Barro, Robert, "Economic Growth in a Cross Section of Countries," *Quarterly Journal of Economics*, May 1991, *106*, 407–43.

Barro, Robert, and Xavier Sala-i-Martin, "Convergence," *Journal of Political Economy*, April 1992, *100*, 223–51.

Barro, Robert, and Xavier Sala-i-Martin, *Economic Growth*. New York: McGraw Hill, 1995.

Baumol, William, "Productivity Growth, Convergence and Welfare: What the Long-Run Data Show," *American Economic Review*, December 1986, *76*, 1072–85.

Ben-David, Dan, "Equalizing Exchange: Trade Liberalization and Convergence," *Quarterly Journal of Economics*, 1993, *108*:3, 653–79.

Ben-David, Dan, and David Papell, "Slow-downs and Meltdowns: Post-War Growth Evidence from 74 countries." Centre for Economic Policy Research Discussion Paper Series No. 1111, February 1995.

Canova, Fabio, and Albert Marcet, "The Poor Stay Poor: Non-Convergence Across Countries and Regions." Centre for Economic Policy Research Discussion Paper No. 1265, November 1995.

Caselli, Franseco, Gerardo Esquivel, and Fernando Lefort, "Reopening the Convergence Debate: A New Look at Cross-Country Growth Empirics," mimeo, Harvard University, 1995.

Chen, Shaohua, Gaurav Datt, and Martin Ravallion, "Is Poverty Increasing in the Developing

World?" World Bank Policy Research Working Paper No. 1146, June 1993.

Clark, Colin, *Population Growth and Land Use*. London: Macmillan, 1977.

De Long, Bradford, "Productivity Growth, Convergence, and Welfare: Comment," *American Economic Review*, December 1988, *78*, 1138–54.

Dollar, David, and Edward Wolff, *Competitiveness, Convergence, and International Specialization*. Cambridge, Mass.: Massachusetts Institute of Technology Press, 1993.

Easterly, William, Michael Kremer, Lant Pritchett, and Lawrence Summers, "Good Policy or Good Luck? Country Growth Performance and Temporary Shocks," *Journal of Monetary Economics*, December 1993, *32:3*, 459–83.

Evans, Paul, "Evaluating Growth Theories Using Panel Data," mimeo, Ohio State University, 1994.

FAO, *Calorie Requirements: Report of the Second Committee on Calorie Requirements*. Rome: FAO, 1957.

FAO, *Handbook on Human Nutritional Requirements*. Rome: Food and Agriculture Organization and World Health Organization, 1974.

de la Fuente, Angel, "The Empirics of Growth and Convergence: A Selective Review." Centre for Economic Policy Research No. 1275, November 1995.

Gerschenkron, Alexander, *Economic Backwardness in Historical Perspective, a Book of Essays*. Cambridge, Mass: Belknap Press, 1962.

Hanson, John R., "Third World Incomes before World War I: Some Comparisons," *Explorations in Economic History*, 1988, *25*, 323–36.

Hanson, John R., "Third World Incomes before World War I: Further Evidence," *Explorations in Economic History*, 1991, *28*, 367–79.

Hill, Kenneth, "The Decline of Childhood Mortality." In Simon, Julian, ed., *The State of Humanity*. Oxford: Blackwell, 1995, pp. 37–50.

International Rice Research Institute, *World Rice Statistics*. Los Banos: International Rice Research Institute, 1987.

Jones, Charles, "R&D Based Models of Economic Growth," *Journal of Political Economy*, August 1995, *103*:4, 759–84.

Kuznets, Simon, *Modern Economic Growth: Rate, Structure and Spread*. New Haven: Yale University Press, 1966.

Kuznets, Simon, *Economic Growth of Nations: Total Output and Production Structure*. Cambridge, Mass.: Belknap Press, 1971.

Livi-Basci, Massimo, *A Concise History of World Population*. Cambridge, Mass: Blackwell, 1992.

Loayza, Norman, "A Test of the International Convergence Hypothesis Using Panel Data." World Bank Policy Research Paper No. 1333, August 1994.

Lucas, Robert, "Ricardian Equilibrium: A Neoclassical Exposition," mimeo, Technion Israel Institute of Technology Economics Workshop Series, June 1996.

Maddison, Angus, "A Comparison of Levels of GDP Per Capita in Developed and Developing Countries, 1700–1980," *Journal of Economic History*, March 1983, *43*, 27–41.

Maddison, Angus, *Dynamic Forces in Capitalistic Development: A Long-Run Comparative View*. New York: Oxford University Press, 1991.

Maddison, Angus, "Explaining the Economic Performance of Nations, 1820–1989." In Baumol, William J., Richard R. Nelson, and Edward N. Wolff, eds., *Convergence of Productivity: Cross-National Studies and Historical Evidence*. New York: Oxford University Press, 1994, pp. 20–61.

Maddison, Angus, *Monitoring the World Economy, 1820–1992*. Paris: Development Centre of the Organisation for Economic Co-operation Development, 1995.

Mankiw, N. Gregory, David Romer, and David Weil, "A Contribution to the Empirics of Economic Growth," *Quarterly Journal of Economics*, May 1992, *107*:2, 407–36.

Nuxoll, Daniel, "Differences in Relative Prices and International Differences in Growth Rates," *American Economic Review*, December 1994, *84*, 1423–36.

Pritchett, Lant, "Where Has All the Education Gone?," mimeo, June 1995a.

Pritchett, Lant, "Population, Factor Accumulation and Productivity." World Bank Policy Research Paper No. 1567, October 1995b.

Pritchett, Lant, and Lawrence H. Summers, "Wealthier is Healthier," *Journal of Human Resources*, 1996, *31*:4, 841–68.

Quah, Danny, "Empirics for Economic Growth and Convergence." Centre for Economic Policy Research Discussion Paper No. 1140, March 1995.

Ravallion, Martin, Gaurav Datt, and Dominique van de Walle, "Quantifying Absolute Poverty in the Developing World," *Review of Income and Wealth*, 1991, *37*:4, 345–61.

Rebelo, Sergio, "Long-Run Policy Analysis and Long-Run Growth," *Journal of Political Economy*, June 1991, *99*, 500–21.

Rostow, W. W., *Theorist of Economic Growth from David Hume to the Present: With a Perspective on the Next Century*. New York: Oxford University Press, 1990.

Sachs, Jeffrey, and Andrew Warner, "Economic Convergence and Economic Policies." NBER Working Paper No. 5039, February 1995.

Sala-i-Martin, Xavier, "Regional Cohesion: Evidence and Theories of Regional Growth and Convergence." Centre for Economic Policy Research Discussion Paper No. 1074, November 1994.

Summers, Robert, and Alan Heston, "The Penn World Tables (Mark 5): An Expanded Set of International Comparisons, 1950–88," *Quarterly Journal of Economics*, 1991, *106*:2, 327–68.

World Bank, *World Development Report: Workers in an Integrating Economy*. Washington, D.C.: Oxford University Press for the World Bank, 1995.

BRANKO MILANOVIC

POPULATION-WEIGHTED INEQUALITY BETWEEN NATIONS: DECREASING IN THE PAST TWENTY YEARS

Figure 1 shows population-weighted international inequality [from 1950 to 2000]. After a significant jump in 1952 when China was added to the sample, and then in 1960 when African countries were included, the weighted international inequality almost constantly slides down, and the decline accelerates in the decade of the 1990s. Between 1965 and 2000, across a

From *Worlds Apart: Measuring International and Global Inequality* (Princeton: Princeton University Press, 2005), pp. 85–93.

practically constant sample of countries, the weighted international inequality decreased from a Gini of 55.7 to 50.5—a 10 percent drop. The decline of the Theil index was even steeper.

What drives the change in the population-weighted Gini? Is it that per capita GDPs in poor and populous countries like China and India grow faster than in rich countries, or perhaps that population growth in rich and middle-income countries is higher even if GDPs per capita grow at the same rate? Or perhaps both? Results shown in figure 2 allow us to dispense

Figure 1. Population-weighted international inequality, 1950–2000.

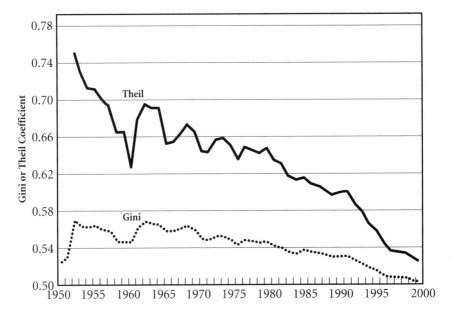

with one possible explanation: that it is the changing population shares between poor and the rich countries that push population-weighted international inequality down. As figure 2 shows, the downward trend in the Gini coefficient is unchanged whether we use the current population shares for each year, or the 1960 or 2000 population shares. There are only very small differences. The Gini coefficients calculated with the 2000 and the current population shares are consistently higher since the mid-1960s than the Ginis obtained using the 1960 population shares—indicating that uneven population growth (that is, faster population growth in poorer countries) increased the *level* of inequality. Yet it also contributed to its faster decline. This can be seen from the fact that the gap between the Ginis calculated using the 2000 and 1960 weights, which widened in the 1970s and 1980s, gradually diminished afterward. In other words, the current-year- and the 2000-population–weighted Ginis both decline faster than the 1960-population–weighted Gini. However, the gap between the various Ginis is hardly significant: at the most, it is a little over one Gini point.

Let us now try to look at other causes behind the decline in weighted international inequality. Figure 3 shows weighted international inequality but excludes India and China. Two important things can be seen. First, when China alone is excluded, weighted international inequality does not show a trend, or rather it shows mild *increasing* trend from the early 1980s onward. Thus, the inclusion or exclusion of China alone makes a huge difference, replacing the strongly decreasing trend of [population-weighted] inequality with a mildly increasing one. Second, when we exclude both India and China, we note an increase in inequality that begins, as in the case of unweighted international inequality, around the mid-1980s. Consequently, it is India's and China's faster growth compared to that of the rich countries at the other pole of income distribution (Western Europe, North America, and Oceania) that is responsible for decreasing weighted international inequality and therefore for the difference in trends between [weighted and unweighted inequality] that is, for what we

Figure 2. International weighted inequality (with different population weights).

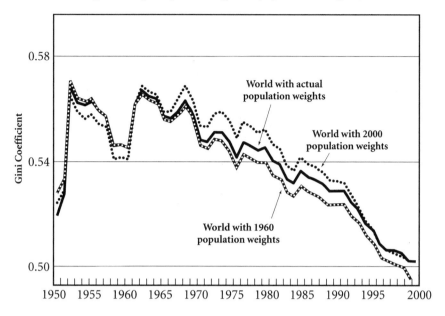

dubbed at the beginning "the mother of all in-equality disputes."

Two additional interesting facts are revealed in figure 3.[1] First, that [population-weighted, between-nation] inequality without China (or without China and India) is, during the past decade, greater than when these two countries are included. In other words, the inclusion of

Figure 3. Weighted international inequality without China and India.

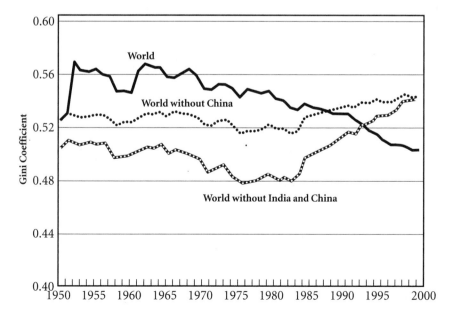

China and India *reduces* weighted international inequality today in contrast to the situation throughout the previous decades. This clearly illustrates the countries' upward movement through income distribution: they are no longer very poor countries. Second, during the recent period, the inclusion or not of India does not seem to make a difference to [population-weighted] inequality. We notice that at the end of the 1990s the population-weighted Gini is practically the same whether we exclude China only, or exclude both China and India. This implies that the presence of China is currently inequality-reducing ***, while the inclusion of India is neutral.[2]

The "Triangle" That Matters: China, India, and the United States

Let us thus consider the "triangle" of China, India, and the United States—the natural candidates for an explanation of [this] declining trend. At the end of the second millennium, these three countries account for about 45 percent of world population, a little over 40 percent of world (PPP) income, and about one-half of [population-weighted, between-nation] inequality. China has experienced tremendously fast

growth since the reforms started in the late 1970s; India has too, even if less impressively, and both must have reduced their distance with respect to the United States. Hence, they should have contributed significantly to the reduction in world inequality.

Table 1 shows three countries' GDP per capita in $PPP terms, their GDPs per capita "normalized" by world (population-weighted) mean GDP per capita, and the distance between such normalized GDPs. Looking at the numbers in the first three columns, we see that China registered fast growth, increasing its GDP per capita by more than one-half between 1965 and 1978, and then quintupling it between 1978 and 2000.[3] China's GDP per capita increased from being equal to 13 percent of the world mean to 60 percent of the world mean.[4]

However, much less impressive—and this is key for the Gini contributions—was the reduction in the world mean-normalized gap between the United States and China: the gap was equal to 4.47 times the mean world GDP per capita in 1965 (16527 − 472 divided by 3589), and despite massive Chinese growth was still 4 times in 2000. This was, of course, due to the significant growth of the United States itself, which, starting from a much higher base, had to grow less in percentage terms in order to maintain the normalized gap unchanged. But since it is the gap

Table 1. China, India, and the United States in 1965, 1978, and 2000

	GDP Per Capita (in $PPP)			GDP Per Capita ("normalized" by world GDP per capita)				"Normalized" Gap Between the Triangle Countries		
	1965	1978	2000	1965	1978	2000		1965	1978	2000
China	472	754	4144	0.13	0.15	0.60	China-India	0.063	0.021	0.35
India	698	857	1693	0.19	0.17	0.25	India-USA	4.410	4.237	4.33
USA	16527	21790	31519	4.60	4.41	4.58	China-USA	4.473	4.258	3.97
World	3589	4940	6883	1.00	1.00	1.00		—	—	—

Note: "Normalized" gap is calculated as the difference between the countries' per capita GDPs divided by the world's mean per capita GDP (all in $PPP terms). World mean income is population-weighted.

that matters in the calculation of the Gini, we can already see that the contribution of the United States–China shrinking gap was much less than it seemed at first. Notice, moreover, that the gap between the United States and India actually *increased* over the recent period (1978 to 2000), and similarly that the gap between India and China also increased (after "changing sign" around 1980 when China overtook India).

But to get the exact contributions of these there countries to the weighted international Gini, we need to weigh the gaps shown in the last three columns of table 1 by the countries' population shares. The first three columns of table 2 give the population shares of China, India, and the United States; the next three, the calculated values of the intercountry terms (ICT) that enter in the calculation of the Gini. The importance of the "triangle" was the greatest in 1965; it decreased significantly between then and 1978, and has stayed since at about the same level. In both 1978 and 2000, the "triangle" contributed over 9 Gini points to total [population-weighted] inequality.[5] It is easy to see why the importance of the interactions among the three most important countries did not change much during the past two decades: the mean-normalized distance between India and the United States went up slightly, the distance between China and the United States decreased, but, by exactly as much, the distance between

China and India—which was practically nil in 1978—increased. This last point illustrates the ambivalence of China's growth "through the ranks" of world income distribution: as its distance from the West diminishes and inequality is thus reduced, it opens up the distance between China and the slower-growing (or stagnating) poor countries and thus contributes to world inequality.

A glance at table 2 shows that the changes within the triangle explained the entire decrease in the [population-weighted, between-nation] inequality between 1965 and 1978. The weighted international inequality decreased between these two years by 1.3 Gini points (from 55.7 to 54.4), while the triangle's contribution was reduced by 1.38 Gini points. Thus, our hypothesis that the interaction within the China–India–United States triangle was crucial is confirmed for the period 1965–78.

However, it is not confirmed for the second period (1978–2000). As we have seen, the contribution of the triangle remained practically unchanged in face of a huge decrease of *** inequality. Between these two years, weighted international inequality went down from a Gini of 54.4 to 50.1. Clearly the explanation for that decline must be sought elsewhere.

Before we move to that search, consider disentangling the effect of changing *income* gaps within the triangle from the effect of changing

Table 2. China, India, the United States: Population Shares and Gini Contributions

.	Population Shares				Gini Points (ICT)		
	1965	*1978*	*2000*		*1965*	*1978*	*2000*
China	0.228	0.236	0.218	China-India	0.22	0.08	1.37
India	0.155	0.162	0.177	India-US	4.24	3.79	3.72
USA	0.062	0.055	0.049	China-US	6.32	5.54	4.20
Total triangle	0.445	0.454	0.443	Total triangle	10.78	9.40	9.29
				Change	—	−1.38	−0.11
				World Gini	55.7	54.4	50.1
				Change	—	−1.3	−4.3

Note: Each ICT, for the country pair (j and i) such that $y_j > y_i$, is equal to $1/\mu \, (y_j - y_i) p_i p_j$.

Table 3. Income and Population Contributions of the Triangle to World Inequality

		Gini Point Contributions with 1965 Population Shares	
	1965	*1978*	*2000*
(1) China-India	0.22	0.07	1.26
(2) India-USA	4.24	4.08	4.17
(3) China-USA	6.23	6.01	5.62
(4) Total triangle	10.78	10.16	11.05
Difference		−0.62	+0.89
		1965–78	*1978–2000*
(5) Total change in triangle contribution (from table 2)		−1.38	−0.11
(6) Due to income		−0.62	+0.89
(7) Due to population (and interaction term)		−0.76	−0.99
(8) Overall Concept 2 Gini change (from table 2)		−1.29	−4.33
Percentage breakdown of triangle contribution			
Due to the triangle (5) : (8)		107.1	2.5
Due to income gaps in the triangle (6) : (8)		48.0	−20.5

population shares. If we apply the 1965 population shares to the actual income gaps, we obtain the values in the first four rows of table 3. We see that between 1965 and 1978, the shrinking of the income gaps between the members of the triangle shaved off 0.62 Gini points of weighted international inequality (10.78 minus 10.16). Since the overall international inequality decreased over the same period by 1.29 Gini points, we conclude that almost one-half of the decrease was due to the shrinking income gaps among the triangle. And as the populations also moved in the "right" direction, the triangle was responsible for more than 100 percent of the overall decrease in international inequality between 1965 and 1978.

But then the situation radically changes. The absolute triangle's contribution to international inequality in 2000 was only 0.11 Gini points less than in 1978 (see line 5 in table 3). This explains 2 percent of the overall Gini decrease between 1978 and 2000, or, in other words, this contribu-

tion is negligible. Moreover, the income gaps between China, India, and the United States did not shrink—they *increased*, thus adding to inequality. It is only because population shares of all three countries went down in 2000 compared to 1978 that the triangle's contribution to international inequality stayed almost unchanged.

So, we need to expand our search for the cause of the decline in weighted international inequality between 1978 and 2000 to countries other than those in the triangle. As we have seen, between 1978 and 2000, weighted international inequality decreased by 4.3 Gini points. China's rapid growth was the key explanatory factor: as China's distance with respect to all richer and populous countries decreased, it reduced the Gini in turn. (However, it should be noticed that China's pulling ahead of India, Bangladesh, and Pakistan *added* to world inequality.) This is depicted in figure 4. Since all the values are normalized by current mean world income, the distance between the lines is the term that

Figure 4. GDP per capita (normalized by current mean world GDP per capita) for five countries. The sharp increase of countries' normalized income in 1952 is due to the addition of (a very poor) China to the sample.

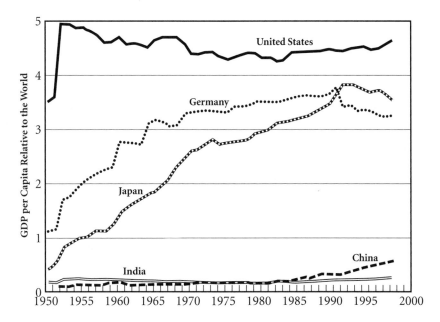

(weighted by the population shares) enters into the Gini calculation. Between 1978 and 2000, the distances among the three rich countries, and between each of them and India, remained about the same.[6] It is only the distance between China (on the one hand), and the United States, Japan, and Germany, on the other, that shrunk—while the distance between China and India increased.

The reduced income distance between China and the six large OECD countries (United States, Japan, Germany, France, United Kingdom, and Italy) lowered the weighted international Gini by a whopping 3.5 Gini points, which is 80 percent of the overall Gini decline between 1978 and 2000 (table 4). When we add the decreasing distance between China and the three large middle-income countries (Brazil, Mexico, and Russia), we end up with more than a full accounting for the Gini decline. The last line of table 4 shows the interaction between China and the large

and poor Third World countries (Pakistan, Bangladesh, Indonesia, and Nigeria). There, as in the interaction between China and India, we see the other side of the coin of China's rapid advance: a contribution to world inequality. Now, of course, assuming that China's advance continues, the positive (inequality-reducing) effects will continue to dominate for quite some time. Yet a point may be reached where the lack of (sufficient) progress in the poor countries and their increasing distance from China may offset (in terms of [population-weighted] inequality) the gains from China's greater proximity to the rich world.

To sum up. For the period 1965–78, the main explanation of the decline in weighted international inequality was the decreasing income gap between the three most important countries (China, India, and the United States). In the second period, however, the entire decrease in weighted international inequality was driven by

Table 4. Gini Points (ICTs): China and the Rest of the World, 1978 and 2000

	1978	2000	Change
China-United States	5.5	4.2	−1.3
China-Japan	1.8	1.3	−0.5
China-Germany	1.5	0.8	−0.7
China-other large OECD countries	2.7	1.7	−1.0
China-(Brazil, Mexico, Russia)	1.8	0.4	−1.4
Total	13.3	8.4	−4.9
World Gini	54.4	50.1	−4.3
China-(poor large Third World countries)	0.27	0.58	+0.34

Note: Other large OECD countries = France, Italy and United Kingdom. Poor large Third World countries are Pakistan, Bangladesh, Indonesia, and Nigeria.

China's growth relative to the rich part of the world.

*   *   *

NOTES

1. The same conclusion holds if instead of Gini, we use Theil index.

2. It may not be quite clear why adding China to the sample of countries reduces (in the 1990s) [population-weighted] inequality while (as we shall see later) China's contribution to overall [population-weighted] inequality is pretty substantial. To explain this, consider the definition of [population-weighted] in inequality

This can be rewritten as

where the entire first right-hand side term is written as *A*, and *k* is the relevant country

(China). All other terms are defined as before. Now, once China is dropped from the sample, all population shares (p_i's) will increase by a factor of β (about 1.29 for the year 2000), and the world mean income will change, too, by a factor α (in the year 2000 if China is dropped, μ will go up by 11 percent). The new Gini will be

The issue then becomes under what conditions equation (9) can be greater than (8). We know that in 2000, the second term in equation (8), summing all absolute income differences between China and all other countries and then normalizing them by mean world income, amounts to 14.6 Gini points. The overall 2000 Gini was 50.2. Thus $A = 50.2 − 14.5 = 35.7$, which, multiplied by $(\beta)^2/\alpha$ [1.48 * $(1.29)^2$/1.1] as per equation (9), gives $G_1 = 52.8$, and $G_1 > G$. The Gini without China is thus indeed shown to be greater than the Gini that includes China (even if China's contribution to inequality is very large).

3. I am using 1965 as the start-up year because it is the year when the steady decline in

[population-weighted] inequality begins. If one were to use 1960, there would have been practically no difference in [population-weighted] inequality between 1960 and 1978.

4. Note as a curiosity that this is the same relative level as that attained by Japan around 1950.

5. Notice that throughout, the interaction within the "triangle" alone explains about a fifth of [population-weighted] international inequality. To get to the overall contribution of China, India, and the United States, we need to include the "interactions" (the ICT terms) between each member of the triangle and all other (100+) countries. Then, the contribution is about one-half of total inequality.

6. More exactly, the distance between the United States and Germany increased by about as much as the distance between the United States and Japan went down, and Japan and Germany switched places. German decline was due to the unification with a poorer country (the former German Democratic Republic).

PAUL COLLIER AND JAN WILLEM GUNNING

WHY HAS AFRICA GROWN SLOWLY?

In the 1960s, Africa's future looked bright. On the basis of Maddison's (1995) estimates of per capita GDP for a sample of countries, during the first half of the century Africa had grown considerably more rapidly than Asia; by 1950, the African sample had overtaken the Asian sample. In the 1950s there were uncertainties of political transition, but after 1960 Africa was increasingly free of colonialism, with the potential for governments that would be more responsive to domestic needs. During the period 1960–73, growth in Africa was more rapid than in the first half of the century. Indeed, for this period, African growth and its composition were indistinguishable from the geographically very different circumstances of south Asia (Collins and Bosworth, 1996). Political self-determination in Africa and economic growth seemed to be proceeding hand-in-hand.

However, during the 1970s both political and economic matters in Africa deteriorated. The leadership of many African nations hardened into autocracy and dictatorship. Africa's economies first faltered and then started to decline. While Africa experienced a growth collapse, nations of south Asia modestly improved their economic performance. A good example of this divergence is the comparison of Nigeria and Indonesia. Until around 1970, the economic performance of Nigeria was broadly superior to that of Indonesia, but over the next quarter-century outcomes diverged markedly, despite the common experience for both countries of an oil boom in a predominantly agricultural economy. Since 1980, aggregate per capita GDP in sub-Saharan Africa has declined at almost 1 percent per annum. The decline has been widespread: 32 countries are poorer now than in 1980. Today, sub-Saharan Africa is the lowest-income region in the world. Figure 1 and Table 1, taken together, offer a snapshot of Africa today. Figure 1 is a map of the continent. Table 1 gives some basic information on population, GDP, standard of living, and growth rates for countries of sub-Saharan Africa. We focus on the sub-

From *Journal of Economic Perspectives*, 13, No. 3 (Summer 1999) pp. 3–22.

Figure 1
The Political Geography of Africa

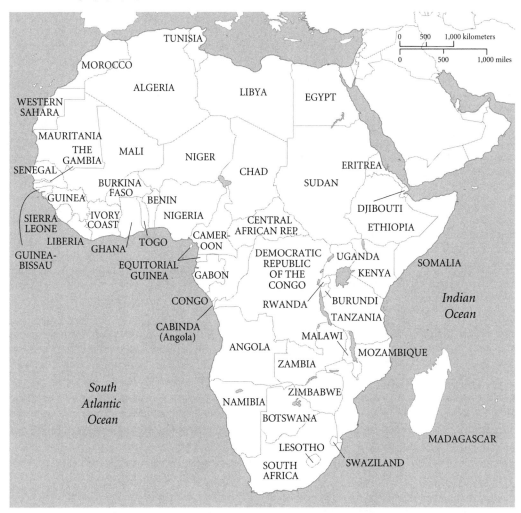

Saharan countries, setting aside the north African countries of Algeria, Egypt, Libya, Morocco and Tunisia. This is conventional for the studies of this area, since the north African countries are part of a different regional economy—the Middle East—with its own distinctive set of economic issues. It is clear that Africa has suffered a chronic failure of economic growth. The problem for analysis is to determine its causes.

The debate on the causes of slow African growth has offered many different explanations.

These can be usefully grouped into a two-by-two matrix, distinguishing on the one hand between policy and exogenous "destiny" and, on the other, between domestic and external factors. Table 2 compares Africa to other developing regions, using this grouping. Until recently it has largely been accepted that the main causes of Africa's slow growth were external, with the debate focusing upon whether external problems were policy-induced or exogenous. Especially during the 1980s, the World Bank, the Interna-

Table 1. The Economies of Sub-Saharan Africa

Country	Population (Millions) 1997	GDP US$m at 1990 Prices 1997	GNP per Capita (PPP $) 1997	GNP Average Annual % Growth per Capita 1965–97	Life Expectancy at Birth (years) 1995	% of Population below $1 a Day (early 1990s)	Trade as % of GDP (in PPP) 1997
Angola	11.6	9,886	728	. . .	48	. . .	77
Benin	5.7	2,540	1,240		48	. . .	17
Botswana	1.5	4,458	7,440	7.7	66	33	. . .
Burkina Faso	11.1	3,643	936	0.9	47	. . .	7
Burundi	6.4	939	661	1.1	51	. . .	5
Cameroon	13.9	11,254	1,739	1.4	57	. . .	13
Cape Verde	0.4	393	. . .	. . .	66	. . .	. . .
Central African Republic	3.4	1,420	1,254	−1.2	50	. . .	10
Chad	6.7	1,492	978	0.1	49	. . .	4
Comoros	0.7	251	. . .	. . .	57	. . .	. . .
Congo	2.7	2,433	1,275	1.7	53	. . .	80
Congo, Dem. Rep.	48.0	6,094	698	−3.7	. . .	. . .	7
Côte d'Ivoire	14.3	13,320	1,676	−0.9	50	18	30
Djibouti	0.4	384	. . .	. . .	49	. . .	. . .
Equatorial Guinea	0.4	541	. . .	. . .	49	. . .	. . .
Eritrea	3.4	1,010	990	. . .	52	. . .	. . .
Ethiopia	60.1	11,327	493	−0.5	49	46	7
Gabon	1.1	7,280	6,480	0.4	55	. . .	58
Gambia	1.0	332	1,372	0.5	46	. . .	30
Ghana	18.3	7,892	1,492	−0.9	57	. . .	19
Guinea	7.6	3,699	1,763	. . .	46	26	14
Guinea-Bissau	1.1	306	1,041	0.1	45	88	13
Kenya	28.4	9,879	1,150	1.3	55	50	16
Lesotho	2.1	998	2,422	3.2	62	49	. . .
Liberia	2.5	. . .	. . .	. . .	57	. . .	. . .
Madagascar	15.8	3,187	892	−1.9	58	72	11
Malawi	10.1	2,480	688	0.5	45	. . .	21
Mali	11.5	3,132	715	0.5	47	. . .	19
Mauritania	2.4	1,346	1,654	−0.2	53	31	28
Mauritius	1.1	3,755	9,147	3.8	71	. . .	37
Mozambique	18.3	2,144	541	−0.1	47	. . .	15
Namibia	1.6	3,141	4,999	0.7	60	. . .	. . .
Niger	9.8	2,776	824	−2.5	48	62	9
Nigeria	118.4	34,418	854	0.0	51	31	23
Rwanda	5.9	1,979	643	0.1	47	46	9
São Tomé & Principe	0.1	56	. . .	. . .	. . .	. . .	. . .
Senegal	8.8	6,708	1,670	−0.5	50	54	11
Seychelles	0.1	435	. . .	. . .	. . .	. . .	. . .

(continued)

Table 1. (continued)

Country	Population (Millions) 1997	GDP US$m at 1990 Prices 1997	GNP per Capita (PPP $) 1997	GNP Average Annual % Growth per Capita 1965–97	Life Expectancy at Birth (years) 1995	% of Population below $1 a Day (early 1990s)	Trade as % of GDP (in PPP) 1997
Sierra Leone	4.4	. . .	401	−1.4	40	. . .	24
Somalia	10.4	. . .	. . .	. . .	48	. . .	. . .
South Africa	43.3	117,089	7,152	0.1	64	24	23
Sudan	27.9	13,119	. . .	−0.2	54	. . .	. . .
Swaziland	0.9	1,031	. . .	. . .	59	. . .	. . .
Tanzania	31.5	4,956	608	. . .	52	11	14
Togo	4.3	1,726	1,408	−0.6	56	. . .	24
Uganda	20.8	6,822	1,131	. . .	44	69	6
Zambia	8.5	3,564	900	−2.0	48	85	26
Zimbabwe	11.7	7,904	2,207	0.5	52	41	21

Sources: *African Development Report* (1998); and *World Development Indicators* (1999).

tional Monetary Fund and bilateral donors came to identify exchange rate and trade policies as the primary causes of slow growth in Africa. Table 2 offers some evidence that official exchange rates in sub-Saharan Africa have been more overvalued relative to (often illegal) market rates than is common for other less developed economies of Asia and Latin America. Tariffs and quantitative trade restrictions have also been higher in Africa than elsewhere. The rival thesis, often favored by African governments, was that the crisis was due to deteriorating and volatile terms of trade, and as Table 2 shows, terms of trade have indeed been more volatile for Africa than for other less developed economies. Jeffrey Sachs and his co-authors have emphasized a further adverse external "destiny" factor: Africa's population is atypically landlocked. As shown in Table 2, a high proportion of the population is remote from the coast or navigable waters.

Recently, attention has shifted to possible domestic causes of slow growth within African nations, but the debate as to the relative importance of policy-induced and exogenous problems has continued. Sachs and his co-authors have at-

tributed slow growth to "the curse of the tropics." Africa's adverse climate causes poor health, and so reduces life expectancy below that in other regions, which puts it at a disadvantage in development. The adverse climate also leads to leached soils and unreliable rainfall, which constrains African agriculture. African nations also appear to have more ethnic diversity than other poor nations of the world, which may make it harder to develop an interconnected economy. In contrast to the domestic destiny argument, Collier and Gunning (1999) have emphasized domestic policy factors such as poor public service delivery. African governments have typically been less democratic and more bureaucratic than their Asian and Latin American counterparts.

Of course, once the conditions for slow growth are established by any combination of these reasons, they can become self-reinforcing in an endogenous process. Weak economic growth helps explain a lower saving rate and a higher proportion of flight capital for Africa compared to the less developed nations of Asia and Africa. Richer countries tend to see their population growth rates drop off, so the poverty

Table 2. Africa Compared With Other Developing Regions

(figures are unweighted country averages)

	Sub-Saharan Africa	Other LDCs
Domestic-Destiny		
Life expectancy in 1970 (years)	45.2	57.3
Income in 1960 (1985 $ PPP-adjusted)	835.5	1855.2
Ethnic Fractionalization	67.6	32.7
Domestic-Policy		
Political Rights, 1973–90	6.0	4.0
Bureaucracy	1.38	1.72
External-Destiny		
Population <100 km from the sea or river (%)	21.0	52.0
Terms of trade volatility	16.4	12.8
External-Policy		
Parallel market exchange rate premium	40.0	26.0
Average tariffs 1996–98 (%)	21.0	13.0
Quantitative Restrictions, 1988–90 (%)	46.0	21.0
Endogenous		
Growth of GDP per capita, 1965–90	0.5	1.7
Investment rate in 1997 (%)	18.0	25.0
Population growth rate, 1980–97 (%)	2.8	1.8
Capital flight/private wealth, 1990 (%)	39.0	14.0

Sources: Life expectancy, World Development Indicators, 1998. Income and growth: Penn World Tables 5.6. The index of ethno-linguistic diversity is on the scale 0–100 with 0 being homogenous (Mauro, 1995). The Gastil index of political rights is on the range 1–7 with 1 being fully democratic.
The index of bureaucracy is on the scale 0–6 with high score indicating better quality (Knack and Keefer, 1995). Population living less than 100 km from the sea or a navigable river, from Bloom and Sachs (1999), Table 2, (other LDCs is the weighted average for Asia and Latin America). Terms of trade volatility is the standard deviation of annual log changes 1965–92, (Collins and Bosworth, 1996). Parallel exchange rate premium (%), (Easterly and Levine, 1997).
Average tariff: simple average, computed by IMF, we would like to thank Robert Sharer for these numbers. QRs: weighted average incidence of non-tariff measures over product lines; other LDCs is simple average of Latin America and East Asia; from Rodrik (1999, Table 12).
Investment rate and population growth rate, World Development Indicators, 1999 Capital flight/private wealth as of 1990 (Collier and Pattillo, 1999).

of Africa has helped to keep its birth rates high, even as compared to the world's other less developed economies. Similarly, poverty may have increased the incidence of Africa's numerous civil wars, as well as being a consequence of them.

In the discussion that follows, we assess the policy/destiny and domestic/external distinctions in various combinations. During the mid-1990s, African performance started to improve, with a few countries growing quite rapidly. We conclude by assessing these different explanations as guides to whether this improvement is likely to be transient or persistent.

Four Types of Explanation

Domestic-Destiny

Africa has several geographic and demographic characteristics which may predispose it to slow growth. First, much of the continent is tropical and this may handicap the economy, partly due to diseases such as malaria and partly due to hostile conditions for livestock and agriculture. Life expectancy has historically been low, with the population in a high-fertility, high infant-mortality equilibrium. With the advent of basic public health measures, population growth became very high. In particular, Africa has not been through the demographic transition whereby fertility rates decline which occurred in Asia and Latin America over the past 40 years. On one estimate, Africa's low life expectancy and high population growth account for almost all of Africa's slow growth (Bloom and Sachs, 1998). The argument is not clear-cut, however. Low life expectancy and high fertility are consequences of low income as well as causes, so the estimates are likely to be biased upwards. The household-level evidence suggests that the effects of poor health on income are small, although these in turn will be biased downwards by the omission of large-scale changes in economic activity which cannot be detected at the household level.

Whether or not Africa's past demographic characteristics have contributed to its slow growth, some African countries seem certain to go through a distinctive and disastrous demographic transition during the next two decades. As a result of AIDS, adult mortality rates will rise dramatically. In Africa, AIDS is a heterosexual disease. During the 1980s in parts of Africa it spread rapidly across the population before the risks became apparent, with up to 20-25 percent of adults now HIV-positive in some countries (World Bank, 1997). This human tragedy will have substantial economic effects during the next decade, especially since infection rates appear to be higher among the more educated, but it does not account for historically slow growth.

A second key characteristic of Africa which may predispose it to slow growth is that soil quality is poor and much of the continent is semi-arid, with rainfall subject to long cycles and unpredictable failure. Soils derive disproportionately from a very old type of rock ("Basement Complex"), which is low in micronutrients

and varies considerably between localities. The application of additional macronutrients, which is the fertilizer package associated with the Green Revolution, is generally ineffective with low levels of micronutrients. Africa probably has scope for its own agricultural revolution, but it will depend upon locality-specific packages of micronutrients (Voortman et al., 1999). Since the 1960s, the semi-arid areas of Africa have been in a phase of declining rainfall (Grove, 1991). While there are no estimates of the output consequences of this decline, it may be significant, since agriculture is typically about one-quarter of GDP in this region. Given the lack of irrigation, the unpredictability of rainfall implies high risks in agriculture. With incomplete insurance and a high rate of time preference, households have to use assets for purposes of consumption-smoothing rather than investment. Households can thus become trapped in low-income, high-liquidity equilibria (Dercon, 1997).

A third relevant characteristic of Africa's economies, which can be seen as a result of these semi-arid conditions, is that the continent has very low population density. One by-product is high costs of transport which in turn have added to risk: poor market integration has hampered the use of trade for risk sharing. Another consequence of low population density is that Africa has relatively high natural resource endowments per capita (Wood and Mayer, 1998). High levels of natural resources can cause several problems. High levels of exported natural resources may lead to an appreciation of the exchange rate, which in turn makes manufacturing less competitive. Yet manufacturing may offer larger growth externalities, such as learning, than natural resource extraction. Natural resources may also increase "loot-seeking" activities. Collier and Hoeffler (1998) find that a dependence on natural resources strongly increases the risk of civil war, which has been a widespread phenomenon in Africa.

A further consequence of low population density is that African countries have much higher ethno-linguistic diversity than other regions; when groups come together less, there is less mingling and merging. Easterly and Levine (1997) find that this high level of diversity is the most important single cause of Africa's slow growth. There are various interpretations of this result. A common perception is that Africa's high ethnic diversity accounts for its high incidence of civil war. This turns out to be false: high levels of ethnic and religious diversity actually make societies significantly safer (Collier and Hoeffler, 1999). The effects of ethnic diversity on growth turn out to be contingent upon the political system; diversity has deleterious effects only when it occurs in the context of governments which are undemocratic. Collier (1999) finds that in democratic societies, ethnic diversity has no effect on either growth or the quality of public projects, but that in dictatorships, high levels of diversity reduce growth rates by 3 percentage points and double the rate of project failure relative to homogeneity. Dictatorships tend not to transcend the ethnic group of the dictator, so that the more ethnically fragmented the society, the more narrowly based a dictatorship will be, whereas democratic governments in such societies must be ethnically cross-cutting. In turn, the more narrowly based the government, the greater the payoff to predation relative to the inducement of generalized growth. Africa's problem was thus not its ethnic diversity but its lack of democracy in the context of diversity.

A fourth characteristic of Africa that may hinder its growth prospects is that because of its colonial heritage, Africa has much smaller countries in terms of population than other regions. Sub-Saharan Africa has a population about half that of India, divided into 48 states. These many states, combined with low levels of income, make Africa's national economies radically smaller than those of other regions. Very small states might be economically disadvantaged for several reasons. If government has some fixed costs, either in its administrative role or as a provider of services, then it may be hard for a small state to perform at minimum cost. Moreover, the society may forfeit much more exten-

sive scale economies if it combines small scale with isolation. Some domestic markets will be too small even for the minimum efficient scale of production of a single producer; all domestic markets taken alone will be less competitive than in larger economies. Small economies are also perceived by investors as significantly more risky (Collier and Dollar, 1999b). Finally, they may have a slower rate of technological innovation; Kremer (1993) argues the incidence of discoveries may be broadly proportional to the population, so that if discoveries cannot readily spread between societies, low-population societies will have less innovation. However, in aggregate these effects cannot be large, because growth regressions generally find that state size does not affect a nation's rate of economic growth.

Domestic-Policy

For much of the post-colonial period, most African governments have been undemocratic. The median African government during the 1970s and 1980s was close to autocracy, and far less democratic than the median non-African developing country (as measured by the Gastil scale of political rights shown in Table 2). A typical pattern was that governments were captured by the educated, urban-resident population, with few agricultural or commercial interests. They expanded the public sector while imposing wide-ranging controls on private activity. These choices have been economically costly.

Public employment was expanded, often as an end in itself. For example, in Ghana by the late 1970s the public sector accounted for three-quarters of formal wage employment (Ghana Central Bureau of Statistics, 1988), and even in a more market-oriented economy like Kenya, the figure was 50 percent as of 1990 (Kenya Central Bureau of Statistics, 1996). Indeed, economic decline may have increased pressure for public sector employment. The large number of public sector employees was reconciled with limited tax revenue by reducing wage rates and non-wage expenditures. The ratio of wage to non-wage expenditures in African governments is double that in Asia, and this has lowered the quality of public services; for example, in education, teaching materials are often lacking. The large, ill-paid public sector became the arena in which ethnic groups struggled for resources. For example, in the Ghanaian public sector, the locally dominant ethnic group received a wage premium of 25 percent over other groups after controlling for worker characteristics, and cognitive skills were completely unrewarded (Collier and Garg, 1999). The combination of low wage levels and payment structures, which rewarded social connections rather than skill, made it difficult for managers to motivate staff, and the difficulties of service delivery were compounded by the low ratio of non-wage to wage expenditures.

Since public sector employment was the main priority, managers were not under severe pressure for actual delivery of services from their political masters. Because of the lack of democracy, neither were they accountable to the broader public. As a result, Africa experienced a paradox of poor public services despite relatively high public expenditure (Pradhan, 1996). Poor service delivery handicapped firms through unreliable transport and power, inadequate telecommunications networks, and unreliable courts. For example, manufacturing firms in Zimbabwe need to hold high levels of inventories, despite high interest rates, due to unreliable delivery of inputs tied to poor transportation infrastructure (Fafchamps et al., 1998). A survey of Ugandan firms found that shortage of electricity was identified as the single most important constraint upon firm growth; indeed, the provision of electricity by firms for their own use was almost as large as the public supply of electricity (Reinikka and Svensson, 1998). A study in Nigeria found that their own generators accounted for three-quarters of the capital equipment of small manufacturers (Lee and Anas, 1991). The poor state of African telecommunications was estimated to reduce African growth rates by 1 percentage point, according to Easterly and

Levine (1997). (However, since telecommunications was the main infrastructure variable which they could quantify, and since lack of different kinds of infrastructure is probably highly correlated, their estimate is probably a proxy for a wider range of infrastructural deficiencies.) African commercial courts are more corrupt than those in other regions (Widner, 1999). As a result, firms face greater problems of contract enforcement. Some firms can overcome these by relying upon their social networks to screen potential clients, but it is common to restrict business to long-standing clients (Bigsten et al., 1999). Ethnic minorities, such as Asians in East Africa and Lebanese in West Africa, tend to have more specialized social networks and so are better able than African firms to screen new clients (Biggs et al., 1996). The problem of contract enforcement thus makes markets less competitive and reduces the potential gains from trade, while tending to perpetuate the dominant position of minorities in business.

Poor public service delivery also handicapped households through inefficient education, health and extension services. A survey of primary education expenditures in Uganda found that, of the non-wage money released by the Ministry of Finance, on average, less than 30 percent actually reached the schools (Ablo and Reinikka, 1998). The expansion of the public sector has reduced private initiative. Since major areas of economic activity were reserved for the public sector—often including transport, marketing and banking—and African elites looked to the public sector rather than the private sector for advancement, Africa was slow to develop indigenous entrepreneurs.

African governments built various economic control regimes. A few nations, such as Ethiopia, Angola and Tanzania, had wide-ranging price controls under which private agents had an incentive to reduce production—at least officially marketed production. These governments often attempted to counterbalance these incentives with coercive production targets, but the net effect was usually dramatic declines in economic activity. More commonly, firms were subject to considerable regulation. For example, for many years manufacturing firms wishing to set up in Kenya had to acquire letters of no objection from existing producers, which resulted in a predictably low level of competition. In Uganda, when the government removed the requirement that coffee could only be transported by rail, the market for road haulage expanded sufficiently to induce new entry, which in turn broke an existing cartel, nearly halving haulage rates. Similarly, in Tanzania during the long period when agricultural marketing was heavily regulated, marketing margins for grain were double what they were both before regulation and after deregulation (Bevan et al., 1993). In this period, food prices became much more volatile: between 1964 and 1980 the coefficient of variation (that is, the ratio of the standard deviation to the mean) of maize prices at regional centers doubled, falling again sharply when markets were liberalized.

Government interventions undermined the functioning of product markets in many countries. Private trading, which was often associated with ethnic minorities such as the Indians in East Africa and the Lebanese in West Africa, was sometimes banned. A particularly damaging intervention, practiced even in relatively market-friendly economies such as Kenya, was to ban private inter-district trade in food. Where government marketing monopolies were focused on ensuring the food supply to urban areas, this provision discouraged farmers from specializing in non-food export crops, since they could not rely on being able to buy food locally.

Since the political base of governments was urban, agriculture was heavily taxed and the public agronomic research needed to promote an African green revolution, based on locally specific packages of micronutrients, was neglected. The main source of agricultural growth has been the gradual adoption of cash crops by smallholders, a process slowed down by government pricing policies (Bevan et al., 1993). While governments favored manufacturing, the basis for industrial growth in this area was also under-

mined, since trade and exchange rate policies induced industrial firms to produce under uncompetitive conditions and only for small and captive domestic markets.

The same urban bias initially led governments to favor the urban wage labor force. In the immediate post-colonial period, minimum wages rose and unions acquired influence, so that wages increased substantially. However, post-independence inflation has usually eroded minimum wages, so that in most of Africa, wage rigidities in the labor market are not currently a significant impediment to the growth process. The exceptions are South Africa, where the labor market may just be going through such a real wage adjustment now, and the low inflation environments of Ethiopia and the countries in the "franc zone," the 13 former colonies of France in west and central Africa which had currencies pegged to the French franc. While high wage levels are not normally a hindrance to African economies, the job matching process appears to be inefficient, so that job mobility offers unusually high returns (Mengistae, 1998). This is an instance of the high costs of market information; for example, newspapers are expensive and have low circulation.

Financial markets were heavily regulated, with bank lending directed to the government, public enterprises or "strategic" sectors, very limited financial intermediation and virtually no competition between financial institutions. A common proxy for the extent of financial intermediation, known as "financial depth," is the broad money supply, M2, relative to GDP. But although Africa has even less financial depth than other developing areas, currently available evidence suggests that this may have had only a modest impact on its growth. For example, Easterly and Levine (1997) estimate that lack of financial depth reduced the annual growth rate by only 0.3 percentage points. Similarly, microeconomic survey evidence on manufacturing firms indicates that the lack of external finance is not currently the binding constraint on industrial investment (Bigsten et al., 1999).

External-Destiny

Africa is better located than Asia for most developed economy markets. However, most Africans live much further from the coast or navigable rivers than in other regions and so face intrinsically higher transport costs for exports (as shown in Table 2). Further, much of the population lives in countries which are land-locked, so that problems of distance are compounded by political barriers. Even a relatively open border like the one between Canada and the United States appears to be a substantial impediment to trade, in the sense that trade across Canadian provinces or across U.S. states is far greater than trade of equal distance between Canada and the United States (McCallum, 1995). Landlocked countries face national borders on all sides, which may constitute an irreducible barrier to trade even if they have good relations with their neighbors. Typically, growth regressions find that being landlocked reduces a nation's annual growth rate by around half of 1 percent.

A further aspect of external destiny is that Africa's exports are concentrated in a narrow range of commodities, with volatile prices that have declined since the 1960s. The deterioration in the terms of trade for such commodities has undoubtedly contributed to Africa's growth slowdown. However, there is controversy over whether its atypical exposure to terms of trade volatility has been damaging. Deaton and Miller (1996) find little evidence of detrimental effects in the short run. However, case study evidence suggests that shocks have often had longer-run deleterious effects. Investment has been concertinaed into short periods, during which construction booms have raised the unit cost of capital, and government budgets have been destabilized, with spending rising during booms but being difficult to reduce subsequently (Schuknecht, 1999; Collier and Gunning, 1999b).

Africa has attracted much more aid per capita than other regions. Donor allocation rules have typically favored countries which have small populations and low incomes, and were re-

cent colonies—and African countries met all three criteria. There has been a long debate as to whether aid has been detrimental or beneficial for the growth process (for recent overviews, see Gwin and Nelson, 1997; World Bank, 1998). Early critics claimed that aid reduced the incentive for good governance (for example, Bauer, 1982). Since the 1980s, the World Bank and the International Monetary Fund have attempted to make policy improvement a condition for the receipt of aid. Econometric work does not find that aid has had a significant effect on policy: to the extent that aid encourages or discourages policy changes, the two effects apparently offset each other. However, the effect of aid on growth has been shown to be policy-dependent. Where policies are good, aid substantially raises growth rates, where they are poor, diminishing returns rapidly set in so that aid cannot significantly contribute to growth. This result holds whether the measure of policy is objective indicators of the fiscal and exchange rate stance (Burnside and Dollar, 1997), or subjective but standardized ratings of a broader range of policies done by the World Bank (Collier and Dollar, 1999a). Until recently, many African policy environments were not good enough for aid to raise growth substantially. Hence, the evidence does not support Bauer's (1982) claim that Africa's large aid receipts were a cause of its slow growth, but does suggest that Africa largely missed the opportunity for enhanced growth which aid provided.

Excluding South Africa and the oil exporters (whose terms of trade have improved), the net aid inflows since 1970 have been around 50 percent greater than the income losses from terms of trade deterioration. The combination was thus somewhat analogous to an increase in export taxation: the terms of trade losses taking money from exporters, while the aid provided money to governments.

External-Policy

In recent decades, African governments adopted exchange rate and trade policies which were atypically anti-export and accumulated large foreign debts. On a range of indicators, Africa has had much higher trade barriers and more misaligned exchange rates than other regions (Dollar, 1992; Sachs and Warner, 1997). Exchange rates were commonly highly overvalued, reflecting the interest of the political elite in cheap imports. Tariffs and export taxes were higher in Africa than in other regions of the world, partly because of the lack of other sources of tax revenue to finance the expansion of the public sector. Exports were sharply reduced as a result of export crop taxation. For example, Dercon (1993) shows that Tanzanian cotton exports would have been 50 percent higher in the absence of taxation. Quantitative restrictions on imports were also used much more extensively, despite yielding no revenue. They often arose because of the difficulties of fine-tuning import demand in a situation where government was attempting to keep exchange rates fixed with few reserves. They probably persisted because they generated large opportunities for corruption, since someone could often be bribed to circumvent the quantitative limits.

The international growth literature has reached a consensus that exchange rate overvaluation and tight trade restrictions are damaging, but controversy continues over the effects of more moderate trade restrictions (Rodrik, 1999). However, there are reasons why Africa's poor export performance may have been particularly damaging. Since 1980, African export revenue per capita has sharply declined, which in turn has induced severe import compression of both capital goods and intermediate inputs. Moreover, because African economies are so much smaller than other economies, external barriers of a given height have been significantly more damaging (Collier and Gunning, 1999).

By the 1990s, several African economies had accumulated unsustainable international debts, largely from public agencies. Clearly, this is one way in which poor decisions of the past become embedded in the present. There is a good theoretical argument that high indebtedness discourages private investment due to the fear of the future tax liability. There is some supporting evidence for this claim, although since poor policies lower GDP, using high debt/GDP as an explanatory variable may simply be a proxy for poor policies more broadly (Elbadawi et al., 1997).

Policy or Destiny?

The dichotomy between policy and destiny is of course an oversimplification: some apparently exogenous features of Africa have often been induced by policy, and conversely, African policies may reflect exogenous factors.

Consider, first, some of the "exogenous" factors that we have discussed under destiny. For example, the claim by Sachs and Warner (1997) that geography and demography almost fully account for Africa's slow growth rests largely upon the lack of a demographic transition to lower fertility rates in Africa, as has happened in most of Latin America and Asia. However, it is more plausible to regard these continuing high fertility rates as a consequence of slow growth than a cause. The lack of employment opportunities for young women has prevented the opportunity cost of children from rising, and the low returns to education in an environment where many of the "good" jobs are allocated by political criteria have reduced the incentive for parents to educate their children.

Similarly, the argument that the concentration of Africa's population in the interior is an external force holding down growth can also be seen as an endogenous outcome; specifically, the population has remained in the interior because of the failure of Africa's coastal cities to grow. In turn, this is partly because the failure to industrialize has slowed urbanization, and partly because policy has often been biased against coastal cities; for example, in both Nigeria and Tanzania the capital was relocated from the coast to the interior. Where policy was less biased, as in the Côte d'Ivoire during the 1970s, the coastal population grew so rapidly that it supported massive emigration from the land-locked economy of Burkina Faso: at its peak, around 40 percent of the Ivorien population were immigrants.

Further, being landlocked need not be an economic disadvantage. Developed landlocked economies, such as Switzerland, have atypically low international transport costs because they have oriented their trade towards their neighbors. By contrast, Africa's landlocked economies trade with Europe, so that neighboring countries are an obstacle rather than a market. These patterns of trade are partly a legacy of the colonial economy, but they also reflect the high trade barriers within Africa erected by post-independence governments, and the slow rate of growth. Ultimately, landlocked economies were faced with neighboring markets that were both inaccessible and unattractive, which did not make it desirable to reorient the economy to trade with them. Finally, Africa's continued export concentration in a narrow range of primary commodities, which we discussed earlier as reflecting the destiny of resource endowments, probably also reflects a number of public policy decisions. Other export activities have been handicapped either directly through overvalued exchange rates, or indirectly, through high transactions costs. Poor policy has given Africa a comparative disadvantage in "transaction-intensive" activities such as manufacturing.

Now consider the reverse situation; that is, how some of the dysfunctional policies that we have discussed can also be considered the outcome of exogenous forces. The anti-export policies which we argue hindered growth can be viewed as a consequence of the fact that most of the population lives far from the coast (Gallup and Sachs, 1999). In such societies, it might be argued that the elasticity of growth with respect to openness is lower and so the incentive for openness is reduced. However, at present Africa offers little evidence for this hypothesis. According to the World Bank's standardized ratings of policy (currently confidential), all five of

the worst-rated countries on the continent are coastal whereas many of the best-rated countries are landlocked. As another example, it is possible that restrictive import policies are adopted, at least initially, in response to trade shocks like those created by an external dependence on commodity exports (Collier and Gunning, 1999b). The prevalence of natural resources may bring forth a variety of other policy errors, as well. For example, it may worsen policy by turning politics into a contest for rents or, through crowding out manufactured exports, prevent the emergence of potentially the most potent lobby for openness.

Along with being endogenous to fixed effects like geography, policies are also affected by experience. Societies which have experienced high levels of economic risk may place a higher priority on income-sharing arrangements such as expanded opportunities of public employment, rather than focusing on income generation. Societies also learn from past failure. The African nations which have recently implemented the strongest economic reforms, such as Ghana and Uganda, tended to be those which had earlier experienced the worst economic crises. However, African countries facing the challenge of reversing economic failure have lacked significant role models within the continent. In east Asia, Hong Kong, Singapore, Taiwan and Korea provided early role models, as did Chile since the late 1970s in Latin America. Within-continent models may be important because the information is both closer to hand and more evidently pertinent. Once Africa develops examples of success, the scope for societal learning across the continent will make it unlikely that Africa is "destined" to poor policies by its geography: although its geographic characteristics may have given it some weak tendencies towards poor policies in the initial post-independence period.

Sorting out the policy effects from the destiny effects is a difficult econometric problem. In the ordinary least squares regressions common in the analysis of African growth, the dependent variable is typically the average growth rate over a long period, and a variety of policy and destiny variables enter as the explanatory variables. Depending upon the specification, either policy or destiny can appear important.

An alternative approach is to consider the extent to which African slow growth has been persistent, to take advantage of the insight that policies have varied, whereas destiny-like geographic disadvantages remain constant over time. Along these lines, Diamond (1998) provides a convincing explanation from a historical perspective of why geographic reasons, such as the north-south axis of the continent, caused African agriculture to develop only slowly prior to European colonization, due to a combination of technological isolation and small scale. However, since colonization gradually relaxed some of these constraints (while introducing others), pre-20th century experience is of limited pertinence for explaining patterns of growth in the last few decades.

More recent experience tends to argue that destiny plays less of a role than policy. After all, the economies of Africa did grow relatively quickly through the first half of the 20th century, and up until the early 1970s, which tends to argue that they were not obviously destined for lower growth. The arrival of slow economic growth in the 1970s coincides with a phase in which African economic policy became both statist and biased against exports. Moreover, the main exception to African economic collapse, Botswana, experienced the most rapid growth in the world despite the seeming exogenous disadvantages of being landlocked and having very low population density.

The most sophisticated econometric test of whether something about Africa seems intrinsically connected to slow growth is the study by Hoeffler (1999). She searches for a continental fixed effect using panel regressions of five-year periods over 1965–90. She first estimates a simple growth model in which the explanatory variables are initial income, investment, population growth, and schooling. She then uses the coefficients on these variables to compute the residu-als, and regresses the residuals on regional dummies. The Africa dummy is small and insignificant, that is, there is no continental fixed effect to explain. However, she does find that both being landlocked and being tropical significantly reduce growth, and these are indeed locational characteristics of much of Africa. Between them they would reduce the African growth rate by around 0.4 percentage points relative to that of other developing regions.

Whereas in the distant past the economies of Africa may well have been intrinsically disadvantaged by factors like less easy access to water transportation or the geography of the continent, the thesis that this has persisted into recent decades is less plausible. Remember that by 1950 Africa had a higher per capita income than south Asia and its subsequent performance was indistinguishable from that region until the mid-1970s. Coastal Africa is not intrinsically markedly worse-endowed in any geographical sense than much of coastal Asia or Brazil, although its soil types pose distinct challenges for agronomic research.

By contrast, it is easy to point to policies which until very recently have been dysfunctional. Even as of 1998, Africa had the worst policy environment in the world according to the World Bank ratings. Microeconomic evidence shows how these policies damaged the growth of firms. Poor infrastructure, poor contract enforcement and volatile policies all make the supply of inputs unreliable. Firms have responded to this risky environment partly by reducing risks: they hold large inventories, invest in electricity generators, and restrict their business relations to known enterprises. They have also responded by reducing investment. A striking implication is the conjunction of a high marginal return on capital and a very low rate of investment, even for firms that are not liquidity constrained. In Africa, the elasticity of investment with respect to profits may be as low as 0.07 (Bigsten et al., 1999). Some of the effects of poor policy are highly persistent. Most notably, the colonial governments of Africa provided little education, especially at the secondary level. Although independent governments rapidly changed these priorities, for the past 30 years Africa has had a markedly lower stock of human capital than other continents. The rapid growth in education has, however, gradually narrowed the gap with other regions.

Even if one disagrees with this view that policy is more important in explaining Africa's slow rate of growth and finds the "destiny" explanations more persuasive, this by no means condemns Africa to growing more slowly than other regions. Some of the economic disadvantages of being tropical may be overcome, for example, by the discovery of vaccines or new strains of crops. Moreover, Africa has two potential growth advantages over other regions which should offset against any locational disadvantage. It has lower per capita income and so could benefit from a convergence effect with richer countries, and it has higher aid inflows and so could benefit from aid-induced growth. If public policies were as good as in other regions, aid and convergence should enable even those countries which are land-locked and tropical to grow more rapidly than other developing regions for several decades. Although the growth regressions would imply that in the long term such countries would converge on a lower steady-state income than more favorably located countries, even this is doubtful. If the coastal African nations grew, then being landlocked would cease to be disadvantageous, since the gains from trading with close neighbors would expand.

Domestic or External?

Until recently, there was broad agreement that Africa's problems were predominantly associated with its external relations, although some analysts emphasized the policy-induced lack of openness and markets, while others attributed poor performance to over-dependence on a few commodities, the prices of which were declining and volatile. In our view, the argument that Africa's poor performance originates in its

overdependence on commodities has looked weaker in recent years: Africa has lost global market share in its major exports, often spectacularly. The focus of the discussion has consequently shifted to underlying reasons for poor domestic performance, and in turn to domestic factors. The domestic factors, as we have argued, can be divided into those that smack of destiny, like the fact that much of Africa has a tropical climate, and those that are related to policy. Indeed, we believe that domestic policies largely unrelated to trade may now be the main obstacles to growth in much of Africa.

To illustrate our argument, we focus on Africa's failure to industrialize. It might appear that Africa is intrinsically uncompetitive in manufactures because of its high natural resource endowments give it a comparative advantage in that area (Wood and Mayer, 1998). But while Africa may have a comparative advantage in natural resources in the long run, at present African wages are often so low that were African manufacturing to have similar levels of productivity to other regions, it would be competitive. Hence, it is low productivity which needs to be explained.

African manufacturing has been in a low-productivity trap. Because African firms are oriented to small domestic markets, they are not able to exploit economies of scale, nor are they exposed to significant competition, and their technology gap with the rest of the world is unusually wide—yielding large opportunities for learning. This suggests that African manufacturing might have atypically large potential to raise productivity through exporting. However, most African firms fail to step onto this productivity escalator. This is because they face high costs for other reasons. As discussed already, transactions costs are unusually high. With transport unreliable, firms typically need to carry very large stocks of inputs to maintain continuity of production, despite higher interest rates than elsewhere. Telecommunications are much worse than other regions. Malfunctioning of the courts makes contract enforcement unreliable, so that firms are reluctant to enter into deals with new partners, in turn making markets less competitive.

These high transactions costs have a relatively large impact on manufacturing. Compared with natural resource extraction, manufacturing tends to have a high share of intermediate inputs and a low share of value-added to final price. Consequently, transactions costs tend to be much larger relative to value-added. Africa's intrinsic comparative advantage in natural resource exports may thus have been reinforced by public policies which have made manufacturing uncompetitive relative to resource extraction. African policies may have given the region a comparative disadvantage in transactions-intensive activities.

Conclusion: Will Africa Grow?

During the mid-1990s, average African growth accelerated and performance became more dispersed. A few countries such as Uganda, Côte d'Ivoire, Ethiopia and Mozambique started to grow very fast, whereas others such as the Democratic Republic of the Congo and Sierra Leone descended into social disorder. "Africa" became less meaningful as a category. Both the improvement in the average performance and the greater dispersion among countries were consistent with what had happened to policy. During the 1990s many of the most egregious exchange rate, fiscal and trade policies were improved. By 1998, although Africa still ranked as the region with the worst policies on the World Bank ratings, it was also the region with by far the greatest policy dispersion.

However, the faster growth coincided not only with better policies but with improvements in the terms of trade. Further, investment in Africa as a share of GDP is currently only 18 percent. This is much lower than other regions: for example, 23 percent in South Asia and 29 percent on average in lower middle-income countries. Even these figures may understate Africa's true investment shortfall. Capital goods are more expensive in

Africa than the international average, so that once the investment share is recalculated at international relative prices it approximately halves. Although it is not pos-sible to disaggregate investment into its public and private components with complete accuracy, estimates suggest that the shortfall in African investment is due to low private investment. Thus, growth may be unsustainable unless there is a substantial increase in private investment.

On an optimistic interpretation of the evidence, Africa's slow growth from the early 1970s into the 1990s has been due to policies which reduced its openness to foreign trade. Since these policies have largely been reversed during the last decade, if this is correct then Africa should be well-placed for continued growth.

The pessimistic interpretation is that Africa's problems are intrinsic, often rooted in geography. This view implies that economic progress in Africa will be dependent upon international efforts to make its environment more favorable, such as research to eradicate tropical diseases, and finance to create transport arteries from the coast to the interior. The thesis that Africa's economic problems are caused by ethnolinguistic fractionalization has similarly intractable implications.

Our own interpretation lies between these extremes. We suggest that while the binding constraint upon Africa's growth may have been externally-oriented policies in the past, those policies have now been softened. Today, the chief problem is those policies which are ostensibly domestically-oriented, notably poor delivery of public services. These problems are much more difficult to correct than exchange rate and trade policies, and so the policy reform effort needs to be intensified. However, even widespread policy reforms in this area might not be sufficient to induce a recovery in private investment, since recent economic reforms are never fully credible. Investment rating services list Africa as the riskiest region in the world. Indeed, there is some evidence that Africa suffers from being perceived by investors as a "bad neighborhood." Analysis of the global risk ratings shows that while they are largely explicable in terms of economic fundamentals, Africa as a whole is rated as significantly more risky than is warranted by these fundamentals (Haque et al., 1999). Similarly, private investment appears to be significantly lower in Africa than is explicable in terms of economic fundamentals (Jaspersen et al., 1999). "Africa" thus seems to be treated as a meaningful category by investors.

The perception of high risk for investing in Africa may partly be corrected by the passage of time, but reforming African governments can also take certain steps to commit themselves to defend economic reforms. Internationally, governments may increasingly make use of rules within the World Trade Organization, and shift their economic relations with the European Union from unreciprocated trade preferences to a wider range of reciprocated commitments. Domestically, there is a trend to freedom of the press, and the creation of independent centers of authority in central banks and revenue authorities, all of which should generally help to reinforce a climate of openness and democracy, which is likely to be supportive of economic reform.

REFERENCES

Ablo, Emanuel and Ritva Reinikka. 1998. "Do Budgets Really Matter? Evidence from Public Spending on Education and Health in Uganda." Policy Research Working Paper No. 1926, World Bank.

African Development Bank. 1998. *African Development Report*. Oxford: Oxford University Press.

Bates, Robert, H. 1983. *Essays in the Political Economy of Rural Africa*. Cambridge: Cambridge University Press.

Bauer, Peter T. 1982. "The Effects of Aid." *Encounter*. November.

Bevan, David L., Paul Collier and Jan Willem Gunning. 1993. *Agriculture and the policy environment: Tanzania and Kenya*. Paris: OECD.

Biggs, T., M. Raturi and P. Srivastava. 1996. "Enforcement of Contracts in an African Credit Market: Working Capital Financing in Kenyan Manufacturing." RPED Discussion Paper, Africa Region, World Bank.

Bigsten, Arne, P. Collier, S. Dercon, B. Gauthier, J. W. Gunning, A. Isaksson, A. Oduro, R. Oostendorp, C. Pattillo, M. Soderbom, M. Sylvain, F. Teal and A. Zeufack. 1999, forthcoming. "Investment by Manufacturing Firms in Africa: a Four-Country Panel Data Analysis." *Oxford Bulletin of Economics and Statistics*.

Bloom, John and Jeffrey Sachs. 1998. "Geography, Demography and Economic Growth in Africa." *Brookings Papers in Economic Activity*. 2, 207–95.

Burnside, Craig and David Dollar. 1997. "Aid, Policies and Growth." Policy Research Working Paper No. 1777, World Bank.

Collier, Paul. 1999. "The Political Economy of Ethnicity," in *Proceedings of the Annual Bank Conference on Development Economics*. Pleskovic, Boris and Joseph E. Stiglitz, eds. World Bank, Washington, D.C.

Collier, Paul and David Dollar. 1999a. "Aid Allocation and Poverty Reduction." Policy Research Working Paper 2041, World Bank, Washington, DC.

Collier, Paul and David Dollar. 1999b. "Aid, Risk and the Special Concerns of Small States." Mimeo, Policy Research Department, World Bank, Washington, DC.

Collier, Paul and Ashish Garg. 1999, forthcoming. "On Kin Groups and Wages in the Ghanaian Labour Market." *Oxford Bulletin of Economics and Statistics*, 61:2, pp. 131–51.

Collier, P. and J. W. Gunning. 1999. "Explaining African Economic Performance." *Journal of Economic Literature*. March, 37:1, 64–111.

Collier, P. and J.W. Gunning. 1999a, forthcoming. "The IMF's Role in Structural Adjustment." *Economic Journal*. World Bank, Washington, DC.

Collier, P. and J.W. Gunning with associates. 1999b. *Trade Shocks in Developing Countries:*

Theory and Evidence. Oxford: Oxford University Press (Clarendon).

Collier, Paul and Anke Hoeffler. 1998. "On the Economic Causes of Civil War." *Oxford Economic Papers.* 50, pp. 563–73.

Collier, Paul and Anke Hoeffler. 1999. "Loot-Seeking and Justice-Seeking in Civil War." Mimeo, Development Research Department, World Bank, Washington DC.

Collier, Paul and Catherine Pattillo, eds. 1999. *Investment and Risk in Africa.* Macmillan: London.

Collins, S. and B. P. Bosworth. 1996. "Economic Growth in East Asia: Accumulation versus Assimilation." *Brookings Papers in Economic Activity,* 2, pp. 135–203.

Deaton, A. and R. Miller. 1996. "International Commodity Prices, Macroeconomic Performance and Politics in Sub-Saharan Africa." *Journal of African Economies.* 5 (Supp.), pp. 99–191.

Dercon, Stefan. 1993. "Peasant supply response and macroeconomic policies: cotton in Tanzania." *Journal of African Economies.* 2, pp. 157–94.

Dercon, Stefan. 1997. "Wealth, Risk and Activity Choice: Cattle in Western Tanzania." *Journal of Development Economics.* 55:1, pp. 1–42.

Diamond, Jared. 1998. *Guns, Germs, and Steel: The Fates of Human Societies.* New York: W. W. Norton & Co.

Dollar, David. 1992. "Outward-Oriented Developing Economies Really do Grow More Rapidly: Evidence from 95 LDCs 1976–85." *Economic Development and Cultural Change.* 40, pp. 523–44.

Easterly, William and Ross Levine. 1997. "Africa's Growth Tragedy: Policies and Ethnic Divisions." *Quarterly Journal of Economics.* CXII, pp. 1203–1250.

Elbadawi, Ibrahim A., Benno J. Ndulu, and Njuguna Ndung'u. 1997. "Debt Overhang and Economic Growth in Sub-Saharan Africa," in *External Finance for Low-Income Countries.* Iqbal, Zubair and Ravi Kanbur, eds. IMF Institute, Washington, DC.

Fafchamps, Marcel, Jan Willem Gunning and Remco Oostendorp. 1998. "Inventories, Liquidity and Contractual Risk in African Manufacturing." Department of Economics, Stanford University, mimeo.

Gallup, John L. and Jeffrey D. Sachs. 1999. "Geography and Economic Growth," in *Proceedings of the Annual World Bank Conference on Development Economics.* Pleskovic, Boris and Joseph E. Stiglitz, eds. World Bank, Washington, DC.

Ghana Central Bureau of Statistics. 1988. *Quarterly Digest of Statistics.* Accra.

Grove, A. T. 1991. "The African Environment," in *Africa 30 Years On.* Rimmer, Douglas, ed. London: James Currey.

Gwin, Catherine and Joan Nelson. 1997. *Perspectives on Aid and Development.* Johns Hopkins for Overseas Development Council, Washington DC.

Haque, Nadeem U., Nelson Mark and Donald J. Mathieson. 1999. "Risk in Africa: its Causes and its Effects on Investment," in *Investment and Risk in Africa.* Collier, Paul and Catherine Pattillo, eds. London: Macmillan.

Hoeffler, Anke A. 1999. "Econometric Studies of Growth, Convergence and Conflicts." D. Phil. Thesis, Oxford University.

Jaspersen, Frederick, Anthony H. Aylward and A. David Cox. 1999. "Risk and Private Investment: Africa Compared with Other Developing Areas," in *Investment and Risk in Africa.* Collier, Paul and Catherine Pattillo, eds. London: Macmillan.

Knack, Stephen and Phillip Keefer. 1995. "Institutions and Economic Performance: Cross-Country Tests Using Alternative Institutional Measures." *Economics and Politics.* 7:3, pp. 207–28.

Kenya Central Bureau of Statistics. 1996. *Statistical Abstract.* Nairobi.

Kremer, Michael. 1993. "Population Growth and Technological Change: One Million B.C. to

1990." *Quarterly Journal of Economics*. 108:3, pp. 681–716.

Lee, K. S. and A. Anas. 1991. "Manufacturers' Responses to Infrastructure Deficiencies in Nigeria: Private Alternatives and Policy Options," in *Economic Reform in Africa*. Chibber, A. and S. Fischer, eds. World Bank, Washington DC.

Maddison, Angus. 1995. *Monitoring the World Economy*. Paris: OECD.

Mauro, P. 1995. "Corruption and Growth." *Quarterly Journal of Economics*. 110, pp. 681–712.

McCallum, J. 1995. "National Borders Matter: Canada-U.S. Regional Trade Patterns." *American Economic Review*. 85, pp. 615–23.

Mengistae, Taye. 1998. "Ethiopia's Urban Economy: Empirical Essays on Enterprise Development and the Labour Market." D.Phil. Thesis, University of Oxford.

Pradhan, Sanjay. 1996. "Evaluating Public Spending." World Bank Discussion Paper 323, Washington DC.

Reinikka, Ritva and Jakob Svensson. 1998. "Investment Response to Structural Reforms and Remaining Constraints: Firm Survey Evidence from Uganda." Mimeo, Africa Region, World Bank.

Rodrik, Dani. 1999. *Making Openness Work: The New Global Economy and the Developing Countries*. Overseas Development Council, Washington DC.

Sachs, J. D. and Mark Warner. 1997. "Sources of Slow Growth in African Economies." *Journal of African Economies*. 6, pp. 335–76.

Schuknecht, Ludger. 1999. "Tying Governments' Hands in Commodity Taxation." *Journal of African Economies*. 8:2, 152–81.

Voortman, R. L., B.G.J.S. Sonneveld and M. A. Keyzer. 1999. "African Land Ecology: Opportunities and Constraints for Agricultural Development." Mimeo, Centre for World Food Studies, Free University, Amsterdam.

Widner, Jennifer, A. 1999. "The Courts as Restraints," in *Investment and Risk in Africa*. Collier, Paul and Catherine Pattillo, eds. London: Macmillan.

Wood, Adrian and J. Mayer. 1998. "Africa's Export Structure in Comparative Perspective," Study No. 4 of the UNCTAD series *Economic Development and Regional Dynamics in Africa: Lessons from the East Asian Experience*.

World Bank. 1997. *Confronting Aids*, Policy Research Report. Oxford University Press.

World Bank. 1998. *Assessing Aid: What Works, What Doesn't, and Why*, Policy Research Report. Oxford University Press.

World Bank. 1999. *World Development Indicators*. Development Data Center, Washington, D.C.

ROBERT J. BARRO

DEMOCRACY: A RECIPE FOR GROWTH?

It sounds nice to try to install democracy in places like Haiti and Somalia, but does it make any sense? Would an increase in political freedom tend to spur economic growth, the key problem in these poor countries? Is there a reasonable prospect that democratic institutions can be maintained in places with such low standards of living? History provides reasonably clear answers to these questions.

From *The Wall Street Journal* (December 1, 1994) p. A18.

More political freedom does not have an important impact on growth, but improvements in the standard of living tend strongly to precede expansions of political freedoms. In particular, democracies that arise in poor countries (sometimes because they are imposed from outside) usually do not last.

Theoretically, the effect of more democracy on growth is ambiguous. The negative effects involve the tendency to enact rich-to-poor redistributions of income (including land reforms) under majority voting and the enhanced role of interest groups in systems with representative legislatures. On the other side, democratic institutions provide a check on governmental power and thereby limit the potential of public officials to amass personal wealth and to carry out unpopular (and perhaps unproductive) projects.

Autocracies avoid some of the problems of democracy, but are adverse to growth if the leaders use their power to steal the nation's wealth and to carry out useless investments. In practice, some dictators have favored economic freedom and growth—including the Pinochet government in Chile, the Fujimori administration in Peru and several previous and current regimes in East Asia. Others have restricted economic freedom and deterred development—including many governments in Africa, some in Latin America, the formerly planned economies of Eastern Europe and the Marcos administration in the Philippines.

From an empirical standpoint, the typical effect of democracy on growth can be ascertained from a statistical analysis of data for about 100 countries at various stages of economic development from 1960 to 1990. My study reveals a number of factors that influence the growth rate of real per-capita gross domestic product. The favorable elements include small distortions of market prices, an inclination and ability of the government to maintain the rule of law, high levels of health and education, low government

If Prosperity Brings Democracy . . .

These countries will be more democratic . . .			These countries will be less democratic . . .		
	1993	2000		1993	2000
Iraq	.00	.21	Hungary	1.00	.81
Haiti	.00	.24	Mauritius	1.00	.81
Sudan	.00	.24	Botswana	.83	.66
Syria	.00	.32	Papua New Guinea	.83	.65
Algeria	.00	.33	Nepal	.83	.60
Swaziland	.17	.35	Bolivia	.83	.58
Iran	.17	.41	Bangladesh	.83	.56
Yugoslavia	.17	.41	Gambia	.83	.54
Indonesia	.00	.43	Benin	.83	.50
South Africa	.33	.47	Pakistan	.67	.48
Peru	.33	.51	Mali	.83	.44
Singapore	.33	.61	Congo	.67	.42
Taiwan	.50	.64	Niger	.67	.37
Hong Kong	.33	.67	Central African Republic	.67	.36
Mexico	.50	.72	Zambia	.67	.35

Note: The democracy index uses a scale from 0 to 1, where 0 means no political rights and 1 means virtually full rights. The figures for 1993 and other years are derived from information presented in Raymond Gastil and followers, *Freedom in the World*, various issues. Their subjective classifications follow the basic definition: "Political rights are rights to participate meaningfully in the political process. In a democracy this means the right of all adults to vote and compete for public office, and for elected representatives to have a decisive vote on public policies." The values shown for 2000 are projections based on the author's statistical analysis.

spending on consumption and a low fertility rate.

If these kinds of variables and the current level of per-capita income are held constant, then the overall effect of more democracy on the growth rate is moderately negative. (Democracy is measured by the index of political rights compiled in the serial publication "Freedom in the World.") There is some indication that more democracy raises growth when political freedoms are low but depresses growth once a moderate amount of freedom has been attained.

The data reveal a stronger linkage between economic development and the propensity to experience democracy. Nondemocratic countries that have achieved high standards of living—measured by real per-capita GDP, life expectancy and schooling—tend to become more democratic over time. Examples include Chile, South Korea, Taiwan, Spain and Portugal. Conversely, democratic countries with low standards of living tend to lose political rights over time. Examples include most of the newly independent African states in the 1970s.

The empirical results can be used to forecast changes in the level of democracy from the last value observed, 1993, into the future. The table [on page 429] displays the cases of especially large projected changes in democracy from 1993 to 2000 (among the 101 countries with the necessary data).

The group with large anticipated increases, on the left side of the table, includes some countries that have virtually no political freedom in 1993. Some of these are among the world's poorest countries, such as Haiti, for which the projected level of democracy in 2000 is also not high. Haiti is expected to raise its democracy (perhaps with the assistance of the U.S.) from zero in 1993 to 0.24 (roughly one-quarter of the way toward a "full representative democracy") in 2000. Some other countries that have essentially no political freedom in 1993 are more well off economically and are therefore forecasted to have greater increases in democracy; for example, the projected value in

2000 is 0.43 for Indonesia, 0.33 for Algeria, and 0.32 for Syria.

Expectations for large increases in democracy also apply to some reasonably prosperous places in which the extent of political freedom lags behind the standard of living. As examples, Singapore is projected to increase its democracy index from 0.33 in 1993 to 0.61 in 2000, Mexico is expected to go from 0.50 to 0.72 (a change that has probably already occurred with the 1994 elections) and Taiwan is forecasted to rise from 0.50 to 0.64.

South Africa is also included on the left side of the table, with a projected increase in the democracy index from 0.33 in 1993 to 0.47 in 2000. However, the political changes in South Africa in 1994 have probably already overshot the mark, and a substantial decline of political freedom is likely after this year.

The examples of large expected decreases in democracy, shown on the right side of the table, consist mainly of relatively poor countries with surprisingly high levels of political freedom in 1993. Many of these are African countries in which the political institutions recently became more democratic: Mali, Benin, Zambia, Central African Republic, Niger and Congo. The model predicts that democracy that gets well ahead of economic development will not last. Three other African countries, The Gambia, Mauritius and Botswana, have maintained democratic institutions for some time, but the analysis still predicts that political freedoms will diminish in these places. (A military coup in July 1994 has already reduced the Gambia's level of political freedom.)

One way to view the findings is that political freedom emerges as a sort of luxury good. Rich places consume more democracy because this good is desirable for its own sake and even though the increased political freedom may have an adverse effect on growth. Basically, rich countries can afford the reduced rate of economic progress.

The analysis has implications for the desirability of exporting democratic institutions from the advanced Western countries to developing nations. Democracy is not the key to economic growth, and political freedoms tend to erode over time if they are out of line with a country's standard of living. Specifically, the U.S. plan to establish democracy in Haiti is a counter-productive policy. It will not improve the standard of living—the main problem in a poor country—and the democracy will almost surely be temporary.

More generally, the advanced Western countries would contribute more to the welfare of poor nations by exporting their economic systems, notably property rights and free markets, rather than their political systems, which typically developed after reasonable standards of living had been attained. If economic freedom were to be established in a poor country, then growth would be encouraged, and the country would tend eventually to become more democratic on its own. Thus, in the long run, the propagation of Western-style economic systems would also be the effective way to expand democracy in the world.

ADAM PRZEWORSKI ET AL.

POLITICAL REGIMES AND ECONOMIC GROWTH

Introduction

With the birth of new nations in Asia and Africa, the fear that democracy would undermine economic growth began to be voiced in the United States. The first statements to that effect were perhaps those by Walter Galenson and by Karl de Schweinitz, who argued, both in 1959, that in poor countries democracy unleashes pressures for immediate consumption, which occurs at the cost of investment, hence of growth. Galenson mentioned both the role of unions and that of governments. He thought that unions "must ordinarily appeal to the worker on an all-out consumptionist platform. No matter how much 'responsibility' the union leader exhibits in his understanding of the limited consumption possi-

From *Democracy and Development: Political Institutions and Well-Being in the World, 1950–1990.* (New York: Cambridge University Press, 2000), pp. 142–74. Some of the authors' notes have been omitted.

bilities existing at the outset of industrialization, he cannot afford to moderate his demands." As for governments, he observed that "the more democratic a government is, . . . the greater the diversion of resources from investment to consumption." According to de Schweinitz (1959: 388), if trade unions and labor parties "are successful in securing a larger share of the national income and limiting the freedom for action of entrepreneurs, they may have the effect of restricting investment surplus so much that the rate of economic growth is inhibited." That argument enjoyed widespread acceptance under the influence of Huntington, who claimed that "the interest of the voters generally leads parties to give the expansion of personal consumption a higher priority via-à-vis investment than it would receive in a non-democratic system" (Huntington and Domiguez 1975: 60; Huntington 1968).

Democracy was thus seen as inimical to economic development. Moreover, via a rather dubious inference, proponents of that view concluded that dictatorships were therefore better able to force savings and launch economic growth. To cite a more recent statement: "Economic development is a process for which huge investments in personnel and material are required. Such investment programs imply cuts in current consumption that would be painful at the low levels of living that exist in almost all developing societies. Governments must resort to strong measures and they enforce them with an iron hand in order to marshal the surpluses needed for investment. If such measures were put to a popular vote, they would surely be defeated. No political party can hope to win a democratic election on a platform of current sacrifices for a *bright future*" (Rao 1984: 75).[1]

The reasoning bears reconstruction. First, that argument assumes that poor people have a higher propensity to consume.[2] This is why democracy may be compatible with growth at high but not at low levels of income. Second, the underlying model of growth attributes it to the increase in the stock of physical capital. Finally, democracy is always responsive to pressures for immediate consumption. The chain of reasoning is thus the following: (1) Poor people want to consume immediately. (2) When workers are able to organize, they drive wages up, reduce profits, and reduce investment (by lowering either the rate of return or the volume of profit or both). (3) When people are allowed to vote, governments tend to distribute income away from investment (either they tax and transfer or they undertake less public investment). (4) Lowering investment slows down growth. Note, as well, that this reasoning implies that the impact of mean-preserving inequality on growth is ambivalent: In the Kaldor-Pasinetti models, inequality promotes growth, as it increases the incomes of those who save more, but in the median-voter models it slows down growth to the extent to which the political system responds to demands for redistribution.

Arguments in favor of democracy are not equally sharp, but they all focus in one form or another on allocative efficiency: Democracies can better allocate the available resources to pro-

ductive uses. One view is that because authoritarian rulers are not accountable to electorates, they have no incentive to maximize total output, but only their own rents. As a result, democracies better protect property rights, thus allowing a longer-term perspective to investors. There is also a vague sense that by permitting a free flow of information, democracies somehow improve the quality of economic decisions.

According to the first view, the state is always ready to prey on the society (North 1990), and only democratic institutions can constrain it to act in a more general interest. Hence, dictatorships, of any stripe, are sources of inefficiency. Barro (1990), Findlay (1990), Olson (1991), and Przeworski (1990) have constructed models that differ in detail but generate the same conclusion. These models assume that some level of government intervention in the economy is optimal for growth. Then they all show that, depending on the details of each model, dictatorships of various stripes can be expected to undersupply or oversupply government activities. One interesting variant of this approach is by Robinson (1995), who thinks that dictators are afraid, at least under some conditions, that development would give rise to political forces that would overturn them, and thus they deliberately abstain from developmentalist policies.

Perhaps the best-known informational argument is based on the Drèze and Sen (1989) observation that no democracy ever experienced a famine, which they attribute to the alarm role of the press and the opposition. Thus, Sen (1994a: 34) observes that "a free press and an active political opposition constitute the best 'early warning system' that a country threatened by famine can possess." He also cites an unlikely source, Mao, reflecting on the great Chinese famine of 1962, to the effect that "without democracy, you have no understanding of what is happening down below." Yet it is not apparent whether this is an argument strictly about avoiding disasters or about average performance.[3]

This summary makes no pretense to being exhaustive. All we want to highlight is that the arguments in favor of dictatorship and those in favor of democracy are not necessarily incompatible. The arguments against democracy claim that it hinders growth by reducing investment; the arguments in its favor maintain that it fosters growth by promoting allocative efficiency. Both may be true: The rate at which productive factors grow may be higher under dictatorship, but the use of resources may be more efficient under democracy. And because these mechanisms work in opposite directions, the net effect may be that there is no difference between the two regimes in the average rates of growth they generate. The patterns of growth may differ, but the average rates of growth may still be the same.

*   *   *

Dictatorships existed predominantly in poor countries: 38.5 percent of annual observations (946 out of 2,481) of dictatorships were in countries with incomes under $1,000, but only 4.5 percent of democracies (75 out of 1,645) were that poor. Democracies flourished in wealthy countries: 46.8 percent of them (769) were observed in countries with incomes above $6,000, whereas only 2.8 percent (68) of dictatorships existed at such income levels. Hence, nearly all our observations of countries with incomes below $1,000, 92.6 percent (946 out of 1,021), are of dictatorships, and nearly all our observations of countries with incomes above $6,000, 91.9 percent (769 out of 837), are of democracies.

Now, examining the rates of growth in countries classified by intervals of $500 of per capita income (Table 1) shows that very poor countries (under $1,000) grow slowly, at about 3.5 percent. Growth accelerates in wealthier economies, reaching a peak of 5.1 percent between $2,000 and $3,000. Then it slows down again to about 3.8 percent when countries reach incomes above $6,000. Hence, in accordance with Quah (1996), incomes diverge among poor countries, until about $2,500, and they converge among wealthy countries.

If very poor and very rich economies both grow slowly regardless of the regime they have, then this pattern does not present a problem. But if poor countries grow slowly because they are ruled by dictatorships, or rich ones because they are democratic, then we cannot make such an inference, for perhaps if the poor countries had been democratic they would have grown faster. In fact, the 75 democratic years at incomes under $1,000 witnessed growth at the rate of 4.22 percent, but dictatorships grew at the rate of 3.46 percent in equally poor countries. Conversely, if the rich countries had been authoritarian, perhaps they would have grown faster. Again, the 68 authoritarian years at incomes above $6,000 enjoyed growth at the rate of 6.05 percent, whereas democracies had a rate of growth of 3.57 percent at those incomes. Our counterfactual procedure matches the regimes for the conditions under which they existed, specifically for their productive inputs and a variety of other conditions. But to find out how a country observed, say, as a dictatorship would have grown had it been a democracy under the same conditions, we use the information about the way these productive inputs are transformed into outputs under each regime. And this information, about production functions, is derived from the actual observations, which means disproportionately from poor dictatorships and rich democracies. Hence these production functions may be different not because of the impact of regimes but because of the effect of wealth.

Thus, to test whether or not the results depend on the samples, we need to estimate production functions separately for different levels of development, as always measured by per capita income. First we consider only countries with incomes under $3,000, which we shall call "poor." Their production functions are almost identical, and regimes make no difference for the average growth rates. Then we take countries with incomes above $3,000, "wealthy," where the difference between the observed growth rates is particularly high, 4.91 percent for dictatorships, and 3.83 for democracies. The difference be-

Table 1. Rate of growth of GDP (YG), by per capita income (LEVEL)

LEVEL	Proportion dictatorships	Rate of growth of GDP [a]		
		All	Dictatorships	Democracies
0–1,000	0.9273	3.519	3.464	4.220
1,001–2,000	0.7472	4.636	4.809	4.123
2,001–3,000	0.6207	5.142	5.633	4.335
3,001–4,000	0.5874	4.740	4.915	4.492
4,001–5,000	0.5424	4.552	4.507	4.606
5,001–6,000	0.4308	4.312	4.772	3.963
6,001–	0.0812	3.770	6.054	3.568
Total (N = 4,128)		4.233	4.424	3.945

[a]All cell entries are based on at least 68 observations.

Moving averages of rates of growth by bands of $500

LEVEL	All	Dictatorships	Democracies
250–750	3.071	3.107	2.380
500–1,000	3.689	3.647	4.164
750–1,250	4.140	4.050	4.724
1,000–1,500	4.505	4.682	3.848
1,250–1,750	4.969	5.381	3.932
1,500–2,000	4.827	5.021	4.396
1,750–2,250	4.972	5.092	4.744
2,000–2,500	5.444	5.664	5.055
2,250–2,750	5.793	6.989	3.993
2,500–3,000	4.827	5.599	3.653
2,750–3,250	4.808	4.955	4.613
3,000–3,500	5.130	5.238	4.977
3,250–3,750	4.594	4.183	5.445
3,500–4,000	4.317	4.565	3.965
3,750–4,250	4.382	5.065	3.491
4,000–4,500	4.984	4.908	5.086
4,250–4,750	4.742	4.771	4.714
4,500–5,000	3.965	3.881	4.050
4,750–5,250	4.558	4.580	4.535
5,000–5,500	4.217	4.360	4.088
5,250–5,750	4.116	4.003	4.194
5,500–6,000	4.418	5.350	3.845
5,750–6,250	3.363	4.479	2.878
6,000–	3.770	6.054	3.568

tween the average values almost vanishes when corrected for selection, but the production functions are quite different. Finally, given that there are very few dictatorships with incomes above $8,000,[4] we need to know if the difference between wealthy dictatorships and wealthy democracies is still due to the composition of the respective samples, so we analyze separately countries within the $3,000–$8,000 income band.

These tests suggest that per capita income of $3,000 is the natural breaking point.[5] The production functions are almost identical in countries with incomes below $3,000, but they differ between regimes in wealthier countries. In particular, the difference between the two regimes becomes visible if we consider only countries within the $3,000–$8,000 income band. Hence, this difference is not due to diminishing returns in wealthy democracies.

Poor Countries

In poor countries, the two regimes are almost identical, with observed rates of growth of 4.34 percent under dictatorship and 4.28 under democracy. The two regimes generate productive inputs at the same rate and use them in identical ways. They invest about 12.5 percent of GDP and increase capital stock at the rate of about 6 percent, and labor force at the rate of about 2.2 percent. An increase of 1 percent in the capital stock raises output by about 0.40 percent under both regimes, and an increase in the labor force by 1 percent augments output by about 0.60 percent.[6] Neither regime benefits much from technical progress, about 0.1 percent per annum; both get 2.8 percent in growth from an increase in capital stock, and 1.4 percent from an increase in labor force. With identical supplies of factors and their identical utilization, they grow at the same rate under the two regimes: The selection-corrected average growth rates are the same.

The idea that democracies in poor countries process pressures for immediate consumption,

resulting in lower investment and slower growth, seemed persuasive at the time it was advanced, and it was not implausible. There appear to be good reasons to think that people in poor countries want to consume more immediately: They cannot afford to make intertemporal trade-offs if they cannot expect to live to benefit from their short-term sacrifices. It is also plausible that unions, particularly if they are decentralized, and political parties, competing for votes, would push forward demands for immediate consumption. Yet, as likely as that view may seem, it simply is not true. Perhaps this only means that democracy is not very effective at processing what people want; perhaps developmental goals are not any more attractive to people under dictatorship than under democracy; perhaps poverty is so constraining that even dictators cannot squeeze savings out of indigent people.

The last explanation is most plausible. One piece of evidence is that very few countries that were very poor when we first observed them ever developed. Of the forty-eight countries that entered our purview with incomes below $1,000, only three made it to above $3,000 by 1990. The two miracles were Taiwan, which had an income of $968 in 1950 and $8,067 in 1990, and South Korea, which went from $814 in 1950 to $6,665 in 1990. Thailand had an income of $815 in 1950 and $3,570 in 1990. Four more countries that began under $1,000 made it to more than $2,000, and eleven more to at least $1,000. But at the end of the period, thirty—out of forty-eight—very poor countries remained within the income band in which they had begun. The experiences of countries that were first observed with incomes between $1,000 and $2,000 were more heterogeneous, but, again, of the forty-five first observed at that level, only five experienced sustained growth: Japan, which went from $1,768 in 1950 to $14,317 in 1990, Singapore from $1,845 in 1965 to 11,698 in 1990, Portugal from $1,314 in 1950 to 7,487 in 1990, Greece from $1,480 in 1950 to $6,768 in 1990, and Malta from $1,377 in 1964 to $6,627 in 1990. Four countries descended to below $1,000, and twelve still had incomes between $1,000 and $2,000 in 1990. In turn, none of the forty-two countries that were first observed with per capita incomes above $2,000 fell below their starting range, and all but seven of them at least doubled their incomes by the end of the period. Because the observation periods were not the same for all countries and typically were shorter for the poorer ones, many of which became independent around 1960, these data are somewhat biased against poor countries. Nevertheless, most countries that we first observed below $2,000 had about thirty years to grow, and yet most remained poor: evidence of a "low-level trap" (Table 2).

Thus, poverty constrains. Whatever the regime, the society is too poor to finance an effective state. Collecting total revenues of $127 per capita, as governments do on the average in countries with incomes under $1,000, can pay for little else than collecting these revenues. Government expenditures add up to $167 per person in these countries, so they run deficits higher than 7 percent of GDP. In countries with incomes between $1,000 and $2,000, governments collect $372 per capita and spend $450, still running deficits over 7 percent. And, like the investment share, government revenue (particularly tax revenue) as a share of GDP increases monot-

onically in per capita income.[7] Thus already in countries with incomes between $2,000 and $3,000, revenues of the central government add to $668 per capita. Between $3,000 and $4,000 they are $904, and above $6,000 they are $2,608. To put it differently, per capita public expenditures in countries with incomes between $3,000 and $4,000 are larger than total per capita incomes in countries with incomes under $1,000; per capita public expenditures in countries with incomes above $6,000 are about the same as total per capita incomes in countries between $3,000 and $4,000.

Poor countries cannot afford a strong state, and when the state is weak, the kind of regime matters little for everyday life. In a village located three days' travel away from the capital, often the only presence of the state is a teacher and occasionally roving uniformed bandits.[8] Just calculate: If a mile of road costs about a million dollars, in a country with per capita income under $1,000 it would take the total government expenditures per 600,000 persons to build 100 miles of road. There is little room for regimes to make a difference when the state is that poor.

Note that we are not arguing that a fiscally large or otherwise large state is necessarily good for development, but only that if the state is to be able to make a difference for better condi-

Table 2. Per capita income at the beginning and end of the period, by bands of $1,000

					Exited							
Entered	0–1	1–2	2–3	3–4	4–5	5–6	6–7	7–8	8–9	9–10	10–	Total
0–1	30	11	4	1	0	0	1	0	1	0	0	48
1–2	4	12	15	6	2	1	2	1	0	0	2	45
2–3	0	0	1	3	3	1	0	1	0	3	1	13
3–4	0	0	0	2	0	2	0	1	0	0	4	9
4–5	0	0	0	0	2	0	1	0	0	0	5	8
5–	0	0	0	0	0	0	1	1	0	0	10	12
Total	34	23	20	12	7	4	5	4	1	3	22	135

Notes: "Entered" stands for 1950 or the year of independence or the first year data were available, and "Exited" for 1990 or in some cases the last year data were available. Per capita incomes are given in thousands (1985 PPP USD). Cell entries are numbers of countries.

tions, it must have resources. The role of the state in economic development is a notoriously controversial issue. Most of the statistical research on this topic has been mindless: Studies that discover that the state is bad for growth simply stick government-consumption expenditures into the equation for growth and discover that its sign is negative. Needless to say, the same would happen if one did that with private-consumption expenditures: We did it and know it to be so. If one thinks that government-consumption expenditures affect growth, the term introduced into the production-function equation should be the change in government consumption, not the share of government consumption in GDP.[9] But the real test of the impact of government is to consider separately the effects of private and public capital stocks. The idea, due to Barro (1990), is that private capital and public capital play different roles in development and that they are complementary, so that even if the production function exhibits diminishing returns in each stock, the joint returns will be constant or even increasing. Moreover, because the ideal combination of private and public capital stocks is one in which their marginal products are equal (with an appropriate correction if public investment is financed by distortionary taxes), for each level of private capital stock (and investment) there is an optimal level of government capital stock (and investment).[10] The state, as measured by the size of the government capital stock, can thus be too small, just right, or too big.

*   *   *

In sum, poor countries are too poor to afford a strong state, and without an effective state there is little difference any regime can make for economic development. Investment is low in poor democracies, but it is not any higher in poor dictatorships. The labor force grows rapidly in both. Development is factor-extensive: Poor countries benefit almost nothing from technical change. Clearly, this does not imply that all poor countries are the same or even that regimes may

not make a difference for other aspects of people's lives; indeed, we show later that they do. But not for economic development in poor countries.

Wealthy Countries

Once countries reach some level of development—somewhere between $2,500 and $3,000, that of Algeria in 1977, Mauritius in 1969, Costa Rica in 1966, South Korea in 1976, Czechoslovakia in 1970, or Portugal in 1966—patterns of economic development under democracy and dictatorship diverge. In countries with incomes above that threshold, regimes do make a difference for how resources are used, for how much people produce and how much they earn.

*   *   *

Conclusion

The main conclusion of this analysis is that there is no trade-off between democracy and development, not even in poor countries. Although not a single study published before 1988 found that democracy promoted growth, and not one published after 1987 concluded in favor of dictatorships (Przeworski and Limongi 1993), there was never solid evidence that democracies were somehow inferior in generating growth—certainly not enough to justify supporting or even condoning dictatorships. We hope to have put the issue to rest. There is little difference in favor of dictatorships in the observed rates of growth. And even that difference vanishes once the conditions under which dictatorships and democracies existed are taken into account. Albeit in omniscient retrospect, the entire controversy seems to have been much ado about nothing.

Poverty appears to leave no room for politics. In countries with incomes below $3,000, the two regimes have almost identical investment shares, almost identical rates of growth of capital stock and of labor force, the same production function, the same contributions of capital, labor, and factor productivity to growth, the same output per worker, the same labor shares, and the same product wages. Poor countries invest little, get little benefit from total factor productivity, and pay low wages. And though a few countries have escaped this bond of poverty, most poor countries, have remained poor. Democracy is highly fragile in such countries, and thus most of them have dictatorial regimes. But regimes make no difference for growth, quantitatively or qualitatively.

Perhaps surprisingly, affluence differentiates regimes. Wealthier dictatorships invest a somewhat larger share of income, experience higher growth of the labor force, have higher capital and lower labor elasticities, derive more growth from capital input and less from labor input and from total factor productivity, have lower output per worker, have a lower labor share, and pay lower wages. Wealthier dictatorships grow by using a lot of labor and paying it little. Because they repress labor, they can pay it little; perhaps because they can pay it little, they care less how it is used. They pay more for capital—the average relative price of investment goods is higher under dictatorships—and they use it well. But because they rely on force to repress workers, they can pay lower wages and use labor inefficiently.

In the end, total output grows at the same rate under the two regimes, both in poor countries and in wealthier countries. But the reasons are different: In poor countries, regimes simply do not matter. In wealthier countries, their average growth rates are the same, but the patterns of growth are different.

*   *   *

NOTES

1. At least Huntington and his collaborators wrote during a period when many dictator-

ships, "authoritarian" and "totalitarian," did grow rapidly. But Rao's assertion was made in 1984, after the failure of several Latin American authoritarian regimes and Eastern European communist regimes was already apparent.

2. Pasinetti (1961) claimed that the propensity to consume is higher for workers than for capitalists, and Kaldor (1956) believed that it is higher for wages than for profits, whereas the scholars discussed here seem to assume that in general the marginal propensity to consume declines with income. Barro and Sala-i-Martin (1995: 77–9) show that in the optimal growth model the savings rate decreases as a result of the substitution effect and increases in income as a consequence of the income effect, the net effect being ambivalent.

3. Sah and Stiglitz (1988) compared the quality of the decisions whether or not to undertake a series of economic projects made under different decision rules. Their conclusions are ambivalent: Although majority rule is conducive to good decisions under many conditions, decisions by smaller groups are better when the costs of information are high, whereas decisions by larger groups are superior when the chances of adopting a bad project are high.

4. The wealthiest dictatorship we observed was Singapore, with an income of $11,698, and the wealthiest democracy in our sample, the United States, had an income of $18,095. There were 200 democratic years with incomes above that of Singapore.

5. We have investigated several more income bands, beginning with $0–$3,000 and moving the lower and upper cutoffs by $1,000, until $8,000–$11,000.

6. This is a constrained estimate. Constrained estimates are cited in the rest of this paragraph.

7. Cheibub (1998) shows that selection-corrected tax revenues are the same for the two regimes.

8. The best portrayal of life under a weak state is by Alvaro Mutis (1996).

9. Ram (1986) has shown that the model that introduces the level of government-consumption expenditures into the production-function equation is misspecified. He has developed a specification that allows an assessment of the impact of government on growth without having explicit information about the public capital stock. We (Cheibub and Przeworski 1997) applied Ram's specification to our data set and discovered that the contribution of the state is positive, but for various reasons we have second thoughts about this approach.

10. It is a different matter whether or not a government, even a benevolent one, would implement it. On the time inconsistency of optimal taxation, see Benhabib and Velasco (1996).

REFERENCES

Barro, Robert J. 1990. Government Spending in a Simple Model of Economic Growth. *Journal of Political Economy* 98(5):103–25.

Barro, Robert J., and Xavier Sala-i-Martin. 1995. *Economic Growth*. New York: McGraw-Hill.

Benhabib, Jess, and Andres Velasco. 1996. On the Optimal and Best Sustainable Taxes in an Open Economy. *European Economic Review* 40(1):134–54.

Cheibub, José Antonio. 1998. Political Regimes and the Extractive Capacity of Governments: Taxation in Democracies and Dictatorships. *World Politics* 50(3): 349–76.

Cheibub, José Antonio, and Adam Przeworski, 1997. Government Spending and Economic Growth under Democracy and Dictatorship. In *Understanding Democracy: Economic and Political Perspectives*, edited by A. Breton, G. Galeotti, P. Salmon, and R. Wintrobe, pp. 107–24. Cambridge University Press.

de Schweinitz, Karl, Jr. 1959. Industrialization, Labor Controls, and Democracy. *Economic Development and Cultural Change* 7(4):385–404.

Drèze, Jean, and Amartya Sen. 1989. *Hunger and Public Action*. Oxford University Press.

Findlay, Ronald. 1990. The New Political Economy: Its Explanatory Power for LDCs. *Economics and Politics* 2(2):193–221.

Galenson, Walter. 1959. *Labor and Economic Development*. New York: Wiley.

Huntington, Samuel P. 1968. *Political Order in Changing Societies*. New Haven, CT: Yale University Press.

Huntington, Samuel P., and Jorge I. Dominguez. 1975. Political Development. In *Macropolitical Theory*, edited by F. I. Greenstein and N. W. Polsby, pp. 1–114. Reading, MA: Addison-Wesley.

Kaldor, Nicolas. 1956. Alternative Theories of Distribution. *Review of Economic Studies* 23:83–100.

Mutis, Alvaro. 1996. *Adventures of Maqroll: Four Novellas*. New York: Harper-Collins.

North, Douglass. 1990. *Institutions, Institutional Change, and Economic Performance*. Cambridge University Press.

Olson, Mancur. 1991. Autocracy, Democracy, and Prosperity. In *Strategy and Choice*, edited by R. J. Zeckhauser, pp. 131–57. Cambridge, MA: MIT Press.

Pasinetti, Luigi. 1961. Rate of Profit and Income Distribution in Relation to the Rate of Economic Growth. *Review of Economic Studies* 29(October):267–79.

Przeworski, Adam. 1990. *The State and the Economy under Capitalism*. Chur, Switzerland: Harwood Academic Publishers.

Quah, Danny T. 1996. Twin Peaks: Growth and Convergence in Models of Distribution Dynamics. *The Economic Journal* 106:1045–55.

Ram, Rati. 1986. Government Size and Economic Growth: A New Framework and Some Evidence from Cross-Section and Time-

Series Data. *American Economic Review* 76:191–203.

Rao, Vaman. 1984. Democracy and Economic Development. *Studies in Comparative International Development* 19(4):67–81.

Robinson, James. 1995. Theories of "Bad Policy." *Policy Reform* 1:1–17.

Sah, Raaj K., and Joseph Stiglitz. 1988. Committees, Hierarchies and Polyarchies. *The Economic Journal* 98(June): 451–70.

Sen, Amartya. 1994a. Freedoms and Needs. *The New Republic*, January 10–7, 31–7.

10 POLITICAL VIOLENCE

In this chapter we look at violence against states and peoples that is not carried out by states themselves. Recall from Chapter 2 that the state is commonly defined as the monopoly of violence over a territory. States use this force at the domestic level to generate stability through such institutions as the law and police. At the international level, armies and diplomacy help generate peace. But, at times, the monopoly of force may escape state control, as in the case of revolutions and terrorism.

In some circumstances, the public may seek to overthrow the current regime through revolution. Theda Skocpol transformed political science with her piece, "France, Russia, China: A Structural Analysis of Social Revolutions" (1976). Expanded in her 1979 book States and Social Revolutions, *Skocpol's thinking on revolution contributed to political science by returning our attention to the state, and* States and Social Revolutions *went on to become one of the most cited works in the field. Why do revolutions, sweeping transformations in existing regime and state institutions, occur? In each case, Skocpol believes that a particular set of conditions in the state and society is necessary to set such revolutions in motion. Her analysis, influenced by Marx, is "structural." That is to say, institutions are central (if not decisive) in shaping the likelihood for dramatic political change.*

Whereas Skocpol emphasizes the importance of institutions in bringing about revolution, Martha Crenshaw's 1981 piece, "The Causes of Terrorism," focuses more on the individual motivations that lead people to resort to terrorist acts. Crenshaw notes that certain structural preconditions can foster terrorism, but this is not enough. Central is the role of a minority or elite group, their grievances and perceived lack of alternatives, and the internal culture they foster. Where Skocpol portrays revolutions as events in which people (even leaders) play a relatively small role, empowered by larger institutional conditions, Crenshaw emphasizes the role of individual and group motivation in carrying out terrorist acts. Overall, it is worth asking oneself how well Crenshaw's work, written twenty years before the attacks of September 11, remains useful in helping us understand current terrorist threats.

*If Skocpol helps us to understand the structural sources of political vio-
lence, and Crenshaw the individual factors, then Buruma and Margalit's "Occidentalism" (2002) helps us to understand the role of ideas and ideology in
these conflicts. Their notion of "Occidentalism" is a hatred of modernity and
the West for its emphasis on materialism, individualism, and the mediocrity
that mass-democratic life inevitably produces. These anti-Western views are
not new, nor did they originate in the Middle East or Islam. Rather, they
emerged from within the West itself in reaction to modernization, and they
can be found at the core of earlier fascist and communist ideologies. The current struggle against terrorism can thus be seen as simply a new variant of an
ongoing struggle against modernity.*

*Our last piece places the discussion of political violence in more specific
context. Sheri Berman's scholarship (2003) has in part focused on the place
of organized political life outside of the state, or what we commonly refer to
as civil society. In this she has provided a useful counterpoint to Putnam's
views on social capital, which have emphasized the need for participation and
organization to sustain democracy in the long run (see Chapter 5). In contrast, Berman has argued that where states are unable to effectively "process"
the demands of civil society, the result can be a threat to the state itself. In
parts of the Middle East, Islamist groups have become a central part of civil
society, fulfilling a role that that state or other groups have failed to play.
This, she argues, may be setting the stage for Islamist revolutions that are
peaceful and incremental, but no less profound.*

THEDA SKOCPOL

FRANCE, RUSSIA, CHINA: A STRUCTURAL
ANALYSIS OF SOCIAL REVOLUTIONS

A revolution," writes Samuel P. Huntington
in *Political Order in Changing Societies*, "is
a rapid, fundamental, and violent domestic

From *Comparative Studies in Society and History*, 18,
no. 2 (April 1976), pp. 175–203. Some of the author's
notes have been omitted.

change in the dominant values and myths of a
society, in its political institutions, social structure, leadership, and government activities
and policies."[1] In *The Two Tactics of Social Democracy in the Democratic Revolution*, Lenin
provides a different, but complementary perspective: "Revolutions," he says, "are the festivals

of the oppressed and the exploited. At no other time are the masses of the people in a position to come forward so actively as creators of a new social order."[2]

Together these two quotes delineate the distinctive features of *social revolutions*. As Huntington points out, social revolutions are rapid, basic transformations of socio-economic and political institutions, and—as Lenin so vividly reminds us—social revolutions are accompanied and in part effectuated through class upheavals from below. It is this combination of thoroughgoing structural transformation and massive class upheavals that sets social revolutions apart from coups, rebellions, and even political revolutions and national independence movements.

If one adopts such a specific definition, then clearly only a handful of successful social revolutions have ever occurred. France, 1789, Russia, 1917, and China, 1911–49, are the most dramatic and clear-cut instances. Yet these momentous upheavals have helped shape the fate of the majority of mankind, and their causes, consequences, and potentials have preoccupied many thoughtful people since the late eighteenth century.

Nevertheless, recently, social scientists have evidenced little interest in the study of social revolutions as such. They have submerged revolutions within more general categories—such as "political violence," "collective behavior," "internal war," or "deviance"—shorn of historical specificity and concern with large-scale social change.[3] The focus has been mostly on styles of behavior common to wide ranges of collective incidents (ranging from riots to coups to revolutions, from panics to hostile outbursts to "value-oriented movements," and from ideological sects to revolutionary parties), any of which might occur in any type of society at any time or place. Revolutions tend increasingly to be viewed not as "locomotives of history," but as extreme forms of one or another sort of behavior that social scientists, along with established authorities everywhere, find problematic and perturbing.

Why this avoidance by social science of the specific problem of social revolution? Ideological bias might be invoked as an explanation, but even if it were involved, it would not suffice. An earlier generation of American social scientists, certainly no more politically radical than the present generation, employed the "natural history" approach to analyze handfuls of cases of great revolutions.[4] In large part, present preoccupation with broader categories can be understood as a reaction against this natural history approach, deemed by its critics too "historical" and "a-theoretical."

In the "Introduction" to a 1964 book entitled *Internal War*, Harry Eckstein defines "a theoretical subject" as a "set of phenomena about which one can develop informative, testable generalizations that hold for all instances of the subject, and some of which apply to those instances alone."[5] He goes on to assert that while "a statement about two or three cases is certainly a generalization in the dictionary sense, a generalization in the methodological sense must usually be based on more; it ought to cover a number of cases large enough for certain rigorous testing procedures like statistical analysis to be used."[6] Even many social scientists who are not statistically oriented would agree with the spirit of this statement: theory in social science should concern itself only with general phenomena; the "unique" should be relegated to "narrative historians."

Apparently it directly follows that no theory specific to social revolution is possible, that the *explanandum* of any theory which sheds light on social revolutions must be something more general than social revolution itself. Hence the efforts to conceptualize revolution as an extreme instance of patterns of belief or behavior which are also present in other situations or events.

This approach, however, allows considerations of technique to define away substantive problems. Revolutions are not just extreme forms of individual or collective behavior. They are distinctive conjunctures of socio-historical structures and processes. One must comprehend them as complex wholes—however few the cases—or not at all.

Fortunately social science is not devoid of a way of confronting this kind of problem. Social revolutions *can* be treated as a "theoretical subject." To test hypotheses about them, one may employ the comparative method, with national historical trajectories as the units of comparison. As many students of society have noted, the comparative method is nothing but that mode of multivariate analysis to which sociologists necessarily resort when experimental manipulations are not possible and when there are "too many variables and not enough cases"—that is, not enough cases for statistical testing of hypotheses.[7] According to this method, one looks for concomitant variations, contrasting cases where the phenomena in which one is interested are present with cases where they are absent, controlling in the process for as many sources of variation as one can, by contrasting positive and negative instances which otherwise are as similar as possible.

Thus, in my inquiry into the conditions for the occurrence and short-term outcomes of the great historical social revolutions in France, Russia and China, I have employed the comparative historical method, specifically contrasting the positive cases with (a) instances of non-social revolutionary modernization, such as occurred in Japan, Germany and Russia (up to 1904), and with (b) instances of abortive social revolutions, in particular Russia in 1905 and Prussia/Germany in 1848. These comparisons have helped me to understand those aspects of events and of structures and processes which distinctively rendered the French, Chinese and Russian Revolutions successful social revolutions. In turn, the absence of conditions identified as positively crucial in France, Russia and China constitutes equally well an explanation of why social revolutions have not occurred, or have failed, in other societies. In this way, hypotheses developed, refined, and tested in the comparative historical analysis of a handful of cases achieve a potentially general significance.

Explaining the Historical Cases: Revolution in Modernizing Agrarian Bureaucracies

Social revolutions in France, Russia and China occurred, during the earlier world-historical phases of modernization, in agrarian bureaucratic societies situated within, or newly incorporated into, international fields dominated by more economically modern nations abroad. In each case, social revolution was a conjuncture of three developments: (1) the collapse or incapacitation of central administrative and military machineries; (2) widespread peasant rebellions; and (3) marginal elite political movements. What each social revolution minimally "accomplished" was the extreme rationalization and centralization of state institutions, the removal of a traditional landed upper class from intermediate (regional and local) quasi-political supervision of the peasantry, and the elimination or diminution of the economic power of a landed upper class.

In the pages that follow, I shall attempt to explain the three great historical social revolutions, first, by discussing the institutional characteristics of agrarian states, and their special vulnerabilities and potentialities during the earlier world-historical phases of modernization, and second, by pointing to the peculiar characteristics of old regimes in France, Russia and China, which made them uniquely vulnerable among the earlier modernizing agrarian states to social-revolutionary transformations. Finally, I shall suggest reasons for similarities and differences in the outcomes of the great historical social revolutions.

An agrarian bureaucracy is an agricultural society in which social control rests on a division of labor and a coordination of effort between a semi-bureaucratic state and a landed upper class.[8] The landed upper class typically retains, as an adjunct to its landed property, considerable (though varying in different cases) undifferentiated local and regional authority over the peasant majority of the population. The partially bureaucratic central state extracts taxes and labor from peasants either indirectly through landlord intermediaries or else directly, but with (at least minimal) reliance upon cooperation from individuals of the landed upper class. In turn, the landed upper class relies upon the backing of a coercive state to extract rents and/or dues from the peasantry. At the political center, autocrat, bureaucracy, and army monopolize decisions, yet (in varying degrees and modes) accommodate the regional and local power of the landed upper class and (again, to varying degrees) recruit individual members of this class into leading positions in the state system.

Agrarian bureaucracies are inherently vulnerable to peasant rebellions. Subject to claims on their surpluses, and perhaps their labor, by landlords and state agents, peasants chronically resent both. To the extent that the agrarian economy is commercialized, merchants are also targets of peasant hostility. In all agrarian bureaucracies at all times, and in France, Russia and China in non-revolutionary times, peasants have had grievances enough to warrant, and recurrently spur, rebellions. Economic crises (which are endemic in semi-commercial agrarian economies anyway) and/or increased demands from above for rents or taxes might substantially enhance the likelihood of rebellions at particular times. But such events ought to be treated as short-term precipitants of peasant unrest, not fundamental underlying causes.

Modernization is best conceived not only as an *intra*societal process of economic development accompanied by lagging or leading changes in non-economic institutional spheres, but also as a world-historic *inter*societal phenomenon. Thus,

> a necessary condition of a society's modernization is its incorporation into the historically unique network of societies that arose first in Western Europe in early modern times and today encompasses enough of the globe's population for the world to be viewed for some purposes as if it consisted of a single network of societies.[9]

Of course, societies have always interacted. What was special about the modernizing intersocietal network that arose in early modern Europe was, first, that it was based upon trade in commodities and manufactures, as well as upon strategic politico-military competition between independent states,[10] and, second, that it incubated the "first (self-propelling) industrialization" of England after she had gained commercial hegemony within the Western European-centered world market.[11]

In the wake of that first commercial-industrial breakthrough, modernizing pressures have reverberated throughout the world. In the first phase of world modernization, England's thoroughgoing commercialization, capture of world market hegemony, and expansion of manufactures (both before and after the technological Industrial Revolution which began in the 1780s), transformed means and stakes in the traditional rivalries of European states and put immediate pressure for reforms, if only to facilitate the financing of competitive armies and navies, upon the other European states and especially upon the ones with less efficient fiscal machineries.[12] In the second phase, as Europe modernized and further expanded its influence around the globe, similar militarily compelling pressures were brought to bear on those non-European societies which escaped immediate colonization, usually the ones with pre-existing differentiated and centralized state institutions.

During these phases of global modernization, independent responses to the dilemmas posed by incorporation into a modernizing world were possible and (in some sense) necessary for governmental elites in agrarian bureaucracies. Demands for more and more efficiently collected taxes; for better and more generously and continuously financed militaries; and for "guided" national economic development, imitating the available foreign models, were voiced within these societies especially by bureaucrats and the educated middle strata. The demands were made compelling by international military competition and threats. At the same time, governmental leaders did have administrative machineries, however rudimentary, at their disposal for the implementation of whatever modernizing reforms seemed necessary and feasible (at given moments in world history). And their countries had not been incorporated into dependent economic and political positions in a world stratification system dominated by a few fully industrialized giants.

But agrarian bureaucracies faced enormous difficulties in meeting the crises of modernization. Governmental leaders' realm of autonomous action tended to be severely limited, because few fiscal or economic reforms could be undertaken which did not encroach upon the advantages of the traditional landed upper classes which constituted the major social base of support for the authority and functions of the state in agrarian bureaucracies. Only so much revenue could be squeezed out of the peasantry, and yet landed upper classes could often raise formidable obstacles to rationalization of tax systems. Economic development might mean more tax revenues and enhanced military prowess, yet it channelled wealth and manpower away from the agrarian sector. Finally, the mobilization of mass popular support for war tended to undermine the traditional, local authority of landlords or landed bureaucrats upon which agrarian bureaucratic societies partly relied for the social control of the peasantry.

Agrarian bureaucracies could not indefinitely "ignore" the very specific crises, in particular fiscal and martial, that grew out of involvement with a modernizing world, yet they could not adapt without undergoing fundamental structural changes. Social revolution helped accomplish "necessary" changes in some but was averted by reform or "revolution from above" in others. Relative stagnation, accompanied by subincorporation into international power spheres, was still another possibility (e.g., Portugal, Spain?). Social revolution was never deliberately "chosen." Societies only "backed into" social revolutions.

All modernizing agrarian bureaucracies have peasants with grievances and face the unavoidable challenges posed by modernization abroad. So, in some sense, potential for social revolution has been built into all modernizing agrarian bureaucracies. Yet, only a handful have succumbed. Why? A major part of the answer, I believe, lies in the insight that "not oppression, but weakness, breeds revolution."[13] It is the breakdown of a societal mode of social control which allows and prompts social revolution to unfold. In the historical cases of France, Russia and China, the unfolding of social revolution depended upon the emergence of revolutionary crises occasioned by the incapacitation of administrative and military organizations. That incapacitation, in turn, is best explained not as a function of mass discontent and mobilization, but as a function of a combination of pressures on state institutions from more modernized countries abroad, and (in two cases out of three) built-in structural incapacities to mobilize increased resources in response to those pressures. France, Russia and China were also special among all agrarian bureaucracies in that their agrarian institutions afforded peasants not only the usual grievances against landlords and state agents but also "structural space" for autonomous collective insurrection. Finally, once administrative/military breakdown occurred in agrarian bureaucracies with such especially insurrection-prone peasantries, then, and only then, could organized revolutionary leaderships have great impact upon their societies' development—though not necessarily in the ways they originally envisaged.

Breakdown of Societal Controls: Foreign Pressures and Administrative/Military Collapse

If a fundamental cause and the crucial trigger for the historical social revolutions was the incapacitation of administrative and military machineries in modernizing agrarian bureaucracies, then how and why did this occur in France, Russia and China? What differentiated these agrarian bureaucracies which succumbed to social revolution from others which managed to respond to modernizing pressures with reforms from above? Many writers attribute differences in response to qualities of will or ability in governmental leaders. From a sociological point of view, a more satisfying approach might focus on the interaction between (a) the magnitude of foreign pressures brought to bear on a modernizing agrarian bureaucracy, and (b) the particular structural characteristics of such societies that underlay contrasting performances by leaders responding to foreign pressures and internal unrest.

Overwhelming foreign pressures on an agrarian bureaucracy could cut short even a generally successful government program of reforms and industrialization "from above." Russia is the obvious case in point. From at least the 1890s onward, the Czarist regime was committed to rapid industrialization, initially government-financed out of resources squeezed from the peasantry, as the only means of rendering Russia militarily competitive with Western nations. Alexander Gerschenkron argues that initial government programs to promote heavy industry had succeeded in the 1890s to such an extent that, when the government was forced to reduce its direct financial and administrative role after 1904, Russia's industrial sector was nevertheless capable of autonomously generating further growth (with the aid of foreign capital investments).[14] Decisive steps to modernize agriculture and free peasant labor for permanent urban migration were taken after the unsuccessful Revolution of 1905.[15] Had she been able to sit out World War I, Russia might have recapitulated the German experience of industrialization facilitated by bureaucratic guidance.

But participation in World War I forced Russia to fully mobilize her population including her restive peasantry. Army officers and men were subjected to years of costly fighting, and civilians to mounting economic privations—all

for nought. For, given Russia's "industrial backwardness . . . enhanced by the fact that Russia was very largely blockaded . . . ," plus the "inferiority of the Russian military machine to the German in everything but sheer numbers . . . , military defeat, with all of its inevitable consequences for the internal condition of the country, was very nearly a foregone conclusion."[16] The result was administrative demoralization and paralysis, and the disintegration of the army. Urban insurrections which brought first middle-strata moderates and then the Bolsheviks to power could not be suppressed, owing to the newly-recruited character and war weariness of the urban garrisons.[17] Peasant grievances were enhanced, young peasant men were politicized through military experiences, and, in consequence, spreading peasant insurrections from the spring of 1917 on could not be controlled.

It is instructive to compare 1917 to the Revolution of 1905. Trotsky called 1905 a "dress rehearsal" for 1917, and, indeed, many of the same social forces with the same grievances and similar political programs took part in each revolutionary drama. *What accounts for the failure of the Revolution of 1905 was the Czarist regime's ultimate ability to rely upon the army to repress popular disturbances.* Skillful tactics were involved: the regime bought time to organize repression and assure military loyalty with well-timed liberal concessions embodied in the October Manifesto of 1905 (and later largely retracted). Yet, it was of crucial importance that the futile 1904–05 war with Japan was, in comparison with the World War I morass, circumscribed, geographically peripheral, less demanding of resources and manpower, and quickly concluded once defeat was apparent.[18] The peace treaty was signed by late 1905, leaving the Czarist government free to bring military reinforcements back from the Far East into European Russia.

The Russian Revolution occurred in 1917 because Russia was too inextricably entangled with foreign powers, friend and foe, economically and militarily more powerful than she. Foreign entanglement must be considered not only to explain the administrative and military incapacitation of 1917, but also entry into World War I. That involvement cannot be considered "accidental." Nor was it "voluntary" in the same sense as Russia's entry into the 1904 war with Japan.[19] Whatever leadership "blunders" were involved, the fact remains that in 1914 both the Russian state and the Russian economy depended heavily on Western loans and capital. Moreover, Russia was an established part of the European state system and could not remain neutral in a conflict that engulfed the whole of that system.[20]

Foreign pressures and involvements so inescapable and overwhelming as those that faced Russia in 1917 constitute an extreme case for the earlier modernizing agrarian bureaucracies we are considering here. For France and China the pressures were surely no more compelling than those faced by agrarian bureaucracies such as Japan, Germany and Russia (1858–1914) which successfully adapted through reforms from above that facilitated the extraordinary mobilization of resources for economic and military development. Why were the Bourbon and Manchu regimes unable to adapt? Were there structural blocks to effective response? First, let me discuss some general characteristics of all agrarian states, and then point to a peculiar structural characteristic shared by Bourbon France and Manchu China which I believe explains these regimes' inability to meet snow-balling crises of modernization until at last their feeble attempts triggered administrative and military disintegration, hence revolutionary crises.

Weber's ideal type of bureaucracy may be taken as an imaginary model of what might logically be the most effective means of purposively organizing social power. According to the ideal type, fully developed bureaucracy involves the existence of an hierarchically arrayed officialdom, where officials are oriented to superior authority in a disciplined manner because they are dependent for jobs, livelihood, status and career-advancement on resources and decisions channeled through that superior authority. But in preindustrial states, monarchs found it difficult to channel sufficient resources through the "center" to pay simultaneously for wars, culture and court life on the one hand, and a fully bureaucratic officialdom on the other. Consequently, they often had to make do with "officials" recruited from wealthy backgrounds, frequently, in practice, landlords. In addition, central state jurisdiction rarely touched local peasants or communities directly; governmental functions were often delegated to landlords in their "private" capacities, or else to non-bureaucratic authoritative organizations run by local landlords.

Inherent in all agrarian bureaucratic regimes were tensions between, on the one hand, state elites interested in preserving, using, and extending the powers of armies and administrative organizations and, on the other hand, landed upper classes interested in defending locally and regionally based social networks, influence over peasants, and powers and privileges associated with the control of land and agrarian surpluses. Such tensions were likely to be exacerbated once the agrarian bureaucracy was forced to adapt to modernization abroad because foreign military pressures gave cause, while foreign economic development offered incentives and models, for state elites to attempt reforms which went counter to the class interests of traditional, landed upper strata. Yet there were important variations in the ability of semi-bureaucratic agrarian states to respond to modernizing pressures with reforms which sharply and quickly increased resources at the disposal of central authorities. What can account for the differences in response?

*   *   *

The Manchu Dynasty proved unable to mobilize resources sufficient to meet credibly the challenges posed by involvement in the modernizing world. "[T]he problem was not merely the very real one of the inadequate resources of the Chinese economy as a whole. In large measure the financial straits in which the Peking government found itself were due to . . . [inability to] command such financial capacity as there was in its empire."[21] Part of the explanation for this inability lay in a characteristic which the Chinese state shared with other agrarian states: lower and middle level officials were recruited from the landed gentry, paid insufficient salaries, and allowed to engage in a certain amount of "normal" corruption, withholding revenues collected as taxes from higher authorities.[22] Yet, if the Manchu Dynasty had encountered the forces of modernization at the height of its powers (say in the early eighteenth century) rather than during its declining phase, it might have controlled or been able to mobilize sufficient resources to finance modern industries and equip a centrally controlled modern army. In that case, officials would never have been allowed to serve in their home provinces, and thus local and regional groups of gentry would have lacked institutional support for concerted opposition against central initiatives. But, as it happened, the Manchu Dynasty was forced to try to cope with wave after wave of imperialist intrusions, engineered by foreign industrial or industrializing nations anxious to tap Chinese markets and finances, immediately after a series of massive mid-nineteenth-century peasant rebellions. The Dynasty had been unable to put down the Taiping Rebellion on its own, and the task had fallen instead to local, gentry-led, self-defense associations and to regional armies led by complexly interrelated gentry who had access to village resources and recruits. In consequence of the gentry's role in putting down rebellion, governmental powers formerly accruing to central authorities or their bureaucratic agents, including, crucially, rights to collect and allocate various taxes, devolved upon local, gentry-dominated, subdistrict governing associations and upon provincial armies and officials increasingly aligned with the provincial gentry against the center.[23]

Unable to force resources from local and regional authorities, it was all Peking could do simply to meet foreign indebtedness, and after 1895 even that proved impossible.

Throughout the period from 1874 to 1894, the ministry [of Revenue in Peking] was engaged in a series of largely unsuccessful efforts to raise funds in order to meet a continuing series of crises—the dispute over Ili with Russia, the Sino-French War [1885], floods and famines, the Sino-Japanese War [1895]. . . . After 1895 the triple pressure of indemnity payments, servicing foreign loans, and military expenditures totally wrecked the rough balance between income and outlay which Peking had maintained [with the aid of foreign loans] until that time.[24]

The Boxer Rebellion of 1900, and subsequent foreign military intervention, only further exacerbated an already desperate situation.

Attempts by dynastic authorities to remedy matters through a series of "reforms" implemented after 1900—abolishing the Confucian educational system and encouraging modern schools;[25] organizing the so-called "New Armies" (which actually formed around the nuclei of the old provincial armies);[26] transferring local governmental functions to provincial bureaus;[27] and creating a series of local and provincial gentry-dominated representative assemblies[28]—only exacerbated the sorry situation, right up to the 1911 breaking point. "Reform destroyed the reforming government."[29] With each reform, dynastic elites thought to create powers to counterbalance entrenched obstructive forces, but new officials and functions were repeatedly absorbed into pre-existing local and (especially) regional cliques of gentry.[30] The last series of reforms, those that created representative assemblies, ironically provided cliques of gentry with legitimate representative organs from which to launch the liberal, decentralizing "Constitutionalist movement" against the Manchus.

What ultimately precipitated the "revolution of 1911" was a final attempt at reform by the central government, one that directly threatened the financial interests of the gentry power groups for the purpose of strengthening central government finances and control over national economic development:

The specific incident that precipitated the Revolution of 1911 was the central government's decision to buy up a [railroad] line in Szechwan in which the local gentry had invested heavily. . . . The Szechwan uprising, led by the moderate constitutionalists of the Railway Protection League, sparked widespread disturbances that often had no connection with the railway issue. . . .[31]

Conspiratorial groups affiliated with Sun Yat Sen's T'eng Meng Hui, and mainly composed of Western-educated students and middle-rank New Army officers, joined the fray to produce a series of military uprisings. Finally,

> . . . the lead in declaring the independence of one province after another was taken by two principal elements: the military governors who commanded the New Army forces and the gentry-official-merchant leaders of the provincial assemblies. These elements had more power and were more conservative than the youthful revolutionarists of the T'eng Meng Hui.[32]

The Chinese "Revolution of 1911" irremediably destroyed the integument of civilian elite ties—traditionally maintained by the operation of Confucian educational institutions and the central bureaucracy's policies for recruiting and deploying educated officials so as to strengthen "cosmopolitan" orientations at the expense of local loyalties—which had until that time provided at least the semblance of unified governance for China. "Warlord" rivalries ensued as gentry interests attached themselves to regional military machines, and this condition of intra-elite disunity and rivalry (only imperfectly and temporarily overcome by Chiang Kai-Shek's regime between 1927 and 1937)[33] condemned China to incessant turmoils and provided openings (as well as cause) for lower-class, especially peasant, rebellions and for Communist attempts to organize and channel popular unrest.

Peasant Insurrections

If administrative and military breakdown in a modernizing agrarian bureaucracy were to inaugurate social revolutionary transformations, rather than merely an interregnum of intra-elite

squabbling, then widespread popular revolts had to coincide with and take advantage of the hiatus of governmental supervision and sanctions. Urban insurrections provided indispensable support during revolutionary interregnums to radical political elites vying against other elites for state power: witness the Parisian *sans culottes'* support for the Jacobins;[34] the Chinese workers' support for the Communists (between 1920 and 1927);[35] and the Russian industrial workers' support for the Bolsheviks. But fundamentally more important in determining final outcomes were the peasant insurrections which in France, Russia and China constituted irreversible attacks on the powers and privileges of the traditional landed upper classes.

Agrarian bureaucracy has been the only historical variety of complex society with differentiated, centralized government that has, in certain instances, incubated a lower-class stratum that was *simultaneously strategic* in the society's economy and polity (as surplus producer, payer of rents and taxes, and as provider of corvée and military manpower), and yet *organizationally autonomous* enough to allow the "will" and "tactical space" for collective insurrection against basic structural arrangements.

How have certain agrarian bureaucracies exemplified such special propensity to peasant rebellion? As Eric Wolf has pointed out, "ultimately, the decisive factor in making a peasant rebellion possible lies in the relation of the peasantry to the field of power which surrounds it. A rebellion cannot start from a situation of complete impotence. . . ."[36] If they are to act upon, rather than silently suffer, their omnipresent grievances, peasants must have "internal leverage" or "tactical mobility." They have this to varying degrees according to their position in the total agrarian social structure. Institutional patterns which relate peasants to landlords and peasants to each other seem to be the co-determinants of degrees of peasant "tactical mobility." Sheer amounts of property held by peasants gain significance only within institutional contexts. If peasants are to be capable of self-initiated rebellion against landlords and state officials, they must have (a) some institutionally based collective solidarity, and (b) autonomy from direct, day-to-day supervision and control by landlords in their work and leisure activities. Agricultural regimes featuring large estates worked by serfs or laborers tend to be inimical to peasant rebellion—witness the East Elbian Junker regime[37]—but the reason is not that serfs and landless laborers are economically poor, rather that they are subject to close and constant supervision and discipline by landlords or their agents. If large-estate agriculture is lacking, an agrarian bureaucracy may still be relatively immune to widespread peasant rebellion if landlords control sanctioning machineries,[38] such as militias and poor relief agencies, at local levels. On the other hand, landlords as a class, and the "system" as a whole, will be relatively vulnerable to peasant rebellion if: (a) sanctioning machineries are centralized; (b) agricultural work and peasant social life are controlled by peasant families and communities themselves. These conditions prevailed in France and Russia and meant that, with the incapacitation of central administrative and military bureaucracies, these societies became susceptible to the spread and intensification of peasant revolts which in more normal circumstances could have been contained and repressed.

It is worth emphasizing that peasant actions in revolutions are not intrinsically different from peasant actions in "mere" rebellions or riots. When peasants "rose" during historical social revolutionary crises, they did so in highly traditional rebellious patterns: bread riots, "defense" of communal lands or customary rights, riots against "hoarding" merchants or landlords, "social banditry." Peasants initially drew upon traditional cultural themes to justify rebellion. Far from becoming revolutionaries through adoption of a radical vision of a desired new society, "revolutionary" peasants have typically been "backward-looking" rebels incorporated by circumstances beyond their control into political

processes occurring independently of them, at the societal "center."[39]

*   *   *

Historians agree that the Russian Emancipation of the serfs in 1861, intended by the Czar as a measure to stabilize the agrarian situation, actually enhanced the rebellious potential of the ex-serfs. Heavy redemption payments and inadequate land allotments fuelled peasant discontent. More important, legal reinforcement of the *obshchina*'s (peasant commune's) authority over families and individuals fettered ever-increasing numbers of peasants to the inadequate lands, reinforced collective solidarity, retarded the internal class differentiation of the peasantry, and left communes largely free to run their own affairs subject only to the collective fulfillment of financial obligations to the state.[40] Estate owners were deprived of most direct authority over peasant communities.[41]

Not surprisingly, given this agrarian situation, widespread peasant rebellions erupted in Russia in 1905, when the Czarist regime simultaneously confronted defeat abroad and an anti-autocratic movement of the middle classes, the liberal gentry, and the working classes at home. "Economic hardship created a need for change; peasant tradition, as well as revolutionary propaganda, suggested the remedy [i.e., attacks on landlords and land seizures]; official preoccupation and indecisiveness invited the storm; and soon the greatest disturbance since the days of Pugachev was under way."[42]

In the wake of the unsuccessful Revolution of 1905, the Czarist regime abandoned its policy of shoring up the peasant commune. It undertook the break-up of repartitional lands into private holdings and implemented measures to facilitate land sales by poorer peasants and purchases by richer ones.[43] Between 1905 and 1917, these measures, in tandem with general economic developments, did something to alleviate agrarian stagnation, promote permanent rural migration to urban industrial areas, and increase class differentiation and individualism in the countryside.[44] However, by 1917, little enough had been accomplished—only one-tenth of all peasant families had been resettled on individual holdings[45]—that peasant communities engaged in solidary actions against both landlords and any rich peasant "separators" who did not join their struggle.

"Any shrewd observer of Russian conditions who weighed the lessons of the agrarian disorders of 1905 could have foreseen that a breakdown of central power and authority was almost certain to bring an even greater upheaval in its train."[46] And, indeed, between the spring and the autumn of 1917, "side by side with the mutiny of the Russian army marched a second great social revolutionary movement: the seizure of the landed estates by the peasantry."[47]

> The peasant movement of 1917 was primarily a drive of the peasantry against the *pomyeschik* class. Among the cases of agrarian disturbance, violent and peaceful, 4,954, overwhelming the largest number, were directed against landlords, as against 324 against the more well-to-do peasants, 235 against the Government and 211 against the clergy.[48]

> The broad general result of the wholesale peasant land seizure of 1917 was a sweeping levelling in Russian agriculture. The big latifundia, even the small estate, ceased to exist. On the other hand landless or nearly landless peasants obtained larger allotments.[49]

For the peasants simply applied traditional communal repartitional procedures to lands seized from the landlords. Their revolt, together with the Bolsheviks' victory, ". . . sealed forever the doom of the old landed aristocracy."[50]

The Chinese case presents decisive contrasts with France and Russia but nevertheless confirms our general insight about the importance of structurally conditioned "tactical space" for peasant insurrection as a crucial factor in the translation of administrative/military breakdown into social revolution.

Except in infertile and marginal highland areas, Chinese peasants, though mostly family smallholders or tenants,[51] did not live in their own village communities clearly apart from landlords.

> The Chinese peasant . . . was a member of two communities: his village and the marketing system to which his village belonged ["typically including fifteen to twenty-five villages . . ." dependent on one of 45,000 market towns]. An important feature of the larger marketing community was its elaborate system of stratification. . . . Those who provided *de facto* leadership within the marketing community *qua* political system and those who gave it collective representation at its interface with larger polities were gentrymen—landed, leisured, and literate. . . . It was artisans, merchants, and other full-time economic specialists, not peasants, who sustained the heartbeat of periodic marketing that kept the community alive. It was priests backed by gentry temple managers . . . who gave religious meaning to peasants' local world.[52]

Voluntary associations, and clans where they flourished, were likewise contained within marketing communities, headed and economically sustained by gentry. Thus kinship, associational and clientage ties cut across class distinctions between peasants and landlords in traditional China. Gentry controlled at local levels a variety of sanctioning machineries, including militias and other organizations which functioned *de facto* as channels of poor relief.[53]

Not surprisingly, therefore, settled Chinese peasant agriculturalists did not initiate class-based revolts against landlords, either in premodern or in revolutionary (1911–49) times. Instead, peasant rebellion manifested itself in the form of accelerating rural, violence and social banditry, spreading outward from the mountainous "border areas" at the edges of the empire or at the intersections of provincial boundaries. Social banditry invariably blossomed during periods of central administrative weakness or collapse and economic deflation and catastrophe. Precisely because normal traditional Chinese agrarian-class relations were significantly commercialized, local prosperity depended upon overall administrative stability, and peasants were not cushioned against economic dislocations by kin or village communal ties. During periods of dynastic decline, local (marketing) communities "closed in" upon themselves normatively, economically, and coercively,[54] and poorer peasants, especially in communities without well-to-do local landed elites, lost property and livelihood, and were forced to migrate. Such impoverished migrants often congregated as bandits or smugglers operating out of "border area" bases and raiding settled communities. Ultimately they might provide (individual or group) recruits for rebel armies led by marginal elites vying for imperial power.[55]

The nineteenth and the first half of the twentieth centuries constituted a period of dynastic decline and interregnum in China, complicated in quite novel ways by Western and Japanese economic and military intrusions. Peasant impoverishment, local community closure, spreading social banditry and military conflicts among local militias, bandit groups, and warlord and/or "ideological" armies, characterized the entire time span, and peaked during the mid-nineteenth and mid-twentieth centuries.

The Communist movement originated as a political tendency among a tiny fraction of China's nationalist and pro-modern intellectual stratum and created its first mass base among Chinese industrial workers concentrated in the treaty ports and to a lesser degree among students and southeast Chinese peasants. But after 1927, the Chinese Communists were forced out of China's cities and wealthier agrarian regions by Kuomintang military and police repression. Would-be imitators of the Bolsheviks were thus forced to come to terms with the Chinese agrarian situation. This they did initially (between 1927 and 1942) by recapitulating the experiences and tactics of traditional rebel elite contenders for imperial power in China. Scattered, disorganized and disoriented Communist leaders, along with military units (which had split off from KMT or warlord armies) of varying degrees of loyalty, retreated to mountainous border areas, there often to ally with already existing bandit groups.[56] Gradually the fruits of raiding expedi-

tions, plus the division and weakness of opposing armies, allowed the "Communist" base areas to expand into administrative regions.

Only after a secure and stable administrative region had finally been established in Northwest China (after 1937) could the Communists finally turn to the intra-market-area and intra-village political organizing that ultimately bypassed and then eliminated the gentry, and so made their drive for power unique in China's history. Before roughly 1940, ideological appeals, whether "Communist" or "Nationalist" played little role in mediating Communist elites' relations to peasants, and spontaneous class struggle, fuelled from below, played virtually no role in achieving whatever (minimal) changes in agrarian class *relations* were accomplished in Communist base areas.[57] To be sure, ideology was important in integrating the Party, an elite organization, and in mediating its relationship with the Red Army. But until Party and Army established relatively secure and stable military and administrative control over a region, Communist cadres were not in a position to penetrate local communities in order to provide organization, leadership, and encouragement for peasants themselves to expropriate land. This finally occurred in North China in the 1940s.[58] Once provided with military and organizational protection from landlord sanctions and influence, peasants often reacted against landlords with a fury that exceeded even what Party policy desired. Perhaps Communist ideological appeals were partially responsible for peasant insurrection. More likely, even at this stage, the Communist organizations' important input to local situations was not a sense of grievances, or their ideological articulation, but rather simply *protection* from traditional social controls: William Hinton's classic *Fanshen: A Documentary of Revolution in a Chinese Village* vividly supports such an interpretation.[59]

Even to gain the military strength they needed to defeat the Kuomintang, the Chinese Communists had to shove aside—or encourage and allow peasants to shove aside—the traditional landed upper class and establish a more direct link to the Chinese peasantry than had ever before been established between an extra-local Chinese rebel movement and local communities.[60] The Chinese Communists also established more direct links to peasants than did radical elites in Russia or France. The Chinese Revolution, at least in its closing stages, thus has more of the aspect of an elite/mass movement than the other great historical social revolutions. Yet the reasons for this peasant mass-mobilizing aspect have little to do with revolutionary ideology (except in retrospect) and everything to do with the "peculiarities" (from a European perspective) of the Chinese agrarian social structure. That structure did not afford settled Chinese peasants institutional autonomy and solidarity against landlords, yet it did, in periods of political-economic crisis, generate marginal poor-peasant outcasts whose activities exacerbated the crises and whose existence provided potential bases of support for oppositional elite-led rebellions or, in the twentieth-century world context, a revolutionary movement. Thus Chinese Communist activities after 1927 and ultimate triumph in 1949 depended directly upon *both* the insurrectionary potentials and the blocks to peasant insurrection built into the traditional Chinese social structure.

Radical Political Movements and Centralizing Outcomes

Although peasant insurrections played a decisive role in each of the great historical social revolutions, nevertheless an exclusive focus on peasants—or on the peasant situation in agrarian bureaucracies—cannot provide a complete explanation for the occurrence of social revolutions, Russia and China were recurrently rocked by massive peasant rebellions,[61] yet peasant uprisings did not fuel structural transformations until the late eighteenth century and after. Obviously agrarian bureaucracies were exposed to additional and unique strains and possibilities once English and then European commercializa-

tion-industrialization became a factor in world history and development. The stage was set for the entry of marginal elites animated by radical nationalist goals.

Who were these marginal elites? What sectors of society provided the social bases for nationalist radicalisms? *Not* the bourgeoisie proper: merchants, financiers and industrialists. These groups have had surprisingly little *direct* effect upon the politics of modernization in any developing nation, from England to the countries of the Third World today. Instead, their activities, commerce and manufacturing, have created and continuously transformed, indeed revolutionized, the national and international *contexts* within which bureaucrats, professionals, politicians, landlords, peasants, and proletarians have engaged in the decisive political struggles. To be sure, in certain times and places, the "bourgeois" commercial or industrial context has been pervasive enough virtually to determine political outcomes, even without the overt political participation of bourgeois actors. But such was not the case in the earlier modernizing agrarian bureaucracies, including France, Russia and China.

Instead, nationalist radicals tended to "precipitate out" of the ranks of those who possessed specialized skills and were oriented to state activities or employments, but either lacked traditionally prestigious attributes such as nobility, landed wealth, or general humanist education, or else found themselves in situations where such attributes were no longer personally or nationally functional. Their situations in political and social life were such as to make them, especially in times of political crises, willing to call for such radical reforms as equalization of mobility opportunities, political democracy, and (anyway, before the revolution) extension of civil liberties. Yet the primary orientation of these marginal elites was toward a broad goal that they shared with all those, including traditionally prestigious bureaucrats, whose careers, livelihoods, and identities were intertwined with state activities: the goal of extension and rationalization of state powers in the name of national welfare and prestige.

*   *   *

In Russia, by 1917, the revolutionary sects, such as the Bolsheviks and the Left Social Revolutionaries, constituted the surviving politically organized representatives of what had earlier been an out-look much more widespread among university-educated Russians: extreme alienation, disgust at Russia's backwardness, preoccupation with public events and yet refusal to become involved in the round of civil life.[62] As Russia underwent rapid industrialization after 1890, opportunities for university education were extended beyond the nobility—a circumstance which helped to ensure that universities would be hotbeds of political radicalism—yet, before long, opportunities for professional and other highly skilled employments also expanded. Especially in the wake of the abortive 1905 Revolution, Russia's university-educated moved toward professional employments and liberal politics.[63] Yet when events overtook Russia in 1917, organized radical leadership was still to be found among the alienated intelligentsia.

In China, as in Russia, radical nationalist modernizers came from the early student generations of university-educated Chinese.[64] Especially at first, most were the children of traditionally wealthy and prestigious families, but urban and "rich peasant" backgrounds, respectively, came to be overrepresented in the (pre-1927) Kuomintang and the Communist elites.[65] With the abolition of the Confucian educational system in 1904, and the collapse of the imperial government in 1911, even traditionally prestigious attributes and connections lost their meaning and usefulness. At the same time, neither warlord regimes, nor the Nationalist government after 1927 offered much scope for modern skills or credentials; advancement in these regimes went only to those with independent wealth or personal ties to military commanders. Gradually, the bulk of China's modern-educated, and especially the young, came to support the Com-

munist movement, some through active commitment in Yenan, others through passive political support in the cities.[66]

Two considerations help to account for the fact that radical leadership in social revolutions came specifically from the ranks of skilled and/or university-educated marginal elites oriented to state employments and activities. First, agrarian bureaucracies are "statist" societies. Even before the era of modernization official employments in these societies constituted both an important route for social mobility and a means for validating traditional status and supplementing landed fortunes. Second, with the advent of economic modernization in the world, state activities acquired greater-than-ever objective import in the agrarian bureaucratic societies which were forced to adapt to modernization abroad. For the concrete effects of modernization abroad first impinged upon the state's sphere, in the form of sharply and suddenly stepped up military competition or threats from more developed nations abroad. And the cultural effects of modernization abroad first impinged upon the relatively highly educated in agrarian bureaucracies, that is upon those who were mostly either employed by the state or else connected or oriented to its activities.

*   *   *

The earlier modernizing agrarian bureaucracies that (to varying degrees) successfully adapted to challenges from abroad did so either through revolution, or basic reforms "from above" or social revolution "from below." Either traditional bureaucrats successfully promoted requisite reforms or else their attempts precipitated splits within the upper class which could, if the peasantry were structurally insurrection-prone, open the door to social revolution. In the context of administrative/military disorganization and spreading peasant rebellions, tiny, organized radical elites that never could have created revolutionary crises on their own gained their moments in history. As peasant insurrections undermined the traditional landed upper classes, and the old regime officials and structures tied to them, radical elites occupied center stage, competing among themselves to see who could seize and build upon the foundations of central state power.

"A complete revolution," writes Samuel Huntington, ". . . involves . . . the creation and institutionalization of a new political order."[67] A social revolution was consummated when one political elite succeeded in creating or capturing political organizations—a revolutionary army, or a revolutionary party controlling an army—capable of restoring minimal order and incorporating the revolutionary masses, especially the peasantry, into national life. No political elite not able or willing to accept the peasants' revolutionary economic gains could hope to emerge victorious from the intra-elite or inter-party conflicts that marked revolutionary interregnums. Elites with close social or politico-military ties to traditional forms of landed upper-class institutional power (i.e., the privileged rentier bourgeoisie of France, the Kerensky regime in Russia, the [post-1927] Kuomintang in China) invariably lost out.

The historical social revolutions did not culminate in more liberal political arrangements. At opening stages of the French, Russian (1905) and Chinese revolutions, landed upper-class/middle-strata political coalitions espoused "parliamentary liberal" programs.[68] But events pushed these groups and programs aside, for the organized elites who provided the ultimately successful leadership in all social revolutions ended up responding to popular turmoil—counterrevolutionary threats at home and abroad, peasant anarchist tendencies, and the international crises faced by their societies—by creating *more* highly centralized, bureaucratized and rationalized state institutions than those that existed prior to the revolutions. This response, moreover, was entirely in character for elites adhering to world views which gave consistent primacy to organized political action in human affairs.[69]

*   *   *

Let me sum up what this essay has attempted to do. To explain the great historical social revolutions, I have, first, conceptualized a certain type of society, the agrarian bureaucracy, in which social control of the lower strata (mainly peasants) rests with institutions locally and regionally controlled by landed upper classes, together with administrative and military machineries centrally controlled; and second, I have discussed differences between agrarian bureaucracies which did and those which did not experience social revolutions in terms of (a) institutional structures which mediate landed upper-class relations to state apparatuses and peasant relations to landed upper classes and (b) types and amounts of international political and economic pressures (especially originating with more developed nations) impinging upon agrarian bureaucracies newly incorporated into the modernizing world. According to my analysis, social revolutions occurred in those modernizing agrarian bureaucracies—France, Russia and China—which *both* incubated peasantries structurally prone to autonomous insurrection *and* experienced severe administrative and military disorganization due to the direct or indirect effects of military competition or threats from more modern nations abroad.

In the process of elucidating this basic argument, I have at one point or another alluded to evidence concerning Prussia (Germany), Japan (and Turkey), and Russia in 1905. Obviously the coverage of these and other "negative" cases has been far from complete. Yet partial explanations have been offered for the avoidance of social revolution by Prussia/Germany, Japan and Russia through 1916. Japan and Russia escaped administrative/military collapse in the face of moderate challenges from abroad because their traditional governmental elites were significantly differentiated from landed upper classes. Prussia lacked a structurally autonomous, insurrection-prone peasantry, and therefore when, in 1848, the King hesitated for a year to use his armies to repress popular disturbances, the Junker-led army, manned by peasants from the estates east of the Elbe, remained loyal and intact until it was finally used to crush the German Revolutions during 1849–50.

This comparative historical analysis has been meant to render plausible a theoretical approach to explaining revolutions which breaks with certain long-established sociological proclivities. While existing theories of revolution focus on discontent, and its articulation by oppositional programs or ideologies, as the fundamental cause of revolutions, I have emphasized mechanisms and dynamics of societal social control through political and class domination. Moreover, while other theories view the impact of modernization (as a cause of revolution) in terms of the effects of processes of economic development on class structures, "system equilibrium," or societal members' levels of satisfaction, my approach focuses on the effects of modernization—viewed also as an intersocietal politico-strategic process—upon adaptive capacities of the agrarian bureaucratic states and upon the opportunities open to political elites who triumph in revolutions.

Obviously, thorough testing of these ideas will require more precise delineation of concepts and the extension of hypotheses derived from this analysis to new cases. But I have made a start. And I hope that especially those who disagree with my conclusions will themselves turn to historical evidence to argue their cases. Social science can best grow through the interplay of theory and historical investigation, and comparative historical analysis represents one indispensable tool for achieving this.

NOTES

1. Samuel P. Huntington, *Political Order in Changing Societies* (New Haven: Yale University Press, 1968), p. 264.

2. Stephan T. Possony, ed., *The Lenin Reader* (Chicago: Henry Regnery Company, 1966), p. 349.

3. For important examples see: Ted Robert Gurr, *Why Men Rebel* (Princeton, New Jersey: Princeton University Press, 1970); Neil

J. Smelser, *Theory of Collective Behavior* (New York: The Free Press of Glencoe, 1963); and Harry Eckstein, "On the Etiology of Internal Wars," *History and Theory* 4(2) (1965).

4. Crane Brinton, *The Anatomy of Revolution* (New York: Vintage Books, 1965; original edition, 1938); Lyford P. Edwards, *The Natural History of Revolution* (Chicago: University of Chicago Press, 1971; originally published in 1927); George Sawyer Petee, *The Process of Revolution* (New York: Harper and Brothers, 1938); and Rex D. Hopper, "The Revolutionary Process," *Social Forces* 28 (March, 1950): 270–9.

5. Harry Eckstein, ed., *Internal War* (New York: The Free Press, 1964), p. 8.

6. *Ibid.*, p. 10.

7. See: Ernest Nagel, ed., *John Stuart Mill's Philosophy of Scientific Method* (New York: Hafner Publishing Co., 1950); Marc Bloch, "Toward a Comparative History of European Societies," in Frederic C. Lane and Jelle C. Riemersma, eds., *Enterprise and Secular Change* (Homewood, Illinois: The Dorsey Press, 1953), pp. 494–521; William H. Sewell, Jr., "Marc Bloch and the Logic of Comparative History," *History and Theory* 6(2) (1967): 208–18; Neil J. Smelser, "The Methodology of Comparative Analysis," (unpublished draft); and S. M. Lipset, *Revolution and Counterrevolution* (New York: Anchor Books, 1970), part I.

8. In formulating the "agrarian bureaucracy" societal type concept, I have drawn especially upon the work and ideas of S. N. Eisenstadt in *The Political Systems of Empires* (New York: The Free Press, 1963); Barrington Moore, Jr., in *Social Origins of Dictatorship and Democracy* (Boston: Beacon Press, 1967); and Morton H. Fried, "On the Evolution of Social Stratification and the State," pp. 713–31 in Stanley Diamond, ed., *Culture in History* (New York: Columbia University Press, 1960). The label "agrarian bureaucracy" is pilfered from Moore. Clear-cut

instances of agrarian bureaucratic societies were China, Russia, France, Prussia, Austria, Spain, Japan, Turkey.

9. Terence K. Hopkins and Immanuel Wallerstein, "The Comparative Study of National Societies," *Social Science Information* 6 (1967), 39.

10. See Immanuel Wallerstein, *The Modern World System: Capitalist Agriculture and the Origins of the European World-Economy in the Sixteenth Century* (New York and London: Academic Press, 1974).

11. E. J. Hobsbawm, *Industry and Empire* (Baltimore, Md.: Penguin Books, 1969).

12. See Walter L. Dorn, *Competition for Empire, 1740–1763* (New York: Harper and Row, 1963; originally, 1940).

13. Christopher Lasch, *The New Radicalism in America* (New York: Vintage Books, 1967), p. 141.

14. Alexander Gerschenkron, "Problems and Patterns of Russian Economic Development," pp. 42–72 in Cyril E. Black, ed., *The Transformation of Russian Society* (Cambridge, Mass.: Harvard University Press, 1960).

15. Geroid Tanquary Robinson, *Rural Russia Under the Old Regime* (Berkeley and Los Angeles: University of California Press, 1969; originally published in 1932), Chap. 11.

16. William Henry Chamberlin, *The Russian Revolution*, Volume I (New York: Grosset and Dunlap, 1963; originally published in 1935), pp. 64–65.

17. Katharine Chorley, *Armies and the Art of Revolution* (London: Faber and Faber, 1943), Chap. 6.

18. *Ibid.*, pp. 118–9.

19. In 1904, "[t]he Minister of Interior, von Plehve, saw a desirable outlet from the [turbulent domestic] situation in a 'little victorious war'" (Chamberlin, *op. cit.*, p. 47).

20. See: Leon Trotsky, *The Russian Revolution* (selected and edited by F. W. Dupee) (New York: Anchor Books, 1959; originally published in 1932), Volume I, Chap. 2; and Rod-

erick E. McGrew, "Some Imperatives of Russian Foreign Policy," pp. 202–29 in Theofanis George Stavrou, ed., *Russia Under the Last Tsar* (Minneapolis: University of Minnesota Press, 1969).

21. Albert Feuerwerker, *China's Early Industrialization* (New York: Atheneum, 1970; originally published in 1958), p. 41.

22. Chung-li Chang, *The Chinese Gentry* (Seattle: University of Washington Press, 1955); Ping-ti Ho, *The Ladder of Success in Imperial China* (New York: Columbia University, Press, 1962); and Franz Michael, "State and Society in Nineteenth Century China," *World Politics* 7 (April, 1955): 419–33.

23. Philip Kuhn, *Rebellion and Its Enemies in Late Imperial China* (Cambridge, Mass.: Harvard University Press, 1970).

24. Feuerwerker, *op. cit.*, pp. 40–41.

25. Mary C. Wright, ed., *China in Revolution: The First Phase, 1900–1913* (New Haven: Yale University Press, 1968), pp. 24–26.

26. Yoshiro Hatano, "The New Armies," pp. 365–82 in Wright, ed., *op. cit.*; and John Gittings, "The Chinese Army," pp. 187–224 in Jack Gray, ed., *Modern China's Search for a Political Form* (London: Oxford University Press, 1969).

27. John Fincher, "Political Provincialism and the National Revolution," in Wright, ed., *op. cit.*, p. 202.

28. Fincher, *op. cit.*; and P'eng-yuan Chang, "The Constitutionalists," in Wright, ed., *op. cit.*

29. Wright, ed., *op. cit.*, p. 50.

30. Fincher, *op. cit.*

31. Wright, ed., *loc. cit.*

32. John King Fairbank, *The United States and China* (Third Edition) (Cambridge, Mass.: Harvard University Press, 1971), p. 132.

33. Martin C. Wilbur, "Military Separatism and the Process of Reunification Under the Nationalist Regime, 1922–1937," pp. 203–63 in Ping-ti Ho and Tang Tsou, eds., *China in Crisis*, Volume I, Book I (Chicago: University of Chicago Press, 1968).

34. Albert Soboul, *The Sans Culottes* (New York: Anchor Books, 1972; originally published in French in 1968); and George Rudé, *The Crowd in the French Revolution* (London: Oxford University Press, 1959).

35. Jean Chesneaux, *The Chinese Labor Movement, 1919–1927* (Stanford: Stanford University Press, 1968).

36. Eric R. Wolf, *Peasant Wars of the Twentieth Century* (New York: Harper and Row, 1969), p. 290.

37. In 1848 the East Elbian region of "Germany" escaped general peasant insurrection, and the Prussian armies that crushed the German Revolutions of 1848 were recruited from the East Elbian estates, officers and rank-and-file alike. See: Theodore Hamerow, *Restoration, Revolution, Recreation* (Princeton, N.J.: Princeton University Press, 1958); and Hajo Holborn, *A History of Modern Germany, 1648–1840* (New York: Alfred A. Knopf, 1963).

38. "Sanctioning machineries" are organizations which control forceful or remunerative sanctions. "Social control" also involves normative pressures, but to be truly binding, especially in hierarchical situations, these must typically be "backed up" by application or credible threat of application of force or manipulation of needed remuneration.

39. See Wolf, *op. cit.*, "Conclusion"; and Moore, *op. cit.*, Chap. 9 and "Epilogue."

40. Terence Emmons, "The Peasant and the Emancipation," and Francis M. Watters, "The Peasant and the Village Commune," both in Wayne S. Vucinich, ed., *The Peasant in Nineteenth-Century Russia* (Stanford: Stanford University Press, 1968); and Robinson, *op. cit.*

41. Jerome Blum, *Lord and Peasant in Russia* (Princeton, New Jersey: Princeton University Press, 1961), pp. 598–9; and Robinson, *op. cit.*, pp. 78–79.

42. Robinson, *op. cit.*, p. 155.

43. *Ibid.*, pp. 188–207.

44. Gerschenkron, *op. cit.*, pp. 42–72.

45. Robinson, *op. cit.*, pp. 225–6.

46. Chamberlin, *op. cit.*, p. 257.

47. *Ibid.*, p. 242.

48. *Ibid.*, p. 252.

49. *Ibid.*, p. 256.

50. *Ibid.*, p. 256.

51. R. H. Tawney, *Land and Labour in China* (Boston: Beacon Press, 1966; originally published in 1932), Chap. 2.

52. G. William Skinner, "Chinese Peasants and the Closed Community: An Open and Shut Case," *Comparative Studies in Society and History* 13(3) (July, 1971), pp. 272–3.

53. Kuhn, *op. cit., passim.*

54. Skinner, *op. cit.*, 278ff.

55. See: Skinner, *op. cit.*, Kuhn, *op. cit.*; and George E. Taylor, "The Taiping Rebellion: Its Economic Background and Social Theory," *Chinese Social and Political Science Review* 16 (1933): 545–614.

56. See: Mark Selden, *The Yenan Way in Revolutionary China* (Cambridge, Mass.: Harvard University Press, 1971), Chaps. 1–2; Dick Wilson, *The Long March 1935* (New York: Avon Books, 1971); and Agnes Smedly, *The Great Road: The Life and Times of Chu Teh* (New York: Monthly Review Press, 1956).

57. Selden, *op. cit.*; Franz Schurmann, *Ideology and Organization in Communist China* (second edition) (Berkeley and Los Angeles: University of California Press, 1968), pp. 412–37; Ilpyong J. Kim, "Mass Mobilization Policies and Techniques Developed in the Period of the Chinese Soviet Republic," pp. 78–98 in A. Doak Barnett, ed., *Chinese Communist Politics in Action* (Seattle: University of Washington Press, 1969).

58. Selden, *op. cit.*; and Schurmann, *op. cit.*

59. William Hinton, *Fanshen: A Documentary of Revolution in a Chinese Village* (New York: Vintage Books, 1968; first published in 1966).

60. Schurmann, *op. cit.*, pp. 425–31.

61. See, for example, Roland Mousnier, *Peasant Uprisings in the Seventeenth Century: France, Russia and China* (New York: Harper and

Row, 1972; originally published in French, 1967).

62. George Fischer, "The Intelligentsia and Russia," pp. 253–73 in Black, ed., *op. cit.*

63. George Fischer, "The Russian Intelligentsia and Liberalism," pp. 317–36 in Hugh McLean, Martin Malia and George Fischer, eds., *Russian Thought and Politics—Harvard Slavic Studies, Volume IV* (Cambridge, Mass.: Harvard University Press, 1957); and Donald W. Treadgold, "Russian Radical Thought, 1894–1917," pp. 69–86 in Stavrou, ed., *op. cit.*

64. John Israel, "Reflections on the Modern Chinese Student Movement," *Daedalus* (Winter, 1968): 229–53; and Robert C. North and Ithiel de Sola Pool, "Kuomintang and Chinese Communist Elites," pp. 319–455 in Harold D. Lasswell and Daniel Lerner, eds., *World Revolutionary Elites* (Cambridge, Mass.: The M.I.T. Press, 1966).

65. North and Pool, *op. cit.*

66. John Israel, *Student Nationalism in China: 1927–1937* (Stanford: Hoover Institute Publications, 1966).

67. Huntington, *op. cit.*, p. 266.

68. See: Hampson, *A Social History* . . . , Chap. 2; Sidney Harcave, *The Russian Revolution of 1905* (London: Collier Books, 1970; first published in 1964); and P'eng-yuan Chang, "The Constitutionalists," pp. 143–83 in Wright, ed., *op. cit.*

69. On the Bolsheviks, see Robert V. Daniels, "Lenin and the Russian Revolutionary Tradition," pp. 339–54 in McLean, Malia and Fischer, eds., *op. cit.* Daniels argues that "the more autocratic societies like pre-revolutionary Russia . . . prompted historical theories which put a premium on individual will, power and ideas . . . ," p. 352.

MARTHA CRENSHAW

THE CAUSES OF TERRORISM

Terrorism occurs both in the context of violent resistance to the state as well as in the service of state interests. If we focus on terrorism directed against governments for purposes of political change, we are considering the premeditated use or threat of symbolic, low-level violence by conspiratorial organizations. Terrorist violence communicates a political message; its ends go beyond damaging an enemy's material resources.[1] The victims or objects of terrorist attack have little intrinsic value to the terrorist group but represent a larger human audience whose reaction the terrorists seek. Violence characterized by spontaneity, mass participation, or a primary intent of physical destruction can therefore be excluded from our investigation.

The study of terrorism can be organized around three questions: why terrorism occurs, how the process of terrorism works, and what its social and political effects are. Here the objective is to outline an approach to the analysis of the causes of terrorism, based on comparison of different cases of terrorism, in order to distinguish

From *Comparative Politics*, 13, no. 4 (July 1981), pp. 379–99.

a common pattern of causation from the historically unique.

The subject of terrorism has inspired a voluminous literature in recent years. However, nowhere among the highly varied treatments does one find a general theoretical analysis of the causes of terrorism. This may be because terrorism has often been approached from historical perspectives, which, if we take Laqueur's work as an example, dismiss explanations that try to take into account more than a single case as "exceedingly vague or altogether wrong."[2] Certainly existing general accounts are often based on assumptions that are neither explicit nor factually demonstrable. We find judgments centering on social factors such as the permissiveness and affluence in which Western youth are raised or the imitation of dramatic models encouraged by television. Alternatively, we encounter political explanations that blame revolutionary ideologies, Marxism-Leninism or nationalism, governmental weakness in giving in to terrorist demands, or conversely government oppression, and the weakness of the regime's opponents. Individual psychopathology is often cited as a culprit.

Even the most persuasive of statements about terrorism are not cast in the form of testable propositions, nor are they broadly comparative in origin or intent. Many are partial analyses, limited in scope to revolutionary terrorism from the Left, not terrorism that is a form of protest or a reaction to political or social change. A narrow historical or geographical focus is also common; the majority of explanations concern modern phenomena. Some focus usefully on terrorism against the Western democracies.[3] In general, propositions about terrorism lack logical comparability, specification of the relationship of variables to each other, and a rank-ordering of variables in terms of explanatory power.

We would not wish to claim that a general explanation of the sources of terrorism is a simple task, but it is possible to make a useful beginning by establishing a theoretical order for different types and levels of causes. We approach terrorism as a form of political behavior resulting from the deliberate choice of a basically rational actor, the terrorist organization. A comprehensive explanation, however, must also take into account the environment in which terrorism occurs and address the question of whether broad political, social, and economic conditions make terrorism more likely in some contexts than in others. What sort of circumstances lead to the formation of a terrorist group? On the other hand, only a few of the people who experience a given situation practice terrorism. Not even all individuals who share the goals of a terrorist organization agree that terrorism is the best means. It is essential to consider the psychological variables that may encourage or inhibit individual participation in terrorist actions. The analysis of these three levels of causation will center first on situational variables, then on the strategy of the terrorist organization, and last on the problem of individual participation.

This paper represents only a preliminary set of ideas about the problem of causation; historical cases of terrorism are used as illustrations, not as demonstrations of hypotheses. The historical examples referred to here are significant terrorist campaigns since the French Revolution of 1789; terrorism is considered as a facet of secular modern politics, principally associated with the rise of nationalism, anarchism, and revolutionary socialism.[4] The term *terrorism* was coined to describe the systematic inducement of fear and anxiety to control and direct a civilian population, and the phenomenon of terrorism as a challenge to the authority of the state grew from the difficulties revolutionaries experienced in trying to recreate the mass uprisings of the French Revolution. Most references provided here are drawn from the best-known and most-documented examples: Narodnaya Volya and the Combat Organization of the Socialist-Revolutionary party in Russia, from 1878 to 1913; anarchist terrorism of the 1890s in Europe, primarily France; the Irish Republican Army (IRA) and its predecessors and successors from 1919 to the present; the Irgun Zwai Leumi in Mandate Palestine from 1937 to 1947; the Front de Libération Nationale (FLN) in Algeria from 1954 to 1962; the Popular Front for the Liberation of Palestine from 1968 to the present; the Rote Armee Fraktion (RAF) and the 2nd June Movement in West Germany since 1968; and the Tupamaros of Uruguay, 1968–1974.

The Setting for Terrorism

An initial obstacle to identification of propitious circumstances for terrorism is the absence of significant empirical studies of relevant cross-national factors. There are a number of quantitative analyses of collective violence, assassination, civil strife, and crime,[5] but none of these phenomena is identical to a campaign of terrorism. Little internal agreement exists among such studies, and the consensus one finds is not particularly useful for the study of terrorism.[6] For example, Ted Robert Gurr found that "modern" states are less violent than developing countries and that legitimacy of the regime inhibits violence. Yet, Western Europe experiences high levels of terrorism. Surprisingly, in the 1961–1970 period, out of 87 countries, the United States was ranked as having the highest number of terrorist campaigns.[7] Although it is impractical to borrow entire theoretical structures from the literature on political and criminal violence, some propositions can be adapted to the analysis of terrorism.

To develop a framework for the analysis of likely settings for terrorism, we must establish conceptual distinctions among different types of factors. First, a significant difference exists between *preconditions*, factors that set the stage for terrorism over the long run, and *precipitants*, specific events that immediately precede the occurrence of terrorism. Second, a further classification divides preconditions into enabling or permissive factors, which provide opportunities for terrorism to happen, and situations that directly inspire and motivate terrorist campaigns.

Precipitants are similar to the direct causes of terrorism.[8] Furthermore, no factor is neatly compartmentalized in a single nation-state; each has a transnational dimension that complicates the analysis.

First, modernization produces an interrelated set of factors that is a significant permissive cause of terrorism, as increased complexity on all levels of society and economy creates opportunities and vulnerabilities. Sophisticated networks of transportation and communication offer mobility and the means of publicity for terrorists. The terrorists of Narodnaya Volya would have been unable to operate without Russia's newly established rail system, and the Popular Front for the Liberation of Palestine could not indulge in hijacking without the jet aircraft. In Algeria, the FLN only adopted a strategy of urban bombings when they were able to acquire plastic explosives. In 1907, the Combat Organization of the Socialist-Revolutionary party paid 20,000 rubles to an inventor who was working on an aircraft in the futile hope of bombing the Russian imperial palaces from the air.[9] Today we fear that terrorists will exploit the potential of nuclear power, but it was in 1867 that Nobel's invention of dynamite made bombings a convenient terrorist tactic.

Urbanization is part of the modern trend toward aggregation and complexity, which increases the number and accessibility of targets and methods. The popular concept of terrorism as "urban guerilla warfare" grew out of the Latin American experience of the late 1960s.[10] Yet, as Hobsbawn has pointed out, cities became the arena for terrorism after the urban renewal projects of the late nineteenth century, such as the boulevards constructed by Baron Haussman in Paris, made them unsuitable for a strategy based on riots and the defense of barricades.[11] In preventing popular insurrections, governments have exposed themselves to terrorism. P.N. Grabosky has recently argued that cities are a significant cause of terrorism in that they provide an opportunity (a multitude of targets, mobility, communications, anonymity, and audiences) and a recruiting ground among the politicized and volatile inhabitants.[12]

Social "facilitation," which Gurr found to be extremely powerful in bringing about civil strife in general, is also an important permissive factor. This concept refers to social habits and historical traditions that sanction the use of violence against the government, making it morally and politically justifiable, and even dictating an appropriate form, such as demonstrations, coups, or terrorism. Social myths, traditions, and habits permit the development of terrorism as an established political custom. An excellent example of such a tradition is the case of Ireland, where the tradition of physical force dates from the eighteenth century, and the legend of Michael Collins in 1919–21 still inspires and partially excuses the much less discriminate and less effective terrorism of the contemporary Provisional IRA in Northern Ireland.

Moreover, broad attitudes and beliefs that condone terrorism are communicated transnationally. Revolutionary ideologies have always crossed borders with ease. In the nineteenth and early twentieth centuries, such ideas were primarily a European preserve, stemming from the French and Bolshevik Revolutions. Since the Second World War, Third World War revolutions—China, Cuba, Algeria—and intellectuals such as Frantz Fanon and Carlos Marighela[13] have significantly influenced terrorist movements in the developed West by promoting the development of terrorism as routine behavior.

The most salient political factor in the category of permissive causes is a government's inability or unwillingness to prevent terrorism. The absence of adequate prevention by police and intelligence services permits the spread of conspiracy. However, since terrorist organizatons are small and clandestine, the majority of states can be placed in the permissive category. Inefficiency or leniency can be found in a broad range of all but the most brutally efficient dictatorships, including incompetent authoritarian states such as tsarist Russia on the eve of the emergence of Narodnaya Volya as well as modern liberal democratic states whose desire to protect civil liberties constrains security measures. The absence of effective security measures is a necessary cause, since our limited information on the subject indicates that terrorism does not occur in the communist dictatorships; and certainly repressive military regimes in Uruguay, Brazil, and Argentina have crushed terrorist organizations. For many governments, however, the cost of disallowing terrorism is too high.

Turning now to a consideration of the direct causes of terrorism, we focus on background conditions that positively encourage resistance to the state. These instigating circumstances go beyond merely creating an environment in which terrorism is possible; they provide motivation and direction for the terrorist movement. We are dealing here with reasons rather than opportunities.

The first condition that can be considered a direct cause of terrorism is the existence of concrete grievances among an identifiable subgroup of a larger population, such as an ethnic minority discriminated against by the majority. A social movement develops in order to redress these grievances and to gain either equal rights or a separate state; terrorism is then the resort of an extremist faction of this broader movement. In practice, terrorism has frequently arisen in such situations: in modern states, separatist nationalism among Basques, Bretons, and Québeçois has motivated terrorism. In the colonial era, nationalist movements commonly turned to terrorism.

This is not to say, however, that the existence of a dissatisfied minority or majority is a necessary or a sufficient cause of terrorism. Not all those who are discriminated against turn to terrorism, nor does terrorism always reflect objective social or economic deprivation. In West Germany, Japan, and Italy, for example, terrorism has been the chosen method of the privileged, not the downtrodden. Some theoretical studies have suggested that the essential ingredient that must be added to real deprivation is the perception on the part of the deprived that this condition is not what they deserve or expect, in short, that discrimination is unjust. An attitude study, for example, found that "the idea of justice or fairness may be more centrally related to attitudes toward violence than are feelings of deprivation. It is the perceived injustice underlying the deprivation that gives rise to anger or frustration."[14] The intervening variables, as we have argued, lie in the terrorists' perceptions. Moreover, it seems likely that for terrorism to occur the government must be singled out to blame for popular suffering.

The second condition that creates motivations for terrorism is the lack of opportunity for political participation. Regimes that deny access to power and persecute dissenters create dissatisfaction. In this case, grievances are primarily political, without social or economic overtones. Discrimination is not directed against any ethnic, religious, or racial subgroup of the population. The terrorist organization is not necessarily part of a broader social movement; indeed, the population may be largely apathetic. In situations where paths to the legal expression of opposition are blocked, but where the regime's repression is inefficient, revolutionary terrorism is doubly likely, as permissive and direct causes coincide. An example of this situation is tsarist Russia in the 1870s.

Context is especially significant as a direct cause of terrorism when it affects an elite, not the mass population. Terrorism is essentially the result of elite disaffection; it represents the strategy of a minority, who may act on behalf of a wider popular constituency who have not been consulted about, and do not necessarily approve of, the terrorists' aims or methods. There is remarkable relevance in E. J. Hobsbawm's comments on the political conspirators of post-Napoleonic Europe: "All revolutionaries regarded themselves, with some justification, as small elites of the emancipated and progressive operating among, and for the eventual benefit of, a vast and inert mass of the ignorant and misled common people, which would no doubt welcome liberation when it came, but could not be expected to take much part in preparing it."[15]

Many terrorists today are young, well-educated, and middle class in background. Such students or young professionals, with prior political experience, are disillusioned with the prospects of changing society and see little chance of access to the system despite their privileged status. Much terrorism has grown out of student unrest; this was the case in nineteenth century Russia as well as post–World War II West Germany, Italy, the United States, Japan, and Uruguay.

Perhaps terrorism is most likely to occur precisely where mass passivity and elite dissatisfaction coincide. Discontent is not generalized or severe enough to provoke the majority of the populace to action against the regime, yet a small minority, without access to the bases of power that would permit overthrow of the government through coup d'état or subversion, seeks radical change. Terrorism may thus be a sign of a stable society rather than a symptom of fragility and impending collapse. Terrorism is the resort of an elite when conditions are not revolutionary. Luigi Bonanate has blamed terrorism on a "blocked society" that is strong enough to preserve itself (presumably through popular inertia) yet resistant to innovation. Such self-perpetuating "immobilisme" invites terrorism.[16]

The last category of situational factors involves the concept of a precipitating event that immediately precedes outbreaks of terrorism. Although it is generally thought that precipitants are the most unpredictable of causes, there does seem to be a common pattern of government actions that act as catalysts for terrorism. Government use of unexpected and unusual force in response to protest or reform attempts often compels terrorist retaliation. The development of such an action-reaction syndrome then establishes the structure of the conflict between the regime and its challengers. There are numerous historical examples of a campaign of terrorism precipitated by a government's reliance on excessive force to quell protest or squash dissent. The tsarist regime's severity in dealing with the populist movement was a factor in the development of Narodaya Volya as a terrorist organization in 1879. The French government's persecution of anarchists was a factor in subsequent anarchist terrorism in the 1890s. The British government's execution of the heros of the Easter Rising set the stage for Michael Collins and the IRA. The Protestant violence that met the Catholic civil rights movement in Northern Ireland in 1969 pushed the Provisional IRA to retaliate. In West Germany, the death of Beno Ohnesorg at the hands of the police in a demonstration against the Shah of Iran in 1968 contributed to the emergence of the RAF.

This analysis of the background conditions for terrorism indicates that we must look at the terrorist organization's perception and interpretation of the situation. Terrorists view the context as permissive, making terrorism a viable option. In a material sense, the means are placed at their disposal by the environment. Circumstances also provide the terrorists with compelling reasons for seeking political change. Finally, an event occurs that snaps the terrorists' patience with the regime. Government action is now seen as intolerably unjust, and terrorism becomes not only a possible decision but a morally acceptable one. The regime has forfeited its status as the standard of legitimacy. For the terrorist, the end may now excuse the means.

The Reasons for Terrorism

Significant campaigns of terrorism depend on rational political choice. As purposeful activity, terrorism is the result of an organization's decision that it is a politically useful means to oppose a government. The argument that terrorist behavior should be analyzed as "rational" is based on the assumption that terrorist organizations possess internally consistent sets of values, beliefs, and images of the environment. Terrorism is seen collectively as a logical means to advance desired ends. The terrorist organization engages in decision-making calculations that an analyst can approximate. In short, the terror-

ist group's reasons for resorting to terrorism constitute an important factor in the process of causation.[17]

Terrorism serves a variety of goals, both revolutionary and subrevolutionary. Terrorists may be revolutionaries (such as the Combat Organization of the Socialist-Revolutionary Party in the nineteenth century or the Tupamaros of the twentieth); nationalists fighting against foreign occupiers (the Algerian FLN, the IRA of 1919–21, or the Irgun); minority separatists combatting indigenous regimes (such as the Corsican, Breton, and Basque movements, and the Provisional IRA); reformists (the bombing of nuclear construction sites, for example, is meant to halt nuclear power, not to overthrow governments); anarchists or millenarians (such as the original anarchist movement of the nineteenth century and modern millenarian groups such as the Red Army faction in West Germany, the Italian Red Brigades, and the Japanese Red Army); or reactionaries acting to prevent change from the top (such as the Secret Army Organization during the Algerian war or the contemporary Ulster Defence Association in Northern Ireland).[18]

Saying that extremist groups resort to terrorism in order to acquire political influence does not mean that all groups have equally precise objectives or that the relationship between means and ends is perfectly clear to an outside observer. Some groups are less realistic about the logic of means and ends than others. The leaders of Narodnaya Volya, for example, lacked a detailed conception of how the assassination of the tsar would force his successor to permit the liberalization they sought. Other terrorist groups are more pragmatic: the IRA of 1919–21 and the Irgun, for instance, shrewdly foresaw the utility of a war of attrition against the British. Menachem Begin, in particular, planned his campaign to take advantage of the "glass house" that Britain operated in.[19] The degree of skill in relating means to ends seems to have little to do with the overall sophistication of the terrorist ideology. The French anarchists of the 1890s, for example, acted in light of a well-developed philosophical doctrine but were much less certain of how violence against the bourgeoisie would bring about freedom. It is possible that anarchist or millenarian terrorists are so preoccupied with the splendor of the future that they lose sight of the present. Less theoretical nationalists who concentrate on the short run have simpler aims but sharper plans.

However diverse the long-run goals of terrorist groups, there is a common pattern of proximate or short-run objectives of a terrorist strategy. Proximate objectives are defined in terms of the reactions that terrorists want to achieve in their different audiences.[20] The most basic reason for terrorism is to gain recognition or attention—what Thornton called advertisement of the cause. Violence and bloodshed always excite human curiosity, and the theatricality, suspense, and threat of danger inherent in terrorism enhance its attention-getting qualities. In fact, publicity may be the highest goal of some groups. For example, terrorists who are fundamentally protesters might be satisfied with airing their grievances before the world. Today, in an interdependent world, the need for international recognition encourages transnational terrorist activities, with escalation to ever more destructive and spectacular violence. As the audience grows larger, more diverse, and more accustomed to terrorism, terrorists must go to extreme lengths to shock.

Terrorism is also often designed to disrupt and discredit the processes of government, by weakening it administratively and impairing normal operations. Terrorism as a direct attack on the regime aims at the insecurity and demoralization of government officials, independent of any impact on public opinion. An excellent example of this strategy is Michael Collins's campaign against the British intelligence system in Ireland in 1919–21. This form of terrorism often accompanies rural guerrilla warfare, as the insurgents try to weaken the government's control over its territory.

Terrorism also affects public attitudes in both a positive and a negative sense, aiming at creating either sympathy in a potential constituency or fear and hostility in an audience identified as the "enemy." These two functions are interrelated, since intimidating the "enemy" impresses both sympathizers and the uncommitted. At the same time, terrorism may be used to enforce obedience in an audience from whom the terrorists demand allegiance. The FLN in Algeria, for example, claimed more Algerian than French victims. Fear and respect were not incompatible with solidarity against the French.[21] When terrorism is part of a struggle between incumbents and challengers, polarization of public opinion undermines the government's legitimacy.

Terrorism may also be intended to provoke a counterreaction from the government, to increase publicity for the terrorists' cause and to demonstrate to the people that their charges against the regime are well founded. The terrorists mean to force the state to show its true repressive face, thereby driving the people into the arms of the challengers. For example, Carlos Marighela argued that the way to win popular support was to provoke the regime to measures of greater repression and persecution.[22] Provocative terrorism is designed to bring about revolutionary conditions rather than to exploit them. The FLN against the French, the Palestinians against Israel, and the RAF against the Federal Republic all appear to have used terrorism as provocation.

In addition, terrorism may serve internal organizational functions of control, discipline, and morale building within the terrorist group and even become an instrument of rivalry among factions in a resistance movement. For example, factional terrorism has frequently characterized the Palestinian resistance movement. Rival groups have competed in a vicious game where the victims are Israeli civilians or anonymous airline passengers, but where the immediate goal is influence within the resistance movement rather than the intimidation of the Israeli public or international recognition of the Palestinian cause.

Terrorism is a logical choice when oppositions have such goals and when the power ratio of government to challenger is high. The observation that terrorism is a weapon of the weak is hackneyed but apt. At least when initially adopted, terrorism is the strategy of a minority that by its own judgment lacks other means. When the group perceives its options as limited, terrorism is attractive because it is a relatively inexpensive and simple alternative, and because its potential reward is high.

Weakness and consequent restriction of choice can stem from different sources. On the one hand, weakness may result from the regime's suppression of opposition. Resistance organizations who lack the means of mounting more extensive violence may then turn to terrorism because legitimate expression of dissent is denied. Lack of popular support at the outset of a conflict does not mean that the terrorists' aims lack general appeal. Even though they cannot immediately mobilize widespread and active support, over the course of the conflict they may acquire the allegiance of the population. For example, the Algerian FLN used terrorism as a significant means of mobilizing mass support.[23]

On the other hand, it is wrong to assume that where there is terrorism there is oppression. Weakness may mean that an extremist organization deliberately rejects nonviolent methods of opposition open to them in a liberal state. Challengers then adopt terrorism because they are impatient with time-consuming legal methods of eliciting support or advertising their cause, because they distrust the regime, or because they are not capable of, or interested in, mobilizing majority support. Most terrorist groups operating in Western Europe and Japan in the past decade illustrate this phenomenon. The new millenarians lack a readily identifiable constituency and espouse causes devoid of mass appeal. Similarly, separatist movements represent at best only a minority of the total population of the state.

Thus, some groups are weak because weakness is imposed on them by the political system they operate in, others because of unpopularity. We are therefore making value judgments about the potential legitimacy of terrorist organizations. In some cases resistance groups are genuinely desperate, in others they have alternatives to violence. Nor do we want to forget that nonviolent resistance has been chosen in other circumstances, for example, by Gandhi and by Martin Luther King. Terrorists may argue that they had no choice, but their perceptions may be flawed.[24]

In addition to weakness, an important rationale in the decision to adopt a strategy of terrorism is impatience. Action becomes imperative. For a variety of reasons, the challenge to the state cannot be left to the future. Given a perception of limited means, the group often sees the choice as between action as survival and inaction as the death of resistance.

One reason for haste is external: the historical moment seems to present a unique chance. For example, the resistance group facing a colonial power recently weakened by a foreign war exploits a temporary vulnerability: the IRA against Britain after World War I, the Irgun against Britain after World War II, and the FLN against France after the Indochina war. We might even suggest that the stalemate between the United States and North Vietnam stimulated the post-1968 wave of anti-imperialist terrorism, especially in Latin America. There may be other pressures or catalysts provided by the regime, such as the violent precipitants discussed earlier or the British decision to introduce conscription in Ireland during World War I.

A sense of urgency may also develop when similar resistance groups have apparently succeeded with terrorism and created a momentum. The contagion effect of terrorism is partially based on an image of success that recommends terrorism to groups who identify with the innovator. The Algerian FLN, for example, was pressured to keep up with nationalists in Tunisia and Morocco, whose violent agitation brought about independence in 1956. Terrorism spread rapidly through Latin America in the post-1968 period as revolutionary groups worked in terms of a continental solidarity.

Dramatic failure of alternative means of obtaining one's ends may also fuel a drive toward terrorism. The Arab defeat in the 1967 war with Israel led Palestinians to realize that they could no longer depend on the Arab states to further their goals. In retrospect, their extreme weakness and the historical tradition of violence in the Middle East made it likely that militant nationalists should turn to terrorism. Since international recognition of the Palestinian cause was a primary aim (given the influence of outside powers in the region) and since attacks on Israeli territory were difficult, terrorism developed into a transnational phenomenon.

These external pressures to act are often intensified by internal politics. Leaders of resistance groups act under constraints imposed by their followers. They are forced to justify the organization's existence, to quell restlessness among the cadres, to satisfy demands for revenge, to prevent splintering of the movement, and to maintain control. Pressures may also come from the terrorists' constituency.

In conclusion, we see that terrorism is an attractive strategy to groups of different ideological persuasions who challenge the state's authority. Groups who want to dramatize a cause, to demoralize the government, to gain popular support, to provoke regime violence, to inspire followers, or to dominate a wider resistance movement, who are weak vis-à-vis the regime, and who are impatient to act, often find terrorism a reasonable choice. This is especially so when conditions are favorable, providing opportunities and making terrorism a simple and rapid option, with immediate and visible payoff.

Individual Motivation and Participation

Terrorism is neither an automatic reaction to conditions nor a purely calculated strategy. What psychological factors motivate the terrorist and influence his or her perceptions and interpretations of reality? Terrorists are only a small minority of people with similar personal backgrounds, experiencing the same conditions, who might thus be expected to reach identical conclusions based on logical reasoning about the utility of terrorism as a technique of political influence.

The relationship between personality and politics is complex and imperfectly understood.[25] Why individuals engage in political violence is a complicated problem, and the question why they engage in terrorism is still more difficult.[26] As most simply and frequently posed, the question of a psychological explanation of terrorism is whether or not there is a "terrorist personality," similar to the authoritarian personality, whose emotional traits we can specify with some exactitude.[27] An identifiable pattern of attitudes and behavior in the terrorism-prone individual would result from a combination of ego-defensive needs, cognitive processes, and socialization, in interaction with a specific situation. In pursuing this line of inquiry, it is important to avoid stereotyping the terrorist or oversimplifying the sources of terrorist actions. No single motivation or personality can be valid for all circumstances.

What limited data we have on individual terrorists (and knowledge must be gleaned from disparate sources that usually neither focus on psychology nor use a comparative approach) suggest that the outstanding common characteristic of terrorists is their normality. Terrorism often seems to be the connecting link among widely varying personalities. Franco Venturi, concentrating on the terrorists of a single small group, observed that "the policy of terrorism united many very different characters and mentalities" and that agreement on using terrorism was the cement that bound the members of Narodnaya Volya together.[28] The West German psychiatrist who conducted a pretrial examination of four members of the RAF concluded that they were "intelligent," even "humorous," and showed no symptoms of psychosis or neurosis and "no particular personality type."[29] Psychoanalysis might penetrate beneath superficial normality to expose some unifying or pathological trait, but this is scarcely a workable research method, even if the likelihood of the existence of such a characteristic could be demonstrated.

Peter Merkl, in his study of the pre-1933 Nazi movement—a study based on much more data than we have on terrorists—abandoned any attempt to classify personality types and instead focused on factors like the level of political understanding.[30] An unbiased examination of conscious attitudes might be more revealing than a study of subconscious predispositions or personalities. For example, if terrorists perceive the state as unjust, morally corrupt, and violent, then terrorism may seem legitimate and justified. For example, Blumenthal and her coauthors found that "the stronger the perception of an act as violence, the more violence is thought to be an appropriate response."[31] The evidence also indicates that many terrorists are activists with prior political experience in nonviolent opposition to the state. How do these experiences in participation influence later attitudes? Furthermore, how do terrorists view their victims? Do we find extreme devaluation, depersonalization, or stereotyping? Is there "us versus them" polarization or ethnic or religious prejudice that might sanction or prompt violence toward an out-group? How do terrorists justify and rationalize violence? Is remorse a theme?

The questions of attitudes toward victims and justifications for terrorism are especially important because different forms of terrorism involve various degrees of selectivity in the choice of victims. Some acts of terrorism are extremely discriminate, while others are broadly indiscriminate. Also, some terrorist acts require more intimate contact between terrorist and victim than others. Thus, the form of terrorism practiced —how selective it is and how much personal domination of the victim it involves—would determine the relevance of different questions.

Analyzing these issues involves serious methodological problems. As the Blumenthal study emphasizes, there are two ways of analyzing the relationship between attitudes and political behavior.[32] If our interest is in identifying potential terrorists by predicting behavior from the existence of certain consciously held attitudes and beliefs, then the best method would be to survey a young age group in a society determined to be susceptible. If terrorism subsequently occurred, we could then see which types of individuals became terrorists. (A problem is that the preconditions would change over time and that precipitants are unpredictable.) The more common and easier way of investigating the attitudes-behavior connection is to select people who have engaged in a particular behavior and ask them questions about their opinions. Yet attitudes may be adopted subsequent, rather than prior, to behavior, and they may serve as rationalizations for behavior engaged in for different reasons, not as genuine motivations. These problems would seem to be particularly acute when the individuals concerned have engaged in illegal forms of political behavior.

Another problem facing the researcher interested in predispositions or attitudes is that terrorists are recruited in different ways. Assuming that people who are in some way personally attracted to terrorism actually engage in such behavior supposes that potential terrorists are presented with an appropriate opportunity, which is a factor over which they have little control.[33] Moreover, terrorist groups often discourage or reject potential recruits who are openly seeking excitement or danger for personal motives. For instance, William Mackey Lomasney, a member of the Clan na Gael or American Fenians in the nineteenth century (who was killed in 1884 in an attempt to blow up London Bridge) condemned the "disgraceful" activities of the hotheaded and impulsive Jeremiah O'Donovan Rossa:

> Were it not that O'Donovan Rossa has openly and unblushingly boasted that he is responsible for those ridiculous and futile efforts . . . we might hesitate to even suspect that any sane man, least of all one professedly friendly to the cause, would for any consideration or desire for notoriety take upon himself such a fearful responsibility, and, that hav-

ing done so, he could engage men so utterly incapable of carrying out his insane designs.[34]

Lomasney complained that the would-be terrorists were:

> such stupid blundering fools that they make our cause appear imbecile and farcical. When the fact becomes known that those half-idiotic attempts have been made by men professing to be patriotic Irishmen what will the world think but that Irish revolutionists are a lot of fools and ignoramuses, men who do not understand the first principles of the art of war, the elements of chemistry or even the amount of explosive material necessary to remove or destroy an ordinary brick or stone wall. Think of the utter madness of men who have no idea of accumulative and destructive forces undertaking with common blasting powder to scare and shatter the Empire.[35]

Not only do serious terrorists scorn the ineptitude of the more excitable, but they find them a serious security risk. Rossa, for example, could not be trusted not to give away the Clan na Gael's plans for terrorism in his New York newspaper articles. In a similar vein, Boris Savinkov, head of the Combat Organization of the Socialist-Revolutionary party in Russia, tried to discourage an aspirant whom he suspected of being drawn to the adventure of terrorism:

> I explained to him that terrorist activity did not consist only of throwing bombs; that it was much more minute, difficult and tedious than might be imagined; that a terrorist is called upon to live a rather dull existence for months at a time, eschewing meeting his own comrades and doing most difficult and unpleasant work—the work of systematic observation.[36]

Similar problems in analyzing the connection between attitudes and behavior are due to the fact that there are role differentiations between leaders and followers. The degree of formal organization varies from the paramilitary hierarchies of the Irgun or the IRA to the semi-autonomous coexistence of small groups in contemporary West Germany or Italy or even to the rejection of central direction in the nineteenth century anarchist movement in France. Yet even

Narodnaya Volya, a self-consciously democratic group, observed distinctions based on authority. There are thus likely to be psychological or background differences between leaders and cadres. For example, a survey of contemporary terrorist movements found that leaders are usually older than their followers, which is not historically unusual.[37] In general, data are scant on individual terrorist leaders, their exercise of authority, the basis for it, and their interactions with their followers.[38] Furthermore, if there is a predisposition to terrorism, the terrorism-prone individual who obtains psychic gratification from the experience is likely to be a follower, not a leader who commands but does not perform the act.

An alternative approach to analyzing the psychology of terrorism is to use a deductive method based on what we know about terrorism as an activity, rather than an inductive method yielding general propositions from statements of the particular. What sort of characteristics would make an individual suited for terrorism? What are the role requirements of the terrorist?

One of the most salient attributes of terrorist activity is that it involves significant personal danger.[39] Furthermore, since terrorism involves premeditated, not impulsive, violence, the terrorist's awareness of the risks is maximized. Thus, although terrorists may simply be people who enjoy or disregard risk,[40] it is more likely that they are people who tolerate high risk because of intense commitment to a cause. Their commitment is strong enough to make the risk of personal harm acceptable and perhaps to outweigh the cost of society's rejection, although defiance of the majority may be a reward in itself. In either case, the violent activity is not gratifying per se.

It is perhaps even more significant that terrorism is a group activity, involving intimate relationships among a small number of people. Interactions among members of the group may be more important in determining behavior than the psychological predispositions of individual members. Terrorists live and make decisions under conditions of extreme stress. As a clandestine minority, the members of a terrorist group are isolated from society, even if they live in what Menachem Begin called the "open underground."[41]

Terrorists can confide in and trust only each other. The nature of their commitment cuts them off from society; they inhabit a closed community that is forsaken only at great cost. Isolation and the perception of a hostile environment intensify shared belief and commitment and make faith in the cause imperative. A pattern of mutual reassurance, solidarity, and comradeship develops, in which the members of the group reinforce each other's self-righteousness, image of a hostile world, and sense of mission. Because of the real danger terrorists confront, the strain they live under, and the moral conflicts they undergo, they value solidarity highly.[42] Terrorists are not necessarily people who seek "belonging" or personal integration through ideological commitment, but once embarked on the path of terrorism, they desperately need the group and the cause. Isolation and internal consensus explain how the beliefs and values of a terrorist group can be so drastically at odds with those of society at large. An example of such a divorce from social and political reality is the idea of the RAF that terrorism would lead to a resurgence of Nazism in West Germany that would in turn spark a workers' revolt.[43]

In their intense commitment, separation from the outside world, and intolerance of internal dissent, terrorist groups resemble religious sects or cults. Michael Barkun has explained the continued commitment of members of millenarian movements, a conviction frequently expressed in proselytizing in order to validate beliefs, in terms of the reinforcement and reassurance of rightness that the individual receives from other members of the organization. He also notes the frequent practice of initiation rites that involve violations of taboos, or "bridge-burning acts," that create guilt and prevent the convert's return to society. Thus the millenarian, like the terrorist group, constitutes "a community of common guilt."[44] J. Bowyer Bell has commented on the religious qualities of dedication and

moral fervor characterizing the IRA: "In the Republican Movement, the two seemingly opposing traditions, one of the revolution and physical force, and the other of pious and puritanical service, combine into a secular vocation."[45]

If there is a single common emotion that drives the individual to become a terrorist, it is vengeance on behalf of comrades or even the constituency the terrorist aspires to represent. (At the same time, the demand for retribution serves as public justification or excuse.) A regime thus encourages terrorism when it creates martyrs to be avenged. Anger at what is perceived as unjust persecution inspires demands for revenge, and as the regime responds to terrorism with greater force, violence escalates out of control.

There are numerous historical demonstrations of the central role vengeance plays as motivation for terrorism. It is seen as one of the principal causes of anarchist terrorism in France in the 1890s. The infamous Ravachol acted to avenge the "martyrs of Clichy," two possibly innocent anarchists who were beaten by the police and sentenced to prison. Subsequent bombings and assassinations, for instance that of President Carnot, were intended to avenge Ravachol's execution.[46] The cruelty of the sentences imposed for minor offenses at the "Trial of the 193," the hanging of eleven southern revolutionaries after Soloviev's unsuccessful attack on the tsar in 1879, and the "Trial of the 16" in 1880 deeply affected the members of Narodnaya Volya. Kravchinski (Stepniak) explained that personal resentment felt after the Trial of the 193 led to killing police spies; it then seemed unreasonable to spare their employers, who were actually responsible for the repression. Thus, intellectually the logic first inspired by resentment compelled them to escalate terrorism by degrees.[47] During the Algerian war, the French execution of FLN prisoners; in Northern Ireland, British troops firing on civil rights demonstrators; in West Germany, the death of a demonstrator at the hands of the police—all served to precipitate terrorism as militants sought to avenge their comrades.

The terrorists' willingness to accept high risks may also be related to the belief that one's death will be avenged. The prospect of retribution gives the act of terrorism and the death of the terrorist meaning and continuity, even fame and immortality. Vengeance may be not only a function of anger but of a desire for transcendence.

Shared guilt is surely a strong force in binding members of the terrorist group together. Almost all terrorists seem compelled to justify their behavior, and this anxiety cannot be explained solely by reference to their desire to create a public image of virtuous sincerity. Terrorists usually show acute concern for morality, especially for sexual purity, and believe that they act in terms of a higher good. Justifications usually focus on past suffering, on the glorious future to be created, and on the regime's illegitimacy and violence, to which terrorism is the only available response. Shared guilt and anxiety increase the group's interdependence and mutual commitment and may also make followers more dependent on leaders and on the common ideology as sources of moral authority.

Guilt may also lead terrorists to seek punishment and danger rather than avoid it. The motive of self-sacrifice notably influenced many Russian terrorists of the nineteenth century. Kaliayev, for example, felt that only his death could atone for the murder he committed. Even to Camus, the risk of death for the terrorist is a form of personal absolution.[48] In other cases of terrorism, individuals much more pragmatic than Kaliayev, admittedly a religious mystic, seemed to welcome capture because it brought release from the strains of underground existence and a sense of content and fulfillment. For example, Meridor, a member of the Irgun High Command, felt "high spirits" and "satisfaction" when arrested by the British because he now shared the suffering that all fighters had to experience. He almost welcomed the opportunity to prove that he was prepared to sacrifice himself for the cause. In fact, until his arrest he had felt "morally uncomfortable," whereas afterwards he

felt "exalted."[49] Menachem Begin expressed similar feelings. Once, waiting as the British searched the hotel where he was staying, he admitted anxiety and fear, but when he knew there was "no way out," his "anxious thoughts evaporated." He "felt a peculiar serenity mixed with incomprehensible happiness" and waited "composedly," but the police passed him by.[50]

Vera Figner, a leader of the Narodnaya Volya, insisted on physically assisting in acts of terrorism, even though her comrades accused her of seeking personal satisfaction instead of allowing the organization to make the best use of her talents. She found it intolerable to bear a moral responsibility for acts that endangered her comrades. She could not encourage others to commit acts she would not herself commit; anything less than full acceptance of the consequences of her decisions would be cowardice.[51]

It is possible that the willingness to face risk is related to what Robert J. Lifton has termed "survivor-guilt" as well as to feelings of group solidarity or of guilt at harming victims.[52] Sometimes individuals who survive disaster or escape punishment when others have suffered feel guilty and may seek relief by courting a similar fate. This guilt may also explain why terrorists often take enormous risks to rescue imprisoned comrades, as well as why they accept danger or arrest with equanimity or even satisfaction.

It is clear that once a terrorist group embarks on a strategy of terrorism, whatever its purpose and whatever its successes or failures, psychological factors make it very difficult to halt. Terrorism as a process gathers its own momentum, independent of external events.

Conclusions

Terrorism per se is not usually a reflection of mass discontent or deep cleavages in society. More often it represents the disaffection of a fragment of the elite, who may take it upon themselves to act on the behalf of a majority unaware of its plight, unwilling to take action to remedy grievances, or unable to express dissent. This discontent, however subjective in origin or minor in scope, is blamed on the government and its supporters. Since the sources of terrorism are manifold, any society or polity that permits opportunities for terrorism is vulnerable. Government reactions that are inconsistent, wavering between tolerance and repression, seem most likely to encourage terrorism.

Given some source of disaffection—and in the centralized modern state with its faceless bureaucracies, lack of responsiveness to demands is ubiquitous—terrorism is an attractive strategy for small organizations of diverse ideological persuasions who want to attract attention for their cause, provoke the government, intimidate opponents, appeal for sympathy, impress an audience, or promote the adherence of the faithful. Terrorists perceive an absence of choice. Whether unable or unwilling to perceive a choice between terrorist and nonterrorist action, whether unpopular or prohibited by the government, the terrorist group reasons that there is no alternative. The ease, simplicity, and rapidity with which terrorism can be implemented and the prominence of models of terrorism strengthen its appeal, especially since terrorist groups are impatient to act. Long-standing social traditions that sanction terrorism against the state, as in Ireland, further enhance its attractiveness.

There are two fundamental questions about the psychological basis of terrorism. The first is why the individual takes the first step and chooses to engage in terrorism: why join? Does the terrorist possess specific psychological predispositions, identifiable in advance, that suit him or her for terrorism? That terrorists are people capable of intense commitment tells us little, and the motivations for terrorism vary immensely. Many individuals are potential terrorists, but few actually make that commitment. To explain why terrorism happens, another question is more appropriate: Why does involvement continue? What are the psychological mechanisms of group interaction? We are not dealing with a situation in which certain types of personalities suddenly turn to terrorism in answer to some inner call. Terrorism is the result of a gradual growth of commitment and opposition, a group development that furthermore depends on government action. The psychological relationships within the terrorist group—the interplay of commitment, risk, solidarity, loyalty, guilt, revenge, and isolation—discourage terrorists from changing the direction they have taken. This may explain why—even if objective circumstances change when, for example, grievances are satisfied, or if the logic of the situation changes when, for example, the terrorists are offered other alternatives for the expression of opposition—terrorism may endure until the terrorist group is physically destroyed.

NOTES

1. For discussions of the meaning of the concept of terrorism, see Thomas P. Thornton, "Terror as a Weapon of Political Agitation," in Harry Eckstein, ed. *Internal War* (New York, 1964), pp. 71–99; Martha Crenshaw Hutchinson, "The Concept of Revolutionary Terrorism," *Revolutionary Terrorism: The FLN in Algeria, 1954–1962* (Stanford: The Hoover Institution Press, 1978) chap. 2; and E. Victor Walter, *Terror and Resistance* (New York, 1969).

2. Walter Laqueur, "Interpretations of Terrorism—Fact, Fiction and Political Science," *Journal of Contemporary History*, 12 (January 1977), 1–42. See also his major work *Terrorism* (London: Weidenfeld and Nicolson, 1977).

3. See, for example, Paul Wilkinson, *Terrorism and the Liberal State* (London: Macmillan, 1977), or J. Bowyer Bell, *A Time of Terror: How Democratic Societies Respond to Revolutionary Violence* (New York, 1978).

4. This is not to deny that some modern terrorist groups, such as those in West Germany, resemble premodern millenarian

movements. See specifically Conor Cruise O'Brien, "Liberty and Terrorism," *International Security*, 2 (1977), 56–67. In general, see Norman Cohn, *The Pursuit of the Millennium* (London: Secker and Warburg, 1957), and E. J. Hobsbawm, *Primitive Rebels: Studies in Archaic Forms of Social Movement in the 19th and 20th Centuries* (Manchester: Manchester University Press, 1971).

5. A sampling would include Douglas Hibbs, Jr., *Mass Political Violence: A Cross-National Causal Analysis* (New York, 1973); William J. Crotty, ed. *Assassinations and the Political Order* (New York, 1971); Ted Robert Gurr, *Why Men Rebel* (Princeton, 1971), and Gurr, Peter N. Grabosky, and Richard C. Hula, *The Politics of Crime and Conflict* (Beverly Hills, 1977).

6. For a summary of these findings, see Gurr, "The Calculus of Civil Conflict," *Journal of Social Issues*, 28 (1972), 27–47.

7. Gurr, "Some Characteristics of Political Terrorism in the 1960s," in Michael Stohl, ed. *The Politics of Terrorism* (New York, 1979), pp. 23–50 and 46–47.

8. A distinction between preconditions and precipitants is found in Eckstein, "On the Etiology of Internal Wars," *History and Theory*, 4 (1965), 133–62. Kenneth Waltz also differentiates between the framework for action as a permissive or underlying cause and special reasons as immediate or efficient causes. In some cases we can say of terrorism, as he says of war, that it occurs because there is nothing to prevent it. See *Man, the State and War* (New York, 1959), p. 232.

9. Boris Savinkov, *Memoirs of a Terrorist*, trans. Joseph Shaplen (New York: A. & C. Boni, 1931), pp. 286–87.

10. The major theoreticians of the transition from the rural to the urban guerrilla are Carlos Marighela, *For the Liberation of Brazil* (Harmondsworth: Penguin Books, 1971), and Abraham Guillen, *Philosophy of the Urban Guerrilla: The Revolutionary Writings of Abraham Guillen*, trans. and edited by Donald C. Hodges (New York, 1973).

11. Hobsbawm, *Revolutionaries: Contemporary Essays* (New York, 1973), pp. 226–27.

12. Grabosky, "The Urban Context of Political Terrorism," in Michael Stohl, ed., pp. 51–76.

13. See Amy Sands Redlick, "The Transnational Flow of Information as a Cause of Terrorism," in Yonah Alexander, David Carlton, and Wilkinson, eds. *Terrorism: Theory and Practice* (Boulder, 1979), pp. 73–95. See also Manus I. Midlarsky, Martha Crenshaw, and Fumihiko Yoshida, "Why Violence Spreads: The Contagion of International Terrorism," *International Studies Quarterly*, 24 (June 1980), 262–98.

14. Monica D. Blumenthal, et al., *More About Justifying Violence: Methodological Studies of Attitudes and Behavior* (Ann Arbor: Survey Research Center, Institute for Social Research, University of Michigan, 1975), p. 108. Similarly, Peter Lupsha, "Explanation of Political Violence: Some Psychological Theories Versus Indignation," *Politics and Society*, 2 (1971), 89–104, contrasts the concept of "indignation" with Gurr's theory of relative deprivation, which holds that expectations exceed rewards (see *Why Men Rebel*, esp. pp. 24–30).

15. Hobsbawm, *Revolutionaries*, p. 143.

16. Luigi Bonanate, "Some Unanticipated Consequences of Terrorism," *Journal of Peace Research*, 16 (1979), 197–211. If this theory is valid, we then need to identify such blocked societies.

17. See Barbara Salert's critique of the rational choice model of revolutionary participation in *Revolutions and Revolutionaries* (New York, 1976). In addition, Abraham Kaplan discusses the distinction between reasons and causes in "The Psychodynamics of Terrorism," *Terrorism—An International Journal*, 1, 3 and 4 (1978), 237–54.

18. For a typology of terrorist organizations, see Wilkinson, *Political Terrorism* (New York, 1975). These classes are not mutually exclusive, and they depend on an outside assessment of goals. For example, the Basque ETA

would consider itself revolutionary as well as separatist. The RAF considered itself a classic national liberation movement, and the Provisional IRA insists that it is combatting a foreign oppressor, not an indigenous regime.

19. Bell presents a succinct analysis of Irgun strategy in "The Palestinian Archetype: Irgun and the Strategy of Leverage," in *On Revolt: Strategies of National Liberation* (Cambridge [Ma.], 1976), chap. 3.

20. See Thornton's analysis of proximate goals in "Terror as a Weapon of Political Agitation," in Eckstein, ed. pp. 82–88.

21. Walter's discussion of the concept of "forced choice" explains how direct audiences, from whom the victims are drawn, may accept terrorism as legitimate; see *Terror and Resistance*, pp. 285–89.

22. See Marighela, *For the Liberation of Brazil*, pp. 94–95. The West German RAF apparently adopted the idea of provocation as part of a general national liberation strategy borrowed from the Third World.

23. See Hutchinson, *Revolutionary Terrorism*, chap. 3, pp. 40–60.

24. See Michael Walzer's analysis of the morality of terrorism in *Just and Unjust Wars* (New York, 1977), pp. 197–206. See also Bernard Avishai, "In Cold Blood," *The New York Review of Books*, March 8, 1979, pp. 41–44, for a critical appraisal of the failure of recent works on terrorism to discuss moral issues. The question of the availability of alternatives to terrorism is related to the problem of discrimination in the selection of victims. Where victims are clearly responsible for a regime's denial of opportunity, terrorism is more justifiable than where they are not.

25. See Fred I. Greenstein, *Personality and Politics: Problems of Evidence, Inference, and Conceptualization* (Chicago, 1969).

26. See Jeffrey Goldstein, *Aggression and Crimes of Violence* (New York, 1975).

27. A study of the West German New Left, for example, concludes that social psychological models of authoritarianism do help explain the dynamics of radicalism and even the transformation from protest to terrorism. See S. Robert Lichter, "A Psychopolitical Study of West German Male Radical Students," *Comparative Politics*, 12 (October 1979), pp. 27–48.

28. Franco Venturi, *Roots of Revolution: A History of the Populist and Socialist Movements in Nineteenth Century Russia* (London: Weidenfeld and Nicolson, 1960), p. 647.

29. Quoted in *Science*, 203, 5 January 1979, p. 34, as part of an account of the proceedings of the International Scientific Conference on Terrorism held in Berlin, December, 1978. Advocates of the "terrorist personality" theory, however, argued that terrorists suffer from faulty vestibular functions in the middle ear or from inconsistent mothering resulting in dysphoria. For another description see John Wykert, "Psychiatry and Terrorism," *Psychiatric News*, 14 (February 2, 1979), 1 and 12–14. A psychologist's study of a single group, the Front de Libération du Québec, is Gustav Morf, *Terror in Quebec: Case Studies of the FLQ* (Toronto: Clarke, Irvin, and Co., 1970).

30. Peter Merkl, *Political Violence Under the Swastika: 581 Early Nazis* (Princeton, 1974), 33–34.

31. Blumenthal, et al., p. 182.

32. Ibid., p. 12. Lichter also recognizes this problem.

33. Ibid., pp. 12–13.

34. William O'Brien and Desmond Ryan, eds. *Devoy's Post Bag*, vol. II (Dublin: C. J. Fallon, Ltd., 1953), p. 51.

35. Ibid., p. 52.

36. Savinkov, *Memoirs*, p. 147.

37. Charles A. Russell and Bowman H. Miller, "Profile of a Terrorist," *Terrorism—An International Journal*, 1 (1977), reprinted in John D. Elliott and Leslie K. Gibson, eds. *Contemporary Terrorism: Selected Readings* (Gaithersburg, Md.: International Association of Chiefs of Police, 1978), pp. 81–95.

38. See Philip Pomper's analysis of the influence of Nechaev over his band of followers: "The People's Revenge," *Sergei Nechaev* (New Brunswick [N.J.], 1979), chap. 4.

39. A Rand Corporation study of kidnappings and barricade-and-hostage incidents concluded that such tactics are not necessarily perilous, while admitting that drawing statistical inferences from a small number of cases in a limited time period (August, 1968 to June, 1975) is hazardous. See Brian Jenkins, Janera Johnson, and David Ronfeldt, *Numbered Lives: Some Statistical Observations from 77 International Hostage Episodes*, Rand Paper P-5905 (Santa Monica: The Rand Corporation, 1977).

40. Psychiatrist Frederick Hacker, for example, argues that terrorists are by nature indifferent to risk; see *Crusaders, Criminals and Crazies* (New York, 1976), p. 13.

41. Menachem Begin, *The Revolt* (London: W. H. Allen, 1951).

42. J. Glenn Gray, "The Enduring Appeals of Battle," *The Warriors: Reflections on Men in Battle* (New York, 1970), chap. 2, describes similar experiences among soldiers in combat.

43. Statements of the beliefs of the leaders of the RAF can be found in *Textes des prisonniers de la Fraction armée rouge et dernières lettres d'Ulrike Meinhof* (Paris: Maspéro, 1977).

44. Michael Barkun, *Disaster and the Millennium* (New Haven, 1974), pp. 14–16. See also Leon Festinger, et al., *When Prophecy Fails* (New York, 1964).

45. Bell, *The Secret Army* (London: Anthony Blond, 1970), p. 379.

46. Jean Maitron, *Histoire du mouvement anarchiste en France (1880–1914)* (Paris: Société universitaire d'éditions et de librairie, 1955), pp. 242–43.

47. S. Stepniak (pseudonym for Kravchimski), *Underground Russia: Revolutionary Profiles and Sketches from Life* (London: Smith, Elder, and Co., 1882), pp. 36–37; see also Venturi, pp. 639 and 707–08.

48. See "Les meurtriers délicats" in *L'Homme Révolté* (Paris: Gallimard, 1965), pp. 571–79.

49. Ya'acov Meridor, *Long is the Road to Freedom* (Tujunga [Ca.]: Barak Publications, 1961), pp. 6 and 9.

50. Begin, p. 111.

51. Vera Figner, *Mémoires d'une révolutionnaire*, trans. Victor Serge (Paris: Gallimard, 1930), pp. 131 and 257–62.

52. Such an argument is applied to Japanese Red Army terrorist Kozo Okamoto by Patricia Steinhof in "Portrait of a Terrorist," *Asian Survey*, 16 (1976), 830–45.

AVISHAI MARGALIT AND IAN BURUMA

OCCIDENTALISM

1.

In 1942, not long after the attack on Pearl Harbor, a group of Japanese philosophers got to-

From *The New York Review of Books* (January 17, 2002).

gether in Kyoto to discuss Japan's role in the world. The project of this ultra-nationalist gathering was, as they put it, to find a way to "overcome modern civilization." Since modern civilization was another term for Western civilization, the conference might just as well have been entitled "Overcoming the West." In a complete reversal of the late-nineteenth-century goal of "leaving Asia and joining the West," Japan was now fighting a "holy war" to liberate Asia from the West and purify Asian minds of Western ideas. Part of the holy war was, as it were, an exercise in philosophical cleansing.

The cleansing agent was a mystical mishmash of German-inspired ethnic nationalism and Zen- and Shinto-based nativism. The Japanese were a "world-historical race" descended from the gods, whose divine task it was to lead all Asians into a new age of Great Harmony, and so on. But what was "the West" which had to be purged? What needed to be "overcome"? The question has gained currency, since the chief characteristics of this Western enemy would have sounded familiar to Osama bin Laden, and other Islamic extremists. They are, not in any particular order, materialism, liberalism, capitalism, individualism, humanism, rationalism, socialism, decadence, and moral laxity. These ills would be overcome by a show of Japanese force, not just military force, but force of will, of spirit, of soul. The key characteristics of the Japanese or "Asian" spirit were self-sacrifice, discipline, austerity, individual submission to the collective good, worship of divine leadership, and a deep faith in the superiority of instinct over reason.

There was of course more at stake in Japan's war with the West, but these were the philosophical underpinnings of Japanese wartime propaganda. The central document of Japan's claim to national divinity was entitled *Cardinal Principles of the National Polity (Kokutai no Hongi)*. Issued in 1937 by the ministry of education, this document claimed that the Japanese were "intrinsically quite different from so-called citizens of Western nations," because the divine imperial bloodlines had remained unbroken, and "we always seek in the emperor the source of our lives and activities." The Japanese spirit was "pure" and "unclouded," whereas the influence of Western culture led to mental confusion and spiritual corruption.

Western, especially German, ideas inspired some of this. A famous right-wing professor, Dr.

Uesugi Shinkichi, began his spiritual life as a Christian, studied statecraft in Wilhelminian Germany, and returned home to write (in 1919): "Subjects have no mind apart from the will of the Emperor. Their individual selves are merged with the Emperor. If they act according to the mind of the Emperor, they can realize their true nature and attain the moral ideal."[1] Of such stuff are holy warriors made.

Similar language—though without the neo-Shintoist associations—was used by German National Socialists and other European fascists. They, too, fought against that list of "soulless" characteristics commonly associated with liberal societies. One of the early critical books about Nazi thinking, by Aurel Kolnai, a Hungarian refugee, was actually entitled *The War Against the West*.[2] Nazi ideologues and Japanese militarist propagandists were fighting the same Western ideas. The West they loathed was a multinational, multicultural place, but the main symbols of hate were republican France, capitalist America, liberal England, and, in Germany more than Japan, the rootless cosmopolitan Jews. Japanese propaganda focused on the "Anglo-American beasts," represented in cartoons of Roosevelt and Churchill wearing plutocratic top hats. To the Nazis "the eternal Jew" represented everything that was hateful about liberalism.

War against the West is partly a war against a particular concept of citizenship and community. Decades before the coming of Hitler, the spiritual godfather of Nazism, Houston Stewart Chamberlain, described France, Britain, and America as hopelessly "Jewified" countries. Citizenship in these places had degenerated into a "purely political concept."[3] In England, he said, "every Basuto nigger" could get a passport. Later he complained that the country had "fallen utterly into the hands of Jews and Americans."[4] Germany in his view, and that of his friend Kaiser Wilhelm II, was the only nation with enough national spirit and racial solidarity to save the West from going under in a sea of decadence and corruption. His "West" was not based on citizenship but on blood and soil.

Oswald Spengler warned in 1933 (of all years) that the main threats to the Occident came from "colored peoples" (*Farbigen*).[5] He prophesied, not entirely without reason, huge uprisings of enraged peoples in the European colonies. He also claimed that after 1918 the Russians had become "Asiatic" again, and that the Japanese Yellow Peril was about to engulf the civilized world. More interesting, however, was Spengler's view that the ruling white races (*Herrenvölker*) were losing their position in Europe. Soon, he said, true Frenchmen would no longer rule France, which was already awash with black soldiers, Polish businessmen, and Spanish farmers. The West, he concluded, would go under because white people had become soft, decadent, addicted to safety and comfort. As he put it: "Jazz music and nigger dances are the death march of a great civilization."

If criticism of the West was influenced by half-baked ideas from Germany, more positive views of the West were also influenced by German ideas. The Slavophiles and the Westernizers, who offered opposing views of the West in nineteenth-century Russia, were both equally inspired by German intellectual currents. Ideas for or against the West are in fact to be found everywhere. The East does not begin at the river Elbe, as Konrad Adenauer believed, nor does the West start in Prague, as Milan Kundera once suggested. East and West are not necessarily geographical territories. Rather, Occidentalism, which played such a large part in the attacks of September 11, is a cluster of images and ideas of the West in the minds of its haters. Four features of Occidentalism can be seen in most versions of it; we can call them the City, the Bourgeois, Reason, and Feminism. Each contains a set of attributes, such as arrogance, feebleness, greed, depravity, and decadence, which are invoked as typically Western, or even American, characteristics.

The things Occidentalists hate about the West are not always the ones that inspire hatred of the US. The two issues should not be conflated. A friend once asked in astonishment: "Why does he hate me? I didn't even help him." Some people hate the US because they were helped by the US, and some because they were not. Some resent the way the US helped their own hateful governments gain or stay in power. Some feel humiliated by the very existence of the US, and some by US foreign policy. With some on the left, hatred of the US is all that remains of their leftism; anti-Americanism is part of their identity. The same goes for right-wing cultural Gaullists. Anti-Americanism is an important political issue, related to Occidentalism but not quite the same thing.

2.

Anti-liberal revolts almost invariably contain a deep hatred of the City, that is to say, everything represented by urban civilization: commerce, mixed populations, artistic freedom, sexual license, scientific pursuits, leisure, personal safety, wealth, and its usual concomitant, power. Mao Zedong, Pol Pot, Hitler, Japanese agrarian fascists, and of course Islamists all extolled the simple life of the pious peasant, pure at heart, uncorrupted by city pleasures, used to hard work and self-denial, tied to the soil, and obedient to authority. Behind the idyll of rural simplicity lies the desire to control masses of people, but also an old religious rage, which goes back at least as far as the ancient superpower Babylon.

The "holy men" of the three monotheistic religions—Christianity, Judaism, and Islam—denounced Babylon as the sinful city-state whose politics, military might, and very urban civilization posed an arrogant challenge to God. The fabled tower of Babylon was a symbol of hubris and idolatry: "Let us build a city and a tower, whose top may reach unto heaven; and let us make us a name" (Genesis 11:4). Indeed, God took it as a challenge to Himself: "And now nothing will be restrained from them, which they imagined to do" (Genesis 11:6). That is, the citizens of this urban superpower will act out their fantasies to become God.

"He loveth not the arrogant," the Koran (16:23) tells us, and goes on to say: "Allah took their structures from their foundation, and the roof fell down on them from above; and the Wrath seized them from directions they did not perceive" (16:26). The prophet Isaiah already prophesied that Babylon, "the glory of all kingdoms," would end up as "Sodom and Gomorrah" (Isaiah 13:19), and that the arrogant would be overthrown so that even an "Arabian pitch tent" would not inhabit the place (13:20). The Book of Revelation goes on to say about Babylon the great, "the mother of harlots and of the abominations of the earth" (17:5), that it "is fallen, is fallen" (18:2).

There is a recurring theme in movies from poor countries in which a young person from a remote village goes to the big city, forced by circumstances or eager to seek a new life in a wider, more affluent world. Things quickly go wrong. The young man or woman is lonely, adrift, and falls into poverty, crime, or prostitution. Usually, the story ends in a gesture of terrible violence, a vengeful attempt to bring down the pillars of the arrogant, indifferent, alien city. There are echoes of this story in Hitler's life in Vienna, Pol Pot's in Paris, Mao's in Beijing, or indeed of many a Muslim youth in Cairo, Haifa, Manchester, or Hamburg.

In our world you don't even have to move to the city to feel its constant presence, through advertising, television, pop music, and videos. The modern city, representing all that shimmers just out of our reach, all the glittering arrogance and harlotry of the West, has found its icon in the Manhattan skyline, reproduced in millions of posters, photographs, and images, plastered all over the world. You cannot escape it. You find it on dusty jukeboxes in Burma, in discothèques in Urumqi, in student dorms in Addis Ababa. It excites longing, envy, and sometimes blinding rage. The Taliban, like the Nazi provincials horrified by "nigger dancing," like Pol Pot, like Mao, have tried to create a world of purity where visions of Babylon can no longer disturb them.

The Taliban, to be sure, have very little idea what the fleshpots of the West are really like.

For them even Kabul sparkled with Occidental sinfulness, exemplified by girls in school and women with uncovered faces populating and defiling the public domain. But the Taliban, like other purists, are much concerned with the private domain too. In big, anonymous cities, separation between the private and the public makes hypocrisy possible. Indeed, in Occidentalist eyes, the image of the West, populated by city-dwellers, is marked by artificiality and hypocrisy, in contrast to the honesty and purity of a Bedouin shepherd's life. Riyadh, and its grandiose Arabian palaces, is the epitome of hypocrisy. Its typical denizens behave like puritanical Wahhabites in public and greedy Westerners at home. To an Islamic radical, then, urban hypocrisy is like keeping the West inside one like a worm rotting the apple from within.

Most great cities are also great marketplaces. Voltaire saw much of what he admired about England in the Royal Exchange, "where the Jew, the Mahometan, and the Christian transact together as tho' they all profess'd the same religion, and give the name of Infidel to none but bankrupts."[6] Those who hate what Voltaire respected, who see the marketplace as the source of greed, selfishness, and foreign corruption, also hate those who are thought to benefit from it most: immigrants and minorities who can only better their fortunes by trade. When purity must be restored, and foreign blood removed from the native soil, it is these people who must be purged: the Chinese from Pol Pot's Phnom Penh, the Indians from Rangoon or Kampala, and the Jews from everywhere.

Sometimes such impurities can extend to nations, or even great powers. In their professed aim to bring back true Asian values to the East, Japanese wartime leaders promised to kick out the white imperialists as one way to "overcome unrestrained market competition."[7] Whatever Israel does, it will remain the alien grit in the eyes of Muslim purists. And the US will always be intolerable to its enemies. In bin Laden's terms, "the crusader-Jewish alliance, led by the US and Israel," cannot do right. The hatred is unconditional. As he observed in a 1998 interview for al-Jazeera TV: "Every grown-up Muslim hates Americans, Jews, and Christians. It is our belief and religion. Since I was a boy I have been at war with and harboring hatred towards the Americans." The September angels of vengeance picked their target carefully. Since the Manhattan skyline is seen as a provocation, its Babylonian towers had to come down.

3.

What did Hitler mean by "Jewish science"? For that matter, what explains the deep loathing of Darwin among Christian fundamentalists? Nazi propagandists argued that scientific truth could not be established by such "Jewish" methods as empirical inquiry or subjecting hypotheses to the experimental test; natural science had to be "spiritual," rooted in the natural spirit of the *Volk*. Jews, it was proposed, approached the natural world through reason, but true Germans reached a higher understanding through creative instinct and a love of nature.

Chairman Mao coined the slogan "Science is simply acting daringly." He purged trained scientists in the 1950s and encouraged Party zealots to embark on crazy experiments, inspired by the equally zany theories of Stalin's pseudoscientist T. D. Lysenko. "There is nothing special," Mao said, "about making nuclear reactors, cyclotrons or rockets. . . . You need to have spirit to feel superior to everyone, as if there was no one beside you."[8] All the sense of envious inferiority that Mao and his fellow Party provincials felt toward people of higher education is contained in these words. Instinct, spirit, daring . . . In 1942, a Japanese professor at Tokyo University argued that a Japanese victory over Anglo-American materialism was assured because the former embodied the "spiritual culture" of the East.

Like those towers of Babel in New York, the "Jewish" idea that "science is international" and human reason, regardless of bloodlines, is the best instrument for scientific inquiry is regarded by enemies of liberal, urban civilization as a form of hubris. Science, like everything else, must be infused with a higher ideal: the German *Volk*, God, Allah, or whatnot. But there may also be something else, something even more primitive, behind this. Worshipers of tribal gods, or even of allegedly universal ones, including Christians, Muslims, and Orthodox Jews, sometimes have a tendency to believe that infidels either have corrupt souls or have no souls at all. It is not for nothing that Christian missionaries speak of saving souls. In extreme cases, this can furnish enough justification to kill unbelievers with impunity.

Soul is a recurring theme of Occidentalism. The nineteenth-century Slavophiles pitted the "big" Russian soul against the mechanical, soulless West. They claimed to stand for deep feelings and profound understanding of suffering. Westerners, on the other hand, were deemed to be mechanically efficient, and to have nothing but an uncanny sense for calculating what is useful. The skeptical intellect, to promoters of soul, is always viewed with suspicion. Occidentalists extol soul or spirit but despise intellectuals and intellectual life. They regard the intellectual life as fragmented, indeed as a higher form of idiocy, with no sense of "totality," the "absolute," and what is truly important in life.

It is a fairly common belief among all peoples that "others" don't have the same feelings that we do. The notion that life is cheap in the Orient, or that coolies feel no pain, is a variation of this, but so is the idea we have heard expressed many times in China, India, Japan, and Egypt that Westerners are dry, rational, cold, and lacking in warm human feelings. It is a mark of parochial ignorance, of course, but it also reflects a way of ordering society. The post-Enlightenment Anglo-Franco-Judeo-American West sees itself as governed by secular political institutions and the behavior of all citizens as bound by secular laws. Religious belief and other matters of the spirit are private. Our politics are not totally divorced from shared values or moral assumptions, and some of our current leaders would like to see more religion brought into our public life; but still the West is not governed by spiritual leaders who seek to mediate between us and the divine world above. Our laws do not come from divine revelation, but are drawn up by jurists.

Societies in which Caesars are also high priests, or act as idols of worship, whether they be Stalinist, monarchical, or Islamist, use a different political language. Again, an example from World War II might be useful. Whereas the Allies, led by the US, fought the Japanese in the name of freedom, the Japanese holy war in Asia was fought in the name of divine justice and peace. "The basic aim of Japan's national policy lies in the firm establishment of world peace in accordance with the lofty spirit of All the World Under One Roof, in which the country was founded." Thus spoke Prime Minister Konoe in 1940. Islamists, too, aim to unite the world under one peaceful roof, once the infidels and their towers have been destroyed.

When politics and religion merge, collective aims, often promoted in the name of love and justice, tend to encompass the whole world, or at least large chunks of it. The state is a secular construct. The Brotherhood of Islam, the Church of Rome, All the World Under One Japanese Roof, world communism, all in their different ways have had religious or millenarian goals. Such goals are not unknown in the supposedly secular states of the West either. Especially in the US, right-wing Christian organizations and other religious pressure groups have sought to inject their religious values and agendas into national politics in ways that would have shocked the Founding Fathers. That Reverend Jerry Falwell described the terrorist attacks on New York and Washington as a kind of punishment for our worldly sins showed that his thinking was not so far removed from that of the Islamists.

But ideally, the US and other Western democracies are examples of what Ferdinand Toennies termed a *Gesellschaft*, whose members are bound by a social contract. The other kind of community, the *Gemeinschaft*, is based on a common faith, or racial kinship, or on deep feelings of one kind or another. Typically, one German thinker, Edgar Jung, described World War I as a clash between the Intellect (the West) and the Soul (Germany).

4.

Enemies of the West usually aspire to be heroes. As Mussolini exhorted his new Romans: "Never cease to be daring!" Islamism, Nazism, fascism, communism are all heroic creeds. Mao's ideal of permanent revolution was a blueprint for continually stirring things up, for a society invigorated by constant heroic violence. The common enemy of revolutionary heroes is the settled bourgeois, the city dweller, the petty clerk, the plump stockbroker, going about his business, the kind of person, in short, who might have been working in an office in the World Trade Center. It is a peculiar trait of the bourgeoisie, perhaps the most successful class in history, at least so far, according to Karl Marx, to be hated so intensely by some of its most formidable sons and daughters, including Marx himself. Lack of heroism in the bourgeois ethos, of committing great deeds, has a great deal to do with this peculiarity. The hero courts death. The bourgeois is addicted to personal safety. The hero counts death tolls, the bourgeois counts money. Bin Laden was asked by his interviewer in 1998 whether he ever feared betrayal from within his own entourage. He replied: "These men left worldly affairs, and came here for jihad."

Intellectuals, themselves only rarely heroic, have often displayed a hatred of the bourgeois and an infatuation with heroism—heroic leaders, heroic creeds. Artists in Mussolini's Italy celebrated speed, youth, energy, instinct, and death-defying derring-do. German social scientists before World War II were fascinated by the juxtaposition of the hero and the bourgeois: Werner Sombart's *Händler und Helden (Mer-*

chants and Heroes) and Bogislav von Selchow's *Der bürgerliche und der heldische Mensch (The Civil and the Heroic Man)* are but two examples of the genre. Von Selchow was one, among many others, by no means all German, who argued that bourgeois liberal society had become cold, fragmented, decadent, mediocre, lifeless. The bourgeois, he wrote, is forever hiding himself in a life without peril. The bourgeois, he said, is anxious to eliminate "fighting against Life, as he lacks the strength necessary to master it in its very nakedness and hardness in a manly fashion."[9]

To the likes of von Selchow or Ernst Jünger, World War I showed a different, more heroic side of man. That is why the Battle of Langemarck, a particularly horrific episode in 1914, in which Jünger himself took part, became such a subject for hero worship. Some 145,000 men died in a sequence of utterly futile attacks. But the young heroes, many of them from elite universities like the Japanese kamikaze pilots thirty years later, were supposed to have rushed to their early graves singing the *Deutschlandied*. The famous words of Theodor Körner, written a century before, were often evoked in remembrance: "Happiness lies only in sacrificial death." In the first week of the current war in Afghanistan, a young Afghan warrior was quoted in a British newspaper. "The Americans," he said, "love Pepsi Cola, but we love death." The sentiments of the Langemarck cult exactly.

Even those who sympathize with the democratic West, such as Alexis de Tocqueville, have pointed out the lack of grandeur, the intellectual conformity, and the cultural mediocrity that is supposed to be inherent in our systems of government. Democracy, Tocqueville warned, could easily become the tyranny of the majority. He noted that there were no great writers in America, or indeed anything that might be described as great. It is a common but somewhat questionable complaint. For it is not at all clear that art and culture in New York is any more mediocre than it is in Damascus or Beijing.

Much in our affluent, market-driven societies is indeed mediocre, and there is nothing admirable about luxury per se, but when contempt for bourgeois creature comforts becomes contempt for life you know the West is under attack. This contempt can come from many sources, but it appeals to those who feel impotent, marginalized, excluded, or denigrated: the intellectual who feels unrecognized, the talentless art student in a city filled with brilliance, the time-serving everyman who disappears into any crowd, the young man from a third-world country who feels mocked by the indifference of a superior West; the list of possible recruits to a cult of death is potentially endless.

Liberalism, wrote an early Nazi theorist, A. Moeller v.d. Bruck, is the "liberty for everybody to be a mediocre man." The way out of mediocrity, say the sirens of the death cult, is to submerge one's petty ego into a mass movement, whose awesome energies will be unleashed to create greatness in the name of the Führer, the Emperor, God, or Allah. The Leader personifies all one's yearnings for grandeur. What is the mere life of one, two, or a thousand men, if higher things are at stake? This is a license for great violence against others: Jews, infidels, bourgeois liberals, Sikhs, Muslims, or whoever must be purged to make way for a greater, grander world. An American chaplain named Francis P. Scott tried to explain to the Tokyo War Crimes Tribunal the extraordinary brutality of Japanese soldiers during the war. After many interviews with former combatants, he concluded that "they had a belief that any enemy of the emperor could not be right, so the more brutally they treated their prisoners, the more loyal to the emperor they were being."[10]

The truest holy warrior, however, is not the torturer but the kamikaze pilot. Self-sacrifice is the highest honor in the war against the West. It is the absolute opposite of the bourgeois fear for his life. And youth is the most capable of sacrificial acts. Most kamikazes were barely out of high school. As bin Laden has said, "The sector between fifteen and twenty-five is the one with ability for jihad and sacrifice."

5.

Aurel Kolnai argued in 1938 in his *War Against the West* that "the trend towards the emancipation of women [is] keenly distinctive of the West." This somewhat sweeping claim seems to be born out by the sentiments of Kolnai's enemies. Here is Alfred Rosenberg, the Nazi propagandist: "Emancipation of woman from the women's emancipation movement is the first demand of a generation of women which would like to save the Volk and the race, the Eternal-Unconscious, the foundation of all culture, from decline and fall."[11] Leaving aside what this woolly-headed thinker could have meant by the Eternal-Unconscious, the meaning is clear enough. Female emancipation leads to bourgeois decadence. The proper role for women is to be breeders of heroic men. One reason the Germans imported such huge numbers of workers from Poland and other countries under Nazi occupation was the dogmatic insistence that German women should stay at home.

Bin Laden is equally obsessed with manliness and women. It is indeed one of his most cherished Occidentalist creeds. "The rulers of that region [the Gulf States] have been deprived of their manhood," he said in 1998. "And they think the people are women. By God, Muslim women refuse to be defended by these American and Jewish prostitutes." The West, in his account, is determined "to deprive us of our manhood. We believe we are men."

Few modern societies were as dominated by males as wartime Japan, and the brutal policy of forcing Korean, Chinese, and Filipina, as well as Japanese, girls to serve in military brothels was a sign of the low status of women in the Japanese empire. And yet, the war itself had the peculiar effect of emancipating Japanese women to a degree that cannot possibly have been intended.

Because most able-bodied men were needed on the battlefronts, women had to take care of their families, trade in the black markets, and work in the factories. Unlike the men, who experienced defeat as a deep humiliation, many Japanese women regarded the Allied victory as a step toward their liberation. One of the most important changes in postwar Japan was that women got the right to vote. They did so in large numbers as early as 1946. A new constitution was drawn up mostly by American jurists, but the articles concerning women's rights were largely the work of a remarkable person called Beate Sirota, who represented most things enemies of the West would have loathed. She was European, educated, a woman, and a Jew.

To all those who see military discipline, self-sacrifice, austerity, and worship of the Leader as the highest social ideals, the power of female sexuality will be seen as a dire threat. From ancient times women are the givers and the guardians of life. Women's freedom is incompatible with a death cult. Indeed, open displays of female sexuality are a provocation, not only to holy men, but to all repressed people whose only way to exaltation is death for a higher cause. Pictures of partly naked Western women advertising Hollywood movies, or soft drinks, or whatever, by suggesting sexual acts, are as ubiquitous in the world as those images of the Manhattan skyline. They are just as frustrating, confusing, and sometimes enraging. For again they promise a sinful, libidinous world of infinite pleasure beyond most people's reach.

6.

There is no clash of civilizations. Most religions, especially monotheistic ones, have the capacity to harbor the anti-Western poison. And varieties of secular fascism can occur in all cultures. The current conflict, therefore, is not between East and West, Anglo-America and the rest, or Judeo-Christianity and Islam. The death cult is a deadly virus which now thrives, for all manner of historical and political reasons, in extreme forms of Islam.

Occidentalism is the creed of Islamist revolutionaries. Their aim is to create one Islamic world guided by the *sharia* (Islamic law), as interpreted by trusted scholars who have proved themselves in jihad (read "revolution"). This is a call to purify the Islamic world of the idolatrous West, exemplified by America. The aim is to strike at American heathen shrines, and show, in the most spectacular fashion, that the US is vulnerable, a "paper tiger" in revolutionary jargon. Through such "propaganda by action" against the arrogant US, the forces of jihad will unite and then impose their revolution on the Islamic world.

Ayatollah Khomeini was a "Stalinist" in the sense that he wanted to stage a revolution in one significant country, Iran, before worrying about exporting it. Bin Laden, by contrast, is a "Trotskyite," who views Afghanistan as a base from which to export revolution right away. There is a tension between the "Stalinists" and the "Trotskyites" within the Islamist movement. September 11 gave the "Trotskyites" an advantage.

Al-Qaeda is making a serious bid to stage an Islamist revolution that would bring down governments from Indonesia to Tunisia. It has not succeeded yet. We can expect more "propaganda by action" against the US and US installations, accompanied by crude Occidentalist propaganda. The West, and not just the geographical West, should counter this intelligently with the full force of calculating bourgeois anti-heroism. Accountants mulling over shady bank accounts and undercover agents bribing their way will be more useful in the long-term struggle than special macho units blasting their way into the caves of Afghanistan. But if one thing is clear in this murky war, it is that we should not counter Occidentalism with a nasty form of Orientalism. Once we fall for that temptation, the virus has infected us too.

NOTES

1. D. C. Holtom, *Modern Japan and Shinto Nationalism* (University of Chicago, 1943), p. 10.
2. Viking, 1938.
3. *Briefe 1882–1924* (Munich: Bruckmann, 1928).
4. *England und Deutschland* (Munich: Bruckmann, 1915).
5. *Jahr der Entscheidung* (Munich: C. H. Beck, 1933).
6. *Letters Concerning the English Nation* (Oxford University Press, 1994), p. 30.
7. Akira Iriye, *Power and Culture: The Japanese-American War 1941–1945* (Harvard University Press, 1981).
8. Jasper Becker, *Hungry Ghosts: Mao's Secret Famine* (Free Press, 1996), p. 62.
9. Quoted in Kolnai, *The War Against the West*, p. 215.
10. Arnold C. Brackman, *The Other Nuremberg: The Untold Story of the Tokyo War Crimes Tribunals* (Morrow, 1987), p. 251.
11. Quoted in George L. Mosse, *Nazi Culture: Intellectual, Cultural and Social Life in the Third Reich* (Grosset and Dunlap, 1966), p. 40.

SHERI BERMAN

ISLAMISM, REVOLUTION, AND CIVIL SOCIETY

Over recent decades, Islamism—the belief that Islam should guide social and political as well as personal life—has become a powerful force throughout much of the Muslim world, especially in Arab countries. Believing that the Islamic community is mired in a state of barbarism, Islamists seek not merely stricter religious observance or a change in political leadership but a revolutionary transformation of their societies. What defines them as members of a coherent movement is not their choice of particular means, but rather the nature and scale of their ends—the establishment of an Islamic state.[1] Since the rise of Islamism has had and will probably continue to have profound social, political, and strategic consequences, understanding its emergence and development is of the utmost practical and intellectual importance.

Popular analyses of Islamism have generally explained it with reference to cultural, religious, or regional concerns: the nature of Arab civilization, the tenets of Islam, the Arab-Israeli conflict. Scholarly treatments of the subject, more sensitive to the problems with using such broad and stable variables to explain a variegated and evolving phenomenon, have dug deeper and perceptively analyzed particular national Islamist movements and the regimes they confront. These studies, however, have rarely been integrated into or informed by wider-ranging literatures and debates in political science. This is unfortunate, since the true contours of the Islamist challenge, both where it conforms to historical norms and where it deviates from them, can be understood only within a broader comparative framework—and political science has at its fingertips impressive bodies of research capable of providing significant analyti-

cal purchase on the phenomenon.

Some scholars, for example, have viewed the rise of Islamism through the lens of the literature on transitions from authoritarianism to democracy. From this perspective, what is most notable about Islamists is their prominent role in civil society organizations and their status as rising oppositions pressing regimes for political change. These factors are often considered to mark Islamists as examples of, or agents for, liberalization.[2] This essay will instead draw on the revolutions literature, arguing that much of what is occurring in the Arab world can be understood as an example of a prerevolutionary situation.[3] In this light, the rise of Islamism appears less benign than it does in much of the transitions-influenced literature, and the movement's pervasive presence in civil society is both more intriguing and less heartening.

Although it may seem an unusual choice, bringing in the revolutions literature makes sense for three reasons. First and most obvious, Islamist movements explicitly state that revolution is their objective, and so it seems logical to take them at their word and view their significance and actions through the prism of previous work on movements with comparable goods.[4] Second, many of the variables highlighted in the revolutions literature seem to play an important role in contemporary Middle Eastern politics. And third, examining Islamism in the context of the revolutions literature provides us with a rare opportunity to analyze a potentially revolutionary process playing out in real time. For the most part, revolutions have been examined after the fact. While nothing is necessary wrong with this, limiting the study of revolutions to those that have already occurred risks introducing a methodological basis into the literature, one that we can and should correct by analyzing cases the display the standard features of a

From *Perspectives on Politics*, 1, no. 2 (2003), pp. 257–272.

prerevolutionary situation but whose outcome remains in doubt.[5] Hence, a study of Islamism holds out the promise of teaching students of revolution some valuable lessons about the applicability and usefulness of existing theories.

This essay, accordingly, will examine the rise of Islamism from an explicitly comparative and theoretical perspective, focusing on the Egyptian case in particular. The fate of Egypt—the largest Arab country, and one of the most influential—has great substantive importance. Furthermore, Egypt has played a special role in the intellectual and political evolution of Islamism. As a result of this and the country's relative openness, events there have been particularly well documented and scholars have produced a number of excellent studies of the rise and rationale of Islamism. Furthermore, to a degree, Egypt can stand in for other Middle Eastern countries, an issue that I will take up later.

What the case demonstrates is that the necessary precondition for the rise of Islamism has been the declining efficacy and legitimacy of the Egyptian state—just as many leading theories on revolutions would predict. This development alone, however, has not been sufficient to turn a potentially revolutionary situation into a successful revolution. Instead, what has occurred in Egypt and other parts of the Arab world is a peculiar kind of stalemate in which the existing regime retains political power while ceding substantial control over the societal and cultural spheres to the revolutionary challenger—an outcome that the revolutions literature does not envision. This stalemate, in turn, is largely a consequence of Islamists' ability to expand their presence in civil society. The expansion of civil society in Egypt and other Arab countries over recent decades is thus best understood as a sign not of benign liberalization but of profound political failure, and as an incubator for illiberal radicalism.[6]

You Say You Want a Revolution

Because of their dramatic nature and consequences, revolutions have always attracted a great deal of attention. The most prominent popular approach to explaining them, and one that is quite often heard in contemporary analyses of Islamism, focuses on social and psychological factors: the accumulation of societal grievances; the development of pervasive discontent, frustration, and (relative) deprivation; a growing discrepancy between the values of an exiting regime and its citizens.[7] These factors are believed to generate "a purposive, broadly based movement . . . which consciously undertakes to overthrow the existing government, and perhaps the entire social order."[8] This perspective focuses, in other words, on "why, when, and how large numbers of individual men and women become discontented"[9] and views revolutions as the work of revolutionary movements generated by widespread social and psychological strains and tension.

Despite its familiarity and superficial plausibility, however, this approach to the study of revolutions has fundamental flaws, the most obvious being a lack of empirical verification. For example, if this theory is correct, then "the ultimate and sufficient condition for revolution is the withdrawal of this consensual support" and "no regime could survive if the masses were consciously disgruntled."[10] But as we know, many do. The theory also leads us to expect revolutions to be fairly common, when in fact they are rare. As Leon Trotsky once noted, "[T]he mere existence of privations is not enough to cause an insurrection; if it were, the masses would always be in revolt."[11]

Such an approach also sidesteps and undertheorizes the most critical component of revolutions—the breakdown of the old order—because it is seen as flowing inexorably from social and psychological strains and tensions among the populace. This failing has been addressed most forcefully by Theda Skocpol, who revolutionized the study of revolutions by insisting that any explanation must be able to account for "the emergence (not 'making') of a revolutionary situation within an old regime."[12] Rather than viewing revolutions as the work of revolutionary movements, Skocpol argues that such movements become significant threats only *after* a revolutionary situation has already begun to emerge.[13] As she has observed, "[T]he fact is that historically no successful revolution has been 'made' by a mass-mobilizing, avowedly revolutionary movement."[14] Revolutionary movements even those "with large, ideologically imbued mass followings," never create the cries they exploit.[15]

How, then, do revolutionary crises emerge? Through the "breakdown of the administrative and coercive powers of an old order."[16] It is not the strength of challengers that analysts should focus on, Skocpol asserts, but rather the weakness of the incumbent regime. But why do states lose power and control over their societies? According to this camp, because they are unable to respond effectively to the challenges they face. Skocpol herself focuses on challenges emanating from the international system: military defeat or geopolitical or economic competition can severely stress inflexible and inefficient political institutions and undermine the authority and legitimacy of weak, vulnerable states. "Modern social revolutions," Skocpol argues, "have happened only in countries situated in disadvantaged positions within international arenas. In particular, the realities of military backwardness or political dependency have crucially affected the occurrence and course of social revolutions."[17]

In complementary analyses, other scholars have explored challenges to states emerging from the domestic sphere. Samuel Huntington, for example, has noted:

> Revolution is . . . an aspect of modernization. It is not something which can occur in any type of society at any period in its history. It is not a universal category but rather an historically limited phenomenon. It will not occur in highly traditional societies with very low levels of social and economic complexity. Nor will it occur in highly modern societies. Like other forms of violence and instability, it is most likely to occur in societies which have experienced some social and economic development and where the processes of political modernization and political development have lagged behind the processes of social and economic change.[18]

In modernizing societies, development has proceeded far enough to offer citizens a glimpse of what modernity has to offer, but not far enough to deliver it; in such societies, states are thus under significant pressure to perform a growing range of functions and satisfy ever-increasing demands. Moreover, since with the onset of development traditional institutions and norms begin to fall apart fairly rapidly but modern ones take a longer time to emerge, modernizing states tend to lack institutional mechanisms capable of handling these growing demands. The weaker, less flexible, and less efficient a country's institutions are, the greater the state's loss of control and legitimacy, and the larger the potential for disorder and violence.[19]

Jack Goldstone, meanwhile, has also focused on the connection between domestic pressures and state breakdown, looking not at modernization but at the chain reactions caused by the inability of state institutions to handle rapid population growth.[20] In the seventeenth century, he notes, large agrarian states

> were not equipped to deal with the impact of the steady growth of population that then began throughout northern Eurasia. . . . The implications of this ecological shift went far beyond mere issues of poverty and population dislocation. Pressure on resources led to persistent price inflation. Because the tax systems of most early modern states were based on fixed rates of taxation on people or land, tax revenues lagged behind prices. States thus had no choice but to seek to expand taxation. . . . Yet attempts to increase state revenues met resistance from the elites and the populace and thus rarely succeeded in offsetting spiraling expenses. As a result, most major states in the seventeenth century were . . . headed for fiscal crisis.[21]

In short, Skocpol and other theorists encourage us to view revolutions as a two-stage process, with the weakening and discrediting of existing political institutions creating a (potentially) revolutionary movements and their attack on the status quo. As we will see, in the Egyptian case the first stage of the revolutionary process has played out by the book. In recent decades, the Egyptian state has faced a variety of challenges, including military defeat, modernization, and rapid population growth. Unable to cope, it has suffered a steady loss of popular support and legitimacy—a problem that has been exacerbated by the regime's resorting to repression as a way of maintaining control. The result has been the opening of a political space for a potential revolutionary challenger.

However, this is only the first stage in any revolutionary process: declining state legitimacy and efficacy can open up a political space that revolutionary movements can exploit, but if we want to know *whether* any movement will be able to do so,[22] or *which movement* will emerge at the forefront, an analysis of the state can get us only so far.[23] If we want to truly understand the trajectories of revolutions in general, and the dynamics of Islamism in Egypt and elsewhere in particular, we need to analyze how and why some movements are able to develop the powerful organizations, cross-class coalitions, and ideologically imbued supporters that we know from previous studies are the hallmarks of successful revolutionary movements.[24] As we will see in the Egyptian case, one way that they do this is to exploit the possibilities offered by civil society—which in these circumstances has played a role quite different from what many of its cheerleaders would expect.

Civil society has become a hot topic in recent years, both inside and outside the academy. Although one can find in the literature almost as many definitions of civil society as there are treatments of it, the term generally refers to all voluntary institutions and associations that exist below the level of the state but above the level of the family:[25] churches, clubs, civic groups, professional organizations, nongovernmental organizations, and so forth.[26] To its many proponents, civil society is both an indicator of and a prerequisite for a healthy democracy and society. Especially after the collapse of the Soviet empire, civil society was seen as "the opposite of despotism"[27] and an embodying "for many an ethical ideal of the social order."[28] Civil society activity is said to produce the "habits of the heart necessary for stable and effective democratic institutions."[29] It is supposed to moderate attitudes, promote social interaction, facilitate trust, and increase solidarity and public spiritedness. Participation in civil society allegedly teaches citizens to be engaged and broad-minded, while at the same time training the activists and leaders that a democracy requires and lays the grounds for successful economic and social development.[30]

Given the dominance of such views in the discipline as a whole, it is not surprising that they have made their way into Middle Eastern studies as well. Many scholars have thus seen the expansion of civil society activity in many parts of the Arab world in recent decades as reason to be optimistic about the region's chances for political liberalization and even democratization. The most prolific and influential observer of the trend, for example, had argued that "the development of civil society is a crucial step toward realizing a freer Middle East."[31] Following such reasoning, major foundations have thrown money at the topic and underwritten research to track the trend's growth and expected beneficent effects.[32]

What the civil society advocates have not sufficiently appreciated, however, is that the nature of civil society's influence is dependent on political context, among other things. Absent strong and healthy political institutions, a rise in civil society activity may be a cause for concern rather than jubilation and may signal and deepen political problems rather than mitigate them.[33] This is what has happened in Egypt and many parts of the Arab world more generally. The expansion of civil society there is best understood as a reflection and cause of local states' declining effectiveness and legitimacy. Civil society has served, moreover, as the base from which Islamist revolutionaries have launched an impressive challenge to the status quo.[34]

The Decline of the State

In Egypt and in many other parts of the Middle East, the 1950s and 1960s represented "the high-water mark of the mass-mobilizing state . . . with its all-pervasive bureaucracy, mass production factory system and official culture."[35] Under Gamal Abdel Nasser's leadership, the Egyptian state undertook a far-reaching program of social and economic development known as Arab socialism, embracing nationalizations, land reform, and giant prestige projects like the Aswan High Dam. In order to maintain support for its ambitious goals, the state entered into a "covenant" with its subjects "in which the subjects relinquished their claims to basic human and civil rights in return for the state undertaking to provide them with education and health care, employment and subsidies."[36] Nasser's international agenda was no less ambitious than his domestic one, as he was the foremost advocate of pan-Arabism—a movement that took as its goal the political unification of all Arab lands and found expression during this era in the League of Arab States, the Arab Federation of Iraq and Jordan, and the United Arab Republic.

By the late 1960s, however, the lofty ambitions and high hopes that Nasser and pan-Arabism inspired came down to earth. Internationally, the Egyptian state and pan-Arabism suffered a number of serious blows, including the breakup of the United Arab Republic, the Yemen civil war, and most importantly, the rout at the hands of the Israelis in 1967. As one observer points out, "That occurrence was the most shattering event in Egypt's contemporary history. 'Why were we so utterly defeated?'—the soul searching question echoed all over the country."[37] Domestically, meanwhile, things were going just as badly. The heavy-handed state-led development model that Nasser embraced in an attempt to modernize the country stifled the private sector and saddled the government with responsibility for everything from education and employment to health care and transportation subsidies. Egypt's economic situation declined dramatically; from the 1970s through the 1990s, unemployment rose steadily while per capita GNP and average real wages fell.

Exacerbating the problems was the simultaneous massive population growth that the country, and indeed the entire region, experienced.[38] As one commentator notes,

> Egypt's social question is a problem of numbers. . . . In 1800 Egypt had a population of about 5 million. . . . [T]oday it is around 60 million—a 1,200 percent increase in less than two centuries. All of this population growth, moreover, has taken place in the fertile valley and delta of the Nile River, a ribbon of territory that makes up only 5 percent of present-day Egypt's total land area. The remainder of the country is a barren and unpopulated desert. . . . [W]ith its birth rate of 28 per 1,000 more than half of Egypt's people are under the age of 20, and the dependency ratio is 4 to 1. To put it another way, these figures mean that no more than a fifth to a quarter of the population is actively and gainfully employed.[39]

These demographic trends were even more alarming from a comparative perspective. Between 1980 and 1995, the Middle East had the highest population growth in the world, twice as high as East Asia and even higher than sub-Saharan Africa.[40] Not surprisingly, population increases have dramatically outpaced the growth of per capita income and GNP. Particularly worrisome has been the extremely rapid increase of the region's "youth rate": in Egypt and in the Arab world generally, approximately 40 percent of the population is under age 15.[41]

Rapid population growth made it impossible for the Egyptian state to live up to the promises it had made to its citizens in return for political support. The government had tried to guarantee education and subsequent public employment, but economic decline made such pledges unsustainable—and indeed, by the 1980s, Egyptian society became flooded by large numbers of secondary school and university graduates who could not find a job. The ones who were fortunate enough to get a job found that their real wages decreased over time. As one analyst comments,

> [T]he regime's ultimate retreat from the entitlement program stirred intense resentment among

would-be recipients who had come to regard state benefits as their "due." In sum . . . the regime deliberately fostered youth dependence on the state but—under conditions of resources scarcity and under-development—ultimately failed to deliver on its promises. The exhaustion of the statist model . . . contributed to the rise of a frustrated stratum of educated, underemployed youth "available" for mobilization by opposition groups.[42]

Alongside the slowdown in state employment, the "safety valve" provided by migration to the oil rich states of the Persian Gulf also began to close. Up through the early 1980s, Egyptians flooded into places like Saudi Arabia, Kuwait, and the Gulf region, but falling oil prices, political disturbances, and the Gulf War severely limited this option.[43] The cumulative result of these trends was a massive rise in unemployment, particularly among the educated.

Thus, by the final quarter of the twentieth century, the Egyptian state had been battered by military defeat and the collapse of pan-Arabism, together with economic failure and overpopulation. It could no longer provide jobs, social services, or a sense of hope and direction to its citizens, and it proved unable or unwilling to respond to the numerous challenges it faced. The government remained relatively resistant to the dramatic liberalizing trends occurring in many other parts of the world and indeed had a tendency to retreat further into an authoritarian and repressive cocoon as problems mounted.[44] Therefore, it became increasingly estranged from its citizens. Surveying the scene in 1995, one observer noted sorrowfully, "At the heart of Egyptian life there lies a terrible sense of disappointment."[45]

The Rise of the Islamists

It was against this background that the contemporary Islamist movement in Egypt emerged. Islamist groups relied on a preexisting network of local mosques, communal ties, and legitimacy;

had access to funding from local supporters (including many wealthy donors and migrant workers in the Persian Gulf) and from foreign governments, particularly Saudi Arabia;[46] and were somewhat insulated from repression (because the state did not want to be seen as attacking religious institutions or organizations)—so they were able to move into the political, social, and economic void that the retreating Egyptian state left behind.[47] Islamist organizations became the main focus of cultural and community life in many parts of Egypt, especially in poorer areas. In addition, private, grass-roots, voluntary associations run by Islamists became important providers of social goods normally associated with the state. As one activist put it, "We provide services for people who are not able to afford it [or] where there are no government services at all."[48] Indeed, Islamist associations grew to handle everything from health care and housing to education and employment help. As a result, the movement came to "play a role in social life governments had once claimed but then abdicated"[49]—with the main difference being that the social services provided by the Islamists tended to be more responsive and efficient. In the words of one observer:

> From my own experience, having visited a number of [institutions run by Egyptian Islamist groups], I can tell you that they are far better equipped, the staff is far more professional, the equipment is much more modern, than things you'll find in the typically run-down government facilities. A perfect example of how the Islamists have responded to social needs with far greater alacrity than the regime was the earthquake in Cairo in 1992. The government was totally paralyzed. [President Hosni] Mubarak was traveling abroad, and for two days the regime did absolutely *nothing*, nothing at all. Within hours, though, the Islamists were on the streets—with tents, with blankets, with food, with alternative housing. The same thing happened in 1994, in Durunka, when flash-floods carried flaming fuel from an army depot through the streets. Once again, the government was simply incapable of coping and the Islamists filled the void.[50]

Along with the help, however, often came a message: "Islam is the way." Sometimes this message was only indirect and implicit, conveyed through the success of Islamic groups in providing services and fulfilling needs that the state could or would not. Even when the groups and associations had no political agenda, "their social services inadvertently highlight[ed] the state's inability to provide such assistance. Thus, they chip[ped] away at the government's credibility."[51] They also "provided the space for a diffuse process of ideological outreach and network building by small clusters of independent activists, expanding the base of reformist and militant Islamic political groups alike."[52] Sometimes, however, the message was delivered explicitly, as when social services were run according to Islamic norms (e.g., gender-segregated health care and interest-free loans),[53] or when schools, tutoring, and other educational services were used to inculcate particular values. Islamist primary schools, for example, offered children not only a rigorous education in relatively uncrowded conditions but also religious indoctrination.[54]

In addition to developing their own civil society organizations, Islamists also became involved in a wide range of existing ones. Thus, beginning in the mid-1970s, Islamist student associations (*jamaat al-Islamiyya*) began to dominate the student unions of most campuses. During the 1970s, the enrollment at Egyptian universities more than doubled while infrastructure and services remained stagnant, and learning conditions as well as job prospects degenerated dramatically. Islamists offered religion as a solution to the crisis, portraying Islam as a "system that was 'complete and total,' that could not only interpret the larger world but also transform it."[55] Backing up this rhetoric were concrete actions, as Islamist associations provided students with everything from photocopied textbooks to low-cost lecture notes to help with housing.

The student associations, furthermore, "were masters at combining practical services with the inculcation of moral standards." For example, in response to a horribly overburdened transportation system, they purchased minibuses to ferry around female students. As this service became increasingly popular, however, Islamists limited it to women who wore the veil. A similar tactic was applied to dress more generally. To students who had trouble affording clothing, Islamists offered "Islamic garments" practically free of charge.[56] And along with practical services, the movement provided "a sense of community and belonging to students who only recently had been drawn away from their familiar surroundings and families."[57]

The same thing happened in many of Egypt's professional associations. By the early 1990s, the Muslim Brotherhood—the largest of Egypt's Islamist groups—had gained control of the doctors', engineers', scientists', pharmacists', and lawyers' syndicates in free and fair elections and provided their constituents with a variety of much-needed services:[58]

> The Islamist-led Engineers' Association [in Egypt] held a conference focused on the needs of the more than 20,000 predominantly young engineers without work. The Islamist leadership of the Medical Association conducted a survey of nearly 25,000 doctors in 12 governorates, in which two-thirds of those interviewed revealed that their salaries were not enough to cover their living costs. The executive boards of the Engineering and Medical Associations have initiated projects in the areas of housing, health care, and insurance, established training programs and pilot small business ventures for new graduates, and exerted pressure on the government to reduce university enrollments.[59]

Indeed, Islamists have been so successful in running these organizations and using them to provide services and a voice to their members that some scholars have argued that under their influence "professional syndicates [became] perhaps the most vibrant institutions of Egyptian civil society."[60]

All this civil society activism has yielded the Islamist movement many benefits. Grass-roots involvement in practically every nook and cranny of Egyptian life has allowed Islamists to gain insight into the needs and demands of a wide range of citizens (including members of the middle class and elites) and craft their appeals and programs appropriately. As Ali E. Hillal Dessouki, currently minister of youth and sport in the Mubarak government, has noted, these groups are "seeking to gain the support of the average Egyptian one by one, inch by inch, through the provision of welfare facilities, Islamic schools, Islamic clinics, technical schools, economic institutions for profit, social insurance, monthly payments for the poor," and so forth.[61] The quality of engagement that the Islamists display in each area, moreover, constitutes "a quiet indictment of the government's inability to provide" basic services to their citizens.[62] By combining their message with concrete social action and offering a real alternative to the existing regime, the Islamists have bolstered their standing and appeal among many different sectors of Egyptian society that feel estranged from and betrayed by the ruling order.

Involvement in civil society has also helped Islamists build a more powerful, flexible, and responsive movement. The infiltration of Egypt's associational life, for example, has helped the movement recruit and train new leaders. As one observer notes:

> The activists who have led the Islamic Trend's [the platform of the Muslim Brotherhood] entry into the professional associations emerged out of the student *gama'at*. . . . These leaders gained valuable experience providing services, propagating Islamic ideology, countering alternative groups on campus, and negotiating with the regime. The professional associations offered them a channel to continue their political activity after graduation. Participation in the *gama'at* also shaped the political consciousness of a much broader circle of university students, thereby creating a constituency upon which the Islamist candidates could draw, first in the student unions and subsequently in the professional associations. One leftist activist in the Engineers' Association explained: "You raise Muslim Brother students in the university, then five years later you have an electoral base for the professional associations. It's like planting seeds on a farm."[63]

The movement has been comparably skillful in using its position in civil society to tape "members' knowledge and organizational skills, financial resources, and access to mosques, newspapers, publishing houses, professional associations, and political parties, to mobilize opposition to government policies or the state."[64] And the dense associational web within which the Islamist movement envelops its supporters has helped build a sense of community and collective identity among them, deepening their commitment to the cause and willingness to sacrifice for it. In a country such as Egypt, where political participation and social activism have generally been discouraged, membership and participation in Islamist associational life has provided many with their first meaningful opportunity to play an active role in their communities and society. One scholar notes (in an assessment that fits in well with the encomiums to civil society so often found in the literature): "Islamists challenged dominant patterns of political alienation and abstention by promoting a new ethic of civic obligation that mandated participation in the public sphere, regardless of its benefits and costs."[65]

The civil society strategy, finally, has to some extent helped Islamists to avoid government prosecution. The dispersed and local nature of their associational life has made it difficult for the Egyptian state to monitor their activities,[66] while the movement's scope and success have made it an unattractive target for government attack. As the author of one of the few statistical studies of the Egyptian nongovernmental sector puts it, "The government could not curtail Islamic charity organizations because they are the most dynamic organizations in civil society, and they reach people and regions that the state cannot."[67]

The Remains of the Day

Particularly after Hosni Mubarak succeeded Anwar Sadat in 1981, the Egyptian state generally responded to the Islamist challenge with a two-pronged strategy, cracking down harshly on the movement's extremists while trying to co-opt moderates and burnish its own Islamic credentials. This meant, in addition to brutal repression, "a discernable retreat on the part of the regime from secular politics and culture."[68] Religious rhetoric began to color official political discourse, and "positions and arguments espoused by different political contenders, including top-ranking state officials, are now often justified or attacked by reference to texts from the Qur'an or the Hadiths."[69] In addition, moderate Islamists were given access to state resources, particularly the media (which they often used to rail against secularism and advocate an Islamic state).[70]

The power of Egypt's leading center of Islamic learning, al-Azhar University, also expanded greatly: "In exchange for conferring Islamic legitimation on the state [the dignitaries of al-Azhar] formulated demands for the Islamization of society, notably in the moral and cultural spheres."[71] They also promoted the Islamization of school curricula and took it upon themselves to pass judgment more generally on what Egyptians read, saw, and learned. As one scholar notes,

> In its efforts to install itself as [society's] supreme censor . . . the Azhar, at first, began by delivering itself through the issuance of fatwas on an increasing number of public issues, then moved to a more obtrusive role, which manifested itself in direct interventions to ban published books on the ground that they violate Islamic principles, and publicly condemned secular authors. Finally, in an attempt to provide for itself a firm legal ground for screening all material intended for broadcasting, the Azhar solicited the "opinion" of the Administrative court in regard to the extent of its legal authority to do so. In a poorly argued decision, the court ruled that indeed the Azhar's jurisdiction is unbounded with respect to all matters "related" to Islam. . . . Since virtually all decisions may be "related" to Islam, the negative consequences for freedom flowing from this view were incalculable.[72]

The result was widespread censorship of information and entertainment and the branding of secular intellectuals as heretics, leading to harassment and even physical attacks. In one particularly notorious example, the secular writer Farag Foda was murdered a few days after he was denounced by the authorities of al-Azhar in 1992.

Although such policies were designed, along with the crackdown, to blunt Islamism's appeal, in practice they had the opposite effect. Moderate Islamists never fully renounced their more radical brethren; indeed, even the Muslim Brotherhood, which openly rejects violence, "continue[d] to act as apologists for [more militant Islamist] groups, portraying them as idealists driven to . . . reprehensible tactics by the government's corruption, its incompetence in dealing with the country's economic problems, and its failure to fulfill its previous commitment to institute Islamic Shari'a as the law of the land."[73] More importantly, by ceding control of broad swaths of civil society and cultural life to Islamists the state not only "legitimize[d] Islamists' demands and encourage[d] them to escalate the pressure for their fulfillment"[74] but also facilitated a profound transformation of Egyptian life.

Blocked from full political participation and allowed much greater freedom in civil society, the Islamist movement set about Islamizing Egypt from below. To put it another way, the Islamists, finding themselves unable to achieve their revolutionary goals directly by conquering the state, turned to gradually remaking Egyptian society and culture.[75] And in this they have been remarkably successful. Not only has the Islamist movement used its network of civil society organizations to put together what is essentially a "counter-society [that can] propagate the movement's ideas, create support networks for them, and show that Islamic values can be implemented in the contemporary world,"[76] but it has also reshaped everyday life. Perhaps the most obvious manifestation of this in both public and private life has been a general growth in religious observance and the role of Islamic norms and values. "According to government estimate, four thousand new mosques were constructed by early 1980s. . . . Religious programming on state radio and television exploded, with both moderate and radical sheikhs spreading their message more effectively than ever. Koranic and religious schools mushroomed, and Islamic mystical orders increased fourfold."[77] In addition, "self-censorship emerged in the production of television programs in response to pressure on the state by popular sentiment, and religious programs increased by 50 percent between 1975 and 1990. Islamic sentiment was particularly expressed in a marked decline of alcohol consumption, bars, liquor stores, and night clubs."[78]

It is important to note that these changes have not been limited to the poor and uneducated but have extended to sectors of the elite: "technocrats, socialists and other presumably secular groups."[79] For example, as one observer of Egypt's changing social and cultural life noted, "[a]t Cairo University, a campus that is representative of middle-class Egyptian society, a majority of female students were veiled. And no matter where I went at noontime, whether it was a bank, an athletic club, the central telephone office, the grand bazaar downtown, or even the government press center, all business stopped for prayer."[80] Indeed, the growing role of Islamic values has impacted everything from gender roles and fertility to consumption habits.[81] It has also led to growing social pressures toward conformity to Islamic norms of dress and behavior, such as veiling for women and beards for young men.[82]

The Islamist movement has also forced dramatic changes in the nature and style of governance in Egypt. Islamists have worked themselves into the public and state sectors, including critical areas such as the educational establishment, and have even gained footholds in the army, the police, and certain government ministries. As one observer noted, "Egypt's Islamist revolution by stealth has burrowed its way into the very heart of the institutions of the

Arab world's largest and most important state."[83] Another says, "Leading institutions, once under complete government control, have begun to erode the state's secularist policies. . . . Major institutions . . . are now in the hands of moderate Islamists [and in] neighborhoods and districts across the country popular sheikhs, free of government control, are making decisions on matters ranging from divorce to land ownership and the role of women in society."[84]

The state itself has been forced to make direct concessions to the Islamists on a whole range of issues—for example, by accepting the Shari'a as the "regulating principle for the community." This particular decision, in turn, has provided Islamists with an opportunity to transform Egypt's judicial system and to use it to attack a wide range of social and cultural norms and practices. "[L]ike other central institutions of Egyptian life, including the universities, al-Azhar, and the professional unions, the court system . . . slipp[ed] away from the secular regime."[85] Perhaps the most (in)famous example generated by the growing Islamization of the judicial system was the case of Abu Zaid, a university professor accused by Islamists of publishing blasphemous works. Backed by Islamist lawyers, Islamists charged Zaid with heresy and argued that as a heretic he could no longer remain married to his Muslim wife. In 1995 the Egyptian Appellate Court agreed with this charge and ordered Zaid to end his marriage. A few weeks later, the couple fled to the Netherlands.[86] After prosecuting Zaid, Islamists turned their attention to using the courts to silence other secular intellectuals and to imposing "Islamic" mores and values on society.

In short, while the Islamist movement has not been able to topple the Egyptian state, it has contributed to isolating it still further from its people and transforming the country's society and culture to such a degree that some scholars refer to what has occurred as the "Islamization of society" or a "cultural revolution." Indeed, the changes in Egypt have been so striking that some have even argued that the country is "already well on its way to becoming a near-Islamic state"[87] and "may indeed be more genuinely Islamized than Iran."[88] A nation "long considered an outpost of democracy and secularism in the Arab world is quietly being transformed into an Islamic order."[89]

A similar pattern can be detected elsewhere in the Arab world. Just as in Egypt, by the late 1960s the implicit social contract struck between many Arab governments and their citizens began to fall apart.[90] Economic decline set in across much of the region; demographic trends exacerbated economic problems and created a large pool of unemployed, frustrated youth along with destabilizing urban migrations; and the military impotence of Arab regimes against Israel was brutally revealed. States proved unable or unwilling to respond to these challenges and so lost popular support and legitimacy. Islamist groups stepped into the political space thus opened and managed to go a long way toward satisfying the basic economic and social needs of many citizens.

In Algeria, for example, the Islamic Salvation Front (FIS) rose to a position where it was poised to win national elections in 1992 as the result of a dynamic similar to the one we saw in Egypt. By the mid 1980s, Algeria was in dire economic straits and more than 60 percent of the population was under 25 years old. The state had largely abdicated its public responsibilities, so most Algerians were left without basic services or hope for the future. The Islamist movement used an extensive associational network to provide the social services, community and recreational groups, and economic support that Algerians desperately needed.[91] Such activities and programs helped the movement attract widespread support while undermining the state's legitimacy, a pattern further displayed when an earthquake hit the country in 1989: "The Islamists were the first to respond and did so effectively. They, rather than the government supplied blankets and medicine, and this scored further points while the government reinforced its image of ineffectiveness."[92]

Algerian Islamist organizations also provided citizens with some of the country's few genuine opportunities for political involvement and debate. As one participant recalls, in such associations Algerians could meet to discuss "all the problems that the Algerian nation was confronting. We spoke about everything . . . the economy . . . all aspects of life."[93] Not surprisingly, the Islamists were able to use such success in civil society to mobilize supporters and construct a powerful political machine. "When [the FIS] became a legal entity in 1989, [the movement's civil society] associations became the support network of the new party."[94] The FIS was able to attract "a broad base of support across the country . . . [and bring] a level of organization and ideological commitment, lacking in other sectors of society, as well as an impressive record of social responsibility and welfare" to the struggle against the existing regime.[95] Only the suspension of the voting and the imposition of martial law prevented the FIS from taking full control of the country.

Lebanon represents another disturbing variation on this theme. The state was never as powerful or centralized as its Egyptian or Algerian counterparts, but its collapse was even more spectacular. As the country descended into civil war in the 1970s, Islamists and Hezbollah in particular moved in to provide desperately needed services to hundreds of thousands of Lebanese—especially Shi'ites, the country's largest and poorest religious group. Hezbollah-affiliated associations now supply citizens with medical care, hospitals, housing, clean water, schools, and more. In addition to providing material aid, Hezbollah also sponsors a wide range of recreational and communal associations that help it attract supporters, spread its ideology, and gradually reshape society from within. At one Hezbollah-supported facility, for example, an American visitor observed "disabled veterans spend[ing] their days weaving baskets, taking computer classes and carving souvenirs with the group's logo that features an AK-47 machine gun clutched in a raised fist." Its civil society activities allow the movement to "keep tabs on the recipients' political feelings and religious observance,"[96] and Hezbollah has thus been able to win "the hearts and minds of new supporters" and build its backing "from the grass roots up."[97]

Something Old, Something New

In comparative historical perspective, three aspects of the Egyptian Islamist case are noteworthy: that state failure preceded the revolutionary challenge, that the state has not collapsed, and that the revolutionary movement has managed to effect a profound social and cultural transformation nonetheless. The first is consistent with reigning theories of revolution and, indeed, just what one would expect to find, given the basic features of the situation. The second highlights lacunae in the state-centric revolutions literature, but also suggests places where the literature's insights can push our understanding forward. The third, finally, is unusual and intriguing and is due to the revolutionaries' clever exploitation of civil society—which in the particular political context found in Egypt and other parts of the Arab world has ended up playing a role quite different than some civil society promoters would predict.[98]

In recent decades political scientists interested in revolutions have been taught to look past colorful challengers and first examine the decrepit incumbents those challengers seek to replace. They have realized, in other words, that the game must be lost by the old regime before it can be won by the new one. Many scholars have come to understand state failure, moreover, in terms of a gap between the challenges a state faces and its ability to respond successfully to them. And common challenges include military weakness, the strains of modernization, and rapid population growth. The rise of Islamism in Egypt, it turns out, is a textbook example of all these variables in action.

Humiliation by a tiny hated enemy (Israel), the collapse of grandiose diplomatic schemes,

dependence on an alien outside power (the United States)—to call the international track record of the Egyptian state from the late 1960s onward unimpressive would be charitable. The one seeming triumph, moreover—the peace treaty with Israel that gained the return of the Sinai Peninsula and a steady stream of American aid—is instead viewed by the Egyptian public as a sign of the state's weakness, an abandonment of the Palestinians, and a cause of increased subordination to the United States.

Domestically, meanwhile, the picture looks even worse. The standard stresses that accompany modernization and capitalist development have been magnified by generally misguided government policies, with the result the continued poverty, unemployment, inequality, and repression have offered little but frustration to an ever-increasing population. By shrinking the world, globalization has only exacerbated the problem. "The new age of globalization," one observer notes, "has hit the Arab world in a very strange way. Its societies are open enough to be disrupted by modernity, but not so open that they can ride the wave. . . . Globalization in the Arab world is the critic's caricature of globalization— a slew of Western products and billboards with little else."[99]

Furthermore, the pervasiveness of repression and authoritarianism (in Egypt and the Arab world more generally) has only contributed to a growing rejection of existing states by their citizens. Leaders in most of these countries are chosen not on the basis of merit or popularity, but because of bloodlines or control over the means of force. Additionally, in response to rising grievances and frustration, the rulers of many of these countries have cracked down further on opposition, thus closing off legitimate alternative channels for the airing of grievances and increasing the use of violence against their citizens. While examples from Algeria to Weimar Germany make clear that political openness and elections alone cannot ward off revolutions, those countries in the Middle East that have experienced some political reform or liberalization (e.g., Morocco, Qatar, Jordan) have been less threatened by extremism than have their more autocratic counterparts. And history has shown time and time again that although authoritarian regimes may be able to control opposition through repression and coercion, denying formal opportunities for political grievances to be voiced does not make the grievances disappear—it only forces them underground or directs them into alternative channels.[100]

The result of these developments, in Egypt and across much of the Arab region, has been the emergence of a classic "Huntingtonian" gap, as mobilization, aspirations, and expectations have increased dramatically while existing state and political institutions have proved unable or unwilling to respond. Accompanying this has been an estrangement of the region's citizens from their governments. As one observer has noted,"Egyptians' attitudes towards their government could be summed up with one word: Animosity. They believe 'that this country is not their country but the country of rich people and thieves. . . . They love Egypt. But they hate the government.'"[101] Under these conditions, the surprise would not be the emergence of some kind of revolutionary challenge, but the absence of one.

The fact remains, however, that despite its demonstrable failure, the Egyptian state—like most of its regional counterparts—has not yet collapsed or been toppled. The state-centric revolutions literature, in other words, helps us understand why a revolutionary movement (Islamism) has emerged in Egypt and other parts of the Arab world, but it is less helpful in predicting whether the challenge to the old regime will be successful. What the Egyptian case highlights, therefore, is a limitation in the state-centric revolutions literature: the ambiguity or indeterminacy of terms like "weakness" or "decline." In historical cases of revolution, we can tell that state strength diminished "far enough" by the presence of a revolution, but this way of assessing the situation is both intellectually and methodologically problematic. In order to in-crease this literature's analytical utility, we need to have ways of determining the value of its independent variable (i.e., the extent of state weakness/decline) separate from its dependent one (revolution or lack thereof).

This is not to say, however, that the state-centric revolutions literature provides no purchase on the phenomenon of regime perseverance in Egypt and other parts of the Arab world in the face of immense declines in efficacy and legitimacy. In particular, Skocpol's admonition that those interested in revolutions pay attention to international factors is very helpful here. Although in most historical cases of revolution a state's ability to retain control over the instruments of repression—its final bulwark against the loss of power—has been intimately linked to its broader domestic power and support, this is generally not true in Arab countries. Egypt's geostrategic importance, for example, has led to massive amounts of American aid and relative indulgence by the international community. Indeed, in the Arab world more generally, windfall oil and gas revenues—together with American aid and the support that authoritarian regimes in the region provide for one another—have acted as a deus ex machina, allowing states to maintain impressive military, police, and domestic intelligence capabilities, as well as relationships with critical social groups, without having to worry too much about widespread declines in societal support and legitimacy. Without these external sources of support, there is every reason to believe that many regimes in the region, including the Egyptian one, would find it much more difficult if not impossible to hold on to power.[102] Skocpol urged consideration of states' international positions and relationships to analyze why some succumb to revolution, so it should hardly be surprising that the same factors can work the other way, to bolster state power.[103]

Given the discontinuous nature of political change as well as the Middle East's many sources of potential volatility, the region's situation could shift at a moment's notice. Withdrawal of American support, the outcome of a war and regime change in Iraq, an escalation of the Israeli-Palestinian conflict—any or all of these things could have a dramatic effect on the various Middle Eastern regimes. Still, regime persistence rather than collapse is the most likely scenario in Egypt and the rest of the Arab world for the foreseeable future. Yet ironically, perhaps, it is at precisely this point that the case becomes most interesting and begins to inform the literature on revolutions, for the situation in Egypt and many other Arab countries appears to have settled into an unusual stalemate. The state is managing to hang on to power but is hollowing out; it has essentially ceded a significant degree of control over society and culture to its revolutionary challenger. Neither a simple success nor a failure for either side, this hybrid situation has received some attention from regionalists,[104] but its larger theoretical and comparative implications remain relatively unexplored.

The key to understanding this unexpected turn of events, I suggest, lies in the particular strategy adopted by Islamist revolutionaries, who have gained a surprising amount of power through the back door by infiltrating their countries' civil societies. If one shortcoming of the state-centric revolutions literature highlighted by the Egyptian case is the indeterminacy of the critical concepts of state weakness and decline, another is the relative lack of attention paid to precisely how revolutionary movements develop the powerful organizations, cross-class coalitions, and ideologically imbued supporters that enable them to pose a viable challenge to existing regimes. In the Egyptian case, a critical component of Islamist success has been the movement's infiltration of civil society. This civil society–based strategy, in turn, has enabled the movement to begin transforming life from the bottom up. Islamic values and norms have permeated almost all sectors of society, affecting everything from gender roles to consumption habits, entertainment to education. Even governance has not been exempt.

What seems to have occurred, in other words, is a reversal of the traditional revolutionary pattern. In most revolutions, political change precedes societal and cultural transformation: the state is captured and the new regime then begins constructing a new order. In Egypt, however, societal and cultural transformation has preceded, and perhaps substituted for, political change: here "a grassroots movement emerg[ed] from the streets . . . to transform the social structure from the bottom-up"[105] One Islamic scholar put it well when he told a Western reporter that "Egypt was undergoing an Islamic revolution that was peaceful and quietist. We don't need to overthrow the state because we are achieving our aims without violent insurrection."[106] What the Egyptian case seems to indicate, then, is that in some ways the capture of civil society can be as powerful an agent of revolutionary change as the capture of the state itself. Hence, those comparativists and regionalists who view the Islamist movement as a failure because it has not captured the state may be missing the larger picture, or at least an important part of it.[107]

Interestingly, the Islamist case is not the first one in which a thoroughly illiberal revolutionary movement has furthered its prospects by exploiting civil society. In the late nineteenth and early twentieth centuries, Germany's civil society expanded in inverse relation to the responsiveness and legitimacy of existing state and (certain) political institutions. The Weimar Republic in particular saw a flowering of associational life, and then—as in much of the Arab world now—the growing strength of civil society activity boded ill rather than well. The infiltration and capture of a wide range of voluntary associations helped a revolutionary challenger—the Nazi party—create a powerful political machine and construct a true cross-class coalition.[108] In Weimar Germany as in Egypt, moreover, it appears that at least one reason the revolutionary challenger adopted a civil society strategy is that it was unable to mount a successful direct challenge to the state. (When Hitler tried this strategy in 1923—the ill-fated Beer Hall Putsch—be found himself in jail, and when Islamists mounted violent attacks in Egypt and elsewhere they were eventually crushed.) What these cases may indicate is that where a revolutionary movement faces a weakened but still functioning state, a civil society approach that allows the gradual accumulation of support, skills, and organization, rather than open confrontation, may be the most logical and efficient strategy.

A final important lesson that the Egyptian case teaches is that at least in certain contexts, the civil society skeptics may have a clearer vision than the boosters. The growth of civil society should not be considered an undisputed good, but a politically neutral multiplier—neither inherently "good" nor "bad," but dependent for its effects on the wider political environment and the values of those who control it.

Where existing political institutions are weak and the regime is perceived as ineffectual and illegitimate, as in Egypt and Weimar Germany, civil society may become an alternative to traditional politics, increasingly absorbing citizens' energies and satisfying their basic needs. In such situations, civil society can work to undermine political stability further by alienating citizens from traditional political structures, deepening dissatisfaction, and providing a rich soil for oppositional and revolutionary movements to mobilize and grow.[109] Furthermore, many of the benefits of associationalism stressed by civil society advocates—providing individuals with political and social skills, creating bonds among citizens, facilitating mobilization, decreasing barriers to collective action, training activists and leaders—do clearly exist, but they can be turned to antidemocratic as well as democratic ends. In short, absent clear specification of the surrounding political context and the character of the groups involved, there is no reason to believe that civil society activity will have democratic, liberal, or even particularly laudable results.

Such a finding has practical and theoretical implications, since the "dogma holding that strengthening civil society is the key to creating and sustaining a healthy polity has come to dominate the thinking of major charitable foundations as well as human rights and humanitarian organizations."[110] Two authorities recently noted, "A term that was scarcely used within the aid community ten years ago has become a ubiquitous concept in discussions and documents about democracy promotion worldwide."[111] Yet if civil society is promoted in the context of weak and illegitimate states, Western donors may find themselves unwillingly or indirectly furthering the cause of revolutionary movements, rather than assisting in a benign process of democratic development.[112]

It seems clear that what Egypt and many other Arab countries need most at this point is not stronger civil societies, but rather more effective and responsive political institutions. Without a state able and willing to respond to the basic needs and demands of its people, all the civil society promotion in the world will have only a limited impact on the life chances of ordinary citizens and may also serve to push countries further down the path of political instability and even violence.[113] While it is certainly much easier to fund social groups and nongovernmental organizations than it is to encourage healthy state development and push authoritarian regimes to undertake real political reform, the latter two efforts are truly necessary if progressive political change and effective economic development are to occur in Egypt and other countries like it.

NOTES

1. Sivan 1990a; Esposito 1999; Esposito et al. 1997; Kepel 1985; Kepel 2002.
2. On the debate over democratic prospects, see Norton 1993; Sadowski 1993; Krämer 1992; Schwedler 1995; Zubaida 1992. Other scholars, however, noting the comparative paucity of democratic systems in the region, have also turned to the transitions literature for insight as to what might make

the Middle East an "exception that proves the rule." Heydemann 2002.

3. Bayat 1998.

4. Whether some Islamist groups advocate violence is irrelevant to their revolutionary status, for the defining feature of revolutions is the degree and scope of change involved, not the way in which change is achieved. This basic point has been obscured by the disproportionate attention paid to cases featuring violent, sudden overthrows of the existing order, such as those of France, Russia, and China. Revolutionary transformations can occur without violence or sudden upheaval, with the ascendancies of Hitler and Mussolini being cases in point.

5. Some skeptics argue that it is inappropriate to apply the revolutions literature to situations where revolutions have not (yet) occurred. It is worth noting that in this case such concerns would apply a fortiori to the democratic transitions literature as well.

6. Bayat 1998; Wickham 2002; Abdo 2000.

7. Goldstone 1980; Goldstone 2001; Eckstein 1965; Feierabend et al. 1972; Gurr 1970; Gurr 1973; Johnson 1966.

8. Skocpol 1994, 111.

9. Tilly 1986, 49.

10. Skocpol 1979, 16.

11. Skocpol 1994, 260. See Trotsky 1980.

12. Skocpol 1994, 18.

13. This insight has also been emphasized by scholars working on less dramatic instances of political change. For example, the literature on social movements focuses on "changing opportunity structures," which incorporate (but are not limited to) changes in the power and policies of existing state and political institutions. McAdam et al. 1996. Wickham 2002, for example, makes use of the social movements literature in her examination of the rise of Islamism in Egypt, which leads her to stress somewhat different factors and dynamics than does analysis presented here.

14. Skocpol 1979, 16.

15. Skocpol 1994, 107.

16. Ibid., 7–8.

17. Skocpol 1979, 23; Dunn 1989. It is worth noting that Skocpol herself attempted to apply this framework to the most importatnt case hitherto of successful Islamic revolution: Iran. Skocpol 1982.

18. Huntington 1968, 265; Goldstone 1986.

19. The critical and innovative aspect of this analysis is not its focus on the social and political changes associated with modernization, but its insistence that these changes become potentially destabilizing only insofar as political institutions and structures lack the capacity and flexibiilty to deal with them. As Charles Tilly has noted, Huntington's theory is made "the more plausible because it appears to dispose of the anomaly that by many standards the relatively peaceful richer countries are also the faster changing." Tilly 1986, 49.

20. Goldstone 1991a; Goldstone 1991b; Goldstone 1986; Goldstone 1999.

21. Goldstone 1991a, 24. See also Foran 1995, 114. Note that for Goldstone it is not population growth itself that matters, but the ability of existing institutions to deal with it. As with Huntington, the crucial variables are the nature and capacities of existing institutions: the weaker and less flexible they are, the less they can deal with the challenges posed by population growth, and the greater the potential for breakdown.

22. For example, it is certainly at least possible to imagine a situation where a severely weakened state exists but no single, coherent revolutionary movement is able to mount a credible challenge. (This description probably fits the situation in many countries in the years before revolutions occur. A good historical example would be several cases in post–World War I Europe, where the revolutions expected to follow on the heels of the Russian Revolution and the

end of the First World War never materialized.) Or, as has happened all too frequently, states can collapse without a coherent revolutionary movement having emerged, leading to chaos and warlordism, rather than a new political order. This latter outcome is much more likely, however, in premodern rather than in transitional societies.

23. Goldstone 1994; Bayat 1998.

24. Goldstone 1991b; Skocpol 1994; Popkin 1979; Wickham-Crowley 1987; Sewell 1980; Sewell 1985; Skocpol 1985.

25. However, see Singerman 1995 and n.d. for an analysis of the role played by familial ties and networks on Egyptian civil society.

26. Eberly 2000. Some have tried to narrow this definition by excluding organizations and associations with explicitly antidemocratic or antiliberal views. The problem with this is that it injects a great deal of subjective judgment into what is ostensibly an objectively defined phenomenon, and it makes arguments about the benign effects of civil society tautological.

    Indeed, some scholars of the Middle East have engaged in precisely this type of reasoning, excluding Islamist groups from their definition of civil society (thereby robbing the sector of its largest and most vital element) and then proclaiming that the weakness of civil society is a main reason for the lack of democracy in the region. Schwedler 1995.

27. Hall 1995, 1.

28. Seligman 1992, x.

29. Putnam 1993, 11. See also Bellah et al. 1985; Tocqueville 1969.

30. The literature claiming to link civil society to myriad positive outcomes is huge. Some good surveys include Diamond 1994; Edwards et al. 2001.

31. Norton 1993, 211. See also Kubba 2000; Sadowski 1993; Krämer 1992 and 1993; Esposito et al. 1999; Ghabra 1991; Sivan 1990b.

32. Both the Ford Foundation and the Social Science Research Council, for example, sponsored initiatives on "Civil Society in the Middle East." The most comprehensive survey of the topic was produced by Norton 1995 and 1996, and summarized in Schwedler 1995. For an overly critical view of this research program, see Kramer 2001.

33. Berman 1997.

34. Wickham 1994; Wickham 2002; Abdo 2000; Bayat 1998; Zaki 1995.

35. Sivan 1990b, 353.

36. Sivan 1998, 9–10.

37. Ayubi 1980, 489.

38. Cordesman 1998 and 1999; United Nations Development Programme 2002.

39. Ibrahim 1996, 125.

40. It should be noted that progress has been made on this front in the last several years.

41. The rate for the developed world is 20 percent; for the developing world in general, 35 percent. A generally accepted estimate identifies 25 percent as a sustainable number for the long term and views anything over 35 percent as "high risk."

42. Wickham 2002, 11–2; see also chapter 3 and Kepel 1985.

43. Wickham, 2002.

44. There was some economic liberalization (the *intifah*), as well as occasional relaxations on political controls. But the former came nowhere close to solving the country's economic problems, and the latter were never allowed to develop far enough to significantly threaten the regime.

45. Ajami 1995, 79.

46. Norton n.d.; Ibrahim 1996; Zaki 1995; Wickham 2002.

47. Bayat 1998; Wickham 2002; Zaki 1995. It is also important to note that other potential challengers, such as secular nationalism and socialism, had already been tried in Egypt and found wanting, so they were not available as the foundation upon which a new revolutionary movement could be built.

48. Karawan 1997, 21.
49. Anderson 1997, 24.
50. Lester 1999. See also Ibrahim 1988.
51. Murphy 2002, 35.
52. Wickham 2002, 102.
53. Sivan 1990b, 359.
54. Denoeux 1993.
55. Kepel 2002, 82.
56. Ibid., 81–2.
57. Denoeux 1993, 151. See also Kepel 2002, chapter 12.
58. Wickham 2002; Ibrahim 1995; Ibrahim 1996.
59. Wickham 1997, 123.
60. Esposito 1999, 100–1. See also Zubaida 1992 and Wickham 2002.
61. Kifner 1986, A2.
62. Esposito et al. 1997, 9.
63. Wickham 1997, 125.
64. Al-Sayyid 1995, 289. See also Dekmejian 1995; Denoeux 1993.
65. Wickham 2002, 120. See also Denoeux 1993; Ibrahim 1980.
66. Wickham 2002; Esposito 1999.
67. Amani Qandil, quoted in Negus 1997.
68. Ajami 1998, 203. See also Flores 1993; Aybui 1982; Dessouki 1981; Sadowski 1987.
69. Zaki 1995, 241.
70. Ibid. See also Ajami 1998, 203; Kepel 2002, chapter 12.
71. Kepel 1985, 19.
72. Zaki 1995. See also Alterman 2000.
73. Zaki 1995, 119.
74. Ibid., 127.
75. Sivan 2000; Kepel 1985.
76. Sivan 1997, 106. See also Sivan 1990a, chapter 4; Dekmejian 1995.
77. Abdo 2000, 14. See also Bayat 1998; Murphy 2002.
78. Bayat 1998, 156.
79. Ayubi 1980, 487–8.
80. Abdo 2000, 4.
81. Sivan 1998.
82. Sivan 1998; Sivan 1990a.
83. Lester 1999, 1. See also Zaki 1995.
84. Abdo 2000, 5–6, 25–6.

85. Abdo 2000, 165.
86. Murphy 2002, 200–11.
87. Dekmejian 1995, 123.
88. Rodenbeck 1998, 185.
89. Abdo 2000, 12. See chapter 8 of the same book for a comparison of trends in Egypt and Iran.
90. On this general pattern, see Norton 1993; Maddy-Weitzman 1996; Khashan 1997; Sivan 1990b; Ibrahim 1995; Ibrahim 1993; Dekmejian 1995; Anderson 1997.
91. Esposito 1999; Entelis 1995; Kepel 2002, chapter 7; Maddy-Weitzman 1996.
92. Esposito 1999, 176.
93. Ibid., 174.
94. Davis 1992, 11.
95. Esposito 1999, 182.
96. Trofimov 2001, 1. See also MacFarquhar 2001.
97. Esposito 1999, 156. See also Norton n.d.; Trofimov 2001; MacFarquhar 2001.
98. Abdo 2000; Wickham 2002; Weaver 1999. Goldstone's most recent work on revolutions, which focuses on efforts to undermine the existing institutions of the state, coincides with the view of Islamist movements presented in this paper. See Goldstone 1994; Goldstone 1999; Goldstone 2001.
99. Zakaria 2001, 30. Although there has been some economic liberalization in Egypt, it has not been nearly enough to tackle the country's continuing major problems.
100. Goodwin 2001.
101. Murphy 2002, 20, quoting attorney Ahmed Saraf Al Din.
102. On a similar point, see Gause 2000 and Goldfrank 1994. This is in some ways the flipside of the well-known argument about how resource extraction has helped keep authoritarianism in place in the Middle East. See, for example, Anderson 1995.
103. Violent Islamists have also been undermined support for the movement more generally by engaging in widespread and indiscriminate slaughter. In both Egypt and Algeria, particularly horrific massacres

aliented many people otherwise sympathetic to the cause.

104. Bayat 1998 interestingly refers to this phenomenon as a "passive revolution." See also Wickham 2002; Abdo 2000.

105. Abdo 2000, 5.

106. Abdo 2000, 199. See also Bayat 1998.

107. This view is held by some of the most perceptive and influential observers of Islamism—e.g., Roy 1994 and Kepel 2002. Such scholars also see Islamism as a failure because it has not come up with distinctive and well-defined political and economic programs for usurping the state's power. However, these criticisms not only pay insufficient attention to the immense societal and cultural changes that Islamist movements have succeeded in effecting; they are also based upon invalid assumptions about how well developed the political and economic plans of revolutionary movements need to be. Almost all revolutionary movements rise to power more on the basis of their critique of the existing order than on their concrete plans for the future, and almost all spend their first years in power experimenting with a variety of politics and institutional arrangements. Once this fact is recognized, Islamists today appear no different from the Russian or Chinese communists or the Nazis on the eves of their ascendancy to power.

108. Berman 1997. Research on other extremist movements also reveals that many have been supported by a vibrant associational infrastructure. See Riley n.d.; Gusfield 1962; Halebsky 1976; Parkin 1968; Wolfinger et al. 1964.

109. Berman 1997.

110. Rieff 1999.

111. Carothers and Ottaway 2000, 3.

112. Not necessarily by unwittingly funding revolutionary movements, but by further undermining support for the state as well as vitiating the state's own need to provide basic services for its own citizens.

113. Huntington 1968.

REFERENCES

Abdo, Geneive. 2000. *No God but God: Egypt and the Triumph of Islam.* New York: Oxford University Press.

Ajami, Fouad. 1995. The sorrows of Egypt. *Foreign Affairs* 75:5, 72–88.

———. 1998. *The Dream Palace of the Arabs: A Generation's Odyssey.* New York: Pantheon Books.

Al–Sayyid, Mustapha K. 1995. A civil society in Egypt? In *Civil Society in the Middle East*, vol. 1, ed. Augustus Richard Norton. New York: E. J. Brill, 269–94.

Alterman, Jon B. 2000. Egypt: Stable, but for how long? *The Washington Quarterly* 23:4, 107–18.

Anderson, Lisa. 1995. Peace and democracy in the Middle East: The constraints of soft budgets. *Journal of International Affairs* 49:1, 25–44.

———. 1997. Fulfilling prophecies: State policy and Islamist radicalism. In *Political Islam: Revolution, Radicalism or Reform?* ed. John L. Esposito. Boulder: Lynne Rienner Publishers, 17–31.

Ayubi, Nazih. 1980. The political revival of Islam: The case of Egypt. *International Journal of Middle East Studies* 12:4, 481–99.

———. 1982. The politics of militant Islamic movements in the Middle East. *Journal of International Affairs* 36 (Fall–Winter), 271–83.

Bayat, Asef. 1998. Revolution without movement, movement without revolution: Comparing Islamic activism in Iran and Egypt. *Comparative Studies in Society and History* 40:1, 136–69.

Bellah, Robert N., Richard Madsen, William M. Sullivan, Ann Swidler, and Steven M. Tipton. 1985. *Habits of the Heart: Individualism and Commitment in American Life.* Berkeley: University of California Press.

Berman, Sheri. 1997. Civil society and the rise of the Weimar Republic. *World Politics* 49:3, 401–29.

Carothers, Thomas, and Marina Ottaway. 2000. The burgeoning world of civil society aid. In

Funding Virtue: Civil Society Aid and Democracy Promotion, eds. Thomas Carothers and Marina Ottaway. Washington, D.C.: Carnegie Endowment for International Peace, 3–18.

Cordesman, Anthony H. 1998. *Demographics and the Coming Youth Explosion in the Gulf.* Washington, D.C.: Center for Strategic and International Studies, 1–56.

———. 1999. *Stability and Instability in the Middle East: Economics, Demography, Energy, and Security.* Washington, D.C.: Center for Strategic and International Studies.

Davis, Hannah. 1992. Taking up space in Tlemcen. The Islamic occupation of urban Alberia: An interview with Rabia Bekkar. *Middle East Report* 179, 11–5.

Dekmejian, R. Hrair. 1995. *Islam in Revolution: Fundamentalism in the Arab World,* 2d ed. Syracuse: Syracuse University Press.

Denoeux, Guilain. 1993. *Urban Unrest in the Middle East: A Comparative Study of Informal Networks in Egypt, Iran, and Lebanon.* Albany: SUNY Press.

Dessouki, Ali E. Hillal. 1981. The resurgence of Islamic organizations in Egypt: An interpretation. In *Islam and Power,* eds. Alexander H. Cudsi and Ali E. Hillal Dessouki. Baltimore: Johns Hopkins University Press, 107–18.

Diamond, Larry. 1994. Rethinking civil society: Toward democratic consolidation. *Journal of Democracy* 5:3, 3–17.

Dunn, John. 1989. *Modern Revolutions: An Introduction to the Analysis of a Political Phenomenon,* 2d. ed. New York: Cambridge University Press.

Eberly, Don E. 2000. The meanings, origins, and applications of civil society. In *The Essential Civil Society Reader,* ed. Don E. Eberly. Lanham, M.D.: Rowman and Littlefield.

Eckstein, Harry. 1965. On the etiology of internal wars. *History and Theory* 4:2, 133–63.

Edwards, Bob, Michael W. Foley, and Mario Diani, eds. 2001. *Beyond Tocqueville: Civil Society and the Social Capital Debate in Comparative Perspective.* Hanover, N.H.: University Press of New England.

Entelis, John. 1995. Civil society and the authoritarian temptation in Algerian politics. In *Civil Society in the Middle East,* vol. 1, ed. Augustus Richard Norton. New York: E. J. Brill, 45–86.

Esposito, John L. 1999. *The Islamic Threat: Myth or Reality?* 3d ed. New York: Oxford University Press.

Esposito, John L., Graham Fuller, Martin Kramer, and Daniel Pipes. 1999. Is Islamism a threat?: A debate. *The Middle East Quarterly* 6:4, 29–41.

Esposito, John L., Robert E. Mazur, and Sibusiso Nkomo. 1997. *Political Islam: Revolution, Radicalism or Reform?* Boulder: Lynne Rienner Publishers.

Feierabend, Ivo K., Rosalind Feierabend, and Ted Robert Gurr, eds. 1972. *Anger, Violence, and Politics: Theories and Research,* Englewood Cliffs, N.J.: Prentice Hall.

Flores, Alexander. 1993. Secularism, integralism and political Islam: The Egyptian debate. *Middle East Report* 183, 32–8.

Foran, John. 1995. Revolutionizing theory/ theorizing revolutions: State, culture, and society in recent works on revolution. In *Debating Revolutions,* ed. Nikki R. Keddie. New York: New York University Press, 112–35.

Gause, F. Gregory. 2000. The persistence of monarchy in the Arabian peninsula: A comparative analysis. In *Middle East Monarchies: The Challenge of Modernity,* ed. Joseph Kostiner. Boulder: Lynne Rienner Publishers, 167–86.

Ghabra, Shafeeq. 1991. Voluntary associations in Kuwait: The foundation of a new system? *Middle East Journal* 45:2, 1999–215.

Goldfrank, Walter L. 1994. The Mexican revolution. In *Revolutions: Theoretical, Comparative, and Historical Studies,* 2d ed., ed. Jack A. Goldstone. Fort Worth: Harcourt Brace College Publishers, 115–27.

Goldstone, Jack A. 1980. Theories of revolution: The third generation. *World Politics* 32:3, 425–53.

———. 1986. The English revolution: A structural-demographic approach. In *Revolutions: Theoretical, Comparative, and Historical Studies*, ed. Jack A. Goldstone. San Diego: Harcourt Brace Jovanovich, 100–14.

———. 1991a. *Revolution and Rebellion in the Early Modern World*. Berkeley: University of California Press.

———. 1991b. An analytical framework. In *Revolutions of the Late Twentieth Century*, eds. Jack A. Goldstone, Ted Robert Gurr, and Farrokh Moshiri. Boulder: Westview Press, 37–51.

———. 1994. The comparative and historical study of revolutions. In *Revolutions: Theoretical, Comparative, and Historical Studies*, 2d ed., ed. Jack A. Goldstone. Forth Worth: Harcourt Brace College Publishers, 1–18.

———. 1999. Population and pivotal states. In *The Pivotal States: A New Framework for U.S. Policy in the Developing World*, eds. Robert Chase, Emily Hill, and Paul M. Kennedy. New York: W. W. Norton, 247–69.

———. 2001. Toward a fourth generation of revolution theory. *Annual Review of Political Science* 4, 139–87.

Goodwin, Jeff. 2001. *No Other Way Out: States and Revolutionary Movements, 1945–1991*. New York: Cambridge University Press.

Gurr, Ted Robert. 1970. *Why Men Rebel*. Princeton: Princeton University Press.

———. 1973. The revolution–social change nexus. *Comparative Politics* 5:3, 359–92.

Gusfield, Joseph R. 1962. Mass society and extremist politics. *American Sociological Review* 27:1, 19–30.

Halebsky, Sandor. 1976. *Mass Society and Political Conflict*. New York: Cambridge University Press.

Hall, John A., ed. 1995. *Civil Society: Theory, History, Comparison*. Cambridge, M.A.: Polity Press.

Heydemann, Steve. 2002. Middle East studies after 9/11: Defending the discipline. *Journal of Democracy* 13:3, 102–8.

Huntington, Samuel P. 1968. *Political Order in Changing Societies*. New Haven: Yale University Press.

Ibrahim, Saad Eddin. 1980. Anatomy of Egypt's militant Islamic groups: Methodological note and preliminary findings. *International Journal of Middle East Studies* 12:4, 423–53.

———. 1988. Egypt's Islamic activism in the 1980s. *Third World Quarterly* 10:2, 632–57.

———. 1993. Crisis, elites and democratization in the Arab world. *Middle East Journal* 47:2, 292–305.

———. 1995. Civil society and prospects for democratization in the Arab world. In *Civil Society in the Middle East*, vol. 1, ed. Augustus Richard Norton. New York: E. J. Brill, 27–54.

———. 1996. Reform and frustration in Egypt. *Journal of Democracy* 7:4, 125–35.

Johnson, Chalmers. 1966. *Revolutionary Change*. Boston: Little, Brown.

Karawan, Ibrahim A. 1997. *The Islamist Impasse*. New York: Oxford University Press.

Kepel, Gilles. 1985. *Muslim Extremism in Egypt: The Prophet and Pharoah*, trans. Jon Rothschild. Berkeley: University of California Press.

———. 2002. *Jihad: The Trail of Political Islam*, trans. Anthony Roberts. Cambridge University Press.

Khashan, Hilal. 1997. The new world order and the tempo of militant Islam. *British Journal of Middle Eastern Studies* 24:1, 5–24.

Kifner, John. 1986. Egypt's new Islamic schools: Setting an example. *The New York Times*, 29 September, A2.

Krämer, Gudrun. 1992. Liberalization and democracy in the Arab world. *Middle East Report* 174, 22–35.

———. 1993. Islamicist notions of democracy. *Middle East Report* 183, 2–8.

Kramer, Martin. 2001. *Ivory Towers on Sand: The Failure of Middle Eastern Studies in America*. Washington, D.C.: The Washington Institute for Near East Policy.

Kubba, Laith. 2000. The awakening of civil society. *Journal of Democracy* 11:3, 84–90.

Lester, Toby. 1999. A conversation with Mary Anne Weaver. *Atlantic Unbound*, 17 February. Available at www.theatlantic.com/

unbound/bookauth/ba990217.htm. Accessed 31 January 2002.

MacFarquhar, Neil. 2001. To U.S., a terrorist group; to Lebanese, a social agency. *The New York Times,* 28 December, A10. Available at www.nytimes.com/2001/12/28/international/middleast/28LEBA.html. Accessed 31 January 2002.

Maddy-Weitzman, Bruce. 1996. The Islamic challenge in North Africa. *Terrorism and Political Violence* 8:2, 171–88.

McAdam, Doug, John D. McCarthy, and Mayer N. Zald, eds. 1996. *Comparative Perspectives on Social Movements: Political Opportunities, Mobilizing Structures, and Cultural Framings.* New York: Cambridge University Press.

Murphy, Caryle. 2002. *Passion for Islam. Shaping the Moden Middle East: The Egyptian Experience.* New York: Scribner.

Negus, Steve. 1997. Down, but not out. . . . The Muslim Brothers keep a low profile, but their main activity—charity work—still goes on. *Cairo Times,* 3 April. Available at www.cairotimes.com/content/issues/Islists/down03.html. Accessed 31 January 2002.

Norton, Augustus Richard. 1993. The future of civil society in the Middle East. *Middle East Journal* 47:2, 205–16.

———, ed. 1995. *Civil Society in the Middle East,* vol. 1. New York: E. J. Brill.

———, ed. 1996. *Civil Society in the Middle East,* vol. 2. New York: E. J. Brill.

———. n.d. The virtue of studying in civil society. In *The Civil Society Debate in Middle Eastern Studies?* eds. Augustus Richard Norton, Roger Owen, Diana Singerman, and James Gelvin. Los Angeles: University of California, Los Angeles, Middle Eastern Identities Colloquium Series.

Parkin, Frank. 1968. *Middle Class Radicalism: The Social Bases of the British Campaign for Nuclear Disarmament.* Manchester, U.K.: Manchester University Press.

Popkin, Samuel L. 1979. *The Rational Peasant: The Political Economy of Rural Society in Vietnam.* Berkeley: University of California Press.

Putnam, Robert D., with Robert Leonardi and Rafaella Y. Nanetti. 1993. *Making Democracy Work: Civic Traditions in Modern Italy.* Princeton: Princeton University Press.

Rieff, David. 1999. The false dawn of civil society: Debatable whether civil society can solve society's problems. *The Nation,* 22 February, 11–8.

Riley, Dylan. n.d. Hegemony and domination: Civil society and authoritarianism in interwar Europe. Unpublished manuscript, University of California, Davis.

Rodenbeck, Max. 1998. Is Islamism losing its thunder? *The Washington Quarterly* 21:2, 177–93.

Roy, Oliver. 1994. *The Failure of Political Islam,* trans. Carol Volk. Cambridge: Harvard University Press.

Sadowski, Yahya. 1987. Egypt's Islamist movement: A new political and economic force. *Middle East Insight* 5:3, 37–44.

———. 1993. The New Orientalism and the democracy debate. *Middle East Report* 183, 14–21, 40.

Schwedler, Jillian. 1995. *Toward Civil Society in the Middle East?: A Primer.* Boulder: Lynne Rienner Publishers.

Seligman, Adam B. 1992. *The Idea of Civil Society.* New York: Free Press.

Sewell, William H., Jr. 1980. *World and Revolution in France: The Language of Labor from the Old Regime to 1848.* New York: Cambridge University Press.

———. 1985. Ideologies and social revolutions: Reflections on the French case. *The Journal of Modern History* 57:1, 57–85.

Singerman, Diane. 1995. *Avenues of Participation: Families, Politics, and Networks in Urban Quarters of Cairo.* Princeton: Princeton University Press.

———. n.d. Civil society in the shadow of the Egyptian state: The role of informal networks in the construction of public life. In *The Civil Society Debate in Middle Eastern*

Studies? eds. Augustus Richard Norton, Roger Owen, Diane Singerman, and James Gelvin. Los Angeles: University of California, Los Angele, Middle Eastern Identities Colloquium Series.

Sivan, Emmanuel. 1990a. *Radical Islam: Medieval Theology and Modern Politics.* New Haven: Yale University Press.

———. 1990b. The Islamic resurgence: Civil society strikes back. *Journal of Contemporary History* 25:2/3, 353–64.

———. 1997. Constraints and opportunities in the Arab world. *Journal of Democracy* 8:2, 103–13.

———. 1998. Why radical Muslims aren't taking over governments. *Middle East Review of International Affairs* 2:2, 9–16.

———. 2000. Illusions of change. *Journal of Democracy* 11:3, 69–83.

Skocpol, Theda. 1979. *States and Social Revolutions: A Comparative Analysis of France, Russia, and China.* New York: Cambridge University Press.

———. 1982. Rentier state and Shi'a Islam in the Iranian revolution. *Theory and Society* 11:3, 265–83.

———. 1985. Cultural idioms and political ideologies in the revolutionary reconstruction of state power: A rejoinder to Sewell. *The Journal of Modern History* 57:1, 86–96.

———. 1994. *Social Revolutions in the Modern World.* New York: Cambridge University Press.

Tilly, Charles. 1986. Does modernization breed revolution? In *Revolutions: Theoretical, Comparative, and Historical Studies,* ed. Jack A. Goldstone. San Diego: Harcourt Brace Jovanovich.

Tocqueville, Alexis de. 1969. *Democracy in America,* ed. J. P. Mayer, trans. George Lawrence. Garden City, N.Y.: Anchor Books.

Trofimov, Yaroslav. 2001. Complex foe: Brandishing weapons and aid, Hezbollah tests U.S. resolve. *The Wall Street Journal,* 17 December, 1.

Trotsky, Leon. 1980. *The History of the Russian Revolution.* New York: Monad Press.

United Nations Development Programme. 2002. *Arab Human Development Report.* New York: United Nations Publications.

Wickham, Carrie Rosefsky. 1994. Beyond democratization: Political change in the Arab World. *PS: Political Science and Politics* 27:3, 507–9.

———. 1997. Islamic mobilization and political change: The Islamic trend in Egypt's professional associations. In *Political Islam,* eds. Joel Beinin and Joe Stork. Berkeley: University of California Press, 120–35.

———. 2002. *Mobilizing Islam: Religion, Activism, and Political Change in Egypt.* New York: Columbia University Press.

Wickham-Crowley, Timothy P. 1987. The rise (and sometimes fall) of guerrilla governments in Latin America. *Sociological Forum* 2:3, 473–99.

Wolfinger, Raymond, Barbara Kaye Wolfinger, Kenneth Prewitt, and Sheilah Rosenhack. 1964. America's radical right. In *Ideology and Discontent,* ed. David E. Apter. New York: Free Press.

Zakaria, Fareed. 2001. The politics of rage: Why do they hate us? *Newsweek,* 15 October, 22–40.

Zaki, Moheb. 1995. *Civil Society and Democratization in Egypt, 1981–1994.* Cairo: Konrad Adenauer Stiftung.

Zubaida, Sami. 1992. Islam, the state, and democracy: Contrasting conceptions of society in Egypt. *Middle East Report* 179, 2–10.

11 GLOBALIZATION

For political scientists, globalization represents the modern intersection between comparative politics (the study of domestic politics across countries) and international relations (the study of foreign relations between countries). As a result, scholars of both international relations and comparative politics have been drawn to this contentious topic. Just as globalization is blurring the lines between the domestic and the international, it is also blurring the lines between comparative politics and international relations.

Stanley Hoffman's "Clash of Globalizations" (2002) takes its name from Samuel Huntington's notion of a "Clash of Civilizations," in which he argued that cultural conflict between civilizations would replace the traditional ideological rivalries between states that marked the twentieth century (see Chapter 3). Hoffman agrees that we are now in a new era but one driven not by cultural divisions that separate civilizations. Rather, all societies now face, in different ways, three distinct forms of globalization—economic, cultural, and political. In each there may be benefits to be gained, but Hoffman is primarily concerned that the negative effects of globalization are likely to outweigh the good, undermining state sovereignty while providing few benefits (or benefits to a few) in return.

Similarly, Richard Florida's piece "The World is Spiky" (2005) is, like Hoffman's, a rejoinder to a popular argument regarding globalization. If Hoffman seeks to challenge Huntington's view of the clash of civilizations, Florida questions the well-known work of Thomas Friedman, who has argued in his book The World Is Flat *that technology has essentially leveled the playing field among countries. In contrast, Florida believes that the world has become a place where highly productive people, cities, and regions are increasingly concentrated and linked to each other while the peoples around them are left out and left behind.*

Not all scholars believe that globalization is so inherently problematic. Jagdish Bhagwati is perhaps the best-known advocate of globalization, and in this short piece (2005) he discusses its strengths and benefits. His main argu-

ment is that opponents of globalization assert that it ignores or even runs counter to social concerns, favoring profits over all other considerations. Bhagwati responds that in fact many of the dangers claimed by opponents of globalization, such as poverty or child labor, are in fact reduced by globalization, rather than exacerbated by it. Where there are problems, he argues, better international oversight can make certain that globalization serves the needs of people everywhere, ensuring the "human face" that he argues is inherent in deepening economic ties.

Of course, all of this assumes that globalization is an unstoppable process. The economic historian Niall Ferguson is not so convinced. In "Sinking Globalization," (2005) he argues that our period is much like the interwar period, marked by imperial overstretch, rivalries between great powers, unstable states, and international terrorism. Moreover, nearly a century later, there appear to be few new mechanisms that are able to manage these risks any more effectively than mechanisms of the past. Ferguson suggests that the end of globalization would be triggered by an economic crisis. Although written before the recent downturn, Ferguson's arguments seem prescient, raising the question that much of the debate over the benefits or costs of globalization may become, for the short term at least, largely academic.

STANLEY HOFFMANN

CLASH OF GLOBALIZATIONS

A New Paradigm?

What is the state of international relations today? In the 1990s, specialists concentrated on the partial disintegration of the global order's traditional foundations: states. During that decade, many countries, often those born of decolonization, revealed themselves to be no more than pseudostates, without solid institutions, internal cohesion, or national consciousness. The end of communist coercion in the former Soviet Union and in the former Yugoslavia also revealed long-hidden ethnic tensions. Minorities that were or considered themselves oppressed demanded independence. In Iraq, Sudan, Afghanistan, and Haiti, rulers waged open warfare against their subjects. These wars increased the importance of humanitarian interventions, which came at the expense of the hallowed principles of national sovereignty and nonintervention. Thus the dominant tension of the decade was the clash between the fragmentation of states (and the state system) and the progress of economic, cultural, and political integration—in other words, globalization.

Everybody has understood the events of September 11 as the beginning of a new era. But what does this break mean? In the conventional

From *Foreign Affairs*, 81, no. 4 (July/August 2002), pp. 104–15.

approach to international relations, war took place among states. But in September, poorly armed individuals suddenly challenged, surprised, and wounded the world's dominant superpower. The attacks also showed that, for all its accomplishments, globalization makes an awful form of violence easily accessible to hopeless fanatics. Terrorism is the bloody link between interstate relations and global society. As countless individuals and groups are becoming global actors along with states, insecurity and vulnerability are rising. To assess today's bleak state of affairs, therefore, several questions are necessary. What concepts help explain the new global order? What is the condition of the interstate part of international relations? And what does the emerging global civil society contribute to world order?

Sound and Fury

Two models made a great deal of noise in the 1990s. The first one—Francis Fukuyama's "End of History" thesis—was not vindicated by events. To be sure, his argument predicted the end of ideological conflicts, not history itself, and the triumph of political and economic liberalism. That point is correct in a narrow sense: the "secular religions" that fought each other so bloodily in the last century are now dead. But Fukuyama failed to note that nationalism remains very much alive. Moreover, he ignored the explosive potential of religious wars that has extended to a large part of the Islamic world.

Fukuyama's academic mentor, the political scientist Samuel Huntington, provided a few years later a gloomier account that saw a very different world. Huntington predicted that violence resulting from international anarchy and the absence of common values and institutions would erupt among civilizations rather than among states or ideologies. But Huntington's conception of what constitutes a civilization was hazy. He failed to take into account sufficiently conflicts within each so-called civilization, and

he overestimated the importance of religion in the behavior of non-Western elites, who are often secularized and Westernized. Hence he could not clearly define the link between a civilization and the foreign policies of its member states.

Other, less sensational models still have adherents. The "realist" orthodoxy insists that nothing has changed in international relations since Thucydides and Machiavelli: a state's military and economic power determines its fate; interdependence and international institutions are secondary and fragile phenomena; and states' objectives are imposed by the threats to their survival or security. Such is the world described by Henry Kissinger. Unfortunately, this venerable model has trouble integrating change, especially globalization and the rise of nonstate actors. Moreover, it overlooks the need for international cooperation that results from such new threats as the proliferation of weapons of mass destruction (WMD). And it ignores what the scholar Raymond Aron called the "germ of a universal consciousness": the liberal, pro-market norms that developed states have come to hold in common.

Taking Aron's point, many scholars today interpret the world in terms of a triumphant globalization that submerges borders through new means of information and communication. In this universe, a state choosing to stay closed invariably faces decline and growing discontent among its subjects, who are eager for material progress. But if it opens up, it must accept a reduced role that is mainly limited to social protection, physical protection against aggression or civil war, and maintaining national identity. The champion of this epic without heroes is *The New York Times* columnist Thomas Friedman. He contrasts barriers with open vistas, obsolescence with modernity, state control with free markets. He sees in globalization the light of dawn, the "golden straitjacket" that will force contentious publics to understand that the logic of globalization is that of peace (since war would interrupt globalization and therefore progress) and democracy (because new technologies increase individual autonomy and encourage initiative).

Back to Reality

These models come up hard against three realities. First, rivalries among great powers (and the capacity of smaller states to exploit such tensions) have most certainly not disappeared. For a while now, however, the existence of nuclear weapons has produced a certain degree of prudence among the powers that have them. The risk of destruction that these weapons hold has moderated the game and turned nuclear arms into instruments of last resort. But the game could heat up as more states seek other WMD as a way of narrowing the gap between the nuclear club and the other powers. The sale of such weapons thus becomes a hugely contentious issue, and efforts to slow down the spread of all WMD, especially to dangerous "rogue" states, can paradoxically become new causes of violence.

Second, if wars between states are becoming less common, wars within them are on the rise—as seen in the former Yugoslavia, Iraq, much of Africa, and Sri Lanka. Uninvolved states first tend to hesitate to get engaged in these complex conflicts, but they then (sometimes) intervene to prevent these conflicts from turning into regional catastrophes. The interveners, in turn, seek the help of the United Nations or regional organizations to rebuild these states, promote stability, and prevent future fragmentation and misery.

Third, states' foreign policies are shaped not only by realist geo-political factors such as economics and military power but by domestic politics. Even in undemocratic regimes, forces such as xenophobic passions, economic grievances, and transnational ethnic solidarity can make policymaking far more complex and less predictable. Many states—especially the United States—have to grapple with the frequent interplay of competing government branches. And the importance of individual leaders and their

personalities is often underestimated in the study of international affairs.

For realists, then, transnational terrorism creates a formidable dilemma. If a state is the victim of private actors such as terrorists, it will try to eliminate these groups by depriving them of sanctuaries and punishing the states that harbor them. The national interest of the attacked state will therefore require either armed interventions against governments supporting terrorists or a course of prudence and discreet pressure on other governments to bring these terrorists to justice. Either option requires a questioning of sovereignty—the holy concept of realist theories. The classical realist universe of Hans Morgenthau and Aron may therefore still be very much alive in a world of states, but it has increasingly hazy contours and offers only difficult choices when it faces the threat of terrorism.

At the same time, the real universe of globalization does not resemble the one that Friedman celebrates. In fact, globalization has three forms, each with its own problems. First is economic globalization, which results from recent revolutions in technology, information, trade, foreign investment, and international business. The main actors are companies, investors, banks, and private services industries, as well as states and international organizations. This present form of capitalism, ironically foreseen by Karl Marx and Friedrich Engels, poses a central dilemma between efficiency and fairness. The specialization and integration of firms make it possible to increase aggregate wealth, but the logic of pure capitalism does not favor social justice. Economic globalization has thus become a formidable cause of inequality among and within states, and the concern for global competitiveness limits the aptitude of states and other actors to address this problem.

Next comes cultural globalization. It stems from the technological revolution and economic globalization, which together foster the flow of cultural goods. Here the key choice is between uniformization (often termed "Americanization") and diversity. The result is both a "disenchantment of the world" (in Max Weber's words) and a reaction against uniformity. The latter takes form in a renaissance of local cultures and languages as well as assaults against Western culture, which is denounced as an arrogant bearer of a secular, revolutionary ideology and a mask for U.S. hegemony.

Finally there is political globalization, a product of the other two. It is characterized by the preponderance of the United States and its political institutions and by a vast array of international and regional organizations and transgovernmental networks (specializing in areas such as policing or migration or justice). It is also marked by private institutions that are neither governmental nor purely national—say, Doctors Without Borders or Amnesty International. But many of these agencies lack democratic accountability and are weak in scope, power, and authority. Furthermore, much uncertainty hangs over the fate of American hegemony, which faces significant resistance abroad and is affected by America's own oscillation between the temptations of domination and isolation.

The benefits of globalization are undeniable. But Friedmanlike optimism rests on very fragile foundations. For one thing, globalization is neither inevitable nor irresistible. Rather, it is largely an American creation, rooted in the period after World War II and based on U.S. economic might. By extension, then, a deep and protracted economic crisis in the United States could have as devastating an effect on globalization as did the Great Depression.

Second, globalization's reach remains limited because it excludes many poor countries, and the states that it does transform react in different ways. This fact stems from the diversity of economic and social conditions at home as well as from partisan politics. The world is far away from a perfect integration of markets, services, and factors of production. Sometimes the simple existence of borders slows down and can even paralyze this integration; at other times it gives integration the flavors and colors of the dominant state (as in the case of the Internet).

Third, international civil society remains embryonic. Many non-governmental organizations reflect only a tiny segment of the populations of their members' states. They largely represent only modernized countries, or those in which the weight of the state is not too heavy. Often, NGOs have little independence from governments.

Fourth, the individual emancipation so dear to Friedman does not quickly succeed in democratizing regimes, as one can see today in China. Nor does emancipation prevent public institutions such as the International Monetary Fund, the World Bank, or the World Trade Organization from remaining opaque in their activities and often arbitrary and unfair in their rulings.

Fifth, the attractive idea of improving the human condition through the abolition of barriers is dubious. Globalization is in fact only a sum of techniques (audio and videocassettes, the Internet, instantaneous communications) that are at the disposal of states or private actors. Self-interest and ideology, not humanitarian reasons, are what drive these actors. Their behavior is quite different from the vision of globalization as an Enlightenment-based utopia that is simultaneously scientific, rational, and universal. For many reasons—misery, injustice, humiliation, attachment to traditions, aspiration to more than just a better standard of living—this "Enlightenment" stereotype of globalization thus provokes revolt and dissatisfaction.

Another contradiction is also at work. On the one hand, international and transnational cooperation is necessary to ensure that globalization will not be undermined by the inequalities resulting from market fluctuations, weak state-sponsored protections, and the incapacity of many states to improve their fates by themselves. On the other hand, cooperation presupposes that many states and rich private players operate altruistically—which is certainly not the essence of international relations—or practice a remarkably generous conception of their long-term interests. But the fact remains that most rich states still refuse to provide sufficient development aid or to intervene in crisis situations such as the genocide in Rwanda. That reluctance compares poorly with the American enthusiasm to pursue the fight against al Qaeda and the Taliban. What is wrong here is not patriotic enthusiasm as such, but the weakness of the humanitarian impulse when the national interest in saving non-American victims is not self-evident.

Imagined Communities

Among the many effects of globalization on international politics, three hold particular importance. The first concerns institutions. Contrary to realist predictions, most states are not perpetually at war with each other. Many regions and countries live in peace; in other cases, violence is internal rather than state-to-state. And since no government can do everything by itself, interstate organisms have emerged. The result, which can be termed "global society," seeks to reduce the potentially destructive effects of national regulations on the forces of integration. But it also seeks to ensure fairness in the world market and create international regulatory regimes in such areas as trade, communications, human rights, migration, and refugees. The main obstacle to this effort is the reluctance of states to accept global directives that might constrain the market or further reduce their sovereignty. Thus the UN's powers remain limited and sometimes only purely theoretical. International criminal justice is still only a spotty and contested last resort. In the world economy—where the market, not global governance, has been the main bene-ficiary of the states retreat—the network of global institutions is fragmented and incomplete. Foreign investment remains ruled by bilateral agreements. Environmental protection is badly ensured, and issues such as migration and population growth are largely ignored. Institutional networks are not powerful enough to address unfettered short-term capital movements, the lack of international regulation on bankruptcy

and competition, and primitive coordination among rich countries. In turn, the global "governance" that does exist is partial and weak at a time when economic globalization deprives many states of independent monetary and fiscal policies, or it obliges them to make cruel choices between economic competitiveness and the preservation of social safety nets. All the while, the United States displays an increasing impatience toward institutions that weigh on American freedom of action. Movement toward a world state looks increasingly unlikely. The more state sovereignty crumbles under the blows of globalization or such recent developments as humanitarian intervention and the fight against terrorism, the more states cling to what is left to them.

Second, globalization has not profoundly challenged the enduring national nature of citizenship. Economic life takes place on a global scale, but human identity remains national—hence the strong resistance to cultural homogenization. Over the centuries, increasingly centralized states have expanded their functions and tried to forge a sense of common identity for their subjects. But no central power in the world can do the same thing today, even in the European Union. There, a single currency and advanced economic coordination have not yet produced a unified economy or strong central institutions endowed with legal autonomy, nor have they resulted in a sense of postnational citizenship. The march from national identity to one that would be both national and European has only just begun. A world very partially unified by technology still has no collective consciousness or collective solidarity. What states are unwilling to do the world market cannot do all by itself, especially in engendering a sense of world citizenship.

Third, there is the relationship between globalization and violence. The traditional state of war, even if it is limited in scope, still persists. There are high risks of regional explosions in the Middle East and in East Asia, and these could seriously affect relations between the major powers. Because of this threat, and because modern arms are increasingly costly, the "anarchical society" of states lacks the resources to correct some of globalization's most flagrant flaws. These very costs, combined with the classic distrust among international actors who prefer to try to preserve their security alone or through traditional alliances, prevent a more satisfactory institutionalization of world politics—for example, an increase of the UN's powers. This step could happen if global society were provided with sufficient forces to prevent a conflict or restore peace—but it is not.

Globalization, far from spreading peace, thus seems to foster conflicts and resentments. The lowering of various barriers celebrated by Friedman, especially the spread of global media, makes it possible for the most deprived or oppressed to compare their fate with that of the free and well-off. These dispossessed then ask for help from others with common resentments, ethnic origin, or religious faith. Insofar as globalization enriches some and uproots many, those who are both poor and uprooted may seek revenge and self-esteem in terrorism.

Globalization and Terror

Terrorism is the poisoned fruit of several forces. It can be the weapon of the weak in a classic conflict among states or within a state, as in Kashmir or the Palestinian territories. But it can also be seen as a product of globalization. Transnational terrorism is made possible by the vast array of communication tools. Islamic terrorism, for example, is not only based on support for the Palestinian struggle and opposition to an invasive American presence. It is also fueled by a resistance to "unjust" economic globalization and to a Western culture deemed threatening to local religions and cultures.

If globalization often facilitates terrorist violence, the fight against this war without borders is potentially disastrous for both economic development and globalization. Antiterrorist measures restrict mobility and financial flows, while new terrorist attacks could lead the way for an antiglobalist reaction comparable to the chauvinistic paroxysms of the 1930s. Global terrorism is not the simple extension of war among states to nonstates. It is the subversion of traditional ways of war because it does not care about the sovereignty of either its enemies or the allies who shelter them. It provokes its victims to take measures that, in the name of legitimate defense, violate knowingly the sovereignty of those states accused of encouraging terror. (After all, it was not the Taliban's infamous domestic violations of human rights that led the United States into Afghanistan; it was the Taliban's support of Osama bin Laden.)

But all those trespasses against the sacred principles of sovereignty do not constitute progress toward global society, which has yet to agree on a common definition of terrorism or on a common policy against it. Indeed, the beneficiaries of the antiterrorist "war" have been the illiberal, poorer states that have lost so much of their sovereignty of late. Now the crackdown on terror allows them to tighten their controls on their own people, products, and money. They can give themselves new reasons to violate individual rights in the name of common defense against insecurity—and thus stop the slow, hesitant march toward international criminal justice.

Another main beneficiary will be the United States, the only actor capable of carrying the war against terrorism into all corners of the world. Despite its power, however, America cannot fully protect itself against future terrorist acts, nor can it fully overcome its ambivalence toward forms of interstate cooperation that might restrict U.S. freedom of action. Thus terrorism is a global phenomenon that ultimately reinforces the enemy—the state—at the same time as it tries to destroy it. The states that are its targets have no interest in applying the laws of war to their fight against terrorists; they have every interest in treating terrorists as outlaws and pariahs. The champions of globalization have sometimes glimpsed the "jungle" aspects of economic globalization, but few observers foresaw similar aspects in global terrorist and antiterrorist violence.

Finally, the unique position of the United States raises a serious question over the future of world affairs. In the realm of interstate problems, American behavior will determine whether the non-superpowers and weak states will continue to look at the United States as a friendly power (or at least a tolerable hegemon), or whether they are provoked by Washington's hubris into coalescing against American preponderance. America may be a hegemon, but combining rhetorical overkill and ill-defined designs is full of risks. Washington has yet to understand that nothing is more dangerous for a "hyperpower" than the temptation of unilateralism. It may well believe that the constraints of international agreements and organizations are not necessary, since U.S. values and power are all that is needed for world order. But in reality, those same international constraints provide far better opportunities for leadership than arrogant demonstrations of contempt for others' views, and they offer useful ways of restraining unilateralist behavior in other states. A hegemon concerned with prolonging its rule should be especially interested in using internationalist methods and institutions, for the gain in influence far exceeds the loss in freedom of action.

In the realm of global society, much will depend on whether the United States will overcome its frequent indifference to the costs that globalization imposes on poorer countries. For now, Washington is too reluctant to make resources available for economic development, and it remains hostile to agencies that monitor and regulate the global market. All too often, the right-leaning tendencies of the American political system push U.S. diplomacy toward an excessive reliance on America's greatest asset—military strength—as well as an excessive reliance on market capitalism and a "sovereigntism" that offends and alienates. That the mighty United States is so afraid of the world's imposing its "inferior" values on Americans is often a source of ridicule and indignation abroad.

Odd Man Out

For all these tensions, it is still possible that the American war on terrorism will be contained by prudence, and that other governments will give priority to the many internal problems created by interstate rivalries and the flaws of globalization. But the world risks being squeezed between a new Scylla and Charybdis. The Charybdis is universal intervention, unilaterally decided by American leaders who are convinced that they have found a global mission provided by a colossal threat. Presentable as an epic contest between good and evil, this struggle offers the best way of rallying the population and overcoming domestic divisions. The Scylla is resignation to universal chaos in the form of new attacks by future bin Ladens, fresh humanitarian disasters, or regional wars that risk escalation. Only through wise judgment can the path between them be charted.

We can analyze the present, but we cannot predict the future. We live in a world where a society of uneven and often virtual states overlaps with a global society burdened by weak public institutions and underdeveloped civil society. A single power dominates, but its economy could become unmanageable or disrupted by future terrorist attacks. Thus to predict the future confidently would be highly incautious or naive. To be sure, the world has survived many crises, but it has done so at a very high price, even in times when WMD were not available.

Precisely because the future is neither decipherable nor determined, students of international relations face two missions. They must try to understand what goes on by taking an inventory of current goods and disentangling the threads of present networks. But the fear of confusing the empirical with the normative should not prevent them from writing as political philosophers at a time when many philosophers are extending their conceptions of just society to international relations. How can one make the global house more livable? The answer presupposes a political philosophy that would be both just and acceptable even to those whose values have other foundations. As the late philosopher Judith Shklar did, we can take as a point of departure and as a guiding thread the fate of the victims of violence, oppression, and misery; as a goal, we should seek material and moral emancipation. While taking into account the formidable constraints of the world as it is, it is possible to loosen them.

RICHARD FLORIDA

THE WORLD IS SPIKY

Globalization Has Changed the Economic Playing Field, but Hasn't Leveled It

The world, according to the title of the *New York Times* columnist Thomas Friedman's book, is flat. Thanks to advances in technology, the global playing field has been leveled, the prizes are there for the taking, and everyone's a player—no matter where on the surface of the earth he or she may reside. "In a flat world," Friedman writes, "you can innovate without having to emigrate."

Friedman is not alone in this belief: for the better part of the past century economists have been writing about the leveling effects of technology. From the invention of the telephone, the automobile, and the airplane to the rise of the personal computer and the Internet, technological progress has steadily eroded the economic importance of geographic place—or so the argument goes.

But in partnership with colleagues at George Mason University and the geographer Tim Culden, of the Center for International and Security Studies, at the University of Maryland, I've begun to chart a very different economic topography.

From *The Atlantic Monthly* (October 2005), pp. 48–51.

Peaks, Hills, and Valleys

When looked at through the lens of economic production, many cities with large populations are diminished and some nearly vanish. Three sorts of places make up the modern economic landscape. First are the cities that generate innovations. These are the tallest peaks; they have the capacity to attract global talent and create new products and industries. They are few in number, and difficult to topple. Second are the economic "hills"—places that manufacture the world's established goods, take its calls, and support its innovation engines. These hills can rise and fall quickly; they are prosperous but insecure. Some, like Dublin and Seoul, are growing into innovative, wealthy peaks; others are declining, eroded by high labor costs and a lack of enduring competitive advantage. Finally there are the vast valleys—places with little connection to the global economy and few immediate prospects.

---

phy. By almost any measure the international economic landscape is not at all flat. On the contrary, our world is amazingly "spiky." In terms of both sheer economic horsepower and cutting-edge innovation, surprisingly few regions truly matter in today's global economy. What's more, the tallest peaks—the cities and regions that drive the world economy—are growing ever higher, while the valleys mostly languish.

————

The most obvious challenge to the flat-world hypothesis is the explosive growth of cities worldwide. More and more people are clustering in urban areas—the world's demographic mountain ranges, so to speak. The share of the world's population living in urban areas, just three percent in 1800, was nearly 30 percent by 1950. Today it stands at about 50 percent; in advanced countries three out of four people live in urban areas. Map A shows the uneven distribution of the world's population. Five megacities currently have more than 20 million inhabitants each. Twenty-four cities have more than 10 million inhabitants, sixty more than 5 million, and 150 more than 2.5 million. Population density is of course a crude indicator of human and economic activity. But in does suggest that at least some of the tectonic forces of economics are concentrating people and resources, and pushing up some places more than others.

Still, differences in population density vastly understate the spikiness of the global economy; the continuing dominance of the world's most productive urban areas is astounding. When it comes to actual economic output, the ten largest U.S. metropolitan areas combined are behind only the United States as a whole and Japan. New York's economy alone is about the size of Russia's or Brazil's, and Chicago's is on a par with Sweden's. Together New York, Los Angeles, Chicago, and Boston have a bigger economy than all of China. If U.S. metropolitan areas were countries, they'd make up forty-seven of the biggest 100 economies in the world.

Unfortunately, no single, comprehensive information source exists for the economic production of all the world's cities. A rough proxy is available, though. Map B shows a variation on the widely circulated view of the world at night, with higher concentrations of light—indicating higher energy use and, presumably, stronger economic production—appearing in greater relief. U.S. regions appear almost Himalayan on this map. From their summits one might look out on a smaller mountain range stretching across Europe, some isolated peaks in Asia, and a few scattered hills throughout the rest of the world.

Population and economic activity are both spiky, but it's innovation—the engine of economic growth—that is most concentrated. The World Intellectual Property Organization recorded about 300,000 patents from resident inventors in more than a hundred nations in 2002 (the most recent year for which statistics are available). Nearly two thirds of them went to

A
Population
Urban areas house half of all the world's people, and continue to grow in both rich and poor countries.[1]

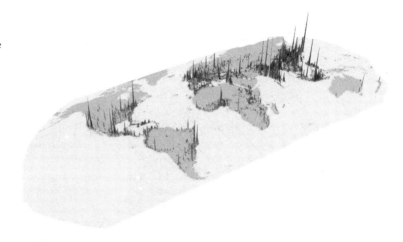

B
Light Emissions
*Economic activity — roughly
estimated here using light-
emissions data — is remarkably
concentrated. Many cities,
despite their large population
barely register.*[2]

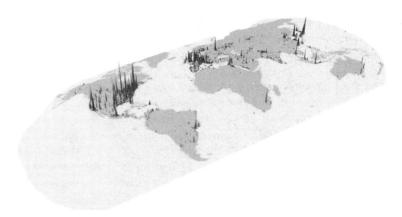

American and Japanese inventors. Eighty-five percent went to the residents of just five countries (Japan, the United States, South Korea, Germany, and Russia).

Worldwide patent statistics can be somewhat misleading, since different countries follow different standards for granting patents. But patents granted in the United States—which receives patent applications for nearly all major innovations worldwide, and holds them to the same strict standards—tell a similar story. Nearly 90,000 of the 170,000 patents granted in the United States in 2002 went to Americans. Some 35,000 went to Japanese inventors, and 11,000 to Germans. The next ten most innovative countries—including the usual suspects in Europe plus Taiwan, South Korea, Israel, and Canada—produced roughly 25,000 more. The rest of the broad, flat world accounted for just five percent of all innovations patented in the United States. In 2003 India generated 341 U.S. patents and China 297. The University of California alone generated more than either country. IBM accounted for five times as many as the two combined.

This is not to say that Indians and Chinese are not innovative. On the contrary, AnnaLee Saxenian, of the University of California at Berkeley, has shown that Indian and Chinese entrepreneurs founded or co-founded roughly 30 percent of all Silicon Valley startups in the late 1990s. But these fundamentally creative

---

The Geography of Innovation

Commercial innovation and scientific advance are both highly concentrated—but not always in the same places. Several cities in East Asia—particularly in Japan—are home to prolific business innovation but still depend disproportionately on scientific breakthroughs made elsewhere. Likewise, some cities excel in scientific research but not in commercial adaptation. The few places that do both well are very strongly positioned in the global economy. These regions have little to fear, and much to gain, from continuing globalization.

---

people had to travel to Silicon Valley and be absorbed into its innovative ecosystem before their ideas became economically viable. Such ecosystems matter, and there aren't many of them.

Map C—which makes use of data from both the World Intellectual Property Organizations and the U.S. Patent and Trademark Office—shows a world composed of innovation peaks and valleys. Tokyo, Seoul, New York, and San Francisco remain the front-runners in the patenting competition. Boston, Seattle, Austin, Toronto, Vancouver, Berlin, Stockholm, Helsinki, London, Osaka, Taipei, and Sydney also stand out.

Map D shows the residence of the 1,200 most heavily cited scientists in leading fields. Scientific advance is even more concentrated than patent production. Most occurs not just in a handful of countries but in a handful of cities—primarily in the United States and Europe. Chi-

C
Patents

Just a few places produce most of the world's innovations. Innovation remains difficult without a critical mass of financiers, entrepreneurs, and scientists, often nourished by world-class universities and flexible corporations.[3]

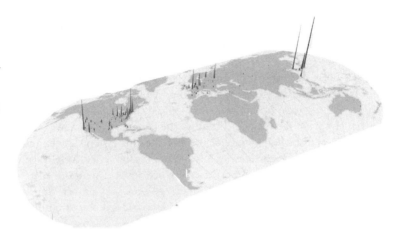

nese and Indian cities do not even register. As far as global innovation is concerned, perhaps a few dozen places worldwide really compete at the cutting edge.

Concentrations of creative and talented people are particularly important for innovation, according to the Nobel Prize–winning economist Robert Lucas. Ideas flow more freely, are honed more sharply, and can be put into practice more quickly when large numbers of innovators, implementers, and financial backers are in constant contact with one another, both in and out of the office. Creative people cluster not simply because they like to be around one another or they prefer cosmopolitan centers with lots of amenities, though both those things count. They and their companies also cluster because of the powerful productivity advantages, economies of scale, and knowledge spillovers such density brings.

So although one might not *have* to emigrate to innovate, it certainly appears that innovation, economic growth, and prosperity occur in those places that attract a critical mass of top creative talent. Because globalization has increased the returns to innovation, by allowing innovative products and services to quickly reach consumers worldwide, it has strengthened the lure that innovation centers hold for our planet's best and brightest, reinforcing the spikiness of wealth and economic production.

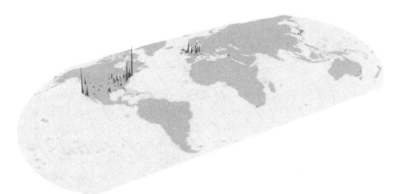

D
Scientific Citations

The world's most prolific and influential scientific researchers overwhelmingly reside in U.S. and European cities.[4]

The main difference between now and even a couple of decades ago is not that the world has become flatter but that the world's peaks have become slightly more dispersed—and that the world's hills, the industrial and service centers that produce mature products and support innovation centers, have proliferated and shifted. For the better part of the twentieth century the United States claimed the lion's share of the global economy's innovation peaks, leaving a few outposts in Europe and Japan. But America has since lost some of those peaks, as such industrial-age powerhouses as Pittsburgh, St. Louis, and Cleveland have eroded. At the same time, a number of regions in Europe, Scandinavia, Canada, and the Pacific Rim have moved up.

The world today looks flat to some because the economic and social distances between peaks worldwide have gotten smaller. Connection between peaks has been strengthened by the easy mobility of the global creative class—about 150 million people worldwide. They participate in a global technology system and a global labor market that allow them to migrate freely among the world's leading cities. In a Brookings Institution study the demographer Robert Lang and the world-cities expert Peter Taylor identify a relatively small group of leading city-regions—London, New York, Paris, Tokyo, Hong Kong, Singapore, Chicago, Los Angeles, and San Francisco among them—that are strongly connected to one another.

But Lang and Taylor also identify a much larger group of city-regions that are far more locally oriented. People in spiky places are often more connected to one another, even from half a world away, than they are to people and places in their veritable back yards.

————

The flat-world theory is not completely misguided. It is a welcome supplement to the widely accepted view (illustrated by the Live 8 concerts and Bono's forays into Africa, by the writings of Jeffrey Sachs and the UN Millennium project)

that the growing divide between rich and poor countries is the fundamental feature of the world economy. Friedman's theory more accurately depicts a developing world with capabilities that translate into economic development. In his view, for example, the emerging economies of India and China combine cost advantages, high-tech skills, and entrepreneurial energy, enabling those countries to compete effectively for industries and jobs. The tensions set in motion as the playing field is leveled affect mainly the advanced countries, which see not only manufacturing work but also higher-end jobs, in fields such as software development and financial services, increasingly threatened by offshoring.

But the flat-world theory blinds us to far more insidious tensions among the world's growing peaks, sinking valleys, and shifting hills. The innovative, talent-attracting "have" regions seem increasingly remote from the talent-exporting "have-not" regions. Second-tier cities, from Detroit and Wolfsburg to Nagoya and Mexico City, are entering an escalating and potentially devastating competition for jobs, talent, and investment. And inequality is growing across the world and within countries.

This is far more barrowing than the flat world Friedman describes, and a good deal more treacherous than the old rich-poor divide. We see its effects in the political backlash against globalization in the advanced world. The recent rejection of the EU constitution by the French, for example, resulted in large part from high rates of "no" votes in suburban and rural quarters, which understandably fear globalization and integration.

But spiky globalization also wreaks havoc on poorer places. China is seeing enormous concentrations of talent and innovation in centers such as Shanghai, Shenzhen, and Beijing, all of which are a world apart from its vast, impoverished rural areas. According to detailed polling by Richard Burkholder, of Callup, average household incomes in urban China are now triple those in rural regions, and they've grown more than three times as fast since 1999; perhaps as a result, urban and rural Chinese now have very different, often conflicting political and lifestyle values. India is growing even more divided, as Bangalore, Hyderabad, and parts of New Delhi and Bombay pull away from the rest of that enormous country, creating destabilizing political tensions. Economic and demographic forces are sorting people around the world into geographically clustered "tribes" so different (and often mutually antagonistic) as to create a somewhat Hobbesian vision.

We are thus confronted with a difficult predicament. Economic progress requires that the peaks grow stronger and taller. But such growth will exacerbate economic and social disparities, fomenting political reactions that could threaten further innovation and economic progress. Managing the disparities between peaks and valleys worldwide—raising the valleys without shearing off the peaks—will be among the top political challenges of the coming decades.

NOTES

1. Map data source: Center for International Earth Science Information Network, Columbia University, and Centro Internacional de Agricultura Tropical.
2. Map data source: U.S. Defense Meteorological Satellite Program.
3. Map data source: World Intellectual Property Organization; U.S. Patent and Trademark Office.
4. Map data source: Michael Batty, Centre for Advanced Spatial Analysis, University College London (www.casa.ucl.ac.uk).

JAGDISH BHAGWATI

IN DEFENSE OF GLOBALIZATION

*   *   *

Let me then turn to the topic of this Lecture: Globalization and the controversies that surround it. Now, the challenge to globalization comes conventionally from protectionists reflecting special producer interests. Ever since Adam Smith wrote about the advantages of free trade, and economists such as David Ricardo and John Stuart Mill elaborated on this demonstration of the gains from specialization and hence from trade, the free traders have had to fight the special interests that seek protection against the general interest of overall economic prosperity.

Today, one sees a return of such conventional protectionism in the United States over outsourcing: the phenomenon of the new trade in services at arm's length where the provider and the user do not have to be in geographical proximity and can transact through snail-mail or the Internet. One also sees it in the resistance in the European Union to the liberalization of agriculture under the ongoing Doha Round of multilateral trade negotiations, the first under the World Trade Organization (WTO) which replaced in 1995 the GATT which had been signed just after the Second World War had ended.

But it would be wrong not to recognize that, in every generation, there has also been some

From 2005 Angelo Costa Lecture, Rome.

dissent from within the economics profession it-self to the proposition that freer trade will pro-duce greater economic prosperity. This dissent, I have observed elsewhere,[1] comes principally from the fact that the case for free trade is based on an extension to the international arena the case for allowing market prices, or Adam Smith's invisible hand, to guide the allocation of resources. But if market prices do not reflect true social costs, the invisible hand may well point in the wrong direction. Such "market fail-ures" need to be corrected for the case for free trade to be restored to full cogency. The correct policy response to this important insight from the postwar theory of commercial policy is, how-ever, to insist that where such market failures exist—e.g. when environmental pollution exists without a "pollution pay tax" in place—the opti-mal policy is not to shift to protectionism but to fix the market failure and then to use free trade to reap the gains from trade.[2] So, there is no real reason for economists today not to be supportive of freer trade.[3]

But today, aside from such conventional pro-tectionism, whether from special producer interests or a handful of economists, we also face massive protectionism, indeed more general anti-globalism, by vast numbers of anti-globalizers worldwide. These critics always say they wish to be stakeholders in the process of globalization. But they divide into two groups: those who wish to drive a stake through the global system, like in Dracula films, because they reject the global system altogether; and those who wish to exercise their stake in the system. The former group takes to the streets; and if you extend a hand to them, they will bite, not shake, it. The latter group, on the other hand, is willing to sit down with us, prepare policy briefs, and to reshape the system. I call the former the *stake-wielding*, the latter the *stake-asserting*, anti-globalization critics.

The stake-wielding groups cannot be talked with; they can only be understood intellectually. But the stake-asserting groups can indeed be en-gaged. The principal task before the proponents of globalization then is to understand what bothers these groups and then to examine their fears and phobias with an open mind, separating the wheat from the chaff. So, I ask: what ails these groups?

Their principal focus is not on the effect of globalization on economic prosperity. They are concerned instead with what I call the "social" effects of "economic" globalization. They fear, indeed claim, that economic globalization is harmful to social agendas such as the reduction of child labour, removal of property, the mainte-nance of rich-country labour and environmental standards, the exercise of national sovereignty and democratic rights, the maintenance of local mainstream and indigenous culture, and women's rights and welfare. With the substantial agitation in that vein worldwide by vast numbers of the stake-asserting anti-globalizers, most politicians can be forgiven for thinking that (eco-nomic) globalization is a phenomenon that im-perils the social agendas that we value.

Thus, Prime Minister Tony Blair, former President Bill Clinton and Chancellor Gerhard Schroeder, the social-democratic proponents of the "Third Way," lament economic globalization, even as they pursue it, as a phenomenon that "needs a human face." Of course, if it needs one, it lacks one. And the former Prime Minister of Ireland, Mrs. Mary Robinson, having finished her term as UN Commissioner for Human Rights, seeks an "ethical globalization," implying that it is not so.

Indeed, in the anti-globalization circles, there is a general tendency to blame globaliza-tion for all shortfalls in social agendas. Typically, many reports in international agencies observe that globalization has increased, that social ills such as poverty exist or have increased, and therefore the former is the cause of the latter. But, like Tina Turner's famous song "What's love got to do with it?" we must ask: what has global-ization to do with it?

The contrary view, which I develop and defend in my just-published book, *In Defense of Globaliza-tion* (Oxford), is that economic globalization *has* a human face. It advances, instead of inhibiting, the achievement of social agendas as wide-ranging as the promotion of gender equality worldwide, reduction of poverty in the poor countries and the shifting of children from work to schools.

The choice between these two assessments of economic globalization—broadly defined as increasing integration of nation states into the international economy via trade, direct foreign investment by chiefly multinational firms, short-term capital flows, cross-border flows of humanity and diffusion and sale of technology—is a matter of the utmost importance. It has immediate implications also for the issue of what I call "appropriate governance."

For, if you believe that globalization lacks a human face, then appropriate governance will encourage policy interventions to restrain globalization. Witness the recent presidential campaign in the United States where the fears over the alleged adverse effects on American workers (which is clearly a "social" issue, one can say) from outsourcing of services led the Democratic presidential aspirants to embrace protectionist policies to tax or prohibit the outsourcing (i.e. import on line) of services by firms whom Senator Kerry of Massachusetts characterized as traitors, never mind that he doubtless joined the company of these traitors when, a man of excellent Yale education and considerable wealth, he probably supped that night on imported French red wine and brie instead of Kraft cheese and Milwaukee beer and watched a BBC Masterpiece Theater play instead of watching an American sitcom.

But if you believe, as I now do, that globalization has a human face, then you will want very different policy interventions—ones that preserve and celebrate the good effects that globalization generally brings out supplement the good outcomes and address the phenomenon's occasional downsides.

This contrast is best seen in relation to child labour in the poor countries. If globalization brings increased incomes to parents, will parents then send more children to work now that their incomes have improved or less because they do not need children to work and can send them to school instead? If the former, then clearly globalization creates a tradeoff between increased prosperity and the reduction of child labour; and policies that inhibit globalization becomes sensible. But if the latter, then we are likely to ask; what can we do to *accelerate* the pace at which child labour will be reduced by globalization? But more of this later when I discuss the nature of Appropriate Governance in greater depth.

The Human Face of Globalization

For the present, let me illustrate with a few examples—you will have to read my book *In Defense of Globalization* for much fuller analysis—how economic globalization has beneficial, not malignant, effects on social agendas.

Child Labour

The anti-globalization critics argue that increased access to foreign markets and resulting increase in poor-family incomes will lead to more child labour: this is the "wicked parents" hypothesis. By contrast, one can hypothesise that increased family incomes among the poor will lead "normal" parents, who do care about their children, to use the opportunity provided by increased incomes to take, say, the fourth child off work and put the child into a primary school instead.

As it happens, economists who have studied child labour empirically have also argued that economic analysis explains why parents act virtuously rather than wickedly. It turns out that the rates of return to primary education are very high in the poor countries. But credit markets are imperfect so that parents are unable to borrow against future income from educated children. These credit constraints are what hold back the education of children and their assignment to work instead. Once incomes improve, that automatically eases the credit constraint through infusion of cash; so education expands and child labour diminishes. Economists have produced a lot of evidence in support of this benign conclusion. Thus, for instance, an econometric study of Vietnam by a husband-wife team of econometricians at Dartmouth College in USA shows that significantly expanded incomes for peasants following liberalization of rice trade led to a significant shift of children from employment into schooling: and a double dividend followed from the fact that the beneficiary children included a number of girls.[4]

So, when globalization leads to increased prosperity, it also leads to less child labour. Indeed, there are many studies, for countries worldwide, that are supportive of this benign-impact outcome.

Poverty in the Poor Countries

Critics also argue that globalization increases, not reduces, poverty in the poor countries. This is a comforting conclusion for those who oppose reducing trade barriers in the rich countries: if you can argue that your protectionism, which is good for yourself, does not harm the victimized abroad but in fact helps them instead, that is fantastic: you can even have a warm good feeling even as you open up with an AK47 on the poor souls! I have heard such self-serving rubbish from the opponents of NAFTA in the United States.

The evidence, however, certainly does not support this bit of sophistry. Globalization helps reduce poverty. Why? We have a two-step argument here. Globalization increases income. Income expansion in turn reduces poverty.

The former relationship is pretty robust, though exceptions can always be found. The economist Arvind Panagariya has shown that, over three decades in the postwar period, on country that has been an "economic miracle" in the sense of having a sustained growth rate of 3% per annum per capita and over, has not had trade also grow rapidly; whereas "economic debacles" with low or declining per capita incomes have also been characterized by similarly declining trade. Can the decline in incomes have come about because of

"exogenously" declining incomes? Yet, sometimes for sure. Thus, civil strife may decimate a country's economic propensity and growth and, in consequence, her trade also: Angola and Sri Lanka could well be examples of this reverse relationship. But, outside of such singular circumstances, the relationship (when sustained over long periods) hardly goes from income to trade, rather than trade to income, in most cases.

But then, has opening up trade further failed to increase income sometimes? Yes, but no one denies this. For instance, you may have infrastructure bottlenecks or civil strife or investment controls that prevent a utilization of the improved trade opportunity. But straw men such as these are constructed by serious people to pretend that the case for free trade is flawed. It is as if the fact that on 9/11 the two flights from Boston to New York crashed into the Twin Towers is used to argue that therefore the introduction of such flights need not lead to an improvement in the ability to get from Boston to New York and back!

The latter relationship, between growth and poverty reduction, is also empirically robust. In the two countries, China and India, where poverty has been immense, this relationship has worked dramatically since the 1980s when both countries retreated [from] autarkic policies and opened to trade and direct foreign investment, more dramatically in China and with more dramatic effects on growth rates and associated poverty reduction. The ability of a rapidly growing economy to suck people up into gainful employment, and thus to make a sustained dent on poverty, has rarely been demonstrated so well. It puts to rest the absurd contention that growth is a conservative, feeble "trickle down" strategy for reducing poverty; I have long argued that it is instead a radical, effective "pull up" strategy for poverty reduction.[5]

Women's Equality

One more example of the benign influence of economic globalization on social agendas comes from the question of women's equality and rights. Two examples suffice to show this.

Consider the effect of globalization on gender pay inequality. That women are paid less than men who are no more qualified is a widespread scandal. This prejudice is however expensive for the employer who indulges in this practice because he then pays more than he should if he hires more expensive men than equally productive women. One can then argue that, in internationally competitive industries, the reduction of such pay inequality will follow because those who fritter away money on indulging such prejudice will yield in competition to those who do not. It turns out that an empirical examination of two decades of experience in US industries shows precisely that the gender pay inequality shrank faster in the traded, than in the non-traded, industries.[6]

A different kind of example comes from the way in which Japanese direct foreign investment in the West in the 1980s and early 1990s led to the acceleration of the assertion of women's rights in Japan. When Japanese firms went abroad, their executives were of course men since women were simply not for recruitment into executive ranks. But the women went to New York, Rome, London and Paris with their husbands and they saw how women were treated a lot better there. That gave them ideas and they became a force for change, as women often do everywhere. Globalization, in shape of multinational investments, had turned out to be a source of beneficial influence for Japan's progress towards women's rights.

Appropriate Governance

Indeed, as one goes down the litany of complaints and fears of the anti-globalizers, the conclusion is inescapable that the effects economic globalization on several social dimensions are benign, on balance, rather than malign. But then we must ask: what institutional policy framework is necessary to improve on the benign out-

comes that globalization fetches?

Evidently, three types of issues matter. First, even if the effect is benign, it is not always so. Therefore, we must devise institutions to deal with downsides, as and when they arise. I have long argued that the developing countries often lack adjustment assistance programs of the kind that the developed countries, which have liberalized trade far more (contrary to Oxfam's ill-informed talk about "double standards" in trade), have evolved over time. But how can the poor countries finance such programs? Evidently, aid agencies such as the World Bank can be mobilized to provide such funds to support trade liberalization. I am happy to note that, after years of exhortation, Mr. James Wolfensohn, the outgoing president of the World Bank, did announce such a scheme to support developing country trade liberalization last year.

Second, we need to ensure that we do not repeat the mistake made by the reformers in Russia, where shock therapy was tried and failed. Maximal speed is not the optimal speed; both economics and politics require cautious adjustment. When the economist Jeffrey Sachs insisted on shock therapy in Russia, he used the analogy: "You cannot cross a chasm in two leaps." The Soviet expert Padma Desai—transparency requires that I reveal that she is my wife—replied: "You cannot cross it in one leap either unless you are Indiana Jones; it is better to drop a bridge." Events proved her right.

Finally, we need to use supplementary policies to accelerate the pace at which the social agendas are advanced. True, child labour will be reduced by the prosperity enhanced by globalization. But then what more can we do to reduce it faster? Here, the unions in the rich countries have taken the view that only trade sanctions have "teeth." This is a myopic and counterproductive view. It is far better, as many intellectuals from the developing countries argue, to use moral suasion today. After all, God gave us a tongue as well; and in today's age, with demo-cratic regimes worldwide, with CNN and with NGOs, a good tongue-lashing is far more powerful than sanctions imposed by governments whose own credentials often are not unblemished.

And so, while globalization has a human face, that face can be made to glow yet better with appropriate governance along these lines. Globalization works; but we can make it work better. That is the chief task before all of us today.

NOTES

1. I have reviewed these dissents from the earliest times since Adam Smith, and the important clarification of the common intellectual basis for these dissents, in my Stockholm Lectures, *Free Trade Today*, also being translated into Italian by Laterza.

2. For a fuller, more nuanced statement of this argument, consult my *Free Trade Today*, ibid., Chapter 1.

3. Nonetheless, there are a couple of economists who play the protectionist role, wittingly or unwittingly, with arguments that are not intellectually compelling. Several of these arguments have been noted and rejected in the Report on *The Future of the WTO* by an expert group, of which I was a member, appointed by the director general of the WTO and released on January 17th 2005.

4. These studies are reviewed in Chapter 6 of *In Defense of Globalization*, ibid. Yet more evidence has accumulated in support of the benign hypothesis since the publication of my book.

5. In my book *In Defense of Globalization*, I do consider several institutional and policy measures to strengthen the impact of growth on poverty. I also consider ways in which a specific growth process might harm the poor, or any specific groups, and how to handle such possible downsides, if and when they arise.

6. This study by the two women economists Elizabeth Brainerd and Sandra Black is discussed in Chapter 7 of *In Defense of Globalization*, ibid. Needless to say, this benign outcome need not hold in every country, particularly if the supply of female labour is perfectly elastic at a given wage and men's wages are at a legislated minimum: conditions that may obtain in some developing countries. The conditions under which the wage differential would go in the perverse direction can be imagined but are improbable in practice.

NIALL FERGUSON

SINKING GLOBALIZATION

Torpedoed

Ninety years ago this May, the German submarine U-20 sank the Cunard liner *Lusitania* off the southern coast of Ireland. Nearly 1,200 people,

From *Foreign Affairs*, 84, no. 2 (March/April 2005), pp. 64–77.

including 128 Americans, lost their lives. Usually remembered for the damage it did to the image of imperial Germany in the United States, the sinking of the *Lusitania* also symbolized the end of the first age of globalization.

From around 1870 until World War I, the world economy thrived in ways that look familiar today. The mobility of commodities, capital, and labor reached record levels; the sea-lanes and telegraphs across the Atlantic had never been busier, as capital and migrants traveled west and raw materials and manufactures traveled east. In relation to output, exports of both merchandise and capital reached volumes not seen again until the 1980s. Total emigration from Europe between 1880 and 1910 was in excess of 25 million. People spoke euphorically of "the annihilation of distance."

Then, between 1914 and 1918, a horrendous war stopped all of this, sinking globalization. Nearly 13 million tons of shipping were sent to the bottom of the ocean by German submarine attacks. International trade, investment, and migration all collapsed. Moreover, the attempt to resuscitate the world economy after the war's end failed. The global economy effectively disintegrated with the onset of the Great Depression and, after that, with an even bigger world war, in which astonishingly high proportions of production went toward perpetrating destruction.

It may seem excessively pessimistic to worry that this scenario could somewhat repeat itself—that our age of globalization could collapse just as our grandparents' did. But it is worth bearing in mind that, despite numerous warnings issued in the early twentieth century about the catastrophic consequences of a war among the European great powers, many people—not least investors, a generally well-informed class—were taken completely by surprise by the outbreak of World War I. The possibility is as real today as it was in 1915 that globalization, like the *Lusitania*, could be sunk.

Back to the Future

The last age of globalization resembled the current one in numerous ways. It was characterized by relatively free trade, limited restrictions on migration, and hardly any regulation of capital flows. Inflation was low. A wave of technological innovation was revolutionizing the communications and energy sectors; the world first discov-

ered the joys of the telephone, the radio, the internal combustion engine, and paved roads. The U.S. economy was the biggest in the world, and the development of its massive internal market had become the principal source of business innovation. China was opening up, raising all kinds of expectations of the West, and Russia was growing rapidly.

World War I wrecked all of this. Global markets were disrupted and disconnected, first by economic warfare, then by postwar protectionism. Prices went haywire: a number of major economies (Germany's among them) suffered from both hyperinflation and steep deflation in the space of a decade. The technological advances of the 1900s petered out: innovation hit a plateau, and stagnating consumption discouraged the development of even existing technologies such as the automobile. After faltering during the war, overheating in the 1920s, and languishing throughout the 1930s in the doldrums of depression, the U.S. economy ceased to be the most dynamic in the world. China succumbed to civil war and foreign invasion, defaulting on its debts and disappointing optimists in the West. Russia suffered revolution, civil war, tyranny, and foreign invasion. Both these giants responded to the crisis by donning the constricting armor of state socialism. They were not alone. By the end of the 1940s, most states in the world, including those that retained political freedoms, had imposed restrictions on trade, migration, and investment as a matter of course. Some achieved autarky, the ideal of a deglobalized society. Consciously or unconsciously, all governments applied in peacetime the economic restrictions that had first been imposed between 1914 and 1918.

The end of globalization after 1914 was not unforeseeable. There was no shortage of voices prophesying Armageddon in the prewar decades. Many popular writers earned a living by predicting a cataclysmic European war. Solemn Marxists had long foretold the collapse of capitalism and imperialism. And Social Darwinists had looked forward eagerly to a conflagration that would weed out the weak and fortify the strong.

Yet most investors were completely caught off guard when the crisis came. Not until the last week of July 1914 was there a desperate dash for liquidity; it happened so suddenly and on such a large scale that the world's major stock markets, New York's included, closed down for the rest of the year. As *The Economist* put it at the time, investors and financial institutions "saw in a flash the meaning of war." The Dow Jones Industrial Average fell by about 25 percent between January 1910 and December 1913 and remained flat through the first half of 1914. European bond markets, which had held up throughout the diplomatic crises of the 1900s, crashed only at the 11th hour, as the lights went out all over Europe.

Some economic historians detect the origins of the deglobalization that followed World War I in the prewar decades. They point, variously, to rising tariffs and restrictions on migration, a slight uptick in inflation starting around 1896, and the chronic vulnerability of the U.S. economy to banking crises. To this list, it might be added that the risk of further Russian and Chinese revolutions should have been fairly apparent after those of 1905 and 1911, respectively.

The trouble is that none of these problems can be said to have caused the great conflagration that was World War I. To be sure, the prewar world was marked by all kinds of economic rivalries—not least between British and German manufacturers—but these did not suffice to cause a disaster. On the contrary, businessmen on both sides agreed that a major war would be an economic calamity. The point seemed so obvious that war came to be seen by some optimistic commentators as all but impossible—a "great illusion," in the famous phrase of the author Norman Angell. Even when the war broke out, many people optimistically clung to the illusion that it would soon be over. Economist John Maynard Keynes said that it could not last more than a year."

With the benefit of hindsight, however, five factors can be seen to have precipitated the global explosion of 1914–18. The first cause was imperial overstretch. By 1914, the British Em-

pire was showing signs of being a "weary Titan," in the words of the poet Matthew Arnold. It lacked the will to build up an army capable of deterring Germany from staging a rival bid for European hegemony (if not world power). As the world's policeman, distracted by old and new commitments in Asia and Africa, the United Kingdom's beat had simply become too big.

Great-power rivalry was another principal cause of the catastrophe. The problem was not so much Anglo-German rivalry at sea as it was Russo-Germany rivalry on land. Fear of a Russian arms buildup convinced the German general staff to fight in 1914 rather than risk waiting any longer.

The third fatal factor was an unstable alliance system. Alliances existed in abundance, but they were shaky. The Germans did not trust the Austrians to stand by them in a crisis, and the Russians worried that the French might lose their nerve. The United Kingdom's actions were impossible to predict because its ententes with France and Russia made no explicit provisions for the eventuality of war in Europe. The associated insecurities encouraged risk-taking diplomacy. In 1908, for example, Austria-Hungary brusquely annexed Bosnia. Three years later, the German government sent the gunboat *Panther* to Agadir to challenge French claims to predominance in Morocco.

The presence of a rogue regime sponsoring terror was a fourth source of instability. The chain of events leading to war, as every schoolchild used to know, began with the assassination of the Austrian Archduke Franz Ferdinand in Sarajevo by a Bosnian Serb, Gavrilo Princip. There were shady links between the assassin's organization and the Serbian government, which had itself come to power not long before in a bloody palace coup.

Finally, the rise of a revolutionary terrorist organization hostile to capitalism turned an international crisis into a backlash against the global free market. The Bolsheviks, who emerged from the 1903 split in the Russian Social Democratic Party, had already established their credentials as a fanatical organization committed to using violence to bring about world revolution. By straining the tsarist system to the breaking point, the war gave Lenin and his confederates their opportunity. They seized it and used the most ruthless terrorist tactics to win the ensuing civil war.

Parallel Universe

There are obvious economic parallels between the first age of globalization and the current one. Today, as in the period before 1914, protectionism periodically challenges the free-trade orthodoxy. By the standards of the pre-1914 United Kingdom, in fact, the major economies are already shamelessly protectionist when it comes to agriculture. Then, the United Kingdom imposed no tariffs on imported agricultural goods, whereas now the United States, the European Union, and Japan all use tariffs and subsidies to protect their farmers from foreign competition.

Today, no one can be sure how stable the international monetary system is, but one thing is certain: it is no more stable than the system that preceded World War I. Although gold is no longer the basis of the monetary system, there are pegged exchange rates, just as there were in 1914. In Europe, there is a monetary union—essentially a deutsche mark zone. In eastern Asia, there is a dollar standard. Both systems, however, are based on fiat currencies. Unlike before 1914, the core central banks in New York and Frankfurt determine the volume of currency produced, and they do so on the basis of an opaque mixture of rules and discretion.

Today, technological innovation shows no sign of slackening. From nanocomputers the size of a pinhead to scramjets that can cross the Atlantic in an hour, there seems no limit to human ingenuity, given sufficient funding of research and development. That is the good news. The bad news is that now technology also helps the enemies of globalization. Before 1914, terrorists had to pursue their bloody trade with Browning revolvers and primitive bombs. These days, an entire city could be obliterated with a single nuclear device.

Today, as before 1914, the U.S. economy is the world's biggest, but it is now much more important as a market for the rest of the world than it was then. Although the United States may enjoy great influence as the "consumer of first resort," this role depends on the willingness of foreigners to fund a widening current account deficit. A rising proportion of Americans may consider themselves to have been "saved" in the Evangelical sense, but they are less good at saving in the economic sense. The personal savings rate among Americans stood at just 0.2 percent of disposable personal income in September 2004, compared with 7.7 percent less than 15 years ago. Whether to finance domestic investment (in the late 1990s) or government borrowing (after 2000), the United States has come to rely increasingly on foreign lending. As the current account deficit has widened (it is now approaching 6 percent of GDP), U.S. net overseas liabilities have risen steeply to around 25 percent of GDP. Half of the publicly held federal debt is now in foreign hands; at the end of August 2004, the combined U.S. Treasury holdings of China, Hong Kong, Japan, Singapore, South Korea, and Taiwan were $1.1 trillion, up by 22 percent from the end of 2003. A large proportion of this increase is a result of immense purchases by eastern Asian monetary authorities, designed to prevent their currencies from appreciating relative to the dollar.

This deficit is the biggest difference between globalization past and globalization present. A hundred years ago, the global hegemon—the United Kingdom—was a net exporter of capital, channeling a high proportion of its savings overseas to finance the construction of infrastructure such as railways and ports in the Americas, Asia, Australasia, and Africa. Today, its successor as an Anglophone empire plays the diametrically opposite role—as the world's debtor rather than the world's creditor, absorbing around three-quarters of the rest of the world's surplus savings.

Does this departure matter? Some claim it does not—that it just reflects the rest of the world's desire to have a piece of the U.S. economic action, whether as owners of low-risk securities or sellers of underpriced exports. This is how Harvard economist Richard Cooper sees it. Assuming that the U.S. economy has a trend rate of growth of 5 percent a year, he argues that a sustained current account deficit of $500 billion per year would translate into external liabilities of 46 percent of GDP after 15 years, but that then U.S. foreign debt would "decline indefinitely."

Well, maybe. But what if those assumptions are wrong? According to the HSBC Group, the current account deficit could reach 8 percent of GDP by the end of the decade. That could push the United States' net external liabilities as high as 90 percent of GDP. When the United Kingdom accumulated net foreign debts of less than half this percentage, it was fighting World War II. In the war's aftermath, the resulting "sterling balances" owned by the rest of the world were one of the reasons the pound declined and lost its reserve currency status.

A sharp depreciation of the dollar relative to Asian currencies might not worry the majority of Americans, whose liabilities are all dollar-denominated. But its effect on Asia would be profound. Asian holders of dollar assets would suffer heavy capital losses in terms of their own currencies, and Asian exporters would lose some of their competitive advantage in the U.S. market. According to Michael Mussa of the Institute for International Economics, lowering the U.S. deficit to 2 percent of GDP over the next few years would require a further 20 percent decline in the dollar. The economists Maurice Obstfeld and Kenneth Rogoff estimate that the fall could be as much as 40 percent. And the University of California at Berkeley's Brad de Long has pointed out that,

[i]f the private market—which knows that with high probability the dollar is going down some-day—decides that that someday has come and that the dollar is going down *now*, then all the Asian

central banks in the world cannot stop it [emphasis in original].

That day may be fast approaching. In the words of Federal Reserve Board Chairman Alan Greenspan last November, "the desire of investors to add dollar claims to their portfolios" must have a limit; a "continued financing even of today's current account deficits . . . doubtless will, at some future point, increase shares of dollar claims in investor portfolios to levels that imply an unacceptable amount of concentration risk."

The domestic effects of a dollar crash would be felt most sharply by the growing numbers of Americans with large mortgage debts who would suddenly face a rise in interest rates. The growth in the share of variable-rate mortgages in the volume of total household debt is seen by some as a sign that the U.S. mortgage market is growing more sophisticated. But it also increases the sensitivity of many American families to rises in the rates. The federal government has a pretty large variable-rate debt, too, given the very short maturities of a large proportion of federal bonds and notes. That fact means that higher rates could quickly affect the deficit itself, creating a dangerous feedback loop. And, of course, higher rates would be likely to lower growth and hence reduce tax revenues. In short, today's international fiat-money system is significantly, and dangerously, crisis-prone.

Another cause for concern is the fragility of China's financial system. This Asian miracle is unlikely to avoid the kind of crisis that marked the Asian miracles of the past. To get a sense of the dangers, consider China's Soviet-style domestic banking system and its puny domestic stock market: how can such rapid growth in manufacturing possibly be sustained with such inadequate financial institutions?

Pre-1914 globalization was remarkably susceptible to the international transmission of crises—what economists call "contagion." So is globalization nowadays. As Andrew Large of the Bank of England pointed out last November, the "search for yield" in an environment of low interest rates is encouraging investors, banks, and hedge funds to converge on similar trading strategies, raising "the prospect of one-way markets developing and market liquidity evaporating in response to a shock."

Ghosts from the Past

As the economic parallels with 1914 suggest, today's globalization shows at least some signs of reversibility. The risks increase when one considers the present political situation, which has the same five flaws as the pre-1914 international order: imperial overstretch, great-power rivalry, an unstable alliance system, rogue regimes sponsoring terror, and the rise of a revolutionary terrorist organization hostile to capitalism.

The United States—an empire in all but name—is manifestly overstretched. Not only is its current account deficit large and growing larger, but the fiscal deficit that lurks behind it also is set to surge as the baby boomers retire and start to claim Social Security and Medicare benefits. The Congressional Budget Office (CBO) projects that over the next four decades, Social Security, Medicaid, and Medicare spending will rise to consume at least an additional 12 percent of GDP per year. The CBO also estimates that the transition costs of President George W. Bush's planned Social Security reform, if enacted, could create a budget shortfall of up to two percent of GDP a year for ten years. Add that to the fiscal consequences of making the president's first-term tax cuts permanent, and it becomes hard to imagine how the country will manage to stem the rising tide of red ink.

The U.S. empire also suffers from a personnel deficit: 500,000 troops is the maximum number that Washington can deploy overseas, and this number is simply not sufficient to win all the small wars the United States currently has (or might have) to wage. Of the 137,000 American troops currently in Iraq, 43 percent are drawn from the reserves or the National Guard. Even

just to maintain the U.S. presence in Iraq, the Army is extending tours of duty and retaining personnel due to be discharged. Such measures seem certain to hurt reenlistment rates.

Above all, the U.S. empire suffers from an attention deficit. Iraq is not a very big war. As one Marine told his parents in a letter home.

> compared to the wars of the past, this is nothing. We're not standing on line in the open—facing German machine guns like the Marines at Belleau Wood or trying to wade ashore in chest-deep water at Tarawa. We're not facing hordes of screaming men at the frozen Chosun Reservoir in Korea or the clever ambushes of Vietcong. We deal with potshots and I.E.D.'s [improvised explosive devices].

He was right; the Iraq war is more like the colonial warfare the British waged 100 years ago. It is dangerous—the author of that letter was killed three weeks after he wrote it—but it is not Vietnam or Korea, much less the Pacific theater in World War II. Yet the Iraq war has become very unpopular very quickly, after relatively few casualties. According to several polls, fewer than half of American voters now support it. And virtually no one seems to want to face the fact that the U.S. presence in Iraq—and the low-intensity conflict that goes with imperial policing—may have to endure for ten years or more if that country is to stand any chance of economic and political stabilization.

Then there is the second problem: great-power rivalry. It is true that the Chinese have no obvious incentive to pick a fight with the United States. But China's ambitions with respect to Taiwan are not about to disappear just because Beijing owns a stack of U.S. Treasury bonds. On the contrary, in the event of an economic crisis, China might be sorely tempted to play the nationalist card by threatening to take over its errant province. Would the United States really be willing to fight China over Taiwan, as it has pledged in the past to do? And what would happen if the Chinese authorities flexed their new financial muscles by dumping U.S. bonds on the world market? To the historian, Taiwan looks somewhat like the Belgium of old: a seemingly inconsequential country over which empires end up fighting to the death. And one should not forget Asia's most dangerous rogue regime, North Korea, which is a little like pre-1914 Serbia with nuclear weapons.

As for Europe, one must not underestimate the extent to which the recent diplomatic "widening of the Atlantic" reflects profound changes in Europe, rather than an alteration in U.S. foreign policy. The combination of economic sclerosis and social senescence means that Europe is bound to stagnate, if not decline. Meanwhile, Muslim immigration and the prospect of Turkey's accession to the European Union are changing the very character of Europe. And the division between Americans and Europeans on Middle Eastern questions is only going to get wider—for example, if the United States dismisses the European attempt to contain Iran's nuclear ambitions by diplomatic means and presses instead for military countermeasures.

These rivalries are one reason the world today also has an unstable alliance system (problem number three). NATO's purpose is no longer clear. Is it just an irrelevant club for the winners of the Cold War, which former Soviet satellites are encouraged to join for primarily symbolic reasons? Have divisions over Iraq rendered it obsolete? To say the least, "coalitions of the willing" are a poor substitute.

None of these problems would necessarily be fatal were it not for the fourth and fifth parallels between 1914 and today: the existence of rogue regimes sponsoring terror—Iran and Syria top the list—and of revolutionary terrorist organizations. It is a big mistake to think of al Qaeda as "Islamo-fascist" (as the journalist Christopher Hitchens and many others called the group after the September 11, 2001, attacks). Al Qaeda's members are much more like "Islamo-Bolshevists," committed to revolution and a reordering of the world along anti-capitalist lines.

Like the Bolsheviks in 1914, these Islamist extremists are part of an underground sect, struggling to land more than the occasional big punch on the enemy. But what if they were to get control of a wealthy state, the way Lenin, Trotsky, and company did in 1917? How would the world look if there were an October Revolution in Saudi Arabia? True, some recent survey data suggest that ordinary Saudis are relatively moderate people by the standards of the Arab world. And high oil prices mean more shopping and fewer disgruntled youths. On the other hand, after what happened in Tehran in 1979, no one can rule out a second Islamist revolution. The Saudi royal family does not look like the kind of regime that will still be in business ten years from now. The only monarchies that survive in modern times are those that give power away.

But is Osama bin Laden really a modern-day Lenin? The comparison is less far-fetched than it seems ("Hereditary Nobleman Vladimir Ulyanov" also came from a wealthy family). In a proclamation to the world before the recent U.S. presidential election, bin Laden declared that his "policy [was] bleeding America to the point of bankruptcy." As he explained, "al Qaeda spent $500,000 on the [September 11 attacks], while America, in the incident and its aftermath, lost—according to the lowest estimate—more than $500 billion. Meaning that every dollar of al Qaeda defeated a million dollars, by the permission of Allah." Bin Laden went on to talk about the U.S. "economic deficit . . . estimated to total more than a trillion dollars" and to make a somewhat uncharacteristic joke:

> [T]hose who say that al Qaeda has won against the administration in the White House or that the administration has lost in this war have not been precise, because when one scrutinizes the results, one cannot say that al Qaeda is the sole factor in achieving those spectacular gains. Rather, the policy of the White House that demands the opening of war fronts to keep busy their various corporations—whether they be working in the field of arms or oil reconstruction—has helped al Qaeda to achieve these enormous results.

Two things are noteworthy about bin Laden's quip: one, the classically Marxist assertion that the war in Iraq was motivated by capitalist economic interests; and two, the rather shrewd—and unfortunately accurate—argument that bin Laden has been getting help in "bleeding America to the point of bankruptcy" from the Bush administration's fiscal policy.

Apocalypse When?

A doomsday scenario is plausible. But is it probable? The difficult thing—indeed the nearly impossible thing—is to predict a cataclysm. Doing so was the challenge investors faced in the first age of globalization. They knew there could be a world war. They knew such a war would have devastating financial consequences (although few anticipated how destructive it would be). But they had no way of knowing when exactly it would happen.

The same problem exists today. We all know that another, bigger September 11 is quite likely; it is, indeed, bin Laden's stated objective. We all know—or should know—that a crisis over Taiwan would send huge shockwaves through the international system; it could even lead to a great-power war. We al know that revolutionary regime change in Saudi Arabia would shake the world even more than the 1917 Bolshevik coup in Russia. We all know that the detonation of a nuclear device in London would dwarf the assassination of Archduke Ferdinand as an act of terrorism.

But what exactly can we do about such contingencies, if, as with the Asian tsunami, we cannot say even approximately when they might occur? The opportunity cost of liquidating our portfolios and inhabiting a subterranean bunker looks too high, even if Armageddon could come tomorrow. In that sense, we seem no better prepared for the worst-case scenario than were the beneficiaries of the last age of globalization, 90 years ago. Like the passengers who boarded the *Lusitania*, all we know is that we may conceivably sink. Still we sail.

CREDITS

Chapter 1: What is Comparative Politics?

p. 3: Mark Irving Lichbach and Alan S. Zuckerman: "Research Traditions and Theory in Comparative Politics: An Introduction," *Comparative Politics: Rationality, Culture, and Structure*, pp. 3–10. © Mark Irving Lichbach and Alan S. Zuckerman 1997. Reprinted with the permission of Cambridge University Press.

p. 7: Francis Fukuyama: "How Academia Failed the Nation: The Decline of Regional Studies," *SAISphere*, Winter 2004. Reprinted by permission of the publisher.

p. 9: Robert Bates: "Area Studies in the Discipline: A Useful Controversy?" *PS: Political Science & Politics*, Vol. 30, Issue 2, June 1997, pp. 166–169. Copyright © 1997 by the American Political Science Association. Reprinted with the permission of Cambridge University Press.

p. 14: Gary King, Robert O. Keohane, and Sidney Verba: "The Science in Social Science," *Designing Social Inquiry: Scientific Inference in Qualitative Research*, pp. 4–12. © 1994 Princeton University Press. Reprinted by permission of Princeton University Press.

Chapter 2: The State

p. 28: Jeffrey Herbst: "War and the State in Africa," *International Security*, 14:4 (Spring, 1990), pp. 117–139. © 1990 by the President and Fellows of Harvard College and the Massachusetts Institute of Technology. Reprinted by permission of MIT Press.

p. 43: Robert Rotberg: "The New Nature of Nation-State Failure," *The Washington Quarterly*, 25:3, Summer 2002, pp. 85–96. Copyright © 2002 by The Center for Strategic and International Studies and the Massachusetts Institute of Technology. Reprinted by permission of the publisher (Taylor & Francis Ltd, http://www.informaworld.com).

p. 51: Stephen D. Krasner: "Sovereignty," *Foreign Policy*, January–February 2001, pp. 20–29. www.foreignpolicy.com. Copyright 2001 by Foreign Policy. Reproduced with permission of Foreign Policy in the format Textbook via Copyright Clearance Center.

p. 58: Mark Juergensmeyer: "The New Religious State," *Comparative Politics*, 27 (July 1995). Reprinted by permission of *Comparative Politics*.

Chapter 3: Nations and Society

p. 68: Eric Hobsbawm: From *The Age of Revolution*, pp. 163–177. © 1996 by Eric Hobsbawm. Reprinted by permission of George Weidenfeld and Nicolson, Ltd., an imprint of The Orion Publishing Group, London.

p. 77: James D. Fearon and David D. Laitin: "Ethnicity, Insurgency, and Civil War," *American Political Science Review*, Vol. 97, No. 1, 2003, pp. 75–76, 77–78, 82–83, 88–89. Copyright © 2003 by the American Political Science Association. Reprinted with the permission of Cambridge University Press.

p. 84: Samuel P. Huntington: "The Clash of Civilizations?" Reprinted by permission of *Foreign Affairs*, Vol. 72, No. 3, Summer 1993. Copyright 1993 by the Council on Foreign Relations, Inc. www.ForeignAffairs.org.

p. 96: Fouad Ajami: "The Summoning." Reprinted by permission of *Foreign Affairs*, Vol. 72, No. 4, September/October 1993. Copyright 1993 by the Council on Foreign Relations, Inc. www.ForeignAffairs.org.

Chapter 4: Political Economy

p. 113: Clive Crook: "Beyond Belief." Copyright 2009, The Atlantic Media Co., as first published in *The Atlantic Magazine*. Distributed by Tribune Media Services. Reprinted with permission.

p. 116: Douglass C. North: "Institutions," *Journal of Economic Perspectives*, Vol. 5, No. 1, Winter 1991, pp. 97–112. Copyright © 1991 by the American Economic Association. Reprinted by permission of the American Economic Association.

p. 128: Daron Acemoglu: "Root Causes," *Finance and Development*, Vol. 40, No. 2, June 2003, pp. 27–30. Copyright © 2003 by the International Monetary Fund. Reprinted by permission of the International Monetary Fund.

Chapter 5: Democratic Regimes

p. 135: Fareed Zakaria: "A Brief History of Human Liberty" from *The Future of Freedom Illiberal Democracy at Home and Abroad* by Fareed Zakaria. Copyright © 2003 by Fareed Zakaria. Used by permission of W.W. Norton & Company, Inc.

p. 151: Phillippe C. Schmitter and Terry Lynn Karl: "What Democracy Is . . . And Is Not," *Journal of Democracy* 2:3 (1991), 75–88. © National Endowment for Democracy and The Johns Hopkins University Press. Reprinted with permission of The Johns Hopkins University Press.

p. 161: Arend Lijphart: "Constitutional Choices for New Democracies," *Journal of Democracy* 2:1 (1991), 72–84. © National Endowment for Democracy and The Johns Hopkins University Press. Reprinted with permission of The Johns Hopkins University Press.

p. 170: Robert Putnam: "Tuning In, Tuning Out: The Strange Disappearance of Social Capital in America," *PS: Political Science & Politics*, Dec. 1995, pp. 664–683. Reprinted by permission of the author.

p. 198: Bryan Caplan: "The Myth of the Rational Voter: Why Democracies Choose Bad Policies," *Cato Unbound*, No. 594. Copyright 2006 by Cato Institute. Reproduced with permission of Cato Institute via Copyright Clearance Center.

Chapter 6: Nondemocratic Regimes

p. 206: Juan J. Linz and Alfred Stepan: "Modern Non-Democratic Regimes," *Problems of Democratic Transition and Consolidation: Southern Europe, South America, and Post-Communist Europe*, pp. 38–54. © 1996 The Johns Hopkins University Press. Reprinted with permission of The Johns Hopkins University Press.

p. 219: Fareed Zakaria: "Islam, Democracy, and Constitutional Liberalism," Reprinted by permission from *Political Science Quarterly*, 119 (Spring 2004): 1–20.

p. 235: Larry Diamond: "The Democratic Rollback: The Resurgence of the Predatory State," adapted from chapters 13 and 14 from the book *The Spirit of Democracy* by Larry Diamond. It was first published in *Foreign Affairs*, March/April 2009. Copyright © 2008 by Larry Diamond. Reprinted by arrangement with Henry Holt and Company, LLC.

p. 241: Erika Weinthal and Pauline Jones Luong: "Combating the Resource Curse: An Alternative Solution to Managing Mineral Wealth," *Perspectives on Politics*, Vol. 4, No. 1, March 2006, pp. 35–38, 43–53. Copyright © 2006 American Political Science Association. Reprinted with the permission of Cambridge University Press.

Chapter 7: Advanced Democracies

p. 268: Seymour M. Lipset: "Economic Development and Democracy," *Political Man: The Social Bases of Politics*, pp. 31–57. Reprinted by permission of the author.

p. 282: Maurice Duverger: "The Number of Parties," from *Les Partis Politiques* (Paris: Armand Colin, 1976), Political Parties: *Their Organization and Activity in the Modern State*, translated by Barbara and Robert North (New York: Wiley, 1954). Reprinted by permission of Armand Colin.

p. 287: Torben Iversen and David Soskice: "Electoral Institution and the Politics of Coalitions: Why Some Democracies Redistribute More Than Others," *American Political Science Review*, Vol. 100, No. 2, May 2006, pp. 165–166, 171–175, 178–179. Copyright © 2006 by the American Political Science Association. Reprinted with the permission of Cambridge University Press.

p. 296: The Economist: "Is Government Disappearing?" *The Economist*, Sept. 27, 2001, pp. 14–18. © 2001 The Economist Newspaper Ltd. All rights reserved. Further reproduction prohibited, www.economist.com.

p. 303: Margarita Estevez-Abe, Torben Iversen, and David Soskice: "Social Protection and the Formation of Skills: A Reinterpretation of the Welfare State." Reproduced from *Varieties of Capitalism: The Institutional Foundations of Comparative Advantage*, eds. Peter A. Hall and David Soskice, © 2001, by permission of Oxford University Press.

Chapter 8: Communism and Postcommunism

p. 336: Valerie J. Bunce: "Rethinking Recent Democratization: Lessons from the Postcommunist Experience," *Journal of Democracy* 55:2 (2003), 167–192. © The Johns Hopkins University Press. Reprinted with permission of The Johns Hopkins University Press.

p. 346: Keith Darden and Anna Maria Grzymala-Busse: "The Great Divide: Literacy, Nationalism, & The Communist Collapse," *World Politics* 59:1 (2006), 83–91, 94–112. © The Johns Hopkins University Press. Reprinted with permission of The Johns Hopkins University Press.

Chapter 9: Less-Developed and Newly Industrializing Countries

Chapter 10: Political Violence